Discovering AutoCAD® 2024

Mark Dix

Paul Riley

Lee Ambrosius

Pearson

Discovering AutoCAD® 2024

Notice of Liability

Credits and acknowledgments borrowed from other sources and reproduced, with permission, in this textbook appear on appropriate page within text.

Acquisitions Editor: Anshul Sharma
Managing Editor: Sandra Schroeder
Project Editor: Charlotte Kughen
Cover Designer: Chuti Prasertsith
Cover Illustration: Givina/Shutterstock
Composition: Bronkella Publishing, LLC
Indexer: Johnna VanHoose Dinse
Proofreader: Rick Kughen
Graphics: tj graham art

Library of Congress Control Number: 2023945867

ISBN 10: 0-13-823237-7
ISBN 13: 978-0-13-823237-5

1 2023

Pearson

Pearson's Commitment to Diversity, Equity, and Inclusion

Pearson is dedicated to creating bias-free content that reflects the diversity of all learners. We embrace the many dimensions of diversity, including but not limited to race, ethnicity, gender, socioeconomic status, ability, age, sexual orientation, and religious or political beliefs.

Education is a powerful force for equity and change in our world. It has the potential to deliver opportunities that improve lives and enable economic mobility. As we work with authors to create content for every product and service, we acknowledge our responsibility to demonstrate inclusivity and incorporate diverse scholarship so that everyone can achieve their potential through learning. As the world's leading learning company, we have a duty to help drive change and live up to our purpose to help more people create a better life for themselves and to create a better world.

Our ambition is to purposefully contribute to a world where:

- Everyone has an equitable and lifelong opportunity to succeed through learning.
- Our educational products and services are inclusive and represent the rich diversity of learners.
- Our educational content accurately reflects the histories and experiences of the learners we serve.
- Our educational content prompts deeper discussions with learners and motivates them to expand their own learning (and worldview).

While we work hard to present unbiased content, we want to hear from you about any concerns or needs with this Pearson product so that we can investigate and address them.

Please contact us with concerns about any potential bias at https://www.pearson.com/report-bias.html.

Preface

Get Active with *Discovering AutoCAD® 2024*

Designed for introductory AutoCAD users, *Discovering AutoCAD 2024* offers a hands-on, activity-based approach to the use of AutoCAD as a drafting tool—complete with techniques, tips, shortcuts, and insights designed to increase efficiency. Topics and tasks are carefully grouped to lead students logically through the AutoCAD command set, with the level of difficulty increasing steadily as skills are acquired through experience and practice. Straightforward explanations focus on what is relevant to actual drawing procedures, and illustrations show exactly what to expect on the computer screen when steps are correctly completed. Each chapter ends with drawing exercises that assess and reinforce the student's understanding of the material.

Features

The book uses a consistent format for each chapter that includes the following:

- Chapter Objectives and Introduction
- Exercises that introduce new commands and techniques
- Exercise instructions clearly set off from the text discussion
- Lots of illustrations with drawings and screenshots
- Twenty end-of-chapter Review Questions
- Four to eight realistic engineering drawing problems—fully dimensioned working drawings

High-quality working drawings include a wide range of applications that focus on mechanical drawings but also include architectural, civil, plumbing, general, and electrical drawings. Appendix A contains 21 drawing projects for additional review and practice. Appendixes B, C, and D cover material not required for drawing practice but highly relevant for any beginning CAD professional. These include information on customization features, basic programming procedures, and a summary of Autodesk cloud-based and file-sharing features.

Acknowledgments

The authors thank the following reviewers for their feedback: John Irwin, Michigan Technological University; Tony Graham, North Carolina A&T State University; Beverly Jaeger, Northeastern University; Daniel McCall, Amarillo College; and Susan Freeman, Northeastern University. Lastly, we would like to thank Jon Page (and his family) for his time in reviewing the content changes made in this edition of the book.

From Lee Ambrosius: I would like to thank my family for being by my side throughout the many stages of my career and during the writing of this book. Along with my family, I would like to give special thanks to my instructors (Gary Magee, Kenneth Schulz, and Tricia Croyle) of the architectural program at Northeast Wisconsin Technical College (NWTC), where it all began. Without them, my career would likely be very different today.

Features New to This Edition

1. Updated to reflect the latest changes to AutoCAD with the 2024 release
2. Updated illustrations representing the newest AutoCAD interface
3. Coverage of the workflow of measuring objects in Chapter 6
4. New sections on counting and replacing blocks in Chapter 10
5. Expanded Appendix D with coverage of design review workflows

Style Conventions in *Discovering AutoCAD® 2024*

Text Element	Example
Key Terms—Boldface and italic on first mention (first letter lowercase, as it appears in the body of the text). Brief definition in margin alongside first mention. Full definition in Glossary available at peachpit.com/Discoverautocad2024.	Views are created by placing ***viewport*** objects in the paper space layout.
AutoCAD commands—Bold and uppercase.	Start the **LINE** command.
Ribbon and panel names, palette names, toolbar names, menu items, and dialog box names—Bold and follow capitalization convention in AutoCAD toolbar or pull-down menu. (Generally, the first letter is capitalized.)	The **Layer Properties Manager** palette
Panel tools, toolbar buttons, and dialog box controls/buttons/input items—Bold and follow the name of the item or the name shown in the AutoCAD tooltip.	Choose the **Line** tool from the **Draw** panel. Choose the **Symbols and Arrows** tab in the **Modify Dimension Style** dialog box. Choose the **New Layer** button in the **Layer Properties Manager** palette. In the **Lines and Arrows** tab, set the **Arrow size:** to **.125**.
AutoCAD prompts—Dynamic input prompts are set in a different font to distinguish them from the text. Command-line prompts are set to look like the text in the command line, including capitalization, brackets, and punctuation. Text following the prompt's colon specifies user input in bold.	*AutoCAD prompts you to specify first point:* `Specify center point for circle or [3P 2P Ttr (tan tan radius)]:` **3.5**
Keyboard Input—Bold with special keys in brackets.	Type **3.5 <Enter>**.

Download Instructor Resources from the Instructor Resource Center

Instructor materials are available from Pearson's Instructor Resource Center. Go to https://www.pearson.com/en-us/highered-educators.html to register or to sign in if you already have an account.

Contents

Appendix D and Glossary are available online at peachpit.com/Discoverautocad2024.

1 chapterone

Lines and Essential Tools

CHAPTER OBJECTIVES

- Get started and create a new drawing
- Explore the drawing window
- Interact with the drawing window
- Explore command entry methods
- Draw, undo, and erase lines
- Save and open drawings
- Get started

Introduction

Drawing in AutoCAD can be a fascinating and highly productive activity. AutoCAD 2024 is full of features you can use to become a very proficient design professional. The main goal here is to get you drawing as quickly and efficiently as possible. Discussion and explanation are limited to what is most useful and relevant at the moment but should also give you an understanding of the program to make you a more powerful user.

This chapter introduces some of the basic tools used when you draw in AutoCAD. You begin by finding your way around the AutoCAD 2024 interface as you learn to control basic elements of the drawing window. You then discover how to produce drawings involving straight lines, undo your last command with the **U** command, and erase individual lines with the **ERASE** command. You finish by saving your drawing, if you wish, using the **SAVE** and **SAVEAS** commands.

Getting Started and Creating a New Drawing

AutoCAD can be customized in many ways, so the exact look and sequence of what you see may be slightly different from what is shown here. It's assumed that you are working with the out-of-the-box settings, but steps are taken to ensure your application resembles the illustrations in this book, and you should have no trouble following the sequences presented here. First, you have to start AutoCAD.

✔ From the Windows desktop, double-click the AutoCAD 2024 icon to start AutoCAD.

If you don't see the icon on the desktop, click the Windows ***Start*** *menu and locate the AutoCAD 2024 folder and the AutoCAD 2024 icon from there.*

✔ Wait . . .

When you see the AutoCAD 2024 ***Start*** *tab and application window, as shown in Figure 1-1, you are ready to begin.*

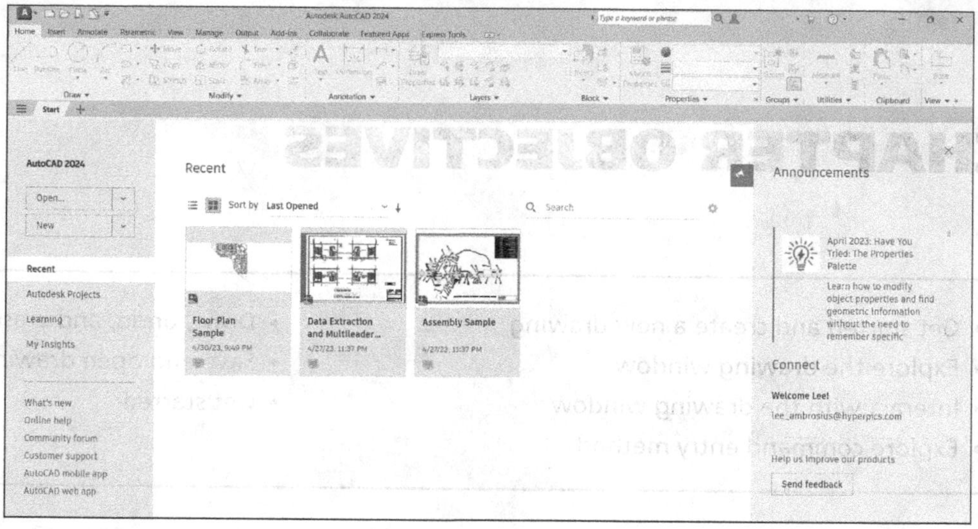

Figure 1-1
AutoCAD **Start** tab

The Start tab

The **Start** tab has a number of options for creating or opening a drawing. These include the use of various templates or opening recent drawings (also sometimes referred to as *documents*). The simplest method for creating a new drawing is to click the **New** button. This creates a new drawing using a default template.

> **TIP**
>
> Following is a general procedure for creating a new drawing:
>
> 1. Display the **Start** tab.
> 2. Choose the template you want from the **New** drop-down list or click the **New** button to use the most recent drawing template.

template: A drawing that contains previously defined settings.

dwt: The file extension given to AutoCAD drawing template files.

In AutoCAD, new drawings are typically created with some form of template. A ***template*** is a drawing that contains previously defined settings, layers, and styles based on established CAD standards. All templates are stored in a **Templates** folder and have a ***.dwt*** extension. The out-of-the-box default template is named **acad.dwt** for imperial drawings or **acadiso.dwt** for metric drawings. The exercises in this book utilize the **acad.dwt** template. To ensure that you use this same template, open the **New** drop-down list to the right of the **New** button.

✔ Using your mouse, move the cursor to the down arrow to the right of the **New** button, as shown in Figure 1-2.

When the cursor is over the down arrow of the ***New*** *drop-down list, the cursor changes from an arrow to a hand, as shown in the figure.*

✔ With the cursor over the down arrow, click the left button on your mouse.

This action opens a short list of templates, as shown in Figure 1-2. It is likely that acad.dwt will be in this list.

✔ Move the cursor down to **Browse Templates** and click the left mouse button.

✔ In the **Select Templates** dialog box, select **acad.dwt** and click **Open**.

This creates a new drawing using the acad.dwt template. Your application should resemble Figure 1-3.

Previously used templates are shown on the **New** drop-down list, so the next time you create a new drawing you can choose it from the list without needing to browse to the template. The most recently used template is also available by clicking the **New** button.

> **TIP**
>
> There are numerous ways to start a new drawing. In addition to using the **New** button, you can execute the **NEW** command by typing **<Ctrl>+N** or by clicking the **New** tool on the **Quick Access toolbar** at the top of the application window. Either of these methods opens the **Select template** dialog box. From here, you can select the template you want and then click **Open**.

Figure 1-2
New drop-down list

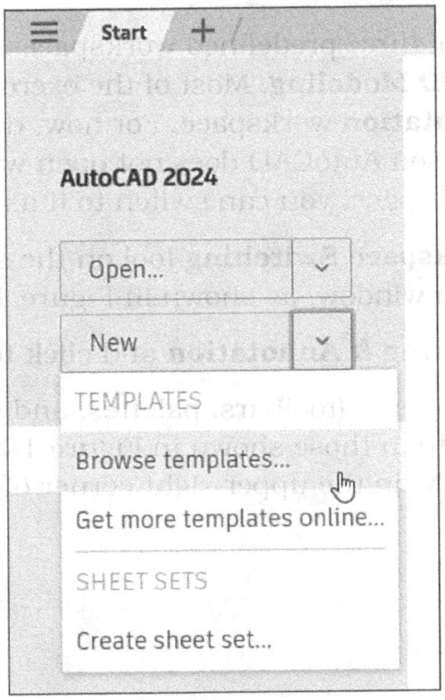

Figure 1-3
Drawing1 created with **acad.dwt**

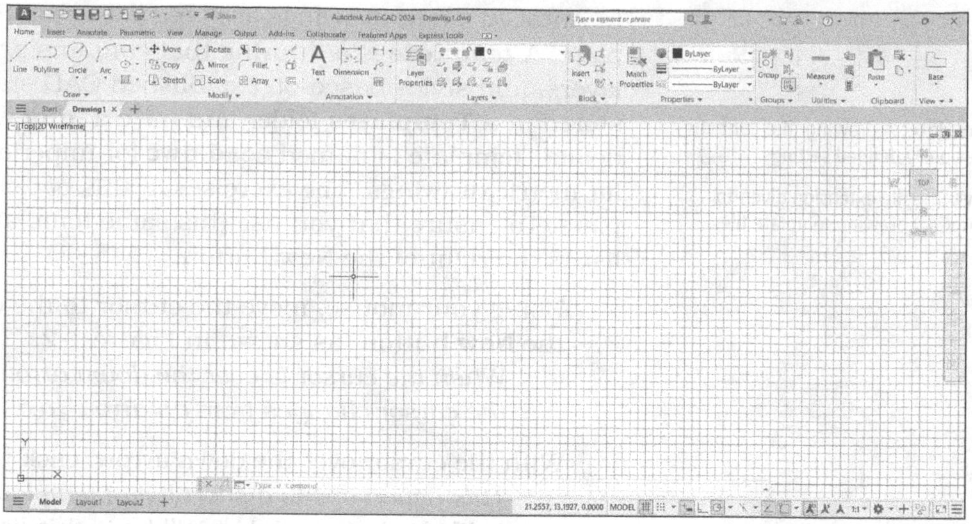

> **TIP**
>
> Along with creating new or opening drawings you recently worked on, the **Start** tab also contains access to the product documentation and community forums that can help you learn more about the product. Links in the lower left of the **Start** tab allow you to learn about new features in the release, access the product's online help, and visit the community forums where you can ask questions and get help from fellow users. The **Recent** tab, located below the **New** button on the left, provides access to not only recently opened drawings but also the **Announcements** panel, which contains notifications about a monthly article focused on different product features. Along with the **Announcement** panel, you can explore the **Learning** tab below the **Recent** tab. The **Learning** tab allows you to access a video library that demonstrates specific product workflows and features and additional learning resources.

Workspaces

workspace: An application setup with a set of toolbar, palettes, and ribbon tabs with panels grouped together to facilitate working on a particular type of drawing. Customized workspaces can be created.

AutoCAD may open with a variety of different appearances, including some settings that you can customize and define as part of a ***workspace***. With typical settings, the **Drafting & Annotation** workspace is current with a drawing that has a generic name such as *Drawing1*, as shown in Figure 1-3.

This is one of three predefined workspaces. The other two are named **3D Basics** and **3D Modeling**. Most of the exercises in this book utilize the **Drafting & Annotation** workspace. For now, do not change workspaces, but if for any reason AutoCAD does not open with the **Drafting & Annotation** workspace, you can switch to it as follows:

- Click the **Workspace Switching** tool on the status bar at the bottom of the application window, as shown in Figure 1-4.
- Highlight **Drafting & Annotation** and click to set the workspace current.
- If there are elements (toolbars, palettes, and so on) in your application window other than those shown in Figure 1-3, close them by clicking the **Close** button **(X)** in the upper-right corner of each unwanted element.

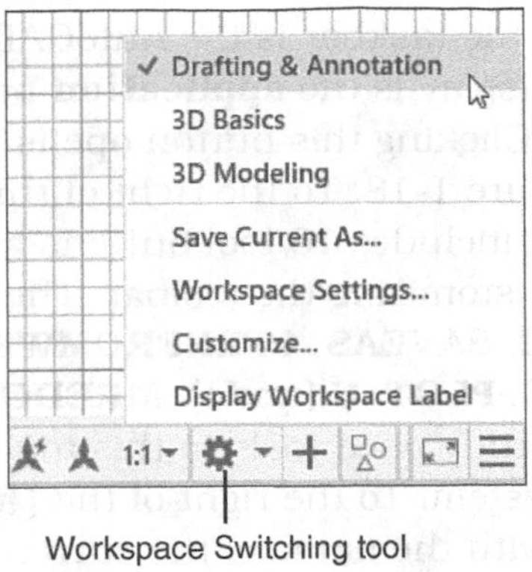

Figure 1-4
Workspace menu

Exploring the Application and Drawing Window

You should be looking at the AutoCAD 2024 application window with the **Drafting & Annotation** workspace current and a drawing based on the **acad.dwt** template. Elements of this workspace are labeled in Figure 1-5. In this section, you get an overview of the essential features of the user interface. If you have worked with other Windows-based applications, such as any of the Microsoft Office programs, you will find the interface familiar.

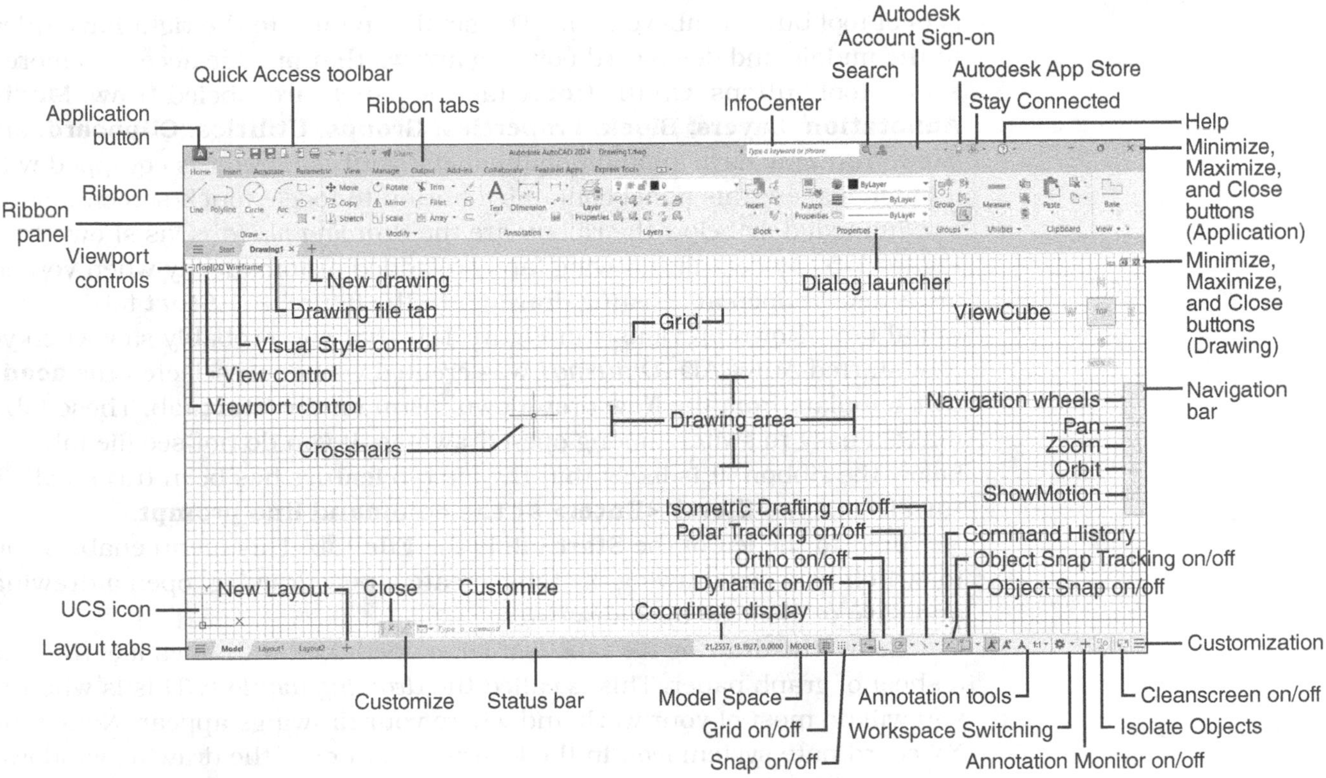

Figure 1-5
Elements of the Drafting & Annotation workspace

At the bottom of your display you see the Windows taskbar, with the **Start** button on the left and buttons for any open applications to the right of that. You should see a button with the AutoCAD icon here, indicating that you have an AutoCAD session running.

application menu: Menu that is opened by clicking the **A** button in the upper-left corner of the application window.

Everything above the taskbar is the AutoCAD application window. In the upper left of the display is the **application button**, which has an image of the AutoCAD icon. Clicking this button opens the ***application menu***, illustrated later in Figure 1-18. To the right of this is the ***Quick Access toolbar***. By default, it includes 10 tool buttons and an arrow that opens a menu of options for customizing the toolbar. The 10 buttons access the **QNEW**, **OPEN**, **QSAVE**, **SAVEAS**, **OPENFROMWEBMOBILE**, **SAVETOWEBMOBILE**, **PLOT**, **U (undo)**, **MREDO**, and **SHARE** commands. It is easy to add frequently used tools to this toolbar, so there may be additional tools on your system. To the right of the **Quick Access toolbar** is the application title bar, with the name of the current drawing. Farther to the right is an area called the **InfoCenter**. Here, you find a search box, an **Autodesk Account** sign-in box, a "cart" that opens the **Autodesk App Stores**, a triangular button that connects to the AutoCAD online community, and a **?** button that provides access to AutoCAD's Help features. Finally, to the right of that are the standard **Minimize**, **Maximize**, and **Close** buttons.

Quick Access toolbar: A standard set of tool buttons located on the title bar at the top of the application window, to the right of the application menu button.

ribbon: A set of tabs, panels, and tool buttons located below the title bar and above the drawing window. The ribbon gives access to many commands and features. Panels and tabs change depending on the workspace and current command.

Moving down, you find the AutoCAD ***ribbon***. The ribbon comprises tabs and panels. There are 11 tabs across the top of the ribbon: **Home**, **Insert**, **Annotate**, **Parametric**, **View**, **Manage**, **Output**, **Add-ins**, **Collaborate**, **Express Tools,** and **Featured Apps**. The **Home** tab, shown in Figure 1-5, has 10 panels. The larger panels to the left have a title at the bottom with sets of tool buttons above them. The smaller panels to the right have titles in the middle and downward pointing arrows that provide access to more sets of tool buttons. On the **Home** tab the panels are labeled **Draw**, **Modify**, **Annotation**, **Layers**, **Block**, **Properties**, **Groups**, **Utilities**, **Clipboard**, and **View**. You may have an additional panel if your computer is equipped with a touch screen; this panel contains a button to toggle touch screen mode.

Immediately below the ribbon are the *drawing file tabs*, as shown in Figure 1-5. By default, drawing tabs are added automatically when you create a new or open an existing drawing. In the figure, the ***Start*** tab is the initial tab, shown previously in Figure 1-1, that you probably saw when you first started AutoCAD. *Drawing1* was created when you selected the **acad.dwt** template from the **New** drop-down menu on the **Start** tab. These tabs make it easy to switch among open drawings. If you do not see file tabs below the ribbon, it is likely that the file tab feature has been turned off. To turn it on, type **filetab <Enter> at the command-line prompt**.

New to AutoCAD 2024

Just to the left of the **Start** tab is the **File** tab. This menu enables you to switch between drawing file tabs, create a new drawing, open a drawing, and save or close all open drawings.

Below the drawing file tabs is a large open area with lines like those on a sheet of graph paper. This is called the *drawing window*. This is where you will do most of your work and where your drawings appear. Notice the XY coordinate system icon in the lower-left corner of the drawing window. This is called the *UCS icon*. In the upper right of the window is a compass-like image called the *ViewCube*, and below this is a vertical strip of tools called the *navigation bar*.

status bar: A set of tool buttons located below the command line and above the Windows taskbar, beginning with the **Model** and **Layout** tabs on the left and ending with the **Customization** button on the right.

At the bottom of the drawing area are the *command line* and just below that the ***status bar***. Typed commands appear on the command line. Typed commands, introduced in the next section, are one of the basic ways of working in AutoCAD.

The status bar gives easy access to a number of critical functions. At the far left, you see the **Model** and **Layout** tabs. These are used to move between modeling procedures and presentation procedures. Using layouts, you can create many different presentations of the same drawing.

New to AutoCAD 2024

Just to the left of the **Model** tab is the **Layout** tab. This menu allows you to switch between layout tabs, create a new layout, manage page setups, select all layout tabs, and control whether the layout tabs are displayed in line with the status bar. If the drawings you work on contain many layouts, you might want to display the layout tabs above the status bar to make them easier to access.

On the right side of the status bar are 16 mode buttons. These are switches for turning on and off some extremely important features of the drawing window (**Model**, **Grid Mode**, **Snap Mode**, **Ortho Mode**, **Polar Tracking**, **Isometric Drafting**, **Object Snap Tracking**, **Object Snap**, three **Annotation buttons** and a list of scales, the **Workspace switching** button, **Annotation Monitor**, **Isolate Objects**, and **Clean Screen**). In addition to the mode buttons, you will find a button named **Customization**. The **Customization** button opens a menu of other mode buttons that may be added to the status bar. Where any of the mode buttons are accompanied by an arrow, clicking the arrow opens a menu with further options.

NOTE

You may also see palettes or toolbars in your drawing window. If so, close each of these by clicking the **X** in its upper-right or -left corner.

Interacting with the Drawing Window

There are many ways to communicate with the drawing window. In this section, you explore the mouse, crosshairs, arrow, and other simple features needed to begin using drawing commands.

The Mouse

Most interactions with the drawing window are communicated through your mouse. Given the graphic interfaces of AutoCAD, a typical two-button mouse is sufficient for most tasks. The exercises of this book assume you have a minimum of two buttons. If you have a digitizer or a more complex pointing device, the two-button functions will be present, along with other functions that are not covered in this book.

On a common two-button mouse, the left button is known as the *pick button*, and it is used to specify points, select objects, and click grips or interface elements. All mouse instructions in this chapter and book refer to the left button unless specifically stated otherwise. So, when you're prompted to specify a point, select an object or item from a list, or click, use the left mouse button.

The right button most often calls up shortcut menus, as in other Windows applications. These are also known as *context menus* because the menu that is displayed depends on what is happening when the right button is pressed. Learning how and when to use these menus can increase your efficiency. As you learn to use commands and interact with the drawing window, you take advantage of these shortcut menus. If you click the right button accidentally and open an unwanted shortcut menu, close it by left-clicking anywhere outside the menu. Your mouse may also have a scroll wheel between the left and right buttons. This wheel has a useful zooming and panning function in AutoCAD. For now, if you happen to roll the mouse wheel forward or backward, just roll it in the opposite direction to reverse the zooming action. Double-clicking the mouse wheel zooms to the extent of the objects in your drawing, while clicking and holding the mouse wheel allows you to pan in your drawing.

Crosshairs

The focus of action in AutoCAD is the crosshairs. This is the cross with a box at its intersection somewhere in the display area within the drawing window. If you do not see it, move your pointing device until it appears. At any time, the point where the two lines of the crosshairs intersect is the point that will be specified by clicking the left button on your mouse. Try it, as follows.

✔ Move the mouse and see how the crosshairs move in coordination with your hand movements.

✔ Move the mouse so that the crosshairs move to the top edge of the display.

When you leave the drawing area, your crosshairs are left behind and you see a standard selection arrow pointing up and to the left. As in other Windows applications, the arrow is used to click tools, tabs, and other user interface elements.

✔ Move the cursor back into the drawing area.

The selection arrow disappears, and the crosshairs move within the drawing area again.

The Coordinate Display and Dynamic Input

The coordinate display and the dynamic input button are not on the status bar by default, but you can easily add them using the **Customization** button at the right end of the status bar.

✔ Move the cursor over the **Customization** button, as shown in Figure 1-6, and click.

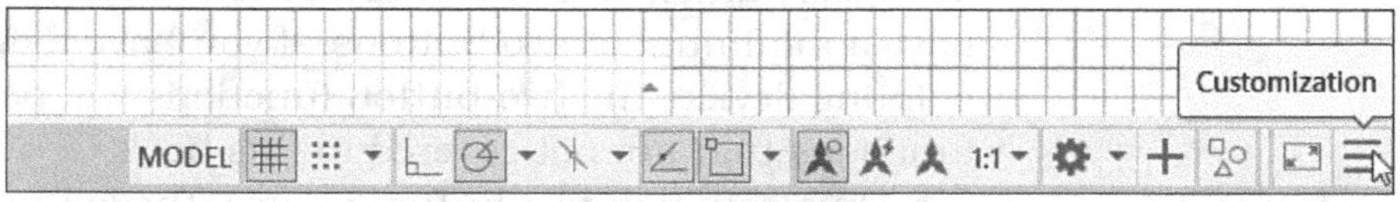

Figure 1-6
Customization button

This displays the ***Customization*** *menu shown in Figure 1-7.*

✔ Click **Coordinates** from the first line on the menu and **Dynamic Input** from the sixth line, as shown in Figure 1-7.

You will now see the coordinate display to the left of the set of status bar tools and the dynamic input button to the right of the **Grid Mode** and **Snap Mode** buttons. The coordinate display keeps track of drawing coordi-

Figure 1-7
Customization menu

Cartesian coordinate system: Based on the concept first described by René Descartes in 1637, a geometric system in which any point on a plane can be identified by values representing its distance from two mutually perpendicular axes.

nates as you move the mouse. AutoCAD uses the ***Cartesian coordinate system*** to identify points in the drawing area. In this system, points are identified by an *x* value, indicating a horizontal position from left to right across the drawing area, and a *y* value, indicating a vertical position from bottom to top on the drawing area. Notice the icon in the lower left of the drawing area. This is the *user coordinate system (UCS) icon*, showing the alignment of the *X*- and *Y*-axes. Typically, a point near the lower left of the drawing area is chosen as the origin, or 0 point, of the coordinate system. Its coordinates are (0,0). Points are specified by pairs of numbers, called *ordered pairs*, in which the horizontal *x* value is first, followed by the vertical *y* value. For example, the point (3,2) identifies a point 3 units over and 2 units up from the origin of the drawing. As you work in AutoCAD, you frequently need to specify or enter ordered pairs. There is also a *z* value in 3D Cartesian coordinates, which measures an imagined distance in front of or behind the 2D drawing area, but that is not used here. For now, the *z* value will always be 0 and can be ignored.

With this in mind, observe the coordinate display as you move the crosshairs.

✔ Move the crosshairs around slowly and keep an eye on the three numbers at the bottom left of the status bar: the coordinate display.

The first two should be moving very rapidly through four-place decimal numbers. When you stop moving, the numbers show coordinates for the location of the crosshairs. Notice the four-place x and y values, which change rapidly, and the z value, which is always 0.0000. Coordinates shown in this form, relative to a fixed coordinate grid, are called ***absolute coordinates****.*

absolute coordinates: Coordinate values given relative to the origin of a coordinate system, so that a point in two dimensions is identified by an *x* value, giving the horizontal distance from the point of origin of the coordinate system, and a *y* value, giving the vertical distance from the same point of origin.

✔ Slowly move the crosshairs horizontally and watch how the first value (*x*) changes and the second value (*y*) stays more or less the same.

✔ Move the crosshairs vertically and watch how the second value (*y*) changes and the first value (*x*) stays more or less the same.

The coordinate display has two different modes. You switch among them by left-clicking directly on the coordinate display.

✔ Move the crosshairs out of the drawing area and down to the **coordinate display** on the status bar.

The crosshairs will be replaced by the selection arrow.

✔ With the arrow over the **coordinate display**, click the left mouse button.

The numbers freeze, and the coordinate display turns gray.

✔ Move the arrow back into the drawing area and continue to move the crosshairs slowly.

Now, as you move the crosshairs you see that the coordinate display does not change. You also notice that it is still grayed out.

✔ Click anywhere near the middle of your drawing area.

Notice that the coordinate display updates to the specified point even though the numbers are grayed out. This is called static mode. In this mode, the coordinate display will change only when you specify a point by clicking in the drawing area. Previously, the coordinate display was in dynamic mode, in which the numbers updated constantly with the movement of the crosshairs.

dynamic input display: A display of coordinate values, lengths, angles, and prompts that moves with the crosshairs and changes with the action being taken. In addition, it also allows you to start commands and selection options, as you will learn a bit later.

You probably will see something else in the drawing area, as shown in Figure 1-8, called the ***dynamic input display****. It is a very powerful feature that in many ways duplicates the function of the coordinate display and command line. You learn about the command line a bit later. However, this display is easier to track because it follows your cursor and it shows linear distances as well as angular values. Also, there are times when it can be used effectively in conjunction with the coordinate display. Dynamic input can be turned on and off using the* ***Dynamic Input*** *button on the status bar.*

Figure 1-8
Dynamic input display

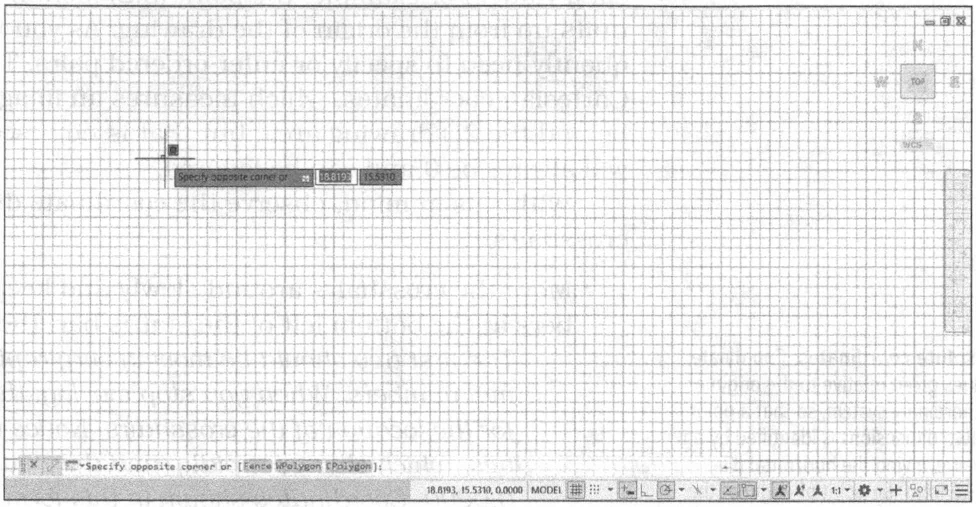

✔ Click the **Dynamic Input** button shown in Figure 1-9.

Figure 1-9
Dynamic Input button

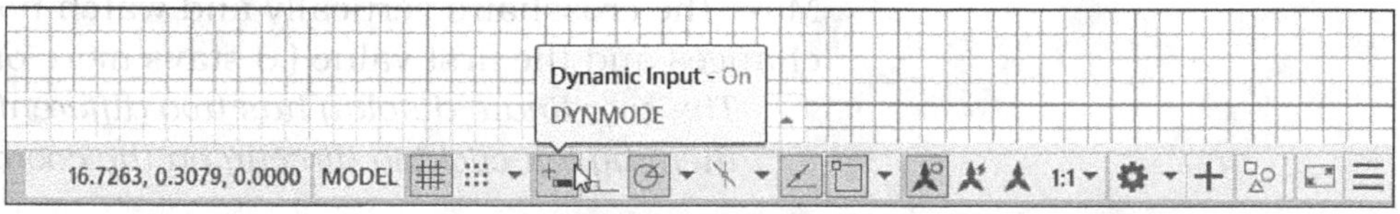

✔ Move your cursor back into the drawing area.

When dynamic input is off, the button appears in gray or white instead of blue. When off, the dynamic input numbers disappear.

✔ Click the **Dynamic Input** button again.

✔ Move the cursor back into the drawing area.

The button appears blue, and the dynamic input display reappears. Currently, the numbers in the dynamic display are x and y coordinates, just as in the coordinate display. The coordinate display on the status bar is static, whereas the dynamic display still moves through values when you move your crosshairs. In other words, the coordinate display indicates the coordinates of the last point you specified with your mouse, and the dynamic input display shows the value of any new point you specify by clicking in the drawing area.

- ✔ Move the crosshairs to another point in the drawing area.

  Something else is happening here that must be mentioned. AutoCAD creates a box in the drawing area, as shown in Figure 1-10. You are not drawing anything with this box. This is the ***object selection window****, used to select objects for editing. It has no effect right now because there are no objects in your drawing. You specify two points to define the window and then it vanishes because there is nothing there to select. Object selection is discussed briefly in the "Drawing, Undoing, and Erasing Lines" section.*

  AutoCAD prompts for the other corner of the selection window. You see the following in the command line and at the dynamic input display:

  ```
  Specify opposite corner or [Fence/WPolygon/CPolygon]:
  ```

object selection window: An area drawn between two points specified by opposite corners of a rectangle. Objects completely within the window are selected for editing.

- ✔ Specify a second point.

  This completes the object selection window and the window vanishes. Notice the change in the static coordinate display numbers.

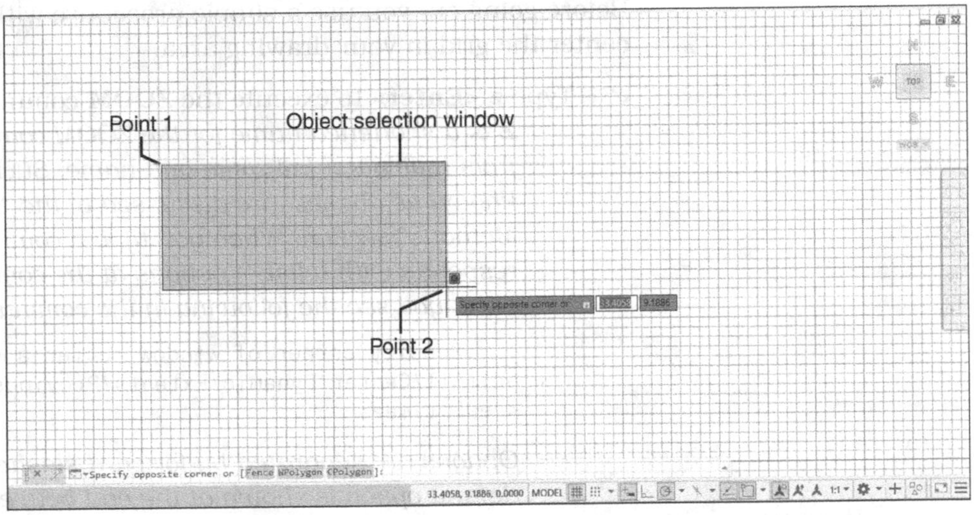

Figure 1-10
Object selection window

The Grid

AutoCAD uses a grid of lines like a sheet of graph paper as a visual aid. The grid shows a matrix of points in its Cartesian coordinate system.

- ✔ Click the **Grid Mode** button on the status bar, the button to the right of **MODEL**, as shown in Figure 1-11, or press **<F7>**.

  This turns off the grid. The grid helps you find your way around the drawing area. It does not appear in your drawing when it is plotted, and it can be turned on and off at will. You can also change the spacing between lines using the ***GRID*** *command. For now, you make one simple adjustment to center the grid in the drawing area.*

> **NOTE**
>
> "Plot" in AutoCAD is "print" in Microsoft Word. You learn to plot your drawing later in this chapter.

Figure 1-11
Grid Mode button

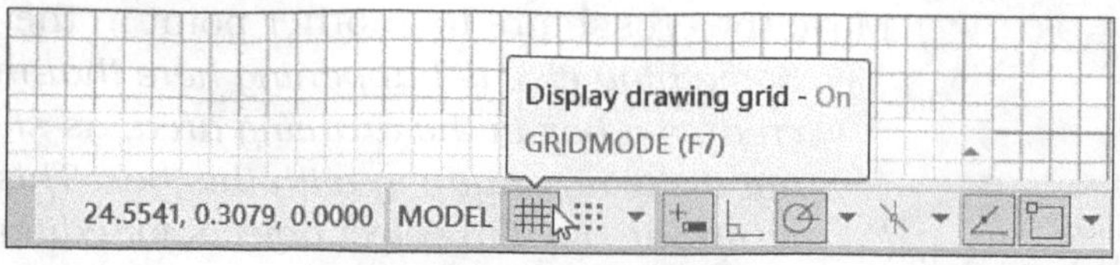

✔ Click the **Grid Mode** button again, or press **<F7>**.

*The grid reappears. With the acad.dwt template, the grid is set up to emulate the shape of an Architectural A-size (12 × 9-inch) sheet of drawing paper, with grid lines at 0.5000 increments. Slightly darker lines are shown at 2.50000 units. The AutoCAD command that controls the outer size and shape of the grid is **LIMITS**. However, by default the grid is set to display beyond the defined limits, so the grid covers the whole drawing area. For now, continue to use the current limits setting.*

Zooming to Center the Grid

Before going on, you use a simple procedure with the **ZOOM** command to center the grid in your drawing area.

✔ Type **z <Enter>** to execute the **ZOOM** command.

***Z** is a shortened name for the ZOOM command, and it saves your from typing the full command name. Such keyboard shortcuts, known as aliases, are discussed in the "Exploring Command Entry Methods" section. When you type a command or an alias, AutoCAD responds with a list of options at the command-line prompt. In this case, you see the following in the command line:*

```
    Specify corner of window, enter a scale factor (nX or nXP),
or [All/Center/Dynamic/Extents/Previous/Scale/Window/Object]
<real time>:
```

*Options are separated by forward slashes or spaces, and the default option is shown at the end between angle brackets. If you press **<Enter>** in response to the prompt, you execute the default option or accept the most recent value. Other options can be executed by typing a letter, indicated by the uppercase blue letter in the option. This is usually the first letter, but not always. Say you want to use the **All** option; you would type **a**. You could also choose an option by clicking it directly from the command line.*

✔ Type **a <Enter>** to zoom in and show the grid within the 12 × 9 limits.

Your grid should now be enlarged and centered in your drawing area, as illustrated in Figure 1-12. The grid is positioned so that the area within the drawing limits between (0,0) and (12,9), is centered in the drawing area. The X-axis is aligned with the bottom of the drawing area, and the origin of the coordinate system (0,0) is at the bottom of the drawing area. The upper limits of the drawing are at the point (12,9), so the top of the grid (where y = 12) is aligned with the top of the drawing area.

Model Space

As you look at the grid and consider its relation to an A-size drawing sheet, you should be aware that there is no need to scale AutoCAD drawings until you are ready to plot and that the size and shape of your grid will be determined by what you are drawing, not by the size of your drawing sheet. You will always draw at full scale, where one unit of length in the drawing area represents one unit of length in real space. This full-scale drawing space is called ***model space***. When plotted, the drawing will be scaled to fit the paper. This process is handled through the creation of a drawing layout in what is called ***paper space***. For now, all your work is done in model space.

model space: The full-scale drawing space, where one unit of length represents one unit of length in real space.

paper space: Use to represent objects in a drawing layout at the scale of the intended drawing sheet.

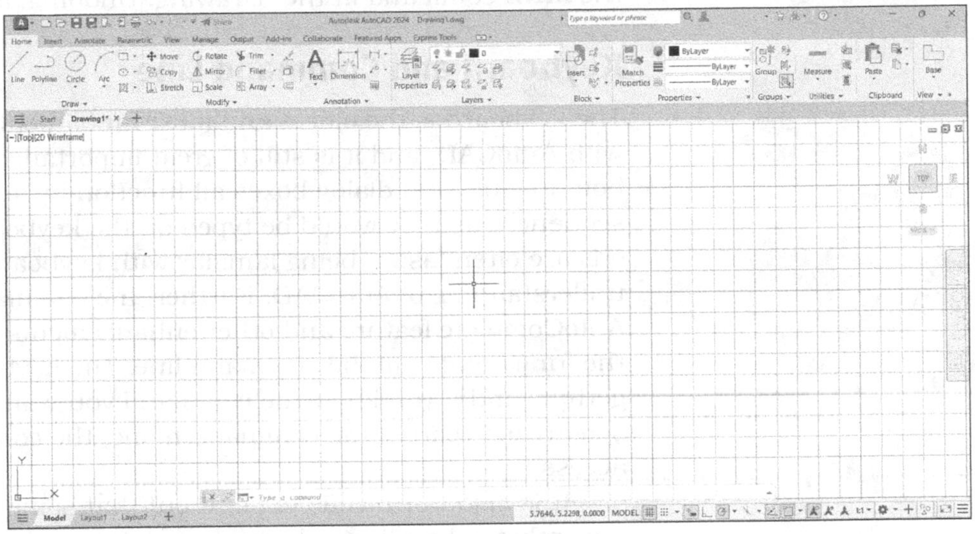

Figure 1-12
Grid enlarged and centered

Other Buttons on the Status Bar

The mode buttons (the 16 small images on the right side of the status bar) are used to turn powerful features on and off. However, some of the features can interfere with your learning and ability to control the cursor when turned on at the wrong time. For this reason, you should keep some features off until you need them. In this chapter, generally, the **Grid mode**, **Snap mode**, and **Dynamic input** buttons should be on, and all other buttons can be off.

Exploring Command Entry Methods

It is characteristic of AutoCAD that most tasks can be accomplished in a variety of ways. For example, you can enter commands by typing or by clicking a button from the ribbon, a shortcut menu, or a dialog box. Each method has its advantages and disadvantages, depending on the situation. Often, a combination of two or more methods is the most efficient way to carry out a complete command sequence. Once you get used to the range of options, you develop your own preferences.

Heads-Up Design

heads-up design: Interface designed to allow the user to remain focused in the main area of the application.

An important concept in the creation of AutoCAD command procedures is termed ***heads-up design***, meaning optimal efficiency is achieved when the CAD operator can keep their hand on the mouse and eyes focused in the drawing area. The less time spent looking away from the drawing area, the better. A major innovation supporting heads-up technique is the dynamic input display. Because this display moves with the cursor, it allows you to stay focused in your drawing area.

In the next section, you learn about each of the basic command and point entry methods. You do not have to try them all out at this time. Read them over to get a feel for the possibilities, and then proceed to exploring the **LINE** command in the "Drawing, Undoing, and Erasing Lines" section.

Keyboard and Command Line

The keyboard is the oldest and most fundamental method of interacting with AutoCAD, and it is still of great importance for all operators. The ribbon, menus, and dialog boxes all function by automating basic command sequences as they would be typed on the keyboard. Although other methods are often faster, being familiar with keyboard procedures increases your understanding of AutoCAD. Further, the command line has an AutoComplete feature and other enhancements that add considerably to the functionality of the command line. The keyboard is literally at your fingertips, and if you know the command you want to use, or even its alias synonym or part of the command name, the command line helps you access it.

It is also worthwhile to point out that some excellent CAD operators may rely too heavily on the keyboard. Do not limit yourself by typing everything. If you know the keyboard sequence, try the other methods to see how they vary and how they can save time and enable you to stay focused on the drawing area. Ultimately, you want to keep your hand on the mouse, type as little as possible, and use the various command entry methods to your advantage.

As you type commands and responses to prompts, the characters you are typing appear on the command line after the colon. If dynamic input is on, they may appear in the drawing area next to the crosshairs instead. Remember that you must press **<Enter>** to complete your commands and responses.

> **TIP**
>
> By pressing **<F2>** (or Fn + F2 on a laptop keyboard) you can expand the command line window to access your command history in the current drawing session. Press **<F2>** again to collapse the command line window and return to the drawing area. A text window can also be displayed instead of expanding the command line window by pressing **<Ctrl>** + **<F2>**. Pressing the Up and Down arrow keys allow you to access previously entered commands or input during the current session.

Many of the frequently used commands, such as **LINE**, **ERASE**, and **CIRCLE**, have aliases. These one- or two-letter shortened names are very handy. A few of the most commonly used aliases are shown in Figure 1-13.

There are also a large number of two- and three-letter aliases that you encounter when working with AutoCAD.

Command Line

The command line sits above the Model and Layout tabs, but can be moved anywhere in the drawing area. The command line also has the quality of ***transparency***, most noticeable when it is moved into the drawing area. Because it is transparent, it interferes only minimally with objects behind it.

When typing commands, the last few command line prompts and responses (by default, the last three) are displayed above the command line, as shown in Figure 1-14. These lines will disappear after a few seconds if no new action is taken. Later, you see that command options can be selected directly from the command line.

Transparency: Objects in AutoCAD have a property called transparency that can be adjusted on a scale from 0 to 90, where 0 is solid/opaque and 90 is extremely faint. Display of transparency can be turned on or off for a whole drawing using the **Transparency** mode button, which is available on the **Customization** menu from the status bar. Along with drawing objects, certain palettes, like the command line, can have a transparency effect applied.

Figure 1-13
Commonly used aliases

COMMAND ALIAS CHART		
LETTER + ENTER		= COMMAND
A	↵	ARC
C	↵	CIRCLE
E	↵	ERASE
F	↵	FILLET
L	↵	LINE
M	↵	MOVE
O	↵	OFFSET
P	↵	PAN
R	↵	REDRAW
S	↵	STRETCH
Z	↵	ZOOM

Figure 1-14
Transparent command line

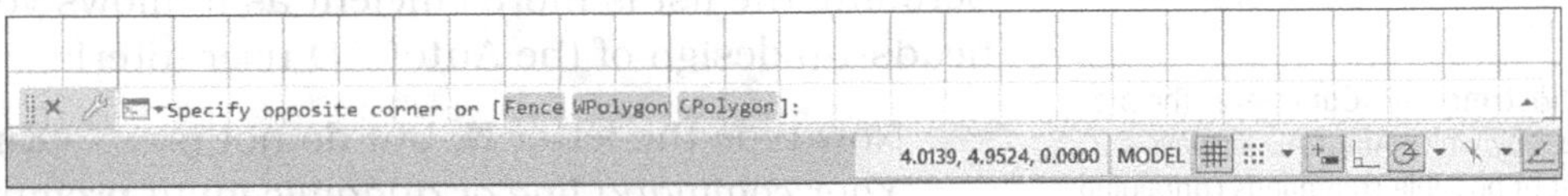

> **TIP**
>
> If you want to see more than the last three lines of command line prompts and responses, press **<F2>** or the up arrow at the right end of the command line. AutoCAD then displays your last 20 lines.

AutoComplete: The process by which AutoCAD displays a list of possible commands after the user has typed one or more letters when a command isn't active. This allows the user to select from the list without typing in the remaining letters to complete the command or system variable name.

AutoComplete and AutoCorrect

The command line also has ***AutoComplete*** and ***AutoCorrect*** features. When these features are turned on, as they are by default, a box with a list of command and system variable choices appears next to the command-line prompt or the dynamic input display as you type when no command is active. Try this:

✔ Type the letter **L,** but do not press **<Enter>**.

You will see a list of possibilities that begin with the letter L, *as shown in Figure 1-15.*

Figure 1-15
AutoComplete

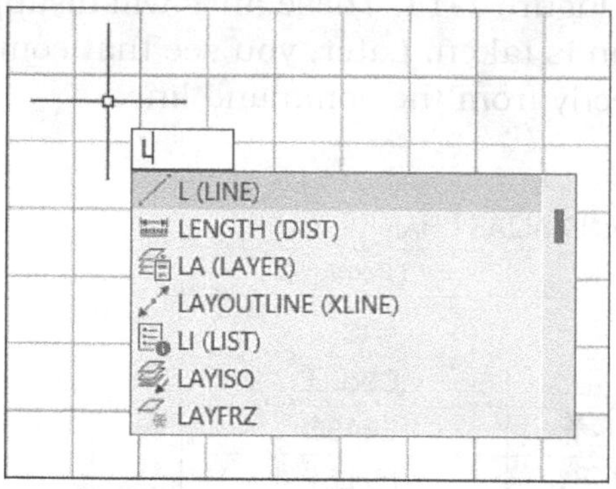

AutoCorrect: The process by which AutoCAD displays a list of possible commands based on the characters entered at the command line after the user has entered only the first few letters, even though there might be no command with the sequence of characters typed. This allows the user to select the correct command from the list without retyping the entry.

Midstring AutoComplete: The process by which AutoCAD displays a list of possible commands containing the characters entered at the command line, including options where the characters do not appear at the beginning of the name.

When AutoCAD presents such a list, you may continue typing to narrow down the list of options, or scroll down the list and select the name of a command or system variable. The suggestions are most useful when you are searching for an obscure command or system variable, when you are uncertain of the name or spelling, or it has a very long name that is inefficient to type. Consider, for example, the system variable **LAYLOCKFADECTL**, you could type its name or select it from the list. Scrolling the list is more efficient as it allows you to take advantage of the heads-up design of the AutoCAD user interface.

✔ Now type the letter **N**, but do not press **<Enter>**.

Your command line or dynamic input prompt should now read ***LN****, and the suggestion box is similar to Figure 1-16. This demonstrates the* ***AutoCorrect*** *feature. There is no AutoCAD command that begins with LN, but instead of replying with Unknown Command, AutoCAD returns a list of possibilities containing these letters. This list is initially based on the profile of an average user, but over time would remember your most frequently executed commands and put these at the top of the list.*

Figure 1-16
AutoCorrect

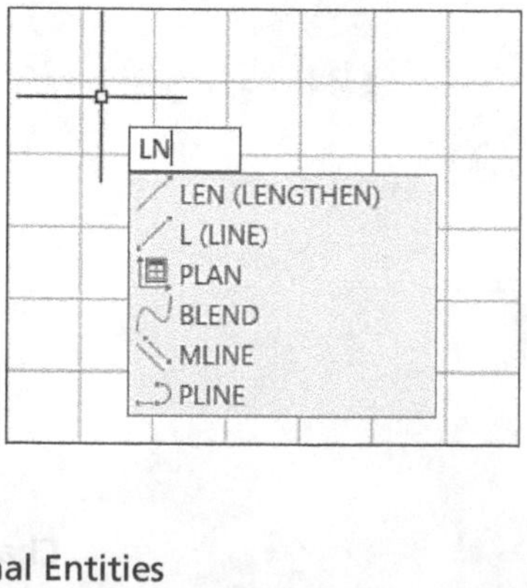

✔ Press the backspace button to remove the letter *N*.

✔ Now add the letters **I** and **N**, so that your command line or dynamic input prompt reads **LIN.**

A suggestion list similar to the one in Figure 1-17 is returned. Notice that an ***E*** *is automatically added. This is an example of the* ***AutoComplete*** *feature. In the suggestion list, you will also see suggestions such as PLINE and LINEFADING. These are examples of* ***Midstring AutoComplete****. Through this feature, AutoCAD returns not only commands and system variable names in which the letters being typed appear at the beginning but also those in which the letters may occur in the middle or at the end.*

Figure 1-17
Midstring AutoComplete

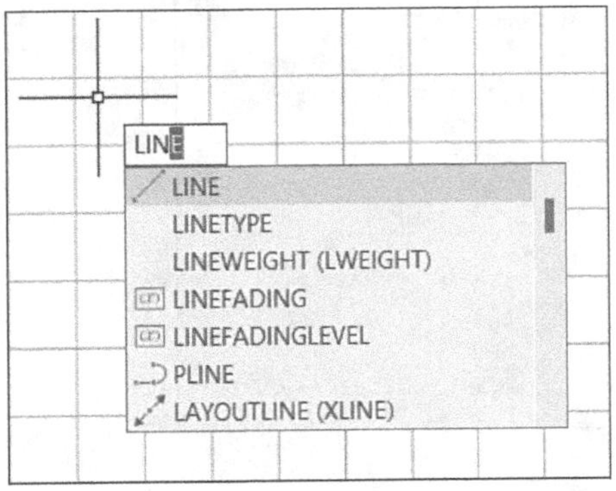

The command line has other features, as well that you learn about as you go along.

The Application Menu

The ribbon, Quick Access toolbar, and shortcut menus offer a great advantage compared to typing commands. You can simply click to select an item without looking away from the display. The application menu provides access to commands for opening, saving, and preparing drawings for plotting and publishing, along with the capability of searching for commands and browsing recently opened drawings:

✔ To open the application menu, click the **A** in the upper-left corner of the application window.

The menu opens, as shown in Figure 1-18. At the left is a list of commands related to drawing preparation. When you hover the cursor over any of the items that have an arrow next to it, a submenu of related commands appears to the right. The application menu also has a search box at the top, for locating commands, and a list of ***Recent Documents*** *or* ***Open Documents*** *at the right.*

NOTE

When entering commands, command aliases, keyboard shortcuts, or command options, uppercase and lowercase letters are equivalent.

Chapter 1

Figure 1-18
Application menu

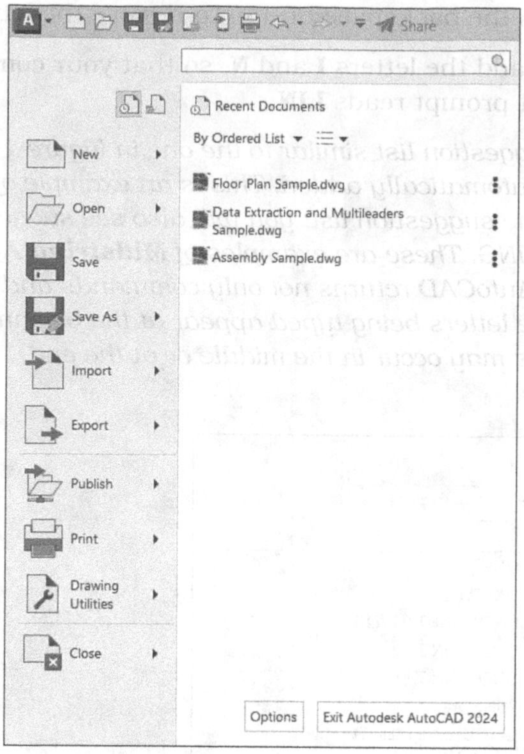

The Ribbon

A large number of commands are on the ribbon. The combination of tabs and panels gives quick access to a large number of commands without cluttering the application and obstructing the drawing area. The many drop-down menus on the ribbon allow access to even more tools. The **Home** tab of the ribbon, which is open by default, contains most of the commands you need in the beginning.

The ribbon contains a convenient **Minimize** button to the right of the row of tabs. Click the up arrow of the **Minimize** button once to collapse the ribbon to show just images for the set of panels on the current tab. When you position your cursor on an image, the tools for that panel appear. Click the up arrow again, and the ribbon collapses further to show just panel labels. Click it a third time, and the panel labels disappear, leaving only the names of the tabs. On the fourth click, the ribbon returns to normal. The advantage of this feature is that it allows you to increase the size of the drawing area. The down arrow to the right of the **Minimize** button opens a drop-down menu showing these same four options.

Tooltips

The buttons, also known as *tools,* are used to represent commands and are a mixed blessing. One picture may be worth a thousand words, but with so many pictures, you may find that a few words can be very helpful as well. As in other Windows applications, you can get information about a tool or command by allowing the cursor arrow to hover over it on the ribbon for a

tooltip: A popup window that opens automatically when the cursor rests over a tool button. Basic tooltips provide a label and a general description. Extended tooltips provide more information and an illustration.

moment without clicking it. These popup windows are called ***tooltips***. There are two levels of information provided by tooltips. Basic tooltips provide the name of the command with a general description. Extended tooltips provide additional information and often include a graphic illustration. Some tools have only basic tooltips.

Try the following:

✔ Position the cursor over the **Line** tool at the left end of the **Draw** panel on the ribbon, as shown in Figure 1-19, but do not click the button.

First, you see a small information window, as shown in Figure 1-20. This is the basic tooltip for the ***LINE*** *command. If you let your cursor hover over the tool longer, you see the extended tooltip shown in Figure 1-21. Once you have practiced with the basic and extended tooltips, it's time to get started drawing!*

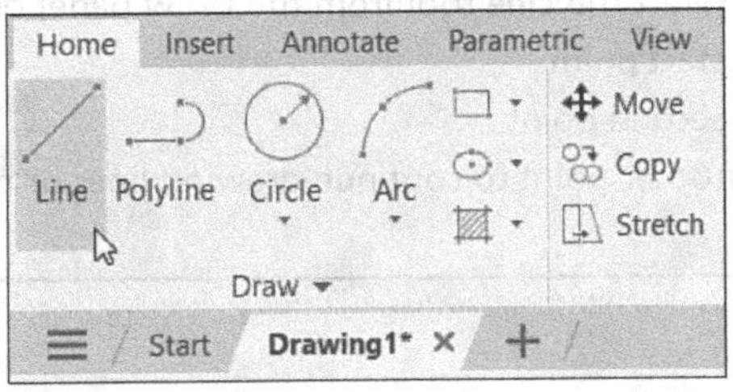

Figure 1-19
Line tool

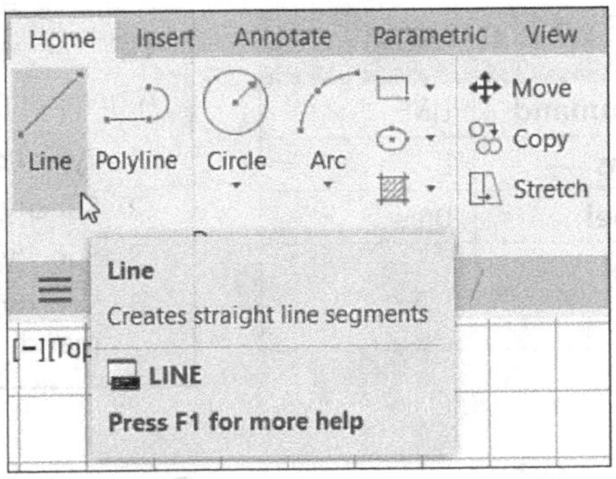

Figure 1-20
Basic tooltip

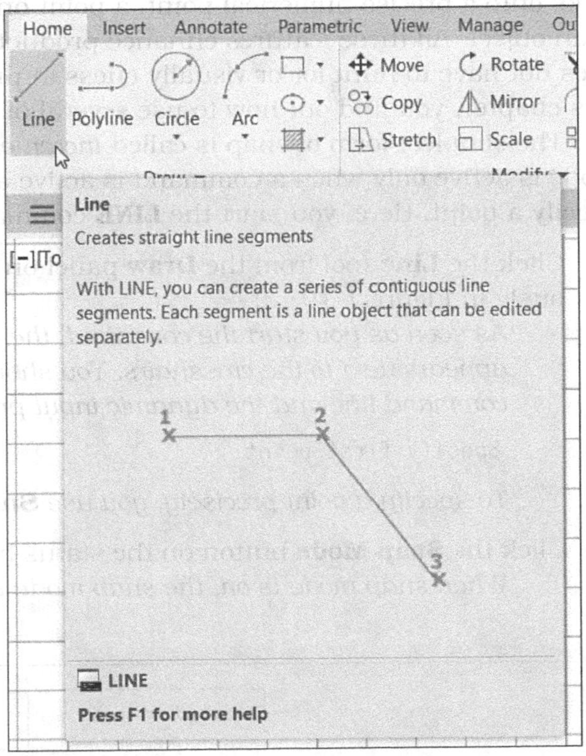

Figure 1-21
Extended tooltip

> **TIP**
>
> If you find the display of tooltips too frequent and distracting, you can increase the time in which basic and extended tooltips are displayed. This is done in the **Options** dialog box with the **OPTIONS** command. Type the command alias **OP <Enter>** to display the dialog box, then click the **Display** tab. Edit boxes for changing the delay time on basic and extended tooltips are under **Show ToolTips** on the left. The default is a 1 second delay for basic tooltips and 2.00 seconds for extended tooltips.

Drawing, Undoing, and Erasing Lines

Drawing lines is a simple matter of starting the **LINE** command and then specifying two or more points. To specify points precisely, you start with **Snap** mode enabled, one of several essential drafting aids.

LINE	
Command	LINE
Alias	L
Panel	Draw
Tool	

> **TIP**
>
> A general procedure for using the **LINE** command is as follows:
>
> 1. Type **l** or select the **Line** tool from the **Draw** panel on the **Home** tab of the ribbon.
> 2. Specify a start point.
> 3. Specify a second point.
> 4. Specify another point to continue drawing lines or press **<Enter>** to exit the command.

Snap

snap: One of a number of several drafting aids that facilitate accurate drawing technique by allowing the software to extrapolate a precise geometric point from an approximate location of the crosshairs.

Snap is an important concept in CAD programs. There are several AutoCAD features through which an approximate location of the crosshairs locks onto a precise numerical point, a point on an object, or the extension of an object. All these features enhance productivity in that the operator does not have to hunt for or visually guess at precise point locations. In this chapter, you find out how to use several of these related techniques.

The simplest form of snap is called *incremental snap* or *grid snap*. **Snap** mode is active only when a command is active and you are prompted to specify a point. Here, you start the **LINE** command.

✔ Click the **Line** tool from the **Draw** panel on the ribbon, as shown previously in Figure 1-19.

As soon as you start the command, the dynamic input prompt appears next to the crosshairs. You should see the following in the command line and the dynamic input prompt:

```
Specify first point:
```

To specify a point precisely, you use ***Snap*** *mode.*

✔ Click the **Snap Mode** button on the status bar, as shown in Figure 1-22.

When snap mode is on, the snap mode button turns blue.

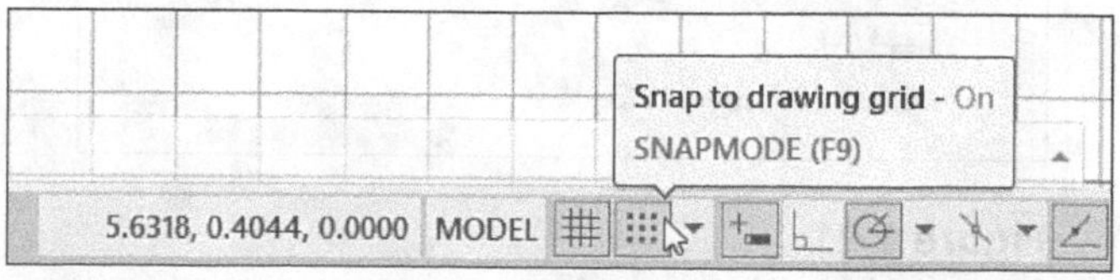

Figure 1-22
Snap Mode button on the status bar

Chapter 1

✔ Move the crosshairs slowly around the drawing area.

Watch closely, and you will see that the crosshairs jump from grid line to grid line. With your grid on, notice that is impossible to make the crosshairs touch a point that is not on the grid. Try it.

✔ If your **coordinate display** is in static mode, click it to switch to dynamic mode.

✔ Move the cursor and watch the coordinate display.

Notice that the coordinate display shows only values ending in .0000 or .5000.

✔ Click the **Snap Mode** button again to turn snap off.

*Snap should now be off, and the **Snap Mode** button is gray.*

If you move the cursor in a circle now, the crosshairs move smoothly without jumping. You also should observe that the coordinate display moves rapidly through a full range of four-place decimal values again.

*With snap off, you can move freely in the drawing area. With snap on, you can move only in predetermined increments. With the acad.dwt template's default settings, snap is set to a value of .5000 so that you can move only in half-unit increments. Later in this chapter, you change this setting using the **SNAP** command. For now, leave the snap settings alone.*

Using an appropriate snap increment is a tremendous time-saver. It also allows for a degree of accuracy that is not possible otherwise. If all the dimensions in a drawing fall into 1-unit increments, for example, there is no reason to deal with points that are not on a 1-unit grid. You can find the points you want much more quickly and accurately if all those in between are temporarily eliminated. The snap setting allows you to do that.

TIP

Incremental snap is more than a convenience. In many cases, it is a necessity. With snap off, it is virtually impossible to locate any point precisely with the mouse. For example, if you try to locate the point (6.5000,6.5000,0.0000) with snap off, you might get close, but the probability is very small that you will actually be able to specify that exact point. Try it.

✔ Click the **Snap Mode** button again to turn it on.

NOTE

Make sure that the mode buttons on your status bar resemble those shown in Figure 1-23. In particular, note that the **Grid Mode**, **Snap Mode**, and **Dynamic Input** buttons are switched on (blue) and that the **Ortho Mode, Polar Tracking, Isometric Tracking, Object Snap Tracking**, and **Object Snap** buttons are all switched off (gray). This keeps things simple and uncluttered for now, which is very important. The remaining buttons will not affect you at this time and may be on or off.

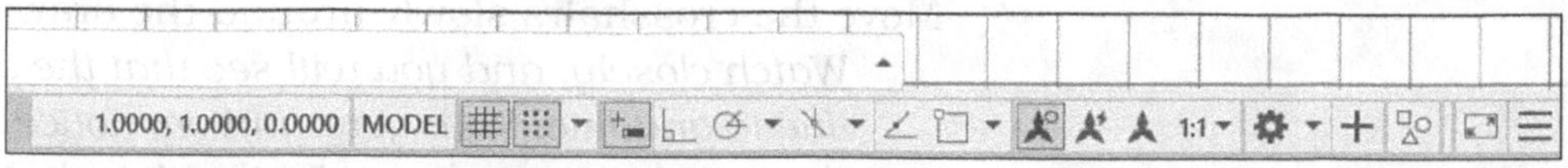

Figure 1-23
Blue color indicates a mode button is on

✔ Move your crosshairs to the point **(1.0000,1.0000)** and click the left mouse button.

AutoCAD registers your point specified and responds with another prompt:

```
Specify next point or [Undo]:
```

*You are now prompted to specify a second point. You learn about the **Undo** option later in this chapter.*

Rubber Band

✔ Move your cursor up toward the center of your drawing area and let it rest, but do not click to specify a point.

There are several other things to be aware of here. The dynamic input display has become much more complex. With typical settings, there will be three new features shown in the drawing area. There is a solid line called the rubber band, stretching from the first point to the new point. There is a linear dimension with a dotted line parallel to and above the rubber band. And there is an angular dimension between the line and the X-axis, as illustrated in Figure 1-24. As you move the cursor, notice that the rubber band stretches, shrinks, or rotates like a tether, keeping you connected to the starting point of the line. Rubber bands have various functions in AutoCAD commands. In this case, the rubber band represents the line you are drawing.

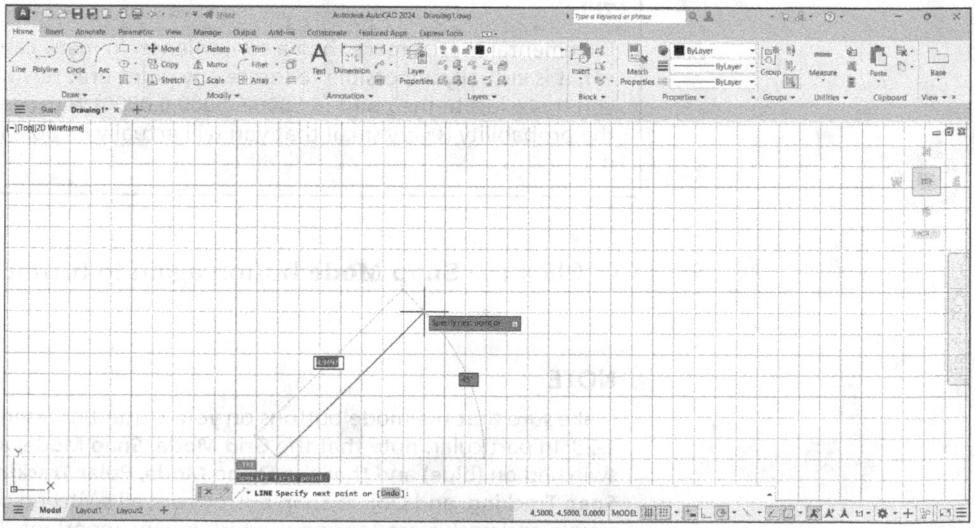

Figure 1-24
Rubber band

Polar Coordinates

polar coordinates: Coordinates that identify a point by giving a distance and an angle from a previous point.

The two dimensions in the dynamic input display show a visual display of ***polar coordinates***. Polar coordinates are given as a linear distance and an angle relative to a starting point. In this case, you see the length of the line you are drawing and its angle from the x-axis straight out to the right.

Working with Absolute and Polar Coordinates

The presence of the coordinate display with the dynamic input display allows you to use absolute (*x, y, z*) coordinates and polar coordinates simultaneously. Try this:

✔ If necessary, click the **coordinate display** until you see dynamic absolute coordinates.

With dynamic absolute coordinates showing, you can use the coordinate display to specify a point in your drawing while the dynamic input display continues to show the polar coordinates of the line you are drawing.

✔ Move the cursor to the point with absolute coordinates **(8.0000,8.0000,0.0000)**.

Notice that the dynamic input display shows that this line is 9.8995 units long and makes a 45° angle with the horizon.

✔ Specify the point **(8.0000,8.0000,0.0000)**.

Your drawing should now resemble Figure 1-25. AutoCAD has drawn a line between (1,1) and (8,8) and is asking for another point:

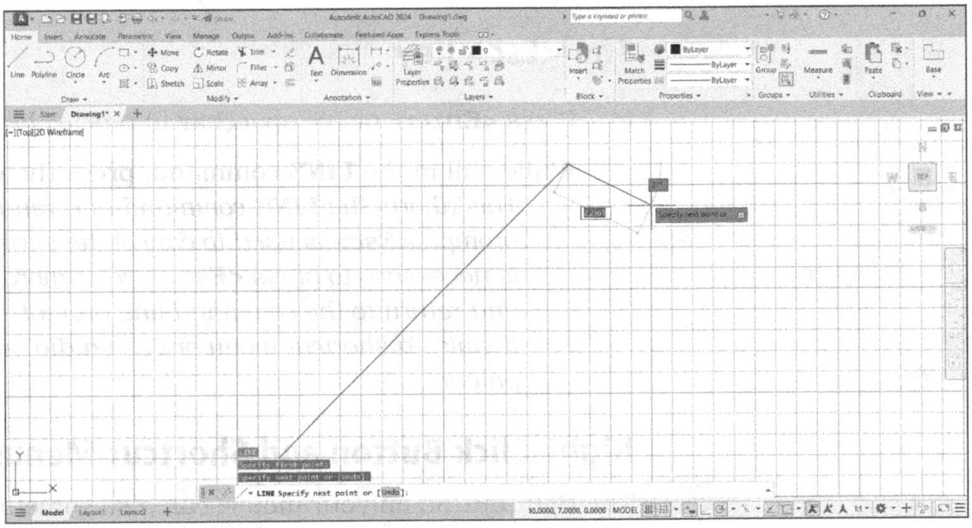

Figure 1-25
Absolute and polar coordinates

```
Specify next point or [eXit/Undo]:
```

*The repetition of this prompt allows you to stay in the **LINE** command to draw a whole series of connected lines if you want. You can draw a single line from point to point, or a series of lines from point to point to point. In either case, you end the command by pressing **<Enter>** or the spacebar.*

NOTE

When you are drawing a continuous series of lines, the polar coordinates on the dynamic input display are given relative to the most recent point, not the original starting point.

✔ Press **<Enter>** or the spacebar to end the **LINE** command.

You should be back to the command-line prompt again, and the dynamic input display disappears.

Spacebar and <Enter> Key

In most cases, AutoCAD allows you to use the spacebar as a substitute for the **<Enter>** key. Although this is one of the oldest AutoCAD features, it is a major contributor to the goal of heads-up drawing. It is a great convenience, because the spacebar is easy to locate with one hand (your left hand if the mouse is on the right side) while the other hand is on the mouse, and your eyes are on the drawing area. The major exception to the use of the spacebar as an **<Enter>** key is when entering text in your drawing. Because a space can be part of a text string, the spacebar must have its usual significance within commands that prompt for text and some dimension commands.

TIP

Another great convenience provided by the spacebar and <Enter> key is that pressing either one at the command-line prompt causes the last command used to be repeated.

The <Esc> Key

✔ Press **<Enter>** or the spacebar to repeat the **LINE** command.

✔ While still in the **LINE** command, press the **<Esc>** (escape) key.

*This aborts the **LINE** command and returns you to the command-line prompt. **<Esc>** is used to cancel the current command. Sometimes it is necessary to press **<Esc>** two or more times to exit a command and return to the command-line prompt. You can also press **<Esc>** to dismiss a shortcut menu or even a dialog box, but not a modeless palette.*

Right-Click Button and Shortcut Menus

The right button on your mouse can also sometimes be used in place of the **<Enter>** key, but in most cases, there will be an intervening step involving a shortcut menu with options. This, too, is a major heads-up feature, which you explore as you go along. For now, the following steps give you an introduction to shortcut menus:

✔ Press the right button on your mouse. (This action is called *right-clicking* from now on.)

*This opens a shortcut menu, as shown in Figure 1-26. The top line is a **Repeat LINE** option that can be used to repeat the **LINE** command. (Remember, you can also do this by pressing the **<Enter>** key* *or spacebar at the command-line prompt.) You have no use for the other options on this shortcut menu for now.*

✔ Specify any point outside the shortcut menu.
The shortcut menu disappears, but AutoCAD takes the specified point as the first point in an object selection window.

✔ Specify any second point to define the object selection window.
In other words, you have to click twice outside the shortcut menu to close it and abort the selection window.

> **TIP**
>
> You can press the **<Esc>** key to dismiss a displayed shortcut menu or cancel the current command.

There are many context-sensitive shortcut menus in AutoCAD. They're not all covered in this book, but explore the ones you encounter along the way. You will find many options and settings simply by right-clicking while in a command or dialog box.

Figure 1-26
Shortcut menu

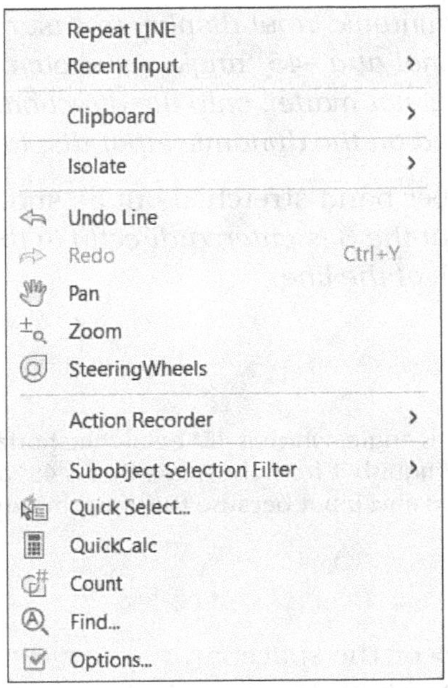

Relative Coordinates and @

relative coordinates: Coordinates given relative to a previously entered point, rather than to the axes of origin of a coordinate system.

Besides typing or specifying points directly in the drawing area, AutoCAD allows you to enter points by typing coordinates relative to the last point. To do this, use the @ symbol and ***relative coordinates***. For example, after specifying the point (1,1) in the previous exercise, you could have specified the point (8,8) by typing **@7,7**, as the second point, which is over 7 units and up 7 units from the first point.

Direct Distance Entry

Values can be entered directly into the dynamic input display. For example, you can specify the first point of a line in the drawing area and then indicate or type the direction of the line segment you want to draw, but instead of specifying the other endpoint in the drawing area, you can type in a value for the length of the line. Try this:

✔ Repeat the **LINE** command by pressing **<Enter>** or the spacebar.

AutoCAD prompts for a first point.

> **TIP**
>
> If you press **<Enter>** or the spacebar at the *Specify first point:* prompt, AutoCAD uses the last point specified, so that you can begin drawing from where you left off.

✔ Press **<Enter>** or the spacebar again to select the point **(8,8,0)**, the endpoint of the previously drawn line.

You are prompted for a second point.

✔ Drag the crosshairs diagonally down to the right at a –45° angle, as shown in Figure 1-27.

Use the dynamic input display to ensure that you are moving along the diagonal at a –45° angle, as shown. The length of the rubber band does not matter, only the direction. Notice that the length is highlighted on the dynamic input display.

✔ With the rubber band stretched out as shown, type **3**.

Notice that the 3 is entered directly in the dynamic input display as the length of the line.

> **NOTE**
>
> In many contexts, this angle, which is 45° below the horizon, must be identified as negative 45° (–45) to distinguish it from the angle that is 45° above the horizon. This convention is ignored in dynamic input because the visual information removes any ambiguity.

✔ Press **<Enter>** or the spacebar.

A 3.0000-unit line segment is drawn at the angle you have specified. You can also use this method to input an angle. Try this:

✔ With the length highlighted in the dynamic input display, type **2**, but do not press **<Enter>**.

*Pressing **<Enter>** would complete the line segment at whatever angle is showing, as you did in the last step. To move from the length value to the angle value in the dynamic input display, use the **<Tab>** key on your keyboard before pressing **<Enter>**.*

Figure 1-27
Direct distance entry

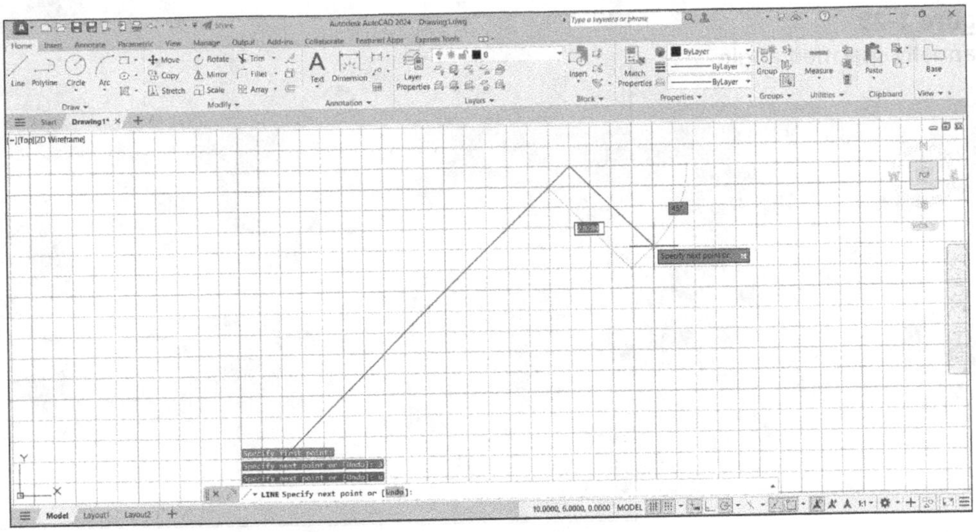

✔ Press the **<Tab>** key once.

The value 2.0000 is locked in as the length, as shown in Figure 1-28. A lock icon is added to the length display, and the rubber band no longer stretches (although it can still be rotated). Now you can manually specify an angle.

Figure 1-28
Length locked at 2.0000

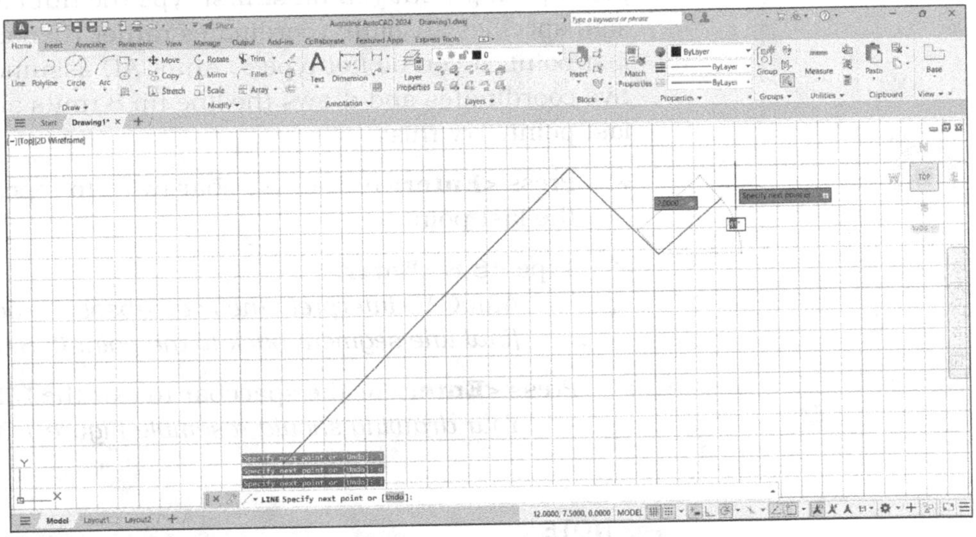

> **NOTE**
>
> Because you are now entering numbers rather than indicating an angle in the drawing area, there is room for ambiguity. If you place the rubber band above the previous point, AutoCAD draws the segment along the positive 45° angle. If you place the rubber band below the previous point, it draws with a negative angle. You can also force a negative angle by typing **–45**.

✔ Place the rubber band above the horizontal.

✔ Type **45 <Enter>**.

✔ Press **<Enter>** or the spacebar to exit the **LINE** command.

Your drawing should resemble Figure 1-29.

Figure 1-29
Manually specified angle

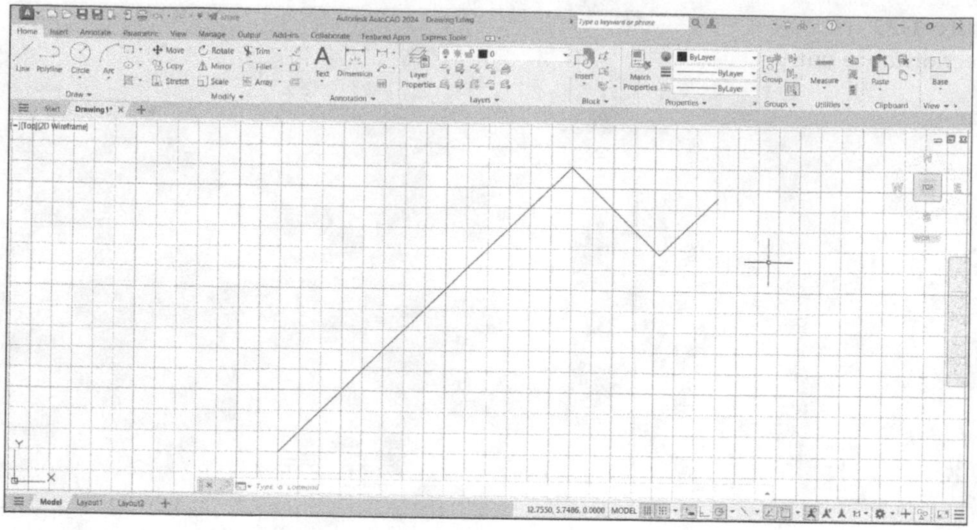

Absolute Coordinates and

Now, suppose that you want to draw a line back to the point (8,8). You could easily do this using **Snap mode** because that point is on a snap point, but you are not restricted to this method. It is important to know that you can also type the absolute coordinates (8,8) at the *Specify second point:* prompt, but you must first type the number or pound **(#)** sign. The # sign specifies absolute coordinates rather than coordinates relative to the last point. If you do not type #, AutoCAD assumes you are specifying relative coordinates and draws the line up 8 units and over 8 units from the last point. Try this:

✔ Press **<Enter>** or the spacebar twice to repeat **LINE** and reconnect to the last point.

✔ Type **#8,8 <Enter>**.
AutoCAD interprets these as absolute coordinates and draws the final line segment back to the point (8,8,0).

✔ Press **<Enter>** or the spacebar to exit the **LINE** command.
Your drawing should resemble Figure 1-30.

NOTE

You use the # sign when entering absolute coordinate values at the dynamic input display. If dynamic input display is off, or you enter an absolute coordinate value at the command line. then you don't need to prefix the absolute coordinate value with the # sign.

Undoing Commands with U

As you create or modify objects, the results might not be as expected. You might create an object with the wrong coordinates or options when creating an object, or you might end up erasing the wrong objects. The **U** command allows you to undo the most recent command.

✔ To undo the line segment you just drew, type **U <Enter>** or click the **Undo** tool on the **Quick Access** toolbar, as shown in Figure 1-31.

U undoes the last command, so if you have done anything else since drawing the line, you need to use the ***U*** *command more than once. This enables you to walk backward through your drawing session, undoing your commands one by one. As mentioned previously, you can use an* ***Undo*** *option within the* ***LINE*** *command to undo the last segment drawn without leaving the command.*

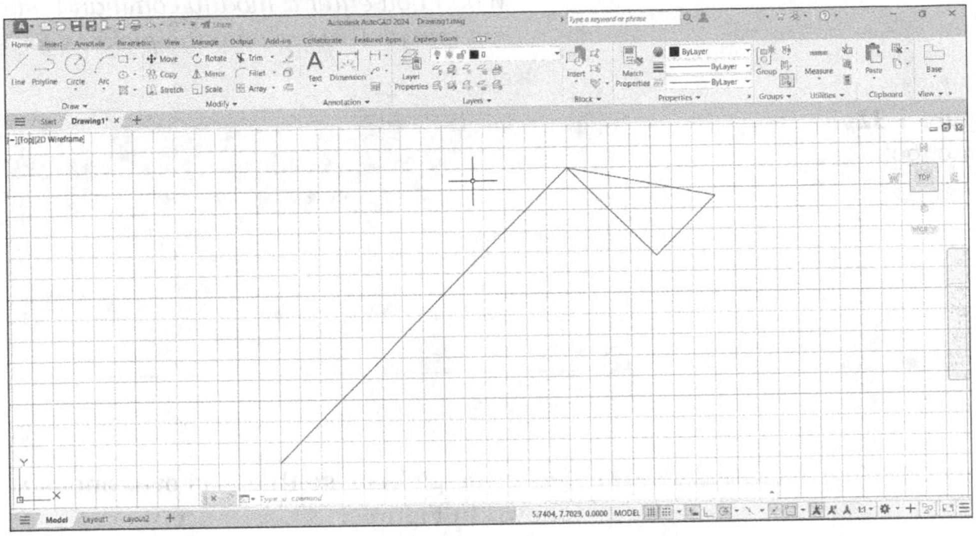

Figure 1-30
Absolute coordinates and the # sign

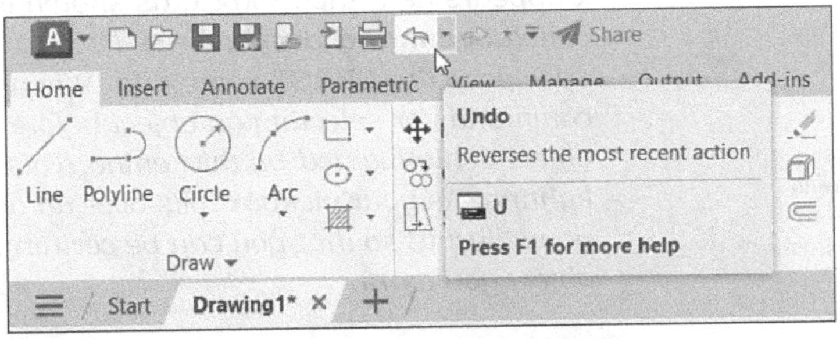

Figure 1-31
Undo tool

NOTE

Typing **U** executes the simple **U** command, which undoes the last command. Selecting the **Undo** tool uses the **UNDO** command. Although the two commands often have the same effect, **U** is not an alias for **UNDO**, which has more elaborate capabilities, as indicated by the options on the command line. **MREDO** can be used to reverse either **U** or **UNDO.** Also, note that **M** or **R** is not an alias for **MREDO**. There is also a **REDO** command; the difference between **REDO** and **MREDO** is that the **MREDO** command allows you to reverse multiple Undo operations at once.

✔ Click the **Redo** tool, which is to the right of the **Undo** tool on the **Quick Access** toolbar.

This redoes the line you have just undone. AutoCAD keeps track of everything undone in a single drawing session, so you can redo a number of undone actions. However, you can use the ***MREDO*** *command immediately only after using the* ***U*** *or* ***UNDO*** *commands.*

Erasing Lines

The **ERASE** command is not explored fully in this chapter, but for now you want to get to know this important command in its simplest form. Using **ERASE** brings up the techniques of object selection that are common to all editing commands. The simplest form of object selection requires that you point to an object and click the left mouse button. Try the following:

✔ Click the **Erase** tool from the **Modify** panel of the ribbon, as shown in Figure 1-32.

*When you enter a modify command, such as **ERASE**, the crosshairs disappear, leaving only the pickbox for selecting objects.*

Figure 1-32
Erase tool

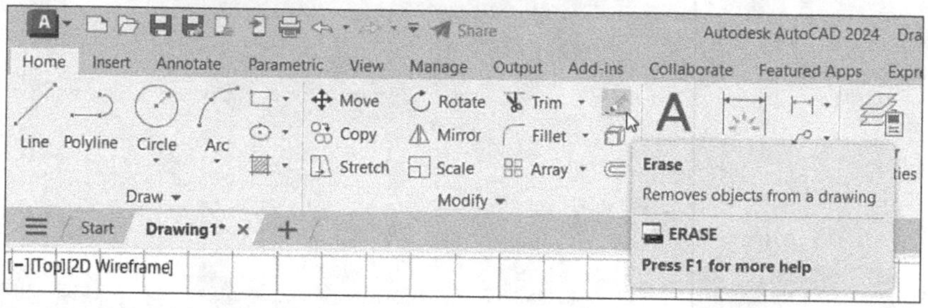

✔ Move the pickbox so that it is over one of the lines in your drawing, as shown in Figure 1-33.

*When the pickbox touches the line, the line is grayed out, and a red x appears near the pickbox, as shown in Figure 1-33. This feature is called **command previewing**. The graying-out and the red **x** are specific to the **ERASE** command. When selecting objects in other commands or selecting an object before executing a command, the object is highlighted by thickening. This is known as rollover highlighting. As your pickbox rolls over an object, it is highlighted before you select it, so that you can be certain that you are selecting the object you want.*

rollover highlighting: A feature that causes geometry in the drawing area to be highlighted when the pickbox passes over it. This is a visual aid in object selection.

Figure 1-33
Rollover highlighting in ERASE

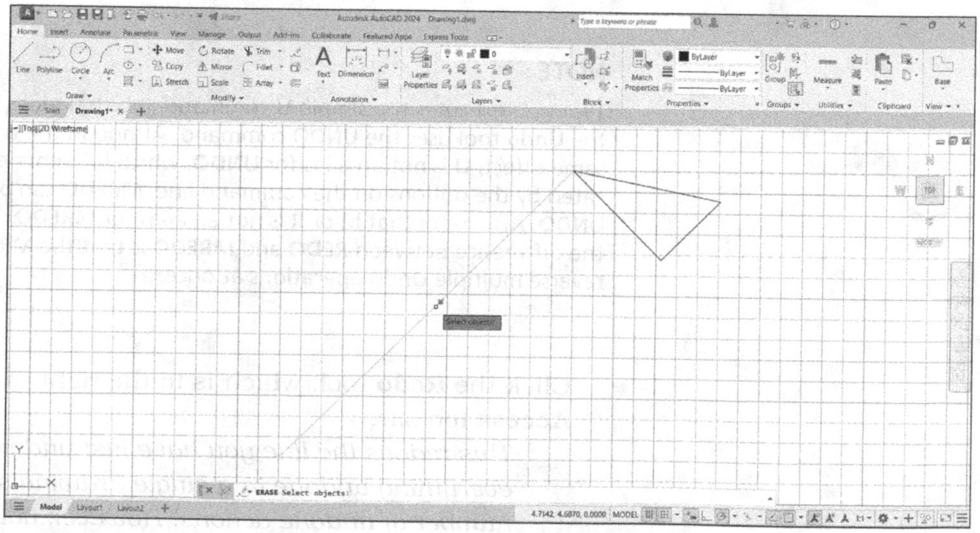

✔ Click the left mouse button to select the line.

*The line remains gray, but the red **x** disappears, indicating that the line has been selected and will be erased when the command is completed.*

✔ Right-click or press **<Enter>** or the spacebar to complete the command.

The line disappears.

✔ Before going on, use **U** or **ERASE** to remove all lines from your drawing, leaving a blank drawing area.

*Be aware that undoing **ERASE** causes a line to reappear.*

Ortho Mode

Before completing this section on drawing lines, give **Ortho** mode and **Polar tracking** a try.

✔ Click the **Line** tool from the **Draw** panel on the ribbon.

✔ Specify a starting point. Any point near the middle of the grid will do.

✔ Click the **Dynamic Input** button to turn off dynamic input display.

*Turning dynamic input display off makes it easier to see what is happening with the **Ortho** and **Polar tracking** modes.*

✔ Click the **Ortho Mode** button to turn **Ortho** on, as shown in Figure 1-34.

✔ Move the cursor slowly in circles.

*Notice how the rubber band jumps between horizontal and vertical without sweeping through any of the angles between. **Ortho** forces the specifying of points with the mouse only along the horizontal and vertical quadrant lines after specifying a starting point. With **Ortho** on, you can specify points at 0°, 90°, 180°, and 270° of rotation from your starting point only (see Figure 1-35).*

Figure 1-34
Ortho Mode button

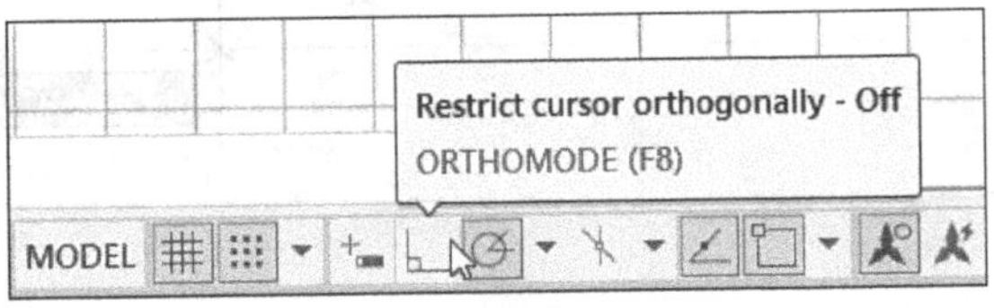

Figure 1-35
Ortho directions

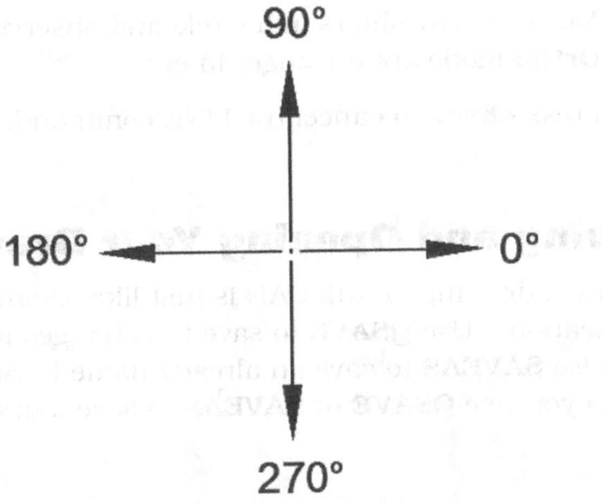

*The advantages of **Ortho** are similar to those of **Snap** mode, except that it limits angular rather than linear increments. It ensures that you get precise and true right angles easily when that is your intent. **Ortho** becomes more important as drawings grow more complex. In this chapter, it is hardly necessary, but it is convenient when working on Drawings 1-1 and 1-3 later in this chapter.*

Polar Tracking

Polar tracking is a feature that can replace **Ortho** mode in many instances. Try it using the following steps:

✔ Click the **Polar Tracking** button, to the right of the **Ortho Mode** button, to turn on polar tracking.

*Notice that **Polar tracking** and **Ortho** are mutually exclusive. They cannot both be on at the same time. When you turn **Polar tracking** on, **Ortho** shuts off automatically.*

✔ Move your cursor in a slow circle around the starting point of your line, just as you did with **Ortho** on.

With polar tracking on, when the rubber band crosses a vertical or horizontal axis (that is, when the rubber band is at 0°, 90°, 180°, or 270°), a green dotted line appears that extends to the edge of the drawing area. You also see a tooltip label, giving a value such as Polar 4.5000<0° (see Figure 1-36). The value is a polar coordinate with the length given first, followed by the angle, with the two separated by the < symbol. By default, polar tracking is set to respond on the orthogonal axes. Polar tracking can be set to track at any angle increment. In fact, if your polar tracking is identifying angles other than 0°, 90°, 180°, and 270°, it means that someone has changed this setting on your system.

Figure 1-36
Polar tracking

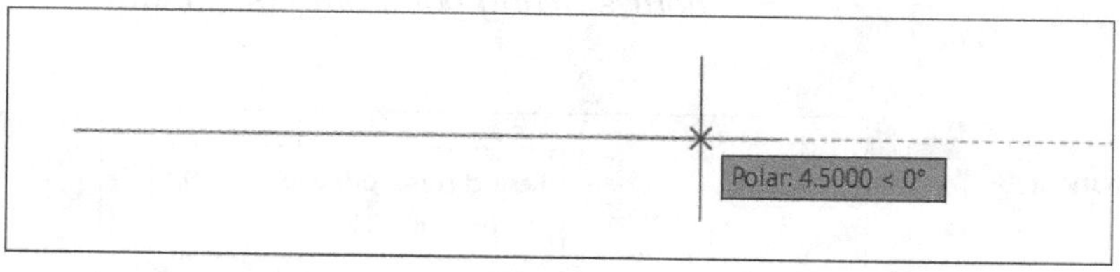

✔ Click the **Polar Tracking** button to turn polar tracking off.

✔ Move the crosshairs in a circle and observe that **polar tracking** and **Ortho** mode are no longer in effect.

✔ Press **<Esc>** to cancel the LINE command.

Saving and Opening Your Drawings

Saving a drawing in AutoCAD is just like saving a file in other Windows applications. Use **QSAVE** to save the changes in the current drawing to a file. Use **SAVEAS** to save an already named drawing under a new name. When you use **QSAVE** or **SAVEAS** to save a drawing the first time, they both prompt you for a name. In all cases, a .dwg extension is added automatically to file names to identify them as drawing files.

The SAVE and SAVEAS Commands

To save your drawing without leaving the drawing window, click the **Save** tool from the **Quick Access** toolbar, as shown in Figure 1-37.

If the current drawing has been previously saved, AutoCAD saves it without an intervening dialog box. If it has not, AutoCAD opens the **Save Drawing As** dialog box, shown in Figure 1-38, and allows you to give the file a new name and location before it is saved. The **Save Drawing As** dialog box is also opened if you select the **Save As** tool, which is to the right of the **Save** tool.

Figure 1-37
Save tool

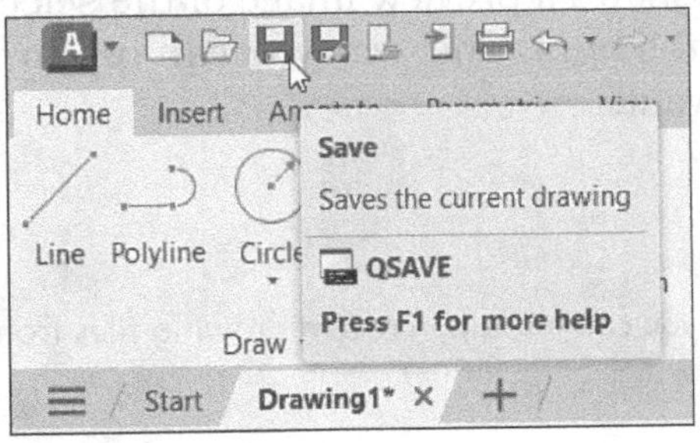

Figure 1-38
Save Drawing As dialog box

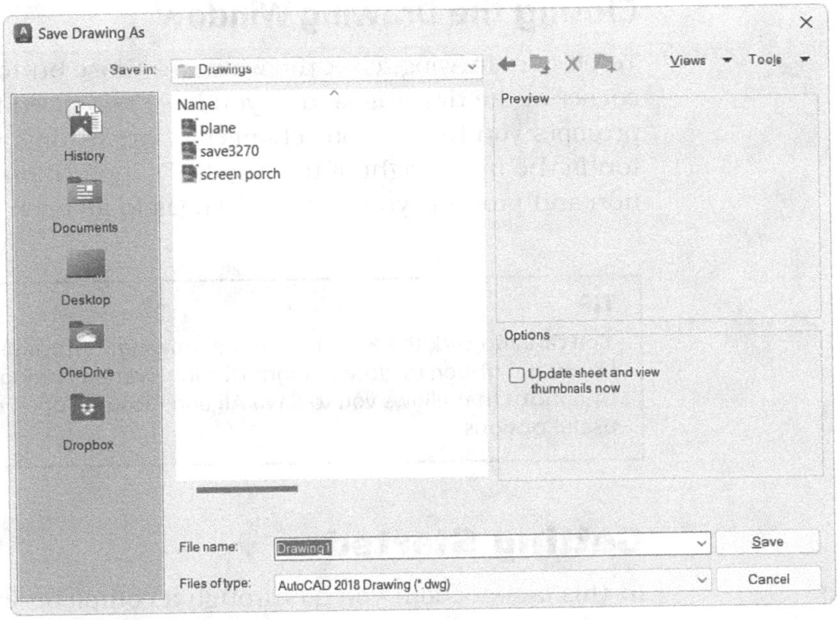

Enter a name in the **File name** box. If necessary, you can browse to a different location by clicking the arrow next to the box at the top labeled **Save in.** A list of drives and folders opens, and you can select a location from the list.

The **Save Drawing As** dialog box is one of several standard file selection dialog boxes. These dialog boxes all have a very similar format. There is a **File name** and a **Files of type** edit box at the bottom, a list of places to look or places to save a file on the left, and a **Look in** or **Save in** list at the top. The places list on the left includes standard locations on your computer. There are **History**, **Documents**, and **Desktop** folders, a **OneDrive** folder for access to Microsoft's online storage system, and a **Dropbox** folder for access to that online storage system.

Opening Saved Drawings

To open a previously saved drawing, select the **Open** tool from the **Quick Access** toolbar, just to the left of the **Save** tool.

This method brings up the **Select File** dialog box. This is another standard file selection dialog box. It is identical to the **Save Drawing As** dialog box, except that **Save in** has been replaced by **Look in**. In this **Select File** dialog box, you can select a file folder or internet location from the places list on the left or from a folder in the middle. When you select a file, AutoCAD shows a preview image of the selected drawing in the **Preview image** box at the right. This way you can be sure that you are opening the drawing you want.

> **NOTE**
>
> As a reminder, you can also open recent drawing files from the application menu and **Start** tab.

Closing the Drawing Window

To close a drawing, click the window's Close button **(X)** in the upper-right corner of the drawing area. If you have not saved the drawing, AutoCAD prompts you to save your changes before exiting. Clicking the Close **(X)** button in the upper right of the AutoCAD application window closes the application and prompts you to save changes to all open drawings one by one.

> **TIP**
>
> You can also click the **X** button on the drawing's associated tab among the **file** tabs below the ribbon to close it. Right-clicking over a drawing **file** tab also brings up a menu of options that allows you to **Save All** and **Close All** open drawings along with other useful options.

Getting Started

In this last section, you go through a complete drawing session. This involves creating a new drawing, making some basic changes to the drawing space, drawing a simple object, saving the drawing, and plotting or printing it. The drawing you complete will be named *Grate* and is shown in Figure 1-39. Most of the necessary procedures have already been covered in this chapter, but some new information will be presented, particularly regarding the **PLOT** command. Discussion will be provided only where necessary to introduce new information. Let's get going:

✔ Assuming **acad.dwt** is the default on your template list, click the **New** button from the **Start tab**. If not, open the **New** drop-down list and select it there or browse to the template.

✔ Click the **Snap Mode** button so that **Snap** mode is on.

✔ Type **z <Enter>**.

✔ Type **a <Enter>**.

✔ Click the **Line** tool from the **Draw** panel on the ribbon's **Home** tab.

✔ Specify the point **(3,1)**.

✔ Specify the point **(9,1)**.

You have now drawn the bottom line of the image in Figure 1-39.

✔ Continuing in the **LINE** command, draw a line from **(9,1)** to **(9,8)**.

✔ Continuing in the **LINE** command, draw a line from **(9,8)** to **(3,8)**.

✔ Type **c <Enter>** for the **Close** option, or right-click and select **Close** from the shortcut menu.

*The **Close** option draws a line back to the first point (3,1). This completes the outer rectangle in Figure 1-39.*

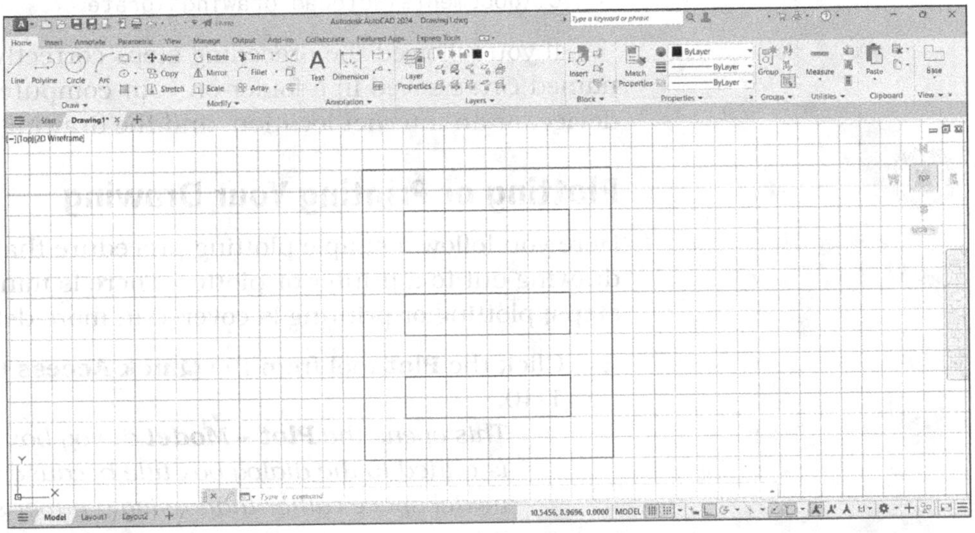

Figure 1-39
Grate drawing

> **TIP**
>
> The **Close** option connects the last in a continuous series of lines back to the starting point of the series. In drawing a rectangle, for instance, you simply type **c** in lieu of drawing the last of the four lines. For this to work, the whole rectangle must be drawn without leaving the **LINE** command.

✔ Press the spacebar to repeat the **LINE** command.

✔ Specify the points **(4,2)**, **(8,2)**, **(8,3)**, and **(4,3)**, and then type **c <Enter>**.

This completes the bottom inner rectangle in Figure 1-39.

✔ Press the spacebar to repeat the **LINE** command.

✔ Specify the points **(4,4)**, **(8,4)**, **(8,5)**, and **(4,5)**, and then type **c <Enter>**.

This completes the middle rectangle in Figure 1-39.

✔ Press the spacebar to repeat the **LINE** command.

✔ Specify the points **(4,6)**, **(8,6)**, **(8,7)**, and **(4,7)**, and then type **c <Enter>**.

This completes the top inner rectangle in Figure 1-39.

Your first drawing is now complete.

✔ Click the **Grid Mode** button to turn off the grid and see your completed drawing.

✔ Click the **Save** tool from the **Quick Access** toolbar.

*At this point, you should get specific directions from your instructor or CAD manager regarding where your drawings should be saved. Please insert the specific path you are instructed to use, open the **Save in** list, and navigate to the location where your drawing is to be saved.*

✔ In the **File name** box, type the drawing name *Grate*, preceded by the path designation you were provided, if necessary. For example:

```
C:\documents\autocad drawings\grate
```

If you followed the preceding steps correctly, you now have a drawing named *Grate* saved in a folder on your computer, an attached storage device, or an internet location, and the drawing remains open.

Plotting or Printing Your Drawing

Here you follow a simple plotting procedure that allows you to get your drawing out to a printer or plotter. There is minimal explanation with the steps; plotting or printing is covered in more detail in later chapters.

✔ Click the **Plot** tool from the **Quick Access** toolbar, as shown in Figure 1-40.

*This opens the **Plot – Model** dialog box shown in Figure 1-41. **Model** is added to the dialog box title because you are plotting directly from model space rather than using a paper space layout.*

Figure 1-40
Plot tool

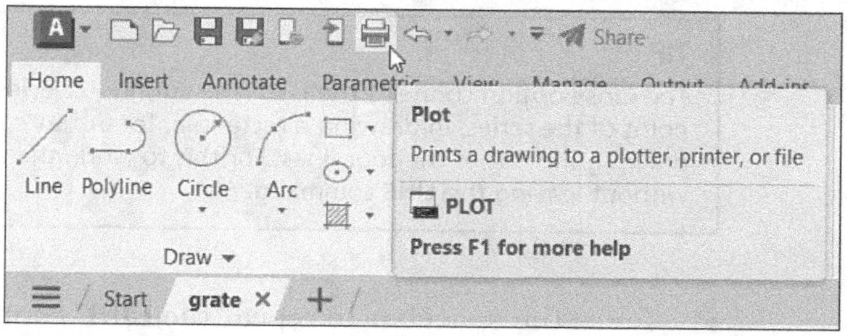

✔ Look at the second panel in the dialog box, labeled **Printer/plotter**. If a printer or plotter is selected, you can move on. If the **Name** box indicates None, open the drop-down list by clicking the arrow at the right and select the name of a plotter or printer connected to your computer or network. If you don't have a plotter or printer available, select **AutoCAD PDF (General Documentation).pc3** from the list.

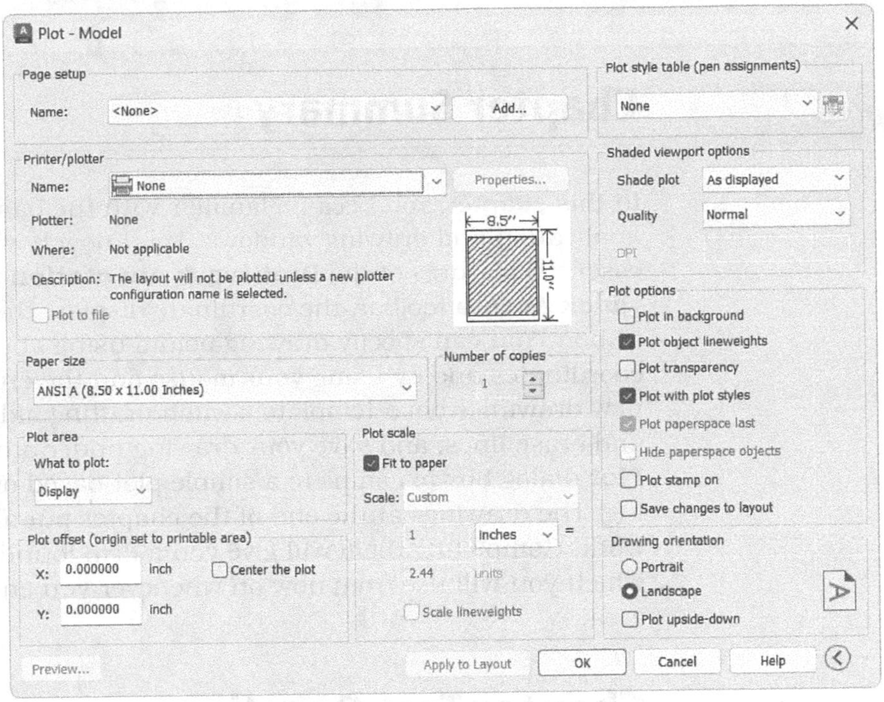

Figure 1-41
Plot – Model dialog box

✔ Look at the list under **What to plot** in the **Plot area** panel and click the arrow to open the drop-down list.

✔ Select **Limits**.

✔ Click the **Preview** button at the bottom of the dialog box.

You should see a preview similar to the one shown in Figure 1-42. This preview shows what your drawing sheet will look like if you choose to send your drawing to a printer or plotter.

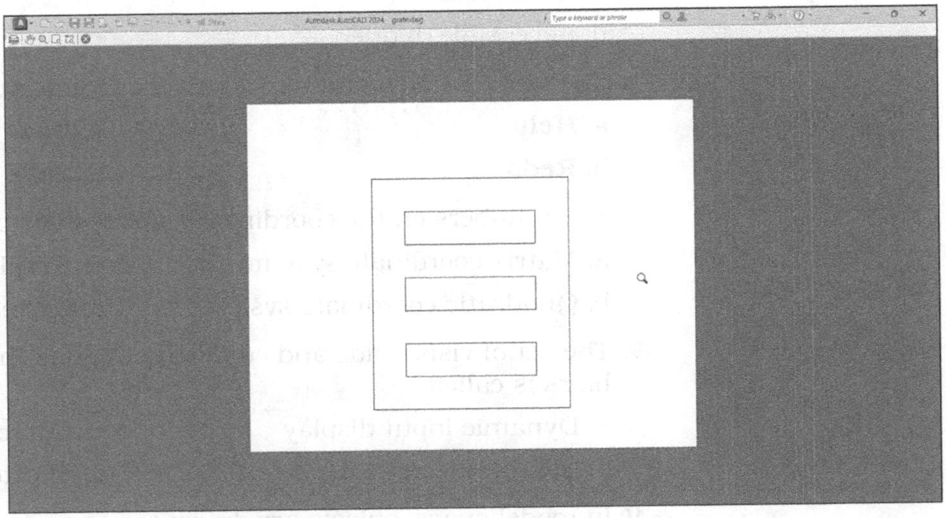

Figure 1-42
Plot preview

✔ Press **<Esc>** to return to the dialog box.

✔ Click **OK** to send the drawing to your plotter or printer or **Cancel** if you do not want to print at this time.

You are now well prepared to complete, save, and plot any of the drawings at the end of this chapter.

chapterone

Chapter Summary

In this chapter, you became familiar with the basic features of the AutoCAD application and drawing windows. You know how to use and control some essential features of the **Drafting & Annotation** workspace, including the **Quick Access** toolbar, the coordinate display, the mode buttons, and the ribbon. You can specify drawing points using absolute, polar, and relative coordinates and by using your mouse and the crosshairs. You can create a new drawing from a template, switch drafting aid modes on and off, draw and erase lines, and save your drawing under a new name. You can use the **Plot** dialog box to complete a simple plot based on the limits of your drawing. The drawings at the end of the chapter put all of these features to work. Completing them will give you a firm foundation in these skills, which you will use from now on whenever you enter the AutoCAD drawing area.

Chapter Test Questions

Multiple Choice

Circle the correct answer.

6. Two modes of the coordinate display are

a. Gray, invisible

b. Static, dynamic

c. Polar, relative

d. Accessible, hidden

7. The tool that does **not** appear on the **Quick Access** toolbar is

a. **Help**

b. **Redo**

c. **New**

d. **Save As**

8. The numbers on the coordinate display show positions in a

a. Matrix coordinate system

b. Quadratic coordinate system

c. Graphic coordinate system

d. Cartesian coordinate system

9. The set of visual aids and command options that move with the crosshairs is called

a. Dynamic input display

b. Coordinate display

c. Cursor

d. Shortcut menu

10. In model space, objects are drawn to

a. Scale

b. Fit

c. Real-world measurements

d. CAD standards

Matching

Write the number of the correct answer on the line.

a. Grid display ______

b. Polar coordinates ______

c. Absolute coordinates ______

d. Relative coordinates ______

e. **Snap** mode ______

1. 6.5 < 45,0
2. (9.54,6.66)
3. Limits point selection
4. Visible but not plotted
5. @7,7

True or False

Circle the correct answer.

1. **True or False**: The command line is the best place to enter AutoCAD commands.
2. **True or False**: Snap makes some points impossible to select with the cursor.
3. **True or False**: The ribbon gives quick access to all AutoCAD commands.
4. **True or False**: The right mouse button calls up shortcut menus according to context.
5. **True or False**: The # sign indicates that you are going to enter polar coordinates.

Questions

1. What are the advantages of using the ribbon to enter commands?
2. What are the two different modes of the coordinate display, and how does each mode appear? How do you switch between modes?
3. What is heads-up design? Give three examples of heads-up design features from this chapter.
4. You have just entered the point **(1,1,0)** and you now want to enter the point 2 units straight up from this point. How would you identify this point using absolute, relative, and polar coordinates?
5. What is the value and limitation of having **Snap** mode on?

Drawing Problems

1. Draw a line from **(3,2)** to **(4,8)** using the keyboard only.
2. Draw a line from **(6,6)** to **(7,5)** using the mouse only.
3. Draw a line from **(6,6)** to **(6,8)** using dynamic input.
4. Undo **(U)** all lines in your drawing area.
5. Draw a square with the corners at **(2,2)**, **(7,2)**, **(7,7)**, and **(2,7)**. Then erase the lines using the **ERASE** command.

Chapter Drawing Projects

> **NOTE**
>
> Units in AutoCAD can represent many different units of measurement. In some cases, the word ***unit*** is generically used when there is no need to refer to specific units such as feet, inches, centimeters, or kilometers.

G Drawing 1-1: *Guide* [BASIC]

Before beginning, look over the drawing page. The first two drawings in this chapter are given without dimensions. Draw them as you see them against the background of a half-unit grid. All these drawings can be done using the default half-unit snap, but all points are found on one-unit increments.

Drawing Suggestions

- If you are beginning a new drawing, open the **Start tab**, check to see that **acad.dwt** is selected on the **New** drop-down list, and click the **New** button.
- Remember to watch the coordinate display or dynamic input display when searching for a point.
- Be sure that **Grid Mode**, **Snap Mode**, and **Dynamic Input** are all turned on and that **Object Snap** and **Object Snap Tracking** are turned off. **Ortho Mode** or **Polar Tracking** can be on or off as you prefer. Other mode buttons have no effect and can also be on or off.
- Draw the outer perimeter first. It is **10** units wide and **7** units high, and its lower left-hand corner is at the point **(1.0000,1.0000)**.
- The **Close** option can be used in all four of the rectangles and squares.

If You Make a Mistake—U

This is a reminder that you can stay in the **LINE** command as you undo the last line you drew, or the last two or three if you have drawn a series.

- Type **U <Enter>**. The last line you drew will be gone or replaced by the rubber band, awaiting a new endpoint. If you want to go back more than one line, type **U** again, as many times as you need to.
- If you have already left the **LINE** command, the **U** command undoes the last continuous series of lines.
- Remember, if you have mistakenly undone something, you can get it back by using the **Redo** tool. You cannot perform other commands between **U** and **MREDO**, but you can redo several **UNDO** commands if they have been done sequentially.

Drawing 1-1
Guide

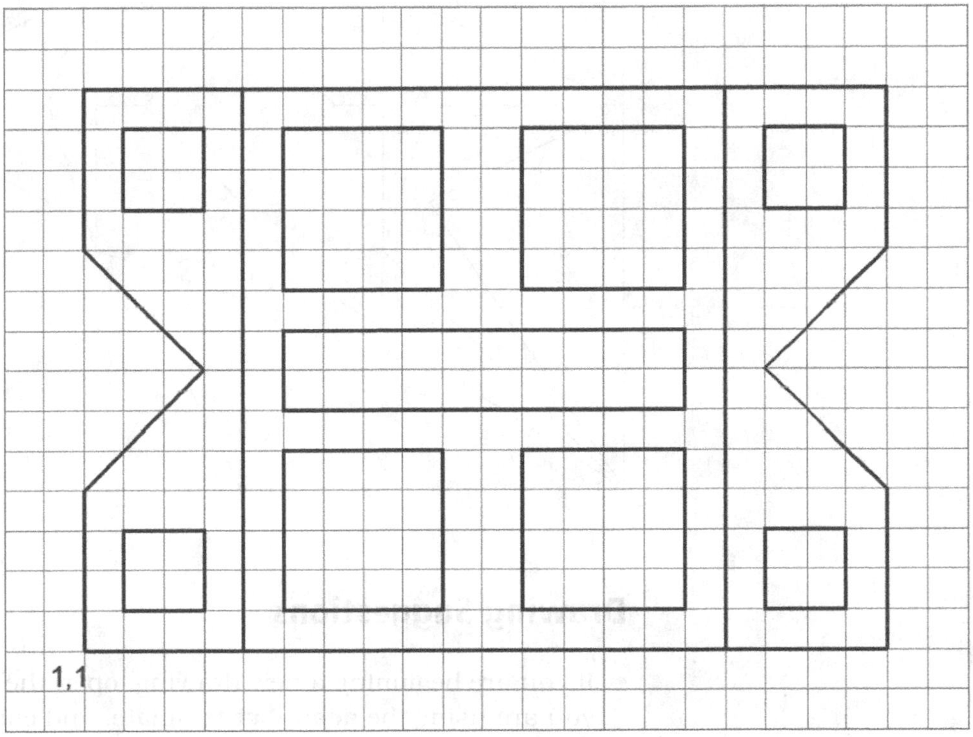

G Drawing 1-2: *Design #1* [BASIC]

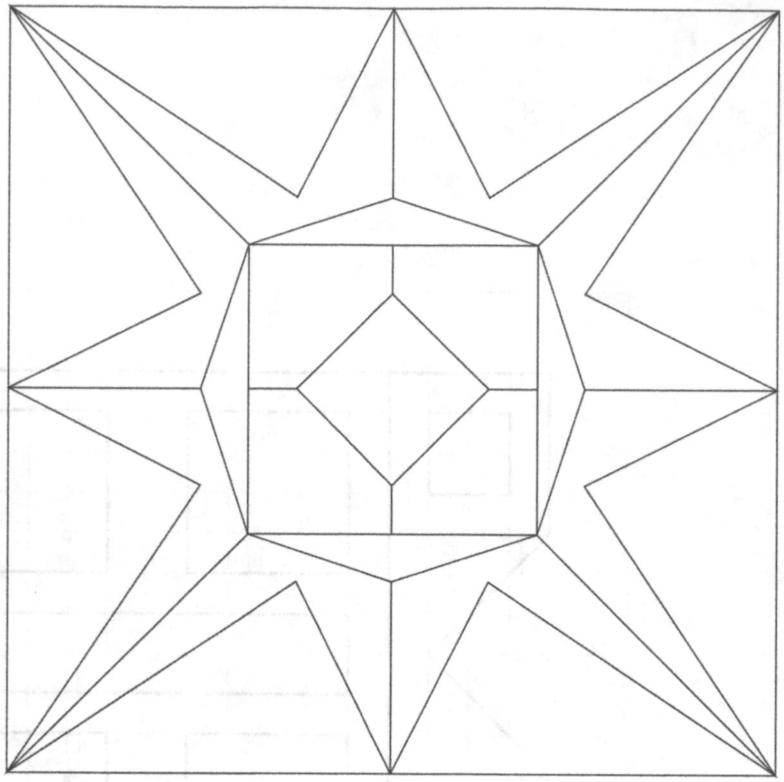

Drawing Suggestions

- If you are beginning a new drawing, open the **Start tab**, check to see that you are using the **acad.dwt** template, and click the **New** button.
- Draw the large outside square starting at **(2.0000,1.0000)**.
- Draw the small inside square.
- Now, connect the lines from the outside square to the inside square.
- Continue connecting lines until the drawing is complete.
- You will need to make sure **Ortho** is off to do this drawing.

Repeating a Command

Remember, you can repeat a command by pressing **<Enter>** or the space-bar at the command line prompt. This is useful in this drawing because you have several sets of lines to draw.

Drawing 1-2
Design #1

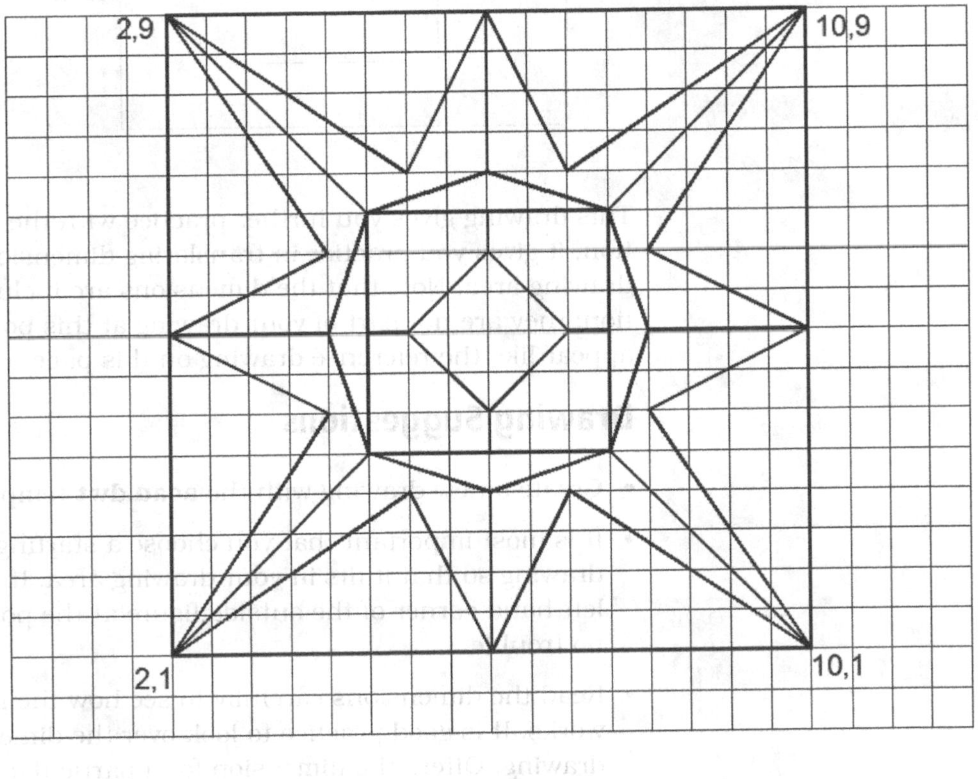

G Drawing 1-3: *Shim* [INTERMEDIATE]

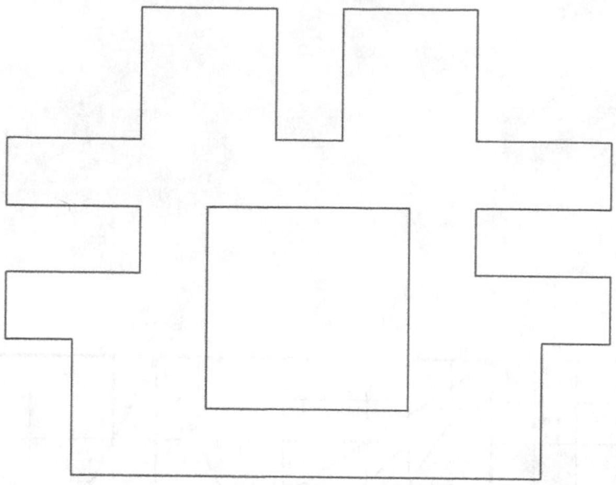

This drawing gives you further practice with the **LINE** command. In addition, it gives you practice in translating dimensions into distances in the drawing area. Note that the dimensions are included only for your information; they are not part of your drawing at this point. Your drawing should appear like the reference drawing on this page.

Drawing Suggestions

- Create a new drawing with the **acad.dwt** template.
- It is most important that you choose a starting point that positions the drawing so that it fits in your drawing area. If you begin with the bottom left-hand corner of the outside figure at the point **(3,1)**, you should have no trouble.
- Read the dimensions carefully to see how the geometry of the drawing works. It is good practice to look over the dimensions before you begin drawing. Often, the dimension for a particular line may be located on another side of the figure or may have to be extrapolated from other dimensions. It is not uncommon to misread, misinterpret, or miscalculate a dimension, so take your time.

Drawing 1-3
Shim

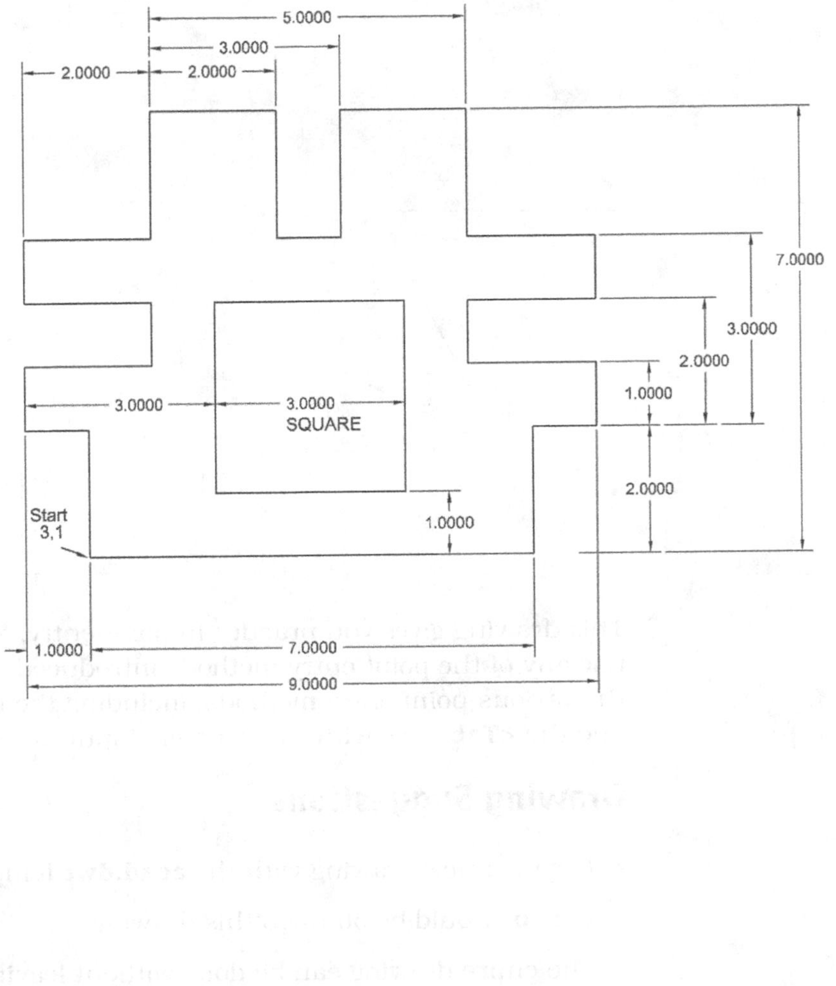

G Drawing 1-4: *Stamp* [INTERMEDIATE]

This drawing gives you practice in point entry. You can begin anywhere and use any of the point entry methods introduced in this chapter. Practice all the various point entry methods, including the use of direct distance entry and the **<Tab>** key with the dynamic input display.

Drawing Suggestions

- Create a new drawing with the **acad.dwt** template.
- **Ortho** should be off to do this drawing.
- The entire drawing can be done without leaving the **LINE** command if you want.
- If you do leave **LINE,** remember that you can repeat **LINE** by pressing **<Enter>** or the spacebar and then select the last point as a new start point by pressing **<Enter>** or the spacebar again.
- Plan to use point selection by typing, by pointing, and by direct distance entry. Make use of absolute, relative, and polar coordinates.

Drawing 1-4
Stamp

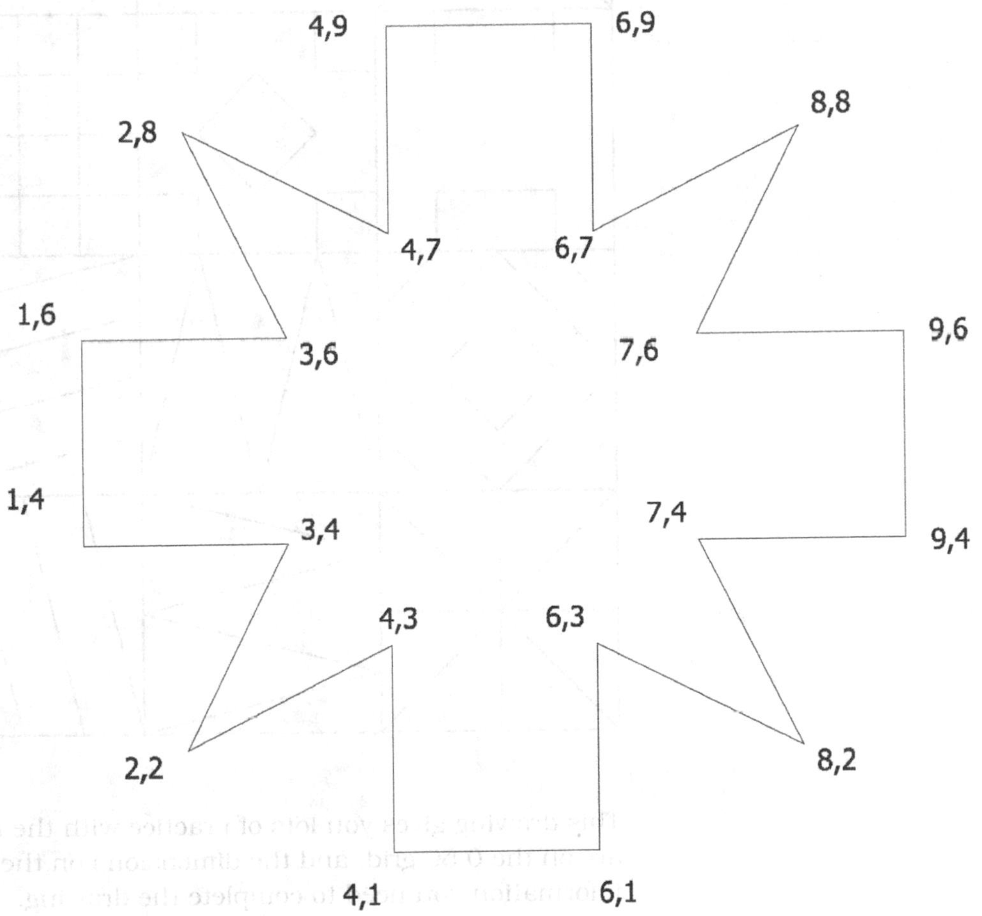

G Drawing 1-5: *Tiles* [ADVANCED]

This drawing gives you lots of practice with the **LINE** command. All points are on the 0.50 grid, and the dimensions on the drawing page give all the information you need to complete the drawing.

Drawing Suggestions

- Begin by drawing an 8 × 8 square.
- Be sure to make frequent use of the spacebar to repeat the **LINE** command.
- Add sixteen 2"-square tile outlines.
- Fill in the geometry in each of the 2" squares.

Drawing 1-5

Tiles

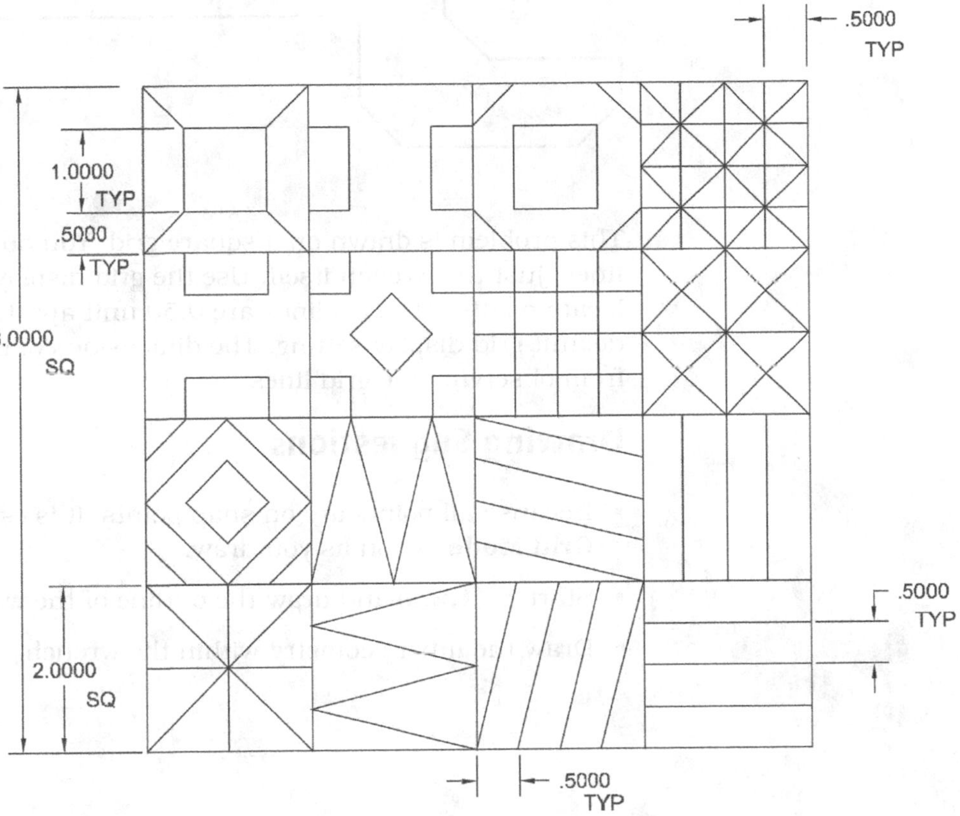

G Drawing 1-6: *Multi Wrench* [ADVANCED]

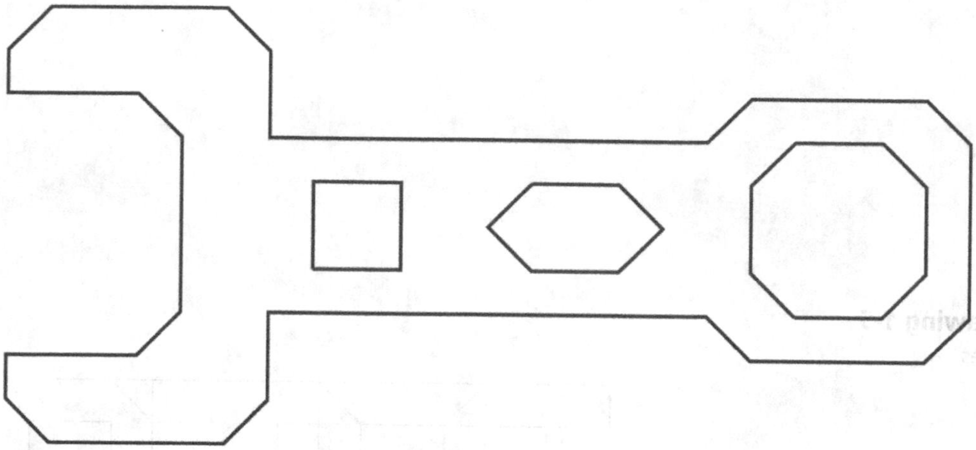

This problem is drawn on a square grid. You do not have to draw the grid lines, just the wrench itself. Use the grid display in place of the grid lines to locate points. The grid lines are 0.50 unit apart, so they will match your default grid display setting. The dimensions of the object can be obtained from observing the grid lines.

Drawing Suggestions

- Because all points are on snap points, it is essential that **Snap Mode** and **Grid Mode** are on as you draw.
- Start at **(1,2.5)** and draw the outline of the wrench first.
- Draw the inner geometry within the wrench.

Drawing 1-6
Multi Wrenc

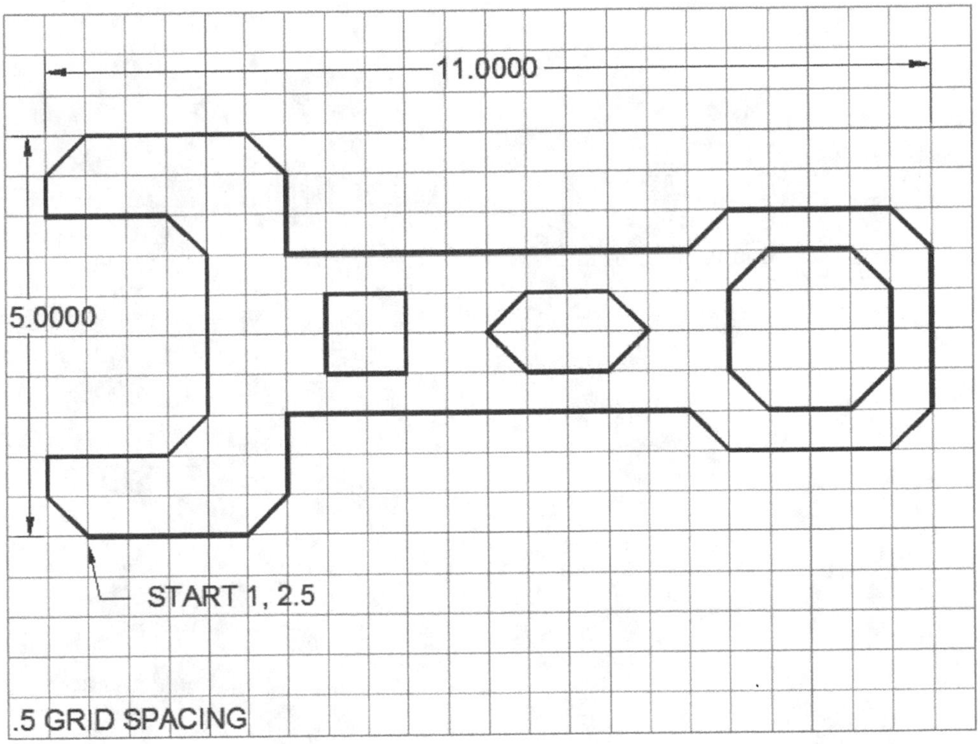

2 chapter two

Circles and Drawing Aids

CHAPTER OBJECTIVES

- Change the grid setting
- Change the snap setting
- Change units
- Draw circles by specifying a center point and a radius
- Draw circles by specifying a center point and a diameter
- Access AutoCAD online Help features
- Use the **ERASE** command
- Use single-point object snap
- Use the **RECTANG** command
- Customize your workspace
- Plot or print a drawing

Introduction

In this chapter, you begin to gain control of your drawing environment by changing the spacing of the grid and snap and the units in which coordinates are displayed. You add to your repertoire of objects by drawing circles with the **CIRCLE** command and rectangles with the **RECTANG** command. You explore the many methods of object selection as you continue to learn editing procedures with the **ERASE** command. You gain access to convenient Help features and begin to learn the extensive plotting and printing features of AutoCAD.

Changing the Grid Setting

> **TIP**
>
> Following is a general procedure for changing the grid spacing at the command line prompt:
>
> 1. Type **grid <Enter>**.
> 2. Enter a new value.

When you begin a new drawing using the acad template, the grid and snap are set with a spacing of 0.5000 unit. You can complete drawings without altering the grid and snap settings from the default value. But usually, you will want to change this to a value that reflects your project. You might want a 10-mile snap for a mapping project or a 0.010" snap for a printed circuit diagram. The grid can match the snap setting or can be set independently.

✔ Create a new drawing by clicking the down arrow on the **New** drop-down list from the **Start** tab and then selecting **acad.dwt**. If **acad.dwt** isn't listed on the drop-down list, click **Browse templates** and select the **acad.dwt** file before clicking **Open**.

*Clicking the **New** button without clicking the down arrow of the drop-down list creates a new drawing with the most recently used drawing template.*

This drawing template ensures that you begin with the settings used for the exercises of this chapter.

✔ Turn on **Snap Mode** and **Grid Display** using the buttons on the status bar.

✔ Type **z <Enter>** to start the **ZOOM** command.

Selecting Options from the Command Line

In this section, you find out how to select an option from the command line. Notice in Figure 2-1 the blue highlighting on the uppercase letters in each option of this prompt from the **ZOOM** command. You can type the letter **A** and press **<Enter>** to execute the **All** option or you can click the word **All** in the command line, as shown in Figure 2-1.

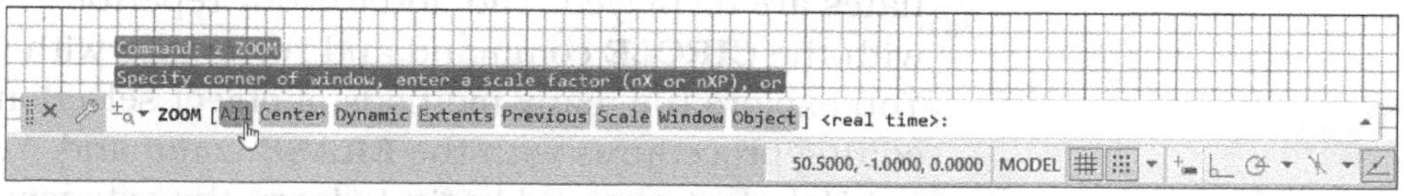

Figure 2-1
Selecting options from the command line

✔ Click the word **All** in the command line, as shown.

The grid is now centered and zoomed to the limits of the drawing. You can select an option from the command line this way any time you have options showing.

- ✔ Type **grid <Enter>**.
  The command-line prompt appears like this, with options separated by spaces:

```
Specify grid spacing(X) or [ON/OFF/Snap/Major/aDaptive/
Limits/Follow/Aspect] <0.5000>:
```

  If dynamic input is on, you also see part of this prompt next to the crosshairs. You can ignore the options for now. The number 0.5000 shows the current setting.

- ✔ To answer the prompt, type **1 <Enter>** and watch what happens.
  The drawing area changes to show a 1-unit grid.

- ✔ Try other grid spacing values. Try **2**, **0.25**, and **0.125**.
  *Remember that you can repeat the last command, **GRID**, by pressing **<Enter>** or the spacebar.*

- ✔ Before going on to the next section, set the grid back to **0.5000**.

Changing the Snap Setting

Grid and snap are similar enough to cause confusion. The grid is only a visual reference. It has no effect on specifying points. Snap is invisible, but it dramatically affects point specification. Grid and snap might not have the same value.

> **TIP**
> Following is a general procedure for changing the snap setting in the **Drafting Settings** dialog box:
>
> 1. Right-click the **Snap Mode** button on the status bar and select **Snap Settings.**
> 2. On the **Snap and Grid** tab, enter a new snap value.
> 3. Click **OK** to exit the dialog box.

Using the Drafting Settings Dialog Box

You can change snap using the **SNAP** command at the command line, as you did with the **GRID** command in the previous section. You also can change both in the **Drafting Settings** dialog box, as you do here.

- ✔ Right-click the **Snap Mode** button on the status bar and select **Snap Settings** from the shortcut menu, as shown in Figure 2-2.

Figure 2-2
Shortcut menu

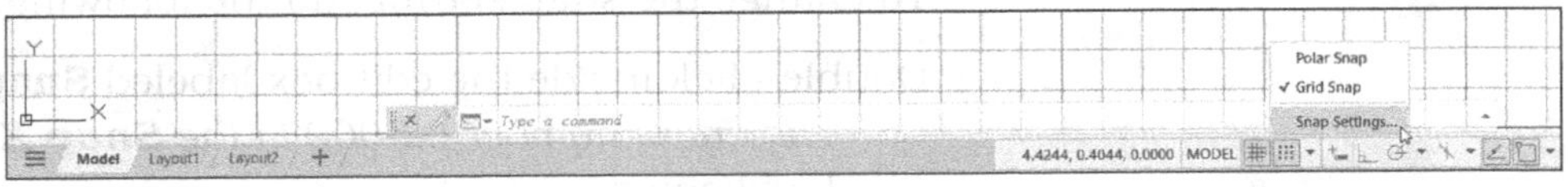

This displays the ***Drafting Settings*** dialog box shown in Figure 2-3. ***DSETTINGS*** is the command that displays this dialog box, and ***DS*** is the command's alias. Look at the dialog box. It contains some common features, including tabs, check boxes, panels, and edit boxes. When you open this dialog box from the **Snap Settings** item on the shortcut menu, the ***Snap and Grid*** tab should be current as shown. If not, click it now.

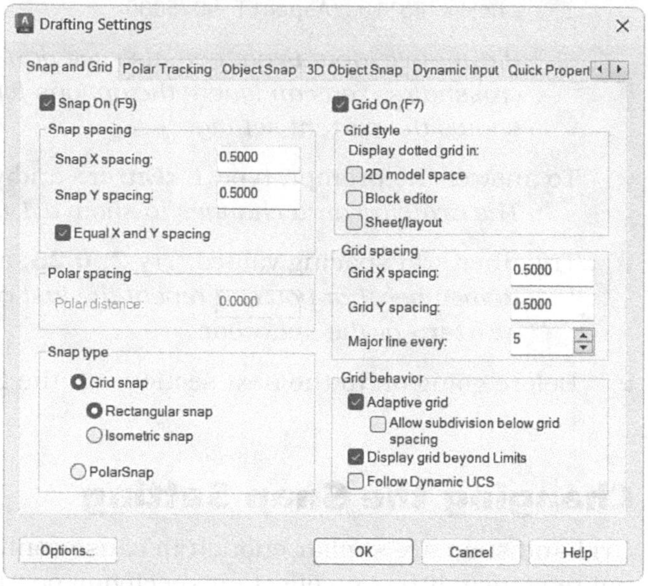

Figure 2-3
Drafting Settings dialog box

✔ If the **Snap and Grid** tab is not current, click the tab.

Below the tabs, you see checkboxes labeled ***Snap On (F9)*** and ***Grid On (F7)***. You can turn snap and grid on and off by selecting the appropriate checkbox. In this dialog box, checkboxes should show that both snap and grid are on.

NOTE

- The dialog box has places to set both *x* and *y* spacing. It is unlikely that you want to have a grid or snap matrix with different horizontal and vertical increments, but the capacity is there if you do.
- Commands that display dialog boxes, like other commands, can be repeated by pressing the spacebar or **<Enter>**.

The snap and grid settings are shown in edit boxes labeled **Snap X spacing**, **Snap Y spacing**, **Grid X spacing**, and **Grid Y spacing**. You can double-click in the edit box to highlight the entire text, or point and click once anywhere inside the box to do partial editing.

To change the snap setting, do the following:

✔ Double-click inside the edit box labeled **Snap X spacing.**

*The entire number 0.5000 in the **Snap X spacing** box should be highlighted.*

✔ Type **1 <Enter>**.

Pressing **<Enter>** at this point is the same as clicking **OK** in the dialog box. It takes you out of the dialog box and back to the drawing area.

Snap is now set at 1, and grid is still at 0.5. This makes the snap setting larger than the grid setting.

✔ Type **L** or click the **Line** tool from the **Draw** panel on the **Home** tab of the ribbon.

*This starts the **LINE** command. A drawing command must be active before snap affects specifying points.*

✔ Move the cursor around the drawing area.

You will see that you can access only half of the grid line intersections. This type of arrangement is not too useful. Try some other settings.

✔ Display the dialog box again by right-clicking the **Snap Mode** button on the status bar and then choosing **Snap Settings** from the shortcut menu.

✔ Change the **Snap X spacing** value to **0.25** and click **OK** to close the dialog box.

Move the cursor slowly and observe the coordinate display. This is a more efficient arrangement. With grid set larger than snap, you can still specify exact points easily, but the grid is not so dense as to be distracting.

✔ Change the **Snap X spacing** value to **0.05**.

✔ Move the cursor and watch the coordinate display.

Observe how the snap setting is reflected in the available coordinates. How small a snap will AutoCAD accept?

✔ Try **0.005**.

Move the cursor and observe the coordinate display.

✔ Try **0.0005**.

You could even try 0.0001, but this would be like turning snap off because the coordinate display is registering four decimal places anyway. Unlike the grid, which is limited by the size and resolution of your screen, you can set snap to any value you like. If you try a grid setting that is too small, AutoCAD will default to a larger grid.

✔ Press **<Esc>** to exit the **LINE** command.

✔ Finally, before you finish this exercise, set the snap back to **0.25** and leave the grid at 0.5.

> **TIP**
>
> If you want to keep snap and grid the same, set the grid to **0** in the **Drafting Settings** dialog box or enter the **GRID** command and type **S** for the **Snap** option. The grid then changes to match the snap and continues to change whenever you reset the snap. To free the grid, just give it its own value again.

Changing Units

UNITS	
Command	UNITS
Alias	Un
Panel	(none)
Tool	0.0

Distances in a drawing are always unitless, so 1 drawing unit could represent a millimeter, an inch, a meter, a foot, a kilometer, or even a mile. For example, architectural drawings commonly express measurements in meters and millimeters or feet and inches, and mechanical drawings use measurements that are commonly expressed in decimal formats. The UNITS command is used to control the display and input format of length and angular values. When the UNITS command is started, it displays the **Drawing Units** dialog box.

> **TIP**
>
> Following is a general procedure for changing units:
>
> 4. Type **Units <Enter>**.
> 5. Respond to the prompts.

The Drawing Units Dialog Box

The **Drawing Units** dialog box makes use of drop-down lists, another common dialog box feature.

✔ Type **Units <Enter>** or click **Application > Drawing Utilities > Units**. (The **Application** menu is located in the upper-left corner of the application).

*This displays the **Drawing Units** dialog box shown in Figure 2-4. This dialog box has six drop-down lists for specifying various characteristics of linear and angular drawing units. Drop-down lists show a current setting next to an arrow that is used to open the list of other possibilities. Your dialog box should show that the current **Length Type** in your drawing is decimal units precise to 0.0000 places, and **Angle Type** is decimal degrees with 0 places. Also notice the **Sample Output** area that gives examples of the current units.*

✔ Under **Type** in the dialog box's **Length** panel, click the arrow to the right of the word.

The resulting drop-down list contains the following options:

Architectural
Decimal
Engineering
Fractional
Scientific

Architectural units display feet and fractional inches (1'-3 ½"), engineering units display feet and decimal inches (1'-3.50"), fractional units display units in a mixed-number format (15 ½), and scientific units use exponential notation for the display of very large or very small numbers (1.55E + 01).

> **NOTE**
>
> With the exception of engineering and architectural formats, these formats can be used with any basic unit of measurement. For example, decimal mode works for metric units as well as imperial units.

In this chapter, you continue to use decimal units. If you are designing a house, you are more likely to use architectural units. If you are building a bridge, you might want engineering units. You might want to use scientific units if you are mapping subatomic particles.

Whatever your application, once you know how to change units, you can do so at any time. However, as a drawing practice, it is best to choose appropriate units when you first begin work on a new drawing.

✔ Select **Decimal** or click anywhere outside the drop-down list to close the list without changing the setting.

Next, you change the precision setting to two-place decimals.

✔ Click the down arrow next to **0.0000** on the **Precision** drop-down list in the **Length** panel.

This opens a list with options ranging from ***0*** *to* ***0.00000000****, as shown in Figure 2-5.*

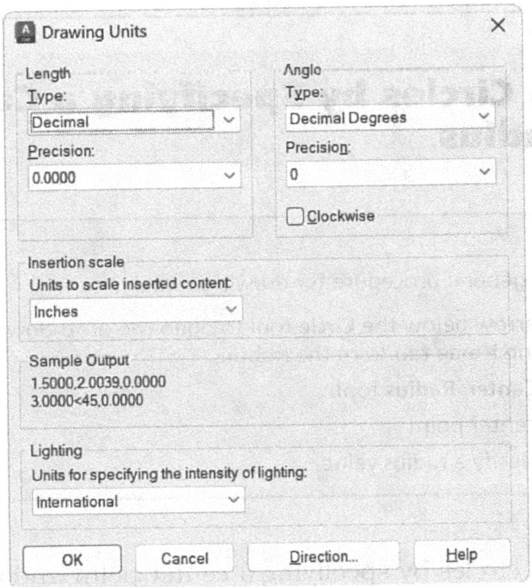

Figure 2-4
Drawing Units dialog box

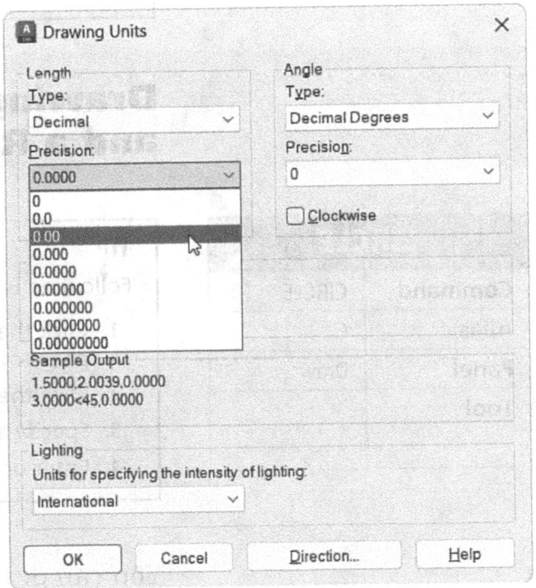

Figure 2-5
Precision list

You select two-place decimals because they are more common than any other choice.

✔ Select **0.00** from the drop-down list, as shown in Figure 2-5.

The list closes, and ***0.00*** *replaces* ***0.0000*** *as the current precision for units of length. Notice that the sample output has also changed to reflect the new setting.*

The settings on the right side of the dialog box allow you to control the units in which angular measurements, including polar coordinates, are displayed. If you open the **Angle Type** drop-down *list, you see the following options:*

Decimal Degrees
Deg/Min/Sec
Grads
Radians
Surveyor's Unit

The default system is standard decimal degrees with 0 decimal places, measured counterclockwise, and with 0° being straight out to the right (3 o'clock), 90° straight up (12 o'clock), 180° to the left (9 o'clock), and 270° straight down (6 o'clock). Leave these settings alone.

✔ Make sure you have two-place decimal units for length and zero-place decimal degree units for angles.

✔ Click **OK** to close the dialog box.

> **TIP**
> All dialog boxes can be moved on screen by clicking and holding down the mouse button on the title area at the top of the dialog box, and then dragging the dialog box across the screen.

Drawing Circles by Specifying a Center Point and a Radius

CIRCLE	
Command	CIRCLE
Alias	C
Panel	Draw
Tool	

> **TIP**
> Following is a general procedure for drawing a circle:
> 1. Click the arrow below the **Circle** tool to open the drop-down menu on the **Draw** panel of the **Home** tab from the ribbon.
> 2. Click the **Center, Radius** tool.
> 3. Specify a center point.
> 4. Enter or specify a radius value.

You can draw circles by specifying a center point and a radius, a center point and a diameter, two points that determine a diameter, three points on the circle's circumference, two tangent points on other objects and a radius, or three tangent points. All these options appear on a drop-down menu below the **Circle** tool on the ribbon. In this chapter, you only use the first two options.

You begin by drawing a circle with a radius 3 and centered at the point (6,5). Then, draw two smaller circles centered at the same point. Later, you erase them using the **ERASE** command.

> **NOTE**
>
> The tool that appears on the ribbon changes with the last option selected. If **Center, Radius** was the last **CIRCLE** command option used, the **Center, Radius** tool is displayed on the ribbon. In this case, **Center, Radius** can be executed without opening the drop-down menu.

✔ Grid should be set to **0.50**, snap to **0.25**, and units to **two-place decimal**.

✔ Click the arrow below the **Circle** tool to open the drop-down menu on the **Draw** panel of the **Home** tab on the ribbon, as illustrated in Figure 2-6.

This opens the drop-down menu shown in the figure. There are many drop-down menus on the ribbon allowing access to more commands and options without them all taking up space on the ribbon. ***Center, Radius*** *is at the top of the menu.*

✔ Click the **Center, Radius** tool from the drop-down menu.

The command line prompt is

```
Specify center point for circle or [3P/2P/Ttr (tan tan radius)]:
```

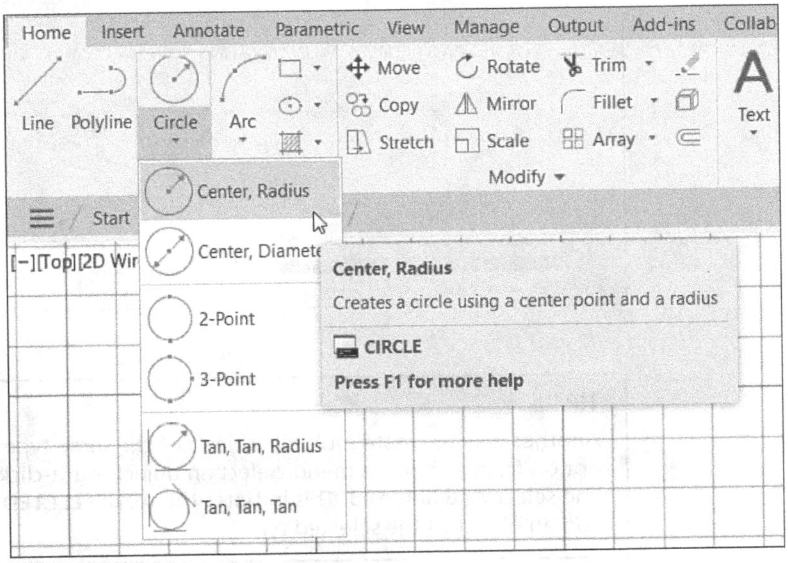

Figure 2-6
Circle tool – drop-down menu

✔ Specify the center point **(6,5)** for the circle.

AutoCAD prompts for a radius or diameter:

```
Specify radius of circle or [Diameter]:
```

If you type or specify a coordinate value now, AutoCAD takes it as a radius because that is the default. Diameter is the only other option still available.

✔ Move your cursor and observe the rubber band and dragged circle. If your dynamic input display is not on, enable it on by clicking the **Dynamic Input** button on the status bar.

Besides the rubber band and the circle, you may also notice that the coordinate display now shows polar coordinates. You will not see this if the coordinate display is in static mode.

✔ If necessary, click the **Coordinates** display on the status bar so that it updates as you move the cursor.

Remember that polar coordinates display a length and an angle. In this case, the length is the length of the radius shown by the rubber band. Dynamic input is also a great feature for drawing circles. It gives you the radius or diameter of the circle being drawn right at the point you are specifying.

✔ Watch the dynamic input display or the coordinate display and specify a point **3.00** units away from the center point, as shown in Figure 2-7.

*Having **Snap** on makes it easy to move exactly 3.00 units at 0°, 90°, 180°, or 270°.*

Your first circle should now be complete.

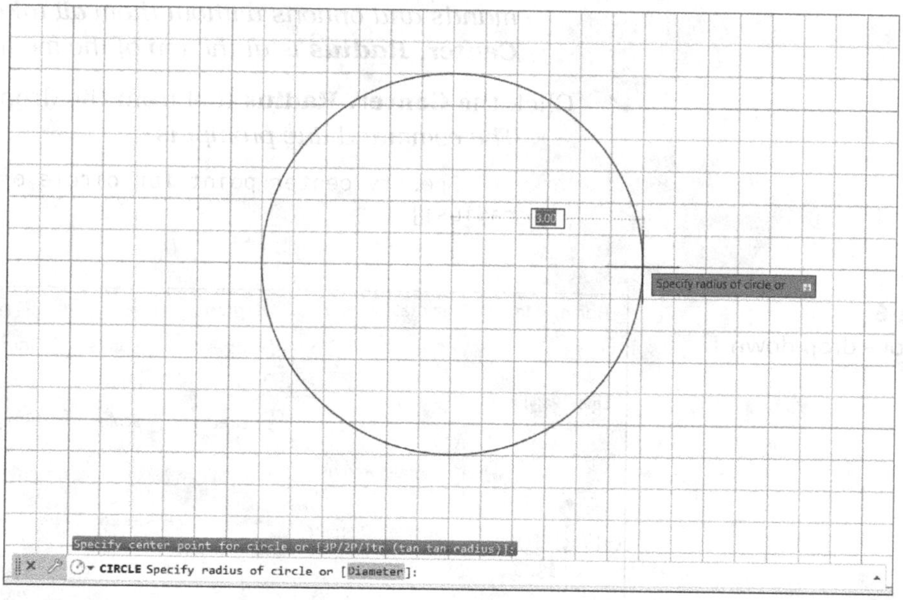

Figure 2-7
Drag circle 3.00 from center point

> **TIP**
>
> Another way to create multiple objects of the same type is to use the **Add Selected** option from a shortcut menu. Select an object, right-click to open the shortcut menu, and select **Add Selected**. This initiates the **ADDSELECTED** command, which allows you to add an object of the selected type.

✔ Draw two more circles using the same center point and radius option. They should be centered at **(6,5)** and have radii of **2.50** and **2.00**. Use the spacebar to repeat the command or click the **Center, Radius** tool from the ribbon again.

The results are shown in Figure 2-8.

Figure 2-8
Circles drawn using **Center, Radius**

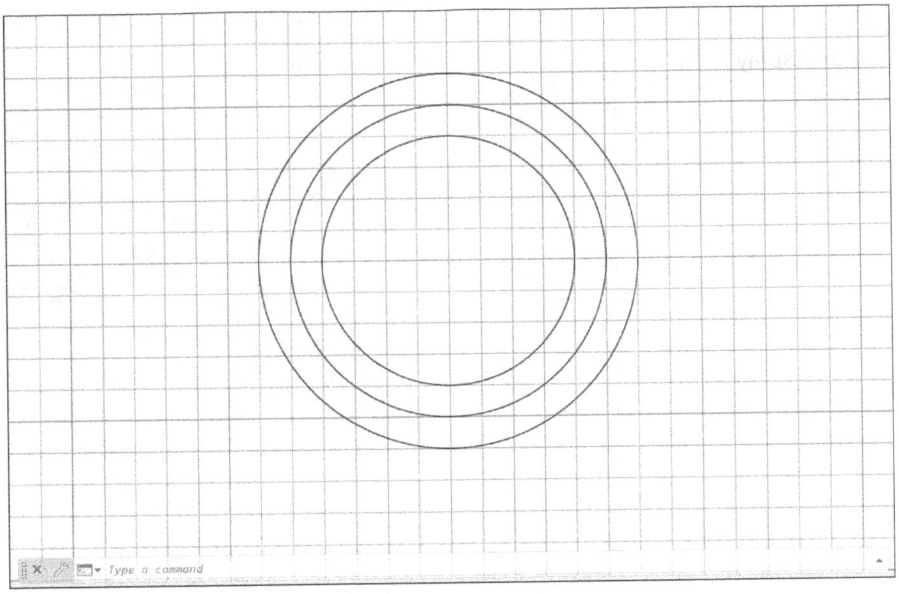

Drawing Circles by Specifying a Center Point and a Diameter

Next, you draw three more circles centered at **(6,5)** having diameters of **1**, **1.5**, and **2**. This option of drawing circles is similar to the radius option, except you see that the rubber band and dynamic input display work differently.

✔ Click the **Circle** drop-down menu on the **Draw** panel of the **Home** tab and click **Center, Diameter**.

✔ Specify the center point at **(6,5)**.

✔ Move the crosshairs away from the center point.

Notice that the crosshairs are now outside the circle you are dragging in the drawing area (see Figure 2-9). This is because AutoCAD is looking for a diameter, but the last point you specified was a center point. So, the diameter (twice the radius) is being measured from the center point out. Also, notice that the dynamic input display has responded to the **Diameter** option and is now measuring the diameter of the circle. Move the cursor around toward and away from the center point to get a feel for this.

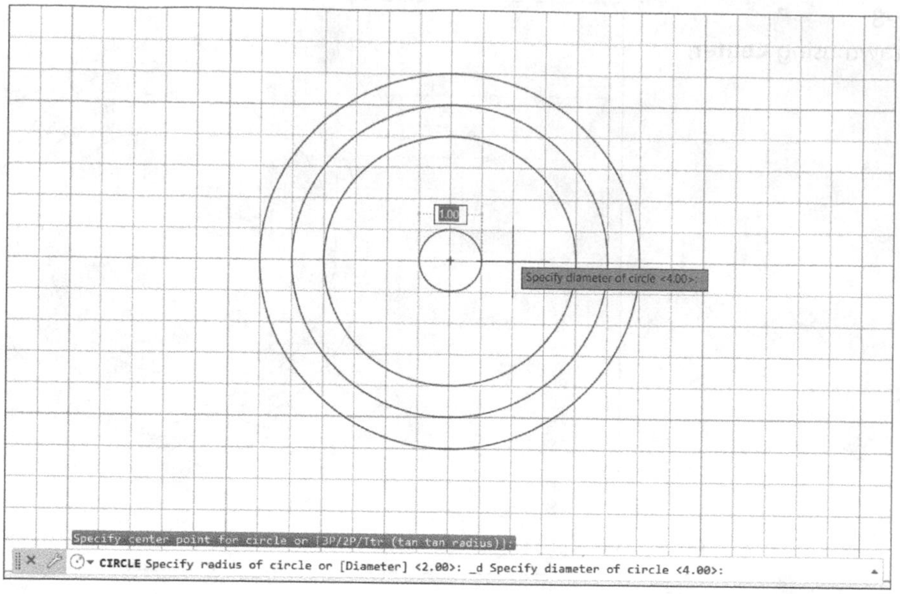
1.00
Specify diameter of circle <4.00>:
Specify center point for circle or [3P/2P/Ttr (tan tan radius)]:
CIRCLE Specify radius of circle or [Diameter] <2.00>: _d Specify diameter of circle <4.00>:

Figure 2-9
Dynamic input display

NOTE

Pressing **<Enter>** or the spacebar to repeat a command will not repeat the option unless it is the default option. In this case, the command defaults to the **Radius** option, not the **Diameter** option.

✔ Specify a distance of **1.00** unit for the circle's diameter.
You should now have four circles.

✔ Draw two more circles with diameters of **1.50** and **2.00**.
*When you are done, your drawing should look like Figure 2-10. Studying Figure 2-11 and using the **HELP** command, as discussed in the next section, will give you a good introduction to the remaining options of the **CIRCLE** command.*

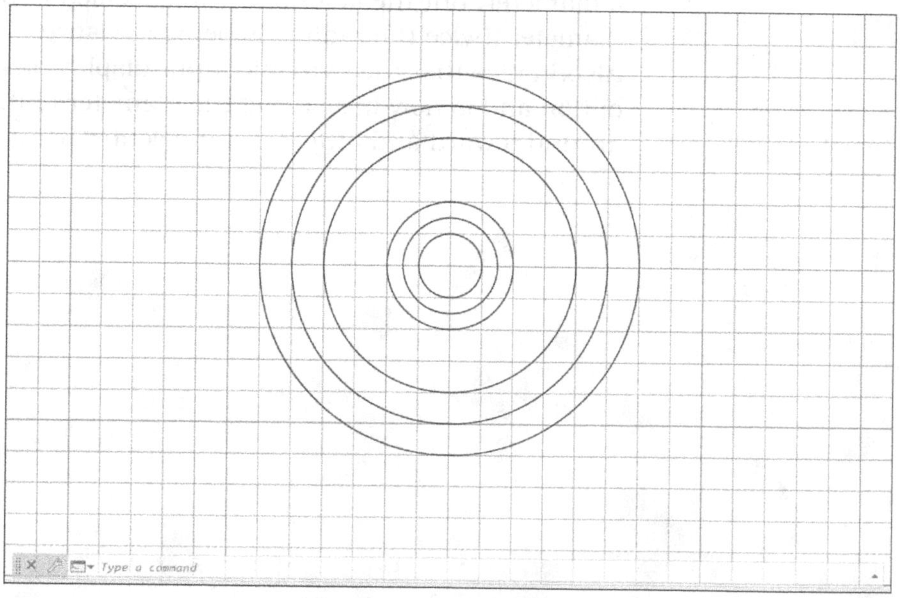
Type a command

Figure 2-10
Six circles

Figure 2-11
Circle options

3P (Three Points)

Creates a circle based on three points on the circumference.

For example:

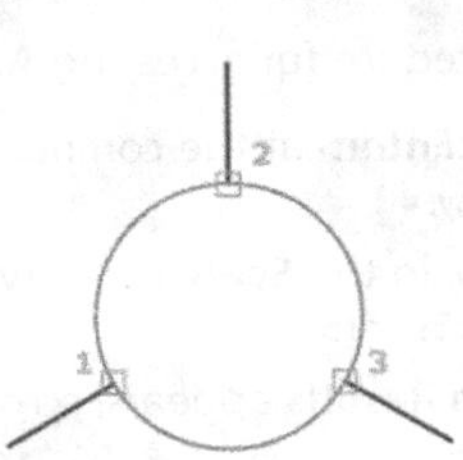

Tan, Tan, Tan

Creates a circle tangent to three objects.

For example:

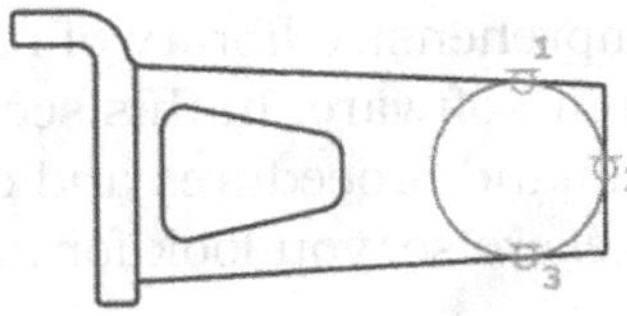

2P (Two Points)

Creates a circle based on two endpoints of the diameter.

For example:

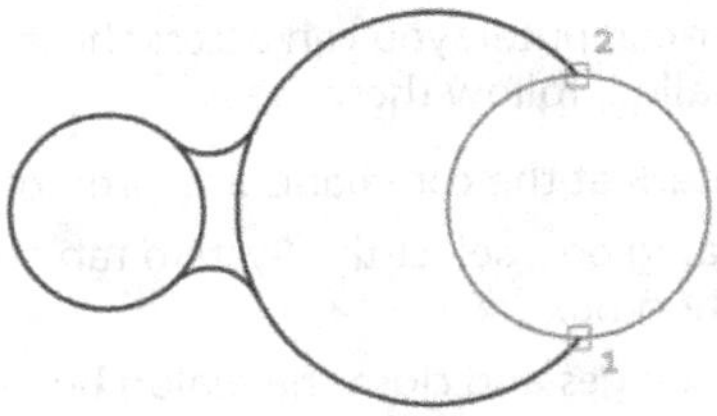

TTR (Tangent, Tangent, Radius)

Creates a circle with a specified radius and tangent to two objects.

Sometimes more than one circle matches the specified criteria. The program draws the circle of the specified radius whose tangent points are closest to the selected points.

For example:

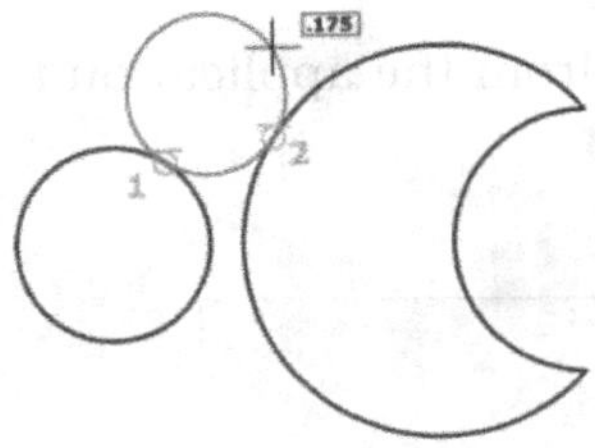

Accessing AutoCAD Online Help Features

TIP

Following is a general procedure for accessing AutoCAD Help features:

1. Press **<F1>**, type **help <Enter>** at the command-line prompt, or click the **Help** tool on the application window.
2. From the **Help** window, in the **Search** box, type the name of the command you want to research and press **<Enter>**.
3. When the list of **Search Results** appears, scroll through the list of topics to the one you want to read.
4. Click the title of the topic you want to read.

If you want information about the active command, press **<F1>** to open the **Help** window and load the topic associated with that command.

The AutoCAD **HELP** command provides access to an extraordinary amount of information in a comprehensive library of resources, available both online and locally in your software. In this section, you learn how to search for information on command procedures and capabilities in the **AutoCAD Help** window. For this exercise, you look for information on the **CIRCLE** command.

NOTE

If you are neither connected to the internet nor have offline Help installed, some of the procedures in the exercise here will not work. If the AutoCAD offline Help files have been installed on your computer, you can access those local Help files instead. To use offline Help once installed, follow these steps:

1. Type **options <Enter>** at the command-line prompt.
2. In the **Options** dialog box, select the **System** tab and clear the **Access online content when available** checkbox.
3. Click **OK** to save changes and close the dialog box.

The following steps provide access to AutoCAD's online Help features.

✔ To begin, you should be at the command-line prompt.

✔ Check to see that you are connected to the internet. If you are unable to connect, refer to the information in the preceding Note.

✔ Click the **Help** tool from the application title bar, as shown in Figure 2-12.

Figure 2-12
Help tool

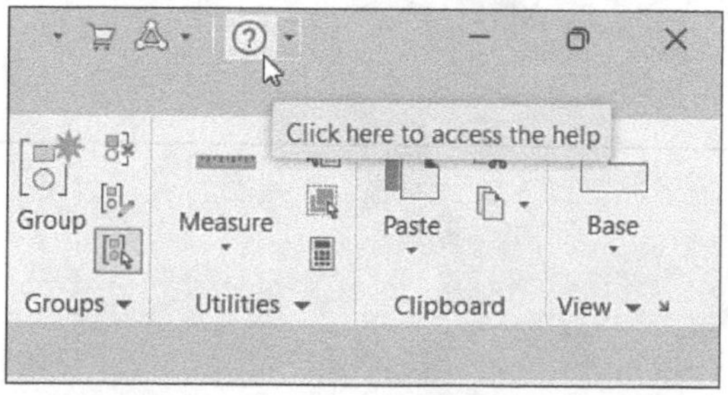

*Assuming you are online, this opens the **AutoCAD Help** window shown in Figure 2-13. Notice the **Search** box at the upper right.*

✔ Type **Circle <Enter>** in the **Search** box.

AutoCAD displays the page shown in Figure 2-14. If you scroll down, you see that this window displays 15 results based on your search. In the search results, click the title of the topic you want to read.

✔ Click the **CIRCLE (Command)** link, third on the list as shown in Figure 2-14.

*AutoCAD Help displays the **CIRCLE (Command)** topic, as shown in Figure 2-15. If you scroll down the page, you find descriptions for all the options of the **CIRCLE** command. Notice that next to the **Circle** icon in the **CIRCLE** (Command) topic is a **Find** link. When clicked, an arrow appears in AutoCAD to help you locate the tool, typically on the ribbon.*

✔ Click the **Find** link, next to the **Circle** tool icon, as shown in Figure 2-15.

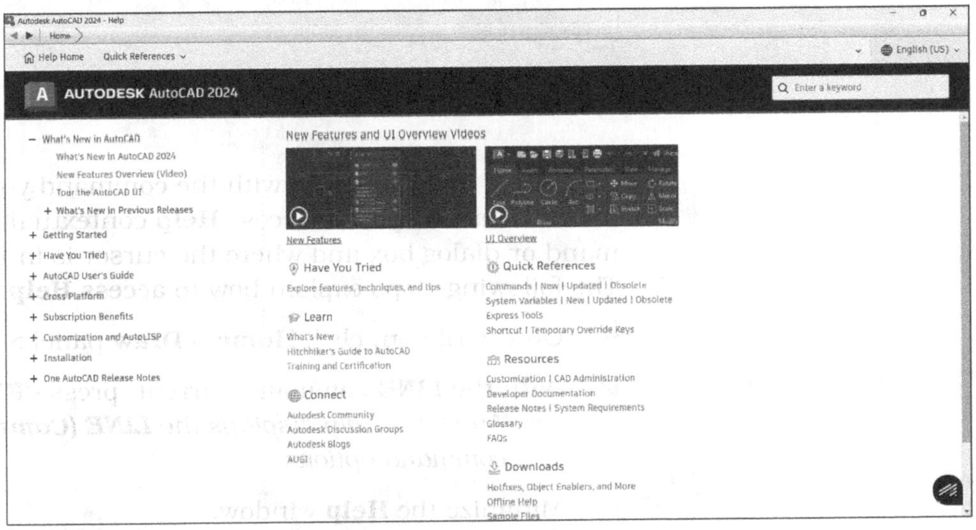

Figure 2-13
AutoCAD **Help**

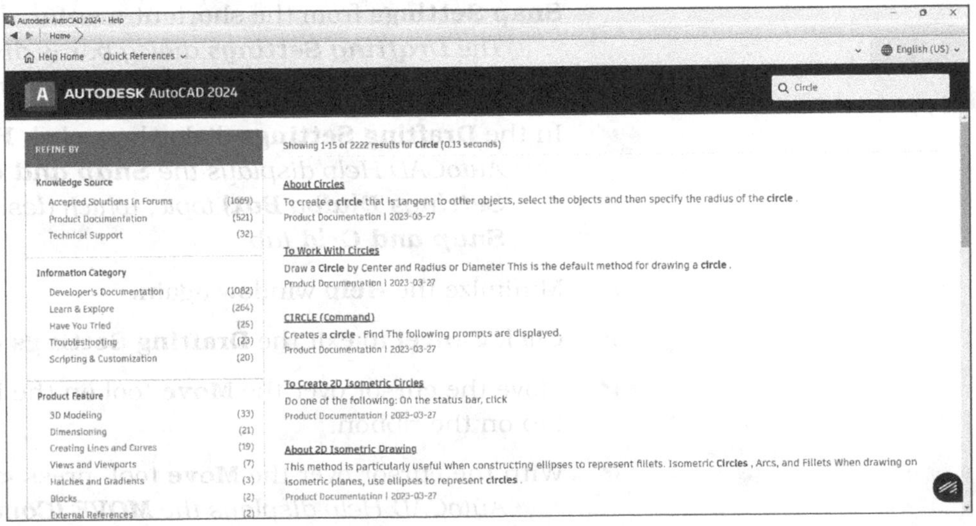

Figure 2-14
Search results page

✔ To exit the **AutoCAD Help** window, click the **Close** button at the top right.

Or you can minimize it and leave it open in the background.

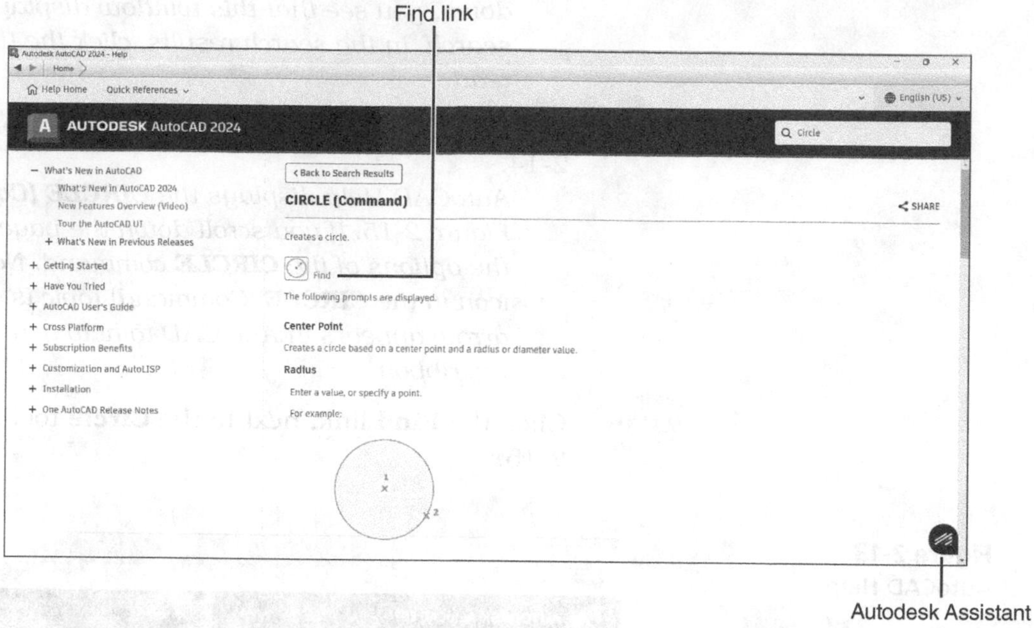

Figure 2-15
CIRCLE (Command) topic

Often, you want help with the command you are currently using. AutoCAD allows you to access **Help** contextually based on the current command or dialog box and where the cursor is in the AutoCAD user interface. The following steps explain how to access **Help** contextually:

✔ On the ribbon, click **Home** > **Draw** panel > **Line**.

✔ With the **LINE** command current, press **<F1>**.

*AutoCAD Help displays the **LINE (Command)** , describing the **LINE** command options.*

✔ Minimize the **Help** window.

✔ Right-click over the **Snap Mode** button on the status bar and select **Snap Settings** from the shortcut menu.

*The **Drafting Settings** dialog box is displayed. This is the same dialog box you used earlier to change grip and snap settings.*

✔ In the **Drafting Settings** dialog box, click **Help** or press **<F1>**.

*AutoCAD Help displays the **Snap and Grid Tab (Drafting Settings Dialog Box)** topic, which describes all settings on the **Snap and Grid** tab.*

✔ Minimize the **Help** window again.

✔ Click **Cancel** to exit the **Drafting Settings** dialog box.

✔ Move the cursor over the **Move** tool on the **Modify** panel of the **Home** tab on the ribbon.

✔ With the cursor over the **Move** tool, press **<F1>**.

*AutoCAD Help displays the **MOVE (Command)** topic, which describes the **MOVE** command.*

✔ Exit the **AutoCAD Help** window by clicking the **Close** button in the top right or minimizing the window.

New to AutoCAD 2023

The **Autodesk Assistant**, located in the lower-right corner of the **Help** window, as shown in Figure 2-15, allows you to ask a product question and find a solution, interact with product support agents, and create a support case for a problem you might be having with AutoCAD. If you don't see the **Autodesk Assistant** icon, this feature might not be available to you. There are some limitations as of this publication that determine whether this feature might be available to you. For a list of these limitations, search for **Autodesk Assistant** in **AutoCAD Help**.

ERASE	
Command	ERASE
Alias	E
Panel	Modify
Tool	

verb/noun: The selection method in which an edit command is started prior to objects being selected for edit.

noun/verb: The selection method in which an object to be edited is selected prior to starting an edit command.

Using the ERASE Command

AutoCAD allows for many different methods of editing. Fundamentally, there are two different sequences for using most edit commands. These are called the ***verb/noun*** and ***noun/verb*** methods.

In this section, you learn to use the verb/noun sequence first and then the noun/verb or "pick first" method along with some of the many options for selecting objects.

> **TIP**
>
> Following is a general procedure for using the **ERASE** command with verb/noun selection:
>
> 1. Click the **Erase** tool from the **Modify** panel on the **Home** tab of the ribbon.
> 2. Select objects.
> 3. Press <**Enter**> to complete the command.

Verb/Noun Editing

✔ To begin this section you should have the six circles in your drawing, as shown previously in Figure 2-10.

You use verb/noun editing to erase the two outer circles. Here, you erase two circles at once.

✔ Click the **Erase** tool from the **Modify** panel on the **Home** tab of the ribbon.

In the command line or dynamic input display, you see the prompt

```
Select objects:
```

This is a very common prompt in all edit commands and many other commands.

✔ Move your cursor, which looks like a box and is known as the *pickbox*, over the outer circle.

The circle is grayed out and a red ***x*** appears.

✔ Click to select the outermost circle.

*The circle remains gray but the red **x** disappears.*

✔ Use the pickbox to select the second circle moving in toward the center.

It, too, should now be grayed out.

✔ Right-click or press **<Enter>** to complete the command.

This is typical of the verb/noun sequence in most edit commands. Once a command has been started and objects have been selected to define a selection set, pressing ***<Enter>*** *or right-clicking is required to complete the command. At this point, the two outer circles should be erased.*

> **TIP**
> In verb/noun edit commands, where pressing **<Enter>** completes the command, it is good heads-up practice to use the right button on your mouse in place of the spacebar or **<Enter>** key.

Noun/Verb Editing

Now, give the noun/verb method a try:

✔ Click the **Undo** tool on the **Quick Access** toolbar or type **u <Enter>** to undo the **ERASE** command and restore the circles.

Notice at the center of your crosshairs is a square; this is the same pickbox you saw when using the verb/noun method with the ERASE command.

grip: In AutoCAD, grips are placed at strategic geometric locations on selected objects in a drawing. Several forms of editing can be accomplished by clicking, dragging, and manipulating grips.

✔ Move your cursor over the outermost circle and click to select it.

The circle is highlighted in blue, and your drawing area should resemble Figure 2-16. Those little blue boxes are called ***grips****. They can be used to edit many AutoCAD objects. For now, you can ignore them.*

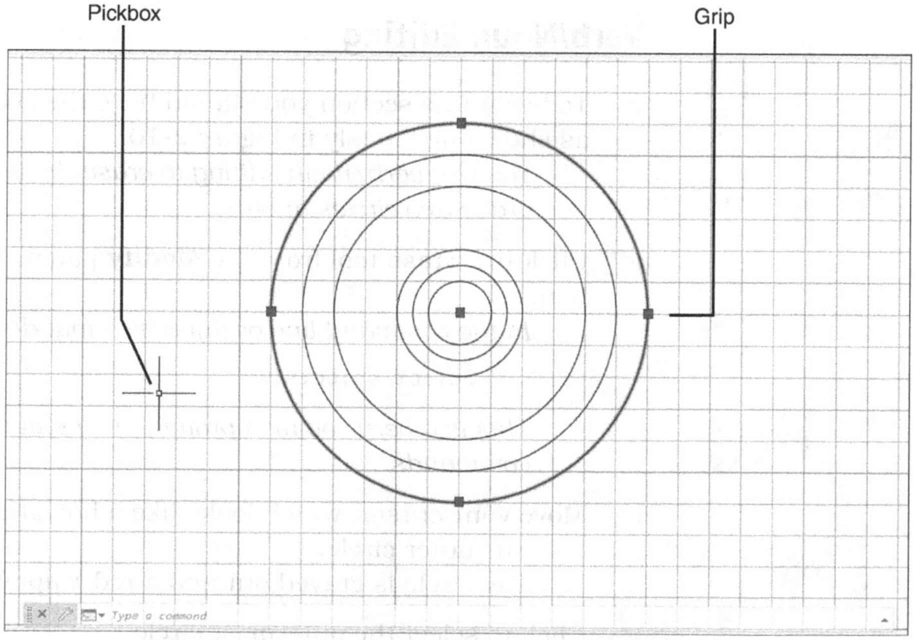

Figure 2-16
Blue grip boxes

✔ Select the second outermost circle in the same fashion.

The second circle also becomes highlighted, and more grips appear.

✔ Click the **Erase** tool on the **Modify** panel of the ribbon's **Home** tab.

*Alternatively, you can type **e <Enter>** or press the **<Del>** key. Your two outermost circles are removed.*

The two outermost circles should now be gone once again. As you can see, there is not much difference between the two methods. One difference that is not immediately apparent is that there are numerous selection methods available in the verb/noun method that cannot be activated when you select objects first. You explore other object selection methods momentarily, but first give the **OOPS** command a try.

> **TIP**
>
> Following is a general procedure for using the **ERASE** command with noun/verb selection:
>
> 1. Select objects.
> 2. Click the **Erase** tool on the **Modify** panel on the ribbon's **Home** tab.

OOPS

✔ Type **oops <Enter>** and watch the drawing area.

*If you make a mistake in your erasure, you can get your objects back by typing **oops**. **OOPS** is to **ERASE** as **REDO** is to **UNDO**. You can use **OOPS** to undo the most recent **ERASE** command, no matter which commands you have done since then as long as you have not performed another **ERASE** in the meantime.*

*You can also use **U** or **Ctrl-Z** to undo an **ERASE**, but notice the difference: **U** simply undoes the last command, whatever it may be; **OOPS** works specifically with **ERASE** to recall the last erased objects. If you have drawn other objects in the meantime, you can still use **OOPS** to recall previously erased objects. However, if you used **U**, you would have to backtrack, undoing any newly drawn objects along the way.*

Other Object Selection Methods

You can select individual entities in the drawing area by selecting them one by one, but in complex drawings this is often inefficient. AutoCAD offers a variety of other selection methods. In this exercise, you select circles with the windowing and crossing methods by indicating **Last** or **L** for the last entity drawn and by indicating **Previous** or **P** for the previous selection set. There are also options to add or remove objects from the current selection set and other variations on windowing and crossing. Take a bit of time to study Figure 2-17 to learn about other methods. The number of selection methods available might seem a bit overwhelming at first, but time learning them is well spent. These same options appear in many editing commands (**MOVE**, **COPY**, **ARRAY**, **ROTATE**, **MIRROR**) and will become part of your CAD vocabulary in no time.

Figure 2-17
Object selection methods chart

OBJECT SELECTION METHOD	DESCRIPTION	ITEMS SELECTED
(W) WINDOW		The entities within the box.
(C) CROSSING		The entities crossed by or within the box.
(P) PREVIOUS		The entities that were previously selected.
(L) LAST		The entity that was drawn last.
(R) REMOVE		Removes entities from the items selected so they will not be part of the selected objects.
(A) ADD		Adds entities that were removed and allows for more selections after the use of remove.
ALL		All the entities currently visible in the drawing.
(F) FENCE		The entities crossed by the fence.
(WP) WPOLYGON		All the entities completely within the window of the polygon.
(CP) CPOLYGON		All the entities crossed by or inside the polygon.

Selection by Window

Window and crossing selections, like individual object selection, can be initiated without entering a command. In other words, they are available for noun/verb selection. Whether you select objects first or enter a command first, you can force a window or crossing selection simply by specifying points in the drawing area that are not on objects. AutoCAD assumes that you want to select by windowing or crossing and prompts for a second point.

Give it a try right now. You erase all the inner circles by defining a temporary selection window around them. The window is defined by two points moving left to right that serve as opposite corners of a rectangular window. Only entities that lie completely within the window are selected (see Figure 2-18).

✔ Specify point 1 in the lower left of the drawing area, as shown.

Any point in the neighborhood of (3.5,1.0) will do. It is particularly important in this case to click and release before moving to specify the second point. Clicking and dragging has a different effect that you explore momentarily.

AutoCAD prompts for another corner:

```
Specify opposite corner:
```

✔ Specify point 2 in the upper right of the drawing area, as shown in Figure 2-18.

Any point in the neighborhood of (9.5,8.5) will do. To see the effect of the window, be sure that it crosses the outside circle, as shown in Figure 2-18.

✔ Click the **Erase** tool from the ribbon or press the **<Del>** key.

The inner circles should now be erased.

✔ Type **oops <Enter>** to restore the circles once more.

*Because **ERASE** was the last command, typing **u** or clicking the **Undo** tool also works.*

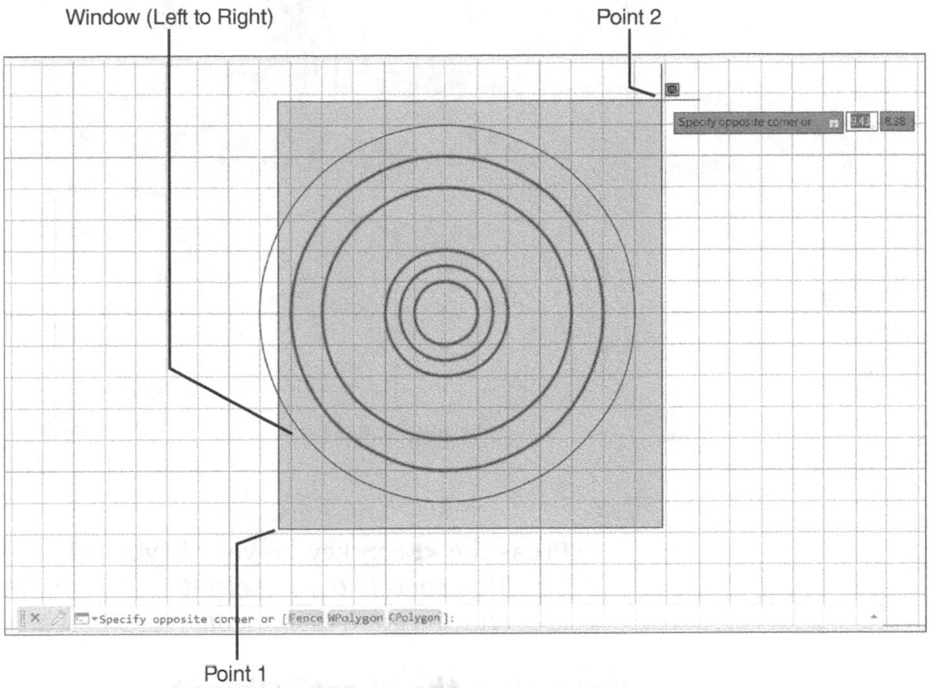

Figure 2-18
Window selection

Selection by Crossing Window

crossing window: A selection window that opens from right to left. Everything within the window is selected, along with anything that crosses the window.

Crossing is an alternative to windowing that is useful in many cases where a standard window selection cannot be performed. The selection method is similar, but a ***crossing window*** opens to the left instead of to the right, and all objects that cross the window are selected, not just those that lie completely inside the window (see Figure 2-19).

Here, you use a crossing window to select the inside circles.

✔ Specify point 1 in the lower right of the drawing area, as shown in Figure 2-19.

*Any point near **(8.0,3.0)** will do.*

AutoCAD prompts:

`Specify opposite corner:`

✔ Specify a point near **(4.0,7.0)**.

The point specified must be done carefully to define a crossing window. Notice that the crossing window is shown with dashed lines and green shading, whereas the window was shown with solid blue lines.

Also, notice how the circles are selected; those that cross and those that are completely contained within the crossing window, but not those that lie outside. Be sure that the crossing window doesn't cross the outside circle, as shown in Figure 2-19.

*At this point you could enter the **ERASE** command to erase the circles, but instead you use the **<Esc>** key to clear object selection.*

Figure 2-19
Crossing window selection

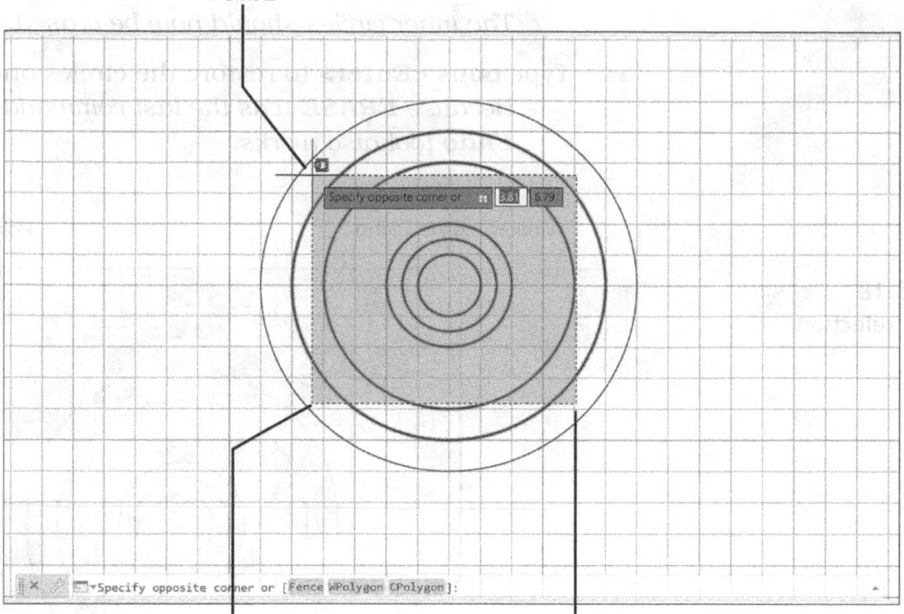

✔ Press the **<Esc>** key on your keyboard.

This cancels object selection. The circles are no longer highlighted, and the grips disappear.

Selecting the "Last" Object

AutoCAD remembers the order in which new objects are drawn during the course of a single drawing session. As long as you do not close the drawing, you can select the last drawn object using the **Last** option.

✔ Click the **Erase** tool.

*Notice that there is no way to specify **Last** before you start a command. This object selection method is available only as part of a command. In other words, it works only with the verb/noun method.*

✔ Type **L <Enter>**.

One of the smaller circles should be highlighted.

✔ Right-click to complete the command.

The circle should be erased.

Selecting the "Previous" Selection Set

The **P** or **Previous** selection method works with the same procedure as **Last**, but it selects the previous selection set rather than the last drawn object.

lasso: A lasso is a series of connected line segments that, together with the rubber band, cross or completely surround objects in the drawing area. Objects crossed or surrounded are selected, depending on the direction of the starting segment.

Window and Crossing Lassos

Window and crossing are two of the most commonly used selection methods, but they can be tough to use in tight places. When selecting objects in tight places, ***lassos*** may be more convenient. Also, because lassos are automatically initiated when you click and drag in the drawing area, it is important to recognize what is occurring and how to use them.

Currently you have five concentric circles in your drawing. Next, you define a window lasso to erase the inner circle and a crossing lasso to erase the two outer circles.

✔ Click and hold at point 1 to the left of the circles, near **(2,5)** as in Figure 2-20.

In this case, it is important that you do not release the mouse button after clicking near point 1.

✔ Hold the mouse button down and drag the cursor over the top of the two smallest circles and then down until the rubber band is just below the inner circle, but crossing the second circle to the release point (point 2 in Figure 2-20).

If done carefully, the innermost circle is highlighted, and the other circles remain unchanged.

Figure 2-20
Window lasso

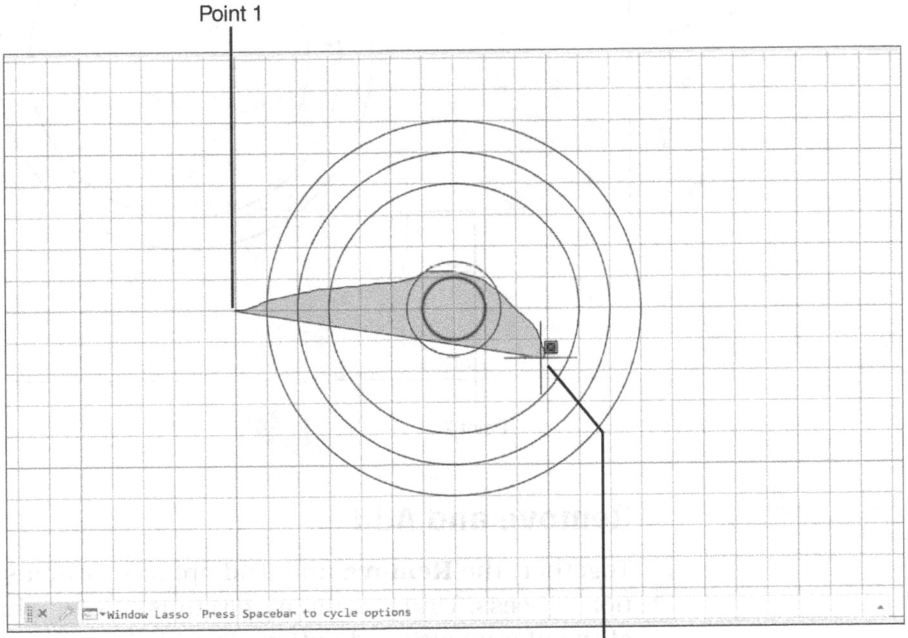

✔ With only the inner circle highlighted, release the mouse button.

The window lasso disappears and the inner circle is highlighted with blue color and grips.

✔ Click the **Erase** tool or press the **<Del>** key to erase the circle.

The inner circle is erased. This is the window lasso. Defined left to right as before, the window lasso selects anything that is completely within the irregular outline defined by the movement of your cursor and the rubber band back to the start point. Next, you define a crossing lasso moving right to left.

✔ Click and hold at point 1 to the right of the circles, near **(10,3)** as in Figure 2-21.

Using a crossing lasso, you can select objects with something near a straight line.

- ✔ Drag the cursor at a slight angle down and to the left to the release point—point 2—near **(2.5,2.5)**. As shown in Figure 2-21, this "line" should cross the two outermost circles only.
- ✔ With the two outermost circles highlighted, release the mouse button. *The two outermost circles are highlighted with dashes and grips.*
- ✔ Click the **Erase** tool or press the **<Del>** key to complete the command. *There are now only two circles remaining.*

Figure 2-21
Crossing lasso

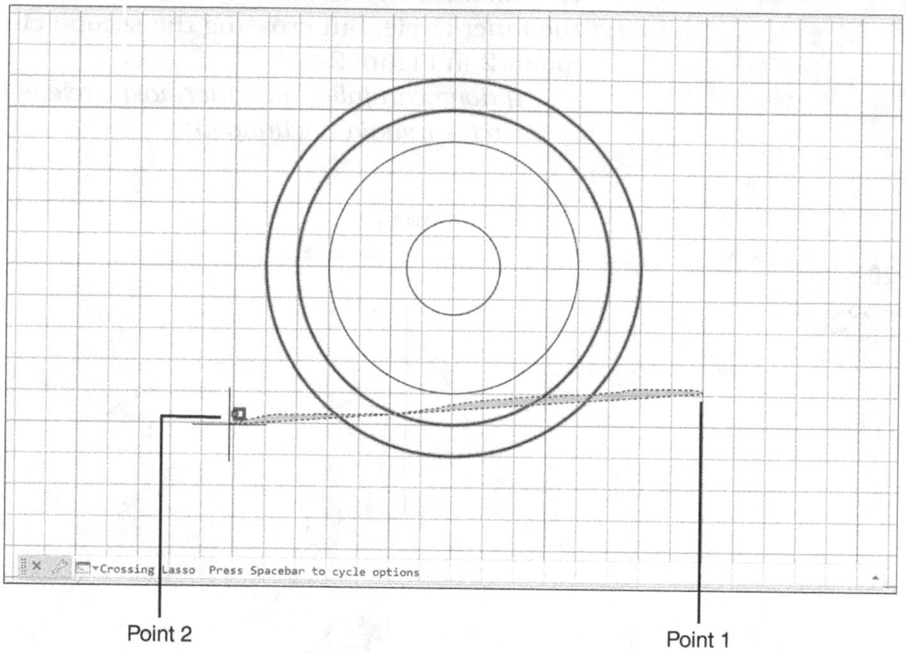

Remove and Add

Together, the **Remove** and **Add** options form a switch in the object selection process. Under ordinary circumstances, whatever you select using any of the aforementioned options is added to a selection set. By typing **r** at the **Select objects** prompt, you switch to a mode in which everything you select is deselected or removed from the selection set. Then, by typing **a**, you can return to the usual mode of adding objects to the set.

> **TIP**
>
> You can hold down the **<Shift>** key to temporarily enter **Remove** mode for object selection. Objects selected while holding **<Shift>** are removed from the current selection set. This can be more efficient than toggling between the **Remove** and **Add** modes.

Undoing a Selection

The **ERASE** command and other edit commands have an internal undo feature, similar to that found in the **LINE** command. By typing **u** at the **Select objects** prompt, you can undo your last selection without leaving the edit command you are in and without undoing previous selections. You can also type **u** several times to undo your most recent selections one by one. This allows you to back up one step at a time without canceling the command and starting all over again.

Select Similar

AutoCAD has a selection feature that allows you to quickly select all similar objects in a drawing after only one object has been selected. Similar objects are those of the same object type, on the same layer, with the same color, and so on. In your drawings, all the circles have the same properties. Try this:

✔ Select the outer circle.

✔ Right-click to open the shortcut menu.

✔ Select **Select Similar** from the menu.

The inner circle will be selected as well. This feature will be most useful when your drawings include a greater variety of objects and properties.

✔ Press **<Esc>** to deselect the circles.

Other Options

If you type **?** at the **Select objects** prompt, you see the following:

```
    Expects a point or Window/Last/Crossing/BOX/ALL/Fence/WPolygon/
CPolygon/Group/Add/Remove/Multiple/Previous/Undo/AUto/Single/SUbobject/
Object
```

Notice that some options require you type two or three letters, as shown by the uppercase letters in the following commands. Along with the options already discussed, **ALL**, **Fence**, **WPolygon**, and **CPolygon** are shown in Figure 2-17. **BOX**, **Multiple**, **AUto**, and **Single** are used primarily in programming customized applications. **SUbobject** and **Object** are used in 3D modeling. Look up the **SELECT** command in the AutoCAD **Help** for additional information on object selection.

> **TIP**
>
> Pressing the **<Ctrl>+A** key combination selects all objects in the drawing that are on unlocked and thawed layers. See Chapter 3 for information on layer states: unlocked, thawed, and more.

Using Single-Point Object Snap

object snap: A snap mode that locates a geometrically definable point on a previously drawn object, such as the midpoint or endpoint of a line.

Now that you have a good foundation of object selection methods, let's turn some focus back to drafting and drawing aids. This section offers a quick introduction to the powerful ***object snap*** feature and single-point object snaps. Instead of snapping to points defined by the coordinate system, this feature snaps to geometrically specifiable points on objects that have already been drawn. It enables you to specify points that you could not locate with the crosshairs or by typing coordinates.

TIP

Following is a general procedure for using single-point object snap:

1. Enter a drawing command, such as **LINE** or **CIRCLE**.
2. Right-click while holding down the **<Shift>** or **<Ctrl>** key.
3. Select an object snap mode from the shortcut menu.
4. Point to a previously drawn object.

quadrant: A point on a curved object along one of the orthogonal axes, at 0°, 90°, 180°, or 270° from a given point, or the area enclosed between any two adjacent axes.

tangent: A line running perpendicular to the radius of a circle and touching at only one point, or the point where the line and circle touch.

You continue to work with the circles you previously drew by drawing a line from one circle tangent to another with the use of the ***quadrant*** and ***tangent*** object snaps.

✔ The **Object Snap** and **Dynamic Input** buttons on the status bar should be off for this exercise.

✔ Enter **LINE** at the command-line prompt.

You draw a line from the quadrant of one circle tangent to another, as shown in Figure 2-22. This requires the use of the ***Tangent*** *object snap. The quadrant point could be easily located without object snap because it is on a grid snap point, but the tangent point could not be located by specifying a point. When AutoCAD prompts for a point, you select an object snap mode from the* ***Object Snap*** *shortcut menu.*

✔ At the **Specify first point** prompt, instead of specifying a point, hold down the **<Shift>** or **<Ctrl>** key and right-click.

This opens the shortcut menu shown in Figure 2-23.

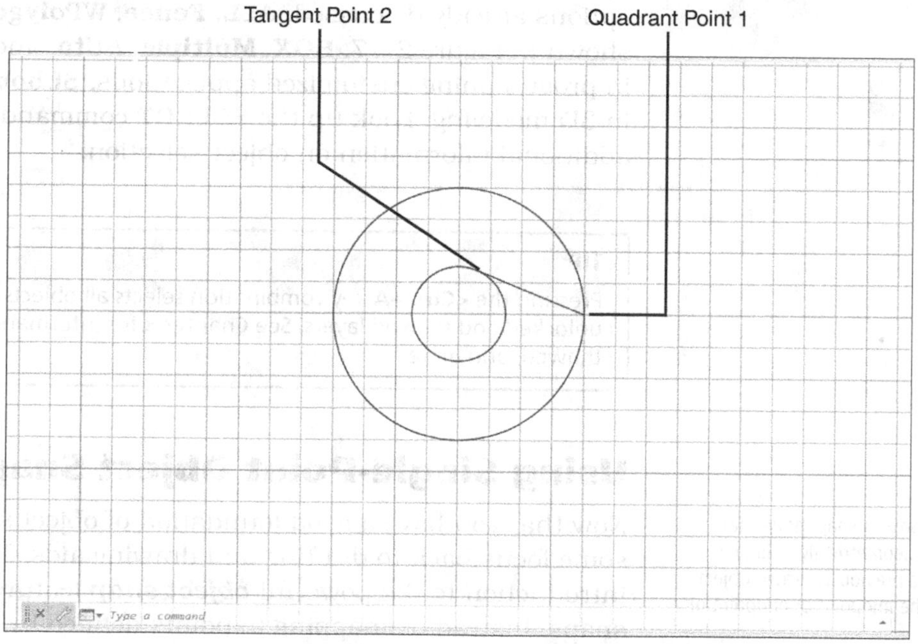

Figure 2-22
Line from quadrant of circle tangent to another

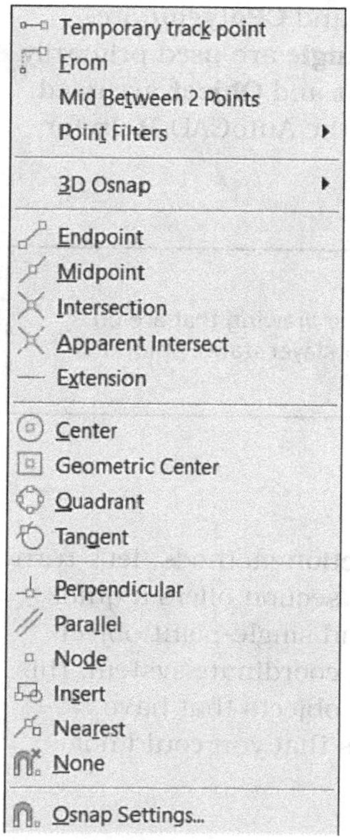

Figure 2-23
Object Snap shortcut menu

✔ Select **Quadrant** from the shortcut menu.

This tells AutoCAD that you are going to select the start point of the line by using a ***Quadrant*** *object snap, rather than by directly specifying or entering a coordinate value.*

✔ Move the crosshairs over the two circles in your drawing.

As you move across the circles, AutoCAD identifies the eight quadrant points and indicates these with a green diamond surrounding each quadrant point. This object snap symbol is called a marker. There are different-shaped markers for each type of object snap. If you let the cursor rest near a marker for a moment, a tooltip appears, naming the type of object snap that has been recognized, as shown in Figure 2-24.

Figure 2-24
Object snap Quadrant point

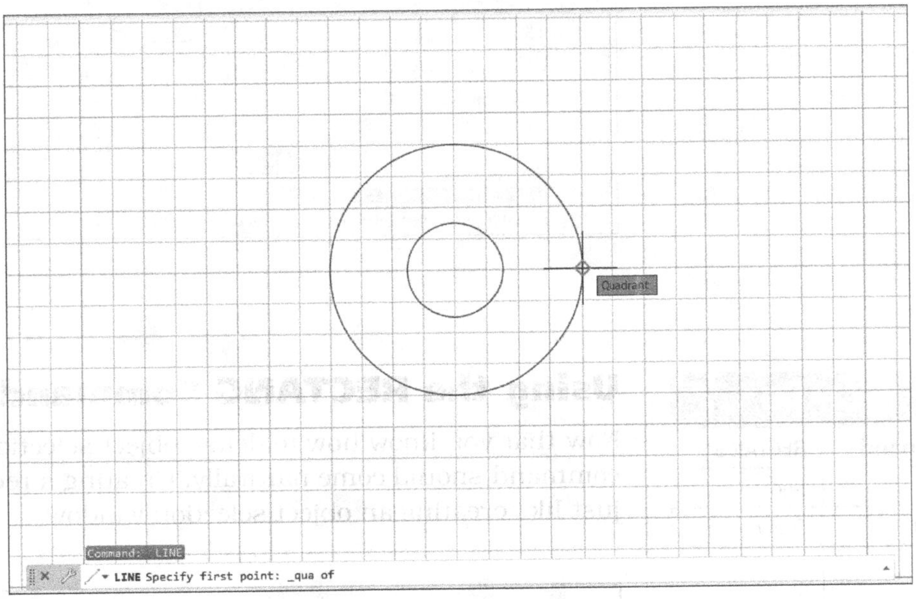

✔ Move the crosshairs near the right quadrant of the larger circle—point 1 in Figure 2-22.

✔ With the quadrant marker showing, click the left mouse button.

The green quadrant marker and the snap-tip disappear, and there is a rubber band stretching from the center of the circle to the crosshairs position. In the command line, you see the ***Specify next point*** *prompt.*

You use a ***Tangent*** *object snap to select the second point.*

✔ At the **Specify next point or [Undo]** prompt, open the shortcut menu again (**<Shift>** + right-click) and select **Tangent**.

✔ Move the cursor up and to the left, positioning the crosshairs so that they are near the right side of the smaller circle.

When you approach the tangent area, you see the green tangent marker, as shown in Figure 2-25. Here again, if you let the cursor rest, you see a tooltip with the object snap type on it.

✔ With the tangent marker showing, click the left mouse button.

AutoCAD locates the tangent point and draws the line. Notice the power of being able to precisely locate the tangent point in this way.

✔ Press <Enter> to complete the **LINE** command.

Your drawing should now resemble Figure 2-22, shown previously.

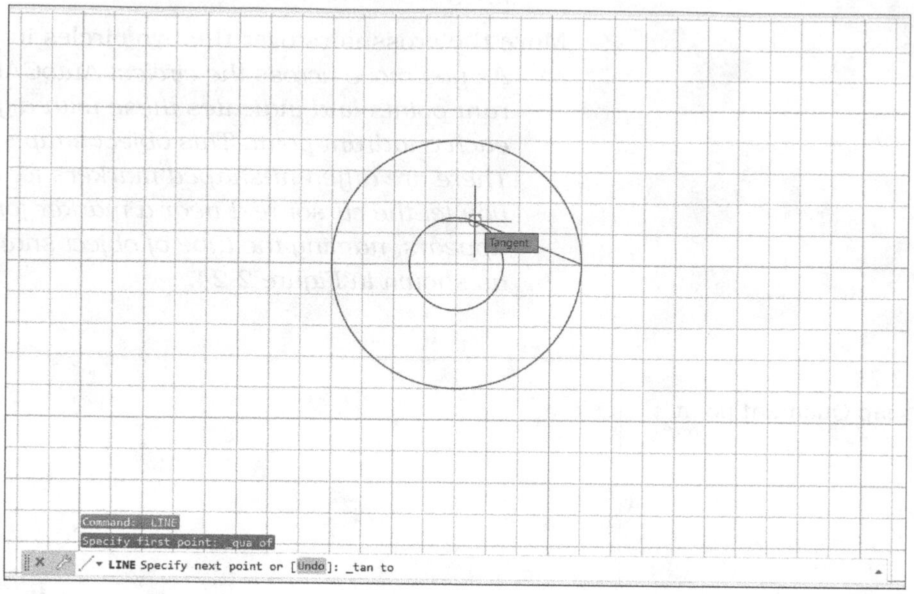

Figure 2-25
Object snap Tangent point

RECTANG	
Command	RECTANG
Alias	Rec
Panel	Draw
Tool	

Using the RECTANG Command

Now that you know how to define object selection windows, the **RECTANG** command should come naturally. Creating a rectangle with **RECTANG** is just like creating an object selection window.

> **TIP**
>
> Following is a general procedure for using the **RECTANG** command:
>
> 1. Click the **Rectangle** tool from the **Rectangle/Polygon** drop-down menu on the **Draw** panel of the **Home** tab.
> 2. Specify the first corner point.
> 3. Specify the opposite corner point.

✔ To prepare for this exercise, erase all objects from your drawing.

✔ Turn on **Snap Mode** and select **Dynamic Input** from the status bar.

✔ Click the **Rectangle** tool from the **Rectangle/Polygon** drop-down menu on the **Draw** panel of the **Home** tab, as shown in Figure 2-26.

AutoCAD prompts for a corner point:

```
Specify first corner point or [Chamfer/Elevation/Fillet/
Thickness/Width]:
```

You can ignore the options for now and proceed with the defaults.

✔ Specify **(3.00,3.00)** for the first corner point, as shown in Figure 2-27.

AutoCAD prompts for another point:

```
Specify other corner point or [Area/Dimensions/Rotation]:
```

Figure 2-26
Rectangle tool

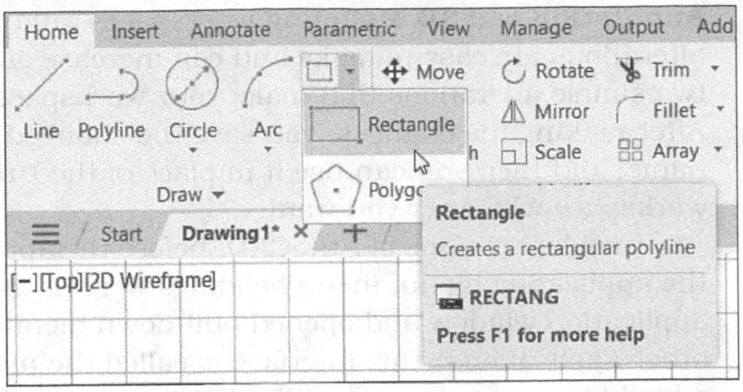

Figure 2-27
A 6 × 3 rectangle

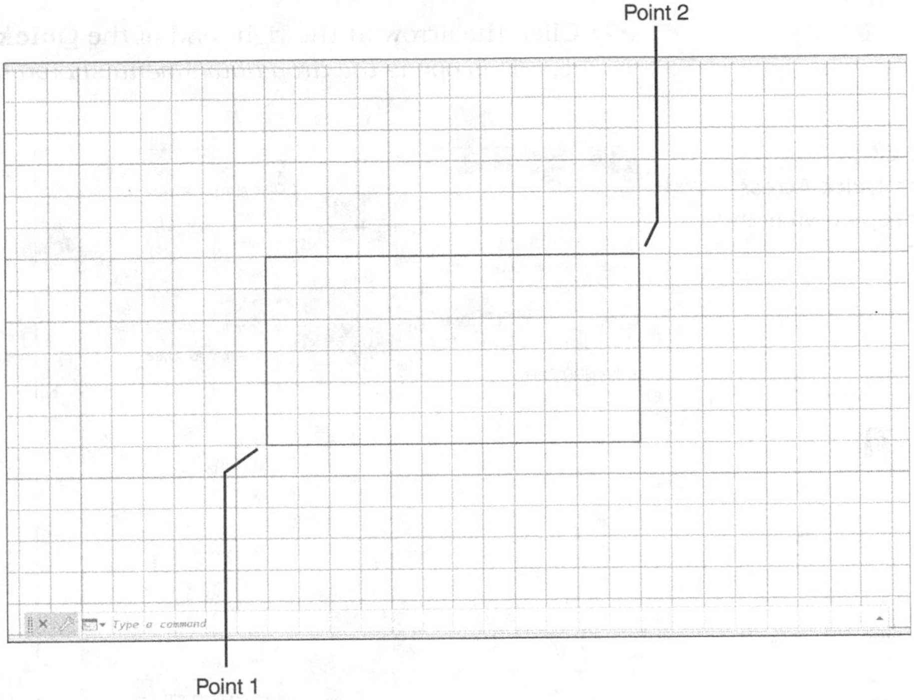

> **TIP**
> Notice how the coordinate display and dynamic input tooltip display work differently after you have entered the **RECTANG** command. The coordinate display continues to show absolute coordinates relative to the display grid. Dynamic input shows absolute coordinates relative to the first corner point of the rectangle.

✔ Specify a second point at **(9.00,6.00)** to create a 6 × 3 rectangle.
As soon as you specify the opposite corner, the rectangle is drawn between the two points and returns you to the command-line prompt. This is a faster way to draw a rectangle than drawing it line by line. Leave the rectangle in your drawing to use with the exercises in the "Plotting or Printing a Drawing" section.

Customizing Your Workspace

There are many ways you can change your workspace to suit your preferences or the needs of a particular type of drawing. The **Drafting &**

Annotation and **3D Modeling** workspaces are usually sufficient, but slight alterations are easy to make and can increase efficiency. Here, you make two simple alterations that make your workspace a little more efficient. After making the changes, you save the changed workspace under a new name, and then you can use it in place of the **Drafting & Annotation** workspace whenever you want.

menu bar: A set of drop-down menus opened from labels displayed horizontally on a bar that appears below the application title bar and above the ribbon. By default the menu bar is not displayed. It can be displayed from the **Quick Access** toolbar.

In older versions of AutoCAD, before the appearance of the ribbon and the application menu, menu headings were positioned across the top of the application window and opened pull-down menus, as is common with many other applications. This interface is called the ***menu bar***, and it can be added to your workspace without giving up much space in your drawing area.

✔ Click the arrow at the right end of the **Quick Access** toolbar.

This opens the drop-down menu shown in Figure 2-28.

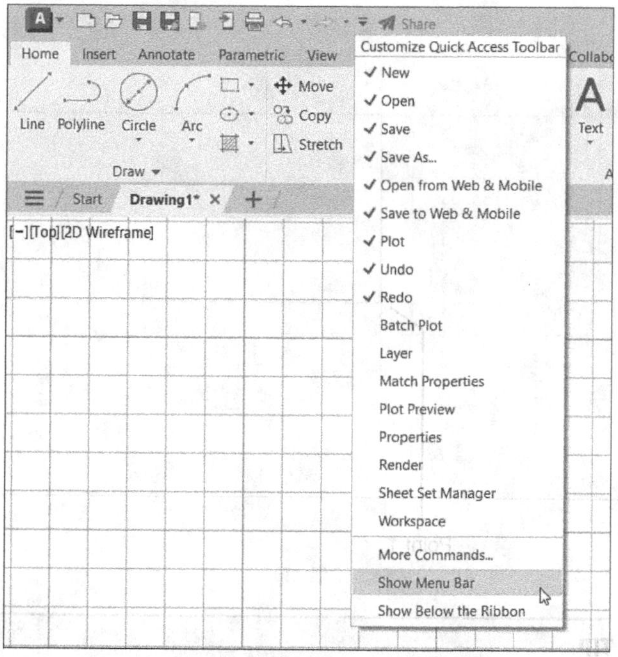

Figure 2-28
Customize Quick Access Toolbar drop-down menu

✔ From the menu, select **Show Menu Bar**.

*The menu bar is added at the top of the application window between the ribbon and the application title bar. Clicking any of the headings (**File**, **Edit**, **View**, **Insert**, etc.) opens a drop-down menu. Many commands and procedures are accessible from these menus. The menu bar can be turned off by reversing this procedure.*

✔ Click the arrow at the right end of the **Quick Access** toolbar again.

✔ From the menu, select **Layer**.

The Layer drop-down list is added to the Quick Access toolbar. This is the same Layer drop-down list on the Layers panel of the Home tab except its available regardless of the ribbon tab that is current.

With the menu bar and Layer drop-down list displayed, you save these changes to the current workspace under a new name. Because the menu bar is open, it will be used to save the workspace.

✔ From the menu bar, select **Tools** > **Workspaces** > **Save Current As**.

This sequence is shown in Figure 2-29. Clicking Save Current As starts the ***WSSAVE*** *command, which allows you to save a new workspace. The* ***Save Workspace*** *dialog box is displayed, as shown in Figure 2-30.*

✔ Type **Custom <Enter>**.

To see that your ***Custom*** *workspace has been saved, select* ***Tools*** *>* ***Workspaces*** *again from the menu bar.* ***Custom*** *is added to the list of workspaces and is highlighted to show that you are currently in this workspace. At any point, you can return to the* ***Drafting & Annotation*** *workspace by selecting it from this* ***Tools*** *menu on the menu bar or selecting it from the* ***Workspace Switching*** *button on the status bar. When you do, the menu bar and the* ***Layer*** *drop-down list on the* ***Quick Access*** *toolbar disappear from the application window.*

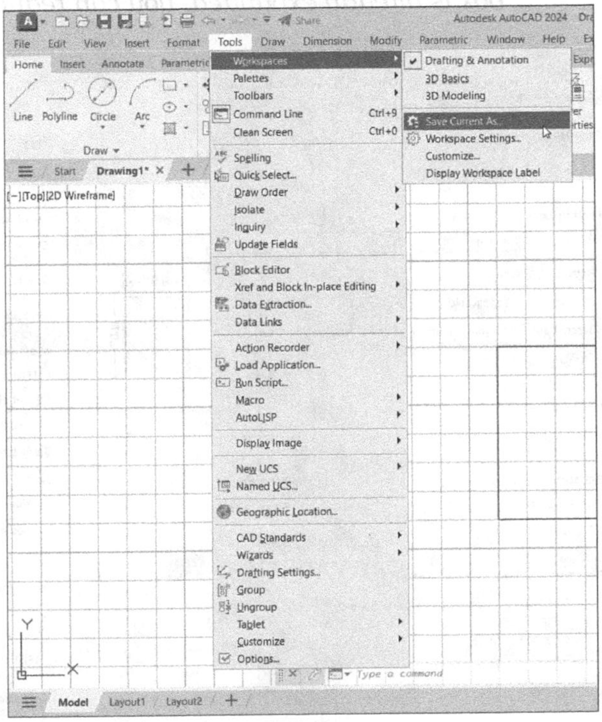

Figure 2-29
Saving the current workspace

Figure 2-30
Save Workspace dialog box

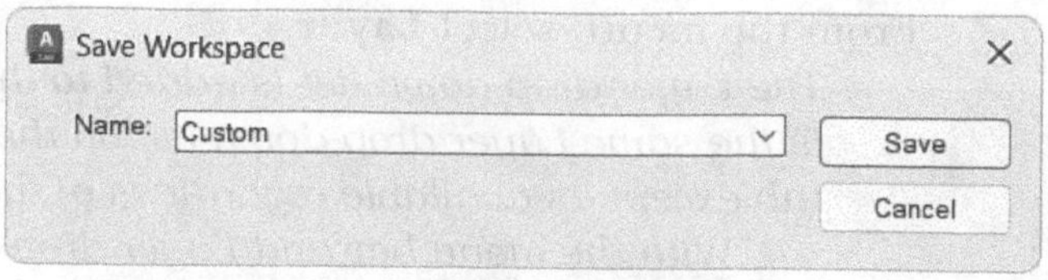

Plotting or Printing a Drawing

AutoCAD's printing and plotting capabilities are extensive and complex. In this section, you perform a very simple type of plot, going directly from your current model space objects to a sheet of drawing paper, changing only one or two plot settings. Different types of plotters and printers work somewhat differently, but the exercise here should achieve reasonably uniform results. It assumes that you do not have to change devices or fundamental configuration details. It should work for all plotters and printers and the drawings from this chapter. Here, you use a window selection to define a plot area and scale this to fit whatever size paper is in your plotter or printer.

✔ Click the **Plot** tool from the **Quick Access** toolbar.

This displays the **Plot** *dialog box shown in Figure 2-31. You will become very familiar with this dialog box as you continue working in AutoCAD. It is one of the most important dialog boxes you encounter. It contains many options and can be expanded to access even more options by clicking the* **>** *button at the bottom right. (If your dialog box is already expanded, you can reduce it by clicking the* **<** *button.)*

Figure 2-31
Plot dialog box

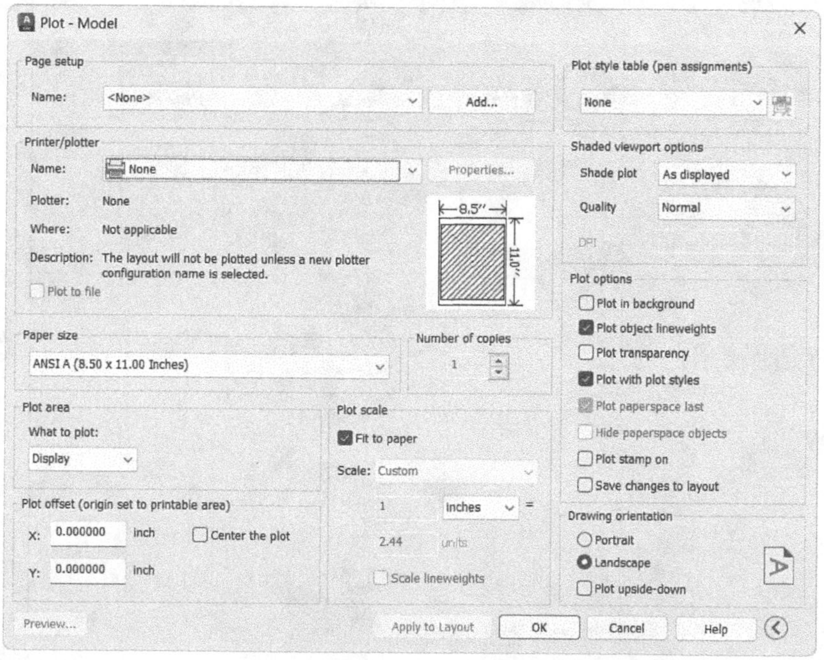

Specifying a Printer

First, you need to specify a plotter or printer. The second panel from the top is **Printer/plotter**. Look to see whether the name of a plotting device is showing in the **Name** list box.

✔ If **None** is displayed in the list box, click the arrow on the right and select a plotter or printer.

If you are unsure what plotter to use, you can work with the AutoCAD PDF (General Documentation).pc3 device, which should be present.

✔ Look at the **Plot scale** panel in the lower right of the reduced dialog box or the lower middle of the expanded dialog box. Locate the **Fit to paper** check box.

If your plot scale is configured to fit your paper, as it should be by default, then AutoCAD plots your drawing at maximum size based on the paper size and the window you specify.

✔ If for any reason **Fit to paper** is not checked, click in the box to check it.

*On the **Custom** line below **Plot scale,** you should see edit boxes with numbers like 1 inches = 2.45. Right now, the plot area is based on the shape of your display area, and these numbers are inaccessible. When you use a window to create a plot area that is somewhat smaller, these scale numbers change automatically. When you use **Scale** rather than **Fit to paper**, these numbers will be accessible, and you can set them manually or select from a list.*

Plot Area

Now look at the panel labeled **Plot area** at the lower left. The **What to plot** drop-down list allows you to choose what area of the drawing to plot; what is currently in the **Display**, the **Extents** or **Limits** of the drawing, or a **Window** you define. **Window** allows you to plot any portion of a drawing by defining an area in the usual way. AutoCAD bases the size and placement of the plot on the window you define.

✔ Click the arrow on the right of the **What to plot** drop-down list and select **Window**.

*The **Plot** dialog box disappears temporarily, giving you access to the drawing. AutoCAD prompts for point selection:*

```
Specify window for printing
Specify first corner:
```

✔ Specify the point **(1.50,1.50)**, as shown in Figure 2-32.

AutoCAD prompts:

```
Specify opposite corner:
```

✔ Specify the point **(10.50,7.50)**, as shown in Figure 2-32.

*As soon as you have specified the second point, AutoCAD displays the **Plot** window again.*

Figure 2-32
Plot window

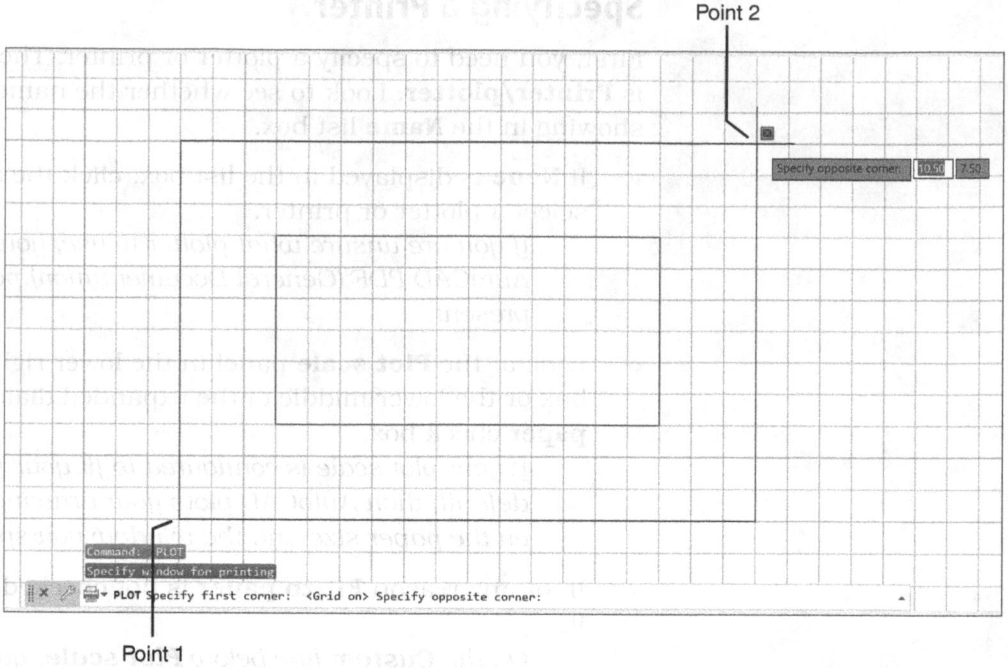

Plot Preview

Plot preview is an essential tool in carrying out efficient plotting and printing. Plot settings are complex, and the odds are good that you will waste time and paper if you print drawings without first previewing them. AutoCAD has two types of previews that help you know exactly what to expect when your drawing reaches a sheet of paper.

Without going to a full preview, you already have a partial preview on the right side of the **Printer/plotter** panel. It shows you an outline of the effective plotting area in relation to the paper size but does not show an image of the plotted drawing. This preview image changes as you change other plot settings, such as plot area and paper size.

The full preview, accessed from the **Preview** button, gives you a complete image of the drawing on a sheet of drawing paper but does not give you the specific information on the effective drawing area available in the partial preview.

✔ Click the **Preview** button in the bottom left of the dialog box.
*You should see a preview image like the one in Figure 2-33. There are more features of the **Plot** dialog box, and you can use full and partial plot previews extensively as you change plot settings. For now, get in the habit of using plot preview. If things are not coming out quite the way you want, you will be able to fix them soon.*

✔ Press **<Esc>** to return to the **Plot** dialog box.

✔ To save your settings, including your plotter selection, click the **Apply to Layout** button.
You are now ready to plot.

✔ If you want to plot or print the rectangle, prepare your plotter and then click **OK**. Otherwise, click **Cancel**.

Figure 2-33
Plot preview

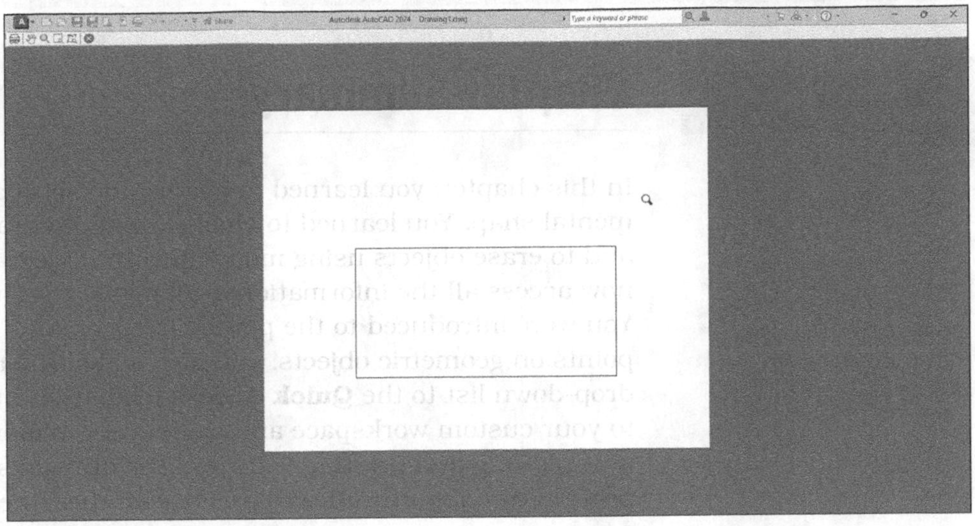

NOTE

Paper sizes are not addressed here. For now, your plot settings should be correctly matched to the paper in your printer or plotter.

Clicking **OK** sends the drawing information to be printed. You can sit back and watch the plotter at work. If you need to cancel for any reason, click **Cancel**.

2 chapter two

Chapter Summary

In this chapter, you learned to change the settings of the grid and the incremental snap. You learned to change units, to draw circles and rectangles, and to erase objects using many different object selection methods. You can now access all the information available in the AutoCAD **Help** resources. You were introduced to the powerful object snap feature for specifying points on geometric objects. You also added the menu bar and the **Layer** drop-down list to the **Quick Access** toolbar and then saved those changes to your custom workspace and began your exploration of AutoCAD's complex plotting and printing features. The drawings at the end of the chapter provide you opportunities to practice all these new skills.

Chapter Test Questions

Multiple Choice

Circle the correct answer.

6. Which of these is the least useful snap and grid setting combination?

a. Snap = **1.0**, grid = **1.0**
b. Snap = **1.0**, grid = **10.0**
c. Snap = **1.0**, grid = **2.0**
d. Snap = **1.0**, grid = **.5**

7. Which of these will **not** open the **Drafting Settings** dialog box?

a. Type **dsettings <Enter>**
b. Type **ds <Enter>**
c. Click the **Drafting Settings** tool from the ribbon
d. Right-click the **Snap Mode** button and select **Snap Settings**

8. To switch from decimal to architectural units

a. Select **architectural** in the **Drawing Units** dialog box
b. Type **architectural <Enter>**
c. Type **drawing units <Enter>**
d. Click **architectural** on the status bar

9. When drawing a circle using the **Diameter** option, the rubber band

a. Stretches from one side of the circle to the other, twice the radius
b. Stretches to the circumference of the circle
c. Stretches from the center point to a point outside the circle
d. Stretches between two points on the circumference

10. To open a crossing window

a. Specify points left to right
b. Specify points that cross the objects you want to select
c. Specify points to create a window around objects you want to select
d. Specify points right to left

Matching

Write the number of the correct answer on the line.

a. Decimal units ______ | 1. 180°
b. Architectural units ______ | 2. 2.3456, 5.4321
c. Horizontal ______ | 3. 270°
d. Vertical ___ | 4. 1'-1/2", 3'-4 3/4"
e. Engineering units ______ | 5. 1'-0.5", 3'-4.75"

True or False

Circle the correct answer.

1. **True or False:** 3 o'clock = 0°.
2. **True or False:** **C** is an alias for **CIRCLE.**
3. **True or False:** **Last** and **Previous** selections are equivalent.
4. **True or False:** The same selection methods are available in noun/verb and verb/noun editing.
5. **True or False:** In AutoCAD, plot settings are affected by your choice of a plotter.

Questions

1. Which is likely to have the smaller setting, grid or snap? Why? What happens if the settings are reversed?
2. Where is 0° located in AutoCAD's default units setup? Where is 270°? Where is −45°?
3. How does AutoCAD know when you want a crossing selection instead of a window selection?
4. What is the difference between noun/verb and verb/noun editing?
5. What aspects of a plot are shown in the preview image in the **Printer/plotter** panel of the **Plot** dialog box?

Drawing Problems

1. Leave the grid at **0.50** and set snap to **0.25**.
2. Use the **3P** option to draw a circle that passes through the points **(2.25,4.25)**, **(3.25,5.25)**, and **(4.25,4.25)**.
3. Use the **2P** option to draw a second circle with a diameter from **(3.25,4.25)** to **(4.25,4.25)**.
4. Draw a third circle centered at **(5.25,4.25)** with a radius of **1.00**.
5. Draw a fourth circle centered at **(4.75,4.25)** with a diameter of **1.00**.

Chapter Drawing Projects

M Drawing 2-1: *Aperture Wheel* [BASIC]

This drawing gives you practice creating circles using the center point, radius method. Refer to the table following the drawing for radius sizes. With snap set at **0.25**, some of the circles can be drawn by pointing and dragging. Other circles have radii that are not on a snap point. These circles can be drawn by typing in the radius.

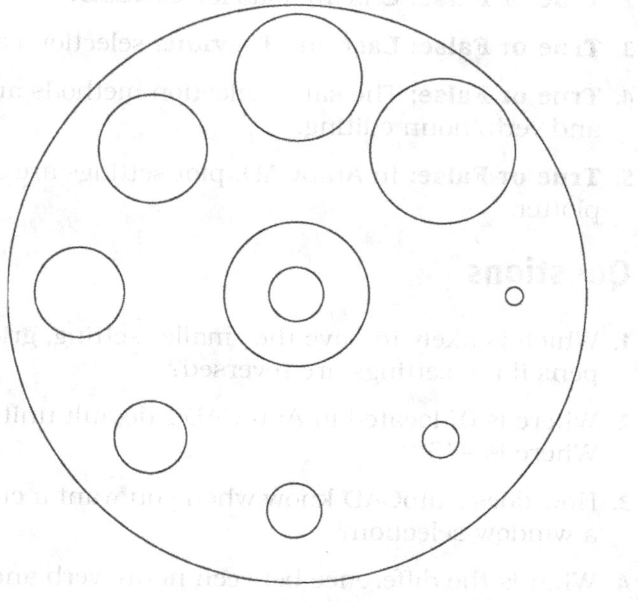

Drawing Suggestions

GRID = 0.50

SNAP = 0.25

- A good sequence for doing this drawing would be to draw the outer circle first, followed by the two inner circles (H and C) in Drawing 2-1. These are all centered on the point **(6.00,4.50)**. Then begin at circle A and work around clockwise, being sure to center each circle correctly.
- Notice that there are two circles C and two circles H. The two circles with the same letter are the same size.
- Remember, you can type any value you like, and AutoCAD gives you a precise graphic image. However, you cannot always show the exact point you want by pointing. Often, it is more efficient to type a few values than to turn snap off or change its setting for a small number of objects.

Drawing 2-1
Aperture wheel

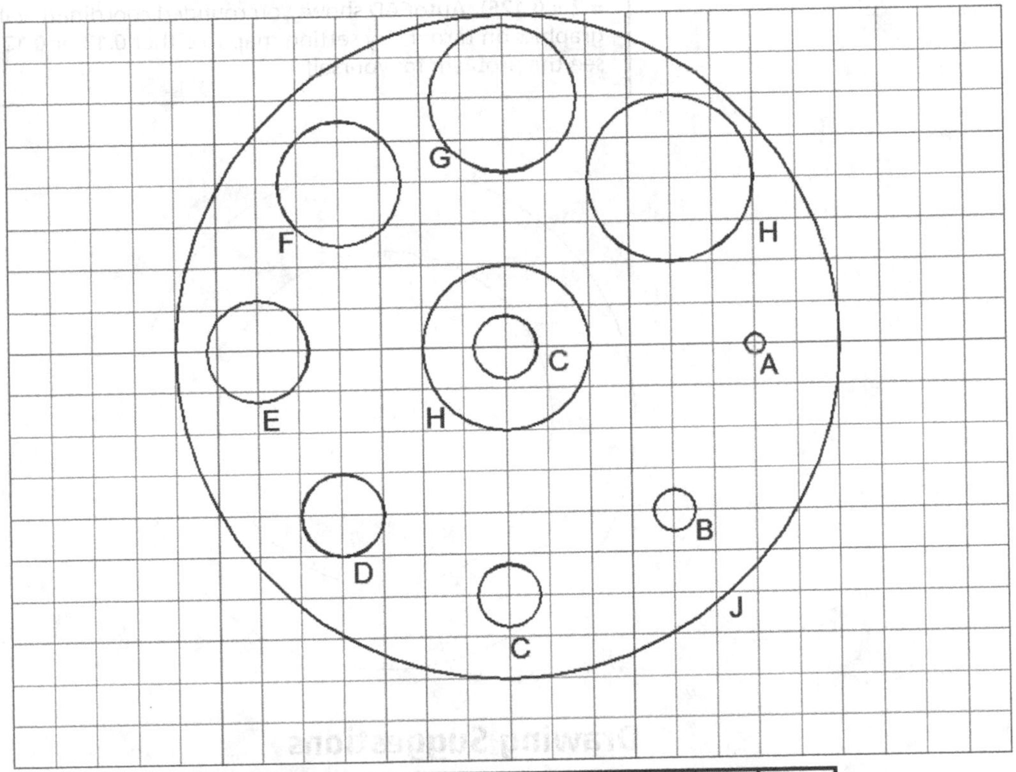

LETTER	A	B	C	D	E	F	G	H	J
RADIUS	.12	.25	.38	.50	.62	.75	.88	1.00	4.00

M Drawing 2-2: *Center Wheel* [BASIC]

This drawing gives you a chance to combine lines and circles and to use the center point, diameter method. It also gives you some experience with smaller objects, a denser grid, and a tighter snap spacing.

> **TIP**
>
> Even though units are set to show only two decimal places, it is important to set the snap using three decimal places **(0.125)** so that the grid is on a multiple of the snap **(0.25 = 2 × 0.125)**. AutoCAD shows you rounded coordinate values, such as **0.13**, but keeps the graphics on target. Try setting snap to either **0.13** or **0.12** instead of **0.125**, and you will see the problem for yourself.

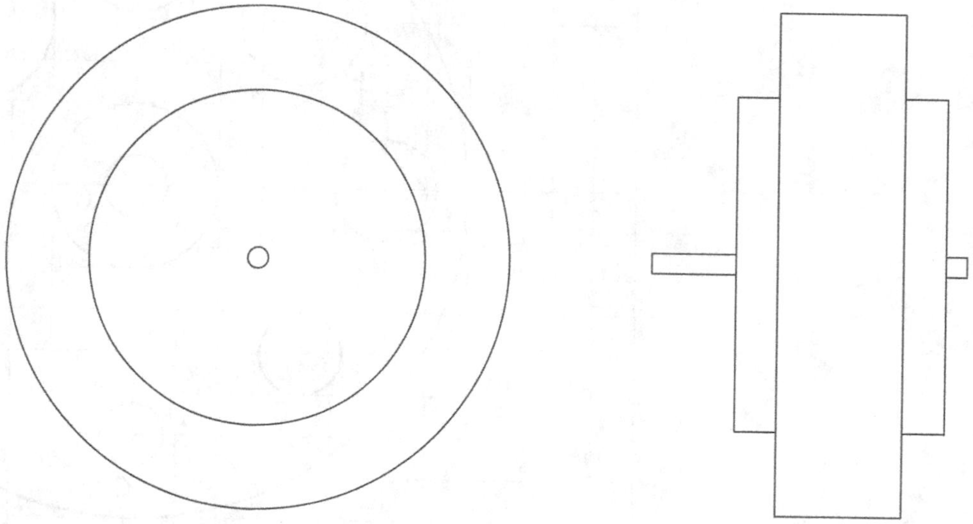

Drawing Suggestions

GRID = 0.25

SNAP = 0.125

- The two views of the center wheel are lined up, making the snap setting essential. Watch the coordinate display as you work and get used to the smaller range of motion.
- Choosing an efficient sequence makes this drawing much easier to complete. Because the two views must line up properly, its suggested to draw the front view first, with circles of diameter **0.25**, **4.00**, and **6.00**. Then, use these circles to position the lines in the right-side view.
- The circles in the front view should be centered in the neighborhood of **(3.50,4.50)**. This puts the lower left-hand corner of the 1 × 1 square at around **(4.50,1.50)**.
- Note the use of the **(Ø)** symbol indicating that circles are given diameter dimensions.

Drawing 2-2
Center wheel

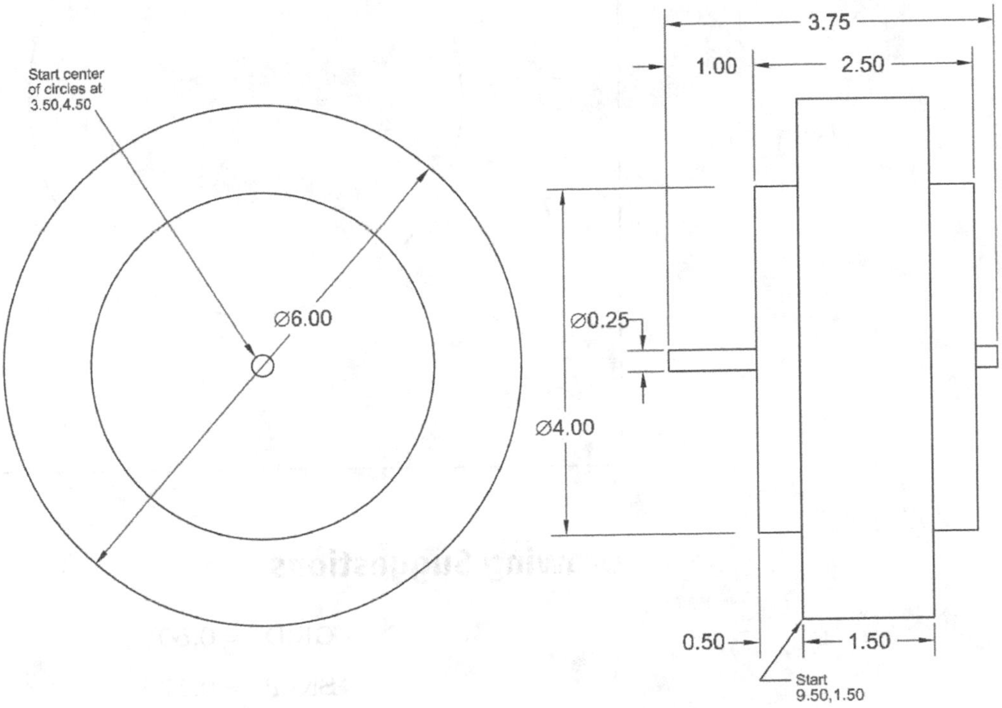

M Drawing 2-3: *Fan Bezel* [INTERMEDIATE]

This drawing should be easy for you at this point. Set grid to **0.50** and snap to **0.125**, as suggested, and everything falls into place nicely.

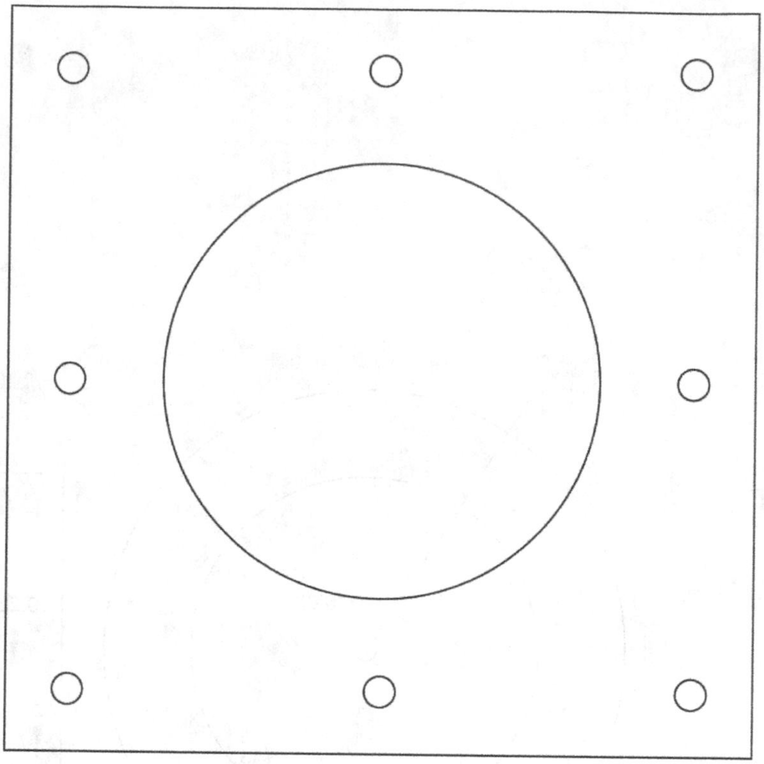

Drawing Suggestions

GRID = 0.50

SNAP = 0.125

- Notice that the outer figure in Drawing 2-3 is a 6 × 6 square and that you are given diameters for the circles, as indicated by the diameter symbol **(Ø)**.
- You should start with the lower-left corner of the square somewhere near the point **(3.00,2.00)** if you want to keep the drawing centered in the drawing area.
- Be careful to center the large inner circle within the square.

Drawing 2-3
Fan bezel

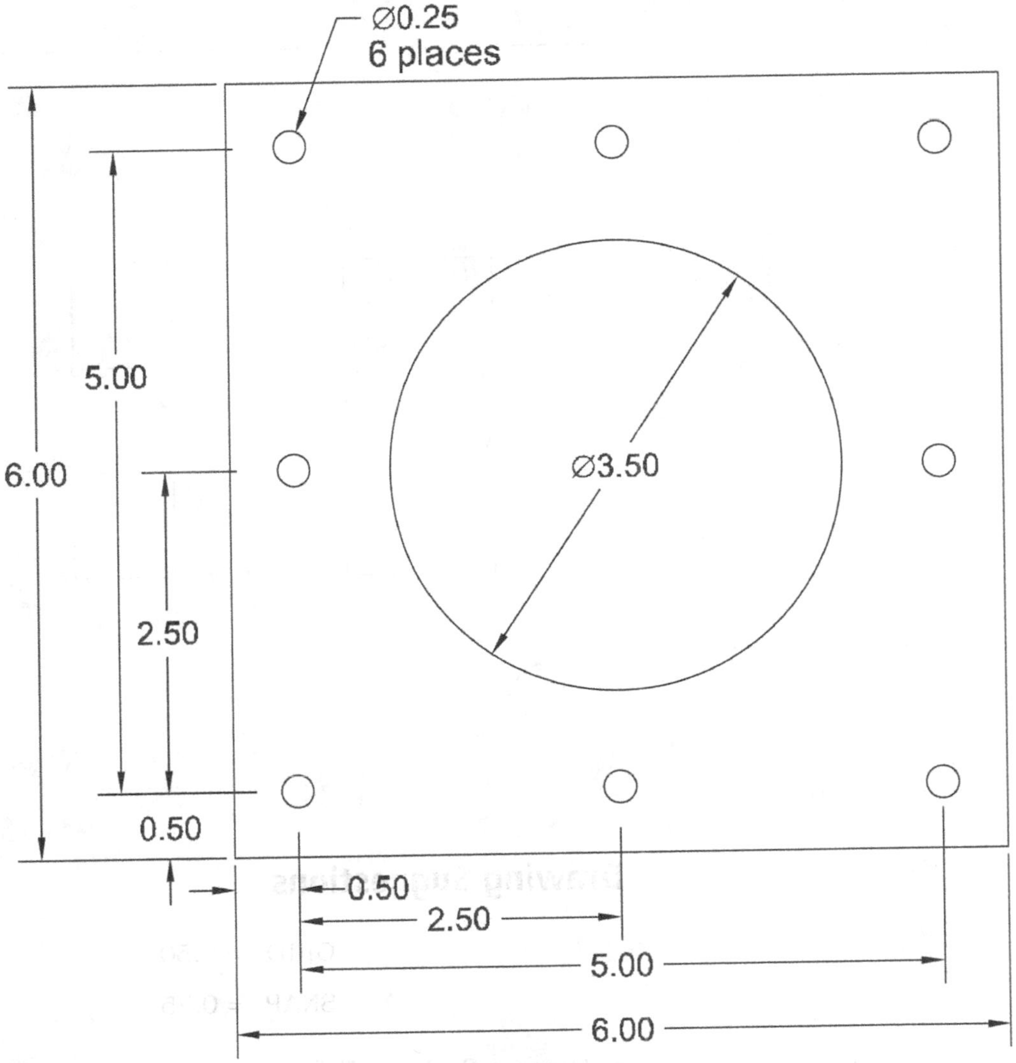

M Drawing 2-4: *Switch Plate* [INTERMEDIATE]

This drawing is similar to the last one, but the dimensions are more difficult, and a number of important points do not fall on the grid. The drawing gives you practice using grid and snap points and the coordinate display. Refer to the table that follows Drawing 2-4 for dimensions of the circles, squares, and rectangles inside the 7 × 10 outer rectangle. The placement of these smaller figures is shown by the dimensions on the drawing itself.

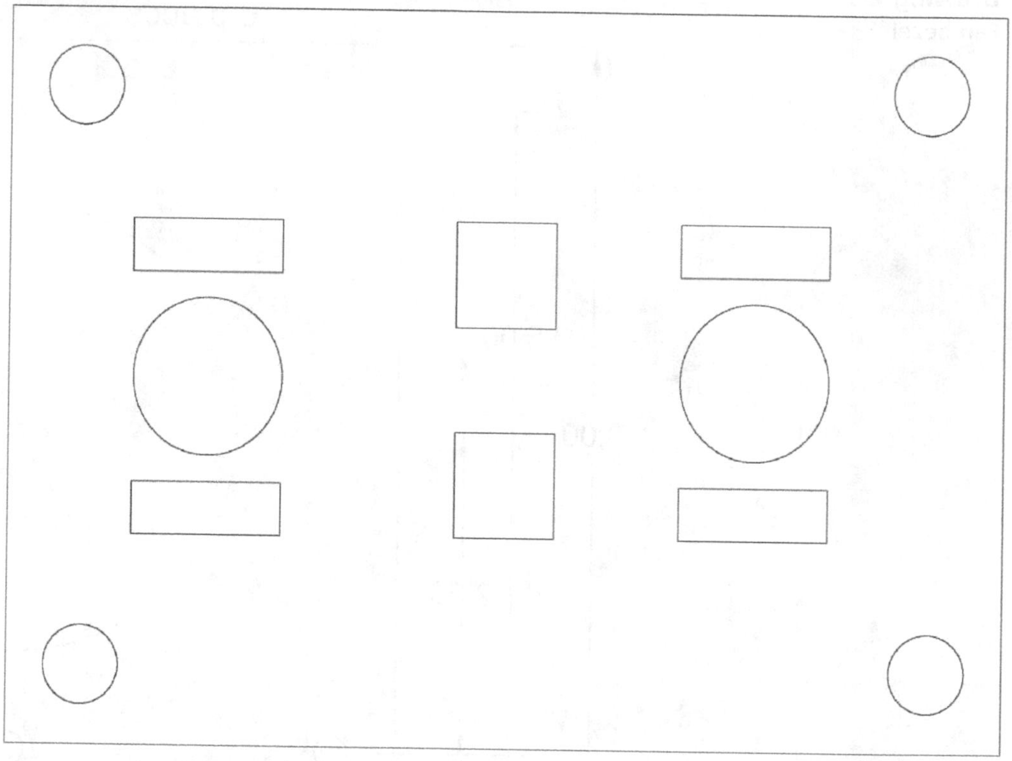

Drawing Suggestions

GRID = 0.50

SNAP = 0.25

- Turn on **Ortho** or **Polar snap** to do this drawing.
- A starting point in the neighborhood of **(1,1)** keeps you well positioned in the drawing area.

Drawing 2-4
Switch plate

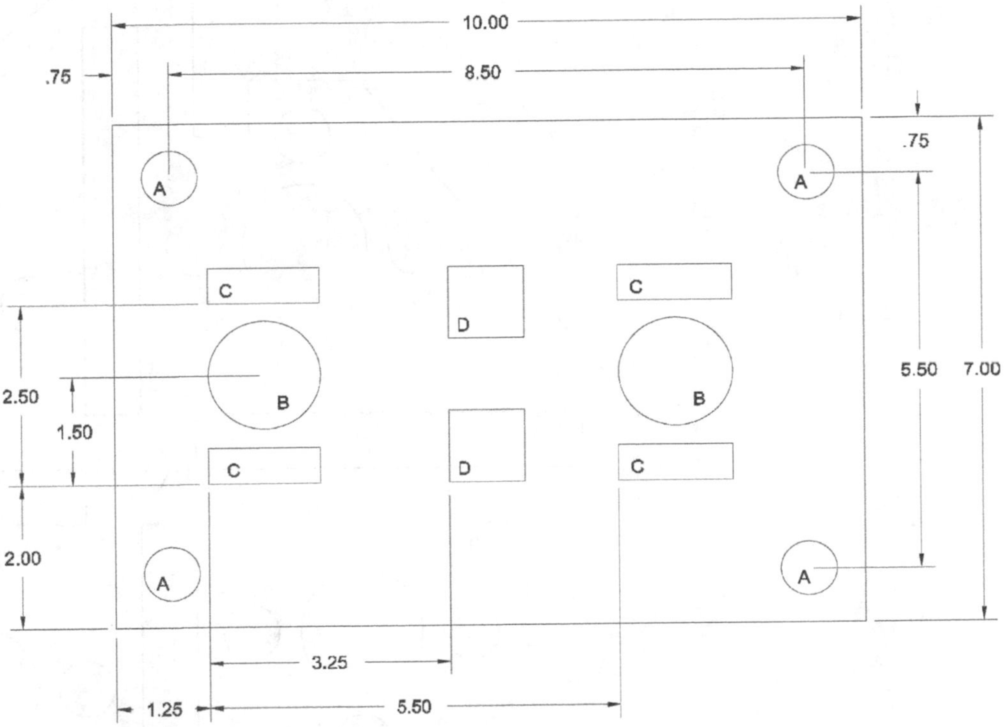

HOLE	SIZE
A	Ø.75
B	Ø1.50
C	.50 H x 1.50 W
D	1.00 SQ

G Drawing 2-5: *Gasket* [ADVANCED]

Drawing 2-5 gives you practice creating simple lines and circles while utilizing grid and snap. The circles in this drawing have a **0.50** and a **1.00** diameter. With snap set at **0.25**, the radii are on a snap point. These circles can be drawn easily by dragging the circle out to show the radius or by typing in the diameter.

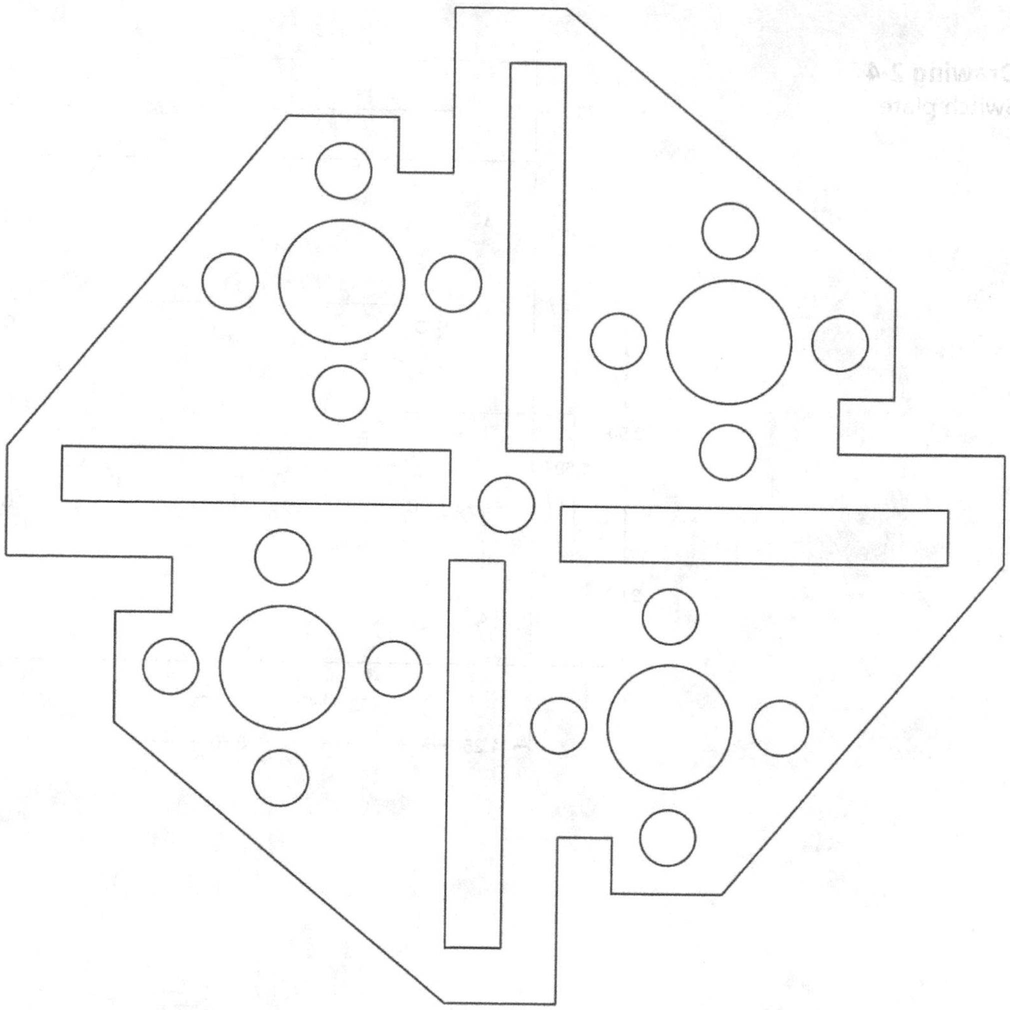

Drawing Suggestions

GRID = 0.50

SNAP = 0.25

- A good sequence for completing this drawing would be to draw the outer lines first, followed by the inner lines and then the circles.
- Notice that all endpoints of all lines fall on grid points; therefore, they are on a snap point.

Drawing 2-5
Gasket

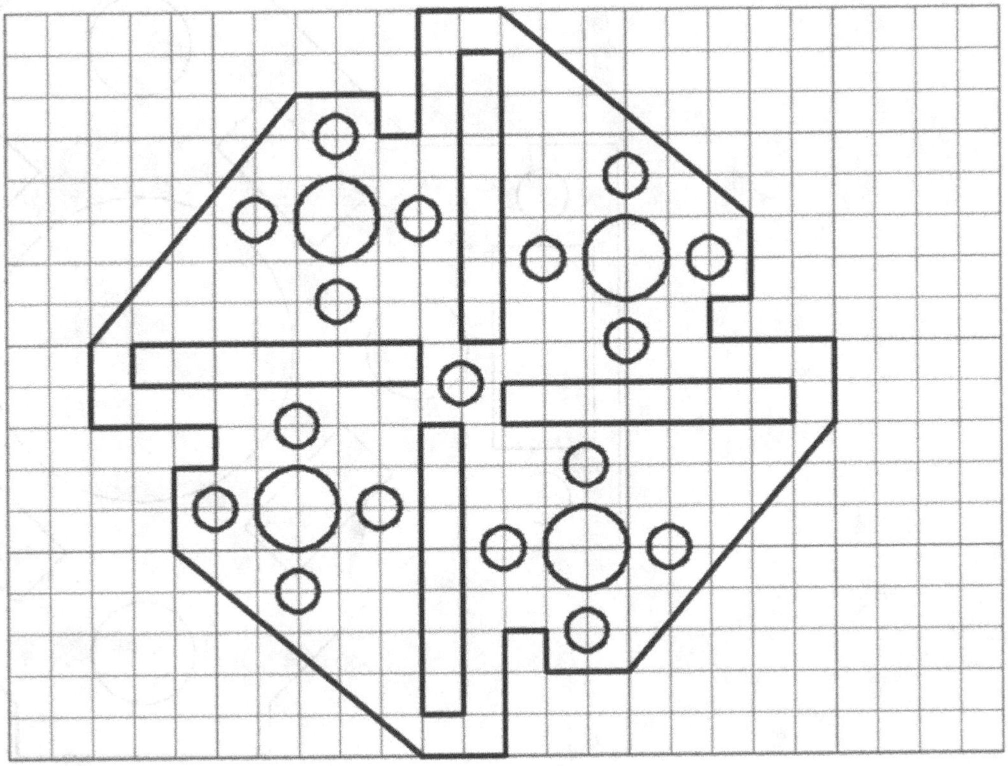

M

Drawing 2-6: *Sheet Metal Stamping* [ADVANCED]

Drawing 2-6 gives you additional practice creating lines and circles while utilizing grid display and **Snap** mode. The circles in this drawing have **0.50**, a **1.00**, and **3.00** diameters. With snap set at **0.25**, the radii are on a snap point but not always on grid line intersections. These circles can be drawn easily by dragging the circle out to show the radius or by typing in the diameter.

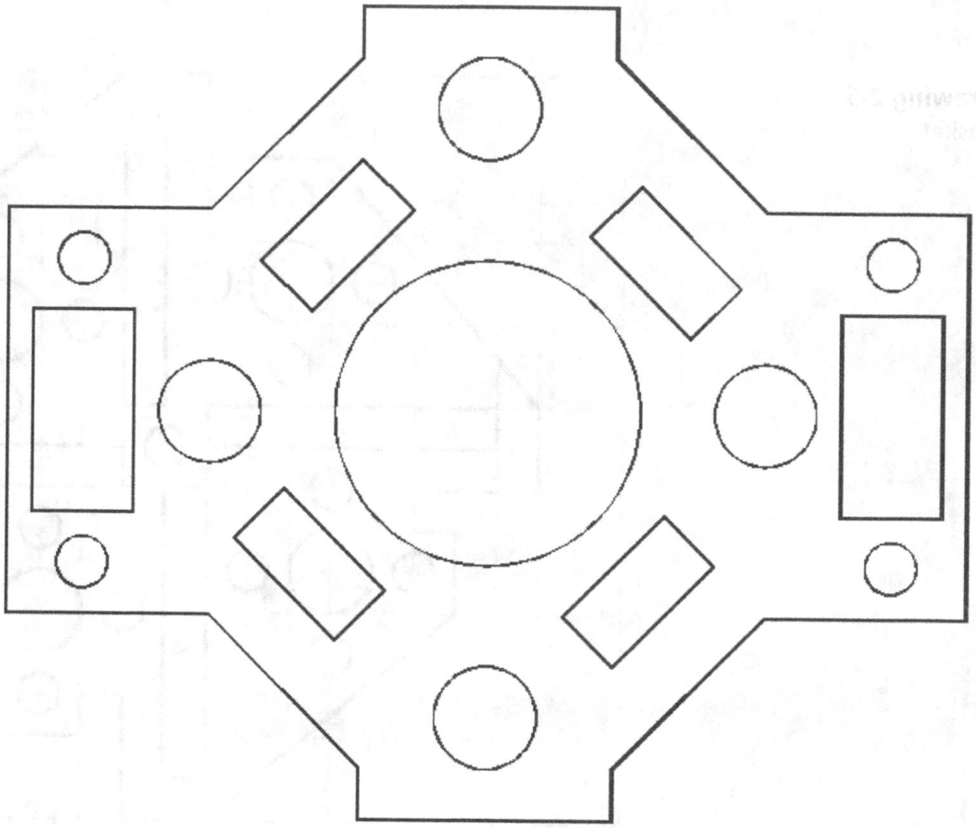

Drawing Suggestions

GRID = 0.50

SNAP = 0.25

- A good sequence for completing this drawing would be to draw the outer lines first, followed by the inner lines, and then the circles.
- Notice that the endpoints of all lines are on snap points but do not always fall on grid line intersections.
- Also, notice that while the placement of most objects in the drawing is symmetrical, the placement of the four smaller rectangles is not.

Drawing 2-6
Sheet metal stamping

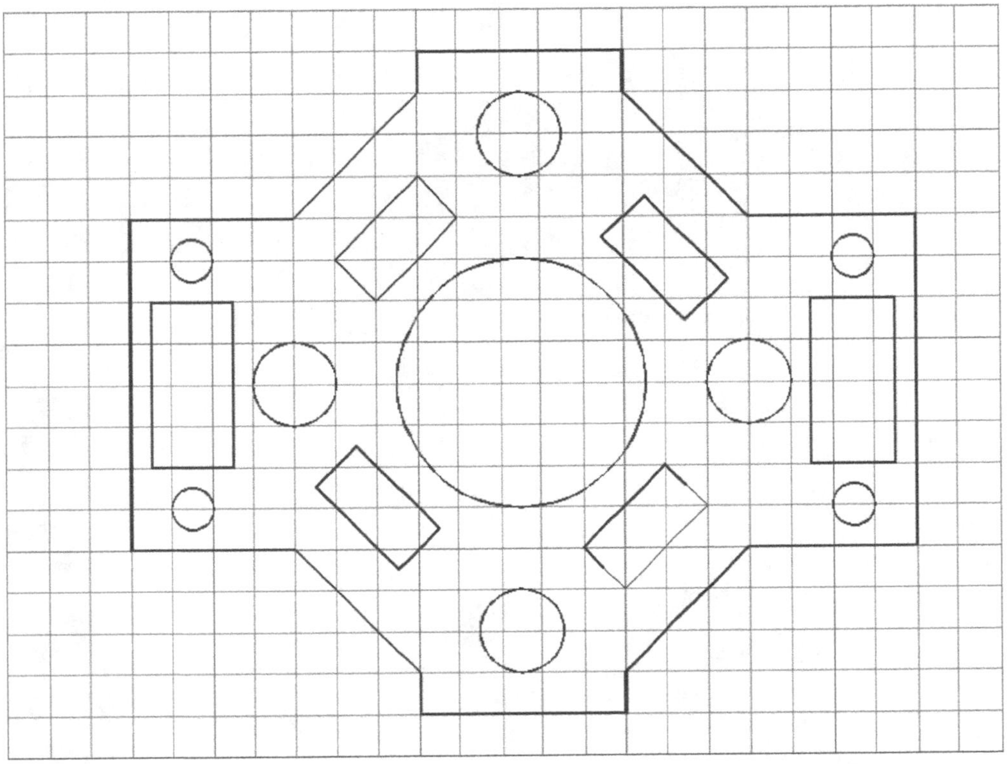

3 chapter three

Layers, Colors, and Linetypes

CHAPTER OBJECTIVES

- Create new layers
- Assign colors to layers
- Assign linetypes
- Assign lineweights
- Change the current layer
- Change linetype scale
- Edit corners using **FILLET**
- Edit corners using **CHAMFER**
- Zoom and pan with the scroll wheel
- Use the **ZOOM** command
- Enter single-line text

Introduction

layer: In CAD practice, a layer is defined with colors, linetypes, and lineweights so that objects of a certain type can be grouped and treated separately from other types of objects.

CAD is much more than a computerized way to do drafting. CAD programs have many powerful features that have no parallel in manual drawing. Layering is a good example. ***Layers*** are like transparent overlays that can be added to or peeled away from a drawing. Layers are used to separate different aspects of a drawing so they can be treated and presented independently. Layers exist in the same space and in the same drawing but can be set up and controlled individually, allowing for greater control, precision, and flexibility. In this chapter, you create and use four new layers, each with its own associated color and linetype.

The **ZOOM** command is another bit of CAD magic, allowing your drawings to accurately represent real-world detail at the largest and smallest scales within the same drawing. In this chapter, you also learn to use the **FILLET** and **CHAMFER** commands on the corners of previously drawn objects and to move between adjacent portions of a drawing with the **PAN** command. All these new techniques add considerably to the professionalism of your developing CAD technique.

LAYER	
Command	LAYER
Alias	La
Panel	Layers
Tool	

Creating New Layers

Layers allow you to treat specialized types of entities in your drawing separately from other types. For example, you can draw dimensions on a special dimension layer so that you can turn them on and off at will. You can then turn off the dimension layer to prepare drawings that are shown without dimensions. When a layer is turned off, all the objects on that layer become invisible, although they are still part of the drawing and can be recalled at any time. In this way, layers can be viewed, edited, manipulated, and plotted independently.

> **TIP**
>
> Following is a general procedure for creating a layer:
>
> 1. Click the **Layer Properties** tool from the **Layers** panel of the **Home** tab on the ribbon.
> 2. Click the **New Layer** button.
> 3. Type a layer name.
> 4. Repeat for other new layers.
> 5. Close the **Layer Properties Manager** palette.

It is common practice to put dimensions on a separate layer, but there are many other uses of layers as well. Fundamentally, layers are used to assign a color and linetype, among other common property values, to all objects on the same layer. These properties, in turn, take on special significance, depending on the drawing application. It is standard drafting practice, for example, to use small, evenly spaced dashes to represent objects or edges that would, in reality, be hidden from view. On a CAD system, these hidden lines can be put on an independent layer so they can be turned on and off and given their own color to make it easy for the designer to remember what layer they are working on.

In this chapter, you start layering with a simple system. You should remember that there are countless possibilities. AutoCAD allows a full range of colors and as many layers as you need.

You should also be aware that linetypes and colors are not restricted to being associated with layers. It is possible to mix linetypes and colors on a single layer. Although this might be useful for certain applications, it is not recommended at this point.

✔ Create a new drawing by clicking the **Start** tab, checking to see that **acad.dwt** is selected in the **Template** drop-down list, and clicking the **New** button. If acad.dwt isn't listed on the drop-down list, click **Browse templates** and select the **acad.dwt** file before clicking **Open**.

✔ If necessary, turn on the **Grid Display**.

✔ Type **z <Enter>** to start the **ZOOM** command and then **a <Enter>** to use the **All** option.

The Layer Properties Manager Palette

You create and specify layers and layer properties through the **Layer Properties Manager** palette. Palettes are like dialog boxes, but they are laid out differently and have some different features. The **Layer Properties Manager** palette consists of a table of layers. Clicking a column cell in a row allows you to change a setting directly or displays a dialog box where a setting can be changed.

✔ Click the **Layer Properties** tool on the **Layers** panel of the **Home** tab, as shown in Figure 3-1.

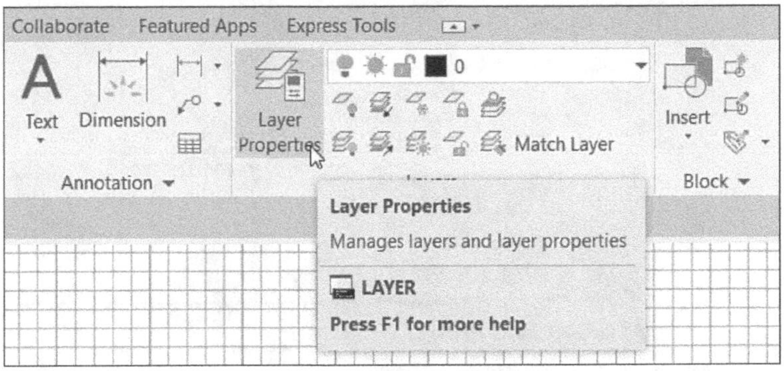

Figure 3-1
Layer Properties tool

*This displays the **Layer Properties Manager** palette as shown in Figure 3-2. The large open area to the right shows the names and properties of all layers defined in the current drawing. Layering systems can become very complex; for this reason, there is a system to limit or filter the layers shown in the **Layer** list. This is controlled through the **Filters** panel and by the two buttons with folder icons in the top left. With the **All** filter specified, the **Layer** list shows all layers, while the **All Used Layers** filter only shows the layers that have objects on them in the drawing. By default, every drawing contains one layer named **0**. The cells on the row, to the right of the layer name, show the current state of its various properties. You learn more about these shortly.*

Now, you create three new layers. AutoCAD makes this easy.

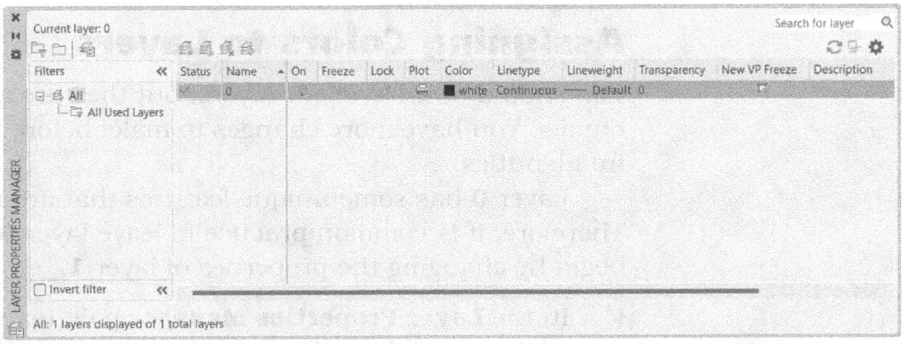

Figure 3-2
Layer Properties Manager palette

✔ Click the **New Layer** button, as shown in Figure 3-3.

*A newly defined layer, Layer1, is created immediately and added to the **Layer** list. The new layer is given the characteristics of layer **0** or whichever layer is currently selected when you click **New Layer**. You alter the layer's properties later in this chapter in the "Assigning Colors to Layers" section. First, however, you give this layer a new name and then define three more layers.*

Layer names can be long or short. In this exercise, single-digit numbers were chosen as layer names because they are easy to type and can be matched to AutoCAD's index color numbering sequence.

Figure 3-3
New Layer button

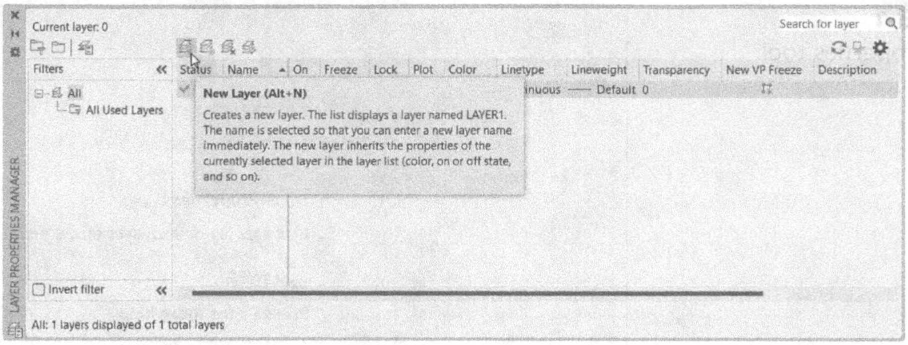

✔ Type **1** for the layer name.

***Layer1** changes to simply **1**. It is not necessary to press **<Enter>** after typing the name.*

✔ Click **New Layer** again.

*A second new layer is added to the list. It again has the default name **Layer1**. Change it to **2**.*

✔ Type **2** for the second layer name.

✔ Click **New Layer** again.

✔ Type **3** for the third layer name and press **<Enter>** to complete the process.

*At this point, your **Layer** list should show the layers **0**, **1**, **2**, and **3**, all which have identical properties.*

Assigning Colors to Layers

You should now have four layers, but they are all the same except for their names. You have more changes to make before these new layers have useful identities.

Layer **0** has some unique features that are not introduced here. Therefore, it is common practice to leave layer **0** defined the way it is. You begin by changing the properties of layer **1**.

✔ In the **Layer Properties Manager** palette, click the white color swatch under the **Color** column in the **layer 1** row.

Clicking the white swatch in the **Color** *column of layer* **1** *selects layer* **1** *and displays the* **Select Color** *dialog box, as shown in Figure 3-4. The three tabs in this dialog box provide three different ways in which colors can be chosen in AutoCAD. By default, the* **Index Color** *tab is probably selected, as shown in Figure 3-4. The* **Index Color** *system is a simple numbered selection of 255 colors and shades. The* **True Color** *and* **Color Books** *color models are standard color systems commonly used by graphic designers. The* **True Color** *tab allows you to define a color with either the Hue, Saturation, and Luminance (HSL) or the Red, Green, Blue (RGB) color models. Both of these color models work by mixing colors and color characteristics. The* **Color Books** *tab gives access to DIC, Pantone, and RAL color books. These standard color sets are also numbered, but they provide many more choices than the AutoCAD Index Color set. In this chapter, you only use the* **Index Color** *tab.*

Figure 3-4
Select Color dialog box

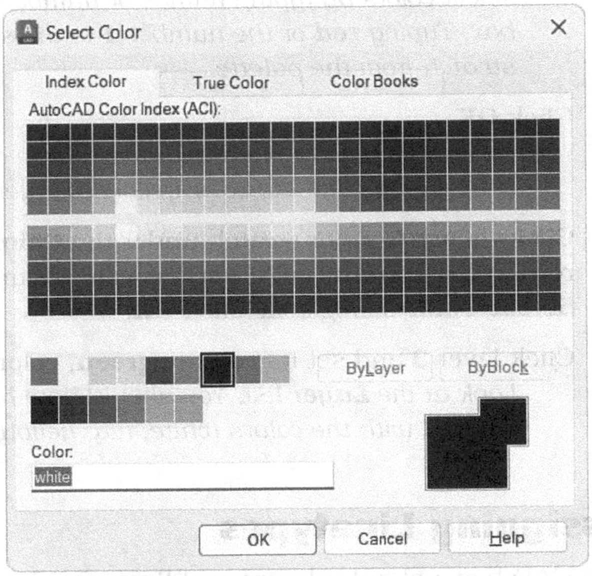

- ✔ If necessary, click the **Index Color** tab.

  The **Index Color** *tab shows the complete selection of 255 colors. At the top is a full palette of shades 10 through 249. Below that are the nine standard colors, numbered 1 through 9, followed by gray shades, numbered 250 through 255.*

- ✔ Move your cursor freely inside the dialog box.

  When your cursor is over a color swatch, it is highlighted with a black and white border.

- ✔ Let your cursor rest over any color swatch.

  Notice that the number of the color is registered under the palette next to the words **Index color***. This is the AutoCAD index color number for the currently highlighted color swatch. Notice also the three numbers on the right, following the words* **Red**, **Green**, *and* **Blue**. *This is the RGB color model equivalent. RGB colors are combinations of red, green, and blue, with 255 shades of each.*

- ✔ Click any color swatch in the palette.

  *When a color swatch is clicked, it is outlined with a black border, and the newly selected color swatch is displayed on the bottom right of the dialog box against a swatch of the current color for comparison. The color is not actually assigned to the layer until you click **OK** to exit the dialog box. For the purposes of this exercise, select the standard red color swatch—color number 1 on the strip in the middle of the dialog box.*

- ✔ Move the cursor to the **red** color swatch, the first of the nine standard colors in the middle of the dialog box.

  *Notice that this is index color number **1**, and its RGB equivalent is **255,0,0**—pure red with no green or blue added.*

- ✔ Click the **red** color swatch.

  *You should see the word **red** and the color red shown in the new color swatch at the bottom of the dialog box. Note that you can also select colors by typing names or numbers directly in the **Color edit** box. Typing **red** or the number **1** is the same as clicking the red color swatch from the palette.*

- ✔ Click **OK.**

  *Layer **1** is now defined with the color red in the **Layer** list. Next, you assign the color yellow to layer **2**.*

- ✔ Click the white color swatch under the **Color** column in the layer **2** row, and assign the color **yellow**, color number **2**, to layer **2** in the **Select Color** dialog box. Click **OK**.

- ✔ Click layer **3** and set its color to **green**, color number **3**.

  *Look at the **Layer** list. You should now have layers **0**, **1**, **2**, and **3** defined with the colors white, red, yellow, and green.*

Assigning Linetypes

AutoCAD has a standard library of linetypes that can easily be assigned to layers. There are 46 standard linetypes. In addition to continuous lines, you use hidden lines and centerlines. You put hidden lines in yellow on layer **2** and centerlines in green on layer **3**. Layers **1** and **0** retain the continuous linetype.

The procedure for assigning linetypes is almost identical to the procedure for assigning colors, except that you have to load linetypes into the drawing before they can be assigned to a layer or even to an object.

- ✔ In the **Layer Properties Manager** palette, click **Continuous** in the **Linetype** column of the layer **2** row.

  *This selects layer **2** and displays the **Select Linetype** dialog box, as shown in Figure 3-5. The dialog box contains a list of loaded linetypes, the only linetype currently is **Continuous**. You can load additional linetypes by clicking the **Load** button at the bottom of the dialog box.*

- ✔ Click **Load.**

  *This displays the **Load or Reload Linetypes** dialog box, as shown in Figure 3-6. Here, you can select from the list of linetypes available* *in the standard acad.lin/acadiso.lin file or from other linetype files if there are any on your system. You also have the option of loading all linetypes from any given file at once. The linetypes are then defined in your current drawing, and you can assign a new linetype to a layer or object at any time. This makes things easier. It does, however, use up more memory.*

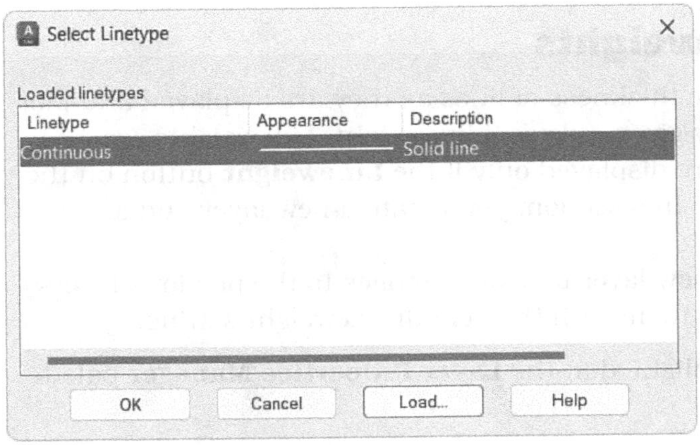

Figure 3-5
Select Linetype dialog box

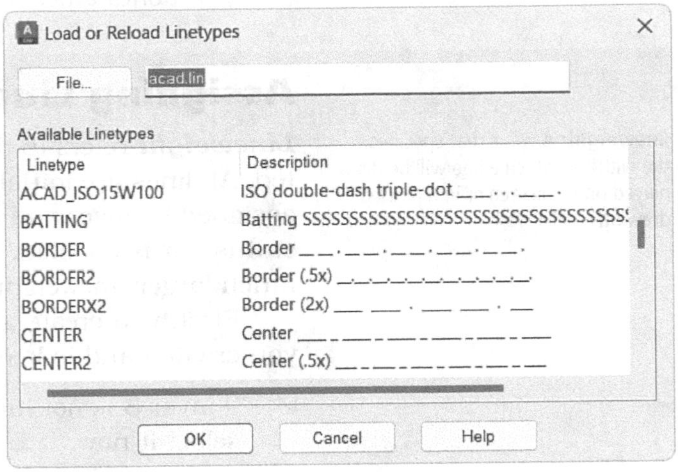

Figure 3-6
Load or Reload Linetypes dialog box

*For the purpose of this exercise, you load only the **Hidden** and **Center** linetypes.*

- ✔ Scroll down until you see the linetype named **CENTER**.
- ✔ Select **CENTER** in the **Linetype** column at the left.
- ✔ Scroll down again until you see the linetype named **HIDDEN**.
- ✔ Hold down the **<Ctrl>** key and select **HIDDEN** in the **Linetype** column.

  *The **<Ctrl>** key lets you select multiple items in a list.*
- ✔ Click **OK** to complete the loading process.

  *You should now see the **Center** and **Hidden** linetypes in the list of loaded linetypes. Now that these are loaded, you can assign them to layers.*

> **NOTE**
>
> Make sure that you actually click the word **Continuous.** If you click one of the cells in the layer **2** row, you might turn the layer off or freeze it so that you cannot draw on it. These properties are discussed at the end of the "Changing the Current Layer" section.

- ✔ Select **HIDDEN** in the **Linetype** column.
- ✔ Click **OK** to close the dialog box.

  *You should see that layer **2** now has the **Hidden** linetype. Next, you assign the **Center** linetype to layer **3**.*

- ✔ Click **Continuous** in the **Linetype** column of the layer **3** row.
- ✔ In the **Select Linetype** dialog box, select the **CENTER** linetype.
- ✔ Click **OK**.

  *Examine your Layer list again. It should show layer **2** with the **Hidden** linetype and layer **3** with the **Center** linetype. Before closing the **Layer Properties Manager** palette, you create one additional layer that utilizes the **Lineweight** feature.*

Assigning Lineweights

lineweight: A value that specifies the width at which a line will be displayed on the screen or in a plotted drawing.

Lineweight refers to the thickness of lines as they are displayed and plotted. All lines are initially given a default lineweight. Lineweights are assigned by layer and are displayed only if the **Lineweight** button on the status bar is enabled. In this section, you create a new layer and assign it a much larger lineweight.

First, you create a new layer to avoid changes to the previous layers you created and to keep them with the default lineweight setting.

- ✔ If layer **3** is not highlighted in the **Layer Properties Manager** palette, select it now.
- ✔ Click the **New Layer** button on the palette.

  *Notice that the new layer takes on the characteristics of the previously highlighted layer. Your last action was to assign the **Center** linetype to or select layer **3**, so your new layer should have the green color and the **Center** linetype along with the other characteristics of layer **3**.*
- ✔ Type **4** for the new layer name.
- ✔ Click **Default** (or **Defa ...**) in the **Lineweight** column of layer **4 row**.

  *This displays the **Lineweight** dialog box, as shown in Figure 3-7. You choose a rather large lineweight to create a clear distinction from other layers. Be aware that plotted lineweights may not exactly match lineweights as shown in the drawing area.*
- ✔ Scroll down until you see **0.50 mm** in the list.
- ✔ Select **0.50 mm**.

Figure 3-7
Lineweight dialog box

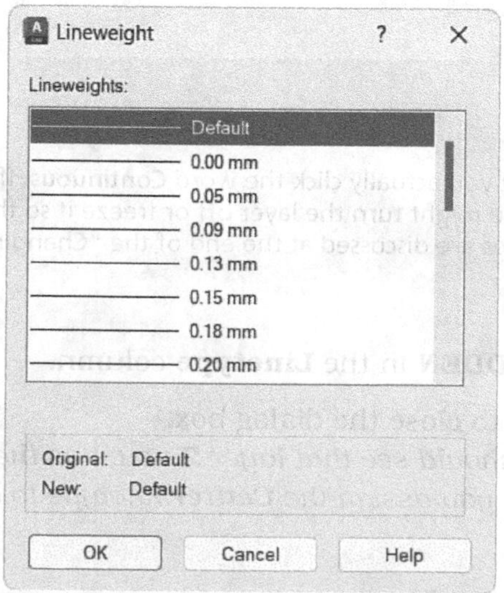

Below the list, you can see that the original specification for the layer was ***Default*** *and is now being changed to* ***0.50 mm.***

> **TIP**
>
> Lineweight settings are most useful when correlated with plotter pen sizes, so that you control the appearance of lines in your plotted drawing. Your pen sizes may be in inches rather than millimeters. To switch from lineweights in mm to inches, use the following procedure:
>
> 1. Type **LWEIGHT <Enter>** at the command line.
> 2. In the **Lineweight Settings** dialog box, select **Inches** in the **Units for Listing** panel.
> 3. Click **OK.**

✔ Click **OK** to return to the **Layer Properties Manager** palette.

It is now time to leave the dialog box and see what you can do with your new layers.

✔ Click the **Close** button **(X)** at the top left of the palette to exit the **Layer Properties Manager** palette.

Before proceeding, you should be back in the drawing area with your new layers defined in your drawing. To verify that you have successfully defined new layers, click the ***Layer*** *drop-down list from the* ***Layers*** *panel of the* ***Home*** *tab on the ribbon, as shown in Figure 3-8. Notice that this is not the label at the bottom of the* ***Layers*** *panel. Clicking that label expands the panel.*

✔ To open the **Layer** list, click the arrow or anywhere on the drop-down list box.

Your list should resemble the one in Figure 3-8.

Figure 3-8
Layer drop-down list

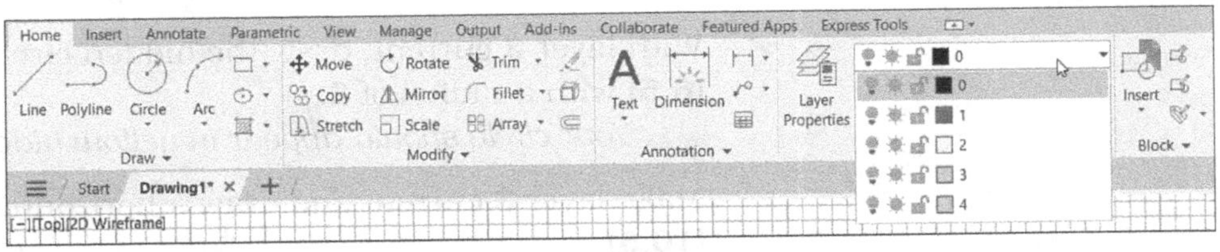

Changing the Current Layer

In this section, you make each of your new layers current and draw objects on them. You can immediately see how much power you have added to your drawing by adding new layers and changing their colors, linetypes, and lineweights.

To draw new entities on a layer, you make it the current layer. Previously drawn objects on other layers are also visible, even though new objects go on the current layer.

There are two quick methods to establish the current layer. The first works the same as any drop-down list. The second makes use of previously drawn objects. Here, you use the first method when drawing the objects in Figure 3-9.

Figure 3-9
Objects on different layers

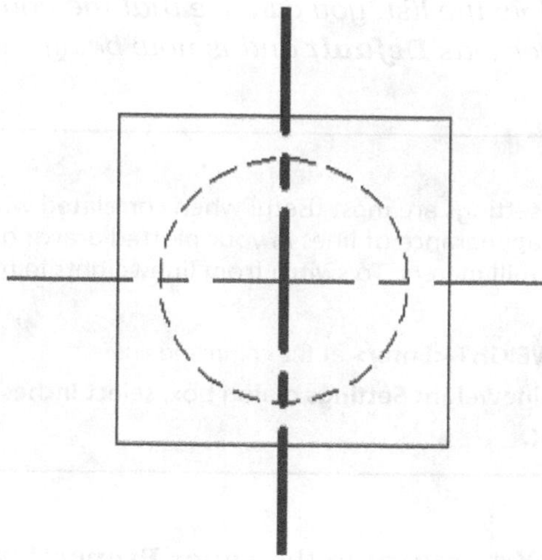

- Click anywhere on the **Layer** drop-down list box from the **Layers** panel on the **Home** tab of the ribbon.
  This opens the list, as shown previously in Figure 3-8.
- Select layer **1** by clicking to the right of its name in the drop-down list.
  *Layer **1** replaces layer **0** as the current layer on the **Layer** drop-down list.*
- Using the **RECTANG** command, draw the 6 × 6 square shown in Figure 3-9, with the first corner at **(3,2)** and the other corner at **(9,8)**.
  *Your square should be shown as red continuous lines on layer **1**.*
- Click anywhere in the **Layer** drop-down list box.
- Click to the right of the name for layer **2**.
  *Layer **2** becomes the current layer.*
- With layer **2** current, draw the hidden circle in Figure 3-9, centered at **(6,5)** with a radius of **2**.
  Your circle should appear in yellow hidden lines.
- Make layer **3** current and draw a horizontal centerline from **(2,5)** to **(10,5)**.
  This line should appear as a green centerline.
- Type **LWDISPLAY <Enter>** to change the **LWDISPLAY** system variable, which allows you to control the display of lineweights.
- Type **on <Enter>** to display lineweights.
- Make layer **4** current and draw a vertical line from **(6,1)** to **(6,9)**.
  This line should appear as a green centerline with noticeable thickness.
- Type **LWDISPLAY <Enter>** again.

✔ Type **off <Enter>** to disable lineweights.

*With **Lineweights** off, the lineweight of the vertical centerline is not displayed.*

Making an Object's Layer Current

Finally, you use another method to make layer **1** current before moving on.

✔ Click the **Make Current** tool from the **Layers** panel on the **Home** tab, as shown in Figure 3-10.

This tool allows you to make a layer current by selecting any object on that layer. AutoCAD shows the following prompt:

```
Select object whose layer will become current:
```

Figure 3-10
Make Current tool

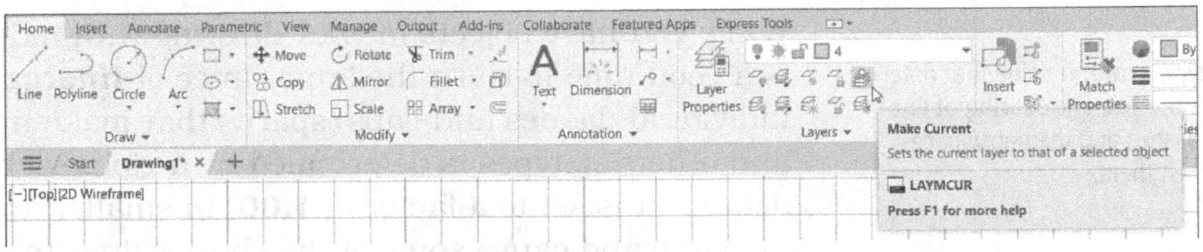

✔ Select the red square drawn on layer **1**.

*Layer **1** replaces layer **4** in the **Layer** drop-down list box on the ribbon.*

Other Properties of Layers

There are several other properties that can be set in the **Layer Properties Manager** palette or, more conveniently, from the **Layer** drop-down list box. These settings probably will not be useful to you in this chapter, but they are introduced briefly here for your information.

On and Off

Layers can be turned on or off, which is indicated by a lightbulb icon. On and off status affects only the visibility of objects on a layer. Objects on layers that are off are not visible or plotted but are still in the drawing, can be selected, and are considered when the drawing is regenerated.

regeneration: The process through which AutoCAD refreshes the drawing image in the drawing area by re-creating the image from the numerical data used to store the geometry of the drawing.

Regeneration is the process by which AutoCAD translates the precise numerical data stored in a drawing file into the less-precise values for on-screen graphics. Regeneration can be a slow process in large, complex drawings. As a result, it may be useful not to regenerate all layers all the time.

Freeze and Thaw

Frozen layers are not only invisible but are also ignored during the regeneration of the drawing and the selection of objects. Thawing a layer reverses this setting. Thawed layers are always regenerated but may not be represented in the drawing area. Freeze and thaw properties are represented by the sun icon, to the right of the lightbulb icon. Layers are thawed by default, as indicated by the yellow sun. When a layer is frozen, the sun icon is replaced with a snowflake.

Lock and Unlock

Next is the lock icon. The **Lock** and **Unlock** settings do not affect visibility but do affect availability of objects for selecting or editing. Objects on locked layers cannot be selected or edited. Unlocking reverses this setting.

Deleting Layers

You can delete layers using the **Delete Layer** tool on the **Layer Properties Manager** palette. This is the button that looks like a stack of papers (layers) with a small red **x** just above the **Name column**. However, you cannot delete layers that have objects drawn on them. Also, you cannot delete the current layer or layer **0**.

Changing Linetype Scale

linetype scale: A value that determines the size and spacing of linetype dashes and the gaps/spaces between them.

While you have objects in your drawing with hidden lines and centerlines, it is a good time to learn the importance of ***linetype scale***. The size of the individual dashes and gaps/spaces that make up hidden lines, centerlines, and other linetypes is determined by a global setting called **LTSCALE**. By default, it is set to a factor of **1.00**. In smaller drawings, this setting may be too large and cause some of the shorter lines to appear continuous regardless of what layer they are on. Or, in some cases, you may want smaller spaces and dashes. To change the linetype scale, use the **LTSCALE** command. Try this:

> **TIP**
>
> Following is a general procedure for changing linetype scale:
>
> 1. Type **lts <Enter>**.
> 2. Enter a new value.

✔ Type **lts <Enter>**.

__lts__, of course, is the alias for __LTSCALE__.

✔ Type **.5 <Enter>**.

Notice the change in the size of dashes and gaps/spaces in your drawing. Both the hidden lines and the centerlines are affected, as shown in Figure 3-11.

Figure 3-11
Effect of changing linetype scale

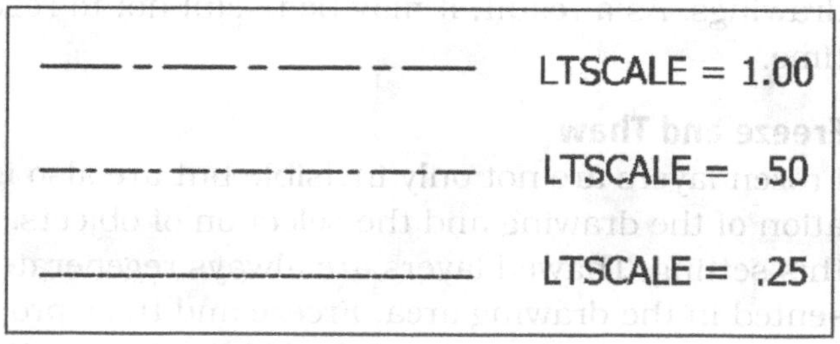

Editing Corners Using FILLET

FILLET	
Command	FILLET
Alias	F
Panel	Modify
Tool	

fillet: In drafting practice, a fillet is a concave curve at the corner of an object. In AutoCAD, the term fillet and the **FILLET** command refer to both concave and convex curves (rounds).

chamfer: An angle cut across the corner of an object.

round: In drafting practice, a convex curve at the corner of an object.

Now that you have a variety of layers to use, you can begin to make more realistic mechanical drawings. Often this requires the ability to create filleted, rounded, or chamfered corners. ***Fillets*** are concave curves on corners and edges, whereas ***rounds*** are convex. AutoCAD uses the **FILLET** command to refer to both. ***Chamfers*** are cut on an angle rather than a curve. The **FILLET** and **CHAMFER** commands work similarly.

> **TIP**
>
> Following is a general procedure for creating fillets:
>
> 1. Click the **Fillet** tool from the **Chamfer/Fillet** drop-down menu on the **Modify** panel of the **Home** tab, or type **f <Enter>**.
> 2. Right-click and select **Radius** from the shortcut menu.
> 3. Enter a radius value.
> 4. Select two lines that meet at a corner.

You modify only the square in this exercise, but instead of erasing the other objects, you turn off the layers those objects are on, as follows:

✔ If you have not already done so, set layer **1** as the current layer.

✔ Click the **Layer** drop-down list box on the **Layers** panel from the **Home** tab of the ribbon, and click the lightbulb for the layers **2**, **3**, and **4** so that the icon turns from yellow to blue, indicating that they are off.

✔ Click anywhere outside the drop-down list box to close it.

When you are finished, you should see only the square. The other objects are still in your drawing and can be displayed anytime simply by turning the layers on again.

You use the square to practice fillets and chamfers.

✔ Type **f <Enter>** or click the **Fillet** tool from the **Chamfer/Fillet** drop-down menu on the **Modify** panel of the **Home** tab, as shown in Figure 3-12.

On the command line, you will see options as follows:

```
Select first object or [Undo/Polyline/Radius/Trim/Multiple]:
```

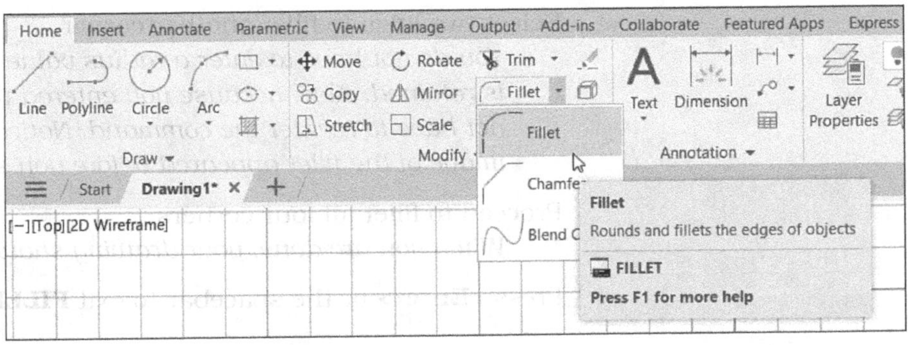

Figure 3-12
Fillet tool

Polylines are not discussed here, but you do get to explore the Polyline option in the next section while learning about the **CHAMFER** command. **Trim** mode is discussed at the end of this exercise.

The first thing you must do is determine the degree of rounding you want. Because fillets appear as arcs, they can be defined by a radius.

✔ Select **Radius** from the command-line options.

AutoCAD prompts:

```
Specify fillet radius <0.00>:
```

*The default is **0.00**.*

✔ Type **.75 <Enter>**.

*You have set **0.75** as the current fillet radius for this drawing. You can change it at any time. Changing the value does not affect previously drawn fillets.*

The prompt is the same as before:

```
Select first object or [Undo/Polyline/Radius/Trim/Multiple]:
```

Notice that you have the pickbox in the drawing area now without the crosshairs.

✔ Select a point on the vertical line on the right near the top corner.

✔ Move the cursor over the horizontal line at the top near the right corner.

The top line is previewed for selection, and a preview image of the fillet appears at the top-right corner. This allows you to see what the fillet will look like before you complete the command.

✔ Select the horizontal line at the top near the top right corner.

*Behold! A fillet! You did not even have to press **<Enter>**. AutoCAD knows that you are done after selecting two lines.*

The Multiple Option

You use the **Multiple** option to fillet the remaining three corners of the square. **Multiple** allows you to create multiple fillets without leaving the **FILLET** command.

✔ Press **<Enter>** or the spacebar to repeat **FILLET**.

✔ Select **Multiple** from the command-line options.

✔ Select two lines to fillet another corner.

*You do not have to enter a radius value again because the last value is retained. Also, because you entered the **Multiple** option, you do not have to reenter the command. Notice again that the preview image of the fillet appeared before you selected the second line.*

✔ Proceed to fillet all four corners.

When you are done, your drawing should resemble Figure 3-13.

✔ Press **<Enter>** or the spacebar to exit **FILLET**.

Chapter 3

Figure 3-13
Multiple fillets on corners

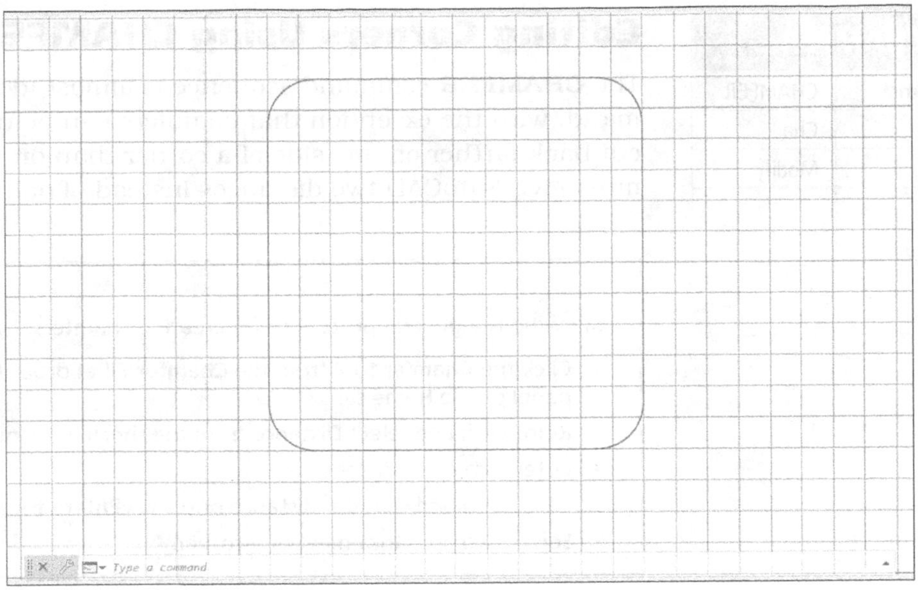

Trim Mode

Trim mode allows you to determine whether you want AutoCAD to remove square corners as it creates fillets and chamfers. Examples of fillets created with **Trim** mode on and off are shown in Figure 3-14. In most cases, you want to leave **Trim** mode on. To turn it off, enter **FILLET** and select **Trim** and then **No Trim** from the command line options.

Figure 3-14
Trim mode on and off

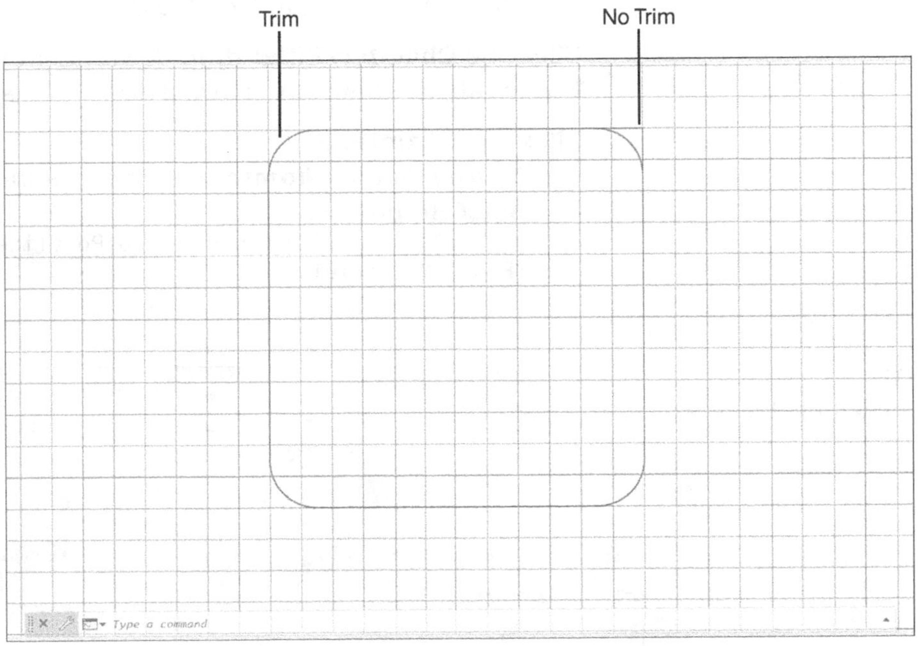

CHAMFER	
Command	CHAMFER
Alias	Cha
Panel	Modify
Tool	

Editing Corners Using CHAMFER

The **CHAMFER** command sequence is almost identical to the **FILLET** command, with the exception that chamfers can be uneven. That is, you can cut back farther on one side of a corner than on the other. To do this, you must give AutoCAD two distances instead of one radius value.

> **TIP**
>
> Following is a general procedure for creating chamfers:
>
> 1. Click the **Chamfer** tool from the **Chamfer/Fillet** drop-down menu on the **Modify** panel of the **Home** tab.
> 2. Right-click and select **Distance** from the shortcut menu.
> 3. Enter a chamfer distance.
> 4. Enter a second chamfer distance or press **<Enter>** for an even chamfer.
> 5. Select two lines that meet at a corner.

In this exercise, you draw even chamfers at the four corners of the square. Using the **Polyline** option, you chamfer all four corners at once.

Accessing the **Chamfer** tool requires opening a simple drop-down menu that has the **Fillet**, **Chamfer**, and **Blend Curves** tools. Blended curves are not covered here.

✔ Undo the fillets drawn in the previous section by clicking the **Undo** button twice or as many times as necessary.

You should have only the red square in your drawing area, as shown previously in Figure 3-9.

✔ Click the **Chamfer/Fillet** drop-down menu on the **Modify** panel of the **Home** tab, as shown in Figure 3-15.

✔ Click the **Chamfer** tool.

*Notice that the **Chamfer** tool replaces the **Fillet** tool on the ribbon. AutoCAD prompts:*

```
    Select first line or [Undo/Polyline/Distance/Angle/Trim/
mEthod/Multiple]:
```

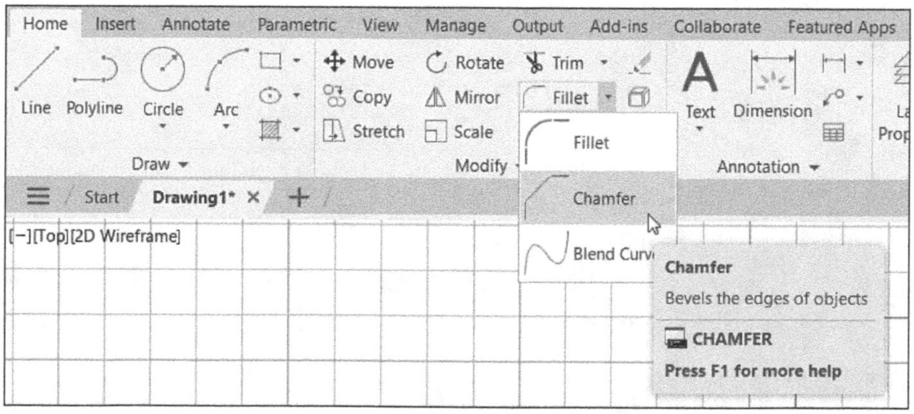

Figure 3-15
Chamfer/Fillet drop-down menu

✔ Select **Distance** from the command-line options.

The next prompt is

```
Specify first chamfer distance <0.00>:
```

✔ Type **1 <Enter>**.

AutoCAD prompts for another distance:

```
Specify second chamfer distance <1.00>:
```

The first distance has become the default and gives you a chamfer cut evenly on both sides. If you want an asymmetrical chamfer, enter a different value for the second distance.

✔ Press **<Enter>** to accept the default, making the chamfer distances symmetrical.

At this point, you could proceed to chamfer each corner of the square independently. However, if you have drawn the square using the ***RECTANG*** *command, you have a quicker option. The* ***RECTANG*** *command draws a closed* **polyline** *in the shape of a rectangle. Polylines are not discussed here, but for now, it is useful to know that a polyline is a single entity comprising multiple straight line and arc segments. If you have drawn a closed polyline and specify the option in the* ***CHAMFER*** *or* ***FILLET*** *command, AutoCAD edits all corners of the object.*

Polyline: A two-dimensional object made of straight line and arc segments that may have varying widths.

✔ Select **Polyline** from the command line options.

AutoCAD prompts:

```
Select 2D polyline or [Distance/Angle/Method]:
```

✔ Move your cursor over any part of the red square.

You see a preview image of the square with chamfers at all four corners.

✔ Select any part of the square.

You should have four even chamfers on your square, and your drawing should resemble Figure 3-16.

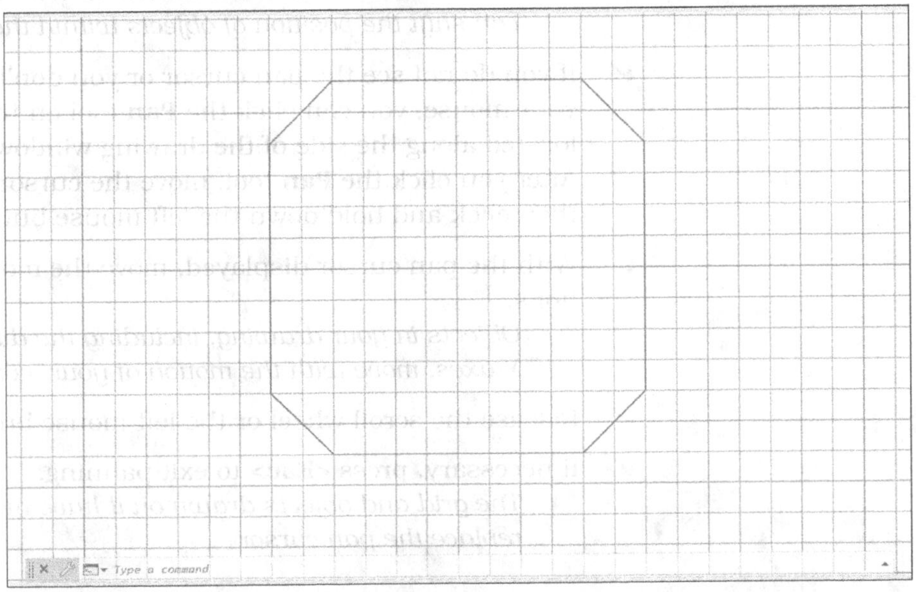

Figure 3-16
Polyline chamfer

Zooming and Panning with the Scroll Wheel

The capability to zoom in and out of a drawing is one of the more impressive benefits of working on a CAD system. When drawings get complex, it often becomes necessary to work in detail on small portions of the drawing. This is done easily with the **ZOOM** command or with the scroll wheel on your mouse. You begin with the convenient scroll wheel technique and then explore the **ZOOM** command in the next section.

✔ You should have a square with chamfered corners in your drawing area from the previous section.

Zooming and panning with the scroll wheel is simple and convenient but less precise than some of the options in the ZOOM command. To better control results, position the crosshairs at or near the center of the objects you want to magnify, and do not move the crosshairs between zooms. AutoCAD zooms in or out centered on the crosshairs' position.

✔ Position the cursor near the center of the chamfered square and roll the scroll wheel forward (away from you) a small amount. If your scroll wheel moves in clicks, one click will do.

Objects in your drawing area are enlarged.

✔ Roll the wheel forward again.

Objects in your drawing area are further enlarged.

✔ Roll the wheel back (toward you) to zoom out.

Panning with the Scroll Wheel

Panning with the mouse is equally simple and does everything the **PAN** command can do. Notice that this technique does not work on every mouse, so you also learn another way to pan. First, try this:

✔ Position the crosshairs anywhere inside or near the chamfered square.

✔ Press and hold down the scroll wheel gently, so that it clicks.

As soon as you do this, the crosshairs are replaced by the pan cursor, which looks like a small hand. With this cursor displayed, you can shift the position of objects within the drawing area.

✔ If you do not see the pan cursor or you don't have a scroll wheel on your mouse, you can click the **Pan** tool on the navigation bar that is located along the side of the drawing window, as shown in Figure 3-17. After you click the **Pan** tool, move the cursor into the drawing area, and then click and hold down the left mouse button .

✔ With the pan cursor displayed, move the mouse slowly in several directions.

Objects in your drawing, including the display grid and the X- and Y-axes, move with the motion of your mouse.

✔ Release the scroll wheel or the left mouse button.

✔ If necessary, press **<Esc>** to exit panning.

The grid and objects drawn on it have moved, and the crosshairs replace the pan cursor.

ZOOM	
Command	ZOOM
Alias	Z
Menu	View
Tool	

Using the ZOOM Command

The **ZOOM** command has many options, a few of which you find out how to use here. Other options have more technical functions. Here, you use the **Extents**, **Window**, **Previous**, and **All** options. These options are readily accessed from the navigation bar along the right side of the drawing window or viewport.

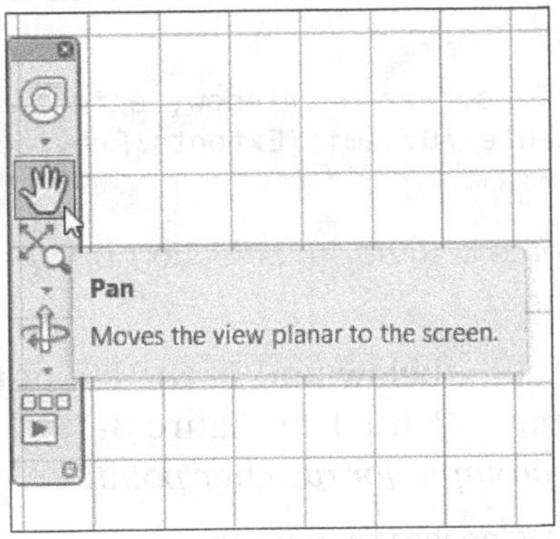

Figure 3-17
Navigation bar

> **NOTE**
>
> In addition to the navigation bar and command line, the **ZOOM** and **PAN** commands can be accessed from the **Navigate** panel of the **View** tab on the ribbon. The **Navigate** panel isn't displayed by default, but if you want to use the tools on this panel, click the **View** tab, right-click anywhere on the ribbon, and select **Show Panels > Navigate.**

Zoom Extents

Extents refers to the area within a drawing that actually contains complete drawn objects. When you **Zoom** to **Extents**, AutoCAD displays only that area of your drawing where you have actually drawn something. You learn this first because it is the default option on the navigation bar. Because it may have been replaced by another option on your navigation bar, you start by opening the **Zoom** drop-down list.

✔ Click the arrow below the **Zoom** tool on your navigation bar.

*The **Zoom** tool is the third tool down on the navigation bar. This opens the drop-down list shown in Figure 3-18. **Zoom Extents** is at the top of the list.*

✔ Click the **Zoom Extents** tool from the navigation bar, as shown in Figure 3-18.

AutoCAD immediately zooms to display an area containing the complete objects in your drawing.

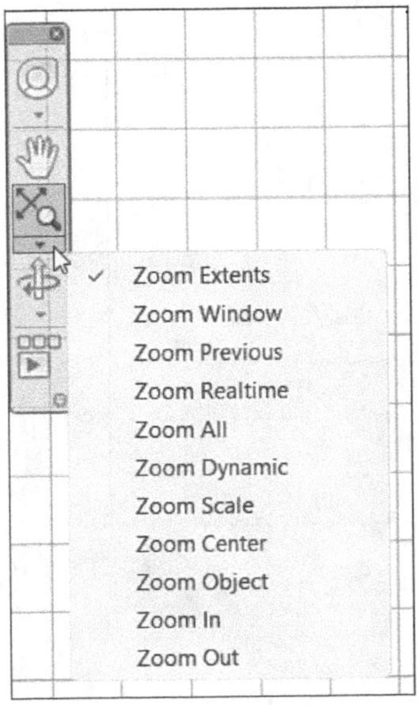

Figure 3-18
Zoom drop-down list

> **NOTE**
>
> - The extents area here is slightly larger than your chamfered square because you have also drawn two lines and a circle on layers that are now turned off. Though these objects are on layers that are turned off and not frozen, they are still considered when AutoCAD calculates drawing extents.
> - If your navigation bar has been turned off, you can turn it on by typing **navbar <Enter>** and then **on <Enter>**.

Zoom Window

A very common option for zooming is to create a window around the objects you want to magnify. You can select the **Zoom Window** tool from the drop-down list, but you can also force a window selection simply by entering the **ZOOM** command and defining a window. Try this:

✔ Type **z <Enter>**.

This alias starts the ***ZOOM*** *command. The prompt that follows looks like this:*

```
    Specify corner of window, enter a scale factor (nX or nXP),
or [All/Center/Dynamic/Extents/Previous/Scale/Window/Object]
<realtime>:
```

You can force a window selection by specifying two points in the drawing area.

✔ Specify a point just below and to the left of the lower-left corner of your chamfered square (Point 1 in Figure 3-19).

AutoCAD prompts for another point:

```
Specify opposite corner:
```

You are being prompted to define a window, just as in the ***ERASE*** *command. This window is the basis for what AutoCAD displays next. Because you are not going to make a window that exactly conforms to the screen size and shape, AutoCAD interprets the window this way: Everything in the window will be shown, plus whatever additional area is needed to fill the drawing area. The center of the window becomes the center of the new display.*

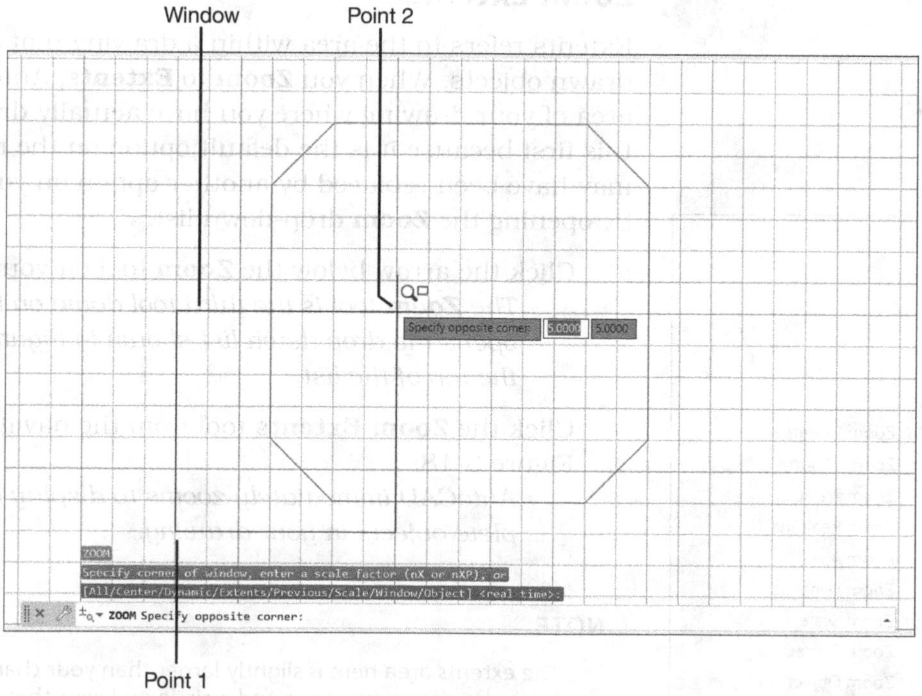

Figure 3-19
Specifying window to zoom

Figure 3-20
Results of **Zoom** window

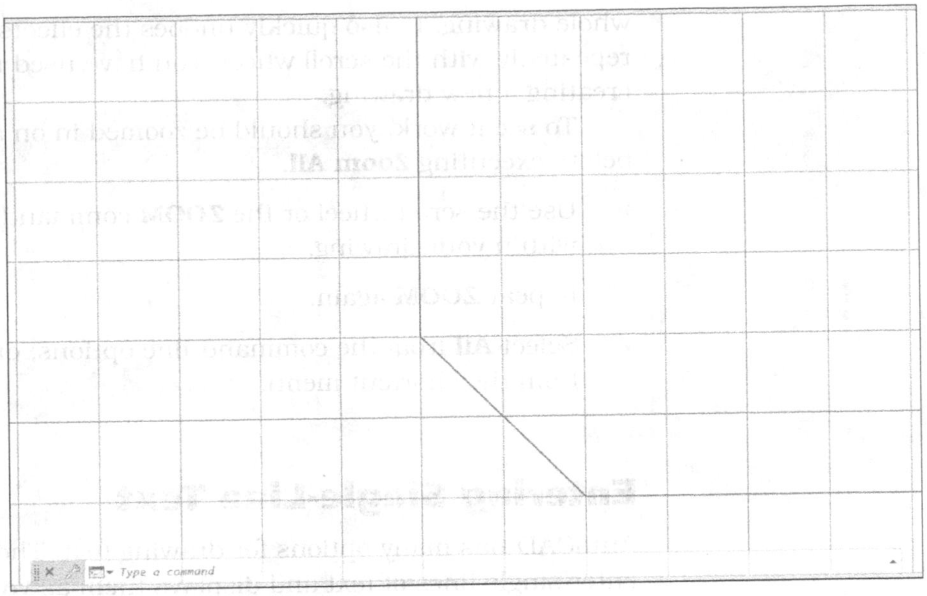

✔ Specify a second point near the center of your square (Point 2 in the figure).

AutoCAD zooms in dynamically until the lower-left corner of the square is enlarged in your drawing area, as shown in Figure 3-20.

✔ Using the same method, try zooming up farther on the chamfered corner of the square. If **Snap** mode is on, you might need to turn it off.

*Remember that you can repeat the **ZOOM** command by pressing **<Enter>** or the spacebar. At this point, most people cannot resist seeing how much magnification they can get by zooming repeatedly on the same corner or angle of a chamfer. Go ahead. After a couple of zooms, the angle does not appear to change, though the placement shifts as the center of your window changes. An angle is the same angle no matter how close you get to it, but what happens to the spacing of the grid and snap as you move in?*

When you are done experimenting with window zooming, try zooming to the previous display, as follows.

Zoom Previous

✔ Press **<Enter>** to repeat the **ZOOM** command.

✔ Select **Previous** from the command-line options.

*You can also select **Zoom Previous** from the drop-down list on the navigation bar. You should now see the previous display.*

✔ **Zoom Previous** as many times as you can until you get a message that says:

```
No previous view saved.
```

Zoom All

Zoom All zooms out to display the limits of the drawing, placing the origin **(0,0)**, at the bottom of the drawing area. It is useful when you have been working in a number of small areas of a drawing and are ready to view the whole drawing. It also quickly undoes the effects of zooming or panning repeatedly with the scroll wheel. You have used this option frequently when creating a new drawing.

To see it work, you should be zoomed in on a portion of your drawing before executing **Zoom All**.

- ✔ Use the scroll wheel or the **ZOOM** command to zoom in on an area within your drawing.
- ✔ Repeat **ZOOM** again.
- ✔ Select **All** from the command-line options, or right-click and select **All** from the shortcut menu.

Entering Single-Line Text

AutoCAD has many options for drawing text. The simplest allows you to enter single lines of text and displays them as you type. You can backspace through lines to make corrections if you do not exit the command. You briefly explore creating text to add labels to a drawing.

For this exercise, you add some simple left-justified text to your drawing. The text "Chamfered Square" is placed on layer **1**, as shown in Figure 3-21.

- ✔ Click the **Text** drop-down menu on the **Annotation** panel of the **Home** tab and then click the **Single Line** text tool, as shown in Figure 3-22. Note that this is the **Annotation** panel on the **Home** tab and not the **Annotate** tab that has more annotation tools not explored here.

Figure 3-21
Text added

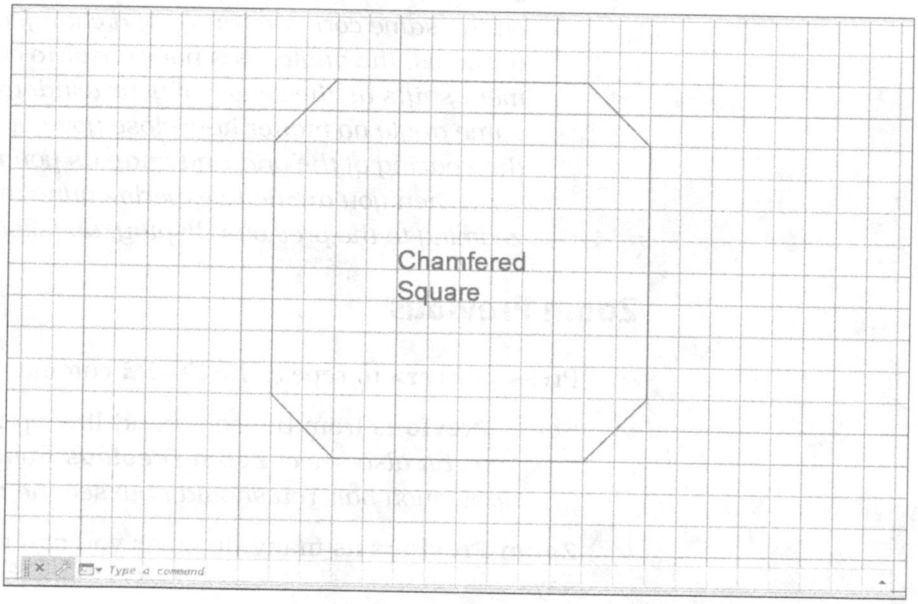

You see a prompt with three options in the command line:

```
Specify start point of text or [Justify/Style]:
```

Here, you use the default method to specify a start point. This gives you standard left-justified text drawn left to right from the specified point.

Figure 3-22
Single Line text tool

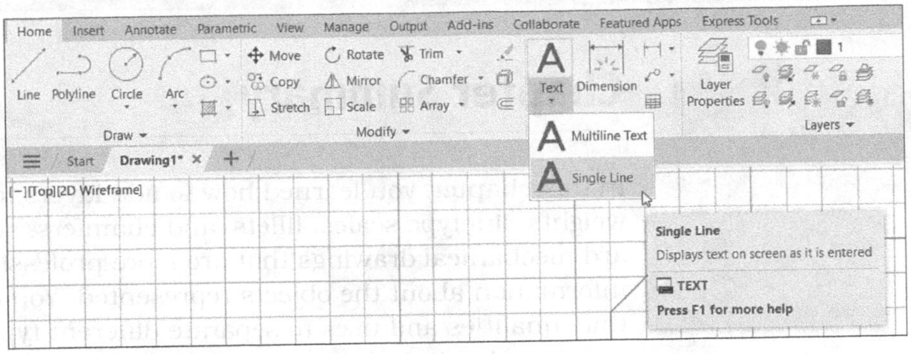

✔ Specify a start point near the middle left of the square, as shown in Figure 3-21, such as the point **(5,5)**.

Study the prompt that follows and be sure that you do not attempt to enter text yet:

```
Specify height <0.20>:
```

This gives you the opportunity to set the text height. The number you type specifies the height of uppercase letters in the units you have specified for the current drawing. Next, you specify a slightly larger text height.

✔ Type **.3 <Enter>**.

The prompt that follows allows you to place text in a rotated position:

```
Specify rotation angle of text <0>:
```

The default of **0°** *orients text in the usual horizontal manner. Other angles can be specified by typing a degree number relative to the polar coordinate system or by showing a point. If you show a point, it is taken as the second point of a baseline, along which the text string is placed. For now, stick to horizontal text.*

✔ Press **<Enter>** to accept the default angle (0).

Now it is time to enter the text itself. There is no prompt for text at the command line. Text is entered directly in the drawing area at the specified start point.

Notice that a blinking cursor appears at the start point. This shows where the first letter you type will be placed. Watch the drawing area as you type, and you can see dynamic text at work.

✔ Type **Chamfered <Enter>**.

Remember, you cannot use the spacebar in place of the **<Enter>** *key when entering text. Notice that the text cursor jumps down a line when you press* **<Enter>**.

✔ Type **Square <Enter>**.

The text cursor jumps down again. This is how AutoCAD allows for easy entry of multiple lines of text directly in the drawing area. To exit the command, press **<Enter>** *again at the prompt.*

✔ Press **<Enter>** to exit the command.

This completes the process and returns you to the command line prompt. Your drawing should resemble Figure 3-21.

chapterthree

Chapter Summary

In this chapter, you learned how to add layers, colors, linetypes, lineweights, linetype scales, fillets, and chamfers, so now you can create standard mechanical drawings that are more professional and contain more information about the objects represented. You can create layers with distinct qualities and uses to separate different types of information and control these layers independently. These layers can be turned on and off, frozen, thawed, locked, styled for plotting, or ignored in plotting. Additionally you can now zoom in or out of your drawing, pan across the area in which you are working, and add single-line text to your drawings.

Chapter Test Questions

Multiple Choice

Circle the correct answer.

1. Which linetype is loaded by default?

a. Solid
b. Center
c. Continuous
d. Diagonal

2. AutoCAD's default color system is

a. Pantone
b. Index
c. RGB
d. True Color

3. Which is **not** entered when you create single-line text?

a. Text height
b. Rotation angle
c. Text location
d. Text color

4. Which of these **cannot** be accomplished using the **Layer** drop-down list?

a. Create new layers
b. Set current layer
c. Turn layers on and off
d. Freeze and thaw

5. How many layers can you create in AutoCAD?

a. 255
b. As many as you like
c. 256
d. It depends on your computer

Matching

Write the number of the correct answer on the line.

a. Fillet ______
b. Off ______
c. Locked ______
d. Layer **0** ______
e. Frozen ______

1. Layer is not visible.
2. Layer cannot be edited.
3. Always symmetric.
4. Cannot be deleted.
5. Not visible, not regenerated.

True or False

Circle the correct answer.

1. **True or False:** You can zoom but not pan with the scroll wheel.
2. **True or False:** Objects on the same layer need not be the same color.
3. **True or False:** It is necessary to match layers and color numbers.
4. **True or False:** Linetypes need to be loaded, but colors do not.
5. **True or False:** You can draw in only one color on one layer.

Questions

1. What linetype is always available when you start a drawing from scratch in AutoCAD? What must you do to access other linetypes?
2. Name three ways to change the current layer.
3. You have been working in the **Layer Properties Manager** palette, and when you return to your drawing you find that some objects are no longer visible. What happened?
4. Describe the use of the scroll wheel for zooming.
5. In single-line text, what values must be specified before entering text content?

Drawing Problems

1. Make layer **3** current and draw a green centerline cross with two perpendicular lines, each 2 units long and intersecting at their midpoints.
2. Make layer **2** current and draw a hidden line circle centered at the intersection of the cross drawn in Step 1, with a diameter of 2 units.
3. Make layer **1** current and draw a red square of 2 units on a side centered on the center of the circle. Its sides run tangent to the circle.
4. Use a window to zoom in on the objects drawn in Steps 1, 2, and 3.
5. Fillet each corner of the square with a **0.125** radius fillet.

chapterthree

Chapter Drawing Projects

M Drawing 3-1: *Mounting Plate* [BASIC]

This drawing gives you experience using centerlines, fillets, and chamfers. Because there are no hidden lines, you have no need for layer **2**, but you continue to use the same numbering system for consistency. Draw the continuous lines in red on layer **1** and the centerlines in green on layer **3**.

> **TIP**
>
> Rather than start each drawing as a new drawing, use the **SAVEAS** command to save drawings under different names so that you don't have to re-create layers in each new drawing.

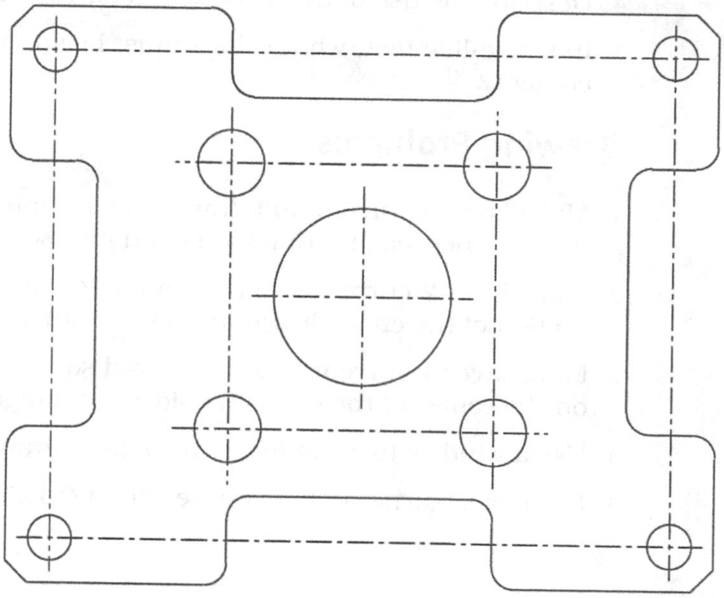

Drawing Suggestions

GRID = 0.5

SNAP = 0.25

LTSCALE = 0.5

- Change linetype scale along with setting grid and snap.
- Pay attention to the linetypes as you draw and change the current layer accordingly.
- Draw the Mounting Plate outline with the **LINE** command. Then chamfer the four corners and fillet all other corners as shown.

Drawing 3-1
Mounting plate

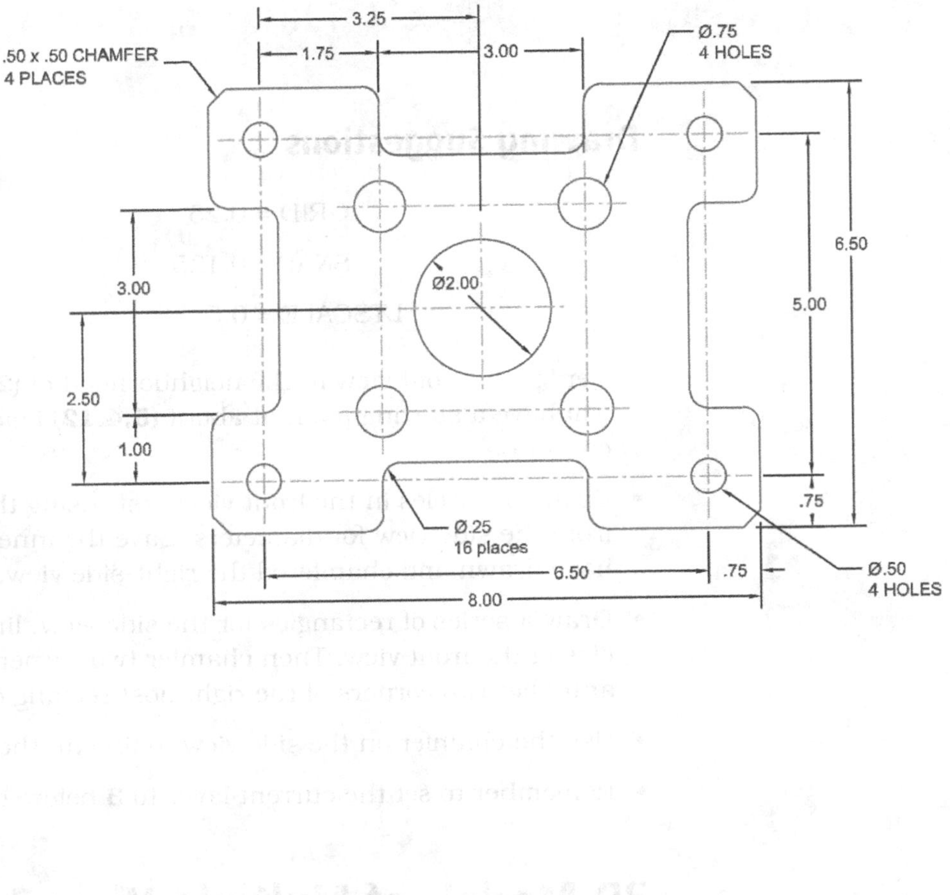

Drawing 3-2: *Stepped Shaft* [INTERMEDIATE]

This two-view drawing uses continuous lines, centerlines, chamfers, and fillets. You may want to zoom in to enlarge the drawing area you are actually working in and pan right and left to work on the two views.

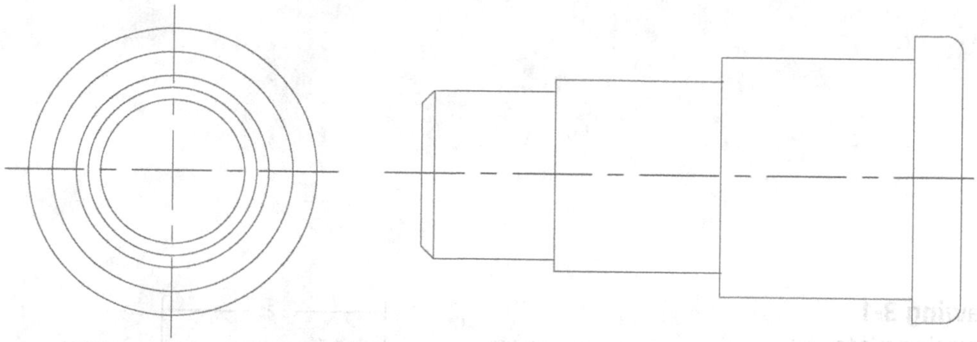

Drawing Suggestions

GRID = 0.25

SNAP = 0.125

LTSCALE = 0.5

- Center the front view in the neighborhood of **(2,5)**. The right-side view will have a starting point at about **(5,4.12)** before the chamfer cuts this corner off.
- Draw the circles in the front view first, using the vertical dimensions from the side view for diameters. Save the inner circle until after you have drawn and chamfered the right-side view.
- Draw a series of rectangles for the side view, lining them up with the circles of the front view. Then chamfer two corners of the leftmost rectangle and fillet two corners of the rightmost rectangle.
- Use the chamfer on the side view to line up the radius of the inner circle.
- Remember to set the current layer to **3** before drawing the centerlines.

3D Models of Multiple-View Drawings

If you have any difficulty visualizing objects in the multiple-view drawings in this chapter, you might want to refer to the images in Drawings 13-5A, B, C, and D. These are 3D solid models derived from 2D drawings.

Drawing 3-2
Stepped shaft

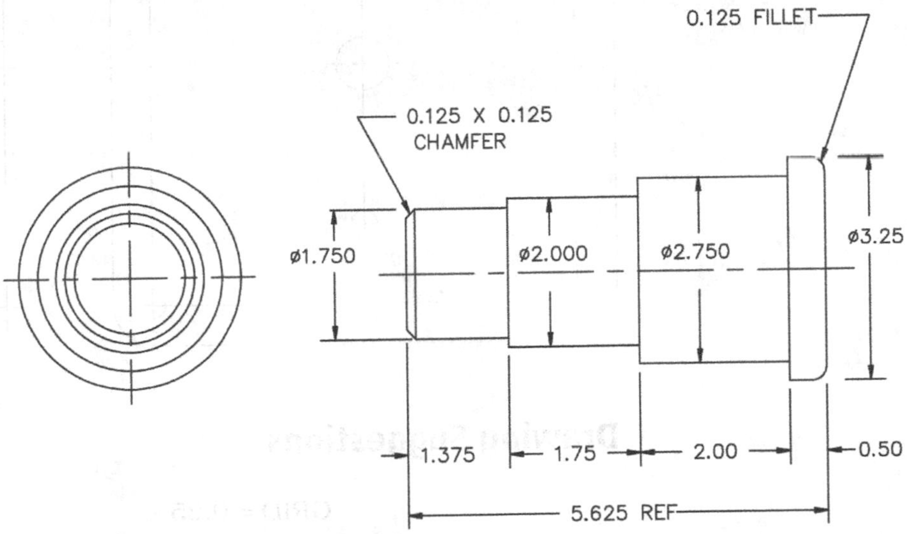

M Drawing 3-3: *Base Plate* [INTERMEDIATE]

This drawing uses continuous lines, hidden lines, centerlines, and fillets. The side view should be quite easy once the front view is drawn. Remember to change layers when you want to change linetypes.

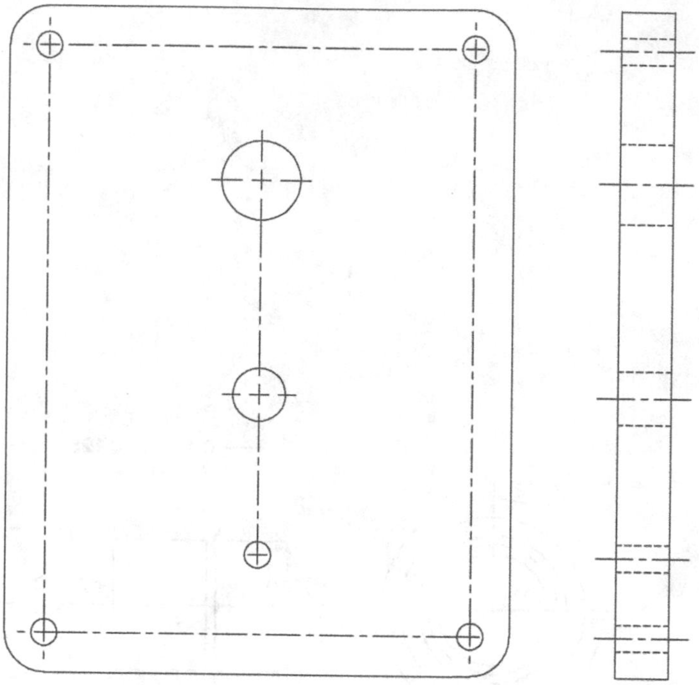

Drawing Suggestions

GRID = 0.25

SNAP = 0.125

LTSCALE = 0.5

- Study the dimensions carefully and remember that every grid increment is **0.25**, and snap points not on the grid are exactly halfway between grid points. The four circles at the corners are **0.38** (actually **0.375** rounded off) over and in from the corner points. This is three snap spaces (**0.375 = 3 × 0.125**).
- Position the three circles along the centerline of the rectangle carefully. Notice that dimensions are given from the center of the screw holes at top and bottom.
- Use the circle perimeters to line up the hidden lines on the side view, and the centers to line up the centerlines.

Drawing 3-3
Base plate

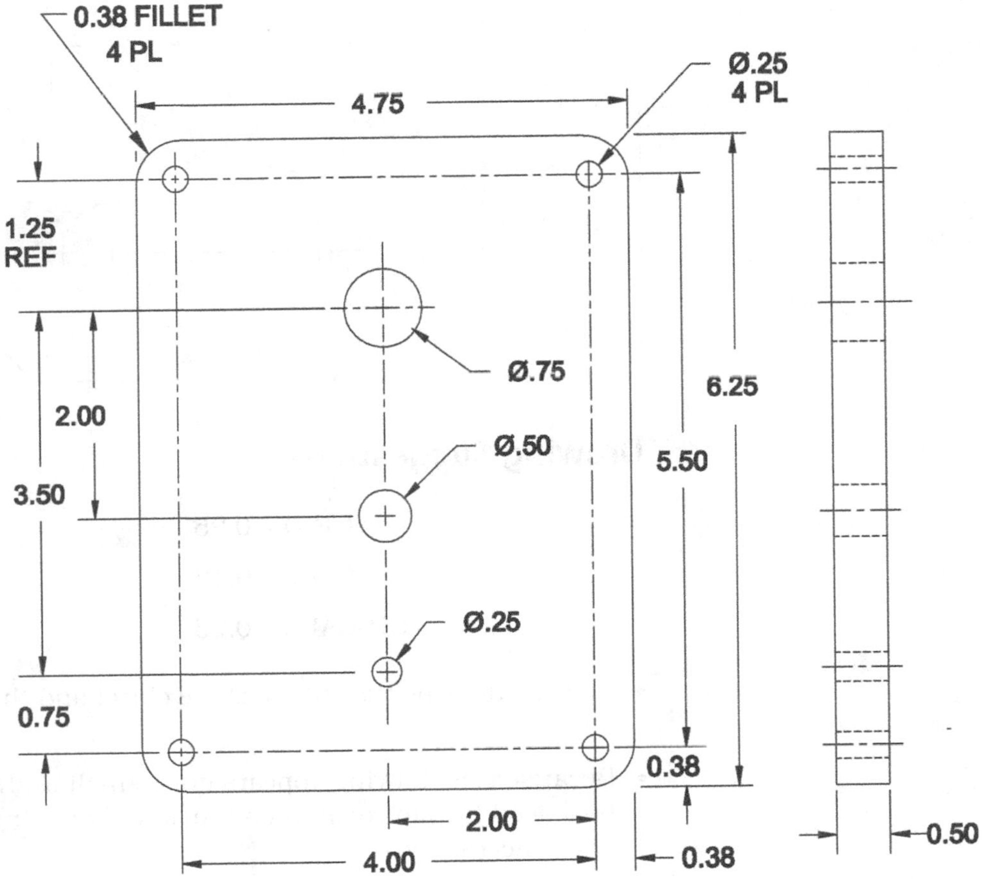

M Drawing 3-4: *Template* [ADVANCED]

This drawing gives you practice with fillets, chamfers, layers, and zooming. Notice that because of the smaller dimensions here, it is recommended to use a smaller **LTSCALE** setting value.

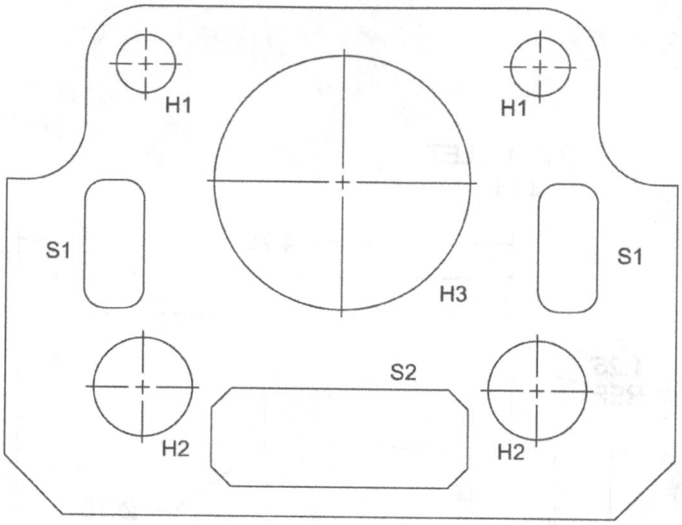

Drawing Suggestions

GRID = 0.25

SNAP = 0.125

LTSCALE = 0.25

- Start by drawing the outline of the object and then fillet and chamfer as shown.
- Because this drawing appears quite small in the drawing area, it would be a good idea to zoom in on the actual drawing space you are using and pan if necessary.
- *Typ* is a standard abbreviation for *typical* and indicates that the dimension is used in multiple locations.
- Draw the cutouts labeled S1 and S2 as rectangles and then fillet and chamfer as shown.
- Label all cutouts as shown using the **TEXT** command.

Regen

When you change a linetype scale setting, you see the message *Regenerating model* in the command line. Regeneration is the process by which AutoCAD translates geometric data into the objects you see in the drawing area. Regeneration happens automatically when certain operations are performed.

Drawing 3-4
Template

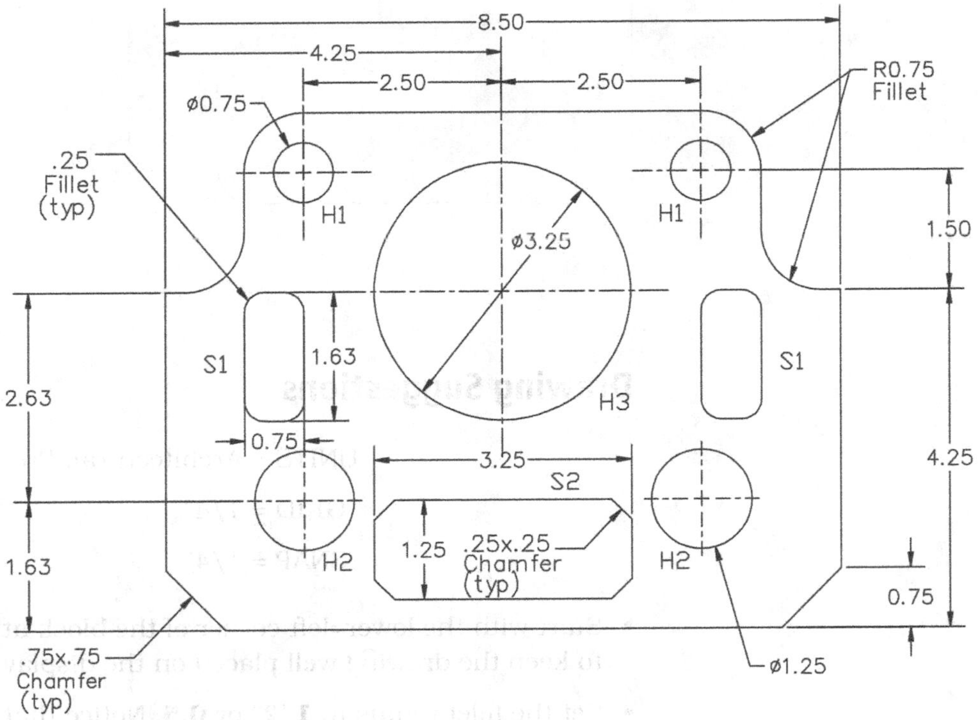

A Drawing 3-5: *Half Block* [INTERMEDIATE]

This cinder block is the first project using architectural units. Set units, grid, and snap as indicated, and everything falls into place nicely.

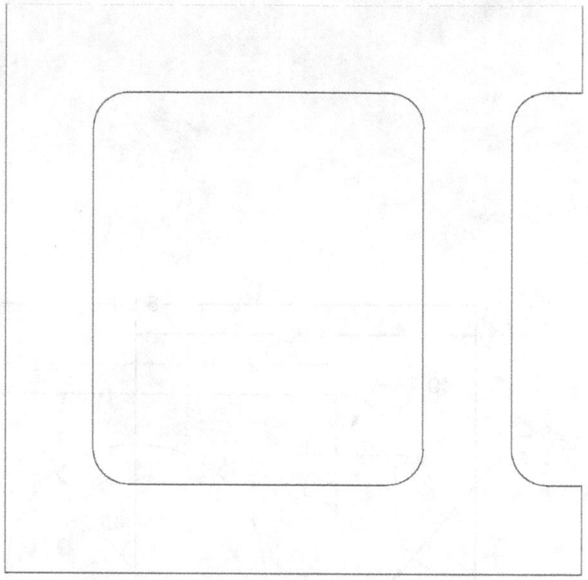

Drawing Suggestions

UNITS = Architectural; Precision = 0'–0 1/4"

GRID = 1/4"

SNAP = 1/4"

- Start with the lower=left corner of the block at the point **(0'–01", 0'–01")** to keep the drawing well placed on the display.
- Set the fillet radius to **1/2"** or **0.5**. Notice that you can use decimal versions of fractions. The advantage is that they are easier to type.

Drawing 3-5
Half block

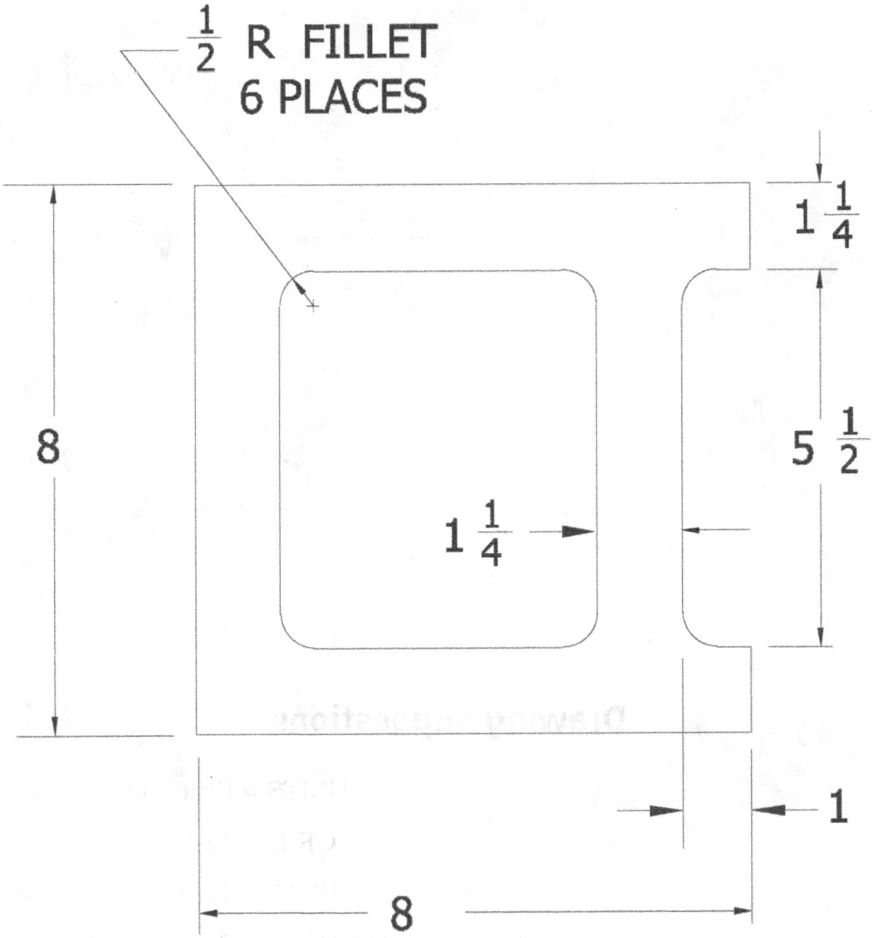

Drawing 3-6: *Packing Flange* [ADVANCED]

This drawing uses continuous lines, hidden lines, centerlines, and fillets. The side view should be quite easy once the top view is drawn. Remember to change layers when you want to change linetypes.

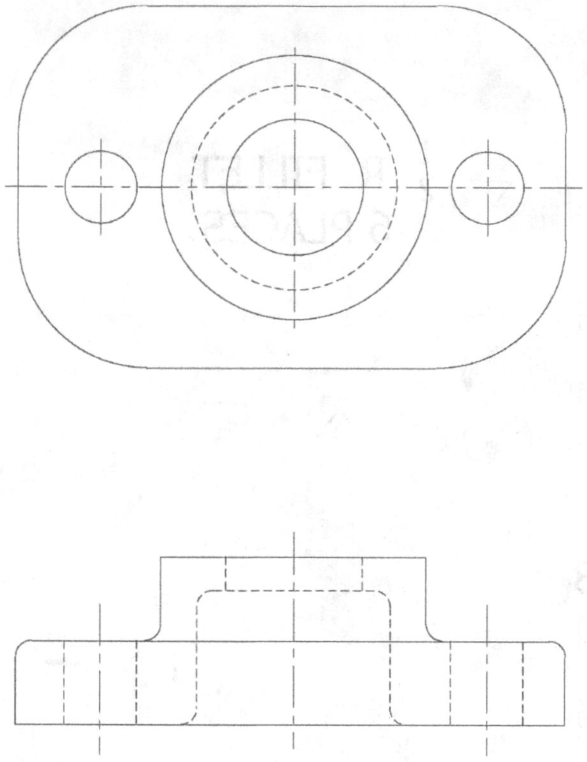

Drawing Suggestions

UNITS = Fractional

GRID = 1/4"

SNAP = 1/16"

LTSCALE = 0.5"

- Study the dimensions carefully, and remember that every grid increment is 1/4", and snap points not on the grid are exactly halfway between grid points. Notice that the units should be set to fractions.
- Begin by drawing the outline and then the three centerlines in the top view. Then proceed by drawing all circles.
- The circles can be drawn using a center point and a diameter. Position the center of the circle where the centerlines cross, and type in the diameter.
- Use the top view to line up all the lines on the side view.

Drawing 3-6
Packing flange

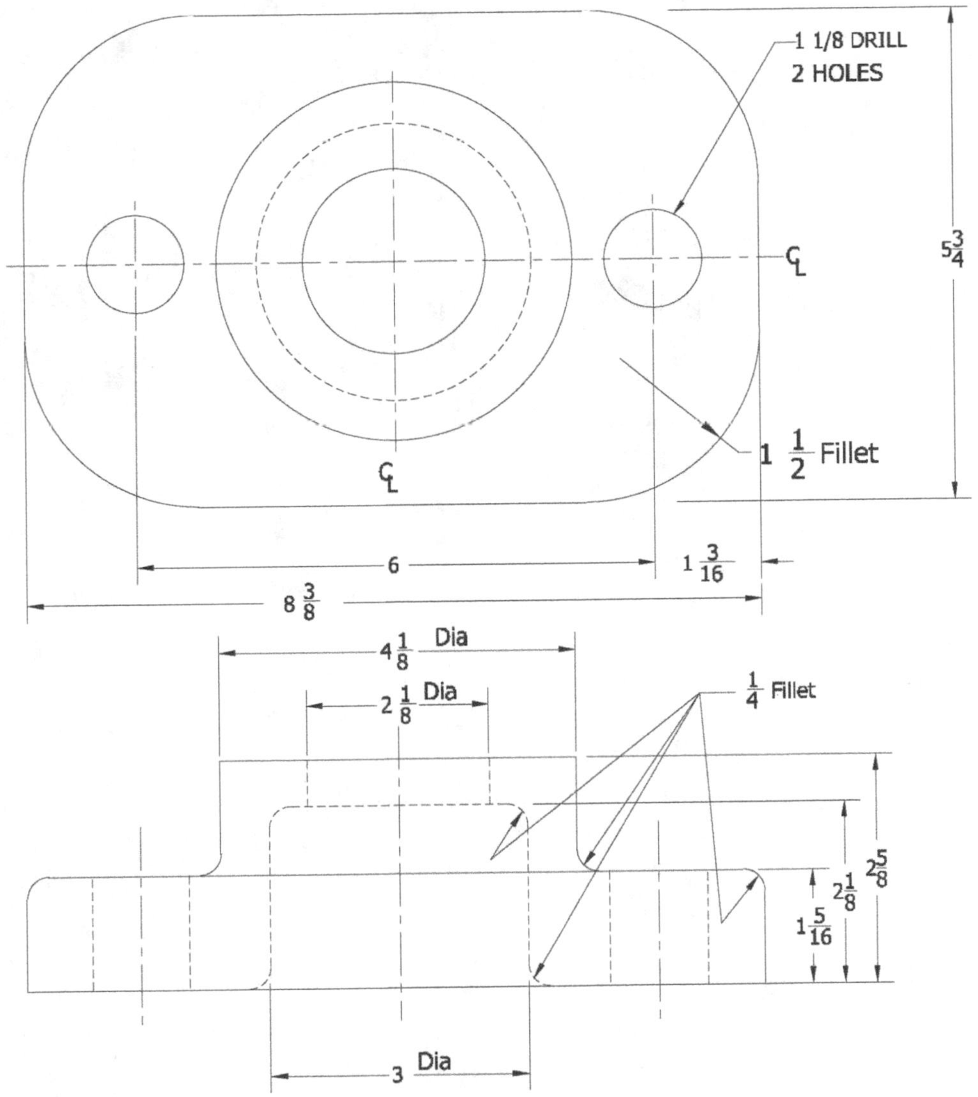

chapter four

Templates, Copies, and Arrays

CHAPTER OBJECTIVES

- Set drawing limits
- Create a template
- Save a drawing template
- Use the **MOVE** command
- Use the **COPY** command
- Use the **ARRAYRECT** command for rectangular arrays
- Create center marks
- Change plot settings

Introduction

In this chapter, you learn some real time-savers. If you are tired of defining the same layers, along with **Units**, **Grid**, **Snap**, and **ltscale**, for each new drawing, read on. You are about to learn how to create your own drawing templates. With templates, you can begin each new drawing with setups you have defined and saved in previous AutoCAD sessions or with a variety of predefined setups included in the software.

In addition, you learn to reshape the drawing grid using the **LIMITS** command and to copy, move, and array objects so that you do not have to draw the same thing multiple times. You begin with the **LIMITS** command because that allows you to change the limits as part of defining your first template.

Setting Drawing Limits

> **TIP**
>
> The following is the general procedure used to change the limits of the drawing grid:
>
> 1. Type **Limits <Enter>** at the command line.
> 2. Enter the coordinates of the lower-left corner.
> 3. Enter the coordinates of the upper-right corner.
> 4. Type **z <Enter>**, and then type **a <Enter>** or select **All** from the command line.

You have changed the density of the drawing grid many times but always within the same space with 12 × 9 ***limits***. Now, you will learn how to set new limits to emulate other sheet sizes or any other space you want to represent; but first, a word about model space and paper space.

Model Space and Paper Space

limits: In AutoCAD, two points that define the outer boundary of the drawing area in a given drawing. The points are defined by ordered pairs in a Cartesian coordinate system, with the first point being the lower-left corner and the second being the upper-right corner of a rectangular space.

layout: A 2D representation of what a drawing will look like when plotted. Layouts are created in paper space, with viewports in which objects drawn in model space can be positioned and scaled for plotting.

Model space is an AutoCAD concept that refers to the imaginary space in which you create and edit objects. In model space, objects are always drawn at full scale (1 drawing unit = 1 unit of length in the real world). The alternative to model space is *paper space*, in which drawing units represent units of length on a piece of paper. You encounter paper space when you begin to use AutoCAD's ***layout*** feature. A layout is like an overlay on your drawing in which you specify a sheet size, scale, and other paper-related options. Layouts also allow you to create multiple views of the same model space objects. To avoid confusion and keep your learning curve on track, layouts are covered later Chapter 6.

In this exercise, you reshape your model space grid to emulate different drawing sheet sizes. This is not necessary in later exercises. With AutoCAD, you can scale your drawing to fit any drawing sheet size when it comes time to plot. Ultimately, model space limits should be determined by the overall size and shape of objects in your drawing, not by the paper you use when you plot.

You begin by creating a new drawing and changing its limits from an Architectural A-size sheet (12 × 9) to an Architectural B-size sheet (18 × 12).

✔ Click the **New** tool from the **Quick Access** toolbar or click the down arrow next to **New** on the **Start** tab to open the template list.

*This brings you to the **Select template** dialog box or the **Template** drop-down list. At this point, you continue to use the **acad.dwt** template. Once you have created your own template, it will appear in this dialog box or list along with all the others.*

✔ In the **Select Template** dialog box, select the **acad.dwt** drawing template and click **Open**, or select **acad.dwt** from the drop-down list.

✔ Type **z <Enter>**.

✔ Type **a <Enter>**.

Thus far, you have always worked with the default settings, which displays the grid beyond limits. By changing this so the grid is displayed only to cover the limits, you will get a better sense of what the limits actually are. Later, you return to the default setting.

✔ Right-click the **Snap Mode** button on the status bar and select **Snap Settings** from the shortcut menu.

*This displays the **Drafting Settings** dialog box, with the **Snap and Grid** tab showing. At the bottom right of this tab, there is a panel labeled **Grid Behavior**.*

✔ In the **Grid Behavior** panel, uncheck the box next to **Display grid beyond Limits**.

✔ Click **OK**.

*Your grid is now displayed only between the current limits of **(0,0)** and **(12,9)**, as shown in Figure 4-1.*

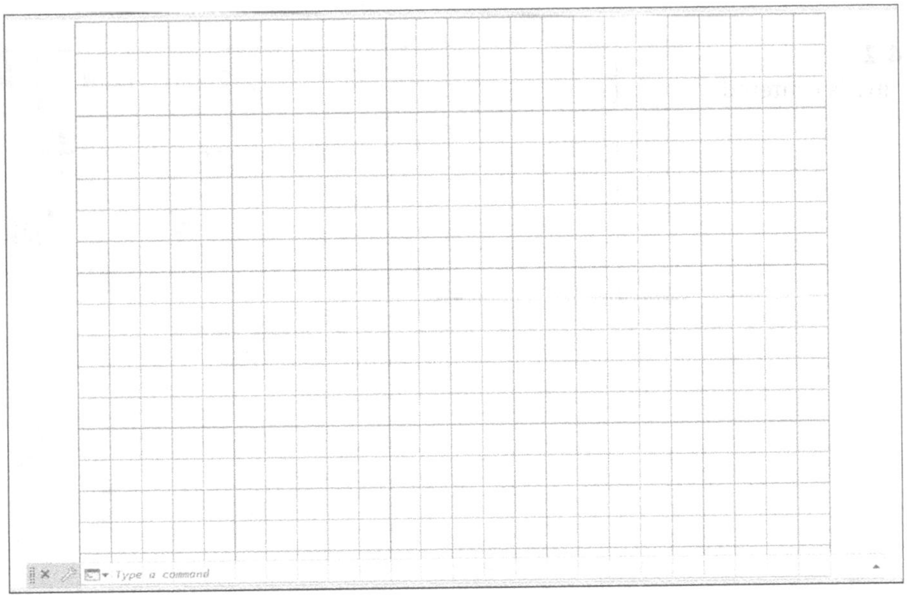

Figure 4-1
Grid displayed between current limits

Setting New Limits

Limits are set using the **LIMITS** command. Unlike most commands, it isn't on the ribbon or the application menu. When you need to change the limits of your drawing, just enter its name at the dynamic input tooltip or command-line prompt.

✔ Type **limits <Enter>**.

You see this prompt:

```
Reset Model Space limits:
Specify lower left corner or [ON/OFF] <0.0000,0.0000>:
```

The on and off options control a feature called limits checking. They determine what happens when you attempt to draw outside the drawing limits. With checking off, nothing happens. With checking on, you get a message that displays "Attempt to draw outside limits", and AutoCAD does not allow you to begin a new object outside of the limits. By default, limits checking is off.

*The default value shows that the current lower-left corner of the grid is at **(0,0)**, where you can leave it.*

✔ Press **<Enter>** to accept the default lower-left corner.

AutoCAD prompts:

```
Specify upper right corner <12.0000,9.0000>:
```

Changing these settings changes the size of your grid.

✔ Type **18,12 <Enter>**.

*Your grid stretches out to the right to reach the new x limit of 12. The usual **Zoom All** procedure enlarges and centers the grid in the drawing area.*

✔ Type **z <Enter>** to enter the **ZOOM** command.

✔ Type **a <Enter>** to **Zoom All**.

You should have an 18 × 12 grid centered in the drawing area, as shown in Figure 4-2.

Figure 4-2
18 × 12 grid is centered

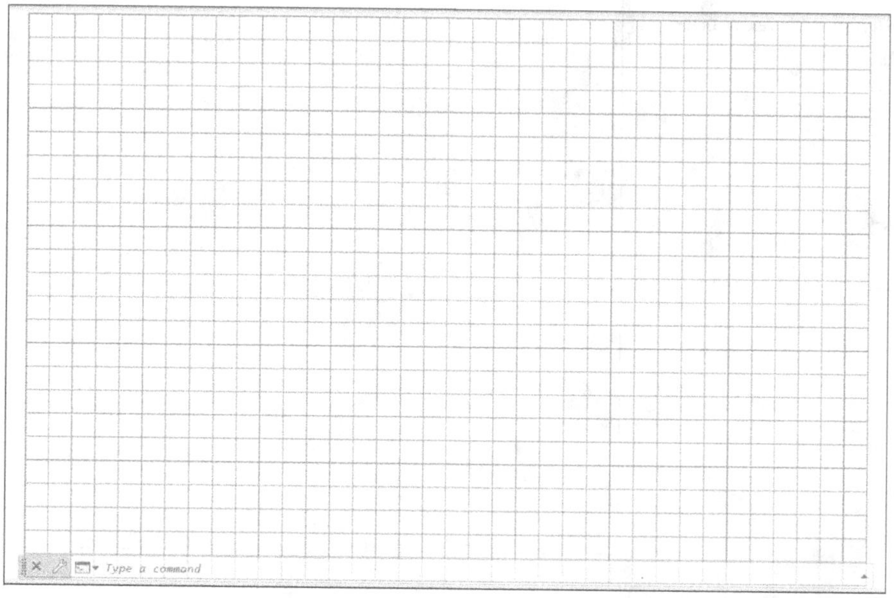

✔ Move the cursor to the upper-right corner to check its coordinates.

This is the grid you use for your B-size drawing template.

It represents a larger area in model space than the 12 × 9 grid.

You might want to experiment with setting limits using some of the possibilities shown in Figure 4-3, which is a table of drawing sheet sizes. It shows the two sets of standard sizes. The standard size you use may be determined by your plotter. For example, some plotters that plot on C-size paper take a 24 × 18 sheet but do not take a 22 × 17 sheet. This information should be programmed into your plotter driver software and appears in the **Plot** dialog box in the image preview area. Though you are currently working in model space, the same procedures for setting limits are relevant to setting up your layout in paper space.

After you are finished exploring the **LIMITS** command, you change the other settings you want and save this drawing as your B-size drawing template. Once you have saved the new template, you can use it any time you want to create a drawing with 18 × 12 limits.

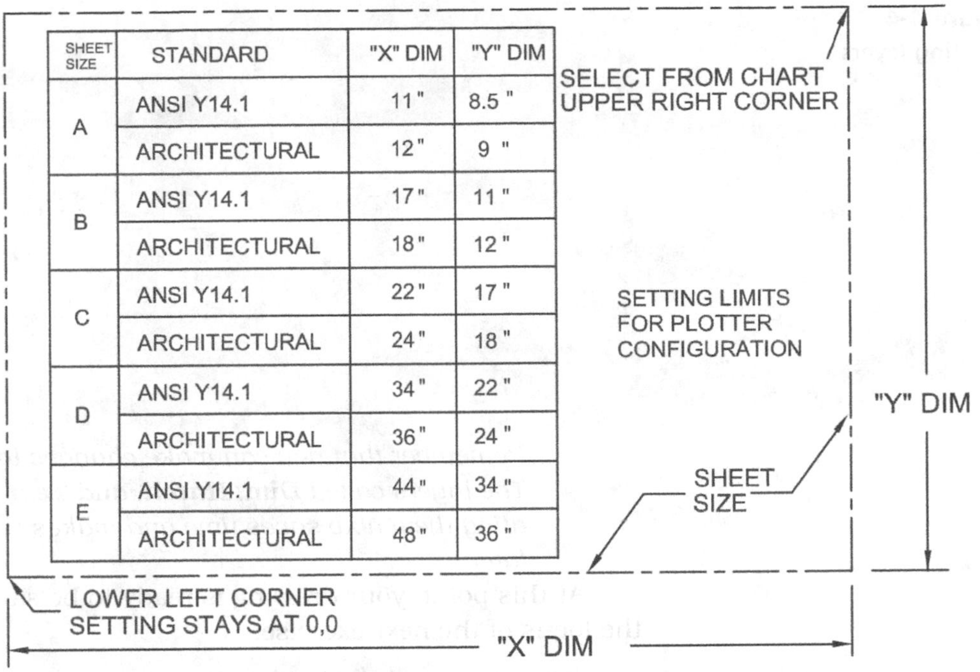

Figure 4-3
Drawing sheet sizes

Creating a Drawing Template

To make your own *template* so that you can begin new drawings with the settings you want, all you have to do is create a drawing that has those settings and then save it as a template.

> **TIP**
>
> The following is a general procedure for creating a template:
>
> 1. Define layers and change settings (**Grid**, **Snap**, **Units**, **Limits**, **ltscale**, etc.) as desired.
> 2. Save the drawing as an **AutoCAD Drawing Template** file.

✔ Make changes to the current drawing as follows:

GRID:	0.50 ON	COORDS:	ON
SNAP:	0.25 ON	LTSCALE:	0.5
UNITS:	2-place decimal	LIMITS:	(0,0) (18,12), displayed beyond limits

> **NOTE**
>
> Do not leave anything drawn in your drawing or it will come up as part of the template each time you create a new drawing. For some applications, this is quite useful, but for now, you want a blank template.

✔ Create layers and associated colors, linetypes, and settings to match those in Figure 4-4.

Figure 4-4
Creating layers

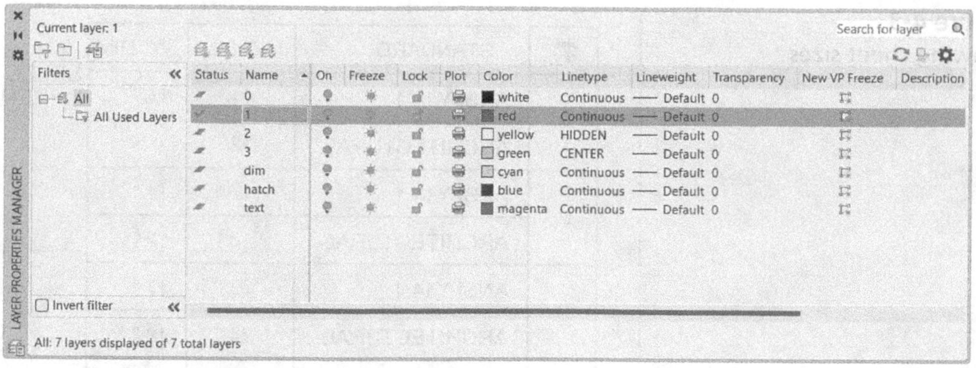

*Remember that you can make changes to your template at any time. The layers called **Dim**, **Hatch**, and **Text** are not used here, but creating them now saves time and makes your template more complete later.*

At this point, your drawing is ready to be saved as a template, which is the focus of the next exercise.

Saving a Drawing Template

A drawing becomes a template when you save it as one. Template files are given a .dwt extension and placed in the **Template** file folder.

> **NOTE**
>
> In situations where multiple users might be using the same computer at different times during the day or week, changing AutoCAD settings might cause confusion. In this case, your instructor or CAD manager might not want you to save a template file or might want it stored in a different location or under a different name. Ask your instructor or CAD manager how it is to be done in your class or CAD environment.

✔ You should be in the drawing created in the last exercise. All the drawing changes should be made as described previously.

✔ Click the **Save As** tool from the **Quick Access** toolbar.

> **NOTE**
>
> The templates included with the AutoCAD program consist of various standard sheet sizes, all with title blocks, borders, and predefined plot styles. These are convenient. At this point, however, they can cause confusion because they are created with paper space in mind and automatically put you into a paper space layout. You have no need for title blocks and borders in this chapter.

Figure 4-5
Save Drawing As dialog box

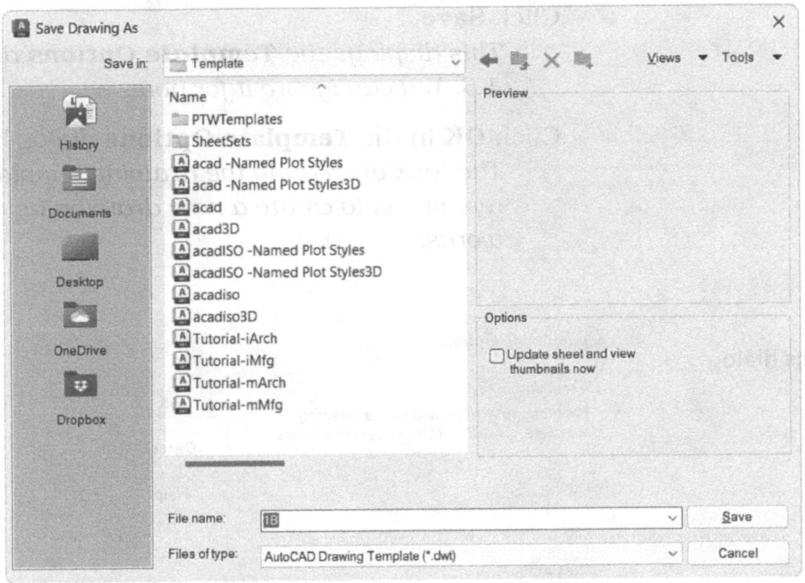

*This displays the **Save Drawing As** dialog box shown in Figure 4-5. The **File name** edit box contains the name of the current drawing. If you have not named the drawing, it is named **Drawing1**, **Drawing2**, and so on.*

*Below the **File name** edit box is the **Files of type** list, which lists options for saving the drawing.*

✔ Open the **Files of type** list by clicking the arrow to the right of the list box.

This opens the list of file-type options.

✔ Select **AutoCAD Drawing Template** (*.**dwt**) file from the list.

*This also the **Template** folder automatically. You see a list of templates commonly seen when creating a new drawing. Many templates are supplied with AutoCAD that might be useful to you later. At this point, it is more important to learn how to create your own.*

✔ If necessary, double-click the **File name** edit box.

✔ Type **1B** for the new name. Or, if others also use your computer, you may want to add your initials to identify this as your template.

ANSI standard: Any of many guidelines and standards created and promulgated by the American National Standards Institute.

> **TIP**
>
> Because template files are listed alphabetically in the **Files** list, it can be convenient to start your template file name with a number so that it appears before the *acad* and ***ANSI standard*** templates that come with the AutoCAD program. Numbers precede letters in the alphanumeric sequence, so your numbered template file appears at the top of the list and saves you the trouble of scrolling down to find it.

*Once you have typed a name for your drawing template in the **File name** edit box and the **Files of type** list shows that **AutoCAD Drawing Template (.dwt)** is selected, you are ready to save.*

✔ Click **Save**.

*This displays the **Template Options** dialog box, as shown in Figure 4-6. You can ignore it for now.*

✔ Click **OK** in the **Template Options** dialog box.

The task of creating the drawing template is now complete. All that remains is to create a new drawing using the template to see how it works.

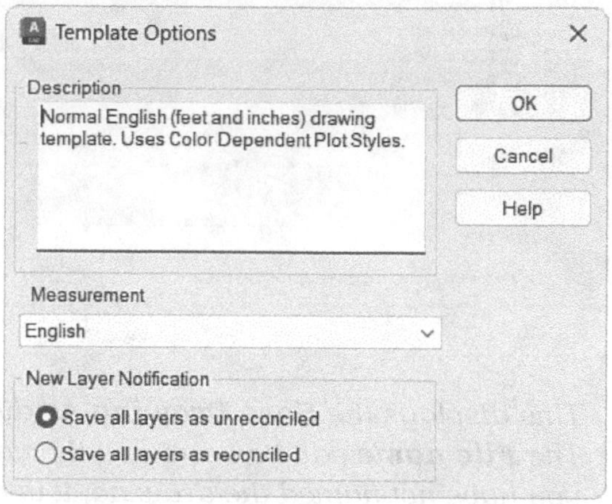

Figure 4-6
Template Options dialog box

NOTE

If **1B** is not at the top of your list after the **PTW Templates** and **Sheet Sets** folders, it might be because your list is sorting in descending order. To reverse the order, click the **Name column**.

✔ Click the **Close** button **(X)** in the upper-right corner of the drawing window.

Be sure to close the current drawing only and not the AutoCAD application window.

✔ Click the **New** tool from the **Quick Access** toolbar.

*This opens the **Select template** dialog box as usual. However, now **1B** is at the top of your list.*

✔ Highlight **1B** or the file name you have used from the list of templates.

✔ Press **<Enter>** or click **Open**.

A new drawing opens with all the settings from 1B already in place. From now on, you can use the 1B template any time you want a drawing with B-size limits along with the layers you have created and the other settings you have specified.

✔ Turn the grid on or off; it's your preference. The figures in this chapter show the grid off for clarity.

MOVE	
Command	MOVE
Alias	M
Panel	Modify
Tool	

Using the MOVE Command

The ability to move and copy objects is one of the great advantages of working on a CAD system. It can be said that CAD is to drafting as word processing is to typing. Nowhere is this analogy more appropriate than in the cut-and-paste capacities that the **MOVE** and **COPY** commands give you.

> **TIP**
>
> The following is a general procedure for using the **MOVE** command:
>
> 1. Click the **Move** tool from the **Modify** panel on the **Home** tab of the ribbon.
> 2. Define a selection set. (If noun/verb selection is enabled, you can reverse Steps 1 and 2.)
> 3. Specify a base point for displacement.
> 4. Specify a second point.

✔ Draw a circle with a radius of **1** near the center of the drawing area **(9,6)**, as shown in Figure 4-7.

✔ Click the **Move** tool from the **Modify** panel on the **Home** tab of the ribbon, as shown in Figure 4-8.

You are prompted to select objects to move.

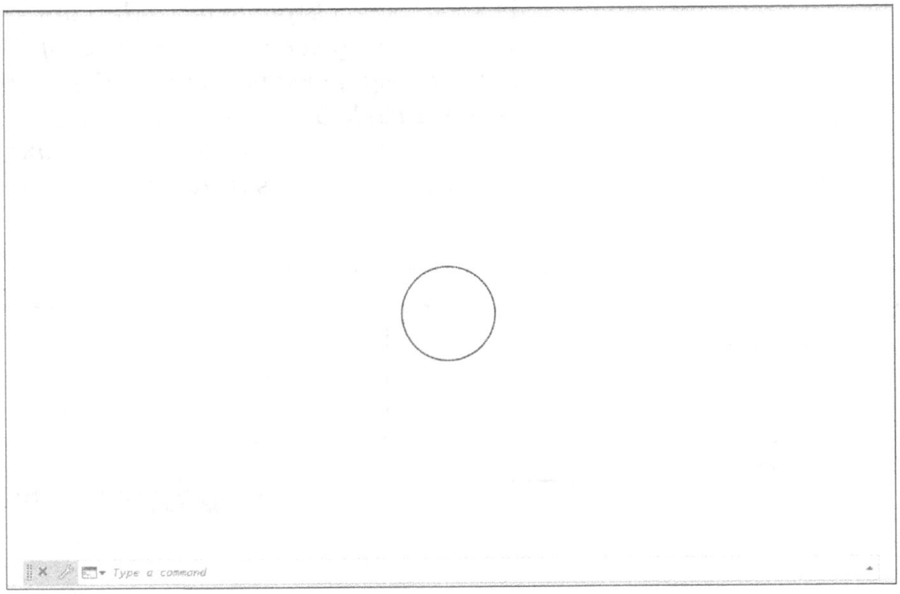

Figure 4-7
Drawing a circle

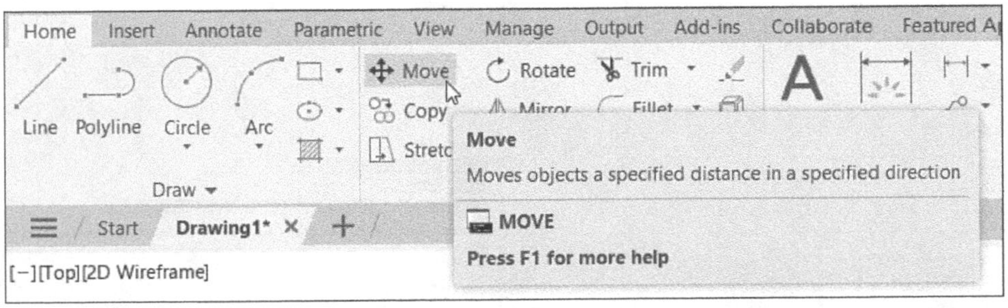

Figure 4-8
Move tool

- ✔ Select the circle.

  Your circle is highlighted in blue.

  In the command line, AutoCAD informs you how many objects have been selected and prompts you to select more.

- ✔ Right-click to end object selection.

  AutoCAD prompts:

  ```
  Specify base point or [Displacement] <displacement>:
  ```

  Most often, you define the movement by specifying two points that give the distance and direction in which you want the objects to be moved. The base point does not have to be on or near the objects you are moving. Any point will do, as long as you can use it to define how you want your objects moved. This might seem strange at first, but it will soon become natural. Of course, you can specify a point on an object if you want. With a circle, the center point might be convenient.

- ✔ If **Snap Mode** is off, turn it on.

- ✔ Specify a point that's not too close to the left edge of the drawing area.

  AutoCAD presents you with a rubber band from the point you specified and prompts for a second point:

  ```
  Specify second point or <use first point as displacement>:
  ```

  As soon as you begin to move the cursor, AutoCAD also draws a circle to drag so you can see the effect of the movement. An example of how this might look is shown in Figure 4-9. Let's say you want to move the circle 3.00 units to the right.

  *Watch the dynamic input tooltip and stretch the rubber band out until the tooltip reads **3.00<0°**.*

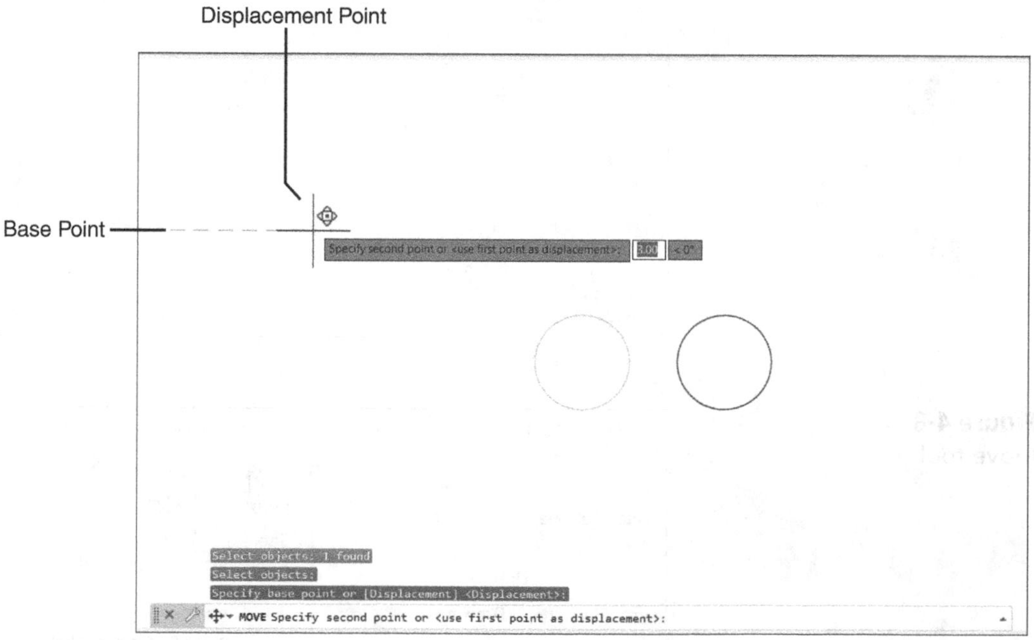

Figure 4-9
Moving the circle horizontally

✔ Specify a point 3.00 units to the right of your base point.

The rubber band and your original circle disappear, leaving you with a circle in the new location.

Now, try a diagonal move.

✔ If **Ortho Mode** is on, turn it off.

✔ Click the **Move** tool from the **Modify** panel on the **Home** tab of the ribbon, or press the spacebar to repeat the command.

AutoCAD follows with the Select objects: prompt.

✔ Select the circle.

✔ Press **<Enter>** or the spacebar to end object selection.

AutoCAD prompts for a base point.

✔ Specify a base point.

✔ Move the circle diagonally in any direction.

Figure 4-10 is an example of how this might look.

✔ Try moving the circle back near the center of the drawing area.

It may help to choose the center point of the circle as a base point this time and use the coordinate display to choose a point at or near ***(9,6)*** *for your second point.*

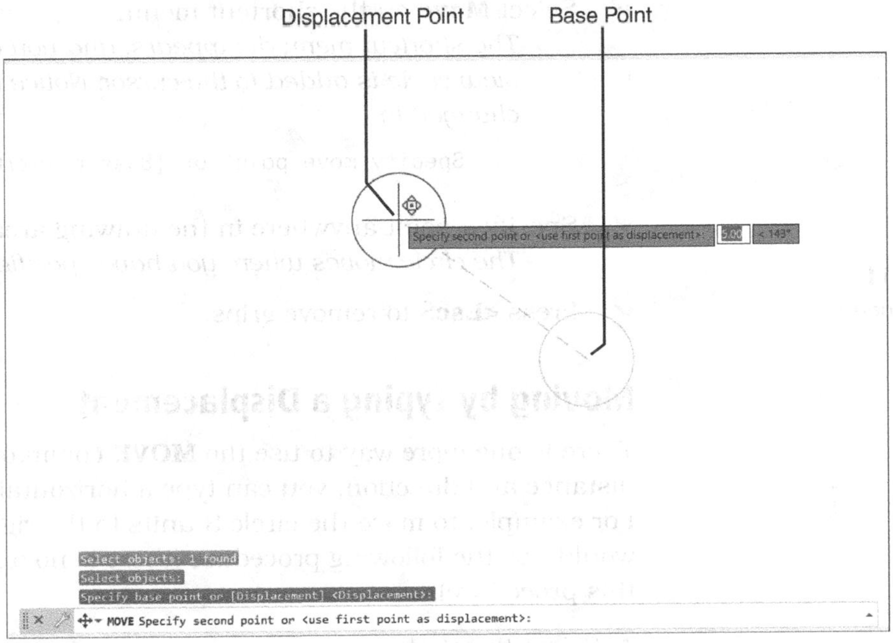

Figure 4-10
Moving the circle diagonally

Moving with Grips

You can use grips to perform numerous editing procedures. This is probably the simplest of all editing methods. It does have some limitations, however. In particular, you can select only by pointing, windowing, or crossing.

✔ Select the circle.

The circle is highlighted, and grips appear.

Notice that grips for a circle are placed at quadrants and at the center. In more involved editing procedures, the choice of which grip or grips to use for editing is significant. In this exercise, you will do fine with any of the grips.

✔ Move the cursor slowly over one of the grips.
If you do this carefully, you notice that the cursor locks onto the grip as it moves over it. When the cursor locks on the grip, the grip turns orange. If you are on one of the quadrant grips, the number ***1.00*** *appears, indicating the radius of the circle.*

✔ When the cursor is locked onto a grip, click.
The color of the selected grip changes again (from orange to red). In the command line, you see

```
Specify stretch point or [Base point/Copy/Undo/eXit]:
```

Stretching is the first of a series of five editing modes that you can activate by selecting grips on objects. The word stretch *has many meanings in AutoCAD, and they are not always what you would expect. The stretch editing mode and the* ***STRETCH*** *commands are not covered here. For now, ignore stretch and use the* ***Move*** *mode.*
AutoCAD has a convenient shortcut menu for use in grip editing.

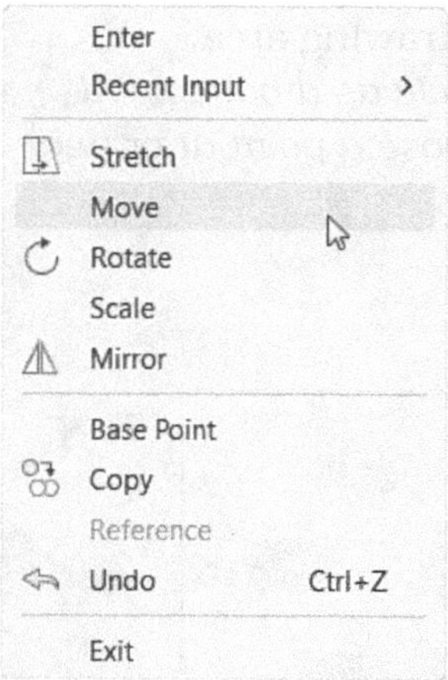

Figure 4-11
Shortcut menu

✔ Right-click in the drawing area.
This opens the shortcut menu shown in Figure 4-11. It contains all the ***Grip Edit*** *modes plus several other options.*

✔ Select **Move** on the shortcut menu.
The shortcut menu disappears, and you are in ***Move*** *mode. A preview circle is added to the cursor. Notice that the prompt has changed to*

```
Specify move point or [Base point/Copy/Undo/eXit]:
```

✔ Specify a point anywhere in the drawing area.
The circle moves where you have specified.

✔ Press **<Esc>** to remove grips.

Moving by Typing a Displacement

There is one more way to use the **MOVE** command. Instead of defining a distance and direction, you can type a horizontal and vertical displacement. For example, to move the circle 3 units to the right and 2 units up, you would use the following procedure (there is no autoediting equivalent for this procedure):

6. Select the circle.
7. Type **m <Enter>** or click the **Move** tool.
8. Type **3,2 <Enter>** in response to the prompt for a base point or displacement.
9. Press **<Enter>** in response to the prompt for a second point.

COPY	
Command	COPY
Alias	Co
Panel	Modify
Tool	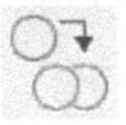

Using the COPY Command

The **COPY** command works much like the **MOVE** command. First, you make several copies of the circle in various positions in the drawing area.

> **TIP**
>
> The following is a general procedure for using the **COPY** command:
>
> 1. Click the **Copy** tool from the **Modify** panel on the **Home** tab of the ribbon.
> 2. Define a selection set. (Steps 1 and 2 can be reversed if noun/verb selection is enabled.)
> 3. Specify a base point.
> 4. Specify a second point.
> 5. Specify another second point or press **<Enter>** to exit the command.

✔ Click the **Copy** tool from the **Modify** panel on the **Home** tab of the ribbon, as shown in Figure 4-12.

*Note that **c** is not an alias for **COPY** (it is the alias for **CIRCLE**).*

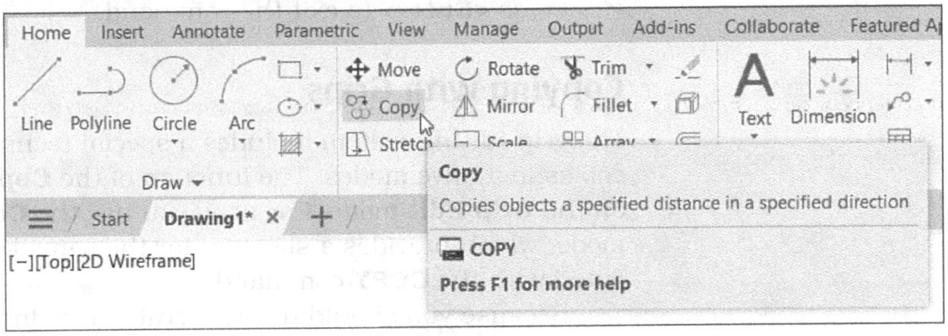

Figure 4-12
Copy tool

✔ Select the circle.

✔ Right-click to end object selection.

AutoCAD prompts for a base point or displacement.

✔ Specify a base point.

*As with the **MOVE** command, AutoCAD prompts for a second point.*

✔ Specify a second point.

*You will see a new copy of the circle. The prompt to specify a second point of displacement has returned in the command line, and another new circle is shown at the end of the rubber band, along with a Copy badge that resembles the **COPY** tool. AutoCAD is waiting for another vector, using the same base point as before.*

✔ Specify another second point.

Repeat this process as many times as you want. If you get into this, you may begin to feel like a magician pulling rings out of thin air and scattering them across the drawing area. When you finish, you should have several copies of the circle in your drawing, as shown in Figure 4-13.

Figure 4-13
Copying the circle

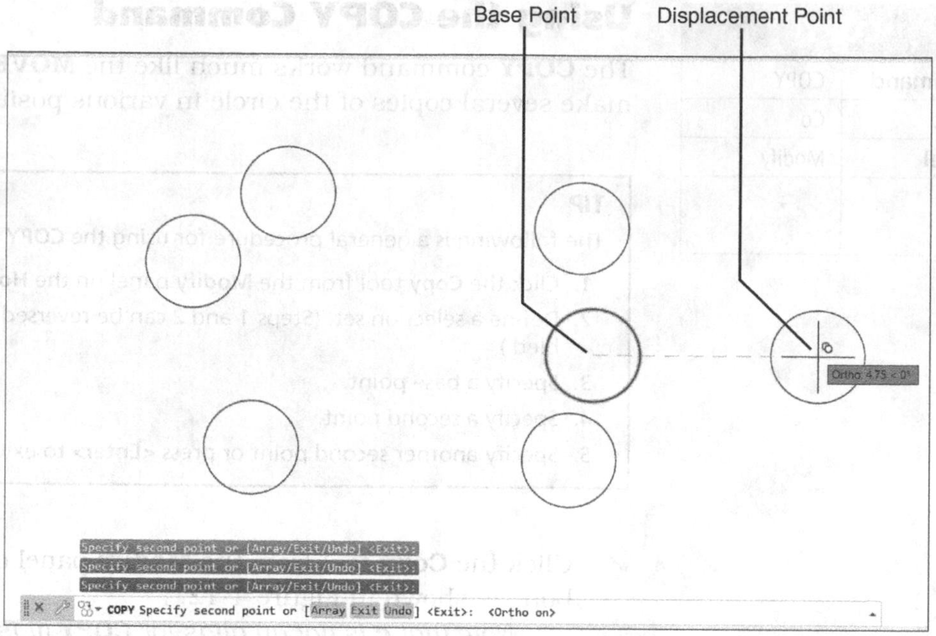

✔ Press **<Enter>** to exit the command.

Copying with Grips

The grip editing system includes a special technique for creating multiple copies in all five modes. The function of the **Copy** option differs depending on the **Grip Edit** mode. For now, you use the **Copy** option with the **Move** mode, which provides a shortcut for the same kind of process you just executed with the **COPY** command.

Because you should have several circles in your drawing now, take the opportunity to learn how to copy or move more than one object at a time using grip editing.

✔ Select any two circles.

The circles you select should be highlighted, and grips should appear on both, as shown in Figure 4-14.

Figure 4-14
Circles highlighted with grips

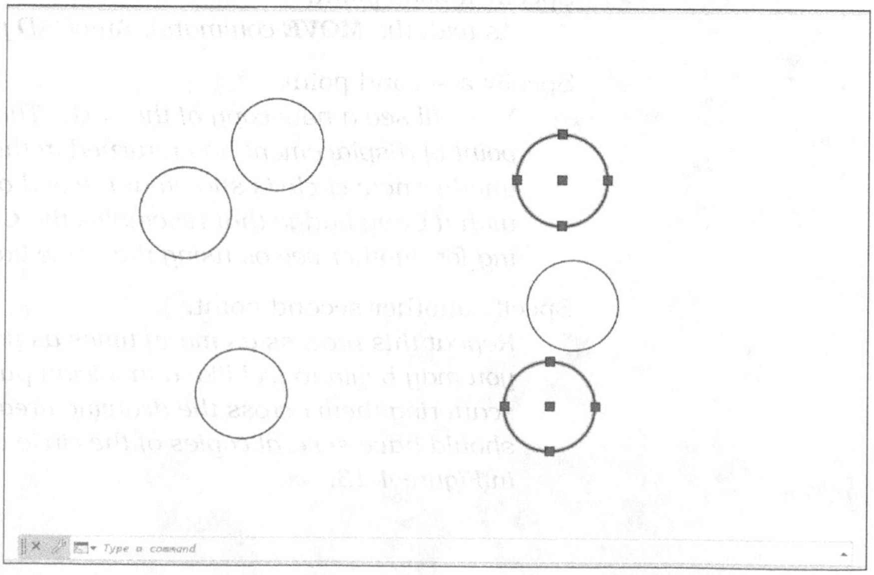

- ✔ Click any grip on either of the two highlighted circles.

  The grip should change color.

- ✔ Right-click and select **Move** from the shortcut menu.

  *This brings you to the **Move** mode prompt:*

  `Specify move point or [Base point/Copy/Undo/eXit]:`

- ✔ Right-click and select **Copy** to initiate copying.

  AutoCAD prompts for a move point again.

  *You will find that all copying in the grip editing system is multiple copying. Once in this mode, you can continue to create copies wherever you specify a point and until you exit by typing **x** or pressing the spacebar.*

- ✔ Move the cursor and observe the two dragged circles.
- ✔ Specify a point to create a copy of the two highlighted circles, as shown in Figure 4-15.
- ✔ Specify another point to create two more copies.
- ✔ Press **<Enter>** or the spacebar to exit the grip editing system.
- ✔ Press **<Esc>** to remove grips.

Figure 4-15
Copying highlighted circles

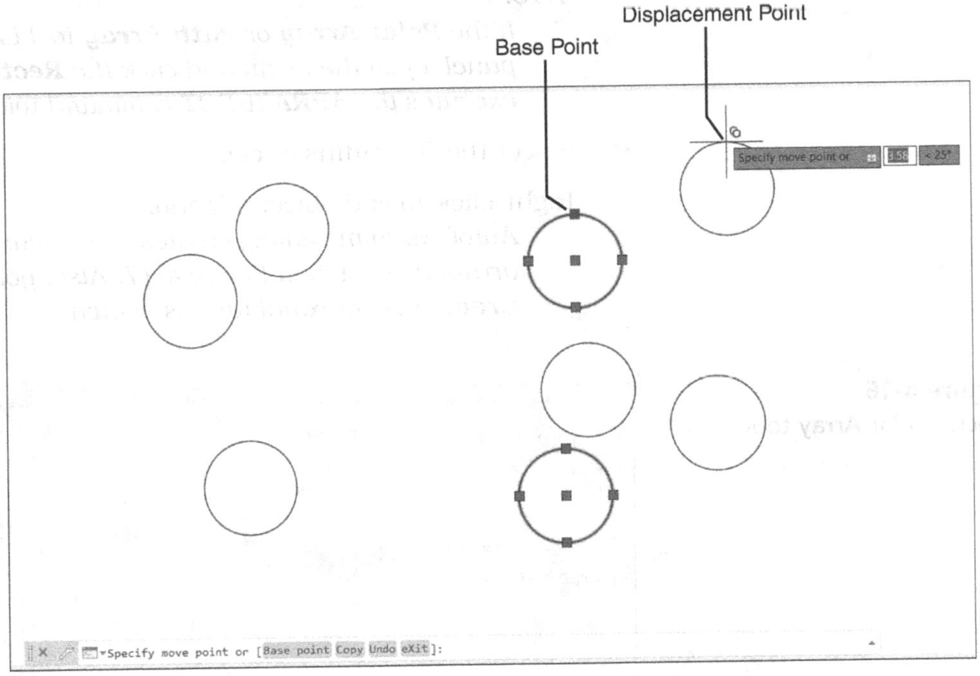

Using the ARRAYRECT Command—Rectangular Arrays

array: A rectangular or circular pattern of objects, or objects along a path.

The **ARRAYRECT** command gives you a powerful alternative to simple copying. An ***array*** is the repetition of an object in matrix form. This command takes an object or group of objects and copies it a specific number of times in mathematically defined, evenly spaced locations. Once defined, an array becomes an abstract template that can be modified in numerous ways.

There are three types of arrays. *Rectangular* arrays are linear and defined by rows and columns. *Polar* arrays are angular and based on the repetition of objects around the circumference of an arc or circle. *Path* arrays are created by copying objects at evenly spaced intervals along any curve, line, or closed figure. The lines on the grid are an example of a rectangular array; the radial lines on any circular dial are an example of a polar array; path arrays can take many shapes and forms. You explore rectangular arrays in this chapter.

Rectangular arrays are defined by a certain number of rows, a certain number of columns, and the spacing between each. In preparation for this exercise, erase all the circles from your drawing. This is a good opportunity to try the **All** selection option of the **ERASE** command.

✔ Click the **Erase** tool from the **Modify** panel on the **Home** tab of the ribbon.

✔ Type **all <Enter>**.

All circles will be grayed out.

✔ Press **<Enter>** again to complete the command.

✔ Now, draw a single circle, radius **0.5**, centered at the point **(2,2)**.

✔ Click the **Rectangular Array** tool from the **Array** drop-down menu of the **Modify** panel on the **Home** tab of the ribbon, as shown in Figure 4-16.

*If the **Polar Array** or **Path Array** tool is shown on the **Modify** panel, open the menu and click the **Rectangular Array** tool. This executes the **ARRAYRECT** command with a **Select objects** prompt.*

✔ Select the 0.5 radius circle.

✔ Right-click to end object selection.

*AutoCAD immediately creates a preview of an evenly spaced 4 × 3 array, as shown in Figure 4-17. Also, you will see the **Array Creation** contextual tab, as shown.*

Figure 4-16
Rectangular Array tool

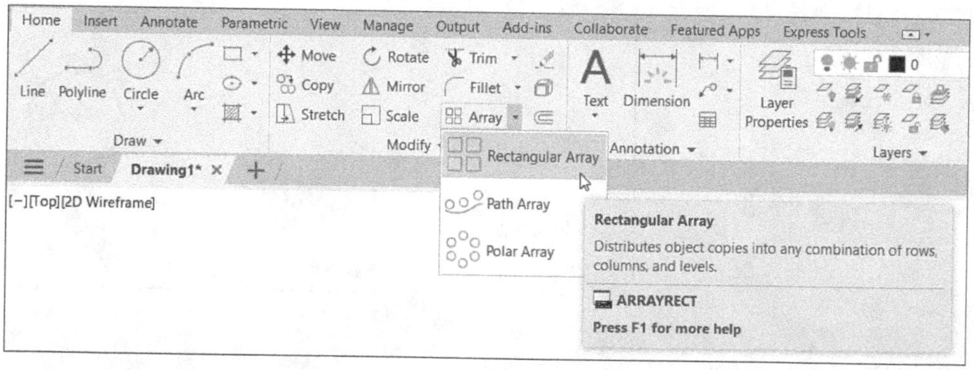

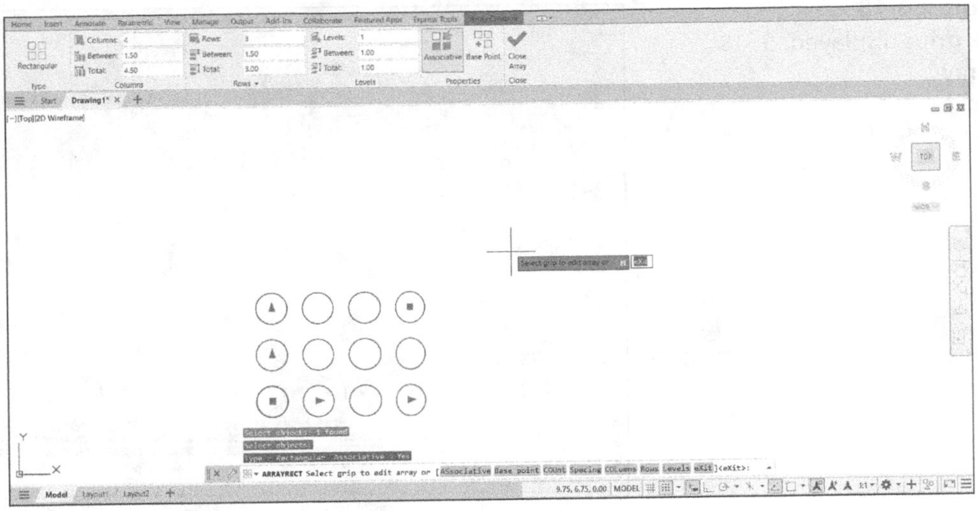

Figure 4-17
4 × 3 preview array and contextual tab

The Array Creation Contextual Tab

contextual tab: A ribbon tab that opens automatically when a certain condition is met. For example, the **Array Creation** tab opens when a previously drawn array is selected.

In certain circumstances, AutoCAD automatically opens a ribbon tab that is not otherwise available. This is called a ***contextual tab***. Here is the first example of a contextual tab; it is displayed after starting the **ARRAYRECT** command. Looking across this tab from left to right, you see the **Type** designation **(Rectangular)** followed by the four panels **Columns**, **Rows**, **Levels**, and **Properties**. In the first three of these are edit boxes for three specifications. If you let your cursor rest in any of these boxes, you will see a tooltip box that identifies the specification. The top is the count, so in your 4 × 3 array are 4 columns, 3 rows, and 1 level. Levels are the third dimension of arrays and will always have a count of 1 when you are in 2D. The second edit box in the **Columns** panel is the spacing between columns. You can see that the column spacing in your preview array is **1.50**. In the **Rows** panel, this will be the spacing between rows, which also is **1.50**. The level spacing is **1.00**, but this has no meaning in your two-dimensional array. The third value is the total distance taken up by the array. It is **4.50** horizontally across the columns and **3.00** vertically along the rows.

To change these values and create an array with your own specifications, you can simply change values in the edit boxes. The following exercise creates a 5 × 3 array with 1.0 unit spacing between rows and columns, as shown in Figure 4-18. This is done by adjusting the values in the contextual tab as shown.

> **NOTE**
>
> If for any reason you have left the **ARRAYRECT** command, you can open the contextual tab again by selecting any item in the array. Selecting an array displays the **Array** contextual tab rather than the **Array Creation** contextual tab. The options are the same on the two tabs; just be aware the name might be different from the exercise steps.

✔ On the **Array Creation** contextual tab, click in the **Columns** edit box and type **5 <Enter>**.

When you press ***<Enter>****, a column will be added, making a total of 5 columns.*

Figure 4-18
Six grips displayed, 5 × 3 array

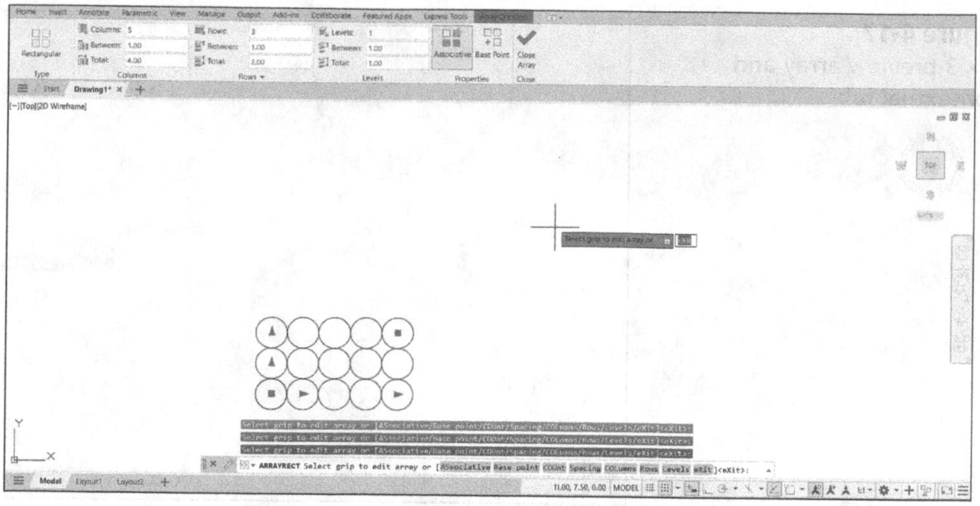

> **NOTE**
> The function symbol that appears at the right of the edit box indicates that you can create arrays based on mathematical relationships and expressions as well as on absolute values.

✔ Click in the **Between** edit box of the **Columns** panel and type **1 <Enter>**.
The spacing between columns will be reduced to ***1.00****.*

✔ Click in the **Between** edit box of the **Rows** panel and type **1 <Enter>**.
The spacing between rows will be reduced to ***1.00****. At this point, your array should resemble Figure 4-18.*

✔ Press **<Enter>** to exit the **ARRAYRECT** command or press **<Esc>** to clear grips if you selected the array for edit.

Using Multifunctional Grips

A more dynamic method for changing array specifications involves the use of multifunctional grips. With the array selected, you also have six grips displayed, as shown in Figure 4-19. You can use these grips to alter the values that define the array. Each grip has a specific purpose and can only be used to edit certain values.

✔ Select the array.

✔ Let the cursor hover over the triangular grip at the lower-right corner of the array, as shown in Figure 4-19.
With the cursor resting on the grip, you see a tooltip with three options. Selecting among these allows you to use this grip to edit the array in three different ways. This is called a ***multifunctional grip****. With the tooltip showing, you can move the cursor over to select among the three options. The top option,* ***Column Count*** *in this case, is the default option.* ***Column Count*** *allows you to add columns to the array without changing the spacing or the number of rows. The second option,* ***Total Column Spacing****, allows you to change the spacing between columns without changing the number of columns. The third option,* ***Axis Angle****, allows you to tilt the columns on an angle.*

multifunctional grip: A grip that can be used to edit objects in multiple ways. When a multifunctional grip is highlighted, AutoCAD displays a list of possible editing modes from which to choose.

Figure 4-19
Multifunctional grips, contextual tab

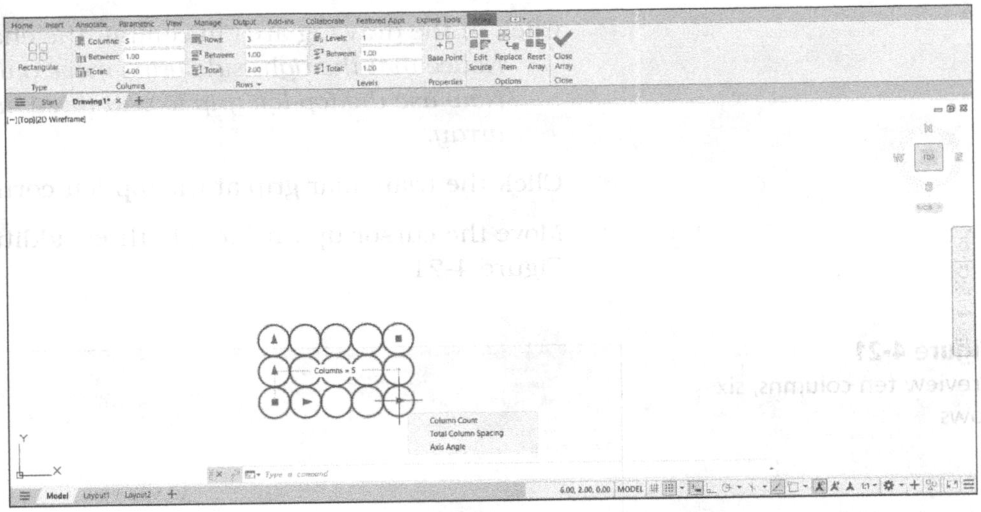

If you let the cursor hover over other grips, you will find that each has its own set of functions. The exceptions are the two grips immediately above and to the right of the lower-left corner. These can only be used to change the row and column spacing. Therefore, these two are not multifunctional and will not call up a box of options.

Here you use the lower-right corner grip to add five additional columns.

✔ Click the triangular grip at the lower-right corner.

A tooltip is shown that indicates the number of columns in the array. Now, as you move the cursor to the right, you see a preview of the columns being added in that direction.

✔ Move the cursor to the right until you have added five additional columns for a total of ten.

Notice the stretched preview grid and the message that displays, ***Columns = 10****, as shown in Figure 4-20.*

Figure 4-20
Preview columns added, multifunction grip list

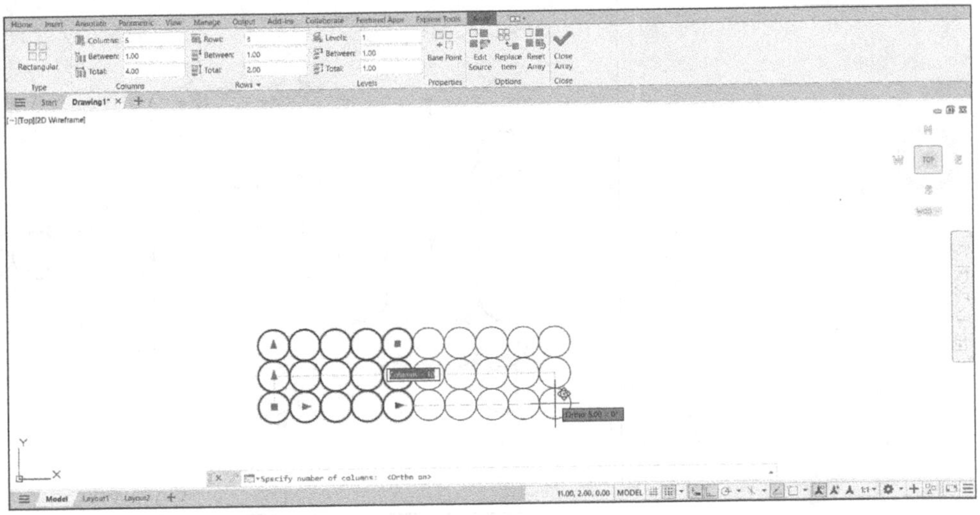

- ✔ Click in the drawing area to commit the change.

  Notice that the right side grips move out to the right side of the array. Now use the top-left grip to add three more rows to the top of the array.

- ✔ Click the triangular grip at the top-left corner of the array.
- ✔ Move the cursor upward to add three additional rows, as shown in Figure 4-21.

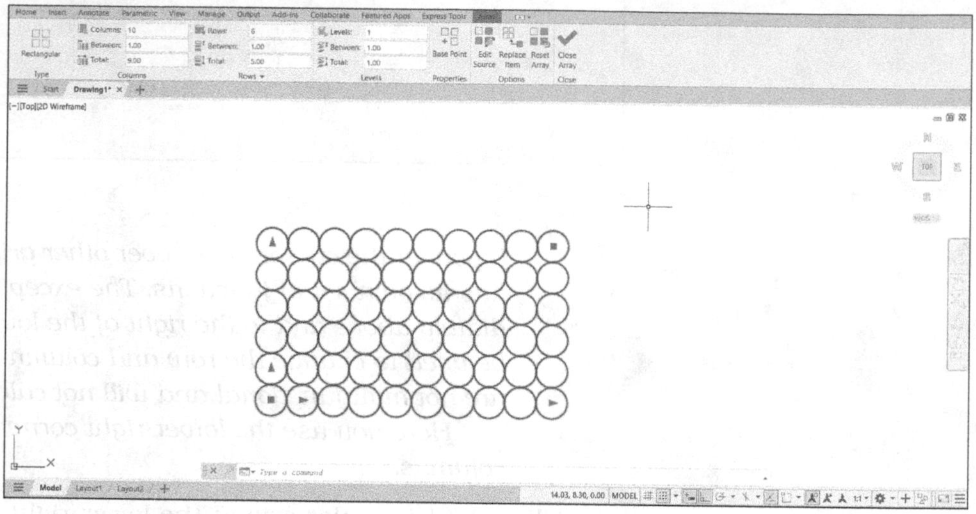

Figure 4-21
Preview ten columns, six rows

- ✔ Now, examine the changes in the contextual ribbon tab.

  You should see 10 for the number of columns and 6 for the number of rows. You end this section by manipulating array values again to create the 15-column, 9-row array shown in Figure 4-22.

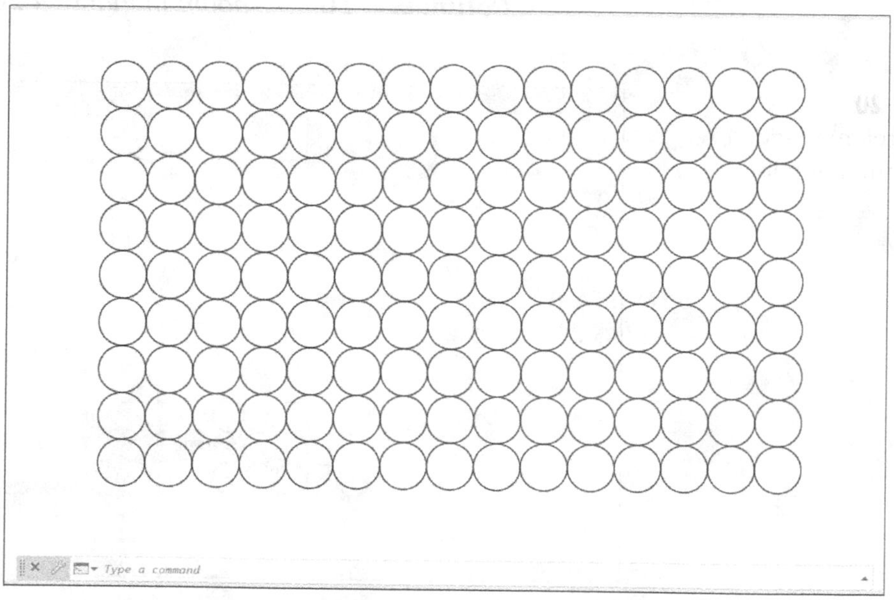

Figure 4-22
Fifteen columns, nine rows

- ✔ Click the triangular grip at the lower-right corner of the array.
- ✔ Move the cursor to the right to add five more columns, for a total of 15.
- ✔ Click the triangular grip at the top-left corner of the array.
- ✔ Move the cursor up to add three more rows, for a total of nine.
- ✔ Press **<Esc>** to remove the grips.
  Your drawing should resemble Figure 4-22.

Array Associativity

By default, arrays are created associatively. This means that all items in the array are defined as members of the array. There are several ways to edit arrays as a whole. Individual items in an array also can be edited separately.

- ✔ Move the cursor over the array.
  Notice that all items in the array are highlighted when the cursor rests on any item. This shows that the array is being treated as a unit.
- ✔ Now hold down the **<Ctrl>** key and move the cursor over the array again.
  *With the **<Ctrl>** key down, you can select individual items in the array, which enables you to edit them independently of the entire array. **However, items edited in this way remain associated with the array**. For example, if you move a single circle and then select the whole array, the moved circle is still selected along with the array. If you want to try this out, a sample procedure would be as follows:*

1. Hold the ***<Ctrl>*** key while selecting a circle from the array.
2. Click the red grip at the center of the circle.
3. Specify a point to move the circle.
4. Press ***<Esc>*** to remove the grips.
5. With the selected item in its altered position, run the cursor over the array. Notice that the entire array is previewed for selection, including the item that was moved.

Creating Center Marks

In this section, you get a quick introduction to a simple dimensioning feature that is used at the end of the chapter. You also conclude the exercise by reviewing the rectangular array procedures previously introduced. All of these techniques will be useful in completing Drawing 4-4, Test Bracket Drawing, at the end of the chapter.

- ✔ To begin this exercise, you should have the array of circles from the last section in your drawing, as shown previously in Figure 4-22.
  *Using the **CENTERMARK** command, you add a simple center mark with centerlines to one circle, as shown in Figure 4-23.*

Figure 4-23
Center mark

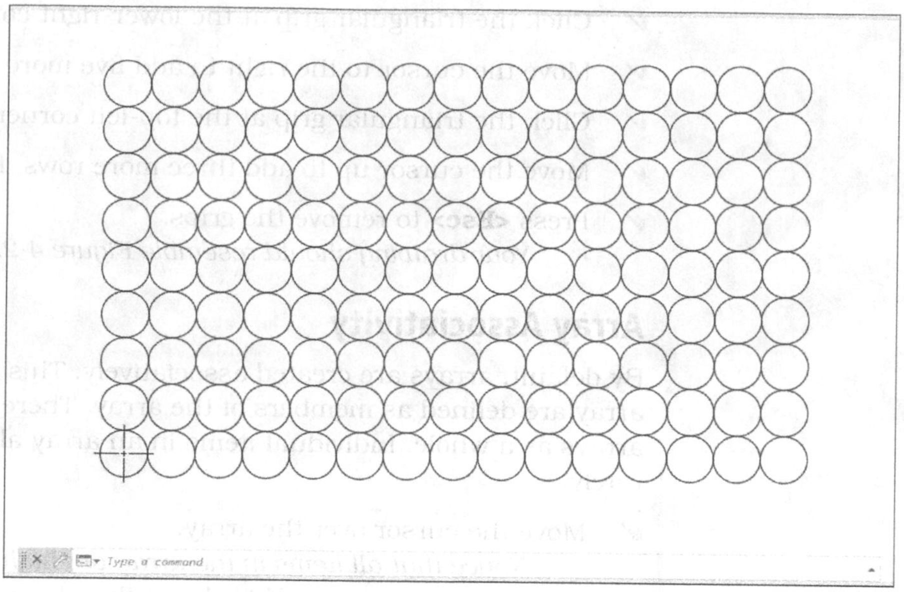

✔ Type **ce <Enter>**.
As you type, the autocomplete feature will call a list of commands beginning with **ce**. *Select* **CENTERMARK** *from the list. AutoCAD prompts:*

`Select circle or arc to add centermark:`

✔ Select the circle at the lower-left corner of the array, as shown in Figure 4-23.
AutoCAD adds a center mark and centerlines as shown in the figure. This is a very simple process. To finish, you array the center marks across the same matrix as the circles in the drawing area. This will put a center mark on each circle. All it requires is that you create a rectangular array using the same specifications as those used to create the array of circles.

✔ Press **<Enter>** to complete the command.

✔ Click the **Rectangular Array** tool from the **Array** drop-down menu on the **Modify** panel of the **Home** tab from the ribbon.
ARRAY *prompts to select objects.*

✔ Type **L <Enter>** to select the last object drawn—the centermark.

✔ Right-click or press **<Enter>** to end object selection.

✔ In the **Columns** panel of the **Array Creation** contextual tab, set the number of columns at **15** and the distance between columns at **1**.

✔ In the **Rows** panel of the **Array Creation** contextual tab, set the number of rows at **9** and the distance between rows at **1**. Press **<Enter>** to complete the command.

✔ Press **<Esc>** to remove the grips.
Your drawing should resemble Figure 4-24. This exact procedure is used to complete Drawing 4-4 at the end of the chapter.

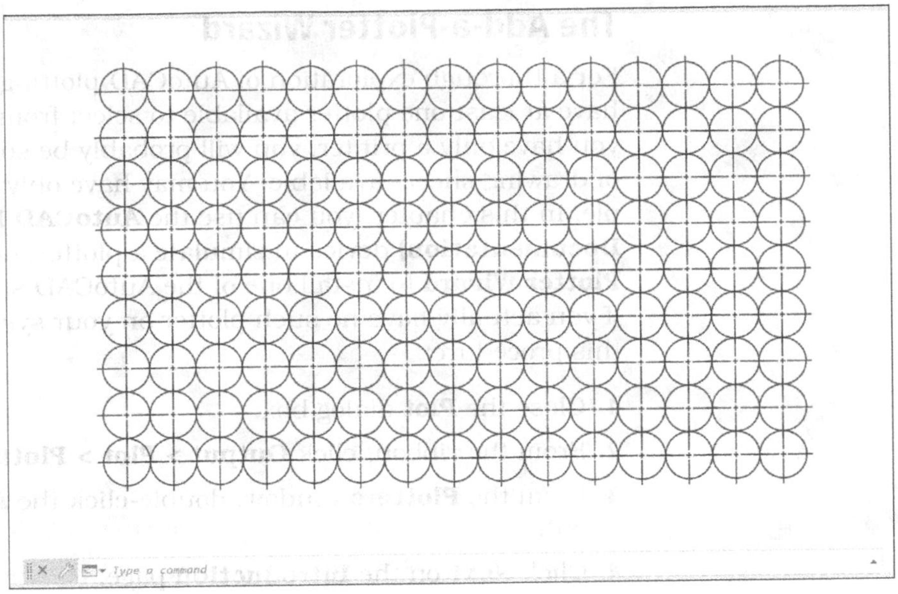

Figure 4-24
Center marks

Changing Plot Settings

In this chapter, you explore various options in the **Plot** dialog box. Using plot previews, you can observe the effects of changing plot settings with any drawing you like and decide at any point whether you actually want to print the results. It is recommended to look at a plot preview after each time you make changes. Plot previewing can save you time and paper and speeds up your learning curve.

✔ To begin this exploration, you should have a drawing or drawn objects in your drawing so that you can observe the effects of various changes you make. The drawing you are in should use the 1B template so that limits are set to 18 × 12. The circles drawn in the last exercise will work fine for this exercise.

✔ Click the **Plot** tool from the **Quick Access** toolbar.

The Printer/Plotter Panel

One of the most basic changes you can make to a plot configuration is your selection of a plotter. Different plotters use different sheet sizes and have different default settings. You begin by looking at the list of available plotting devices and add a plotter to the list.

✔ Click the arrow to the right of the **Name** drop-down list in the **Printer/plotter** panel.

The list you see depends on your system and may include printers, plotters, and any electronic output devices you have configured, along with ***AutoCAD PDF (General Documentation).pc3****, which can be used to send a drawing in an email or post it online.*

The Add-a-Plotter Wizard

For a thorough exploration of AutoCAD plotting, it is important that you have at least one plotter available to select from the **Printer/plotter** list. If you have only a printer, you will probably be somewhat limited in the range of drawing sheets available. You may have only an A-size option, for example. In this chapter, you can use the **AutoCAD PDF (General Documentation)** device to simulate a plotter, or you can use the **Add-a-Plotter Wizard** to install one of the AutoCAD standard plotter drivers, even if you actually have no such plotter on your system. To add a plotter, follow this procedure:

1. Close the **Plot** dialog box.
2. From the ribbon, click **Output > Plot > Plotter Manager**.
3. From the **Plotters** window, double-click the **Add-a-Plotter Wizard** shortcut.
4. Click **Next** on the **Introduction** page.
5. Check to see that **My Computer** is selected on the **Add Plotter – Begin** page, and then click **Next**.
6. On the **Plotter Model** page, select a manufacturer and model and then click **Next**.
7. Click **Next** on the **Ports** page.
8. Click **Next** on the **Plotter Name** page.
9. Click **Finish** on the **Finish** page.

When the wizard is done, the new plotting device will be available from the list of plotting devices in the **Plot** dialog box.

✔ If you closed the **Plot** dialog box to install a plotter driver, redisplay it. In the **Plot** dialog box, click the **Name** drop-down list in the **Printer/plotter** panel.

✔ From the **Name** drop-down list, select a plotter or the **AutoCAD PDF (General Documentation).pc3** to simulate a plotter.

Paper Size

Now that you have a plotter selected, you should have a number of paper size options.

✔ From the drop-down list in the **Paper size panel**, select a B-size drawing sheet.

The exact size depends on the plotter you have selected. An ANSI B 17 × 11 sheet is a common choice.

Drawing Orientation

Drawing orientation choices are found on the expanded **Plot** dialog box, as shown in Figure 4-25.

Figure 4-25
Plot dialog box expanded

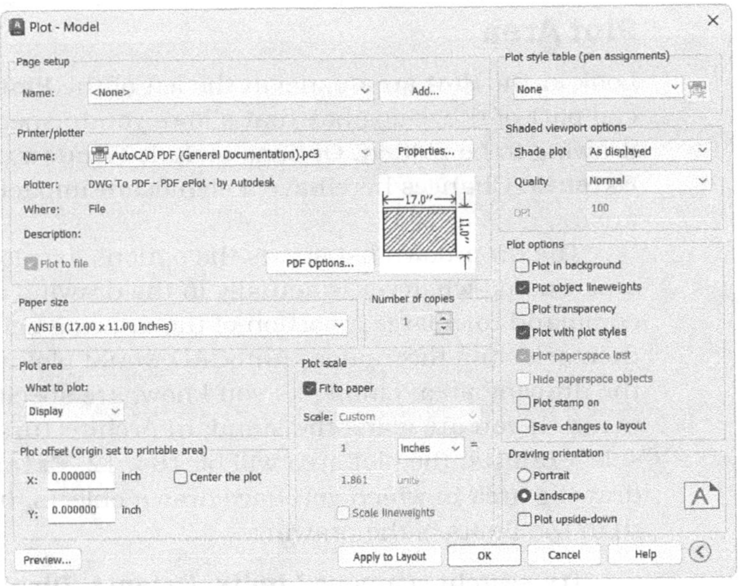

✔ If your dialog box is not already expanded, click the right arrow button (>) at the bottom right of the dialog box.

There are basically two options for drawing orientation: portrait, in which the short edge of the paper is across the bottom, and landscape, in which the long edge is across the bottom. Portrait is typical of a letter or printed sheet of text, and landscape is typical of a drawing sheet. Your plotting device has a default orientation, but you can print either way using the radio buttons. Drawing orientation obviously has a major impact on how the plotting area of the page is used, so be sure to check out the partial preview any time you switch orientations. Try the following:

✔ Click the **Preview** button to see how your current drawing orientation is interpreted.

✔ Press **<Esc>** or **<Enter>** to return to the **Plot** dialog box.

✔ Switch from **Landscape** to the **Portrait orientation setting**, or vice versa.

✔ Click the **Preview** button again to see how drawing orientation changes the plot.

> **TIP**
>
> On some plotters, you have a choice of different paper orientations. For example, you might have an 11 × 17 and a 17 × 11 option. In this case, there should be a correlation between the paper you choose and the drawing orientation. If you are plotting in landscape, select the 17 × 11; in portrait, select the 11 × 17. Otherwise, your paper settings will be 90° off from your drawing orientation, and things will get confusing.

✔ For the following exercise, set the drawing orientation to **Landscape**.

This is the default for most plotters.

Plot Area

Look at the **Plot area** panel at the left of the **Plot** dialog box. This is a crucial part of the dialog box that allows you to specify the portion of your drawing to be plotted. Options include **Window**, **Display**, **Limits**, and **Extents**. Changes here have a significant impact on the effective plotting area.

The drop-down list shows the options for plotting area. **Display** creates a plot using whatever is actually in the drawing area. If you used the **ZOOM** command to enlarge a portion of the drawing before entering **PLOT** and then selecting this option, AutoCAD would plot whatever was showing in the drawing area. Limits, as you know, are specified using the **LIMITS** command. If you are using the standard Architectural B-size template and select **Limits**, the plot area will be 18 × 12. **Extents** refers to the actual drawing area in which you have drawn objects. It can be larger or smaller than the limits of the drawing.

✔ Try switching among **Limits**, **Extents**, **Display**, and **Window** selections, and click the **Preview** button to see the results.

*Whenever you make a change, also observe the changes in the **Plot scale** boxes showing inches = units. Assuming that **Fit to paper** is checked, you will see significant changes in these scale ratios as AutoCAD adjusts scales according to the area specified.*

Plot Offset

The **Plot offset** panel is at the bottom left of the **Plot** dialog box. **Plot offset** determines the way the plot area is positioned on the drawing sheet. Specifically, it determines where the plot origin is placed. The default locates the origin point **(0,0)** at the lower left of the plotted area and determines other locations from there. If you enter a different offset specification—**(2,3)**, for example—the origin point of the drawing area is positioned at this point instead, and plot locations are determined from there. This has a dramatic effect on the placement of objects on paper.

The other option in **Plot offset** is to **Center the plot**. In this case, AutoCAD positions the drawing so that the center point of the plot area coincides with the center point of the drawing sheet.

✔ Try various plot offset combinations, including **Center the plot**, and click the **Preview** button to see the results.

4 chapterfour

Chapter Summary

The ability to create and save drawing templates is a very significant addition to your set of drawing skills. It allows you to skip many steps in drawing setup and to create your own library of predefined drawing setups for different types of drawings. An essential factor in setting up any drawing or template is the specification of limits that define the size and outer frame of your drawing area in whatever units are appropriate for your application. You have also gained the very significant skill of moving and copying objects you have drawn so that objects do not have to be drawn twice. Or, if many identical objects are to be created in a regular configuration of rows and columns, you can draw one object and multiply it across the desired matrix using the **ARRAYRECT** command. Also, you have learned to add center marks and centerlines to circles and to change various plot settings in the **Plot** dialog box. The drawings at the end of this chapter draw on all these new skills.

Chapter Test Questions

Multiple Choice

Circle the correct answer.

1. To facilitate creating new drawings from a previous drawing

   a. Save it in the **Template** folder

   b. Save it in the **Save Drawing As** folder

   c. Save it as a drawing template

   d. Save it with all the settings you want, but no objects drawn

2. In the **MOVE** command, after defining a selection set, you will

   a. Specify a move location

   b. Specify an endpoint

   c. Define a displacement vector

   d. Define a vector location

3. In grip editing, you can't select objects by

   a. Windowing

   b. Typing **L** for **last**

   c. Crossing

   d. Pointing with the pickbox

4. To remove grips

   e. Press **Cancel**

   f. Specify any point not on an object

   g. Double-click in the drawing area

   h. Press **<Esc>**

5. To access the **Grip Edit** shortcut menu:
   a. Right-click after selecting objects
   b. Click the **Grip Edit** tool
   c. Right-click the **Grip Edit** button
   d. Right-click on an object you want to edit

Matching

Write the number of the correct answer on the line.

a. Clock face _____	**1.** Template
b. Grid _____	**2.** Polar array
c. 17 × 11_____	**3.** Vertical
d. dwt _____	**4.** ANSI B
e. Portrait _____	**5.** Rectangular array

True or False

Circle the correct answer.

1. **True or False**: Any drawing may be saved as a drawing template.
2. **True or False**: By default, the **COPY** command creates multiple copies of selected objects.
3. **True or False**: Rows are horizontal; columns are vertical.
4. **True or False**: When **LIMITS** are changed AutoCAD automatically zooms out to center the grid.
5. **True or False**: It is usually unnecessary to perform a full plot preview.

Questions

1. Name at least five settings that would typically be included in a drawing template.
2. Where are drawing templates stored in a standard AutoCAD file configuration? What extension is given to drawing template file names?
3. What is the value of using a drawing template?
4. How do you access the **Grip Edit** shortcut menu?
5. What is a rectangular array? What is a polar array? What is a path array?

Drawing Problems

1. Create a C-size drawing template using an ANSI standard sheet size, layers, and other settings as shown in this chapter. Start with your 1B template settings to make this process easier.
2. Open a drawing with your new C-size template and draw a circle. Set the radius to **2** with the center at **(11, 8)**.
3. Using grips, make four copies of the circle, centered at **(15,8)**, **(11,12)**, **(7,8)**, and **(11,4)**.
4. Switch to layer **2** and draw a **1 × 1** square with its lower-left corner at **(1,1)**.
5. Create a rectangular array of the square with **14** rows and **20** columns, **1** unit between rows, and **1** unit between columns.

chapter four

Chapter Drawing Projects

E Drawing 4-1: *7-Pin Trailer Wiring Diagram* [BASIC]

All the drawings in this chapter use the 1B template. Do not expect, however, never to need to change settings. Layers stay the same, but limits change from time to time, and grid and snap change frequently.
This drawing gives you practice using the **COPY** command. There are numerous ways in which the drawing can be done. All locations are approximate except where dimensioned. Set up a layer for each wire color and draw the wire, box, circle, and text using the color layer that matches.

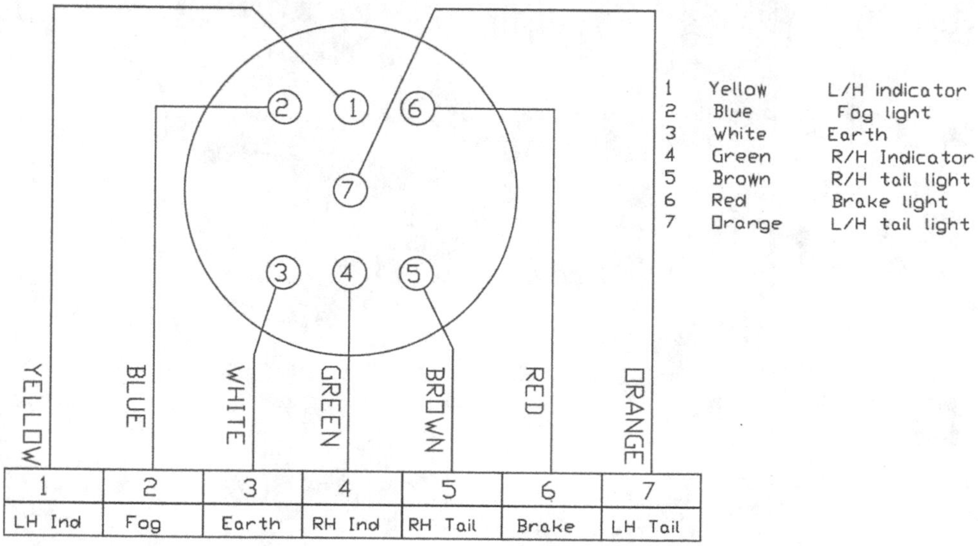

Drawing Suggestions

GRID = 0.5

SNAP = 0.25

TEXT HEIGHT = .25 for the larger text and .18 for the smaller

- Begin with a **0.25 × 1.50** rectangle starting at **(3.00,3.00)**. Array the rectangle to get the **2 × 7** array. Then draw the circles and connect the wires.
- Use the **Nearest** object snap to get the wire lines to touch the circles.
- Add all text in approximate locations.

Drawing 4-1
7-Pin Trailer Wiring diagram

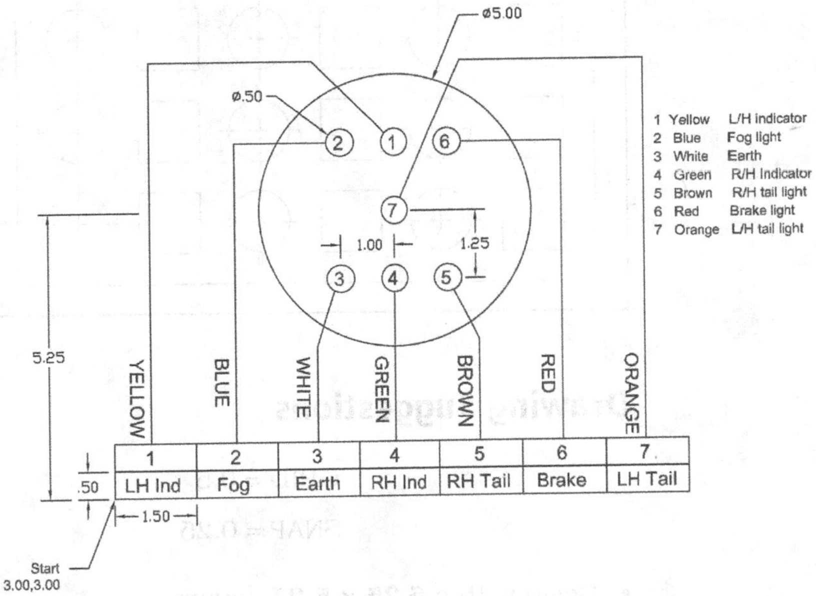

G Drawing 4-2: *Grill* [BASIC]

This drawing should go very quickly if you use the **ARRAYRECT** command and set the **DIMCEN** system variable to **0.09**.

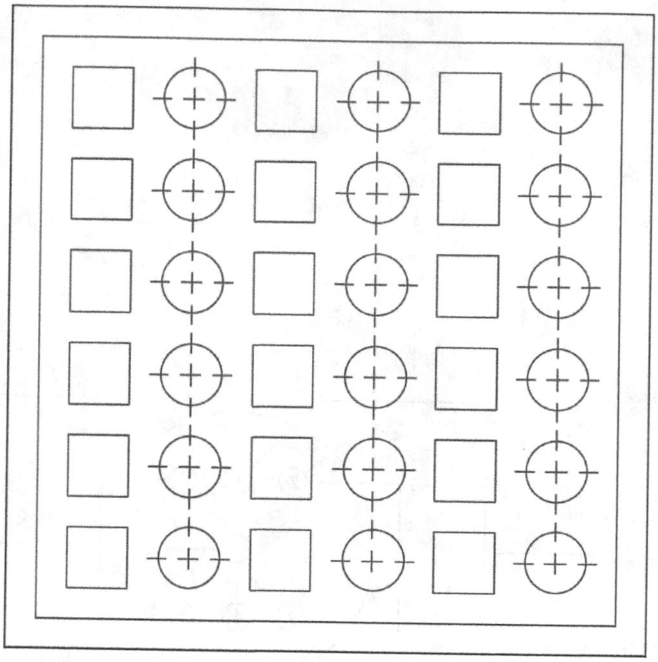

Drawing Suggestions

GRID = 0.5

SNAP = 0.25

- Begin with a **5.25 × 5.25** square.
- Move in **0.25** all around to create the inside square.
- Draw the small square and the circle with centerlines in the lower-left corner first, and then use the **ARRAYRECT** command to create the rest.
- Type **dimcen <Enter>** and change the system variable to **0.09**.
- Then type **dimcenter <Enter>** and **cen <Enter>** to draw the centerlines on the circle. Be sure to do this before arraying the square and the circle.
- Also remember that you can undo a misplaced array using the **U** command.

Drawing 4-2
Grill

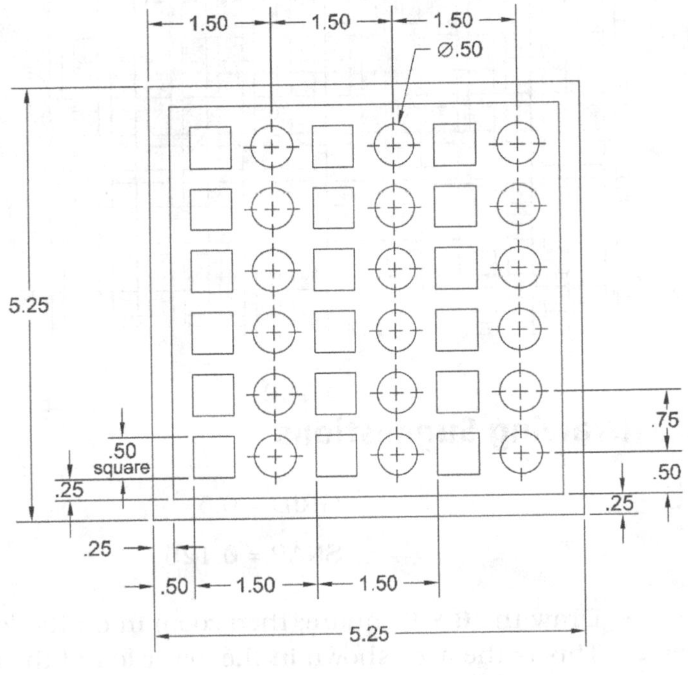

G Drawing 4-3: *Weave* [INTERMEDIATE]

As you do this drawing, watch AutoCAD work for you and think about how long it would take to do this by hand! The finished drawing looks like the representation shown. For clarity, the drawing shows only one cell of the array and its dimensions.

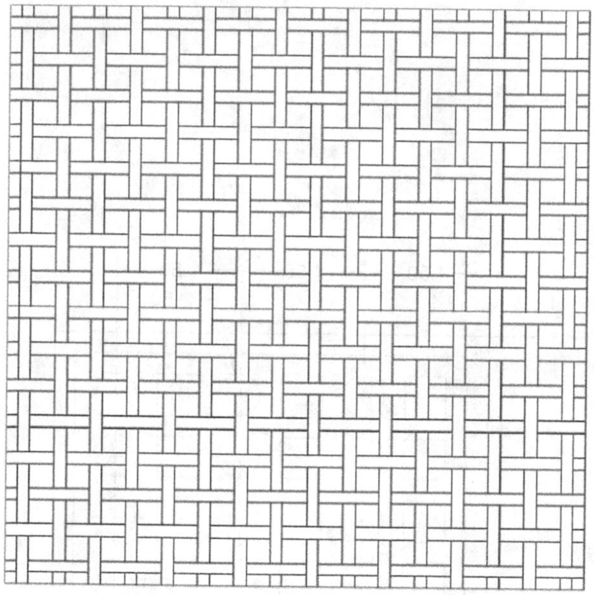

Drawing Suggestions

GRID = 0.5

SNAP = 0.125

- Draw the **6 × 6** square; then zoom in on the lower-left using a window. This is the area shown in the lower left of the dimensioned drawing.
- Observe the dimensions and draw the line patterns for the lower-left corner of the weave. You could use the **COPY** command in several places if you'd like, but the time gained would be minimal. Don't worry if you have to fuss with this a little to get it correct; once you have it right, the rest will be easy.
- Use **ARRAY** to repeat the lower-left cell in an **8 × 8** matrix.
- If you get it wrong, use **U** and try again.

Drawing 4-3
Weave

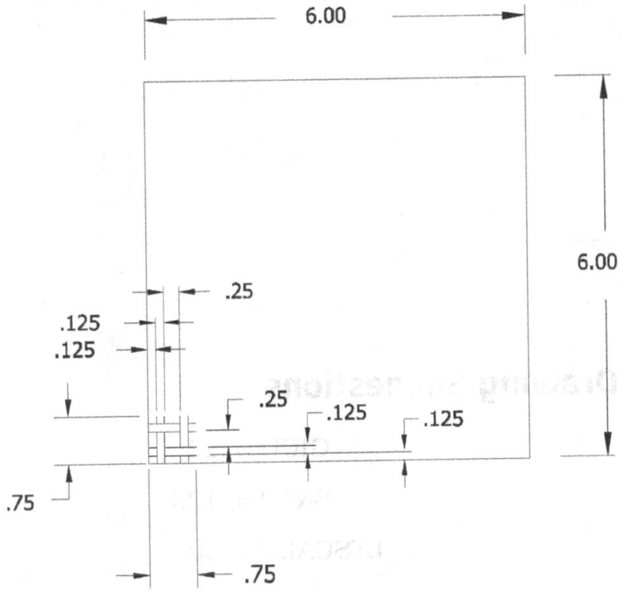

M Drawing 4-4: *Test Bracket* [INTERMEDIATE]

This is a great drawing for practicing much of what you have learned up to this point. Notice the suggested snap, grid, ltscale, and limit settings, and use the **ARRAYRECT** command along with the **0.09** centerline dimension to draw the **25** circles on the front view.

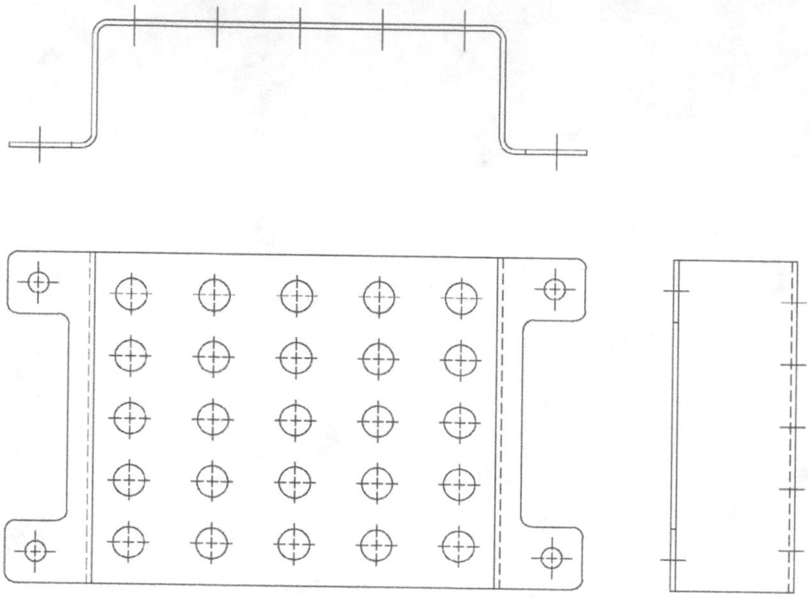

Drawing Suggestions

GRID = .25

SNAP = .125

LTSCALE = .50

LIMITS = (0,0)(24,18)

- Be careful to draw all lines on the correct layers, according to their linetypes.
- Draw centerlines through the circles before copying or arraying them; otherwise, you will have to go back and draw them on each individual circle or repeat the array process.
- A multiple copy works nicely for the four **0.50**-diameter holes. A rectangular array is definitely desirable for the twenty-five **0.75**-diameter holes.
- If you have not already done so, change the **DIMCEN** system variable to **0.09**.
- After drawing your first circle and before arraying it, type **dimcenter <Enter>** and add centerlines to the circle.
- Create the rectangular array of circles with centerlines as shown.

Drawing 4-4
Test Bracket

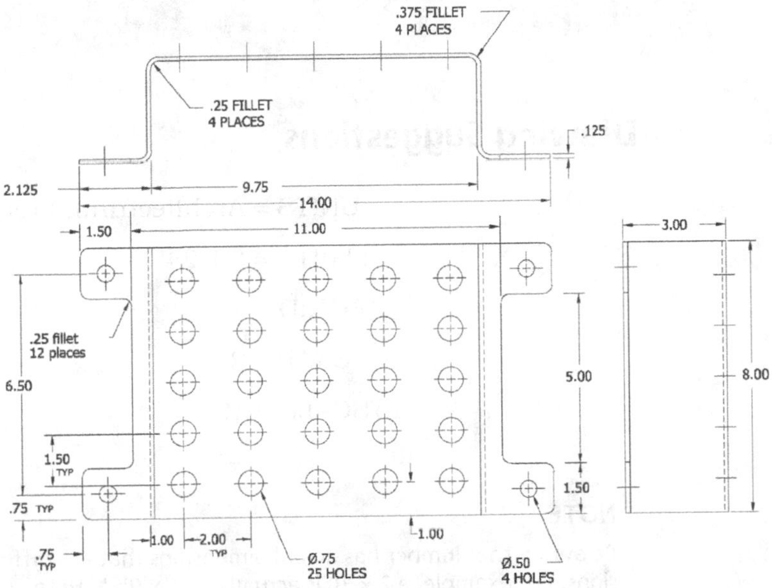

A Drawing 4-5: *Floor Framing* [ADVANCED]

This architectural drawing requires changes in many features of your drawing setup. Pay close attention to the suggested settings.

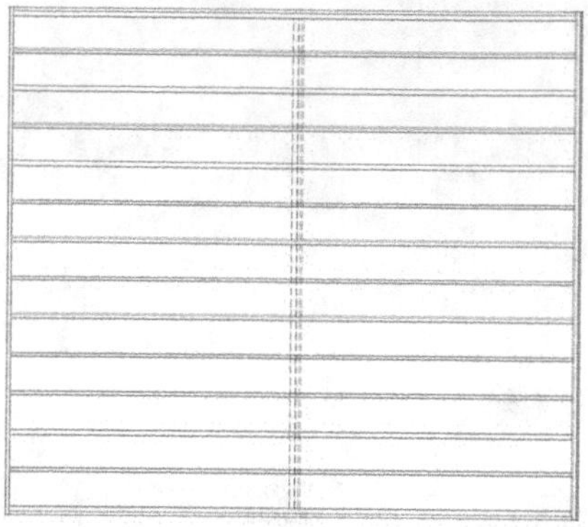

Drawing Suggestions

UNITS = Architectural; Precision = 0'-00"

LIMITS = 36',24'

GRID = 1'

SNAP = 2"

LTSCALE = 12

> **NOTE**
> Be aware that lumber has actual dimensions that are different from the nominal dimensions. For example, a 2 × 10 is actually 1½" × 9¼". Here, you use nominal dimensions in all drawings.

- Be sure to use foot (') and inch (") symbols when setting limits, grid, and snap (but not ltscale).
- Begin by drawing the **20' × 17'-10"** rectangle, with the lower-left corner somewhere in the neighborhood of **(4',4')**.
- Complete the left and right **2 × 10** joists by copying the vertical **17'-10"** lines **2"** in from each side.
- Draw a **19'-8"** horizontal line **2"** up from the bottom and copy it **2"** higher to complete the double joists.
- Array the inner **2 × 10**s in a **14**-row by **1**-column array, with **16"** between rows.
- Set to Layer **2**, and draw the three hidden lines down the center.

Drawing 4-5
Floor Framing

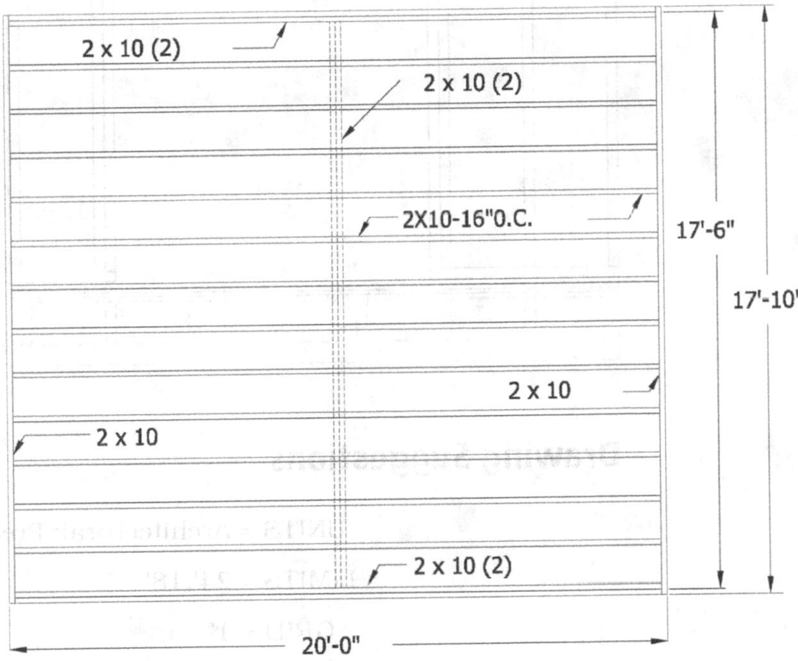

A Drawing 4-6: *Wall Framing* [ADVANCED]

This architectural drawing incorporates rectangular **ARRAYRECT**, **COPY**, and **MOVE** commands. As in the previous drawing, pay close attention to the drawing setup and remember to use nominal sizes as dimensions indicate.

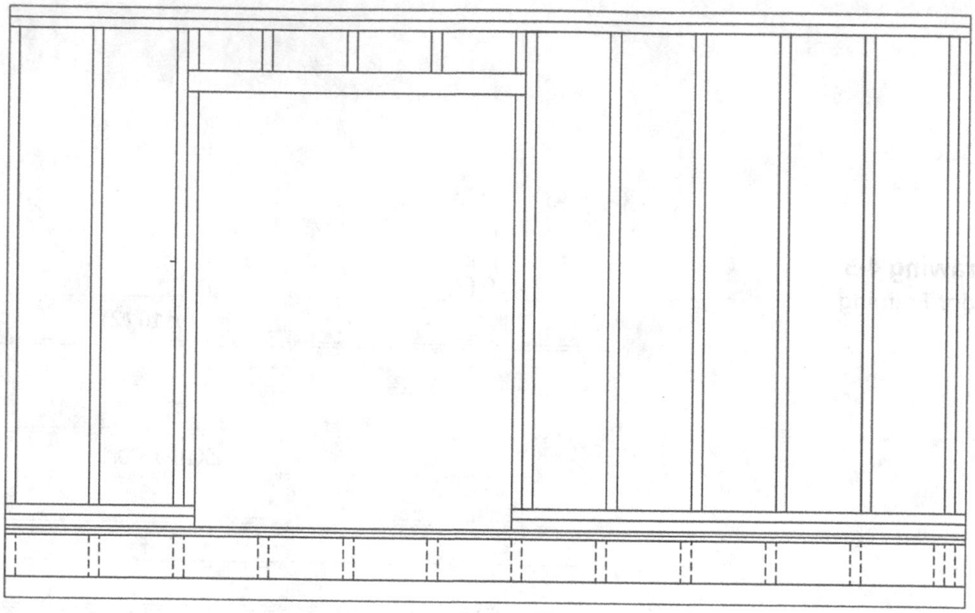

Drawing Suggestions

UNITS = Architectural; Precision = 0'-00"

LIMITS = 24',18'

GRID = 1'

SNAP = 1'

LTSCALE = 6

- Be sure to use foot (') and inch (") symbols when setting limits, grid, and snap (but not ltscale).
- Begin by drawing the **15'-2" × 9'-4"** rectangle, with the lower-left corner at **(4',4')**.
- Build the drawing up from the bottom by next drawing the **4" × 6"** sill.
- Make layer **2** current and draw a hidden line **2" × 10"** floor joist on the far left.
- Array the **2" × 10"** floor joists in a **1**-row by **12**-column array, with **16"** between rows.
- Continue building the drawing from bottom to top.

Drawing 4-6
Wall Framing

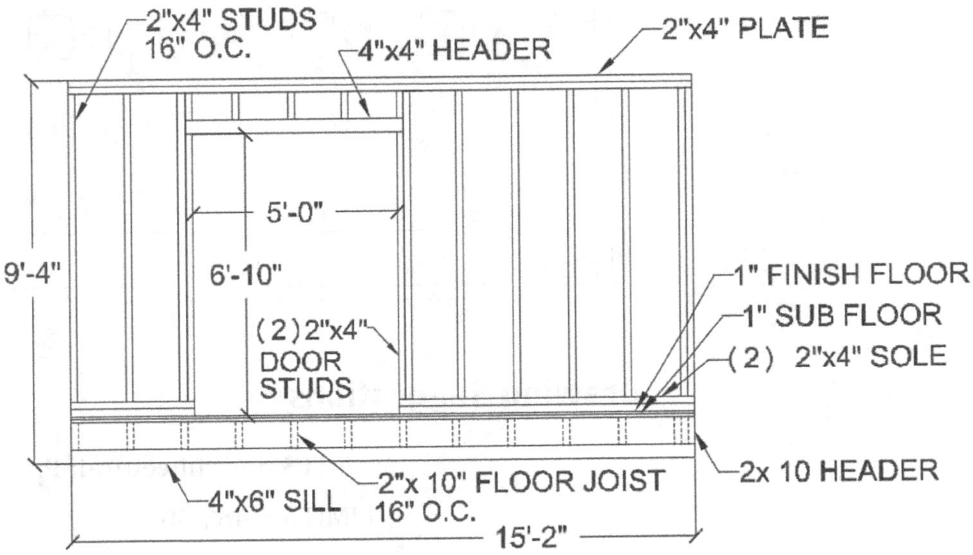

A

Drawing 4-7: *Classroom – Floor Plan* [ADVANCED]

This architectural drawing incorporates rectangular **ARRAYRECT**, **COPY**, and **MOVE** commands. Pay close attention to the drawing setup and remember to use nominal sizes as dimensions indicate.

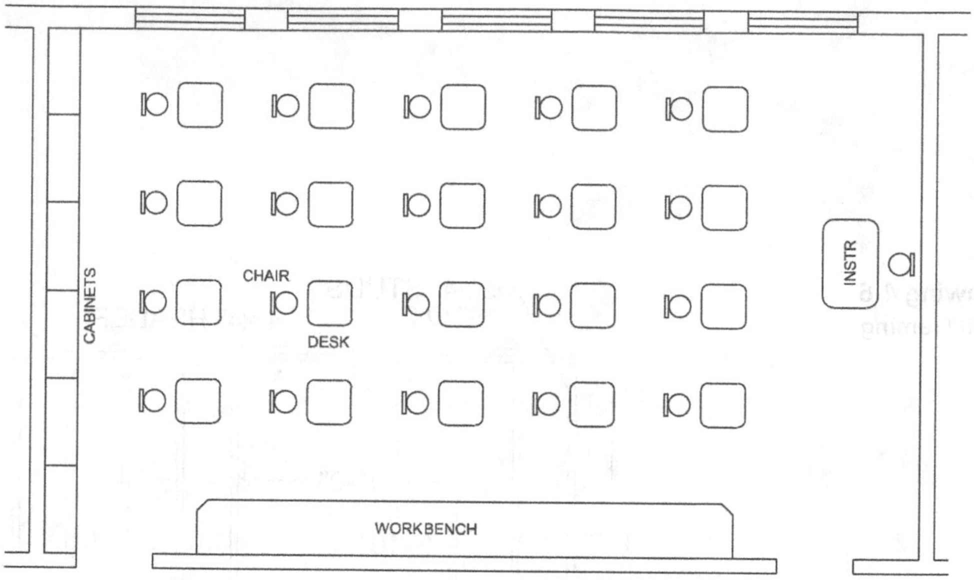

Drawing Suggestions

UNITS = Architectural; Precision = 0'-00"

LIMITS = 48', 36'

GRID = 1'

SNAP = 6'

- Be sure to use foot (') and inch (") symbols when setting limits, grid, and snap.
- Begin by drawing the outer walls, with the lower left line at **(4',4')**. When you get to the wall with the windows, you can draw the windows separately or draw one and array five columns.
- Draw the lower-left chair and desk and then array to create the room with **20** desks and chairs.
- Continue by drawing the cabinets, bench, and instructor's desk and chair.

Drawing 4-7
Classroom – Floor Plan

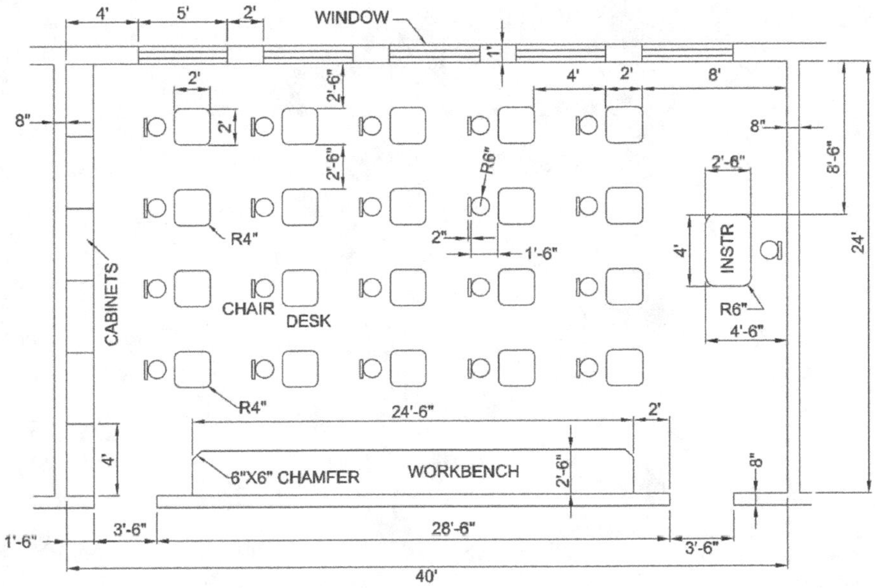

chapter five

Arcs and Polar Arrays

CHAPTER OBJECTIVES

- Create polar arrays
- Draw arcs
- Use the **ROTATE** command
- Use polar tracking at any angle
- Create mirror images of objects
- Create page setups

Introduction

Lines and circles are two main object types used in most drawings. In this chapter, you learn a third object type, the arc. In addition, you expand your ability to manipulate objects. You learn to rotate objects and create their mirror images. You learn to save plot settings as named page setups. First, however, you see how to create polar arrays.

Creating Polar Arrays

ARRAY	
Command	ARRAY
Alias	Ar
Panel	Modify
Tool	

Defining a polar array requires more steps than a rectangular array does. There are three qualities that define a polar array, but two are sufficient. A polar array is defined by any combination of two of the following: a certain number of items, an angle that these items span, and an angle between each item and the next. You also have to tell AutoCAD whether to rotate the newly created objects as they are copied.

✔ Create a new drawing with drawing limits set to **18 × 12**. You can do this using the 1B template if you have it.

- ✔ Turn the grid on or off according to your preference. The figures in this drawing show the grid off for clarity.
- ✔ In preparation for this exercise, draw a vertical **0.75-unit** line at the bottom center of the drawing, with the lower end at **(9.00,4.25)**, as shown in Figure 5-1.
- ✔ Select the line.
- ✔ Open the **Array** drop-down menu on the **Modify** panel of the **Home** tab and click the **Polar Array** tool, as shown in Figure 5-2.

Figure 5-1
Drawing a vertical line

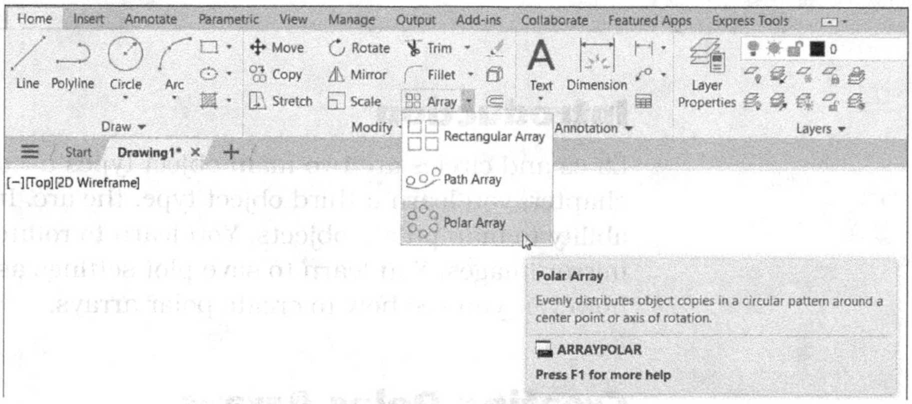

Figure 5-2
Polar Array tool

To define a polar array, you need to specify a center point. Polar arrays are created by copying objects around the circumferences of circles or arcs, so you need to specify one of these.

- ✔ Specify the point **(9.00,7.00)** directly above the line and somewhat below the center of the drawing area.

  As soon as you specify the point, a preview array with six evenly spaced items in a 360° polar array is displayed, as shown in Figure 5-3. Also you see the ***Array Creation*** *contextual tab, as shown.*

This tab works like the tab of the same name when creating a rectangular array, except that the specifications to be made are different. In the ***Items*** *tab, you see the three values required to define a polar array:* ***Items***, ***Between***, *and* ***Fill***. *The third panel is named* ***Rows***, *just as on the tab when you created a rectangular array. The next panel is for 3D levels, as also seen when creating rectangular arrays.*

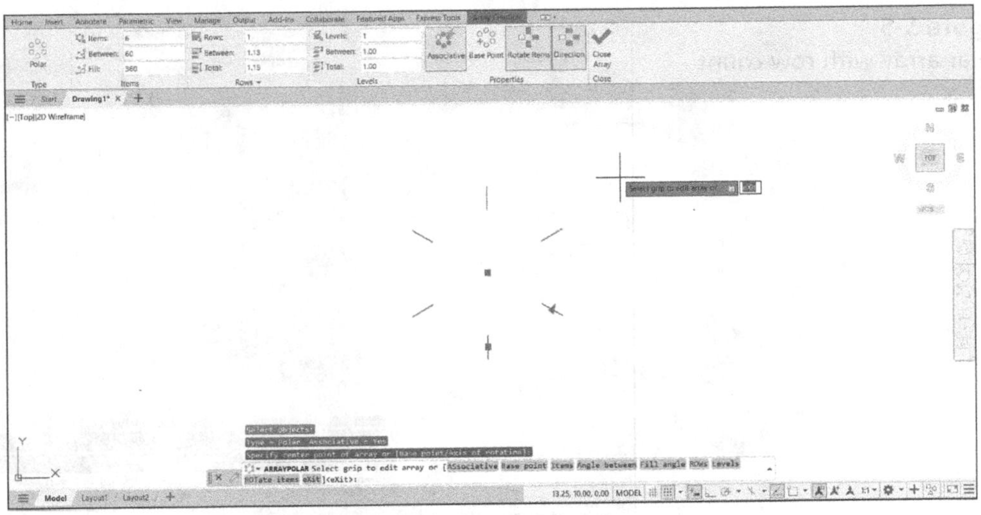

Figure 5-3
Preview array

As you see in the drawing area and on the contextual tab, the preview array has six items by default, and they are spaced 60° apart to fill a complete circle of 360°. Changing any of these values will generate a new array.

✔ Click in the **Items** edit box and type **12 <Enter>**.

A preview array with 12 items is displayed, as shown in Figure 5-4. In the tab's edit boxes you see that the 60° spacing has been adjusted to 30°, maintaining a fill angle of 360°.

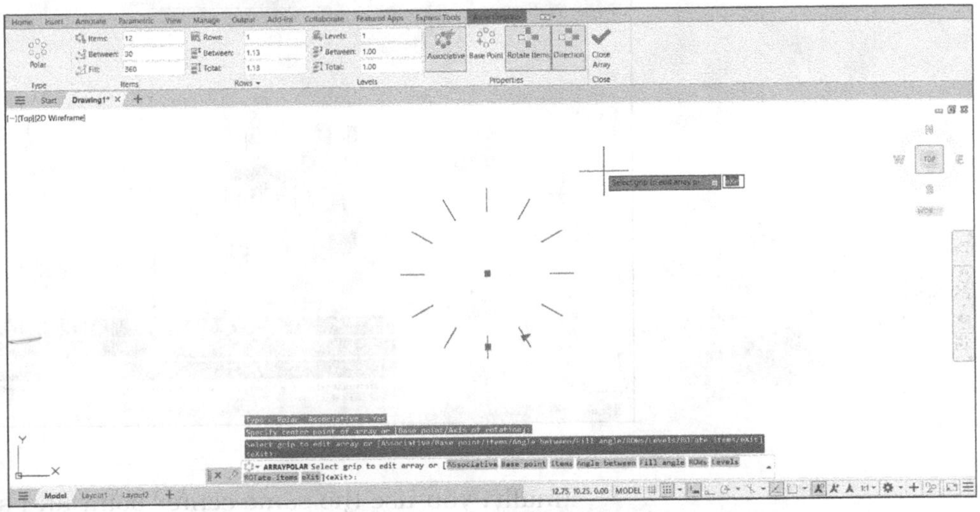

Figure 5-4
Preview array with 12 items

With this array in your drawing, you can set polar rows and use the **Rotate Items** function. Rows in polar arrays radiate outward from the center point. By changing from the default of one row to three, you create the array shown in Figure 5-5.

✔ Click in the **Rows** edit box, on the top line of the **Rows** panel, and type **3 <Enter>**.

Your drawing should resemble Figure 5-5.

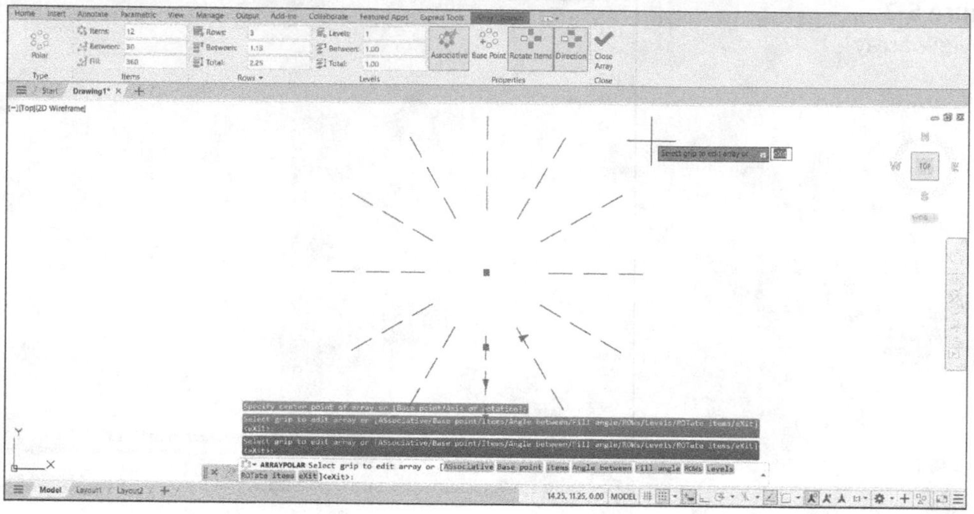

Figure 5-5
Polar array with row count 3

✔ Click the **Rotate Items** button, as shown in Figure 5-5.

*In the default option, objects are rotated as they are copied to form the array. With **Rotate Items** off, they maintain the orientation of the original object.*

✔ Press **<Enter>** to complete the **ARRAYPOLAR** command.

Your drawing should resemble Figure 5-6.

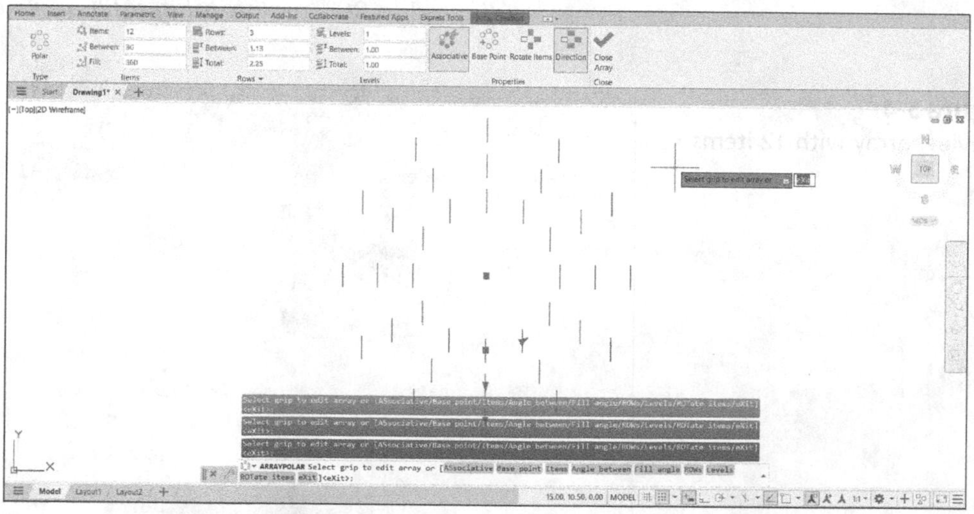

Figure 5-6
Rotate Items button

Finally, you use the same center point and source object to define an array that has 20 items placed 15° apart and not rotated when they are copied. This time, you select options from the shortcut menu or the command line rather than using the contextual tab.

- ✔ Undo the last array, so you have the single line shown previously in Figure 5-1.
- ✔ Click the **Polar Array** tool from the ribbon.
- ✔ Select the line.
- ✔ Right-click to end object selection.
- ✔ Specify **(9,7)** for the center point.

  A preview array with six items, filling 360°, as previously shown in Figure 5-3.
- ✔ Right-click and select **Angle between** from the shortcut menu, or select **Angle between** from the command line.
- ✔ Type **15 <Enter>** for the angle between items.

  A preview array with 15° between the six preview items is shown. Using the arrow-shaped grip at the top right, you can add more items while maintaining the 15° between.
- ✔ Click the arrow-shaped grip at the right and drag the rubber band around 270° to the left quadrant at 9 o'clock.

  This will bring you to a y value on the coordinate display of ***(5.00)****, even with the center of the array. Notice that there are now 19 items in the array, spaced 15°, and filling the angle of 270°.*
- ✔ Right-click and select **ROTate items** from the shortcut menu, or select **ROTate items** from the command line.
- ✔ Type **n <Enter>** to not rotate the items.
- ✔ Press **<Enter>** to end the command.

  Your drawing should now resemble Figure 5-7.

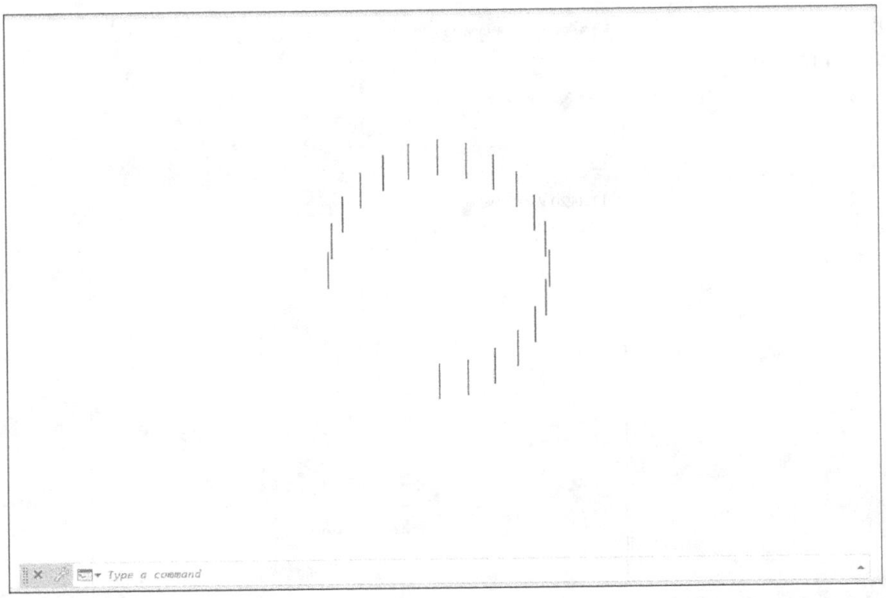

Figure 5-7
Array with 19 items, spaced 15 degrees

With the options AutoCAD gives you, there are many possibilities that you can try. As always, experimentation is encouraged.

ARC	
Command	ARC
Alias	A
Panel	Draw
Tool	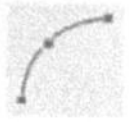

Drawing Arcs

> **TIP**
>
> The following is a general procedure for using the **ARC** command:
>
> 1. Click an **Arc** tool from the **Arc** drop-down menu on the **Draw** panel of the **Home** tab on the ribbon.
> 2. Type or specify where to start the arc, where to end it, and what circle it is a portion of, using any of the 11 available methods.

Learning the **ARC** command is an exercise in geometry. In this section, you get a firm foundation in understanding and drawing arcs so that you are not confused by all the available options. The information provided should be more than enough to do the drawings in this chapter and most drawings you encounter elsewhere. Refer to the AutoCAD Online Help system and the chart at the end of this section (Figure 5-9) if you need additional information.

AutoCAD gives you eight distinct ways to draw arcs (11 if you count variations in order). With so many choices, some generalizations are helpful.

First, every option requires you to specify three pieces of information: where to begin the arc, where to end it, and what circle it is theoretically a part of. To get a handle on the range of options, look at the options on the **Arc** drop-down menu.

✔ Erase any objects left in your drawing from the previous section.

✔ Open the **Arc** drop-down menu from the **Draw** panel of the ribbon's **Home** tab, as shown in Figure 5-8.

Figure 5-8
Arc drop-down menu

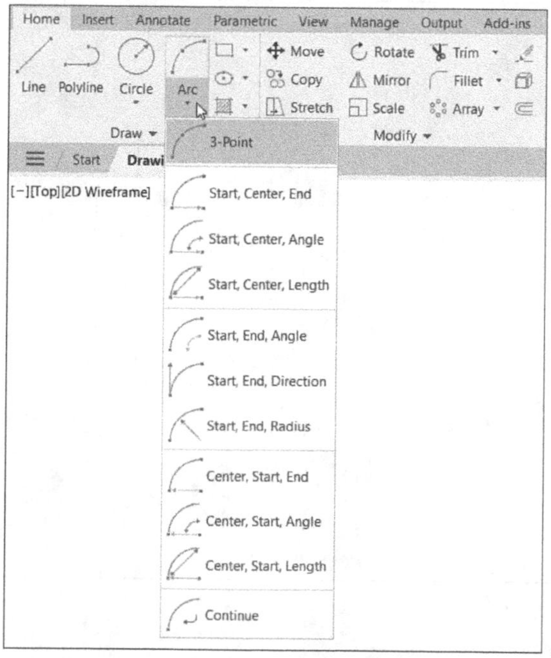

Notice that the options in the fourth panel down (**Center**, **Start**, **End**, etc.) are simply reordered versions of those in the second panel (**Start**, **Center**, **End**, etc.). This is how there are 11 options instead of 8.

More importantly, **Start** is always included. In every option, a starting point must be specified, although it does not have to be the first point specified.

The options arise from the different ways you can specify the end and the circle from which the arc is cut. The end can be shown as an actual point (all **End** options) or inferred from a specified angle or length of chord (all **Angle** and **Length** options).

The circle that the arc is part of can be specified directly by its center point (all **Center** options) or inferred from other information, such as a radius length (**Radius** option), an angle between two given points (**Angle** options), or a tangent direction (the **Start**, **End**, **Direction**, and **Continue** options).

The 3P Option

With this framework in mind, you begin by drawing an arc using the simplest method, which is also the default: the three-point option. The geometric key to this method is that any three points not on the same line determine a circle or an arc of a circle. AutoCAD uses this in the **CIRCLE** command (the **3P** option) as well as in the **ARC** command.

✔ Select **3-Point** from the top of the **Arc** drop-down menu.

AutoCAD's response is this prompt:

```
Specify start point of arc or [Center]:
```

Accepting the default by specifying a point leaves open all those options in which the start point is specified first.

If you instead type **c <Enter>** *or select* **Center** *from the shortcut menu, AutoCAD prompts for a center point and follows with those options that begin with a center.*

✔ Specify a start point near the center of the drawing area.

AutoCAD prompts:

```
Specify second point of arc or [Center/End]:
```

You continue to follow the default three-point sequence by specifying a second point. You may want to refer to Figure 5-9 as you draw this arc.

✔ Specify any point one or two units away from the previous point. Exact coordinates are not important right now.

Once AutoCAD has two points, it gives you an arc to drag. By moving the cursor slowly in a circle and in and out, you can see the range of arc the third point will produce.

AutoCAD also knows now that you have to provide an endpoint to complete the arc, so the prompt has only one option:

```
Specify end point of arc:
```

Any point you specify will do, as long as it produces an arc that fits in the current view.

✔ Specify an endpoint.

As you can see, three-point arcs are easy to draw. The procedure is much like drawing a line, except that you have to specify three points instead of two. In practice, however, you do not always have three points to use this way. This necessitates the broad range of options in the **ARC** command. The dimensions you are given and the objects already drawn determine what options are useful to you.

Figure 5-9
Arc options

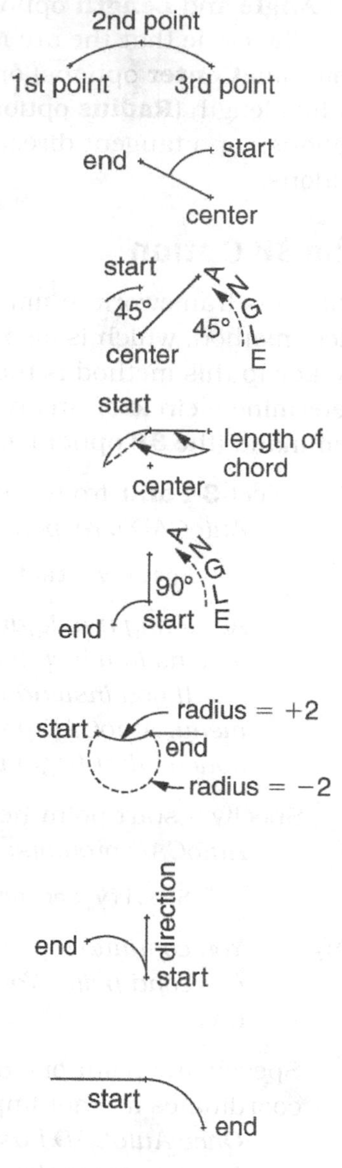

TYPE	APPEARANCE	DESCRIPTION
3-point	2nd point / 1st point / 3rd point	Clockwise or counterclockwise
S, C, E (start, center, end)	end / start / center	Counterclockwise Radial rubber band indicates angle only, length is insignificant
S, C, A (start, center, angle)	start / 45° / 45° / center / ANGLE	+ angle = CCW − angle = CW Rubber band shows angle only, starting from horizontal
S, C, L (start, center, length of chord)	start / length of chord / center	Counterclockwise "Chord" rubber band shows length of chord only, direction is insignificant
S, E, A (start, end, angle)	ANGLE / 90° / end / start	+ angle = CCW − angle = CW Rubber band shows angle only, starting from horizontal
S, E, R (start, end, radius)	radius = +2 / start / end / radius = −2	Counterclockwise + radius = minor arc − radius = major arc Rubber band shows + radius values only, For − radius (type value)
S, E, D (start, end, direction)	direction / end / start	Direction of rubber band is a line tangent to the arc being constructed and runs through the start point
CONTIN: (continuous from line)	start / end	Arc begins at end point of previous line or arc and is tangent to it; Rubber band is a chord from start point to end point

Start, Center, End

Next, you create an arc using the start, center, end method, the second option illustrated in Figure 5-9.

✔ Type **u <Enter>** or click the **Undo** tool on the **Quick Access** toolbar to undo the three-point arc.

✔ Click the **Start**, **Center**, **End** tool from the **Arc** drop-down menu.

✔ Specify a point near the center of the drawing area as a start point.

*The following prompt is the same as for the three-point option, but the **Center** option has been entered for you.*

```
Specify second point of arc (hold Ctrl to switch direction)
or [Center/End]: _c
Specify center point of arc:
```

✔ Specify any point roughly one to three units away from the start point.

The circle from which the arc is to be cut is now clearly determined. All that is left is to specify how much of the circle to take, which can be done in one of three ways, as the following prompt indicates:

```
Specify end point of arc (hold Ctrl to switch direction) or
[Angle/chord Length]:
```

Specify an endpoint. First, however, try this:

✔ Move the cursor slowly in a circle and in and out to see how this method works.

As before, there is an arc to drag, and now there is a radial direction rubber band as well. If you specify a point anywhere along this rubber band, AutoCAD assumes that you want the point where it crosses the circumference of the circle.

*As with the polar arrays in this chapter, AutoCAD creates arcs counterclockwise, consistent with its coordinate system. This is the default. However, as indicated in the prompt, you have the option of switching to creating clockwise arcs from the same start point and curving around the circle to the endpoint. This is accomplished by pressing and holding the **<Ctrl>** key. Try this:*

✔ Hold down the **<Ctrl>** key and move the crosshairs slightly.

✔ Figure 5-10 shows an example of switching between counterclockwise and clockwise arcs.

Figure 5-10
Counterclockwise and clockwise arcs

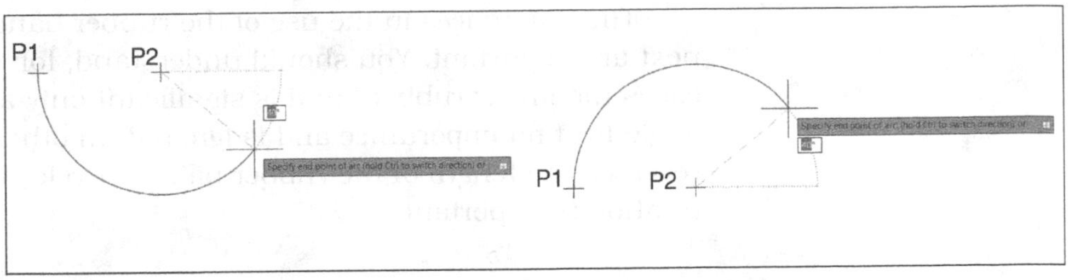

Counter clockwise

Hold Ctrl for Clockwise

✔ Release the **<Ctrl>** key and the counterclockwise arc returns.

Whichever arc is showing when you specify an endpoint will be the one retained in your drawing.

✔ Specify an endpoint to complete the arc.

Start, Center, Angle

You learn to draw one more arc, using the start, center, angle method, before moving on. This method has some peculiarities in the use of the rubber band that are typical of the **ARC** command, and they can be confusing. An example of how the start, center, angle method might look is shown in Figure 5-9.

✔ Undo the last arc.

✔ Click the **Start, Center, Angle** tool from the **Arc** drop-down menu.

AutoCAD prompts for a start point:

```
Specify start point of arc or [Center]:
```

✔ Specify a start point near the center of the drawing area.

AutoCAD prompts:

```
Specify second point of arc or [Center/End]:_c Specify
center point of arc:
```

✔ Specify a center point 1 to 3 units below the start point.

*AutoCAD prompts with the **Angle** option:*

```
Specify end point of arc (hold Ctrl to switch direction) or
[Angle/chord Length]:_a Specify included angle:
```

You can type an angle specification or specify an angle in the drawing area. Notice that the rubber band now displays an angle only; its length is insignificant. The indicated angle is being measured from the horizontal, but the actual arc begins at the start point and continues counterclockwise, as illustrated in Figure 5-9.

✔ Type **45 <Enter>** or show an angle of 45°.

Now that you have tried three of the basic methods for creating an arc, study the chart in Figure 5-9 and then try the other methods, along with switching to clockwise arcs using the **<Ctrl>** key. The notes in the right-hand column serve as a guide.

The differences in the use of the rubber band from one method to the next are important. You should understand, for instance, that in some cases the linear rubber band is significant only as a distance indicator; its angle is of no importance and is ignored. In other cases, it is just the reverse: The length of the rubber band is irrelevant, whereas its angle of rotation is important.

> **TIP**
>
> One additional trick you should try as you experiment with arcs is as follows: If you press **<Enter>** or the spacebar at the *Specify start point of arc or [Center]:* prompt, AutoCAD uses the endpoint of the last line or arc you drew as the starting point for the new arc and creates the arc tangent to it. This is the same as the **Continue** tool at the bottom of the **Arc** drop-down menu.

This completes the discussion of the **ARC** command. Creating arcs can be tricky. Another option that is available and often useful is to draw a complete circle and then use the **TRIM** command to cut out the arc you want.

Using the ROTATE Command

ROTATE	
Command	ROTATE
Alias	Ro
Panel	Modify
Tool	

ROTATE is a fairly straightforward command, and it has some uses that may not be immediately apparent. For example, it frequently is easier to draw an object in a horizontal or vertical position and then rotate it into position than to draw it at an angle.

In addition to the **ROTATE** command, the **Grip Edit** system includes a **Rotate** mode, which is introduced later in this section.

✔ In preparation for this exercise, clear your drawing and draw a three-point arc using the points **(9,6)**, **(11.50,5)**, and **(14,6)**, as in Figure 5-11.

You begin by rotating the arc to the position shown in Figure 5-12.

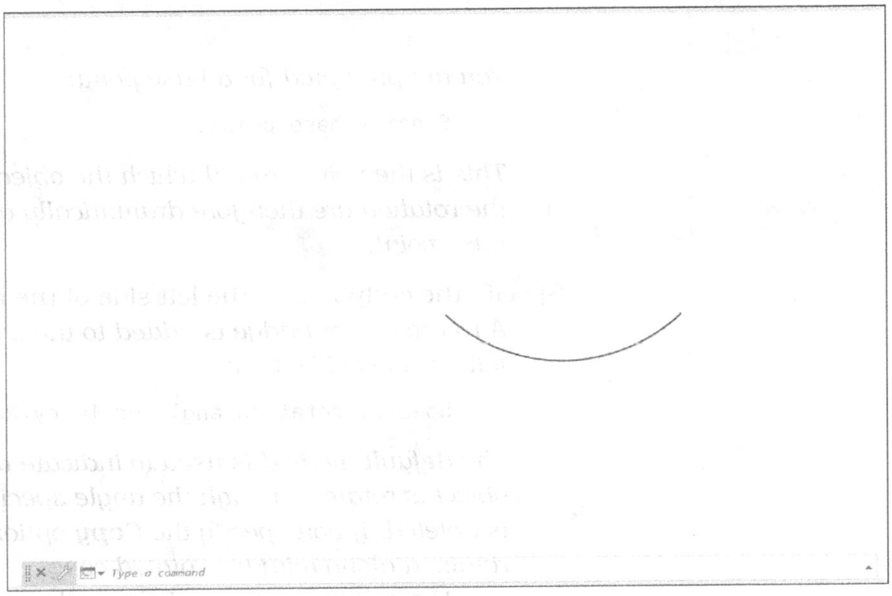

Figure 5-11
Drawing a three-point arc

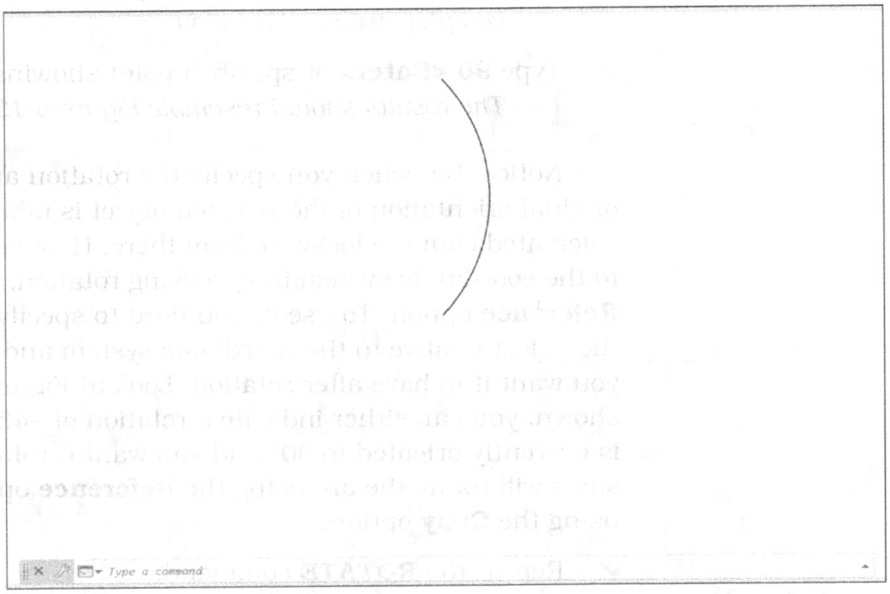

Figure 5-12
Rotating the arc

- ✔ Select the arc.
- ✔ Click the **Rotate** tool from the **Modify** panel on the ribbon's **Home** tab, as shown in Figure 5-13.

Figure 5-13
Rotate tool

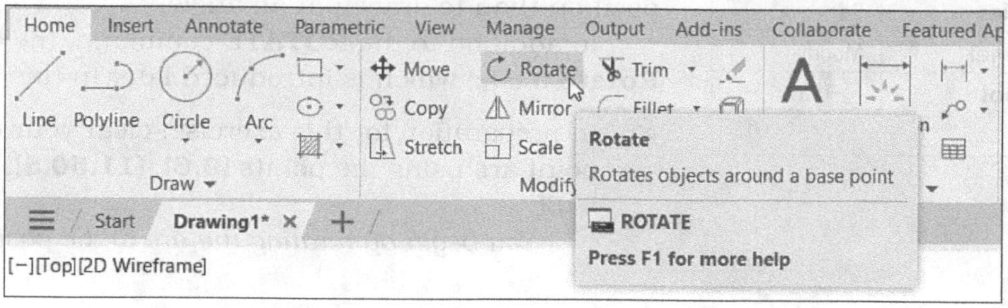

You are prompted for a base point:

```
Specify base point:
```

This is the point around which the object is rotated. The results of the rotation are therefore dramatically affected by your choice of base point.

- ✔ Specify the endpoint on the left side of the arc.

A rotate cursor badge is added to the crosshairs and the prompt that follows looks like this:

```
Specify rotation angle or [Copy/Reference] <0>:
```

The default method is used to indicate a rotation angle directly. The object is rotated through the angle specified, and the original object is deleted. If you specify the ***Copy*** *option, the original object is retained along with the rotated copy.*

Move the cursor in a circle, and you will see that you have an arc to drag into place visually. If ***Ortho*** *is on, turn it off to see the complete range of rotation.*

- ✔ Type **90 <Enter>** or specify a point showing a rotation of 90°.

The results should resemble Figure 5-12.

Notice that when you specify the rotation angle directly like this, the original orientation of the selected object is taken to be 0°. The rotation is calculated counterclockwise from there. However, you might want to refer to the coordinate system in specifying rotation. This is the purpose of the **Reference** option. To use it, you need to specify the present orientation of the object relative to the coordinate system and then specify the orientation you want it to have after rotation. Look at Figure 5-14. To rotate the arc as shown, you can either indicate a rotation of −45° or inform AutoCAD that it is currently oriented to 90° and you want it rotated to 45°. The following steps will rotate the arc using the **Reference** option and retain the original using the **Copy** option.

- ✔ Repeat the **ROTATE** command.
- ✔ Select the arc.
- ✔ Right-click to end object selection.

- ✔ Specify a base point at the lower endpoint of the arc.
- ✔ Type **c <Enter>** or select **Copy** from the command line.
- ✔ Type **r <Enter>** or select **Reference** from the command line.

  Notice that both options can be active at once.

  AutoCAD prompts for a reference angle:

```
Specify the reference angle <0>:
```

- ✔ Type **90 <Enter>**.

  AutoCAD prompts:

```
Specify the new angle or [Points]:
```

- ✔ Type **45 <Enter>**.

  Your drawing should now include both arcs shown in Figure 5-14.

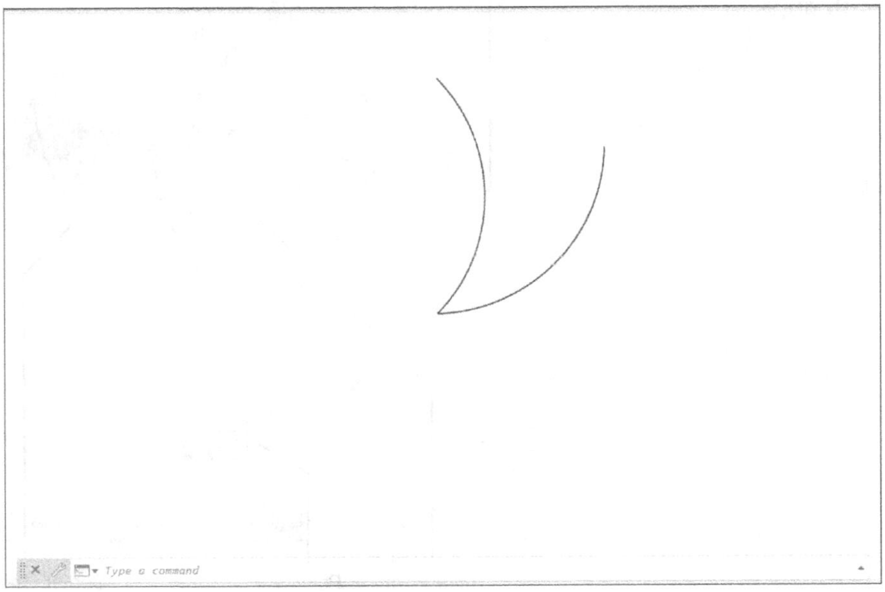

Figure 5-14
Arc rotated 45 degrees

Rotating with Grips

Rotating with grips is simple, but your choice of object selection methods is limited, as always—pointing, windowing, and lassoing. Complete the following steps:

- ✔ Select the two arcs.

  The arcs are highlighted and their grips appear. These grips are especially designed for arcs. If you let the cursor rest on the grips in the middle and the endpoints of each arc, you will see that these grips are multifunctional. The grips at the centers and base point have only one function.

- ✔ Click the grip in the middle of either arc.
- ✔ Right-click to open the **Grip Edit** shortcut menu.
- ✔ Select **Rotate**.

  Move your cursor in a circle, and you see the arcs rotating around the grip you selected.

- ✔ Right-click again and select **Base Point** from the shortcut menu, or select **Base Point** from the command line.

  Base Point *allows you to specify a base point other than the selected grip.*

- ✔ Specify a base point to the left of the arcs, as shown in Figure 5-15.

  Move your cursor in circles again. You can see the arcs rotating around the new base point.

- ✔ Type **c <Enter>** or select **Copy** from the command line.
- ✔ Specify a point to define a rotation angle of 90°, as illustrated by the top two arcs in Figure 5-15.

Figure 5-15
Arc rotated with grips

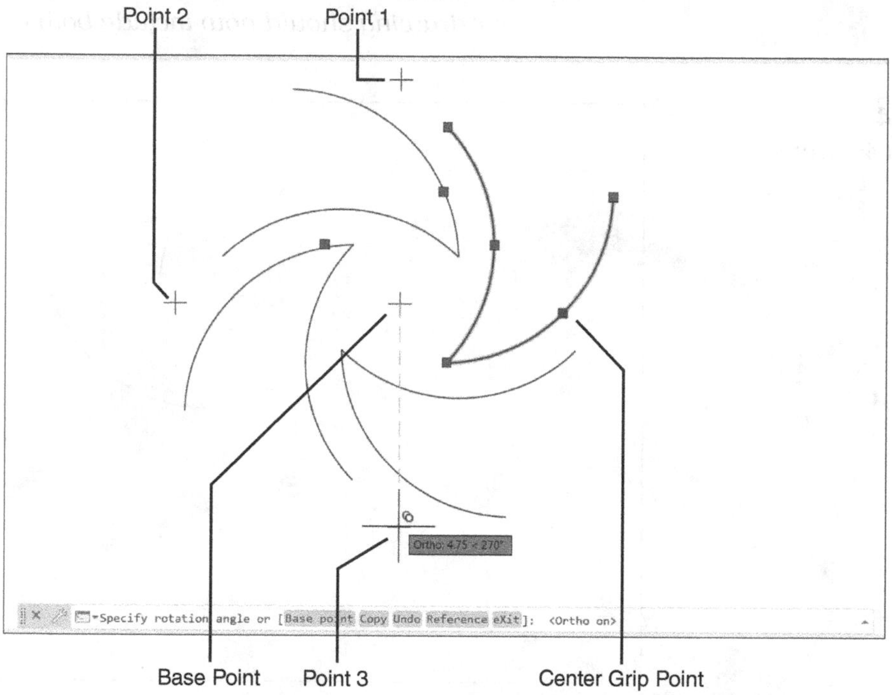

- ✔ Specify a second point to define a rotation angle of 180°, as illustrated by the arcs at the left in the figure.
- ✔ Specify point 3 at 270° to complete the design shown in Figure 5-15.
- ✔ Press **<Enter>** or the spacebar to exit the **Grip Edit** mode.
- ✔ Press **<Esc>** to clear grips.

The capability to create rotated copies is very useful, as you will find when you do the drawings at the end of this chapter.

Using Polar Tracking at Any Angle

polar tracking: The AutoCAD feature that displays tracking lines at a regular specified angle.

You might have noticed that using **Ortho** or ***Polar tracking*** to force or snap to the 90°, 180°, and 270° angles in the last exercise would make the process more efficient. With polar tracking, you can extend this concept to include angular increments other than the standard 90° orthogonal angles. This feature combined with the rotate copy technique facilitates the creation of rotated copies at regular angles. For example, you use this process to create Figure 5-16.

To begin this task, erase all but one arc in your drawing. This is a good opportunity to use the **Remove** option when selecting objects.

- ✔ Type **e <Enter>** or click the **Erase** tool from the **Modify** panel of the **Home** tab on the ribbon.
- ✔ Select all the arcs with a window, crossing window, or lasso.
- ✔ Type **r <Enter>** to enter the **Remove** option.
  Right-clicking to use the shortcut menu doesn't work here because the right-click completes the command and erases the arcs.

Figure 5-16
Using polar tracking with rotate and copy

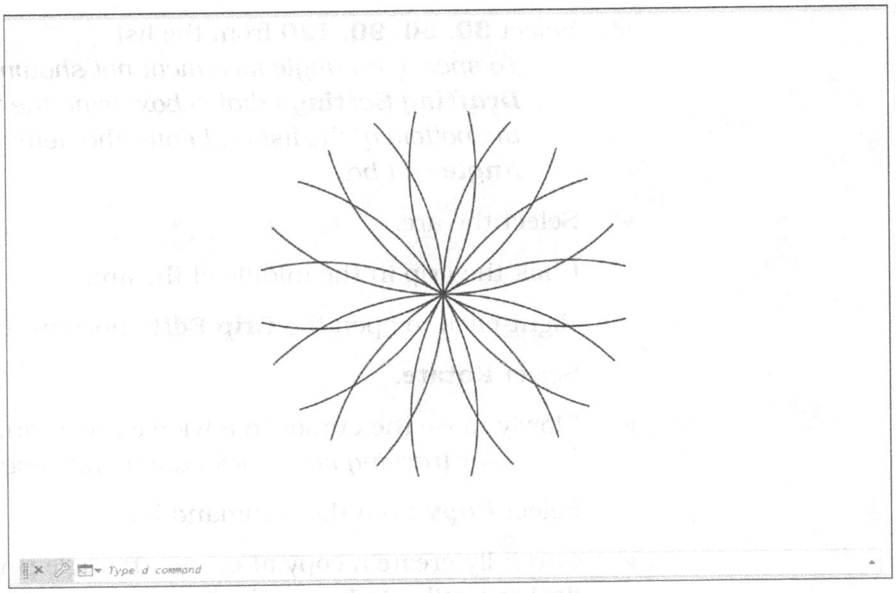

- ✔ Select the original arc, which is now rotated to 90°.
- ✔ Press **<Enter>** or right-click in the drawing area to complete the command.
  You are left with one vertically oriented arc.
- ✔ If necessary, move the arc near the center of the drawing area.
  Before you rotate and copy this arc, set polar tracking to track at 30° angles.
- ✔ Turn **Snap Mode** off.
- ✔ Click the **Polar Tracking** button on the status bar so that polar tracking is on.
- ✔ Right-click the **Polar Tracking** button.
  This opens the list shown in Figure 5-17.

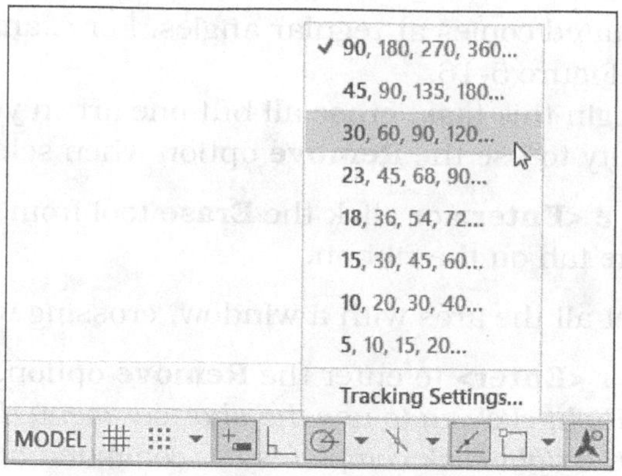

Figure 5-17
Polar Tracking shortcut menu

- ✔ Select **30**, **60**, **90**, **120** from the list.
  *To specify an angle increment not shown on the list, display the **Drafting Settings** dialog box using the **Track Settings** option at the bottom of the list and enter the new angle in the **Increment Angle** edit box.*
- ✔ Select the arc.
- ✔ Click the grip in the middle of the arc.
- ✔ Right-click to open the **Grip Edit** shortcut menu.
- ✔ Select **Rotate**.
- ✔ Slowly move the cursor in a wide circle around the selected grip.
  Polar tracking now tracks and snaps every 30° angular increment.
- ✔ Select **Copy** from the command line.
- ✔ Carefully create a copy at every 30° angle until you have created a design similar to Figure 5-16.
- ✔ Press **<Enter>** to exit **Grip Edit** mode.
- ✔ Press **<Esc>** to clear grips.
  Your drawing should resemble Figure 5-16.

Creating Mirror Images of Objects

MIRROR	
Command	MIRROR
Alias	Mi
Panel	Modify
Tool	

The **MIRROR** command creates a copy of an original object across an imaginary mirror line, so that every point on the object has a corresponding point on the opposite side of the mirror line at an equal distance from the line.

There is also a **Mirror** mode in the **Grip Edit** system, which you explore a bit later in this section.

- ✔ To begin this exercise, erase all but the horizontal arc in the drawing area, as shown in Figure 5-18.
  *Here is another opportunity to use the **Remove** option, as described in the previous section.*
- ✔ Turn **Snap Mode** on.
- ✔ Keep **Polar Tracking** or **Ortho Mode** on to do this exercise.

✔ Select the arc.

✔ Click the **Mirror** tool from the **Modify** panel on the ribbon's **Home** tab, as shown in Figure 5-19.

Now AutoCAD prompts you for the first point of a mirror line:

```
Specify first point of mirror line:
```

A mirror line is just what you would expect; the line serves as the mirror, and all points on your original object are reflected across the line at an equal distance and opposite orientation.

You use a mirror line along the horizontal between the endpoints of the arc, so that the endpoints of the mirror images touch.

Figure 5-18
Original arc

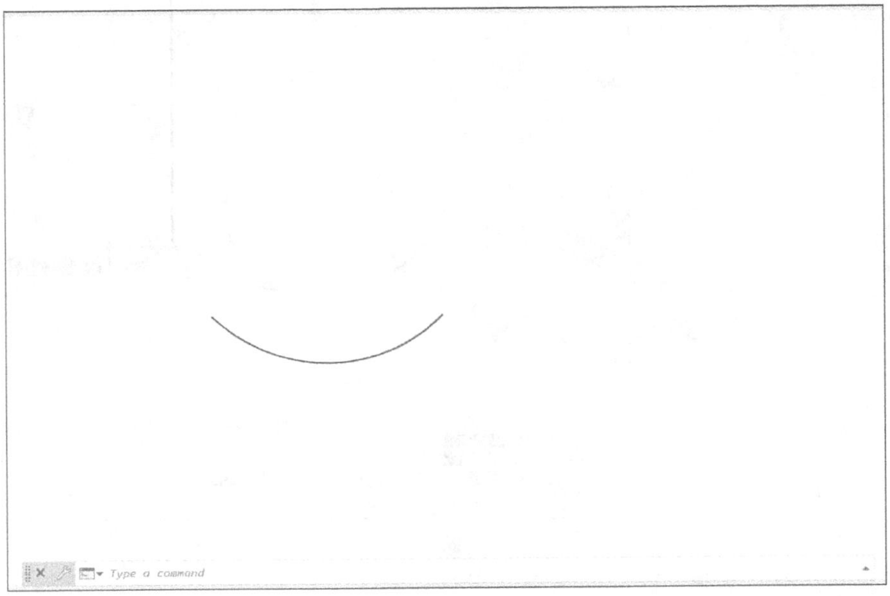

Figure 5-19
Mirror tool

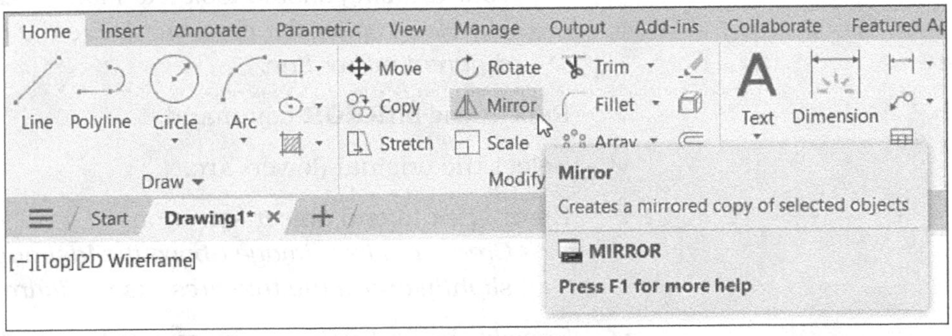

✔ Specify a point anywhere to the left side of the arc, along the horizontal between the arc endpoints, as in Figure 5-20.

You are prompted to specify the other endpoint of the mirror line:

```
Specify second point of mirror line:
```

The length of the mirror line is not important. Only orientation matters. Move the cursor slowly in a circle, and you see an inverted copy of the arc moving with you to show the different mirror images that are possible given the first point you specified.

- ✔ Specify a point at 0° from the first point, so that the mirror image is directly above the original arc and touching at the endpoints, as in Figure 5-20.

  The dragged object disappears until you respond to the next prompt, which prompts you to decide whether you want to delete the original object:

```
Erase source objects? [Yes/No] <N>:
```

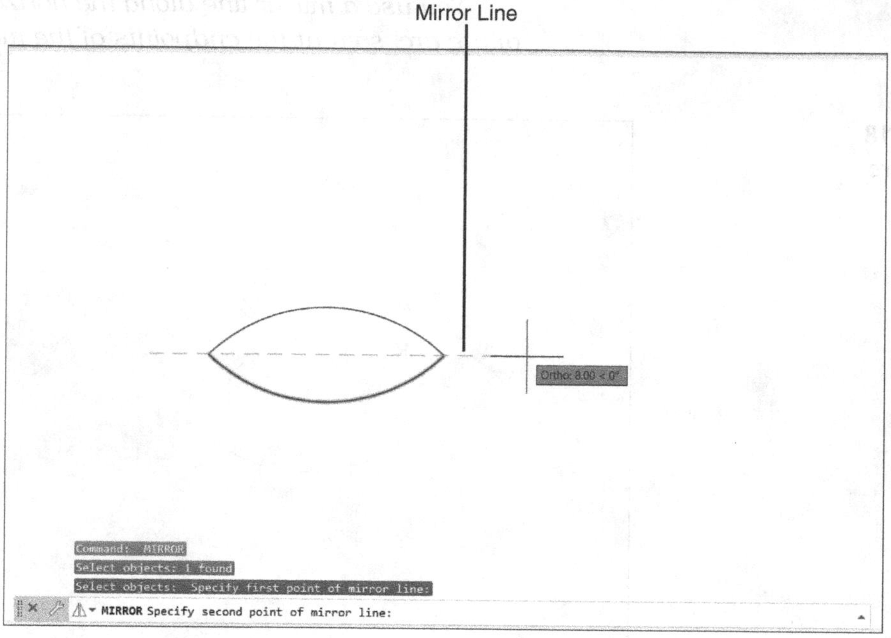

Figure 5-20
Mirror line between arc endpoints

- ✔ Press **<Enter>** to retain the source object.

  Your drawing should look like Figure 5-20, without the mirror line.

  Now repeat the process, delete the original this time and use a different mirror line.

- ✔ Repeat the **MIRROR** command.
- ✔ Select the original (lower) arc.
- ✔ Right-click to end object selection.

  Create a mirror image above the last one by choosing a mirror line slightly above the two arcs, as in Figure 5-21.

- ✔ Specify the first point of the mirror line slightly above and to the left of the figure.
- ✔ Specify the second point at 0° to the right of the first point.
- ✔ Type **y <Enter>** or select **Yes** from the command line.

  Your drawing should now resemble Figure 5-22.

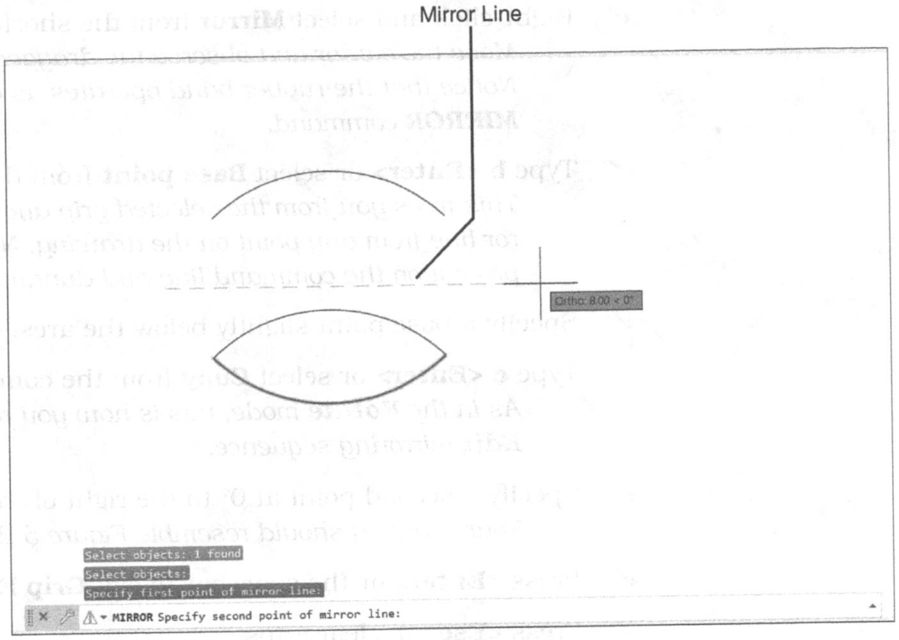

Figure 5-21
Mirror line above arc

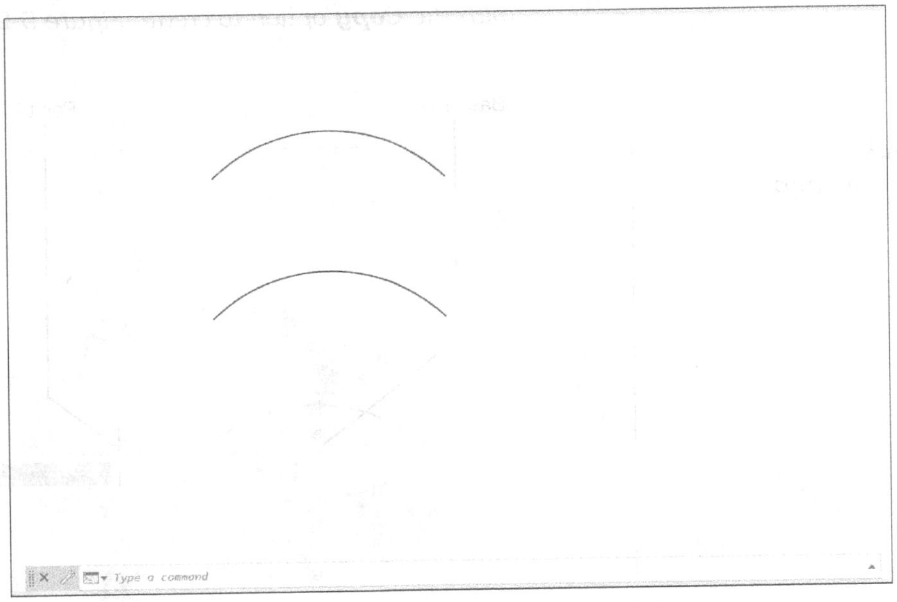

Figure 5-22
Results of mirror

Mirroring with Grips

In the **Mirror Grip Edit** mode, the rubber band shows you a mirror line instead of a rotation angle. The option to retain or delete the original is selected through the **Copy** option, just as in the other **Grip Edit** modes.

- ✔ Select the two arcs in the drawing area by pointing or using a crossing window or lasso.

  The arcs are highlighted, and the grips are showing.

- ✔ If necessary, turn **Ortho Mode** off.

- ✔ Click any of the grips.

✔ Right-click and select **Mirror** from the shortcut menu.

*Move the cursor and observe the dragged mirror images of the arcs. Notice that the rubber band operates as a mirror line, just as in the **MIRROR** command.*

✔ Type **b <Enter>** or select **Base point** from the command line.

This frees you from the selected grip and allows you to create a mirror line from any point on the drawing. Notice the Specify base point: *prompt on the command line and dynamic input tooltip.*

✔ Specify a base point slightly below the arcs.

✔ Type **c <Enter>** or select **Copy** from the command line.

*As in the **Rotate** mode, this is how you retain the original in a **Grip Edit** mirroring sequence.*

✔ Specify a second point at 0° to the right of the first.

Your drawing should resemble Figure 5-23.

✔ Press **<Enter>** or the spacebar to exit **Grip Edit** mode.

✔ Press **<Esc>** to clear grips.

*Try completing this exercise by using the **Mirror Grip Edit** mode with the **Copy** option to create Figure 5-24.*

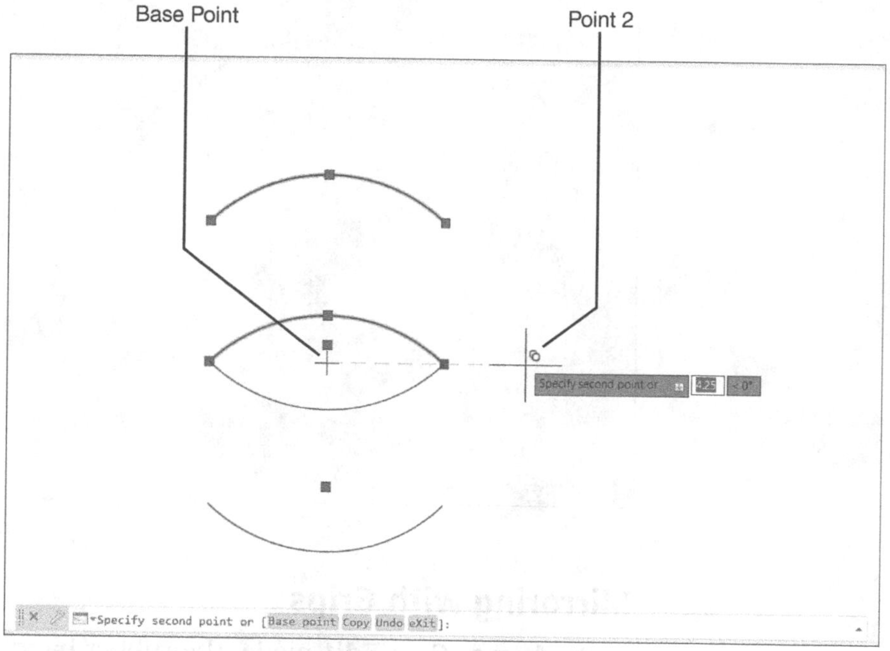

Figure 5-23
Mirroring with grips

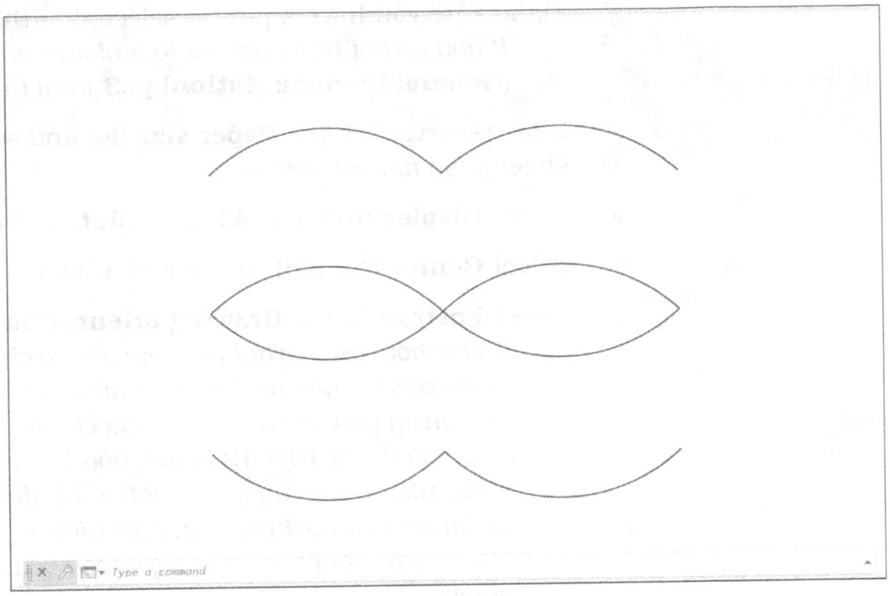

Figure 5-24
Completed mirror

Creating Page Setups

In this chapter, you move to another level in your exploration of AutoCAD plotting. Rather than confining yourself to plot configurations tied directly to objects visible in your model space drawing area, you continue to plot from model space but introduce the concept and technique of ***page setup***. With page setups, you can name and save different plot configurations so that one drawing can produce several different types of output. You define two simple page setups. You do not need to learn any new options, but you do learn to save settings of the options you have learned so far so that you can reuse them as part of a page setup.

page setup: A group of plot settings applied to a drawing or drawing layout that is named and saved. Page setups can be applied to drawings other than the one in which they are created.

✔ To begin the exercises in this section, you should be in a drawing with 18 × 12 limits.

You continue with the objects drawn in the "Creating Mirror Images of Objects" section.

The Page Setup Dialog Box

A page setup is nothing more than a group of plot settings, like the ones you have previously specified. The only difference is that you give the settings a name and save it to a list of setups. Once named, the plot settings can be restored by selecting the name, and they can even be exported to other drawings.

You can define a page setup from the **Plot** dialog box or **Page Setup** dialog box, accessible through the **Page Setup Manager**. There is little difference between the two methods. Here, you continue to use the **Plot** dialog box.

✔ Click the **Plot** tool from the **Quick Access** toolbar.

*You should now be in the **Plot** dialog box. You make a few changes to the settings and then give this page setup a name.*

You create a portrait setup and a landscape setup. Besides the difference in orientation, the only difference in settings between the two is that the portrait setup is centered, whereas the landscape setup is plotted from the origin.

- ✔ Make sure you have a plotter selected in the **Printer/plotter** list.
  If you do not have access to a plotter or printer, select **AutoCAD PDF (General Documentation).pc3** *from the list.*
- ✔ If necessary, click the **Paper size** list and select an A-size 8.50 × 11.00 sheet (also named Letter).
- ✔ Select **Display** from the **What to plot** list in the **Plot area** panel.
- ✔ Select **Center the plot** in the **Plot offset** panel.
- ✔ Select **Portrait** in the **Drawing orientation** panel.
  Notice how the partial preview image changes. Pause for a moment to make sure you understand why the preview looks this way. Assuming you are using the objects drawn in this chapter or another drawing using 18 × 12 limits, you have model space limits set to 18 × 12. You are plotting to an 8.5 × 11 sheet of paper. The 18 × 12 limits have been positioned in portrait orientation, placed across the effective area of the drawing sheet, scaled to fit, and centered on the paper.
  Now, you name this page setup.
- ✔ Click the **Add** button next to the **Name** list in the **Page setup** panel.
  This opens the ***Add Page Setup*** *dialog box shown in Figure 5-25.*
- ✔ Type **Portrait** as the page setup name.

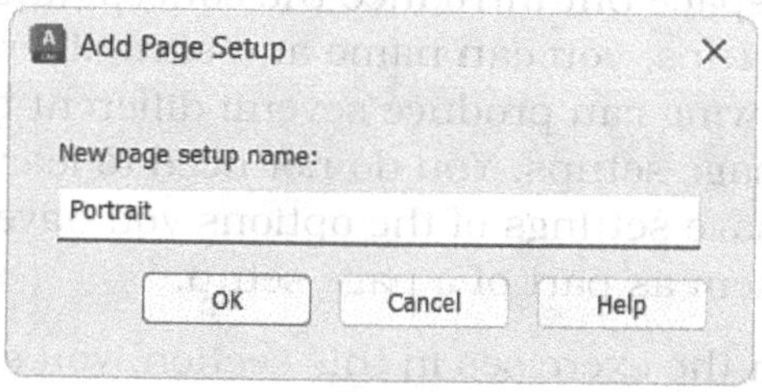

Figure 5-25
Add Page Setup dialog box

- ✔ Press **<Enter>** or click **OK**.
  This brings you back to the ***Plot*** *dialog box.* ***Portrait*** *is now entered in the* ***Name*** *list of the* ***Page setup*** *panel. That's all there is to it. The portrait page setup information is now part of the current drawing.*
  Next, you define a landscape page setup and add it to the list as well. This setup puts the drawing in landscape orientation and positions it from the origin rather than from the center.
- ✔ Select **Landscape** in the **Drawing orientation** panel.
  Notice that ***Portrait*** *is no longer in the* ***Name*** *list of the* ***Page setup*** *panel now that you have changed a setting.*
- ✔ Deselect **Center the plot**.
  The page's preview image stays in the portrait position even though the plot will be landscape. This is because the sheet size is 8.5 × 11. If you wanted to rotate this image to horizontal, you would need to select an 11 × 8.5 sheet. Now you have the 18 ×12 limits aligned with the left edge of the page, positioned at the origin of the printable area and scaled to fit. Give this setup a name.
- ✔ Click **Add** again from the **Page setup** panel.

NOTE

Once you have defined page setups, you can access them through the **Page Setup Manager**, displayed from the **Output** tab. This dialog box allows you to select page setups from a list. It will then take you to the **Page Setup** dialog box to modify existing page setups or create new ones. You also can import page setups from other drawings, as described in the next section.

✔ Type **Landscape** in the **Add Page Setup** box.

✔ Press **<Enter>** or click **OK**.

*Back in the **Plot** dialog box, you see that **Landscape** is now the current page setup. You should now restore the portrait settings.*

✔ Click the **Name** drop-down list in the **Page setup** panel and select **Portrait**.

*Your portrait settings, including the **Portrait** radio button and **Center the plot**, are restored.*

✔ Click the **Preview** button.

You should see a preview similar to Figure 5-26.

✔ Press **<Esc>** or **<Enter>** to return to the **Plot** dialog box.

✔ Click the **Name** drop-down list again and select **Landscape**.

Your landscape settings are restored.

✔ Click the **Preview** button.

You should see a preview similar to Figure 5-27. Notice that the paper image is turned to the landscape orientation in the full preview.

*Although this exercise was simple, keep in mind that everything from the sheet size to the plotter you are using and all the settings in the **Plot** or **Page Setup** dialog boxes can be included in a named page setup.*

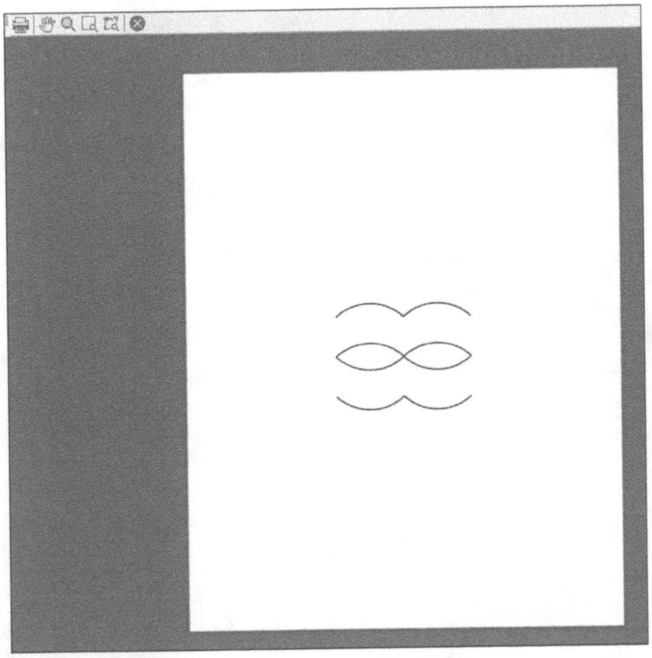

Figure 5-26
Plot preview in portrait orientation

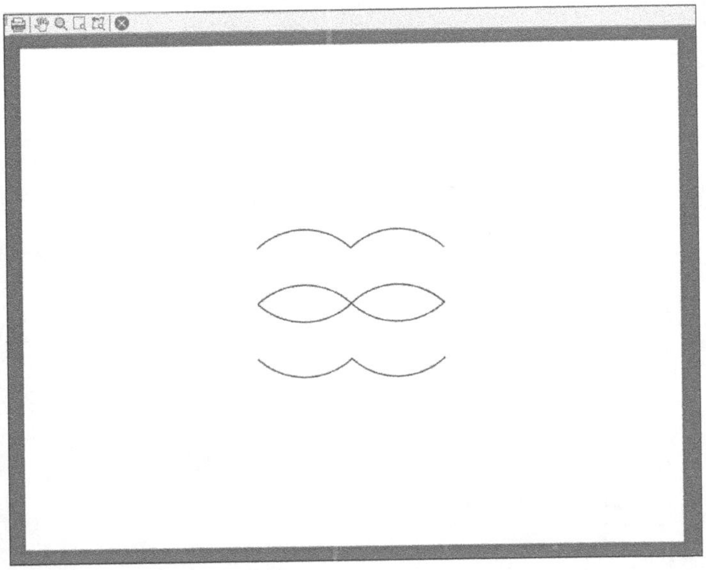

Figure 5-27
Plot preview in landscape orientation

> **NOTE**
>
> Page setups are defined in either model space or paper space as part of a layout. If you create a page setup in model space and then go into a paper space layout, you will not see it on your list. Also, if you define a page setup as part of a paper space layout, you will not see it if you begin a plot from model space.

✔ Press **<Esc>** to return to the **Plot** dialog box.

✔ You can click **OK** to plot the drawing or **Cancel** to exit the dialog box. *Either way your page setups will be saved.*

Importing Page Setups

A powerful feature of page setups is that they can be exchanged among drawings using the **PSETUPIN** command. This allows you to import page setups from a known drawing into the current drawing. The procedure is as follows:

6. From a drawing into which you would like to import a page setup, click **Output** > **Plot** > **Page Setup Manager**.
7. In the **Page Setup Manager**, click the **Import** button.
8. In the **Select Page Setup From File** dialog box, navigate to the drawing file from which you would like to import a page setup and select it.
9. In the **Import Page Setup** dialog box, select the name of the page setup you want to import and click **OK**.
10. Display the **Plot** or **Page Setup** dialog box and click the **Name** list in the **Page setup** panel. The imported page setup should be there.

5 chapter five

Chapter Summary

In this chapter, you learned more about drawing and editing objects based on circles and circular frames. You can now create polar arrays of objects copied around an imaginary arc or circle. You learned how to draw arcs, using 11 combinations of three essential types of information. Once drawn, any object may be rotated, or you can create rotated copies and place them at regular angles using polar tracking. You also learned how to create mirror images of drawn objects. Finally, you began to use page setups so that the work you do in defining plot settings can be named, saved, and used again for other drawings.

Chapter Test Questions

Multiple Choice

Circle the correct answer.

1. Which of these is **not** required to define a polar array?

a. Number of items
b. Start point
c. Angle between items
d. Angle to fill

2. Which of the following is always specified in defining an arc?

a. Arc length
b. Length of chord
c. Center point
d. Start point

3. You are rotating an object from its current position at 45° to a new position at 30° using the **Reference** option. The reference angle will be

a. 30°
b. 45°
c. 15°
d. 75°

4. The **Continue** option will begin an arc

a. At the endpoint of the last arc drawn
b. Perpendicular to the last arc drawn
c. Tangent to the last arc drawn
d. At the start point of the last arc drawn

5. Polar tracking can be set to track

a. At any angle
b. At 30°
c. At orthogonal angles only
d. At 90°

Matching

Write the number of the correct answer on the line.

a. Base point ______	1. Plot
b. Mirror line ______	2. **ARC**
c. Angle between items ______	3. **ARRAYPOLAR**
d. Start point ______	4. **ROTATE**
e. Page setup ______	5. **MIRROR**

True or False

Circle the correct answer.

1. **True or False:** It is not possible to plot a landscape-oriented plot on a printer.
2. **True or False:** AutoCAD will not send a plot to a printer or plotter if the drawing limits exceed the sheet size.
3. **True or False:** Polar arrays can be defined around circles or arcs.
4. **True or False:** In order to define an arc, you must first specify a start point.
5. **True or False:** In defining an arc, the rubber band indicates the end-point.

Questions

1. What factors define a polar array? How many are needed to define an array?
2. What factors define an arc? How many are needed for any single method?
3. How would you use the **Reference** option to rotate a line from 60° to 90°? How would you accomplish the same rotation without using a reference?
4. What is the purpose of the **Base Point** option in the **Rotate Grip Edit** mode?
5. What would happen if a drawing created with 18 × 12 limits were printed with a 1:1 scale on an A-size printer? What feature of the **Plot Setup** or **Page Setup** dialog box would you use to find out if you weren't sure?

Drawing Problems

1. Draw an arc starting at **(10,6)** and passing through **(12,6.5)** and **(14,6)**.
2. Create a mirrored copy of the arc across the horizontal line passing through **(10,6)**.
3. Rotate the pair of arcs from Step 2 **45°** around the point **(9,6)**.
4. Create a mirrored copy of the pair of arcs mirrored across a vertical line passing through **(9,6)**.
5. Create mirrored copies of both pairs of arcs mirrored across a horizontal line passing through **(9,6)**.
6. Erase any three of the four pairs of arcs in your drawing and re-create them using a polar array.

chapter five

Chapter Drawing Projects

A Drawing 5-1: *Hearth* [BASIC]

Once you have completed this architectural drawing as it is shown, you might want to experiment with filling in a pattern of firebrick in the center of the hearth. The drawing itself is not complicated, but little errors become very noticeable when you try to make the row of 4 × 8 bricks across the bottom fit with the arc of bricks across the top, so work carefully.

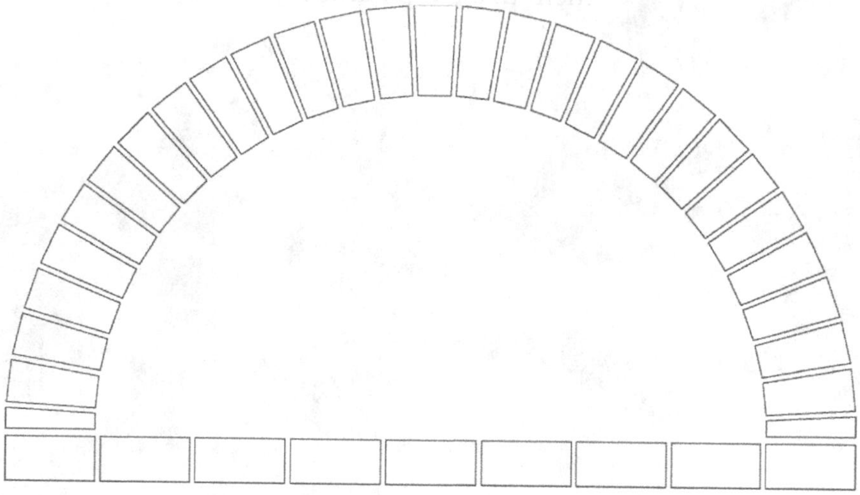

Drawing Suggestions

UNITS = Architectural

PRECISION = 0'–0 1/8"

LIMITS = (0,0) (12',9')

GRID = 1'

SNAP = 1/8'

- Zoom in to draw the wedge-shaped brick indicated by the arrow on the right of the dimensioned drawing. Draw half of the brick only and mirror it across the centerline as shown. (Notice that the centerline is for reference only.) It is very important that you use **MIRROR** so that you can erase half of the brick later.
- Array the brick in a 29-item, 180° polar array.
- Erase the bottom halves of the end bricks at each end.
- Draw a new horizontal bottom line on each of the two end bricks.
- Draw a 4 × 8 brick directly below the half brick at the left end.
- Array the 4 × 8 brick in a one-row, nine-column array, with 8.5" between columns.

Drawing 5-1
Hearth

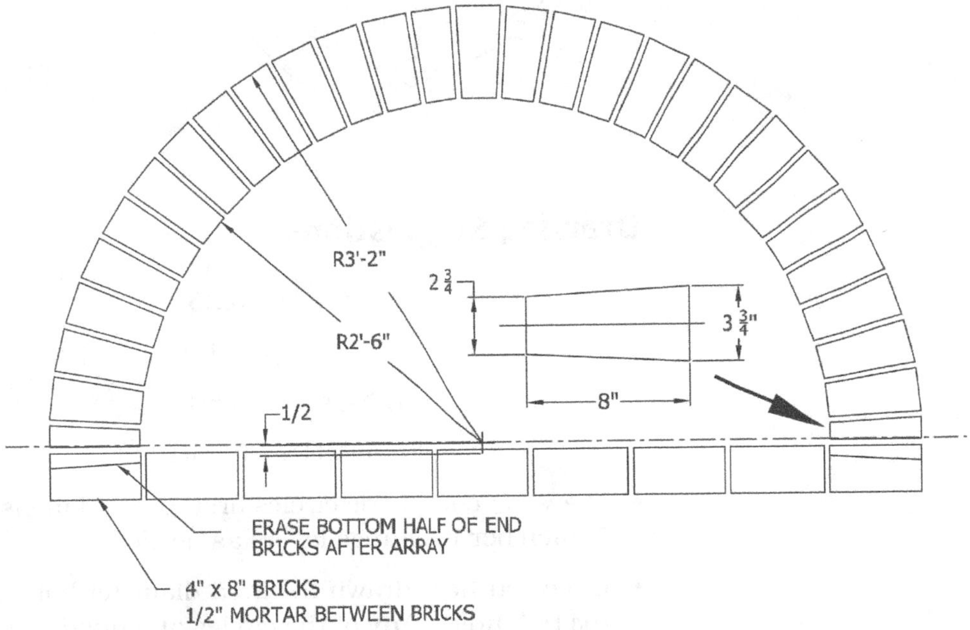

M Drawing 5-2: *Flanged Bushing* [INTERMEDIATE]

This drawing makes use of a polar array to draw eight screw holes in a circle. It also reviews the use of layers and linetypes.

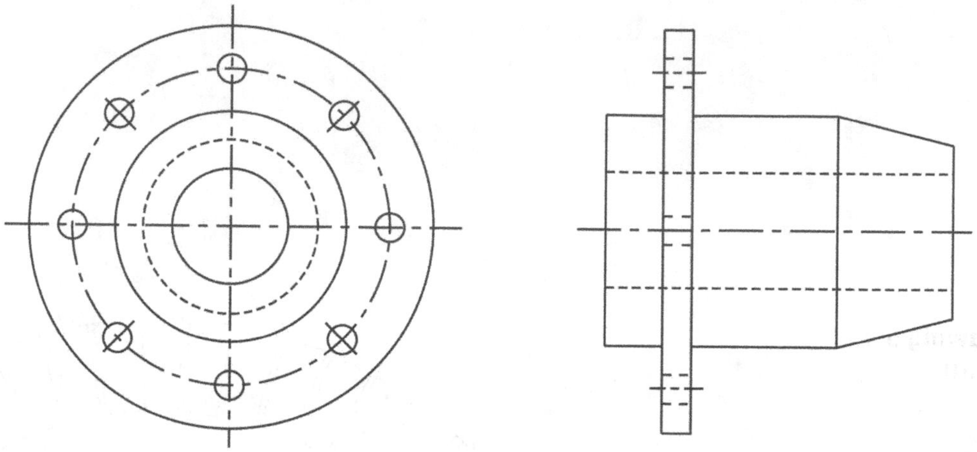

Drawing Suggestions

GRID = 0.25

SNAP = 0.125

LTSCALE = 0.50

LIMITS = (0,0)(12,9)

- Draw the concentric circles first, using dimensions from both views. Remember to change layers as needed.
- Once you have drawn the 2.75-diameter bolt circle, use it to locate one of the bolt holes. Any of the circles at a quadrant point (0°, 90°, 180°, or 270°) will do.
- Draw a centerline across the bolt hole, and then array the hole and centerline 360°. Be sure to rotate the objects as they are copied; otherwise, you will get strange results from your centerlines.

Drawing 5-2
Flanged Bushing

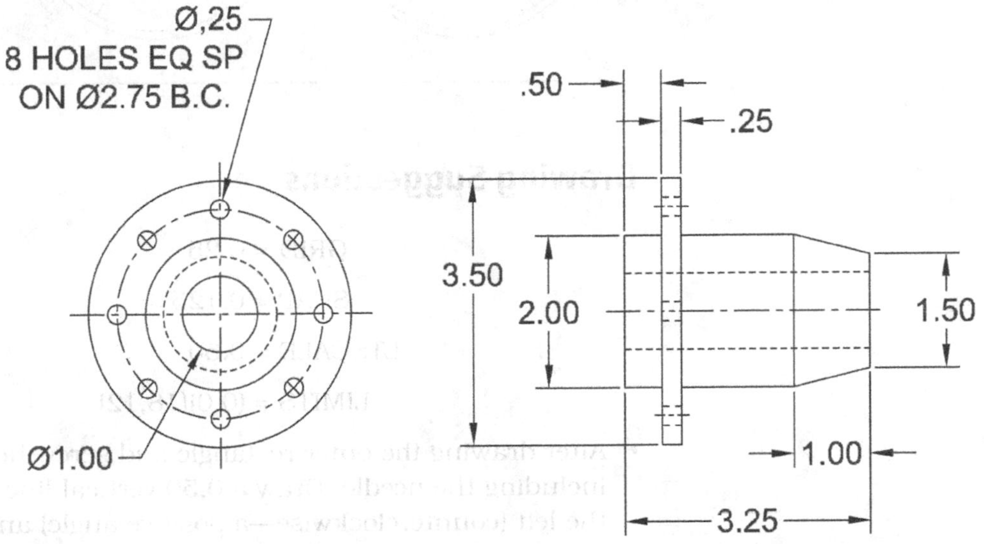

M

Drawing 5-3: *Dials* [INTERMEDIATE]

This is a relatively simple drawing that gives you some good practice with polar arrays and the **ROTATE** and **COPY** commands. Notice that the needle drawn at the top of the next page is for reference only; the actual drawing includes only the plate and the three dials with their needles.

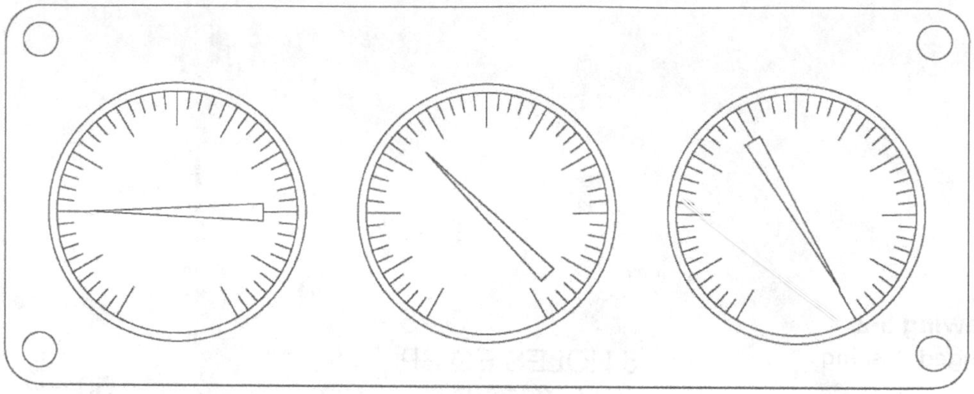

Drawing Suggestions

GRID = 0.25

SNAP = 0.125

LTSCALE = 0.50

LIMITS = (0,0)(18,12)

- After drawing the outer rectangle and screw holes, draw the leftmost dial, including the needle. Draw a 0.50 vertical line at the top and array it to the left (counterclockwise—a positive angle) and to the right (negative) to create the 11 larger lines on the dial. How many lines in each of these left and right arrays do you need to end up with 11?
- Draw a 0.25 line on top of the 0.50 line at the top of the dial. Then, use right and left arrays with a **Last** selection to create the 40 small markings. How many lines are in each of these two arrays?
- Complete the first dial, and then use a multiple copy to produce two more dials at the center and right in the drawing area. Be sure to use a window to select the entire dial.
- Finally, use the **ROTATE** command to rotate the needles as indicated on the new dials.

Drawing 5-3
Dials

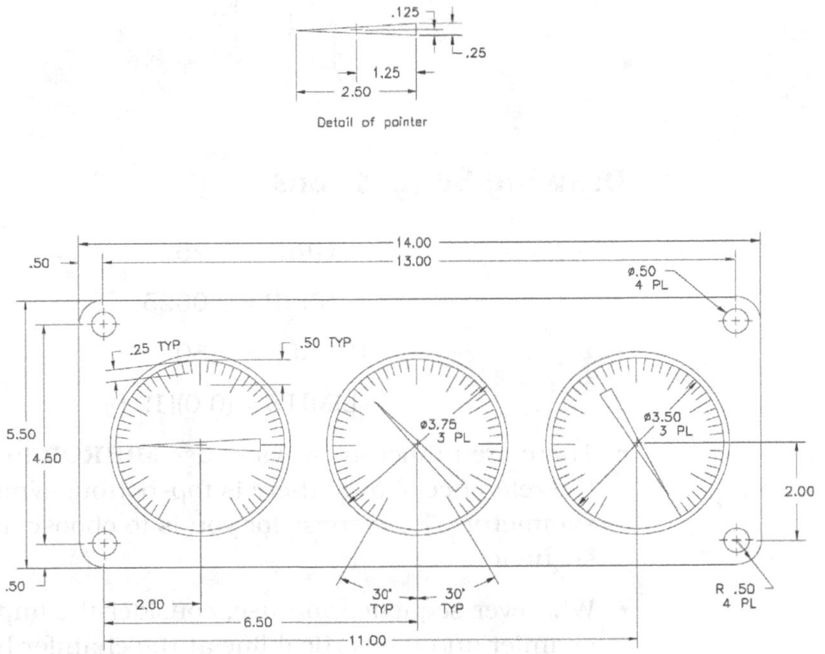

M

Drawing 5-4: *Alignment Wheel* [INTERMEDIATE]

This drawing shows a typical use of the **MIRROR** command. Carefully mirroring sides of the symmetrical front view saves you from duplicating some of your drawing efforts.

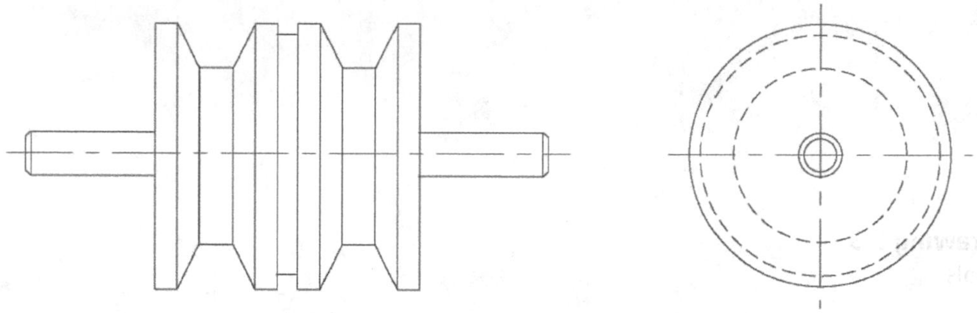

Drawing Suggestions

GRID = 0.25

SNAP = 0.0625

LTSCALE = 0.50

LIMITS = (0,0)(12,9)

- There are numerous ways to use **MIRROR** in drawing the front view. As the reference shows, there is top–bottom symmetry as well as left–right symmetry. The exercise for you is to choose an efficient mirroring sequence.
- Whatever sequence you use, consider the importance of creating the chamfer and the vertical line at the chamfer before mirroring this part of the object.
- Be careful when drawing the vertical line representing the vertical display of the chamfer. Though the chamfer may appear to fall on a snap point, it does not. Zoom in to check this out. Consider using the **Endpoint object** snap to locate the ends of the chamfer.
- Once the front view is drawn, the right-side view is easy. Remember to change layers for center and hidden lines and to line up the small inner circle with the chamfer.

Drawing 5-4
Alignment Wheel

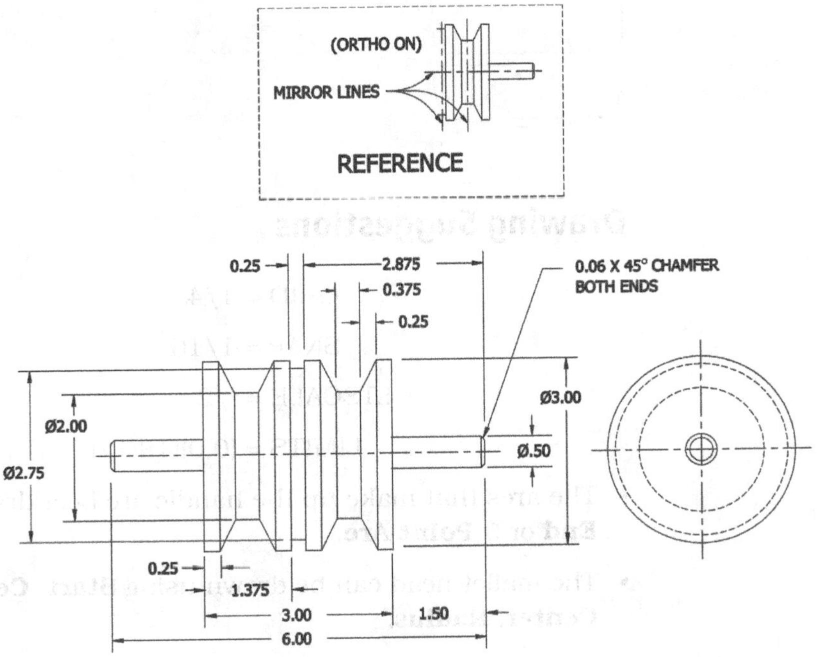

M Drawing 5-5: *Mallet* [ADVANCED]

There are many arcs in this drawing, all of which can be created using the 3-Point technique of the **ARC** command. Look at the overall design of the mallet and find ways to use the **MIRROR** command as well.

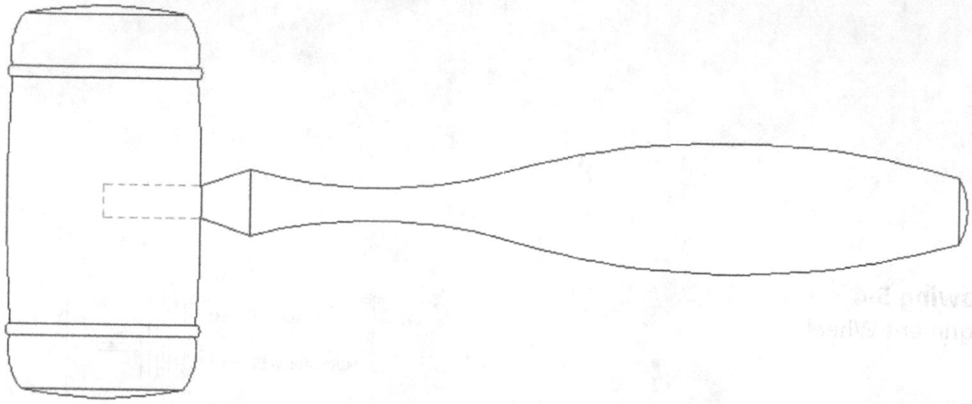

Drawing Suggestions

GRID = 1/4

SNAP = 1/16

LTSCALE =1/2

LIMITS = (0,0)(18,12)

- The arcs that make up the handle are best drawn using **Start**, **Center**, **End** or **3-Point Arc**.
- The mallet head can be drawn using **Start**, **Center**, **End** and **Start**, **Center**, **Radius**.

Drawing 5-5
Mallet

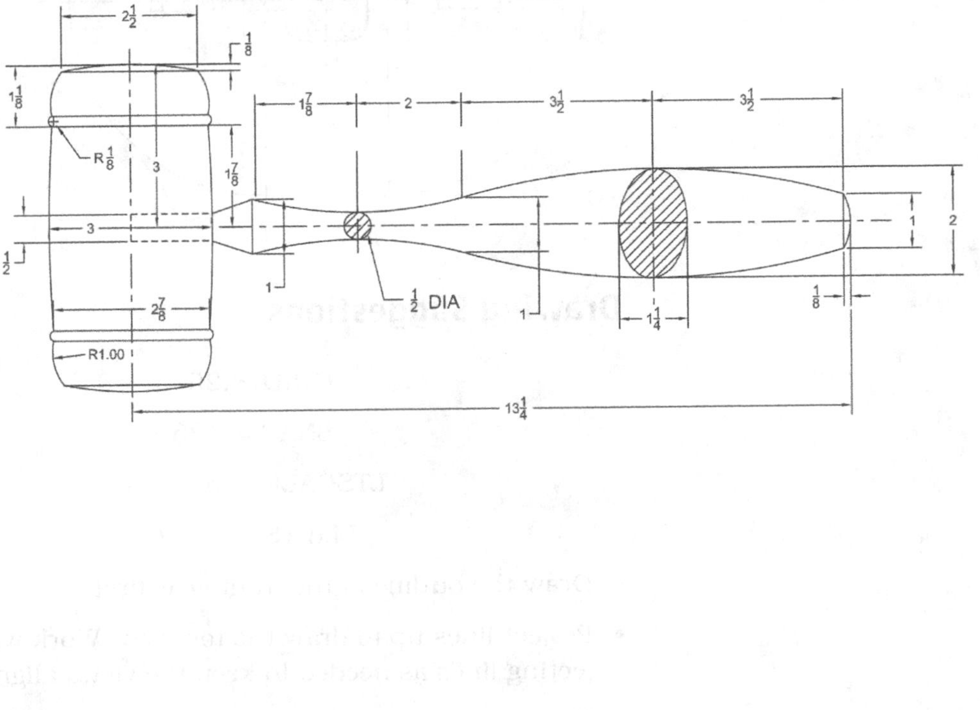

M Drawing 5-6: *Index Guide* [ADVANCED]

This drawing will give you additional practice drawing polar arrays and arcs and working with two views of an object.

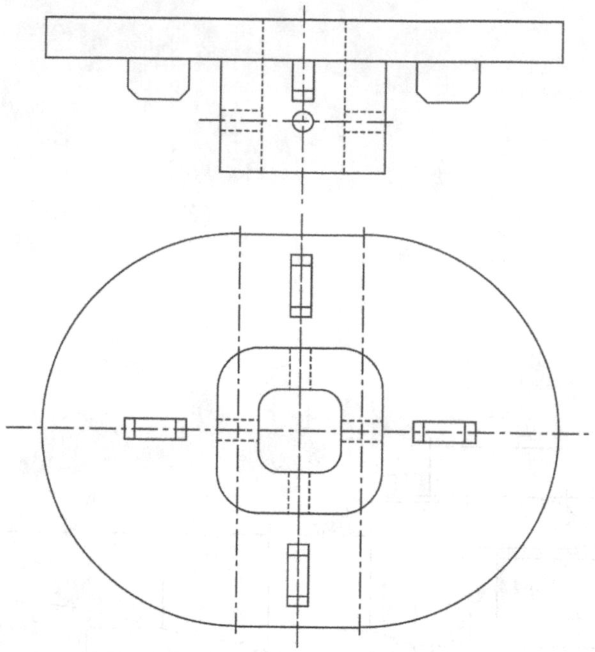

Drawing Suggestions

GRID = .25

SNAP = .125

LTSCALE = .5

LIMITS = 18,12

- Draw the outline of the front view first.
- Project lines up to draw the top view. Work with both views together, projecting lines as needed to keep the views aligned.
- Draw the arc on the right using **Start**, **End**, **Radius**.
- Draw the 1.50-unit lines. Then draw the arc on the left.
- At the center of the object, draw the inner and outer squares, using the **RECTANG** command. Chamfer them using the **Polyline** option.
- Draw the small rectangular tabs in the top view; then chamfer and project lines into the front view.
- After completing the rectangular tabs in the front view, create a polar array.
- Draw all hidden lines as shown. Explore ways to use another polar array.

Drawing 5-6
Index Guide

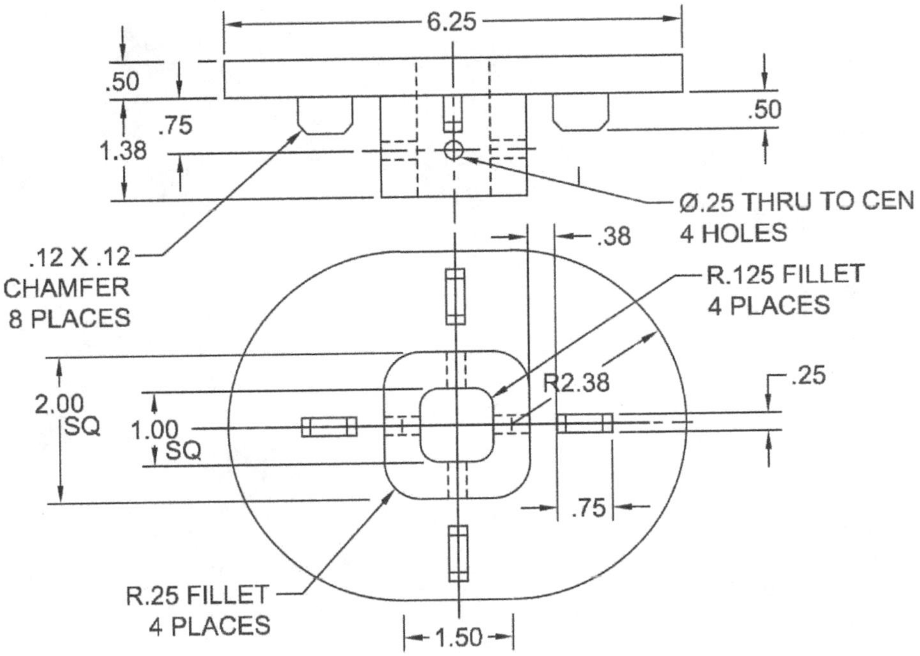

6 chapter six

Object Snaps and Resized Objects

CHAPTER OBJECTIVES

- Select points with object snap (single-point override)
- Select points with running object snap
- Use object snap tracking
- Use the **OFFSET** command (create parallel objects with **OFFSET**)
- Shorten objects with the **TRIM** command
- Extend objects with the **EXTEND** command
- Use the **STRETCH** command to alter objects connected to other objects
- Measure distances and calculate areas with the **MEASUREGEOM** command
- Create plot layouts

Introduction

In this chapter, you learn about AutoCAD's very powerful object snap and object tracking features. These take you to a new level of accuracy and efficiency as a CAD operator. You also learn to shorten objects at intersections with other objects using the **TRIM** command or to lengthen them with the **EXTEND** command. You use the **STRETCH** command, which lengthens some objects and shortens others, allowing you, for example, to move windows within walls. After learning to shorten and lengthen objects, you use the **MEASUREGEOM** command to get the distance or area of drawn objects. Finally, you move into the world of paper space as you begin to use AutoCAD's layout and multiple viewport system.

Selecting Points with Object Snap (Single-Point Override)

In this section, you learn to use the single-point override procedure. In the next section, you move onto the use of running object snaps.

> **TIP**
>
> The following is a general procedure for using single-point object snap:
>
> 1. Enter a drawing command, such as **LINE**, **CIRCLE**, or **ARC**.
> 2. Right-click while holding down the **<Shift>** or **<Ctrl>** key.
> 3. Select an object snap mode from the shortcut menu.
> 4. Move your cursor over a previously drawn object.

✔ To prepare for this exercise, begin a new drawing using a template with B-size (18 × 12) limits. You can use the 1B template if you have it.

✔ Turn the grid on or off. The figures in this drawing show the grid off for clarity.

✔ Draw a 6 × 6 square with a 1.50-radius circle centered inside, as in Figure 6-1.

To keep the circle centered, draw the square with the ***RECTANG*** *command with corners at (6,3) and (12,9). Then, center the circle at (9,6).*

✔ The **Polar Tracking**, **Object Snap**, and **Snap Mode** buttons should be off for the rest of this exercise.

✔ Enter the **LINE** command.

Next, you draw a line from the lower-left corner of the square to a point on a line tangent to the circle, as shown in Figure 6-2. The corner is easy to locate because you have drawn it on a snap point, but the tangent will not be.

Figure 6-1
Square and circle

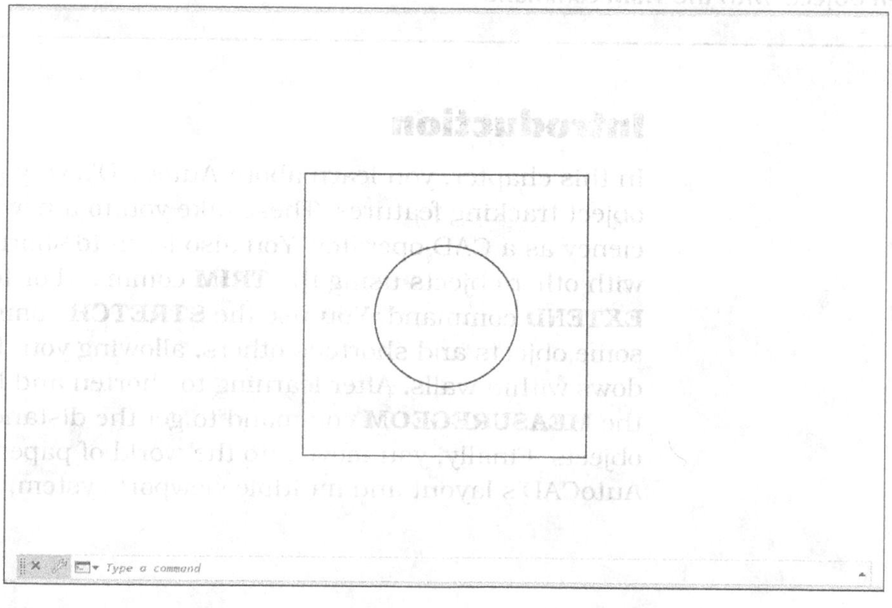

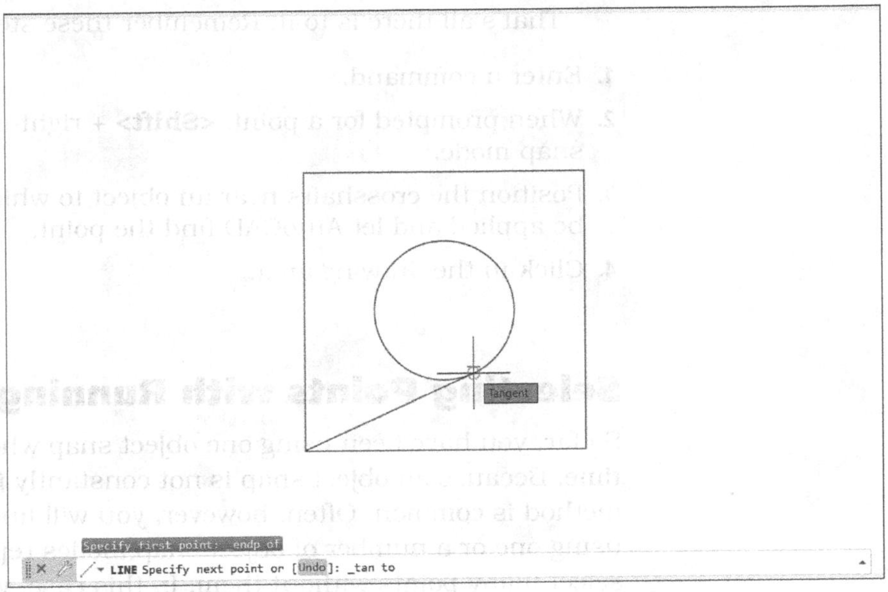

Figure 6-2
Endpoint and **Tangent** object snaps

You use the **Endpoint** object snap to locate the corner of the square and the **Tangent** object snap to locate the tangent point on the circle.

- ✔ At the **Specify first point** prompt, instead of specifying a point, hold down the **<Shift>** or **<Ctrl>** key and right-click.

  *This opens the **Object Snap** shortcut menu.*

- ✔ Select **Endpoint.**
- ✔ Move the cursor near the lower-left corner of the square.

  *The **Endpoint** object snap marker appears as a green box surrounding the endpoint.*

- ✔ With the **Endpoint** object snap marker showing, click in the drawing area.

  *The green endpoint box and the snap-tip disappear, and there is a rubber band stretching from the lower-left corner of the square to the crosshairs position. In the command line, you see the **Specify next point** prompt.*

  *You use a **Tangent** object snap to select the second point.*

- ✔ At the **Specify next point or [Undo]** prompt, **<Shift>** + right-click and select **Tangent.**
- ✔ Move the cursor to the right and position the crosshairs so that they are near the lower-right side of the circle.

  When you approach the tangent area, you see the green tangent object snap marker.

- ✔ With the tangent marker showing, click in the drawing area.

  AutoCAD locates the tangent point and draws the line.

- ✔ Press **<Enter>** to exit the **LINE** command.

  Your drawing should now resemble Figure 6-2.

That's all there is to it. Remember these steps:

1. Enter a command.
2. When prompted for a point, **<Shift>** + right-click and select an object snap mode.
3. Position the crosshairs near an object to which the object snap mode can be applied and let AutoCAD find the point.
4. Click in the drawing area.

Selecting Points with Running Object Snaps

So far, you have been using one object snap when specifying one point at a time. Because an object snap is not constantly in use, this single-point method is common. Often, however, you will find that you are going to be using one or a number of object snap modes repeatedly and do not need to select many points without them. In this case, you can keep object snap modes on so that they affect all points specified. This is called *running object snaps*. You use this method to complete the drawing shown in Figure 6-3. Notice how each line is drawn from a midpoint or corner to a tangent point on the circle. This is easily done with running object snaps.

> **TIP**
>
> The following is a general procedure for using running object snap:
>
> 1. Click the **Object Snap** button on the status bar so that it is on.
> 2. Right-click the **Object Snap** button, and select **Object Snap Settings** to open the **Drafting Settings** dialog box.
> 3. Select object snap modes on the **Object Snap** tab from the **Drafting Settings** dialog box.
> 4. Enter drawing commands.
> 5. If there is more than one object snap choice in the area, cycle through them using the **<Tab>** key.

✔ Click the **Object Snap** button on the status bar to enable it.

*When the button is blue, you are using running object snaps. The modes that are in effect depend on the AutoCAD default settings, or whatever settings were last selected. To change settings or to see what settings are on, you open the **Drafting Settings** dialog box.*

✔ Right-click over the **Object Snap** button on the status bar.

*The shortcut menu shown in Figure 6-4 opens. The object snap icons and names here allow you to turn object snap modes on and off without opening the **Drafting Settings** dialog box. For this exercise, though, you use the dialog box instead.*

Figure 6-3
Running Object Snap mode

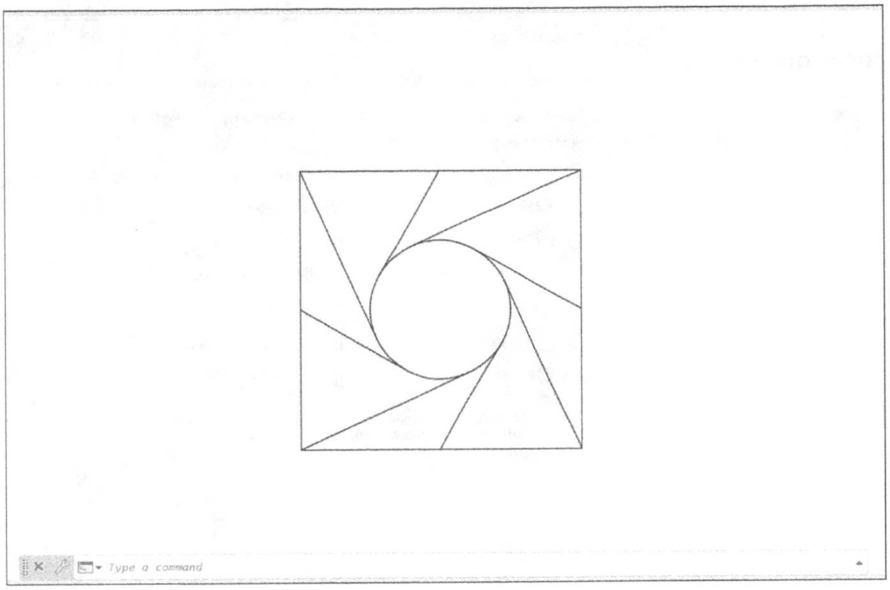

Figure 6-4
Object Snap shortcut menu

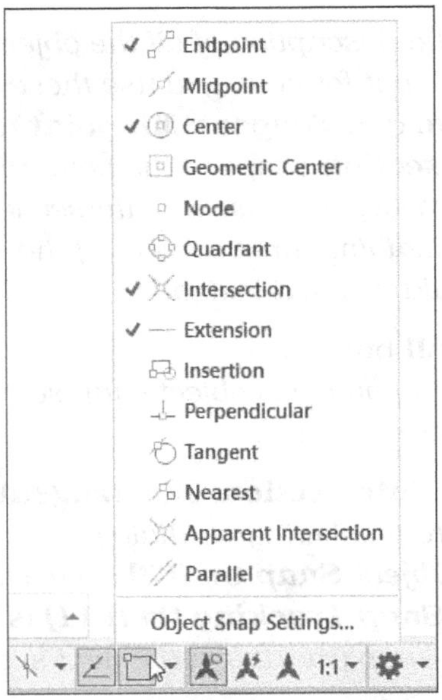

> **TIP**
>
> Once you have specified object snap modes, you can turn individual object snap modes on or off by right-clicking the **Object Snap** button on the status bar and selecting an object snap mode from the shortcut menu shown in Figure 6-4.

✔ Select **Object Snap Settings** from the bottom of the shortcut menu.

*This executes the **OSNAP** command and opens the **Drafting Settings** dialog box with the **Object Snap** tab selected, as shown in Figure 6-5.*

Figure 6-5
Drafting Settings dialog box

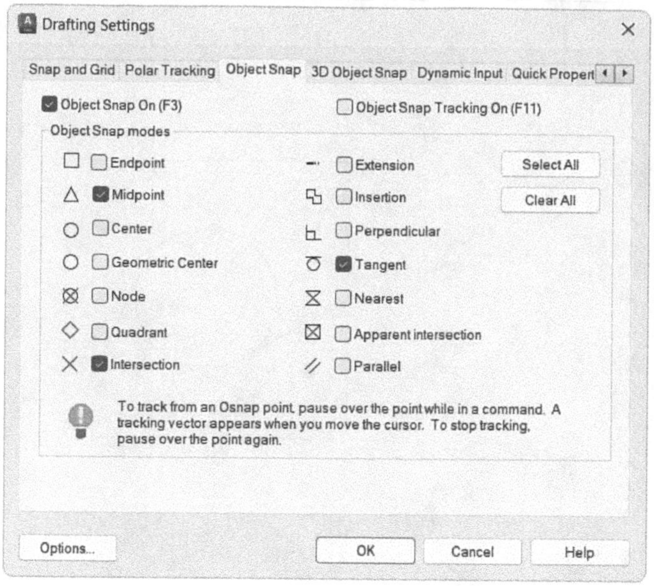

You can find a description of all the object snap modes on the chart in Figure 6-6, but for now, you use these three: ***Midpoint***, ***Intersection***, *and* ***Tangent***. ***Midpoint*** *and* ***Tangent*** *you already know.* ***Intersection*** *snaps to the point where two entities meet or cross. For practice, you use an intersection instead of an endpoint to select the remaining three corners of the square, even though an endpoint could be used instead.*

✔ Click the **Clear All** button.

This clears any previous object snap selections that may have been made on your system.

✔ Select **Midpoint**, **Intersection**, and **Tangent**.

When you are finished, your dialog box should resemble Figure 6-5. Notice that ***Object Snap On (F3)*** *is checked at the top of the box, and* ***Object Snap Tracking On (F11)*** *is not checked. You learn about object snap tracking in the next section.*

✔ Click the **OK** button.

✔ Enter the **LINE** command.

✔ Position the crosshairs along the bottom line of the square.

A green triangle—the midpoint object snap marker—appears.

✔ With the midpoint marker showing, click in the drawing area.

AutoCAD selects the midpoint of the line and gives you the rubber band and the prompt for the next point.

✔ Move the crosshairs up and along the lower-right side of the circle until the tangent object snap marker appears.

✔ With the tangent marker showing, click in the drawing area.

AutoCAD constructs a new tangent from the midpoint to the circle.

Figure 6-6
Object Snap options

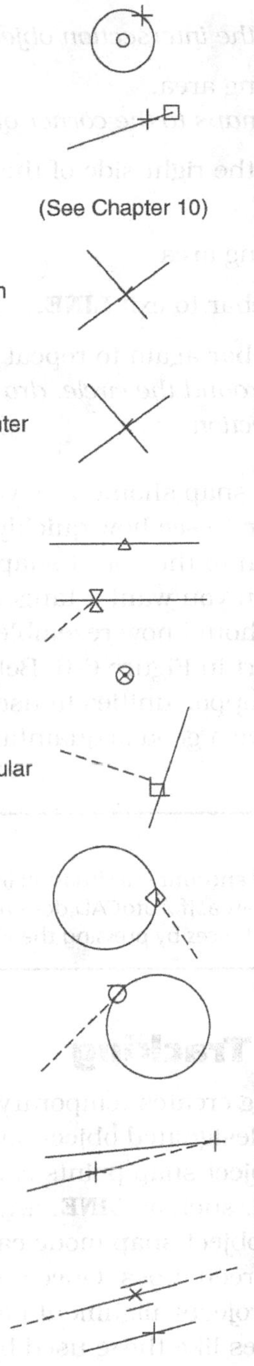

TYPE	APPEARANCE	DESCRIPTION
CENter		Snaps to the center of an arc, circle, ellipse, or elliptical arc.
ENDpoint		Snaps to the closest endpoint of an arc, elliptical arc, line, mline, polyline, ray, or to the closest corner of a trace, solid, or 3D face.
INSertion	(See Chapter 10)	Snaps to the insertion point of a block, attribute, shape, or text.
INTersection		Snaps to crossing or meeting point of arcs, lines, circles, ellipses, elliptical arcs, mlines, polylines, rays, splines, or xlines.
APParent Inter		Snaps to apparent crossing or meeting point of arcs, lines, circles, ellipses, elliptical arcs, mlines, polylines, rays, splines, or xlines. If apparent intersection and intersection are on at the same time, varying results may occur.
MIDpoint		Snaps to the midpoint of an arc, circle, ellipse, elliptical arc, line, mline, polyline, solid, spline, or xline.
NEArest		Snaps to the nearest point on an arc, circle, ellipse, elliptical arc, line, mline point, polyline, spline, or xline.
NODe		Snaps to a point object.
PERpendicular		Snaps to a point on an arc, circle, ellipse, elliptical arc, line, mline, ray, solid, spline, or xline.
QUAdrant		Snaps to nearest quadrant point of an arc, circle, ellipse, or elliptical arc. 0, 90, 180, or 270 degrees
TANgent		Snaps to the tangent of an arc, circle, ellipse, or elliptical arc.
EXTension		Snaps to the extension point of an object. Establish an extension path by moving the cursor over the endpoint of an object. A marker is placed on the endpoint. While the endpoint is marked, the cursor snaps to the extension path of the endpoint.
PARallel		Snaps to extension parallel with an object. When the cursor is moved over the endpoint of an object, the endpoint is marked and the cursor snaps to the parallel alignment path to that object. The alignment path is calculated from the current "from point" of the command.

✔ Press the spacebar to complete the **LINE** command.

✔ Press the spacebar again to repeat **LINE** so you can begin with a new start point.

You continue to move counterclockwise around the circle. This should begin to be easy now. There are four steps.

1. *Repeat the command.*
2. *Specify a midpoint or corner intersection on the square.*
3. *Specify a tangent point on the circle.*
4. *End the command.*

- ✔ Position the crosshairs so that the bottom-right corner of the square is within the box.
  A green X, the intersection object snap marker, appears.
- ✔ Click the drawing area.
  AutoCAD snaps to the corner of the square.
- ✔ Move up along the right side of the circle so that the tangent marker appears.
- ✔ Click the drawing area.
- ✔ Press the spacebar to exit **LINE**.
- ✔ Press the spacebar again to repeat **LINE**.
  Continue around the circle, drawing tangents from each midpoint and intersection.

Running object snap should give you both speed and accuracy, so push yourself a little to see how quickly you can complete the figure. Be sure to pay attention to the object snap markers so that you do not select an intersection when you want a tangent, for example.

Your drawing should now resemble Figure 6-3. Before going on, study the object snap chart in Figure 6-6. Before you can effectively analyze situations and look for opportunities to use object snaps and object snap tracking, you need to have a good acquaintance with all the object snap modes.

> **TIP**
>
> Occasionally, you may encounter a situation in which there are several possible object snap points in a tight area. If AutoCAD does not recognize the one you want, you can cycle through all the choices by pressing the <Tab> key repeatedly.

Object Snap Tracking

alignment path: A dotted line used as a visual and snap aid, constructed through an acquired object snap point and extending to the edge of the display horizontally or vertically.

acquired point: An object snap point identified and highlighted in object snap tracking mode.

Object snap tracking creates temporary construction lines, called ***alignment paths***, from designated object snap points. Alignment paths are constructed through object snap points called ***acquired points***. Once you are in a draw command, such as **LINE**, any object snap point that can be identified by a running object snap mode can be acquired. An acquired point is highlighted with a green cross. Once a point is acquired, object snap tracking automatically projects alignment path lines from this point. Alignment paths are dotted lines like those used by polar tracking. They are visual snap aids that extend to the edge of the display horizontally and vertically from the acquired point. They will also pick up specified polar tracking angles. Try the following:

To begin this exercise, running object snap mode should be on with **Endpoint** in effect; all other object snaps from the last exercise should be turned off.

NOTE

Remember the following steps:

1. Right-click the **Object Snap** button on the status bar.
2. Select **Object Snap Settings**.
3. Click **Clear All** in the dialog box.
4. Check **Endpoint**.
5. Click **OK**.

✔ Click the **Dynamic Input** button to turn dynamic input off.
This is technically not necessary, but you will be able to see other things happening more easily with the dynamic input display turned off.

✔ Click the **Object Snap Tracking** button (next to the **Object Snap** button) on the status bar so that it is on.

✔ Enter the **LINE** command.

✔ Select a first point to the left of the square and circle, as shown by point 1 in Figure 6-7.

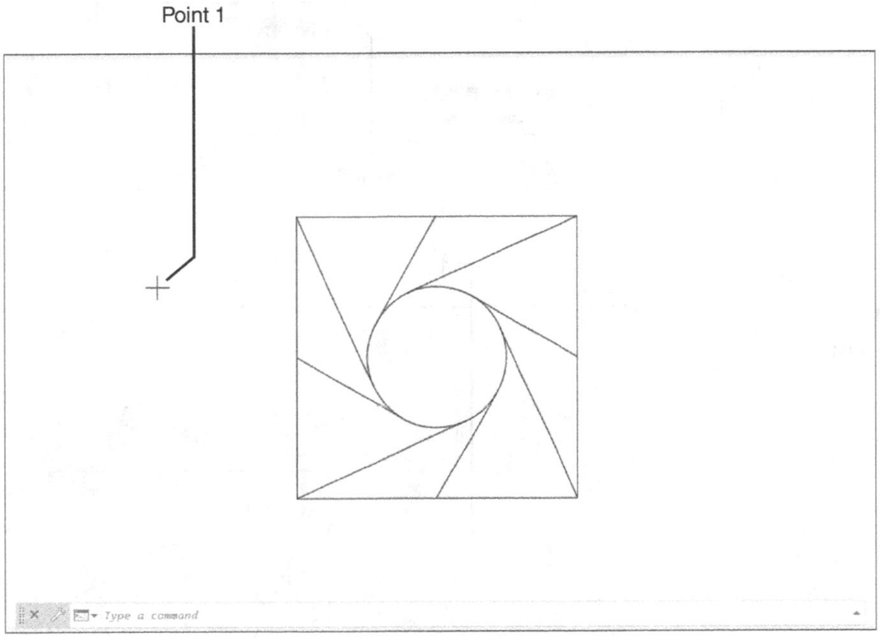

Figure 6-7
Selecting point 1

Point Acquisition

point acquisition: The process by which object snap points are acquired for use in object snap tracking. An acquired point is marked by a small green cross.

To take the next step, you need to learn a new technique called ***point acquisition***. Before a point can be used for object snap tracking, it must be acquired, which is a form of selection. To acquire a point, move the cursor over it so that the object snap marker appears, and pause for about a second without clicking. Try it with the following steps:

✔ Move the cursor over the lower-left corner of the square, point 2 in Figure 6-8, so that the endpoint object snap marker appears, but do not click to snap to the corner of the square.

✔ Pause.

✔ Now, move the cursor away from the corner.

If you have done this correctly, a small green cross appears at the corner intersection, as shown in Figure 6-9, indicating that this point has been acquired for object snap tracking. (Repeating this procedure over the same point removes the cross.)

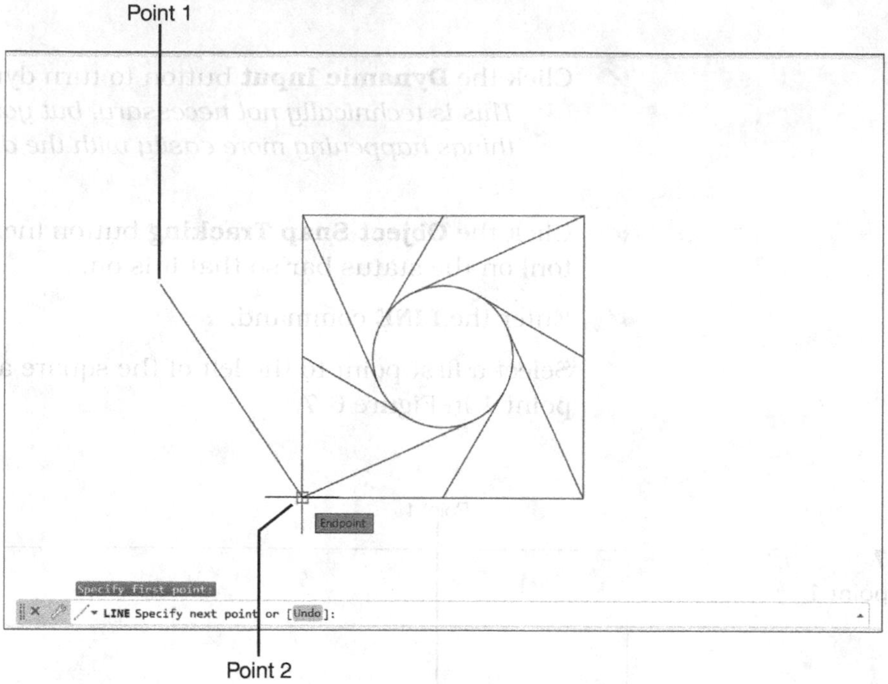

Figure 6-8
Endpoint marker

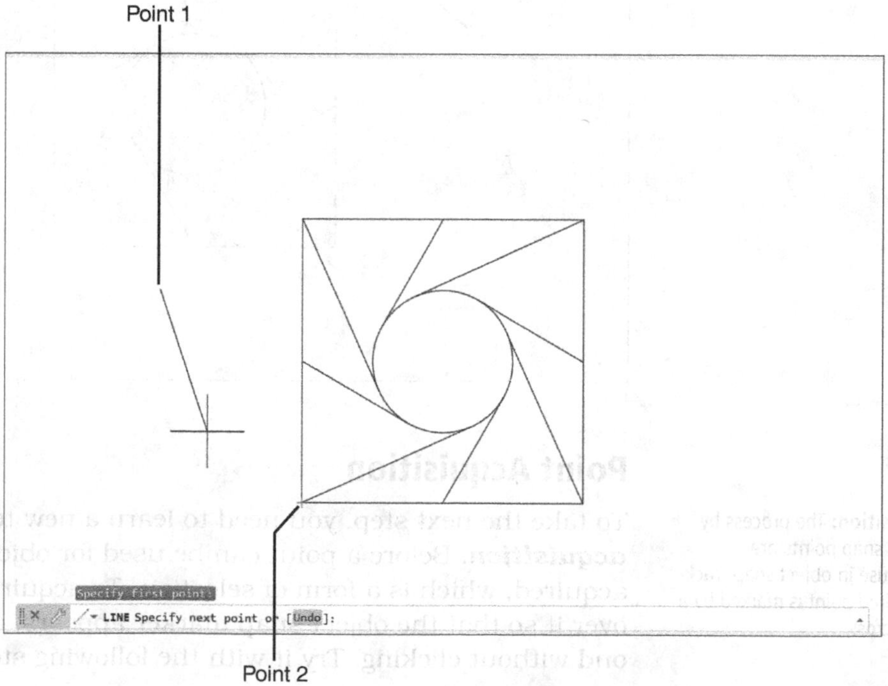

Figure 6-9
Acquired point

- ✔ Move the cursor to a position left of point 2 and even with the horizontal lower side of the square, as shown in Figure 6-10.

  You see a horizontal alignment path and a tracking tip like those shown in Figure 6-10.

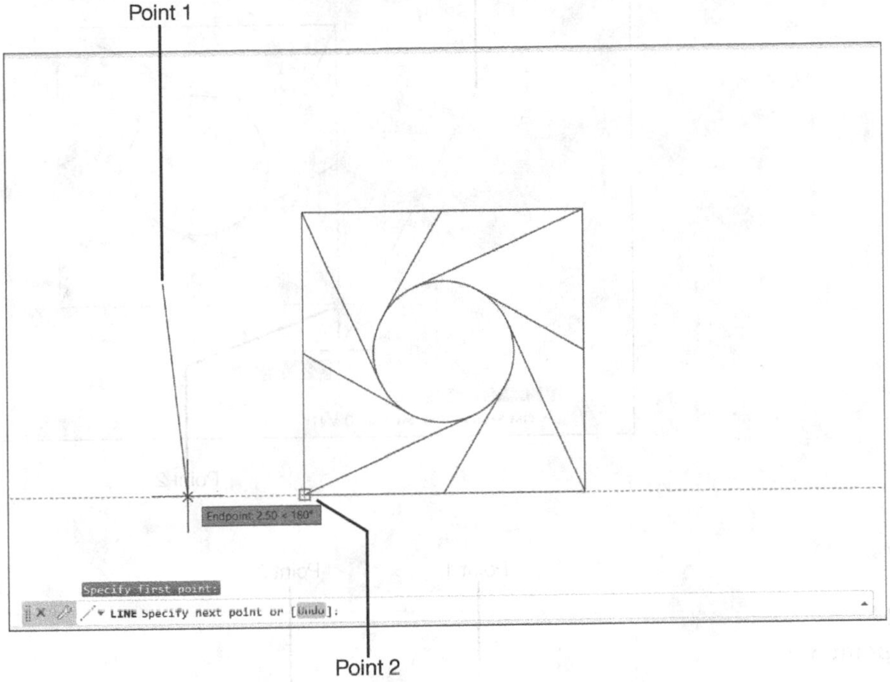

Figure 6-10
Horizontal alignment path and tracking tip

- ✔ Move the cursor over and down to a position even with and below the vertical left side of the square, as shown in Figure 6-11.

  You see a vertical alignment path and tracking tip like those shown in Figure 6-11.

  These paths are interesting, but they do not accomplish a great deal because your square is constructed on grid snap points anyway. Let's try something more difficult and a lot more interesting. Here, you use two acquired points to locate a point that currently is not specifiable in either object snap or incremental snap.

- ✔ Move the cursor up and acquire point 3, as shown in Figure 6-12.

  Point 3 is the lower endpoint of the line previously drawn from the midpoint of the top side of the square to a point tangent to the circle. You should now have two acquired points with two green crosses showing: one at point 2 and one at point 3.

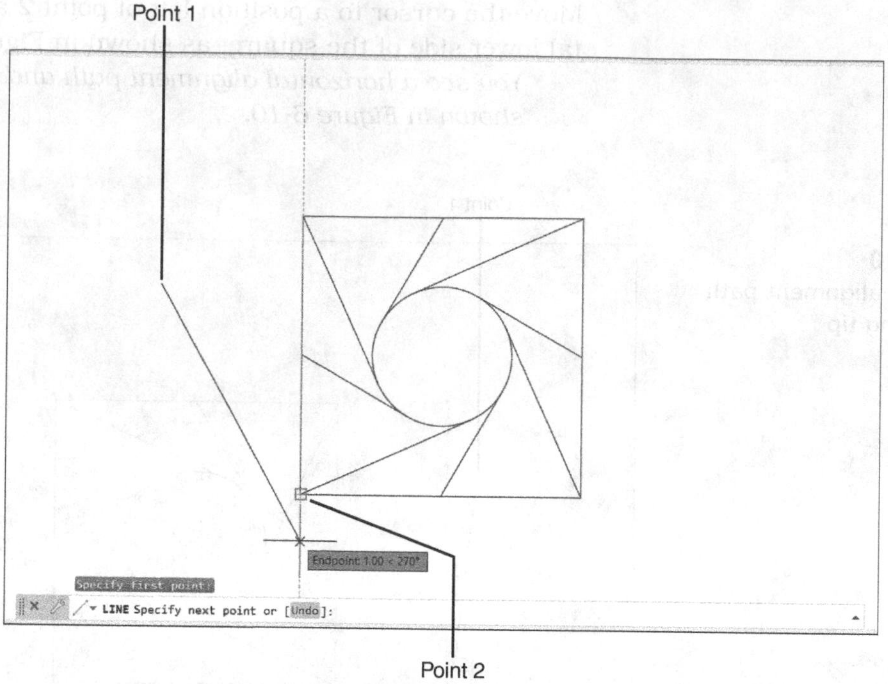

Figure 6-11
Vertical alignment path

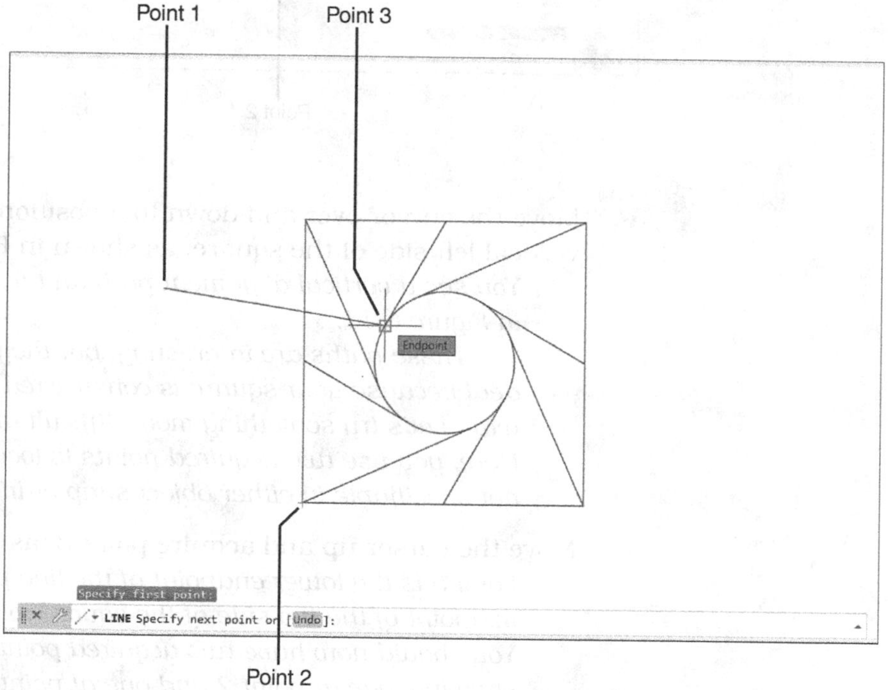

Figure 6-12
Acquiring point 3

- ✔ Move the cursor slowly along the left side of the square.
  You are looking for point 4, the point where the vertical alignment path from point 2 intersects the horizontal path from point 3. When you approach it, your drawing area should resemble Figure 6-13. Notice the double tracking tip, ***Endpoint: <90, Endpoint: <180***.

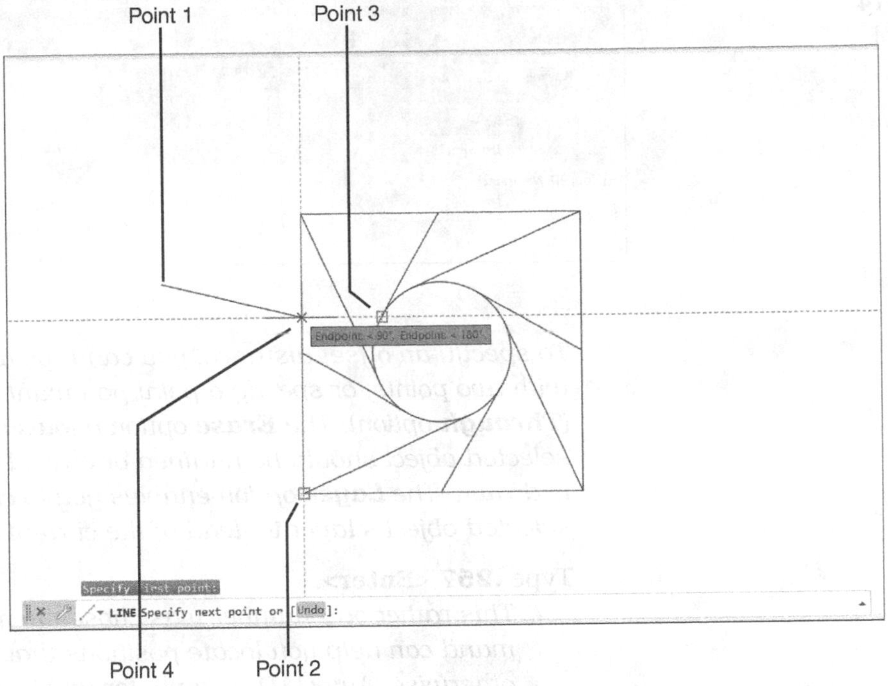

Figure 6-13
Double tracking tip

✔ With the double tracking tooltip and the two alignment paths showing, click in the drawing area.

A line is drawn from point 1 to point 4.

✔ Press **<Enter>** or the spacebar to exit the **LINE** command.

Before going on, you need to turn off the running object snap mode.

✔ Click the **Object Snap** button or press **<F3>** to turn off running object snap mode.

If you have followed this exercise closely, you have already greatly increased your understanding of CAD techniques. You will find many opportunities to use object snap and object snap tracking from now on.

Next, you move on to a very powerful editing command called **OFFSET**. Before leaving object snaps behind for now, be sure you have studied the chart in Figure 6-6, which shows examples of all the object snap modes.

Using the OFFSET Command (Creating Parallel Objects with OFFSET)

OFFSET	
Command	OFFSET
Alias	O
Panel	Modify
Tool	

OFFSET is one of the most useful editing commands in AutoCAD. With the combination of object snap and the **OFFSET** command, you can become completely free of incremental snap and grid points. Any point in the drawing space can be precisely located. Essentially, **OFFSET** creates parallel copies of lines, circles, arcs, or polylines. You can find a number of typical applications in the drawings at the end of this chapter. In this brief exercise, you perform an offset operation to draw some lines through points that would be very difficult to locate without **OFFSET**.

✔ Click the **Offset** tool from the **Modify** panel on the ribbon's **Home** tab, as shown in Figure 6-14. AutoCAD prompts:

```
Specify offset distance or [Through/Erase/Layer] <Through>:
```

Figure 6-14
Offset tool

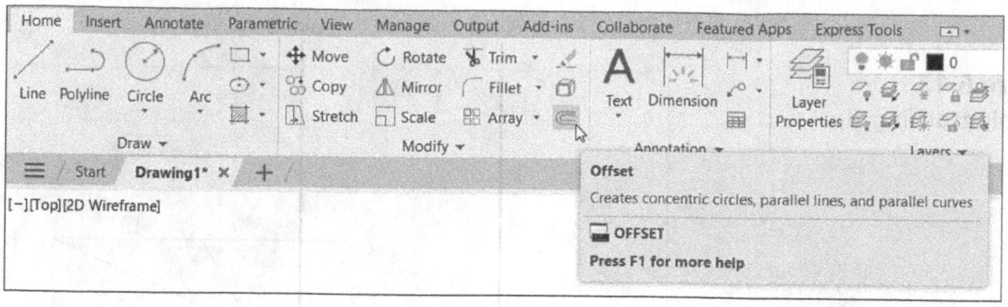

- ✔ *To specify an offset distance, you can type a number, define a distance with two points, or specify a point you want the new copy to run through (**Through** option). The **Erase** option allows you to specify whether the selected object should be retained or erased when the new offset object is drawn. The **Layer** option enables you to create the new object on the selected object's layer instead of the current layer.*
- ✔ Type **.257 <Enter>**.

  This rather odd number was chosen to make the point that this command can help you locate positions that would be difficult to find otherwise. AutoCAD prompts for an object:

  ```
  Select object to offset or <exit>:
  ```

- ✔ Select the diagonal line drawn in the last exercise.

  AutoCAD creates a preview offset, but needs to know whether to create the offset image above or below the line:

  ```
  Specify point on side to offset:
  ```

- ✔ Specify a point anywhere below the line.

  Your drawing should now resemble Figure 6-15. AutoCAD continues to prompt for objects to offset using the same offset distance. You can continue to create offset objects at the same offset distance by pointing and clicking.

- ✔ Select the line just created.
- ✔ Specify any point below the line.

  *A second offset line is added, as shown in Figure 6-15. As long as you stay within the **OFFSET** command, you can select any object to offset using the same offset distance.*

- ✔ Select the circle in the square.
- ✔ Specify any point inside the circle.

  An offset circle is added, as shown in Figure 6-16.

- ✔ Continue selecting and clicking to create additional offset circles, as shown in Figure 6-16.

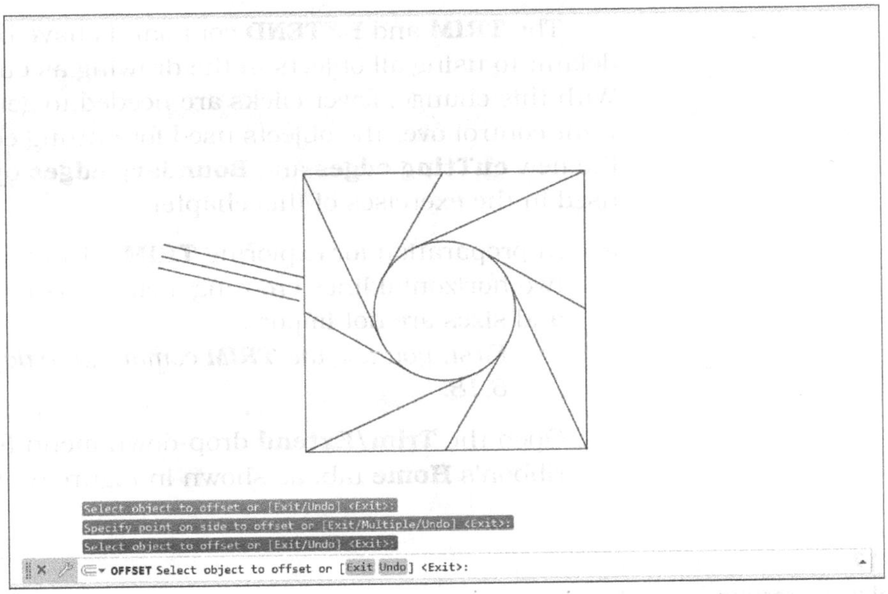

Figure 6-15
Offset line

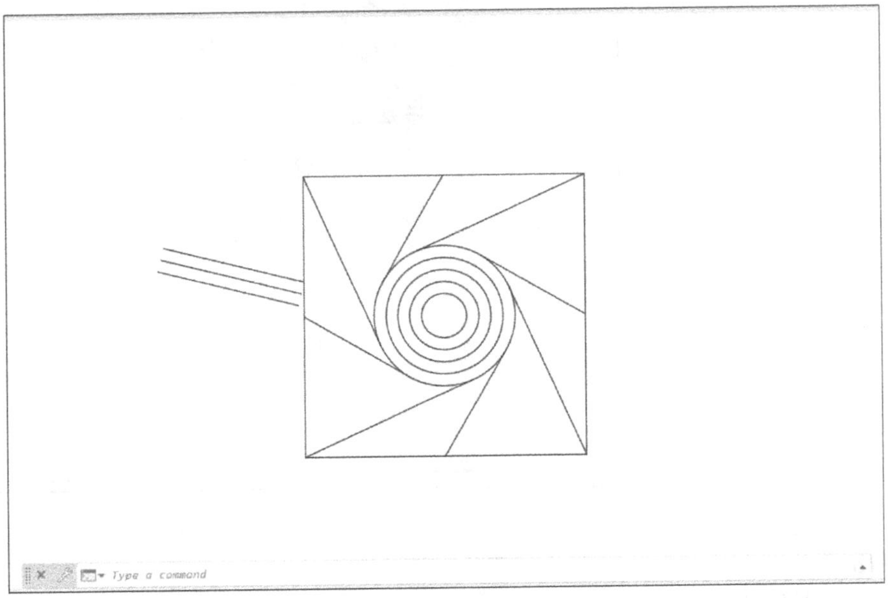

Figure 6-16
Offset line and circles

✔ Press **<Enter>** to exit the **OFFSET** command.

*When you exit **OFFSET**, the offset distance is retained as the default, so you can return to the command and continue using the same distance.*

Shortening Objects with the TRIM Command

TRIM	
Command	TRIM
Alias	Tr
Panel	Modify
Tool	

In the next three sections, you explore edit commands that allow you to shorten and lengthen objects in your drawing. The **TRIM** command works wonders in many situations where you want to shorten objects at their intersections with other objects. It works with lines, circles, arcs, and polylines. The only limitations are that you must have at least two objects, and they must cross or meet.

New to AutoCAD 2021

The **TRIM** and **EXTEND** commands have been simplified and now default to using all objects in the drawing as cutting edges or boundaries. With this change, fewer clicks are needed to get the desired results. If you want control over the objects used for cutting edges or boundaries, you use the new **cuTting edges** and **Boundary edges** options. Both techniques are used in the exercises of this chapter.

✔ In preparation for exploring **TRIM**, clear your drawing and then draw two horizontal lines crossing a circle, as in Figure 6-17. Exact locations and sizes are not important.

First, you use the ***TRIM*** *command to go from Figure 6-17 to Figure 6-18.*

✔ Open the **Trim/Extend** drop-down menu from the **Modify** panel on the ribbon's **Home** tab, as shown in Figure 6-19.

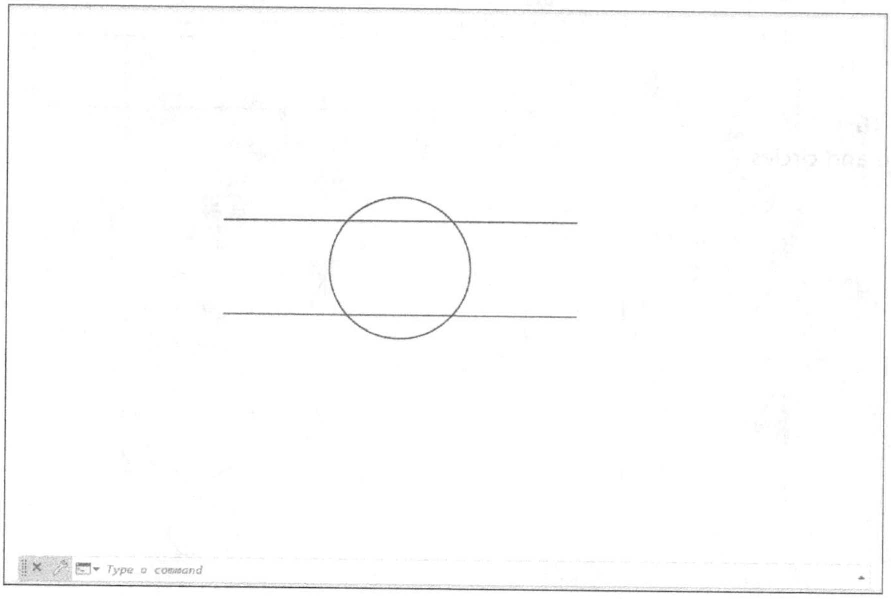

Figure 6-17
Horizontal lines crossing circle

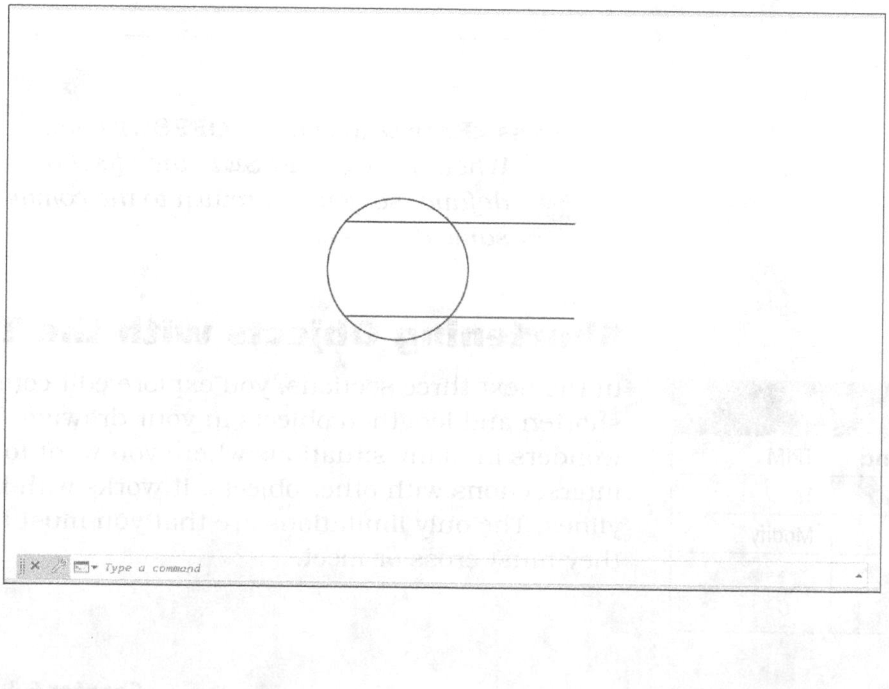

Figure 6-18
Trimming lines at circle

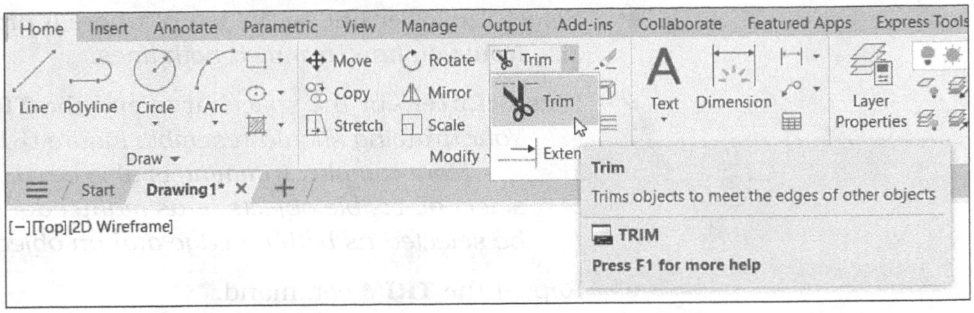

Figure 6-19
Trim from the **Trim/Extend** drop-down menu

✔ From the drop-down menu, click the **Trim** tool, as shown.

You begin by selecting at least one cutting edge. A cutting edge is an entity you use to trim another entity—you want the trimmed entity to end at its intersection with the cutting edge.

You are prompted for an object to trim:

```
Select object to trim or shift-select to extend or
[cuTting edges/Crossing/mOde/Project/eRase]:
```

✔ Type **t <Enter>** or select **cuTting edges** at the command line.

The prompt asks you to select objects to use as cutting edges, or press ***<Enter>*** *for the* ***Select All*** *option. In a bit, you'll use all objects as cutting edges, which is the default behavior and doesn't require the use of the* ***cuTting edges*** *option.*

For now, select the circle as an edge and use it to trim the upper line.

✔ Select the circle.

The circle becomes highlighted and remains so until you leave the ***TRIM*** *command. AutoCAD prompts for more objects until you indicate that you are finished selecting edges.*

✔ Right-click to end the selection of cutting edges.

You are prompted for an object to trim:

```
Select object to trim or shift-select to extend or
[cuTting edges/Crossing/mOde/Project/eRase]:
```

This prompt allows you to shift over to the ***EXTEND*** *command by holding down the* ***<Shift>*** *key. Otherwise, you select objects to trim using the given options. You follow a simple procedure to trim off the segment of the upper line that lies outside the circle on the left. Make sure to point to the part of the object to be removed, as shown in Figure 6-18.*

✔ Point to the upper line to the left of where it crosses the circle.

Notice the red X at the crosshairs and the gray highlight indicating the segment you are choosing to trim.

✔ Left-click to complete the trim.

The line is trimmed immediately and AutoCAD continues to prompt for more objects to trim.

Note that an ***Undo*** *option is added to the prompt, so if the trim does not turn out the way you wanted, you can back up without having to leave the command and start over. Also notice the* ***eRase*** *option, which allows you to erase objects without leaving the* ***TRIM*** *command.*

✔ Select the lower line to the left of where it crosses the circle.

Now you have trimmed both lines.

✔ Press **<Enter>** or the spacebar to end the **TRIM** operation.

Your drawing should resemble Figure 6-18.

More complex trimming is also easy. The key is that you can select all visible objects or as many edges as you like. An entity can be selected as both an edge and an object to trim.

✔ Repeat the **TRIM** command.

In this case, you won't use the ***cuTting edges*** *option and proceed to select the objects to trim.*

✔ Point to each of the remaining two line segments that lie outside the circle on the right and to the top and bottom arcs of the circle to produce the bandage-shaped object in Figure 6-20.

✔ Press **<Enter>** to exit the **TRIM** command.

Figure 6-20
Trimmed lines and circle

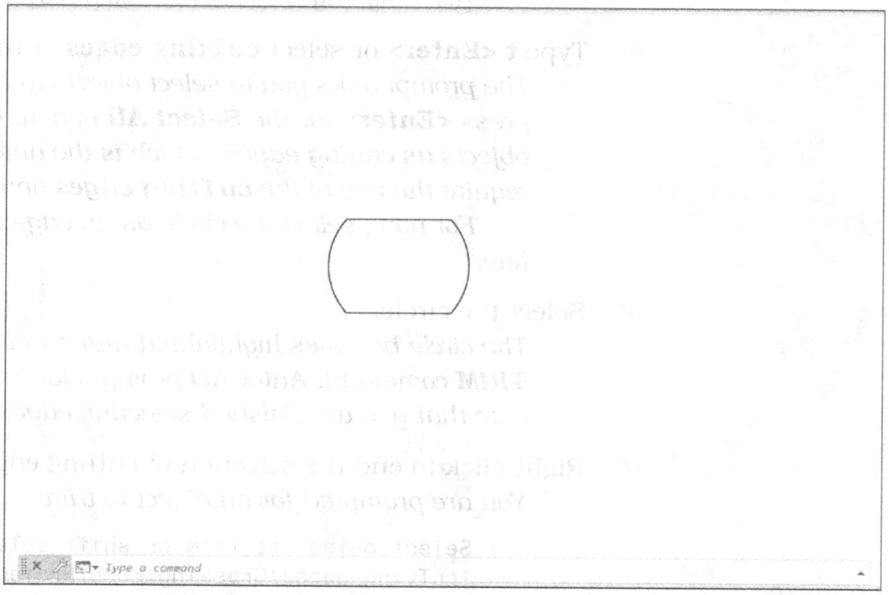

Extending Objects with the EXTEND Command

EXTEND	
Command	EXTEND
Alias	Ex
Panel	Modify
Tool	

The procedure for using the **EXTEND** command is the same as for the **TRIM** command, but instead of selecting cutting edges, you select boundaries to which objects are extended. **TRIM** and **EXTEND** are conceptually related, and you can switch from one to the other without leaving the command.

> **TIP**
> It is sometimes efficient to draw a temporary cutting edge or boundary in your drawing and erase it after using **TRIM** or **EXTEND**.

✔ Leave the bandage in your drawing, shown in Figure 6-20, and draw a vertical line to the right of it, as in Figure 6-21.

You use this line as a boundary to which to extend the two horizontal lines, as shown in Figure 6-22.

Figure 6-21 Drawing vertical boundary line

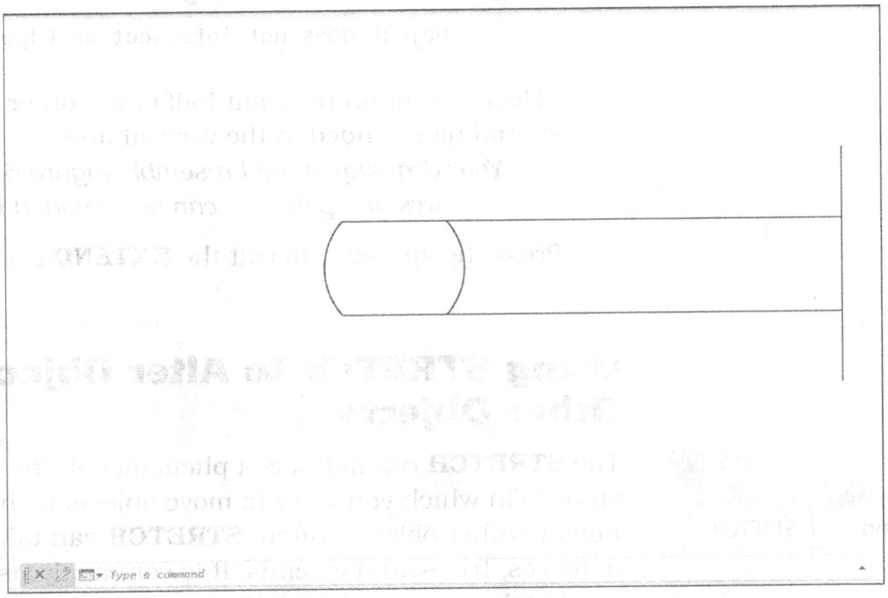

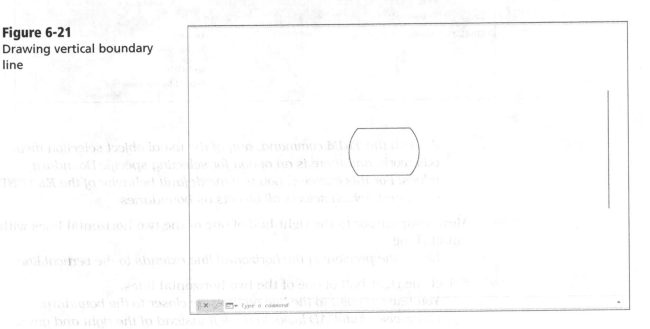

Figure 6-22 Extending the horizontal lines

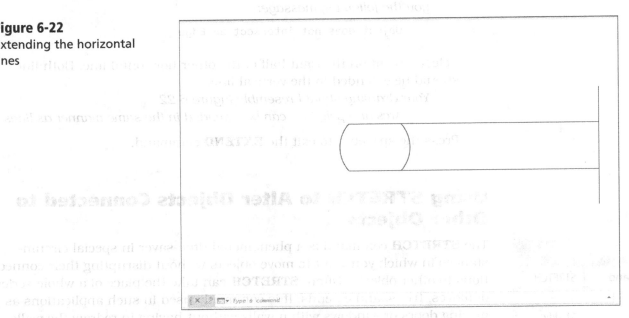

✔ From the **Trim/Extend** drop-down menu on the ribbon, click the **Extend** tool, as shown in Figure 6-23.

You are prompted to select the objects to extend:

```
Select object to extend or shift-select to trim or
[Boundary edges/Crossing/mOde/Project]:
```

Figure 6-23
Extend from the **Trim/ Extend** drop-down menu

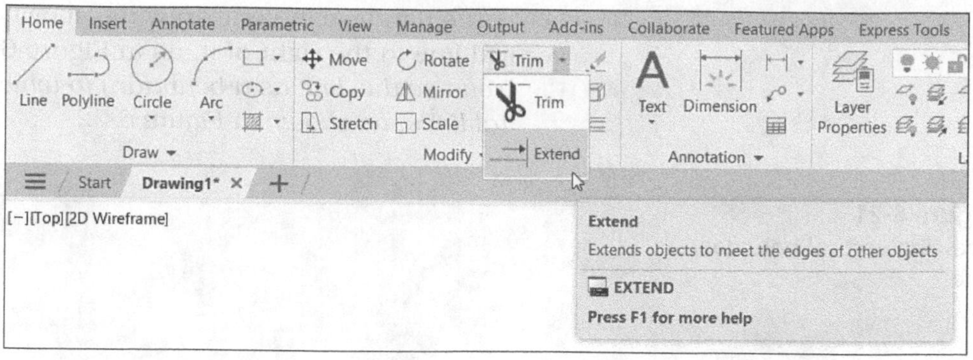

*As with the **TRIM** command, any of the usual object selection methods work, and there is an option for selecting specific Boundary edges. For this exercise, you use the default behavior of the **EXTEND** command, which selects all objects as boundaries.*

✔ Move your cursor to the right half of one of the two horizontal lines without clicking.

Notice the preview of the horizontal line extends to the vertical line.

✔ Select the right half of one of the two horizontal lines.

You have to point to the line on the side closer to the boundary. Otherwise, AutoCAD looks to the left instead of the right and gives you the following message:

```
Object does not intersect an Edge
```

✔ Select a point on the right half of the other horizontal line. Both lines should be extended to the vertical line.

Your drawing should resemble Figure 6-22.

Arcs and polylines can be extended in the same manner as lines.

✔ Press the spacebar to exit the **EXTEND** command.

Using STRETCH to Alter Objects Connected to Other Objects

STRETCH	
Command	STRETCH
Alias	S
Panel	Modify
Tool	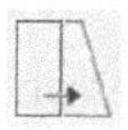

The **STRETCH** command is a phenomenal time-saver in special circumstances in which you want to move objects without disrupting their connections to other objects. Often, **STRETCH** can take the place of a whole series of moves, trims, and extends. It is commonly used in such applications as moving doors or windows within walls without having to redraw the walls.

The term *stretch* must be understood to have a special meaning in AutoCAD. When a typical stretch is performed, some objects are lengthened, others are shortened, and others are simply moved.

There is also a **Stretch** mode in the grip edit system, as you have seen previously. It functions very differently from the **STRETCH** command. You look at stretching objects with grips later in this section.

First, you do a simple stretch on the objects you drew in previous sections.

✔ Click the **Stretch** tool from the **Modify** panel on the ribbon's **Home** tab, as shown in Figure 6-24.

Figure 6-24
Stretch tool

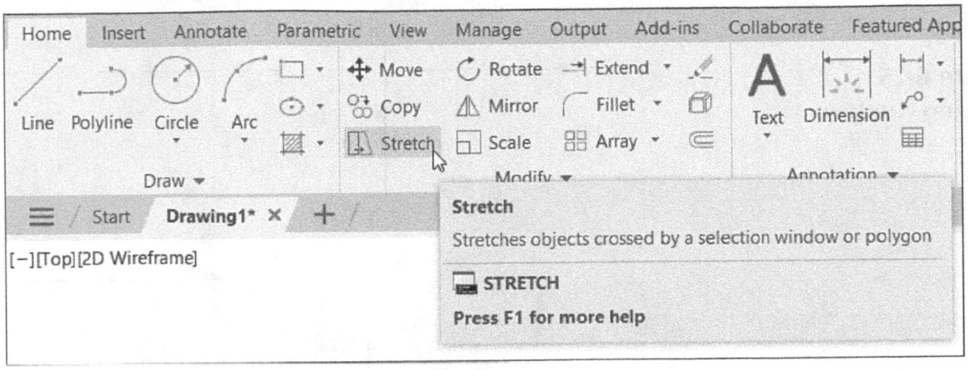

AutoCAD prompts for objects to stretch.

For a stretch procedure to be effective, you will want to use at least one crossing-window or crossing-polygon selection in your selection set. Objects crossed by the window or polygon will be stretched, whereas objects within the window or selected individually will simply be moved. If it is not your intent to stretch or shorten some of the objects in your selection set, you probably should be using a different modifying command.

✔ Specify the first corner of a crossing window, as shown by Point 1 in Figure 6-25.

AutoCAD prompts for a second corner:

```
Specify opposite corner:
```

✔ Specify the opposite corner of the window, as shown by Point 2 in Figure 6-25.

AutoCAD continues to prompt for objects, continue selecting objects or end selection.

✔ Right-click to end the selection process.

Now, you need to provide the degree and direction of stretch you want. In effect, you specify how far to move the objects that are completely within the window. Objects that cross the window are extended or shrunk so they remain connected to the objects that move.

The prompt sequence for this action is the same as the sequence for a move:

```
Specify base point or [Displacement] <Displacement>:
```

✔ Specify any point near the middle of the drawing area, leaving room to indicate a horizontal displacement to the right, as illustrated in Figure 6-26.

AutoCAD prompts:

```
Specify second point of displacement <or use first point as
displacement>:
```

Figure 6-25
Crossing window

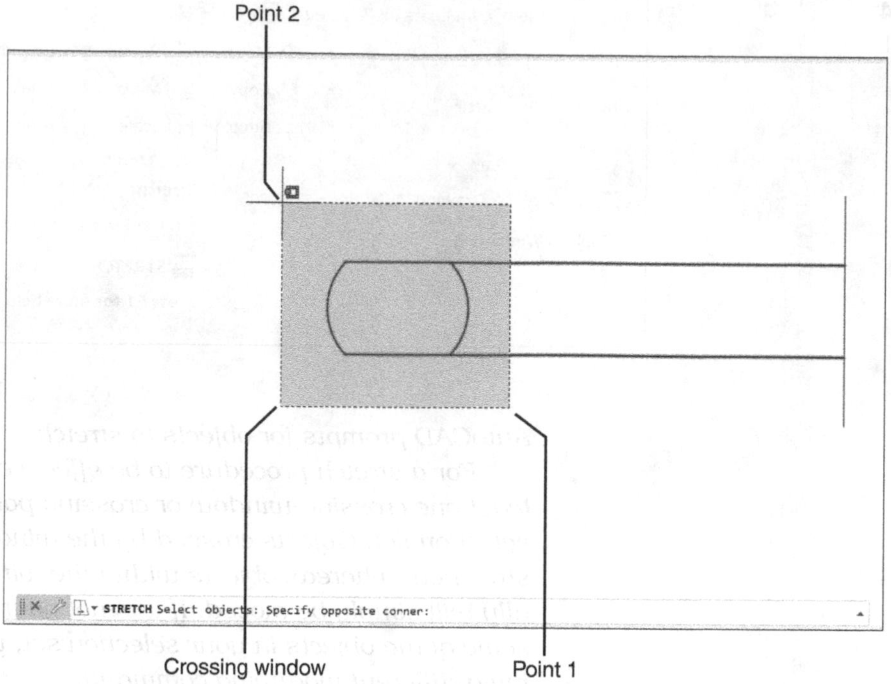

Figure 6-26
Horizontal stretch

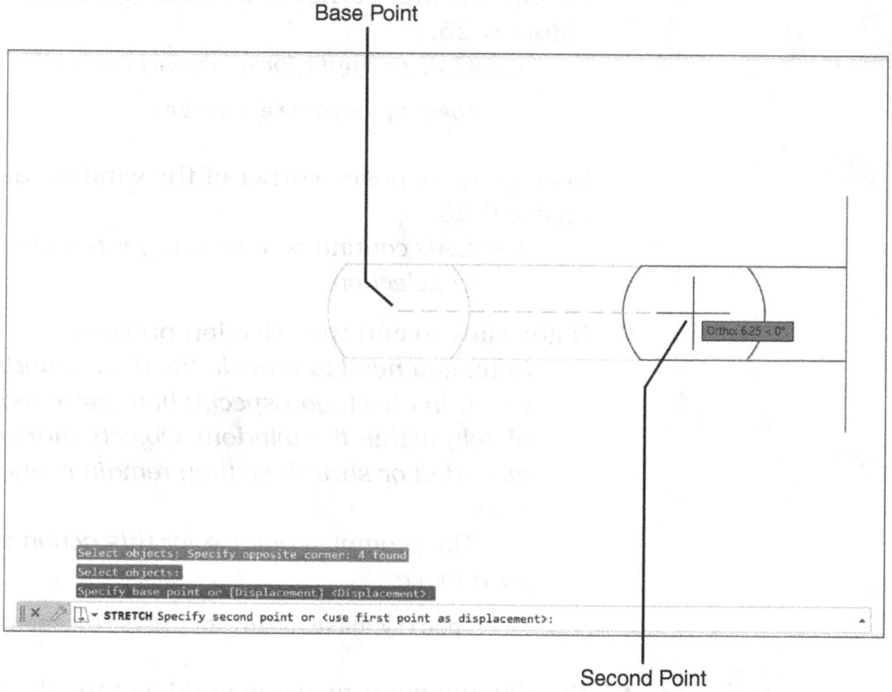

- ✔ Specify a second point to the right of the first, as shown in Figure 6-26.

  Having ***Ortho*** *on ensures a horizontal move.*

  The arcs are moved to the right, and the horizontal lines are shrunk as shown. Notice that nothing here is literally being stretched. The arcs are being moved, and the lines are being compressed.

- ✔ Try performing another stretch like the one illustrated in Figures 6-27 and 6-28.

  Here, the lines are being lengthened while one arc moves and the other stays put, so that the original bandage is indeed stretched.

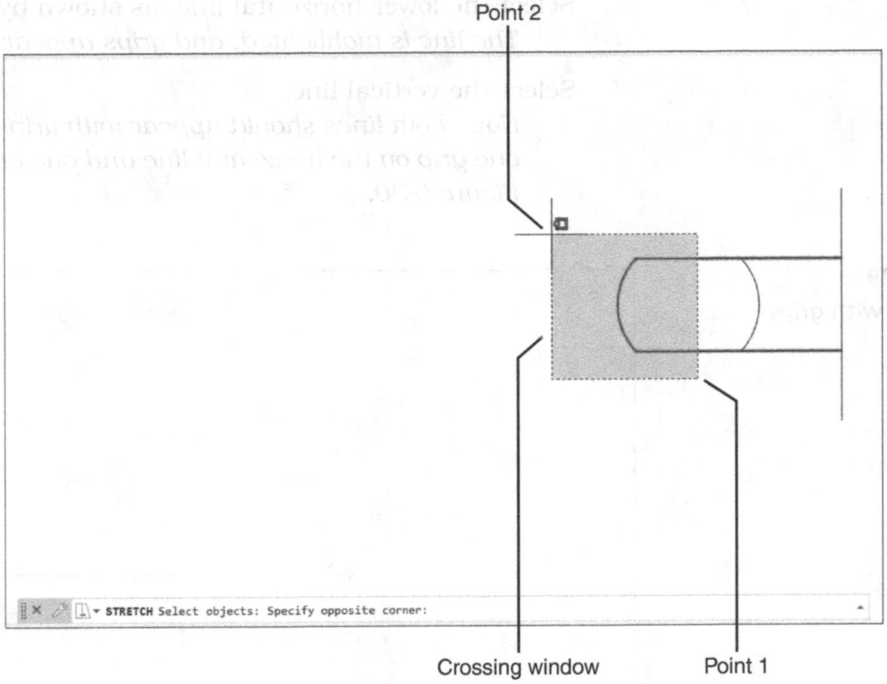

Figure 6-27
Crossing window

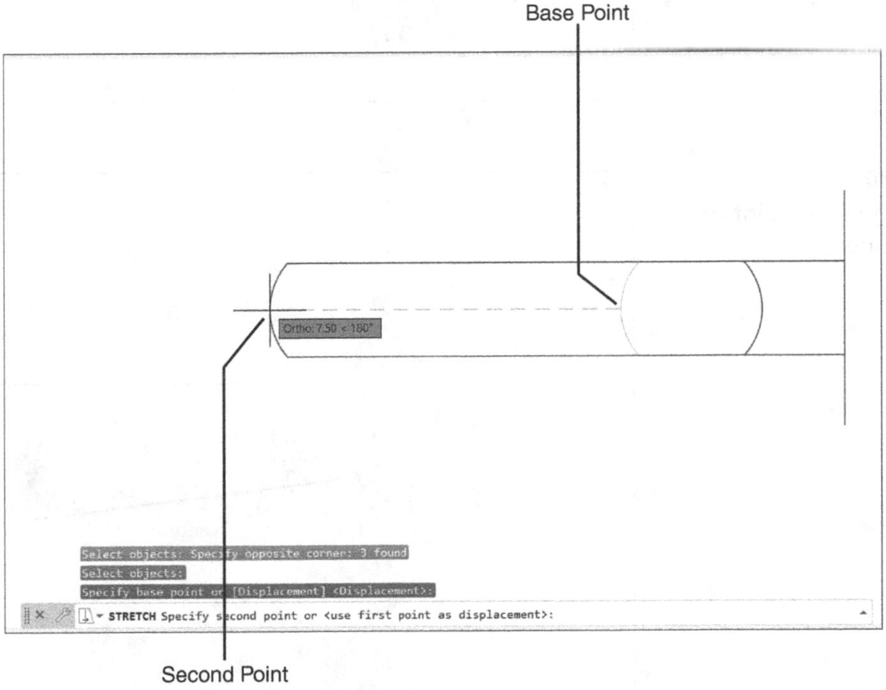

Figure 6-28
Stretched object

Stretching with Grips

Stretching with grips is a simple operation best reserved for simple stretches. Stretches like the ones you just performed with the **STRETCH** command are possible in grip editing, but they require careful selection of multiple grips. The results are not always what you might expect, and it takes more time to complete the process. The type of stretch that works best with grips is illustrated in the following exercise:

- ✔ Select the lower horizontal line, as shown by the grips in Figure 6-29.

  The line is highlighted, and grips appear.

- ✔ Select the vertical line.

  Now, both lines should appear with grips, as in Figure 6-29. You use one grip on the horizontal line and one on the vertical line to create Figure 6-30.

Figure 6-29
Stretching with grips

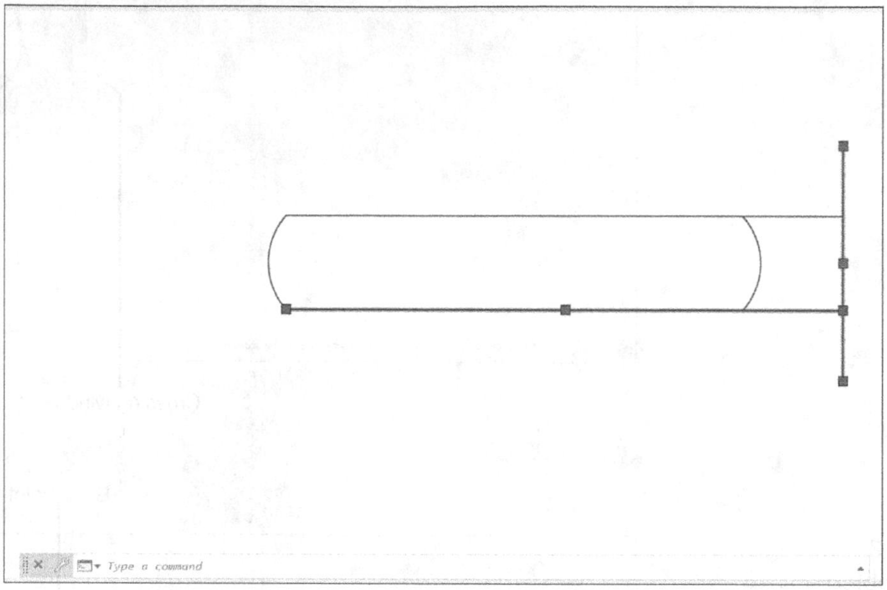

Figure 6-30
Stretching the endpoint of the lower line

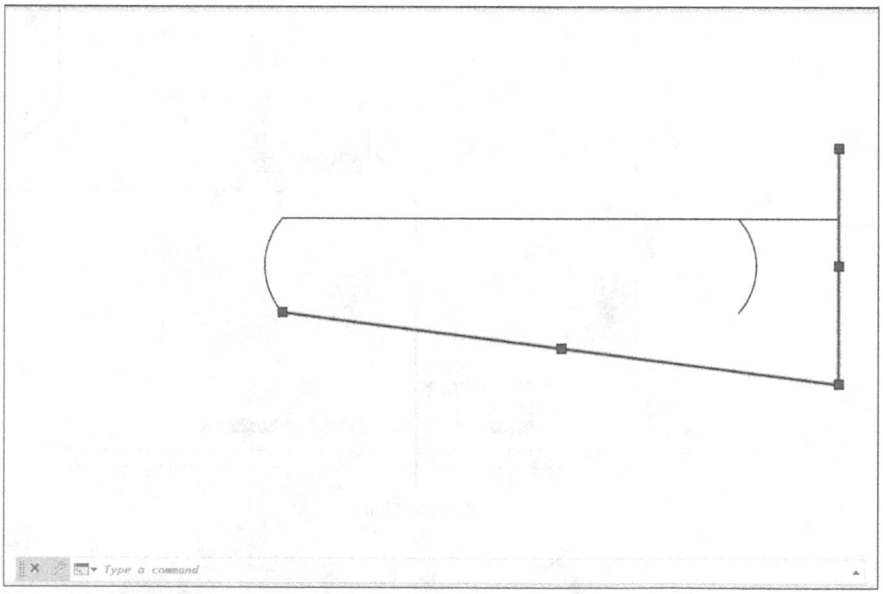

- ✔ Click the grip at the right end of the horizontal line.

  As soon as you click, the grip edit system puts you into ***Stretch*** *mode, and the selected grip changes color.*

  In the command line, you see the following:

```
Specify stretch point or [Base point/Copy/Undo/eXit]:
```

You stretch the line to end at the lower endpoint of the vertical line.

✔ Move the crosshairs slowly downward, and observe the objects being stretched.

*If **Ortho** is off, you see two rubber bands. One represents the line you are stretching, and the other connects the crosshairs to the grip you are manipulating.*

NOTE

If, by chance, you have constructed the design so that the grip on the end of the horizontal line coincides with the midpoint grip on the vertical line, you will see that the line moves with the grip, making the next step impossible.

✔ Click the grip at the bottom of the vertical line.

Your drawing should resemble Figure 6-30. Notice how the grip on the vertical line works like an object snap point.

✔ Press **<Esc>** to clear the grips from the objects.

✔ Try one more grip stretch to create Figure 6-31. Stretch the endpoint of the upper line just as you did the lower.

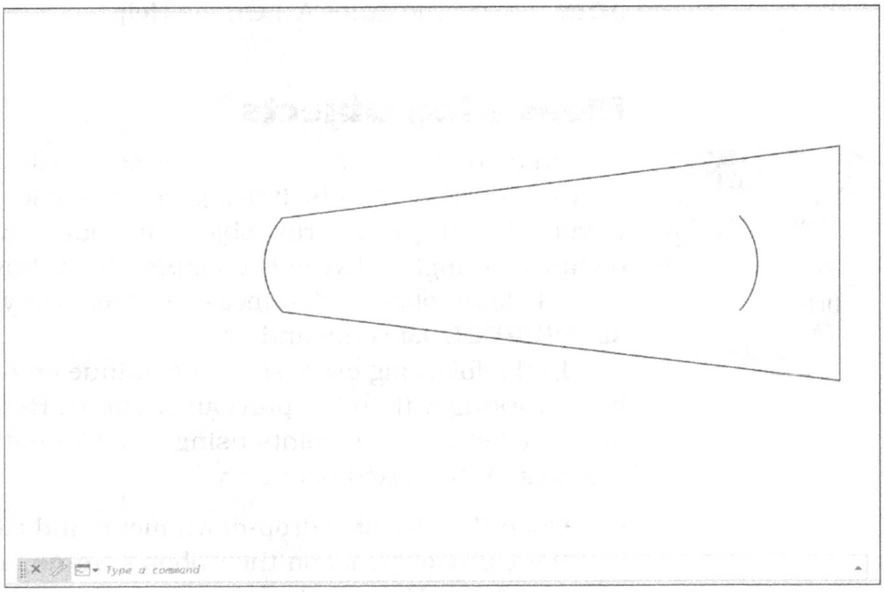

Figure 6-31
Stretching the endpoint of the upper line

Lengthen, Break, and Join

Four additional commands related to those introduced in the previous three sections are **LENGTHEN**, **BREAKATPOINT**, **BREAK**, and **JOIN**. They are not required to complete any of the drawings in this chapter, but you should know about them. **LENGTHEN** allows you to lengthen or shorten lines, arcs, and polylines. You can find the **Lengthen** tool by expanding the **Modify** panel on the **Home** tab. The panel is expanded by clicking the arrow next to the title on the panel's title bar. After starting the command, specify a lengthening option and then select objects to modify. There are four lengthening options. **Delta** lengthens by a specified amount (specifying a negative amount causes shortening). **Percent** lengthens objects by a percentage of their current length. **Total** adjusts selected objects to a new total length, regardless of their current length. **Dynamic** allows you to adjust length dynamically with cursor movement.

New to AutoCAD 2021

With the **BREAKATPOINT** command, you can break a selected object into separate objects. You can do this without erasing anything, in which case, there is no visible difference in your drawing, but you will be able to manipulate parts of the broken object independently. To break without creating a gap, use the **Break at Point** tool from the expanded area of the **Modify** panel.

You can also use the **BREAK** command to create a gap between the newly separated objects without needing to define cutting edges and trim the object. To break with a gap, use the **Break** tool from the expanded area of the **Modify** panel extension. The **Break** tool can also be used to shorten lines by picking the second point of the "gap" beyond the end of the line.

The **JOIN** command is the reverse of the **BREAKATPOINT** and **BREAK** commands. You can join arcs, elliptical arcs, lines, polylines, and splines that are linear, touch end to end, and are coplanar to each other. When selecting objects, the first object is the source object and the next objects selected are joined to it. The **JOIN** command also allows you to close an arc or elliptical arc into a circle or ellipse object. To join objects, use the **Join** tool from the expanded area of the **Modify** panel extension.

For more information on **LENGTHEN**, **BREAKATPOINT**, **BREAK**, or **JOIN**, access the AutoCAD Online Help.

Measuring Objects

MEASUREGEOM	
Command	MEASUREGEOM
Alias	Mea
Panel	Utilities
Tool	

Now that you know how to specify precise points on objects using object snaps and resize objects, it is a good time to learn how to measure objects in your drawing. Measuring objects in your drawing allows you to find the distance or angle between two points, the radius of an arc or circle, or the area of closed objects. You measure objects in your drawing using the **MEASUREGEOM** command.

In the following exercise, you continue on with the drawing you have been working with in the previous sections. Here you learn to measure the distance between two points using two different techniques and calculate the area of the closed boundary.

✔ Open the **Measure** drop-down menu and click the **Distance** tool from the **Utilities** panel on the ribbon's **Home** tab, as shown in Figure 6-32.

AutoCAD prompts for a point.

```
Specify first point:
```

✔ Specify the first endpoint of the bottom line, as shown by Point 1 in Figure 6-33.

AutoCAD prompts for a second corner:

```
Specify opposite corner:
```

✔ Specify the second endpoint of the bottom line, as shown by Point 2 in Figure 6-33.

Figure 6-32
Distance tool

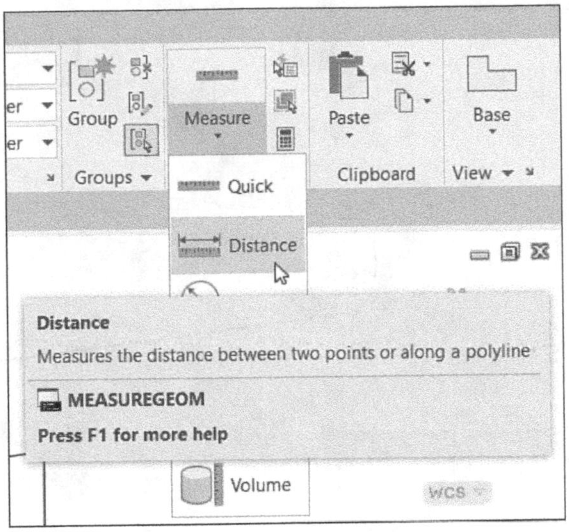

Figure 6-33
Measuring a distance between two points

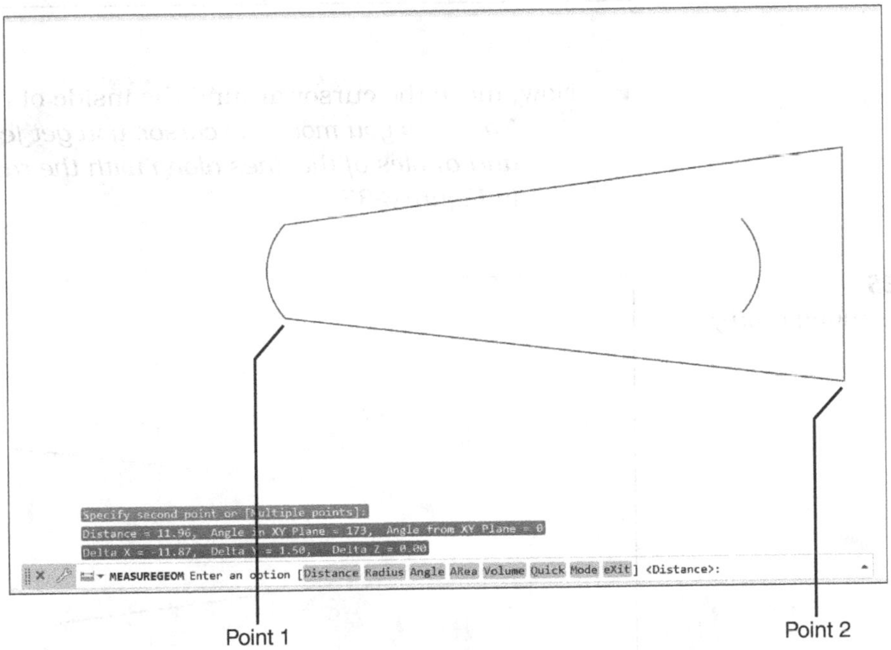

The distance—and even the angle—between the two points is calculated and displayed in the command line. Press F2 to expand the command line if you don't see the calculated values.

- ✔ Type **x <Enter>** or select **eXit** from the command line to exit the command.
- ✔ Open the **Measure** drop-down menu again from the **Utilities** panel on the **Home** tab; this time, click the **Quick** tool.

  AutoCAD prompts you to move the cursor in the drawing area:

  ```
  Move cursor or [Distance/Radius/Angle/ARea/Volume/Quick/
  Mode/eXit] <eXit>:
  ```
- ✔ Move the cursor near the bottom line of the drawing.

  Notice you immediately get feedback in the form of the line's length, as shown in Figure 6-34.

Figure 6-34
Measuring the length of a line dynamically

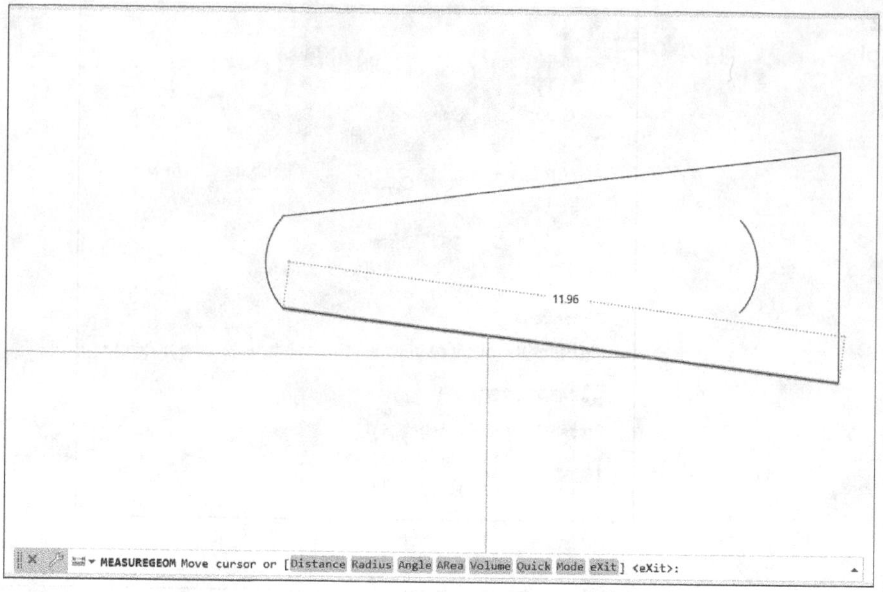

✔ Now, move the cursor around the inside of the closed area.

Notice as you move the cursor, you get feedback about the lengths and angles of the lines along with the radius of the arcs, as shown in Figure 6-35.

Figure 6-35
Quickly measuring nearby objects

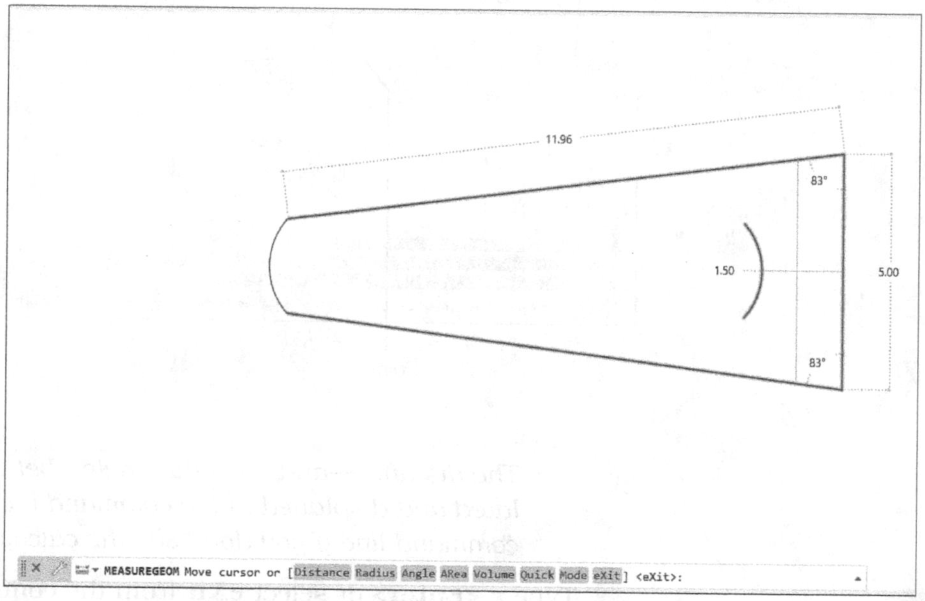

✔ With the cursor inside the closed object, click and don't move the cursor.

The area and perimeter of the closed object are calculated. These values are shown temporarily in the drawing area and output to the command line, as shown in Figure 6-36. If you move your cursor, the command returns to ***Quick mode*** *again.*

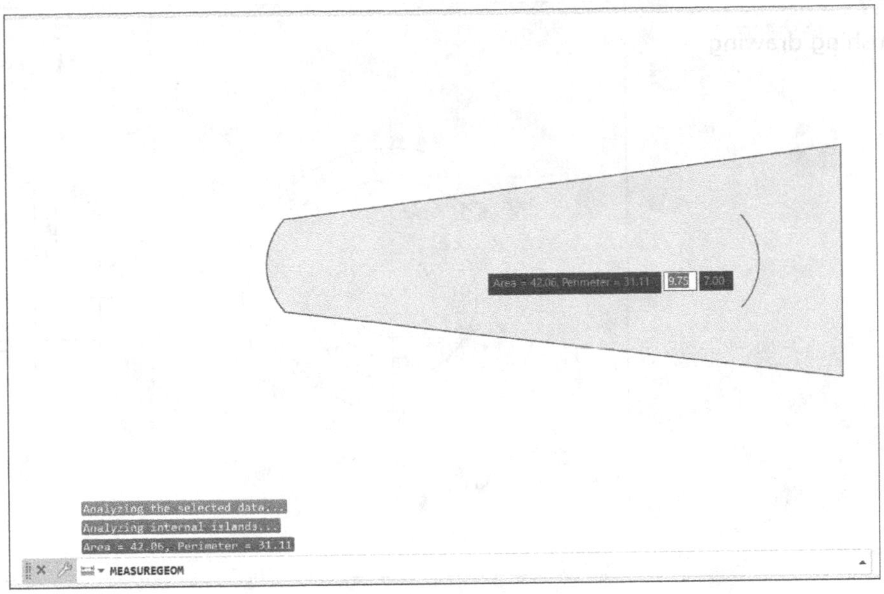

Figure 6-36
Measuring the area of a closed object

✔ Press **<Enter>** to exit the command.

Try some of the other options available on the **Measure** drop-down menu or with **MEASUREGEOM** at the command line. In addition to the **MEASUREGEOM** command, you can use the **DIST**, **AREA**, and **LIST** commands to inquire about the geometric measurements of objects in your drawing. For more information on the **MEASUREGEOM**, **DIST**, **AREA**, and **LIST** commands, see the AutoCAD Online Help system.

Creating Plot Layouts

Plotting from model space has its uses, particularly in the early stages of the design process. However, when your focus shifts from modeling issues to presentation issues, paper space layouts have much more to offer. The separation of model space and paper space in AutoCAD allows you to focus entirely on modeling and real-world dimensions when you are drawing and then shift your focus to paper output issues when you plot. On the drafting board, all drawings are committed to paper from the start. People doing manual drafting are inevitably conscious of scale, paper size, and rotation from start to finish. When draftspersons first begin using CAD systems, they might still tend to think in terms of the final hard copy their plotter will produce even as they are creating lines in a drawing. The AutoCAD plotting system takes full advantage of the powers of a CAD system, allowing you to ignore scale and other drawing paper issues entirely, if you wish, until it is time to plot.

In addition, the paper space world allows you to create multiple views of the same objects without copying or redrawing them and to plot these viewports simultaneously. In this exercise, you create two layouts of the flanged bushing shown in Figure 6-37. The first layout contains only one viewport. The second is used to demonstrate some basic principles of working with multiple viewports.

Figure 6-37
Flanged bushing drawing

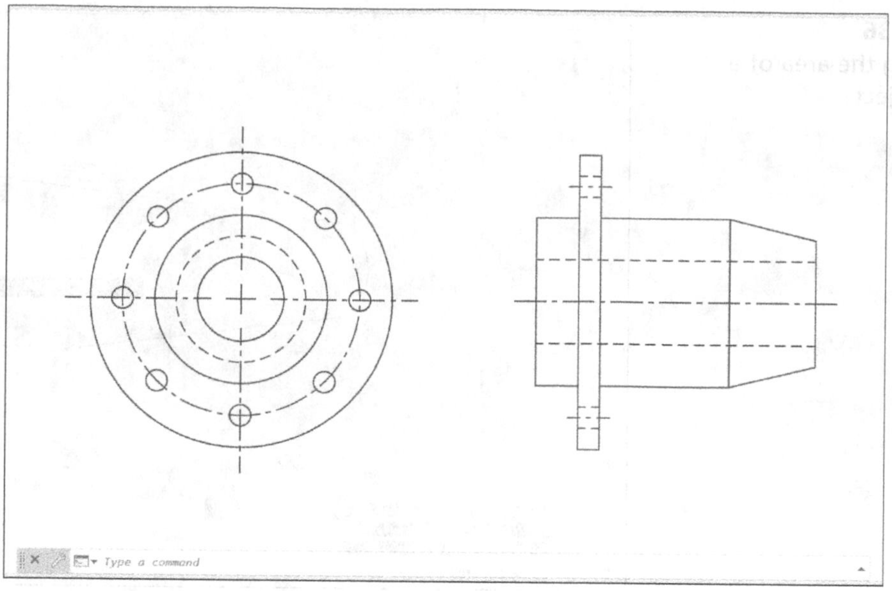

Opening Layout

✔ To begin this exercise, create an approximation of the bushing shown in Figure 6-37, or open this drawing if you have saved it.

To approximate the drawing, follow these steps:

1. *Erase all objects from your drawing.*
2. *Set limits to* ***(0,0)*** *and* ***(12,9)****. This is critical. If you use different limits, the exercise is difficult to follow.*
3. *Draw a circle with diameter* ***3.50*** *centered at* ***(3.00,4.00)****.*
4. *Draw a second circle with diameter* ***2.50*** *centered at the same point.*
5. *Draw a rectangle with the first corner at* ***(6.50,2.75)*** *and the second corner at* ***(10.00,5.25)****.*

✔ Before leaving model space, turn off the grid.

✔ Click the **Layout1** tab on the status bar, as shown in Figure 6-38.

You see an image similar to the one in Figure 6-39. When clicked, AutoCAD automatically creates a single viewport determined by the extents of your drawing. Paper space viewports are sometimes called floating viewports because they can be moved and reshaped. They are like windows from paper space into model space.

Figure 6-38
Layout1 tab

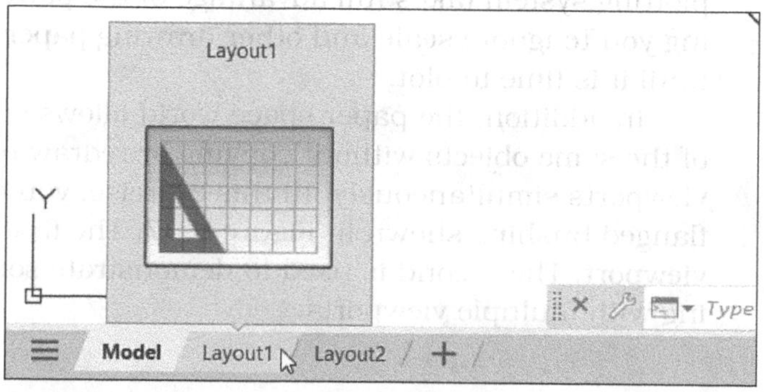

Figure 6-39
Paper space viewport

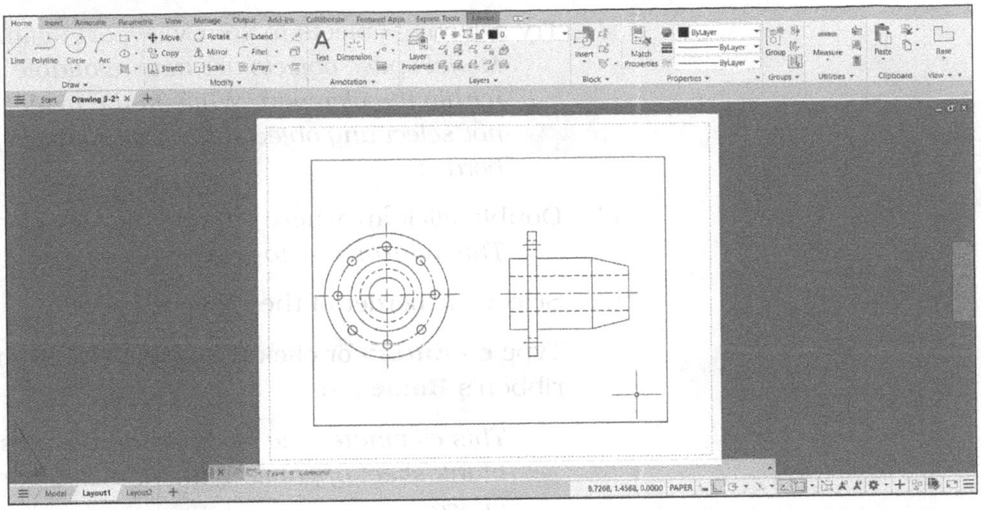

Viewports are also AutoCAD objects and are treated and stored as such. You can move them, stretch them, copy them, and erase them. Editing the viewport does not affect the model space objects within the viewport. When a viewport is selected, the border is highlighted, and grips are shown at each corner.

Switching Between Paper Space and Model Space

✔ Try selecting the viewport border, just as you would select any AutoCAD object.

If you are unable to select the viewport border, you are still in model space. Whether you have entered Layout1 in model space or paper space depends on recent AutoCAD activity. If you are still in model space, double-clicking anywhere outside the viewport border puts you into paper space.

✔ If necessary, double-click outside the viewport border to enter paper space.

✔ Try selecting the viewport border again.

When you are in paper space, you can select the viewport border but not the objects inside.

✔ Try to select any of the objects within the viewport.

You cannot. As long as you are in paper space, model space objects are not accessible. To gain access to model space objects while on a layout, you must double-click inside a viewport.

✔ Double-click anywhere within the viewport.

The border of the viewport takes on a bold outline, and the ***ViewCube*** *and navigation bar appear inside the viewport.*

You are now in model space within the viewport. Notice the difference between working within a viewport in a layout and switching into model space by clicking the ***Model*** *tab. If you click the* ***Model*** *tab, the layout disappears, and you are back in the familiar model space drawing area.*

- ✔ Try selecting objects in your viewport again.

  Model space objects are now available for editing or positioning within the viewport. While in the model space of a viewport, you cannot select any objects drawn in paper space, including the viewport border.

- ✔ Double-click anywhere outside the viewport border.

  This returns you to paper space.

- ✔ Select the border of the viewport.

- ✔ Type **e <Enter>** or click the **Erase** tool from the **Modify** panel on the ribbon's **Home** tab.

  This eliminates the viewport and leaves you with the image of a blank sheet of paper. Without a viewport, you have no view of model space.

Next, you create a more complex layout by adding your own viewports.

Modifying a Layout

Layouts can be modified in numerous ways and can be accessed from the **Layout** tabs at the bottom of the drawing area. You are looking at Layout1, which is based on the 12 × 9 drawing limits of the bushing drawing or the approximation you created at the beginning of this section. You modify the page setup to represent an ANSI D-size drawing sheet and then add three new viewports to the layout.

- ✔ Click **Output tab** > **Plot panel** > **Page Setup Manager** tool from the ribbon or **Print** > **Page Setup** tool from the application menu.

  This displays the ***Page Setup Manager*** *dialog box shown in Figure 6-40. Layout1 should be highlighted in the current page setup list.*

- ✔ Click the **Modify** button on the right.

  This opens the ***Page Setup – Layout1*** *dialog box shown in Figure 6-41. This is a version of the* ***Plot*** *dialog box.*

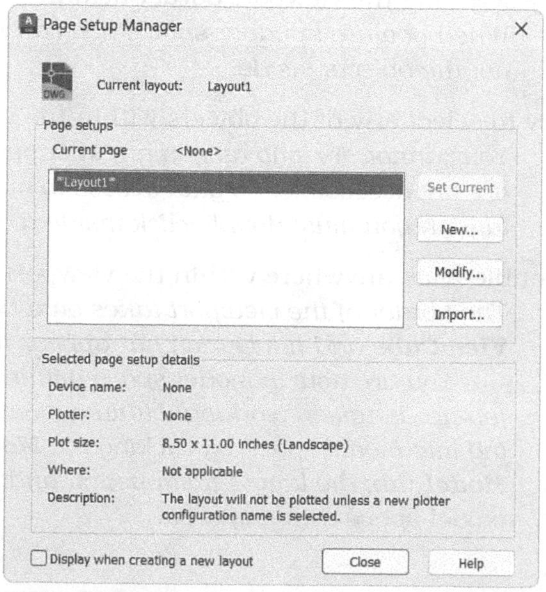

Figure 6-40
Page Setup Manager dialog box

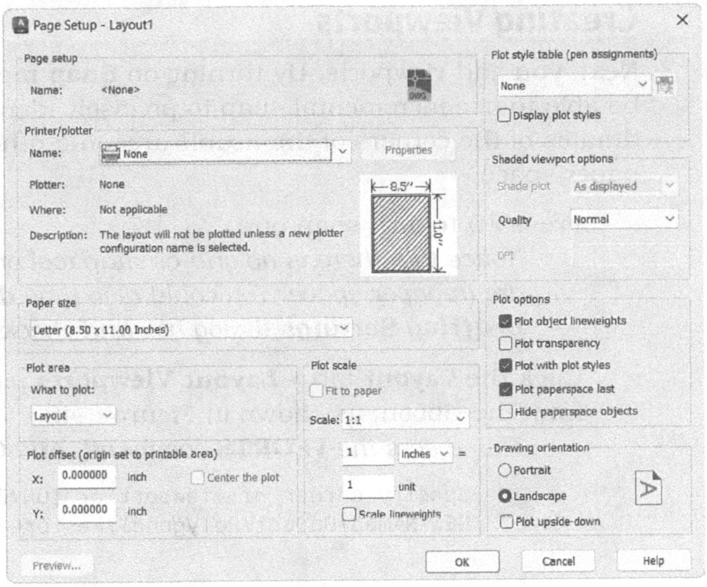

Figure 6-41
Page Setup – Layout1 dialog box

In this exercise, you use a D-size drawing sheet for your layout. If you do not have a D-size plotter, you can use the AutoCAD PDF (General Documentation).pc3 device, which is designed to create electronic plots that can be sent out over the internet or a local network. If you prefer to use a different-size paper, you have to make adjustments as you go along. If you use A-size, for example, most specifications can be divided by four. A-size specifications are included at critical points in case you don't have access to a D-size plotter or want to use a printer.

✔ In the **Printer/plotter** panel, select a plotting device that has a D-size sheet option, such as AutoCAD PDF (General Documentation).pc3.

✔ In the **Paper size** panel, select an ANSI D (34 × 22) paper size.

*The **Layout** is now the default selection in the **What to plot** list. You have not encountered this selection before because it is not present when you enter the **Plot** dialog box from model space.*

✔ If necessary, select **Landscape** in the **Drawing orientation** panel.

✔ Click **OK**.

*You return to the **Page Setup Manager**. Notice the changes in the panel labeled **Selected page setup details**.*

✔ Click the **Close** button.

AutoCAD adjusts the layout image to represent a D-size drawing sheet in landscape.

Your drawing is now truly representative of a drawing sheet. The rectangle of dotted lines within the white square of the paper indicates the *effective drawing* area of the sheet. Move your cursor to the upper-right corner to see the new limits.

Creating Viewports

Next, you add viewports. By turning on **Snap mode** in paper space, you will be able to use incremental snap to precisely identify the paper space coordinates of the corners of the usable area and other coordinate points in paper space.

✔ Press **F9** to turn snap on.

Notice that there is no grid or snap tool on the status bar when you are in paper space. You could also type **ds <Enter>** *to display the* ***Drafting Settings*** *dialog box and check the* ***Snap on*** *check box.*

✔ Click the **Layout** tab > **Layout Viewports** panel > **Rectangular** tool from the ribbon, as shown in Figure 6-42.

This enters the ***VPORTS*** *command. AutoCAD prompts:*

```
Specify corner of viewport or [ON/OFF/Fit/Shadeplot/Lock/
NEw/NAmed/Object/Polygonal/Restore/LAyer/2/3/4] <Fit>:
```

Figure 6-42
Viewports, Rectangular tool

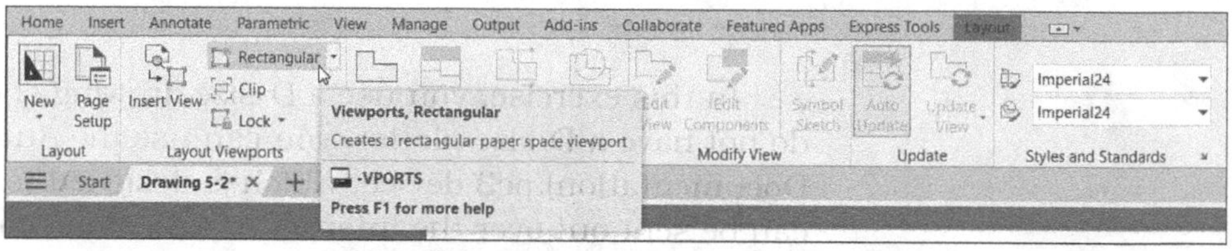

You only use the ***Specify corner*** *option in this exercise. With this option, you create a viewport just as you would a selection window. But first, check the coordinates of your usable paper space.*

✔ Move the cursor over the lower-left corner of the usable area of paper, the point **(0,0)**.

This is the origin of the plot, indicated by the corner of the effective drawing area.

✔ Move the cursor to the upper-right corner of the effective drawing area.

The exact point depends on your plotter. With the AutoCAD PDF (General Documentation).pc3 device and D-size paper, it is ***(33.50,20.50)****.*

Now you define a window for your first paper space viewport.

✔ Specify the point **(1.00,1.00)** the lower-left part of your drawing, as shown in Figure 6-43.

If you are not using a D-size paper, it is fine to make your viewports resemble those in Figure 6-43 but with a modified size, shape, and location.

✔ Specify an opposite corner, as shown in Figure 6-43. This is **(20,13)** on a D-size sheet.

Your viewport is drawn with the drawing extents from model space at maximum scale centered within the viewport.

Now, you create a second viewport to the right of the first.

Figure 6-43
Creating viewports

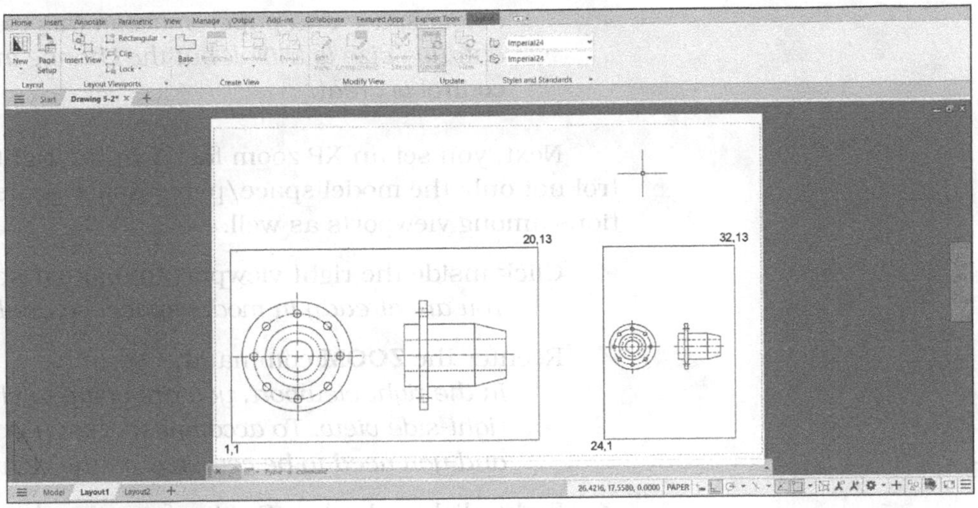

✔ Repeat **VPORTS**.

✔ Specify the point **(24.00,1.00)**, as shown in Figure 6-43.

✔ Specify the point **(32.00,13.00)**, as shown.

Zooming XP

You have now created a second viewport. Notice that the objects in the two viewports are drawn at different scales. Each is drawn to fit within its viewport. This can create problems later when you add dimensions and text. You want to maintain control over the scale of objects within viewports and have a clear knowledge of the relationships among scales in different viewports. For this, you can use the **Scale** feature of the **ZOOM** command. You create different zoom magnifications inside the two viewports.

✔ Double-click inside the left viewport.

This takes you into model space within the left viewport. You are going to zoom so that the two-view drawing is in a precise and known scale relation to paper space.

✔ Type **z <Enter>**.

*Notice the **ZOOM** command prompt:*

```
Specify corner of window, enter a scale factor (nX or nXP), or
[All/Center/Dynamic/Extents/Previous/Scale/Window/Object]
<real time>:
```

*In this exercise, you use two new options, the paper space scale factor option **(nXP)** and the **Center** option.*

✔ Type **2xp <Enter>** (on A-size paper divide these factors by four, so you will use **.5xp**).

This results in only a slight change in the left viewport. XP means "times paper." It allows you to zoom relative to paper space units. If you zoom 1xp, then a model space unit takes on the size of a current paper space unit, which, in turn, equals 1" of drawing paper. You zoomed 2xp. This means 1 unit in the viewport equals 2 paper space units or 2" on paper. You now have a precise relationship between model space and paper space in this viewport. The change in presentation size is trivial, but the change in terms of understanding and control is great.

Next, you set an XP zoom factor in the right viewport so that you control not only the model space/paper space scale relations but the scale relations among viewports as well.

✔ Click inside the right viewport to make it active.

You are already in model space, so double-clicking is unnecessary.

✔ Reenter the **ZOOM** command.

In the right viewport, you are going to show a close-up image of the right-side view. To accomplish this, you need a larger zoom factor, and you need to be centered on the right-side view.

✔ Right-click and select **Center** from the shortcut menu, or select **Center** from the command line.

AutoCAD prompts you to specify a center point.

✔ Specify a point on the centerline near the center of the flange—the midpoint of the vertical left side of the rectangle.

Look at Figure 6-44. The point you select becomes the center point of the right viewport when AutoCAD zooms in.

```
AutoCAD prompts:
Enter magnification or height <13.57>:
```

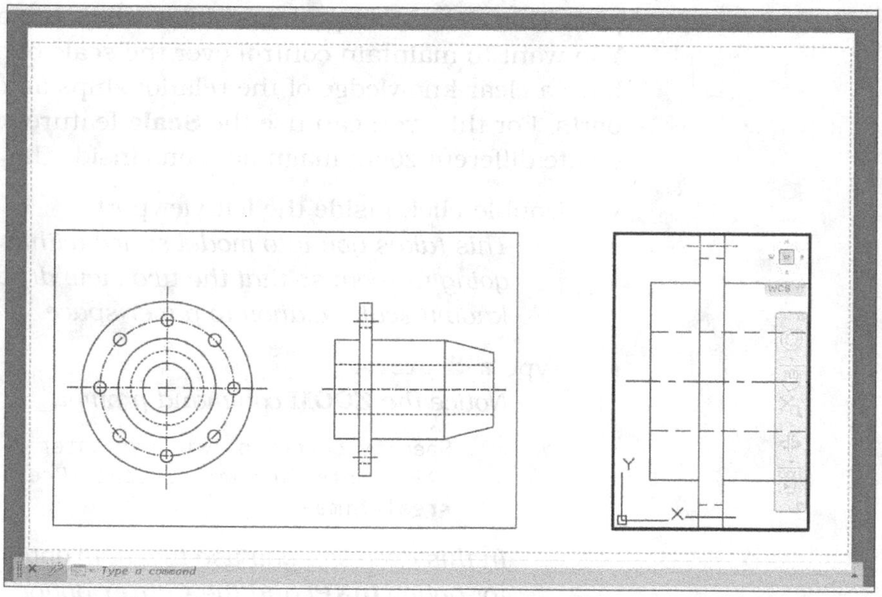

Figure 6-44
Zooming 4xp

Accepting the default would simply center the image in the viewport. You specify an XP value here.

✔ Type **4xp <Enter>**.

Your right viewport is dynamically magnified to resemble the one in Figure 6-44. In this enlarged image, 1 model space unit equals 4" in the drawing sheet (1 = 1 on A-size).

> **TIP**
>
> In addition to using the **Scale** feature of the **ZOOM** command to adjust the scale of objects in a viewport, you can also use the **Viewport Scale** drop-down list on the status bar.

Now that you know the technique, create one more viewport, focusing this time on one of the circle of holes in the flange.

✔ Type **mv <Enter>** to enter the **MVIEW** command.
AutoCAD automatically returns you to paper space temporarily.

✔ Specify the point **(1.00,14.00)**.

✔ Specify the point **(9.00,20.00)**.
You are now in model space in the new viewport.

✔ Using techniques you used with the previous viewport, zoom to the center in the new viewport, centering on the lower quadrant of the inner circle in the front view, at six times paper (6xp).
*This may require the use of a **Center** or **Quadrant** object snap. Remember that you can access a single-point object snap by holding down **<Shift>**, right-clicking in the drawing area, and then selecting from the **Object Snap** shortcut menu.*
Your drawing should resemble Figure 6-45.
Before proceeding to plot, try a print preview to ensure that you are ready.

✔ Double-click outside all viewports to return to paper space.

Figure 6-45
Three viewports

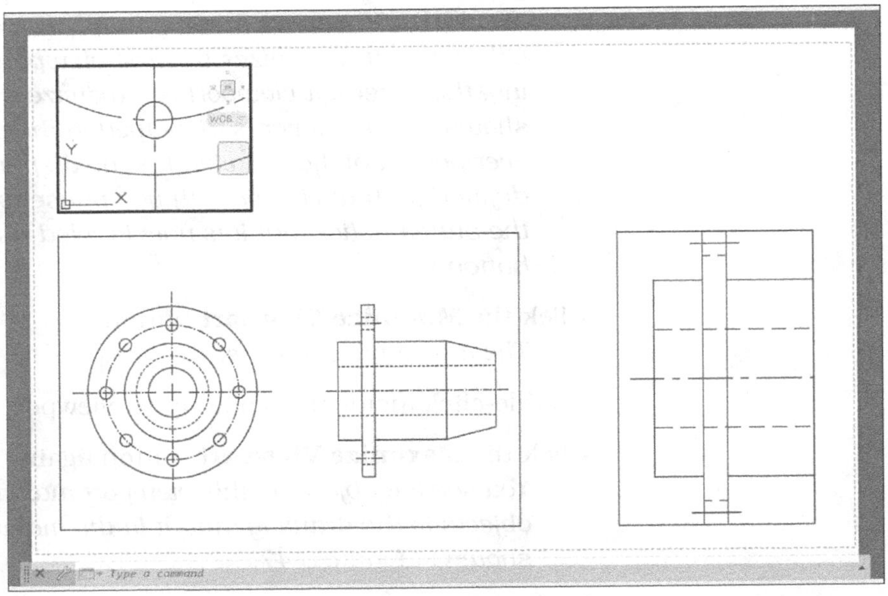

> **TIP**
>
> After the scale of all your viewports has been set, it is recommended to lock the viewports to ensure their assigned scale isn't accidentally changed while you're working in the model space of the viewport. To lock a viewport, select the viewport(s) to lock and then click the **Viewport Lock** button on the status bar or right-click and select **Display Locked** > **Yes** from the shortcut menu. Press **<Esc>** to clear the grips from the viewports.

✔ Click the **Plot** tool on the **Quick Access** toolbar.

✔ Click the **Preview** button in the **Plot** dialog box.

This full preview should look very much like the layout image. This is the beauty of the AutoCAD plotting system. You have a great deal of control and the ability to assess exactly what your paper output will be before you actually plot the drawing.

✔ Press **<Esc>** or **<Enter>** to exit the preview.

✔ Click **Cancel** to exit the **Plot** dialog box.

Maximize Viewport Button

Before going on, you learn about the **Maximize Viewport** button on the status bar. This button not only allows you to switch into model space in any viewport but also maximizes that viewport to fit the display. Once you have maximized a viewport, you can cycle through other viewports and maximize them one at a time. Try this:

✔ Click the **Maximize Viewport** button on the status bar, shown in Figure 6-46.

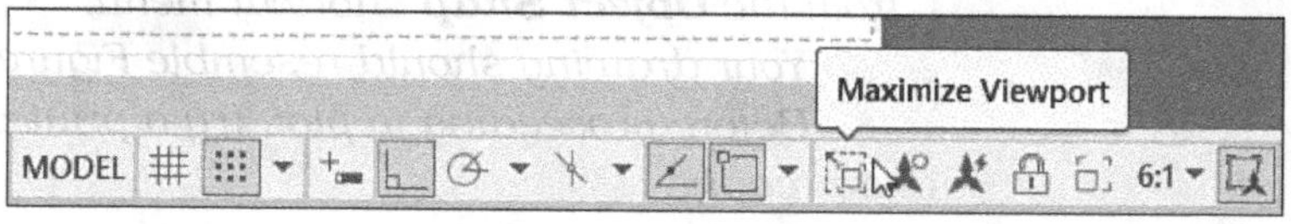

Figure 6-46
Maximize Viewport button

If you entered the model space of a viewport before clicking the ***Maximize Viewport*** *button, AutoCAD maximizes that viewport. Otherwise, it maximizes the first viewport you defined. In this drawing, the lower-left viewport is maximized. The maximized viewport shows you whatever is displayed in the viewport, along with whatever portion of the drawing fits the display at the magnification defined for that viewport. (If you pause with the selection arrow on the button notice that it is now labeled as the* ***Minimize Viewport*** *button.)*

✔ Click the **Minimize Viewport** button.

The layout view returns.

✔ Double-click inside the small upper viewport.

✔ Click the **Maximize Viewport** button again.

You see the objects in this viewport maximized along with other objects in the drawing that fit in the maximized drawing area, as shown in Figure 6-47.

✔ When you are done, click the **Minimize Viewport** button again.

This returns you to the paper space layout.

Figure 6-47
Viewport maximized

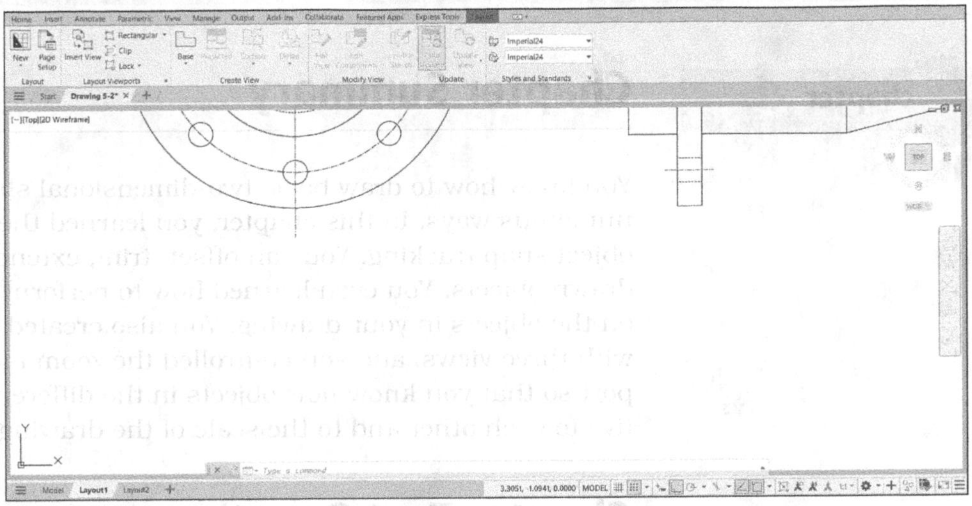

Plotting the Multiple-View Drawing

Now you are ready to plot. Plotting a multiple-viewport drawing is no different from plotting from a single view. Just make sure you are in the layout before entering the **PLOT** command.

✔ With Layout1 current, click the **Plot** tool on the **Quick Access** toolbar.

At this point, you should have no need to adjust settings within the ***Plot*** *dialog box because you have already made adjustments to the page setup and the plotting device. Notice the settings that are now included in the layout.*

NOTE

If you have done this exercise using the AutoCAD PDF (General Documentation).pc3 device, note that AutoCAD sends your plot to a file rather than to a plotter. Any drawing can be saved to a file to be plotted later or emailed to someone who needs to review the design.

✔ Prepare your plotter. (Make sure you use the right size paper.)

✔ Click **OK**.

Important: Be sure to save this drawing with its multiple-viewport, three-view layout before leaving this chapter. You may need it later.

6 chapter**six**

Chapter Summary

You know how to draw basic two-dimensional shapes and to edit them in numerous ways. In this chapter, you learned the power of object snap and object snap tracking. You can offset, trim, extend, and stretch previously drawn objects. You even learned how to perform geometric measurements on the objects in your drawing. You also created your first drawing layout with three views, and you controlled the zoom magnification in each viewport so that you know how objects in the different viewports are scaled relative to each other and to the scale of the drawing sheet.

Chapter Test Questions

Multiple Choice

Circle the correct answer.

1. To initiate a single-point object snap,

a. Enter an object snap mode at the *Select objects:* prompt.

b. Click the **Object Snap** button from the status bar.

c. Right-click the **Object Snap** button and select **Single Point**.

d. Enter an object snap mode when AutoCAD prompts for point selection.

2. To access the **Object Snap** shortcut menu,

a. Right-click when AutoCAD prompts for point selection.

b. Right-click after entering a draw command.

c. Click the **Object Snap** button.

d. Click the **Object Snap Tracking** button.

3. An acquired point will be

a. Saved in your drawing

b. An object snap point

c. Marked with a small green cross

d. Specified by pressing the left mouse button

4. In paper space, the typical plot scale is

a. Scaled to paper size

b. Scaled to fit

c. 1:1

d. Plot dependent

5. To coordinate layout scales with viewport scales use

a. **Viewport Scale**

b. **Zoom XP**

c. **Zoom Scale**

d. **Zoom Viewport**

Matching

Write the number of the correct answer on the line.

a. Cutting edge ______
b. Boundary edge ______
c. Intersection ______
d. Acquired point ______
e. Crossing window ______

1. Trim
2. Object snap tracking
3. Stretch
4. Object snap
5. Extend

True or False

Circle the correct answer.

1. **True or False**: It is not possible to plot a landscape-oriented plot on a printer.
2. **True or False**: Like incremental snap, object snap doesn't interfere with ordinary point selection.
3. **True or False**: When using the **TRIM** command, trimmed objects may also serve as cutting edges.
4. **True or False**: In the **Stretch** grip edit mode and the **STRETCH** command, it is necessary to select objects with a crossing window.
5. **True or False**: AutoCAD layouts are always created in paper space.

Questions

1. How do you access the **Object Snap** shortcut menu?
2. You have selected a line to extend and a boundary to extend it to, but AutoCAD gives you the message, "Object does not intersect an edge." What happened?
3. What selection method is always required when you use the **STRETCH** command?
4. Why is it usual practice to plot **1:1** in paper space?
5. Why do you use the **Zoom XP** option when zooming in floating model space viewports?

Drawing Problems

1. Draw a line from **(6,2)** to **(11,6)**. Draw a second line perpendicular to the first starting at **(6,6)**.
2. Break the first line at its intersection with the second.
3. There are now three lines in the drawing. Draw a circle centered at their intersection and passing through the midpoint of the line going up and to the right of the intersection.
4. Trim all the lines to the circumference of the circle.
5. Erase what is left of the line to the right of the intersection, and trim the portion of the circle to the left, between the two remaining lines.

Chapter Drawing Projects

G Drawing 6-1: *Sprocket* [INTERMEDIATE]

This drawing can be done with the tools you now have. It makes use of **Object Snap**, **TRIM**, **OFFSET**, and polar array. Be sure to set the limits large, as suggested.

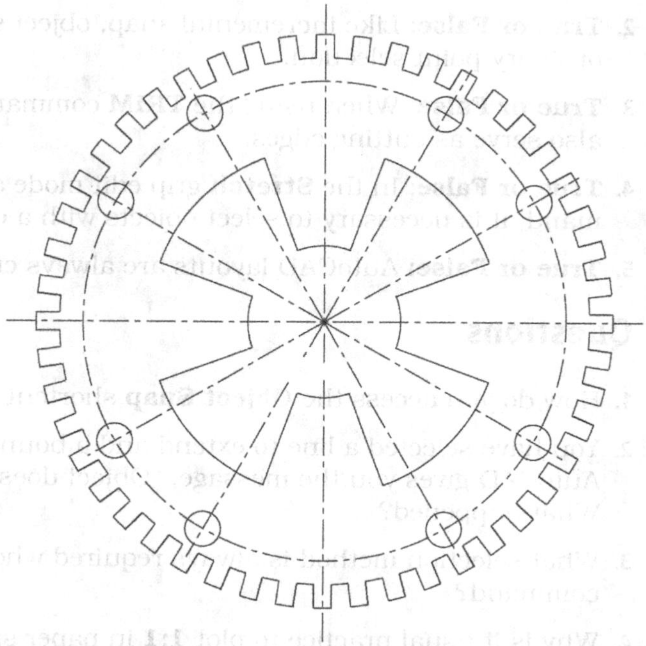

Drawing Suggestions

GRID = .25

SNAP = 0.0625

LIMITS = (0,0)(24,18)

- Begin by drawing the **12.25**- and **11.25**-diameter circles centered on the same point near the middle of your display.
- To construct the sprocket teeth, draw a line using the **Quadrant** object snap to locate the point at the top of the **12.25**-diameter circle. The second point can be straight down so that the line crosses the **11.25**-diameter circle. The exact length is insignificant because you will trim the line back to the inner circle.
- Offset this line **.1875** on both sides.

- Trim the first line, and trim and extend the other two lines to the inner and outer circles.
- Create a polar array of these lines and trim them to create the teeth.
- Draw the **10.25 B.C.** on the **Centerline** layer.
- Draw a line from the center to the quadrant.
- Use grips to rotate and copy the line to 30° and 60° for the **0.75**-diameter circles, and 20° and 70° for the inside cutout.
- Draw two circles where the centerline intersects with the bolt circle.
- Construct a polar array to get the proper hole pattern.
- Draw the **7.44**-diameter circle and the **3.25**-diameter circle.
- Trim to construct the cutout geometry.

Drawing 6-1
Sprocket

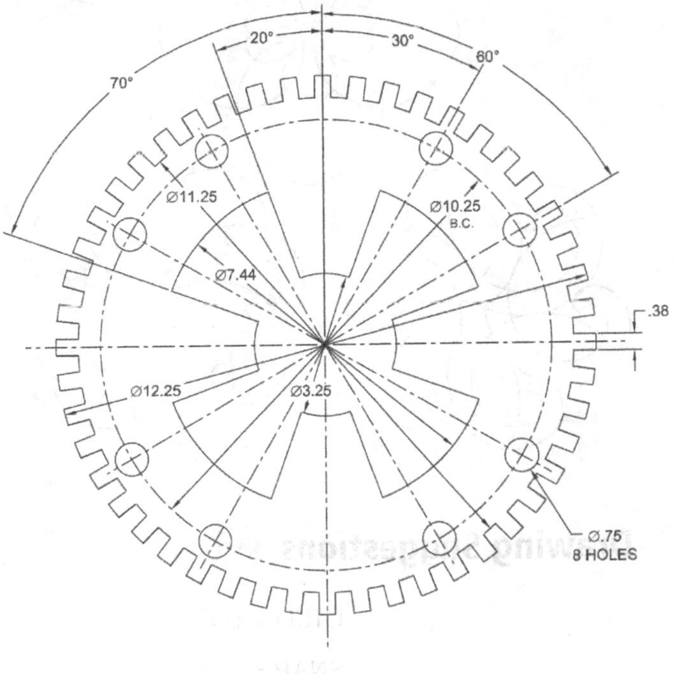

G

Drawing 6-2: *Archimedes Spiral* [INTERMEDIATE]

The designs in this drawing are not technical drawings, but they give you valuable experience with important CAD commands. First, you create an accurate Archimedes spiral using a radial grid of circles and lines as a guide. Once the spiral is done, turn off the grid layers and use the spiral to create the designs in the reference drawing.

Drawing Suggestions

GRID = 0.5

SNAP = 0.25

LIMITS = (0,0)(18,12)

LTSCALE = 0.5

- The alternating continuous and hidden lines work as a drawing aid. If you use different colors and layers, they are more helpful. Because all circles are offset **0.50**, you can draw one continuous and one hidden circle and then use the **OFFSET** command to create all the others.
- Begin by drawing one of the continuous circles on layer **0**, centered near the middle of your display; then offset all the other continuous circles.
- Draw the continuous horizontal line across the middle of your six circles, and then array it in a three-item polar array.

- Set to layer **2**, and draw one of the hidden circles, then the other hidden circles.
- Draw a vertical hidden line and array it as you did the horizontal continuous line.
- Set to layer **1** for the spiral itself.
- Turn on a running object snap to **Intersection** mode and construct a series of three-point arcs. Be sure to turn off any other modes that might get in your way. Start points and endpoints will be on continuous line intersections; second points always will fall on hidden line intersections.
- When the spiral is complete, turn off layers **0** and **2**. There should be nothing left in your drawing but the spiral itself.
- Once the spiral is complete, use only edit commands to create the designs. For the designs there are no dimensions. Don't be too concerned with precision. Some of your designs might come out slightly different from those in this chapter. When this happens, try to analyze the differences. To place all designs in one view, you will need to increase the limits.

Drawing 6-2
Archimedes Spiral

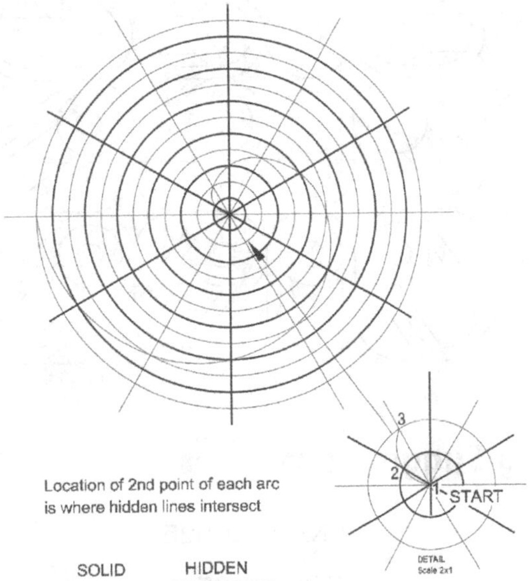

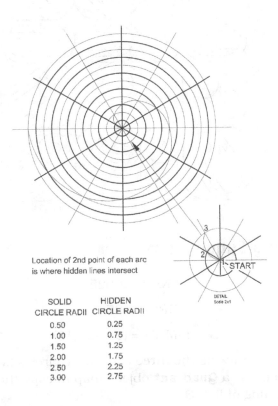

Location of 2nd point of each arc is where hidden lines intersect

SOLID CIRCLE RADII	HIDDEN CIRCLE RADII
0.50	0.25
1.00	0.75
1.50	1.25
2.00	1.75
2.50	2.25
3.00	2.75

G Drawing 6-3: *Link Design* [INTERMEDIATE]

This drawing provides a mental challenge and makes use of many commands and object snap modes with which you are now familiar. As is typical, there are numerous ways to reach the visual result shown. In all methods, you need to think carefully about the geometry of the links and how they are positioned relative to one another. The drawing suggestions here get you started but leave you with some puzzles to solve. The letters shown are labels for different styles of links; the numbers in the drawing suggest an order of steps you might take.

Drawing Suggestions

SNAP = .0625

GRID = .25

LIMITS = (0,0)(24,18)

- Start by drawing the three concentric circles labeled A above the number 1; then use a **Quadrant** object snap to copy these vertically to create the beginning of link B.
- Make another copy of the three circles up **.875**.
- Draw lines tangent to tangent from the middle and outer circles of the link. The final two vertical lines of link B are offset from a line between the centers of the upper and lower circles.
- Trim lines and circles to complete link B.

- Copy link B up so that the copy is at the upper quadrant point of link B. This becomes link C. Stretch the copy to create link C, in which the distance between the lower center and the upper center is **1.25**.
- Create a polar array of links B and C with circles A in the center to create a cross pattern.
- The rectangles and squares in Steps 2 and 3 are created by drawing lines from different quadrant points on the links in the array. Fillet the corners of these boxes to the **0.875** radius.
- The diagonal links inside the boxes can be created in a manner similar to links B and C and then copied in polar arrays.

Drawing 6-3
Link Design

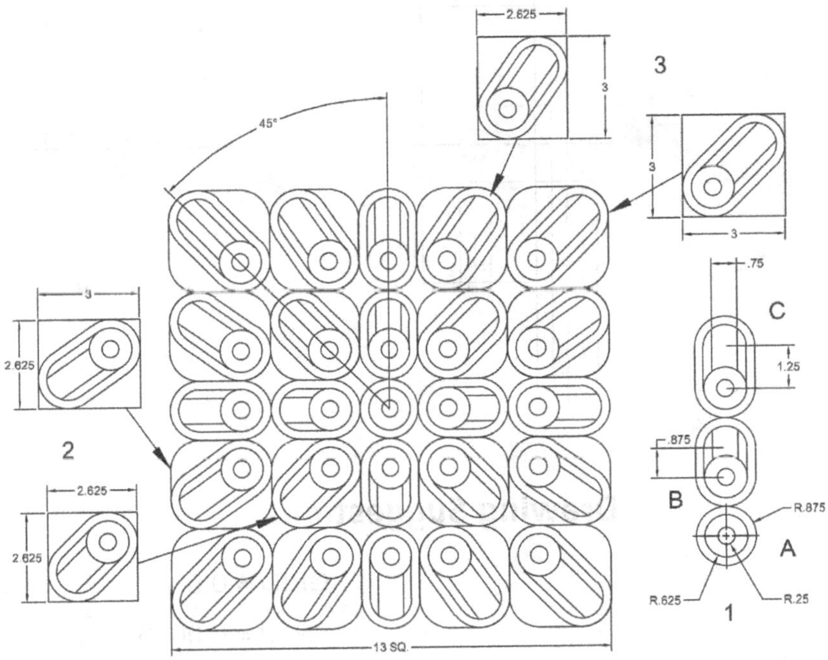

M Drawing 6-4: *Grooved Hub* [INTERMEDIATE]

This drawing includes another typical application of the rotation techniques just discussed. The hidden lines in the front view must be rotated 120° and a copy retained in the original position. There are also good opportunities to use **MIRROR**, object snap, object snap tracking, and **TRIM**.

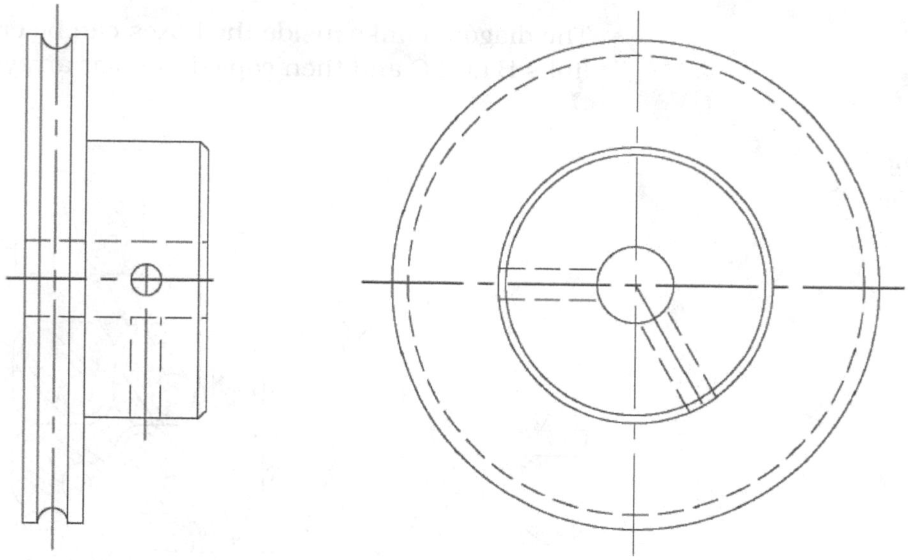

Drawing Suggestions

GRID = 0.5

SNAP = 0.0625

LIMITS = (0,0)(12,9)

LTSCALE = 1

- Draw the circles in the front view, and use these to line up the horizontal lines in the left-side view. This is a good opportunity to use object snap tracking. By acquiring the quadrant of a circle in the front view, you can track along the horizontal construction lines to the left-side view.
- There are several different planes of symmetry in the left-side view, which suggests the use of mirroring. It is left up to you to choose an efficient sequence.
- A quick method for drawing the horizontal hidden lines in the left-side view is to acquire the upper and lower quadrant points of the **0.625**-diameter circle in the front view to track horizontal construction lines. Draw the lines in the left-side view longer than actual length, and then use **TRIM** to erase the excess on both sides of the left-side view.

- The same method can be used to draw the two horizontal hidden lines in the front view. A slightly different method that does not use object tracking is to snap lines directly to the top and bottom quadrants of the **0.25**-diameter circle in the left-side view as a guide and draw them all the way through the front view. Then trim to the **2.25**-diameter circle and the **0.62**-diameter circle.
- Once these hidden lines are drawn, rotate them, retaining a copy in the original position.

Creating the Multiple-View Layout

Use this drawing to create the multiple-view layout shown below the dimensioned drawing. This three-view layout is very similar to the one created in the "Creating Plot Layouts" section. Exact dimensions of the viewports are not given. You should create them depending on the paper size you want to use. What should remain consistent is the scale relationships among the three viewports. On an A sheet, for example, if the largest viewport is zoomed **0.5xp**, then the left close-up is **1.0xp**, and the top close-up is **1.5xp**. These ratios must be adjusted for other sheet sizes.

Drawing 6-4
Grooved Hub

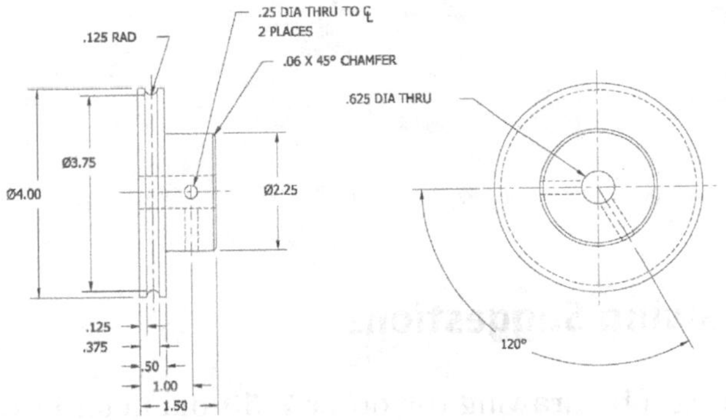

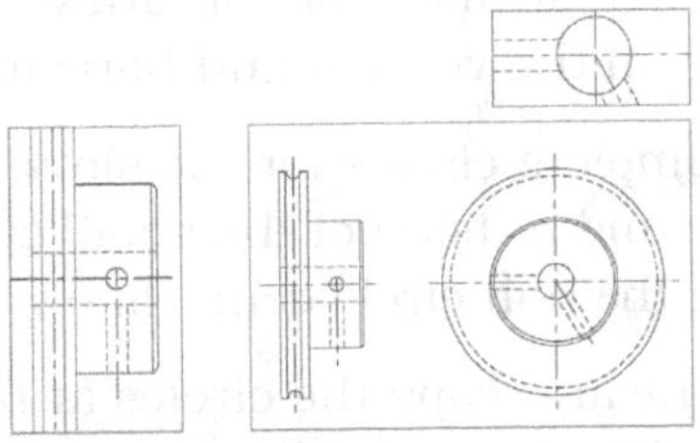

M Drawing 6-5: *Slotted Flange* [ADVANCED]

This drawing includes a typical application of polar arrays, **ROTATE**, and **TRIM**. The finished drawing should consist of the 2D top view and front view, not the 3D view shown on the drawing page. The centerlines and outline of the large circle in the top view are shown in the reference drawing. Use the 3D view as a reference to draw the 2D top and front views.

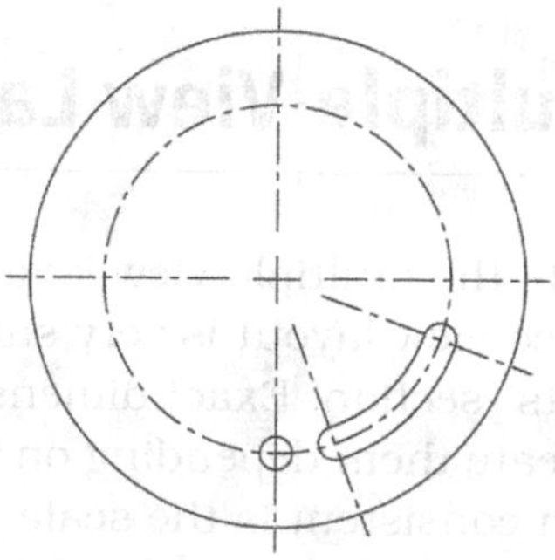

Location of Top View

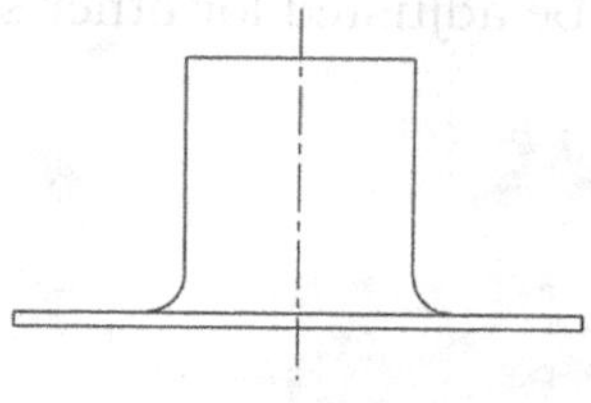

Location of Front View

Drawing Suggestions

- Begin by drawing the outer **7.50**-diameter circle. Then draw the three circles on the centerline for the center bored hole in the top view.
- Figure out the placement of and draw the bolt circle diameter for the four small circles on the vertical and horizontal centerlines in the top view.
- Draw two complete circles for the slots. These circles should run tangent to the inside and outside of the small circles, or they can be constructed by offsetting the bolt circle centerline.
- You can rotate and copy the circles at the end of the slots into place using grips; then trim what is not needed.
- Complete the front view, making sure to line up the circles and centerlines in the top view with the vertical lines in the front view.

Drawing 6-5
Slotted Flange

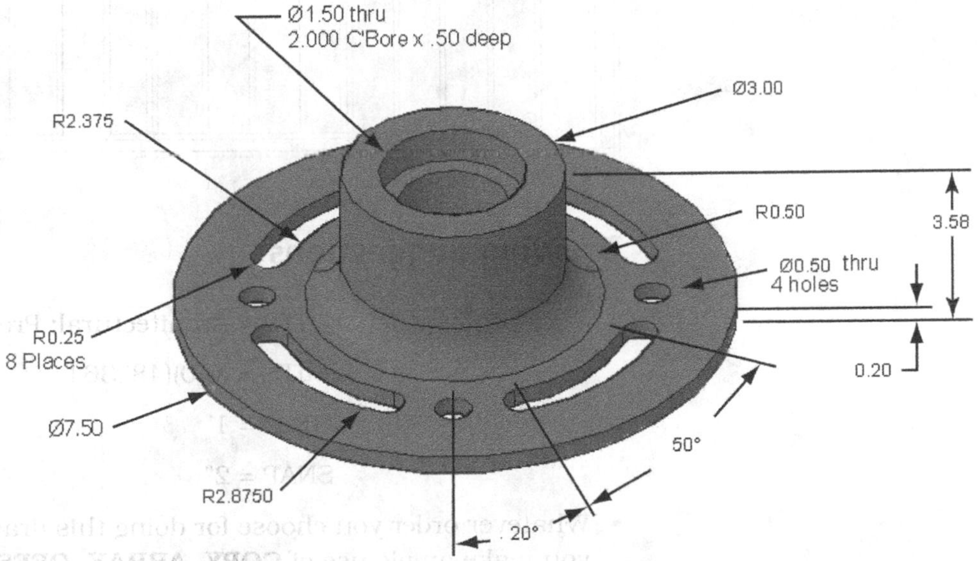

A Drawing 6-6: *Deck Framing* [INTERMEDIATE]

This architectural drawing may take some time, although there is nothing in it you have not done before. Be sure to make the suggested adjustments to your drawing setup before beginning.

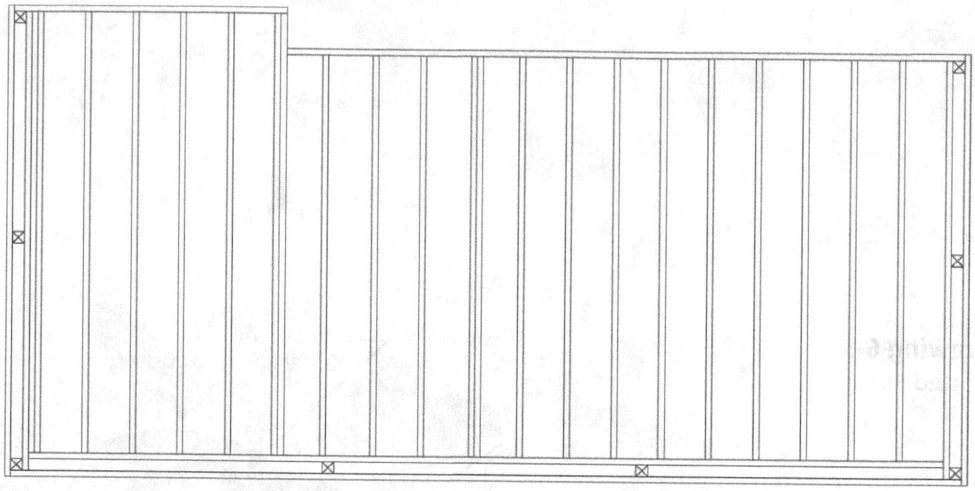

Drawing Suggestions

UNITS = Architectural; Precision = 0'-0"

LIMITS = (0,0)(48',36')

GRID = 1'

SNAP = 2"

- Whatever order you choose for doing this drawing, it is suggested that you make ample use of **COPY**, **ARRAY**, **OFFSET**, and **TRIM**.
- Keep **Ortho** on, except to draw the lines across the middle of the squares, representing upright posts.
- With snap set at 2", it is easy to copy lines 2" apart, as you have to do frequently to draw the 2 × 8 studs.
- You may need to turn **Snap Mode** off when you are selecting lines to copy, but be sure to turn it on again to specify displacements.
- Notice that you can use **ARRAY** effectively, but there are three separate arrays. They are all 16" on center, but the double boards in several places make it inadvisable to do a single array of studs all the way across the deck. What you can do, however, is draw, copy, and array all the "vertical" studs at the maximum length first and then go back and trim them to their various actual lengths using the "horizontal" boards as cutting edges.

Drawing 6-6
Deck Framing

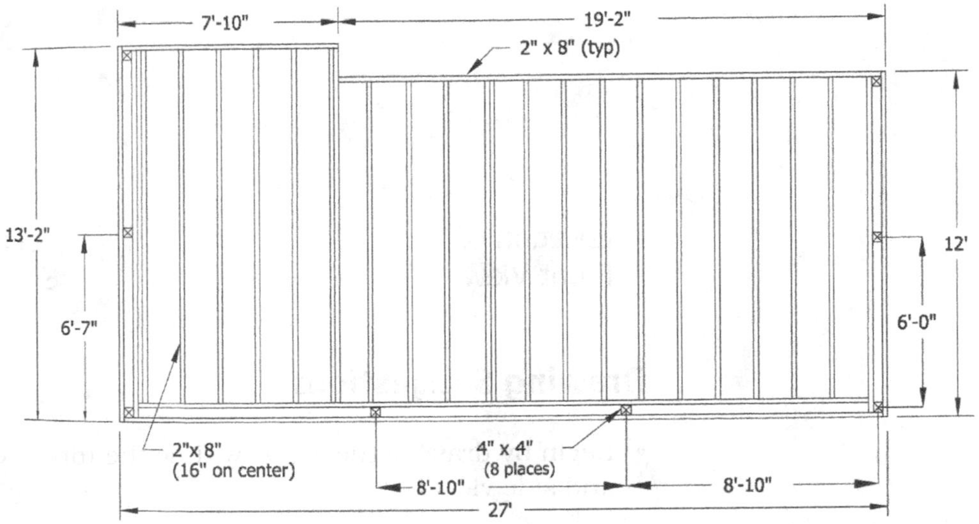

Drawing 6-7: *Tool Block* [ADVANCED]

In this drawing, you take information from a 3D drawing and develop it into a three-view drawing. The finished drawing should be composed of the top view, front view, and side view. The reference drawing shows a portion of each view to be developed. You are to complete these views.

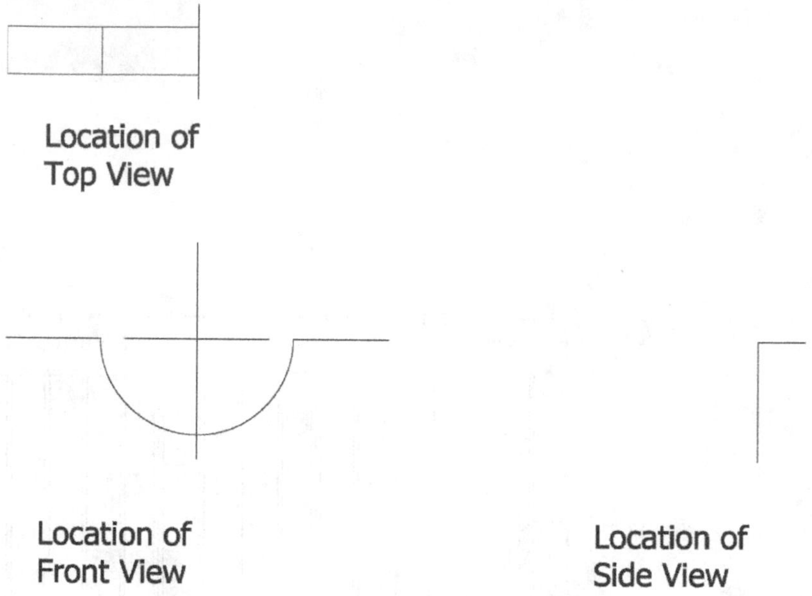

Drawing Suggestions

- Begin by drawing the top view. Use the top view to line up the front view and side view.
- The slot with the angular lines must be drawn in the front view before the other views. These lines can then be lined up with the top and side views and used as guides to draw the hidden lines.
- Be sure to include all the necessary hidden lines and centerlines in each view.

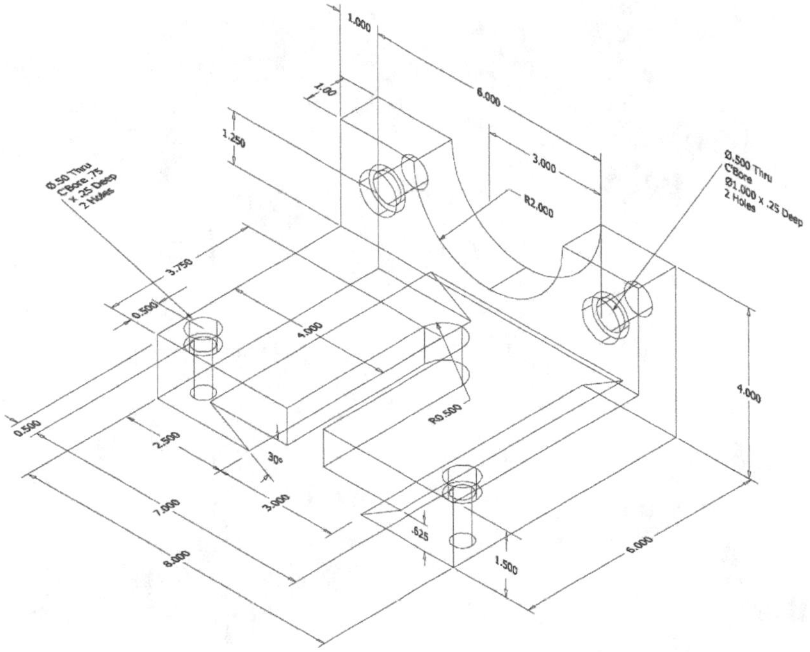

1.000
6.000
1.250
3.000
R2.000
Ø.50 Thru
C'Bore .75
x .25 Deep
2 Holes
Ø.500 Thru
C'Bore
Ø1.000 x .25 Deep
2 Holes
3.750
0.500
4.000
4.000
R0.500
0.500
2.500
30°
3.000
7.000
8.000
.525
1.500
6.000

7 chapterseven

Text

CHAPTER OBJECTIVES

- Enter single-line text with justification options
- Enter text on an angle and enter text using character codes
- Enter multiline text using **MTEXT**
- Edit text in place with **TEXTEDIT**
- Modify text with the **Quick Properties** palette
- Use the **SPELL** and **FIND** commands
- Change fonts and styles
- Change properties with **MATCHPROP**
- Scale previously drawn entities
- Create tables and fields
- Use drawing templates, borders, and title blocks

Introduction

Now, it's time for a discussion of adding text to your drawings. In this chapter, you learn to find your way around AutoCAD's **TEXT** and **MTEXT** commands. In addition, you discover many new editing commands often used with text but equally important for editing other objects.

Entering Single-Line Text with Justification Options

TEXT	
Command	TEXT
Alias	(none)
Panel	Text
Tool	A

AutoCAD provides two commands for entering text in a drawing. **TEXT** allows you to enter single lines of text and displays them as you type. **MTEXT** allows you to type multiple lines of text in a special text editor and positions them in a windowed area of your drawing. Both commands provide numerous options for placing and formatting text. Named styles can be created and applied to text to enforce consistent appearance across your drawing. You probably are already familiar with entering single lines of left-justified text. Here, you begin to include other forms of single-line text.

✔ To prepare for this exercise, create a new drawing using B-size (18 × 12) limits, turn off grid display, and draw a 4.00-unit horizontal line beginning at (1,1). Then, create five copies of the line 2.00 units apart, as shown in Figure 7-1.

These lines are for orientation in this exercise only; they are not essential for drawing text. Your first step is a quick review of left-justified text.

✔ Click the **Annotate** tab > **Text** panel > **Text** drop-down menu > **Single Line** text tool.

✔ Specify a start point at the left end of the upper line.

✔ Press **<Enter>** to accept the default height (0.2000).

✔ Press **<Enter>** to accept the default angle (0).

✔ Type **Left <Enter>**.

Notice that the text cursor jumps below the line when you press ***<Enter>***.

✔ Type **Justified <Enter>**.

The text cursor jumps down again, and another ***Enter text*** *prompt appears. To exit the command, you need to press* ***<Enter>*** *at the prompt.*

✔ Press **<Enter>** to exit the command.

This completes the process and returns you to the command-line prompt.

Figure 7-2 shows the left-justified text you have just drawn.

TIP

Single-line and multiline text is commonly placed on specific layers. You can use the text layer override setting to put any new annotation you create on a specific layer for text without having to first change the current layer. To change the text layer override setting, do one of the following:

- Click the **Annotate** tab, expand the **Text** panel, and select a layer from the **Text Layer Override** drop-down list.
- Enter the **TEXTLAYER** system variable at the command line and type the name of the layer you want to use.

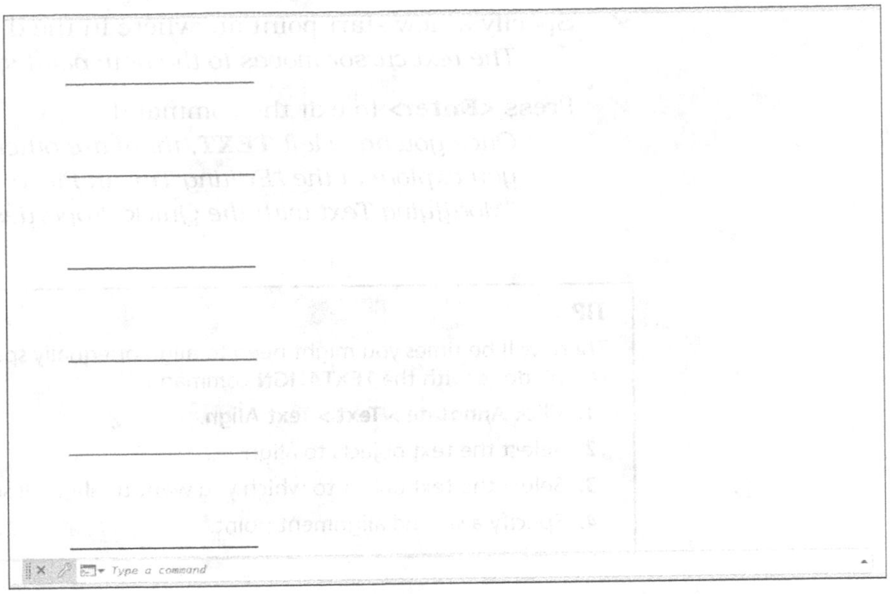

Figure 7-1
Drawing six lines

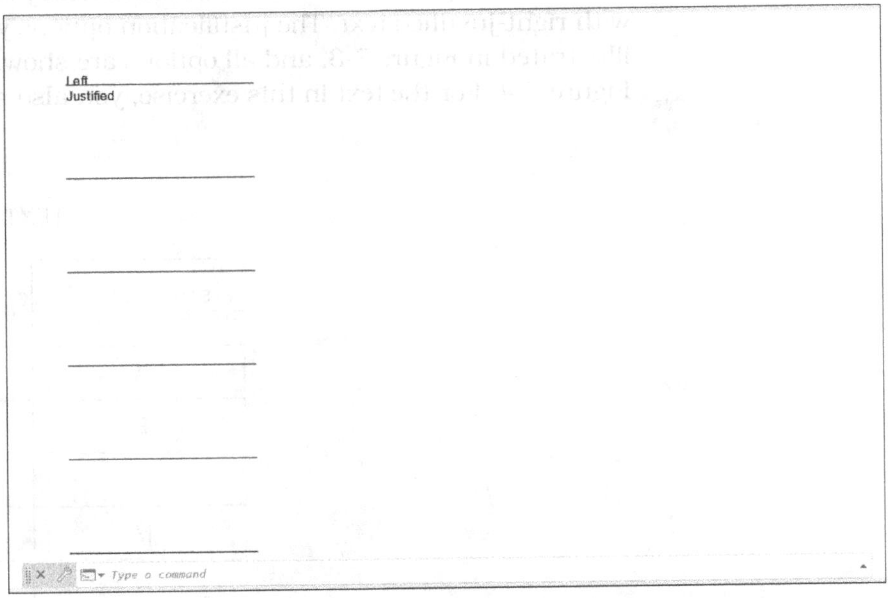

Figure 7-2
Left-justified text

Before proceeding with other text justification options, you should know about one additional feature of **TEXT**:

✔ Press **<Enter>** to repeat the **TEXT** command.
*If you press **<Enter>** again at this point instead of specifying a new start point or selecting a justification option, you go right back to the **Enter text** prompt as if you had never left the command. Try it.*

✔ Press **<Enter>** again.
*You see the **Enter text** prompt in the command line, and the text cursor reappears just below the word **Justified**.*

✔ Type **Text <Enter>**.
*Anytime you have the **Specify start point** prompt in the command line, you can also move the text cursor to another point. Try it.*

- ✔ Specify a new start point anywhere in the drawing.

  The text cursor moves to the new point specified.

- ✔ Press **<Enter>** to exit the command.

  *Once you have left **TEXT**, there are other ways to edit text, which you explore in the "Editing Text in Place with TEXTEDIT" and "Modifying Text with the Quick Properties Palette" sections.*

> **TIP**
>
> There will be times you might need to align or equally space multiple text objects. This can be done with the **TEXTALIGN** command.
>
> 1. Click **Annotate** > **Text** > **Text Align**.
> 2. Select the text objects to align.
> 3. Select the text object to which you want to align all selected text objects.
> 4. Specify a second alignment point.

You now proceed to some of the other text justification options, beginning with right-justified text. The justification options you try in this exercise are illustrated in Figure 7-3, and all options are shown in the complete chart in Figure 7-4. For the text in this exercise, you also specify a change in height.

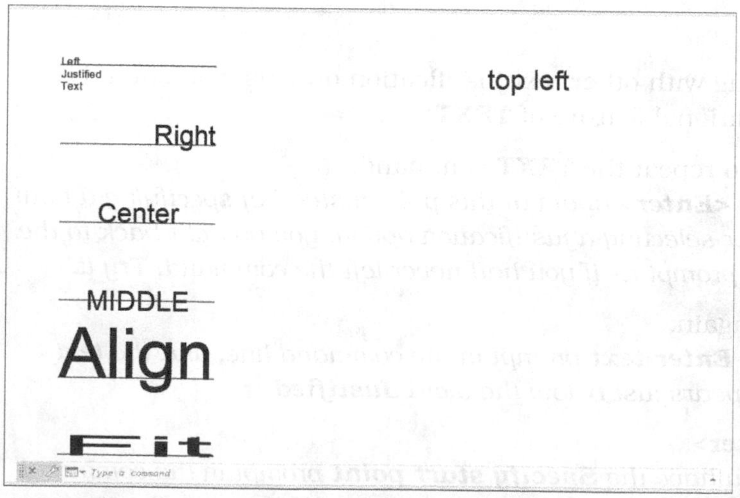

Figure 7-3
Examples of text justification options

TEXT JUSTIFICATION	
START POINT TYPE ABBREVIATION	TEXT POSITION + INDICATES START POINT OR PICK POINT
A	ALIGN
F	FIT
C	CENTER
M	MIDDLE
R	RIGHT
TL	TOP LEFT
TC	TOP CENTER
TR	TOP RIGHT
ML	MIDDLE LEFT
MC	MIDDLE CENTER
MR	MIDDLE RIGHT
BL	BOTTOM LEFT
BC	BOTTOM CENTER
BR	BOTTOM RIGHT

Figure 7-4
Text options

Right-Justified Text

Right-justified text is constructed from an endpoint backing up, right to left.

✔ Repeat the **TEXT** command.

✔ Right-click and select **Justify** from the shortcut menu shown in Figure 7-5.

If Dynamic Input is open, this calls up a dynamic input list.

✔ If **Dynamic Input** is open, select **Right** from the menu. Otherwise, select **Right** from the command line.

You are prompted for an endpoint instead of a start point:

```
Specify right endpoint of text baseline:
```

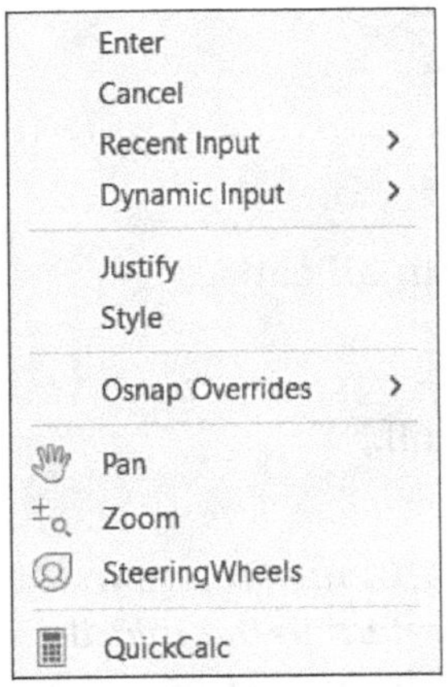

Figure 7-5
Shortcut menu

✔ Specify the right end of the second line.

The prompt requests you to specify a text height. This time you change the height to ***0.50****.*

✔ Type **.5 <Enter>**.

✔ Press **<Enter>** to retain 0° of rotation.

Notice the larger text cursor at the right end of the second line.

✔ Type **Right <Enter>**.

You should have the word "Right" right-justified on the second line.

✔ Press **<Enter>** to exit the command.

Your drawing should now include the second line of text in right-justified position, as shown in Figure 7-3.

Centered Text

Centered text is justified from the bottom center of the text.

✔ Repeat the **TEXT** command.

✔ Select **Justify** from the command line.

✔ Select **Center** from the command line or **Dynamic Input** list.

AutoCAD prompts:

```
Specify center point of text:
```

✔ Specify the midpoint of the third line.

✔ Press **<Enter>** to retain the current height, which is now set to **0.50**.

✔ Press **<Enter>** to retain 0° of rotation.

✔ Type **Center <Enter>**.

✔ Press **<Enter>** again to complete the command.

The word "Center" should now be centered, as shown in Figure 7-3.

Middle Text

Middle text is justified from the middle of the text both horizontally and vertically, rather than from the bottom center. Previously you have selected justification options from the command line and shortcut menu; this time you skip these steps by typing in the initial for the option. Also, for this text, you enter it in uppercase letters, which is common in most drawings.

✔ Repeat **TEXT**.

✔ Type **m <Enter>**.
AutoCAD prompts:

```
Specify middle point of text:
```

✔ Specify the midpoint of the fourth line.

✔ Press **<Enter>** to retain the current height of 0.50.

✔ Press **<Enter>** to retain 0° of rotation.

✔ Press **<Caps Lock>** on your keyboard to enter text in all caps.

✔ Type **MIDDLE <Enter>**.

✔ Press **<Caps Lock>** on your keyboard to turn caps off.

✔ Press **<Enter>** again to complete the command.
Notice the difference between center and middle. Center refers to the midpoint of the baseline below the text. Middle refers to the middle of the text itself, so that the line now runs through the text.

Aligned Text

Aligned text is placed between two specified points. The height of the text is calculated proportional to the distance between the two points, and the text is drawn along the line between the two points.

✔ Repeat **TEXT**.

✔ Type **a <Enter>**.
AutoCAD prompts:

```
Specify first endpoint of text baseline:
```

✔ Specify the left end of the fifth line.
AutoCAD prompts for another point:

```
Specify second endpoint of text baseline:
```

✔ Specify the right end of the fifth line.
Notice that there is no prompt for height. AutoCAD calculates a height based on the space between the points you chose. There is also no prompt for an angle because the angle between the two points (in this case, 0) is used.

✔ Type **Align <Enter>**.
The text initially appears very large, but as you type, the text size is adjusted with the addition of each letter.

- ✔ Press **<Enter>** again to complete the command.

  Notice that the text is sized to fill the space between the two points you selected.

Text Drawn to Fit Between Two Points

The **Fit** option is similar to the **Align** option, except that the specified text height is retained.

- ✔ Repeat **TEXT**.
- ✔ Type **f <Enter>**.

  You are prompted for two points, as in the ***Align*** *option.*
- ✔ Specify the left end of the sixth line.
- ✔ Specify the right end of the sixth line.
- ✔ Press **<Enter>** to retain the current height.

  As with the ***Align*** *option, there is no prompt for an angle of rotation.*
- ✔ Type **Fit <Enter>**.

  Once again, the text size is adjusted as you type, but this time, only the width changes.
- ✔ Press **<Enter>** again to complete the command.

  This time, the text is stretched horizontally to fill the line without a change in height. This is the difference between ***Fit*** *and* ***Align****. In the* ***Align*** *option, the text height is determined by the width you show. With* ***Fit****, the specified height is retained, and the text is stretched or compressed to fill the given space.*

Other Justification Options

Before proceeding to the next exercise, take a moment to look at the complete list of justification options. The command-line prompt looks like this:

```
Enter an option [Left/Center/Right/Align/Middle/Fit/TL/TC/TR/ML/MC/
MR/BL/BC/BR]:
```

The same options are on the dynamic input list and are spelled out in the chart shown in Figure 7-4. You have already explored the first six justification options. For the others, study the figure. As shown on the chart, *T* is for top, *M* is for middle, and *B* is for bottom. *L*, *C*, and *R* stand for left, center, and right, respectively. Let's try one:

- ✔ Repeat **TEXT** and then type **tl <Enter>** for the **Top Left** option, or select **TL** from the dynamic input list or command line.

  AutoCAD gives you the ***Specify top-left point of text*** *prompt. As shown in Figure 7-4, "top left" refers to the highest potential text point at the left of the word.*
- ✔ Specify a top-left point to place the text, as shown in Figure 7-3.
- ✔ Press **<Enter>** twice to accept the height and rotation angle settings and arrive at the ***Text*** prompt.

✔ Type **top left <Enter>**.

The text is entered from the top-left position.

✔ Press **<Enter>** again to complete the command.

Your drawing should now resemble Figure 7-3.

Entering Text on an Angle and Text Using Character Codes

In this section, you explore **TEXT** further by entering several lines on an angle and adding special character symbols along the way. You create three lines of left-justified text, one below the other and all rotated 45°, as shown in Figure 7-6.

✔ Repeat the **TEXT** command.

AutoCAD retains your most recent choice of options, so if you have not used other text options, you see the prompt for a top-left point. This option is fine for the purpose of this exercise but is not necessary.

```
Specify top-left point of text or [Justify/Style]:
```

✔ Specify a point near (12.00,8.00), as shown in Figure 7-6.

✔ Type **.3 <Enter>** to specify a smaller text size.

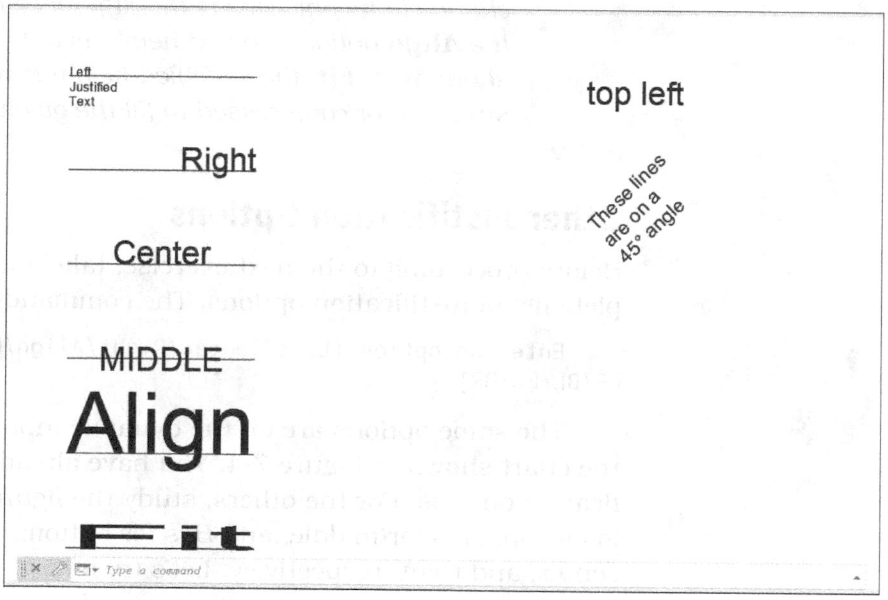

Figure 7-6
Text on an angle

✔ Type **45 <Enter>** to set an angle of 45°.

Notice that the text cursor is shown at the specified angle.

✔ Type **These lines <Enter>**.

The text is drawn in your drawing at a 45° angle, and the cursor moves down to the next line. Notice that the text cursor is still at the specified angle.

✔ Type **are on a <Enter>**.

The Degree Symbol and Other Special Characters

The next line contains a degree symbol. Because you do not have this character on your keyboard, AutoCAD provides a special method for adding it to the single-line text object. Type the text with the **%%** signs, as shown in the first step and then study Figure 7-7, which lists other special characters that can be drawn in the same way.

Figure 7-7
Control codes and special characters

Control Codes and Special Characters	
Type at Text Prompt	Text in Drawing
%%OOVERSCORE	OVERSCORE
%%UUNDERSCORE	UNDERSCORE
180%%D	180°
2.00 %%P.01	2.00 ±.01
%%C4.00	Ø4.00
37.5%%%	37.5%

✔ Type **45%%d.**

TEXT *initially displays the percent symbols directly in the text editor, just as you have typed them. When you type the* ***d****, the character code is translated and redrawn as a degree symbol.*

✔ Add a space and then type **angle <Enter>**.

✔ Press **<Enter>** again to complete the command sequence.

Your drawing should now resemble Figure 7-6.

Entering Multiline Text Using MTEXT

MTEXT	
Command	MTEXT
Alias	T
Panel	Text
Tool	A

The **MTEXT** command allows you to create multiple lines of text as a single object in a text editor and position them within a defined window in your drawing. Like **TEXT**, **MTEXT** has nine options for text justification and its own set of character codes.

You begin by creating a simple left-justified block of text.

✔ Click the **Multiline Text** tool from the **Text** drop-down list on the **Text** panel of the **Annotate** tab, as shown in Figure 7-8.

You see the following prompt in the command line:

```
Specify first corner:
```

Also, notice that a multiline text symbol, "abc", has been added to the crosshairs.

Figure 7-8
Multiline Text tool

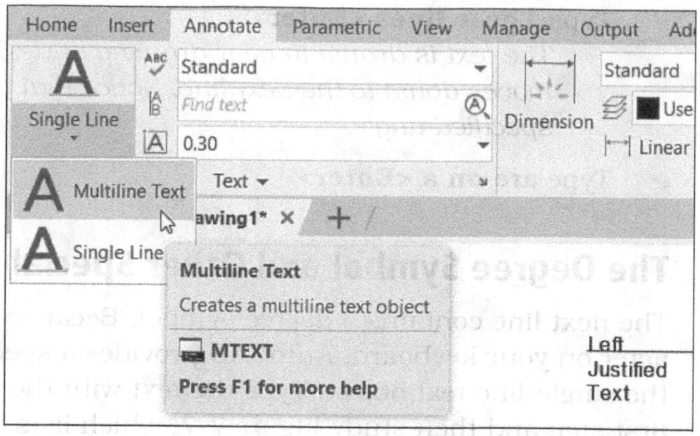

Fundamentally, **MTEXT** lets you define the width of a group of text lines that you create in a special text editor. As the text is entered, AutoCAD formats it to conform to the specified width and justification options and draws it. The width can be defined in several ways. The default method for specifying a width is to draw a window in the drawing, but this can be misleading. **MTEXT** does not attempt to place the complete text inside that window but only within its width. The first point of the window becomes the insertion point of the text. How AutoCAD uses this insertion point depends on the justification option. The second window point defines the width and the text flow direction (that is, whether the text lines should be drawn above or below and to the left or right of the insertion point). Exactly how this is interpreted is also dependent on the justification option.

✔ Specify an insertion point near the middle of your drawing area, in the neighborhood of (12.00,5.00).

AutoCAD begins a window at the selected point and gives you a new prompt:

```
Specify opposite corner or
[Height/Justify/Line spacing/Rotation/Style/Width/Columns]:
```

Continue with the default options by specifying a second corner. For purposes of this exercise, a window 2.00 units wide is drawn down and to the right from the insertion point.

✔ Specify a second point 2.00 units to the right and about 1.00 unit below the insertion point.

When you specify the opposite corner, AutoCAD opens the ***Multiline Text In-place Editor*** *at the insertion point in your drawing. At the same time, the* ***Text Editor*** *contextual tab is added to the ribbon, as illustrated in Figure 7-9. The panels on the* ***Text Editor*** *tab give you the capacity to change text styles and fonts (see the "Changing Fonts and Styles" section) and text height, along with many other text features, such as bolding and underlining. When you enter text in the editor, it wraps around as it will be displayed in your drawing, according to the width you have specified. This width is represented by the small ruler at the top of the text editor. Using the small L along the left side of the ruler, you can also set first-line indent and hanging indent tabs for paragraph formatting. If you let the cursor* *rest along the right side of the ruler, you see a double-arrow cursor that indicates you can adjust the width of the window. Letting the cursor rest at the bottom edge of the text editor, you see two vertical arrows that indicate you can adjust the height of the window.*

Figure 7-9
Multiline Text In-place Editor

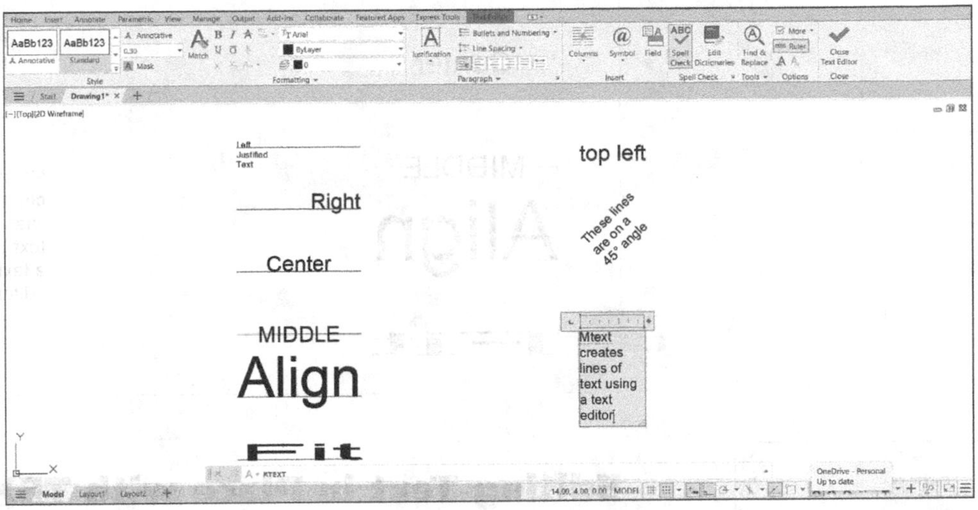

The text editor is placed at the actual text location, and the text is shown in the editor at the same size as it will appear in the drawing, unless this would make it either too large or too small for convenient editing. In such cases, the text size is adjusted to a reasonable size for editing, and the actual size is shown only when the command is completed.

✔ Type **Mtext creates lines of text using a text editor**.

Text appears in the text editor, as shown in Figure 7-9.

✔ Specify a point outside the text editor to leave the editor and complete the command.

You are returned to the drawing window. The ***Annotate*** *tab is set as current again, and the new text is added, as shown in Figure 7-10. Notice that the text you typed has been wrapped around to fit within the 2.00-width window; the 0.30 height of the text has been retained; and the 1.00 height of the text window you defined has been ignored.*

In a moment, you explore other multiline text (mtext) justification options. First, however, you do some simple text editing with ***TEXTEDIT****.*

TIP

Multiple single-line and multiline text (mtext) objects can be combined into a single mtext object. To combine multiple text objects, type **txt2mtxt <Enter>** at the command prompt and follow the prompts.

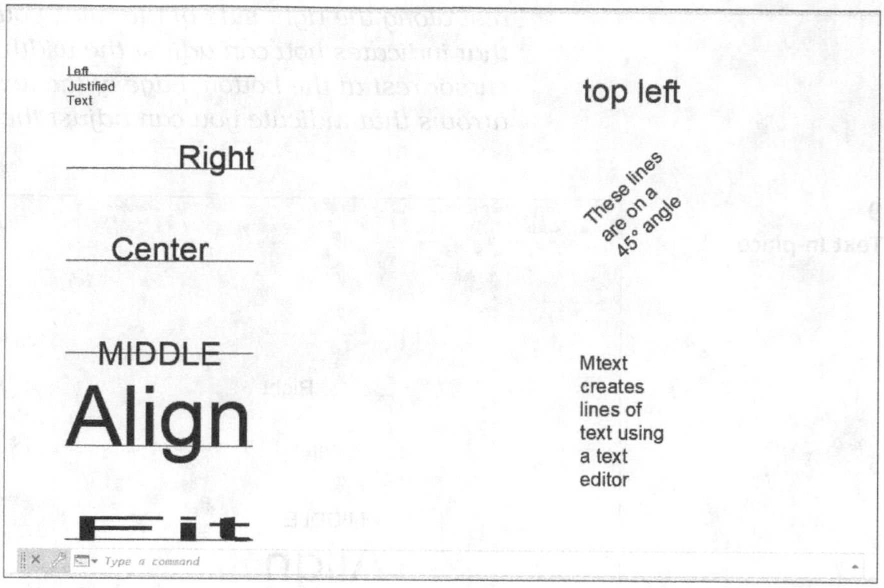

Figure 7-10
New text added

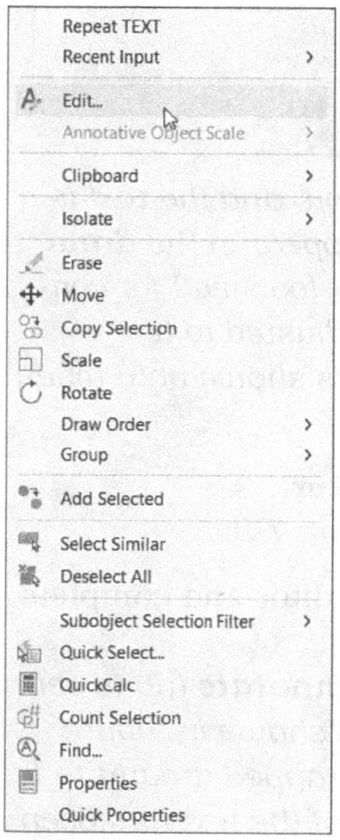

Figure 7-11
Shortcut menu

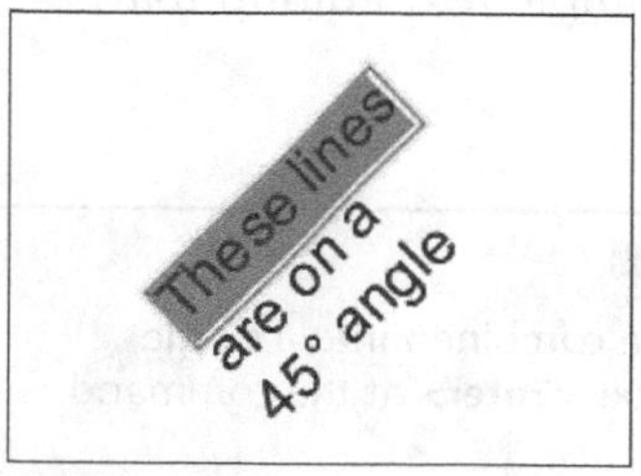

Figure 7-12
Selecting text on an angle

Editing Text in Place with TEXTEDIT

There are several ways to modify the existing text in your drawing. You can change wording and spelling and properties such as layer, style, and justification. For simple text wording changes, use the **TEXTEDIT** command, which you can access by selecting a text object and selecting **Edit/Mtext Edit** from the shortcut menu or double-clicking a text object; for property changes, use the **Quick Properties** palette discussed in the next section.

In this exercise, you perform some simple text editing with **TEXTEDIT**. Start by selecting the first line of the angled text.

✔ Select the words "These lines" by clicking any of the letters.

The words "These lines" are highlighted, and two grips appear at the start point of the line, indicating that this single line of text has been selected.

✔ Right-click to open the shortcut menu shown in Figure 7-11.

✔ Select **Edit** from the shortcut menu, as shown.

*When you make this selection, the shortcut menu disappears, and you see the selected text line highlighted, as shown in Figure 7-12. This is how **TEXTEDIT** functions for text created with **TEXT**. If you had selected text created with **MTEXT**, AutoCAD would have put you in the text editor instead.*

You add the word "three" to the middle of the selected line, as follows.

✔ Move the cursor to the center of the text between "These" and "lines" and click.

A flashing cursor should now be present, indicating where text will be added if you begin typing.

✔ Type **three** and add a space so that the line reads "These three lines", (see Figure 7-13).

✔ Press <Enter> **twice to complete the edits and exit the command.**

The cursor and highlighting disappears.

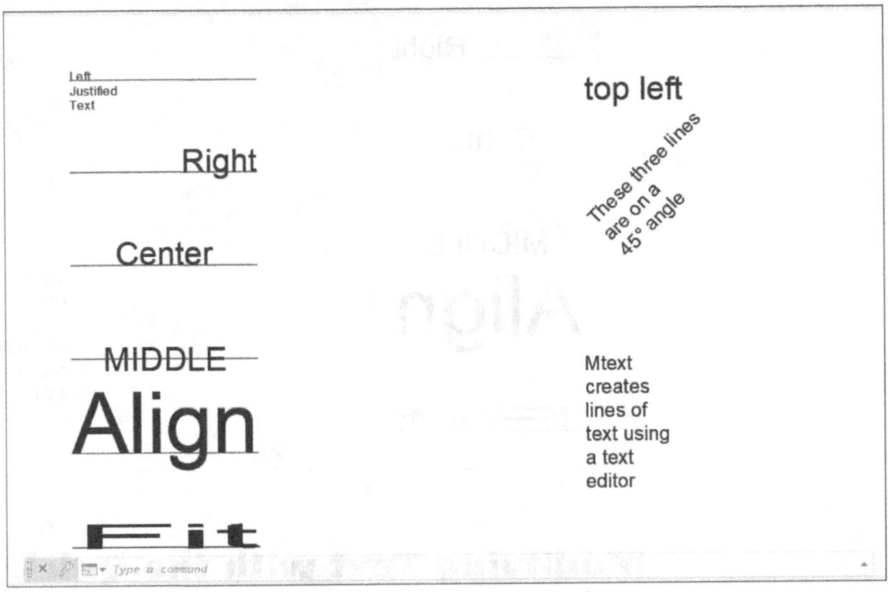

Figure 7-13
Adding text

Now you are going to edit the text you created with **MTEXT**. The first difference you notice is that because **MTEXT** creates multiple lines of text as a group, you cannot select a single line of text. When you double-click or select the object, all lines are selected.

✔ Double-click the text that begins with "Mtext creates."

__TEXTEDIT__ recognizes that you have chosen text created with __MTEXT__ and opens the __Multiline Text In-place Editor__, with the text window around the chosen paragraph. The __Text Editor__ tab also appears on the ribbon. In the in-place text editor, the cursor is placed in the line where you double-clicked.

✔ Point and click just to the left of the word "lines" in the in-place text editor.

You should see a white cursor blinking at the beginning of the line.

✔ Type **multiple** so that the text reads "Mtext creates multiple lines of text using a text editor".

You may also notice that "Mtext" is underlined in red dashes. This indicates that the in-place text editor does not recognize this word, and it may be misspelled. You explore the __SPELL__ command later in this chapter in the "Using the SPELL and FIND Commands" section.

✔ Move the cursor anywhere outside the in-place text editor and click to exit the **Multiline Text Editor**.

You return to the drawing window with the new text added, as shown in Figure 7-14. Next, you explore the __Quick Properties__ palette, along with the mtext justification options.

Figure 7-14
Multiline text added

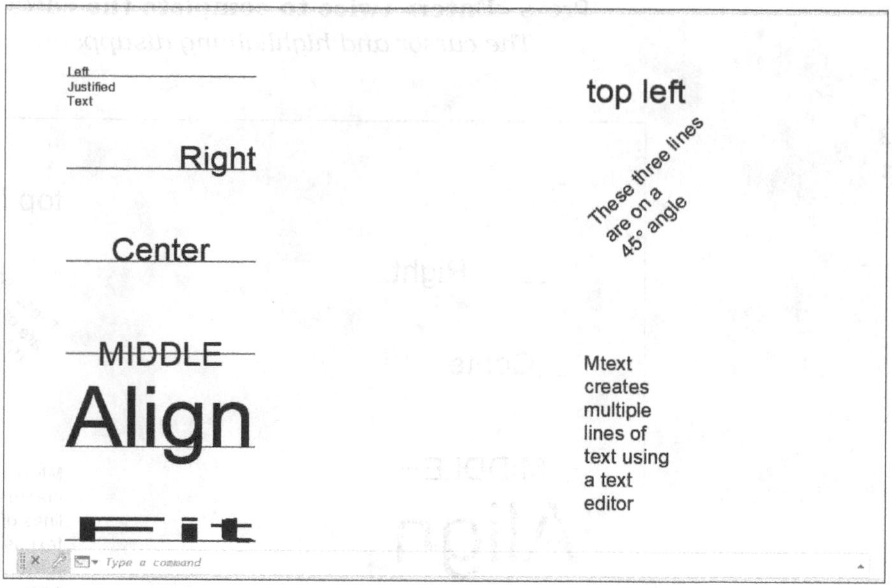

Modifying Text with the Quick Properties Palette

properties: Characteristics of an object that determine how and where an object is displayed in a drawing. Some properties are common to all objects (layer, color, linetype, or lineweight), whereas others apply only to a particular type of object (radius of a circle or endpoint of a line).

All objects in a drawing have characteristics called ***properties***. Standard properties for lines include color, layer, linetype, lineweight, and length. Depending on the type of object, there are many additional properties. Properties for text include layer, content, justification, height, and rotation. There is also a property named Annotative, which is explained later in this book. In this exercise, you learn how to change the justification property of mtext. Other properties can be changed using the efficient **Quick Properties** palette found on the status bar. Begin by drawing a visual reference line, so that changes in justification will be clear.

> **TIP**
> The following is a general procedure for modifying properties:
> 1. If necessary, select **Quick Properties** from the **Customization** menu on the status bar.
> 2. Select an object or objects.
> 3. Click the **Quick Properties** button on the status bar.
> 4. Use the **Quick Properties** palette to change property values.
> 5. Close the **Quick Properties** palette.

✔ Draw a 2.00 line just above the mtext paragraph, as shown in Figure 7-15.

This line will make the placement of different justification options clearer. It should begin at the same snap point as the insertion point for the text. The left end of the line shows the insertion point, and the length shows the width of the paragraph.

✔ If necessary, click the **Customization** button at the right end of the status bar and select **Quick Properties** from near the bottom of the menu, as shown in Figure 7-16.

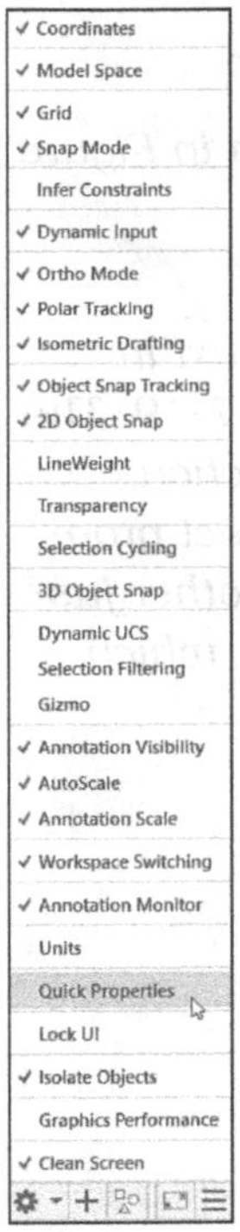

Figure 7-16
Quick Properties tool

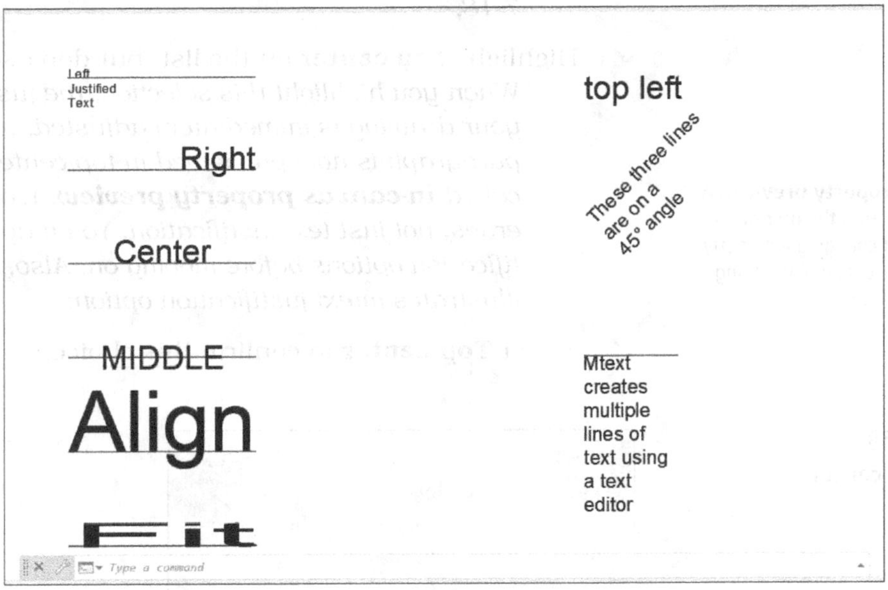

Figure 7-15
Draw a 2.00 line

*This places the **Quick Properties** button on the status bar, as shown.*

✔ Select the mtext object with the text "Mtext creates."

The text is highlighted, with grips at the top and bottom of the text window.

✔ Click the **Quick Properties** button on the status bar.

*With the **Quick Properties** tool on, you see the palette shown in Figure 7-17. It is a floating window, so it may appear at a different location on your screen. You can move it by clicking and dragging the right or left border. The palette is in the form of a two-column table, with properties listed on the left and their current values on the right. Some property values are changed by typing as you would in an edit box; others are changed by selecting from a drop-down list.*

Figure 7-17
Quick Properties tool palette

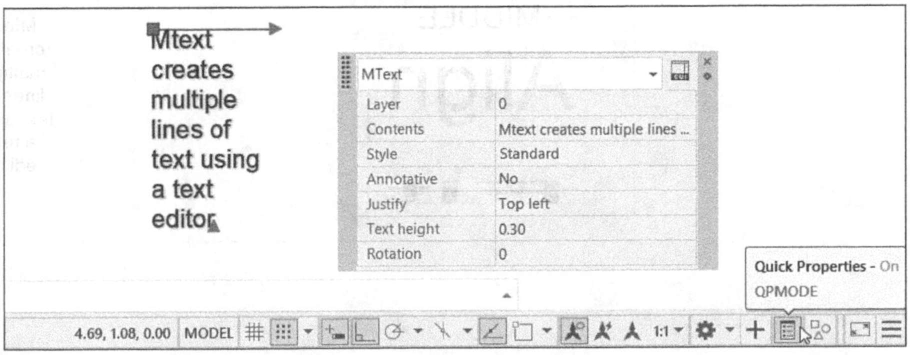

- ✔ Select the **Top left** value in the right column opposite the **Justify property**.
- ✔ Click the arrow at the right to open the drop-down list.

  This opens the drop-down list of justification options shown in Figure 7-18.
- ✔ Highlight **Top center** on the list, but don't select it.

  *When you highlight this selection, the justification of the mtext in your drawing is immediately adjusted, as shown in Figure 7-19. The paragraph is now previewed in top-centered format. This action, called **in-canvas property preview**, works with many object properties, not just text justification. You may want to highlight other justification options before moving on. Also, study Figure 7-20, which illustrates mtext justification options.*
- ✔ Select **Top center** to confirm this choice.

in-canvas property preview: A feature that allows the user to see the effect that changing a property will have prior to actually making the property change.

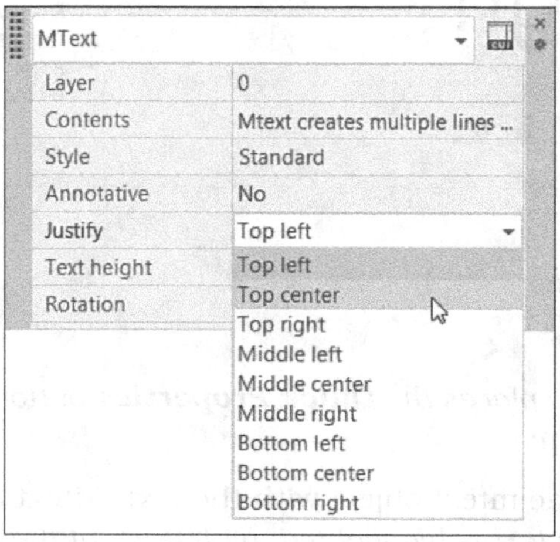

Figure 7-18
Select **Top center**

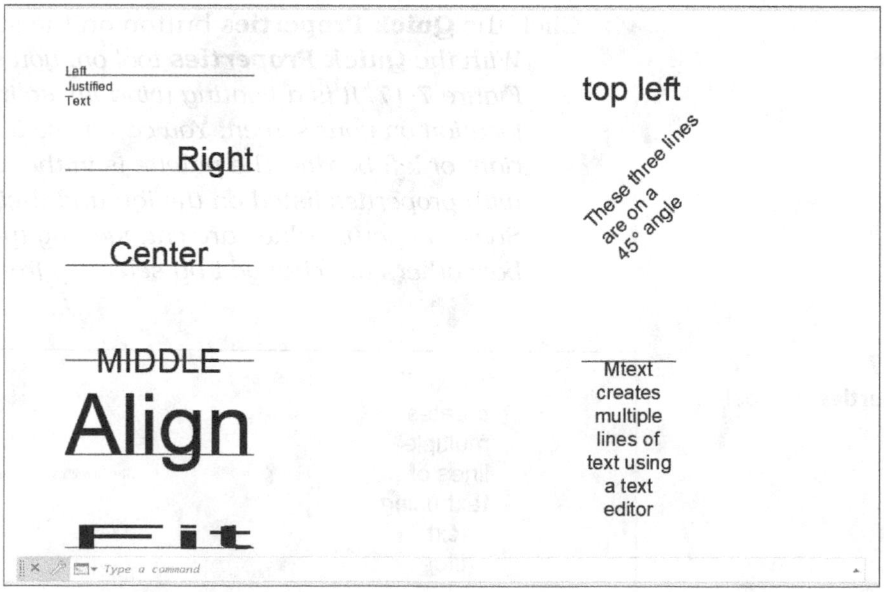

Figure 7-19
Text centered

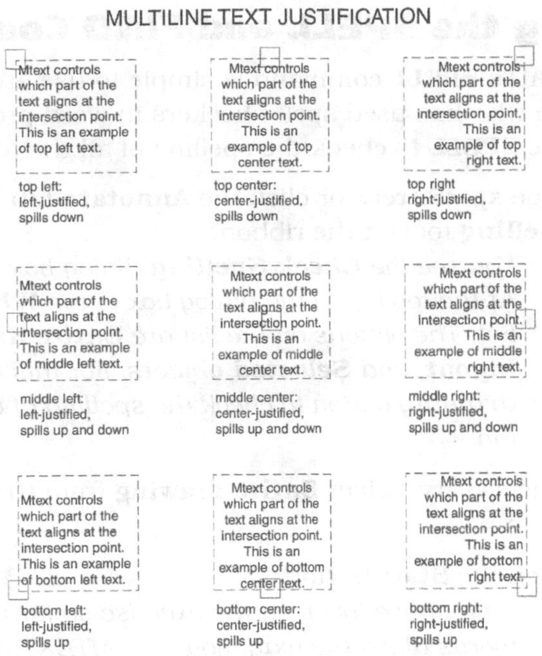

Figure 7-20
Multiline text justification

- ✔ To close the palette, click the **Quick Properties** button on the status bar.

  This closes the palette and leaves it closed while you continue to edit your drawing.

  *Before going on, take a look at the **Quick Properties** palette for a line.*

- ✔ Press **<Esc>** to clear grips.
- ✔ Select any of the lines in your drawing.
- ✔ Click the **Quick Properties** button on the status bar.

  You see a palette like the one shown in Figure 7-21. Look over the palette and the four properties shown there.

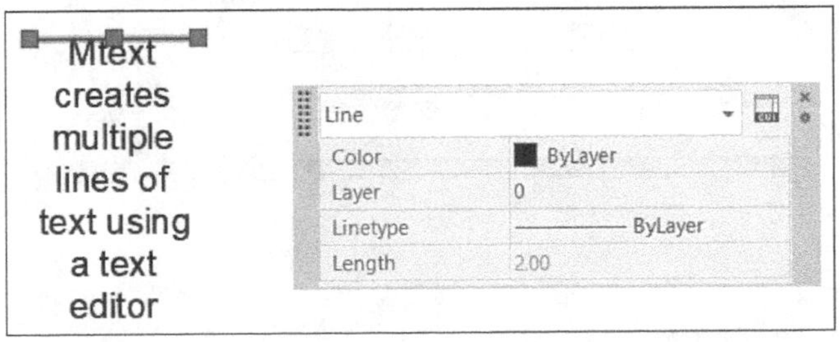

Figure 7-21
Modify line using **Quick Properties**

- ✔ Click the **Quick Properties** button on the status bar to close the *palette.*
- ✔ Press **<Esc>** to clear grips.

Using the SPELL and FIND Commands

SPELL	
Command	SPELL
Alias	Sp
Panel	Text
Tool	

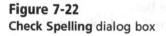

AutoCAD's **SPELL** command is simple to use and will appear familiar to anyone who has used spell-checkers in word processing programs. Here, you use **SPELL** to check the spelling of all the text you have drawn so far.

✔ Type **sp <Enter>** or click the **Annotate** tab > **Text** panel > **Check Spelling** tool on the ribbon.

*You see the **Check Spelling** dialog box shown in Figure 7-22.*
*At the top left of the dialog box is the **Where to check** drop-down list. The options on the list are **Entire drawing**, **Current space/ layout**, and **Selected objects**. For this exercise, use the **Entire drawing** option to check the spelling of all text objects in the drawing.*

✔ If necessary, select **Entire drawing** from the **Where to check** drop-down list.

✔ Click the **Start** button.

*If you have followed the exercise so far without misspelling any words along the way, you see "MTEXT" in the **Not in dictionary** box and "TEXT" as a suggested correction. Ignore this change; but before you leave **SPELL**, look at what is available: You can ignore a word the checker does not recognize or change it. You can change a single instance of a word or all instances in the currently selected text. You can add a word to the main dictionary or change to another dictionary. Click the **Settings** button in the lower-left corner; here, you can control the types of objects to check for spelling along with options to control the type of words to be ignored. If you clicked the **Settings** button, click **Cancel** to return to the **Check Spelling** dialog box.*

Figure 7-22
Check Spelling dialog box

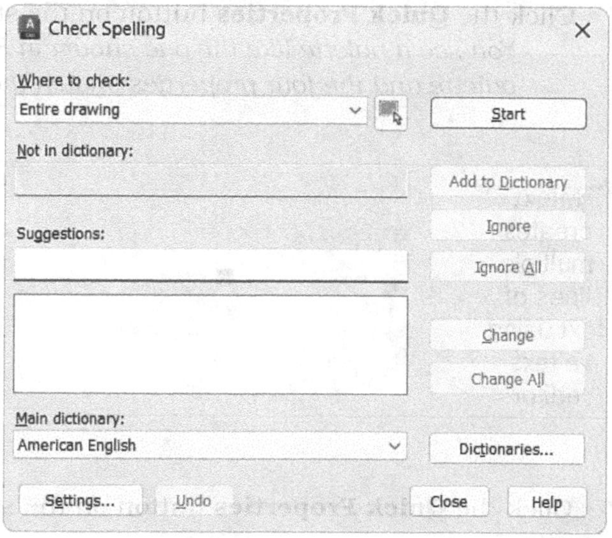

✔ Click **Ignore**.

If your drawing does not contain other spelling irregularities, you should now see an AutoCAD message that reads

```
Spelling check complete.
```

✔ Click **OK** to close the message box.

✔ Click **Close** to complete the **SPELL** command.

If you have made any corrections in spelling, they are applied to your drawing at this point.

FIND	
Command	FIND
Alias	(none)
Panel	Text
Tool	

The **FIND** command allows you to do what its name implies—find something. In this case, it's to find a text string in your drawing and unfortunately not your car keys or phone (but wouldn't that be great?). After you provide a text string to find, AutoCAD zooms to the location of the first text object it finds with the matching text string to give you the context in which the text string appears. Once it finds a match, you can choose to replace the text string with a new text string or go to the next match found.

✔ Type **find <Enter>** or enter a text string to find in the **Find Text** box on the **Text** panel on the ribbon's **Annotate** tab and press **<Enter>**.

*You see the **Find and Replace** dialog box shown in Figure 7-23. At the top left of the box is the **Find where** drop-down list, which has the same options as the **Where to check** drop-down list in the **Check Spelling** dialog box.*

✔ In the **Find what** edit box, type **text**, which is the text string to find.

✔ If necessary, select **Entire drawing** from the **Find where** drop-down list.

✔ Click the **Find** button.

*AutoCAD zooms to the first text object it finds with the text string. At this time, you could type a value in the Replace with edit box and click **Replace** to replace the text string with a new text string. You could also click **Replace All** to replace all instances of the text string in the **Find what** edit box found in the drawing. Clicking **Find Next** goes to the next text object that contains the text string. You can control the type of objects that are searched for the text string and search options by clicking the **More Options** button in the lower-left corner of the dialog box.*

Figure 7-23
Find and Replace dialog box

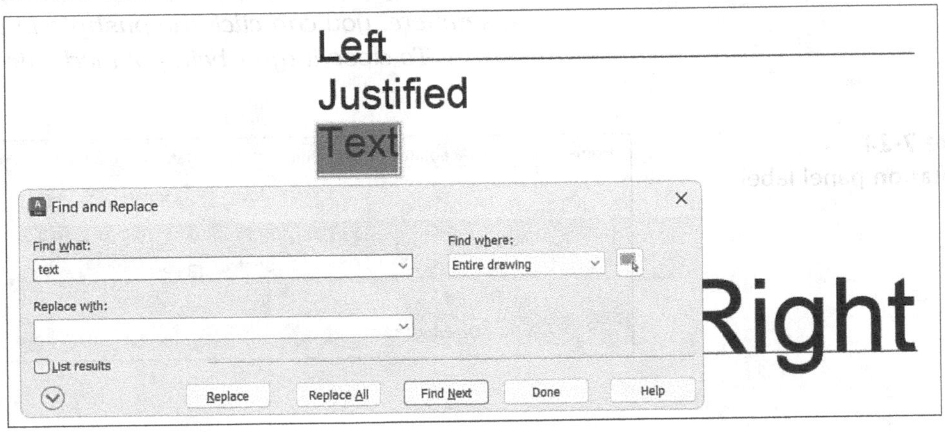

✔ Click **Done** to complete the **FIND** command.

The dialog box closes and you are returned to the drawing area.

Changing Fonts and Styles

By default, the current text style in any AutoCAD drawing is called **Standard**. It uses the Arial true-type font, which is the same one you might use in a word processing program. All the text you have entered so far has been drawn with this Standard text style.

annotative: In AutoCAD, text and dimensions with the **Annotative** property can be automatically scaled to match the scale of viewports in a drawing layout.

Also predefined in all AutoCAD drawings is a style named ***Annotative***. The **Annotative** style is the same as **Standard** in all ways except that it has the **Annotative** property enabled. This property allows you to create text that can be automatically scaled to match the scale of different viewports within the same layout.

Fonts are the basic patterns of character and symbol shapes that can be used with the **TEXT** and **MTEXT** commands. *Styles* are variations in the size, orientation, and spacing of the characters in those fonts. It is possible to create your own fonts, but for most of us, this is an esoteric activity. In contrast, creating your own styles is easy and practical. Text styles are also used with dimension, multileader, and table styles that are explained later in this and other chapters.

Expanded Ribbon Panels

You begin by creating a variation of the **Standard** style you have been using. This process also introduces you to the panel slideouts feature of the ribbon. Notice that there is a small triangle facing downward on the right side of most panel label names. Clicking anywhere along the label bar of a panel expands it to reveal additional tools. You have been using the tools on the **Text** panel of the **Annotate** tab in this chapter so far. For this next exercise, you work with the tools on the **Annotation** panel of the **Home** tab.

✔ Click the **Home** tab and then the label of the **Annotation** panel, as shown in Figure 7-24.

*This expands the **Annotation** panel shown in Figure 7-25. If you move the cursor away from the panel, it closes immediately. If you let the cursor rest anywhere on the expanded area, the panel remains open. To keep the panel expanded while moving the cursor elsewhere, you can click the pushpin in the lower-left corner of the panel. To close it after being pinned, click the pushpin again.*

Figure 7-24
Annotation panel label

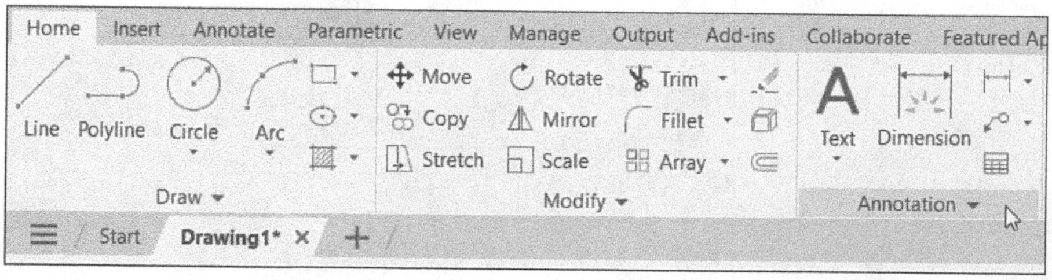

Figure 7-25
Annotation panel expanded

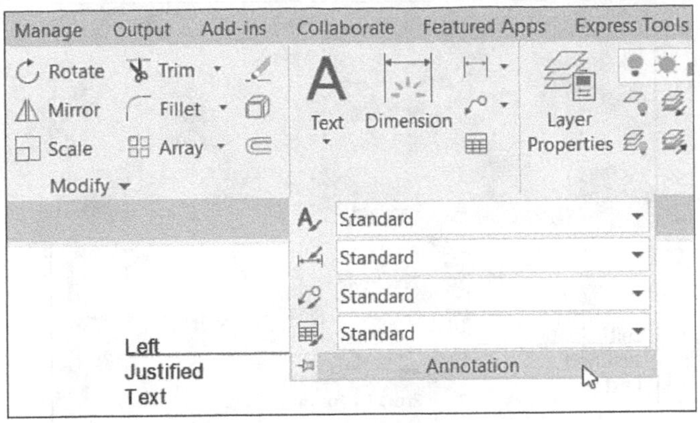

With the **Annotation** panel expanded, you can see there are four drop-down lists. Each list gives access to a different type of annotation style. Text style, dimension style, and table style are all introduced in this chapter. Multileader styles are covered in a later chapter.

NOTE

There is also a **Text Style** drop-down list on the **Text** panel of the **Annotate** tab. Make sure that you are clear about the difference between the **Annotate** tab and the **Annotation** panel on the **Home** tab, but either of these locations can be used to access text styles.

✔ From the expanded **Annotation** panel, click the **Text Style** tool, as shown in Figure 7-26.

*You see the **Text Style** dialog box shown in Figure 7-27. You see **Annotative** and **Standard** listed in the **Styles** list box. It is possible that other styles are listed. **Standard** should be selected.*

*You create a new style and assign it a different font than Arial. The new style will be named **Vertical** because it will be drawn downward instead of across.*

✔ Click the **New** button.

AutoCAD opens a smaller dialog box that prompts for a name of the new text style.

✔ Type **vertical <Enter>**.

*This returns you to the **Text Style** dialog box, with the new style listed in the **Styles** list box. Next, you assign the txt.shx font and the vertical text effect to make this style different. The vertical text option is not available when the Arial font is assigned to a style.*

Figure 7-26
Text Style tool

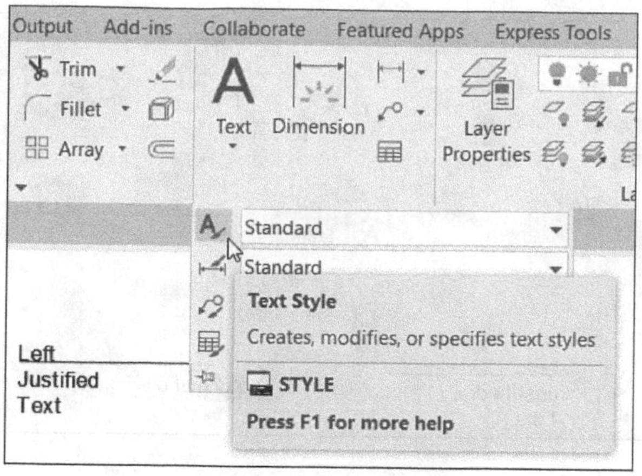

Figure 7-27
Text Style dialog box

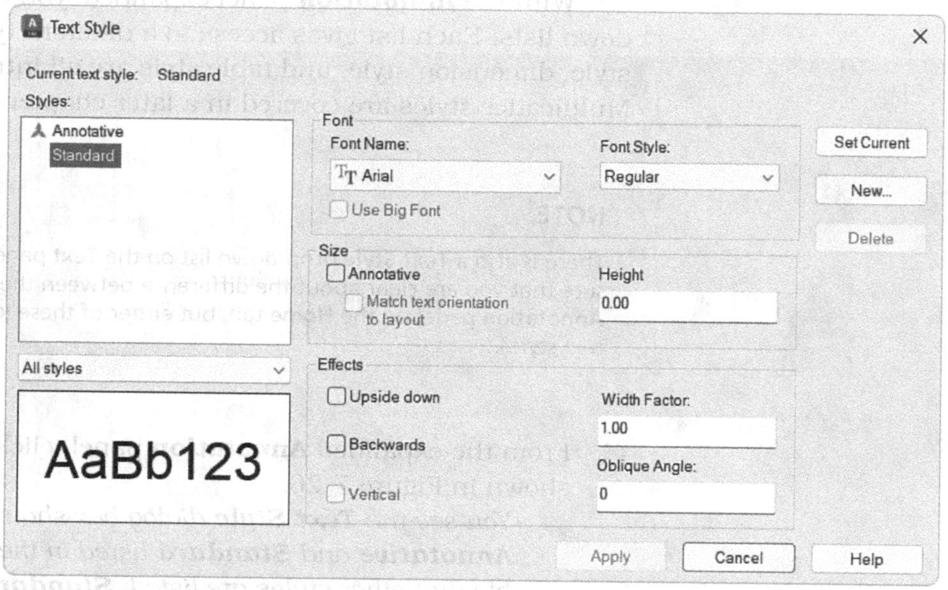

✔ Click the **Font Name** drop-down list and scroll down to **txt.shx**.
A lengthy list of fonts is available.

✔ Select **txt.shx** to set it as the font for the style.
*The **Vertical** option is now accessible in the **Effects** panel at the lower middle of the dialog box.*

✔ Click the **Vertical** check box in the **Effects** panel.
*Notice the change to vertically oriented text in the **Preview** panel at the lower left of the dialog box.*

Next, you give this style a fixed height and width factor. Notice that the current height is 0.00. This does not mean that your characters will be drawn 0.00 units high. It means that there will be no fixed height, so you can specify a height whenever you use this style. Standard currently has no fixed height, so Vertical has inherited this setting.

✔ Double-click in the **Height** edit box and type **.5**.

✔ Double-click in the **Width Factor** edit box and type **2**.

*Vertical should be automatically set as the current text style. If not, you can make it current by highlighting it in the **Styles** list box and clicking the **Set Current** button at the right.*

✔ If necessary, click the **Set Current** button to make **Vertical** the current text style.

*If you see a message box indicating that you have made changes to the text style, click **Yes** to save changes.*

✔ Click the **Close** button to exit the **Text Style** dialog box.

*The new **Vertical** style is now current. To see it in action, you need to enter some text.*

✔ Click **Home** > **Annotation** > **Text** > **Single Line** on the ribbon.

✔ Specify a start point, as shown by the placement of the letter *V* in Figure 7-28.

Notice that you are not prompted for a height because the current style has a fixed height of 0.50. Also notice that the default rotation angle is set to 270. Your vertical text is entered going downward at 270°.

✔ Press **<Enter>** to retain 270° of rotation.

✔ Type **Vertical <Enter>**.

✔ Press **<Enter>** again to end the **TEXT** command.

Your drawing should resemble Figure 7-28.

*Next, you create another style using a different font and some of the other style options. Watch the **Preview** panel in the dialog box; it updates automatically to show your changes.*

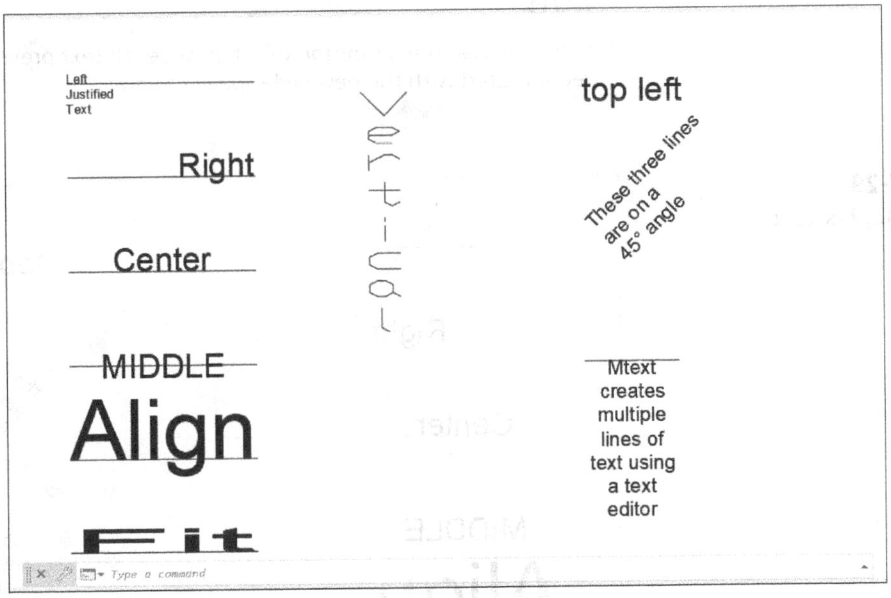

Figure 7-28
Vertical text

- ✔ On the **Home** tab, expand the **Annotation** panel and click the **Text Style** tool.
- ✔ Click the **New** button.
- ✔ In the **New Text Style** dialog box, name the style **Slanted**.
- ✔ Click **OK** to close the **New Text Style** box.
- ✔ Click the **Font Name** drop-down list by clicking the arrow.
- ✔ Scroll to **romand.shx** and stop.

  Romand stands for Roman Duplex, an AutoCAD font.
- ✔ Select **romand.shx**.
- ✔ Clear the **Vertical** checkbox.
- ✔ Set the text **Height** to **0.00**.
- ✔ Set the **Width Factor** to **1**.
- ✔ Set **Oblique Angle** to **45**.

  This causes your text to be slanted 45° to the right. For a left slant, you would type a negative number.
- ✔ Click the **Close** button to exit the **Text Style** dialog box.
- ✔ Click the **Yes** button to save your changes.

  Enter some text to see how the Slanted style looks.
- ✔ Click the **Single Line** text tool and respond to the prompts to draw the words "Roman Duplex" with a 0.50 height and 0 degree rotation, as shown in Figure 7-29.

> **NOTE**
>
> If you change the definition of a text style, all text previously drawn in that style will be regenerated with the new style specifications.

Figure 7-29
Roman Duplex text

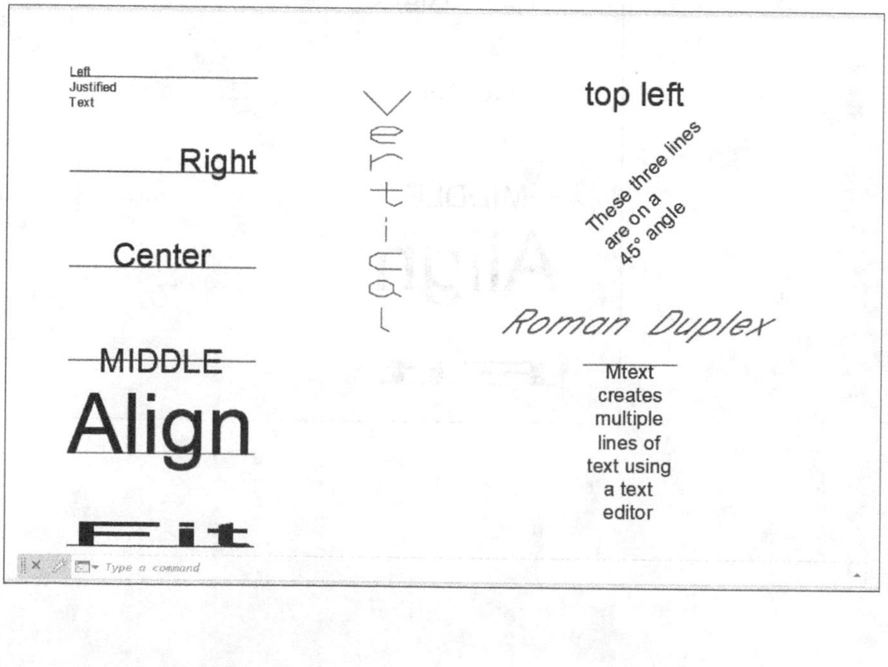

Switching the Current Style

All new text is created with the current style. The style of previously drawn text can be changed. Once you have a number of styles defined in a drawing, you can switch from one to another by using the **Style** option of the **TEXT** and **MTEXT** commands or by selecting a text style from the **Text Style** drop-down list. Expand the **Annotation** panel, click the arrow at the right of the text style and select the style from the drop-down list. All the defined text styles in the drawing are available from this list.

Changing Properties with MATCHPROP

MATCHPROP	
Command	MATCHPROP
Alias	Ma
Panel	Properties
Tool	

MATCHPROP is an efficient command that lets you match all or some of the property values of an object to those of another object. Property values that can be transferred from one object to others include Layer, Linetype, Color, and Linetype scale. These properties are common to all AutoCAD entities. Other properties that relate to only specific types of entities are Thickness, Text Style, Dimension Style, and Hatch Style. In all cases, the procedure is the same.

> **TIP**
>
> The following is a general procedure for changing property values with **MATCHPROP**:
>
> 1. Click the **Match Properties** tool from the **Properties** panel on the **Home** tab of the ribbon.
> 2. Select a source object with the property values you want to transfer to another object.
> 3. If necessary, specify which properties you want to match with the **Settings** option.
> 4. Select destination objects.
> 5. Press **<Enter>** to end object selection.

Here you use **MATCHPROP** to change the style of some previously drawn text to the new **Slanted** style.

✔ Click the **Match Properties** tool from the **Properties** panel on the **Home** tab of the ribbon, as shown in Figure 7-30.

AutoCAD prompts

```
Select source object:
```

You can have many destination objects, but only one source object.

✔ Select the “Roman Duplex” text, drawn in the last exercise with the **Slanted** style.

*AutoCAD switches to the **Match Properties** cursor, shown in Figure 7-31.*

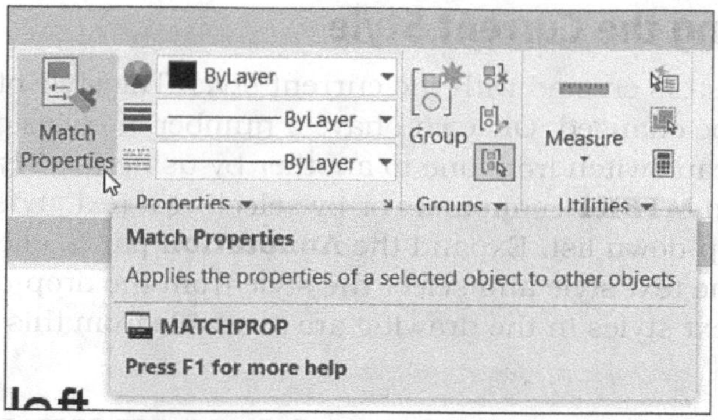

Figure 7-30
Match Properties tool

Figure 7-31
Match Properties cursor

```
Select destination object(s) or [Settings]:
```

*At this point, you can limit the properties you want to match with the **Settings** option, or you can select destination objects, in which case all properties are matched.*

✔ Select **Settings** from the command line.

*This opens the **Property Settings** dialog box shown in Figure 7-32. The **Basic Properties** panel shows properties that can be changed and the settings that will be used based on the source object you have selected.*

*At the bottom, you see nine other properties in the **Special Properties** panel. These refer to properties and styles that have been defined in your drawing. If any one of these is not selected, **Match Properties** ignores it and matches only the properties selected.*

Figure 7-32
Property Settings dialog box

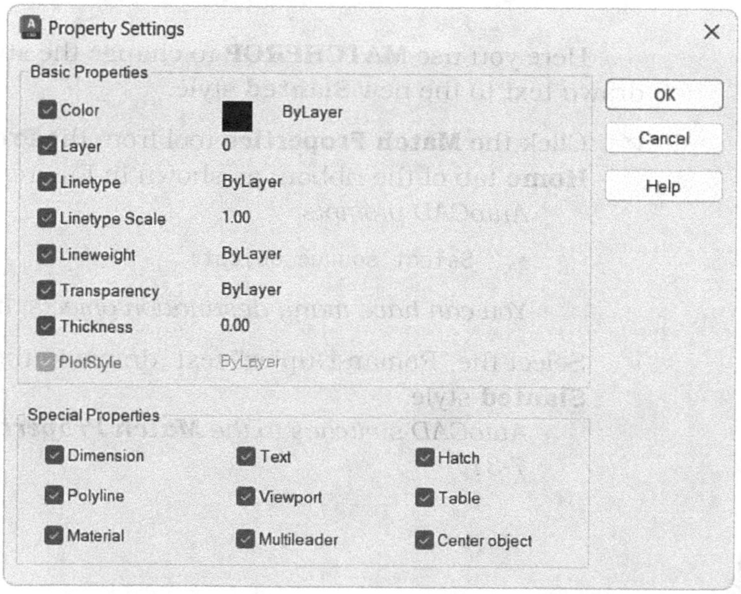

✔ Click **OK** to exit the dialog box.

AutoCAD returns to the drawing area with the same prompt as before.

- ✔ Move your cursor over any of the text in your drawing.

  AutoCAD previews how the text would appear in the ***Slanted*** *text style.*

- ✔ Select the text objects with the text "Align" and "Vertical" in your drawing.

  These two text objects are redrawn in the Slanted style, as shown in Figure 7-33. AutoCAD returns the ***Select destination object(s)*** *prompt so that you can continue to select objects.*

- ✔ Press **<Enter>** to exit the command.

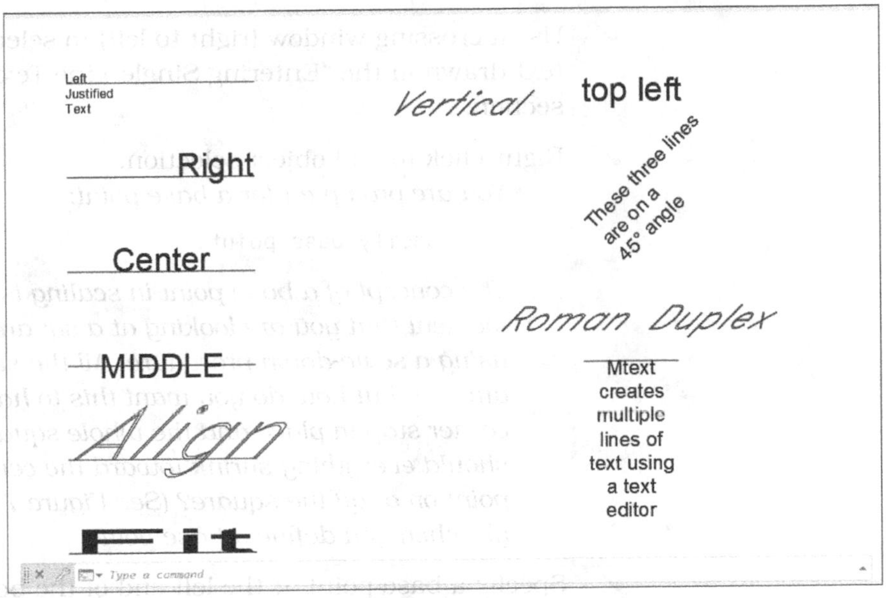

Figure 7-33
Align and **Vertical** text slanted

Scaling Previously Drawn Entities

SCALE	
Command	SCALE
Alias	Sc
Panel	Modify
Tool	

Any object or group of objects can be scaled up or down using the **SCALE** command or the **Scale** grip edit mode. In this exercise, you practice scaling some of the text and lines that you have drawn. Remember, however, that there is no special relationship between **SCALE** and text and that other types of entities can be scaled just as easily.

- ✔ Click the **Scale** tool from the **Modify** panel on the ribbon's **Home** tab, as shown in Figure 7-34.

  AutoCAD prompts you to select objects.

> **TIP**
>
> The following is a general procedure for changing the scale of objects:
>
> 1. Click the **Scale** tool from the **Modify** panel on the ribbon's **Home** tab.
> 2. Select objects.
> 3. Specify a base point.
> 4. Enter a scale factor.

Figure 7-34
Scale tool

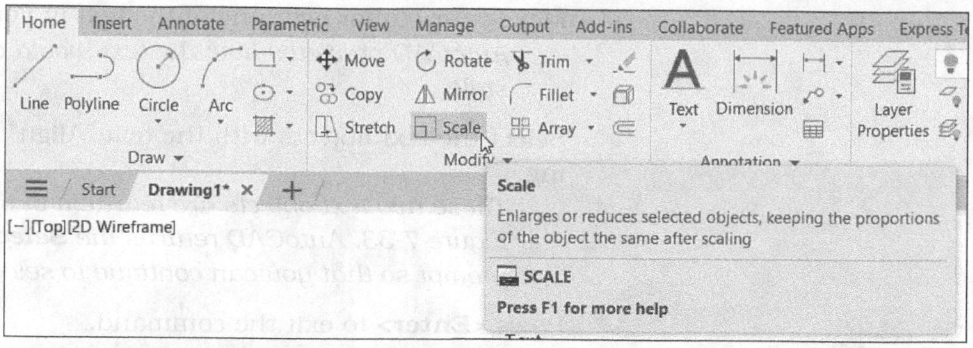

✔ Use a crossing window (right to left) to select the set of six lines and text drawn in the "Entering Single-Line Text with Justification Options" section.

✔ Right-click to end object selection.

You are prompted for a base point:

```
Specify base point:
```

The concept of a base point in scaling is critical. Imagine for a moment that you are looking at a square and you want to shrink it using a scale-down procedure. All the sides will be shrunk the same amount, but how do you want this to happen? Should the lower-left corner stay in place and the whole square shrink toward it? Or should everything shrink toward the center? Or toward some other point on or off the square? (See Figure 7-35.) This is what you specify when you define a base point.

✔ Specify a base point at the left end of the bottom line of the selected objects (shown as base point in Figure 7-36).

AutoCAD now needs to know how much to shrink or enlarge the objects you have selected:

```
Specify scale factor or [Copy/Reference] <1.00>:
```

Figure 7-35
Base point concept

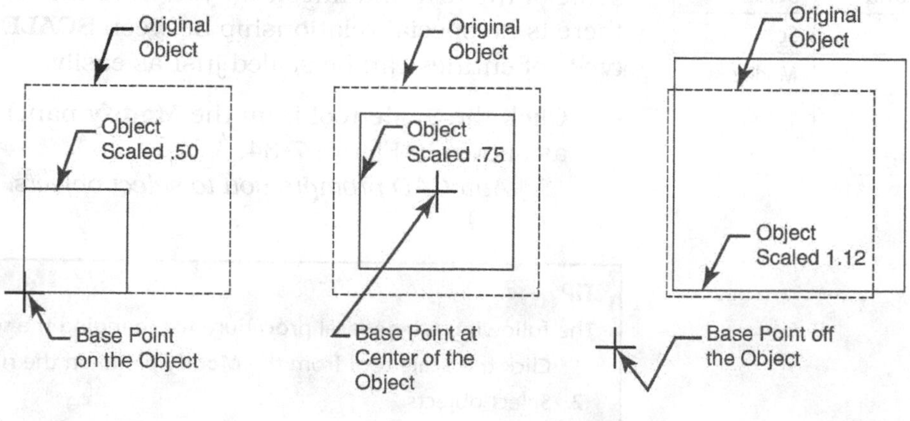

The **Copy** option allows you to retain the selected objects at their original scale and create copied objects at a new scale. Objects can be scaled by reference, which is covered in a moment. When you enter a scale factor, all lengths, heights, and diameters of the selected objects are multiplied by that factor and redrawn accordingly. Scale factors are based on a unit of 1. If you enter **0.5**, objects are reduced to half their original size. If you enter **2**, objects become twice as large.

✔ Type **.5 <Enter>**.

Your drawing should now resemble Figure 7-36.

Figure 7-36
Base point

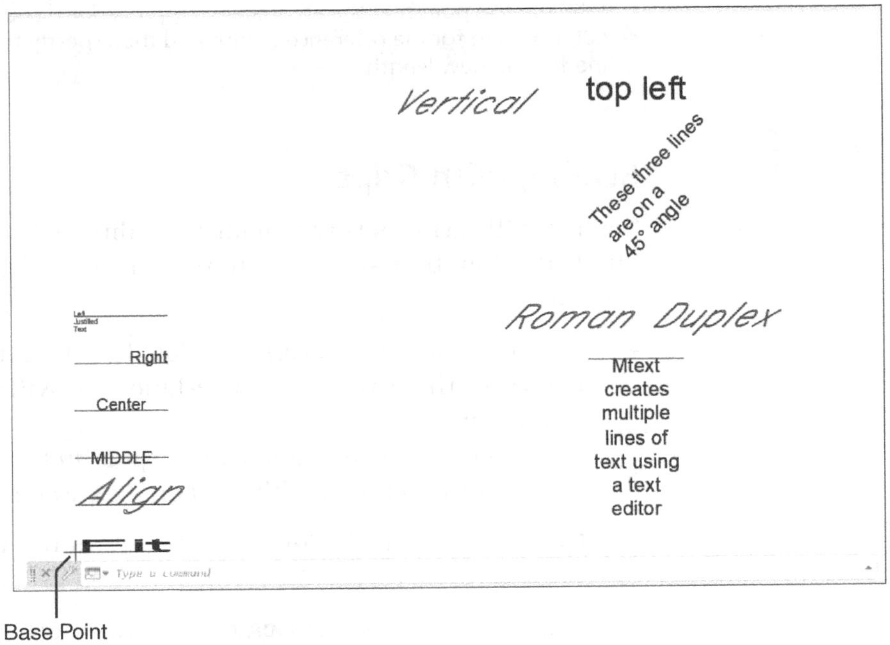

> **TIP**
>
> While text objects can be scaled with the **SCALE** command, there is also a specialized command to resize text objects. The **SCALETEXT** command scales each selected text object from its insertion point, rather than a common base point, which doesn't cause the text object to be moved while being scaled.

Scaling by Reference

This option can save you from doing the arithmetic to figure out scale factors. It is useful when you have a given length and you know the desired length after the scaling is done. For example, you know that the length of the lines you just scaled are now 2.00 because they were drawn at a length of 4 and scaled down by a factor of 0.5. Let's say you want to scale the objects again so that the length becomes 2.33. This would be a scale factor of 1.165 (2.33 divided by 2.00), but who wants to stop and figure that out? This can be done using the following procedure:

6. Enter the **SCALE** command.
7. Select the line and text objects again.
8. Specify a base point.
9. Type **r <Enter>** or right-click and select **Reference** from the shortcut menu.

10.Type **2 <Enter>** for the reference length.
11.Type **2.33 <Enter>** for the new length.

> **NOTE**
>
> You can also perform reference scaling by specifying two points and using the distance between the points. In the accompanying procedure, you can specify the ends of the 2.00-unit line for the reference length and then specify the two endpoints of a 2.33-unit line for the new length.

Scaling with Grips

Scaling with grips is very similar to scaling with the **SCALE** command. To illustrate this, try using grips to return the text you just scaled back to its original size.

✔ Use a window or crossing window to select the six lines and the text drawn in the "Entering Single-Line Text with Justification Options" section again.

There are several grips that appear in the drawing: three on each line and two on most of the text entities. Some of these overlap each other.

✔ Click the grip at the lower-left corner of the word "Fit"—the same point used as a base point in the last scaling procedure.

✔ Right-click and select **Scale** from the shortcut menu.

✔ Move the cursor slowly and observe the dragged image.

AutoCAD uses the selected grip point as the base point for scaling unless you specify that you want to use a different base point. Notice that you also have a ***Reference*** *option, as in the* ***SCALE*** *command.*

As in ***SCALE****, the default method is to specify a scale factor by specifying points or typing.*

✔ Type **2 <Enter>** or specify two points that have a distance of 2.00 units between them. (The objects were previously reduced by a factor of 0.5, so they need to be enlarged by a factor of 2 to return them to their original size.)

Your text returns to its original size, and your drawing should resemble Figure 7-33 again.

✔ Press **<Esc>** to clear grips.

Creating Tables and Fields

TABLE	
Command	TABLE
Alias	(none)
Panel	Table
Tool	

AutoCAD has many features for creating and managing tables and table data. Table styles can be created and named. Cells can be formatted with text, numerical data, formulas, and fields that update automatically. Data can be extracted from the current drawing into a table or from an external spreadsheet. In this exercise, you create a basic table with three date and time formats and control their appearances. The table will include a title, two columns with headers, and three rows of data. In addition to using a table, you learn about fields which can be inserted and easily updated when the information they hold changes.

✔ To begin this exercise you can be in any AutoCAD drawing.

You continue to use the drawing with the text objects created earlier in this chapter, but zoom into the area where the table can be inserted.

✔ Zoom in to an empty window of space (approximately 5.00 by 5.00) in your drawing.

✔ Click the **Table** tool from the **Annotation** panel on the **Home** tab of the ribbon, as shown in Figure 7-37.

*Additional tools related to working with tables and table data are on the **Tables** panel of the **Annotate** tab.*

Figure 7-37
Table tool

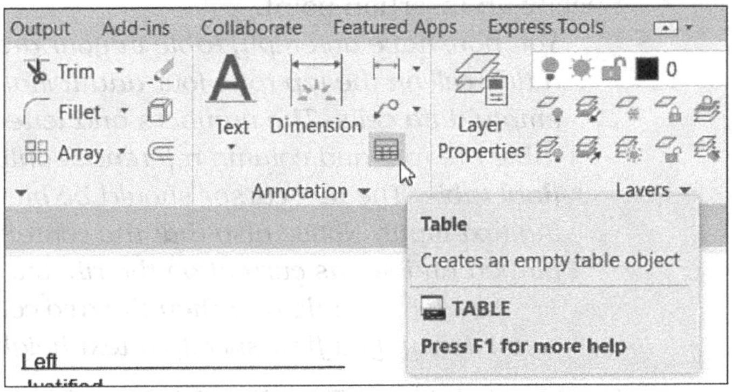

*This opens the **Insert Table** dialog box, as shown in Figure 7-38. Before inserting a table, you specify its size, shape, and style. The **Standard** table style has a title row, a header row, and any number of rows and columns of data. The table you insert will use the **Standard** style and have three rows and two columns.*

Figure 7-38
Insert Table dialog box

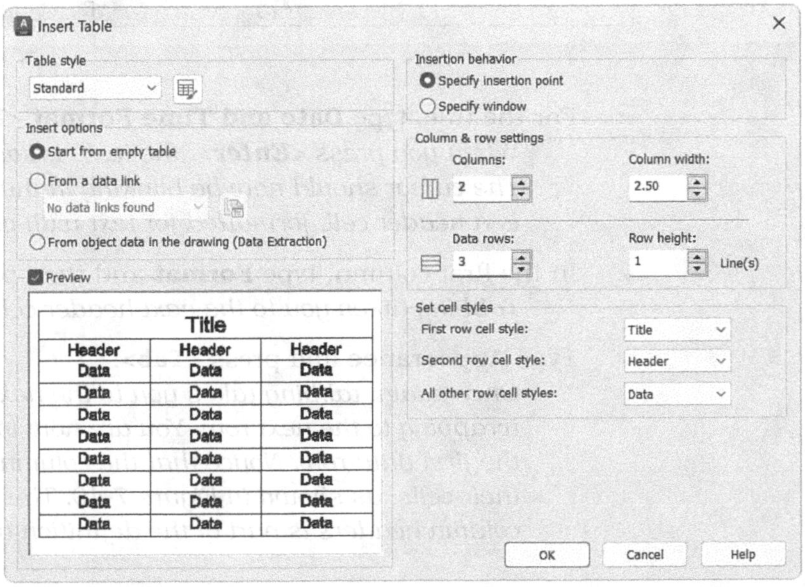

✔ Check to see that **Standard** is listed in the **Table style** drop-down list, **Specify insertion point** is selected in the **Insertion behavior** panel, and **Start from empty table** is selected in the **Insert options** panel.

✔ In the **Column & row settings** panel, use the arrows or the edit box to specify **2** columns.

✔ If necessary, set the column width to **2.50**.

✔ Use the arrows or the edit box to specify **3** rows.

✔ If necessary, set row height to **1** line.

When you are done, the dialog box should resemble Figure 7-38.

✔ Click **OK**.

AutoCAD closes the dialog box and shows a table that moves with your crosshairs as you drag it into place.

✔ Specify an insertion point.

*You now have an empty table in your drawing. In this table, you see a title cell on the top row, four additional rows, and two columns of empty data cells. The numbers and letters at the left and top of the table are row and column references only; they are not part of the final table. The text cursor should be blinking in the title cell, awaiting text input. Notice also that the contextual **Text Editor** tab is displayed and set as current on the ribbon.*

You fill in a title and then the two column headers. To ensure consistency, you first specify a text height.

✔ Double-click in the **Text Height** drop-down list box on the **Style** panel of the **Text Editor** tab, as shown in Figure 7-39, and type **0.20 <Enter>**.

The text height is now 0.20.

Figure 7-39
Text Height

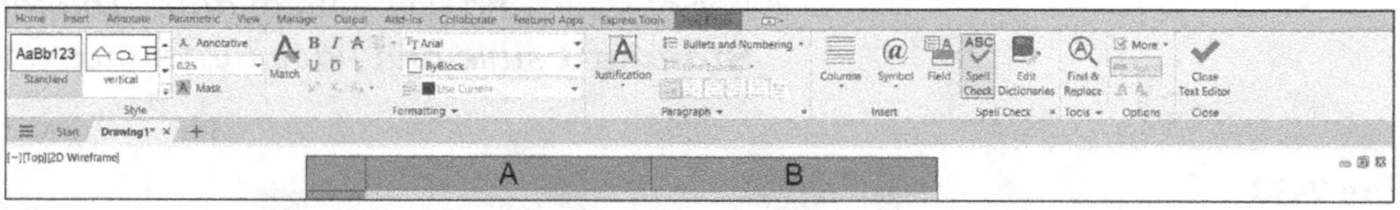

✔ For the title, type **Date and Time Format <Enter>**.

*When you press **<Enter>**, the text cursor moves to row 2, column A. The cursor should now be blinking in the 2A cell, awaiting input. 2A is a header cell, formatted for text with center justification.*

✔ In the first column, type **Format** and then press **<Tab>**.

Tabbing takes you to the next header cell.

✔ Type **Appearance** and press **<Tab>**.

*Once again, tabbing takes you to the next table cell—in this case, wrapping to the next row. You are now in the third row of column A, the first data row. Notice that the column headings are centered in their cells, as shown in Figure 7-40. This center justification for the column headers is part of the definition of the **Standard** table style.*

> **TIP**
> When entering data in table cells, you can move sequentially through cells using the **<Tab>** key. To reverse direction and move backward, hold down **<Shift>** while pressing **<Tab>**. You can also use the arrow keys on your keyboard to move between table cells.

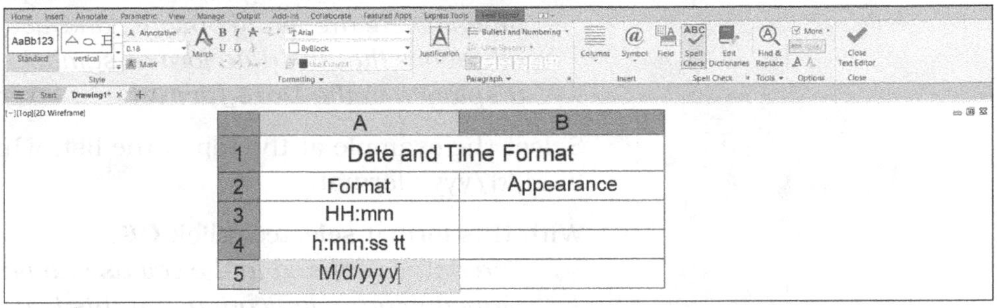

Figure 7-40
Entering text

As part of the data in the table, you enter date and time format definitions in the **Format** column and the corresponding date and time fields in the **Appearance** column. The text in the **Appearance** column will be inserted as fields that can be updated automatically. Dates and times are used in this exercise because they update very readily.

✔ In the first data row, first column, as shown in Figure 7-40, type **HH:mm <Enter>**.

This is the common symbol for time in hours and minutes format. The uppercase HH indicates that this is 24-hour time (2:00 P.M. will appear as 14:00). Pressing **<Enter>** *takes you to row 4, column A.*

✔ Type **h:mm:ss tt <Enter>**.

This symbolizes time in hours, minutes, and seconds. The **tt** *stands for A.M. or P.M. You will see more of these symbols in a moment.*

✔ In cell 5A type **M/d/yyyy** and press **<Tab>** once.

This represents a date in month, day, year format, with a four-place number for the year.

Inserting Fields

You are now in cell 5B of the table and instead of typing text here, you insert a date field, in month, day, year format to match the **Format** column. Then you return to the other rows in this column and enter time fields.

✔ From the **Insert** panel on the ribbon's **Text Editor** tab, click the **Field** tool shown in Figure 7-41.

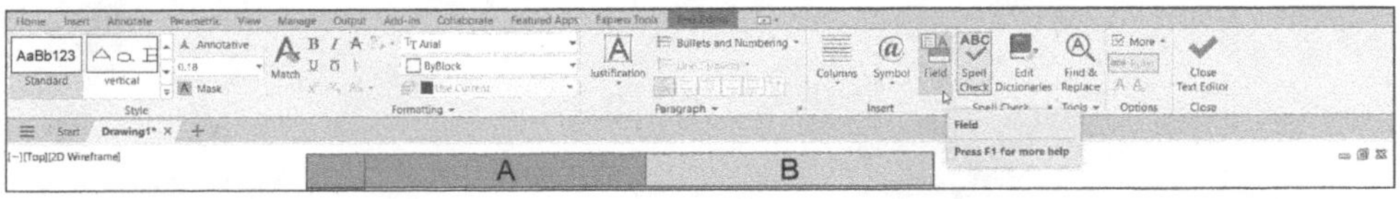

Figure 7-41
Insert Field tool

*This opens the **Field** dialog box shown in Figure 7-42. There are many types of predefined fields shown in the **Field names** list box on the left. What appears in the **Examples** list box in the middle depends on the type of field selected.*

✔ Select **Date** in the **Field names** list box.

*With **Date** selected, you see the example formats for dates and times. There are many options, and you have to scroll to see them all. Notice that the date format symbols for the selected format are displayed in the **Date format** edit box above the examples.*

✔ Select the example at the top of the list, which will be the current date in M/d/yyyy format.

✔ With this format selected, click **OK**.

The date is entered in the cell as shown in Figure 7-43. It is displayed in gray, indicating that this is a field, not ordinary text. If this drawing were to be plotted, the gray would not appear in the plot.

At this point, exit the table and return to the drawing.

Figure 7-42
Field dialog box

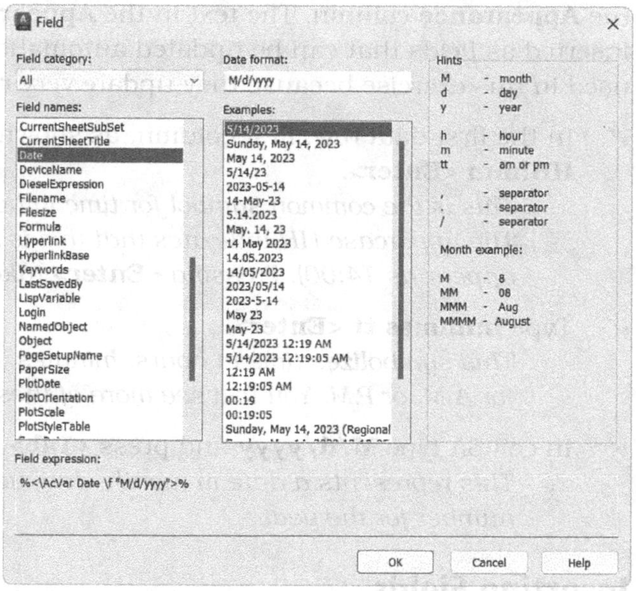

Figure 7-43
Date entered in cell

Date and Time Format	
Format	Appearance
HH:mm	
h:mm:ss tt	
M/d/yyyy	5/14/2023

NOTE

You can insert fields anywhere in a drawing. To insert a field without a table, click the **Field** tool from the **Data** panel on the **Insert** tab of the ribbon. This displays the **Field** dialog box, and the rest of the process previously described remains the same.

✔ To return to the drawing, click outside of the table.

Your table should now resemble Figure 7-43.

You could have filled out all the table cells without leaving the table, but it is important to know how to enter data after a table has already been created. Different selection sequences select cells in different ways. For example, clicking a cell selects it and the **Table Cell** tab is displayed on the ribbon. Double-clicking within a cell displays the **Text Editor** tab on the ribbon.

✔ Click once inside the first data row, second column, below the **Appearance** header.

*The cell is highlighted, and the **Table Cell** tab appears on the ribbon.*

✔ On the **Table Cell** tab, click the **Field** tool from the ribbon's **Insert** panel.

*The **Field** dialog box opens with **Date** selected in the **Field names** list box. Select the **HH:mm** example to match the format indicated in the **Format** column. You will find this selection seventh up from the bottom of the **Examples** list box. It will have hours and minutes in 24-hour format, with no A.M. or P.M. designation.*

✔ Highlight the **HH:mm** date format example, seventh up from the bottom of the list.

*When it is highlighted, **HH:mm** appears in the **Date format** edit box.*

✔ Click **OK**.

Finally, repeat the process to insert a field in the remaining cell.

✔ Press the down arrow on your keyboard to move down one row.

✔ Click the **Field** tool again.

✔ Select the **h:mm:ss tt** format from the **Examples** list.

This is just above the HH:mm date format.

✔ Click **OK**.

✔ Press **<Esc>** to clear the grips of the selected cell.

Your table should now resemble Figure 7-44 with three fields in the three right-hand data cells. You probably will notice a time difference between cells 3B and 4B.

Figure 7-44
Three fields in data cells

Date and Time Format	
Format	Appearance
HH:mm	00:21
h:mm:ss tt	12:21:01 AM
M/d/yyyy	5/14/2023

Updating Fields

Fields may be updated manually or automatically, and individually or in groups. To update an individual field, double-click the field text and right-click to open the shortcut menu. Select **Update field** from the shortcut menu. This also works with individual fields that are not in a table.

For this exercise, you update all fields in your table at once.

✔ Select any border of the table.

This selects the entire table. Grips are added.

✔ With the entire table selected, click the **Insert** tab > **Data** panel > **Update Fields** tool from the ribbon, as shown in Figure 7-45.

Notice how the two time fields are updated while the date field remains the same.

Fields also update automatically when certain events occur, as controlled by settings on the ***User Preferences*** *tab of the* ***Options*** *dialog box. To reach these settings, right-click an empty area of the drawing window and select* ***Options*** *from the bottom of the shortcut menu. Click the* ***User Preferences*** *tab and then the* ***Field Update Settings*** *button in the* ***Fields*** *panel. Fields may be automatically updated when a file is opened, saved, plotted, regenerated, or transmitted over the Internet. Any combination of these may be selected. By default, all are selected.*

Figure 7-45
Update Fields tool

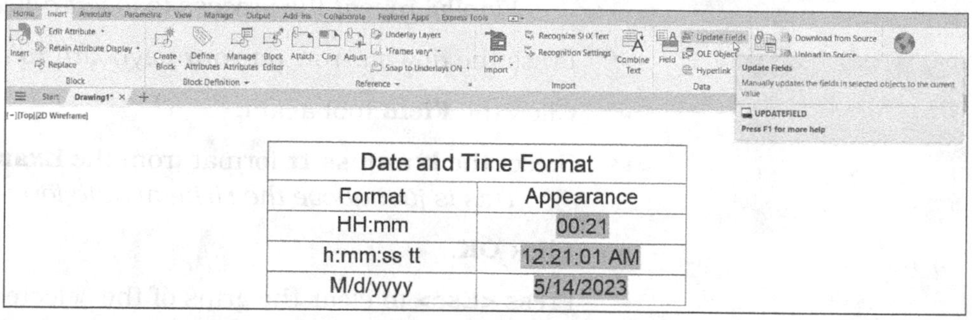

Using Drawing Templates, Borders, and Title Blocks

With knowledge of how to create text and how to use paper space layouts, you can take full advantage of the drawing templates with predrawn borders and title blocks. In this exercise, you create a new drawing using a D-size drawing template, add some simple geometry, and add some text to the title block. The work you do here can be saved and used as a start to completing Drawing 7-2, the gauges at the end of the chapter.

✔ Click the **New** tool from the **Quick Access** toolbar.

✔ In the **Select template** dialog box, select **Tutorial-iMfg**.

✔ With **Tutorial-iMfg** in the **File name** box, click **Open**.

This opens a new drawing layout with a predrawn border and title block, as shown in Figure 7-46. Notice the paper space icon in the lower-left corner in the drawing window and the ***Paper*** *button that has replaced the* ***Model*** *button on the status bar. Also, notice the window with blue borders that outlines a model space viewport. Next, you enter this viewport and draw a circle to begin the geometry of the drawing.*

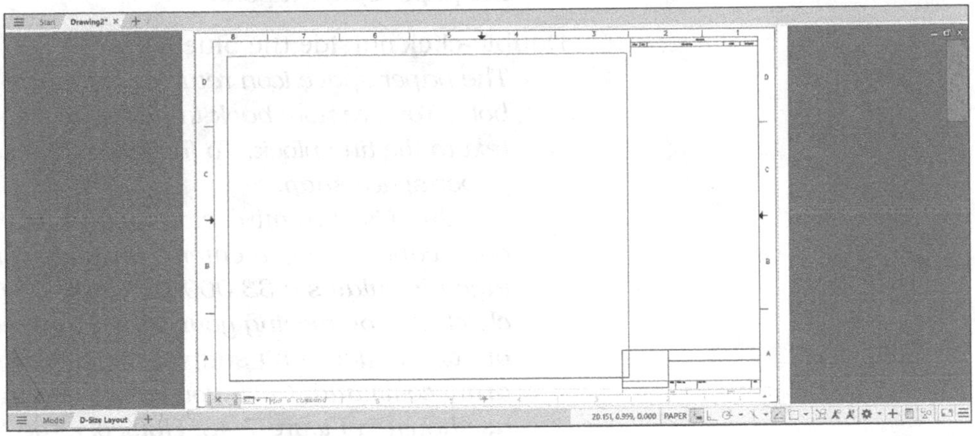

Figure 7-46
New drawing layout

✔ Double-click inside the blue borders to enter model space in this viewport.

The borders thicken. Turning on the grid gives you a better sense of the drawing space in this viewport.

✔ Turn on the grid in this viewport.

✔ If necessary, right-click the **Snap Mode** button on the status bar, select **Snap Settings**, and select **Display grid beyond Limits** from the dialog box, so that the grid fills the viewport.

✔ Enter the **CIRCLE** command.

✔ Create a **2.50**-radius circle with center point at **(3.00,5.00)**, as shown in Figure 7-47.

As you do this, notice also that having started this drawing with a different template, you have a whole different set of layers, and the units are three-place decimal.

Figure 7-47
Creating a circle

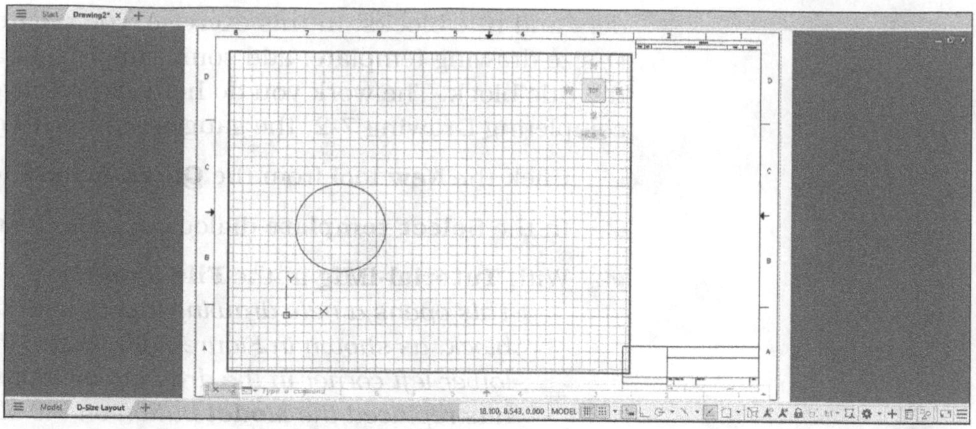

✔ Turn off the grid in the viewport.

You will not want the model space grid showing when you return to the paper space layout.

✔ Double-click outside the blue border.

The paper space icon returns, and the viewport border is no longer bold. You are now back in paper space. Next, you add two items of text to the title block. To facilitate these entries, you change to the paper space snap.

Snap is currently set to .500 in this template, but this is not observable until you enter a drawing command. Notice that the layout emulates a 33.000 × 21.000 D-size drawing sheet. You can check this by moving your cursor to the corners of the effective area, but again, you can't snap to these points exactly without entering a draw command. Next, you create text in two areas of the title block, as shown in Figure 7-48. However, the current snap setting makes this difficult.

✔ Type **snap <Enter>**.

✔ Select **On** from the command line.

✔ Press **<Enter>** to repeat **SNAP**.

Figure 7-48
Adding text

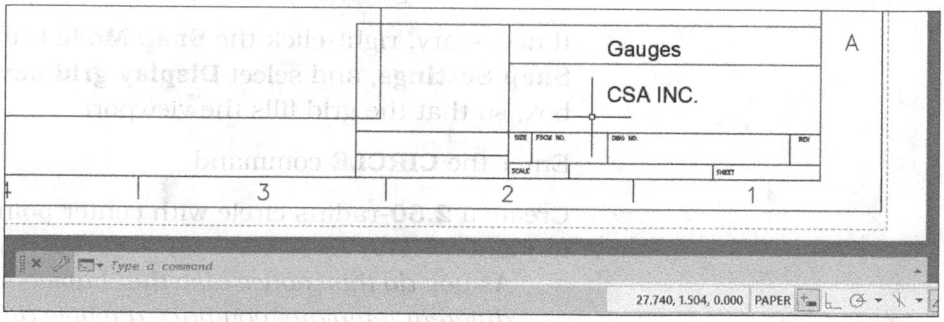

✔ Type **.250 <Enter>** to change the snap setting.

✔ Type **z <Enter>** and then use a window to zoom into the title block, as shown in Figure 7-48.

You are now ready to add text.

- ✔ Click the **Single Line** text tool from the **Text** drop-down menu on the **Annotation** panel of the **Home** tab on the ribbon.
- ✔ Specify a start point near **(28.000,2.500)**, as shown.
- ✔ Specify a text height of **.25** and a rotation angle of **0**.
- ✔ Type **Gauges <Enter>**.
- ✔ Press **<Enter>** again to exit **TEXT**.
- ✔ Repeat **TEXT** and type **CSA INC.** at **(28.000,1.750)**, as shown in Figure 7-48.
- ✔ Press **<Enter>** twice to exit **TEXT**.
- ✔ Type **z <Enter>** and then type **a <Enter>** to view the complete layout.

  There you go. You are well on your way to finishing Drawing 7-2, complete with title block.

7 chapterseven

Chapter Summary

This chapter dramatically increased your skill at working with text in AutoCAD. You have gone from entering simple single-line text to creating paragraph text, text with special characters and symbols, and text in a variety of fonts and styles. You learned to alter the properties of text and other objects, edit text in place in a drawing, check spelling and find text, and scale any drawing object. You learned to create tables with any number of cells, rows, and columns and populate cells with text, numbers, or fields that can be updated automatically or manually. Finally, you created your first layout using a drawing template with a title block and border and added text to that title block.

Chapter Test Questions

Multiple Choice

Circle the correct answer.

1. To enter single-line text you must first enter all of the following **except**

a. Alignment
b. Rotation angle
c. Start point
d. Text height

2. To enter multiline text, click the **Multiline Text** tool and then

a. Open the **Multiline Text Editor**
b. Enter two points
c. Specify a start point
d. Select a justification style

3. **TEXTEDIT** can be used to change

a. Text height
b. Text location
c. Text content
d. Text style

4. Borders and title blocks that come with AutoCAD can be found in the

a. **Border** folder
b. **Layout** tab
c. Acad.dwt template
d. **Template** folder

5. **MATCHPROP cannot** be used to match

a. Text style
b. Text height
c. Layer
d. Transparency

Matching

Write the number of the correct answer on the line.

a. Degree symbol _____	1. **Contextual** tab
b. Diameter symbol _____	2. **Grip Edit** mode
c. **Text Editor** _____	3. %%d
d. tt _____	4. %%c
e. **Scale** _____	5. A.M.

True or False

Circle the correct answer.

1. **True or False:** Objects can be scaled from different base points with different results.
2. **True or False:** MTEXT is drawn within a rectangular box defined by the user.
3. **True or False:** Fields can be updated each time a file is opened.
4. **True or False:** Center-justified text and middle-justified text are two names for the same thing.
5. **True or False**: Fonts are created based on text styles.

Questions

1. What is the difference between center-justified text and middle-justified text?
2. What is the purpose of %% in text entry?
3. What is the difference between a font and a style?
4. How would you use **SCALE** to change a 3.00 line to 2.75?
5. You want to use an AutoCAD-provided border and title block for your drawing. Where would you find the one you want to use?

Drawing Problems

1. Draw a 6 × 6 square. Create text with the word "Top" above the square, 0.4 unit high, and centered at the midpoint of the top side of the square.
2. Create text with the word "Left" 0.4 unit high and centered at the midpoint along the outer left side of the square.
3. Create text with the word "Right" 0.4 unit high and centered at the midpoint along the outer right side of the square.
4. Create text with the word "Bottom" 0.4 unit high, and below the square so that the top of the text is centered on the midpoint of the bottom side of the square.
5. Create text with the words "This is the middle" inside the square, 0.4 unit high, so the complete text wraps around within a 2-unit width and is centered on the center point of the square.

7 chapterseven

Chapter Drawing Projects

G Drawing 7-1: *Title Block* [INTERMEDIATE]

This title block gives you practice in using a variety of text styles and sizes. You may want to save it and use it as a title block for future drawings.

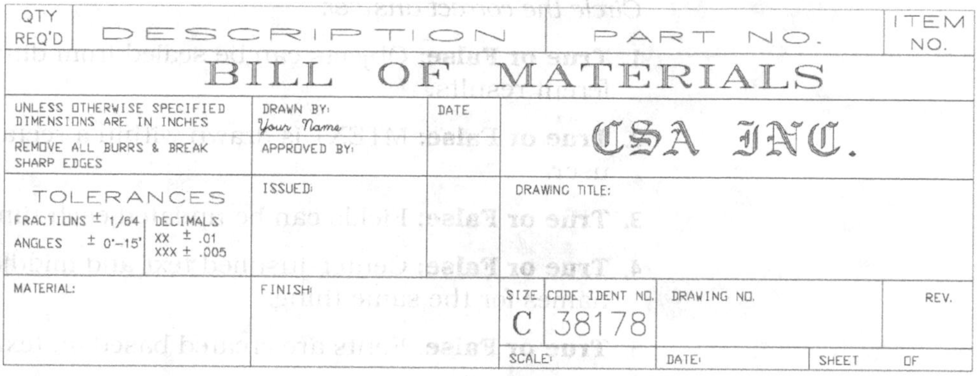

QTY REQ'D
DESCRIPTION
PART NO.
ITEM NO.
BILL OF MATERIALS
UNLESS OTHERWISE SPECIFIED DIMENSIONS ARE IN INCHES
REMOVE ALL BURRS & BREAK SHARP EDGES
DRAWN BY:
Your Name
APPROVED BY:
DATE
CSA INC.
TOLERANCES
FRACTIONS ± 1/64
ANGLES ± 0°-15'
DECIMALS
XX ± .01
XXX ± .005
ISSUED:
DRAWING TITLE:
MATERIAL:
FINISH:
SIZE
C
CODE IDENT NO.
38178
DRAWING NO.
REV.
SCALE:
DATE:
SHEET
OF

Drawing Suggestions

GRID = 1

SNAP = 0.0625

- Make ample use of **TRIM** as you draw the line patterns of the title block. Take your time and make sure that at least the major divisions are in place before you start entering text into the boxes.
- Set to the text layer current before creating text.
- Use **TEXT** when creating the **Standard**, 0.09, and left-justified text.
- Remember that once you have defined a style, you can make it current in the **TEXT** command. This saves you from restyling more than necessary.
- Use **%%D** for the degree symbol and **%%P** for the plus or minus symbol.

Drawing 7-1
Title Block

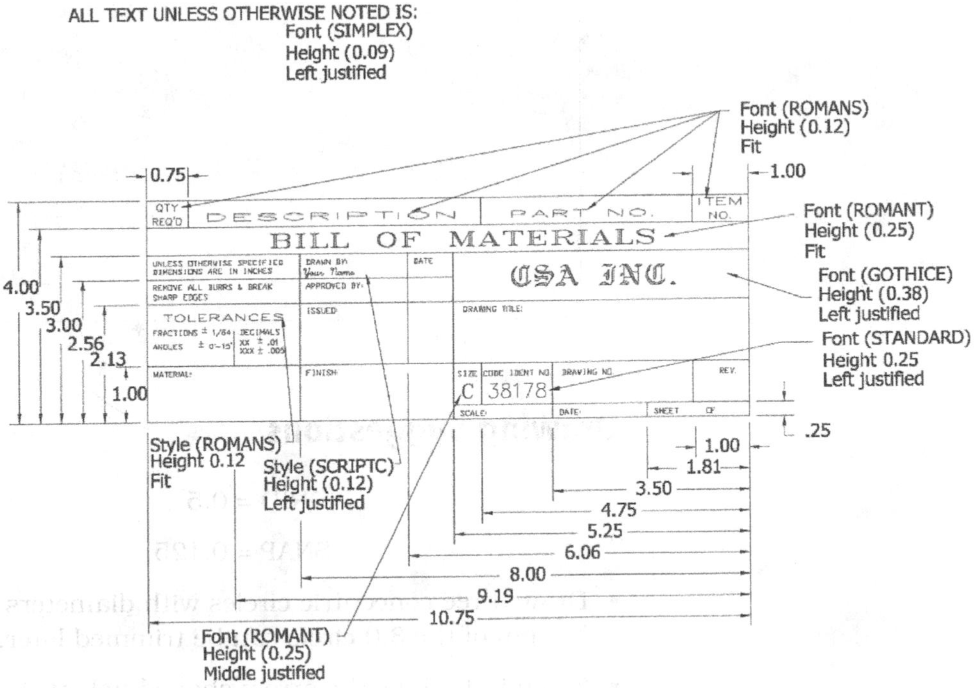

ALL TEXT UNLESS OTHERWISE NOTED IS:
Font (SIMPLEX)
Height (0.09)
Left justified
Font (ROMANS)
Height (0.12)
Fit
0.75
1.00
QTY REQ'D
DESCRIPTION
PART NO.
ITEM NO.
Font (ROMANT)
Height (0.25)
Fit
BILL OF MATERIALS
USA INC.
Font (GOTHICE)
Height (0.38)
Left justified
TOLERANCES
DRAWING TITLE:
Font (STANDARD)
Height 0.25
Left justified
MATERIAL:
FINISH
ISSUED
SIZE
C
38178
REV.
SCALE:
DATE:
SHEET
OF
4.00
3.50
3.00
2.56
2.13
1.00
.25
Style (ROMANS)
Height 0.12
Fit
Style (SCRIPTC)
Height (0.12)
Left justified
1.00
1.81
3.50
4.75
5.25
6.06
8.00
9.19
10.75
Font (ROMANT)
Height (0.25)
Middle justified

G Drawing 7-2: *Gauges* [INTERMEDIATE]

This drawing teaches you some typical uses of the **SCALE** and **TEXTEDIT** commands. Some of the techniques used are not obvious, so read the suggestions carefully.

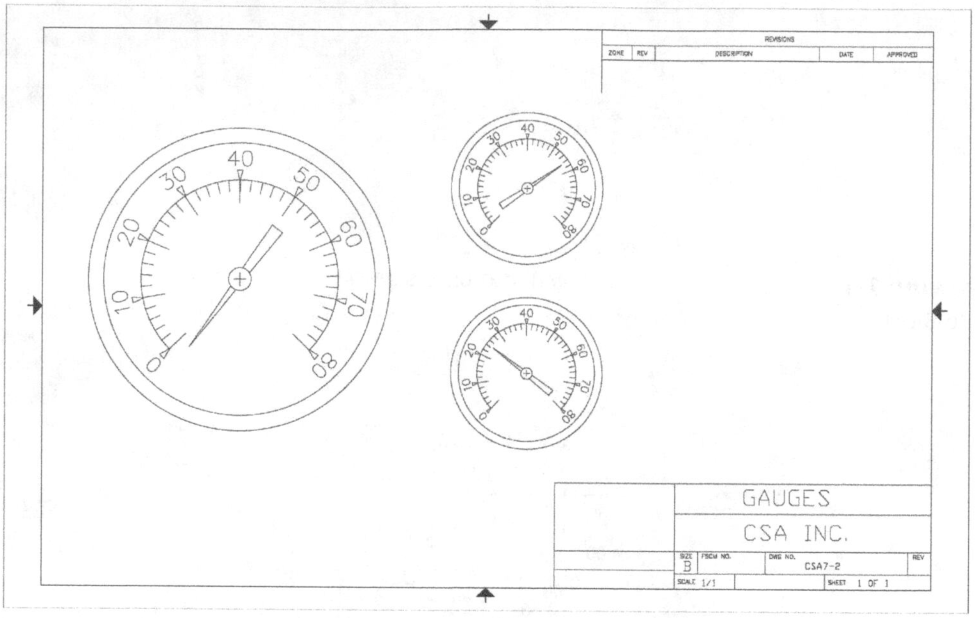

Drawing Suggestions

GRID = 0.5

SNAP = 0.125

- Draw three concentric circles with diameters of 5.0, 4.5, and 3.0. The bottom of the 3.0 circle can be trimmed later.
- Zoom in to draw the arrow-shaped tick at the top of the 3.0 circle. Then draw the 0.50 vertical line directly below it and the number 40 (middle-justified text) above it.
- These three objects can be arrayed to the left and right around the perimeter of the 3.0 circle using angles of 135° and −135°, as shown.
- Use **TEXTEDIT** to change the arrayed numbers to 0, 10, 20, 30, and so on. You can do all of these without leaving the command.
- Draw the 0.25 vertical tick directly on top of the 0.50 mark at the top center and array it left and right. There should be 20 marks each way.
- Draw the needle horizontally across the middle of the dial.
- Make two copies of the dial; use **SCALE** to scale them down as shown. Then move them into their correct positions.
- Rotate the three needles into positions as shown.

Drawing 7-2
Gauges

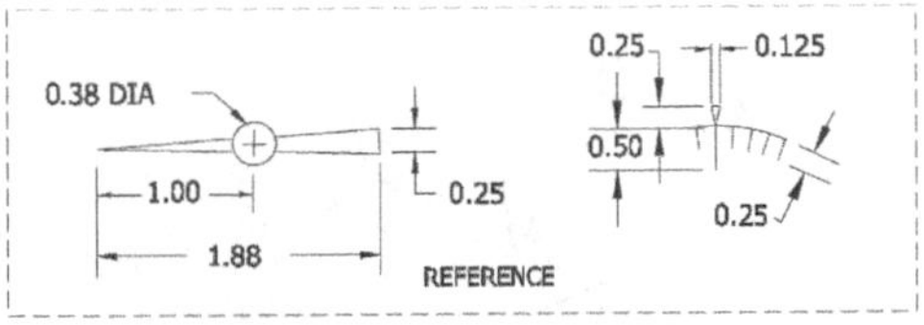

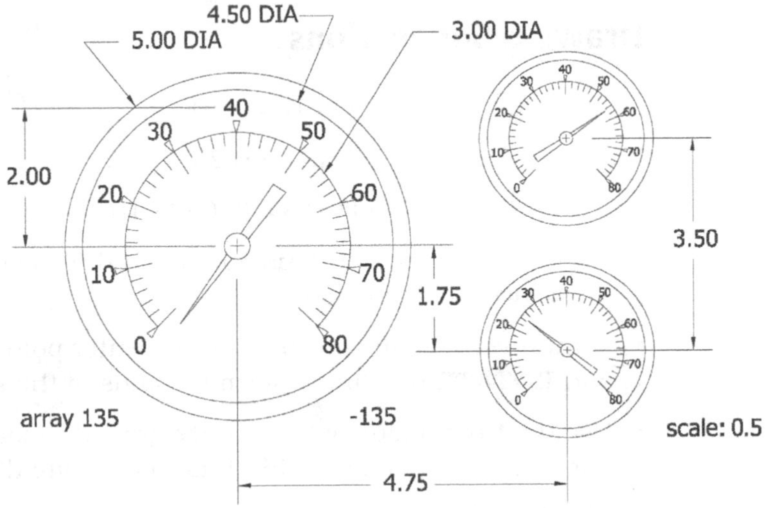

G Drawing 7-3: *Stamping* [INTERMEDIATE]

This drawing is trickier than it appears. There are many ways that it can be done and make use of a number of commands and techniques with which you are familiar. Notice that a change in limits is needed to take advantage of some of the suggestions.

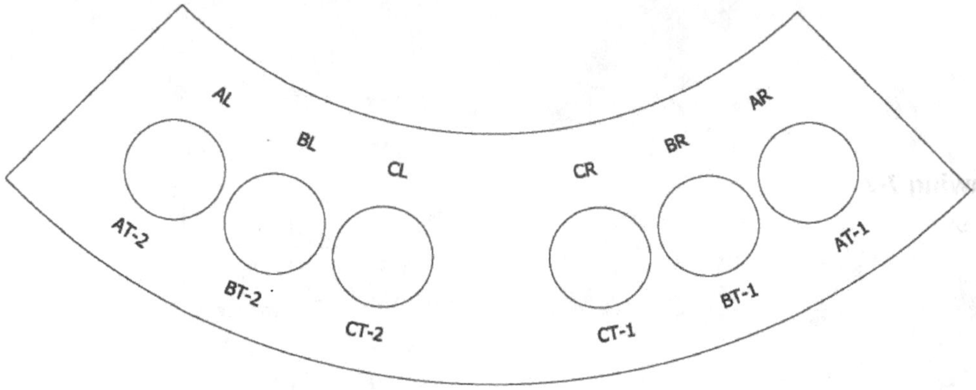

Drawing Suggestions

GRID = 0.50

SNAP = 0.25

LIMITS = (0,0)(24,18)

- Draw two circles, of radius 10.25 and 6.50, centered at about (13,15). These are trimmed later.
- Draw a vertical line down from the center point to the outer circle. **COPY** and **ROTATE** this line to form the ends of the stamping.
- Use the **Copy** mode of the **Rotate** grip edit mode to create copies of the line rotated at 45° and –45°. (The coordinate display shows 315°.)
- **TRIM** the lines and the circles to form the outline of the stamping.
- Draw a 1.50-diameter circle in the center of the stamping, 8.50 down from **(13,15)**. Draw middle-justified text, AR, 7.25 down, and AT-1 down from 9.75 (13,15).
- Follow the procedure given in the next subsection to create offset copies of the circle and text; then, use **TEXTEDIT** to modify all text to agree with the drawing.

Grip Copy Mode with Offset Snap Locations

Here is a good opportunity to try another grip edit feature. If you hold down the **<Shift>** key while specifying multiple copy points, AutoCAD is constrained to place copies only at points offset from each other the same distance as your first two points. For example, try the following steps:

1. Select the circle and text.
2. Select any grip to initiate grip editing.
3. Select **Rotate** from the shortcut menu.
4. Type **b** or select **Base point** from the shortcut menu.
5. Specify the center of the stamping **(13,15)** as the base point.
6. Type **c** or select **Copy** from the shortcut menu.
7. Hold down the **<Shift>** key and move the cursor to rotate a copy 11° from the original.
8. Keep holding down the **<Shift>** key as you move the cursor to create additional copies. All copies are offset 11°.

Drawing 7-3
Stamping

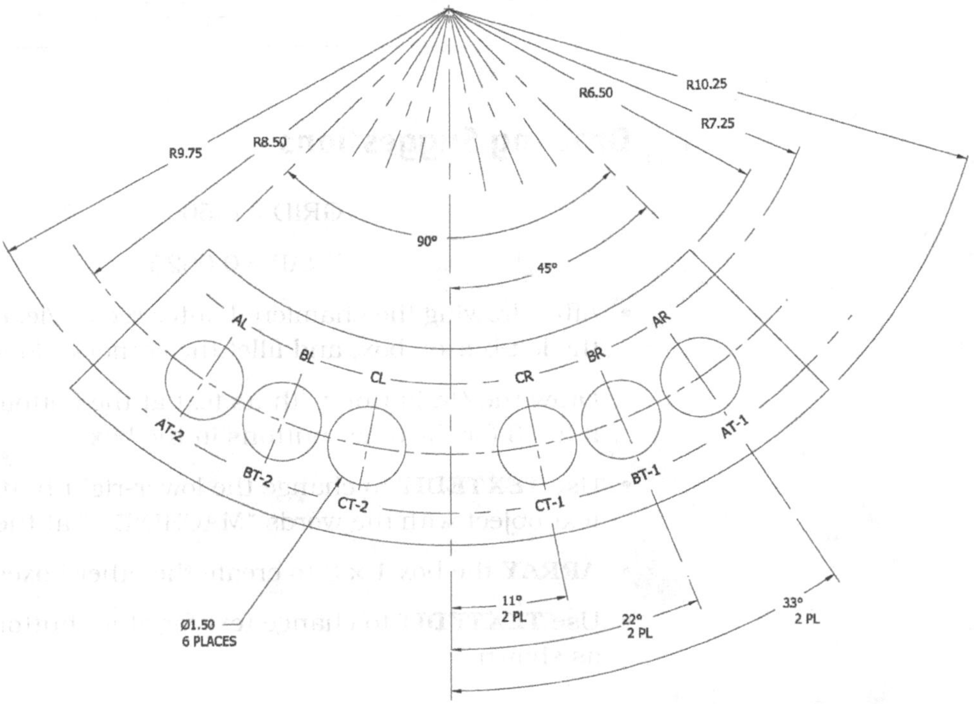

Drawing 7-4: *Control Panel* [INTERMEDIATE]

Done correctly, this drawing gives you a good feel for the power of the commands you now have available to you. Be sure to take advantage of combinations of **ARRAY** and **TEXTEDIT** as described. Also, read the suggestion on moving the origin before you begin. Moving the origin in this drawing makes it easier to read the dimensions, which are given in ordinate form measured from the (0,0) point at the lower-left corner of the object.

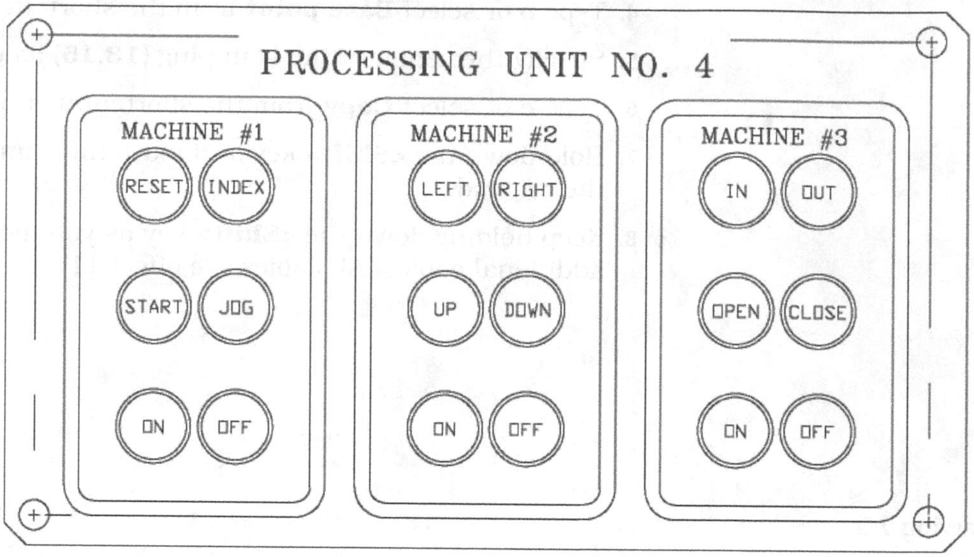

Drawing Suggestions

GRID = 0.50

SNAP = 0.0625

- After drawing the chamfered outer rectangle, draw the double outline of the left button box, and fillet the corners. Notice the different fillet radii.
- Draw the **On** button with its text at the bottom left of the box. Then array it 2 × 3 for the other buttons in the box.
- Use **TEXTEDIT** to change the lower-right button text to **Off** and create a text object with the words "MACHINE #" at the top of the box.
- **ARRAY** the box 1 × 3 to create the other boxes.
- Use **TEXTEDIT** to change text for other buttons and machine numbers as shown.

Moving the Origin with the UCS Command

The dimensions of this drawing are shown in ordinate type, measured from a single point of origin in the lower-left corner. In effect, this establishes a new coordinate origin. If you move the origin to match this point, you can read dimension values directly from the coordinate display. This can be done by setting the lower-left limits to (–1, –1). However, it can be completed more efficiently using the **UCS** command to establish a user coordinate system with the origin at a point you specify. User coordinate systems are not discussed in depth here. For now, here is a simple procedure:

1. Type **ucs <Enter> at the command-line prompt**.
2. Type **o <Enter>** or select **Origin** from the command line.
3. Specify a point for the new origin.

That's all there is to it. Move your cursor to the new origin and watch the coordinate display. It should show 0.00,0.00,0.00, and all values are measured from there.

Drawing 7-4
Control Panel

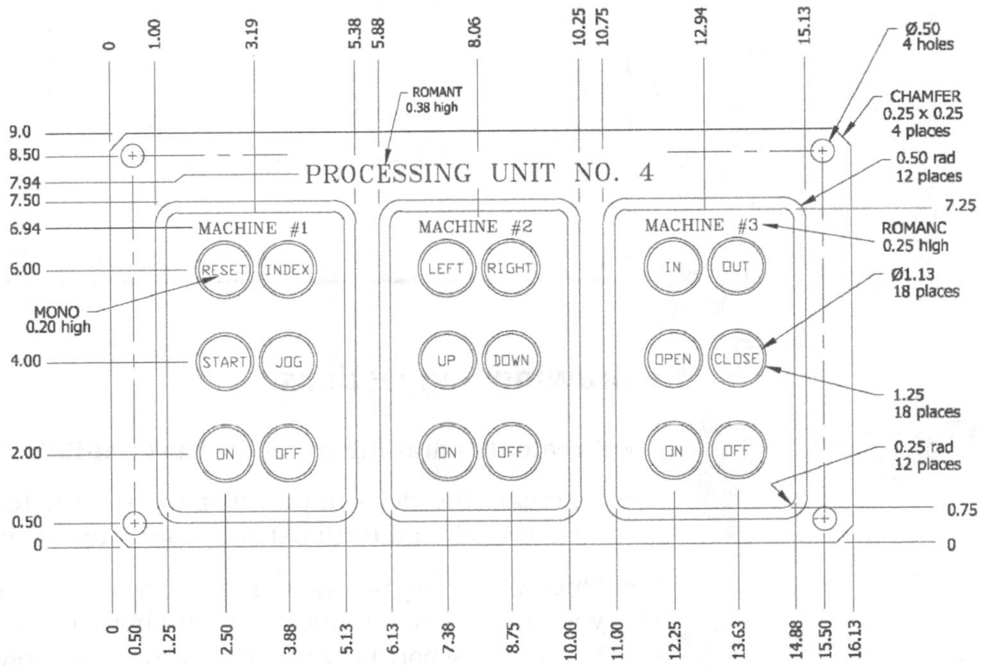

M Drawing 7-5: *Angle Bracket* [ADVANCED]

This drawing gives you practice with multiline text (mtext) and with using a drawing template with a title block and border. The drawing is a three-view drawing that is created in model space, but it appears in a floating viewport on a paper space layout. The multiline text is drawn in the layout view in paper space and not model space.

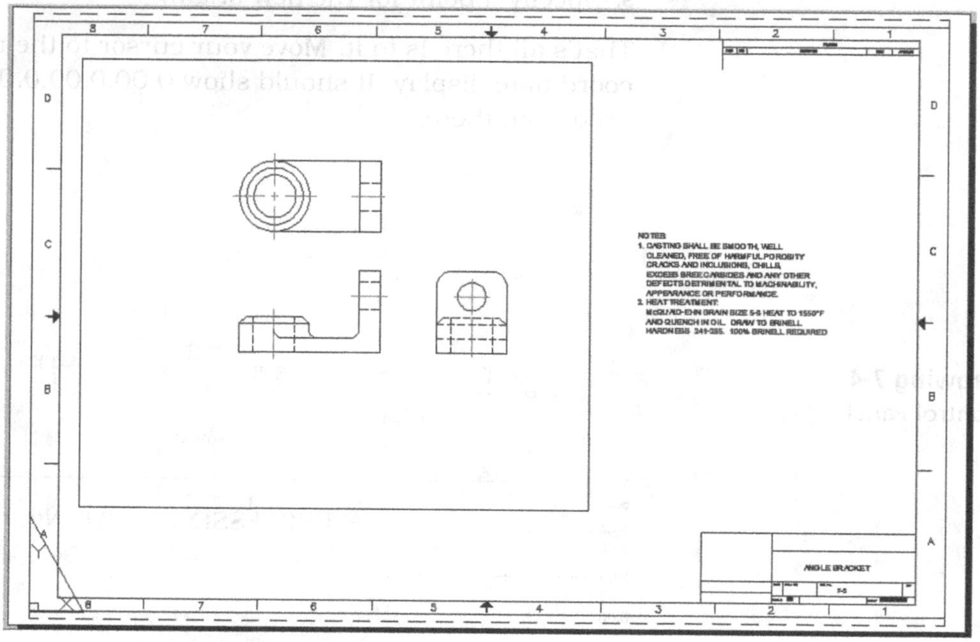

NOTES:
1. CASTING SHALL BE SMOOTH, WELL CLEANED, FREE OF HARMFUL POROSITY CRACKS AND INCLUSIONS, CHILLS,
DEFECTS DETRIMENTAL TO MACHINABILITY, APPEARANCE OR PERFORMANCE.
2. HEAT TREATMENT:
HEAT TO 1550°F AND QUENCH IN OIL. DRAW TO BRINELL
100% BRINELL REQUIRED
ANGLE BRACKET

Drawing Suggestions

- Create this drawing using the **Tutorial-iMfg** drawing template.
- To create the views in model space and the text in paper space, you switch back and forth between model space and the layout view.
- Once you have the drawing open with the D-Size Layout layout current, you should see the title block and border. Use **MVIEW** to create a single floating viewport for your three views, as shown in the reference drawing.
- Add the two notes in paper space on the layout using **MTEXT**.
- The dimensions in the drawing are for reference only; they are not part of the final design.

Drawing 7-5
Angle Bracket

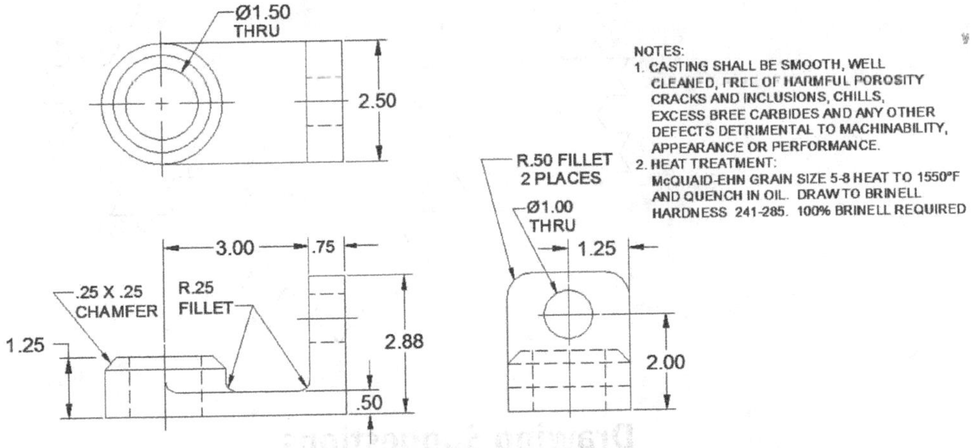
Ø1.50
THRU
2.50
R.50 FILLET
2 PLACES
Ø1.00
THRU
3.00
.75
1.25
.25 X .25
CHAMFER
R.25
FILLET
1.25
2.88
.50
2.00
NOTES:
1. CASTING SHALL BE SMOOTH, WELL CLEANED, FREE OF HARMFUL POROSITY CRACKS AND INCLUSIONS, CHILLS, EXCESS BREE CARBIDES AND ANY OTHER DEFECTS DETRIMENTAL TO MACHINABILITY, APPEARANCE OR PERFORMANCE.
2. HEAT TREATMENT:
McQUAID-EHN GRAIN SIZE 5-8 HEAT TO 1550°F AND QUENCH IN OIL. DRAW TO BRINELL HARDNESS 241-285. 100% BRINELL REQUIRED

G

Drawing 7-6: *Koch Snowflake* [ADVANCED]

The Koch snowflake design can be done in numerous ways, all involving similar techniques of reference scaling, rotating, and polar arraying. A few suggestions and hints are given here, but you are largely on your own in solving this visual design puzzle.

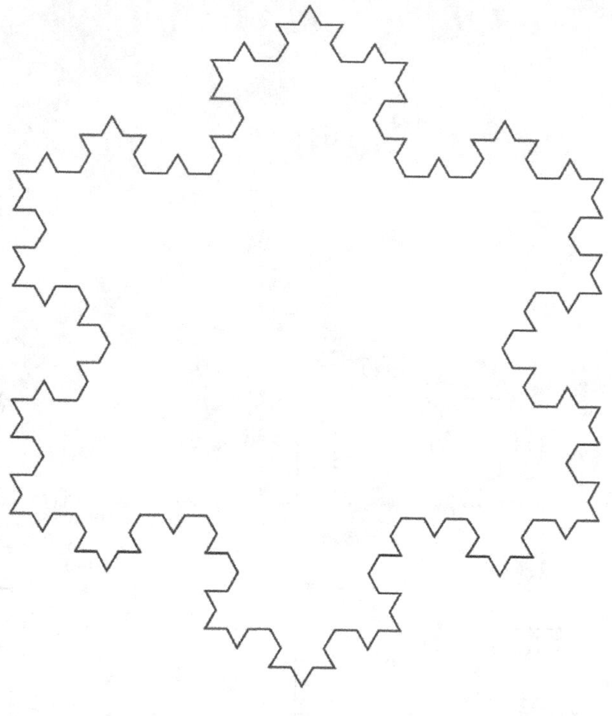

Drawing Suggestions

- Begin by creating an equilateral triangle. Because it is important to know the center point of this triangle, construct it from a circle, as shown. The radial lines are drawn by arraying a single line from the center point three times in a 360° polar array.
- After drawing the initial equilateral triangle, you make frequent use of reference scaling.
- The number 3 is important throughout this design. Consider how you will use the number 3 in the reference scaling option.
- You will have frequent use for **Center**, **Intersection**, and **Midpoint** object snaps.
- Do not move the original triangle, so that you can always locate its center point. There are at least two ways to find the center point of other triangles you create. One involves constructing a 3P circle, and another involves three construction lines.
- A lot of trimming and erasing is required to create the final design.

Drawing 7-6
Koch Snowflake

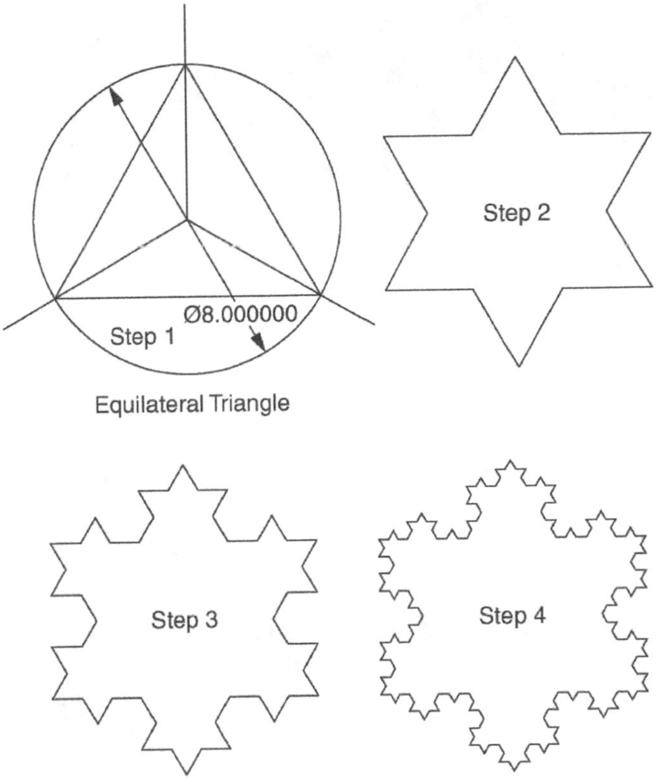

8 chapter eight
Dimensions

CHAPTER OBJECTIVES

- Create and save a dimension style
- Draw linear dimensions
- Draw multiple linear dimensions using **QDIM**
- Draw ordinate dimensions
- Draw angular dimensions
- Dimension arcs and circles
- Dimension with multileaders
- Change dimension text
- Use associative dimensions
- Use the **HATCH** command
- Scale dimensions between paper space and model space

Introduction

The ability to dimension your drawings and add crosshatch patterns greatly enhances the professional appearance and utility of your work. AutoCAD's dimensioning features form a complex system of commands, subcommands, and variables that automatically measure objects and draw dimension text and extension lines. With AutoCAD's dimensioning tools and variables, you can create dimensions in a wide variety of formats, and these formats can be saved as styles. The time saved by not drawing each dimension object line by line is among the most significant advantages of CAD.

Creating and Saving a Dimension Style

Dimensioning objects in AutoCAD is simplified compared with manual dimensioning. Although creating dimensions is relatively straightforward, defining dimension styles used to control the appearance of dimensions is necessarily complex because of the flexibility required to cover all dimension styles. In the exercises that follow, you learn the workflows to manage dimension styles, use some of the options available, and get a solid foundation for understanding how to get what you want from AutoCAD dimensioning. You find out how to create a basic dimension style and use it to draw standard dimensions and tolerances. Many possible variations are left to you to explore.

dimension style: A set of dimension variable settings that controls the text and geometry of all available dimension types.

In AutoCAD, it is best to begin by naming and defining a dimension style. A ***dimension style*** is a set of dimension variable settings that control the text and geometry of all available dimension types. It's recommended that you create new dimension styles in your drawing template and save it so that you do not have to make these changes again when you start a new drawing.

✔ To begin this exercise, create a new drawing with 18 × 12 limits (or open the 1B template drawing if you have it).

You make changes to dimension style settings so that all dimensions showing distances are presented with two decimal places, and angular dimensions have no decimals.

> **TIP**
>
> If you make changes to a dimension style in a drawing template, these changes become the default dimension settings for any drawing created from that template.
>
> Remember, you find drawing template files in the **Template** folder. Use the **OPEN** command to access the **Select File** dialog box. Select **Drawing Template (*.dwt)** from the **Files of type:** drop-down list. This automatically opens the **Template** folder. Select the template file you want from the list, and click **Open**.

✔ Turn the grid on or off, your preference.

For clarity, the figures in this chapter are shown with the grid off.

✔ Click the **Annotate** tab on the ribbon.

*This displays the set of **Annotate** ribbon panels, as shown in Figure 8-1. The **Annotate** tab is used frequently throughout this chapter.*

Figure 8-1
Annotate tab

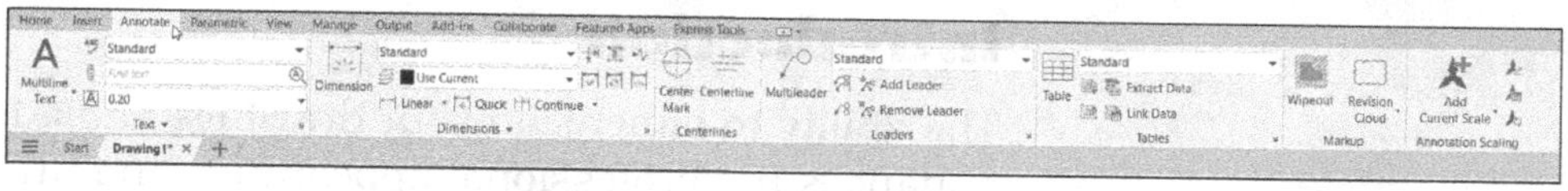

✔ Click the diagonal arrow on the **Dimensions** panel of the ribbon, as shown in Figure 8-2.

*This is the small arrow on the right side of the **Dimensions** panel title bar. Notice that the **Text**, **Dimensions**, **Leaders**, and **Tables** panels all have these type of arrows, which are known as a panel dialog box launcher.*

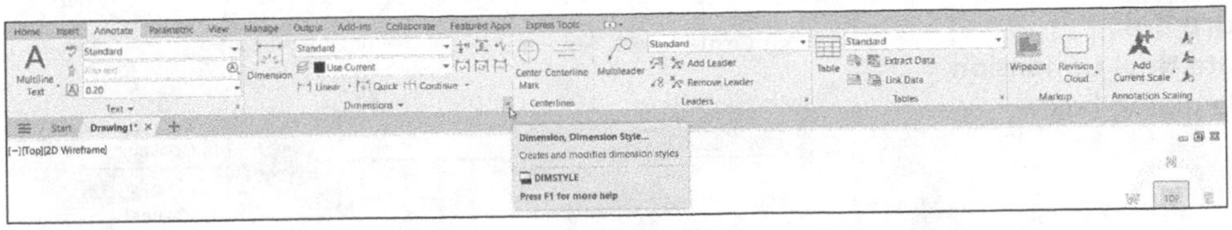

Figure 8-2
Dimensions diagonal arrow

This opens the ***Dimension Style Manager*** *shown in Figure 8-3. The current dimension style is named* ***Standard****. As with text styles, the other predefined style is* ***Annotative****. The* ***Annotative*** *property allows dimensions and other annotative objects to be scaled to show at the correct size in paper layouts. The only difference between the* ***Standard*** *and* ***Annotative*** *styles is the value of the* ***Annotative*** *property. You explore this feature later in this chapter in the "Scaling Dimensions Between Paper Space and Model Space" section.*

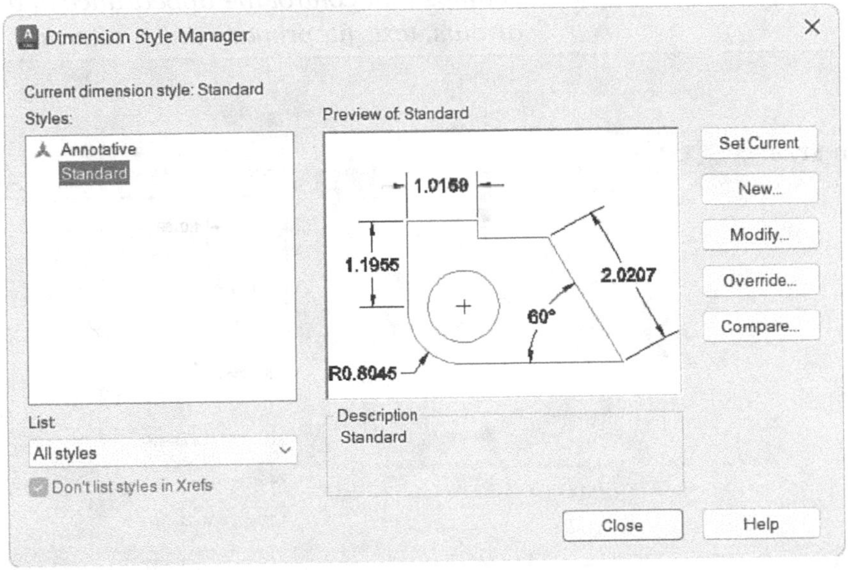

Figure 8-3
Dimension Style Manager dialog box

To the right of the **Styles** list is a preview that presents a sample image showing many of the dimension variable settings of the style highlighted in the **Styles** list. The style being previewed is also named at the top of the dialog box. The preview image is updated any time you make a change to a dimension setting.

Below the preview image is a **Description** box. Right now, the description simply indicates that the style is **Standard**.

✔ Check to see that **Standard** is selected in the **Styles** list.

Now, you proceed to create a new style based on the ***Standard*** *style. To the right of the preview is a set of five buttons, the second of which is the* ***New*** *button.*

✔ Click the **New** button.

This opens the ***Create New Dimension Style*** *dialog box shown in Figure 8-4.*

If necessary, double-click in the ***New Style Name*** *edit box to highlight the text* ***Copy of Standard****.*

Figure 8-4
Create New Dimension Style dialog box

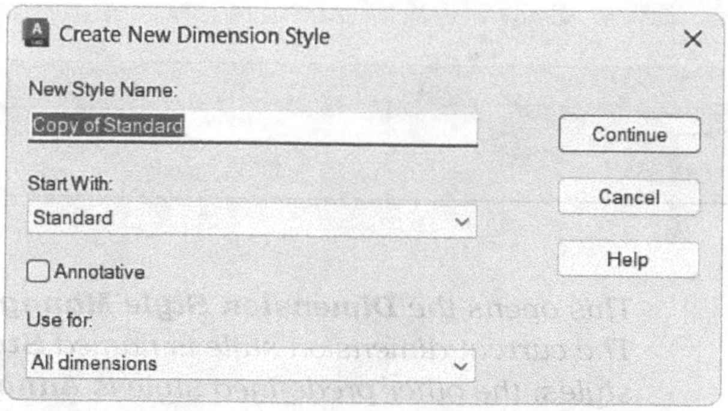

✔ Type a name, such as **MyStyle**, for the new dimension style and click **Continue**.

This creates the new dimension style and takes you to the ***New Dimension Style*** *dialog box shown in Figure 8-5. Here, there are seven tabs that allow you to make many changes to the dimension settings that control the appearance of dimension lines, symbols and arrows, text, fit, primary units, alternate units, and tolerances.*

Figure 8-5
New Dimension Style dialog box

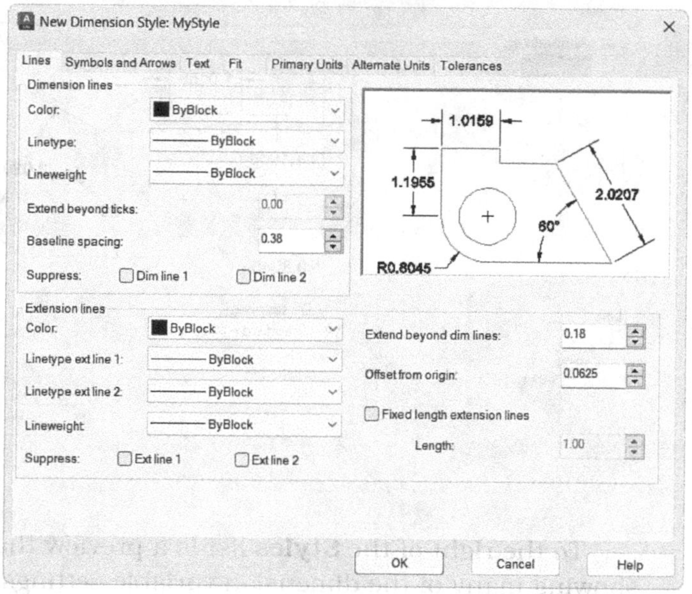

✔ Click the **Primary Units** tab.

This ***Primary Units*** *tab is displayed, as shown in Figure 8-6. There are settings available for linear and angular units. The* ***Unit format*** *and* ***Precision*** *drop-down lists under the* ***Linear dimensions*** *and* ***Angular dimensions*** *panels are similar to the lists used in the* ***Drawing Units*** *dialog box. Notice, however, that dimension units are completely separate from drawing units. They must be set independently and may or may not have the same settings. In the* ***Linear dimensions*** *panel,* ***Unit format*** *should show* ***Decimal****. In the* ***Angular dimensions*** *panel,* ***Units format*** *should show* ***Decimal Degrees****. If these are not the current values in your dialog box, make these changes now. For this exercise, all you should need* *to change is the number of decimal places showing in the* ***Precision*** *drop-down list on the* ***Linear dimensions*** *panel. By default, it is* ***0.0000****. Change it to* ***0.00****.*

Figure 8-6
Primary Units tab

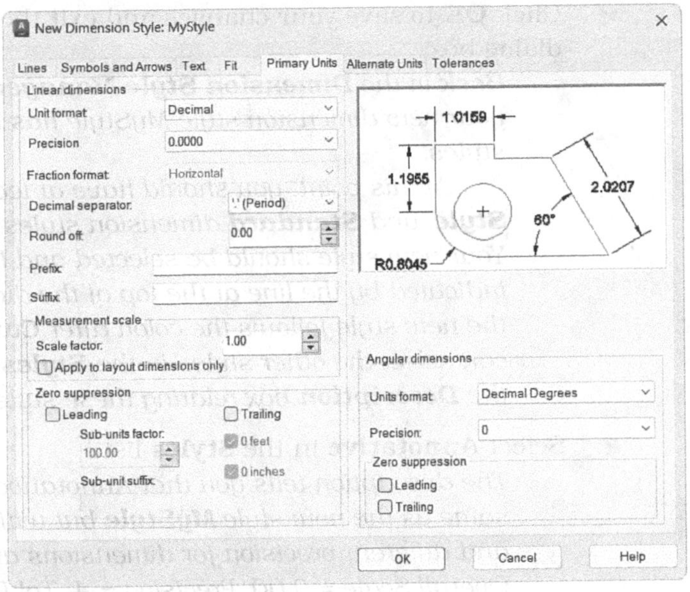

- ✔ Click the **Precision** drop-down list in the **Linear dimensions** panel.
- ✔ *This opens a list of precision settings ranging from 0 to 0.00000000.*
- ✔ Select **0.00** from the drop-down list.

This closes the drop-down list and shows ***0.00*** *as the selected precision. Notice the change in the preview image, which now shows two-place decimals. At this point, you are ready to complete this part of the procedure by returning to the* ***Dimension Style Manager****.*

Before leaving the ***New Dimension Style*** *dialog box, click each of the other tabs and look at the large variety of dimension variable settings you can adjust. You also can change dimension variables at the command line by typing in their names and entering a new value, but the dialog box makes the process much easier, and the preview image give you immediate visual feedback upon the changing of a dimension variable setting.*

On the ***Lines*** *and* ***Symbols and Arrows*** *tabs, you find options for changing the size and positioning of dimension geometry. On the* ***Text*** *tab, you can adjust the look and placement of dimension text. This tab includes the option of selecting from different text styles previously defined in the drawing. On the* ***Fit*** *tab, you can tell AutoCAD how to manage situations in which there is a tight fit that creates some ambiguity about how dimension geometry and text should be arranged. This is also where the* ***Annotative*** *property can be changed.* ***Primary Units****, as you know, lets you specify the units in which dimensions are displayed.* ***Alternate Units*** *allows you to include a secondary unit specification along with the primary dimension unit. For example, you can use these dimension variable settings to display dimension values in both inches and centimeters.*

*Tolerances are added to dimension specifications to give them a range of acceptable values, for example, a machining process. The **Tolerances** tab gives several options for how tolerances are displayed.*

✔ Click **OK** to save your changes and exit the **New Dimension Style** dialog box.

*Back in the **Dimension Style Manager** dialog box, you can see that your new dimension style MyStyle has been added to the list of styles.*

*At this point, you should have at least the **Annotative**, **MyStyle**, and **Standard** dimension styles defined in your drawing. Your new style should be selected and be the current style. This is indicated by the line at the top of the dialog box where the name of the new style follows the colon after **Current dimension style**. You can select the other styles in the **Styles** list and see descriptions in the **Description** box relating these styles to the current style. Try it.*

✔ Select **Annotative** in the **Styles** list.

*The description tells you that Annotative for the most part is the same as the new style **MyStyle** but with a variable overall scale and different precision for dimensions and tolerances, "New + Overall Scale = 0.00, Precision = 4, Tol Precision = 4."*

*Conversely, if you set **Annotative** as the current style, the description of the new style will be relative to **Annotative**. Try it.*

✔ With **Annotative** selected in the **Styles** list, click the **Set Current** button.

*Annotative now appears in the **Description** box.*

✔ Select your new style, **MyStyle**, in the **Styles** list.

*The description now reads, "Annotative + Overall Scale = 1.0000, Precision = 2, Tol Precision = 2." The new style is the same as **Annotative** but with a fixed scale and precision of two-places.*

✔ Click **Set Current** to set the new style, **MyStyle**, as the current dimension style again.

✔ Click **Close** to exit the **Dimension Style Manager** dialog box.

✔ If you are working in a template drawing, save your changes and close the drawing. Otherwise, move on to the next section.

✔ If you have modified a template, create a new drawing using the modified template.

*If the new drawing is created from the modified template, **MyStyle** should be the current dimension style. Its name appears in the **Dimension Style** drop-down list on the ribbon's **Dimensions** panel.*

Drawing Linear Dimensions

AutoCAD has many commands and features that aid in the drawing of dimensions. In this exercise, you create some basic linear dimensions formatted with the newly created dimension style.

TIP

Following is a general procedure for drawing linear dimensions:

1. Click the **Linear** tool from the **Dimensions** panel on the **Annotate** tab of the ribbon.
2. Select an object or specify two origin points for the extension lines.
3. Specify a point for the placement of the dimension line.

✔ To prepare for this exercise, draw a (3.00,4.00,5.00) triangle, a 4.00 vertical line, and a 6.00 horizontal line above the middle of the display, as shown in Figure 8-7.

You begin by adding dimensions to the triangle.

DIMLINEAR	
Command	DIMLINEAR
Alias	Dli
Panel	Dimensions
Tool	

✔ If your drawing has a layer for dimensions, click the **Layer** drop-down list on the **Home** tab's **Layers** panel, and make that layer current.

The dimensioning commands are streamlined and efficient. Their full names, however, are long. They all begin with ***DIM*** *and are followed by the name of a type of dimension (e.g.,* ***DIMLINEAR***, ***DIMALIGNED****, and* ***DIMANGULAR****). Use the ribbon to avoid typing these names.*

TIP

The **Dimensions** panel on the ribbon's **Annotate** tab contains a **Dim Layer Override** control. This control is used to set the layer on which new dimensions should be created—a specific named layer or to use the current drawing layer. So, if you always place your dimensions on layer named **dims**, you could set that layer current here.

Figure 8-7
Drawing triangle and lines

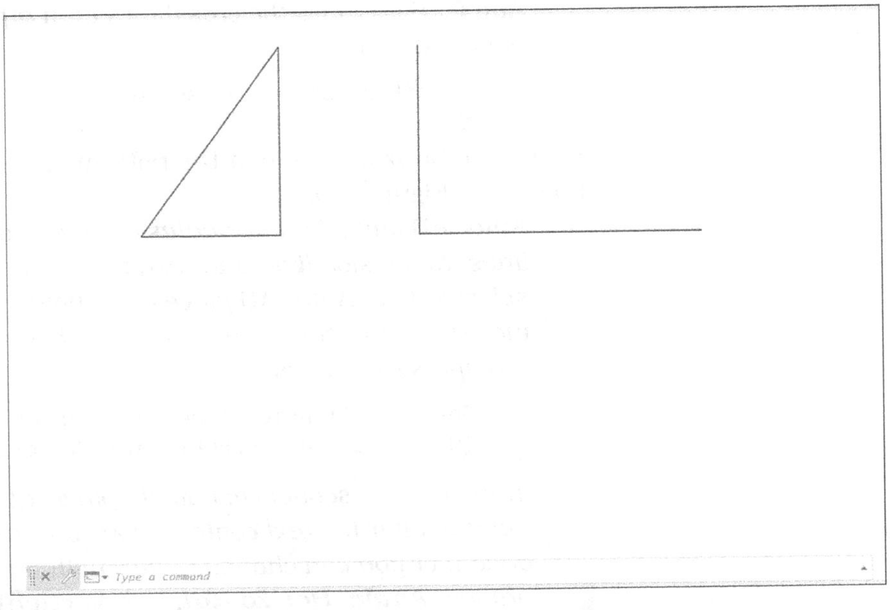

You begin by placing a linear dimension below the base of the triangle.

✔ Click the **Annotate** tab on the ribbon, and click the **Linear** tool from the **Dimensions** panel, as shown in Figure 8-8.

*The ribbon places the last dimension command used at the top of the drop-down list, so it may be necessary to open the drop-down list to access the **Linear** tool.*

Figure 8-8
Linear tool

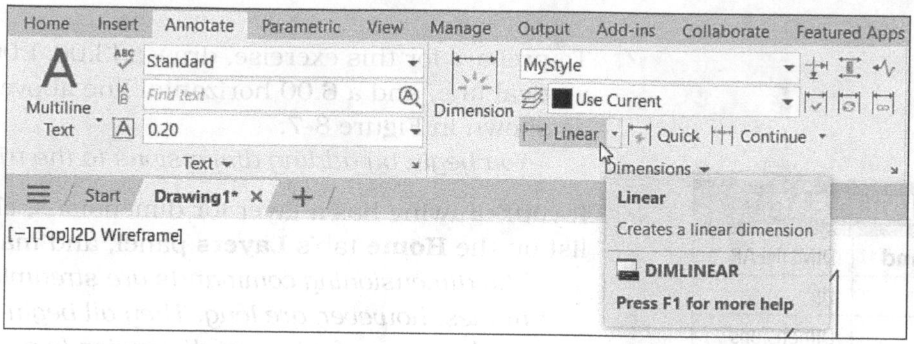

*This starts the **DIMLINEAR** command, with the following prompt appearing in the command line:*

```
Specify first extension line origin or <select object>:
```

There are two ways to proceed at this point. One is to specify where the extension lines should begin, and the other is to select the object you want to dimension and let AutoCAD position the extension lines. In most simple applications, the latter method is faster.

✔ Press **<Enter>** to allow you to select an object.

AutoCAD replaces the crosshairs with a pickbox and prompts for your selection:

```
Select object to dimension:
```

✔ Select the horizontal line at the bottom of the triangle, as shown by Point 1 in Figure 8-9.

AutoCAD immediately creates a dimension, including extension lines, dimension line, and text, that you can drag away from the selected line. AutoCAD places the dimension line and text where you indicate but keeps the text centered between the extension lines. The prompt is as follows:

```
Specify dimension line location or
[Mtext/Text/Angle/Horizontal/Vertical/Rotated]:
```

*In the default sequence, you simply locate the dimension line. If you want to alter the text content, you can do so using the **Mtext** or **Text** option, or you can change it later with the **DIMEDIT** command named. **Angle**, **Horizontal**, and **Vertical** allow you to define the orientation of the text. Horizontal text is the default for linear dimensions. **Rotated** allows you to rotate the complete dimension so that the extension lines move out at an angle from the object being dimensioned. (Text remains horizontal.)*

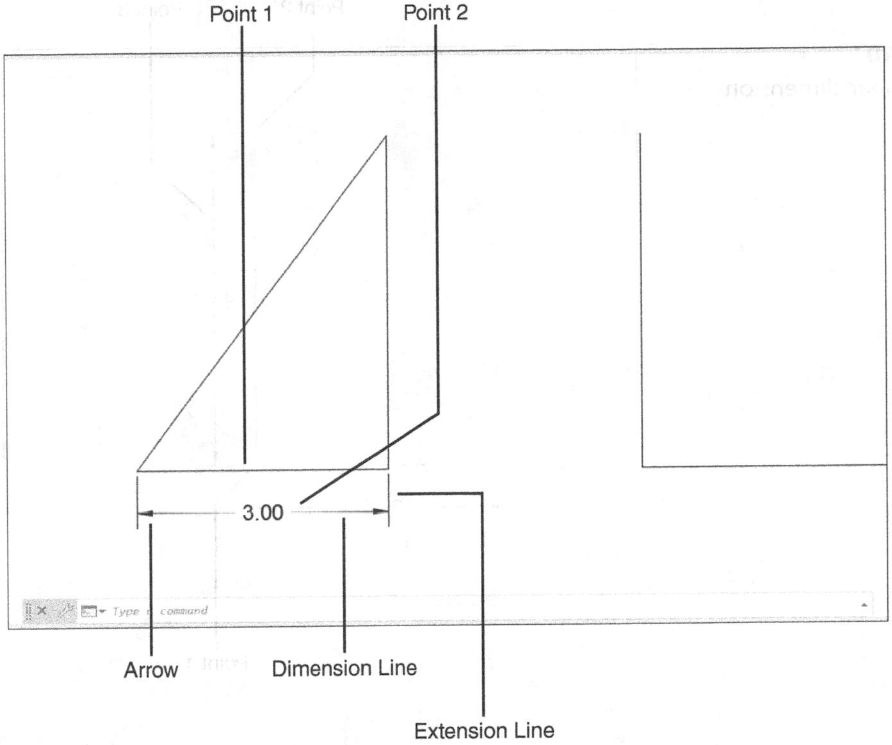

Figure 8-9
Horizontal linear dimension

✔ Specify a location about 0.50 units below the triangle, as shown by Point 2 in Figure 8-9.

Bravo! You have completed your first dimension. (Notice that the figure and others in this chapter are shown zoomed in on the relevant object for the sake of clarity. You can zoom or not, as you like.)

At this point, take a good look at the dimension you have just drawn to see what it consists of. As in Figure 8-9, you should see the following components: two extension lines, two arrows, a dimension line on each side of the text, and the text itself.

Notice also that AutoCAD has automatically placed the extension line origins a short distance away from the triangle base. (You may need to zoom in to see this.) This distance is controlled by a dimension variable named **DIMEXO**, which can be changed in the **Modify Dimension Style** dialog box with the **Offset from origin** option on the **Lines** tab.

Next, you place a vertical dimension on the right side of the triangle. You can see that **DIMLINEAR** handles both horizontal and vertical dimensions.

✔ Repeat the **DIMLINEAR** command.
You are prompted for extension line origins as before:

```
Specify first extension line origin or <select object>:
```

This time, manually specify the origin of the extension lines.

✔ Specify the first origin at the right-angle corner in the lower right of the triangle—Point 1 in Figure 8-10.
AutoCAD prompts for a second point:

```
Specify second extension line origin:
```

Figure 8-10
Vertical linear dimension

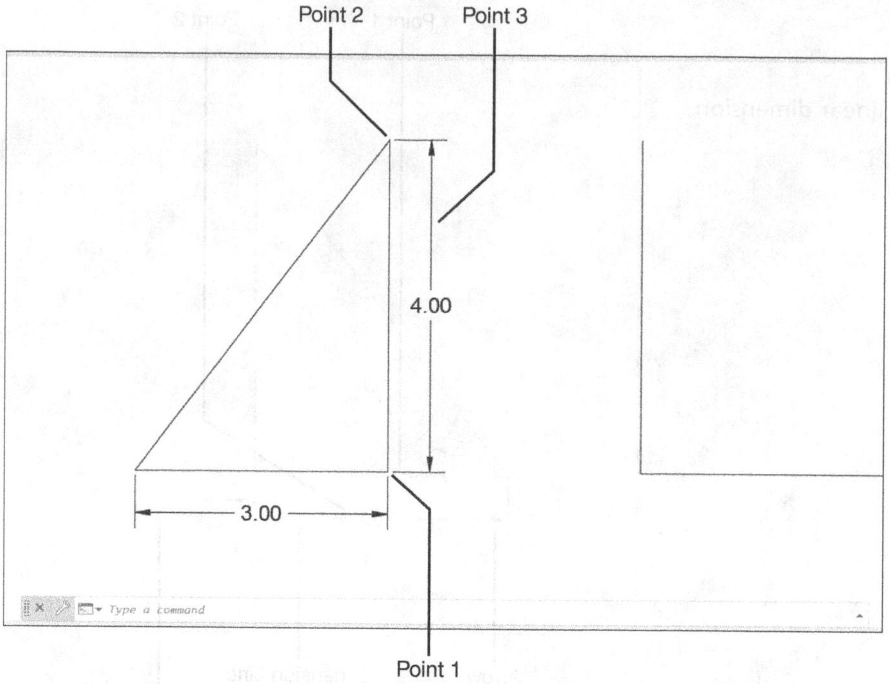

✔ Specify a second origin at the top intersection of the triangle—Point 2 in Figure 8-10.

From here on, the procedure is the same as before. You should have a dimension to drag into place, and the following prompt:

```
Specify dimension line location or
[Mtext/Text/Angle/Horizontal/Vertical/Rotated]:
```

✔ Specify a location about 0.50 units to the right of the triangle—Point 3 in Figure 8-10.

Your drawing should now include the vertical dimension, as shown in Figure 8-10.

Now, let's place a dimension on the diagonal side of the triangle. For this, you need the **DIMALIGNED** command. The **Aligned** dimension tool is on the drop-down menu opened by clicking the down arrow next to the **Linear** dimension tool.

✔ On the **Annotate** tab, open the **Dimension** tool drop-down menu on the **Dimensions** panel and click the **Aligned** tool, as shown in Figure 8-11.

✔ Press **<Enter>**, indicating that you will select an object.

AutoCAD provides you with the pickbox and prompts you to select an object to dimension.

✔ Select the hypotenuse of the triangle.

✔ Specify a location approximately 0.50 above and to the left of the line.

Your drawing should resemble Figure 8-12. Notice that AutoCAD retains horizontal text in aligned and vertical dimensions as the default.

Chapter 8

Figure 8-11
Aligned dimension tool

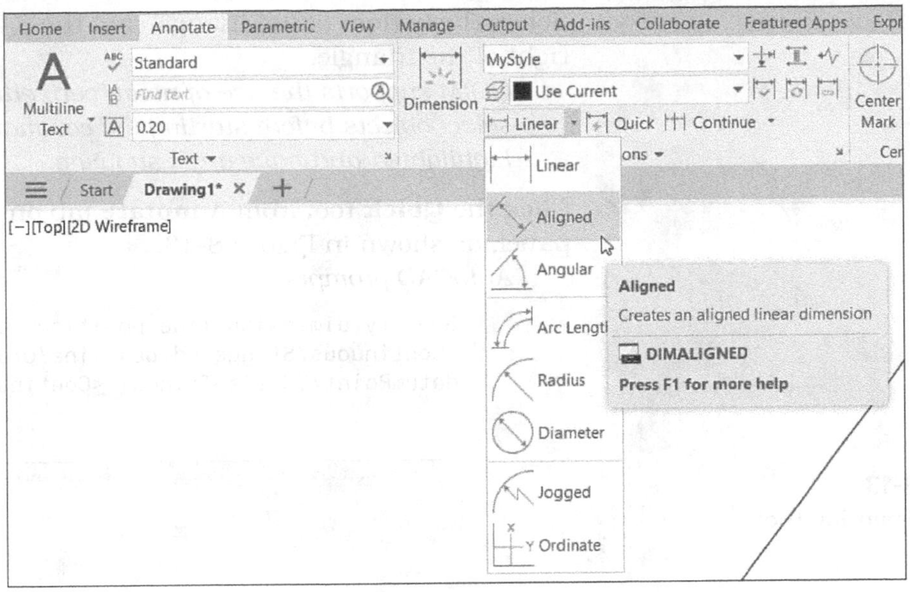

Figure 8-12
Aligned dimension

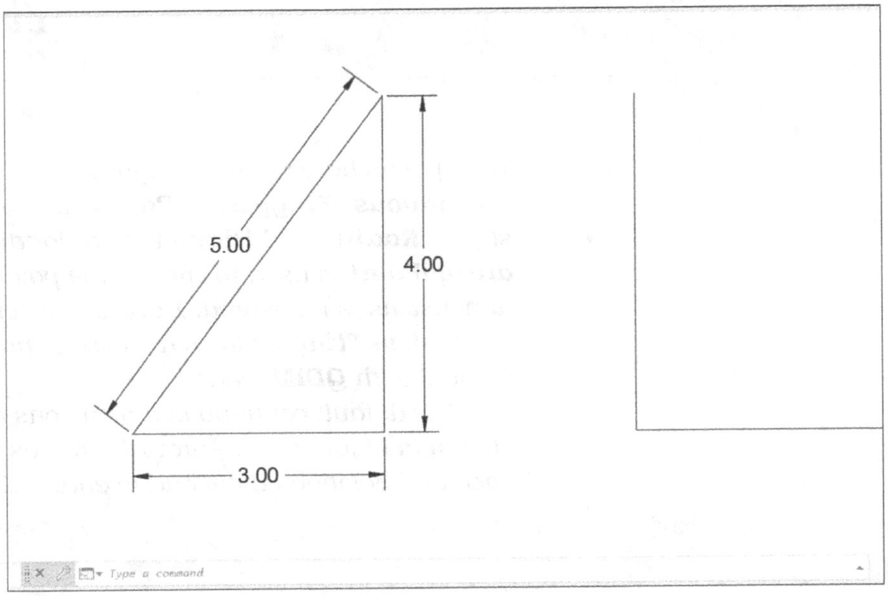

Drawing Multiple Linear Dimensions Using QDIM

QDIM	
Command	QDIM
Alias	(none)
Panel	Dimensions
Tool	

QDIM automates the creation of multiple dimensions of certain types. With this command, you can create a whole series of related dimensions with a few clicks. As an introduction to **QDIM**, you dimension the bottom of the triangle, the space between the triangle and the horizontal line, and the length of the line itself. Then you specify several points along the line to dimension. Finally, you change the dimensions on the line from a continuous series to a baseline series. In later exercises, you use **QDIM** to create other types of dimensions.

✔ Erase the 3.00 dimension from the bottom of the triangle.

✔ Select the bottom of the triangle and the 6.00 horizontal line to the right of the triangle.

QDIM supports the use of noun/verb editing, which allows you to select objects before starting the command. Your selected lines are highlighted and have grips showing.

✔ Click the **Quick** tool from **Annotate** tab on the ribbon's **Dimensions** panel, as shown in Figure 8-13.

AutoCAD prompts:

```
Specify dimension line position, or
[Continuous/Staggered/Baseline/Ordinate/Radius/Diameter/
datumPoint/Edit/seTtings] <Continuous>:
```

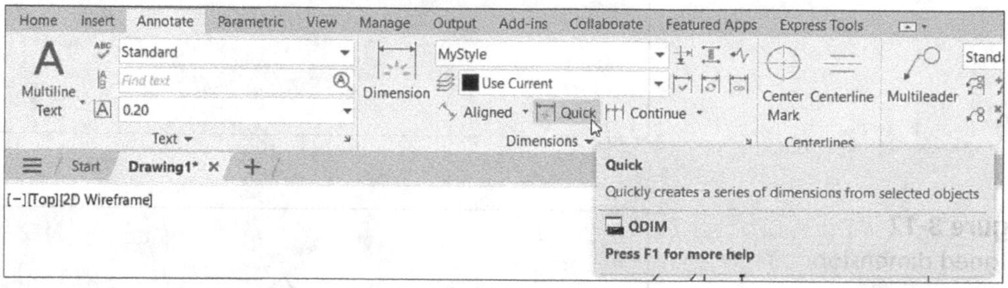

Figure 8-13
Quick Dimension tool

*The options here are various forms of multiple dimensions. **Continuous**, **Staggered**, **Baseline**, and **Ordinate** are all linear styles. **Radius** and **Diameter** are for dimensioning circles and arcs. **datumPoint** is used to change the point from which a set of linear dimensions is measured. **Edit** has several functions you explore in a moment. **seTtings** allows a choice of how associated dimensions created with **QDIM** work.*

The default continuous dimensions are positioned end to end, as shown in Figure 8-14. AutoCAD creates three linear dimensions at once and positions them end to end.

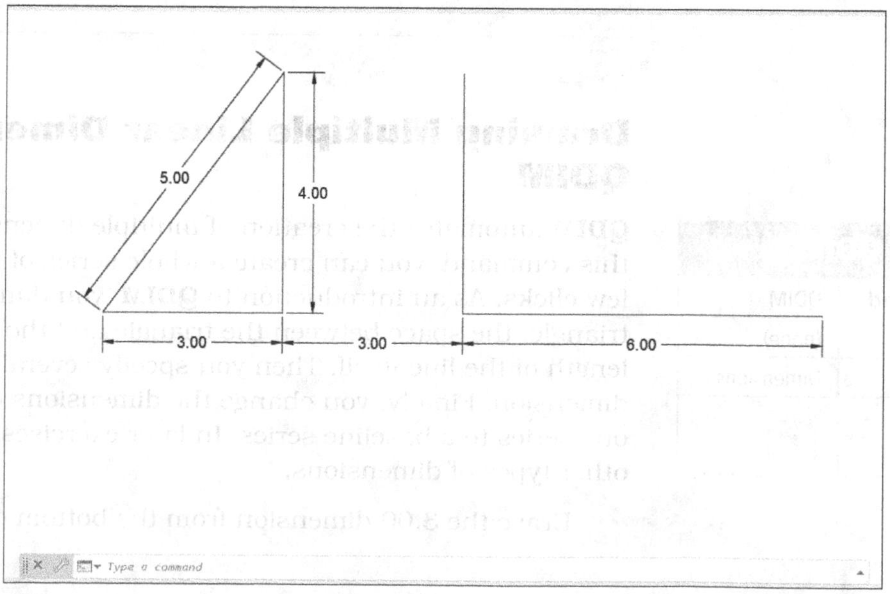

Figure 8-14
Continuous dimensions

> **NOTE**
>
> The objects selected for the **QDIM** command can be dimensions or objects to be dimensioned. If you select objects, **QDIM** creates new dimensions for these objects; if you select dimensions, **QDIM** edits or re-creates these dimensions depending on the options you select.

✔ Specify a location about 0.5 units below the triangle, as shown in Figure 8-14.

Next, you edit the horizontal dimension on the right, so that the line length is measured to several different lengths.

✔ Repeat **QDIM**.

✔ Select the dimension at the right, below the 6.00 line.

Notice that this dimension can be selected independently. The three continuous dimensions were created as separate objects, even though they were created simultaneously.

✔ Right-click to end object selection.

AutoCAD gives you a single dimension to drag into place. If you specify a point now, the selected 6.00 dimension is re-created at the point chosen. You do something more interesting than just re-create the dimension, though.

✔ Select **Edit** from the command line.

***QDIM** adds Xs at the two endpoints of the dimensioned line and prompts:*

```
Indicate dimension point to remove, or [Add/eXit] <eXit>:
```

The Xs indicate dimension points. You can add other points to dimension the line.

✔ Select **Add** from the command line.

The prompt changes slightly, as follows:

```
Indicate dimension point to add, or [Remove/eXit] <eXit>:
```

✔ Specify Point 1, as shown in Figure 8-15.

*This point is 2 units from the left endpoint of the line. **QDIM** continues to prompt for points.*

✔ Specify Point 2, as shown in Figure 8-15.

This point is 2 units from the right endpoint of the line.

✔ Press **<Enter>** or the spacebar to end point selection.

***QDIM** now divides the single 6.00 dimension into a series of three continuous 2.00 dimensions. You are not done yet; instead of continuous dimensions, you will draw these three dimensions as the baseline type.*

✔ Select **Baseline** from the command line.

***QDIM** immediately switches the three dragged dimensions to a baseline form.*

Figure 8-15
Baseline dimensions

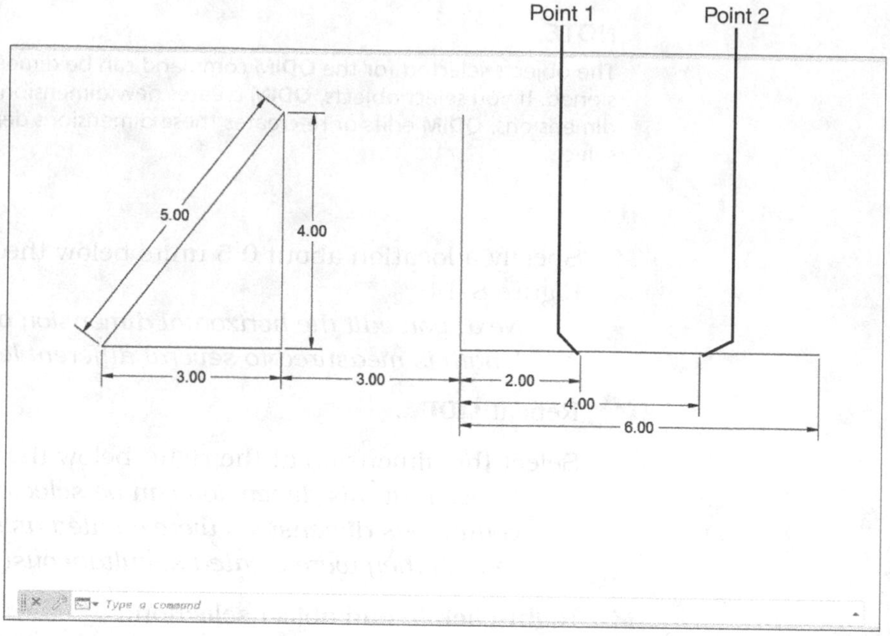

> **NOTE**
>
> AutoCAD retains the last option used for drawing dimensions with **QDIM**, so if you were to enter the command now, it would default to **Baseline** rather than **Continuous** dimensions.

✔ Specify a point so that the top, shortest dimension of the three is located about 0.5 units below the line.

Your drawing should now have three baseline dimensions, as shown in Figure 8-15, instead of the original 6.00 linear dimension shown in Figure 8-14. You learn more about this powerful command later. In the next exercise, you use it to create ordinate dimensions.

DIMBASELINE and DIMCONTINUE

Baseline and continuous dimensions can also be created one at a time using individual commands. The following general procedure is used with these commands:

1. Create an initial linear dimension.
2. Click the **Baseline** or **Continue** tool from the **Dimensions** panel on the ribbon's **Annotate** tab.
3. Specify a second extension line origin.
4. Specify another extension line origin.
5. Press **<Enter>** to exit the command.

NOTE

Baseline and continued dimensions may be drawn either in the current dimension style or in the style of the selected dimension (assuming it is different from the current style). This depends on the setting of the **DIMCONTINUEMODE** system variable. When set to **0**, the default, the current style is used; when set to **1**, the style of the selected dimension is used.

Chapter 8

Drawing Ordinate Dimensions

ordinate dimension: A dimension given relative to a fixed point of origin rather than through direct measurement of the objects being dimensioned.

Ordinate dimensions are another way to specify linear dimensions. They are used to show multiple horizontal and vertical distances from a single point, often the corner of an object in a design. Because these fall readily into a coordinate system, it is efficient to show these dimensions as the *x* and *y* displacements from a single point of origin.

There are two ways to create ordinate dimensions. AutoCAD ordinarily specifies points based on the point (0,0) in your drawing. Using **QDIM**, you can specify a new datum point that serves as the origin for a set of ordinate dimensions. Using **DIMORDINATE**, it is necessary to temporarily move the origin of the coordinate system to the point from which you want dimensions to be specified. In this exercise, you learn to use both methods.

QDIM and the Datum Point Option

You use ordinate dimensions to specify a series of horizontal and vertical distances from the intersection of the two lines to the right of the triangle. First, you use **QDIM** to add ordinate dimensions along the 4.00 vertical line. Then, you use **DIMORDINATE** to add ordinate dimensions to the 6.00 horizontal line.

✔ Click the **Quick** tool from the **Dimensions** panel on the ribbon's **Annotate** tab.

✔ Select the vertical line.

✔ Right-click to end object selection.

✔ Select **Ordinate** from the command line.

✔ Specify a location about 0.5 units to the left of the line, as shown in Figure 8-16.

*The two dimensions you see are at the ends of the line and show the y value of each endpoint. Whether in the ordinate option of **QDIM** or in **DIMORDINATE**, AutoCAD automatically chooses the x or y value, depending on the object you choose. Because the values you see are measured from the origin at the lower-left corner of the grid, they are not particularly useful. A more common use is to measure points from the intersection of the two lines. To complete this set of dimensions, you go back into **QDIM**, select a new datum point, and add and remove dimension points, as shown in Figure 8-17.*

Figure 8-16
Quick Dimension vertical line

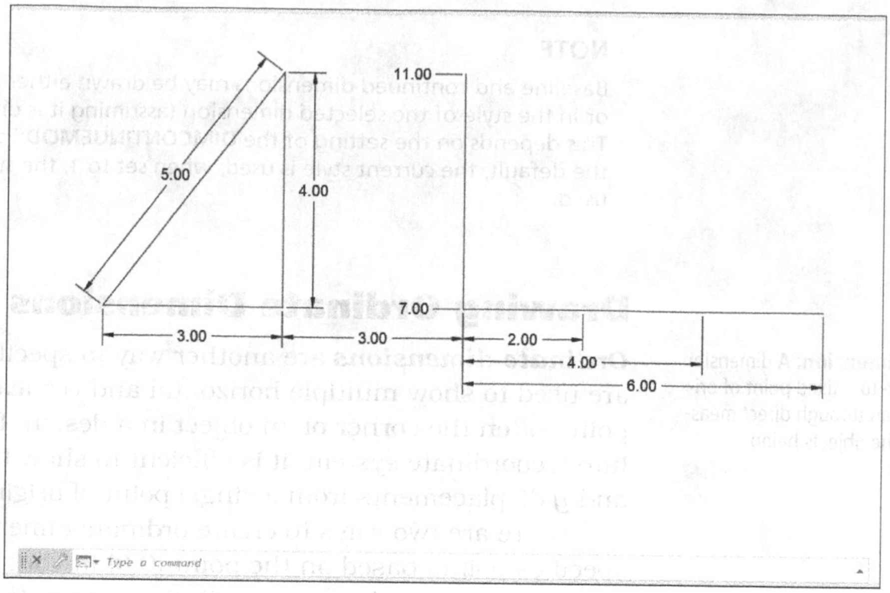

Figure 8-17
Datum point

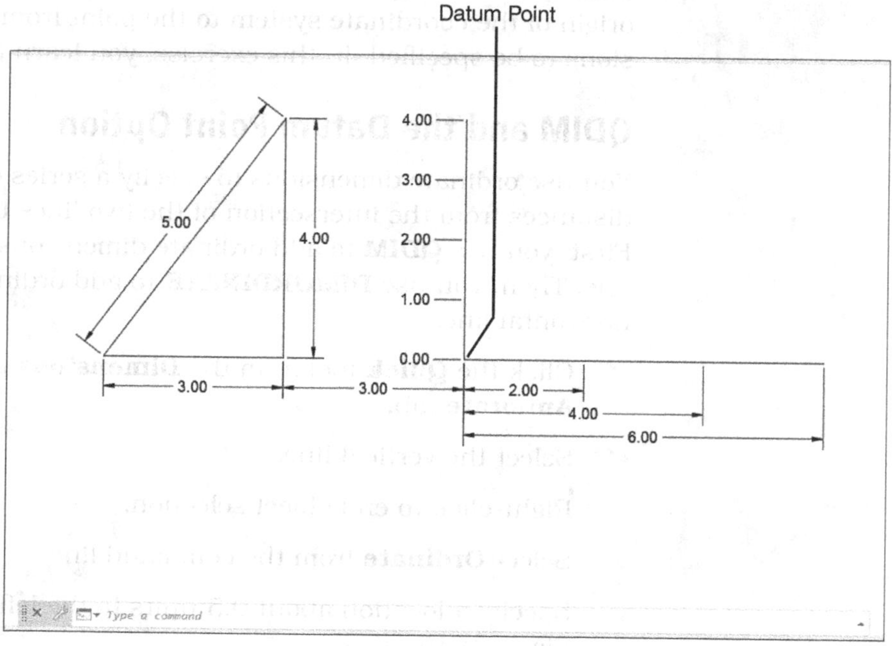

- ✔ Repeat **QDIM**.
- ✔ Select the bottom ordinate dimension (**7.00** in Figure 8-17).
- ✔ Select the top ordinate dimension (**11.00** in Figure 8-17).
  Notice that these need to be selected separately.
- ✔ Right-click to end geometry selection.
- ✔ Select **Ordinate** from the command line.
- ✔ Select **datumPoint** from the command line.
  ***QDIM** prompts:*

```
Select new datum point:
```

✔ Select the intersection of the two lines, as shown in Figure 8-17.
*The new datum point is now established. You add three new dimension points and remove one before leaving **QDIM**.*

✔ Select **Edit** from the command line.

✔ Select **Add** from the command line.

✔ Specify points 1.00, 2.00, and 3.00 up from the bottom of the vertical line.
As you specify the points to add, they are marked by Xs.

✔ Select **Remove** from the command line.

✔ Remove the point at the intersection of the two lines.

✔ Press **<Enter>** or the spacebar to end the specifying of points.

✔ Specify a point about 0.5 units to the left of the vertical line, as before.
*Your drawing should resemble Figure 8-17. Notice that the top dimension is automatically updated to reflect the new datum point. Next, you dimension the horizontal line using the **DIMORDINATE** command.*

DIMORDINATE and the UCS Command

You use **DIMORDINATE** to create a series of ordinate dimensions above the horizontal 6.00 line. This method requires you to create a new origin for the coordinate system using the **UCS** command. User coordinate systems are most important in 3D drawings and are not explored in depth here. Although **DIMORDINATE** creates only one dimension at a time, it does have some advantages over the **QDIM** system. To begin with, you do not have to go back and edit the dimension to add and remove points. Additionally, you can create a variety of leader shapes.

✔ If your UCS icon is not visible, turn it on by typing **ucsicon <Enter>**, and selecting **On**.

✔ Type **ucs <Enter>**.
*This executes the **UCS** command and presents a distinctive dashed yellow rubber band from the lower-left corner of the drawing area or the origin of the grid to the position of the crosshairs. Specifying a new coordinate system by moving the point of origin is the default and is the simplest of many options in the **UCS** command. AutoCAD prompts:*

```
Specify origin of UCS or
[Face/Named/Object/Previous/View/World/X/Y/Z/ZAxis]
<World>:
```

✔ Specify the intersection of the two lines.
AutoCAD prompts:

```
Specify point on X-axis or <accept>:
```

✔ Move the cursor in a slow circle around the intersection.
*You see the previewed axis in the new coordinate system you are specifying. If you specify a third point, it will become a point on the new axis. However, if you complete the command by pressing **<Enter>**, the orientation of the current coordinate system is maintained.*

✔ Press **<Enter>** to accept the new origin.

The lower-left corner (origin) of your grid moves to the new origin point. If you move your cursor to the intersection and watch the coordinate display, you can see that this point is now read as (0.00,0.00,0.00). If your user coordinate system icon is on and set to move to the origin, it moves to the new point. Also, if your grid is on, the origin moves to the new origin point.

✔ Select **Annotate** > **Dimension**, as shown in Figure 8-18.

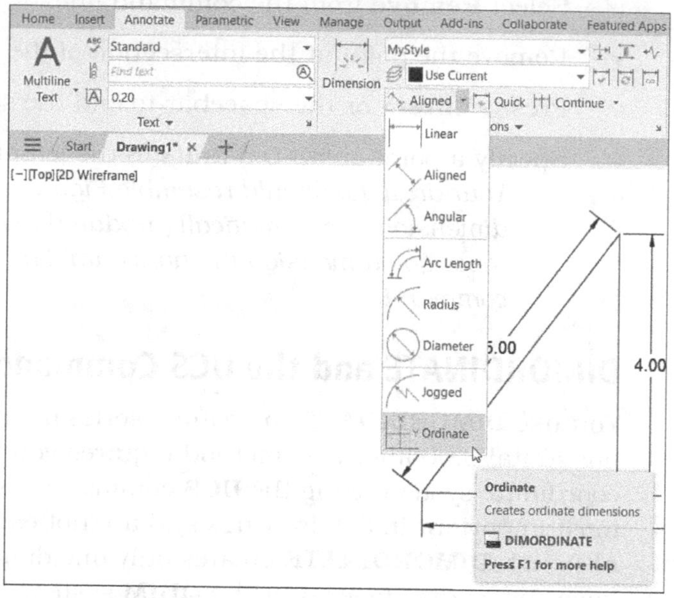

Figure 8-18
Ordinate dimension tool

✔ Click the **Ordinate** dimension tool from the drop-down menu, as shown.

AutoCAD prompts:

```
Specify feature location:
```

In actuality, all you do is specify a point and then an endpoint for a leader. Depending on where the endpoint is located relative to the first point, the dimension text reflects either an x or a y displacement from the origin of the current coordinate system.

✔ Specify a point along the 6.00 line, 1.00 to the right of the intersection, as shown in Figure 8-19.

In the new coordinate system, this point will be (1,0).

AutoCAD prompts:

```
Non-associative dimension created
Specify leader end point or [Xdatum/Ydatum/Mtext/Text/
Angle]:
```

Figure 8-19
Ordinate Dimension horizontal line

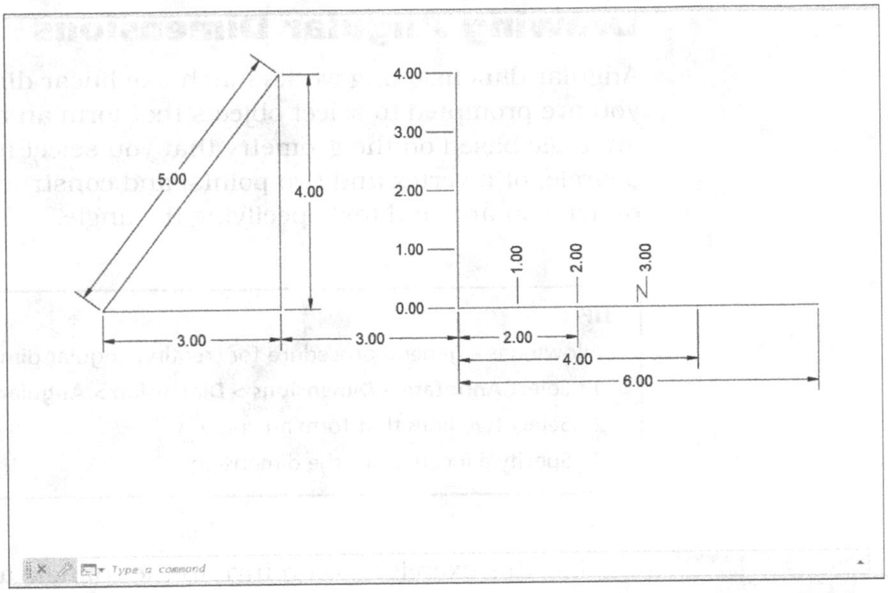

✔ *The first line tells you that ordinate dimensions created in this fashion are nonassociative. Associativity is discussed in the "Using Associative Dimensions" section later in this chapter. The second line prompts you to specify a leader endpoint. You can manually indicate whether you want the dimension text to show the x or y coordinate by typing* ***x*** *or* ***y****. However, if you choose the endpoint correctly, AutoCAD picks the right coordinate automatically. You could also provide your own text, but that would defeat the purpose of setting up a coordinate system that automatically gives you the distances from the intersection of the two lines.*

✔ Specify an endpoint 0.50 units directly above the line, as shown in Figure 8-19.

Your drawing should now include the 1.00 ordinate dimension shown in Figure 8-19.

✔ Repeat **DIMORDINATE** and add the second ordinate dimension at a point 2.00 units from the origin.

This will be at the point (2,0).

✔ Repeat **DIMORDINATE** once more.

✔ Specify a point on the line 3.00 units from the origin. The point is (3,0).

✔ Move your cursor left and right to see some of the leader shapes that **DIMORDINATE** creates depending on the endpoint of the leader.

✔ Specify an endpoint slightly to the right of the dimensioned point to create a broken leader similar to the one in Figure 8-19.

When you are done, you should return to the world coordinate system. This is the default coordinate system and the one you have been using all along.

✔ Type **ucs <Enter>**.

✔ Select **World** from the command line.

This returns the origin to its original position at the lower left of your drawing window.

Drawing Angular Dimensions

Angular dimensioning works much like linear dimensioning, except that you are prompted to select objects that form an angle. AutoCAD computes an angle based on the geometry that you select (two lines, an arc, a part of a circle, or a vertex and two points) and constructs extension lines, a dimension arc, and text specifying the angle.

> **TIP**
>
> Following is a general procedure for creating angular dimensions:
>
> 1. Select **Annotate > Dimensions > Dimension > Angular**.
> 2. Select two lines that form an angle.
> 3. Specify a location for the dimension.

DIMANGULAR	
Command	DIMANG
Alias	Dan
Panel	Dimensions
Tool	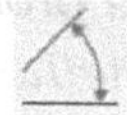

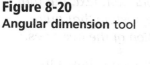

For this exercise, you return to the triangle and add angular dimensions to two of the angles.

✔ From the **Annotate** ribbon tab, open the **Dimension** tools drop-down menu on the **Dimensions** panel and click the **Angular** tool, as shown in Figure 8-20.

The first prompt is

```
Select arc, circle, line, or <specify vertex>:
```

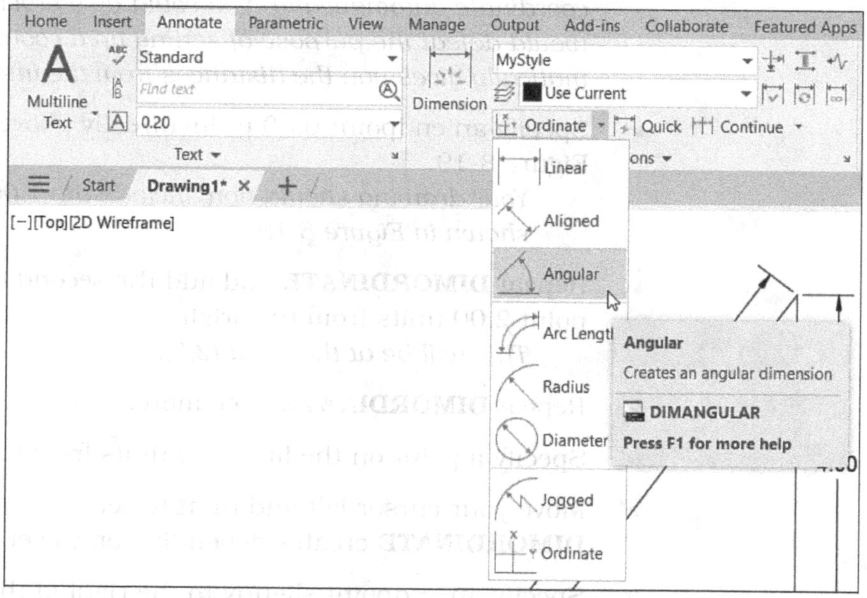

Figure 8-20
Angular dimension tool

*The prompt shows that you can use **DIMANGULAR** to dimension angles formed by arcs and portions of circles as well as angles formed by lines. If you press **<Enter>**, you can specify an angle manually by picking its vertex and a point on each side of the angle. You begin by picking lines.*

✔ Select the base of the triangle.

You are prompted for another line:

```
Select second line:
```

✔ Select the hypotenuse.

As with linear dimensioning, AutoCAD now shows you the dimension line and lets you drag it into place. The prompt asks for a dimension arc location and also allows you the option of changing the text or the text angle:

```
Specify dimension arc line location or [Mtext/Text/Angle/
Quadrant]:
```

✔ Move the cursor around to see how the dimension can be placed, and then specify a point between the two selected lines, as shown in Figure 8-21.

The lower-left angle of your triangle should now be dimensioned, as in Figure 8-21. Notice that the degree symbol is added by default in angular dimension text.

✔ *Next, dimension the upper angle by specifying its vertex.*

✔ Repeat the **DIMANGULAR** command.

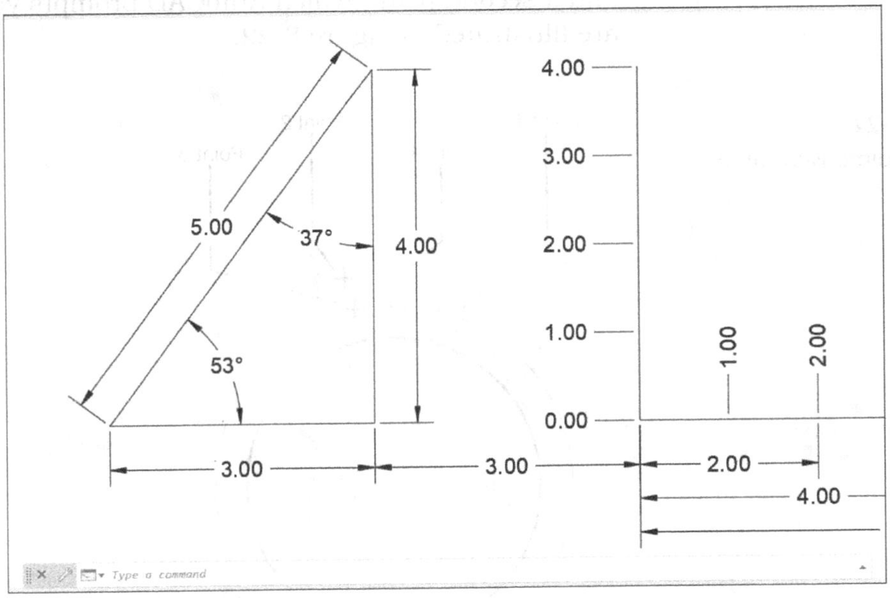

Figure 8-21
Dimension angles

✔ Press **<Enter>**.

AutoCAD prompts for an angle vertex.

✔ If necessary, click the **Snap Mode** button to enable **Snap** mode.

✔ Specify the intersection point at the top of the triangle as the vertex of the angle.

AutoCAD prompts:

```
Specify first angle endpoint:
```

✔ Specify a point along the hypotenuse.

To be precise, this should be a snap point. The most dependable one is the lower-left corner of the triangle. AutoCAD prompts:

```
Specify second angle endpoint:
```

✔ Specify any point along the vertical side of the triangle.

All available points on the vertical line should be snap points.

✔ Move the cursor slowly up and down within the triangle.

Notice how AutoCAD places the arrows outside the angle when you approach the vertex, and things get crowded. Also notice that if you move outside the angle, AutoCAD switches to the outer angle.

✔ Specify a location for the dimension arc, as shown in Figure 8-21.

Angular Dimensions on Arcs and Circles

You can also place angular dimensions on arcs and circles. In both cases, AutoCAD creates extension lines and a dimension arc. When you dimension an arc with an angular dimension, the center of the arc becomes the vertex of the dimension angle, and the endpoints of the arc become the start points of the extension lines. In a circle, the same format is used, but the dimension line origins are determined by the point used to select the circle and a second point, which AutoCAD prompts you to select. These options are illustrated in Figure 8-22.

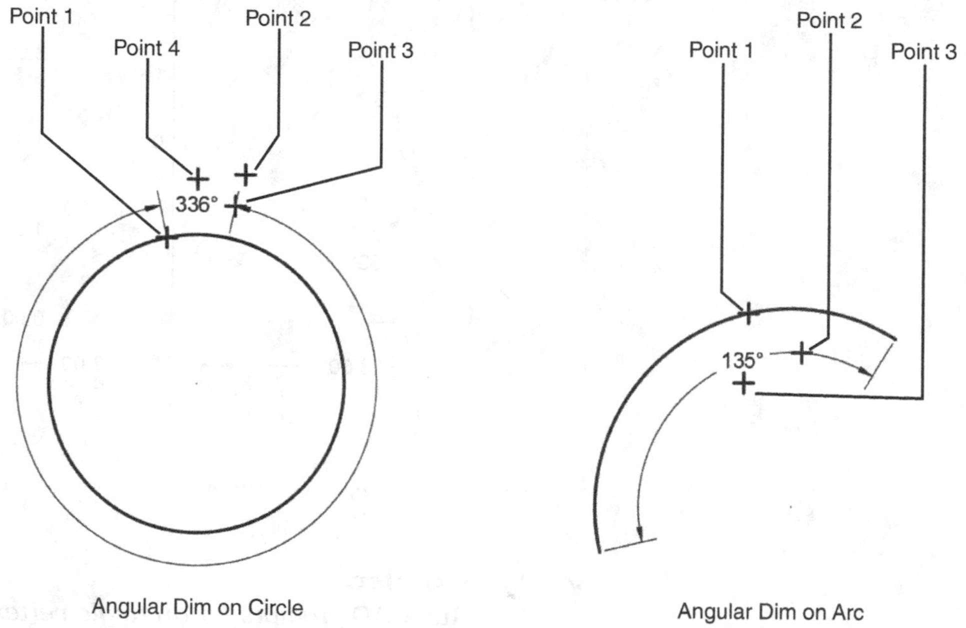

Figure 8-22
Angular dimension on arcs and circles

Dimensioning Arcs and Circles

The basic process for dimensioning circles and arcs is as simple as those that have already been covered. It can get tricky, however, when AutoCAD does not place the dimension where you want it. Text placement can be controlled by adjusting dimension variables. In this exercise, you create a center mark and some diameter and radius dimensions.

> **TIP**
> Following is a general procedure for dimensioning arcs and circles:
> 1. Select **Annotate** > **Dimensions** > **Dimension** > **Radius** or **Diameter**.
> 2. Select an arc or a circle.
> 3. Specify a location for the leader line endpoint.

✔ To prepare for this exercise, draw two circles, with radii of 2.00 and 1.50, as shown in Figure 8-23. If your drawing has multiple layers, the circles should not be drawn on the dimension layer.

✔ If necessary, return to the dimension layer.

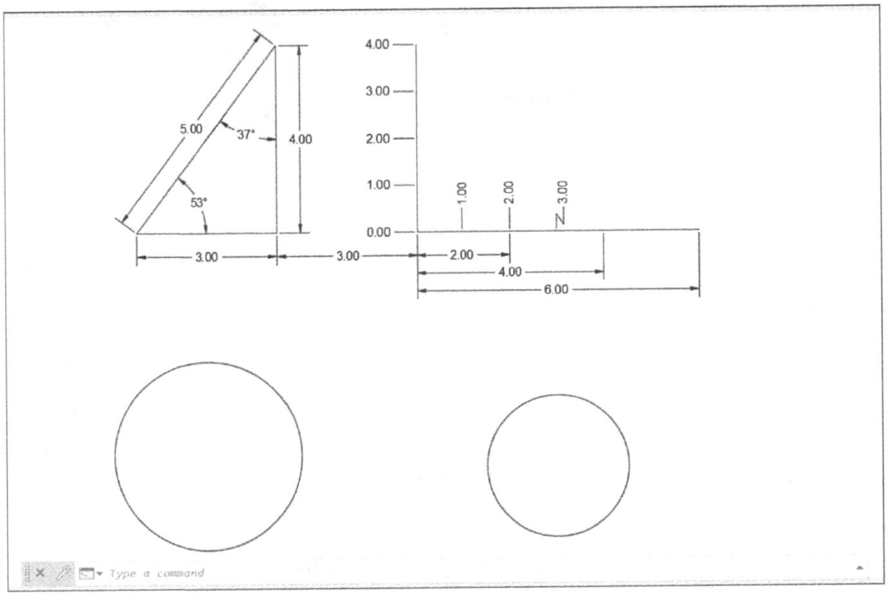

Figure 8-23
Drawing two circles

Diameter Dimensions

You begin by adding a diameter dimension to the 2.00 radius circle on the left, as shown in Figure 8-24.

✔ Select **Annotate** > **Dimensions** > **Dimension** > **Diameter**, as shown in Figure 8-25.

AutoCAD prompts:

```
Select arc or circle:
```

Figure 8-24
Dimensioning diameter and radius

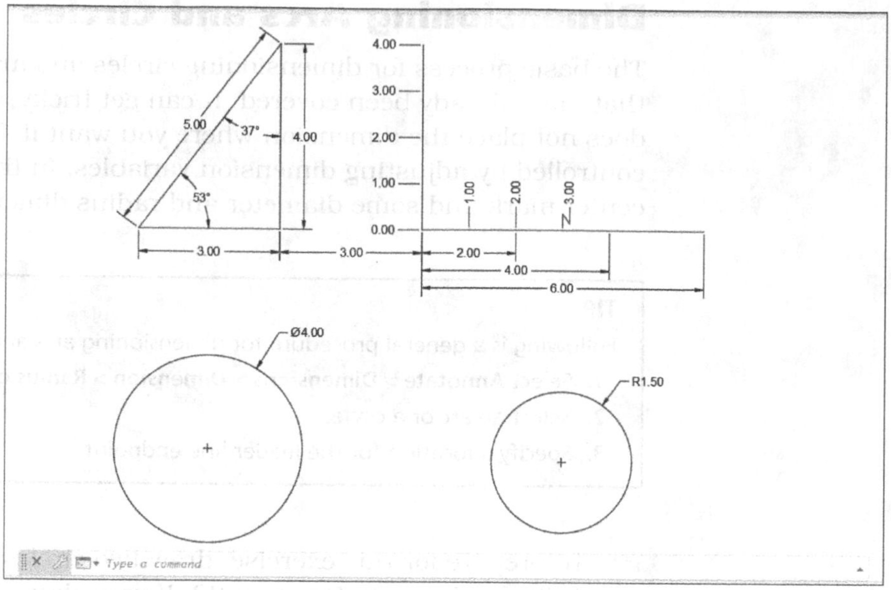

Figure 8-25
Diameter tool

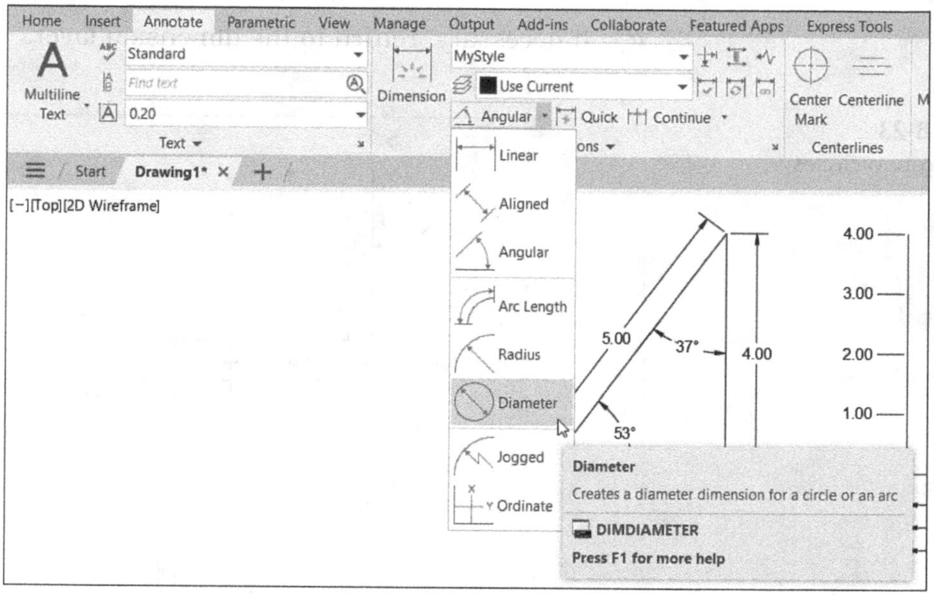

✔ Select the larger circle.

AutoCAD shows a diameter dimension and asks for a dimension line location with the following prompt:

```
Specify dimension line location or [Mtext/Text/Angle]:
```

The ***Text*** *and* ***Angle*** *options enable you to change the dimension text or put it at an angle. If you move your cursor around, you see that you can position the dimension line anywhere around or inside the circle.*

✔ Specify a location for the dimension line near the top of the 2.00 circle so that your drawing resembles Figure 8-24.

Notice that the diameter symbol prefix and the center mark are added automatically by default.

Radius Dimensions

The procedure for placing radius dimensions is exactly the same as for diameter dimensions, and the results look the same. The only differences are the radius value of the text and the use of R for radius in place of the diameter symbol.

Draw a radius dimension on the smaller circle.

✔ Click the **Radius** tool from the **Dimension** tools drop-down menu on the **Annotate** tab of the ribbon.

✔ Select the 1.50 (smaller) circle.

✔ Move the cursor around the circle, inside and outside.

✔ Specify a location for the dimension line to complete the dimension, as shown in Figure 8-24.

The R for radius and the center mark are added automatically.

Annotating with Multileaders

MLEADER	
Command	MLEADER
Alias	Mld
Panel	Leaders
Tool	

multileader: An object with an arrowhead and one or more leaders connecting annotation text or symbols to annotated objects.

Radius and diameter dimensions, along with ordinate dimensions, make use of leaders to connect dimension text to the object being dimensioned. Leaders or ***multileaders*** can also be created independently to attach annotation to all kinds of objects. Unlike other dimension types, in which you select an object or show a length, a leader is simply a line or series of lines with an arrow at the end to visually connect an object to its annotation. Thus, when you create a leader, AutoCAD does not recognize and measure any selected object or distance. You need to know the dimension text or annotation you want to use before you begin.

> **TIP**
>
> Following is a general procedure for dimensioning with multileaders:
>
> 1. On the ribbon's Annotate tab, click the **Multileader** tool from the **Leaders** panel.
> 2. Specify a point for the leader arrowhead.
> 3. Specify a location for the leader landing.
> 4. Type dimension text.

You begin by adding a multileader with attached text to annotate the circle at the right. Multileaders appear the same as leaders in other dimension objects, but there are multileader commands, styles and procedures that do not apply to dimension leaders.

✔ Select **Annotate > Leaders > Multileader**, as shown in Figure 8-26.

AutoCAD prompts for an arrowhead location:

```
Specify leader arrowhead location or [pre enter Text/leader
Landing first/Content first/Options] <Options>:
```

Figure 8-26
Multileader tool

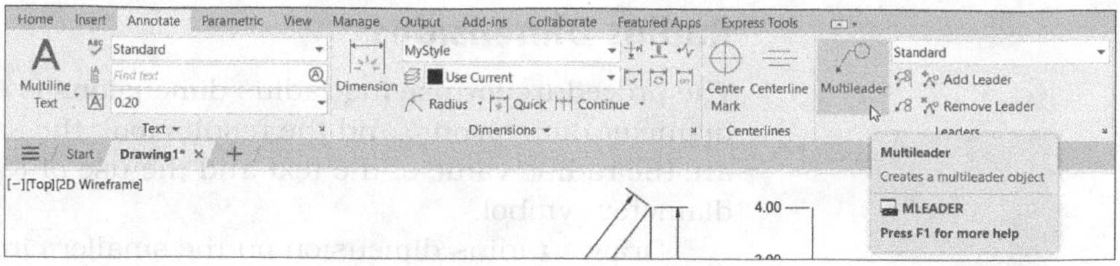

Leaders consist of an arrowhead, a leader line, and a short landing line connecting the leader to the text or annotation symbol. The options allow you to change the order in which these elements are specified.

*To attach the arrow to the circle, use the **Nearest** object snap.*

✔ Hold down **<Shift>** and right-click your mouse to open the **Object Snap** shortcut menu.

✔ Select **Nearest** from the shortcut menu.

*The **Nearest** object snap allows you to snap to the nearest point on an object when you click. If you have not used this object snap before, take a moment to get familiar with it. As you move around the drawing, you see the **Nearest** object snap marker whenever the crosshairs approaches an object. If you allow the crosshairs to rest on an object, the **Nearest** tooltip label appears in place of the dynamic input prompt.*

✔ Specify a point for the leader arrowhead on the upper-right side of the larger, 2.00-radius circle.

✔ Specify a location for the leader landing about 45° and 1.00 units up and to the right of the first point.

> **TIP**
>
> Use polar tracking to precisely draw the angle of a leader line. This will give your leaders a consistent look. You can enable polar tracking using the **Polar Tracking** button on the status bar or by pressing **<F10>**.

*The **Text Editor** contextual tab appears on the ribbon. The two arrows just above where your text will be entered allow you to specify a width for the text you will enter.*

✔ Position your cursor within the small gray box with two arrows, as shown in Figure 8-27.

✔ Click and drag the arrows of the in-place text editor to adjust the width of the box to about 2.50 units to the right, and then release the mouse button.

✔ Type **This circle is 4.00 inches in diameter** and press **<Enter>**.

Chapter 8

Figure 8-27
Text Editor resizing arrows

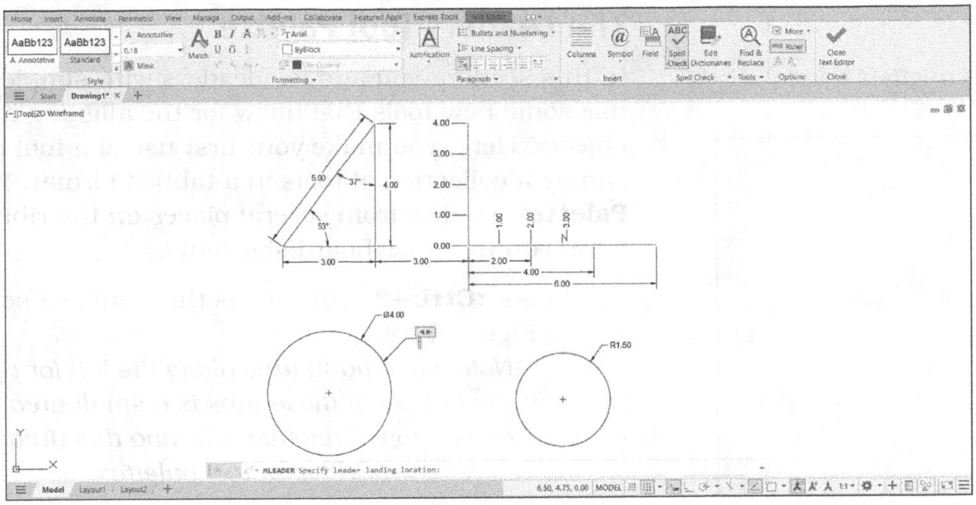

✔ Click outside the in-place text editor to complete the command.

Your drawing should now resemble Figure 8-28. This is a multileader object, and the text is mtext. The entire object, lines, arrow, and text can be selected as a single object.

Next, you add a multileader object with an annotation symbol to the smaller circle.

Figure 8-28
Leader and text added

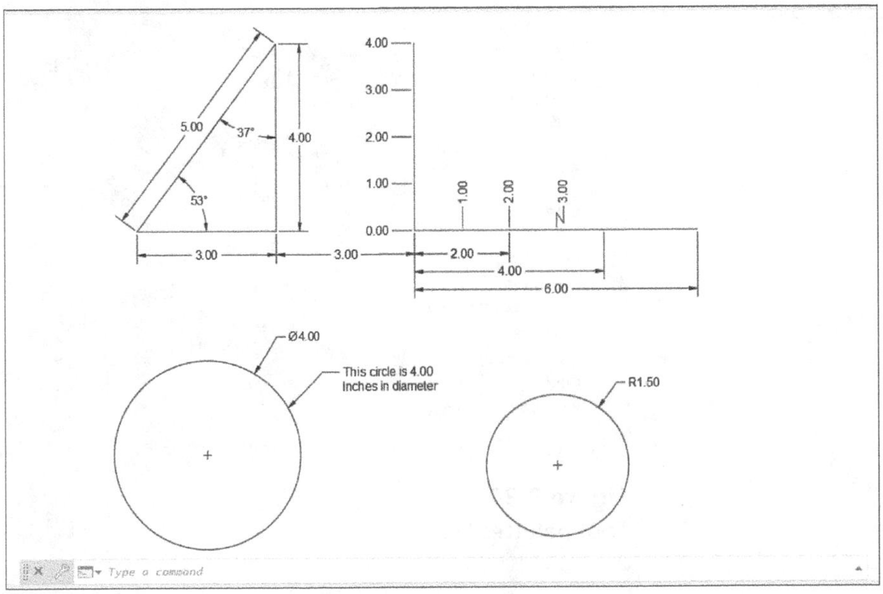

New to AutoCAD 2023

TIP

The **MLEADER** command supports the ability to convert an MText object to a multileader with the selected MText object as its content. To convert an existing MText object to a multileader, follow these steps:

1. Start the **MLEADER** command.
2. Select the **Content first** option and then select the **select Mtext** suboption.
3. When prompted, select the MText object to convert.
4. Specify the location of the arrowhead.

The Leaders Tool Palette

tool palette: A collection of tools in a tabbed format.

In this section, you add two leaders with simple tag annotations and then use some new tools that allow for the aligning and gathering of multileader objects. Here, you make your first use of a tool palette. A ***tool palette*** is simply a collection of tools in a tabbed format. You can open the **Tool Palettes** window from several places on the ribbon or the menu bar, but here, you use a keyboard shortcut.

✔ Press **<Ctrl>+3**. This opens the complete set of tool palettes, as shown in Figure 8-29.

Notice the many tabs along the left (or right) side of the palette. At the bottom of these tabs is a small area that looks like multiple tabs, one on top of another. Clicking this area opens a list that gives access to additional tool palettes.

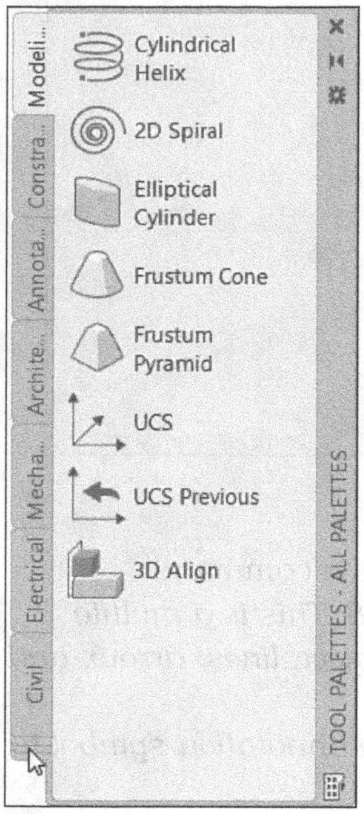

Figure 8-29
Tool palettes–all palettes

✔ Click in the area at the bottom of the tool palettes tabs, below the tabs, as shown in Figure 8-30.

This opens the list of available tool palettes shown at the left in the figure.

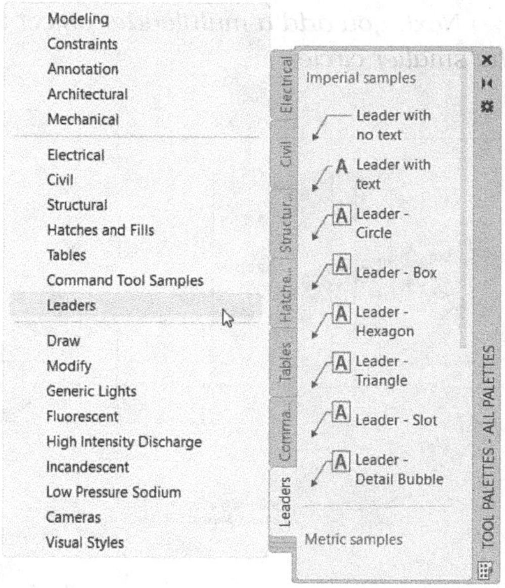

Figure 8-30
Tool palettes list

✔ Select **Leaders** from the list.

*This opens the **Leaders** tool palette, as shown in Figure 8-31.*

This palette contains two sets of leader styles: imperial styles at the top and metric styles at the bottom. There are eight of each, and the lists are identical except for variations in size. Here, you use the metric **Leader–Circle** style tool.

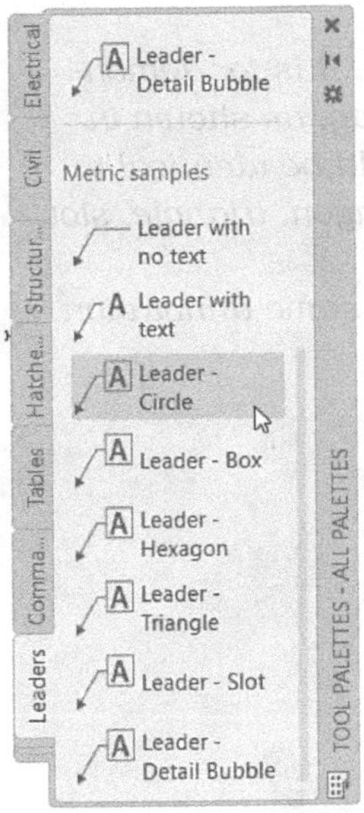

Figure 8-31
Leaders tool palette

✔ Click the **Leader – Circle** style tool from the Metric samples portion of the tool palette, as shown in Figure 8-31.

AutoCAD prompts for an arrowhead location or option, as before:

```
Specify leader arrowhead location or
[pre enter Text/leader Landing first/Content first/Options]
<Options>:
```

✔ *Using the **Leader – Circle** style tool, you can tag the 1.50-radius circle with a number. Nothing is being dimensioned by this leader. It is simply a tag such as might be applied to call out or number an object in a drawing.*

✔ Hold down **<Shift>** and right-click your mouse to open the **Object Snap** shortcut menu.

✔ Select **Nearest** from the shortcut menu.

✔ Move the crosshairs over the upper right of the 1.50-radius circle and click.

The leader is snapped to the circle, and a rubber band appears, extending to the crosshairs. AutoCAD prompts for a second point:

```
Specify leader landing location:
```

✔ Specify a location for the leader, at a 45° angle up and to the right of the first point, as shown in Figure 8-32.

*AutoCAD draws a leader, landing line, and circle, as shown, and opens the **Edit Attributes** dialog box with a prompt to enter a tag number, as shown in Figure 8-33. Attributes consist of information stored and attached to blocks in a drawing. They can be any form of data, such as a part number or name, that can be retrieved from the drawing database.*

Figure 8-32
Leader with text in circle

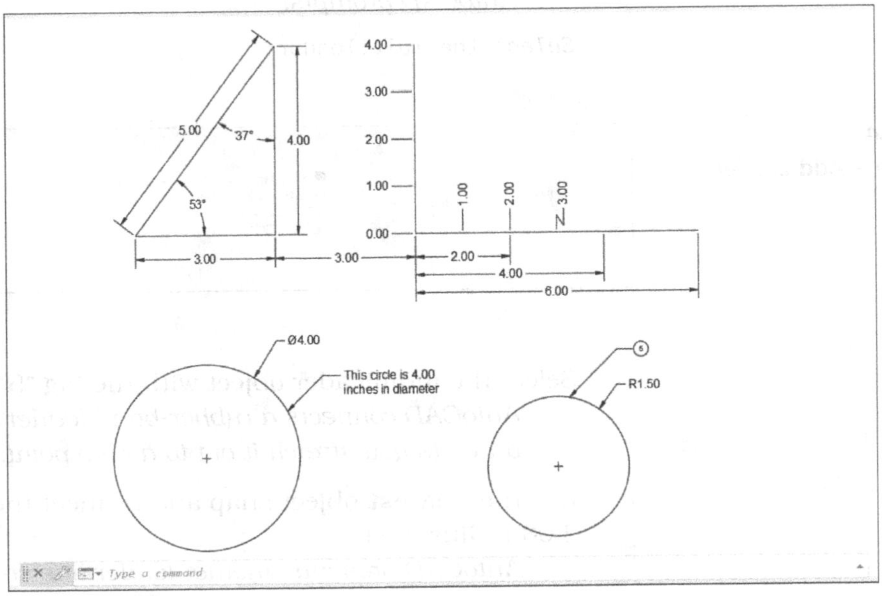

✔ Type **5** and click **OK**.

The number 5 has no particular significance here. It is for demonstration only. The number is added to the circle tag, as shown in Figure 8-32. Many of the other leader styles would be identical to this one except for the shape of the tag (box, hexagon, triangle, slot, or detail bubble).

Next, you add a second multileader from the same annotation tag, connecting to the other circle.

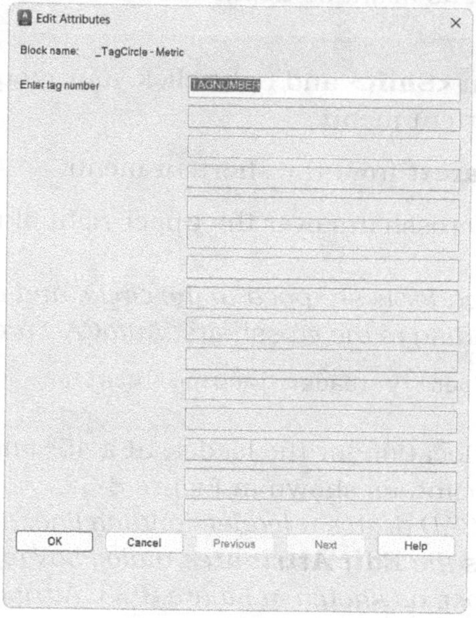

Figure 8-33
Edit Attributes dialog box

✔ From the **Leaders** panel on the **Annotate** tab, click the **Add Leader** tool, as shown in Figure 8-34.

AutoCAD prompts:

```
Select the multileader:
```

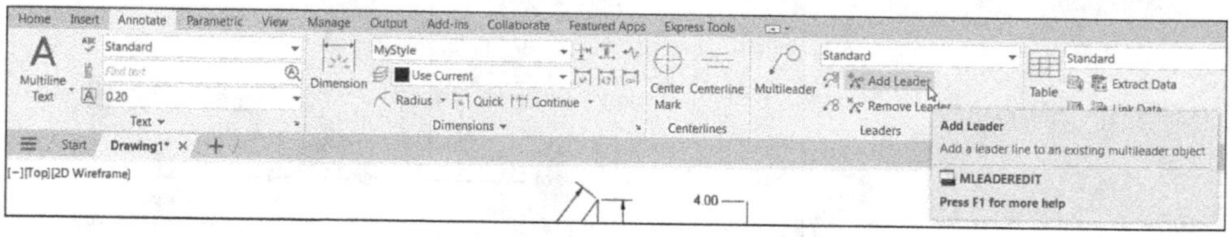

Figure 8-34
Multileader – Add Leader tool

✔ Select the multileader object with the tag "5".

AutoCAD connects a rubber-band leader to the original landing line and lets you stretch it out to a new point.

✔ Use the **Nearest** object snap and connect the added leader line to the 2.00 radius circle.

AutoCAD presents another leader line so that you can continue to add leader lines to this multileader group.

✔ Press **<Enter>** to end the command.

Your drawing should resemble Figure 8-35.

Finally, you use a special multileader alignment command to align the radius dimension on the smaller circle with the multileader annotation tag. This will require replacing the radius dimension with a multileader object.

✔ Erase the **R1.50** dimension from the smaller circle.

✔ Click the **Multileader** tool from the **Leaders** panel on the **Annotate** tab.

✔ **<Shift>** + right-click and select **Nearest** from the **Object Snap** shortcut menu.

✔ Specify a point on the circle near where the previous radius dimension was attached.

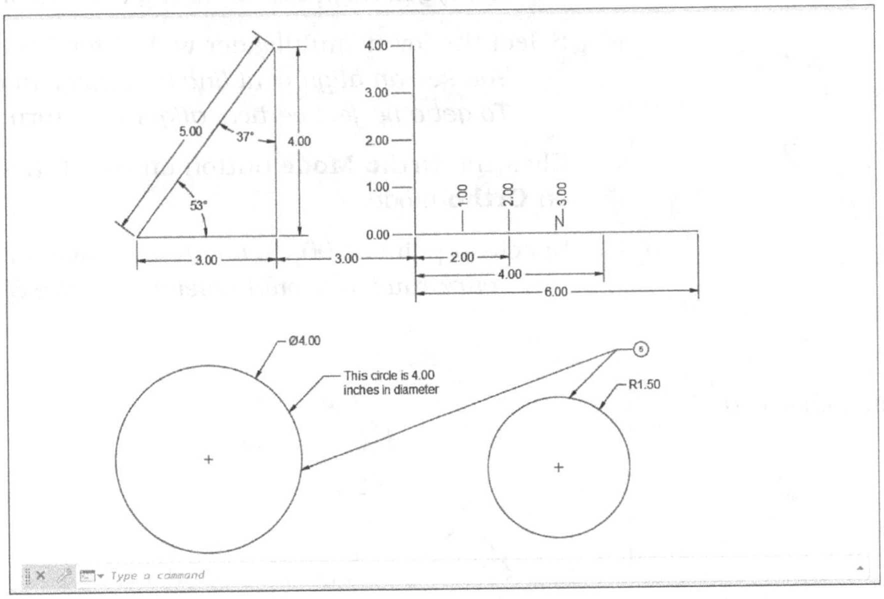

Figure 8-35
Leader stretched out

✔ Specify a location for the leader landing so that the leader text is positioned near where the previous dimension was located.

✔ Type **R1.50 <Enter>**.

✔ Click outside the in-place text editor to complete the text.

If you have done this correctly, your drawing will still resemble Figure 8-35, except the center mark will no longer be at the center of the circle.

✔ Click the **Align** tool from the **Leaders** panel on the **Annotate** tab, as shown in Figure 8-36.

AutoCAD prompts:

```
Select multileaders:
```

Figure 8-36
Multileader Align tool

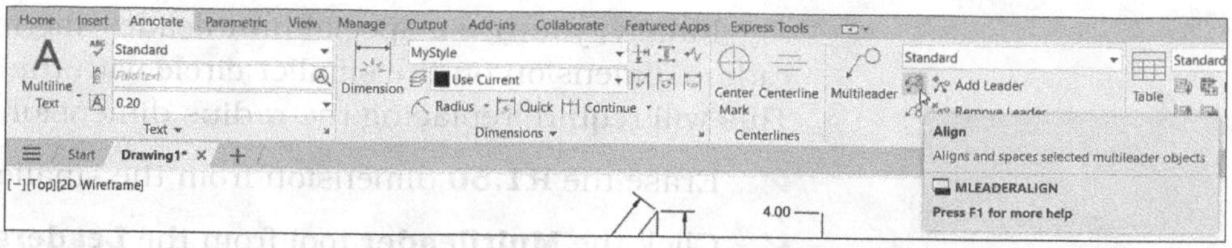

✔ Select the multileader with tag 5 and the R1.50 multileader.

✔ Right-click to end object selection.
AutoCAD prompts:

```
Select multileader to align to or [Options]:
```

Here, you align the upper tag with the lower text.

✔ Select the lower multileader with the R1.50 text.
*You see an alignment line that you can move to align at any angle. To get a perfect vertical alignment, turn on **Ortho** mode.*

✔ Click the **Ortho Mode** button on the status bar or press **<F8>** to turn on **Ortho** mode.

✔ Specify a point at 90° to create a vertical alignment.
Your drawing should resemble Figure 8-37.

Figure 8-37
Multileaders are aligned

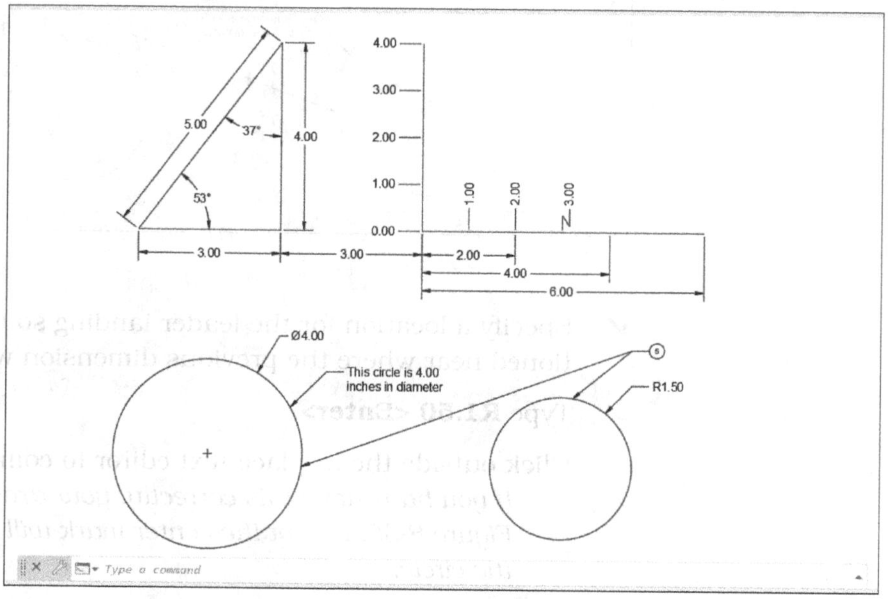

Changing Dimension Text

Dimensions can be edited in many of the same ways that other objects are edited. They can be moved, copied, stretched, rotated, trimmed, extended, and so on. There are numerous ways to change dimension text and placement. Grips can be used effectively to accomplish most changes in placement. Here, you learn two different ways to change dimension text.

The DIMEDIT Command

✔ Type **dimedit <Enter>**.

AutoCAD prompts with options:

```
Enter type of dimension editing [Home/New/Rotate/Oblique]
<Home>:
```

If dynamic input is on, you also see these options on a list. ***Home, Rotate****, and* ***Oblique*** *are placement and orientation options;* ***New*** *refers to new text content.*

✔ Select **New** from the dynamic input list.

AutoCAD opens the ***Text Editor*** *contextual tab on the ribbon and waits for you to enter text. You see a small blue edit box floating in the middle of the drawing area; this is the in-place text editor. You can enter text here and then indicate which dimensions you want to apply it to.*

You change the 5.00 aligned dimension to read 5.00 cm.

✔ Delete the text inside the in-place text editor.

✔ Type **5.00 cm**.

The new text appears in the in-place text editor.

✔ Click anywhere outside the in-place text editor to close it and return to the drawing area.

AutoCAD prompts for objects to receive the new text:

```
Select Objects:
```

✔ Select the 5.00 aligned dimension on the hypotenuse of the triangle.

✔ Press **<Enter>** or right-click to end object selection.

The text is redrawn, as shown in Figure 8-38.

Figure 8-38
Text changed to 5.00 cm

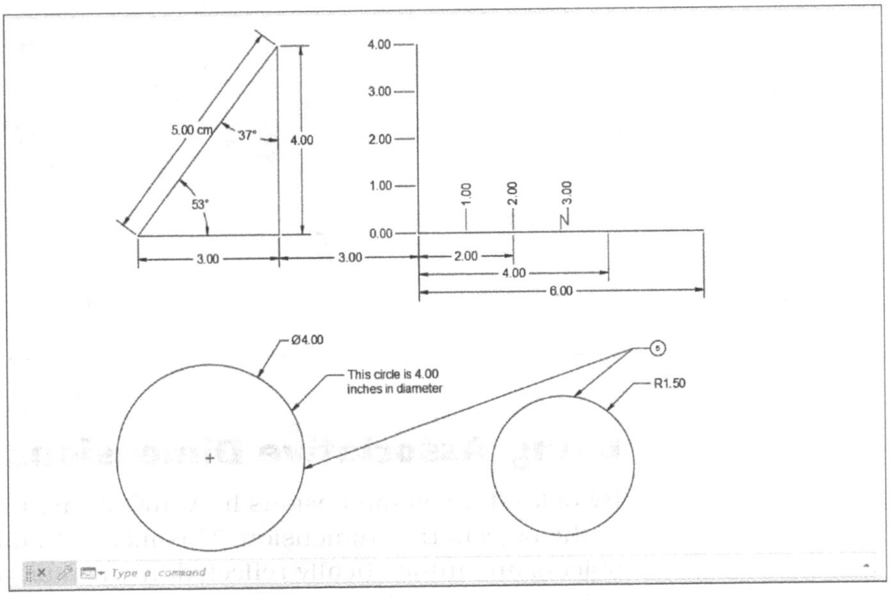

The Quick Properties and Properties Palettes

The **Quick Properties** and **Properties** palettes provide you with other ways to change dimension text content. Try the following:

✔ Select the lower baseline dimension on the 6.00 line.

✔ Right-click in the drawing area and select **Quick Properties** or click the **Quick Properties** tool on the status bar. (If necessary, select **Quick Properties** from the **Customization** menu on the status bar.)

✔ Click in the **Text override** field.

✔ Type **6.00 cm** in the edit box.

✔ Close the **Quick Properties palette**.

✔ Press **<Esc>** to clear grips.

Your dimension is redrawn with the text shown in Figure 8-39.

> **TIP**
>
> In addition to just replacing a dimension value with static text, you can add text before or after a dimension value with the **New** option of the **DIMEDIT** command or in the **Text Override** field of the **Quick Properties/Properties** palettes. The characters <> in the text string represents the dimension value. As an example, you could enter **<> cm** to add cm after the dimension value in the previous exercise.

Figure 8-39
Text changed to 6.00 cm

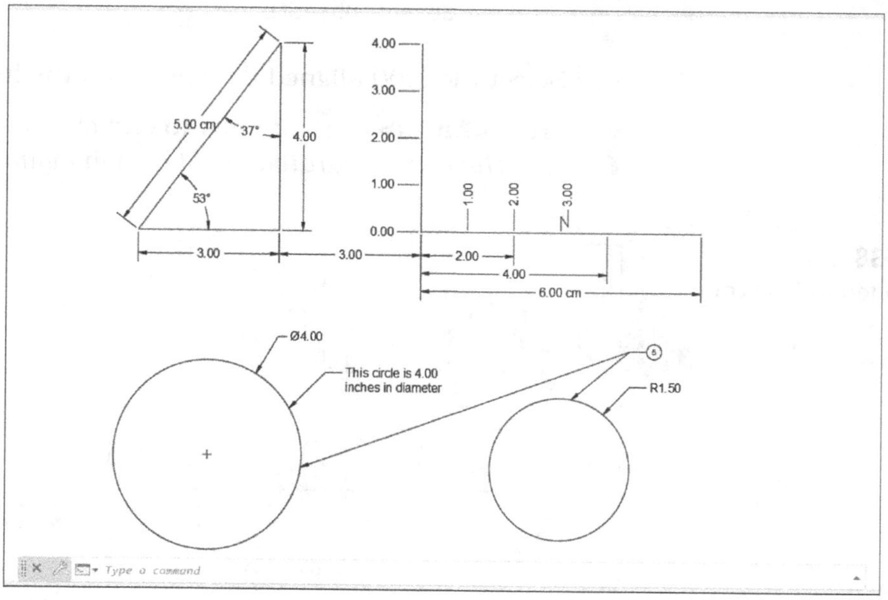

Using Associative Dimensions

By default, most dimensions in AutoCAD are associative with the geometry of the objects they dimension. This means that changes in the dimensioned objects are automatically reflected by the dimensions. If a dimensioned object is moved, the dimensions associated with it move as well. If a

associative dimension: A dimension that is associated with the object it dimensions, so that if the object moves or changes size, the dimension changes with the object.

dimensioned object is scaled, the position and measurements associated with that object change to reflect the new size of the object. The following exercise illustrates several points about ***associative dimensions***.

✔ Select the 2.00-radius circle.

✔ Click the center grip, move the circle about 2.00 units to the left, and click again to complete the move.

Your drawing should resemble Figure 8-40. Notice that the 4.00-diameter dimension moves with the circle, and the leaders from the mtext dimension text and the multileader tag stretch to maintain connection with the circle, but the text and tag do not move. You learn more in a moment, but first, try the following steps:

Figure 8-40
Results when circle is moved

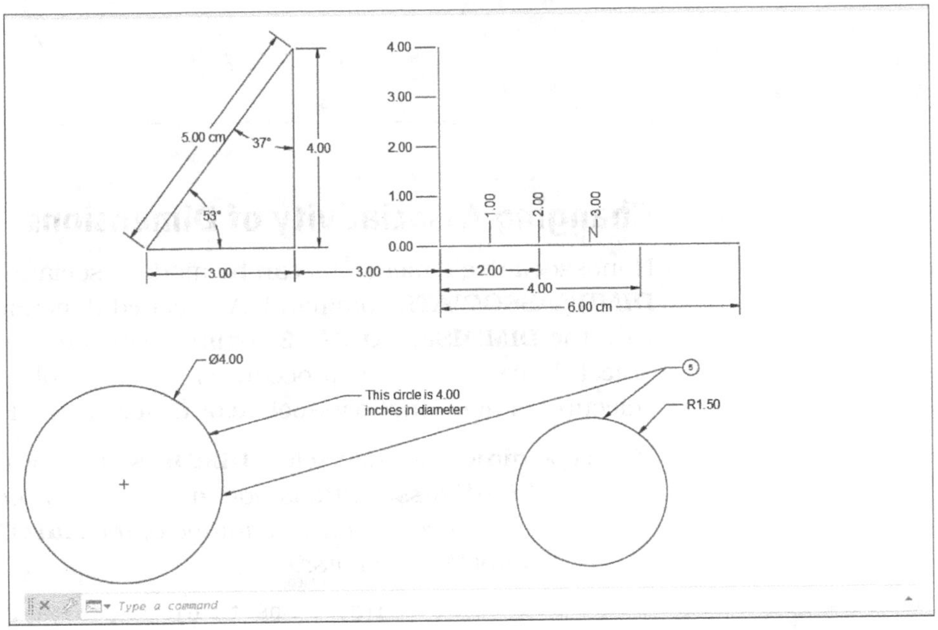

✔ Select any of the grips.

✔ Right-click to open the **Grip** shortcut menu.

✔ Select **Scale**.

✔ Type **.5 <Enter>** for a scale factor.

✔ Press **<Esc>** to clear grips.

Your circle is redrawn to resemble Figure 8-41. Notice now that the scale factor is reflected in the diameter dimension (4.00 has changed to 2.00) but not in the leadered text. The diameter dimension is a true associative dimension; it moves and updates to reflect changes in the circle. In the multileadered text, the connection point of the leadered dimension is associated with the circle, but the text is not. Therefore, the leader stretches to stay connected to the circle, but the text does not move or change with the circle.

Figure 8-41
Results when circle is scaled

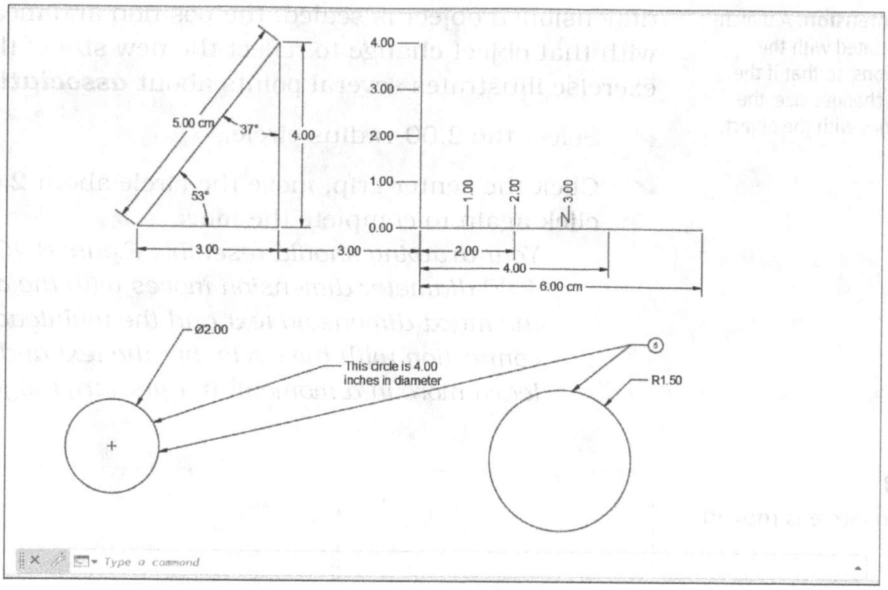

Changing Associativity of Dimensions

Nonassociative dimensions can be made associative using the **DIMREASSOCIATE** command. Associated dimensions can be disassociated with the **DIMDISASSOCIATE** command or the result of copying a dimension object. In each case, the procedure is a matter of entering the command and selecting dimensions to associate or disassociate. For example, try the following:

✔ Type **dimd** and then select **DIMDISSOCIATE** from the **AutoComplete** list.
__Dimdisassociate__ is not on any ribbon panel or menu, so this is a great time to take advantage of the __AutoComplete__ feature.
AutoCAD prompts:

```
Select dimensions to disassociate . . .
Select objects:
```

✔ Select the 2.00-diameter dimension.

✔ Right-click to end object selection.
Now, try moving the circle again to observe the changes.

✔ Select the circle, click the center grip, and move the circle to the right.
This time, the 2.00 diameter does not move with the circle, as shown in Figure 8-42. The multileaders adjust as before to stay attached to the circle, but the diameter dimension is currently not associated to the circle. To reassociate it, use the __DIMREASSOCIATE__ command, as follows:

✔ Type **dimr** and select **DIMREASSOCIATE** from the **AutoComplete** list, or select **Annotate** > **Dimensions** > **Reassociate** from the ribbon, as shown in Figure 8-43.

✔ Select the 2.00-diameter dimension.

✔ Press **<Enter>** to end object selection.
AutoCAD recognizes that this is a diameter dimension and prompts for a circle or arc to attach it to. Notice that this means you can associate the dimension to any arc or circle, not just the one to which it was previously attached.

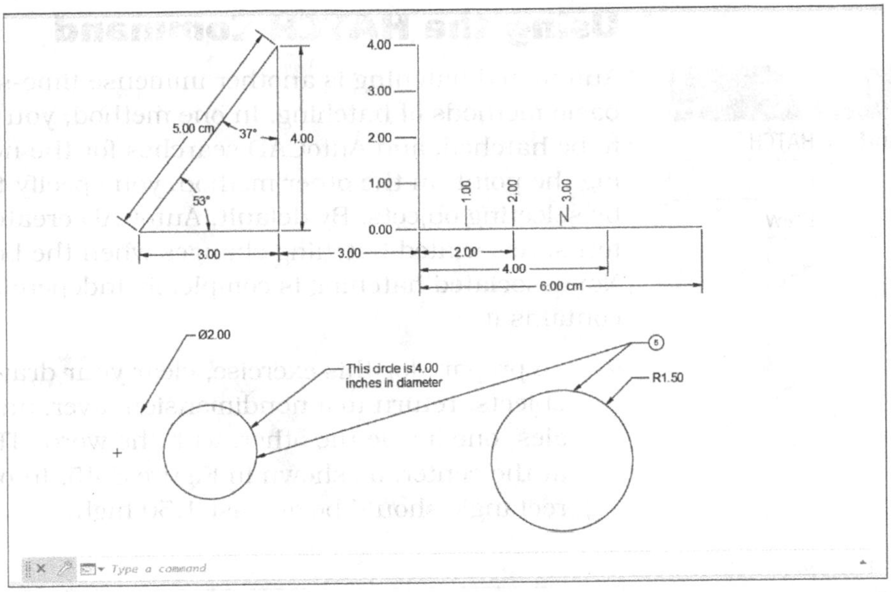

Figure 8-42
Results of disassociated dimension

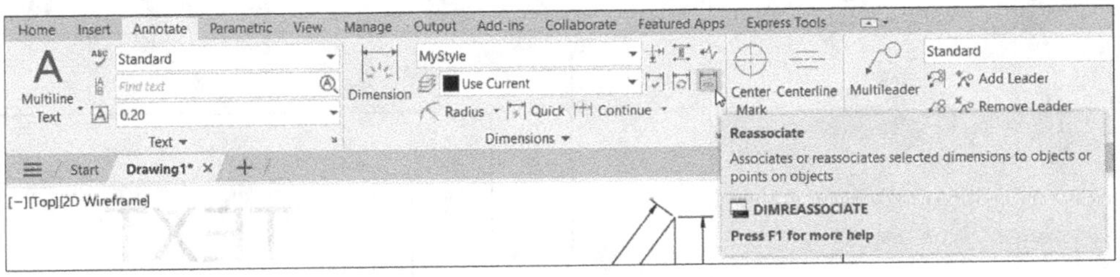

Figure 8-43
Reassociate tool

✔ Select the circle on the left again.

The diameter dimension moves and attaches to the 2.00-radius circle again, as shown in Figure 8-44.

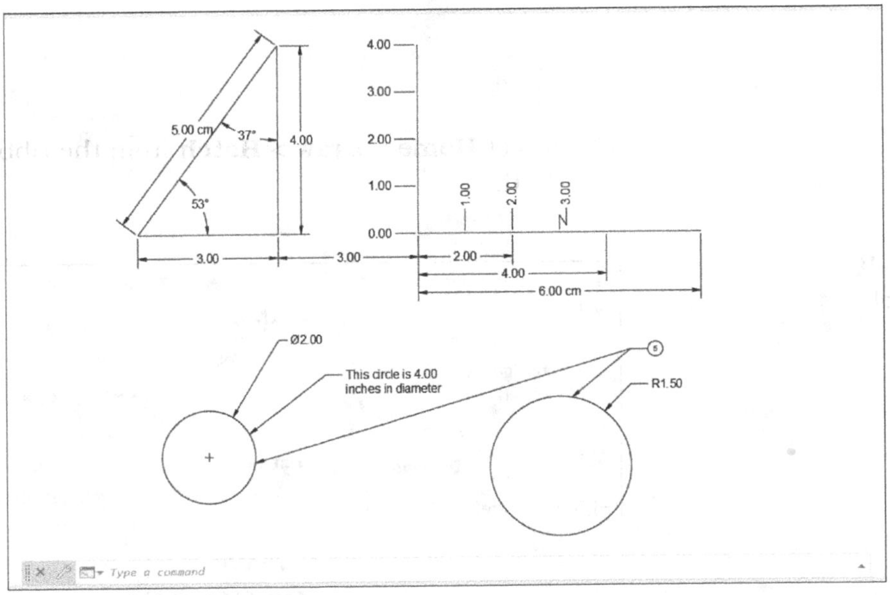

Figure 8-44
Results of reassociated dimension

Using the HATCH Command

HATCH	
Command	HATCH
Alias	H
Panel	Draw
Tool	

Automated hatching is another immense time-saver. AutoCAD has two basic methods of hatching. In one method, you select a point within an area to be hatched, and AutoCAD searches for the nearest boundary surrounding the point. In the other method, you specify the boundaries themselves by selecting objects. By default, AutoCAD creates associated hatch patterns. Associated hatching changes when the boundaries around it change. Nonassociated hatching is completely independent of the geometry that contains it.

✔ To prepare for this exercise, clear your drawing of all previously drawn objects, return to a nondimension layer, and then draw three rectangles, one inside the other, with the word "TEXT" with a height of 1.00 at the center, as shown in Figure 8-45. In order to do this, your inner rectangle should be at least 1.50 high.

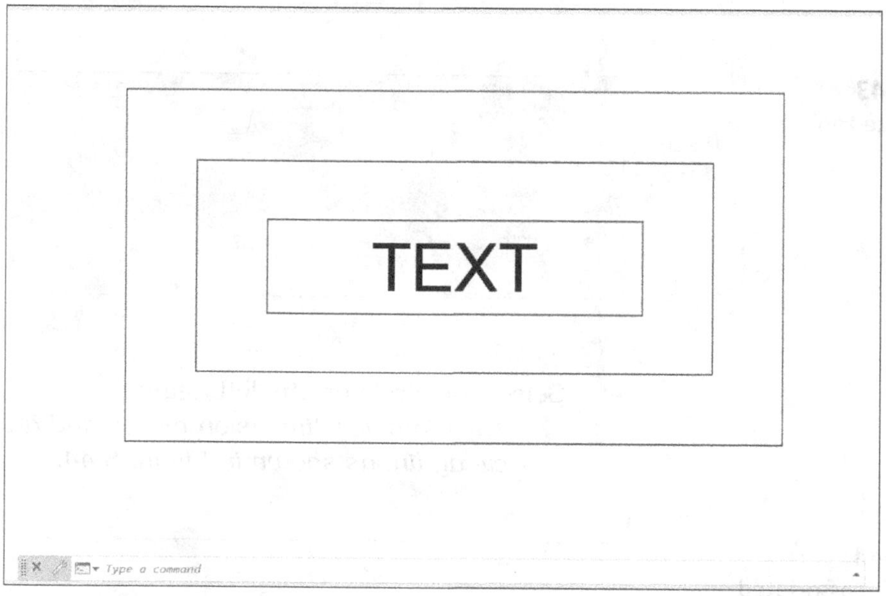

Figure 8-45
Drawing three rectangles

✔ Select **Home** > **Draw** > **Hatch** from the ribbon, as shown in Figure 8-46.

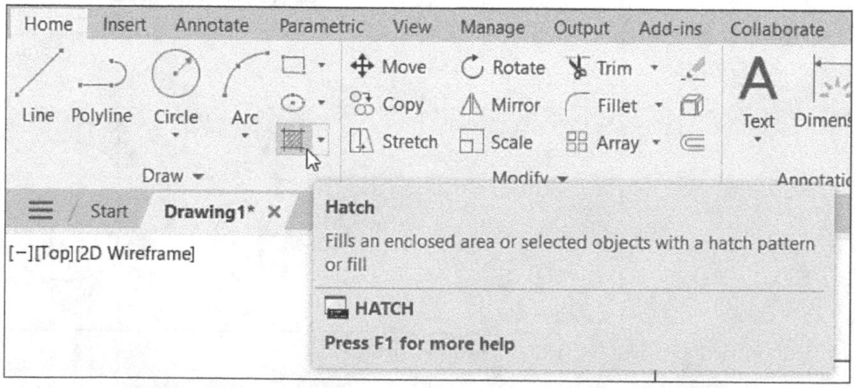

Figure 8-46
Hatch tool

*This initiates the **HATCH** command, which displays the **Hatch Creation** contextual tab shown in Figure 8-47. The tools on this ribbon tab give you many options for creating hatch and fill patterns, including 50 standard predefined patterns, solid color fills, and gradient fills. The default pattern is **ANSI31**, a simple pattern of crosshatch lines on a 45° angle. If this pattern is not showing and highlighted on the **Pattern** panel, you need to scroll to find it.*

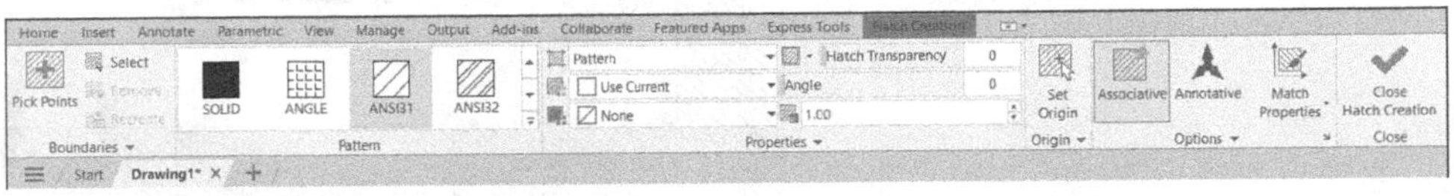

Figure 8-47
Hatch Creation contextual tab

✔ If necessary, scroll the list of patterns, using the up and down arrows on the right side of the panel. Because the list is in alphabetic order, except for **Solid**, try scrolling up in the list.

✔ If necessary, select the **ANSI31** pattern image, as shown in Figure 8-47.
AutoCAD prompts:

```
Pick internal points or [Select objects/Undo/seTtings]:
```

*This indicates that the default method, picking internal points, is in operation. Typing **S** switches to the select boundary objects method; typing **T** displays the **Hatch and Gradient** dialog box. When you move the cursor into a boundaried area, AutoCAD analyzes the drawing for a closed area under the crosshairs before showing a preview of the area hatched or filled in the current pattern. In this case, that is **ANSI31**.*

NOTE

The **HATCH** command remembers the most recent settings. If someone has recently drawn a hatch pattern by selecting objects rather than with internal points, **Select objects** may be the default setting. In this case, simply select picK **internal points** from the command line.

✔ Move the crosshairs into the area between the largest and the second largest rectangle and pause.
You see a preview image similar to Figure 8-48.

✔ Move the crosshairs into the area between the second largest and the smallest rectangle and pause.
You see a preview with this area hatched. Notice in each case that AutoCAD recognizes internal and external boundaries.

✔ Move the crosshairs into the inner rectangle and pause.
Notice in this preview image that AutoCAD also recognizes text within the boundary and automatically leaves space around the text.

✔ Now move the crosshairs outside all of the rectangles.
*You are still in the **HATCH** command, but no crosshatching has actually been applied to your drawing yet.*

Figure 8-48
Preview ANSI31 hatch pattern

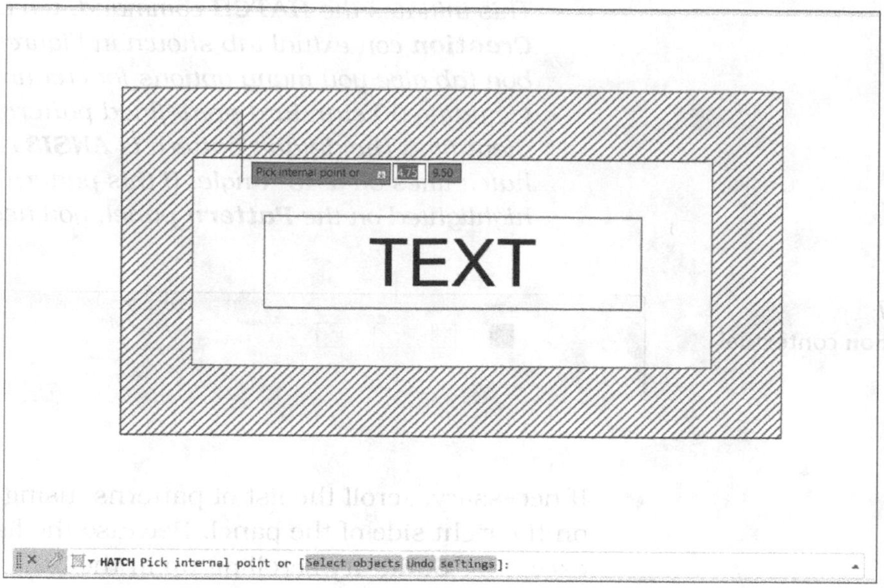

Other Predefined Patterns

AutoCAD's standard library of predefined hatch patterns includes 82 patterns that you can access from the **Pattern** panel. The arrows on the right side of the panel allow you to scroll through the pattern images. The bottom arrow allows you to open a larger window with four rows of images and its own scroll bar on the right. Here, you open the window and scroll down to the Escher pattern, as shown Figure 8-49.

✔ Click the down arrow at the bottom right of the **Pattern** panel.

Notice this is the bottom arrow, not the middle arrow, which also points down and can also be used to scroll down through rows of four patterns at a time. Using the bottom arrow, you see the window of patterns shown in Figure 8-49.

Figure 8-49
Selecting Escher pattern

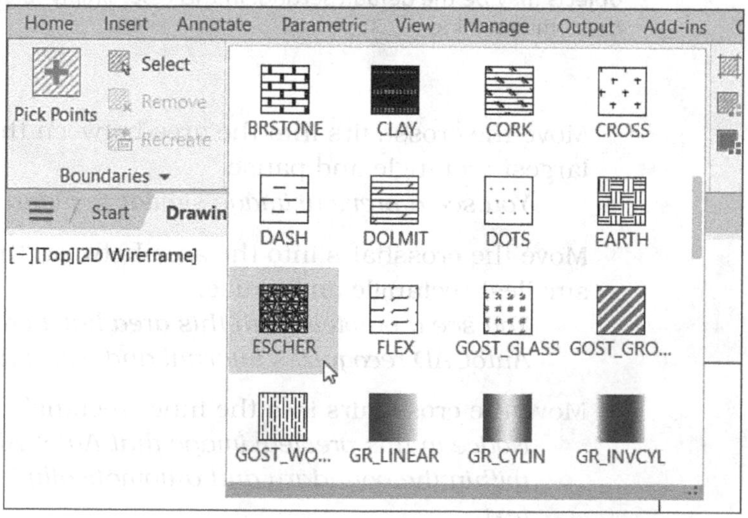

Chapter 8

✔ Scroll down to the Escher pattern and select it.

*The window closes, and the row containing the Escher pattern is displayed on the **Pattern** panel with **Escher** selected. Apply this pattern to the inner and outer rectangles, as shown in Figure 8-50.*

Figure 8-50
Preview of Escher hatch pattern

✔ Move the cursor into the area between the largest and second-largest rectangles, and specify a point inside the closed area.

*The area is filled with the Escher pattern. To also hatch the inner rectangle, you have to leave and then reenter the **HATCH** command. This is necessary because the inner rectangle boundaries are within the boundaries of the outer rectangle. To hatch separated areas, you could continue without leaving the command.*

✔ Press **<Enter>** to complete the command.

✔ Press **<Enter>** again to reenter **HATCH**.

✔ Move the crosshairs inside the inner rectangle, specify a point inside the closed area, and press **<Enter>** to complete the command.

Your drawing should resemble Figure 8-50.

> **TIP**
> When hatching an area that includes text, it is always a good idea to draw the text first. If the text is present, AutoCAD leaves space around it when hatching. Otherwise, you need to draw a temporary boundary around the text, **TRIM** to the boundary, and then **ERASE** it.

Gradient Fill

Next, you add a ***gradient*** fill pattern to the area between the inner and outer rectangles, as shown in Figure 8-51. You can do this in exactly the same way you choose any predefined hatch pattern or in a slightly different way by using the drop-down list at the top left of the **Properties** panel of the **Hatch Creation** contextual tab. To use the former method, open the **Pattern** window and scroll to the gradient fill you want. Using the latter method, click the **Hatch Type** drop-down list on the **Properties** panel and select **Gradient** to go automatically to the gradient patterns in the **Patterns** panel.

gradient: In AutoCAD, a fill pattern in which there is a smooth transition between one color or tint and another color or tint.

Figure 8-51
Preview of GR_SPHER gradient fill

✔ Press **<Enter>** to reenter the **HATCH** command.

This opens the ***Hatch Creation*** *contextual tab shown in Figure 8-52.*

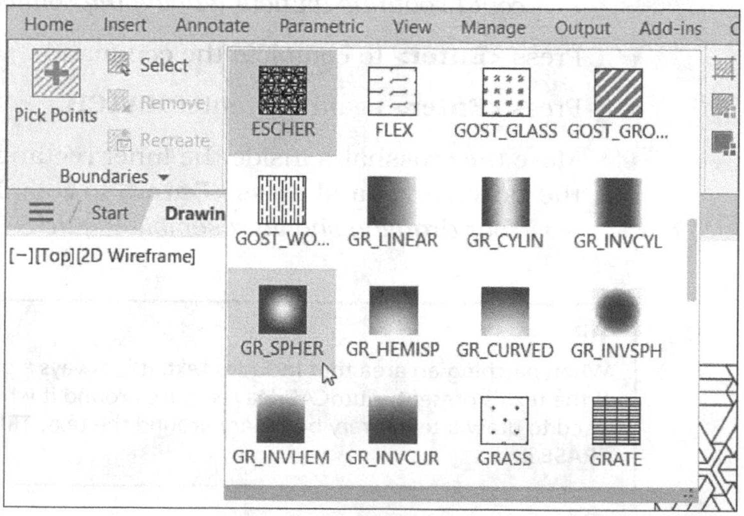

Figure 8-52
Selecting GR_SPHER gradient fill

✔ Open the **Hatch Type** drop-down list at the top of the **Properties** panel, as shown in Figure 8-53.

This drop-down list gives access to solid fills of various colors and user-defined hatch patterns and allows you to change the colors in gradient fills.

Figure 8-53
Hatch Type drop-down list

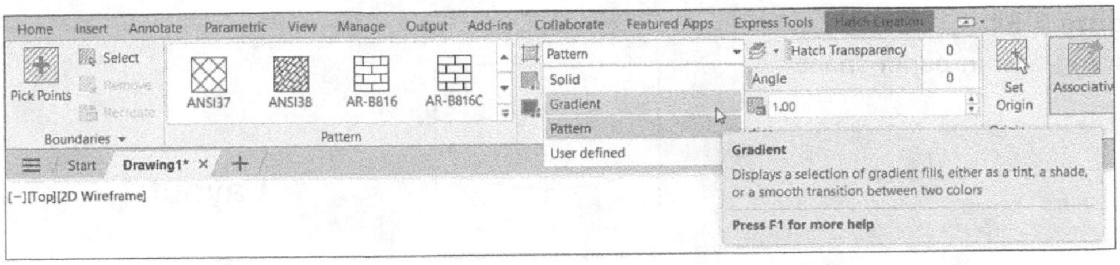

✔ Select **Gradient** from the list.

✔ On the **Pattern** panel, scroll down using the bottom arrow on the right.

✔ Select the **GR_SPHER** gradient pattern, the first pattern in the second row, as shown in Figure 8-52.

✔ Specify a point in the closed area between the inner and outer rectangles to create the image shown previously in Figure 8-51.

✔ Press **<Enter>** to exit **HATCH**.

Scaling Dimensions Between Paper Space and Model Space

You probably already know how to create multiple-viewport layouts. Now that you will be adding text and dimensions to your drawings, new questions arise about scale relationships between model space and paper space. The **Zoom XP** feature allows you to create precise scale relationships between floating model space viewports and paper space units. To simplify this process, you can use the **Annotative** property of annotation objects and styles to assist in matching dimension and text sizes to those zoom factors.

✔ If you have Drawing 5-2, the Flanged Bushing, as shown in Figure 8-54, open it. Otherwise, create an approximation as described below. Then click the **Layout1** tab.

1. Set limits to **(0,0)** and **(12,9)**. This is critical. If you use different limits, the exercise is difficult to follow.
2. Draw a circle with a diameter of 3.50 units centered at (3.00,4.00).
3. Draw a second circle with a diameter of 2.50 units centered at the same point.
4. Draw a small 0.25-diameter circle at the lower quadrant of the 2.50 diameter circle.
5. Draw a rectangle with the first corner at (6.50,2.75) and the second corner at (10.00,5.25).
6. Open **Layout1** and create a layout with D-size limits, using the **Page Setup Manager**. (Click the **Output** tab, select the **Plot** panel, and choose the **Page Setup Manager** tool.)

Figure 8-54
Adding text in paper space

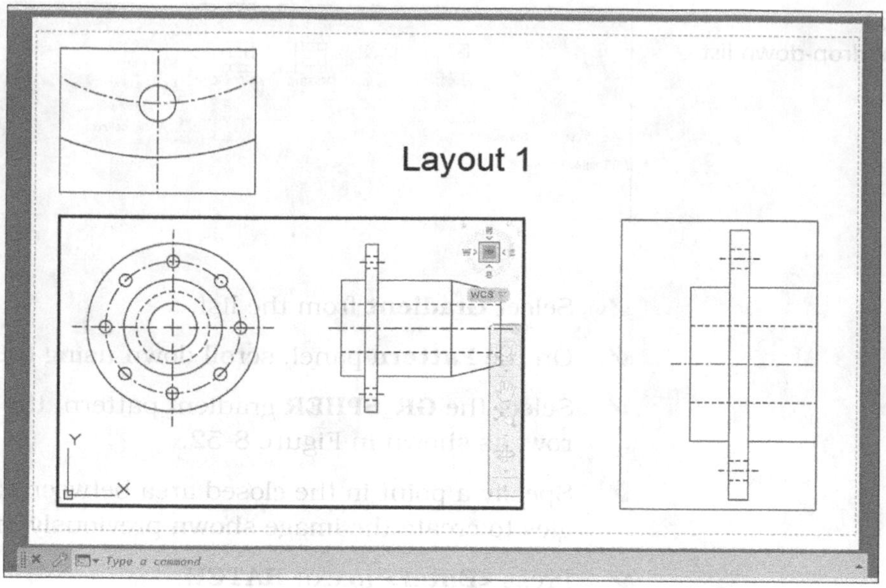

7. Create three viewports, positioned as shown in Figure 8-54. The coordinates of the corners of the lower-left viewport are (1,1) and (20,13). Those of the lower-right viewport are (22,1) and (32,13). The upper viewport stretches from (1,14) to (9,20). The zoom factor for the large viewport should be 2xp. The smaller viewport to the right should be at 4xp, centered on the midpoint of the left side of the rectangle, and the smallest viewport at the top should be at 6xp, centered on the small circle at the quadrant of the 2.50 circle.

Text in Paper Space and Model Space

Text drawn in paper space can be drawn at the 1:1 scale of the layout. Text drawn within viewports will be affected by the viewport scale. Try this:

✔ Double-click anywhere outside the viewports to ensure that you are in paper space.

✔ Select **Annotate** > **Text** > **Single Line** from the ribbon.

✔ Specify a start point outside any of the viewports at about (15,15).
This places the text about 2.00 units above the right side of the left viewport, as shown in Figure 8-54.

✔ Type **1 <Enter>** for a text height of 1 unit.
This assumes that you are using the D-size paper space limits. If not, you have to adjust for your own settings. On A-size paper, the text height is about 0.25.

✔ Press **<Enter>** for 0° rotation.

✔ Type **Layout 1 <Enter>**.

✔ Press **<Enter>** again to exit.
Your drawing should have text added, as shown in Figure 8-54.

✔ Double-click in the lower-left, largest viewport to enter model space in this viewport.

✔ Enter the **TEXT** command again.

✔ Specify a start point below the left view in the viewport, as shown in Figure 8-55.

Figure 8-55
Adding text in model space

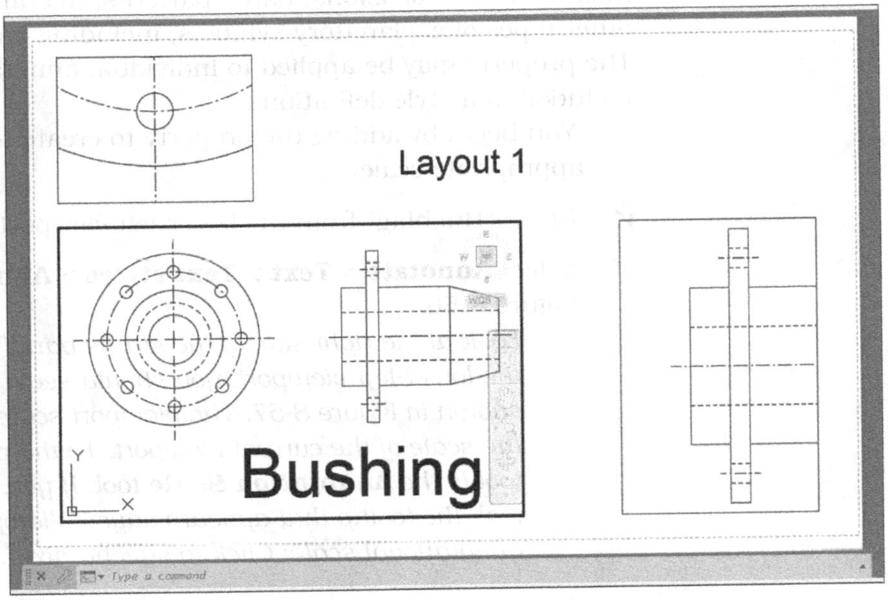

✔ Press **<Enter>** to retain a height of 1.00 unit.

✔ Press **<Enter>** for 0° rotation.

✔ Type **Bushing <Enter>**.

✔ Press **<Enter>** again to exit the command.

You may need to move objects in the viewport to make room for the text. You can do this using PAN in the viewport to make your drawing resemble Figure 8-55.

What has happened here? Why is "Bushing" drawn twice as big as "Layout 1"? Do you remember the **Zoom XP** scale factor you used in this viewport? This viewport is enlarged by two times paper space, so any text drawn inside it is enlarged by a factor of 2 as well. If you want, try drawing text in either of the other two viewports. You will find that text in the right viewport is magnified four times the paper space size, and text in the uppermost viewport is magnified six times.

You can compensate for these enlargements by dividing text height by factors of 2, 4, and 6, but that can become very cumbersome. Furthermore, if you decide to change the zoom factor at a later date, you would have to re-create any text drawn within the altered viewport. Otherwise, your text sizes in the overall drawing would become inconsistent. The purpose of the annotative property is to add control in situations such as this.

The Annotative Property

All types of objects used to annotate drawings can be defined as annotative. This annotative property allows you to attach one or more scales to the object. With the property and the correct scale, the scale of the object will match the scale of the viewport, and the annotation will appear at the desired size in paper space. Objects that can have the annotative property include text, dimensions, hatch patterns, tolerances, leaders, symbols, and other types of explanatory symbols, including ones you may define yourself. The property may be applied to individual annotative objects or may be included in a style definition.

You begin by adding the property to create text in the lower viewport at the appropriate scale.

✔ Erase "Bushing" from the lower-left viewport.

✔ Select **Annotate** > **Text** > **Text styles** > **Annotative**, as shown in Figure 8-56.

Look at the right side of the status bar. If you are in model space in the lower-left viewport, you should see a viewport scale indicator, as shown in Figure 8-57. The viewport scale should be 2:1, matching the scale of the current viewport. To the right of the ***Viewport Scale*** *tool is the* ***Annotation Scale*** *tool. If you rest your cursor on this tool, the tooltip that appears says, "Viewport scale is not equal to annotational scale: Click to synchronize".*

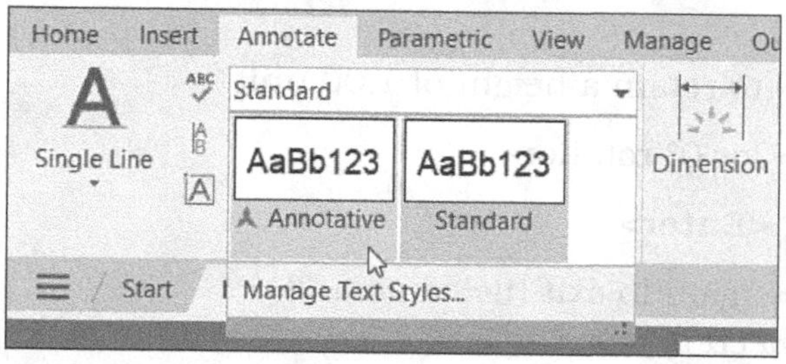

Figure 8-56
Annotative text style

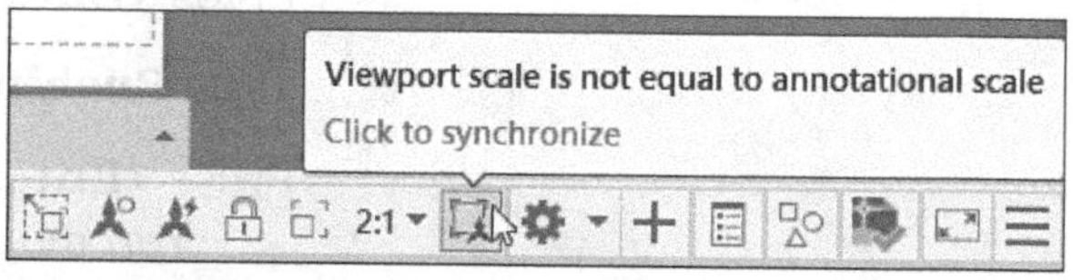

Figure 8-57
Viewport Scale Sync tool

By synchronizing the annotation scale with the viewport scale, you cause annotative objects in the viewport to be scaled automatically.

✔ On the status bar, click the **Viewport Scale Sync** tool.

Notice that the viewport scale changes to 1:1. The current scale factor in paper space is 1:1, as usual. To synchronize the viewport scale, AutoCAD changes the viewport scale to match the paper scale. Notice the change in the viewport. You want to return it to 2:1.

✔ On the status bar, click the **Viewport Scale** tool and select **2:1** from the long menu.

The viewport image returns to its previous size. It may seem as though nothing has changed, but now that the annotation and viewport scales are synchronized, annotative text will be adjusted to match paper space units.

Now, you draw text in the Annotative style in the left viewport.

✔ Click the **Single Line** text tool from the **Text** panel of the ribbon's **Annotate** tab.

✔ Specify a start point below the objects in the lower-left viewport.

✔ Type **1 <Enter>** for a text height.

✔ Press **<Enter>** for 0° rotation.

✔ Type **Bushing <Enter>**.

✔ Press **<Enter>** again to exit the command.

Your drawing should resemble Figure 8-58.

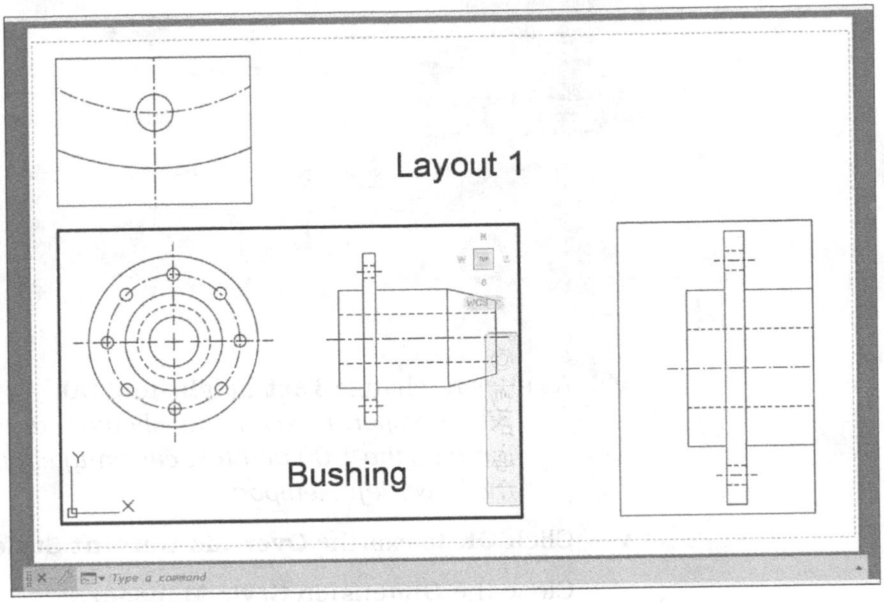

Figure 8-58
Results of **Annotation Scale**

> **TIP**
> After you have set the scales of your viewports on a layout, you want to make sure the scale doesn't accidentally change in the viewport. You can lock the scale of a viewport by selecting the viewports to be locked and clicking the **Viewport Lock** tool on the status bar or right-clicking and selecting **Display Locked > Yes** from the shortcut menu.

Controlling Annotation Scale Visibility

Next, you add some dimensions to your viewports and learn more about how scales and viewports can be managed. First, you switch to the Annotative dimension style and override the text of the style. This is a temporary override; it does not change the default definition of the style.

✔ Select **Annotate > Dimensions > Dimension Style > Manage Dimension Styles**.

✔ In the **Dimension Style Manager**, double-click **Annotative** from the **Styles** list to set it current.

*The **Current dimension** style label above the **Styles** list should now be proceeded by the name **Annotative**.*

✔ Click the **Override** button on the right.

✔ In the **Override Current Style** dialog box, click the **Text** tab.

*The **Text** tab is shown in Figure 8-59.*

Figure 8-59
Override Current Style dialog box

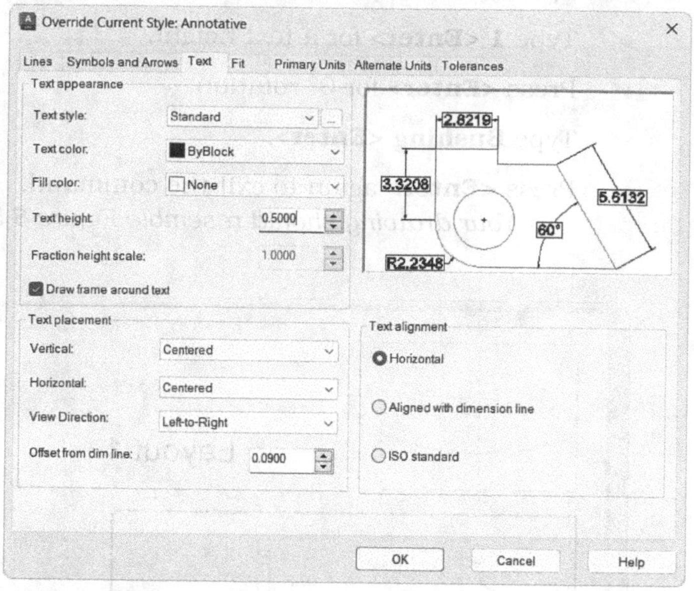

✔ As shown, change **Text height** to **0.50**.

When properly scaled, this should make your dimension text half as large as the 1.00 unit text currently showing in paper space and in the lower-left viewport.

✔ Click **OK** to exit the **Override Current Style** dialog box.

✔ Close the **Dimension Style Manager**.

✔ Click the **Dimension** tools drop-down menu and click the **Diameter** tool on the **Dimensions** panel on the ribbon's **Annotate** tab.

✔ Click the small bolt-hole circle at the bottom quadrant of the bushing, as shown in Figure 8-60.

Figure 8-60
Picking the small bolt -hole circle

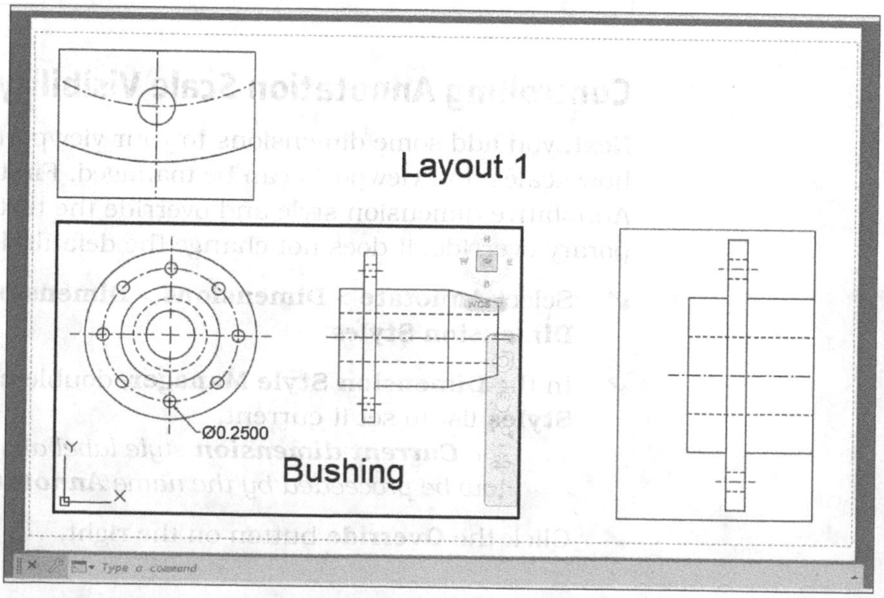

✔ Specify a location for the dimension as shown.

Your drawing should resemble Figure 8-60. Notice that the dimension just added does not appear in the top viewport, even though the bolt hole being dimensioned is clearly visible in that viewport. The ***Annotative*** *property of the text style has also made this possible.*

Look at the right side of the status bar again. Four icons to the left of the ***Annotation Scale*** *tool, you see the tool illustrated in Figure 8-61. This is the AutoCAD annotation symbol with a tiny gray circle behind it. The tooltip for this tool will display,* ***Show annotation objects – At current scale.***

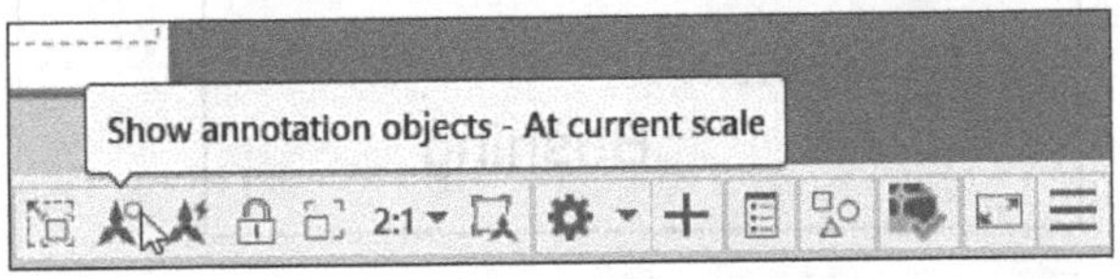

Figure 8-61
Annotation Visibility tool

✔ Click the **Annotation Visibility** tool.

The tool changes to blue. The tooltip now displays, ***Show annotative objects – Always****. Look closely at the upper-left viewport. A large dimension leader has been added. If you were to pan to see the dimension text, you would see that it is 1.50 units high, three times the 0.50 unit height of the text in the lower-left viewport. Once again, this is the result of the viewport scales, with the lower viewport at 2:1 and the upper viewport at 6:1.*

Annotative Objects with Multiple Scales

But what if you want a dimension or other annotative object to appear in two different viewports and still retain the correct size in relation to paper space? This can be handled by assigning more than one scale to an annotative object or group of annotative objects. To complete this exploration, you add a linear dimension to the lower-left viewport and assign it two scales, so that it appears at the same height in the right viewport.

✔ You should be in the lower-left viewport to begin this exercise.

✔ Select **Annotate** > **Dimensions** > **Dimension** > **Linear**.

✔ Press **<Enter>** or right-click to select an object to dimension.

✔ Select the vertical side of the right view of the bushing, as shown in Figure 8-62.

✔ Specify a location for the dimension line, as shown.

Your drawing should resemble Figure 8-63. You have the familiar problem that the dimension text appears twice as large in the right viewport, where the viewport scale is 4:1 instead of 2:1, as it is in the lower-left viewport. Your goal is to display this dimension in both viewports at the same size. This will require two changes. First, you match the annotation scale to the viewport scale in this viewport. Second, you add a second scale to the dimension object so that it can be displayed at both scales.

Figure 8-62
Dimensioning right view of bushing

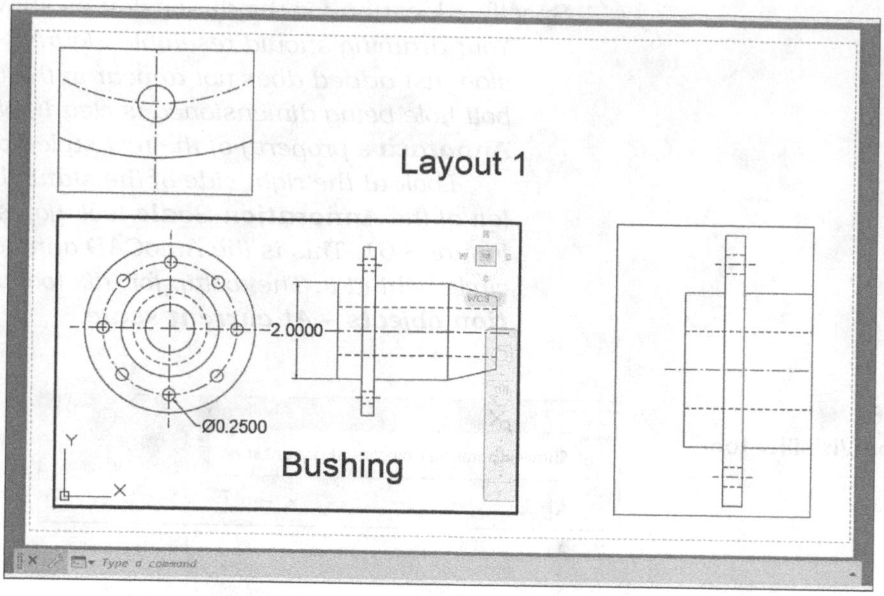

Figure 8-63
Text appears twice as large

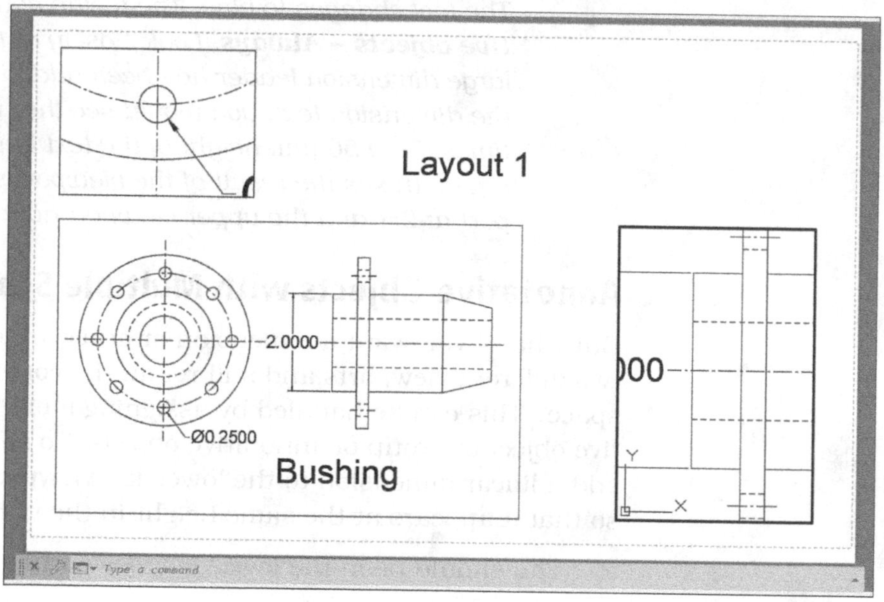

✔ Double-click in the right viewport.

*Notice here that the **Viewport Scale** tool on the status bar shows 4:1.*

✔ Click the **Viewport Scale Sync** tool to the right of the **Viewport Scale** indicator.

The viewport scale changes to 1:1 to synchronize with the annotation scale, shrinking the objects in the viewport.

✔ Click the **Viewport Scale** tool and select **4:1** from the list.

Though it appears you have not accomplished anything, you now have a match between the viewport scale and the annotation scale in this viewport, but the dimension is still twice as large as in the left viewport.

✔ Select the dimension.

When the dimension is selected, you see grips in both viewports.

✔ Right-click to open the shortcut menu.

✔ Highlight **Annotative Object Scale** and then select **Add/Delete Scales**, as shown in Figure 8-64.

*This displays the **Annotation Object Scale** dialog box shown in Figure 8-65. Notice that **2:1** is the only scale showing in the **Object Scale List**.*

✔ Click the **Add** button.

*You see the **Add Scales to Object** dialog box shown in Figure 8-66.*

✔ Select **4:1**, as shown.

✔ Click **OK**.

***4:1** is added to the **Object Scale List** below **2:1**.*

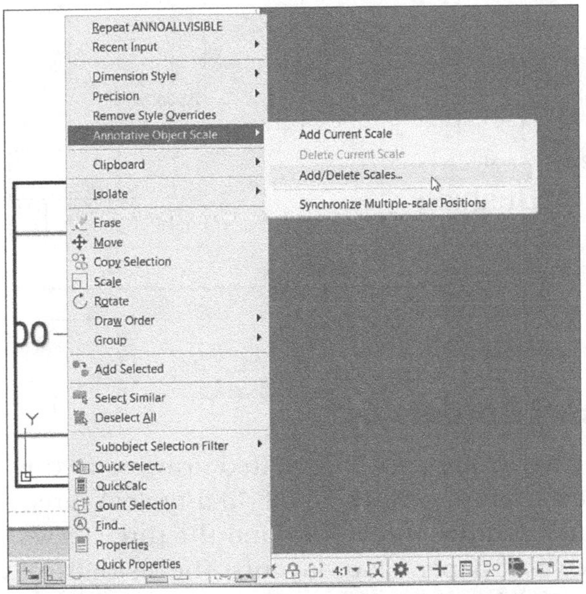

Figure 8-64
Add/Delete Scales

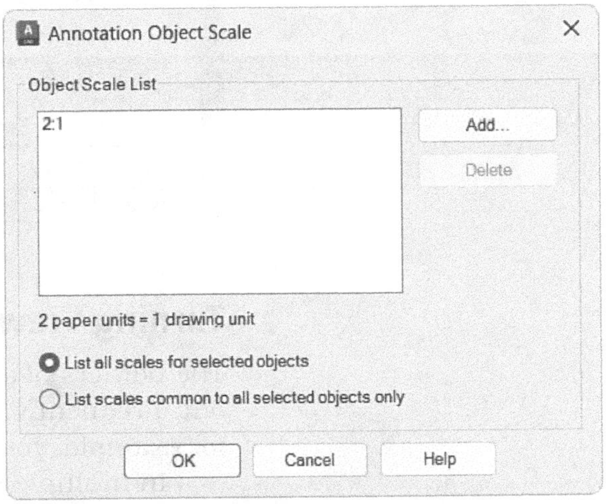

Figure 8-65
Annotation Object Scale dialog box

Figure 8-66
Add Scales to Object dialog box

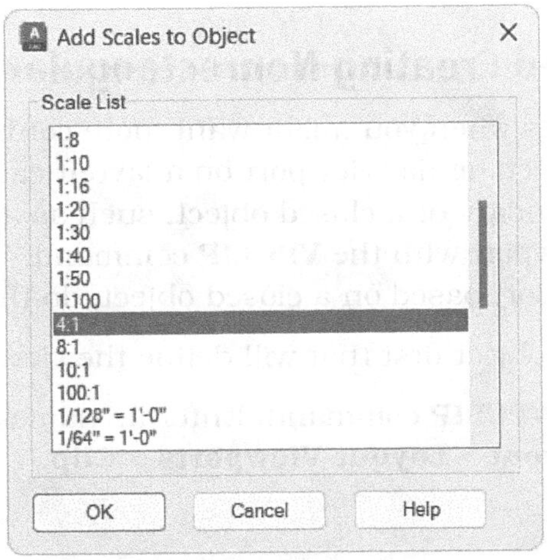

- ✔ Click **OK** to return to the drawing.

  The dimension in the right viewport is adjusted to the 4:1 scale in the right viewport.

- ✔ Finally, click the **Annotation Visibility** tool again.

  The dimension in the upper viewport vanishes, but the scaled dimension in the right viewport remains. Your drawing resembles Figure 8-67.

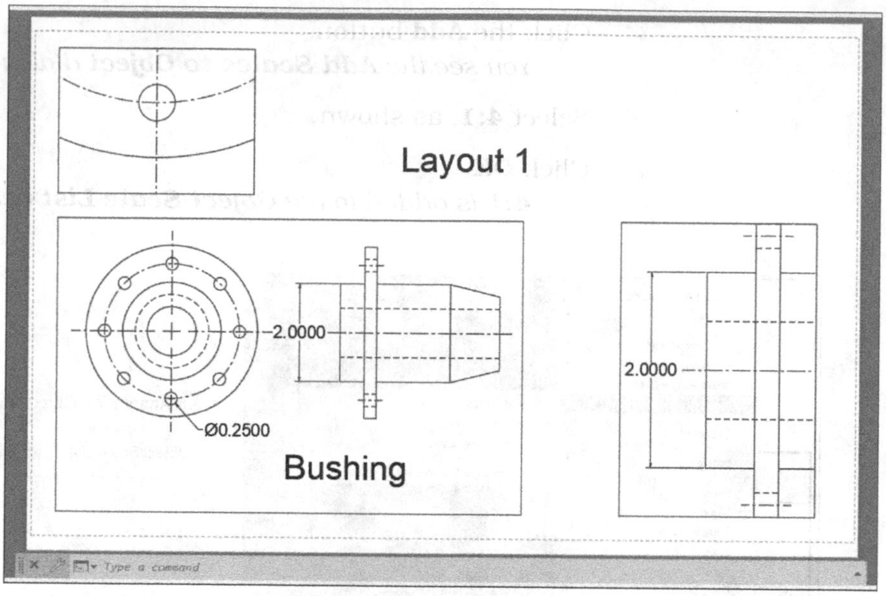

Figure 8-67
Scale is adjusted in right viewport

Turning Viewport Borders Off

The borders of a viewport are part of a plotted drawing in this drawing layout. Frequently, you want to turn them off. In a typical three-view drawing, for example, you do not draw borders around the three views.

In multiple-viewport paper space layouts, the visibility of viewport borders is easily controlled by putting the viewports on a separate layer and then turning the layer off before plotting. You can make a "border" layer, for example, and make it current while you create viewports. You can also use the **Quick Properties** palette to move viewports to the border layer later.

Clipping and Creating Nonrectangular Viewports

There are times when you might want more control over the shape of your viewports. A rectangular viewport on a layout can be clipped based on a polygonal boundary or a closed object, such as a polyline, circle, or ellipse. You clip a viewport with the **VPCLIP** command.

To clip a viewport based on a closed object, do the following:

- ✔ Draw the object first that will define the viewport's new border.
- ✔ Start the **VPCLIP** command. Enter its name at the command line or select **Layout** > **Layout Viewports** > **Clip**.

- ✔ Select the viewport to clip.
- ✔ Select the object that will define the viewport's new border.

  The viewport is now clipped to the selected object.

Once a viewport has been clipped, you can remove its clipped boundary. Start the **VPCLIP** command, select the clipped viewport, and then select the **Delete** option.

8 chapter eight

Chapter Summary

You now have a solid foundation of AutoCAD's extensive dimensioning capabilities. You can create and save dimension styles much as you previously created text styles. You can create dimensions in numerous common types including linear and aligned dimensions, radius and diameter dimensions, baseline or continued dimensions, and dimensions using leaders and multileaders. You can place several dimensions at once using **QDIM**; and you can edit dimension placement, dimension text content, and dimension properties. To further enhance your drawings, you also know how to add hatch and gradient patterns to your drawings. Finally, you learned the uses of associative dimensions and of the **Annotative** property, which allows you to control the scaling of text so that it is consistent among viewports and in paper space.

Chapter Test Questions

Multiple Choice

Circle the correct answer.

1. To move the origin point of a drawing use the
   a. **MOVE** command
   b. **ORIGIN** command
   c. **UCS** command
   d. **UCSICON** command
2. Which of the following does **not** adjust when an object with associative dimensions is moved?
   a. Start point of a leader
   b. Text of a radius dimension
   c. Text of a linear dimension
   d. Multileader text
3. Which of the following **cannot** be hatched using the **HATCH** command?
   a. A 355° arc
   b. A rectangle
   c. A circle
   d. An irregular quadrilateral
4. Dimension units are set in the
   a. **Units** dialog box
   b. **Dimension Style** dialog box
   c. **Dimension Units** dialog box
   d. **Annotation** dialog box
5. The default dimension style is called
   a. Annotative
   b. Linear
   c. Standard
   d. Dimstyle

Matching

Write the number of the correct answer on the line.

a. Multiple dimension ________
b. Datum point ________
c. UCS origin ________
d. Vertex ________
e. Annotative dimension ________

1. Viewport scale
2. Baseline
3. **DIMORDINATE**
4. **DIMANGULAR**
5. **QDIM**

True or False

Circle the correct answer.

1. **True or False**: By default, dimension style units are the same as drawing units.
2. **True or False**: Mtext is drawn within a rectangular box defined by the user.
3. **True or False**: The default dimension style is Annotative.
4. **True or False**: Center-justified text and middle-justified text are two names for the same thing.
5. **True or False**: Fonts are created based on text styles.

Questions

1. You are working in a drawing with units set to architectural, but when you begin dimensioning, AutoCAD provides four-place decimal units. What is the problem? What do you need to do so that your dimensioning units match your drawing units?
2. What is a **Nearest** object snap, and why is it important when dimensioning with leaders?
3. Why is it useful to move the origin of the coordinate system to make good use of ordinate dimensioning? What option to do this is available in the **QDIM** command?
4. What is associative dimensioning? What command makes a nonassociative dimension associative?
5. Paper space is at a 1:1 plotting scale; two viewports in a layout are at 8:1 and 2:1 viewport scales. What do you have to do so that a single annotation object will appear at the same scale in both viewports?

Drawing Problems

1. Create a new dimension style called Dim-2. Dim-2 uses architectural units with ½" precision for all units except angles, which use two-place decimals. Text in Dim-2 is 0.5 unit high.
2. Draw an isosceles triangle with vertexes at (4,3), (14,3), and (9,11). Draw a 2-unit circle centered at the center of the triangle.
3. Dimension the base and one side of the triangle using the Dim-2 dimension style.
4. Add a diameter dimension to the circle, and change a dimension variable so that the circle is dimensioned with a diameter line drawn inside the circle.
5. Add an angle dimension to one of the base angles of the triangle. Make sure the dimension is placed outside the triangle.
6. Hatch the area inside the triangle and outside the circle using any predefined crosshatch pattern.

8 chaptereight

Chapter Drawing Projects

M Drawing 8-1: *Tool Block* [INTERMEDIATE]

In this drawing, the dimensions should work well without editing. The hatch is a simple user-defined pattern used to indicate that the front and right views are sectioned views.

Drawing Suggestions

GRID = 1.0

SNAP = 0.125

HATCH line spacing = 0.125

- As a general rule, complete the drawing first, including all crosshatching, and then add dimensions and text at the end.
- Place all hatching on the **hatch** layer. When hatching is complete, set to the **dim** layer and turn the hatch layer off so that **hatch** lines do not interfere when you select lines for dimensioning.
- The section lines in this drawing can be easily drawn as leaders. Set the dimension arrow size to **0.38** first. Check to see that **Ortho** is on; then begin the leader at the tip of the arrow and make a right angle as shown. After picking the other endpoint of the leader, press **<Enter>** to bring up the first line of annotation prompt. Type a space and press **<Enter>**, so you have no text. Press **<Enter>** again to exit.
- You need to set the **DIMTIX** variable to **On** to place the 3.25-diameter dimension at the center of the circle in the top view and **Off** to create the leader style diameter dimension in the front section.

Drawing 8-1
Tool Block

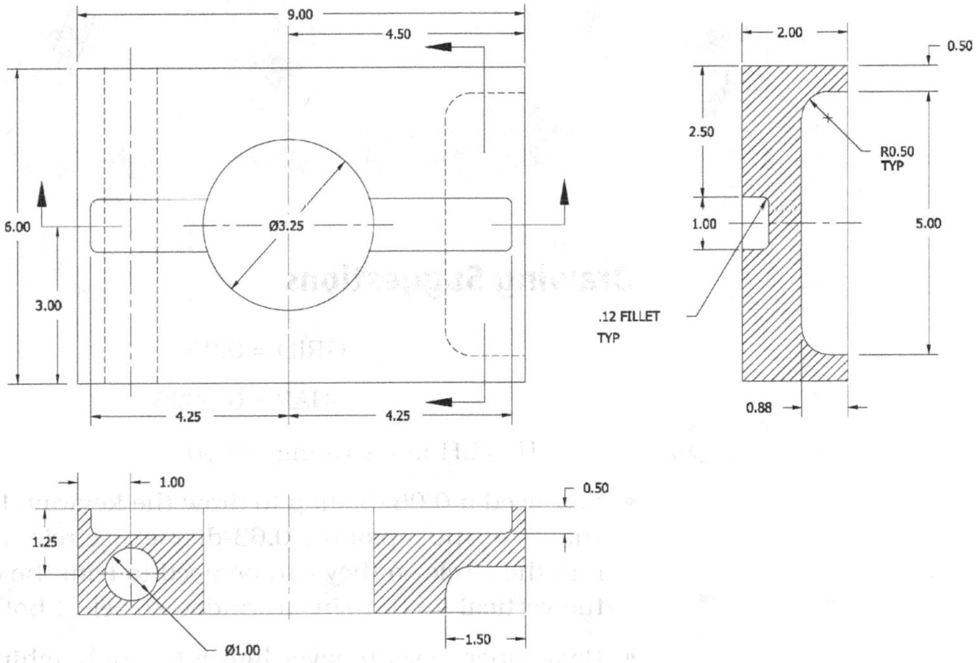

M Drawing 8-2: *Flanged Wheel* [INTERMEDIATE]

Most of the objects in this drawing are straightforward. The keyway is easily done using the **TRIM** command. If necessary, use the **Edit** shortcut menu or grips to move the diameter dimension, as shown in the reference.

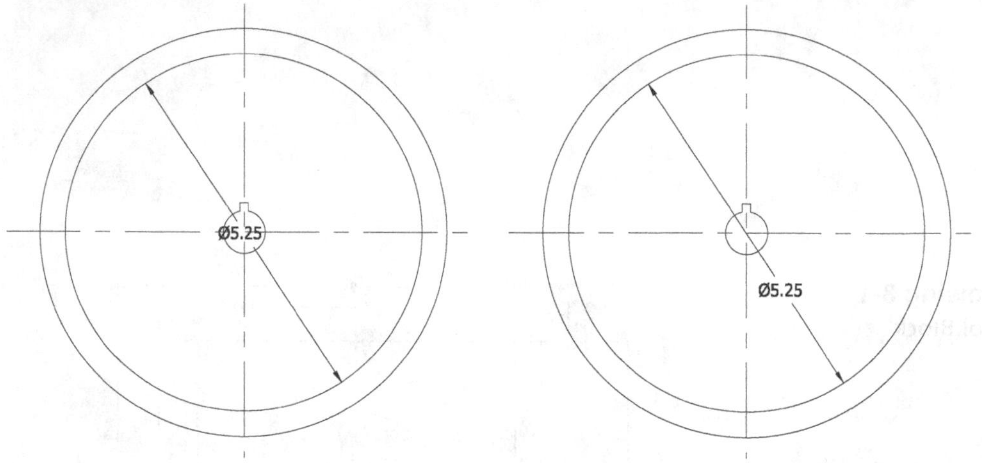

Drawing Suggestions

GRID = 0.25

SNAP = 0.0625

HATCH line spacing = 0.50

- You need a 0.0625 snap to draw the keyway. Draw a 0.125 × 0.125 square at the top of the 0.63-diameter circle. Drop the vertical lines down into the circle so they can be used to trim the circle. **TRIM** the circle and the vertical lines, using a window to select both as cutting edges.
- Remember to set to layer **hatch** before hatching, layer **text** before adding text, and layer **dim** before dimensioning.

Drawing 8-2
Flanged Wheel

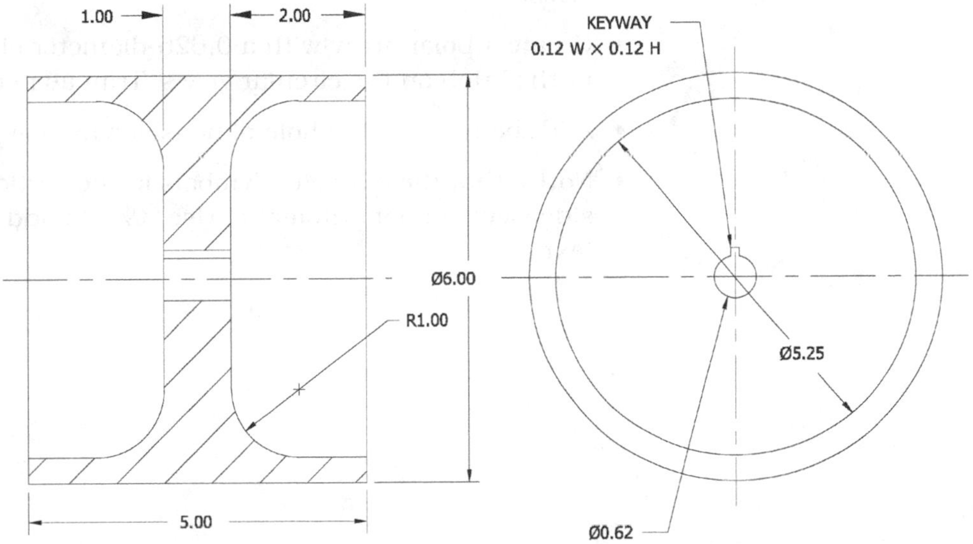

M Drawing 8-3: *Knob* [INTERMEDIATE]

This drawing makes use of the procedures for hatching and dimensioning you learned in the last two drawings. In addition, it uses an angular dimension, leaders, and %%c for the diameter symbol.

Drawing Suggestions

GRID = 0.125

SNAP = 0.0625

HATCH line spacing = 0.25

- You can save some time on this drawing by using **MIRROR** to create half of the right-side view. Notice, however, that you cannot hatch before mirroring because the **MIRROR** command reverses the angle of the hatch lines.
- Create a polar array with a 0.625-diameter circle to get the indentations in the knob on the circular views. Trim as necessary.
- Add the notes to the hole dimensions by using the **DIMEDIT** command.
- Notice that the diameter symbols in the vertical dimensions on the right-side view are not automatic. Use %%c to add the diameter symbol to the text.

Drawing 8-3
Knob

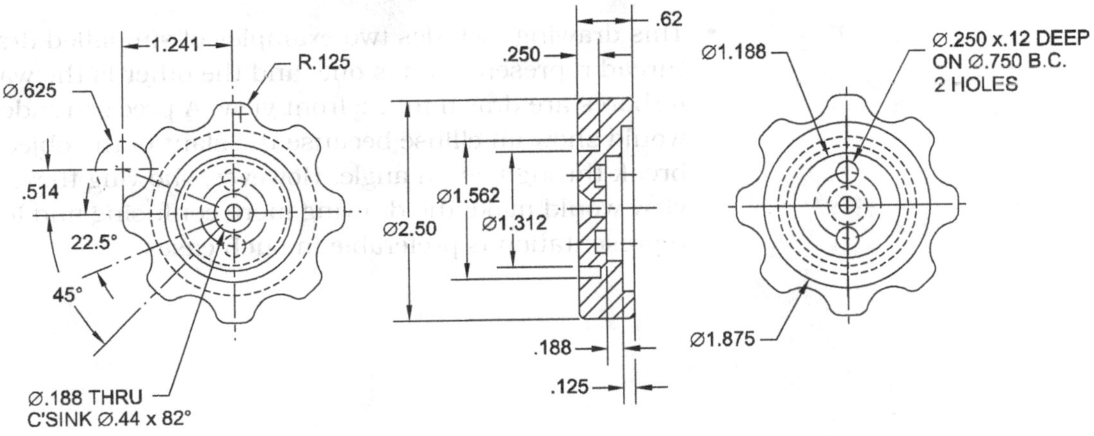

M Drawing 8-4: *Nose Adapter* [INTERMEDIATE]

Make ample use of **ZOOM** to work on the details of this drawing. Notice that the limits are set larger than usual, and the snap is rather fine by comparison.

Drawing Suggestions

LIMITS = (0,0) (36,24)

GRID = 0.25

SNAP = 0.125

HATCH line spacing = 0.25

- You need a 0.125 snap to draw the thread representation shown in the reference. Understand that this is nothing more than a standard representation for screw threads; it does not show actual dimensions. Zoom in close to draw it, and you should have no trouble.
- This drawing includes two examples of simplified drafting practice. The thread representation is one, and the other is the way in which the counterbores are drawn in the front view. A precise rendering of these holes would show an ellipse because the slant of the object dictates that they break through on an angle. However, showing these ellipses in the front view would make the drawing more confusing and less useful. Simplified representation is preferable in such cases.

Drawing 8-4
Nose Adapter

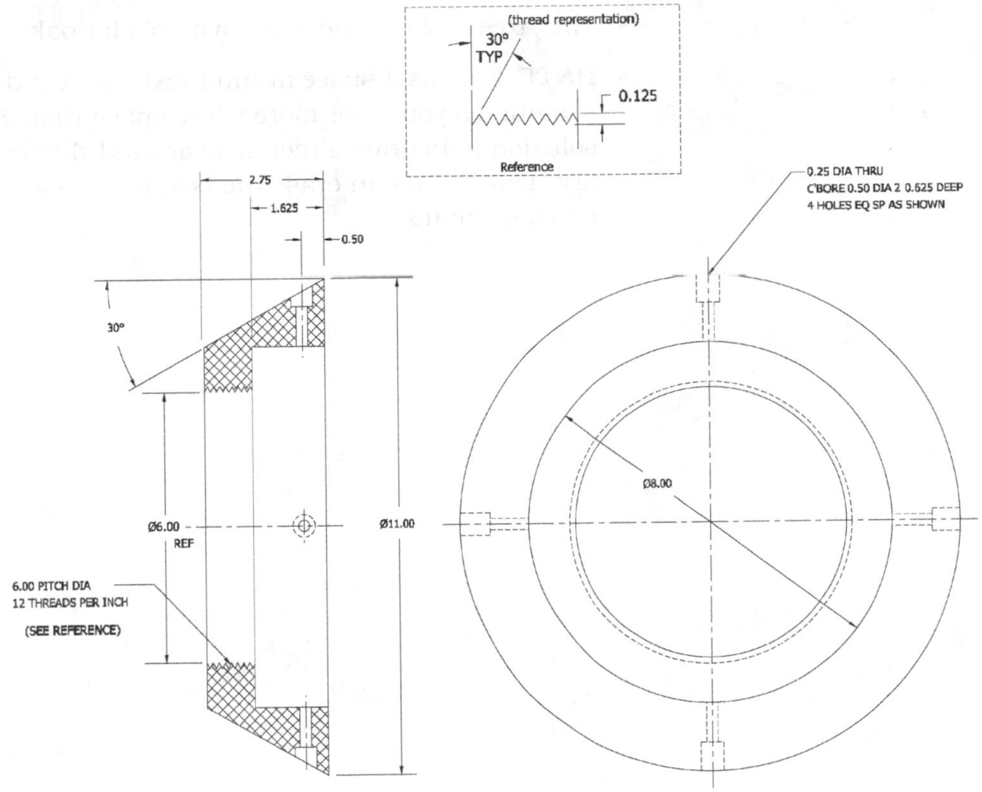

A

Drawing 8-5: *Plot Plan* [INTERMEDIATE]

This architectural drawing makes use of three hatch patterns and several dimension variable changes. Be sure to make these settings as shown.

Drawing Suggestions

GRID = 10'

SNAP = 1'

LIMITS = (0',0') (180',120')

LTSCALE = 2'

- The "trees" shown here are symbols for oaks, willows, and evergreens.
- **HATCH** opens a space around text inside a defined boundary; however, sometimes you want more white space than **HATCH** leaves. A simple solution is to draw a rectangle around the text area as an inner boundary. Later, you can erase the box, leaving an island of white space around the text.

Drawing 8-5
Plot Plan

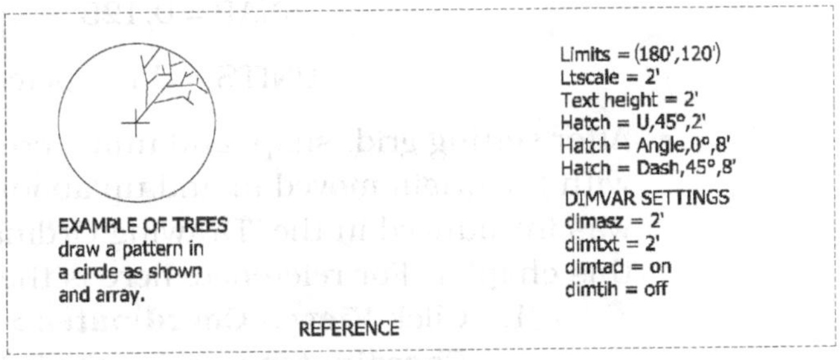

EXAMPLE OF TREES
draw a pattern in
a circle as shown
and array.
REFERENCE
Limits = (180',120')
Ltscale = 2'
Text height = 2'
Hatch = U,45°,2'
Hatch = Angle,0°,8'
Hatch = Dash,45°,8'
DIMVAR SETTINGS
dimasz = 2'
dimtxt = 2'
dimtad = on
dimtih = off

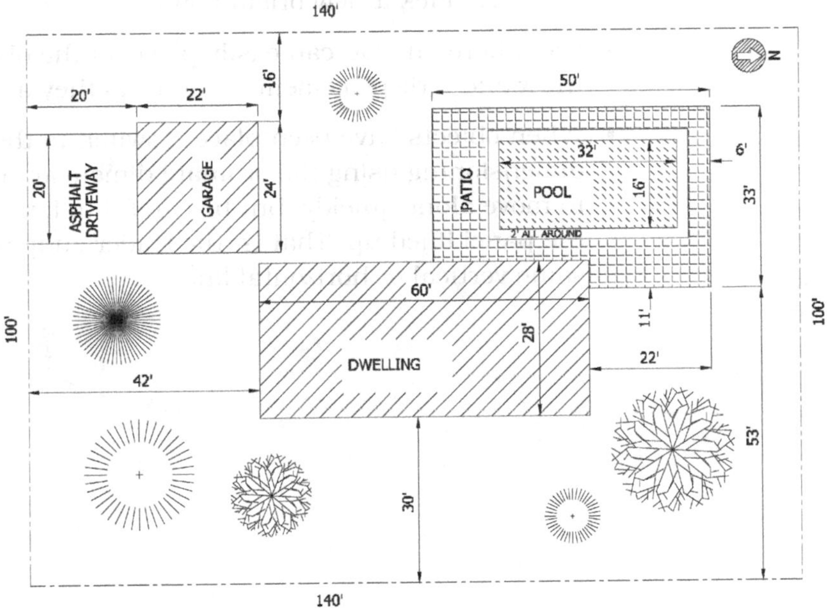

140'
N
16'
20'
22'
50'
32'
6'
20'
ASPHALT
DRIVEWAY
GARAGE
24'
PATIO
POOL
16'
33'
2' ALL AROUND
60'
100'
100'
11'
28'
DWELLING
22'
42'
53'
30'
140'

G Drawing 8-6: *Panel* [ADVANCED]

This drawing is primarily an exercise in using ordinate dimensions. Both the drawing of the objects and the adding of dimensions are facilitated dramatically by this powerful feature.

Drawing Suggestions

GRID = 0.50

SNAP = 0.125

UNITS = three-place decimal

- After setting grid, snap, and units, create a new user coordinate system with the origin moved in and up about 1 unit each way. This technique was introduced in the "Drawing Ordinate Dimensions" section earlier in this chapter. For reference, here is the procedure:
    1. Click **View** > **Coordinates** > **Origin** from the ribbon. (If the **Coordinates** panel isn't visible, right-click over the **View** tab and select **Show Panels** > **Coordinates**.)
    2. Pick a new origin point.
- From here on, you can easily place all the objects in the drawing using the *x* and *y* displacements exactly as they are shown in the drawing.
- When objects have been placed, switch to the **dim** layer and begin dimensioning using the ordinate dimension feature. You should be able to move along quickly, but be careful to keep dimensions on each side of the panel lined up. That is, the leader endpoints should end along the same vertical or horizontal line.

Drawing 8-6
Panel

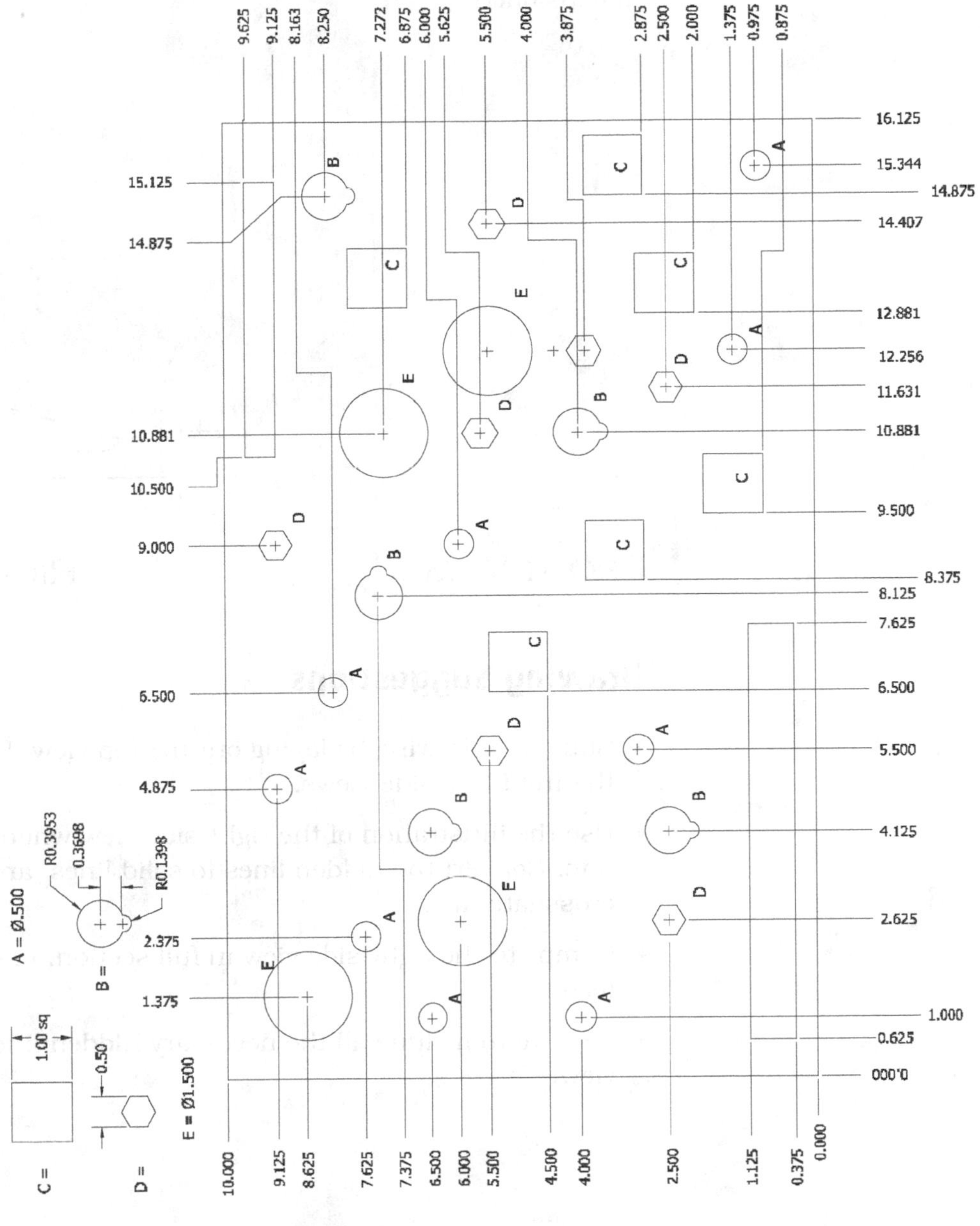

Drawing 8-7: *Angle Support* [ADVANCED]

In this drawing, you are expected to use the 3D view to create three orthographic views. Draw a front view, top view, and side view. The front and top views are drawn showing all necessary hidden lines, and the right-side view is drawn in full section. The finished multiview drawing should be fully dimensioned.

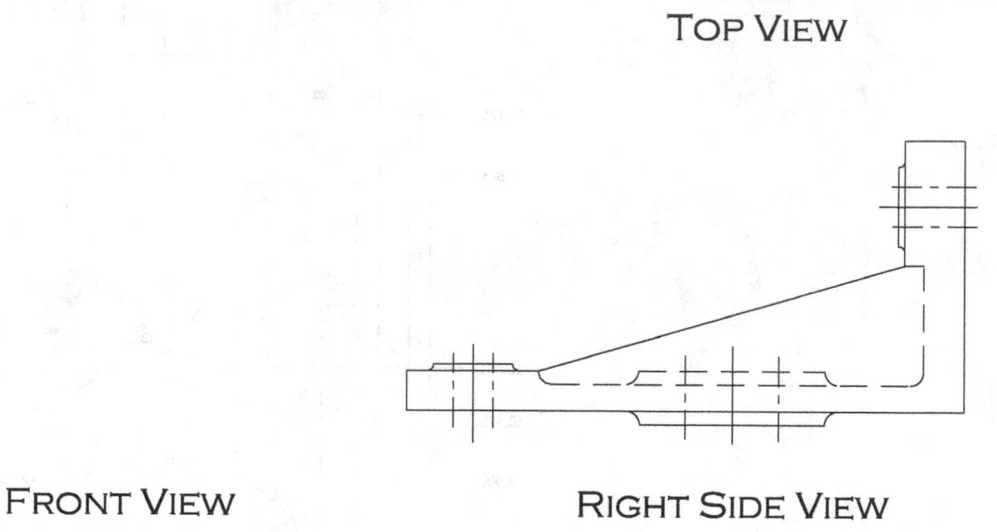

Drawing Suggestions

- Start this drawing by laying out the top view. Use the top view to line up the front and side views.
- Use the illustration of the right-side view when planning out the full section. Convert the hidden lines to solid lines, and use **HATCH** to create crosshatching.
- Complete the right-side view in full section, using the **ANSI31** hatch pattern.
- Be sure to include all the necessary hidden lines and centerlines in each view.

Drawing 8-7
Angle Support

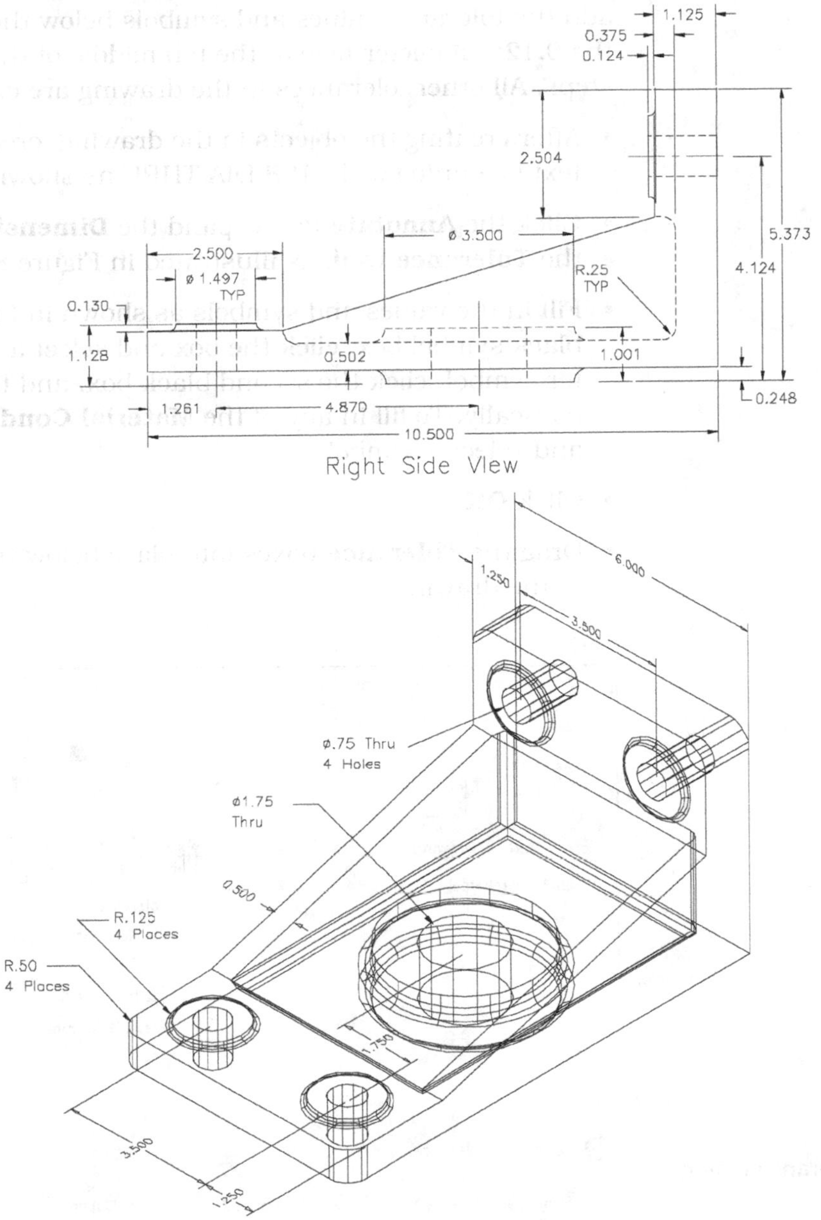

M

Drawing 8-8: *Mirror Mounting Plate* [ADVANCED]

This drawing introduces AutoCAD's geometric tolerancing capability, an additional feature of the dimension system. Geometric tolerancing symbols and values are added using a simple dialog box interface. For example, to add the tolerance values and symbols below the leadered dimension text on the 0.128-diameter hole at the top middle of the drawing, follow these steps. All other tolerances in the drawing are created in the same manner.

- After creating the objects in the drawing, create the leadered dimension text beginning with .128 DIA THRU as shown.
- Click the **Annotate** tab, expand the **Dimensions** panel, and then click the **Tolerance tool**, as illustrated in Figure 8-68.
- Fill in the values and symbols as shown in Figure 8-69. To fill in the first black symbol box, click the box and select a symbol. To fill in the diameter symbol, click the second black box, and the symbol is filled in automatically. To fill in any of the **Material Condition** boxes, click the box and select a symbol.
- Click **OK**.
- Drag the **Tolerance** boxes into place below the dimension text, as shown in the drawing.

Figure 8-68
Tolerance tool

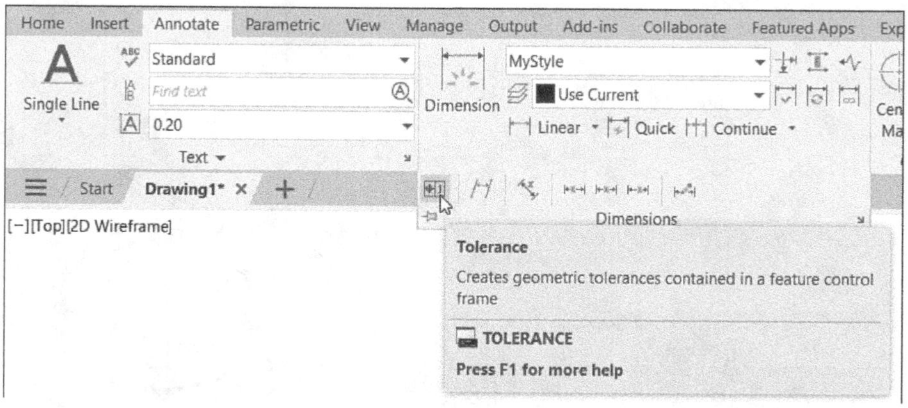

Figure 8-69
Geometric Tolerance dialog box

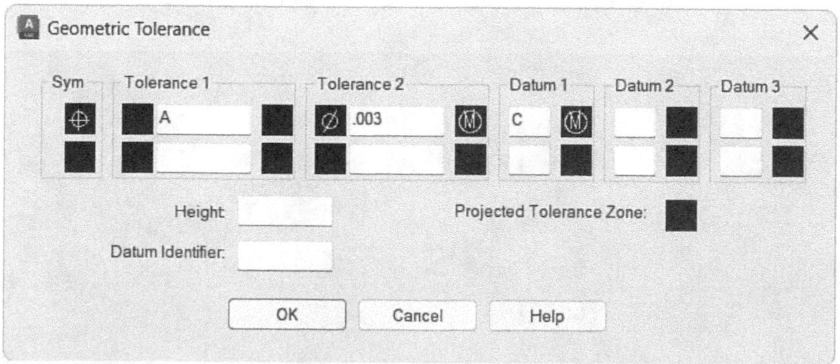

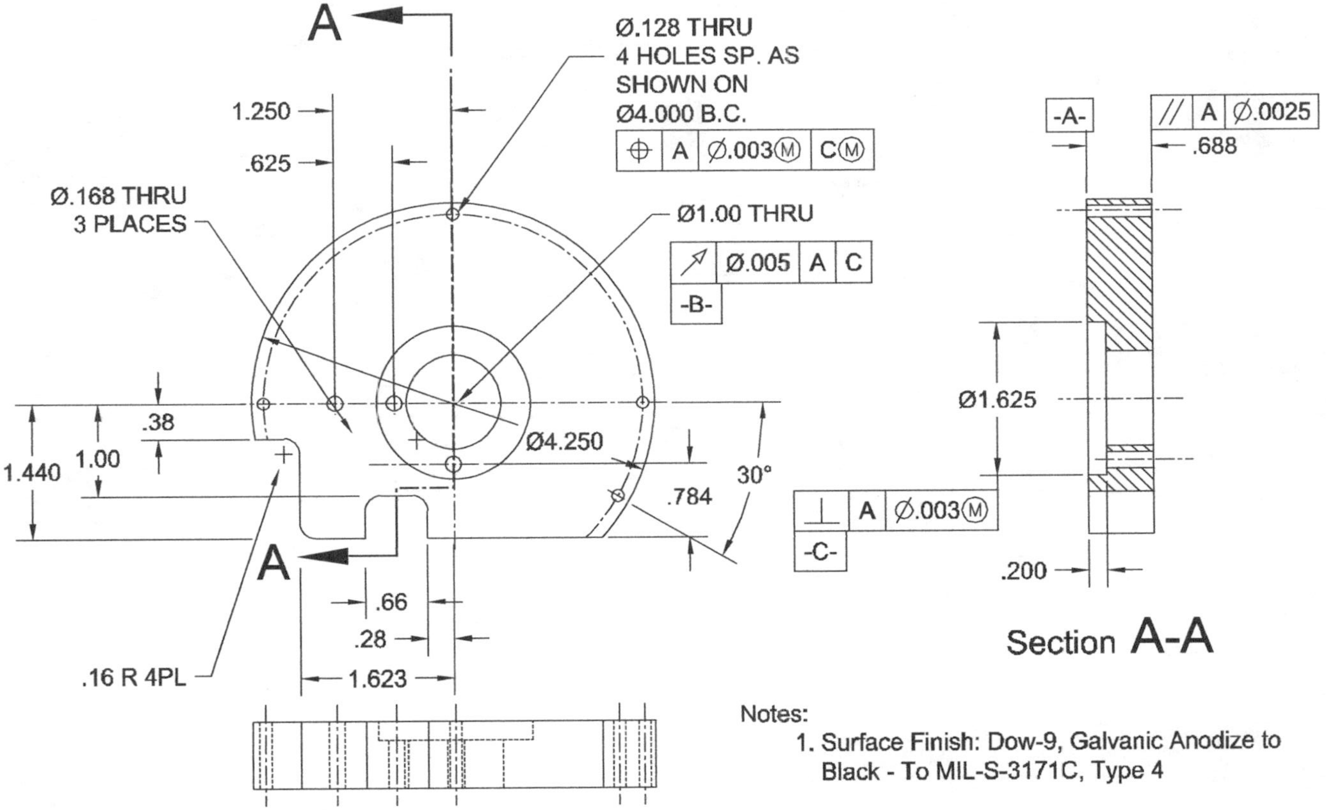

Notes:

1. Surface Finish: Dow-9, Galvanic Anodize to Black - To MIL-S-3171C, Type 4

Drawing 8-8
Mirror Mounting Plate

chapter nine

Polylines

CHAPTER OBJECTIVES

- Draw polygons
- Draw donuts
- Use the **FILL** command
- Draw straight polyline segments
- Draw polyline arc segments
- Edit polylines with **PEDIT**
- Draw splines
- Create path arrays
- Draw revision clouds
- Draw points
- Use constraint parameters
- Use **AutoConstrain** and inferred constraints

Introduction

This chapter should be fun because you will be learning a large number of new commands. You will see new things happening in your drawing with each command. The commands in this chapter are used to create special objects, some of which cannot be drawn any other way. All of them are made up of multiple line and/or arc segments and stored and treated as singular objects. Some of them, such as polygons and donuts, are familiar geometric figures, whereas others, such as polylines, are peculiar to CAD. You also return to the **ARRAY** command to create arrays along curved paths. In addition to these new types of objects, this chapter covers a new drawing method in which you apply geometric and dimensional constraints to previously drawn objects to achieve design objectives.

Drawing Polygons

POLYGON	
Command	POLYGON
Alias	Pol
Panel	Draw
Tool	

Among the most interesting and flexible of the objects you can create in AutoCAD is the *polyline*, a two-dimensional object made of lines and arcs that may have varying widths. In this chapter, you begin with two regularly shaped polyline objects: polygons and donuts. These objects have their own special commands, separate from the general **PLINE** command ("Drawing Straight Polyline Segments" and "Drawing Polyline Arc Segments" sections), but are created as polylines and can be edited just as any other polyline would be.

> **TIP**
>
> The following is a general procedure for drawing polygons:
>
> 1. On the **Home** tab of the ribbon, in the **Draw** panel, click the **Polygon** tool from the **Rectangle/Polygon** drop-down menu.
> 2. Type the number of sides.
> 3. Specify a center point.
> 4. Indicate inscribed or circumscribed.
> 5. Specify the radius of the circle.

Polygons with any number of sides can be drawn using the **POLYGON** command. In the default sequence, polygons are created based on the number of sides, a center point, and a radius. Optionally, the **Edge** option allows you to specify the number of sides and the length and position of one side (see Figure 9-1).

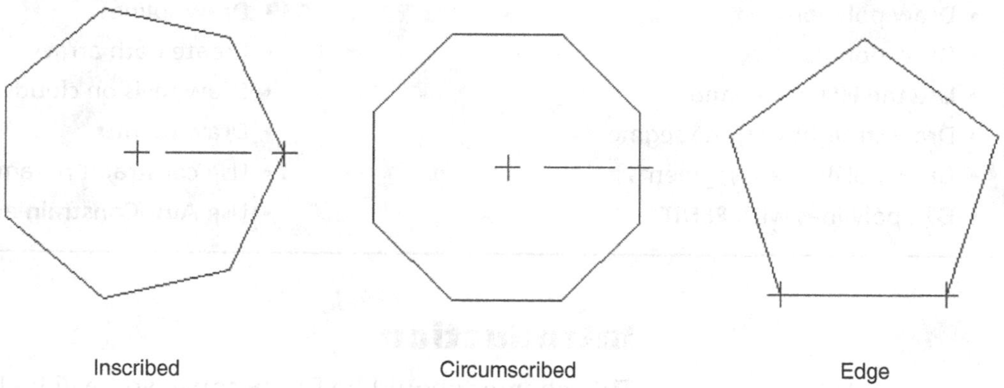

Figure 9-1
Polygon drawing methods

✔ Create a new drawing with 18 × 12 limits.

✔ On the **Home** tab of the ribbon, in the **Draw** panel, click the **Polygon** tool from the **Rectangle/Polygon** drop-down menu, as shown in Figure 9-2.

AutoCAD's first prompt is for the number of sides:

```
Enter number of sides <4>:
```

Figure 9-2
Polygon tool

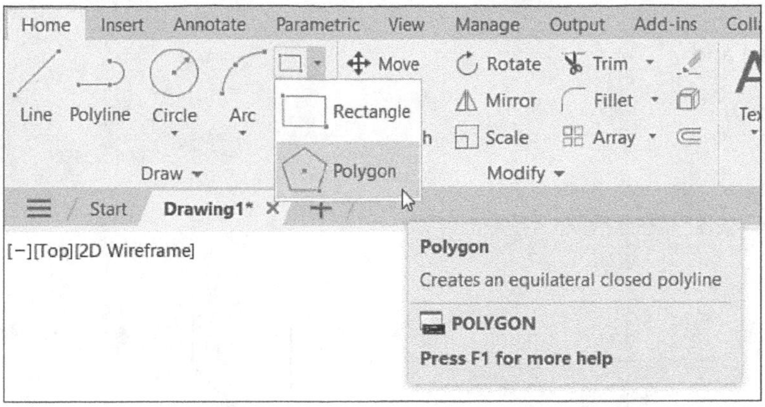

✔ Type **8 <Enter>**.

Next, you are prompted to specify either a center point or the first point of one edge:

```
Specify center of polygon or [Edge]:
```

✔ Specify a center point, as shown by the center mark on the left in Figure 9-3.

From here, the size of the polygon can be specified in one of two ways, as shown in Figure 9-1. The radius of a circle is given, and the polygon is drawn either inside or outside the imaginary circle. In the case of the inscribed polygon, this means that the radius is measured from the center to a vertex of the polygon. In the circumscribed polygon, the radius is measured from the center to the midpoint of a side. You indicate which option you want by typing ***i*** *or* ***c*** *or selecting from the dynamic input menu. The prompt is*

```
Enter an option [Inscribed in circle/Circumscribed about
circle]:
```

Inscribed *is the default. You use the* ***Circumscribed*** *option instead.*

✔ Type **c <Enter>** or select **Circumscribed about circle** from the dynamic input menu.

Now, you are prompted to show a radius of this imaginary circle (that is, a line from the center to the midpoint of a side):

```
Specify radius of circle:
```

✔ Specify a radius similar to the one in Figure 9-3.

Feel free to try the ***Inscribed*** *option. Next, you draw one more polygon, using the* ***Edge*** *option.*

Figure 9-3
Polygon **Circumscribed** and **Edge** options

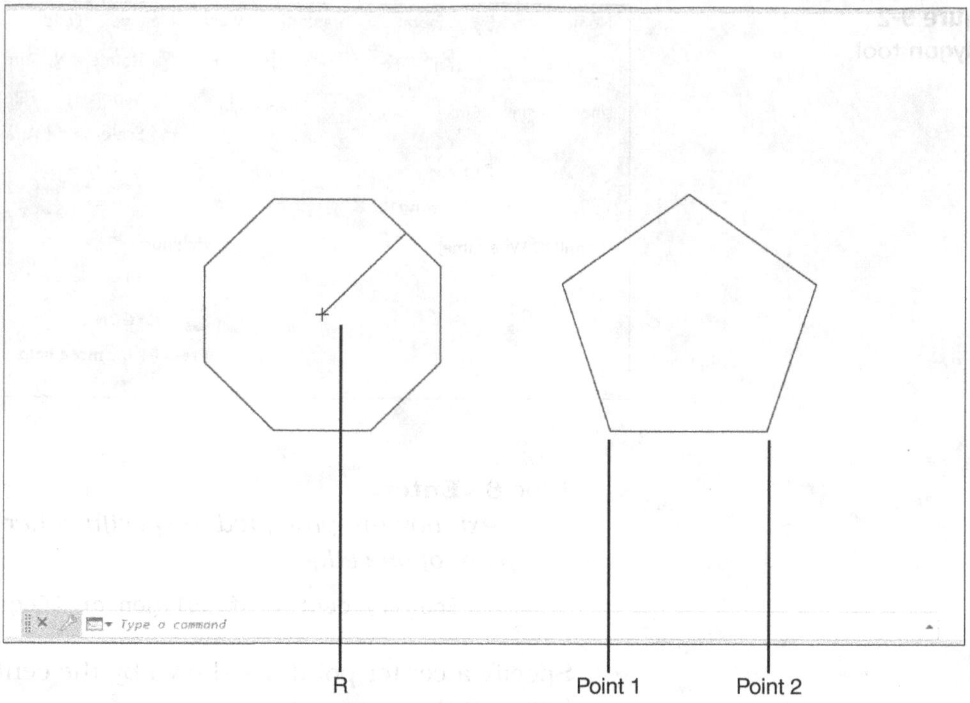

- ✔ Press **<Enter>** or the spacebar to repeat the **POLYGON** command.
- ✔ Type **5 <Enter>** for the number of sides.
- ✔ Type **e <Enter>** or select **Edge** from the command line.
  AutoCAD issues a different series of prompts:

  ```
  Specify first endpoint of edge:
  ```

- ✔ Specify point 1, as shown on the right in Figure 9-3.
  AutoCAD prompts:

  ```
  Specify second endpoint of edge:
  ```

- ✔ Specify a second point as shown.
  Your drawing should resemble Figure 9-3.

Drawing Donuts

DONUT	
Command	DONUT
Alias	Do
Panel	Draw
Tool	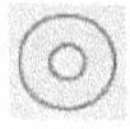

A donut in AutoCAD is a polyline object represented by two arcs that appear to form concentric circles. The area between the two concentric circles is filled like a polyline with a width.

> **TIP**
>
> The following is a general procedure for drawing donuts:
>
> 1. On the ribbon's **Home** tab, expand the **Draw** panel and click the **Donut** tool.
> 2. Type or specify an inside diameter.
> 3. Type or specify an outside diameter.
> 4. Specify a center point.
> 5. Specify another center point.
> 6. Press **<Enter>** to exit the command.

The **DONUT** command is logical and easy to use. You specify a center point and inside and outside diameters and then draw as many donut-shaped objects of the set size as you like.

✔ Erase all the polygons in your drawing before continuing.

✔ On the ribbon's **Home** tab, expand the **Draw** panel and click the **Donut** tool, as shown in Figure 9-4.

AutoCAD prompts:

```
Specify inside diameter of donut <0.50>:
```

You change the inside diameter to 1.00.

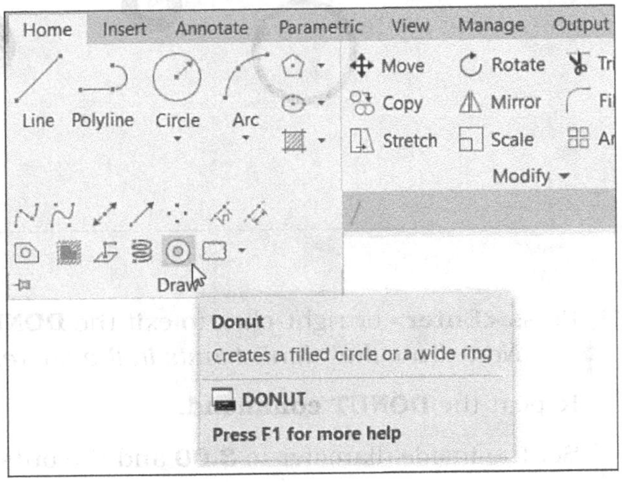

Figure 9-4
Donut tool

✔ Type **1 <Enter>**.

AutoCAD prompts:

```
Specify outside diameter of donut <1.00>:
```

You change the outside diameter to 2.00.

✔ Type **2 <Enter>**.

AutoCAD prompts:

```
Specify center of donut or [exit]:
```

✔ Specify any point in the drawing.

A donut is drawn around the chosen point, as shown by the "fat" donuts in Figure 9-5. (If your donut is not filled, see the next section, "Using the FILL Command.")

*AutoCAD stays in the **DONUT** command, allowing you to continue drawing donuts.*

✔ Specify a second center point.

✔ Specify a third center point.

You should now have three "fat" donuts in your drawing, as shown in Figure 9-5.

Figure 9-5
Donuts drawn with **FILL** on

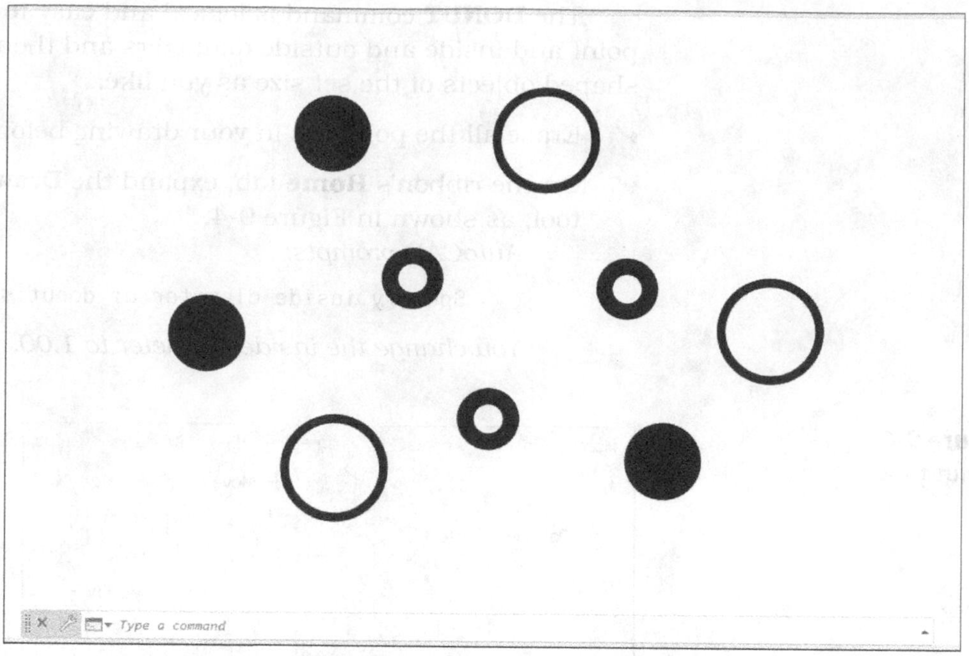

- ✔ Press **<Enter>** or right-click to exit the **DONUT** command.
  Now draw the "thin" donuts in the figure.
- ✔ Repeat the **DONUT command.**
- ✔ Set the inside diameter to **3.00** and the outside diameter to **3.25**.
- ✔ Draw three or four "thin" donuts, as shown in Figure 9-5.
  *When you are done, leave the donuts in the drawing so that you can see how they are affected by the **FILL** command.*

> **TIP**
> If you specify an inside diameter of **0 (zero)**, the center of the donut will be closed, as shown in Figure 9-5.

Using the FILL Command

Donuts and polylines with a width (in the "Drawing Straight Polyline Segments" and "Drawing Polyline Arc Segments" sections) are all affected by **FILL**. With **FILL** on, these objects are displayed and plotted as solid filled objects. With **FILL** off, only the outer boundaries are displayed. (Donuts are shown with radial lines between the inner and outer circles.)

> **TIP**
> The following is a general procedure for turning **FILL** on and off:
> 1. Type **fill <Enter>** at the command prompt.
> 2. Type **on** or **off <Enter>**, or select one of the options from the command line.
> 3. Type **regen <Enter>** at the command prompt.

✔ For this exercise, you should have at least one donut in your drawing from the "Drawing Donuts" section.

✔ Type **fill <Enter>** at the command prompt.

AutoCAD prompts:

```
Enter Mode [ON/OFF] <ON>:
```

These options are also shown on the dynamic input menu.

✔ Select **OFF** from the dynamic input menu.

You do not see any immediate change in your display when you do this. To see the effect, you have to regenerate your drawing.

✔ Type **regen <Enter>** at the command prompt.

*Your drawing is regenerated with **FILL** off and should resemble Figure 9-6. Many of the special objects discussed in the remainder of this chapter can be filled, so make sure to continue to experiment with **FILL** as you go along.*

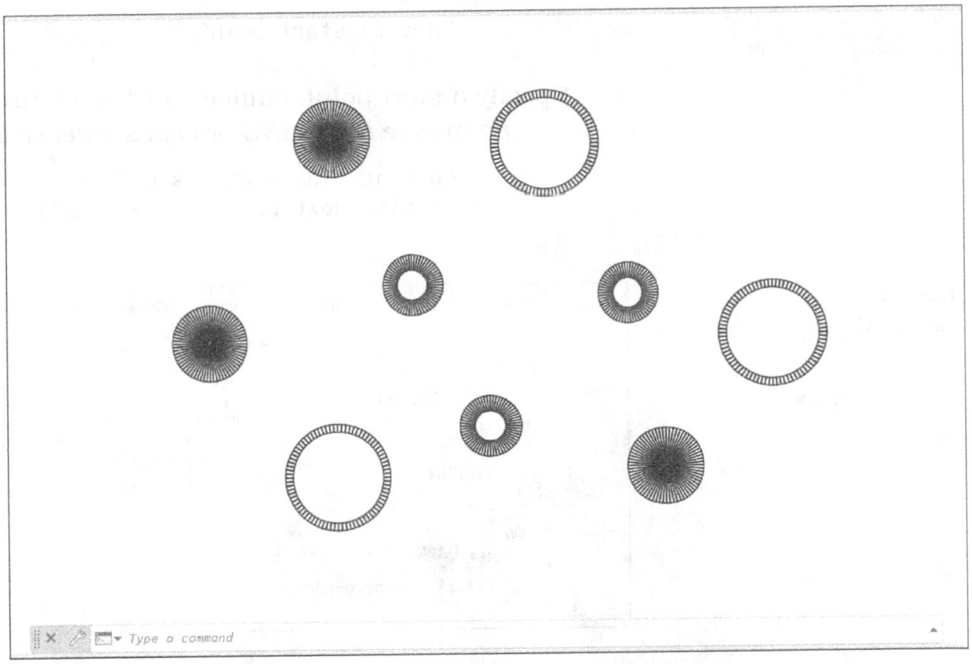

Figure 9-6
Donuts drawn with **FILL** off

Drawing Straight Polyline Segments

PLINE	
Command	PLINE
Alias	Pl
Panel	Draw
Tool	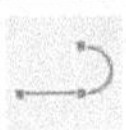

Text, dimensions, and hatch patterns are all created from multiple objects that are combined into a single complex object. In these next sections, you focus on polylines. You have already drawn several polylines without using the **PLINE** command. Donuts and polygons both are drawn as polylines and therefore can be edited using the same edit commands that work on polylines. You can, for instance, fillet all the corners of a polygon at once, using the **Polyline** option of the **FILLET** command. Using the **PLINE** command itself, you can draw anything from a simple line to a series of lines and arcs with varying widths. Most important, you can edit polylines using many of the ordinary edit commands and a set of specialized editing procedures found in the **PEDIT** command.

TIP

The following is a general procedure for drawing straight polylines:

1. Click **Home** tab > **Draw** panel > **Polyline** tool on the ribbon.
2. Specify a start point.
3. Type or select **Width**, **Halfwidth**, or other options from the command line.
4. Specify other points.

You begin by creating a simple polyline rectangle. The process is much like drawing a rectangular outline with the **LINE** command, but the result is a single object rather than four distinct line segments.

✔ Erase the donuts from your drawing before continuing.

✔ Click **Home** tab > **Draw** panel > **Polyline** tool on the ribbon, as shown in Figure 9-7.

AutoCAD begins with a prompt for a starting point, like the ***LINE*** *command:*

```
Specify start point:
```

✔ Specify a start point, similar to P1 in Figure 9-8.

From here the ***PLINE*** *prompt sequence becomes more complicated:*

```
Current line width is 0.00
Specify next point or [Arc/Halfwidth/Length/Undo/Width]:
```

Figure 9-7
Polyline tool

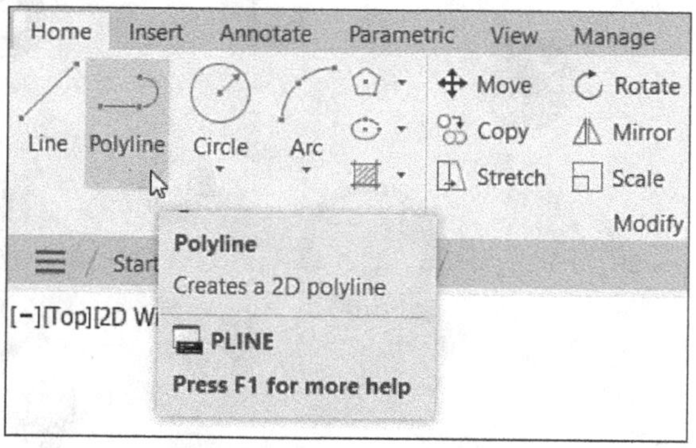

The prompt begins by giving you the current line width, left over from the previous use of the ***PLINE*** *command in the open drawing.*

Then, the prompt offers options in the usual format. The ***Arc*** *option leads you to another set of options that deals with drawing polyline arcs. You learn to draw polyline arcs in the next section. Before then, you learn about other options momentarily.*

Here, you draw a series of 0-width segments, just as you would with the ***LINE*** *command.*

Figure 9-8
Drawing a closed polyline rectangle

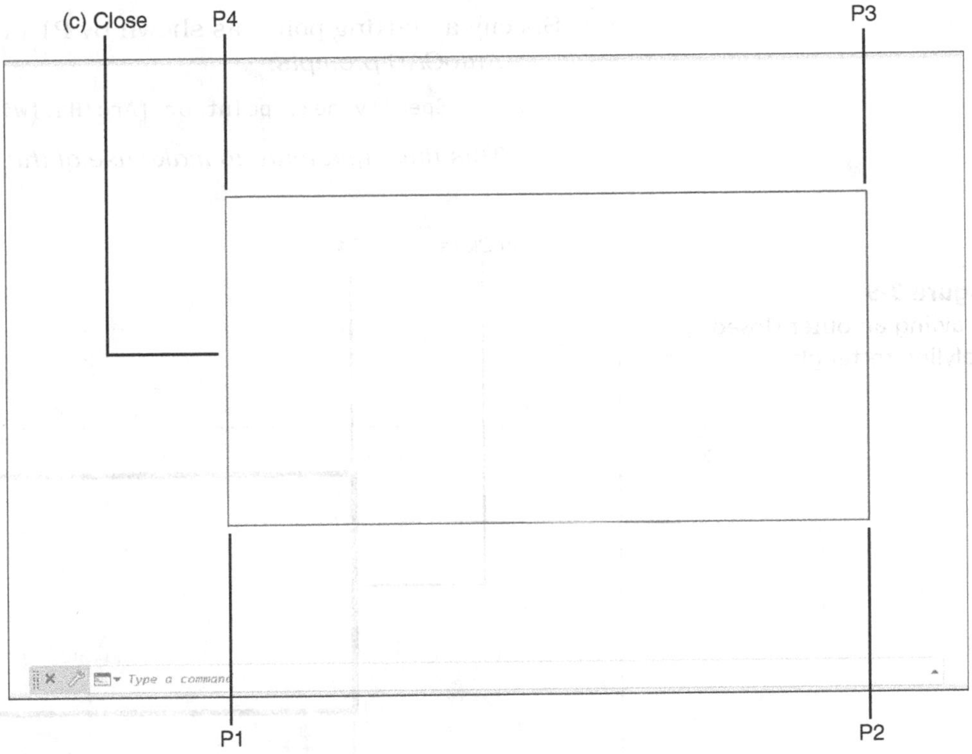

> **NOTE**
> The **Close** option is very important in drawing closed polylines. AutoCAD recognizes the polyline as a closed object only if you use the **Close** option.
> The **Halfwidth** option differs from the **Width** option only in that the width of the line to be drawn is measured from the center out. With either option, you can specify by showing a width rather than typing a value.

✔ Specify a point, similar to P2 in Figure 9-8.

*AutoCAD draws the segment and repeats the prompt. Notice that after you have specified two points, the **Close** option is added to the command prompt.*

✔ Specify another point, P3 in Figure 9-8.

✔ Specify another point, P4 in Figure 9-8.

✔ Type **c <Enter>** or right-click and select **Close** from the shortcut menu to complete the rectangle, as shown in Figure 9-8.

✔ Now, move the cursor over any part of the polyline rectangle.

You can see that the entire rectangle is highlighted, rather than only the line segment under the crosshairs being highlighted. This means all line segments drawn are part of the same object. Because of this, you could fillet or chamfer all four corners of the rectangle at once.

Now, let's create a rectangle with wider lines.

✔ Repeat the **PLINE** command.

✔ Specify a starting point, as shown by P1 in Figure 9-9.

AutoCAD prompts:

```
Specify next point or [Arc/Halfwidth/Length/Undo/Width]:
```

This time, you want to make use of the ***Width*** *option.*

Figure 9-9
Drawing an outer closed polyline rectangle

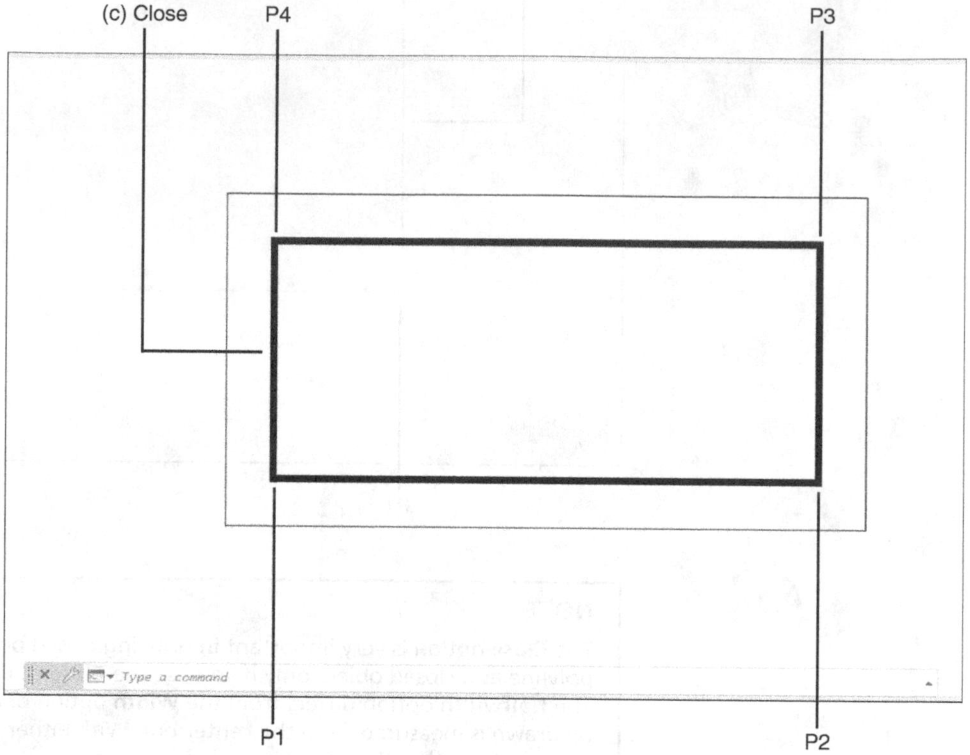

✔ Type **w <Enter>** or select **Width** from the command line.

AutoCAD shows a dashed and yellow-colored rubber band and responds with this prompt:

```
Specify starting width <0.00>:
```

You are prompted for starting and ending widths. This makes it possible to draw tapered lines. For this exercise, the lines have the same starting and ending width.

✔ Type **.25 <Enter>**.

AutoCAD prompts:

```
Specify ending width <0.25>:
```

Notice that the starting width has become the default for the ending width. To draw a polyline of uniform width, accept this default.

✔ Press **<Enter>** or the spacebar to keep the starting width and ending width the same.

AutoCAD returns to the previous prompt and gives you a .25-wide rubber band to drag in the drawing area.

✔ Specify a point, as shown by P2 in Figure 9-9.

- ✔ Continue specifying points P3 and P4 to draw a second rectangle, as shown in Figure 9-9. Use the **Close** option to draw the last side.

  *When the rectangle is complete, AutoCAD joins the endpoint of the last segment to the start point of the first segment drawn. If you do not close the last side but draw a line segment to the start point, the last and first segments drawn intersect and are not joined. Be aware also that once a polyline has been given a width, it is affected by the **FILL** setting, which was demonstrated in the previous section with donuts.*

The only options that have not been discussed in this exercise are **Length** and **Undo**. **Length** allows you to type or specify a value and then draw a segment of that length starting from the endpoint of the previous segment and continuing in the same direction. (If the last segment was an arc, the length is drawn tangent to the arc.) **Undo** undoes the last segment, just as in **LINE**.

In the next section, you draw polyline arc segments.

Drawing Polyline Arc Segments

A word of caution: Because of the flexibility and power of the **PLINE** command, it is tempting to think of polylines as always having weird shapes, tapered lines, and strange sequences of lines and arcs. Remember, **PLINE** may also be used to create simple sets of lines, polygons, or arcs.

> **TIP**
>
> The following is a general procedure for drawing a polyline with arcs:
>
> 1. Enter the **PLINE** command.
> 2. Specify a start point.
> 3. Specify a width.
> 4. Type a <Enter> or select **Arc** from the command line.
> 5. Type or select options or specify a point.

Having said that, you proceed to construct your own weird shape to show what can be done. Here you draw a polyline with three arc segments and one tapered line segment that looks similar to a goosenecked funnel, as shown in Figure 9-10. You may have seen something like it at your local garage.

- ✔ Enter the **PLINE** command.
- ✔ Specify a start point, as shown by P1 in Figure 9-10.
- ✔ Type **w <Enter>** or select **Width** from the command line to set new widths.
- ✔ Type **0 <Enter>** for the starting width.
- ✔ Type **.5 <Enter>** for the ending width.

  AutoCAD shows a wedge-shaped rubber band and prompts for the next point.

- ✔ Move your cursor toward P2 to define the arc direction, as shown in Figure 9-10.

Figure 9-10
Drawing a goosenecked funnel

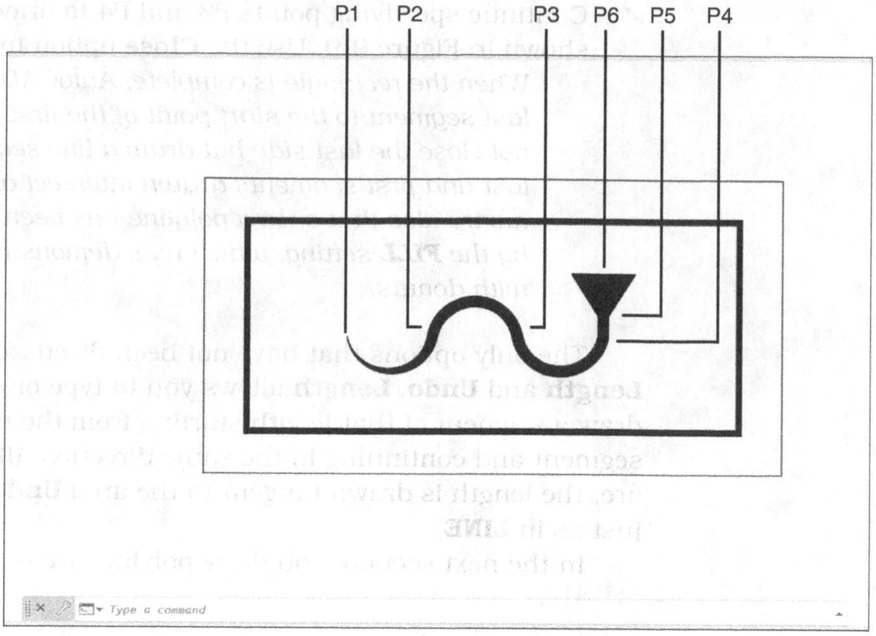

✔ Type **a <Enter>** or right-click and select **Arc** from the shortcut menu.

This opens the arc prompt, which looks like this:

```
Specify endpoint of arc (hold Ctrl to switch direction) or
[Angle/Center/Direction/Halfwidth/Line/Radius/Secondpt/Undo/
Width]:
```

Let's look at this prompt for a moment. To begin with, there are four options that are familiar from the previous prompt. ***Halfwidth***, ***Undo***, *and* ***Width*** *all function exactly as they would in drawing straight polyline segments. The* ***Line*** *option returns you to the previous prompt so that you can continue drawing straight line segments after drawing arc segments.*

The other options, ***Angle***, ***CEnter***, ***Direction***, ***Radius***, ***Secondpt***, *and* ***Endpoint of arc***, *allow you to specify arcs in ways similar to those in the* ***ARC*** *command. AutoCAD assumes that the arc you are constructing will be tangent to the last polyline segment entered. You can override this assumption with the* ***CEnter*** *and* ***Direction*** *options, which allow you to establish different directions.*

✔ Specify a point to the right, as shown by P2 in Figure 9-10, to complete the first arc segment.

TIP

If you did not follow the order shown in the figures and drew your previous rectangle clockwise, or if you drew other polylines in the meantime, you may find that the arc does not curve below the horizontal, as shown in Figure 9-10. This is because AutoCAD starts arcs tangent to the last polyline segment drawn. Fix this by using the **Direction** option. Type **d <Enter>** and then specify a point straight down. Now, you can specify an endpoint to the right, as shown.

AutoCAD prompts again:

```
Specify endpoint of arc or
[Angle/Center/Close/Direction/Halfwidth/Line/Radius/
Secondpt/Undo/Width]:
```

For the remaining two arc segments, retain a uniform width of 0.50.

✔ Specify points P3 and P4 to draw the remaining two arc segments as shown.

Next, you draw two straight segments to complete the polyline.

✔ Right-click and select **Line** from the shortcut menu.

This takes you back to the original prompt.

✔ Specify P5 straight up about 1.00 unit, as shown.

✔ Right-click and select **Width** from the shortcut menu.

✔ Press **<Enter>** to retain 0.50 as the starting width.

✔ Type **3 <Enter>** for the ending width.

✔ Specify a point up about 2.00 units, as shown by P6.

✔ Press **<Enter>** or the spacebar to exit the command.

Your drawing should resemble Figure 9-10.

PEDIT	
Command	PEDIT
Alias	Pe
Panel	Modify
Tool	

Editing Polylines with PEDIT

The **PEDIT** command provides a subsystem of special editing capabilities that work only on polylines. All those options are not covered here. Most important is that you be aware of the possibilities so that when you find yourself in a situation calling for a **PEDIT** procedure, you know what to look for. After executing the following steps, study Figure 9-14, the **PEDIT** chart.

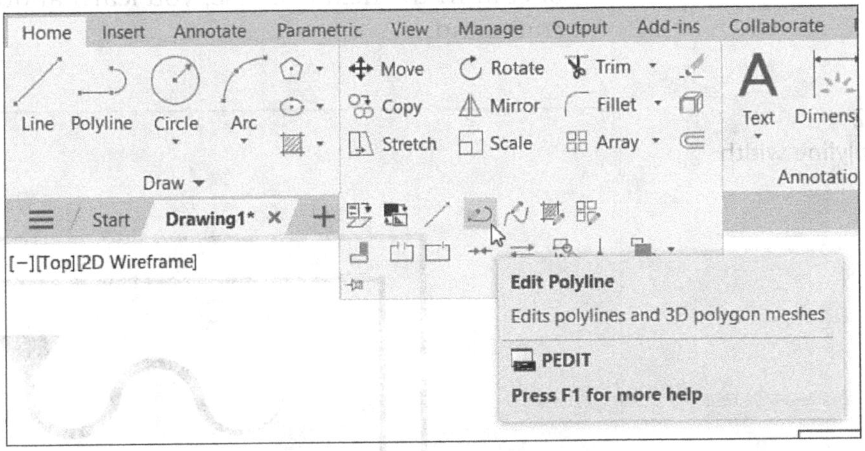

Figure 9-11
Edit Polyline tool

Here, you perform two edits on the polylines already drawn.

✔ On the **Home** tab, expand the **Modify** panel and click **Edit Polyline** tool, as shown in Figure 9-11.

*This starts the **PEDIT** command. You are prompted to select a polyline:*

```
Select polyline or [Multiple]:
```

- ✔ Select the outer 0-width polyline rectangle drawn in the "Drawing Straight Polyline Segments" section.

  *Notice that **PEDIT** works on only one object at a time by default. If you want to modify more than one polyline at a time, use the **Multiple** option. You are prompted as follows:*

```
Enter an option [Open/Join/Width/Edit
vertex/Fit/Spline/Decurve/Ltype gen/Reverse/Undo]:
```

  *These same options are displayed in a drop-down menu on the dynamic input display. **Open** is replaced by **Close** if your polyline has not been closed. **Undo** is self-explanatory. Other options are illustrated in Figure 9-14. **Edit vertex** brings up the subset of options shown on the right side of the chart. When you do vertex editing, AutoCAD marks one vertex at a time with an X. You can move the X to other vertices by pressing **<Enter>** or typing **n** **<Enter>**.*

  Now, you can edit the selected polyline by changing its width.

- ✔ Type **w <Enter>** or select **Width** from the command line.

  This option allows you to set a new uniform width for an entire polyline. All tapering and variation are removed when this edit is performed.

  AutoCAD prompts:

```
Specify new width for all segments:
```

- ✔ Type **.25 <Enter>**.

  Your drawing should now resemble Figure 9-12.

  *The prompt is returned, and the polyline is still selected so that you can continue modifying it with other **PEDIT** options.*

- ✔ Press **<Enter>** or the spacebar to exit **PEDIT**. This exiting and reentering is necessary to select another polyline to edit, using a different type of edit. In the next exercise, you learn another way to enter the **PEDIT** command.

Figure 9-12
Changed polyline width

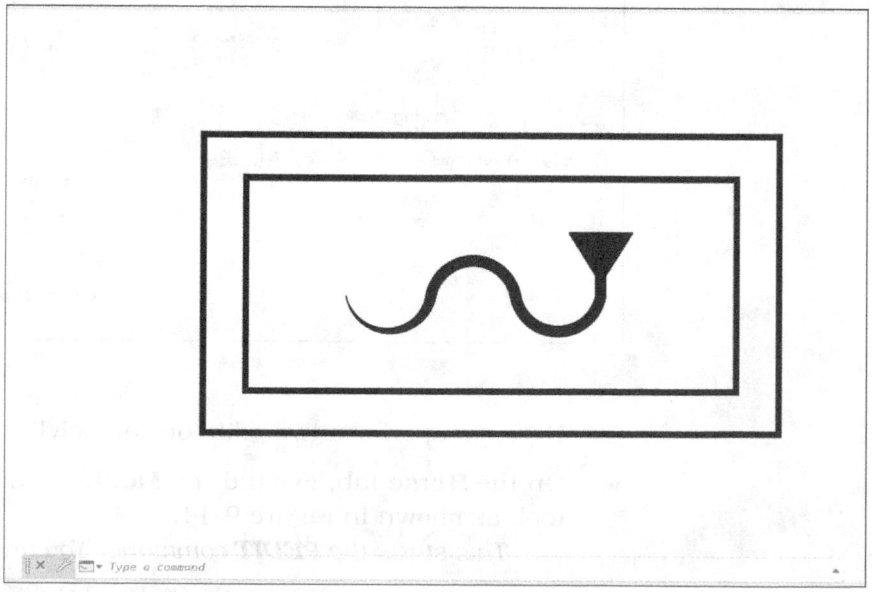

Figure 9-13
Decurved polyline

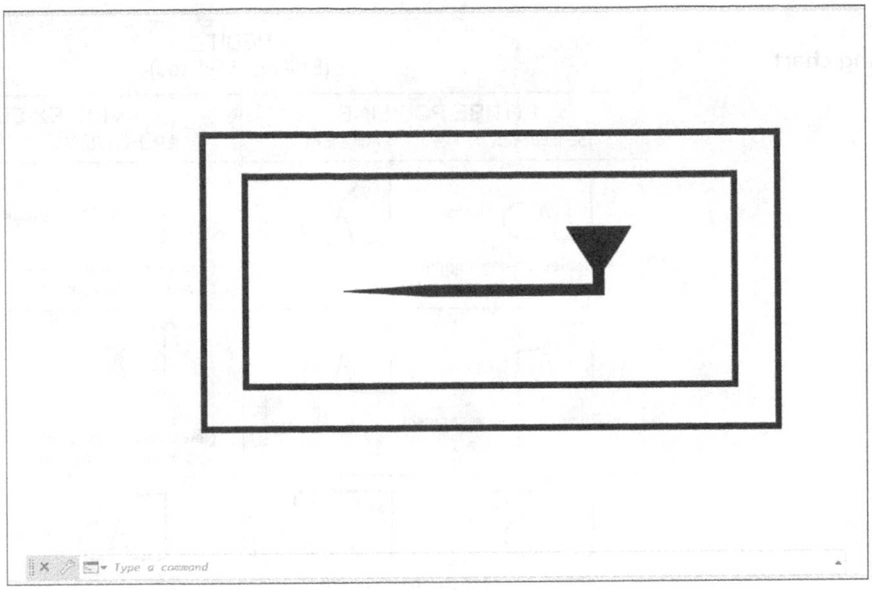

- ✔ Select the polyline that represents the goosenecked funnel.
- ✔ Right-click to open the shortcut menu.
- ✔ Highlight **Polyline** and select **Decurve** from the submenu.
  This time, try the ***Decurve*** *option, which straightens all curves within the selected polyline.*
- ✔ Press **<Esc>** to deselect the polyline.
  Your drawing should resemble Figure 9-13.

To complete this exercise, try some of the other editing options. In particular, you can get interesting results from **Fit** and **Spline**. Be sure to study the **PEDIT** chart (Figure 9-14) before going on to the next exercise.

New to AutoCAD 2023

The end vertices of a polyline can now be extended with grip editing. This allows you to add a new vertex at the beginning or end of a polyline without having to first reverse its direction. Select a polyline to display its grips and then move the cursor over the polyline's first or last grip point, but don't click yet. From the grip menu, select **Extend Vertex** and specify a new point to add a new vertex to the polyline.

Figure 9-14
Polyline editing chart

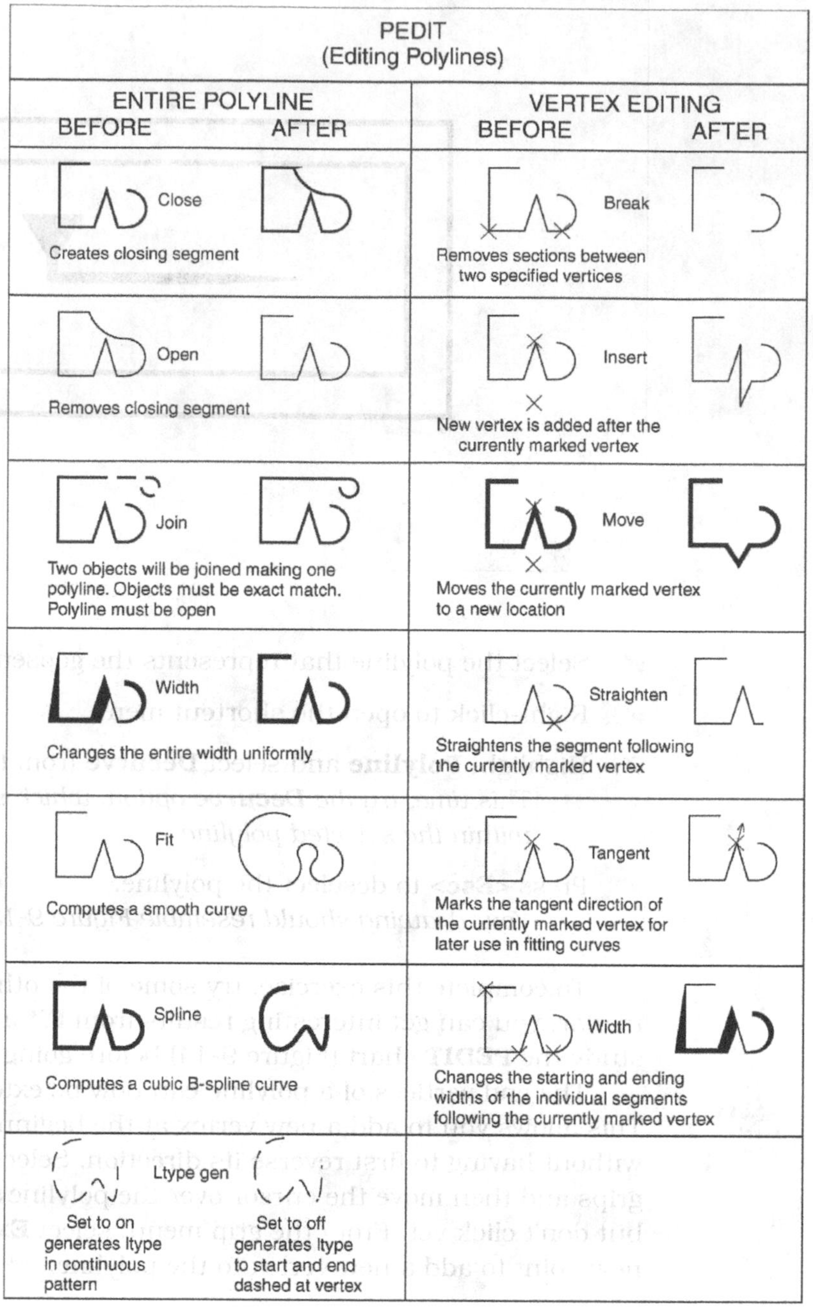
PEDIT
(Editing Polylines)
ENTIRE POLYLINE
BEFORE
AFTER
VERTEX EDITING
BEFORE
AFTER
Close
Creates closing segment
Break
Removes sections between two specified vertices
Open
Removes closing segment
Insert
New vertex is added after the currently marked vertex
Join
Two objects will be joined making one polyline. Objects must be exact match. Polyline must be open
Move
Moves the currently marked vertex to a new location
Width
Changes the entire width uniformly
Straighten
Straightens the segment following the currently marked vertex
Fit
Computes a smooth curve
Tangent
Marks the tangent direction of the currently marked vertex for later use in fitting curves
Spline
Computes a cubic B-spline curve
Width
Changes the starting and ending widths of the individual segments following the currently marked vertex
Ltype gen
Set to on generates ltype in continuous pattern
Set to off generates ltype to start and end dashed at vertex

Drawing Splines

SPLINE	
Command	SPLINE
Alias	Spl
Panel	Draw
Tool	

A ***spline*** is a smooth curve passing through or near a specified set of points. In AutoCAD, splines are created in a precise mathematical form called *nonuniform rational B-spline* (NURBS). Splines can be drawn to fit the specified points or to be controlled by a framework of vertices. In either case, you can draw splines with varying degrees of tolerance, meaning the degree to which the curve is constrained by the defining points. In addition to tolerance and the set of points needed to define a spline, you can specify

spline: A smooth curve passing through or near a specified set of points according to a mathematical formula.

tangent directions for the starting and ending portions of the curve. You can use splines to create any smooth curve that can be defined by a set of control points. In this exercise, you use a simple **SPLINE** with fit points to draw a curve surrounding the polylines drawn in previous sections.

TIP

The following is a general procedure for drawing spline curves:

1. On the ribbon's **Home** tab, expand the **Draw** panel and click the **Spline Fit** tool.
2. Specify points.
3. Close or specify start and end tangent directions.

✔ On the ribbon's **Home** tab, expand the **Draw** panel and click the **Spline Fit** tool, as shown in Figure 9-15.

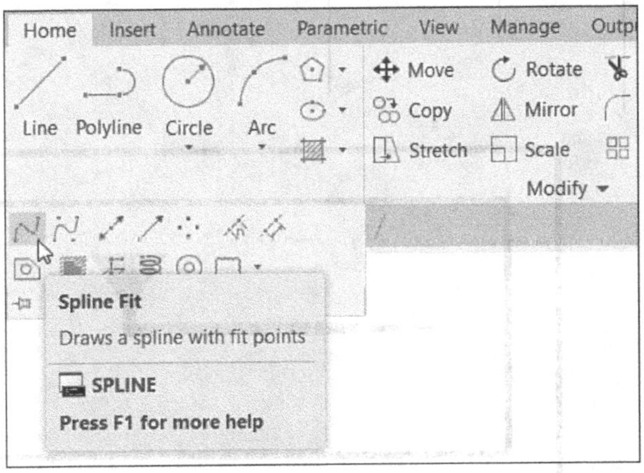

Figure 9-15
Spline Fit tool

AutoCAD prompts:

```
Specify first point or [Method/Knots/Object]:
```

Specify a point. The ***Method*** *option allows you to switch from the fit point method to a control vertices method.* ***Knots*** *gives you a choice among three ways in which the spline curve may fit the specified points. Based on distinct mathematical formulae, each yields a slightly different curve.* ***Object*** *converts polylines to equivalent splines.*

NOTE

Next to the **Spline Fit** tool on the **Modify** panel is the **Spline CV** tool. With **Spline CV**, you can create a spline curve using control points, or control vertices, instead of fit points. In this case, the spline curve is drawn with mathematical tendencies in the direction of all control points but may not pass through these points.

✔ Specify a point roughly 1.00 unit to the left of the top element of the horizontal polyline, P1, as shown in Figure 9-16.

AutoCAD prompts:

```
Enter next point or [start Tangency/tolerance/Undo]:
```

You can continue to enter fit points, specify a tangent direction for the beginning of the curve, or specify a tolerance value.

✔ Specify a second point about 1.00 unit above the left side of the horizontal polyline, P2, as shown in Figure 9-16.

As soon as you have two points, AutoCAD shows a spline as you specify a third point. The prompt also changes:

```
Enter next point or [end Tangency/tolerance/Undo]:
```

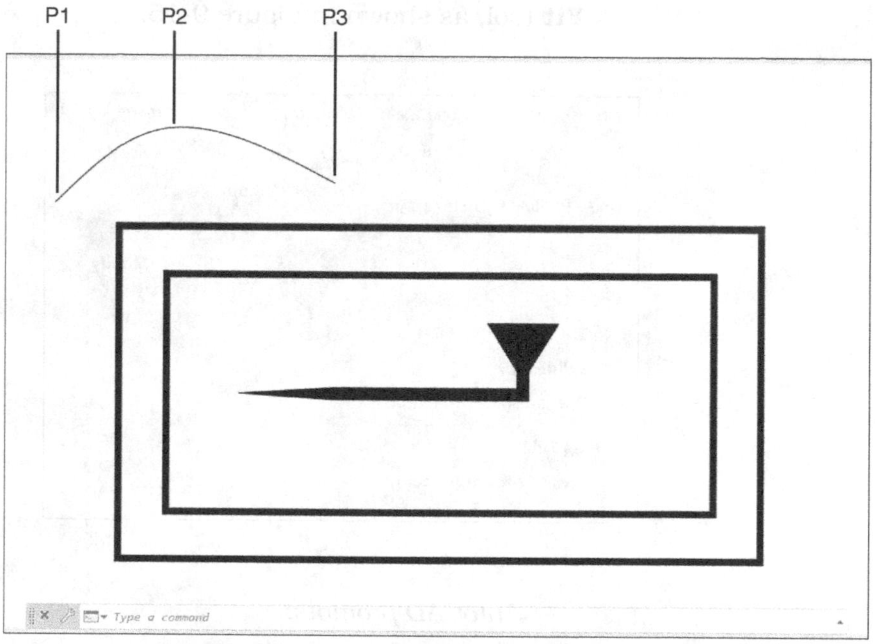

Figure 9-16
Specify points P1, P2, P3 then press **<Enter>**

End Tangency *has replaced* ***start Tangency****;* ***toLerance*** *is still available for change, and you can undo your last segment.*

✔ Specify a third point, P3, as shown in Figure 9-16.

Now that you have three points, the ***Close*** *option is added. From here on, you are on your own as you continue entering points to surround the polylines. No attempt to specify precise points was made in this exercise. 12 points were used to go all the way around without crossing the polylines, as shown in Figure 9-17. The exact number of points you choose is not important for this exercise.*

Figure 9-17
Specify points P1 to P12 then press <Enter>

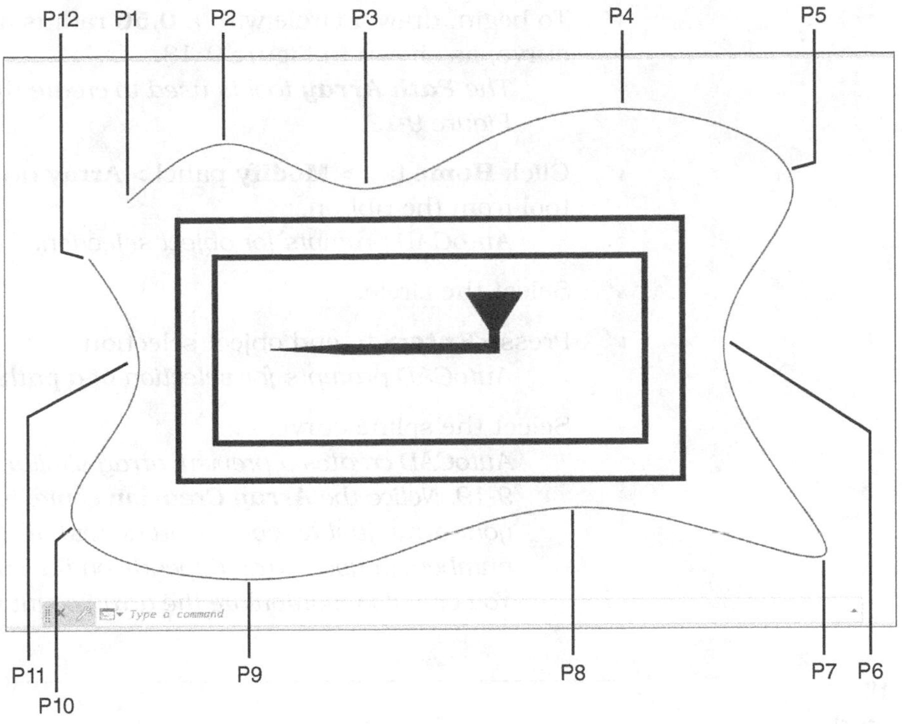

✔ Continue specifying points to surround the polylines without touching them.

✔ After you reach and specify a point similar to P12 in Figure 9-17, press **<Enter>** or the spacebar.

This indicates that you are finished specifying points.

Your drawing should now resemble Figure 9-17.

Editing Splines

Splines can be edited in the usual ways, but they also have their own specialized edit command, **SPLINEDIT**. Because splines are defined by sets of points, one useful option is to use grips to move those points. The **SPLINEDIT** command gives you additional options, including options to change the tolerance, add fit points for greater definition, or delete unnecessary points. An open spline can be closed, or the start and end tangent directions can be changed. To access **SPLINEDIT**, expand the **Modify** panel on the **Home** tab and click the **Edit Spline** tool.

Creating Path Arrays

path array: An array created by copying objects repeatedly at regular intervals along a selected linear or curved path.

Spline curves and polylines present good opportunities to create ***path arrays***. You already know how to draw rectangular and polar arrays. Path arrays are very similar but are drawn along a path rather than in a rectangular or circular matrix. For this quick demonstration, you add a circle to the drawing and array it along the spline curve you have just drawn. Much of what you know about arrays applies equally to path arrays.

✔ To begin, draw a circle with a **0.50** radius at the lower end of the spline curve, as shown in Figure 9-18.

*The **Path Array** tool is used to create the array of circles shown in Figure 9-19.*

✔ Click **Home** tab > **Modify** panel > **Array** drop-down menu > **Path Array** tool from the ribbon.

AutoCAD prompts for object selection.

✔ Select the circle.

✔ Press **<Enter>** to end object selection.

AutoCAD prompts for selection of a path curve.

✔ Select the spline curve.

*AutoCAD creates a preview array similar to the one shown in Figure 9-19. Notice the **Array Creation** contextual tab. Here, you can modify your array just as you would do with rectangular and polar arrays. The numbers in your array depends on the size and shape of your curve. You can also manipulate the array count using the arrow-shaped grip.*

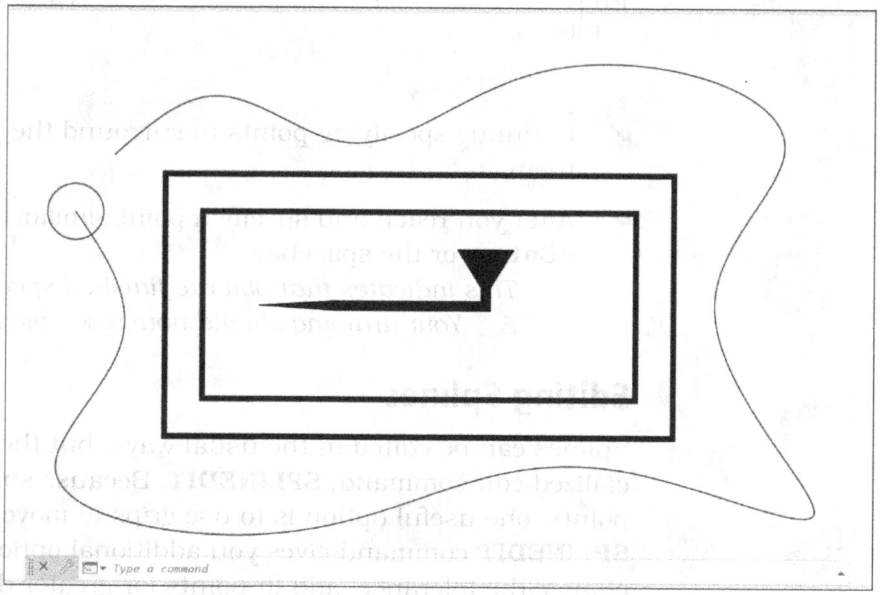

Figure 9-18
Drawing a circle

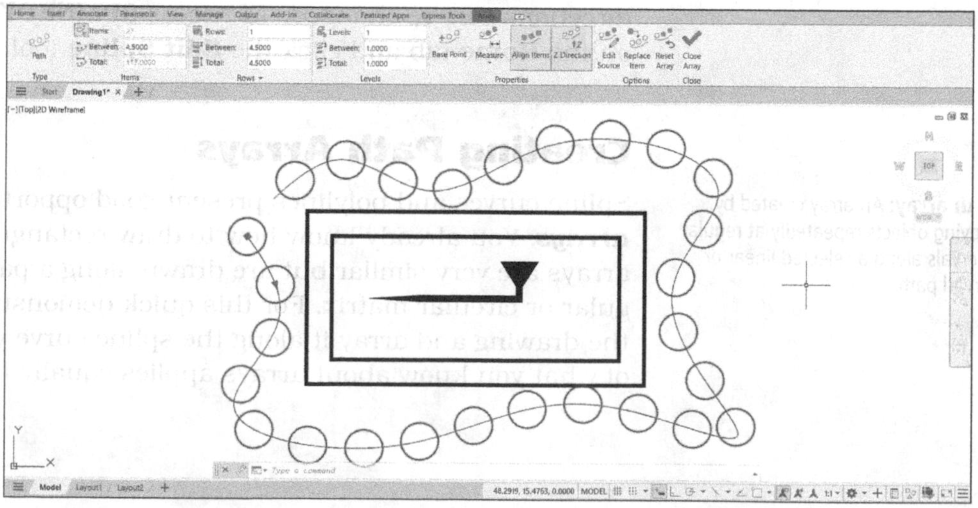

Figure 9-19
Path array preview

- ✔ Try using the edit boxes on the contextual tab or the arrow-shaped grip to create a path array with 10 items, about 5.0 units apart, similar to Figure 9-20.

Figure 9-20
Path array with ten items

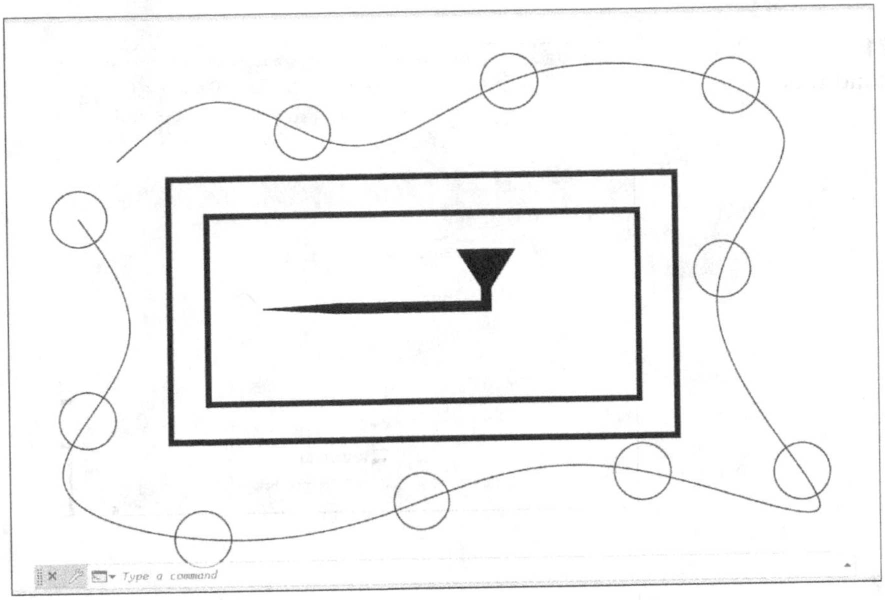

REVCLOUD	
Command	REVCLOUD
Alias	(none)
Panel	Draw
Tool	

revision cloud: A closed object made of many small arcs typically used to surround an area in a drawing to indicate that it has been edited.

Drawing Revision Clouds

Revision clouds are a simple graphical means of highlighting areas in a drawing that have been or need to be edited. They are primarily used in large projects where a number of people are working on a drawing or a set of drawings. Revision clouds can be very quickly created to highlight an error or a place where changes have been made. Their shape is very unlikely to be confused with any actual geometry in your drawing. Try this:

> **TIP**
> The following is a general procedure for drawing a revision cloud:
> 1. Expand the **Draw** panel on the **Home** tab and click the **Freehand** tool from the **Revision Cloud** drop-down menu.
> 2. Specify a start point and draw a rough circle around the desired area.
> 3. Bring the cloud outline back to the start point, and let AutoCAD close the cloud automatically.

- ✔ Expand the **Draw** panel on the **Home** tab and click the **Freehand** tool from the **Revision Cloud** drop-down menu, as shown in Figure 9-21.

  AutoCAD prompts:

```
Specify start point or [Arc length/Object/Rectangular/
Polygonal/Freehand/Style/Modify] <Object>:
```

  Drawing a freehand revision cloud is a simple matter of moving the crosshairs in a circular fashion around an area, as if you were circling an area with a pencil on a paper drawing. You draw a cloud around the open end of the spline curve.

✔ Specify any point about 1.00 unit away from the open left end of the spline curve, as shown in Figure 9-22.

AutoCAD prompts:

```
Guide crosshairs along cloud path...
```

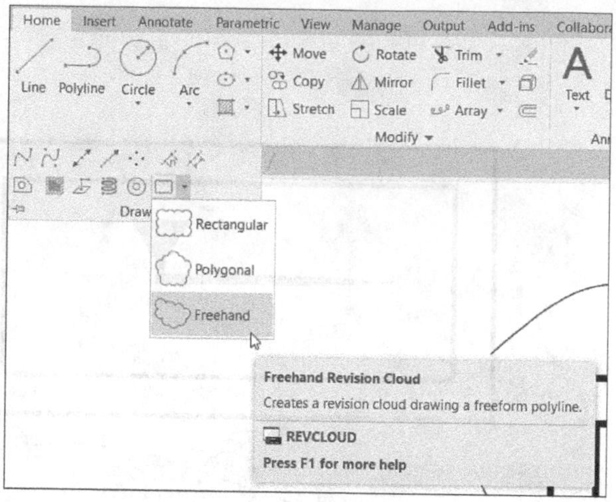

Figure 9-21
Revision Cloud tool

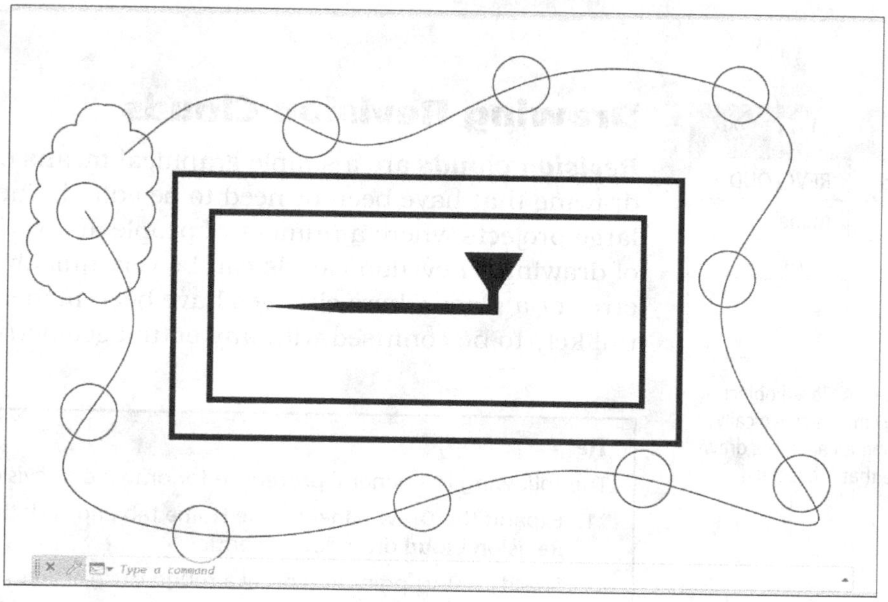

Figure 9-22
Creating a revision cloud

✔ Move the cursor in a rough circle around the open ends of the spline curve to create a cloud similar to the one shown in Figure 9-22.

If snap is on, AutoCAD temporarily turns it off. When you come near the starting point, the cloud closes automatically. Your drawing should resemble Figure 9-22.

Creating Revision Clouds from Drawn Objects

That revision cloud is adequate, but what if you want to create a neater, more precise-looking revision cloud? Revision clouds can be created from circles, rectangles, polygons, or other closed 2D objects. These can be drawn in the usual manner and then converted to clouds using the **Object** option. The **Arc length** option allows you to change the size of the individual arcs that make up the cloud. As you might expect, a completed revision cloud is a polyline. Good practice may require that you create revision clouds on a special layer. You complete this section by creating a revision cloud from a circle and then reversing the small arcs that make up the revision cloud.

- ✔ **Erase** or **Undo** the revision cloud around the open end of the spline curve.
- ✔ Enter the **CIRCLE** command and draw a circle centered between the two endpoints of the curve.
- ✔ Expand the **Draw** panel on the **Home** tab and click any of the **Revision Cloud** tools from the **Revision Cloud** drop-down menu.
- ✔ Press **<Enter>** or the spacebar for the **Object** option.
- ✔ Select the circle.

  AutoCAD converts the circle to a revision cloud and offers you the option of reversing the direction of the arcs.
- ✔ Select **Yes** from the dynamic input display menu.

  Your drawing should resemble Figure 9-23.

Finally, you can create a revision cloud from previously drawn polylines, as long as they are closed.

- ✔ Expand the **Draw** panel on the **Home** tab and click any of the **Revision Cloud** tools from the **Revision Cloud** drop-down menu.
- ✔ Press **<Enter>** or the spacebar for the **Object** option.
- ✔ Select the outer rectangle, created previously in the "Drawing Straight Polyline Segments" section.
- ✔ Press **<Enter>** to complete the command without reversing the arcs.

  Your drawing should resemble Figure 9-24.

Figure 9-23
Converting a circle to a revision cloud

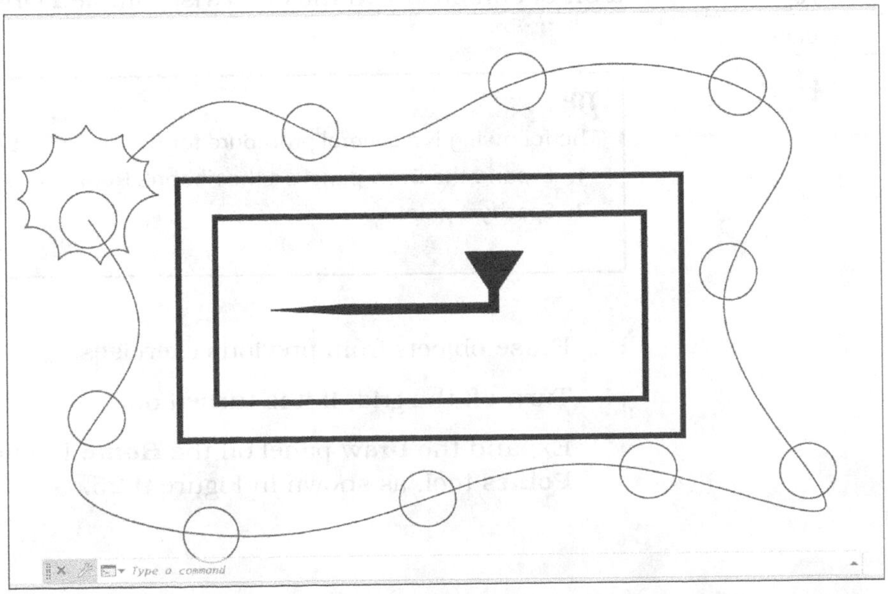

Figure 9-24
Converting a polyline to a revision cloud

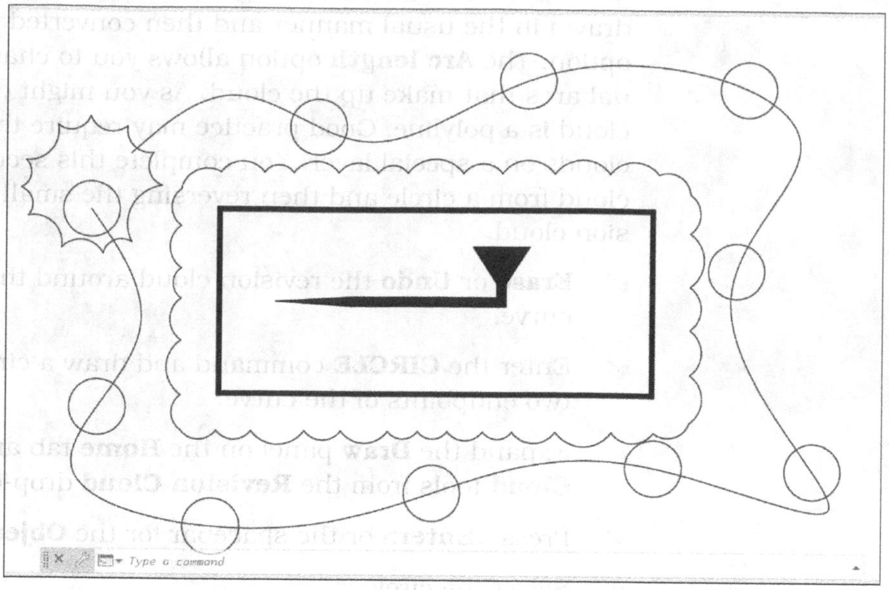

New to AutoCAD 2023

Revision clouds have been updated to make them easier to create and modify. You can now do the following:

- ✔ Set a single arc length value to create more consistency with the arcs in a revision cloud. If you want to have greater variance in the arcs of your revision clouds, try changing the **REVCLOUDARCVARIANCE** system variable.
- ✔ Change the properties of a revision cloud using the **Properties** palette.
- ✔ Reshape a revision cloud with grip editing.

Drawing Points

POINT	
Command	POINT
Alias	Po
Panel	Draw
Tool	

On the surface, this is the simplest draw command in AutoCAD. However, if you look at Figure 9-25, you can see figures that were drawn with the **POINT** command that do not look like ordinary points. This capability adds a bit of complexity to the otherwise simple **POINT** command.

> **TIP**
> The following is a general procedure for drawing point objects:
> 1. Expand the **Draw** panel on the ribbon's **Home** tab and click the **Multiple Points** tool.
> 2. Specify a point.

- ✔ Erase objects from previous exercises.
- ✔ Turn off the grid, if it is turned on.
- ✔ Expand the **Draw** panel on the **Home** tab and click the **Multiple Points** tool, as shown in Figure 9-25.

Figure 9-25
Multiple Points tool

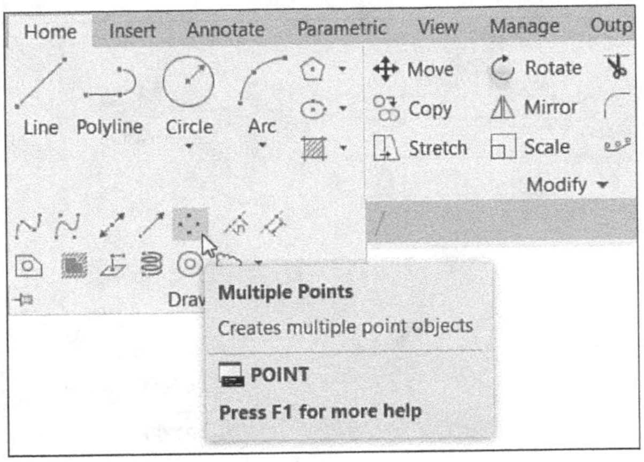

✔ Specify a point anywhere in the drawing area.

AutoCAD places a point at the specified location and prompts for another point. Look closely, and you can see the point you have drawn. Besides those odd instances in which you may need to draw tiny dots like this, points can also serve as object snap nodes and used to divide and measure lines.

What about those circles and crosses in Figure 9-26? AutoCAD has 18 other simple forms that can be drawn as points.

Figure 9-26
Drawing points

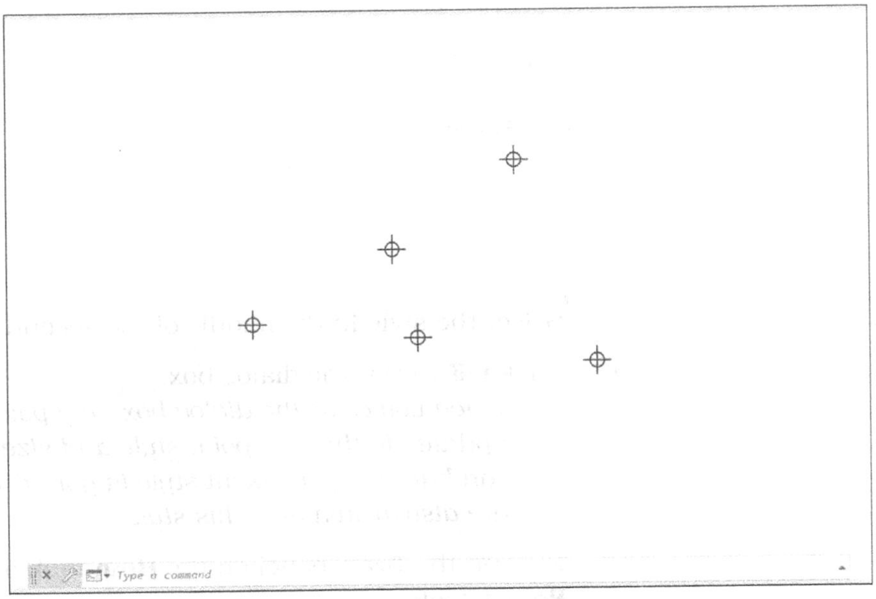

✔ Expand the **Utilities** panel on the **Home** tab and click the **Point Style** tool, as shown in Figure 9-27.

AutoCAD displays the ***Point Style*** *dialog box, which offers a preview of the available styles, as shown in Figure 9-28. Select the point style you want to use and change the size of the points using the* ***Point Size*** *edit box.*

Figure 9-27
Point Style tool

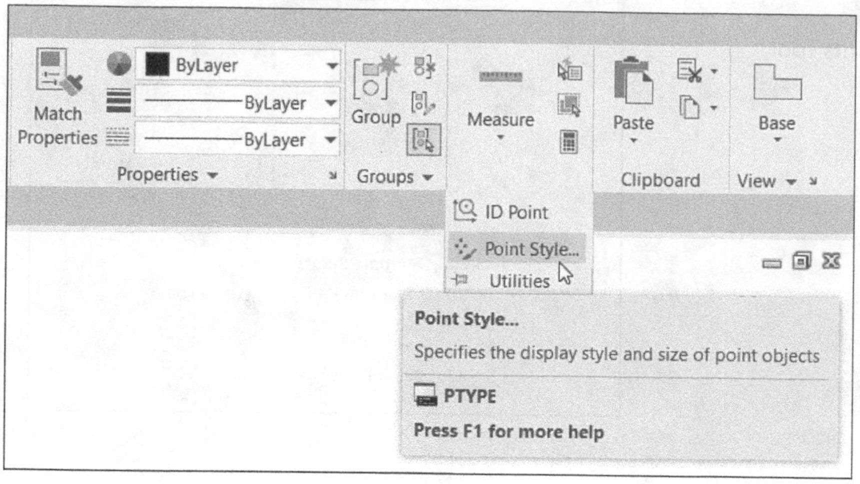

Figure 9-28
Point Style dialog box

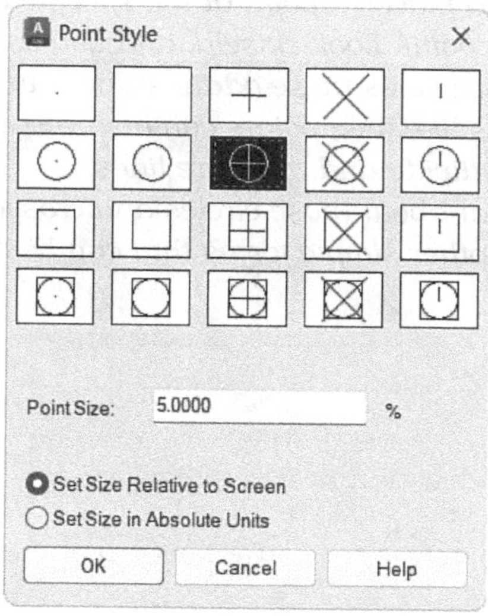

- ✔ Select the style in the middle of the second row.
- ✔ Click **OK** to exit the dialog box.

  When you close the dialog box, any points previously drawn are updated to the new point style and size. Notice that this means you can have only one point style in your drawing at a time. New points are also drawn with this style.

- ✔ Expand the **Draw** panel on the **Home** tab and click the **Multiple Points** tool.
- ✔ Specify a point anywhere in the drawing area.

  AutoCAD draws a point in the chosen style, as shown previously in Figure 9-26.

  *If you clicked the **Multiple Points** tool from the ribbon, AutoCAD continues to prompt for a point until you press **<Esc>** to exit the command. If you entered **POINT** at the command line, you have to repeat the command to draw more points.*

- ✔ Specify another point.

  Draw a few more points or return to the dialog box to try another style.

- ✔ Press **<Esc>** to exit the **POINT** command.

  *Notice that you cannot exit **POINT** by pressing **<Enter>** or the spacebar.*

Using Constraint Parameters

parametric design: The set of processes involved in creating design drawings based on defined relationships and related dimensional values among aspects of a design. Typically, drawings created in this manner can be altered and adjusted when parameter values change.

In this section, you explore an entirely new way to draw in AutoCAD using geometric and dimensional constraints. ***Parametric design*** provides you with a new set of drawing tools and a different way to approach the drawing area. Typically, drawing objects involves specifying points, distances, and angles within a two- or three-dimensional coordinate system. Instead of beginning with specifiable values, in parametric design, you specify a set of geometric ideas and relationships that define the shape you want to draw. The shape is constrained by these values and relationships, but shapes drawn in this way can be updated to show the effect of changing one or more values. When values change, the objects update while maintaining the defined relationships. In essence, this is the approach taken by a designer who wants to create an object fulfilling certain numeric requirements.

In this exercise, you use geometric and dimensional constraints and parameters to draw a parallelogram with two sides double the length of the other two. You do not start with distances and angles—just with these geometric and numeric concepts.

- ✔ To begin, erase all the objects in your drawing.
- ✔ Turn off all the mode buttons on the status bar.

  You should have an empty drawing with none of the usual landmarks and drawing aids active.

- ✔ Enter the **PLINE** command and draw a rough parallelogram like the one shown in Figure 9-29. It may be any size and angle, but be sure to **Close** it.

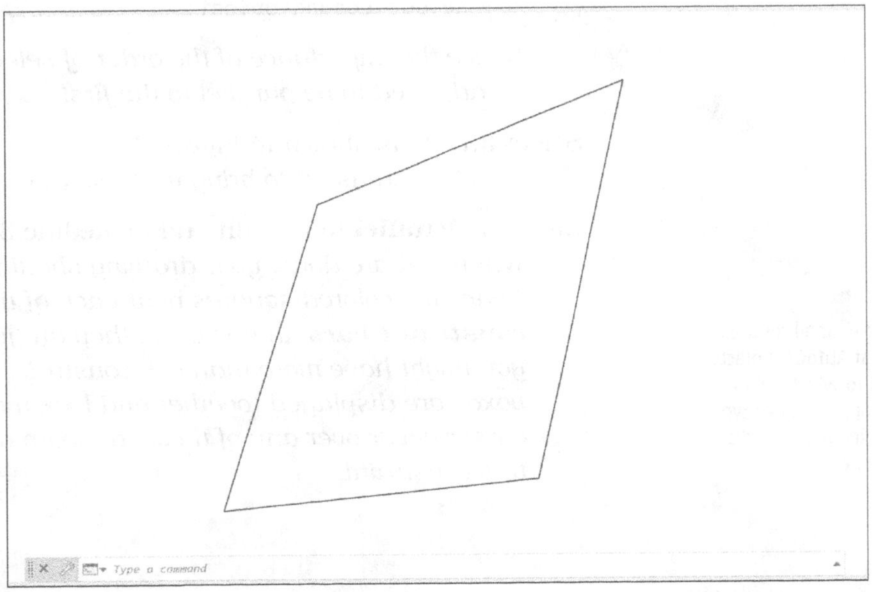

Figure 9-29
Drawing a rough parallelogram

Geometric Constraints

This figure was made very rough on purpose. No doubt, you can draw one that looks a lot more like a parallelogram. However, without snap or other aids, your lines may look parallel but probably are not. Now that you have the basic outline of the shape, you can specify geometric relationships or constraints to turn the sketch into a clearly defined and precise object. For this, you need new tools that are accessible on the **Parametric** tab. On this tab, there are 12 ***geometric constraints*** used to set relationships between drawing objects.

geometric constraint: A property that limits the placement and size of an object in a drawing through specification of its relationship to other objects or to its geometric environment.

✔ Click the **Parametric** tab and then click the **Parallel** tool from the **Geometric** panel, as shown in Figure 9-30.

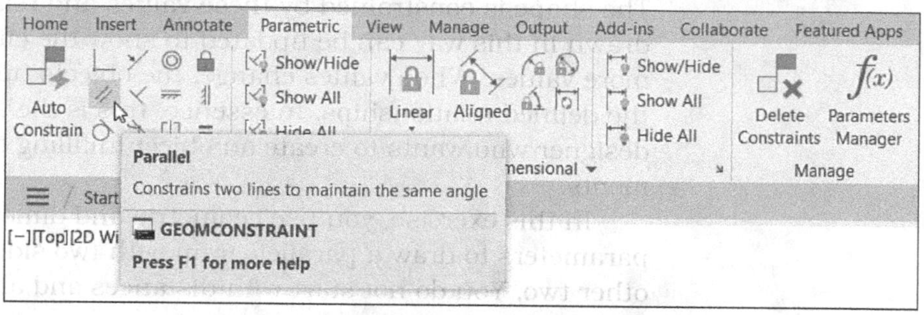

Figure 9-30
Parallel geometric constraint tool

*Observe the **Parametric** tab. There are three panels, covering geometric constraints, dimensional constraints, and constraint management. You use the **Parallel** constraint to make your figure into a true parallelogram. At the command prompt, you see*

```
Select first object:
```

✔ Select line 1, as shown in Figure 9-31.

AutoCAD prompts for a second object:

```
Select second object:
```

Notice the importance of the order of selection. The second object will be adjusted to be parallel to the first.

✔ Select line 2, as shown in Figure 9-31.

Line 2 is adjusted to bring it parallel to line 1.

✔ Click the **Parallel** tool again and make line 3 parallel to line 4.

*When you are done, your drawing should resemble Figure 9-32. Notice the colored squares near each of the lines. These are called **constraint bars**. In this case, they are just single boxes, but often, you might have more than one constraint applied, and then the boxes are displayed together and look more like bars. If you let your cursor hover over any of these, a tooltip appears with the label for this constraint.*

constraint bar: A small square or set of squares that AutoCAD places next to an object to which a constraint has been applied. Each type of constraint has its own icon displayed in the square.

Figure 9-31
Line 2 is adjusted to bring it parallel to Line 1

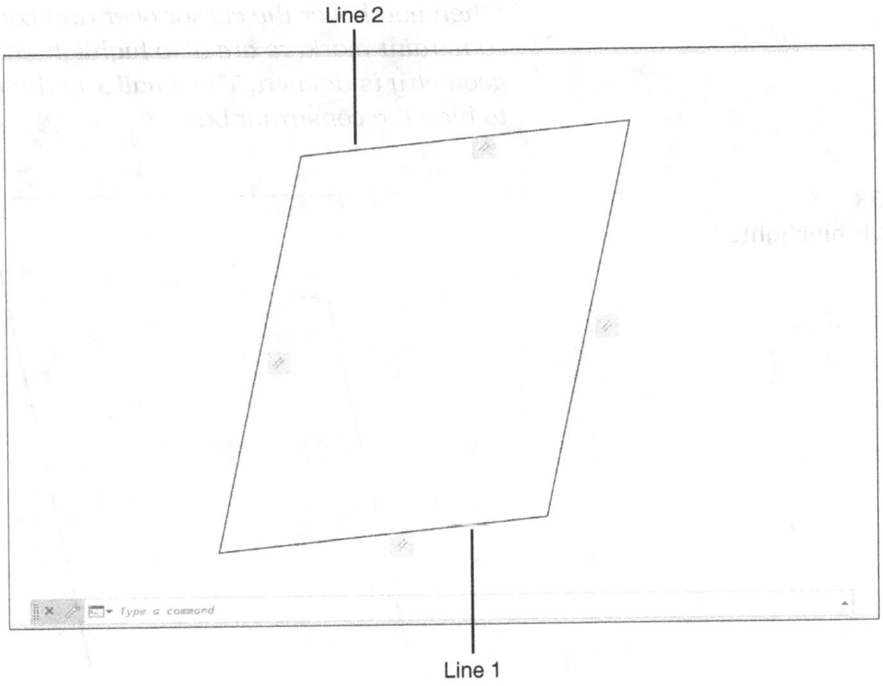

Figure 9-32
Parallel constraint markers

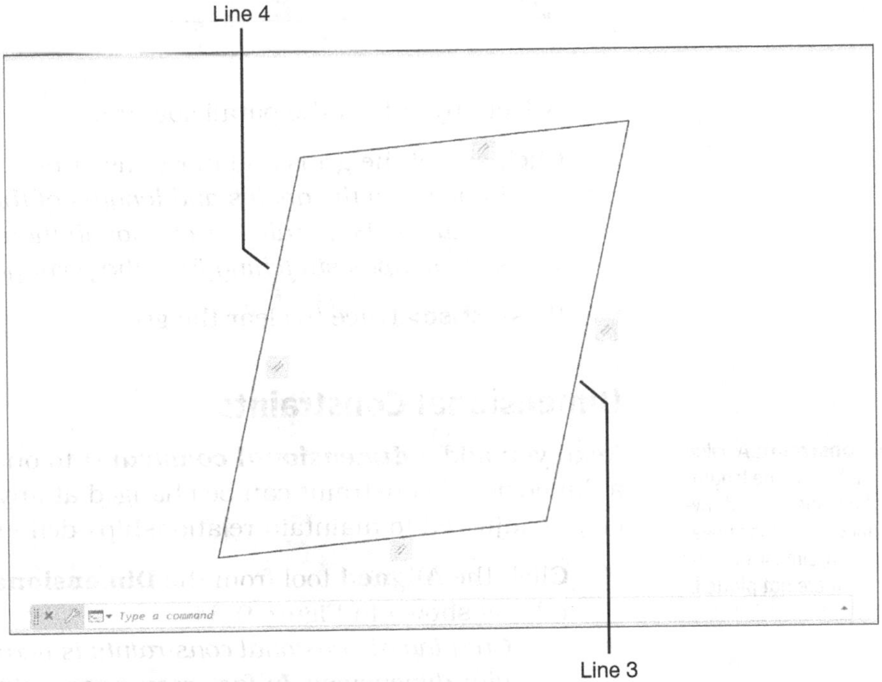

*Each of the geometric constraint tools has its own icon that appears on constraint bars as an indication that these constraints have been applied. Geometric constraints can be shown or hidden in a drawing. If yours are not visible, click the **Show All** tool on the **Geometric** panel.*

✔ Hover your cursor over one of the parallel constraint icons.
The constraint is highlighted, along with the marker on the opposite, parallel side, and the two parallel lines, as shown in Figure 9-33.

When you hover the cursor over any constraint marker, the related constraint markers are also highlighted so you can see how the geometry is defined. The small x to the right of the bar can be used to hide the constraint bar.

Figure 9-33
Constraint is highlighted

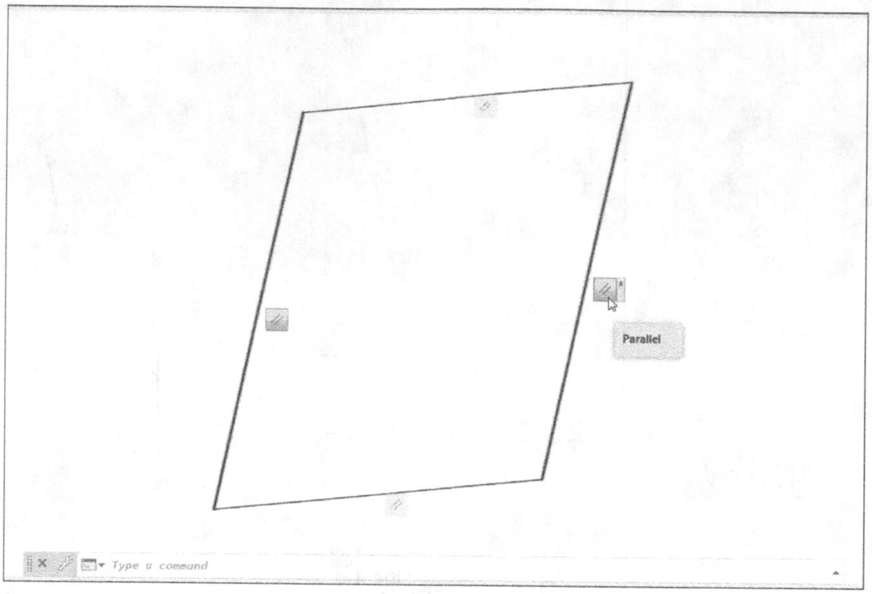

✔ Select any side of the parallelogram.

✔ Click any of the grips and move the cursor.
Notice how the angles and lengths of the sides are now constrained to always be parallel, even though there are still a great many possible shapes stretching from the point you selected.

✔ Press **<Esc>** twice to clear the grips.

Dimensional Constraints

dimensional constraint: A value or expression that limits the length and position of an object in a drawing. Dimensional constraints appear in the drawing area, similar to standard dimensions but are not plotted.

Next, you add a ***dimensional constraint*** to one of the sides. Once defined, a dimensional constraint can be changed at any time, and all related geometry is adjusted to maintain relationships defined by the constraints.

✔ Click the **Aligned** tool from the **Dimensional** panel of the **Parametric** tab, as shown in Figure 9-34.
Creating dimensional constraints is nearly the same as creating regular dimensions. In fact, regular associative dimensions can be converted to dimensional constraints.
AutoCAD prompts:

```
Specify first constraint point or [Object/Point &
line/2Lines] <Object>:
```

✔ Press **<Enter>** to indicate that an object will be selected.

✔ Select line 1, as shown in Figure 9-35.
AutoCAD prompts for a dimension line location.

Figure 9-34
Aligned dimensional constraint tool

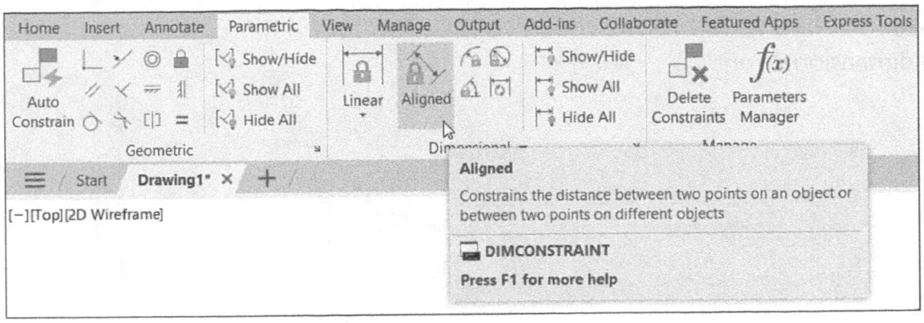

✔ Position the dimensional constraint below line 1, as shown, and then click to place the constraint.

Notice that the text for the dimension is highlighted, and unlike a regular dimension, this constraint has a name (d1).

Figure 9-35
Dimensional constraint

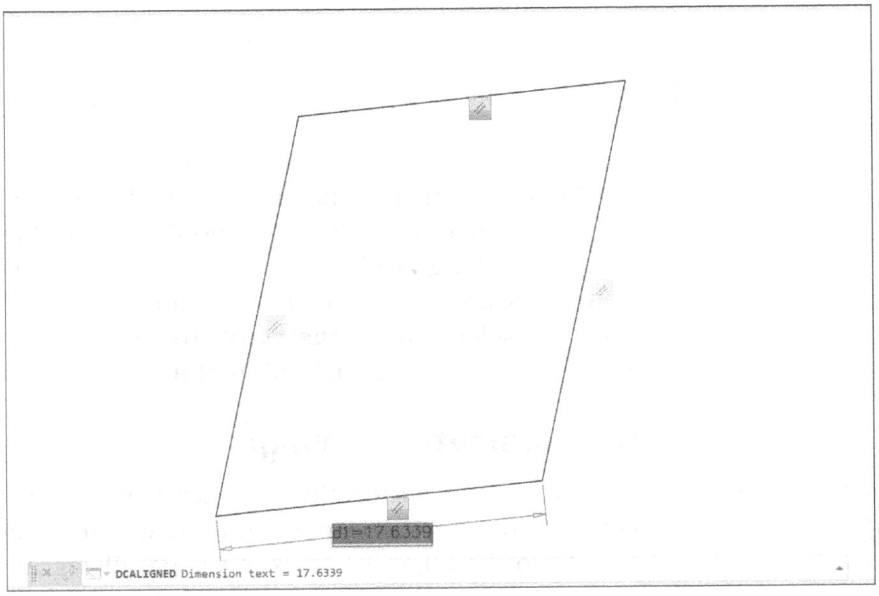

Here, the dimension constraint shows d1 = 17.6339. Yours will likely be different, but you will fix that. Often, you want to change this value because the ability to manipulate the dimension is the purpose of the dimensional constraint. You can change it now or come back to it later. You change it in this exercise.

> **NOTE**
>
> Dimensional constraints, like geometric constraints, can be shown or hidden in your drawing. If your constraint disappears when you press **<Enter>**, click the **Show Dynamic Constraints** tool on the **Dimensional** panel on the **Parametric** panel.

✔ Type **10 <Enter>**.

Your drawing should resemble Figure 9-36.

Figure 9-36
Changing dimensional constraint to 10

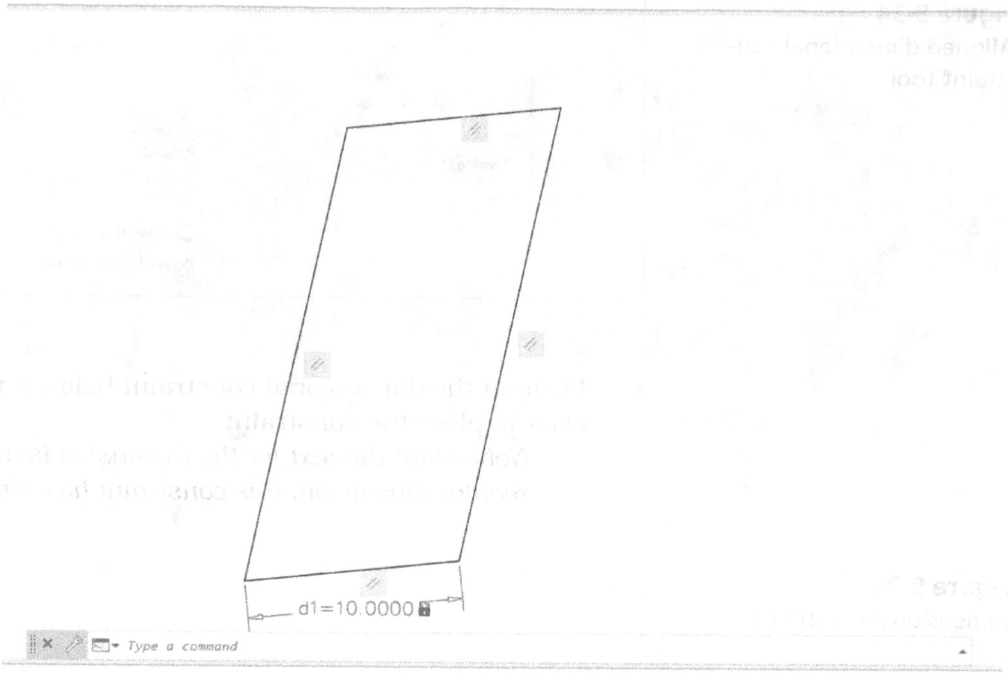

Your drawing now has two types of constraints. The two pairs of sides are constrained to be parallel, and the lower side, line 1, is constrained to be 10 units long until that value is changed. One way to change the value is to select the dimensional constraint, right-click to open a shortcut menu, and then select **Edit Constraint** from the menu. When you do this, the dimension text is highlighted, just as if you had never left the constraint.

The Parameters Manager

parameter: A value that can be varied from one representation of an object to another.

Here, you change the value another way, using the **Parameters Manager**. This also provides the opportunity to create a new ***parameter*** that can be applied to the adjacent sides of the parallelogram.

✔ Click the **Parameters Manager** tool from the **Manage** panel on the **Parametric** tab, as shown in Figure 9-37.

Figure 9-37
Parameters Manager tool

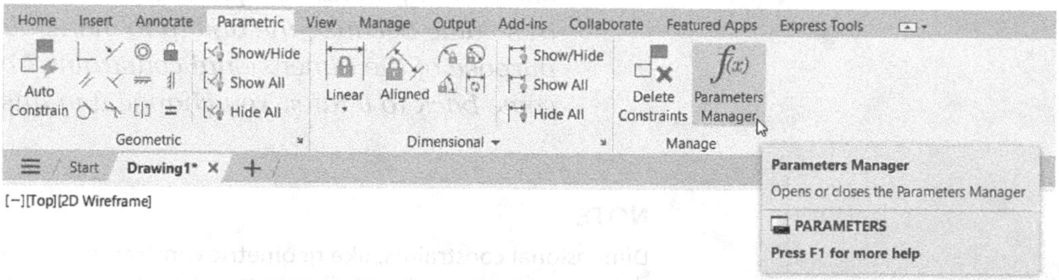

*This opens the **Parameters Manager** palette shown in Figure 9-38. It is a simple table of parameters. For each parameter, there is a name followed by an expression or a value. If the value is a constant, then the expression and the value are the same. You change the name to something more useful and then create a second dimensional constraint defined by an expression.*

✔ Double-click the name **d1**.
"d1" should be highlighted in blue.

✔ Type **side1 <Enter>**.
The name in the table is changed from d1 to side1. It is also changed in the drawing.

Next, you create a dimensional constraint so that the sides adjacent to side1 will be half as long as side1.

✔ Click the **Creates a new user parameter** button on the **Parameters Manager** palette, as shown in Figure 9-39.
*New data are added to the table, setting up a new section for user-defined parameters, meaning they are defined in the **Parameters Manager** but not necessarily in the drawing. This parameter will be named side2.*

✔ Double-click on the **user1** name and change it to **side2**.

✔ Double-click in the **Expression** column of side2 and type **side1/2 <Enter>**.
*side2 is now 5, or half the length of side1, as shown in the **Parameters Manager** in Figure 9-40. However, this does not affect the drawing because side2 has not been applied to any geometry in the drawing yet.*

✔ Click the **Aligned** tool from the **Dimensional** panel on the **Parametric** tab.

✔ Press **<Enter>**.

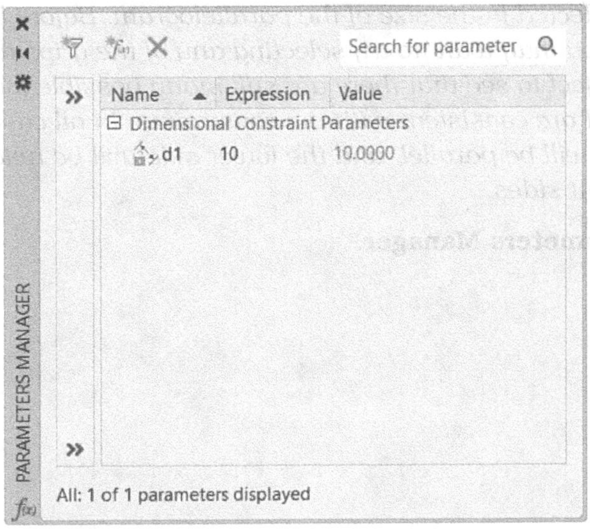

Figure 9-38
Parameters Manager palette

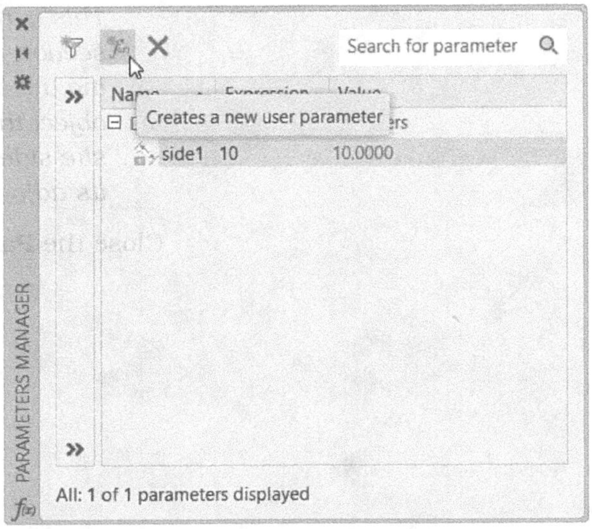

Figure 9-39
Creates a new user parameter button

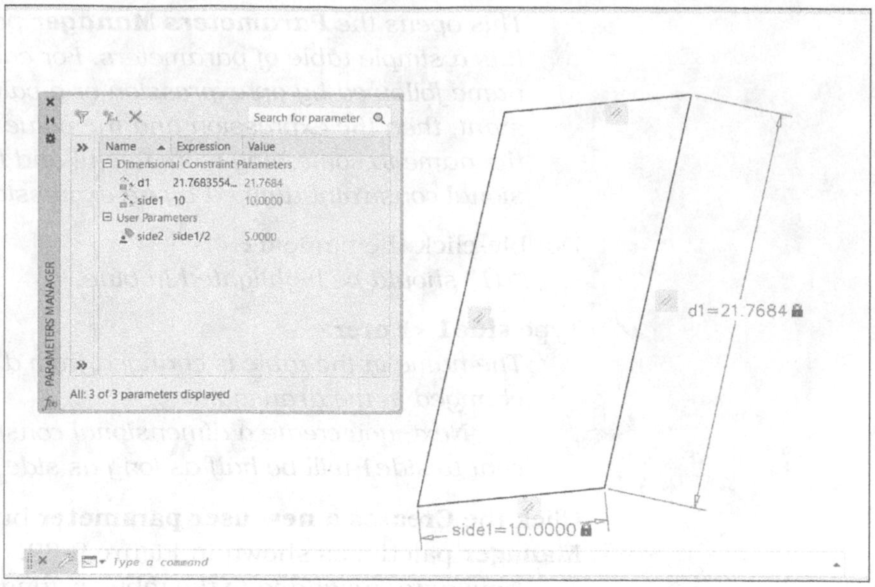

Figure 9-40
Dimensional constraints side1

✔ Select line 3.

✔ Position the dimensional constraint away from line 3 and then click to place the constraint, as shown in Figure 9-40.

Notice the dimension text. Here, the figure shows d1 = 21.7684.

✔ Type **side2 <Enter>**.

*The line at side2 is now evaluated with the expression that defines the side2 variable. The dimension now reads **fx:d1=side2**, and your drawing resembles Figure 9-41. Before closing the **Parameters Manager**, change the value of side1 and see how it is interpreted in the drawing.*

✔ Double-click the number **10** in the **Expression** column.

✔ Type **20 <Enter>**.

*In the **Parameters Manager**, side1 is now 20, and side2 is now 10. This is reflected in the size of the parallelogram. Before leaving this section, you may want to try selecting any of the grips and stretching the object to see that there are still many possible forms for this object that are consistent with the constraints. In all cases, the opposite sides will be parallel, and the lower side will be twice as long as its adjacent sides.*

✔ Close the **Parameters Manager**.

Figure 9-41
d1 = side2

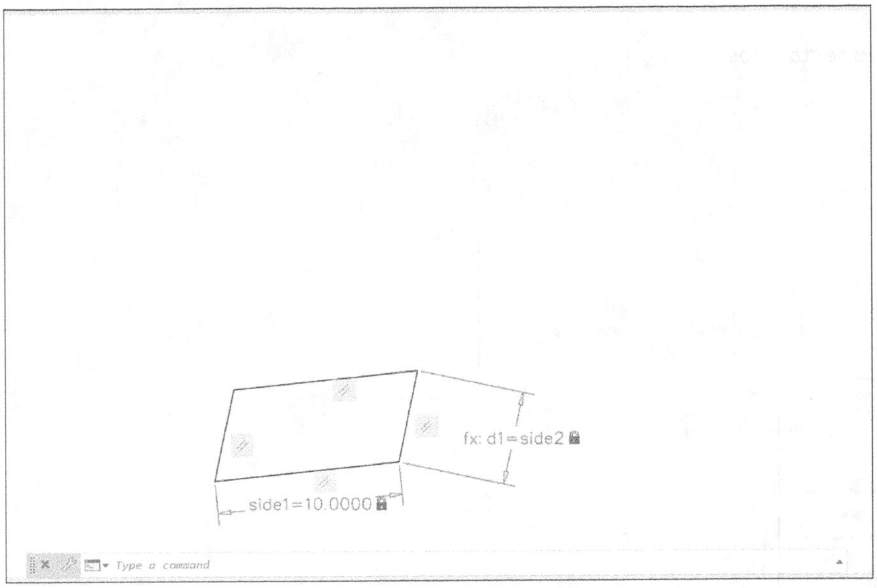

Using AutoConstrain and Inferred Constraints

In the previous section, you defined and applied geometric and dimensional constraints manually, one at a time. AutoCAD can also apply geometric constraints automatically, based on its analysis of selected geometry. This can be done as objects are drawn, by turning on the **Infer Constraints** button on the status bar. It can also be done after objects have been drawn, using the **AutoConstrain** tool on the **Parametric** tab of the ribbon. As an example of what this means, when you draw a rectangle, you assume that adjacent sides are perpendicular and opposite sides are equal. But what happens when you begin editing the rectangle? Stretching a rectangle ignores these relationships unless constraints are applied.

✔ To begin this exercise, erase all objects from the drawing.

✔ Using the **RECTANG** command, draw a single rectangle, as shown by the rectangle on the left in Figure 9-42. The exact size and location are not critical.

This is a normal, unconstrained rectangle. Next, you draw the rectangle on the right with inferred constraints.

✔ Click the **Customization** button on the status bar and select **Infer Constraints**, as shown in Figure 9-43.

*The **Infer Constraints** button appears on the status bar to the right of the **Grid Mode** and **Snap Mode** buttons.*

✔ Click the **Infer Constraints** button from the status bar, as shown in Figure 9-44.

***Infer Constraints** should now be on.*

✔ Using the **RECTANG** command, draw a second rectangle, as shown in Figure 9-42.

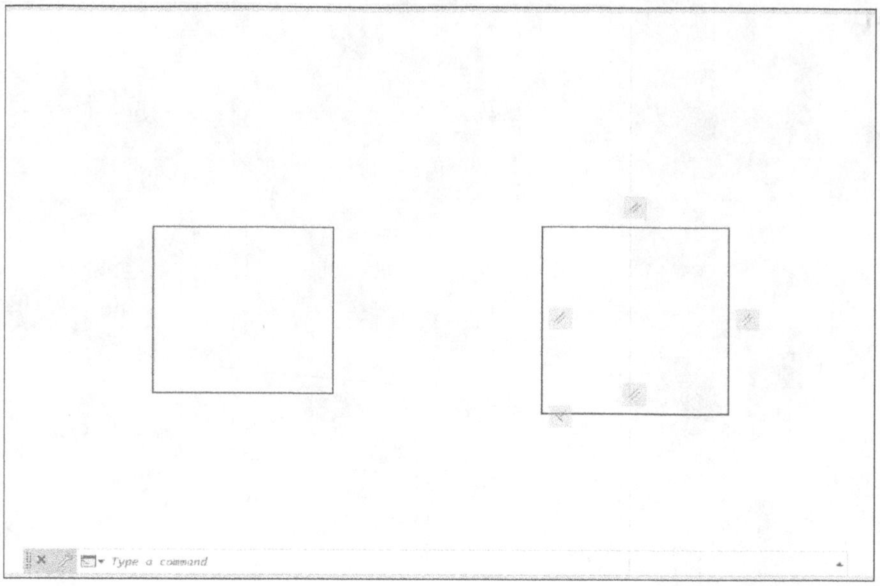

Figure 9-42
Drawing two rectangles

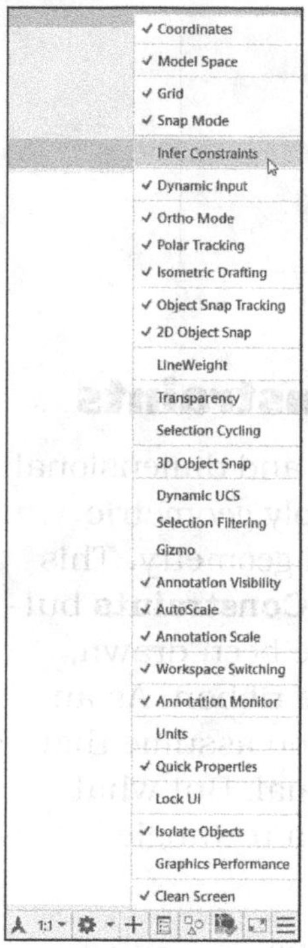

Figure 9-43
Customization menu

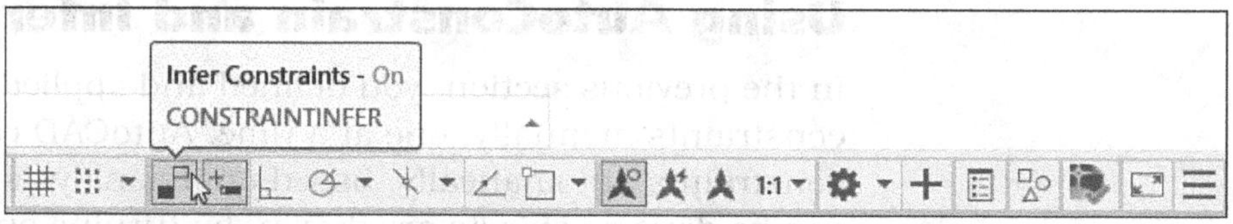

Figure 9-44
Infer Constraints button

Along the sides of this rectangle, you see five constraint bars. The constraint bars at the top and bottom and on the two sides are parallel constraints, showing that these opposite sides are constrained to be parallel. The constraint bar on the line near the top-left corner shows that the lines meeting at this corner are constrained to be perpendicular. A little geometry will convince you that if the opposite sides are parallel and the lines at this corner are perpendicular, then the other corners are perpendicular intersections also. So, additional constraint bars would be redundant. Next, you stretch both rectangles using grips.

✔ Select both rectangles so grips appear.
The grips on both rectangles are identical.

✔ Click the upper-left corner grip on the left rectangle and stretch the vertex up and to the left, as shown in Figure 9-45.

Figure 9-45
Stretching the rectangles

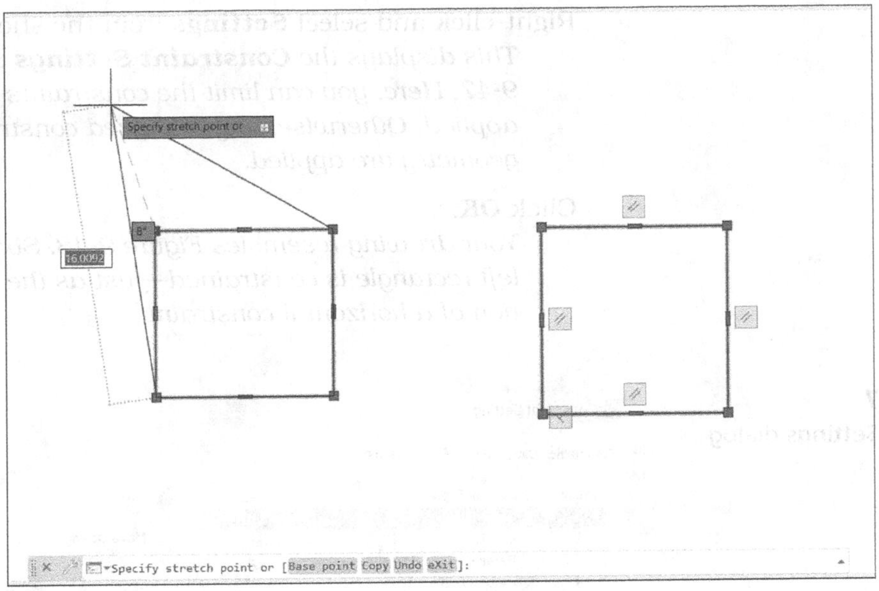

✔ Click the upper-left corner grip on the right rectangle and stretch the rectangle up and to the left, as shown.

Notice the difference. The unconstrained rectangle is stretched to form an irregular quadrilateral. The constrained rectangle retains its rectangular shape.

✔ Undo the two stretches.

Your drawing should resemble Figure 9-42 again.

Using AutoConstrain

You now use the **AutoConstrain** tool to add geometric constraints to the rectangle on the left.

✔ Click the **Parametric** tab > **Geometric** panel > **AutoConstrain** tool from the ribbon, as shown in Figure 9-46.

Figure 9-46
AutoConstrain tool

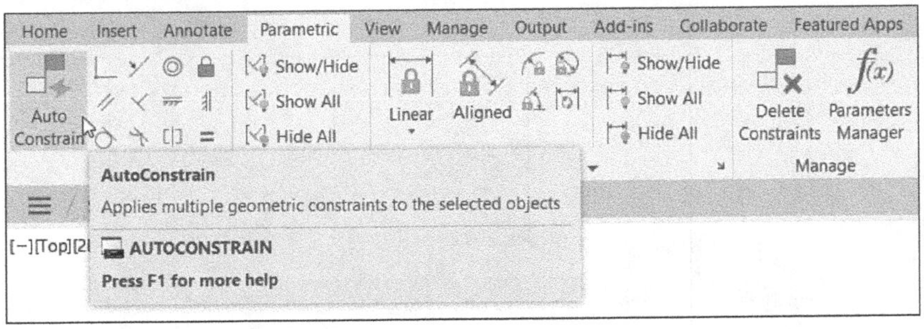

AutoCAD prompts:

```
Select objects or [Settings]:
```

✔ Select the rectangle on the left.

*AutoCAD prompts for more objects, but instead, let's look at the **Settings** option.*

✔ Right-click and select **Settings** from the shortcut menu.

This displays the ***Constraint Settings*** *dialog box shown in Figure 9-47. Here, you can limit the constraints that are automatically applied. Otherwise, any analyzed constraints based on the selected geometry are applied.*

✔ Click **OK**.

Your drawing resembles Figure 9-48. Six constraints are added. The left rectangle is constrained—just as the right one is—with the addition of a horizontal constraint.

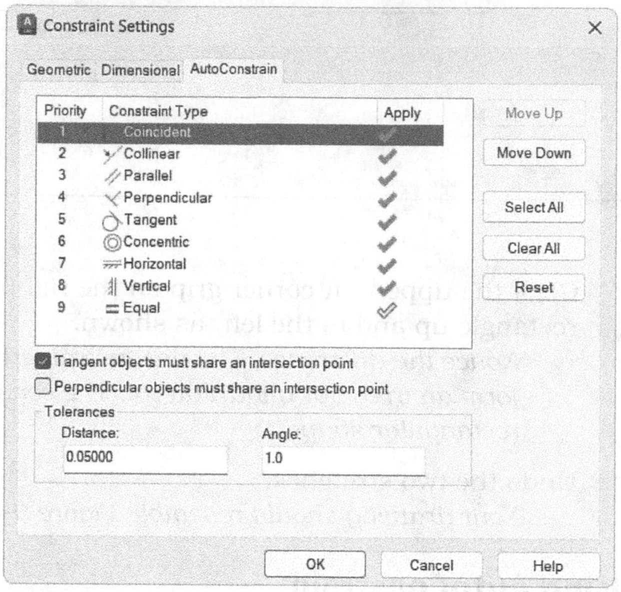

Figure 9-47
Constraint Settings dialog box

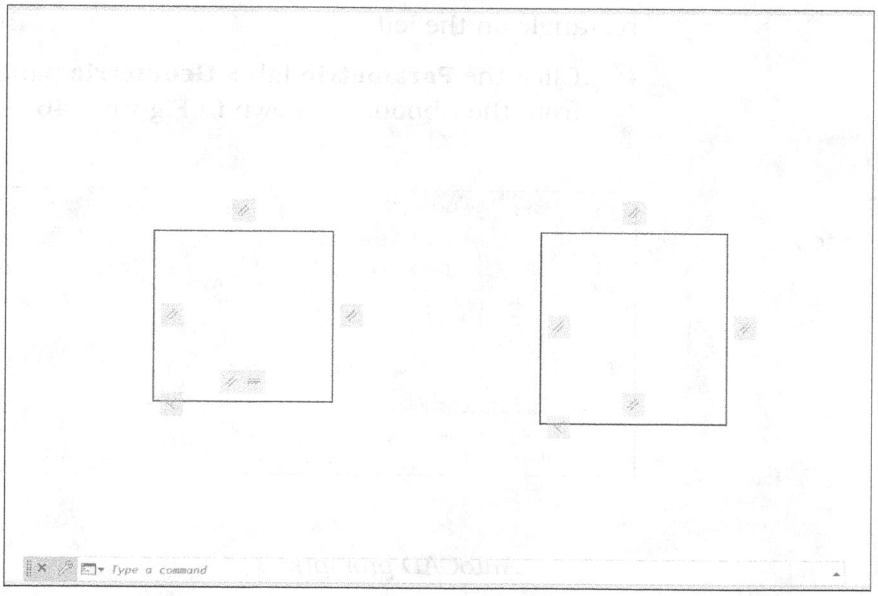

Figure 9-48
Six constraints are added

9 chapternine

Chapter Summary

You now have at your disposal a large number of new commands for drawing and editing complex objects consisting of various shapes made of straight and curved segments. Polygons, donuts, and polylines drawn with the **POLYGON**, **DONUT**, and **PLINE** commands all create polyline objects that you can edit with the **PEDIT** command. You can also create splines, which have their own editing features: path arrays, which can be drawn along spline or polyline paths; points, which can be created in 19 different styles; and revision clouds, which are primarily used in marking up designs but may be creatively applied as part of a drawing as well. At this point, you know how to draw most of AutoCAD's two-dimensional entities, and you have had your first experience using geometric and dimensional constraints, along with AutoConstrain and inferred constraints, to draw objects consistent with specific design objectives.

Chapter Test Questions

Multiple Choice

Circle the correct answer.

7. Which of these **cannot** be given a width using **PEDIT**?
   a. Rectangle
   b. Circle
   c. Polygon
   d. Polyline

8. A polygon can be drawn around the outside of a circle using which option?
   a. **Radius**
   b. **Inscribed**
   c. **Circumscribed**
   d. **Edge**

9. Polyline arcs are drawn
   a. Tangent to the rubber band
   b. Tangent to the last polyline selected
   c. Tangent to the last polyline arc segment
   d. Tangent to the last polyline drawn

10. Geometric constraints cannot be added:
   a. Using **PEDIT**
   b. Using AutoConstrain
   c. Using inferred constraints
   d. By selecting objects
11. Dimensional constraints cannot be added:
   a. Using inferred constraints
   b. By selecting an object
   c. Using AutoConstrain
   d. By selecting constraint points

Matching

Write the number of the correct answer on the line.

a. **Circumscribed** ______	1. Polyline
b. Outer radius ______	2. Polygon
c. **Halfwidth** ______	3. Polyline arc
d. **Direction** ______	4. Spline
e. **Fit tolerance** ______	5. Donut

True or False

Circle the correct answer.

1. **True or False:** When drawing a polyline, using the **Close** option has the same effect as using an **Endpoint** object snap to snap back to the first point.
2. **True or False:** Polylines, donuts, splines, and polygons can all be edited with **PEDIT**.
3. **True or False:** Revision clouds can be drawn freehand or created from previously drawn objects.
4. **True or False:** Spline curves touch each point you specify.
5. **True or False:** Geometric and dimensional constraints are maintained when an object is edited.

Questions

1. Why does **PLINE** prompt for two different widths?
2. Why is it important to use the **Close** option when drawing closed polygons using the **PLINE** command?
3. How does AutoCAD decide in which direction to draw a polyline arc?
4. What is the difference between a spline curve constructed with a 0 tolerance and one with a 0.5 tolerance?
5. What is the difference between a geometric constraint and a dimensional constraint? Which can be applied using the **AutoConstrain** tool?

Drawing Problems

1. Draw a regular six-sided polygon centered at (9,6) with a circumscribed radius of 3.0 units. The top and bottom sides should be horizontal.
2. Fillet all corners of the hexagon with a single execution of the **FILLET** command, giving a 0.25-unit radius.
3. Give the sides of the hexagon a 0.25-unit uniform width.
4. Draw a 0.50-width polyline from the midpoint of one angled side of the hexagon to the midpoint of the diagonally opposite side.
5. Draw a second 0.50-width polyline, using the other two angled sides so that the two polylines cross in the middle.
6. Draw a 1.50 radius circle centered at (9,6).
7. Convert this circle to a revision cloud.

9 chapternine

Chapter Drawing Projects

G Drawing 9-1: *Backgammon Board* [INTERMEDIATE]

This drawing should go very quickly. It is a good warm-up that gives you practice with **PLINE**. Remember that the dimensions are always part of your drawing now, unless otherwise indicated.

Drawing Suggestions

GRID = 1.0

SNAP = 0.125

- First, create the 15.50 × 17.50 polyline frame as shown.
- Draw a 0-width 15.50 × 13.50 polyline rectangle and then **OFFSET** it 0.125 to the inside. The inner polyline is actually 0.25 wide, but it is drawn on center, so the offset must be half the width.
- Enter the **PEDIT** command and change the width of the inner polyline to 0.25. This gives you your wide filled border.
- Draw the four triangles at the left of the board and then array them across. The filled triangles are drawn with the **PLINE** command (starting width 0 and ending width 1.00); the others are just outlines drawn with **LINE** or **PLINE**. (Notice that you cannot draw some polylines filled and others not filled.)
- The dimensions in this drawing are straightforward and should give you no trouble. Remember to set to layer **dim** before dimensioning.

Drawing 9-1
Backgammon Board

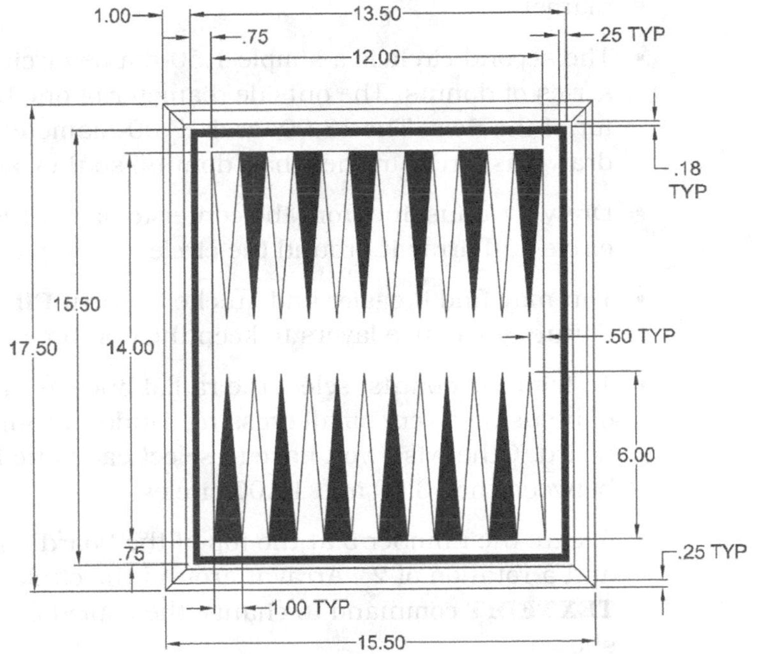

G Drawing 9-2: *Dartboard* [INTERMEDIATE]

Although this drawing may seem to resemble the previous one, it is quite a bit more complex and is drawn in an entirely different way. It is suggested to use donuts and trim them along the radial lines. Using **PLINE** to create the filled areas here would be less efficient.

Drawing Suggestions

LIMITS = (0,0)(24,18)

GRID = 1.00

SNAP = 0.125

- The filled inner circle is a donut with 0 inner diameter and 0.62 outer diameter.
- The second circle is a simple 1.50-diameter circle. From here, draw a series of donuts. The outside diameter of one becomes the inside diameter of the next. The 13.00- and 17.00-diameter outer circles must be drawn as circles rather than donuts, so they are not filled.
- Draw a radius line from the center to one of the quadrants of the outer circle and array it around the circle.
- You may find it easier and quicker to turn **FILL** off before trimming the donuts. Also, use layers to keep the donuts, separated visually by color.
- To trim the donuts, select the radial lines as cutting edges. This is easily done using a very small crossing window around the center point of the board. Otherwise, you have to select each line individually in the area between the 13.00 and 17.00 circles.
- Create the number 5 at the top of the board using a middle text position and a rotation of 2°. Array it around the circle, and then use the **TEXTEDIT** command to change the copied 5s to the other numbers shown.

Drawing 9-2
Dartboard

DIAMETERS
Ø.62
Ø1.50
Ø7.50
Ø8.25
Ø13.00
Ø17.00

E

Drawing 9-3: *Printed Circuit Board* [ADVANCED]

This drawing uses donuts and polylines. Also notice the ordinate dimensions.

Drawing Suggestions

UNITS = 4-place decimal

LIMITS = (0,0)(18,12)

GRID = 0.5000

SNAP = 0.1250

- Because this drawing uses ordinate dimensions, moving the 0 point of the grid using the **UCS** command makes the placement of figures very easy.
- The 26 rectangular tabs at the bottom can be drawn as polylines.
- After placing the donuts according to the dimensions, draw the connections to them using polyline arcs and line segments. These are simple polylines of uniform 0.03125 half-widths. The triangular tabs are added later.
- Remember, all polyline arcs begin tangent to the last segment drawn. Often, this is not what you want. One way to correct this is to begin with a line segment that establishes the direction for the arc. The line segment can be extremely short and still accomplish your purpose. Thus, many of these polylines consist of a line segment, followed by an arc, and then another line segment.
- There are two sizes of the triangular tabs, one on top of the rectangular tabs and one at each donut. Draw one of each size in place and then use multiple **COPY**, **MOVE**, and **ROTATE** commands to create all the others.

Drawing 9-3
Printed Circuit Board

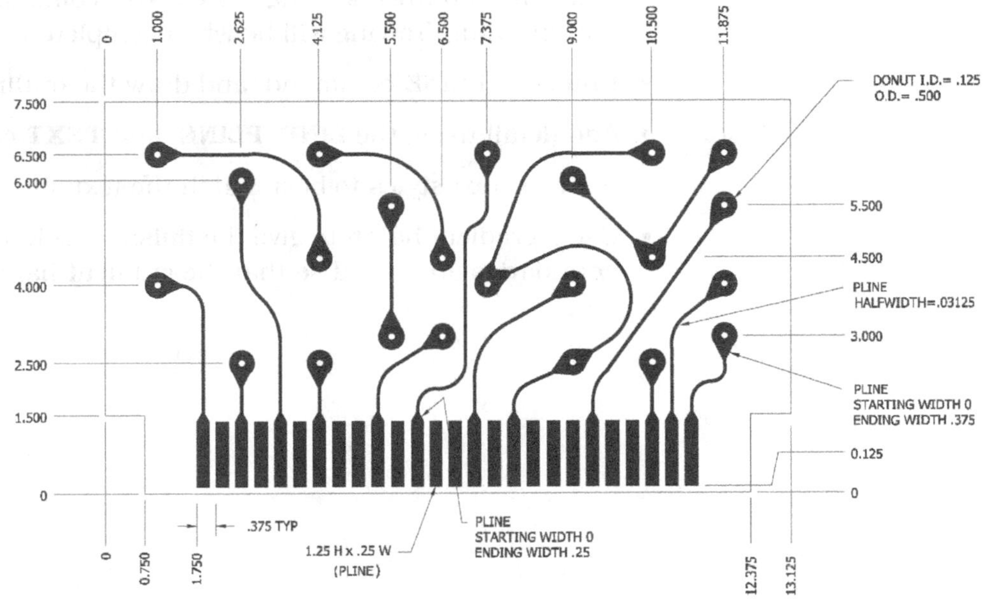

G Drawing 9-4: *Race Car* [ADVANCED]

This is an attractive drawing that requires creating shapes using donuts and polylines, along with text in different styles and a gradient hatch to fill and form details of the race car. The drawing does not have to be exact in all details, but you should try to make it a close approximation of the race car shown.

Drawing Suggestions

- Measure and scale this drawing using the grid of squares as a guide. Determine what size you want to draw the race car in your drawing, and set your grid accordingly. The corner of each square on the page will be represented by a grid point in your drawing.
- Draw the two wheels using the **DONUT** command; this will determine how big your drawing will be when completed.
- Enter the **PLINE** command, and draw the outline of the race car.
- Add detail using the **LINE**, **PLINE**, and **TEXT** commands.
- Set your text styles to best match the text shown on this drawing.
- Use a gradient hatch to give the finished look to the car. Be sure your boundaries are closed so that the gradient hatch works properly.

Drawing 9-4
Race Car

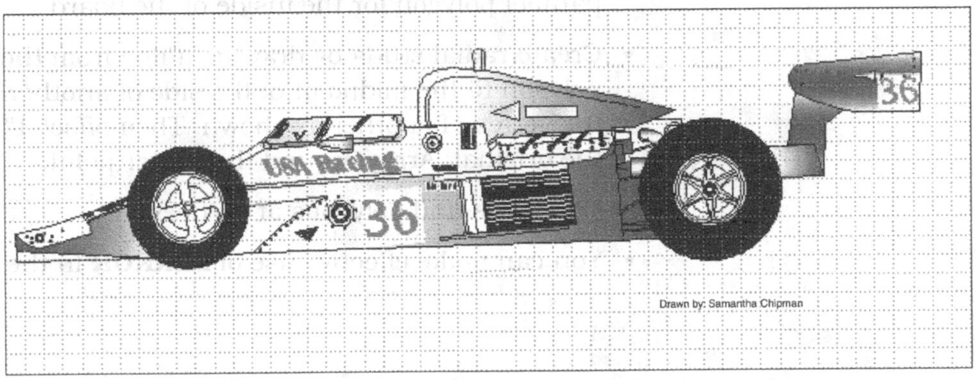

A

Drawing 9-5: *Gazebo* [INTERMEDIATE]

This architectural drawing makes extensive use of both the **POLYGON** command and the **OFFSET** command.

Drawing Suggestions

UNITS = Architectural

GRID = 1'

SNAP = 2"

LIMITS = (0',0')(48',36')

- All radii except the 6" polygon are given from the center point to the midpoint of a side. In other words, the 6" polygon is inscribed, whereas all the others are circumscribed.
- Notice that all polygon radii dimensions are given to the outside of the 2" × 4" construction/framing lumber. Offset to the inside to create the parallel polygon for the inside of the board.
- Create radial studs by drawing a line from the midpoint of one side of a polygon to the midpoint of the side of another or the midpoint of one to the vertex of another as shown. Then offset 1" from each side and erase the original. Array around the center point.
- Trim lines and polygons at vertices.
- You can make effective use of **MIRROR** in the elevation.

Drawing 9-5
Gazebo

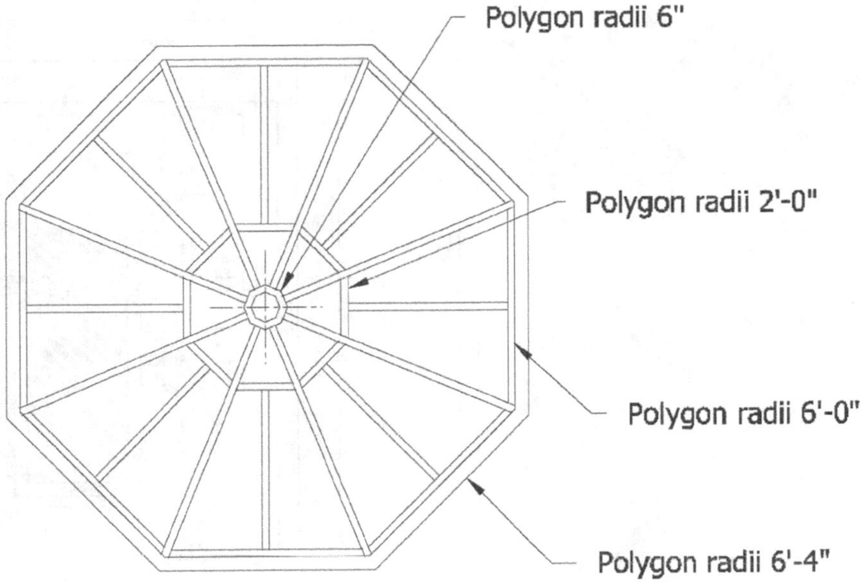

ROOF FRAMING

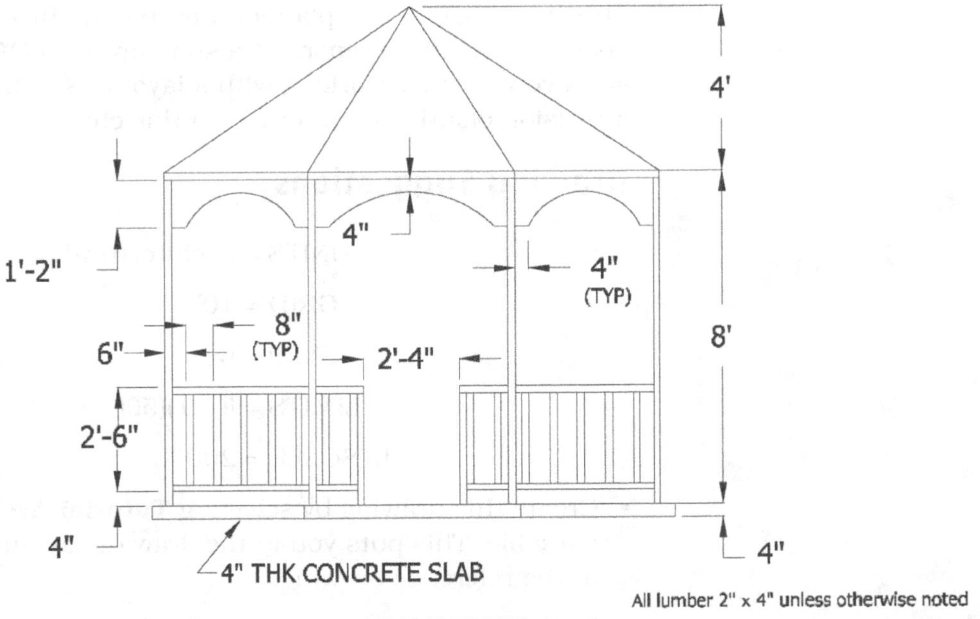

FRONT ELEVATION

C Drawing 9-6: *Office Building* [ADVANCED]

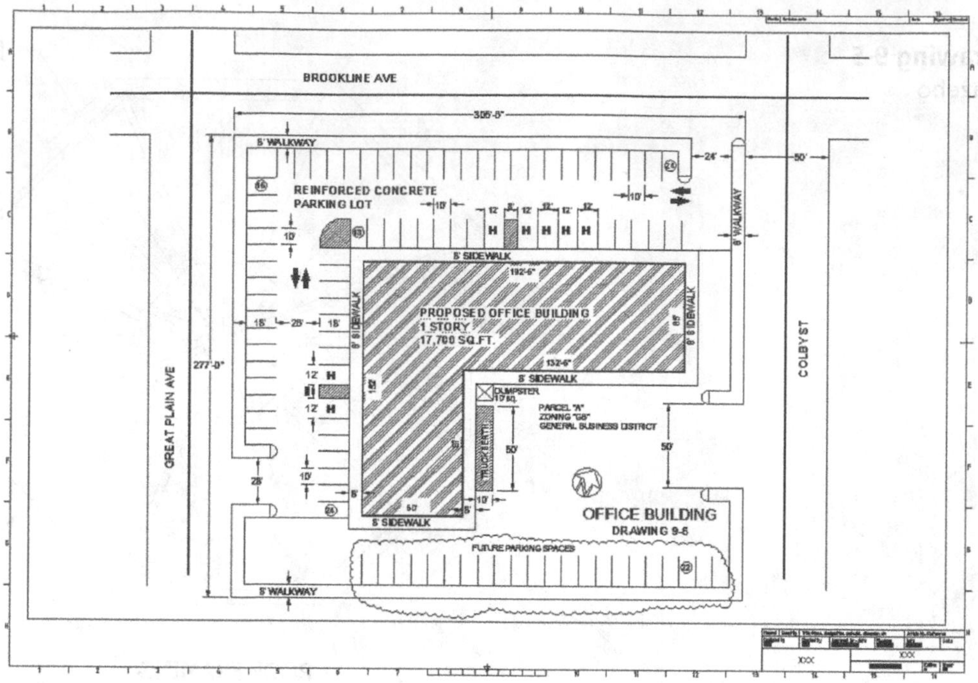

This drawing of a plot plan for a proposed office building is drawn in model space in a single viewport on a standard AutoCAD architectural layout. It gives you practice working with a layout as well as with using polylines and a revision cloud, as introduced in this chapter.

Drawing Suggestions

UNITS = Architectural

GRID = 10'

SNAP = 6'

LIMITS = (0',0')(500',400')

LTSCALE = 200

- Create this drawing by selecting **Tutorial-Arch.dwt** as the drawing template file. This puts you in the drawing layout with the title block shown in the reference drawing.
- Switch to model space and make the changes to the drawing setup listed here.
- Use polylines for the walkways and road lines and for the direction arrows and building outlines.
- Use **REVCLOUD** to draw the outline around future parking.
- Return to the paper space layout to plot with the title block.

Drawing 9-6
Office Building

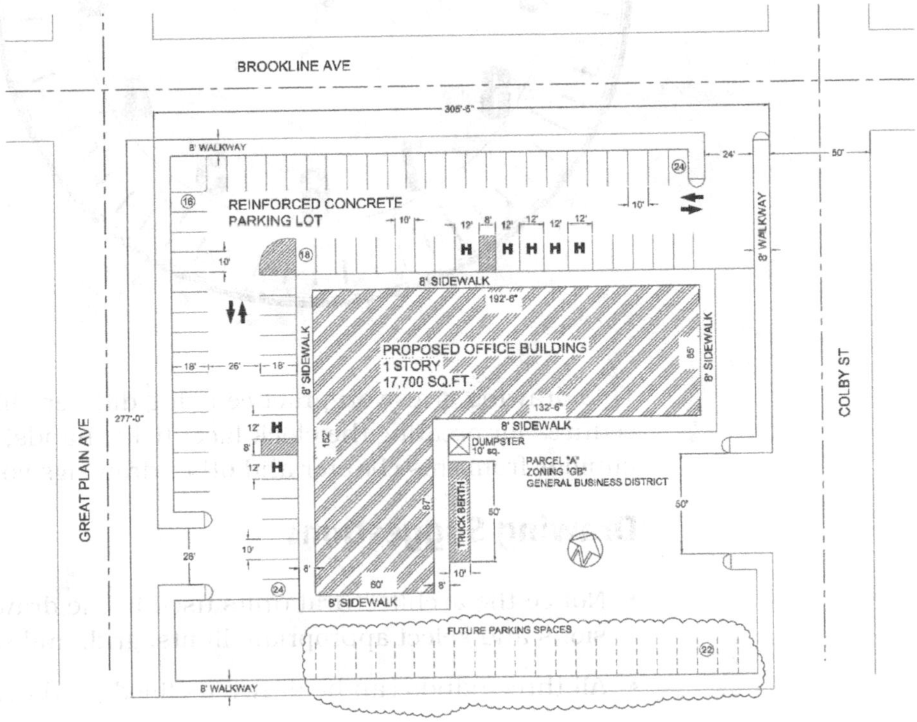

G

Drawing 9-7: *Clock Face* [ADVANCED]

This drawing gives you practice using different filled polyline forms. All procedures for creating the clock face, ticks, hands, and numbers should be familiar from this chapter and other drawings you may have done.

Drawing Suggestions

- Notice the architectural units used in the drawing. Observe the dimensions and select appropriate limits, grid, and snap settings.
- All three hands can be drawn as filled polylines.
- Clock ticks are also filled polylines.
- The font is Impact.

Drawing 9-7
Clock Face

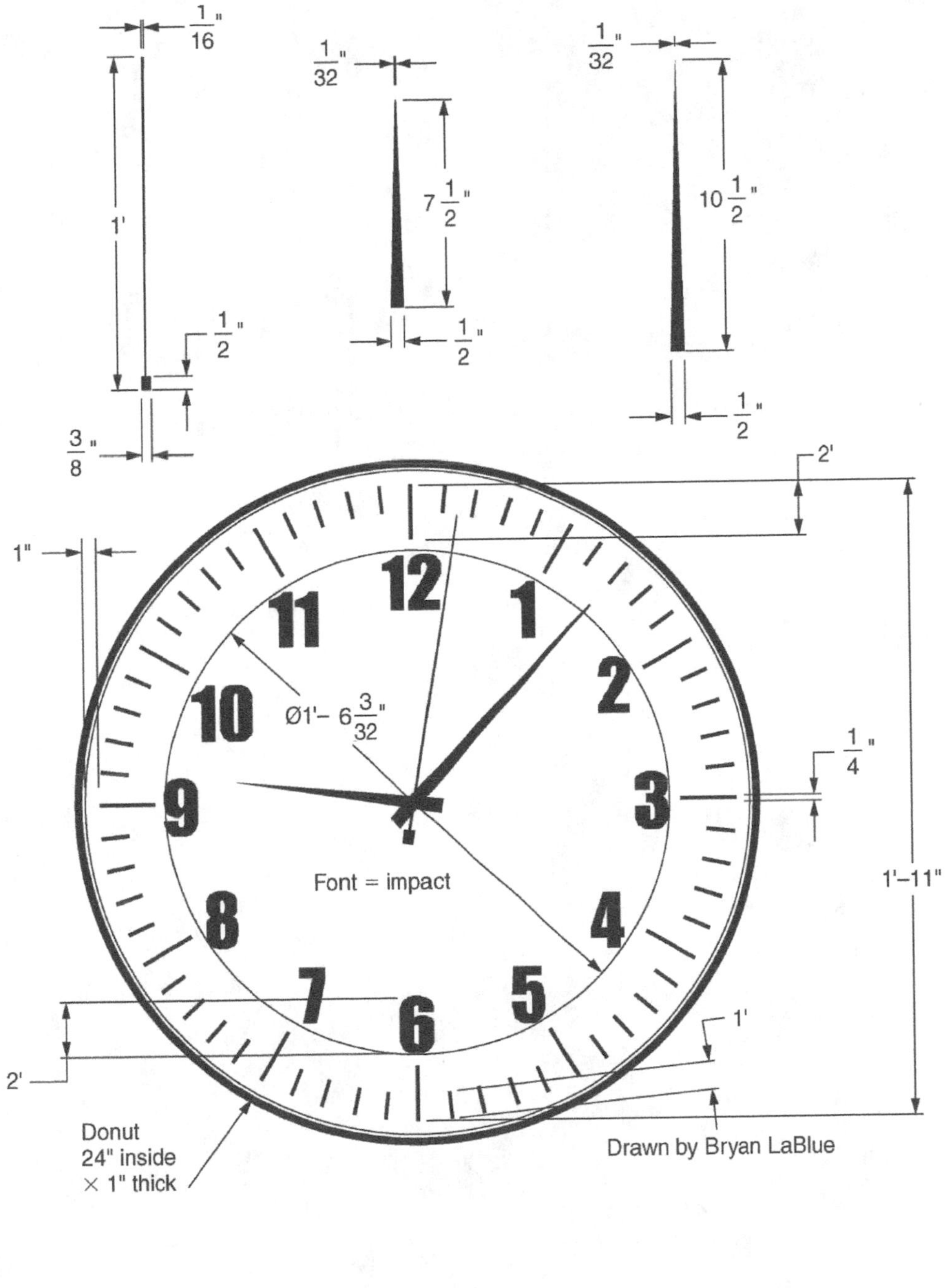

10 chapter ten

Blocks, Attributes, and External References

CHAPTER OBJECTIVES

- Create groups
- Create blocks
- Insert blocks into the current drawing
- Create dynamic blocks
- Add constraints to dynamic blocks
- Access data in a block table
- Use the Windows Clipboard
- Insert blocks and external references into other drawings
- Use the AutoCAD **DesignCenter**
- Define attributes
- Work with external references
- Extract data from attributes
- Count blocks
- Replace blocks
- Create tool palettes
- Explode blocks
- Purge unused blocks and named objects

Introduction

Working effectively in a professional design environment requires more than proficiency in drafting techniques. Most design work is done in collaboration with other designers, engineers, managers, and clients. This chapter begins to introduce you to some of the techniques and features that allow you to communicate and share the powers of AutoCAD with others.

group: A set of objects defined as a single entity that can be selected, named, and manipulated collectively.

block: A set of objects defined as a single entity and saved so that it can be scaled and inserted repeatedly and potentially used in other drawings.

To begin, you learn to create groups and blocks. A ***group*** is a set of objects defined as a single entity that can be selected, named, and manipulated collectively. A ***block*** is a set of objects defined as a single entity and saved so that it can be scaled and inserted repeatedly and potentially used in other drawings. Blocks become part of the content of a drawing that can

xref: Short for external reference.

attribute: In AutoCAD, a value that can be defined with a block definition to give textual or numeric information about an inserted block reference.

be browsed, viewed, and manipulated within and between drawings using the AutoCAD **DesignCenter**. **DesignCenter** and other functions, including the Windows Clipboard and externally referenced drawings (***xrefs***), allow AutoCAD objects and drawings to be used in other drawings and shared with other applications. This information can be accessed by CAD operators that are on the same local network or from the Internet. This chapter also introduces block attributes. An ***attribute*** is an item of information attached to a block, such as a part number or price, that is defined with a block definition. All the information stored in attributes can be extracted from a drawing into a spreadsheet or database program and used to produce itemized reports. Like text and dimensions, attributes and blocks have the **Annotative** property and are scaled automatically to match a viewport scale.

The procedures introduced in this chapter are among the most complex you will encounter. Follow the text and instructions closely and to save your work if you do not complete the exercise in one session. This is particularly important in the exercises where you are working with two drawings.

Creating Groups

The simplest way to create a collective entity from previously drawn entities is to group them into a unit with the **GROUP** command. Groups can be given names and can be selected for all editing processes.

> **TIP**
>
> The following is a general procedure for creating groups:
>
> 1. Click **Home** > **Groups** > **Group** from the ribbon.
> 2. Select objects to be included in the group definition.
> 3. Use the **Name** options to name the group, if desired.
> 4. Press **<Enter>** or the spacebar to complete the command.

In this exercise, you draw some objects to use for creating groups. You'll use the same objects later to define blocks. In this way, you get a feel for the different functions of these two features of creating collections of objects. You begin by creating a simple representation of a computer, monitor, digitizer, and keyboard. Take your time getting these right because once created, you can insert them when you complete Drawing 10-1 at the end of the chapter.

Create a new drawing and make the following changes, if necessary, in the drawing setup:

8. Set layer **0** as the current layer. (The reason for doing this is discussed in the note accompanying this list.)
9. Change to architectural units with precision = 0'–0". Using architectural units facilitates, move on to Drawing 10-1, which is an architectural layout of a CAD room.
10. Set GRID = **1'**.

11. Set SNAP = **1"**.

12. Set LIMITS = **(0',0') (12',9')**. Be sure to include the feet symbol.

13. Set CONSTRAINTINFER = **0**.

14. At the Command prompt, type **ZOOM <Enter>** and then select the **All** option from the command line.

> **NOTE**
>
> Objects created on layer **0** and defined in a block inherit the properties of the current layer when the block is inserted. Objects created on any other layer stay on the layer on which they were created. Inserting blocks is discussed in the "Inserting Blocks into the Current Drawing" section later in this chapter.

✔ Turn the grid on or off—your preference.

The figures in this chapter are shown with the grid off for clarity.

✔ Draw the four objects shown in Figure 10-1.

Draw the geometry only; the text and dimensions in the figure are for your reference only and should not be added to the drawing. Notice that the computer is a simple rectangular representation of an old-style computer CPU that lays horizontally under the monitor. Later, you will modify the definition of this block so that it has the flexibility to also represent a more typical tower-style computer.

Figure 10-1
Draw objects

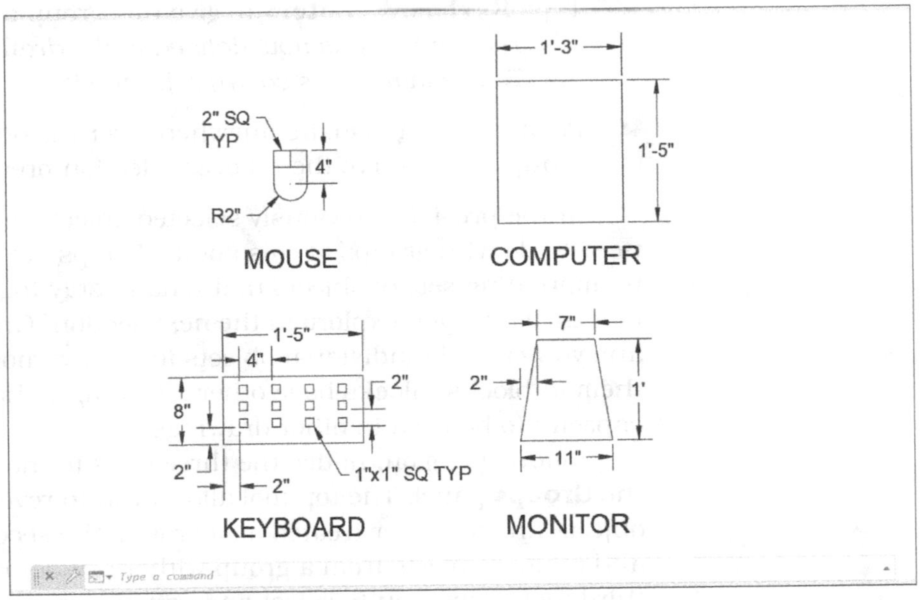

✔ Save this drawing as **Source**.

You work with two drawings later in this chapter, and naming them Source and Target helps with clarity. Source will have 12' × 9', A size architectural limits, and Target will have 18 × 12 decimal units. This will give you experience in some important issues about working with multiple drawings. For now, continue working in Source and hold off on creating Target until later.

Next, you define the keyboard as a group.

✔ Click the **Group** tool from the **Groups** panel of the ribbon's **Home** tab, as shown in Figure 10-2.

AutoCAD prompts:

```
Select objects or [Name/Description]:
```

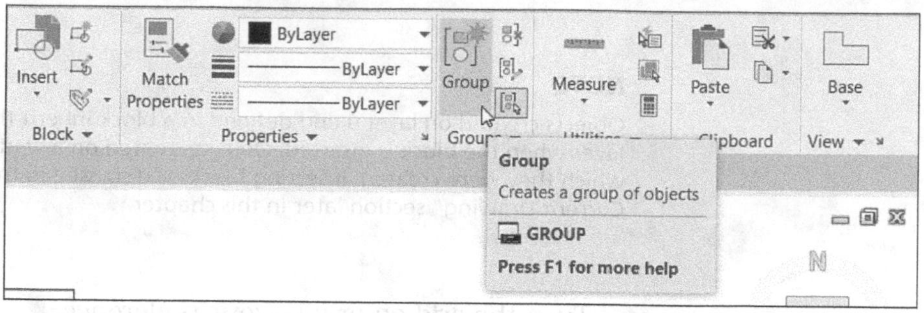

Figure 10-2
Group tool

*Groups can be named and saved. Descriptions may be added to help identify previously defined groups. You use the **GROUP** command when you want to create a grouping of objects that can be selected as one object.*

✔ Select the keyboard outer rectangle and small rectangles using a window.

✔ Select **Name** from the command line.

✔ Type **Keyboard <Enter>** to give this group a name.

The keyboard is now defined in the drawing as a selectable group. To see that this is so, try selecting it.

✔ Position the crosshairs anywhere over the objects in the **Keyboard** group and observe the rollover selection preview.

In the preview, previously selected objects are grouped. That is all you need to do with groups at this point. Groups are useful for copying and manipulating sets of objects that tend to stay together. Groups resemble blocks, which you explore in the next section. Groups are easier to define, and you can edit individual objects in groups more easily than you can edit them in blocks. Blocks have other advantages, however, including the capacity to be used in other drawings.

Before going on, notice the three tools to the right of the **Group** tool on the **Groups** panel. The top tool allows you to reverse the process so that objects are no longer treated as a group. The second tool allows you to add and remove objects from a group without undoing the group definition. The third tool allows you to select and edit objects within a group while the group is still defined. You can expand the **Groups** panel by clicking its title bar, which enables you to manage the groups in your drawing as well as control the display of group bounding boxes.

Creating Blocks

BLOCK	
Command	BLOCK
Alias	B
Panel	Block
Tool	

Blocks are defined as part of an individual drawing or as separate drawings. You can insert them into the drawing in which they were defined or into other drawings. You can scale and rotate blocks as you insert them. In AutoCAD, blocks can also be defined as *dynamic*, meaning that they are flexible and can be altered in specific ways to represent variations of the basic geometry of the block.

In general, the most useful blocks are those that can be used repeatedly in many drawings and, therefore, can become part of a library of predrawn objects. In mechanical drawings, for instance, you might want a set of screws drawn to standard sizes. If you are doing architectural drafting, you might find a library of doors and windows useful. You see examples of predefined block libraries later in this chapter when you explore the AutoCAD **DesignCenter** and tool palettes.

> **TIP**
>
> The following is a general procedure for creating blocks:
>
> 1. Click the **Create** tool from the **Block** panel on the ribbon's **Home** tab.
> 2. Type a name.
> 3. Specify an insertion point.
> 4. Select objects to be included in the block definition.
> 5. Click **OK** to define the block.

You create the first block from the "computer" in your drawing.

✔ Click the **Create** tool from the **Block** panel on the ribbon's **Home** tab, as shown in Figure 10-3.

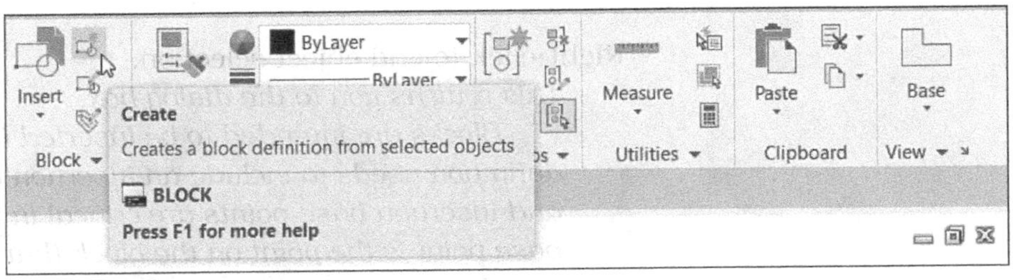

Figure 10-3
Create Block tool

This starts the ***BLOCK*** *command and displays the* ***Block Definition*** *dialog box, as shown in Figure 10-4.*

✔ Type **computer** in the **Name** box.

Next, you select objects to define as the block.

✔ Click the **Select objects** button in the middle of the dialog box.

It may be necessary to clear the checkmark from the ***Specify On-screen*** *box before you can do this. If this box is checked, the* ***Select objects*** *button is not accessible, and you will be returned to the command-line prompt for object selection.*

The dialog box disappears, giving you access to objects in the drawing.

Figure 10-4
Block Definition dialog box

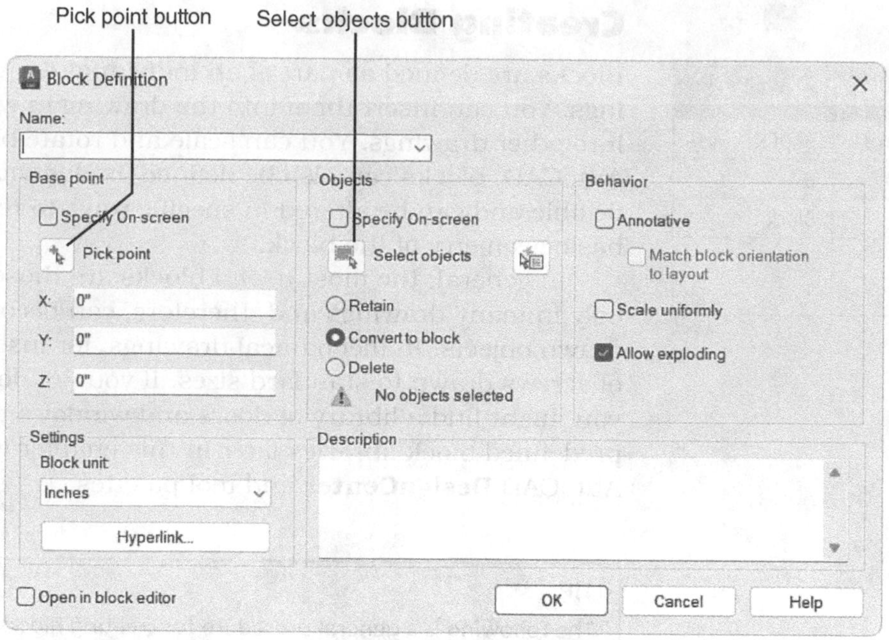

✔ Select the rectangle that represents the computer.
AutoCAD continues to prompt for object selection.

NOTE

Be sure to use the **Select objects** button, not the **Quick Select** button. **Quick Select** executes the **QSELECT** command and opens the **Quick Select** dialog box. The purpose of this dialog box is to establish filtering criteria so that defined types of objects can be selected more quickly in a complex drawing, filtering out objects that do not meet the selection criteria.

✔ Right-click to end object selection.
This returns you to the dialog box.

Blocks are intended to be inserted into drawings, so any block definition needs to include an insertion base point. Insertion points and insertion base points are critical in using blocks. The insertion base point is the point on the block that is at the intersection of the crosshairs when you insert the block. Therefore, when defining a block, try to anticipate the point on the block you will most likely use to position the block in the drawing. If you do not define an insertion base point, AutoCAD uses the origin of the coordinate system, which may be quite inconvenient.

✔ Click the **Pick point** button on the left side of the dialog box.
Here again, you may need to clear the check mark from the ***Specify On-screen*** *box first.*

✔ Hold down **<Shift>** and right-click to open the **Object Snap** menu.

✔ Use a **Midpoint** object snap to specify the middle of the bottom line of the computer for its insertion point, as shown in Figure 10-5.

*When creating blocks, you have three choices regarding what happens to objects included in the block definition, shown by the three buttons in the **Objects** panel just below the **Select objects** button. Objects can be retained in the drawing, converted to an instance of the new block, or deleted from the drawing. In all instances, the objects are defined in the drawing as a block definition.*

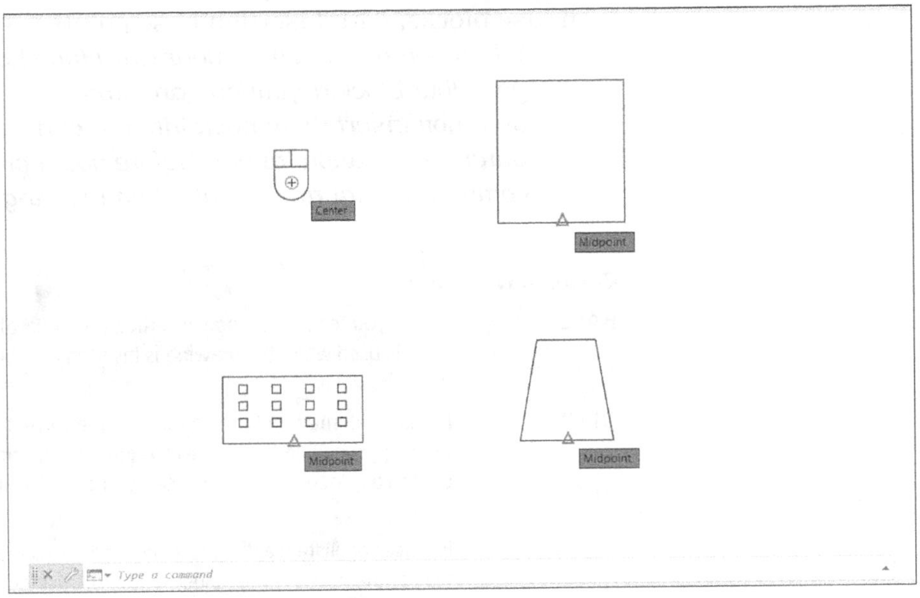

Figure 10-5
Define objects as blocks

*A common practice is to create a number of blocks, one after the other, and then insert them at the end. To facilitate this method, select the **Delete** button. With this setting, selected objects are erased from the drawing automatically. They can be retrieved using **OOPS** if necessary (but not **U**, as this would undo the block definition). In this case, removing the selected objects as you define blocks helps to make a clearer distinction among the objects remaining in your drawing.*

✔ Select the **Delete** button.

The selected objects will be removed from the drawing when the block definition is completed.

✔ Click **OK** to close the dialog box and create the block definition.

*You have created a block definition named Computer. The objects selected to define the computer are removed from your drawing, but the new block definition can be inserted using the **INSERT** command, which you turn to momentarily. Now, repeat the **BLOCK** process to make a keyboard block.*

✔ Repeat **BLOCK**.

✔ Type **keyboard** in the block **Name** box.

✔ Click the **Select objects** button.

✔ Select the keyboard group defined in the previous section.

✔ Right-click to end object selection.

✔ Click the **Pick point** button.

✔ Specify the midpoint of the bottom line of the keyboard as the insertion base point, using a **Midpoint** object snap, if necessary.

✔ Click **OK**.

✔ Repeat the create block process two more times to define monitor and mouse blocks, with insertion base points, as shown in Figure 10-5.

When you are finished, your drawing should be empty. At this point, your four block definitions are stored in the drawing. In the next section, you insert them back into the current drawing to create a computer workstation layout. Before going on, take a look at these other commands that are useful when working with blocks.

Command	Usage
BASE	Allows you to specify a new insertion base point for an entire drawing. The base point is used when the drawing is inserted as a block or attached as an xref into other drawings.
DBLIST	Displays information for all entities in the current drawing database. Information includes type of entity and layer. Additional information depends on the type of entity. For blocks, it includes insertion point, *x* scale, *y* scale, rotation, and attribute values.
EXPLODE	Replaces an instance of a block inserted into a drawing with the individual objects that define its associated block definition. Exploding a block reference has no effect on the block definition.
LIST	Lists information about a single block or entity. Information listed is the same as that in **DBLIST**, but for the selected entities only.
PURGE	Removes unused blocks, layers, linetypes, shapes, dimension styles, and text styles from a drawing.
WBLOCK	Saves a block to a separate file so it can be inserted into other drawings. Does not save unused blocks or layers and therefore can be used to reduce drawing file size.

Inserting Blocks into the Current Drawing

INSERT	
Command	INSERT
Alias	I
Panel	Block
Tool	

The **INSERT** command is used to add block references in a drawing. Here, you begin to distinguish between block definitions, which are not visible and reside in the drawing database, and block references, which are instances of a block definition inserted into a drawing. The four block definitions you created in the "Creating Blocks" section are part of the drawing database and can be inserted into this drawing or any other drawing. In this section, you focus on inserting blocks into the current drawing. In the next section, you explore sharing blocks between drawings.

> **TIP**
>
> The following is a general procedure for inserting blocks:
>
> 1. Click the **Insert** tool from the **Block** panel of the **Insert** tab on the ribbon.
> 2. Select a block name.
> 3. Specify an insertion point.
> 4. Respond to the prompts for x and y scale and rotation angles.

Among other things, these procedures are useful in creating complex drawings that represent assemblies of machines or buildings. You can efficiently insert blocks using appropriate object snap modes to place blocks in precise relation to other objects.

In this section, you insert the computer, monitor, keyboard, and mouse back into the drawing to create the workstation assembly shown in Figure 10-6.

✔ If you are still on layer **0**, you may want to create and switch to another layer.

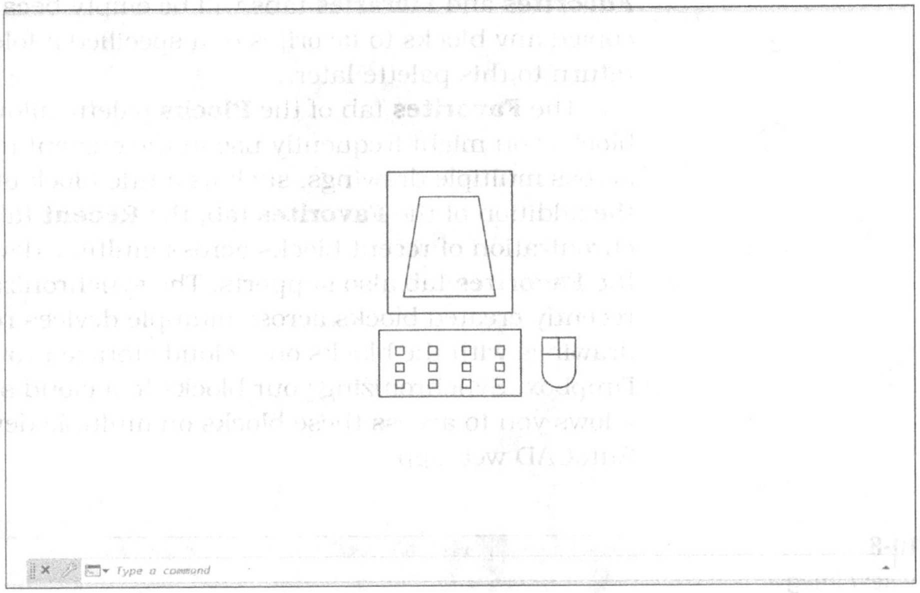

Figure 10-6
Inserted blocks

The Insert Tab

There is an **Insert** tool just to the left of the **Create** tool on the **Block** panel on the ribbon's **Home** tab. But there is a more complete set of tools related to blocks and external references available on the **Insert** tab. Switch to that tab now.

✔ Click the **Insert** tab on the ribbon.

*This opens a new set of tools, as shown in Figure 10-7. Notice the **Insert** tool on the **Block** panel at the far left and the **Create Block** and **Block Editor** tools on the **Block Definition** panel.*

Figure 10-7
Insert tool

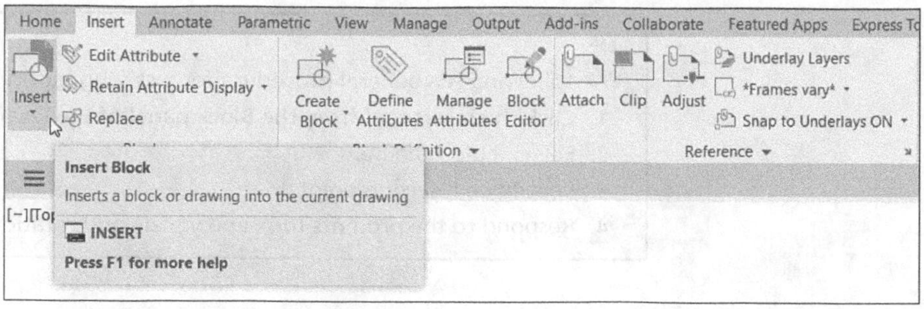

✔ Click the **Insert** tool from the **Block** panel on the ribbon, as shown in Figure 10-7.

*This starts the **INSERT** command and opens the gallery of block previews shown in Figure 10-8.*

These are the blocks defined in the current drawing. Notice the three options below these preview images. Choose one of the top two options to open the ***Blocks*** palette shown in Figure 10-9. As shown, the ***Recent*** tab shows the same set of blocks as those on the ***Current Drawing*** tab. The ***Favorites*** and **Libraries** tabs will be empty because you likely have not copied any blocks to favorites or a specified a folder as a library yet. You return to this palette later.

New to AutoCAD 2021

The **Favorites** tab of the **Blocks** palette allows you to quickly access blocks you might frequently use in the current drawing or want to access across multiple drawings, such as a title block or viewport label. Along with the addition of the **Favorites** tab, the **Recent** tab now supports the synchronization of recent blocks across multiple devices, which is something the **Favorites** tab also supports. The synchronization of your favorite and recently created blocks across multiple devices requires you to store your drawings with the blocks on a cloud storage provider like OneDrive or Dropbox. Synchronizing your blocks to a cloud storage provider not only allows you to access these blocks on multiple devices but also with the AutoCAD web app.

Figure 10-8
Block preview images

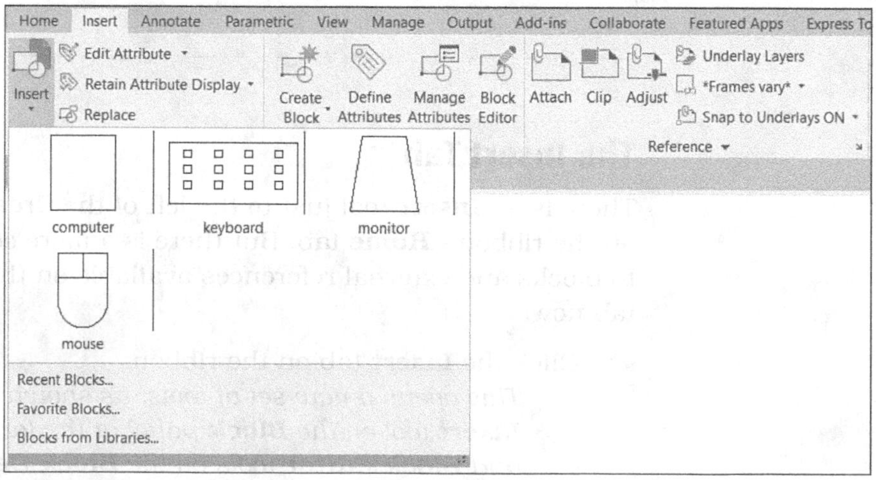

Figure 10-9
Blocks palette

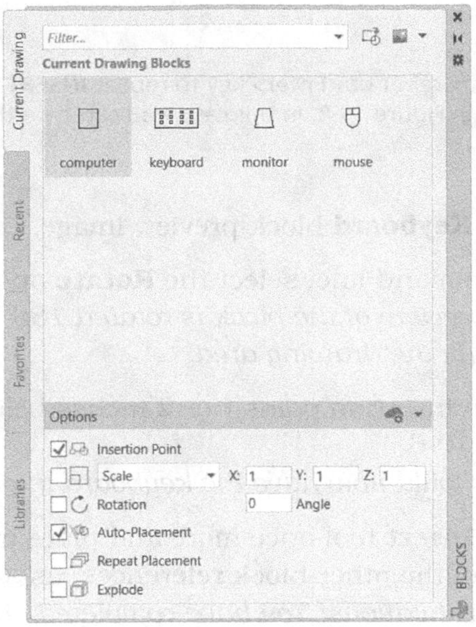

- ✔ Click the **Computer** block image.

  From here on, you follow prompts from the command line or dynamic input display. AutoCAD now needs to know where to insert the computer, and you see this prompt:

  `Specify insertion point or [Basepoint/Scale/X/Y/Z/Rotate]:`

  AutoCAD gives you a block to drag into place. Notice that it is positioned with the block's insertion base point at the intersection of the crosshairs.

- ✔ Specify a point near the middle of the drawing area, as shown previously in Figure 10-6.

  *If your current layer is other than layer **0**, notice that the block is inserted on the current layer even though it was created on layer **0**. Remember that this works only with blocks drawn on layer **0**. Blocks drawn on other layers stay on the layer on which they were drawn when they are inserted. This not only creates some inflexibility but also may add unwanted layers if the block was drawn on a layer that does not exist in the new drawing.*

  Now, let's add a monitor.

- ✔ Click the **Insert** tool again on the ribbon.

  *Notice that the last block inserted is retained as the default block name in the block **Name** box. This facilitates procedures in which you insert the same block in several different places in a drawing.*

- ✔ Click **Monitor** from the set of preview images.
- ✔ Specify an insertion point 2 or 3 inches above the insertion point of the computer, as shown in Figure 10-6. Remember that **Object Snap Tracking** can help you specify a point from an object snap point.

  You should now have the monitor sitting on top of the computer and be back at the command-line prompt. You next insert the keyboard, as shown in Figure 10-6.

- ✔ Again, click the **Insert** tool from the ribbon.

> **NOTE**
>
> If you use the spacebar or <**Enter**> key to repeat **INSERT**, you will not see the thumbnail images shown in Figure 10-8. In this case, you can type the name of the block.

✔ Click the **Keyboard** block preview image.

✔ At the command line, select the **Rotate** option and type **180 <Enter>**.
The preview of the block is rotated 180° and is now below the cross-hairs in the drawing area.

✔ Specify an insertion point 1 or 2 inches below the computer, as shown in Figure 10-6.
You should now have the keyboard in place.

✔ Click the **Insert** tool once more and place a mouse block reference to the right of the other block references, as shown in Figure 10-6.
Congratulations! You have completed your first design using blocks. Next, you modify the definition of the computer block so that it becomes dynamic and may be used to represent different styles and sizes of computers.

The Blocks Palette

While the previous steps focused on using the gallery of blocks from the **Insert** tool on the ribbon, the **Blocks** palette shown in Figure 10-9 offers more flexibility to insert blocks in everyday drafting. Along with clicking one of the three options below the gallery of block to open the **Blocks** palette, you can also open the palette by clicking **View** > **Palettes** > **Blocks**.

Notice the **Insertion Options** at the bottom of the palette. These options are used to assist in the placement of block reference. The **Insertion Point** option allows you place a block by specifying a point in the drawing area or providing **X**, **Y**, and **Z** values in the palette.

Unlike the **SCALE** command, which automatically scales uniformly in the directions of the x-axis and y-axis, blocks can be stretched or shrunk in either direction independently as you insert them. You can enter an X scale factor or specify both an x and a y scale factor. Use of the Z scale is reserved for 3D modeling. The **Uniform Scale** option from the **Scale** drop-down list sets the scales x, y, and z uniformly. This is also the default option, with **X**, **Y**, and **Z** at a scale of **1**.

The **Rotation** option allows you to specify the angle at which the block is inserted. This is similar to using the **ROTATE** command to rotate objects around a specified base point.

New to AutoCAD 2024

The **AutoPlacement** option utilizes machine-learning to help insert a block based on previous instances of that block inserted into the drawing. As you insert a block, AutoCAD suggests an insertion point, scale and/or rotation based on the geometry around the block being inserted. When a suggestion is being made, geometry near the block being dragged is highlighted in yellow and the block snaps into place based on that suggestion, as shown in Figure 10-10.

Figure 10-10
Insertion of block based on **AutoPlacement** suggestion

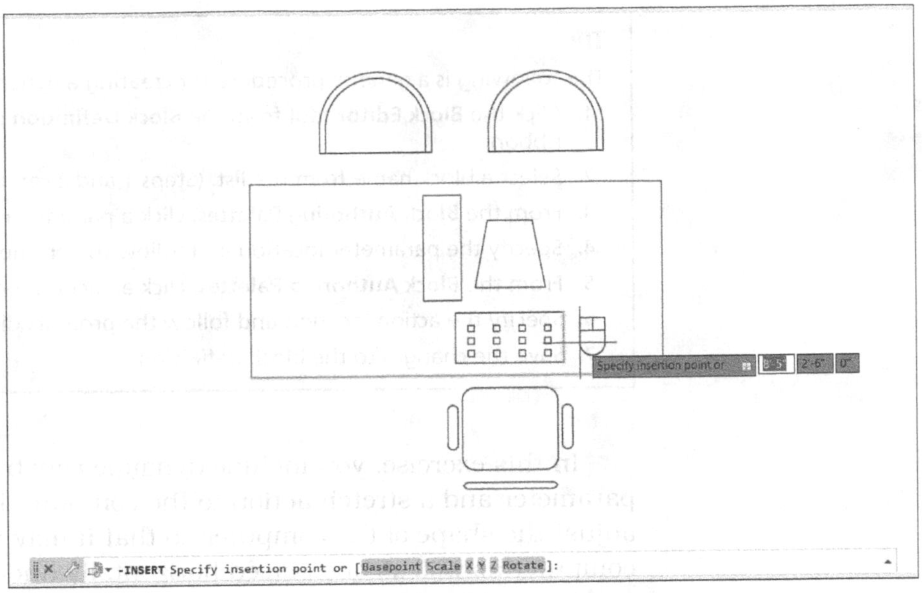

TIP
When inserting a block with the **AutoPlacement** option enabled, press and hold **<Shift>+W** or **<Shift>+]** to temporarily disable placement suggestions.

The final two options under **Insertion Options** at the bottom of the **Blocks** palette allow you to insert multiple instances of a block and explode the block after it has been inserted. These options are named **Repeat Placement** and **Explode**, respectively.

Creating Dynamic Blocks

dynamic block: In AutoCAD, a block defined with variable parameters that can be specified in any individual block reference.

Dynamic blocks are blocks that can be altered without redefining the block. They are created using the **Block Editor**. The editor is a whole subsystem of windows, symbols, and commands that enables you to add dynamic parameters and actions to newly or previously defined blocks. Here, a *parameter* is an aspect of the geometry of a block definition that may be designated as a variable. Parameters are always associated with *actions*. When a dynamic block is inserted, it takes the standard form of its original definition. Unlike other blocks, however, once a dynamic block is inserted, it can be selected and altered in specific ways. The ways in which a dynamic block can be altered depend on the parameters and actions that have been added to the definition. Parameters and actions are effective for creating blocks that may be adjusted through various simple editing procedures. When the goal is to define more complex relationships among different geometric and dimensional features of a block object, dynamic blocks can be defined with geometric and dimensional constraints (constraint parameters), which can be manipulated like other constraints.

> **TIP**
>
> The following is a general procedure for creating a dynamic block:
>
> 1. Click the **Block Editor** tool from the **Block Definition** panel on the **Insert** tab of the ribbon.
> 2. Select a block name from the list. (Steps 1 and 2 can be reversed.)
> 3. From the **Block Authoring Palettes**, click a parameter tool.
> 4. Specify the parameter location and follow the prompts displayed.
> 5. From the **Block Authoring Palettes**, click an action tool.
> 6. Specify the action location and follow the prompts displayed.
> 7. Save the changes to the block definition.

In this exercise, you include dynamic capabilities by adding a linear parameter and a stretch action to the computer block. This will allow you to adjust the shape of the computer so that it may represent a tower-style computer as well as one placed horizontally under the monitor. In the next section, you apply constraint parameters to make the monitor block dynamic, while ensuring that certain relationships are maintained.

✔ To begin this task, you should be in your *Source* drawing with the four blocks inserted in the last section, as shown in Figure 10-6.

✔ Select the computer block.

✔ Click the **Block Editor** tool from the **Block Definition** panel on the **Insert** tab of the ribbon, as shown in Figure 10-11.

This starts the ***BEDIT*** *command and displays the* ***Edit Block Definition*** *dialog box shown in Figure 10-12. Because you selected the computer block before entering the dialog box, the computer block should be selected in the block list, and an image of the block should be displayed in the* ***Preview*** *box. Once inside the* ***Block Editor****, you have access to a set of commands and procedures that cannot be accessed anywhere else. All these commands begin with the letter B and work on the block that was selected for editing.*

Figure 10-11
Block Editor tool

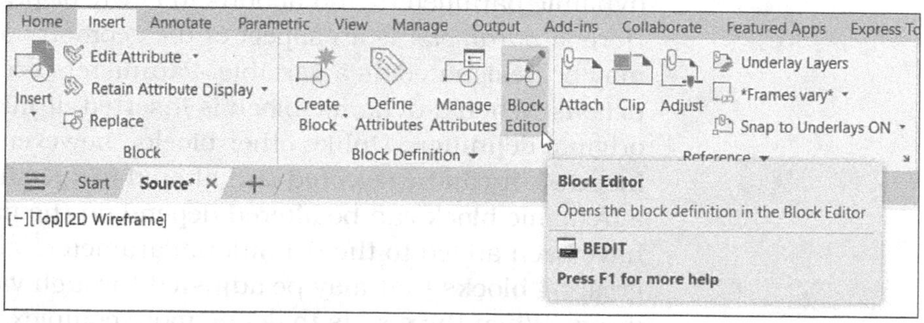

Figure 10-12
Edit Block Definition dialog box

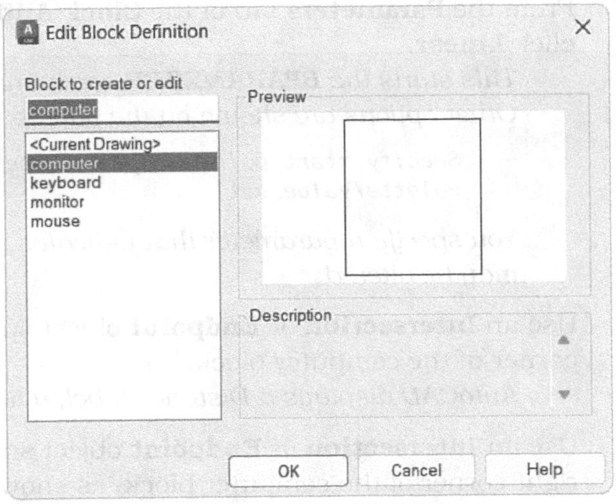

✔ Click **OK**.

This brings you into the Block editor with the ***Block Authoring Palettes*** *window and the* ***Block Editor*** *contextual tab of panels shown in Figure 10-13. On the right is the block itself in a special editing window where you can work directly on the block geometry. The light-gray hue distinguishes this window from the regular drawing area. On the left, there are the four tabs of the* ***Block Authoring Palettes****. The first is for defining parameters; the second is for actions; the third is for sets of parameters and actions that are frequently paired; and the fourth is for geometric constraints. Here, you add a linear parameter so that the width of the block can be altered; then you add a stretch action to show how the parameter can be edited after it is inserted.*

Figure 10-13
Block Authoring Palettes

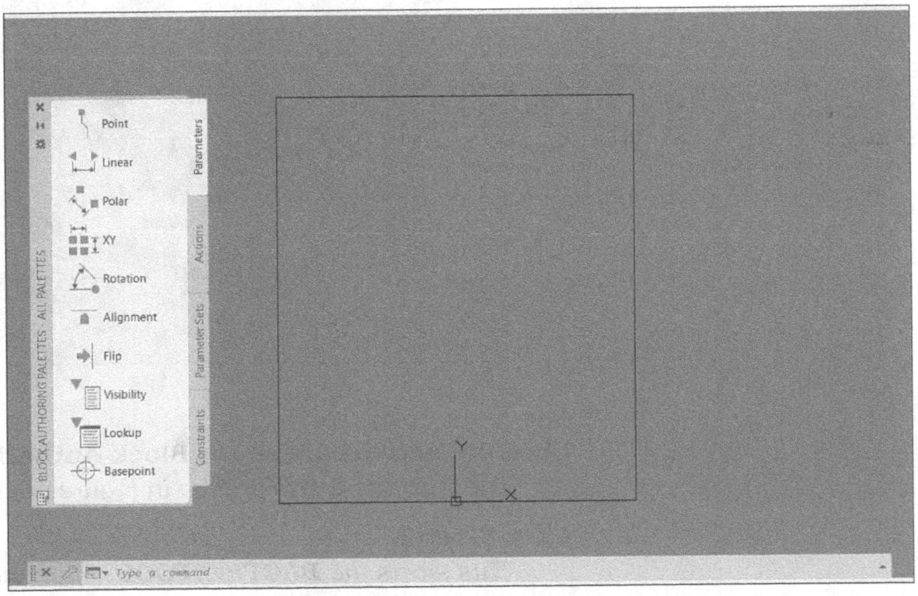

✔ From the **Parameters** tab of the **Block Authoring Palettes** window, click **Linear**.

*This starts the **BPARAMETER** command with the **Linear** option. Other options are shown on the palette. AutoCAD prompts:*

```
Specify start point or [Name/Label/Chain/Description/Base/
Palette/Value set]:
```

You specify a parameter that indicates the width of the computer may be altered.

✔ Use an **Intersection** or **Endpoint** object snap to specify the upper-left corner of the computer block.

AutoCAD displays a Distance label, a line, and two arrows.

✔ Use an **Intersection** or **Endpoint** object snap to specify the upper-right corner of the computer block, as shown by the triangular grip in Figure 10-14.

The length of the parameter is now established. AutoCAD prompts you to specify a label location.

✔ Specify a location point for the **Distance1** parameter label, as shown in Figure 10-14.

The parameter is now defined, but it is incomplete because there is no action defined for altering the parameter. The yellow box with the exclamation point is an alert to remind you of this.

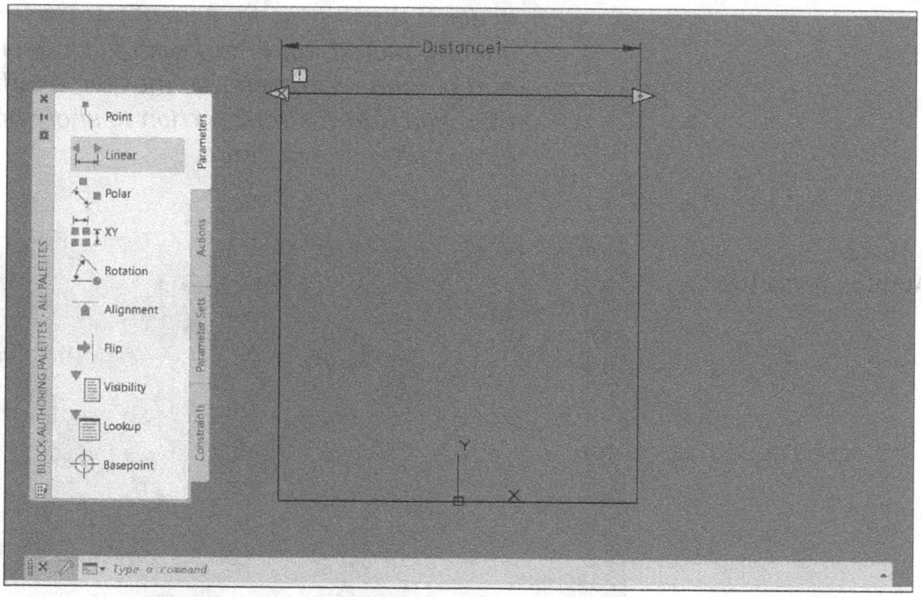

Figure 10-14
Distance label

✔ Click the **Actions** tab on the **Block Authoring Palettes** window.

*The **Actions** tab is shown in Figure 10-15.*

✔ Click **Stretch**.

*This starts the **BACTIONTOOL** command with the **Stretch** option. AutoCAD prompts:*

```
Select Parameter:
```

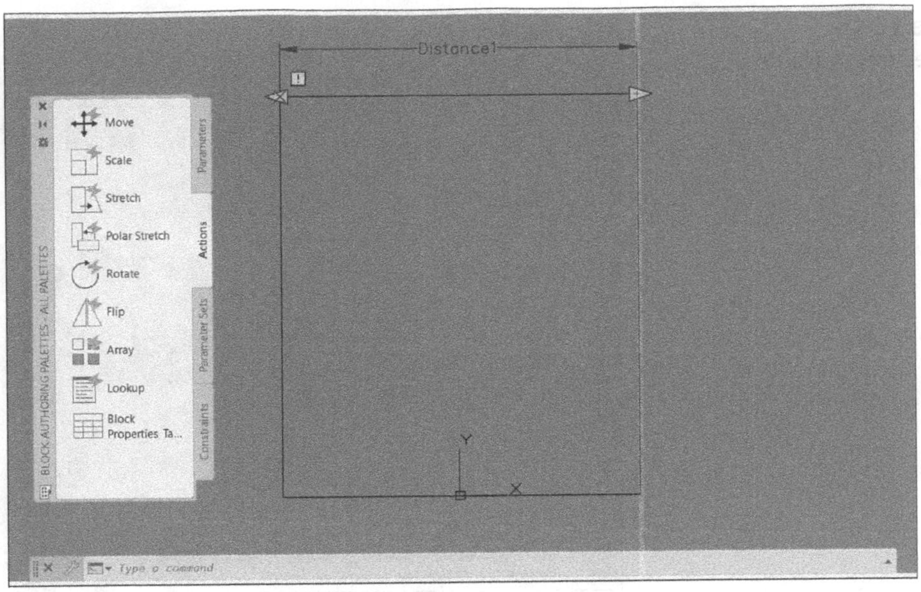

Figure 10-15
Actions tab

- ✔ Select any part of the parameter or its label.

  AutoCAD prompts:

  ```
  Specify parameter point to associate with action
  or enter [sTart point/Second point] <Start>:
  ```

  The points you can specify are the two triangles at the top corners of the block. These are the start point and the endpoint of the linear parameter. The behavior of the geometry is dependent on the point you specify.

- ✔ Specify the endpoint on the right.

  With this point specified, you are able to alter the width of the rectangle from the right side. AutoCAD now prompts you to define a stretch frame, just as you would do in the ***STRETCH*** *command.*

  ```
  Specify first corner of stretch frame or [CPolygon]:
  ```

  This window will frame the portion of the rectangle to be stretched.

- ✔ Specify two points to define a stretch frame around the right side of the rectangle, as shown in Figure 10-16.

  AutoCAD now prompts you to select objects.

- ✔ Select the objects that form the computer rectangle that cross or are inside the stretch frame.

- ✔ Right-click or press **<Enter>** to end object selection.

Figure 10-16
Define stretch frame

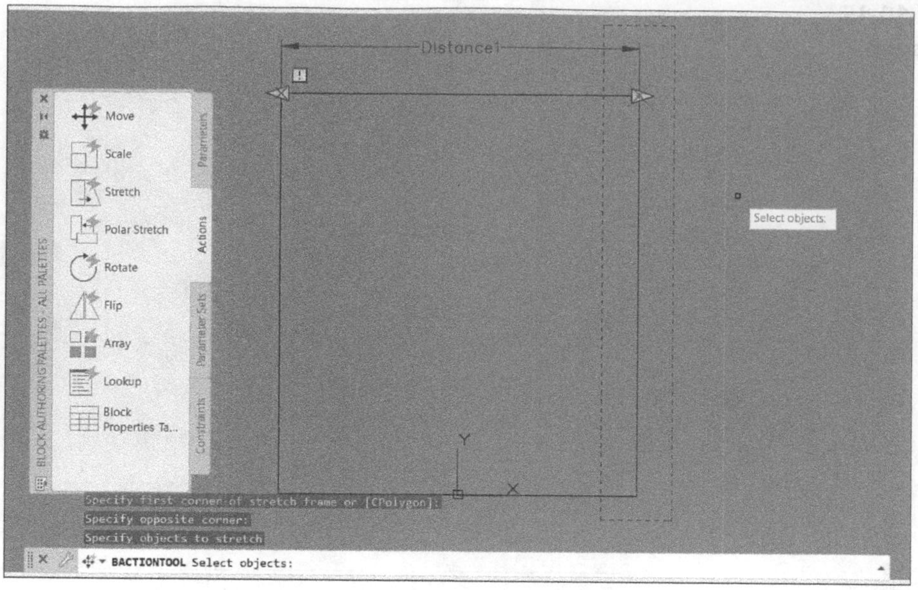

A stretch action icon is added to the block in the area of the stretch, as shown in Figure 10-17. If you let your cursor rest on the icon, you see that it is named *Stretch*.

The Test Block Window

The block now has a linear parameter with a stretch action. You can use the **Test Block** window to see how this works before leaving the **Block Editor**.

Figure 10-17
Stretch action symbol

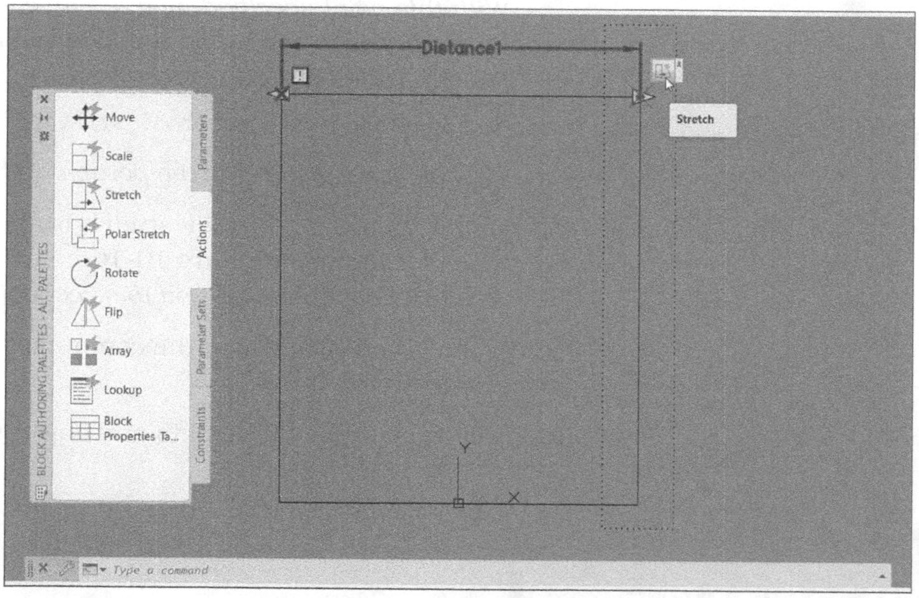

- ✔ Click the **Test Block** tool from the **Open/Save** panel on the ribbon's **Block Editor** contextual tab, as shown in Figure 10-18.

  This opens a simple window with the same light-gray background, but only the block is showing. It is more efficient to test the block here than to leave the ***Block Editor*** *and return to the drawing.*

Chapter 10

Figure 10-18
Test Block tool

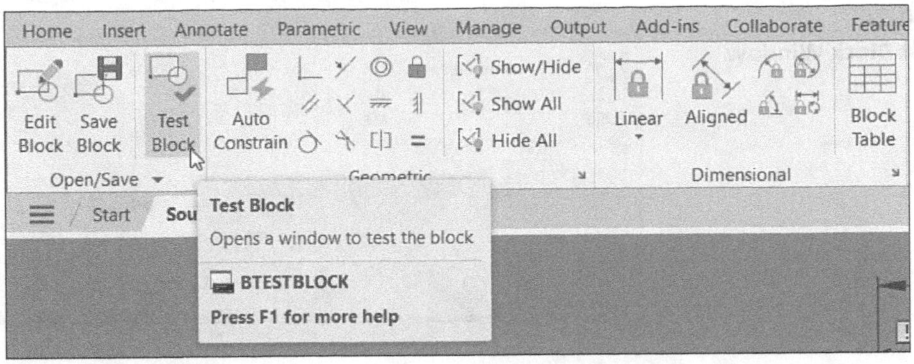

✔ Select the block.

The block is highlighted and an arrow at the point associated with the stretch action is displayed, as shown in Figure 10-19. The grip at the bottom shows the insertion point of the block.

✔ Click the arrow point at the upper-right corner of the block.

Figure 10-19
Stretch action arrow

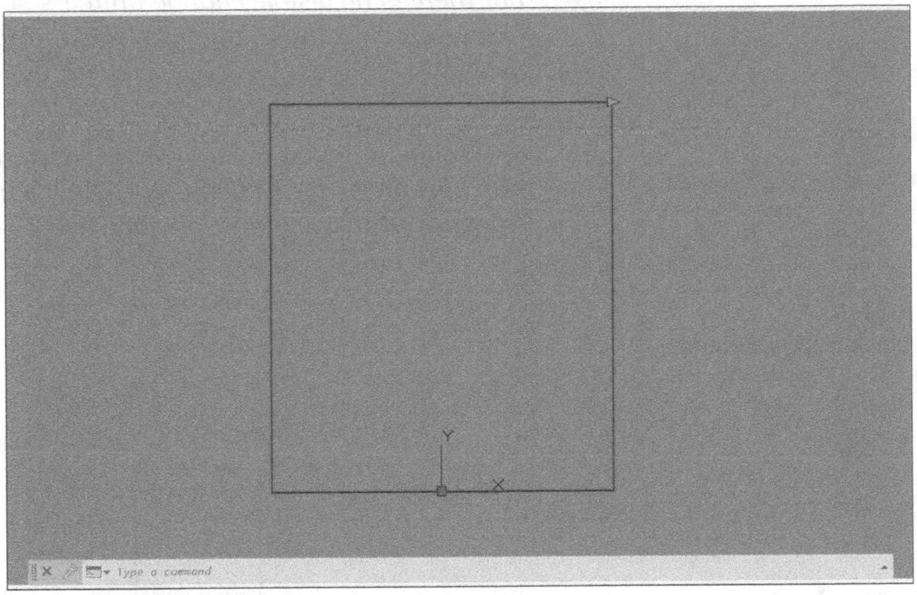

✔ Stretch the block right and left to see how the block can be stretched.

You can stretch the block horizontally to any length. This is just a test, however; nothing you do here will be saved.

✔ Specify any point to complete the stretch.

Next, you exit the ***Test Block*** *window and return to the* ***Block Editor****.*

✔ Click the **Close Test Block** tool, as shown in Figure 10-20.

This returns you to the ***Block Editor****. You are ready to return to the drawing. Like the* ***Close Test Block*** *tool, the* ***Close Block Editor*** *tool is at the right of the ribbon.*

Figure 10-20
Close Test Block Window tool

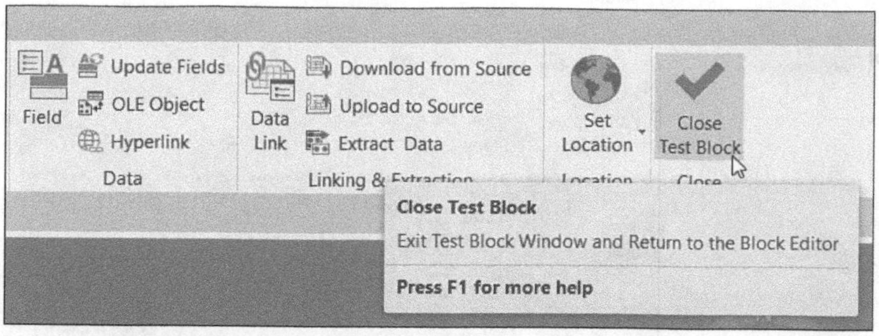

✔ Click the **Close Block Editor** tool to exit the block editing system.

AutoCAD displays a message prompting whether you want to save changes to the block.

✔ Click **Save the changes to computer** to save the changes to the block definition.

This returns you to the drawing editor. The four block references are displayed there as before. The computer block has been updated, but there is no visible change until it's selected. To complete this exercise, select the computer block and use the new dynamic behavior.

✔ Select the computer block.

The computer block is highlighted, and the new dynamic block grip has been added to indicate the linear parameter, just as it was in the ***Test Block*** *window, as shown in Figure 10-21.*

Figure 10-21
Dynamic block grip is added

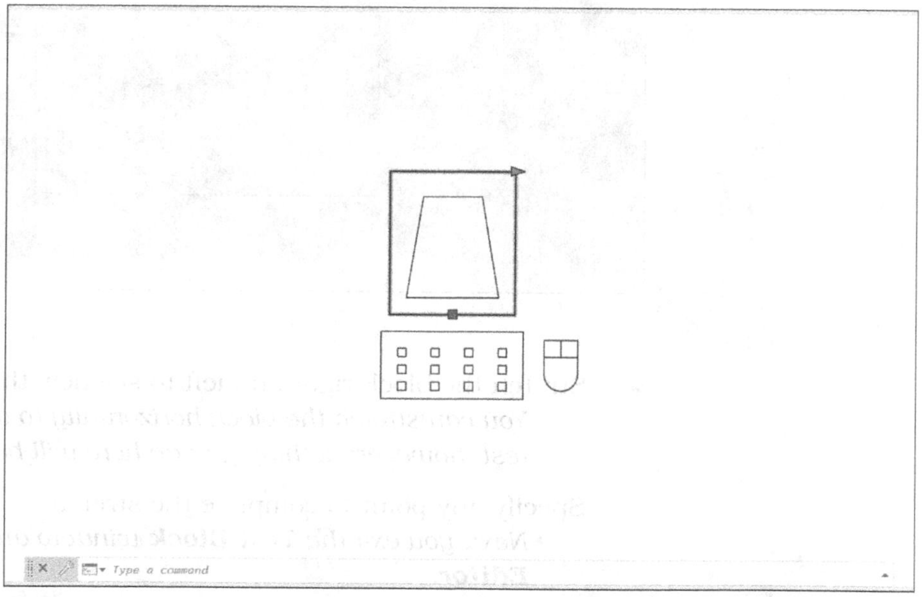

✔ Click the dynamic block grip at the upper-right corner of the computer block.

✔ Move your cursor to the left to shrink the computer block to a 6" width.

You now have a narrowed version of the computer block, which represents a tower-style computer. All you need to do is to move it over to the left.

✔ Click the square grip and move the computer 6" to the left, as shown in Figure 10-22.

✔ Press **<Esc>** to clear grips.

Your drawing should now resemble Figure 10-22.

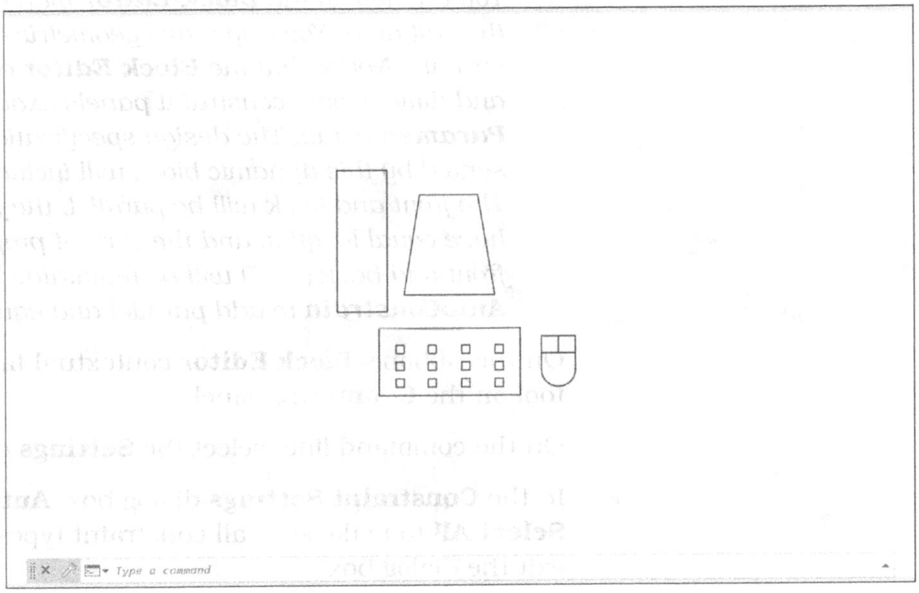

Figure 10-22
Computer shape has changed

This has been a brief introduction to the capabilities of dynamic blocks of the ***Block Editor****. In the next section, you add geometric and dimensional constraints to the monitor block, so that it can represent different-sized monitors.*

Adding Constraints to Dynamic Blocks

Constraint parameters provide the capability to create dynamic blocks in which geometric and dimensional relationships among different aspects of the block are carefully controlled. Once defined in this way, it also becomes possible to insert blocks with numeric data that exactly define the object, while adhering to general design specifications. In this section, you add constraints to the monitor block so that it becomes dynamic and may be used to represent different-sized monitors without losing its overall shape. You begin by entering the **Block Editor** with the monitor block selected.

> **TIP**
>
> The following is a general procedure for adding constraints to a dynamic block:
>
> 1. Click the **Block Editor** tool from the **Block Definition** panel on the ribbon's **Insert** tab.
> 2. Select a block. (Steps 1 and 2 can be reversed.)
> 3. In the **Block Editor**, add geometric and dimensional constraints.
> 4. Test the block.
> 5. Close the **Block Editor**.

- ✔ Select the monitor block.
- ✔ Click the **Block Editor** tool from the **Block Definition** panel on the ribbon's **Insert** tab.
- ✔ Press **<Enter>** in the **Edit Block Definition** dialog box.

  *You are now in the **Block Editor** with the monitor block showing in the edit area. You apply two geometric and two dimensional constraints. Notice that the **Block Editor** contextual tab has geometric and dimensional constraint panels exactly like those on the **Parametric** tab. The design specifications of the monitors represented by this dynamic block will include the following constraints: The front and back will be parallel, the front and the two sides will have equal lengths, and the current proportion in the widths of the front and back (11:7) will be maintained. First, you use **AutoConstrain** to add parallel and equal constraints.*

- ✔ On the ribbon's **Block Editor** contextual tab, click the **AutoConstrain** tool on the **Geometric** panel
- ✔ On the command line, select the **Settings** option.
- ✔ In the **Constraint Settings** dialog box, **AutoConstrain** tab, click **Select All** to make sure all constraint types are selected. Click **OK** to exit the dialog box.

  The Equal constraint isn't selected by default.

- ✔ Select the objects that define the monitor.
- ✔ Press **<Enter>** to end object selection.

  The front and back sides are constrained to be parallel, and the sides are constrained to be equal. Notice also that a horizontal constraint has been added, as shown in Figure 10-23. Because you might want the freedom to insert a monitor that is not horizontal, you want to eliminate this constraint.

> **NOTE**
>
> If you have not drawn the sides of the monitor equal, you can remedy this by clicking the **Equal** constraint tool and selecting the two sides.

- ✔ Right-click on the horizontal constraint and select **Delete** from the shortcut menu.

  The horizontal constraint disappears, leaving the other constraints in place.

Figure 10-23
Geometric constraints

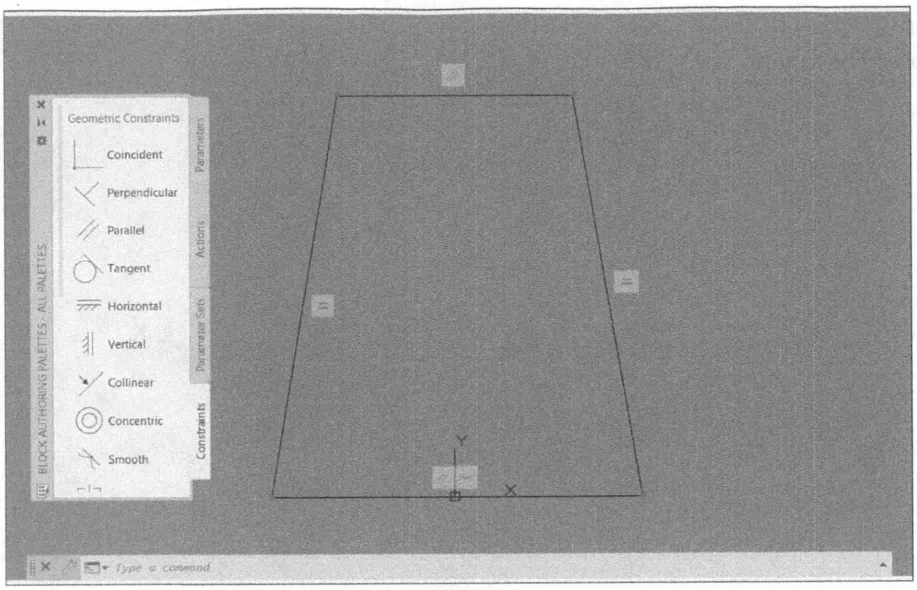

Next, you add a constraint to make the front and the two sides equal. Because the two sides are already equal, you need to select only one side.

✔ Click the **Equal** constraint tool from the **Geometric** panel.

✔ Select the 11" front edge of the monitor for the first object.

AutoCAD prompts:

```
Select second object:
```

✔ Select either of the two sides.

An equal constraint marker is added to the front, and the length of the two sides adjusts to be equal to the front edge, as shown in Figure 10-23. Notice that there are now two constraints applied to the front edge.

Next, you add dimensional constraints to the front and back.

✔ Click the **Linear** tool from the **Dimensional** panel.

✔ Select the 11" front edge near its endpoint on the left side.

Before you select the line, you should see a small red circle with an X at the endpoint.

✔ Now, select the 11" front edge near its other endpoint on the right side.

✔ Specify a dimension line location below the monitor, as shown in Figure 10-24.

✔ Press **<Enter>** to accept the name and value of the constraint.

The constraint is added, as shown in Figure 10-24.

✔ Click the **Linear** tool from the **Dimensional** panel again.

✔ Press **<Enter>** so you can select an object.

✔ Select the 7" back edge.

✔ Specify a dimension line location above the monitor, as shown in Figure 10-24.

Figure 10-24
Dimensional constraints

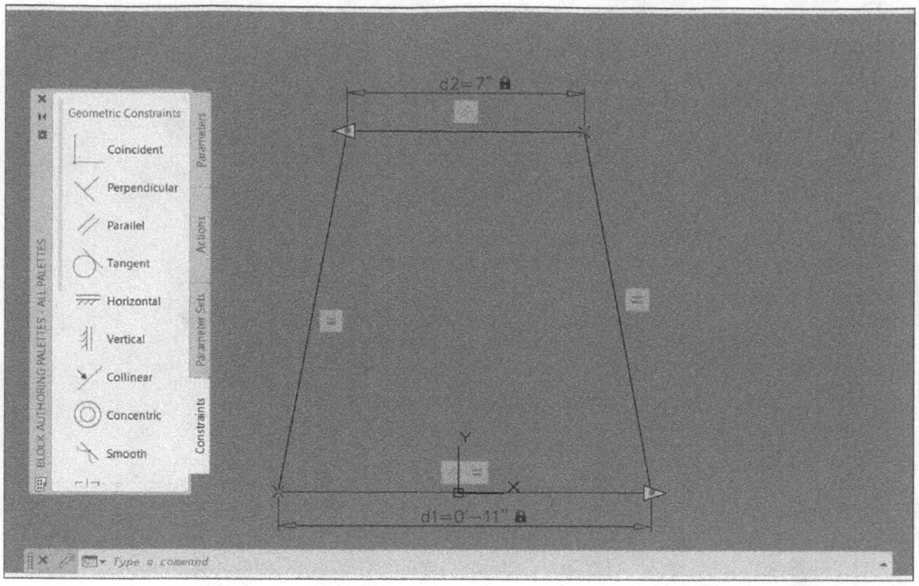

✔ Press <Enter> to accept the name and value.

Finally, you open the ***Parameters Manager*** *and specify a proportional relationship between the front and back.*

✔ Click the **Parameters Manager** tool from the **Manage** panel on the **Block Editor** contextual tab of the ribbon.

The ***Parameters Manager*** *position depends on its most recent use. It may be located at the left, covering part of the ribbon. It may be floating within the drawing window, or it may also be collapsed if the* ***Auto-hide*** *feature has been activated. In any case, when you open it, you see a table with* ***d1*** *and* ***d2*** *defined as shown in Figure 10-25. You create the proportion directly in the constraint entry for* ***d2****.*

✔ Double-click in the **Expression** column of the row for **d2**.

✔ Type **d1*7/11 <Enter>**.

*This expression ensures that the current proportion between front and back edges will be maintained at all sizes. The label on the constraint changes to "d2 = d1*7/11".*

Figure 10-25
Parameters Manager

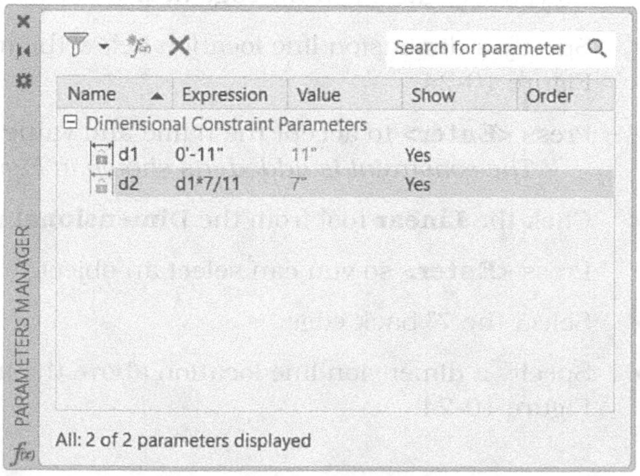

*The block now has all the constraints required by the design specifications. You move to the **Test Block** window to try it out before leaving the **Block Editor**.*

- ✔ Close the **Parameters Manager**.
- ✔ Click the **Test Block** tool from the **Open/Save** panel.
- ✔ Select the monitor.
- ✔ Click the arrow-shaped grip at the front right of the monitor.
- ✔ Stretch the monitor larger and smaller.
  You see that all of the constraints are maintained at all sizes of the monitor.
- ✔ Specify any point to complete the stretch.
- ✔ Close the **Test Block** window.
- ✔ Close the **Block Editor**.
  AutoCAD warns you that the edited block is not fully constrained.
- ✔ Click **Save changes** and exit the **Block Editor**.
  The monitor block reference is updated and adjusted slightly.
- ✔ Select the monitor block and use the grip to see that you can vary the size of the monitor, just as you did in the **Test Block** window.

Accessing Data in a Block Table

The addition of constraints to dynamic blocks adds the capability to specify variable block dimensions in a block table. Once a table of block variations is defined, all you have to do is click a grip on the block to open a shortcut menu where you can select from the list of block variations. To do this, you open the monitor block in the **Block Editor** again, add a block table, and define three more size variations. Then you return to the drawing and select one of these new sizes from the **Block Table** shortcut menu.

- ✔ To begin, you should be in the ***Source*** drawing.
  There are four blocks in your drawing. Two of them—the computer and the monitor—are dynamic blocks.
- ✔ Select the monitor block.
- ✔ Click **Insert** > **Block Definition** > **Block Editor**.
- ✔ Press **<Enter>** or click **OK** to edit the monitor block.

  *You are in the **Block Editor** contextual tab with the **Block Authoring Palettes** window and the monitor block showing in the editing area. The two dimensional parameters are shown. Block tables hold parameter information for the selected block. First, you must attach a table to the block and then add data to it.*

- ✔ Click the **Block Table** tool from the **Dimensional** panel on the ribbon's **Block Editor** contextual tab, as shown in Figure 10-26.

  AutoCAD prompts:

  ```
  Specify parameter location or [Palette]:
  ```

  Before you can create a block table, you need to specify a point from where the table and associated shortcut menu can be opened.

Figure 10-26
Block Table tool

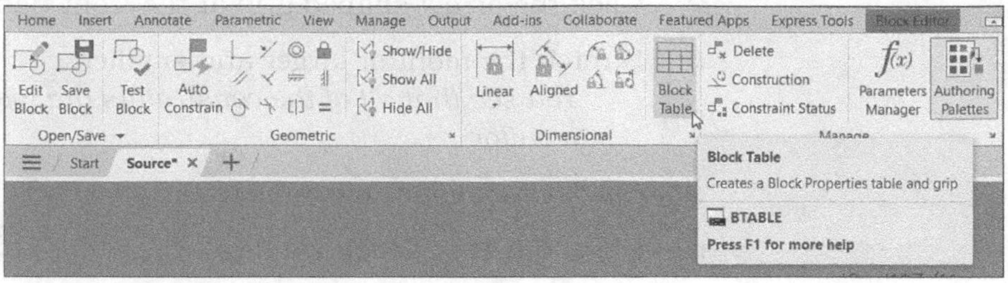

- ✔ Specify a point in the middle of the block, as shown in Figure 10-27.

  The prompt gives you the opportunity to have either no grip or one grip added to the block.

Figure 10-27
Specify point

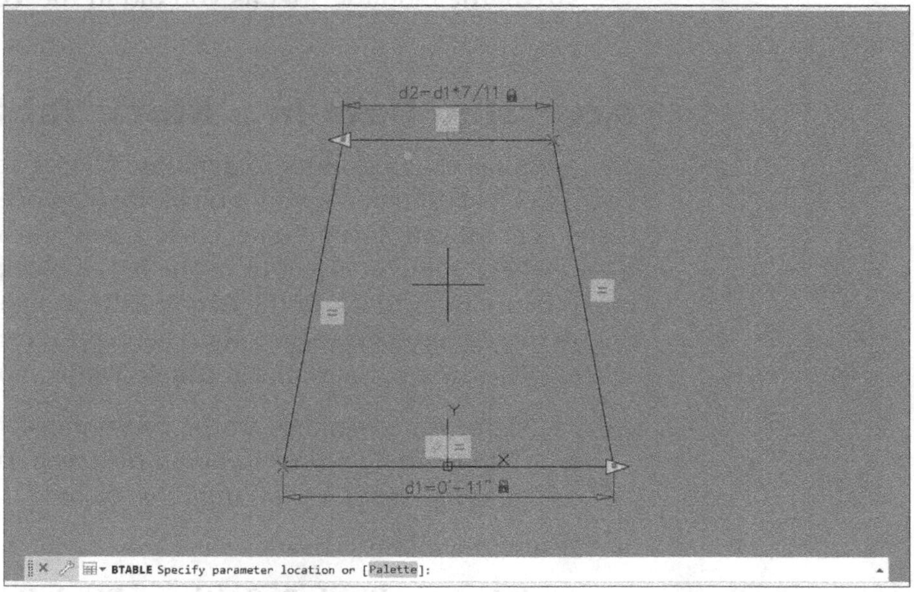

- ✔ Press **<Enter>** to accept one grip.

  *This opens the **Block Properties Table** dialog box, shown in Figure 10-28. It is blank until you take steps to add properties to it.*

- ✔ Click the **Adds properties** button, as shown.

  *You see the **Add Parameter Properties** dialog box, shown in Figure 10-29. It shows the two distance parameters defined in the last section.*

Figure 10-28
Block Properties Table

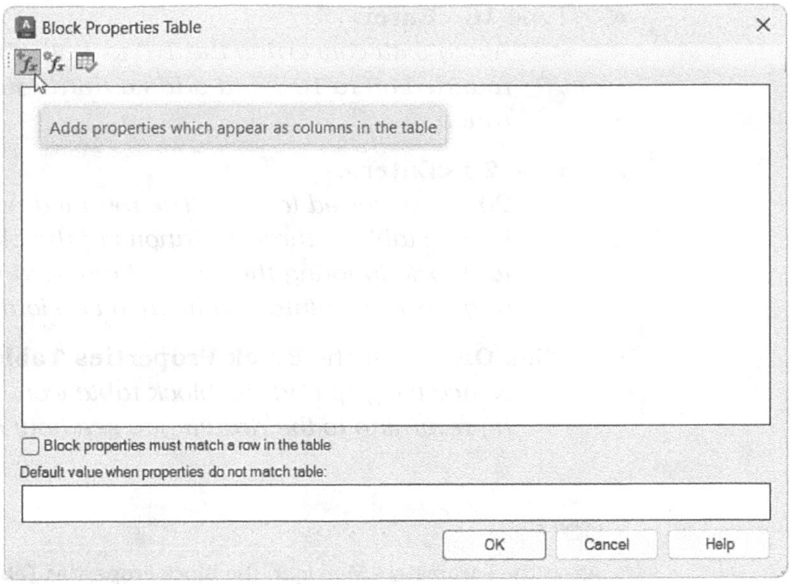

Figure 10-29
Add Parameter Properties dialog box

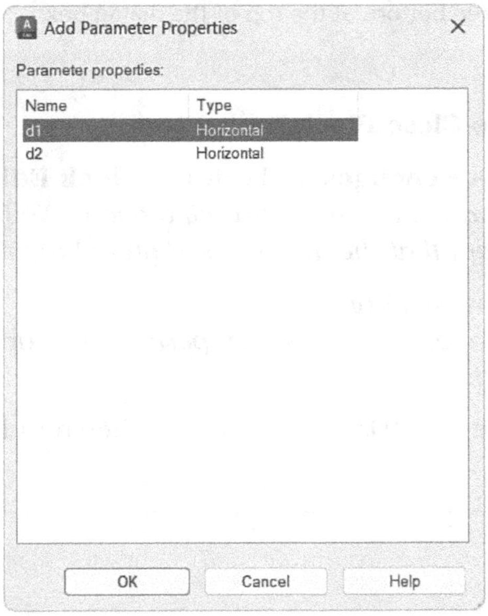

✔ Hold down the **<Shift>** key and select **d1** and **d2**.

✔ Click **OK**.

You are now back in the ***Block Properties Table*** dialog box, *with d1 and d2 showing as column headers. Each row represents a different configuration of the block constraints, by varying the values under d1 and d2. Try this:*

✔ Click once in the cell below **d1**.

✔ Type **12 <Enter>**.

*Three things happen. The value in column d1 is rewritten as 1′. The value in column d2 is calculated from the expression = d1*7/11. Your units are set to 0 decimal places precision, so the result is rounded to 8″. Finally, a second row is added. You add a second configuration.*

✔ Type **16 <Enter>**.

Along with converting the 16" to 1'-4", the table calculates d2, rounded off to 10", and adds a third row. You add one more configuration.

✔ Type **20 <Enter>**.

20" is converted to 1'-8". The rounded value for d2 is 1'-1". You now have a table of three variations of the block parameters for the monitor block. Ignoring the issue of rounded values, the dimensional constraints are maintained in each version.

✔ Click **OK** to exit the **Block Properties Table** dialog box.

Notice the grip and the block table icon. You complete this exercise by returning to the drawing to see how it works.

> **NOTE**
>
> As on the **Parameters Manager**, the **Block Properties Table** allows you to create new parameters that are not yet defined in the drawing. You would do this by clicking the **New User Parameter** button to the right of the **Adds properties** button—that is, the middle of the three buttons at the top of the dialog box.

✔ Click the **Close Block Editor** tool.

✔ Click **Save changes** and exit the **Block Editor**.

You are back in the drawing again. Nothing has changed visually, except that the monitor is slightly larger.

✔ Select the monitor.

There is a new block properties table grip near the middle of the block.

✔ Click the new triangular grip, as shown in Figure 10-30.

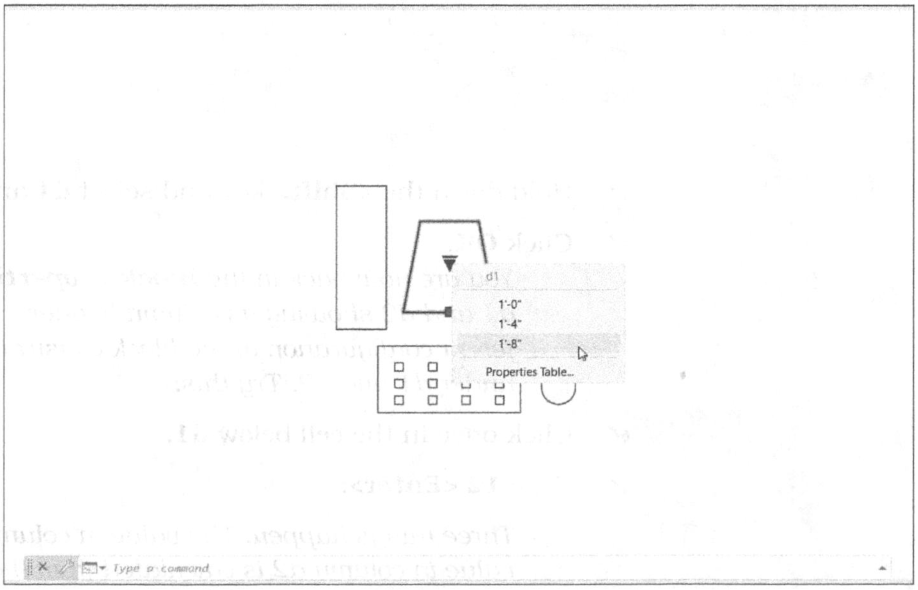

Figure 10-30
Triangular grip opens a shortcut menu

This opens the shortcut menu, as shown. The menu shows the three values of d1 you entered in the table. The complete table, as shown previously, can be accessed from the bottom of the menu.

✔ Select **1'-8"**.

The monitor is resized, as shown in Figure 10-31. You may need to use the grips to adjust its position and that of the mouse and keyboard.

✔ Press **<Esc>** to clear grips.

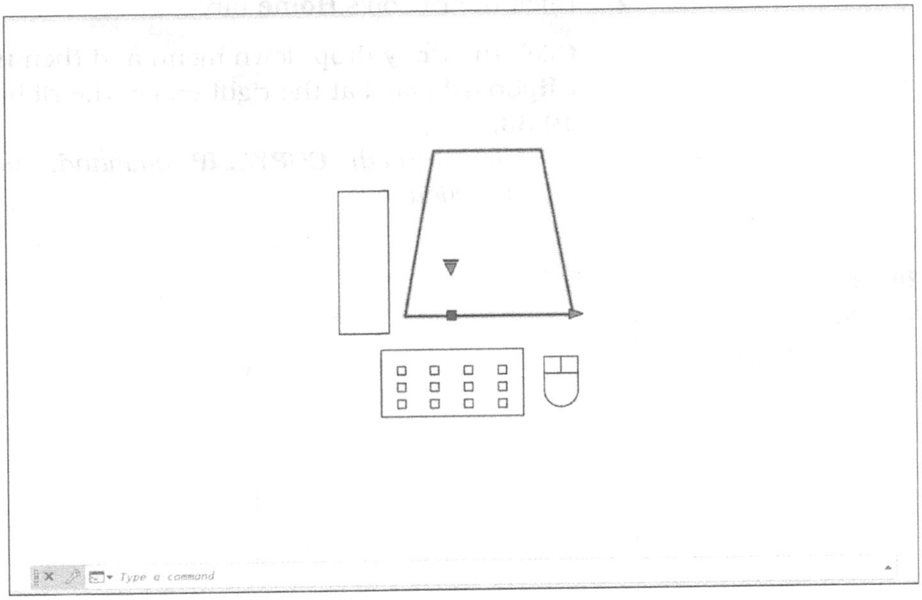

Figure 10-31
Resizing monitor

In the next two sections, you explore copying drawn objects between applications using the Windows Clipboard and copying blocks between drawings.

Using the Windows Clipboard

COPYCLIP	
Command	COPYCLIP
Shortcut	<Ctrl> + C
Panel	Clipboard
Tool	

In this section, you begin your exploration of sharing blocks and other data among drawings. The Windows Clipboard makes it very easy to copy objects from one AutoCAD drawing to another or into other Windows applications. **CUTCLIP** and **CUTBASE** remove selected objects from your AutoCAD drawing, whereas **COPYCLIP** and **COPYBASE** leave them in place. The differences between the commands that end with "CLIP" versus "BASE" is that the two commands that end with "BASE" prompt for a base point that is used when pasting the objects back into a drawing. When you send blocks to another AutoCAD drawing via the Windows Clipboard, they are defined as blocks in the new drawing as well. Block names and definitions are maintained, but there is no option to scale the blocks as they are being pasted, as there is when you **INSERT** blocks.

New to AutoCAD 2023

The **CUTBASE** command copies selected objects to the Windows Clipboard and then removes those same objects from a drawing. Prior to the introduction of the **CUTBASE** command, you would use the **COPYBASE** command and follow that with the **ERASE** command.

In this section, you create a new drawing called *Target* and copy the blocks that make up the workstation into it. The steps would be the same to copy the objects into another Windows application. The procedure is very simple and works with any Windows application that supports Windows object linking and embedding (OLE).

✔ To begin this exercise, you should be in the *Source* drawing with the inserted blocks in your drawing, resembling Figure 10-32.

To access the ***COPYCLIP*** *and* ***CUTCLIP*** *commands, you return to the ribbon's* ***Home*** *tab.*

✔ Click the ribbon's **Home** tab.

✔ Click the **Copy** drop-down menu and then the **Copy Clip** tool from the **Clipboard** panel at the right end of the ribbon, as shown in Figure 10-33.

This starts the ***COPYCLIP*** *command. AutoCAD prompts for object selection.*

Figure 10-32
Source drawing

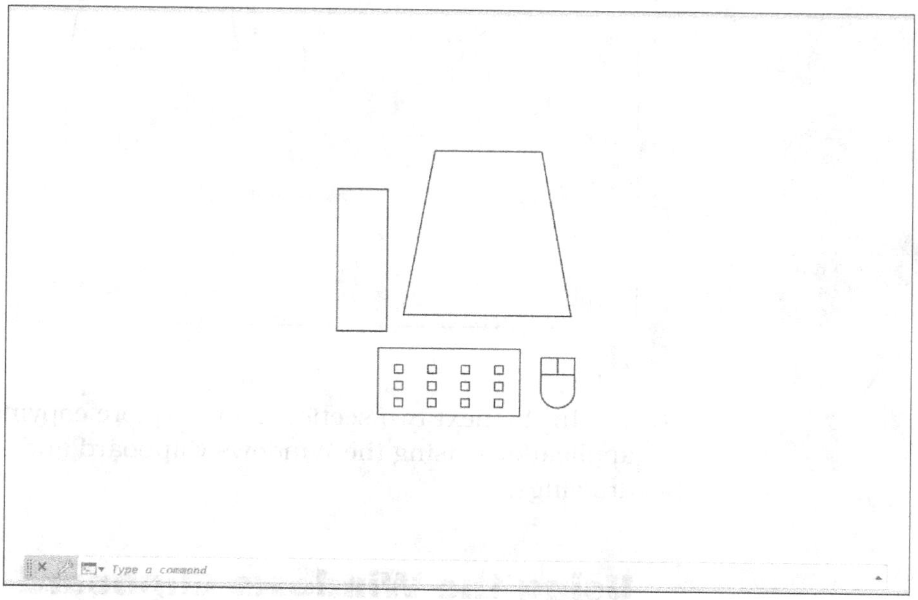

Figure 10-33
Copy Clip tool

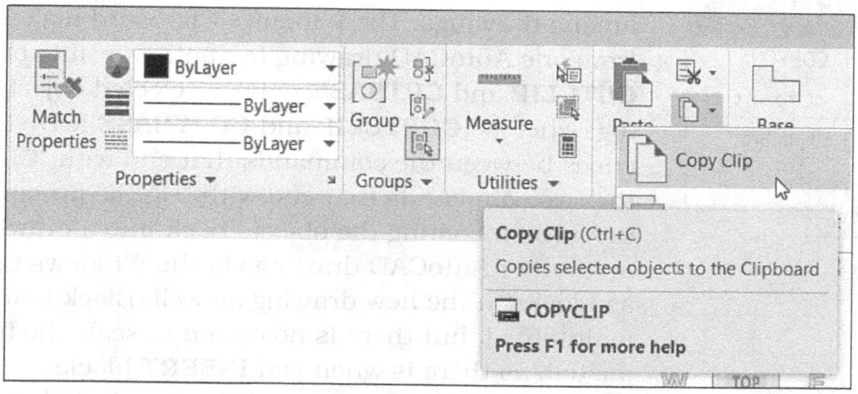

✔ Using a window or lasso selection, select all the objects in the computer workstation created in the "Inserting Blocks into the Current Drawing" section.

✔ Right-click to end object selection.

AutoCAD adds the selected objects to the Windows Clipboard. Nothing happens to the selected objects, but they are stored and can be pasted back into this drawing, another AutoCAD drawing, or another Windows application. Next, you create a new drawing.

✔ Create a new drawing with 18 × 12 limits and decimal units. The 1B template is effective if you have it.

You name this drawing Target. Notice that you can have multiple drawings open in a single AutoCAD session.

✔ Save the new drawing, giving it the name ***Target***.

Target should now be the current drawing with Source also open in the background. To see this, you use the drawing file tabs, which become useful whenever you have more than one drawing open.

✔ Move your cursor and let it rest on the **Source** drawing file tab, as shown in Figure 10-34.

This opens a thumbnail image representing the Source *drawing and two drawing layouts, which haven't been initialized yet, so they are represented with a standard layout icon. For now, these thumbnails are hardly necessary. You can switch between the two open drawings simply by clicking the* ***Source*** *tab or the* ***Target*** *tab to activate whichever drawing you want to set current.*

You stay with the current drawing, Target.

Figure 10-34
Source drawing file tab

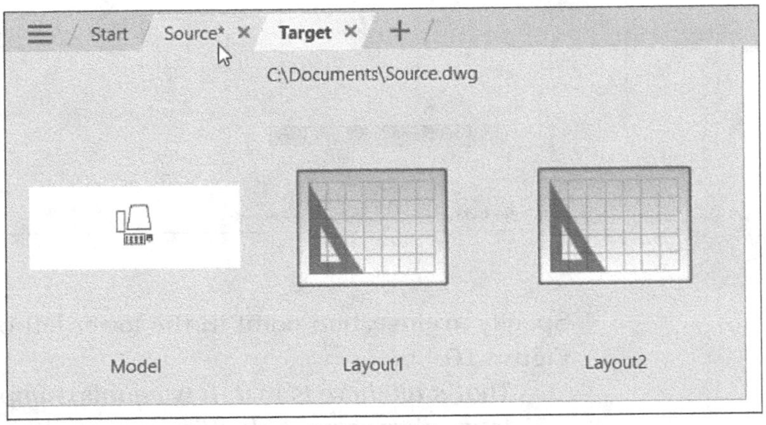

✔ Move your cursor away from the drawing file tabs to keep *Target* the current drawing.

✔ In *Target*, click the **Paste** tool from the **Paste** drop-down menu on the **Clipboard** panel, as shown in Figure 10-35.

AutoCAD prompts for an insertion point and presents you with the objects to drag into place. You see a very large keyboard in the drawing area, as shown in Figure 10-36. Actually, the whole workstation is there, but the computer, monitor, and mouse are outside the current view of the drawing. They are so large because the view scale of this drawing is very different from the one the objects were drawn in. The original drawing has been set up with different limits. In the new drawing, the limits are set to 18 × 12 and the keyboard is coming in at 17", covering most of the current drawing view. Without the scaling capacity of the ***INSERT*** *command, you have no control over this interpretation.*

Figure 10-35
Paste tool

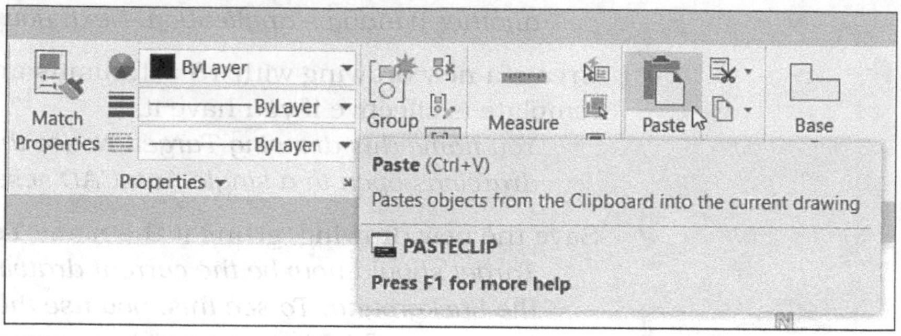

Figure 10-36
Specify insertion point

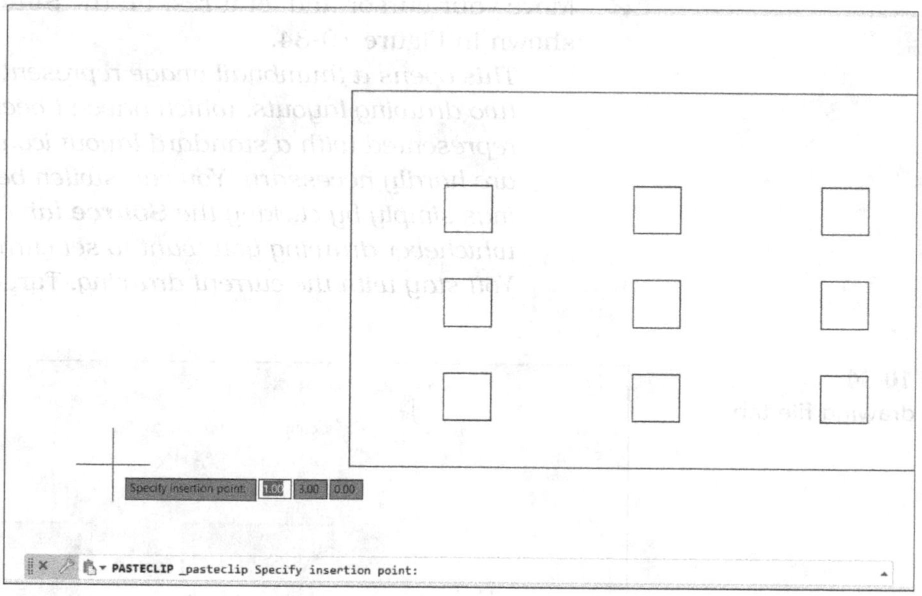

✔ Specify an insertion point in the lower left of your drawing, as shown in Figure 10-36.

That's all there is to it. It is equally simple to paste text and images from other compatible Windows applications into AutoCAD. Just reverse the process, cutting or copying from another application and pasting into AutoCAD.

You undo this paste before moving on.

✔ Press **U** until everything has been undone in *Target*.

The issue of scaling is handled differently when you paste AutoCAD objects into other applications. In those cases, objects are automatically scaled to fit in the document that receives them. Most applications have their own sizing feature, which allows you to adjust the size of the objects after they have been pasted.

Along with the **Paste** tool, which starts the **PASTECLIP** command, there are additional commands that allow you to paste objects from the Windows Clipboard into AutoCAD. From the **Paste** drop-down menu on the **Clipboard** panel, you can paste copied drawing objects as a block with the **Paste as Block** tool (**PASTEBLOCK** command) and drawing objects can be pasted to their original coordinates using the **Paste to Original Coordinates** tool (**PASTEORIG** command). If you are pasting objects from the Windows Clipboard that were copied from another Windows application, the **Paste Special** tool (**PASTESPEC** command) can give you some control over how that data is converted to drawing objects as it is pasted into a drawing.

Inserting Blocks and External References into Other Drawings

Any drawing can be inserted as a block or attached as an external reference into another drawing. The process is much like inserting a block within a drawing, but you need to specify the drawing location. In this exercise, you attach *Source* as an external reference in *Target*. The process for inserting blocks into other drawings is similar to attaching an external reference, but the result is different.

> **TIP**
>
> The following is a general procedure for inserting or attaching a drawing into another drawing:
>
> 1. Prepare a drawing to be inserted or attached into another drawing.
> 2. Enter the **INSERT** or **XATTACH** command.
> 3. Browse to the drawing to be inserted or attached.
> 4. Provide values in the dialog box or prompts displayed for insertion, scale, and rotation.

External References

external reference: In AutoCAD, a reference that points to a drawing that is not in the database of the current drawing, so that information for the external reference is available within the current drawing but is maintained in another drawing file.

An ***external reference*** is a bit of information within one drawing that provides a link to another drawing. If the path to the external drawing is clear and accessible, objects from the referenced drawing appear in the current drawing just as if they had been created or inserted there.

> **NOTE**
>
> The use of external references requires careful project and file management. Creating a dependency of one drawing on another opens up possibilities for confusion. If a file is moved or renamed, for example, the path to the external reference could be lost.

Externally referencing a drawing is a powerful alternative to inserting it as a block. Because attaching a reference loads only enough information to point to and access data from the externally referenced drawing, it does not increase the size of the current drawing file as significantly as defining the objects in the drawing and then inserting them as a block with **INSERT**.

Most important, if the referenced drawing is changed, the changes are reflected in the current drawing the next time it is loaded or when the **Reload** option of the **External Manager** is used. This allows designers at remote locations to work on different aspects of a single master drawing, which can be updated as changes are made in the various referenced drawings.

✔ You should be in *Target* to begin this exercise, with everything undone.

At this point, you return to the Source *drawing. To switch back, use the drawing file tab.*

✔ Click the **Source** drawing file tab to bring this drawing back into the foreground.

Now, you are back in your original drawing with the computer workstation objects displayed as shown previously in Figure 10-32. You could use this drawing as a block or external reference without further adjustment, but using the ***BASE*** *command to adjust the insertion base point of the drawing is convenient.* ***BASE*** *works to move the insertion point from the origin of the drawing and impacts the inserting or attaching of the drawing.*

✔ Click the ribbon's **Home** tab and then click the **Block** panel's title bar to expand it. From the expanded **Block** panel, click the **Set Base Point** tool, as shown in Figure 10-37.

This tool is also available by expanding the ***Block*** *panel of the* ***Insert*** *tab.*

AutoCAD prompts:

```
Enter base point, <0'-0", 0'-0", 0'-0">:
```

This indicates that the current base point is at the origin of the grid. Here, you relocate it to the lower-left corner of the keyboard.

Figure 10-37
Set Base Point tool

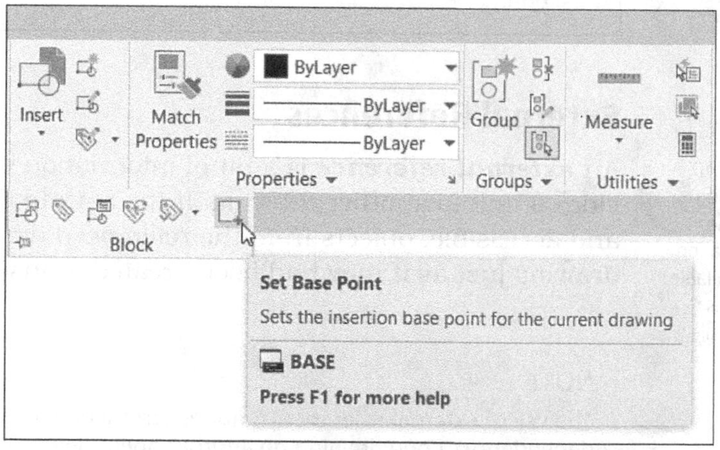

✔ Specify the lower-left corner of the keyboard.

The new base point is registered, but there is no visible change in the drawing. To see what you have accomplished, you have to save Source *and return to* Target.

NOTE

Be sure to pay attention to where you are saving the ***Source*** drawing so you can easily find it again. If you are uncertain, use the **Save As** tool on the **Quick Access** toolbar instead of the **Save** tool. You can also right-click on a drawing file tab and select **Open File Location** to open File Explorer to the location of the drawing.

✔ Save **Source**.

If you don't save the drawing after changing the base point, the base point is not used when the drawing is attached.

✔ Click the **Target** drawing file tab.

This returns you to your Target *drawing. There should be no objects in this drawing. You use the* **XATTACH** *command here to attach* Source *as an external reference in* Target.

✔ Click **Insert** > **Reference** > **Attach** tool, as shown in Figure 10-38.

This opens the ***Select Reference File*** *dialog box, as shown in Figure 10-39. This is basically the same dialog box you see when you enter any command in which you select a file.*

Figure 10-38
Attach tool

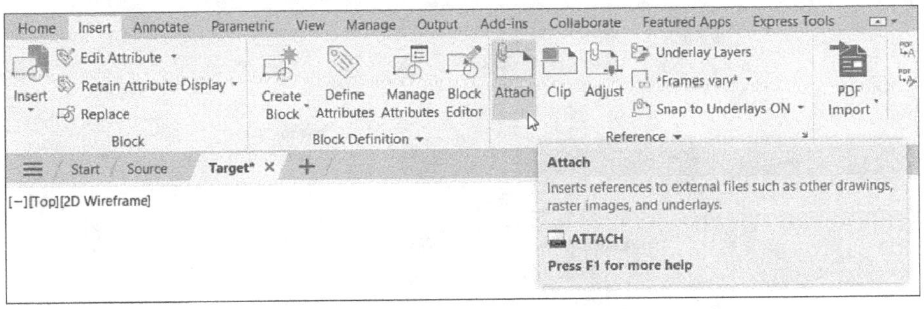

Figure 10-39
Select Reference File dialog box

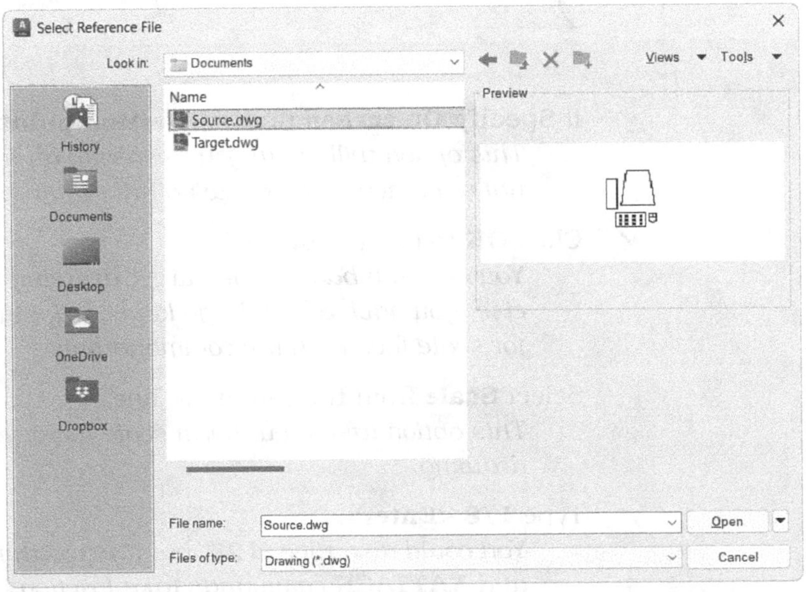

✔ Make sure that **Drawing (*.dwg)** is selected in the **Files of type** list.
This will facilitate finding your drawing.

✔ Navigate to the folder that contains *Source*, using the **Look In** drop-down list, **Up One Level** button, the **Place** buttons on the left, or the **Find** feature under **Tools**, if necessary, to locate *Source*.

✔ Select ***Source*** from the list of files or from the thumbnail gallery, depending on your operating system and settings.

✔ Click **Open**.
This opens the ***Attach External Reference*** *dialog box, shown in Figure 10-40.* ***Source*** *should be entered in the* **Name** *drop-down list. Notice that* Source *is already open, so you are not actually opening the drawing at this point but attaching it to* Target.

Figure 10-40
Attach External Reference
dialog box

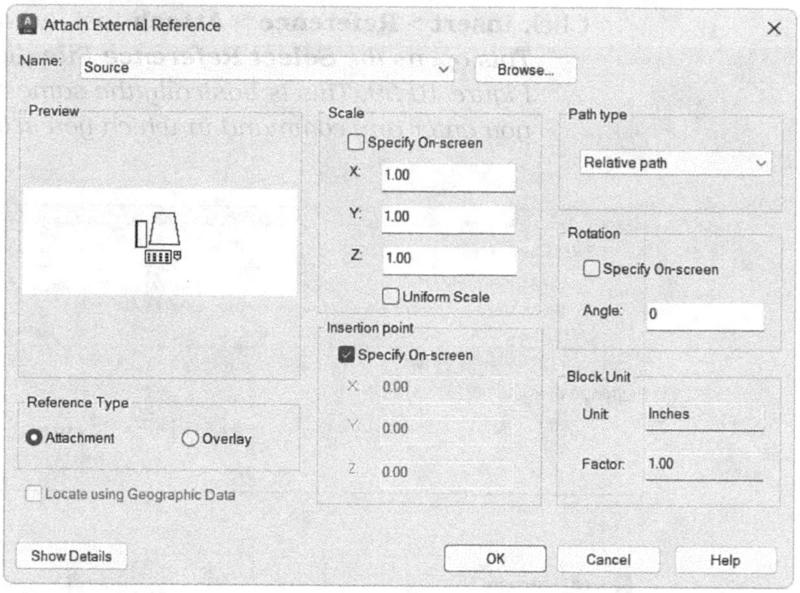

✔ If **Specify On-screen** under **Insertion point** is not checked, click it.
This option will allow you to specify an insertion point for the external reference in the drawing area after exiting the dialog box.

✔ Click **OK** to exit the dialog box.
You are now back to the Target *drawing window. As in the last exercise, you have a very large keyboard, but this time there is a prompt for scale factors in the command line.*

✔ Select **Scale** from the command line.
This option takes a uniform scale factor for the complete inserted drawing.

✔ Type **1/8 <Enter>**.
You could also type ***.125****, but it is worth noting that the* ***INSERT*** *and* ***XATTACH*** *commands take fractions or scale ratios at the scale factor prompt.*

✔ Specify an insertion point near the middle of the drawing area.

At this scale, the workstation appears in the drawing area much as it does in the Source drawing. The slightly faded objects remind you that this is an external reference.

Stop for a moment to consider your two drawings. *Source* is open in the background but has been attached as an external reference in *Target*. *Source* has the architectural units and 12' × 9' limits established at the beginning of the chapter. It has four separate blocks currently that make up a workstation. *Target* has decimal units and 18 × 12 limits and has one instance of *Source* attached as an external reference, scaled down to 1/8. In the exercises that follow, you continue to make changes to these drawings. Later, you see those changes in *Source* are reflected in *Target*. In the next exercise, you are introduced to another powerful tool for managing drawing data, AutoCAD **DesignCenter**.

Using AutoCAD DesignCenter

DesignCenter: In AutoCAD, a palette that provides access to content in open or closed drawing files on local or in remote locations.

AutoCAD ***DesignCenter*** enables you to manipulate drawing content similar to the way File Explorer in Windows handles files and folders. The interface is familiar, with a tree view on the left and a list of content on the right. The difference is the data types available. With **DesignCenter** you can access the contents of open or closed drawing files and easily copy or insert content into other open drawings. Blocks, external references, layers, linetypes, dimension styles, text styles, table styles, and page layouts are all examples of content defined in a drawing that can be copied or inserted into another drawing to reduce duplicated effort and increase consistency in your designs.

In this exercise, you begin by opening **DesignCenter** and examining some of the available content.

✔ Make sure you have ***Target*** open and is the current drawing.

✔ Press **<Ctrl>+2** or click **View** > **Palettes** > **DesignCenter** from the ribbon, as shown in Figure 10-41.

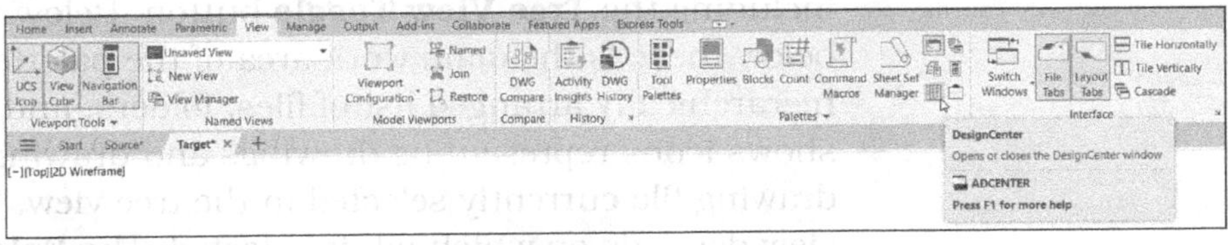

Figure 10-41
DesignCenter tool

*This starts the **ADCENTER** command and displays the **DesignCenter** palette shown in Figure 10-42. If you or someone else has used **DesignCenter** on your computer, you might see something slightly different from the illustration because the **DesignCenter** remembers changes and resizing adjustments. In particular, if you do not see the tree view on the left as shown, you will need to click the **Tree View Toggle** button to restore the tree view before going on.*

Figure 10-42
DesignCenter palette

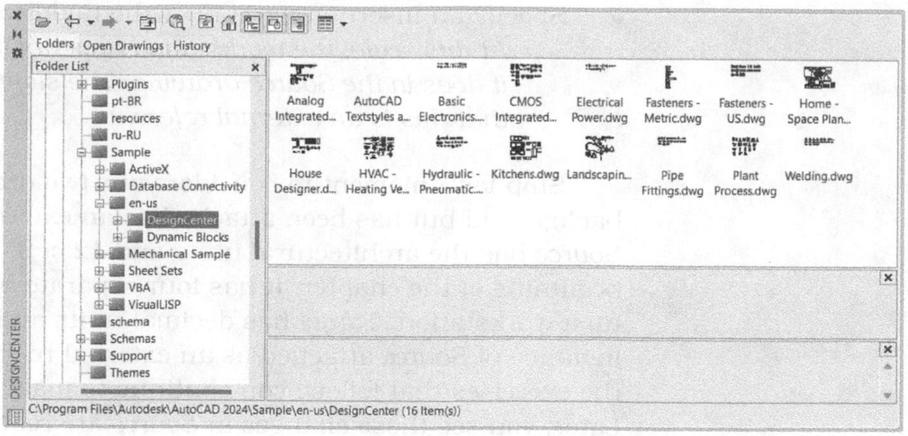

✔ If necessary, click the **Tree View Toggle** button, as shown in Figure 10-43.

*Your **DesignCenter** has a tree view on the left and a content area on the right.*

Figure 10-43
Tree View Toggle button

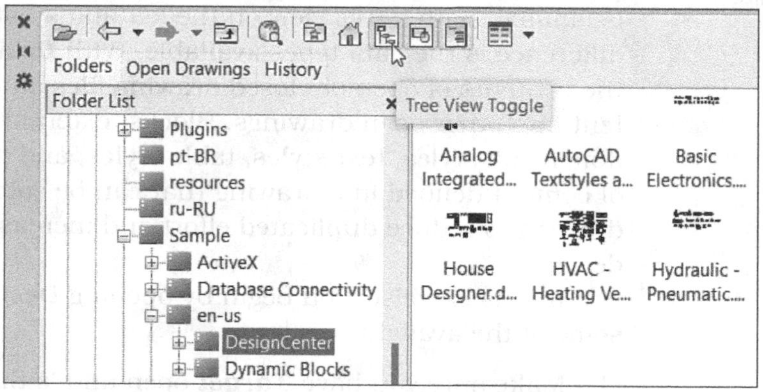

DesignCenter is a complex palette that gives you access to a vast array of resources. There is a toolbar-like set of buttons at the top of the palette, including the **Tree View Toggle** button. Below these are three tabs, and below these is the main work area of the palette. The tree view area shows a hierarchically arranged list of files, folders, and locations. The content area shows icons representing drawings and drawing content of the folder or drawing file currently selected in the tree view. What appears in the tree view depends on which tab is selected. The **Folders** tab shows the complete desktop hierarchy of your computer. The **Open Drawings** tab lists only open AutoCAD drawings. The **History** tab shows a history of drawing files that have been specifically opened in **DesignCenter**. You begin by clicking the **Open Drawings** tab and seeing what **DesignCenter** shows in regard to your current drawing.

✔ Click the **Open Drawings** tab.

Now, you have a very simple tree view showing the open drawings and content types along with the content area, as shown in Figure 10-44.

Figure 10-44
Open Drawings tab

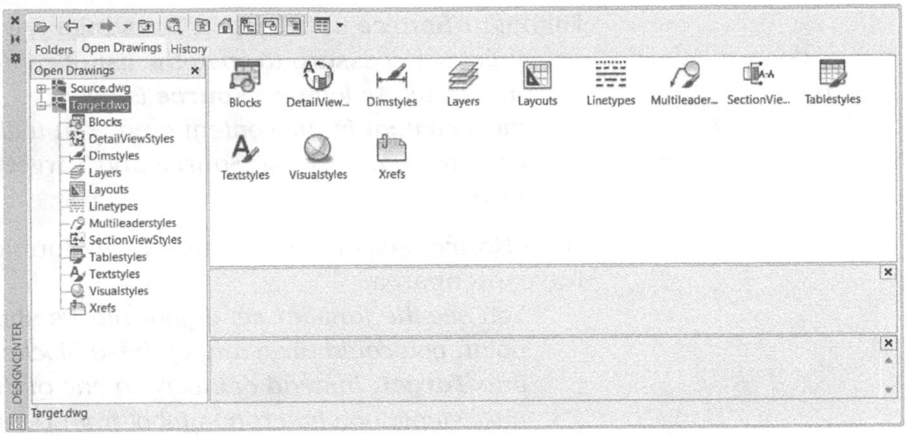

You see icons representing standard content types: **Blocks**, **DetailViewStyles**, **Dimstyles**, **Layers**, **Layouts**, **Linetypes**, **Multileaderstyles**, **SectionViewStyles**, **Tablestyles**, **Textstyles**, **Visualstyles**, and **Xrefs** (external references). All drawings show the same list, although not all drawings have content defined in each category.

In the tree view, the list of types is as far as you can go. In the palette, however, there is another level.

✔ If necessary, highlight **Target.dwg** in the tree view and click the **+** sign to open the tree view list.

✔ Select **Xrefs** in the tree view at the end of the list.

*You see an icon representing the attached **Source** drawing in the content area, as shown in Figure 10-45. If you'd like, check out the other contents as well. Select **Dimstyles**, for example, and you see the **Standard**, **Annotative**, and any other style defined in this drawing.*

*Now try looking into **Source**. It is still open, but notice that its contents would still be accessible in the **DesignCenter** if it were closed. You would just have to browse to it in the **Folders** tab.*

Figure 10-45
Attached ***Source*** drawing icon

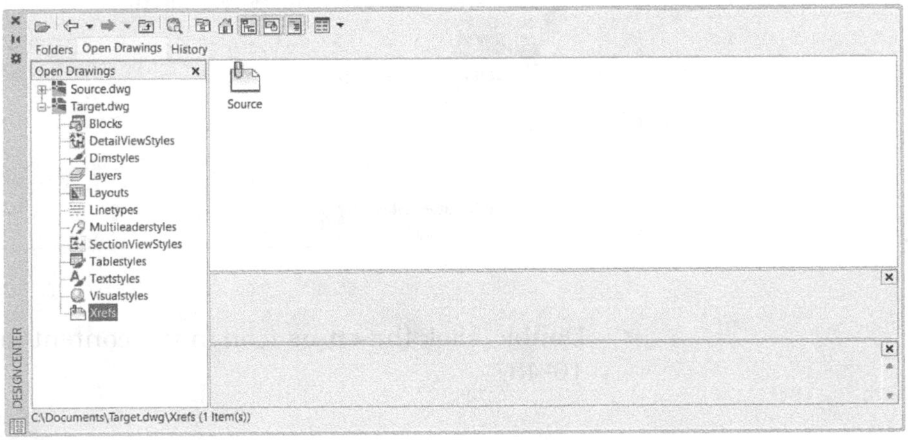

✔ Highlight **Source** in the **Open Drawings** tab.

It is not necessary to open the list of contents under ***Source*** *in the tree view. As long as* ***Source*** *is selected, you can access the drawing's content in the content area. You will notice no difference in the content area because* Source *and* Target *have the same content elements.*

✔ With **Source** selected in the tree view, double-click the **Blocks** icon in the content area.

You see the familiar set of four blocks shown in Figure 10-46. At this point, you could drag any of these blocks right off the palette and into ***Target****. Instead of inserting one of these blocks again, in the next steps, you insert a symbol from* ***DesignCenter****'s sample blocks. These are easily located using the* ***Home*** *button.*

✔ Click the **Home** button at the top of the **DesignCenter** palette, as shown in Figure 10-47.

Figure 10-46
Four blocks shown

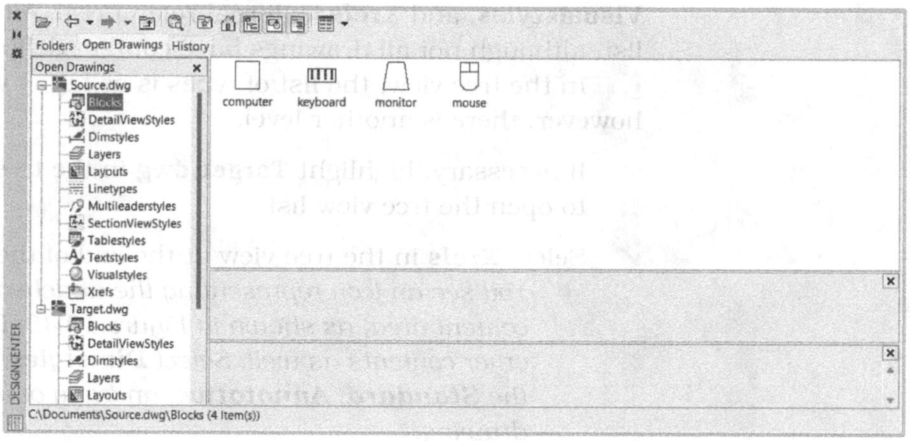

Figure 10-47
Home button

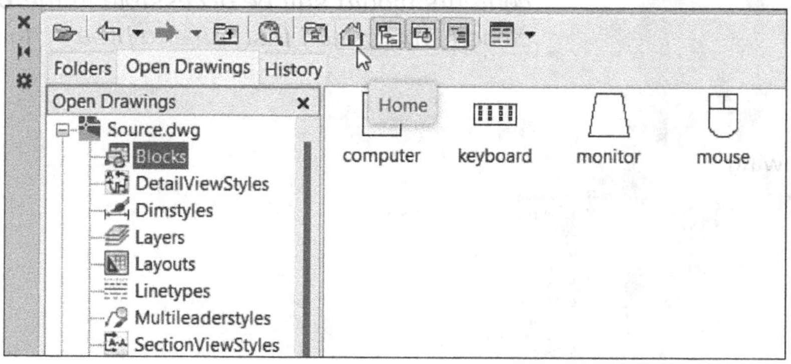

✔ Double-click the **en-us** icon in the content area, as shown in Figure 10-48.

Figure 10-48
en-us icon

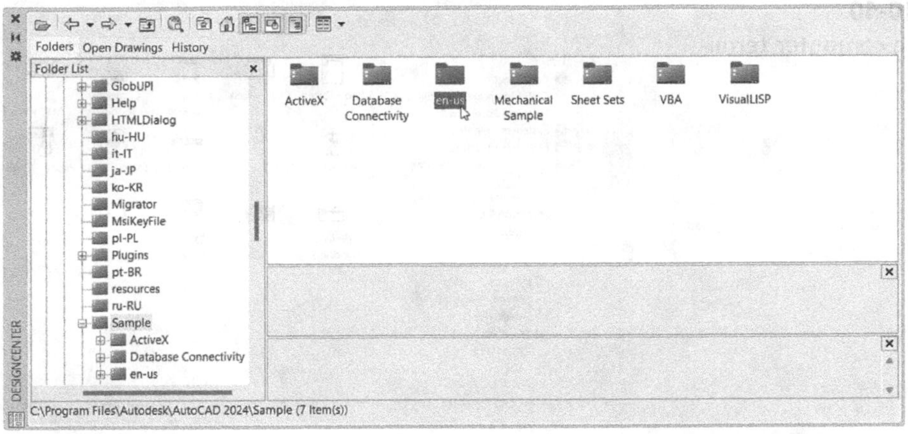

✔ Double click the **DesignCenter** icon in the content area.

*This takes you to the **DesignCenter** folder, which contains sample drawings and blocks, as illustrated in Figure 10-49. In the content area, you see a set of sample drawing thumbnails.*

✔ Double-click **Home - Space Planner.dwg**.

When you select this drawing, you again see the familiar set of icons for standard drawing content.

Figure 10-49
Sample drawings and blocks

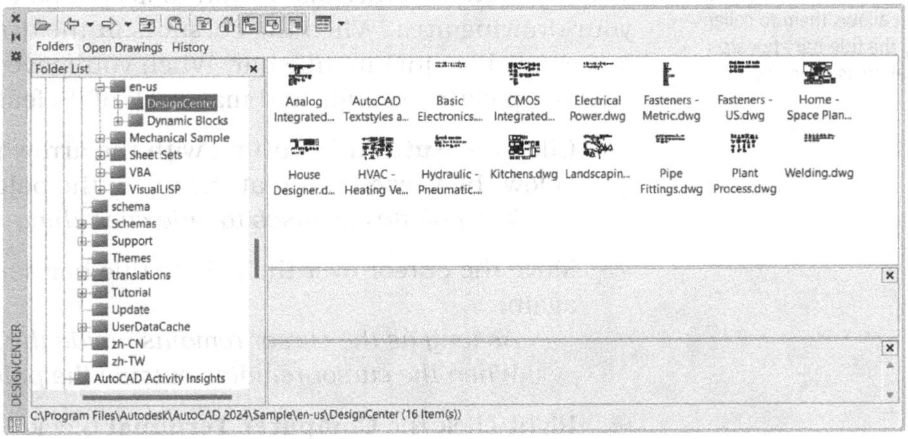

✔ Double-click the **Blocks** icon in the content area.

Now, you see a set of blocks representing household furniture, as shown in Figure 10-50. Look for the computer terminal. You insert this symbol, which is similar to your own workstation symbol, into Target.

*Blocks can be inserted from **DesignCenter** by dragging, but there are some limitations, as you will see.*

✔ Select the **Computer Terminal** block in the palette.

✔ Click and drag the computer terminal block slowly into the *Target* drawing area.

As soon as you are in the drawing area, you see a very large image of the computer block. This is a now-familiar scaling problem.

Figure 10-50
Select the computer terminal

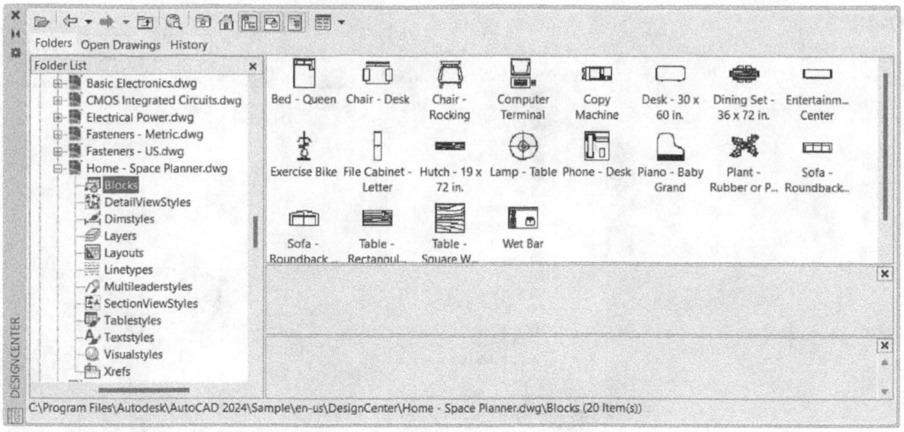

✔ Return your cursor to the palette without releasing the left mouse button until your cursor is back over the palette.

*There is a more precise and dependable method for inserting blocks from **DesignCenter**. This second method allows you to scale the block as you insert it. First, however, it is convenient to put the **DesignCenter** palette in **Auto-hide** mode.*

Auto-hide

Auto-hide: A feature of AutoCAD palettes that allows them to collapse so that only the title bar appears when the palette is open but not in use.

The ***Auto-hide*** feature allows you to keep a palette open without cluttering your drawing area. When the cursor is in the drawing area, the palette collapses to show just its title bar. When you move the cursor over the title bar, the palette expands and makes all of its features accessible.

✔ Click the **Auto-hide** button, with the arrow pointing to the left just below the **Close** button at the top of the palette title bar.

The palette collapses to hide everything but the title bar.

✔ Move the cursor over the palette title bar so that the palette opens again.

As long as the cursor remains inside the palette, it remains open. When the cursor remains outside the palette, it collapses again.

✔ Right-click the **Computer Terminal** block.

This opens a shortcut menu.

✔ Select **Insert Block**.

*The **Insert** dialog box is displayed with **Computer Terminal** in the **Name** edit box. From here on, the procedure is just like inserting a block within its original drawing.*

✔ If necessary, select the **Uniform Scale** checkbox.

✔ If necessary, select the **Specify On-Screen** checkbox on the left of the dialog box under **Insertion Point**.

✔ If necessary, clear the check mark for the **Specify On-screen** box in the middle of the dialog box under **Scale**.

✔ Enter **1/8** or **.125** in the **X scale** box in the middle of the dialog box.

*Be sure that you enter this in the **X scale** box, not the box on the left for specifying an insertion point.*

✔ Click **OK**.

As the dialog box closes, the ***Auto-hide*** *feature activates, and* ***DesignCenter*** *collapses so that only the title bar remains. This makes it easy to specify an insertion point in the drawing area.*

✔ Select an insertion point above or below the workstation Xref, as shown in Figure 10-51.

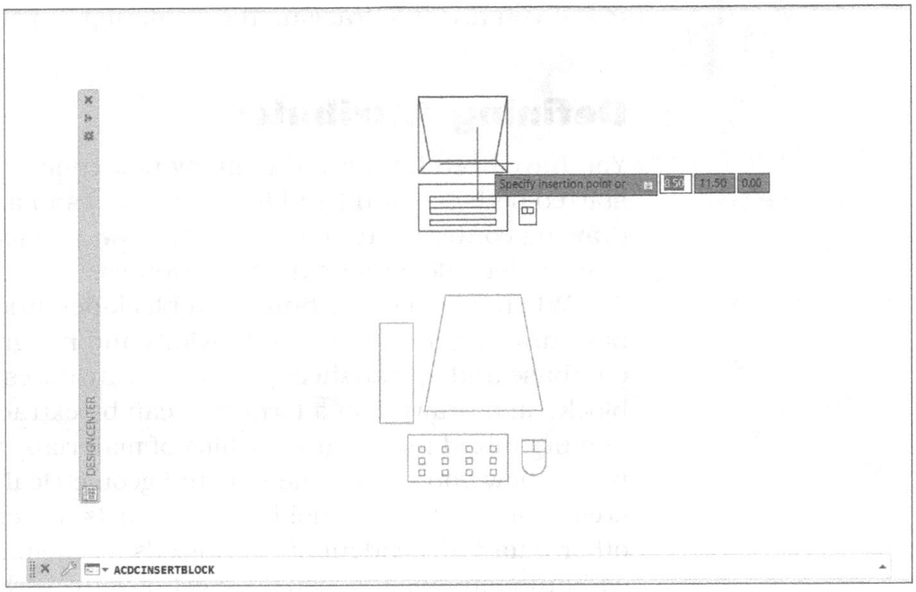

Figure 10-51
Specify the insertion point

✔ Move the cursor back onto the **DesignCenter** title bar.

The palette opens again.

✔ Click the **Open Drawings** tab.

✔ Highlight **Target.dwg**.

✔ Double-click the **Blocks** icon in the palette.

You see that the ***Computer Terminal*** *block definition from the* Home - Space Planner *drawing is now in* Target.

Other Features of DesignCenter

Before leaving **DesignCenter**, a few more features are controlled by the buttons at the top. Across the toolbar, the **Load** button opens a standard file selection dialog box where you can load any folder or drawing file into **DesignCenter**. The **Back** and **Forward** buttons take you to previous tree view and content area displays. The **Up** button takes you up one level in whatever folder hierarchy you are exploring. The **Search** button opens a **Search** dialog box, allowing you to search for files, folders, and text in a variety of ways familiar in Windows applications. The **Favorites** button takes you to a defined favorite location. By default, this folder is empty until you add a file or folder to your favorites. You add a file or folder to **Favorites** by selecting it in the tree view, right-clicking it, and then selecting **Add to Favorites**. The **Home** button, as you have seen, takes you directly to the **DesignCenter** folder. The **Tree View Toggle** button opens and closes the tree view panel. With the panel closed, there is more room to view content. The **Preview** button opens and closes a panel below the content area that shows a preview image of the selected content. The **Description** button opens and closes a panel below the **Preview** panel that displays text describing a selected block. Finally, the **Views** button allows for a choice over the style in which content is displayed in the content area. Before moving on, close the **DesignCenter** palette.

✔ Click the **Close** button at the top of the **DesignCenter** title bar.

✔ If you are still dragging the Computer Terminal block, press **<Esc>**.

Defining Attributes

You have been introduced to many new concepts in this chapter. You started off by creating and inserting blocks in a single drawing to sharing drawing content between drawings. Now, you learn to add variable information to block definitions using attributes.

When you add attributes to a block definition, you create the ability to pass drawing data between drawings and nongraphic applications, typically database and spreadsheet programs. Attributes hold information about blocks in a drawing in a form that can be extracted out to other programs and organized into reports or bills of materials, whereas dynamic block features allow you to vary the size and geometrical relationships in a block reference, and attributes hold specific labels, descriptions, part numbers, and other data independent of the object's mathematical form. For example, without changing the visual aspect of your workstation, you can define it as a block and use it to represent different hardware configurations. One instance of the workstation block could represent a computer with a Core 7 processor and a 20" CRT monitor, whereas another instance of the same block could represent a computer with an 8-Core processor and a 24" LCD monitor. Those descriptive labels—Core 7, 8-Core, 20" CRT, 24" LCD—can all be handled as attributes. If you want, you can look ahead to Figure 10-55 to get an idea of what this looks like.

TIP

The following is a general procedure for defining attributes:

1. On the **Insert** tab, click the **Define Attributes** tool from the **Block Definition** panel of the ribbon.
2. Select attribute modes.
3. Type an attribute tag.
4. Type an attribute prompt.
5. If desired, type a default attribute value.
6. Specify a location for the attribute in a block definition.

In this exercise, you create variable and visible attributes for computer processors and monitors, along with a constant and invisible attribute to label the mouse in each workstation. Once you have defined these attributes, you create a block called *workstation* that includes the whole computer workstation assembly and its attributes. To accomplish this, you return to *Source* and add attributes to your workstation assembly there. Because *Source* is now attached to *Target* as an external reference, you can later return to *Target* and update it with the changes made to *Source*.

Assuming you are still in *Target* from the previous section, you begin this exercise by using the **XOPEN** command, which allows you to quickly open an Xref from within a drawing without searching through a file hierarchy to locate the referenced drawing.

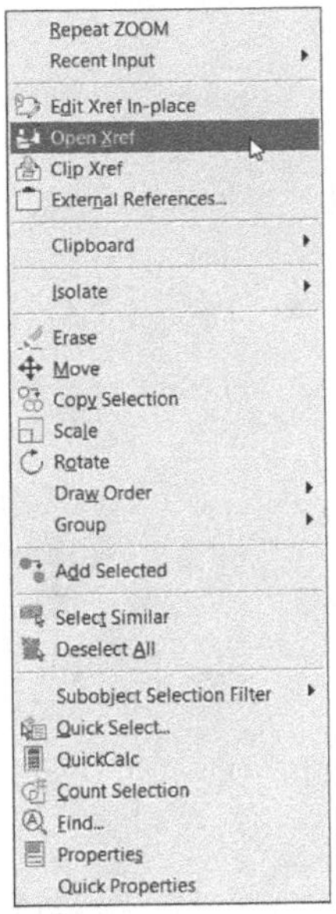

Figure 10-52
Xref shortcut menu

✔ Select the computer workstation in *Target* that you originally drew in *Source* and attached to *Target* as an external reference.

The workstation is highlighted, and a grip is placed at the previously defined insertion base point.

✔ With the external reference highlighted, right-click it.

This opens the lengthy shortcut menu shown in Figure 10-52.

✔ Select **Open Xref**.

This is a convenient way to open an externally referenced drawing from within the drawing where it is attached. Source *opens in the drawing area. You should see the original workstation assembly on layer 0 in this drawing, just as you created it in the "Creating Blocks" section.* Source *is open just as if you had opened it using the* **OPEN** *command. You now have the two drawings open again.* Source *is current, with* Target *open in the background.*

You are going to add attributes to these blocks in Source *and then define the whole assembly and its attributes as a single block called* workstation. *First, you define an attribute that allows you to specify the type of processor in any individual reference of the workstation block.*

✔ On the **Insert** tab, click the **Define Attributes** tool from the **Block Definition** panel, as shown in Figure 10-53.

Figure 10-53
Define Attributes tool

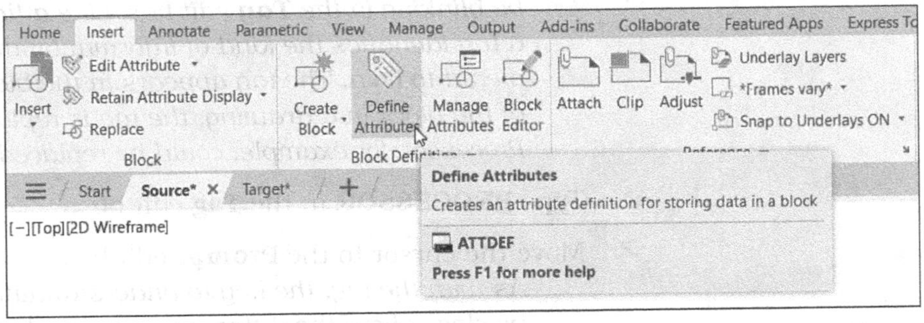

This starts the **ATTDEF** *command and displays the* **Attribute Definition** *dialog box shown in Figure 10-54.*

Figure 10-54
Attribute Definition dialog box

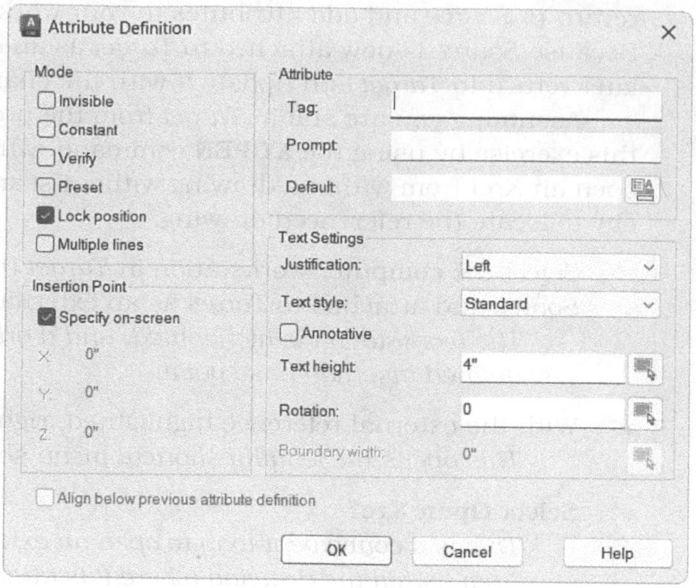

Look first at the checkboxes at the top left in the ***Mode*** *panel. For the purposes of this chapter, only* ***Lock position*** *should be checked. These are the default settings, which you use to create the first attribute definition. When your* workstation assembly *block is inserted, the processor attribute value will be visible in the drawing (because* ***Invisible*** *is not selected), variable with each insertion of the block (because* ***Constant*** *is not selected), not verified (****Verify*** *is not selected), and not preset to a value (****Preset*** *is not selected). You won't be able to reposition the attribute within the block, because* ***Lock position*** *is selected by default. The attribute will also be formatted as single-line text, because* ***Multiple lines*** *is not selected.*

Next, look at the ***Attribute*** *panel to the right. The cursor should be blinking in the* ***Tag*** *edit box. Like a field name in a database, a tag identifies the kind of information this particular attribute is meant to hold. The tag appears in the block definition. In instances of the block in a drawing, the tag is replaced by a specific value. Processor, for example, could be replaced by Core 7.*

✔ Type **PROCESSOR** in the **Tag** edit box.

✔ Move the cursor to the **Prompt** edit box.

As with the tag, the key to understanding the attribute prompt is to be clear about the difference between block definitions and block references. Right now, you are defining an attribute definition. The attribute definition becomes part of the definition of the workstation block and is used whenever a workstation is inserted. With the attribute definition you are creating, there is a prompt for the processor whenever you insert the workstation block.

✔ Type **Specify processor type**.

You also have the opportunity to specify a default attribute value, if you want, by typing in the ***Default*** *value edit box. Here, you can leave this edit box empty, specifying no default value in your attribute definition.*

The panel labeled ***Text Settings*** *allows you to specify text parameters as you would with the* ***TEXT*** *command. Visible attributes appear as text in the drawing. Therefore, the appearance of the text needs to be specified. You can specify a height and also enable the annotative property so that the text scales to appear at an appropriate height within a layout viewport.*

✔ Click the check box next to **Annotative**.

✔ Double-click in the edit box to the right of **Text height** and then type **4**.

If you click the ***Text height*** *button to the right, the dialog box disappears so that you can indicate a height by specifying two points in the drawing.*

Finally, AutoCAD needs to know where to place the visible attribute definition in the drawing. You can type in x-, y-, *and* z-*coordinate values, but you are more likely to specify a point in the drawing.*

✔ Check to see that **Specify on-screen** is selected in the **Insertion Point** panel.

✔ Click **OK**.

The dialog box disappears to allow access to the drawing area. You see a preview of the 4" PROCESSOR *attribute tag and a* ***Start point*** *prompt in the command line.*

Place the attribute about 3" below the keyboard.

> **NOTE**
> The button to the right of the **Default** value edit box allows you to insert a field as the attribute value. In that case, the attribute would automatically update when the field data changed.

✔ Specify a start point 3" below the left side of the keyboard (see Figure 10-55).

The dialog box disappears, and the PROCESSOR *attribute tag is added as shown. Remember, this is an attribute definition, not an occurrence of the attribute.* PROCESSOR *is the attribute tag. After you define the workstation as a block and the block is inserted, answer the* ***Specify processor type*** *prompt with the name of a processor type, and the name will be shown in the drawing rather than this tag.*

You proceed to define two more attributes using some different options.

✔ Repeat **ATTDEF**.

You use all the default modes but provide a default monitor value in this attribute definition.

✔ Type **MONITOR** for the attribute tag.

✔ Type **Specify monitor type** for the attribute prompt.

Figure 10-55
Attribute tags

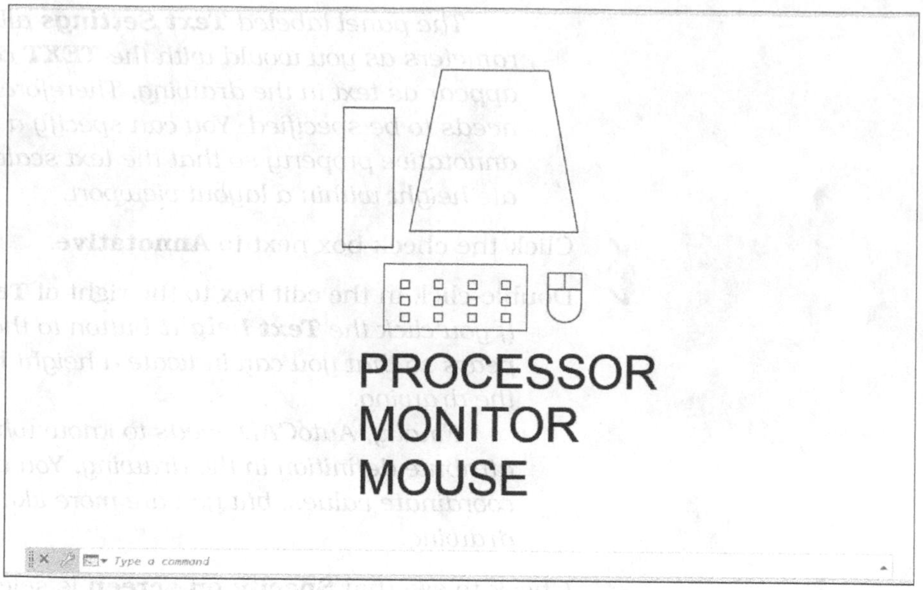

✔ Type **20" LCD** for the default attribute value.

*Now, when AutoCAD shows the prompt for a monitor type, it also shows **20" LCD** as the default value, as you will see.*

*You can align a series of attributes by selecting the **Align below previous attribute definition** checkbox at the lower left of the dialog box.*

✔ Select the **Align below previous attribute definition** checkbox.

✔ Click **OK** to create the attribute definition and exit the dialog box.

*The **MONITOR** attribute tag should be added to the workstation below the **PROCESSOR** tag, as shown in Figure 10-55.*

Next, you add an invisible preset attribute for the mouse, meaning the attribute text is not visible when the block is inserted, although the information is in the database and can be extracted. Preset means that the attribute has a default value and does not issue a prompt to change it.

✔ Repeat **ATTDEF**.

✔ Select the **Invisible** checkbox.

✔ Select the **Preset** checkbox.

✔ Type **MOUSE** for the attribute tag.

You do not need a prompt because the preset attribute is automatically set to the default value. There is no need to add the annotative property because the attribute is not visible when the drawing is plotted.

✔ Type **MS Mouse** in the **Default** value edit box.

✔ Select the **Align below previous attribute definition** check box to position the attribute below **MONITOR** in the drawing.

✔ Click **OK** to complete the dialog.

*The **MOUSE** attribute tag should be added to your drawing, as shown in Figure 10-55. When a workstation block is inserted, the **MS Mouse** attribute value is written into the database, but nothing appears in the drawing area because the attribute is defined as invisible.*

Finally comes the most important step of all: You must define the workstation as a block that includes all your attribute definitions.

✔ Click the **Create Block** tool from the **Block Definition** panel.

✔ Type **workstation** for the block name.

✔ Click the **Select objects** button.

✔ Use a selection window to select the individual blocks of the workstation and the three attribute definition tags.

✔ Right-click to end object selection.

✔ Click the **Pick point** button.

✔ Specify an insertion base point at the midpoint of the bottom of the keyboard.

✔ If necessary, select the **Delete** option.

✔ Click **OK** to close the dialog box.

The newly defined block disappears from the drawing area.

The workstation block with its three attribute definitions is now present in the *Source* drawing database. Before moving on, you insert three instances of the block and edit their attribute values.

Inserting Blocks with Attributes

Inserting blocks with attributes is no different from inserting any block, except that you are prompted for attribute values.

✔ To complete this exercise, insert three of the workstation blocks, using the following procedure (note the attribute prompts):

1. Type **insert <Enter>** or click the **Insert** tool from the ribbon's **Block** panel.
2. Select **workstation** from the set of block images. You may have to scroll down to see the block.
3. Specify an insertion point.
4. Fill in the boxes to specify monitors and processors.

Specify two different configurations for this exercise, as shown in Figure 10-56. The first two are Core i5 processors with the default 20" LCD monitor. The third is a Core i9 processor with a 27" LED monitor. This exercise will be easier to follow if you use the same attribute values. Notice that you are not prompted for mouse specifications because that attribute is preset.

When you are done, your drawing should resemble Figure 10-56.

Figure 10-56
Blocks with attributes

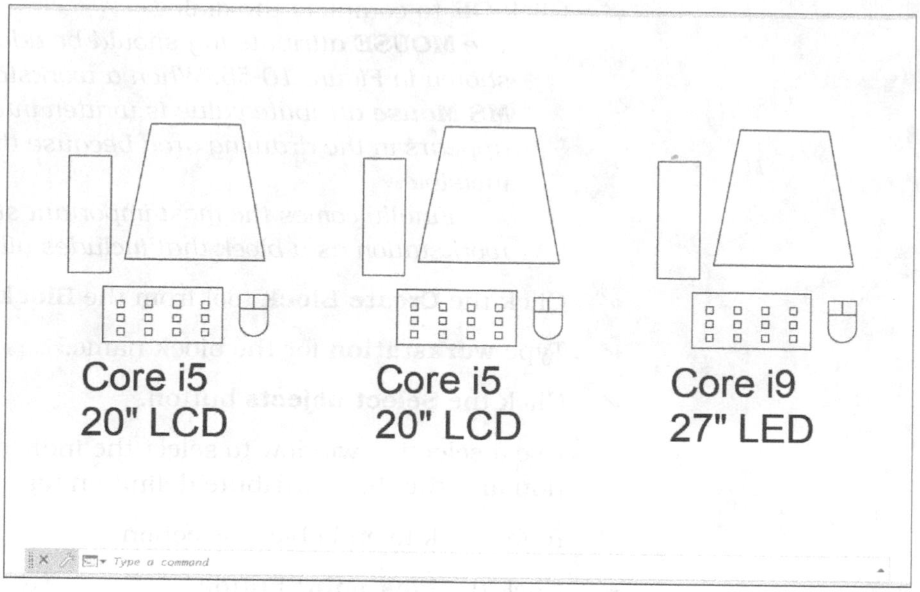

Editing Attribute Values and Definitions

Once you begin to work with attributes in blocks, you may have to edit them. The first thing to consider when you edit attributes is whether you want to edit attribute values in a block reference or edit the actual attribute definition. Editing an attribute value merely replaces an attribute value in one instance of the block inserted into your drawing. Editing the attribute definition changes the block definition itself, so that all new instances of the block inserted in the future are changed. Attributes of existing instances of the block inserted into the drawing remain unchanged unless you use the **ATTSYNC** command. There are four other major commands used to edit attributes. **ATTDISP**, **ATTEDIT**, and **EATTEDIT** work on attribute values in blocks that have been inserted, whereas **BATTMAN** works directly on attribute definitions. The following chart explains their uses.

Command	Usage
ATTDISP	Allows control of the visibility of all attribute values in inserted blocks, regardless of their defined visibility mode. There are three options. **Normal** means that visible attributes are visible, and invisible attributes are invisible. **On** makes all attributes visible. **Off** makes all attributes invisible.
ATTEDIT	Allows single or global editing of attribute values from the command line. Global editing allows editing text strings in all attribute values that fit criteria you define.
ATTSYNC	Synchronizes the attribute definitions in a block definition with all references of a block inserted into a drawing. Use this command after adding or removing attributes to a block definition.
EATTEDIT	Opens the **Enhanced Attribute Editor** dialog box for editing individual attribute values in inserted blocks. It allows you to change individual attribute values, text position, height, angle, style, layer, and color of attribute values.
BATTMAN	Opens the **Block Attribute Manager** and allows editing of attribute definitions. In this dialog box you can edit tags, prompts, default values, and modes for attribute definitions of any block defined in a drawing. Changes are made directly to the block definition and reflected in blocks subsequently inserted.

> **NOTE**
>
> If you insert a block with attributes and are not prompted to enter a value for the attributes, check the value of the **ATTREQ** system variable. By default, **ATTREQ** should be set to **1**, so you are prompted to enter values for each attribute that doesn't have the modes Preset or Constant.

Working with External References

You have made numerous changes to the drawing named *Source*. You've added attributes, created a workstation block, and inserted three references of the new block into the drawing, with attached attribute values. This provides a good opportunity to turn attention back to *Target* and look at the *Source* external reference there to see how Xrefs work in action.

✔ Before leaving *Source*, click the **Save** tool on the **Quick Access** toolbar to save your changes.

This is not just to safeguard changes. It is necessary to save changes to an Xref before the changes can be read into another drawing.

✔ Click the **Target** drawing file tab.

You should now be back in Target *with a single workstation Xref and a computer terminal block in your drawing, as shown previously in Figure 10-51. You should also see a notification balloon in the lower-right corner of the status bar, as shown in Figure 10-57, indicating that an externally referenced drawing has been changed and giving you the name of the Xref. To clearly appreciate the use of this notification, imagine for a moment that you are working with a team of designers. The focus of the project is a master drawing that contains references to several external drawings, and these drawings are being created or edited by designers at various locations connected by a network or the Internet. The external reference update notification instantly informs anyone looking at the master drawing that one or more of the external references have changed and should be reloaded to keep things up to date. Be aware that this notification would not appear if the changes made to* Source *had not been saved.*

Figure 10-57
External reference notification balloon

The first thing you need to do is reload the Source *Xref to bring your changes into* Target.

- ✔ Click the checkmark for the **Compare the changes** option in the notification balloon; the checkmark should now be cleared.

  The ***Compare the changes*** *option allows you to view the differences between two versions of the* Source *external reference; the one currently loaded and the one being loaded. Comparing external references is covered a bit later in this chapter.*

- ✔ Click the blue underlined **Source** link in the notification balloon.

  This updates the external reference to Source, *which now includes all three references of the workstation block.* Target *is updated to reflect the changes in Source, as shown in* Figure 10-58. *Following are a few notes on working with external references.*

Figure 10-58
Updated *Target* drawing

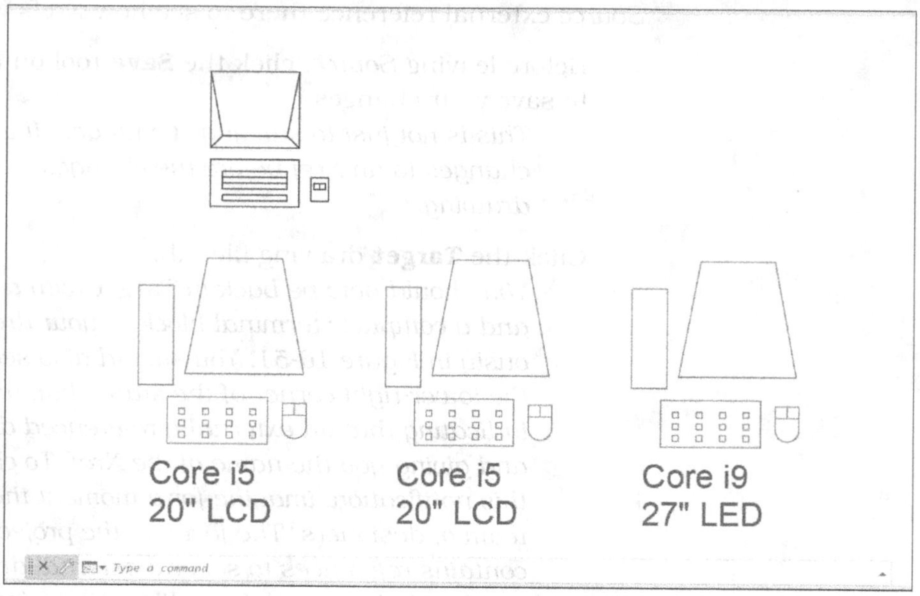

Reloading Attached References

If you need to update an attached reference when the notification balloon is not showing, follow these steps:

1. Click **View** > **Palettes** > **External References Palette** on the ribbon.
2. In the **External references** palette, select the external reference you want to reload.
3. Right-click and select **Reload** from the shortcut menu.

Editing External References in Place

You can edit external references within the current drawing and even use them to update the original referenced drawing. This should be done sparingly and for simple edits only; otherwise, the current drawing expands to take up more memory, and the point of using an external reference instead of a block reference is lost. To edit a block or external reference in place, select the external reference, then right-click and select **Edit Xref In-place** from the shortcut menu. If you select a block reference and right-click, select **Edit Block In-place** to edit the block definition in the drawing window rather than the **Block Editor**.

Clipping External References

External references can also be clipped so that only a portion of the referenced drawing is actually displayed in the current drawing. This allows different users on the same network to share portions of their drawings without altering the original drawings. Clipping boundaries can be defined by a rectangular window, a polygon window, or an existing polyline. Clipping is performed with the **XCLIP** command and can be used on block references as well as external references. To clip a reference, select it, right-click, and select **Clip Xref** from the shortcut menu.

For example, you could clip the attributes in *Target* so that only the workstations remain visible. The process would be as follows:

1. In *Target*, select the three workstation references of ***Source***.
2. Right-click to open the shortcut menu.
3. Select **Clip Xref**.
4. Press **<Enter>** to accept the default, rectangular boundary.
5. Specify two points to define a window around the workstations but not around the attributes.

Clipping an instance of an Xref does not alter the Xref definition; it only suppresses the display of the objects outside the clipping boundary.

Compare External References

New to AutoCAD 2021

When an Xref is changed and before it's reloaded, you have the opportunity to compare the Xref as it is defined in your drawing right now against the drawing which the Xref is defined. As part of the Xref notification balloon, as shown in Figure 10-57, you can choose to compare changes. If **Compare the changes** is checked and you click the **Reload** link, **Xref Compare** mode is enabled. While in **Xref Compare** mode, a thick blue boundary appears in the drawing area to let you know you are not in a standard drawing area. The **Xref Compare** toolbar also appears at the top of the drawing area along with the differences between the Xrefs reflected in the drawing area, as shown in Figure 10-59.

Objects in the current Xref are red in color, while objects being loaded from the updated Xref are green in color with a revision cloud drawn around them. Objects in gray are common between the two Xrefs. Use the **Next** and **Previous** buttons on the **Xref Compare** toolbar to navigate the differences. Once done, click the gray **X** button to exit the comparison mode. Use the **Settings** button on the left side of the **Xref Compare** toolbar to change the colors used to reflect the differences between the two Xrefs, as well as other settings.

In the next section, you return to working with the attribute values in block references.

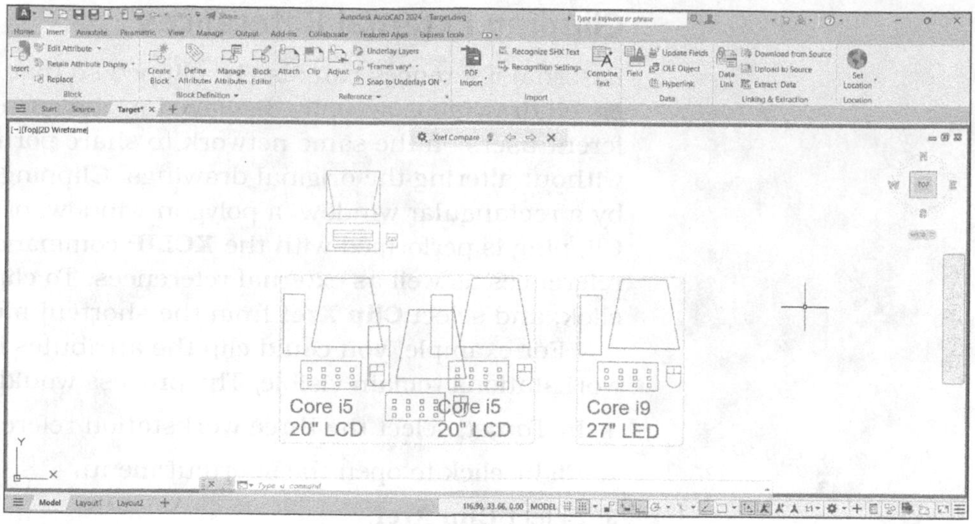

Figure 10-59
Comparing Xrefs

Extracting Data from Attributes

Many types of data can be extracted from a drawing and quickly formatted into tables or linked to external applications. Extracted data can be transferred to spreadsheet or database programs for use in the preparation of parts lists, bills of material, and other documentation. For example, with a well-managed system of parts and attributes, you can do a drawing of a construction project and get a complete price breakdown and supply list directly from the drawing database, all processed by your computer. To accomplish this, you need carefully defined blocks with attributes and a program such as Microsoft Excel that is capable of receiving the extracted data and formatting it into a useful report.

In this exercise, you extract attribute values from the blocks in *Source* and place it in an AutoCAD table, which you insert back into the drawing. The steps are the same as if you were exporting the values for use in a spreadsheet or database program but can be completed successfully without leaving AutoCAD. If you are in *Target* from the previous task, you start by switching back to *Source*.

✔ Click the **Source** drawing file tab to make *Source* the current drawing.

You should see the three workstation blocks and their attribute values now.

✔ Click the **Data Extraction** tool from the **Linking & Extraction** panel on the ribbon's **Insert** tab, as shown in Figure 10-60.

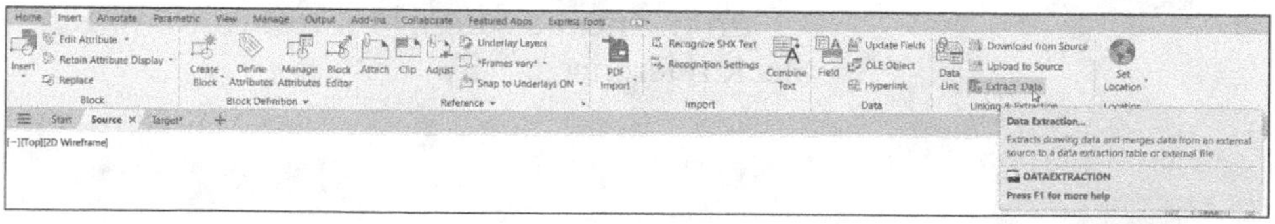

Figure 10-60
Data Extraction tool

You see the ***Data Extraction*** *wizard, as shown in Figure 10-61. This wizard takes you through eight steps of selecting data to extract and creating a table that can be exported or inserted.*

The first step in this wizard is to select a data extraction template file or to create a file from scratch. The template can be a previous extraction file that defines the attributes to be extracted from your blocks.

Figure 10-61
Data Extraction wizard

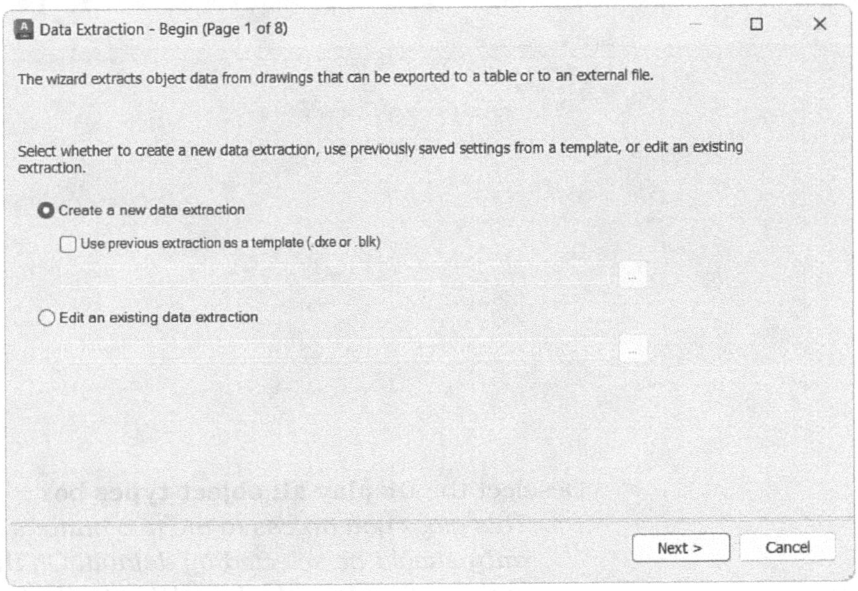

✔ If necessary, select the **Create a new data extraction** button.

✔ Click **Next**.
This brings you to the ***Save Data Extraction As*** *dialog box. This is a standard save file dialog box. The extracted data must first be saved to a file with a .dxe extension. This is true even if you are going to insert it back into your current drawing.*

✔ Type **workstation data <Enter>** in the **File name** box.
This takes you to the ***Data Extraction – Define Data Source*** *dialog box shown in Figure 10-62. In the* ***Data source*** *panel of this dialog box, you can choose to extract data from the current drawing and/or drawing sheet set or from selected objects only. The panel below that gives the path of the current drawing.* ***Drawings/Sheet set*** *and* ***Include current drawing*** *should be selected in this box.*

✔ Click **Next**.

This brings you to the **Data Extraction — Select Objects** dialog box shown in Figure 10-63. Here, you begin to narrow down the type of data to extract. Currently, all objects in the drawing are displayed. However, all that needs to be extracted is just the attribute values from the three workstation blocks in the drawing.

Figure 10-62
Data Extraction – Define Data Source dialog box

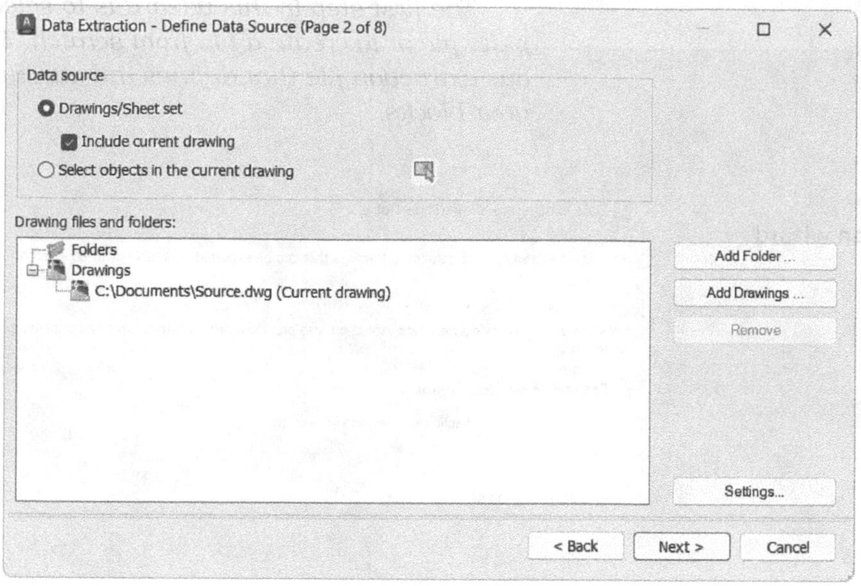

- ✔ Deselect the **Display all object types** box.

  This gives you access to the two buttons below. ***Display blocks only*** *should be selected by default. On the right are two other options:* ***Display blocks with attributes only*** *and* ***Display objects currently in-use only****.*

Figure 10-63
Data Extraction – Select Objects dialog box

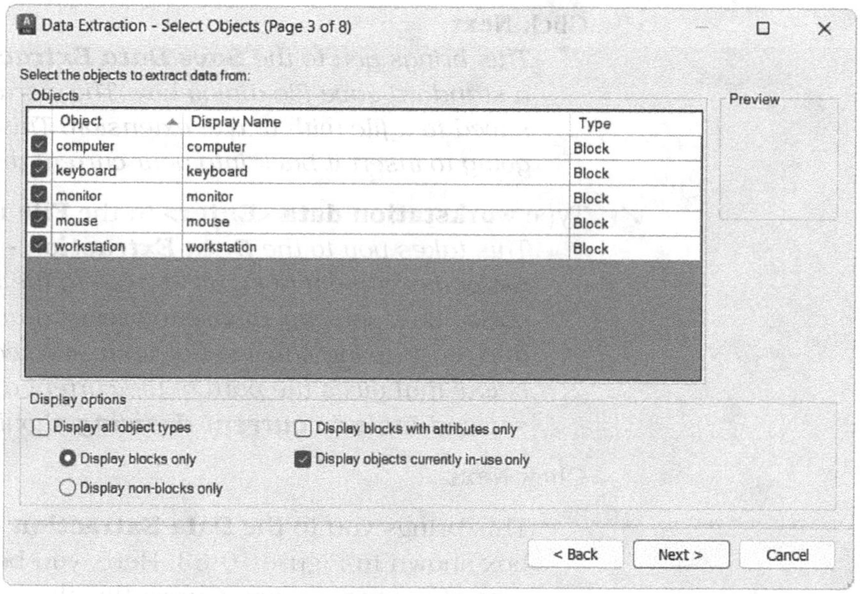

- ✔ Select **Display blocks with attributes only**.

  At this time, the only thing that should be displayed in the ***Objects*** *list is the workstation block.*

- ✔ Click **Next**.

  Now, you see the ***Data Extraction – Select Properties*** *dialog box shown in Figure 10-64. The* ***Category filter*** *on the right allows you to narrow down to attributes only.*

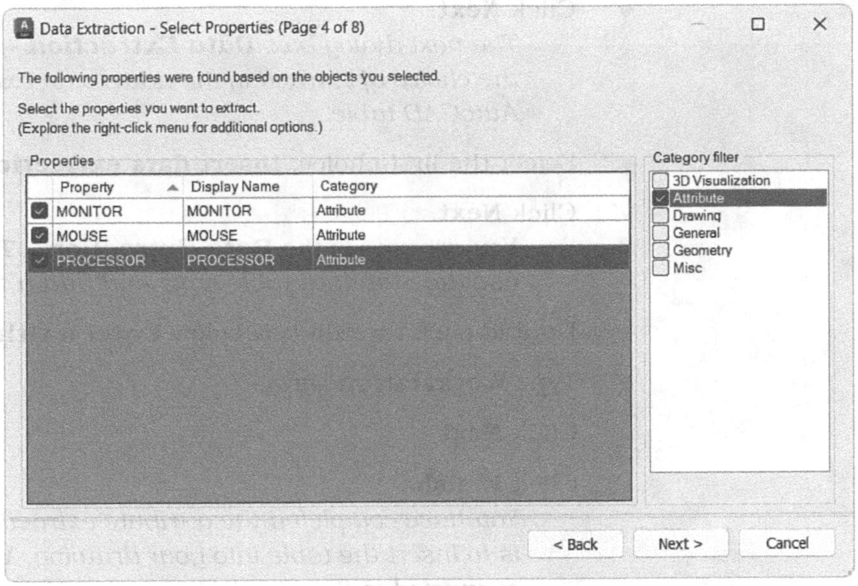

Figure 10-64
Data Extraction – Select Properties dialog box

✔ Deselect all the categories except **Attribute**, as shown in the figure.

*You should see only the **Monitor**, **Mouse**, and **Processor** attributes in the **Properties** list, as shown.*

✔ If necessary, select the **Monitor**, **Mouse**, and **Processor** property boxes on the left.

✔ Click **Next**.

*In the **Data Extraction – Refine Data** dialog box shown in Figure 10-65, the data is displayed and grouped according to the selections made in the three boxes at the bottom: **Combine identical rows**, **Show count column**, and **Show name column**. They should all be selected by default.*

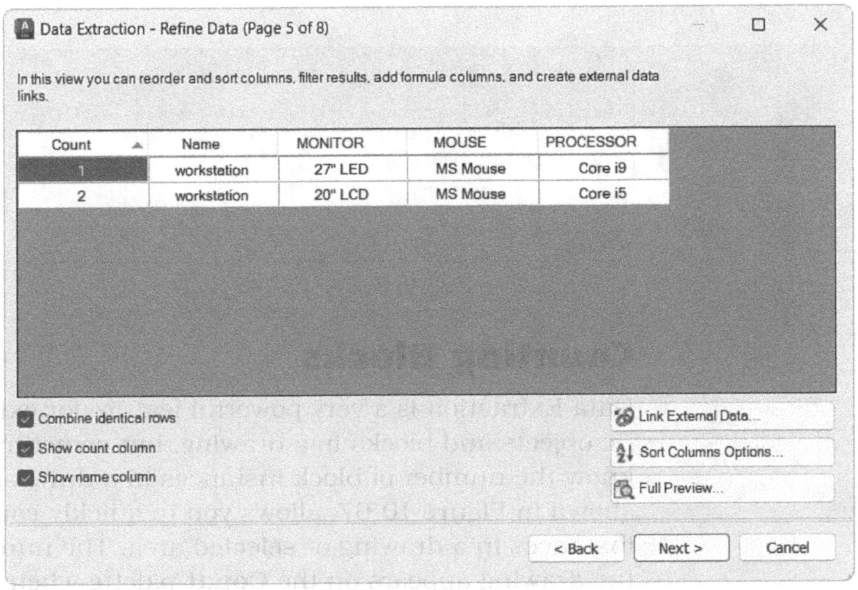

Figure 10-65
Data Extraction – Refine Data dialog box

✔ Click **Next**.

*The next dialog box, **Data Extraction – Choose Output**, gives you the choice of extracting the data to an external file and/or to an AutoCAD table.*

✔ Select the first choice, **Insert data extraction table into drawing**.

✔ Click **Next**.

*You are now in the **Data Extraction – Table Style** dialog box. You use the Standard table style and add a title.*

✔ Double-click the edit box below **Enter a title for your table**.

✔ Type **Workstation Data**.

✔ Click **Next**.

✔ Click **Finish**.

You have completed the attribute extraction process; all that remains is to insert the table into your drawing. You see a very small table connected to the crosshairs.

✔ Specify a point in your drawing below the middle block reference.

✔ Zoom into a window around the inserted table.

Your drawing should resemble Figure 10-66.

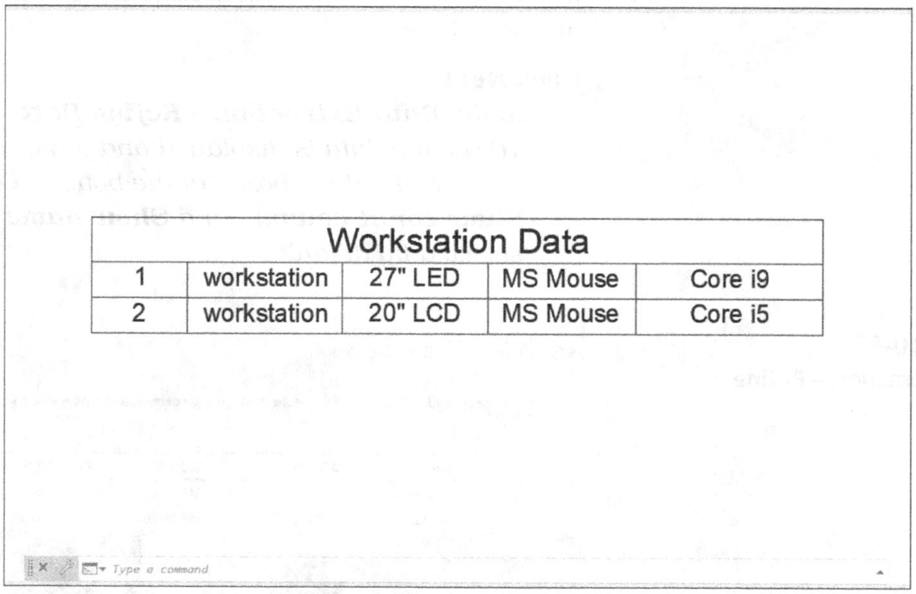

Figure 10-66
Inserted table

Counting Blocks

New to AutoCAD 2021

Data Extraction is a very powerful feature for extracting data from geometric objects and blocks in a drawing, but sometimes, you might just need to know the number of block instances in a drawing. The **Count** palette, as shown in Figure 10-67, allows you to quickly count the number of block instances in a drawing or selected area. The number of block instances in the drawing appears on the **Count** palette when displayed, and selecting one of the blocks from the palette enables **Count** mode. While in **Count** mode, a thick blue boundary appears in the drawing area to let you know you are not in the standard drawing mode. The **Count** toolbar also is displayed at the top of the drawing window.

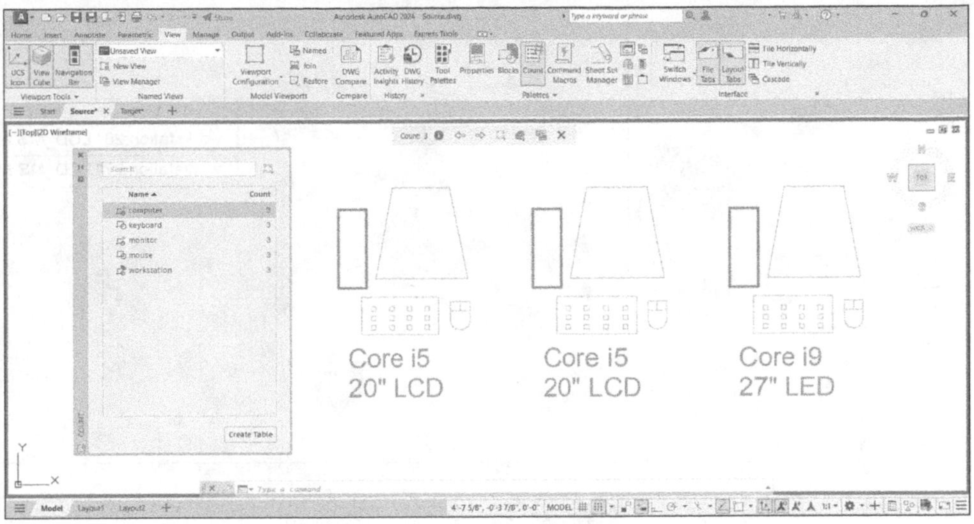

Figure 10-67
Count palette and Count mode

After **Count** mode is enabled, the block instances associated with the selected item on the **Count** palette are highlighted in the drawing, and you are able to utilize the various tools on the **Count** toolbar. The first button on the **Count** toolbar allows you to display details about the selected block on the **Count** palette. In large drawings, you can utilize the **Next** and **Previous** buttons on the **Count** toolbar to zoom one at a time to each block instance of the selected item, which can be helpful if you might need to remove or update a block instance.

By default, blocks are counted in the entire drawing, but you can choose to only count the blocks in a specific area of a drawing. Clicking the **Specify Area** button on the **Count** toolbar allows you to define the area of the drawing to perform the count. Next to the **Specify Area** button is the **Select Count** button, which you can use to create a selection set from the counted blocks so they can be modified if needed. Lastly, the **Insert Count Field** button allows you to insert an Mtext object with the current count value, and you use the gray **X** button to exit **Count** mode.

Once you have defined the area to count, you see a total of the block instances that were counted on the **Count** palette. You can right-click over an item to further break down the count by properties like layer, scale, and even attribute values. In addition to seeing the counts on the **Count** palette, you can also insert a table of the counted items into your drawing, as shown in Figure 10-68. At the bottom of the **Count** palette is the **Create Table** button. Click this button to choose which blocks and their counts should be used to create and insert a table into the drawing. The counts in the table are updated as blocks are added to or removed from the drawing or specified area for which the count was performed.

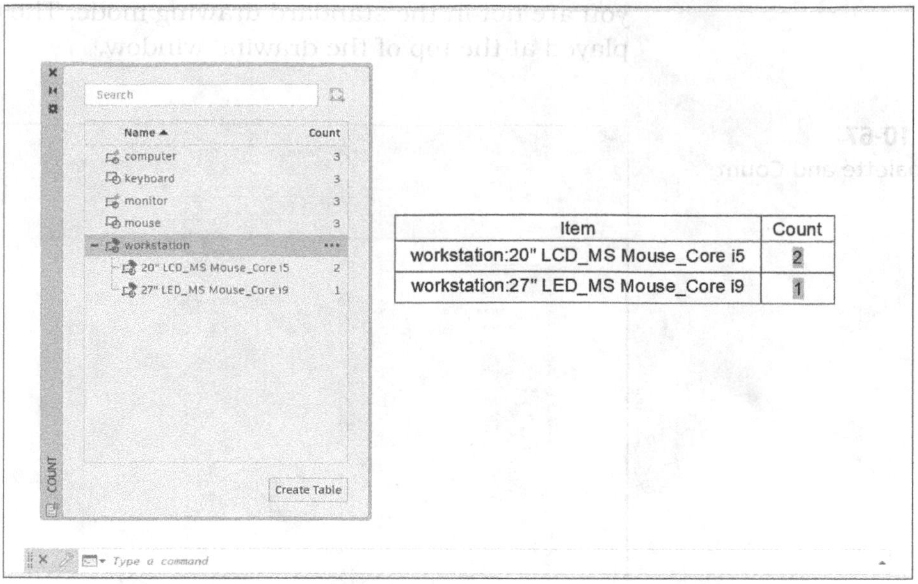

Figure 10-68
Table of counted blocks

Replacing Blocks

New to AutoCAD 2024

From time to time, you may want to replace or substitute one block for another. For example, you might initially insert a block of a chair with arms throughout a drawing but are later asked to replace those blocks with a block that represents a chair without arms. To replace a block, you use the **BREPLACE** command. When prompted to select the blocks to replace, you can select as many blocks references as you want, but they can't be references of different block definitions.

Creating Tool Palettes

Given your knowledge of blocks, Xrefs, and **DesignCenter**, at this point, you also have use for another AutoCAD feature. *Tool palettes* are collections of blocks placed very accessibly in a format that is much simpler to use than the **DesignCenter** palette.

The real power of tool palettes comes from the ease with which you can populate them with your own content. Try this:

✔ Click the **DesignCenter** tool from the **Palettes** panel on the **View** tab.

✔ If necessary, click the **Open Drawings** tab.

✔ If necessary, select ***Source.dwg*** and open the **Source** list.

✔ Double-click the **Blocks** icon.

You can see the set of blocks in Source, *including the workstation, computer, keyboard, monitor, and mouse blocks.*

✔ Right-click anywhere in the content area.

✔ From the shortcut menu, select **Create Tool Palette** at the bottom of the shortcut menu.

The Tool Palettes window opens with a new tab, labeled **Source**, *from the name of the drawing. This palette tab has the five blocks from* Source, *as shown in Figure 10-69. It's that simple. You now*

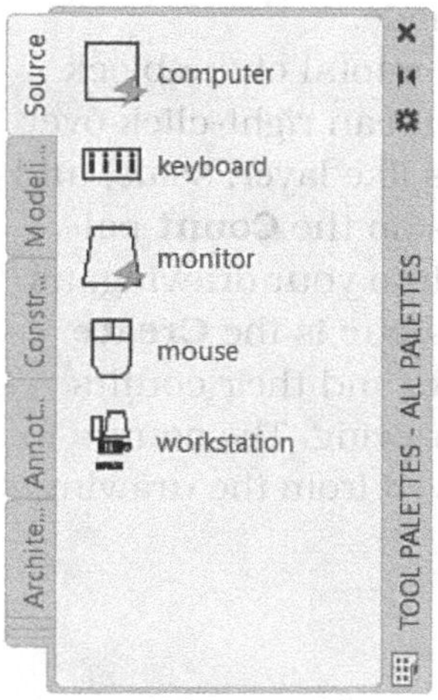

Figure 10-69
Source tool palette created

have your own tool palette to work with. The blocks on this tab can be clicked or dragged into the drawing. Clicking a block allows you to use object snaps to precisely place the block.

Keep in mind that the tools on a tool palette are accessible only as long as the reference is clear. If they originate from an externally referenced drawing, the reference path must be clear and accessible. If the referenced drawing is moved, deleted, or renamed, the tool will no longer be available.

TIP

If your **Source** tool palette does not open automatically, click **View > Palettes > Tool Palettes**. This opens the whole set of tool palettes, with the **Source** tab open at the top.

✔ Close the **Tool Palettes** window and **DesignCenter**.

NOTE

You can drag most types of geometry and annotation from the drawing area onto a tool palette to create a tool that allows you to create that type of object with the original objects property values. This can be helpful to create annotation of the same style throughout a drawing or project.

In the next and final section of this chapter, you learn how to reverse the block definition process.

Exploding Blocks

EXPLODE	
Command	EXPLODE
Alias	X
Panel	Modify
Tool	

The **EXPLODE** command undoes the work of the **BLOCK** command. It takes a set of objects that have been defined as a block and re-creates them as independent objects. **EXPLODE** works on dimensions, mtext, polylines, hatch patterns, and associative arrays as well as on blocks created with the **BLOCK** command or tools on a tool palette. It does not work on externally referenced drawings until they have been bound permanently through the **Bind** option of the **External References** palette.

TIP

The following is a general procedure for exploding blocks:

1. Type **explode <Enter>**, or click the **Explode** tool from the **Modify** panel on the **Home** tab of the ribbon.
2. Select objects.
3. Right-click to end object selection and complete the command.

NOTE

Exploding only affects the topmost block reference. If a block is made up of several blocks, these "nested" blocks remain as block references after exploding. Attribute value information is removed by exploding, leaving the attribute definitions instead.

✔ To begin this exercise, you should have **Source** open as the current drawing.

Try exploding a workstation.

✔ If necessary, type **zoom <Enter>** and select the **All** option at the command line to see the complete drawing.

✔ Click **Home > Modify > Explode** from the ribbon, as shown in Figure 10-70. You are prompted to select objects.

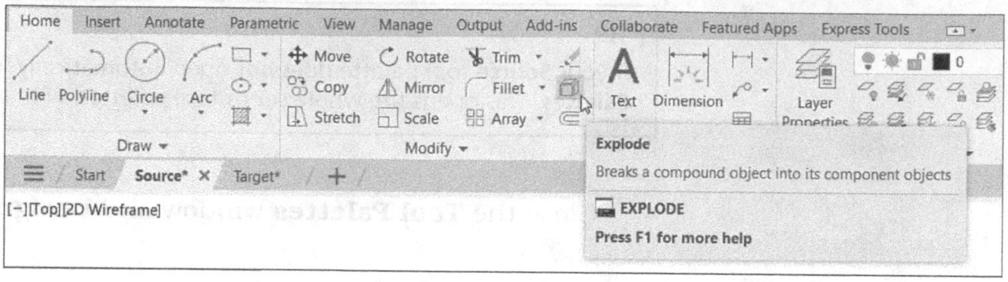

Figure 10-70
Explode tool

✔ Select the center workstation.

✔ Right-click to end object selection and complete the command.

You should notice immediately that the attribute values are replaced by attribute definitions. Move your cursor over any part of the workstation and observe the preview highlighting.

All the component parts of the previously blocked workstation can now be selected separately, including the attribute definitions. If you select the computer rectangle, you see that the parameter and action are once again accessible. If you select the monitor, you see the constraint parameter and block table markers. If you select the keyboard and mouse, you see they are still defined as separate blocks.

Purging Content from a Drawing

EXPLODE reverses the blocking process to return items in a block reference to independent objects. However, to remove unused block definitions from the drawing database requires a different process using the **PURGE** command. Only items that are in the drawing database but are not used can be purged. This includes unused blocks, layers, dimension styles, groups, and all the other types of content shown in the tree view on the left in Figure 10-71.

The **PURGE** command (click **Manage > Cleanup > Purge**) displays this dialog box with two options, indicated by the two buttons at the top, shown in Figure 10-71. When the **Purgeable Items** button is selected, the tree view on the left is labeled **Named Items Not Used**. These are the items that can be purged. A plus sign next to a category indicates that there are items of this type that can be purged. To select an item to purge, open the list and check the box next to the purgeable item. Purge the selected items by clicking the **Purge Checked Items** at the bottom of the dialog box.

When **Find Non-Purgeable Items** is selected, as it is in Figure 10-71, the tree view is labeled **Named Items in Use**. The categories are the same, but plus signs appear in different places depending on what is or is not in use in the current drawing. Opening a category list in this view produces a list of items that cannot be purged. Checking one of these boxes calls an explanation on the right in the **Possible Reasons** section. In the figure, the **Possible Reasons** section explains that the **Keyboard** block cannot be purged because it is nested in another block definition and has been inserted into the current drawing.

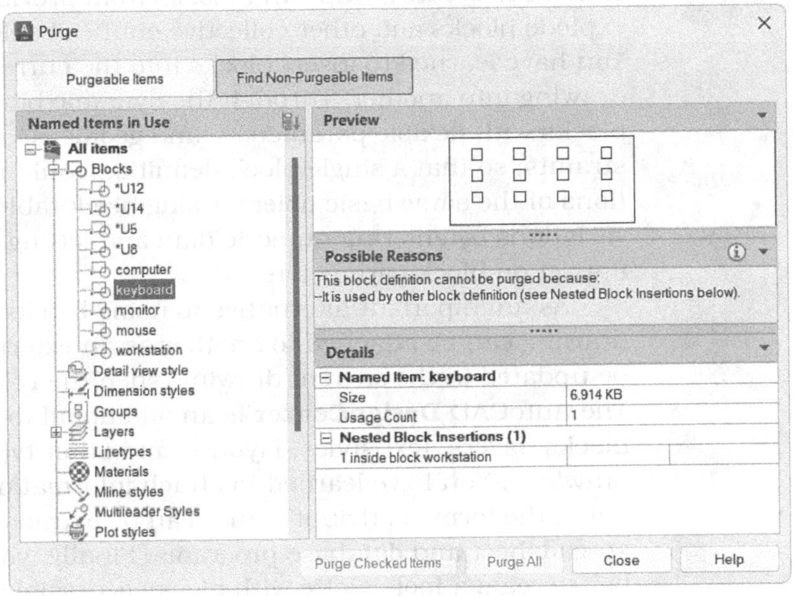

Figure 10-71
Purge dialog box

10 chapter ten

Chapter Summary

Congratulations! This has been a tough chapter with a lot of new information and procedures to learn. You have gained a greater sense of the tools available for using AutoCAD in collaborative work environments. You have learned to create groups and blocks from previously drawn objects and to explode blocks and other collective entities back into independent objects. You have learned to insert blocks into the current drawing and to insert one drawing into another. Through the dynamic block feature, you created blocks with flexible parameters, and geometric and dimensional constraints, so that a single block definition could represent different variations of the same basic object. Using block tables, you created a set of these variations by entering numeric data and letting AutoCAD extrapolate the impact on block parameters.

As an important alternative to using blocks, you have seen how one drawing can be attached to another as an external reference (Xref) that can be updated in the current drawing when the referenced drawing changes. The AutoCAD **DesignCenter** is an additional tool that allows you to share blocks, layers, text styles, layouts, and other types of content between drawings. You have learned to attach information to objects in your drawing in the form of attributes that can be extracted and manipulated in spreadsheet and database programs. Finally, you have seen how easy it can be to create a tool palette with blocks accessible from your current drawing. For simpler applications, objects can be saved to the Windows Clipboard and then inserted into other AutoCAD drawings or other types of documents. Through these new techniques, you should appreciate that AutoCAD has powerful features that go well beyond the one-person, one-workstation arena to include collaboration among individuals, companies, and work sites around the globe.

Chapter Test Questions

Multiple Choice

Circle the correct answer.

1. Which of these **cannot** be found in the AutoCAD **DesignCenter**?
   a. Layers
   b. Blocks
   c. External references
   d. Block tables
2. If a base point is **not** defined in an inserted drawing, the base will be the
   a. Midpoint of the block
   b. Insertion point
   c. Origin point
   d. Datum point

3. While blocks are inserted, xrefs are
   a. Linked
   b. Attached
   c. Referenced
   d. Hyperlinked
4. Every parameter in a dynamic block must have
   a. An action
   b. A constraint
   c. A base point
   d. A block table
5. The name that identifies an attribute in an attribute definition is called a(n)
   a. **ATTDEF**
   b. Field
   c. Tag
   d. Attribute prompt

Matching

Write the number of the correct answer on the line.

a. Insert ______________
b. Attach ______________
c. Tag ______________
d. Parameter ______________
e. Tree view ______________

1. Attribute
2. Block
3. Block table
4. **DesignCenter**
5. Xref

True or False

Circle the correct answer.

1. **True or False:** Base points are included in block definitions, and insertion points are included in block references.
2. **True or False:** External references are updated automatically when the referenced drawing changes.
3. **True or False:** Parameters, actions, constraints, and block tables are added to dynamic blocks in the **Block Editor** contextual tab.
4. **True or False:** To redefine a block as separate entities, you must return to the block definition.
5. **True or False:** A block table has attribute fields that can be updated.

Questions

1. Why is it usually a good idea to create blocks on layer **0**?
2. What would you have to do to create blocks with geometry that could be edited after they were inserted?
3. What is the purpose of the yellow exclamation point that appears whenever you add a parameter to a block?
4. What other complex entities can be exploded besides blocks?
5. What happens to attribute values when a block is exploded?

Drawing Problems

1. Open a new drawing with **18 × 12** limits and create a hexagon circumscribed around a circle with a **1.0**-unit radius.
2. Define an attribute to go with the hexagon and circle. The tag should identify the two as a hex bolt; the prompt should ask for a hex bolt diameter. The attribute should be visible in the drawing, center justified **0.5** unit below the block, and text **0.3** unit high.
3. Create a block with the bolt and its attribute. Leave a clear drawing area when you are done.
4. Draw a rectangle with the lower-left corner at **(0,4)** and upper-right corner at **(18,8)**.
5. Insert **0.5**-diameter hex bolts centered at **(2,6)** and **(16,6)**. Insert a **1.0**-unit hex bolt centered at **(9,6)**. The size of each hex bolt should appear beneath the bolt.

Chapter Drawing Projects

A Drawing 10-1: *CAD Room* [INTERMEDIATE]

This architectural drawing is primarily an exercise in using blocks and attributes. Use your workstation block and its attributes to fill in the workstations and text after you draw the walls and countertop. New blocks should be created for the plotters and printers, as described subsequently. The drawing setup is consistent with *Source* from the chapter so that blocks can be easily inserted without scaling. When you have completed this drawing, you might want to try extracting the attribute information to a word processor or Microsoft Excel file.

Drawing Suggestions

UNITS = Architectural; Precision = 0'-0'

GRID = 1'

SNAP = 1'

LIMITS = (0',0')(48',36')

- The "plotter" block is a 1 × 3 rectangle, with two visible, variable attributes (all the default attribute modes). The first attribute is for a manufacturer, and the second is for a model. The "printer" is 2 × 2.5 with the same type of attributes. Draw the rectangles, define their attributes 8" below them, create the block definitions, and then insert the plotter and printer as shown.

NOTE

Do not include the labels "plotter" and "laser printer" in the block because text in a block is rotated with the block. This would give you inverted text on the front countertop. Insert the blocks and add the text afterward. The attribute text can be handled differently, using the **MIRRTEXT** system variable.

- The largest "plotter" was inserted with a *y* scale factor of 1.25.

The MIRRTEXT System Variable

The four workstations on the front counter could be inserted with a rotation angle of 180°, but then the attribute text would be inverted also and would have to be turned around using **EATTEDIT**. Instead, you reset the **MIRRTEXT** system variable so that you can mirror blocks without inverting attribute text:

1. Type **mirrtext**.
2. Type **0**.

Now, you can mirror objects on the back counter to create those on the front. With the **MIRRTEXT** system variable set to **0**, text included in a **MIRROR** procedure is not inverted, as it would be with **MIRRTEXT** set to **1**. This applies to attribute text as well as ordinary text. However, it does not apply to ordinary text included in a block definition.

Drawing 10-1
CAD Room

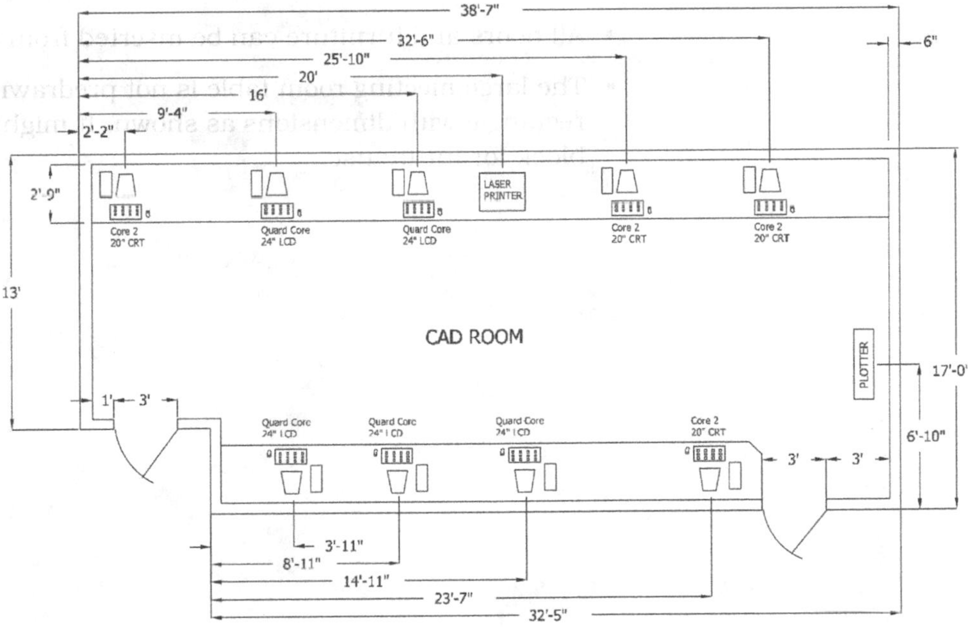

A Drawing 10-2: *Office Plan* [INTERMEDIATE]

This drawing is primarily an exercise in the use of predrawn blocks and symbols. With a few exceptions, everything in the drawing can be inserted from the AutoCAD **DesignCenter**.

Drawing Suggestions

- Observe the overall 62' × 33' dimensions of the office space and choose appropriate architectural limits, snap settings, and grid settings for the drawing.
- Dimensions are not provided for the interior spaces, so you are free to choose dimensions as you wish.
- All walls can be drawn as 60"-wide filled polylines.
- All doors and furniture can be inserted from the **DesignCenter**.
- The large meeting room table is not predrawn. Create a simple filleted rectangle with dimensions as shown. It might be defined and saved as a block for future use.

Drawing 10-2
Office Plan

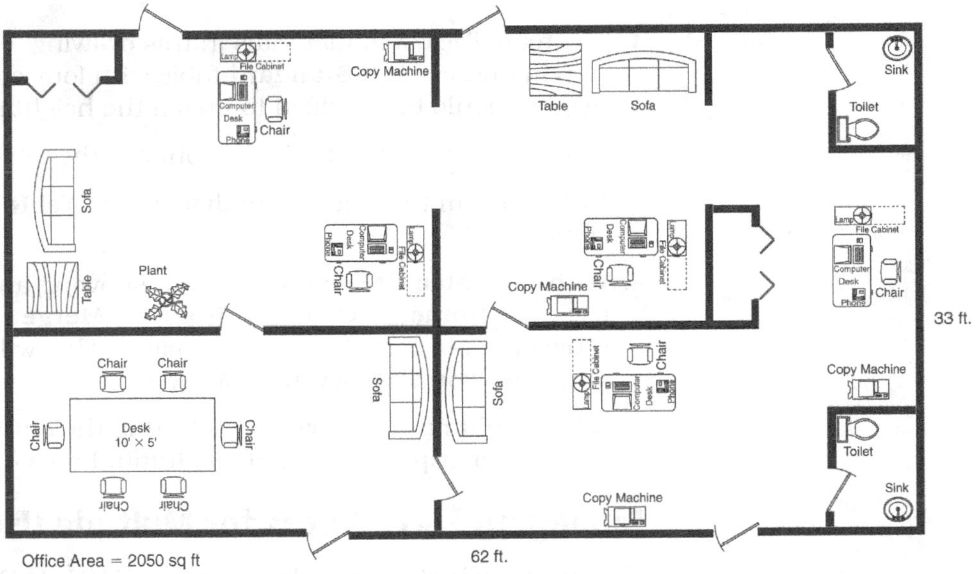

M Drawing 10-3: *Base Assembly* [INTERMEDIATE]

This is a good exercise in assembly drawing procedures. You draw each of the numbered part details and then assemble them into the base assembly.

Drawing Suggestions

Units, grid, snap, and limit settings are not provided here. You can determine what you need by looking over the drawing and its dimensions. Remember that you can always change a setting later if necessary.

You can either create your own title block from scratch or develop one from a previous drawing. Once created and saved or wblocked, a title block can be inserted and scaled to fit any drawing. AutoCAD also comes with drawing templates that have borders and title blocks.

Using Table to Create a Bill of Materials

1. To create the bill of materials in this drawing, click the **Table** tool from the ribbon and insert a **Standard** table with four columns and five rows. Row height should be specified to match the height shown in the drawing.
2. Once the table is inserted, click outside the table to complete the command.
3. Click once in the title row to display the **Table Cell** contextual tab on the ribbon.
4. With the **Table Cell** contextual tab showing and the title row highlighted, click the **Unmerge Cells** tool from the **Merge** panel. Click outside the table again to complete the command. This will eliminate the title row and leave you with seven data rows.
5. Adjust column width by first selecting the entire table, then clicking and dragging a grip at the top of a column. Press **<Esc>** to remove grips.

Managing Parts Blocks for Multiple Use

You draw each of the numbered parts (B101-1, B101-2, etc.) and then assemble them. In an industrial application, the individual part details would be sent to different manufacturers or manufacturing departments, so they must exist as separate, completely dimensioned drawings as well as blocks that can be used in creating the assembly. An efficient method is to create three separate blocks for each part detail: one for dimensions and one for each view in the assembly. The dimensioned part drawings include both views. The blocks of the two views have dimensions, hidden lines, and centerlines erased.

Think carefully about the way you name blocks. You may want to adopt a naming system such as the following: B101-1D for the dimensioned drawing, B101-IT for a top view without dimensions, and B101-1F for a front view without dimensions. Such a system makes it easy to call out all the top view parts for the top view assembly, for example.

Notice that the assembly requires you to do a considerable amount of trimming away of lines from the blocks you insert. This can be easily completed, but you must remember to explode the inserted blocks first.

Drawing 10-3
Base Assembly

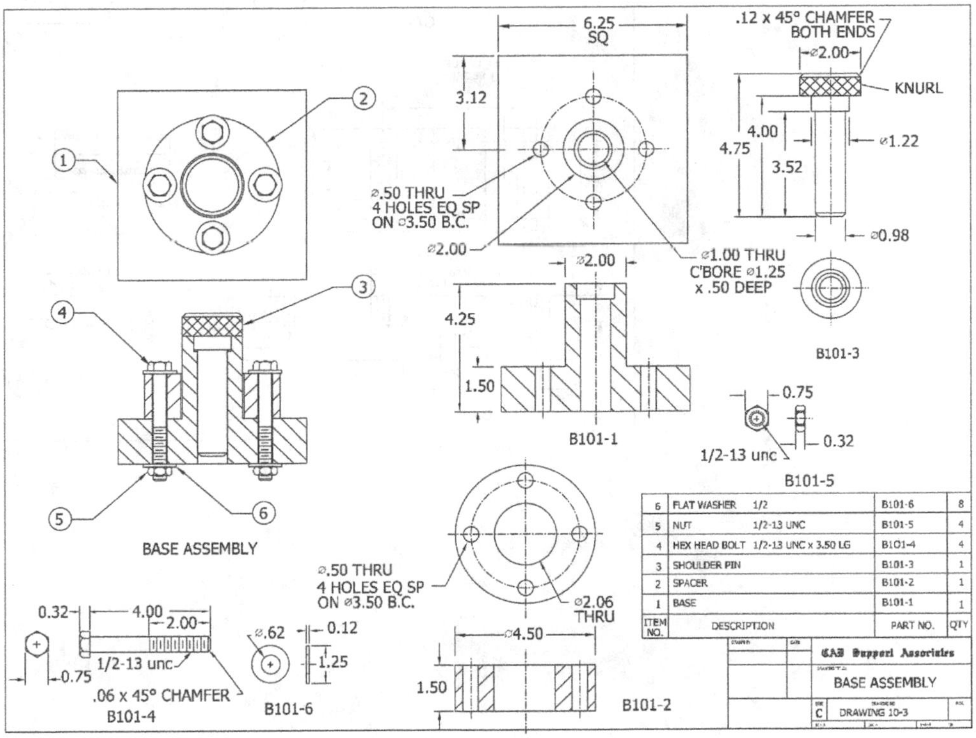

6.25
SQ
3.12
⌀.50 THRU
4 HOLES EQ SP
ON ⌀3.50 B.C.
⌀2.00
⌀2.00
⌀1.00 THRU
C'BORE ⌀1.25
x .50 DEEP
4.25
1.50
B101-1
.12 x 45° CHAMFER
BOTH ENDS
⌀2.00
KNURL
4.00
4.75
3.52
⌀1.22
⌀0.98
B101-3
0.75
0.32
1/2-13 unc
B101-5
BASE ASSEMBLY
⌀.50 THRU
4 HOLES EQ SP
ON ⌀3.50 B.C.
⌀2.06
THRU
⌀4.50
1.50
B101-2
0.32
4.00
2.00
1/2-13 unc
0.75
.06 x 45° CHAMFER
B101-4
⌀.62
0.12
1.25
B101-6
6 FLAT WASHER 1/2 B101-6 8
5 NUT 1/2-13 UNC B101-5 4
4 HEX HEAD BOLT 1/2-13 UNC x 3.50 LG B101-4 4
3 SHOULDER PIN B101-3 1
2 SPACER B101-2 1
1 BASE B101-1 1
ITEM NO. DESCRIPTION PART NO. QTY
CAD Support Associates
BASE ASSEMBLY
C DRAWING 10-3

M Drawing 10-4: *Double Bearing Assembly* [ADVANCED]

Drawing 10-4

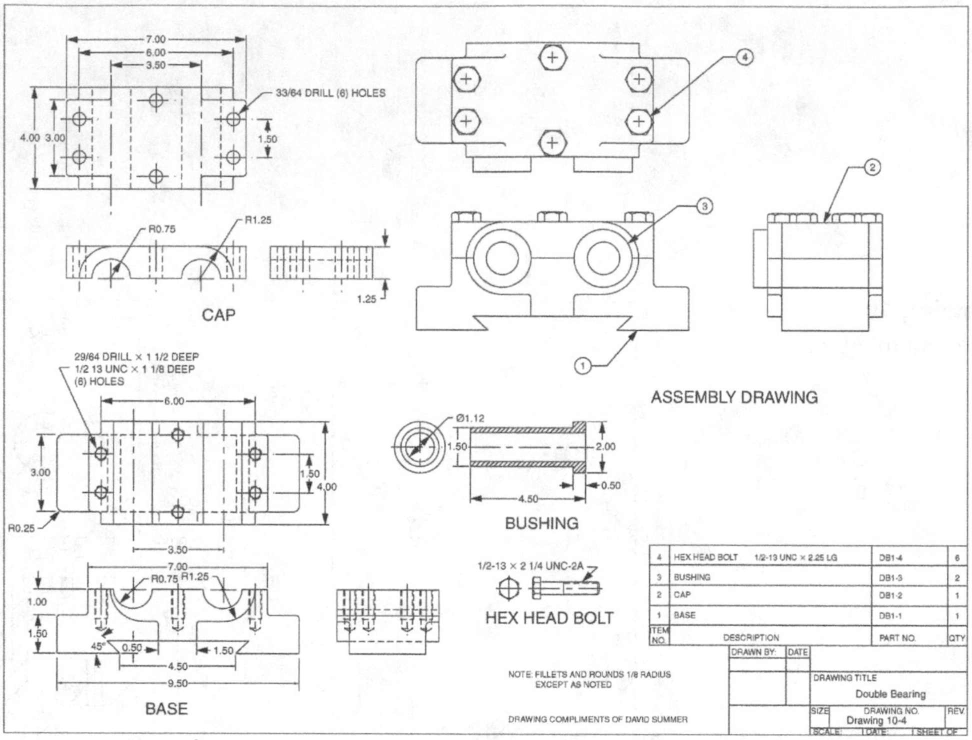

M Drawing 10-5: *Scooter Assembly* [ADVANCED]

Drawing 10-5
Sheet 1 of 2 (assembly drawing)

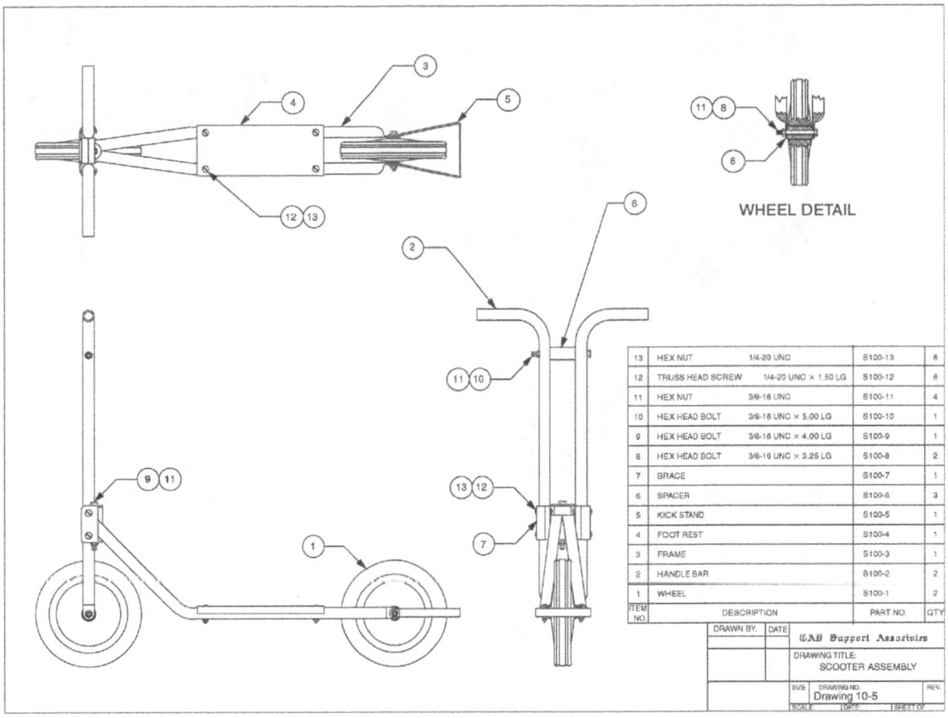

ITEM NO.	DESCRIPTION		PART NO.	QTY
13	HEX NUT	1/4-20 UNC	S100-13	8
12	TRUSS HEAD SCREW	1/4-20 UNC × 1.50 LG	S100-12	8
11	HEX NUT	3/8-16 UNC	S100-11	4
10	HEX HEAD BOLT	3/8-16 UNC × 5.00 LG	S100-10	1
9	HEX HEAD BOLT	3/8-16 UNC × 4.00 LG	S100-9	1
8	HEX HEAD BOLT	3/8-16 UNC × 3.25 LG	S100-8	2
7	BRACE		S100-7	1
6	SPACER		S100-6	3
5	KICK STAND		S100-5	1
4	FOOT REST		S100-4	1
3	FRAME		S100-3	1
2	HANDLE BAR		S100-2	2
1	WHEEL		S100-1	2

Drawing 10-5
Sheet 2 of 2 (details drawings)

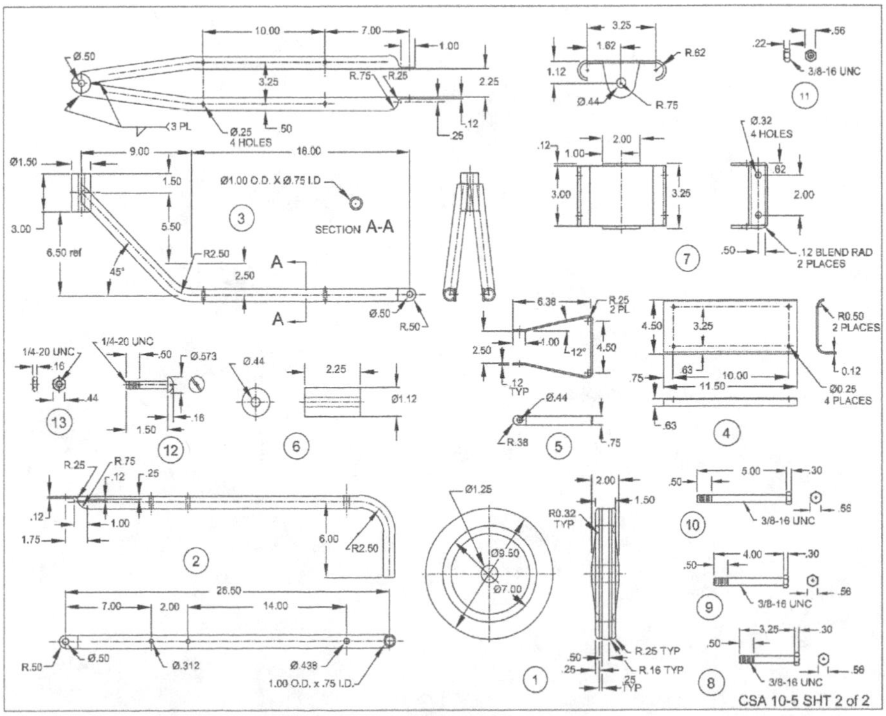

chapter eleven

Isometric Drawing

CHAPTER OBJECTIVES

- Use isometric snap
- Switch isometric planes
- Use **COPY** and other edit commands
- Draw isometric circles with **ELLIPSE**
- Draw text aligned with isometric planes
- Draw ellipses in orthographic views
- Save and restore displays with **VIEW**

Introduction

Learning to create isometric drawings should be a pleasure at this point. There are very few new commands to learn, and anything you already know about manual isometric drawing makes it that much easier on the computer. Once you know how to get into the isometric mode in AutoCAD and change from plane to plane, you can rely on previously learned skills and techniques. Many of the commands from early chapters in this book will work readily, and you will find that using the isometric drawing planes is an excellent warm-up for 3D wireframe and solid modeling.

Using Isometric Snap

To begin drawing isometrically, you need to switch to the isometric snap style. You will find the grid and crosshairs behaving in ways that might seem odd at first, but you will quickly get used to them.

TIP

The following is a general procedure for entering isometric snap mode:

1. Click the **ISODRAFT** tool from the status bar.
2. Press **<F5>** to cycle through the three isoplanes.

✔ Begin a new drawing using decimal units and 18 × 12 limits. Use the *1B* template if you have it; otherwise, be sure to use the *acad.dwt* template.

✔ Check to see that the **Grid Mode** and **Snap Mode** tools are on.

✔ Click the **ISODRAFT** tool from the status bar, as shown in Figure 11-1.

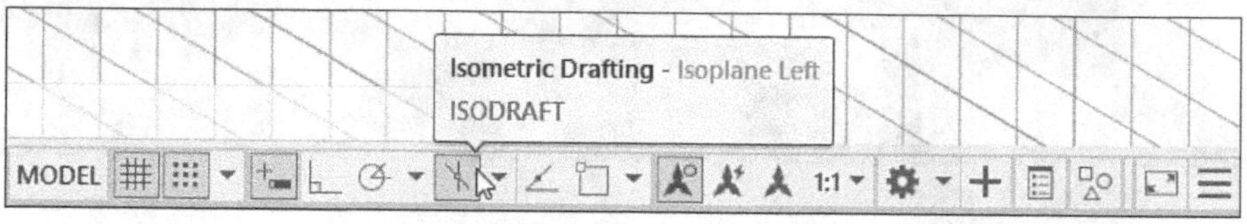

Figure 11-1
ISODRAFT tool

NOTE

Because isoplane settings are retained within the current session, it is possible that your crosshairs may be turned to the top or right isoplane instead of the left, as shown. It is not necessary to change the setting in this exercise.

At this point, your grid and crosshairs are reoriented, resembling Figure 11-2. *This is the 2D model space grid in isometric mode. Gridlines are drawn at 30°, 90°, and 150° angles from the horizontal, depending on which isoplane is being represented. The crosshairs are initially turned to define the left isometric plane, and gridlines are drawn to represent the left isoplane, with lines at 90° and 150°. The three* ***isoplanes*** *are discussed in the "Switching Isometric Planes" section.*

isoplane: One of three planes used for isometric drawing. In AutoCAD, these planes are named left, right, and top.

✔ To get a feeling for how this snap style works, start the **LINE** command and draw some boxes, as shown in Figure 11-3.

Make sure ***Ortho*** *is off and* ***Snap*** *is on, or you will be unable to draw the lines shown.*

Figure 11-2
Isometric grid, left isoplane

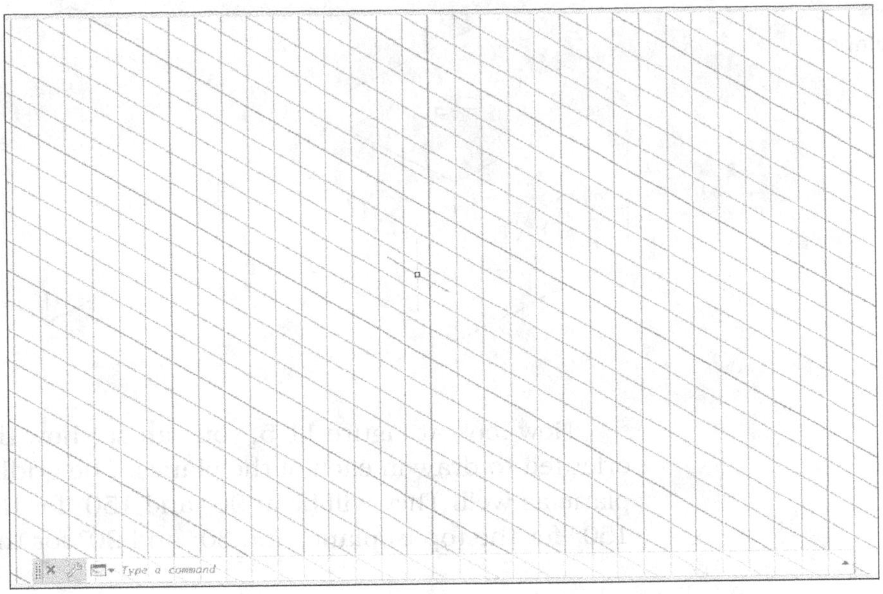

Figure 11-3
Isometric boxes

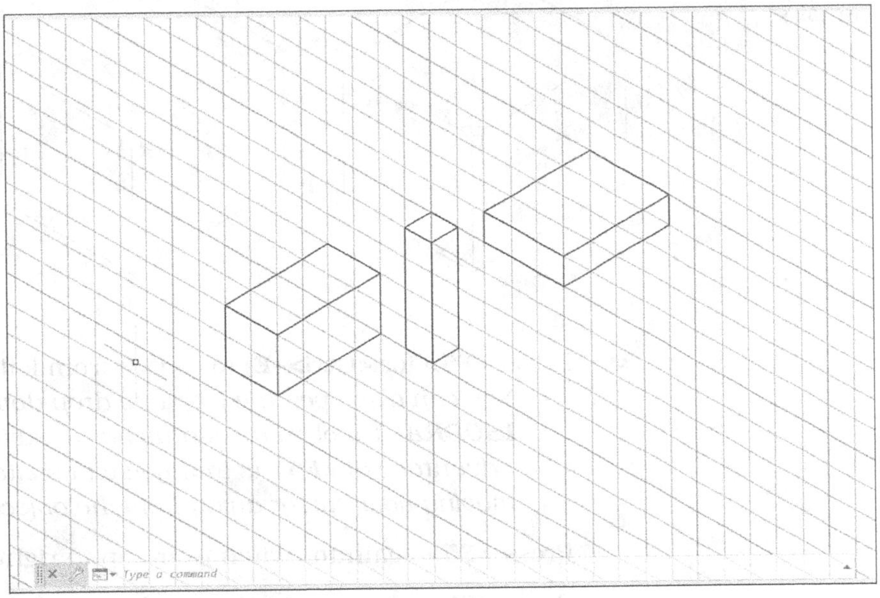

Switching Isometric Planes

If you tried to draw the boxes in the preceding section with **Ortho** on, you discovered that it is impossible. Without changing the orientation of the crosshairs, you can draw in only two of the three isometric planes. To utilize **Ortho** for accuracy and speed, you have to be able to switch planes. There are several ways to do this, but the simplest, quickest, and most convenient way is to use the **<F5>** key (or **<Ctrl>+E**).

Before beginning, take a look at Figure 11-4, which shows the three planes of a standard isometric drawing. These planes are often referred to as top, front, and right. However, AutoCAD's terminology is top, left, and right. While there are differences in the naming of the isometric planes, in this chapter, the AutoCAD terminology is used when referring to the isometric planes.

Figure 11-4
Isometric planes

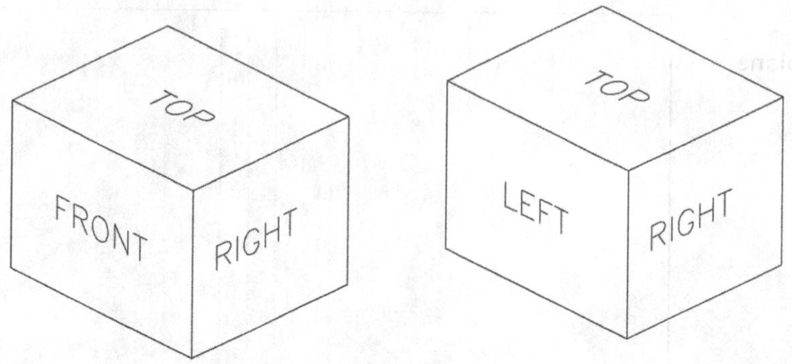

Now look at Figure 11-5, you can see how the isometric crosshairs are oriented to draw in each of the planes. The gridlines change for each isoplane as well. They will be at 90° and 150° for the left isoplane, 30° and 150° for the top isoplane, and 30° and 90° for the right isoplane.

Figure 11-5
Isometric crosshairs

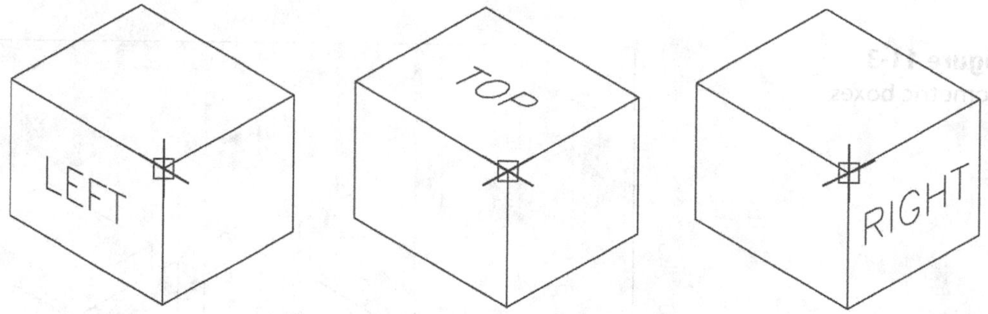

✔ Press **<F5>** (or **<Ctrl>**+**E**) to switch from left to top.

*You can also open the Isoplane drop-down menu to the right of the **ISODRAFT** tool on the status bar to switch among the planes. The advantage of **<F5>** is that you can switch while drawing without moving your cursor away from the object you are drawing.*

✔ Press **<F5>** again to switch from top to right.

✔ Press **<F5>** once more to switch back to left.

✔ Now turn **Ortho** on and draw a box outline like the one in Figure 11-6.

*You need to switch planes several times to accomplish this. Notice that you can switch planes using **<F5>** without interrupting the **LINE** command. If you find that you are in the wrong plane to construct a line, switch planes. Because every plane allows movement in two of the three directions, you can always move in the direction you want with one switch. However, you may not be able to hit the snap point you want. If you cannot, switch planes again.*

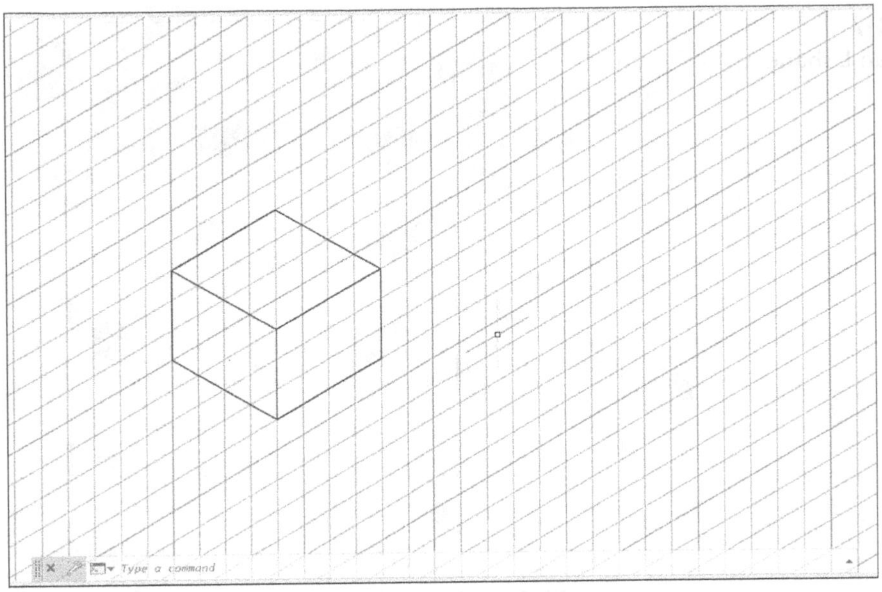

Figure 11-6
Isometric box outline

Using COPY and Other Edit Commands

Most commands work in the isometric planes just as they do in standard orthographic views. In this exercise, you construct an isometric view of a bracket using **LINE** and **COPY**. Then you draw angled corners using **CHAMFER**. In the next exercise, you will draw a hole in the bracket with **ELLIPSE**, **COPY**, and **TRIM**.

✔ Erase the boxes you previously drew and check to see that **Ortho** mode is on.

✔ Switch to the left isoplane.

✔ Click the **Line** tool on the ribbon.

✔ Draw the L-shaped object shown in Figure 11-7.
Notice that this is drawn in the left isoplane and that it is 3.00 units high by 4.00 units long by 1.00 unit wide.

✔ Next, you copy this object 4.00 units back to the right to create the back surface of the bracket.

✔ Click the **Copy** tool on the ribbon.

✔ Select all the lines in the L.

✔ Right-click to end object selection.

✔ Specify a base point at the inside corner of the L.
*It is a good exercise to keep **Ortho** on, switch planes, and move the object around in each plane. You can move in two directions in each isoplane. To move the object back to the right, as shown in Figure 11-8, you must be in either the top or the right isoplane.*

Figure 11-7
Drawing an L shape

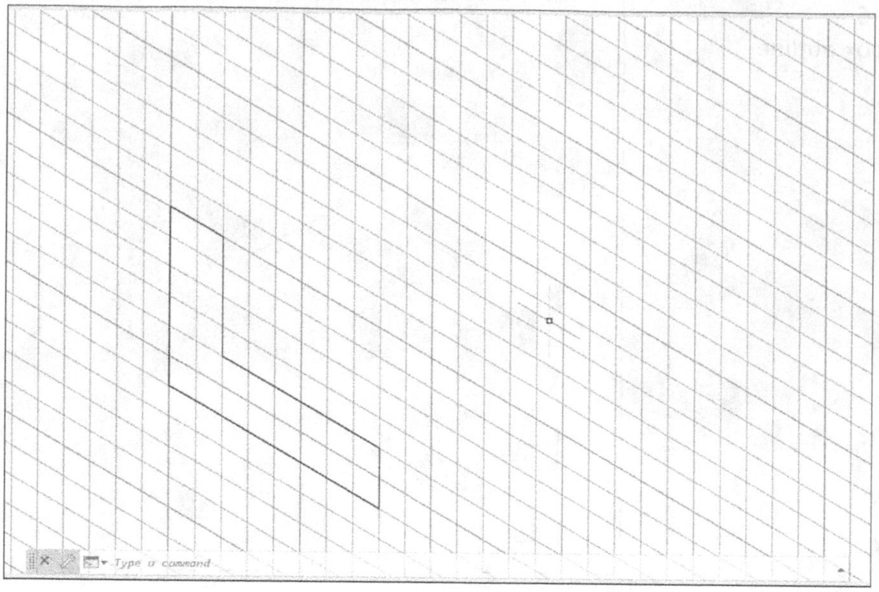

- ✔ Switch to the top or right isoplane and specify a second point of displacement 4.00 units back to the right, as shown in Figure 11-8.
- ✔ Press **<Enter>** to exit **COPY**.
- ✔ Enter the **LINE** command again and draw the connecting lines in the right plane, as shown in Figure 11-9.

Figure 11-8
Copying the L shape

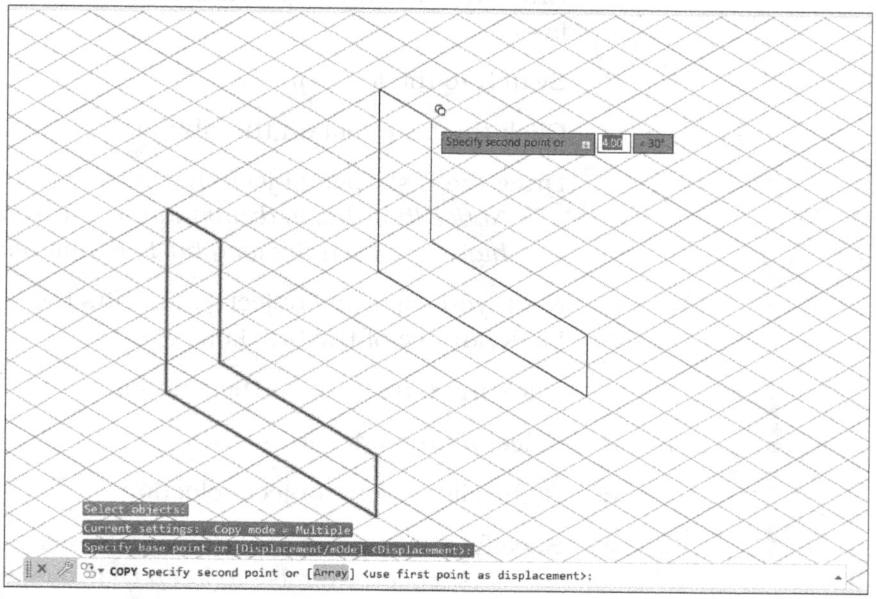

Figure 11-9
Drawing connecting lines

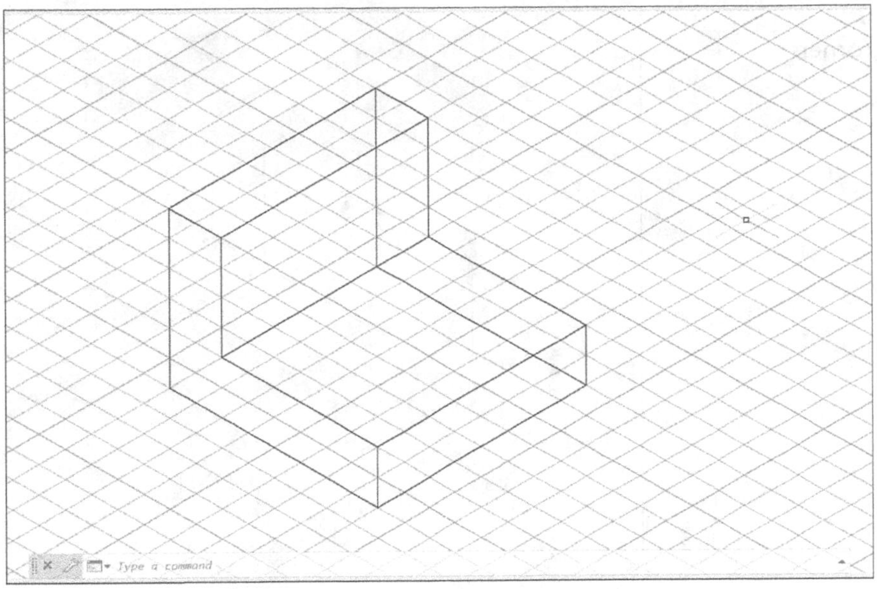

Creating Chamfers in an Isometric View

Keep in mind that inclined edges in an isometric view do not show true lengths. Edges of inclined planes must be drawn between endpoints located along vertical or horizontal paths in one of the three drawing planes. In this exercise, you create inclined edges by using the **CHAMFER** command to cut the corners of the bracket. This is no different from using **CHAMFER** in orthographic views.

✔ Click the **Chamfer** tool from the **Fillet/Chamfer** drop-down menu on the **Modify** panel on the ribbon's **Home** tab.

✔ Right-click and select **Distance** from the shortcut menu.
AutoCAD prompts for a first chamfer distance.

✔ Type **1 <Enter>**.

✔ Press **<Enter>** to accept 1.00 as the second chamfer distance.

✔ Select the top and left back edges of the bracket to create a chamfer, as shown in Figure 11-10.

✔ Repeat the **CHAMFER command.**

✔ Chamfer the other edges so that your drawing resembles Figure 11-10.

✔ To complete the bracket, start the **LINE** command and draw lines between the new chamfer edges.

✔ Finally, erase the two unseen lines on the back surface and the two corner lines left "in space" from the creation of the chamfers to produce what's shown in Figure 11-11.

Figure 11-10
Chamfering corners

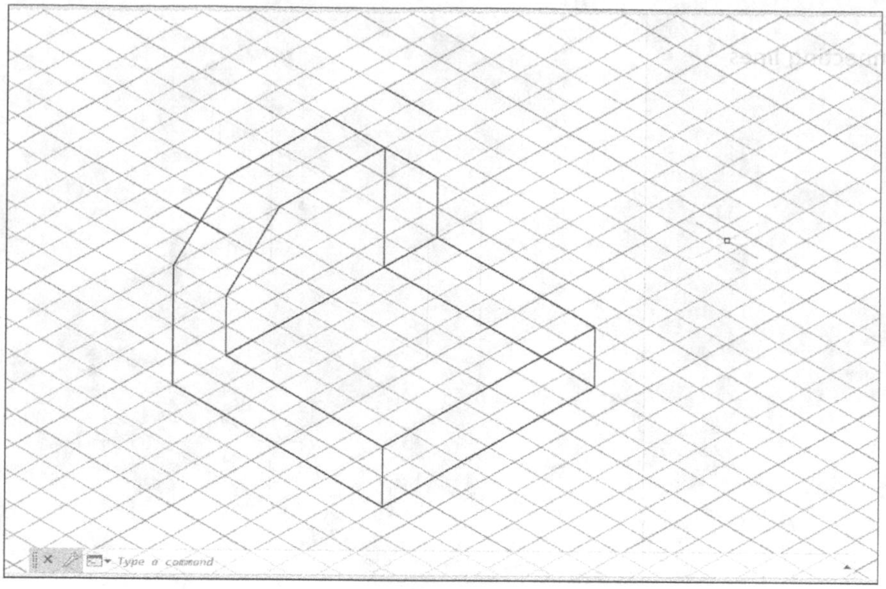

Figure 11-11
Finishing the chamfer and edges

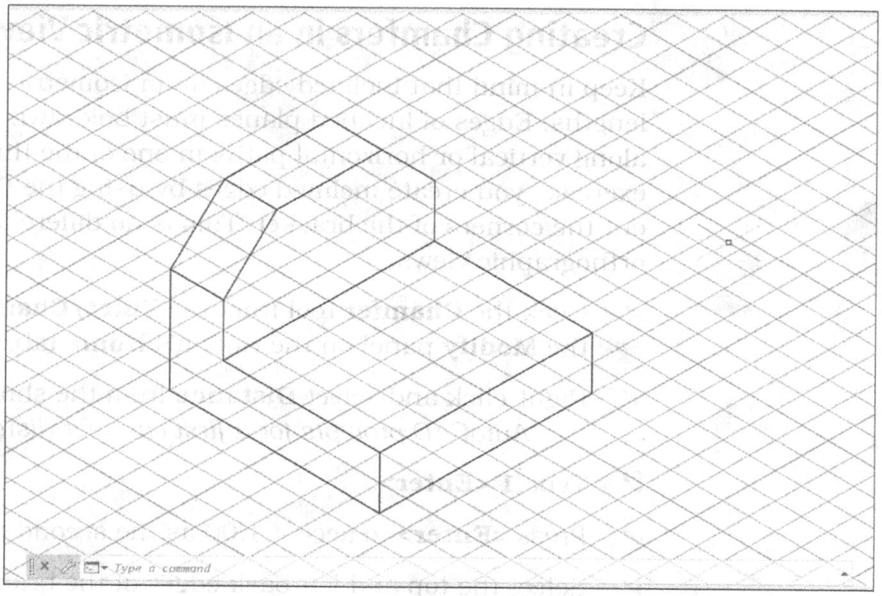

ELLIPSE	
Command	ELLIPSE
Alias	El
Panel	Draw
Tool	

isocircle: The elliptical representation of a circle in an isometric drawing.

Drawing Isometric Circles with ELLIPSE

You can use the **ELLIPSE** command to draw true ellipses in orthographic views or ellipses that appear to be circles in isometric views (called ***isocircles*** in AutoCAD). In this exercise, you use the latter capability to construct a hole in the bracket.

✔ To begin, you should have the bracket shown in Figure 11-11 in your drawing.

*To draw an isocircle, you need a center point. Often, it is necessary to locate this point carefully using temporary lines, object snap tracking, or point filters. You must be sure that you can locate the center point before entering the **ELLIPSE** command.*

In this case, it is easy because the center point is on a snap point.

✔ Type **ellipse <Enter>** at the Command prompt.

*There is an **Ellipse** tool on the ribbon, but this automates an initial option and does not give you access to the **Isocircle** option.*

AutoCAD prompts:

```
Specify axis endpoint of ellipse or [Arc/Center/Isocircle]:
```

*The option you want is **Isocircle**. Ignore the others for the time being.*

✔ Select **Isocircle** from the command line, or right-click and select **Isocircle** from the shortcut menu.

AutoCAD prompts:

```
Specify center of isocircle:
```

If you could not locate the center point, you would have to exit the command now and start over.

✔ Use the **Snap Mode** and **Grid Mode** tools to specify the center of the ellipse, as shown in Figure 11-12. If you have drawn your object with the suggested dimensions, the center point will be over 2 units and back 2 units from the top-front corner of the bracket.

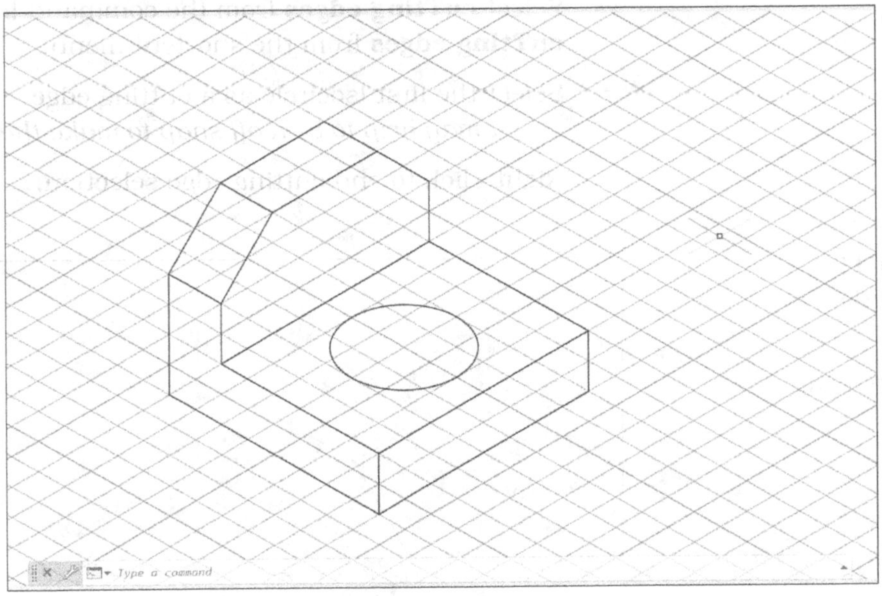

Figure 11-12
Ellipse isocircle

*AutoCAD presents you with an isocircle to drag, as in the **CIRCLE** command. The isocircle you see depends on the isoplane you are in. To understand this, try switching planes to see how the preview changes.*

✔ Drag the cursor to define the radius of the isocircle and then press **<F5>** to switch isoplanes. Observe the isocircle. Try this two or three times.

✔ Switch to the top isoplane before moving on.

AutoCAD prompts for a radius or diameter:

```
Specify radius of isocircle or [Diameter]:
```

*A radius specification is the default here, as it is in the **CIRCLE** command.*

✔ Specify a point so that your isocircle resembles the one in Figure 11-12.

*Next, you use the **COPY** and **TRIM** commands to create the bottom of the hole.*

✔ Start the **COPY** command.

✔ Select the isocircle.

✔ Right-click to end object selection.

✔ Specify the top-front corner of the bracket.

Any point can be used as the base point. By specifying the top-front corner, the bottom-front corner gives you the exact thickness of the bracket.

✔ Specify the bottom-front corner. Make sure you are in an isoplane that allows movement from top to bottom (the left or right isoplanes).

Your drawing should now resemble Figure 11-13. The last thing you must do is trim the hidden portion of the bottom of the hole.

✔ Press **<Enter>** to exit **COPY**.

✔ Start the **TRIM** command.

✔ Select **cuTting edges** from the command line, or right-click and select **cuTting edges** from the shortcut menu.

✔ Select the first isocircle as a cutting edge.

It may help to turn off snap to make these selections.

✔ Right-click to end cutting edge selection.

Figure 11-13
Copy isocircle

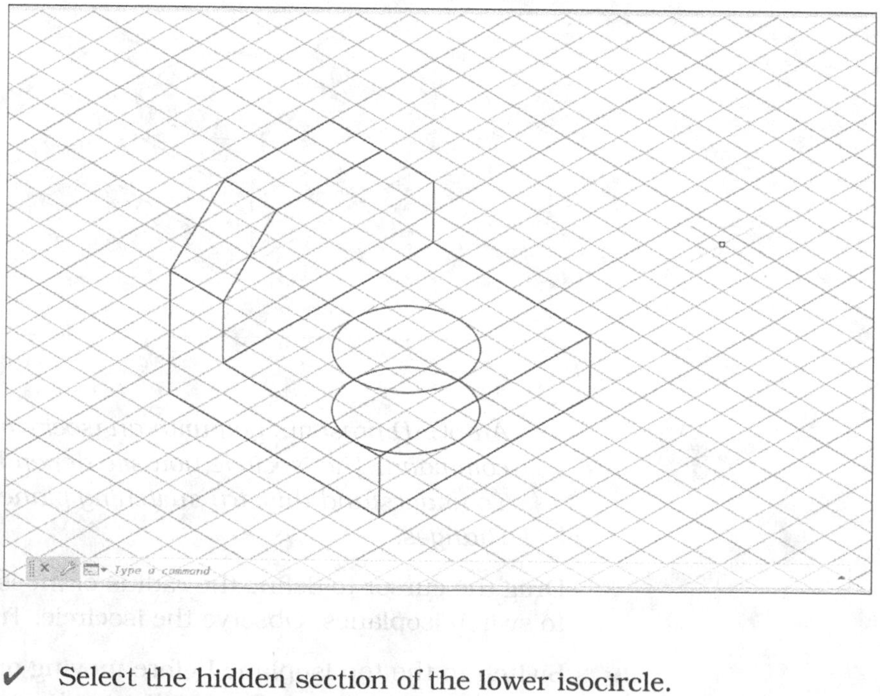

✔ Select the hidden section of the lower isocircle.

✔ Press **<Enter>** to exit **TRIM**.

The bracket is now complete, and your drawing should resemble Figure 11-14.

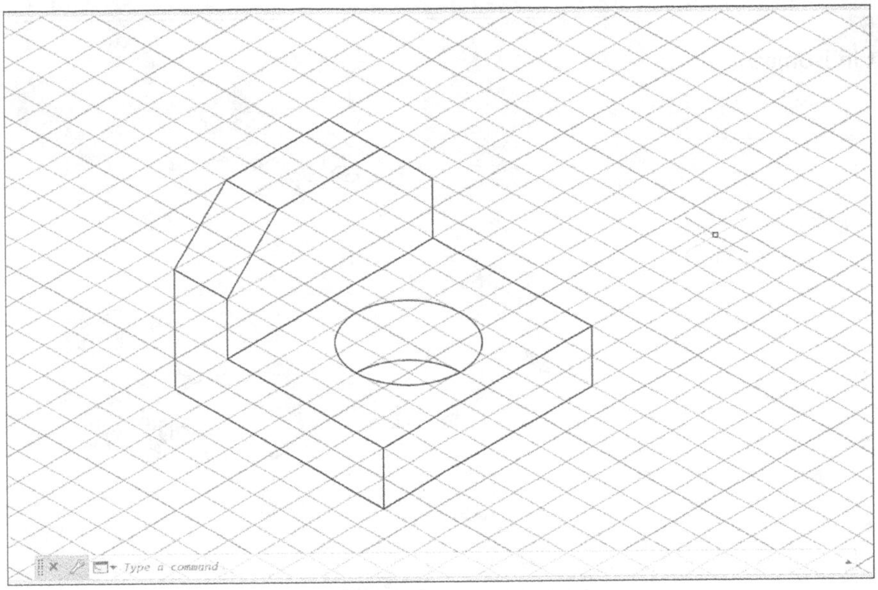

Figure 11-14
Trimming lower isocircle

Drawing Text Aligned with Isometric Planes

Adding text to isometric drawings has some challenges you may not have encountered previously. To create the appearance that text aligns with an isometric plane, it needs to be altered in two ways. First, the whole line of text needs to be rotated to align with one side of the plane. Second, the obliquing angle of individual characters needs to be adjusted to match the plane's tilt. Rotation angle, you recall, is handled through the command sequence of the **TEXT** command. Obliquing angle is set as a text style characteristic using the **STYLE** command.

Typically, text in an isometric drawing aligns with one of the three isometric planes. In order to demonstrate how this works, you add a single-line text object to each of the planes of the bracket, as shown in Figure 11-15. Though you will be drawing on three planes, you can accomplish this with only two new text styles. These will be simple variations of the Standard text style, with the oblique angles needed for isometric alignment. The right isoplane will use a 30° oblique angle, while the top and left planes will use a –30° angle.

✔ To begin, you should be in the bracket drawing created in the previous sections. Isometric snap and grid modes should be enabled.

✔ Click the **Home** tab, expand the **Annotation** panel, and then click the **Text Style** tool in the top left, next to the name of the current text style (**Standard**).

This opens the ***Text Style*** *dialog box. The first new text style you create will be used for drawing text on the right isoplane. If you look at Figure 11-15, you can see that this text (the word* Right*) is rotated along the 30° X-axis of the isoplane. What may be less obvious is that the individual characters are also drawn at a 30° oblique angle. You enter the rotation angle when creating the text. Here, you set the oblique angle for this plane.*

Figure 11-15
Drawing text in isometric view

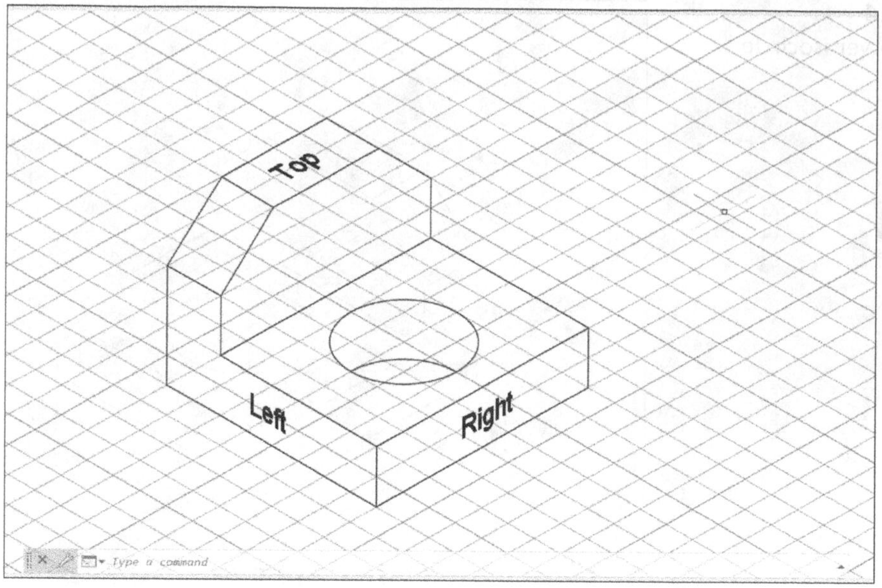

- ✔ In the **Text Style** dialog box, click the **New** button.
- ✔ In the **New Text Style** dialog box, type **isotext30**.
- ✔ Click **OK**.
- ✔ Change the **Oblique Angle** to **30**.
- ✔ Click **Apply**.

  You repeat these steps to create a style with –30° obliquing angle.
- ✔ Click the **New** button.
- ✔ In the **New Text Style** dialog box, type **isotext-30**.
- ✔ Click **OK**.
- ✔ Change the **Oblique Angle** to **–30**.
- ✔ Click **Apply**.
- ✔ Highlight **isotext30** in the **Styles** list.
- ✔ If you see a message saying the current text style has been modified, click **Yes**.

  *You should now be back in the drawing with **isotext30** as the current text style. You are now ready to add the single-line text.*
- ✔ Click the **Set Current** button.
- ✔ Click **Close**.
- ✔ Make sure to be on the right isoplane. Press **<F5>** to cycle through the isoplanes until you get to the right isoplane.
- ✔ On the **Annotation** panel, click the **Multiline Text/Single-line** text drop-down menu and choose the **Single Line** text tool.
- ✔ Use the **Justify** option and set the justification for the new text to **Middle Center (MC)**.

- ✔ Specify the middle point on the right front of the bracket, as shown by the placement of the word *Right* in Figure 11-15.
- ✔ Specify a text height of **.30**.
- ✔ Type **30 <Enter>** for the rotation angle.
- ✔ Type **Right <Enter>**.
- ✔ Press **<Enter>**.

  The word Right *should be drawn on the bracket, as shown in Figure 11-15. Now draw the word* Left *on the left isoplane, as shown. This will use the* ***isotext-30*** *style and a rotation angle of –30°.*

- ✔ Expand the **Annotation** panel and select **isotext-30** from the **Text Style** drop-down list.
- ✔ Press **<F5>** to set the left isoplane current.
- ✔ Click the **Single Line** text tool from the **Annotation** panel.
- ✔ Specify the middle point on the left side of the bracket, as shown by the placement of the word *Left* in Figure 11-15.
- ✔ Specify a text height of **.30**.
- ✔ Type **–30 <Enter>** for the rotation angle.
- ✔ Type **Left <Enter>**.
- ✔ Press **<Enter>**.

Finally, for text in the top isoplane, use **isotext-30** with a rotation angle of +30°.

- ✔ Press **<F5>** to set the top isoplane current.
- ✔ Click the **Single Line** text tool from the **Annotation** panel.
- ✔ Specify the middle point on the top of the bracket, as shown by the placement of the word *Top* in Figure 11-15.
- ✔ Press **<Enter>** for a text height of **.30**.
- ✔ Type **30 <Enter>** for the rotation angle.
- ✔ Type **Top <Enter>**.
- ✔ Press **<Enter>**.

  Your drawing should resemble Figure 11-15.

This completes the present discussion of isometric drawing. You can find more in the drawing suggestions at the end of this chapter.

Next, you go on to exploring the nonisometric use of the **ELLIPSE** command and saving named views with the **VIEW** command.

Drawing Ellipses in Orthographic Views

orthographic view: One of six standard views in which the observer's point of view is normal to the front, back, left, right, top, or bottom of the drawing plane.

The **ELLIPSE** command is important not only for drawing isocircles but also for drawing true ellipses in ***orthographic views***. There is also an option to create elliptical arcs.

An ellipse is determined by a center point and two perpendicular axes of differing lengths. In AutoCAD, these specifications can be shown in two nearly identical ways, each requiring you to show three points (see Figure 11-16). In the default method, you show two endpoints of an axis and then show half the length of the other axis, from the midpoint of the first axis out. (The midpoint of an axis is also the center of the ellipse.) The other method allows you to specify the center point of the ellipse first, then the endpoint of one axis, followed by half the length of the other axis.

✔ In preparation for this exercise, return to the standard **Snap** mode and **Grid** mode by clicking the **ISODRAFT** tool on the status bar to turn off the **Isometric Snap** mode.

Your grid is returned to the standard pattern of lines, and the crosshairs are horizontal and vertical again. Notice that this does not affect the isometric bracket you have just drawn.

*You briefly explore the **ELLIPSE** command and draw some standard ellipses.*

Figure 11-16
Ellipse axis and center

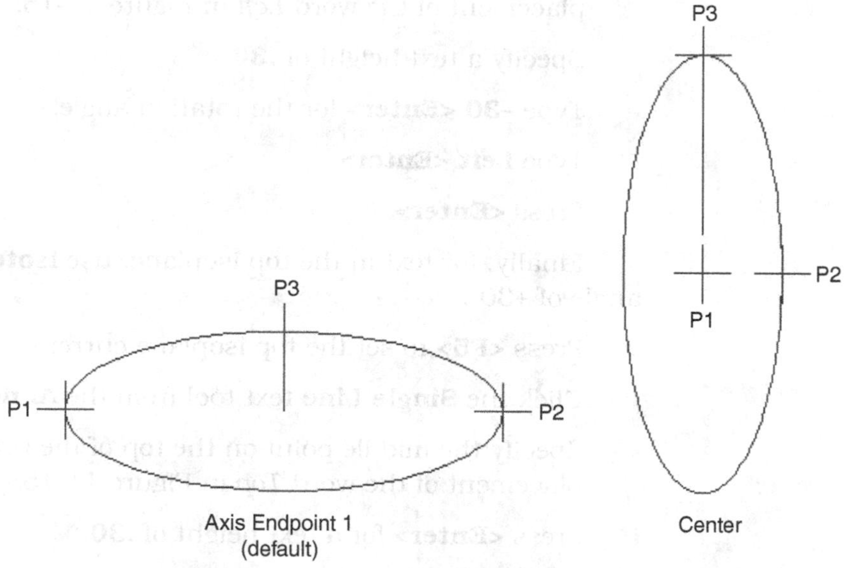

✔ **Ortho** should be off for this exercise.

✔ On the **Home** tab, click the **Ellipse** drop-down menu on the **Draw** panel and then select the **Axis, End** tool, as shown in Figure 11-17.

AutoCAD prompts:

```
Specify axis endpoint of ellipse or [Arc/Center]:
```

✔ Specify the axis endpoint, as shown by P1 on the ellipse at the lower left in Figure 11-18.

AutoCAD prompts for the other endpoint:

```
Specify other endpoint of axis:
```

✔ Specify the second endpoint, as shown by P2.

As you drag the rubber band, a preview of the ellipse is updated to show the length of the other axis. Only the length of the rubber band is significant; the angle is already determined to be perpendicular to the first axis. Because of this, the third point falls on the ellipse only if the rubber band happens to be exactly perpendicular to the first axis.

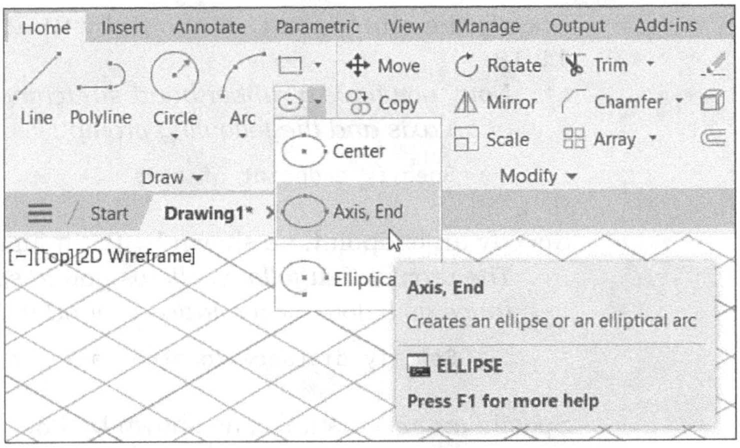

Figure 11-17
Ellipse Axis, End tool

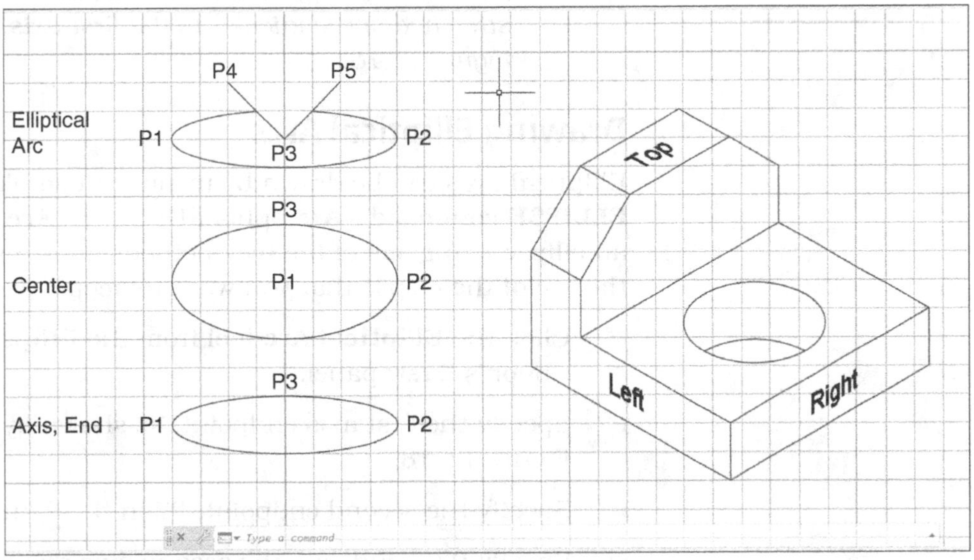

Figure 11-18
Drawing standard ellipses

As before, the following prompt allows you to specify the second axis distance or a rotation around the first axis:

```
Specify distance to other axis or [Rotation]:
```

The ***Rotation*** *option is awkward to use and is not explored here; see the AutoCAD Command Reference for more information.*

✔ Specify P3 as shown.

This point shows half the length of the other axis.

The first ellipse should now be complete. Next, you draw one by specifying the center point first, using the **Center** ellipse tool from the ribbon.

✔ Click the **Center** tool from the **Ellipse** drop-down menu on the ribbon's **Draw** panel.

*This uses the **Center** option.*

AutoCAD prompts you for a center point:

```
Specify center of ellipse:
```

✔ Specify the center point, as shown by P1 at the middle left in Figure 11-18.

Now, you have a rubber band stretching from the center to the end of an axis and the following prompt:

```
Specify endpoint of axis:
```

✔ Specify an endpoint, as shown by P2 in Figure 11-18.

The prompt that follows allows you to specify the second axis distance as before, or a rotation around the first axis:

```
Specify distance to other axis or [Rotation]:
```

✔ Specify an axis distance, as shown by P3.

Here again, the rubber band is significant for distance only. The point you specify falls on the ellipse only if the rubber band is stretched perpendicular to the first axis. Notice that it is not so in Figure 11-18.

Drawing Elliptical Arcs

Elliptical arcs can be drawn by trimming complete ellipses or using the **ELLIPSE** command's **Arc** option. Using the **Arc** option, you first construct an ellipse using one of the two methods shown previously and then define the arc of the ellipse that you want to keep.

✔ Click the **Elliptical Arc** tool from the **Ellipse** drop-down menu on the ribbon's **Draw** panel.

✔ Specify the first axis endpoint, as shown by P1 at the upper left in Figure 11-18.

✔ Specify the second endpoint, P2 in the figure.

✔ Specify P3 to indicate the second axis distance.

*AutoCAD draws an ellipse as you have specified, but the object is only temporary. Now, you need to show the arc you want drawn. The two options are **Parameter** and **Included angle**. **Parameter** takes you into more options that allow you to specify your arc in different ways, similar to the options of the **ARC** command. Stick with the default option here.*

✔ Specify P4 to indicate the angle at which the elliptical arc begins.

Move the cursor slowly along the ellipse's preview, and you can see all the arcs that are possible, starting from this angle.

✔ Specify P5 to indicate the end angle and complete the ellipse.

Saving and Restoring Displays with VIEW

VIEW	
Command	VIEW
Alias	V
Panel	Views
Tool	

The word *view* in connection with the **VIEW** command has a special significance in a drawing. It refers to any set of display boundaries that have been named and saved using the **VIEW** command. It also refers to a defined 3D viewpoint that has been saved with a name. Saved views can be restored by direct reference rather than by redefining the location, size, or viewpoint of the area to be displayed. **VIEW** can be useful in creating drawing layouts and when you know you will be returning frequently to a certain area of a large drawing. It saves you from having to zoom out to look at the complete drawing and then zoom in again on the area you want. It can also save time in creating a 3D viewpoint. In this chapter, you learn to use 2D views only.

Imagine that you have to complete some detail work on the area around the hole in the bracket and also on the top corner. You can define each of these as a view and jump back and forth at will.

✔ To begin this exercise, you should have the bracket in your drawing, as shown in Figure 11-19.

✔ Type **view <Enter>** or click **View** > **Named Views** > **View Manager** from the ribbon, as shown in Figure 11-20.

*This displays the **View Manager** dialog box shown in Figure 11-21. At the left is a list of views, including **Current**, **Model Views**, **Layout Views**, and **Preset Views**. In this chapter, you only work with the **Current** view, which you define and name.*

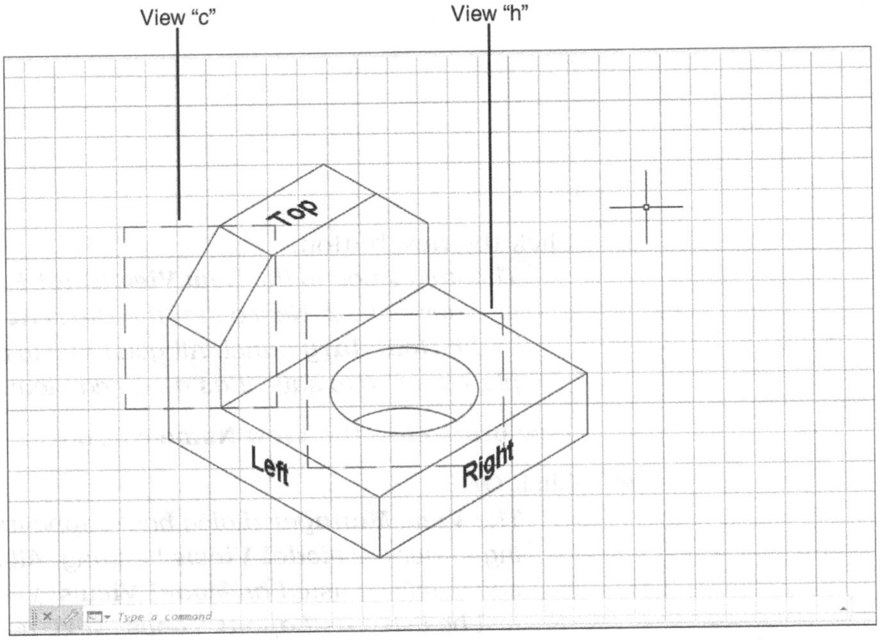

Figure 11-19
Defining views

Figure 11-20
View Manager tool

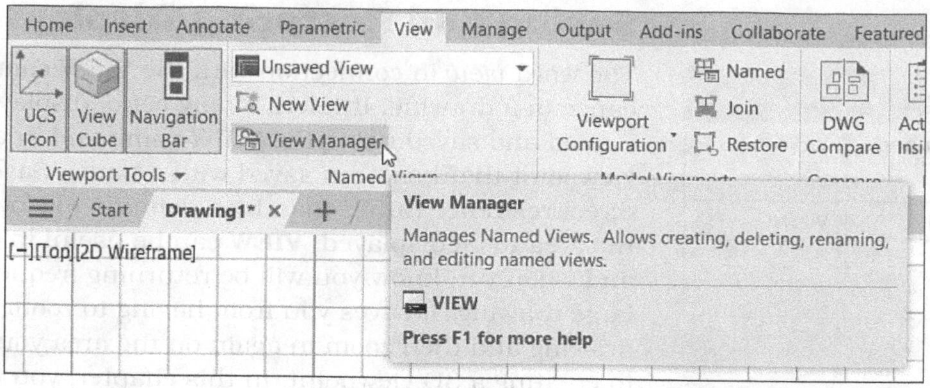

Figure 11-21
View Manager dialog box

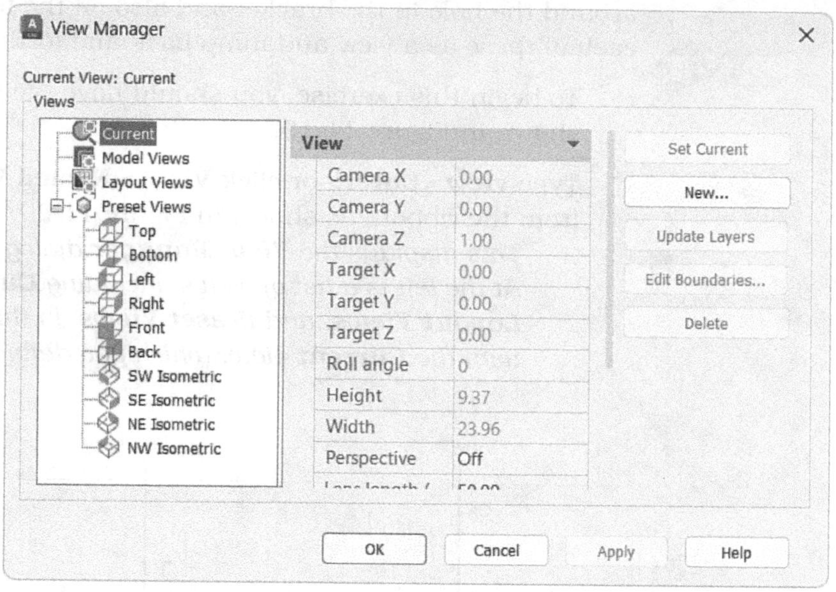

✔ Click the **New** button.

This takes you to the ***New View/Shot Properties*** *dialog box shown in Figure 11-22. Notice that the* ***Current Display*** *option is selected in the* ***Boundary*** *panel. All you have to do is give the current display a name to save it as a named view.*

✔ Type **bracket** in the **View Name** edit box.

✔ Click **OK**.

The ***View Manager*** *dialog box reappears, with* ***bracket*** *now showing under the* ***Model Views*** *heading. All views defined in model space will be listed as* ***Model Views****. Views defined in paper space will be listed as* ***Layout Views****. Next, you use a window to define a model space with a smaller area as a view.*

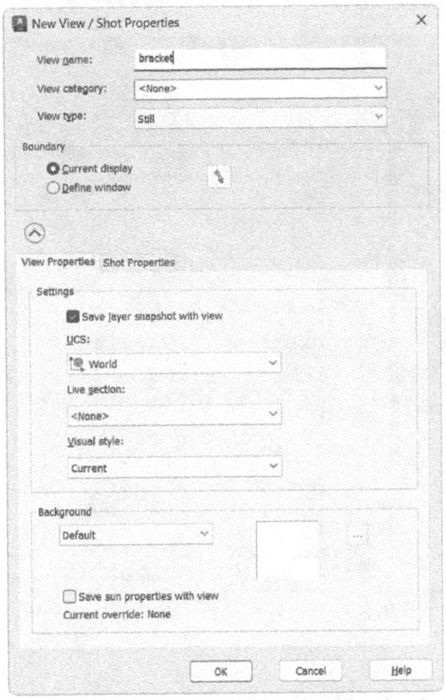

Figure 11-22
New View/Shot Properties dialog box

- ✔ Click the **New** button to return to the **New View/Shot Properties** dialog box.
- ✔ Type **hole** in the **View Name** edit box.
  This view zooms in on the hole.
- ✔ Select the **Define Window** option in the **Boundary** panel.
  The dialog box closes, giving you access to the drawing area where the current view is outlined. The rest of the drawing is grayed out.
- ✔ Specify the first and second corners to define a window around the hole in the bracket, as shown previously in Figure 11-19.
  A window outline of the new view is shown, with the rest of the drawing grayed out.
- ✔ Press **<Enter>** to return to the **New View/Shot Properties** dialog box.
- ✔ Click **OK** to save the named view.
  *You are now back in the **View Manager** dialog box with **bracket** and **hole** in the list of **Model Views**. Define one more view to show the upper-left corner of the bracket, as shown in Figure 11-19.*
- ✔ Click the **New** button.
- ✔ Type **corner** for the view name.
- ✔ Select the **Define Window** option.
- ✔ Define a window, as shown in Figure 11-19.
- ✔ Press **<Enter>** to return to the dialog box.
- ✔ Click **OK** to close the **New View/Shot Properties** dialog box.
  *You have now defined three model views. To see the views in action, you must set them as current. Notice that the new view names are now displayed in a list on the **Views** panel, as shown in Figure 11-23.*

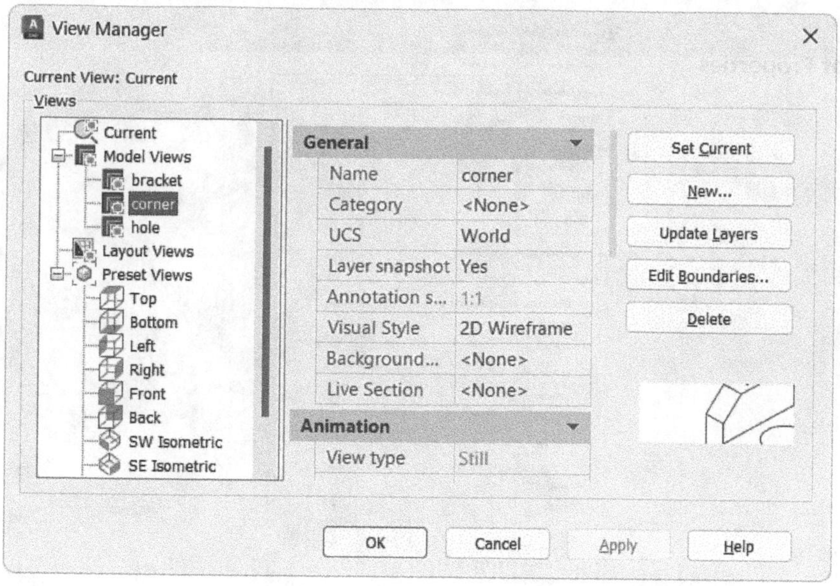

Figure 11-23
New view list on the **Views** panel

- ✔ Double-click **hole** in the **Views** list.
- ✔ *Click* **OK**.

  Your drawing should resemble Figure 11-24.

  Now, switch to the corner view.

- ✔ Instead of using the **View Manager** again to set a view current, click the **Views** drop-down list on the ribbon's **Named Views** panel.
- ✔ Select **corner** from the **Views** list.

  Your drawing should resemble Figure 11-25.

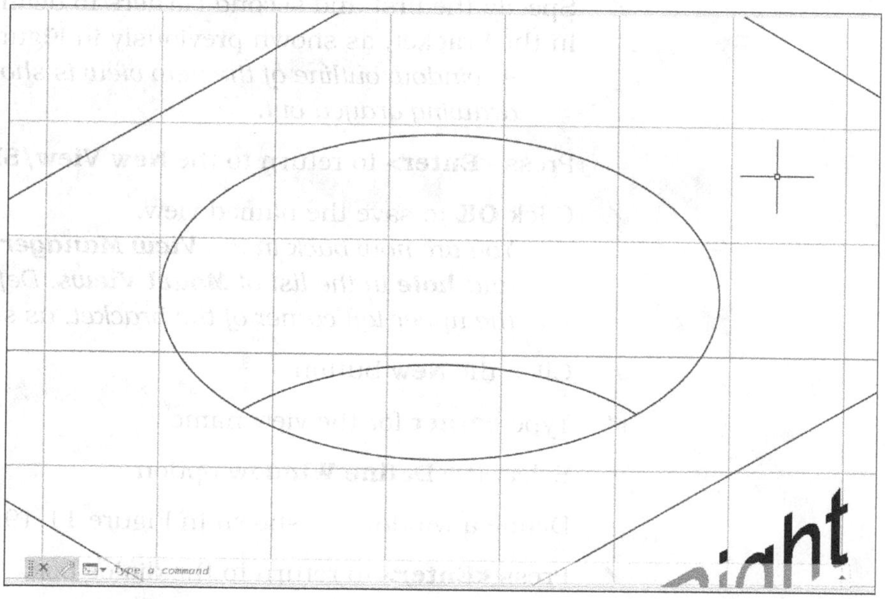

Figure 11-24
Hole view

Figure 11-25
Corner view

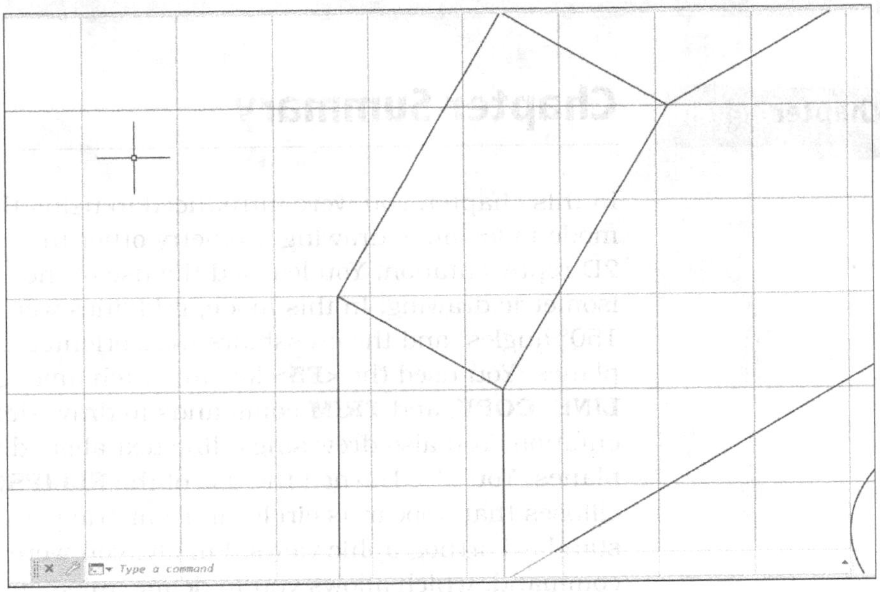

11 chapter eleven

Chapter Summary

In this chapter, you were introduced to using the grid display and **Snap** mode to facilitate drawing geometry other than the standard orthographic 2D representation. You learned the use of the isometric grid to create an isometric drawing. In this mode, grid lines were shown at 30°, 90°, and 150° angles, and the crosshairs were oriented to the top, left, and right isoplanes. You used the **<F5>** key to switch among these planes, and the **LINE**, **COPY**, and **TRIM** commands to draw simple objects in isometric orientation. You also drew single-line text aligned with each of the three isoplanes. You also learned the use of the **ELLIPSE** command to create ellipses that appear as circles in isometric planes and also drew ellipses in standard orthographic views. Finally, you were introduced to the **VIEW** command, which allows you to define any display as a named view that can be restored at any time.

Chapter Test Questions

Multiple Choice

Circle the correct answer.

6. Change to this to align the grid with isometric planes:

a. Change grid to polar
b. Change grid to isometric
c. Change grid to 2D model space
d. Change snap to 2D model space

7. Which of these does **not** name an isoplane in AutoCAD?

a. Right
b. Left
c. Front
d. Top

8. The command used to draw circles in isometric views is

a. **ISOCIRCLE**
b. **ELLIPSE**
c. **ISOPLANE**
d. **CIRCLE**

9. To align text with isometric planes, make changes to

a. Rotation and oblique angles
b. Text style and alignment
c. Alignment style and rotation
d. Rotation angle and grid style

10. The minimum number of points required to define an elliptical arc are

a. 2
b. 3
c. 4
d. 5

Matching

Write the number of the correct answer on the line.

a. Isoplane switch ______
b. Isocircle ______
c. Right isoplane text ______
d. Top isoplane text ______
e. Default view ______

1. Ellipse
2. 30°, 30°
3. 30°, –30°
4. **<F5>**
5. Current display

True or False

Circle the correct answer.

1. **True or False:** Isometric drawings are two-dimensional.
2. **True or False:** Isometric drawings show no true distances.
3. **True or False:** To draw an isometric circle, it is necessary to specify a center point.
4. **True or False:** To switch isoplanes, you must open the **Drafting Settings** dialog box.
5. **True or False:** Drawing isocircles is the same as drawing ellipses in orthographic views.

Questions

1. What are the angles of the crosshairs and grid lines in an isometric grid?
2. What are the names for the isometric planes in AutoCAD?
3. What is an isocircle? Why are isocircles drawn with the **ELLIPSE** command?
4. How many different isocircles can you draw with the same radius and the same center point?
5. What rotation angle and oblique angle are used to align text with each of the three isoplanes?

Drawing Problems

1. Using the isometric grid, draw a 4 × 4 square in the right isoplane.
2. Copy the square back 4.00 units along the left isoplane.
3. Connect the corners of the two squares to form an isometric cube. Erase any lines that would be hidden in this object.
4. Use text rotation and obliquing to draw the word *Top* in the top plane of the cube so that the text is centered on the face and aligned with its edges. The text should be 0.5-unit high.
5. In a similar manner, draw the word *Left* at the center of the left side and the word *Right* at the center of the right side. All text should align with the face on which it is located.

11 chaptereleven

Chapter Drawing Projects

M Drawing 11-1: *Isometric Projects* [INTERMEDIATE]

This drawing is a direct extension of the exercises in the chapter. It gives you practice in basic AutoCAD isometrics and in transferring dimensions from orthographic to isometric views.

Drawing Suggestions

- Set your grid to **.50** and your snap to **.25** to create all the objects in this project. Your grid should match the grid of this drawing. Notice that some lines do not fall on grid points, but halfway between.
- There is no **Arc** option when you use **ELLIPSE** to draw isocircles, so semicircles such as those at the back of the holes must be constructed by first drawing isocircles and then trimming or erasing unwanted portions.
- To draw the portion of the isocircle that shows the depth of a circle, copy the isocircle down or back, snapping from endpoint to endpoint of other lines in the view that show the depth.
- Often, when you try to select a group of objects to copy, there are many crossing lines that you do not want to include in the copy. This is an ideal time to use the **Remove** option in object selection. First, window the objects you want along with those nearby that are unavoidable, and then remove the unwanted objects one by one.
- Sometimes, you may get unexpected results when you try to trim an object in an isometric view. For example, AutoCAD divides an ellipse into a series of arcs and trims only a portion. If you do not get the results you want, use a **Nearest** object snap to control how the object is trimmed.

Drawing 11-1
Isometric projects

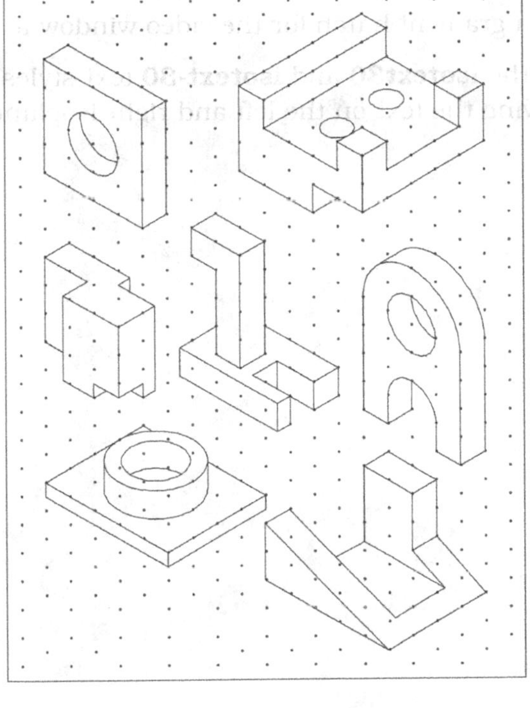

M

Drawing 11-2: *MP3 Player* [ADVANCED]

This drawing introduces text and combines a complete set of 2D views with an isometric representation of the object. Placing objects on different layers so they can be turned on and off during **TRIM** and **ERASE** procedures makes things considerably less messy.

Drawing Suggestions

- Use the box method to create the isometric view of this drawing. That is, begin with an isometric box according to the overall outside dimensions of the MP3 player. Then trim and add the details.
- The dial is made from isocircles with copies to show thickness. You can use the **Tangent** object snap to draw the front-to-back connecting lines.
- Use a gradient hatch for the video window area.
- Use the **isotext30** and **isotext-30** text styles created in this chapter for drawing the text on the left and right isoplanes, as shown.

Drawing 11-2
MP3 player

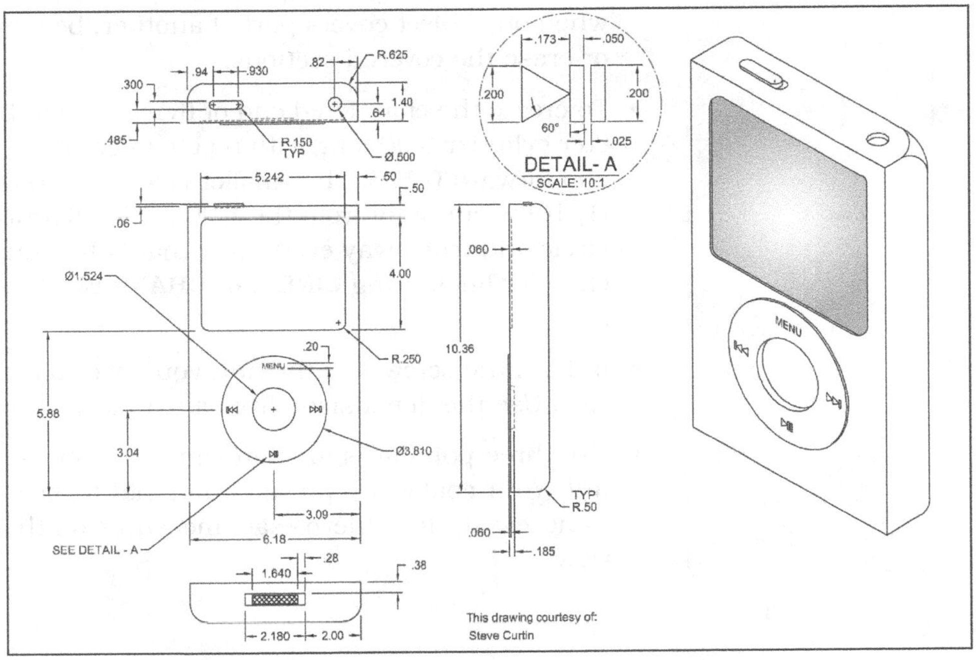

M Drawing 11-3: *Fixture Assembly* [ADVANCED]

This is a difficult drawing. It takes time and patience but teaches you a great deal about isometric drawing in AutoCAD.

Drawing Suggestions

- This drawing can be completed either by drawing everything in place as you see it or by drawing the parts and moving them into place along the common centerline that runs through the middle of all the items. If you use the former method, draw the centerline first and use it to locate the center points of isocircles and as base points for other measures.
- As you go, look for pieces of objects that can be copied from other objects. Avoid duplicating efforts by editing before copying. In particular, when one object covers part of another, be sure to copy it before you trim or erase the covered sections.
- To create the chamfered end of Item 4, begin by drawing the 1.00-diameter cylinder 3.00 long with no chamfer. Then, copy the isocircle at the end forward 0.125. The smaller isocircle is 0.875 (7/8) because 0.0625 (1/16) is cut away from the 1.00 circle all around. Draw this smaller isocircle and trim away everything that is hidden. Then draw the slanted chamfer lines using **LINE**, not **CHAMFER**. Use the same method for Item 5.
- In both the screw and the nut, you need to create hexes around isocircles. Use the dimensions from a standard bolt chart.
- Use three-point arcs to approximate the curves on the screw bolt and the nut. Your goal is a representation that looks correct. It is impractical and unnecessary to achieve exact measures on these objects in the isometric view.

Drawing 11-3
Fixture assembly

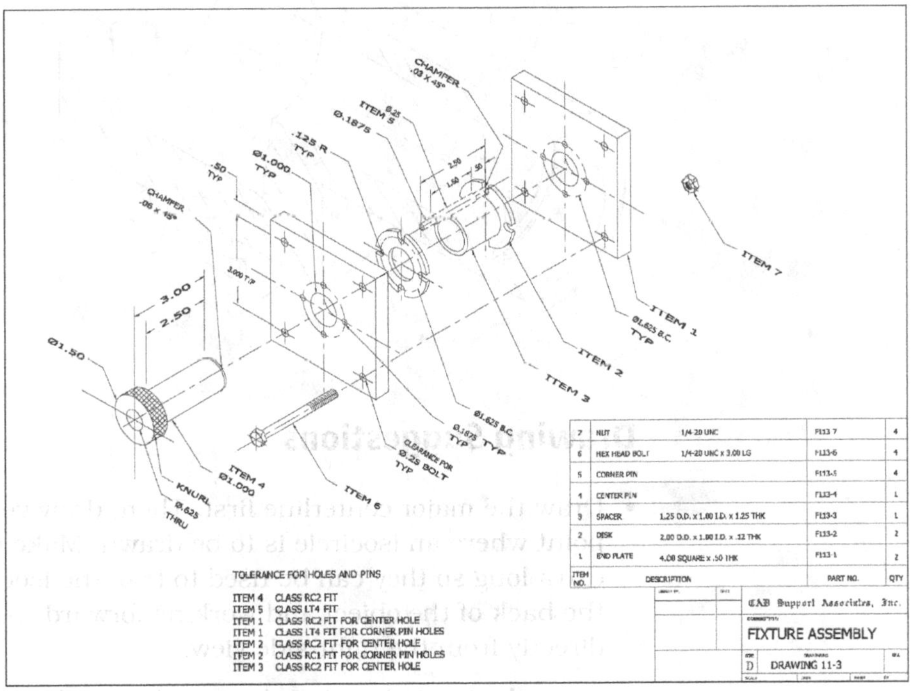

ITEM NO.	DESCRIPTION		PART NO.	QTY
7	NUT	1/4-20 UNC	F113 7	4
6	HEX HEAD BOLT	1/4-20 UNC x 3.00 LG	F113-6	4
5	CORNER PIN		F113-5	4
4	CENTER PIN		F113-4	1
3	SPACER	1.25 O.D. x 1.00 I.D. x 1.25 THK	F113-3	1
2	DISK	2.00 O.D. x 1.00 I.D. x .12 THK	F113-2	2
1	END PLATE	4.00 SQUARE x .50 THK	F113-1	2

M Drawing 11-4: *Flanged Coupling* [ADVANCED]

The isometric view in this three-view drawing must be completed working off the centerline.

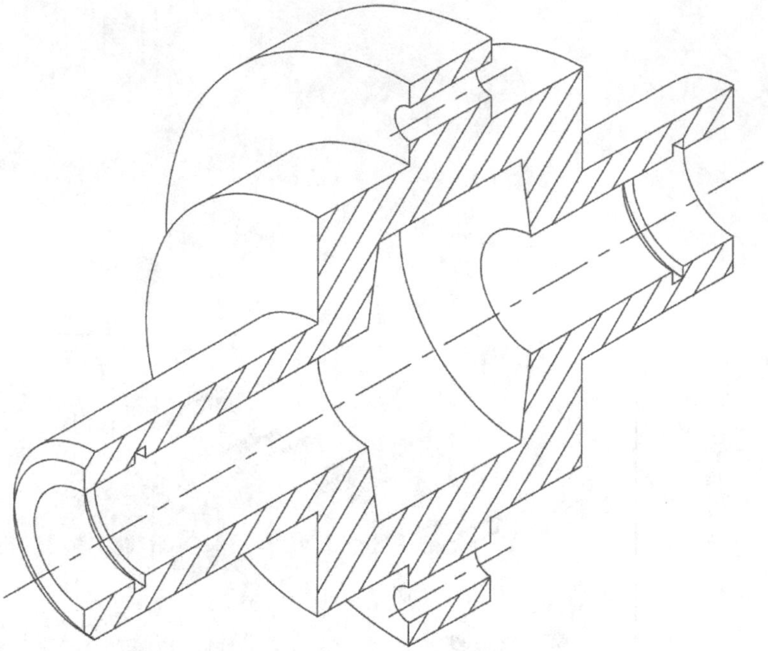

Drawing Suggestions

- Draw the major centerline first. Then, draw vertical centerlines at every point where an isocircle is to be drawn. Make sure to draw these lines extra long so they can be used to trim the isocircles in half. By starting at the back of the object and working forward, you can take dimensions directly from the right-side view.
- Draw the isocircles at each centerline and then trim them to represent semicircles.
- Use the **Endpoint**, **Intersection**, and **Tangent** object snaps to draw horizontal lines.
- Trim away all obstructed lines and parts of isocircles.
- Draw the four slanted lines in the middle as vertical lines first. Then, with **Ortho** off, change their endpoints, moving them 0.125 closer.
- Remember, **MIRROR** does not work in the isometric view, although it can be used effectively in the right-side view.
- Use **HATCH** to create the crosshatching.
- If you have made a mistake in measuring along the major centerline, **STRETCH** can be used to correct it. Make sure **Ortho** is on and you are in an isoplane that lets you move the way you want.

Drawing 11-4
Flanged coupling

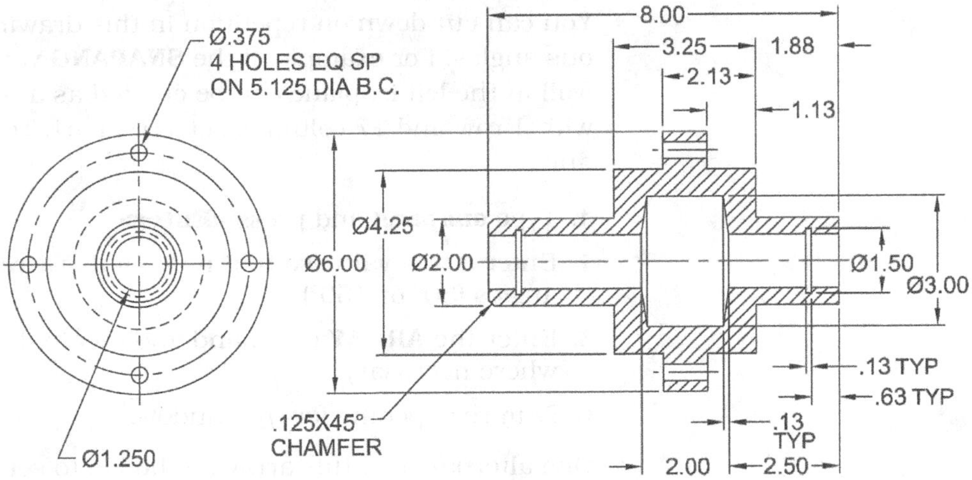

A

Drawing 11-5: *Garage Framing* [ADVANCED]

This is a fairly complex drawing that takes lots of trimming and careful work. Changing the **SNAPANG** (snap angle) variable so that you can draw slanted arrays is a method that can be used frequently in isometric drawing.

Drawing Suggestions

- You will find yourself using **COPY**, **ZOOM**, and **TRIM** a great deal. **OFFSET** also works well.
- You may want to create some new layers with different colors. Keeping different parts of the construction walls, rafters, and joists on different layers allows you to have more control over them and adds a lot of clarity to what you see on the screen. Turning layers on and off can considerably simplify trimming operations.
- You can cut down on repetition in this drawing by using arrays on various angles. For example, if the **SNAPANG** variable is set to 150°, the 229 wall in the left isoplane can be created as a rectangular array of studs with 1 row and 17 columns set 160 apart. To do so, follow this procedure:

  1. Type **snapang** and press **<Enter>**.
  2. Enter a new value so that rectangular arrays are created at isometric angles (30° or 150°).
  3. Enter the **ARRAY** command and create the array. Use negative values where necessary.
  4. Trim the opening for the window.

- One alternative to this array method is to set your snap to **16"** temporarily and use **COPY** to create the columns of studs, rafters, and joists. Another alternative is to use the grip edit offset snap method beginning with an offset snap of 16" (i.e., press **<Shift>** when you show the first copy displacement and continue to hold down **<Shift>** as you make other copies).
- The cutaway in the roof that shows the joists and the back door is drawn using the standard nonisometric **ELLIPSE** command. Then, the rafters are trimmed to the ellipse, and the ellipse is erased. Do this procedure before you draw the joists and the back wall. Otherwise, you will need to trim these as well.
- Use **CHAMFER** to create the chamfered corners on the joists.

Drawing 11-5
Garage framing

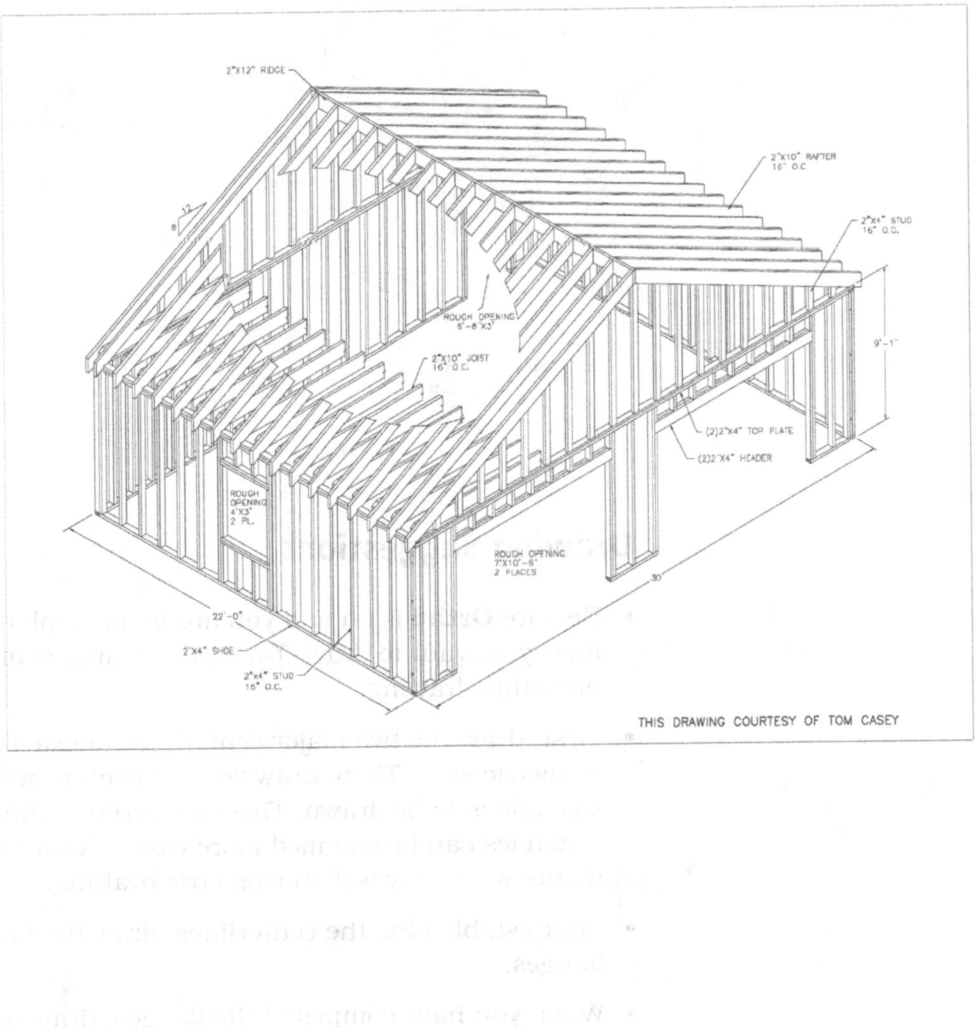

P Drawing 11-6: *Cast Iron Tee* [ADVANCED]

The objective of this exercise is to complete the isometric view of the tee using dimensions from the three-view drawing. Begin this isometric by working off the centerline.

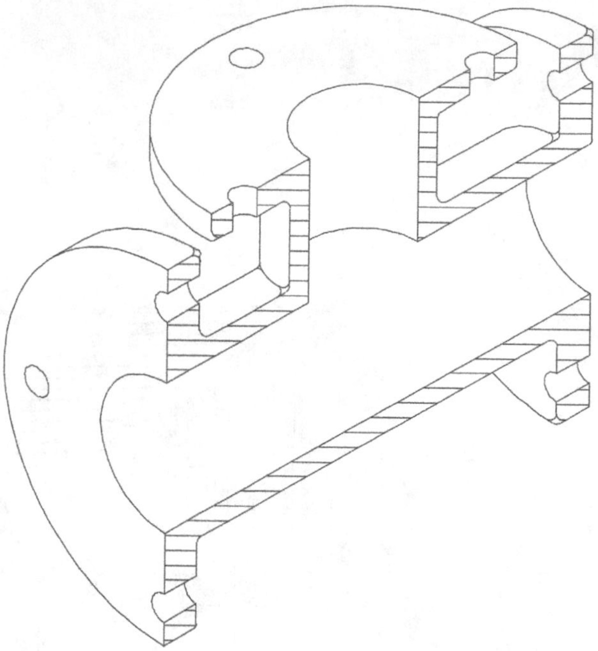

Drawing Suggestions

- Be sure **Ortho** is on and you are in an isoplane that is correct for the lines you want to draw. Take full advantage of object snaps as you complete this drawing.
- First, draw the two major centerlines to exact length, as shown in the isometric view. Then, draw vertical centerlines at every point where an isocircle is to be drawn. These centerlines should be drawn longer so the isocircles can be trimmed more easily. Notice that **OFFSET** and **MIRROR** do not work very well in isometric drafting.
- After establishing the centerlines, draw the isocircles for the three flanges.
- When you have completed the flanges, draw the isocircles for the wall of the tee.
- Draw all horizontal and vertical lines and trim away all nonvisible lines and parts of the isocircles. Fillet the required intersections.
- After completing the outline of the tee, use **HATCH** to create the cross-hatching.

Drawing 11-6
Cast iron tee

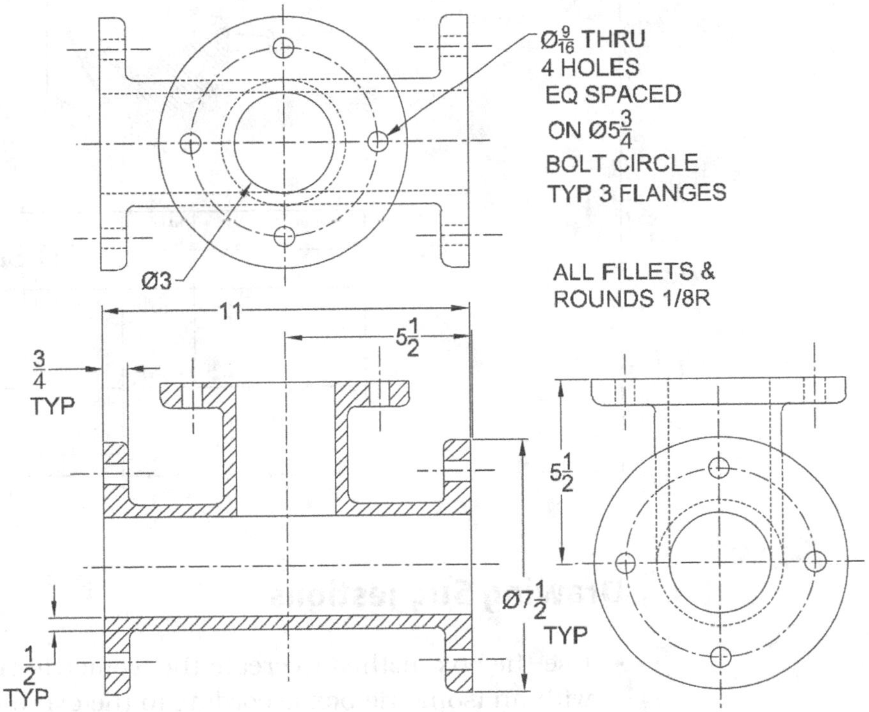

P

Drawing 11-7: *Valve* [ADVANCED]

For the purposes of this chapter, the isometric view is most important. The three detail views, the title block, and the border can be included or not, as assigned.

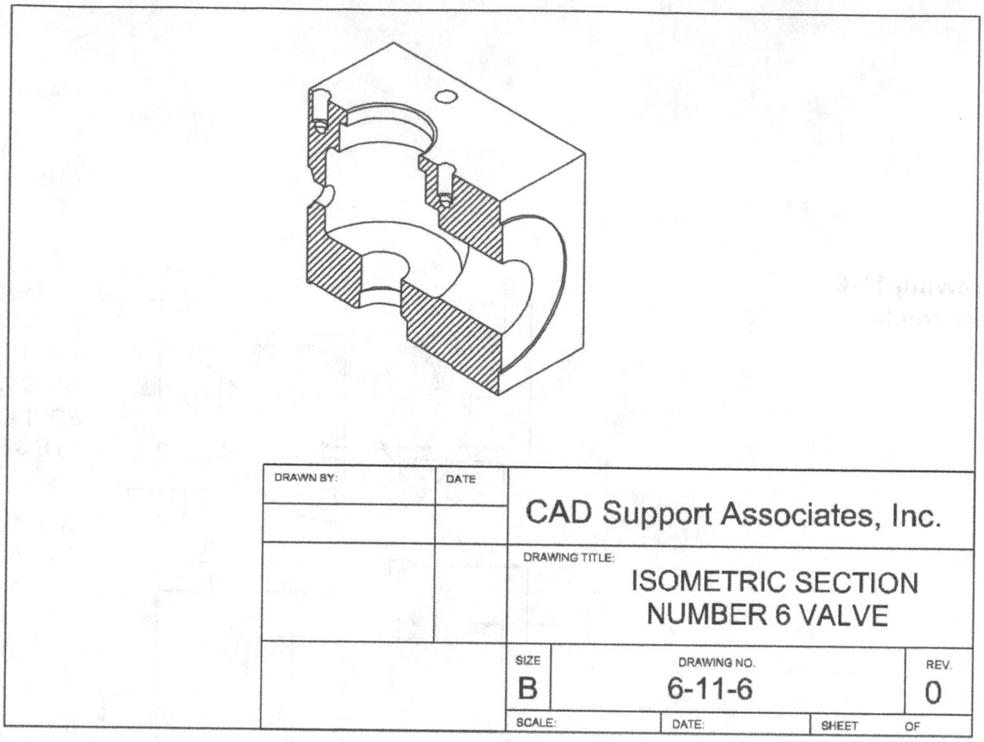

DRAWN BY:
DATE
CAD Support Associates, Inc.
DRAWING TITLE:
ISOMETRIC SECTION
NUMBER 6 VALVE
SIZE
B
DRAWING NO.
6-11-6
REV.
0
SCALE:
DATE:
SHEET
OF

Drawing Suggestions

- Use the box method to create the isometric view in this drawing. Begin with an isometric box according to the overall outside dimensions of the valve. Then go back and cut away the excess so the drawing becomes half the valve, exposing the interior details of the object.
- As in all section drawings, no hidden lines are shown.
- In addition to flat surfaces indicated by hatching, the interior is made up of isocircles of different sizes on different planes.
- Keep all construction lines and centerlines until the drawing is complete. (Draw them on a separate layer, and you can turn off that layer when you no longer need them.)
- The tapped holes are drawn with a series of isocircles that can be arrayed. This is only a representation of a screw thread, so it is not drawn to precise dimensions. Draw one thread, and copy it to the other side.

Drawing 11-7
Valve

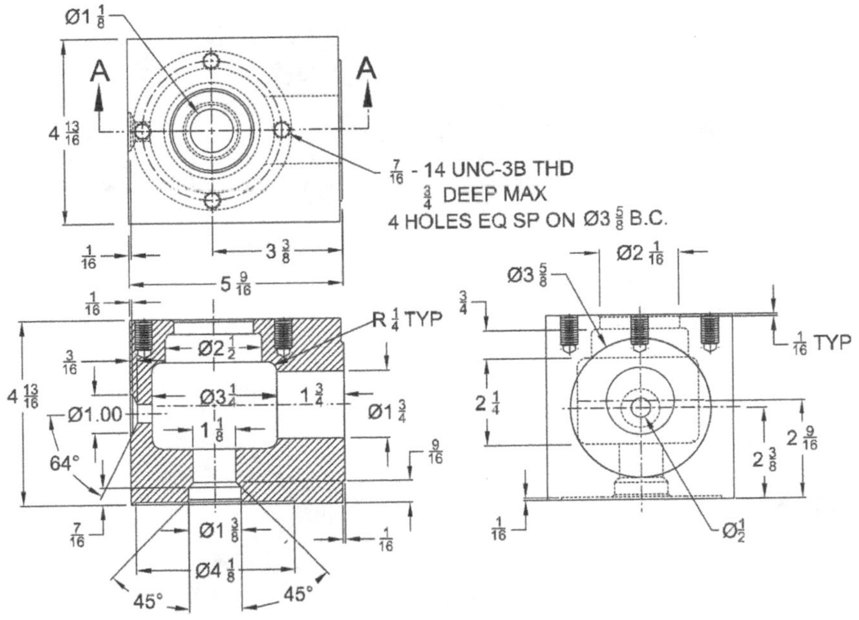

SECTION A-A

12 chapter twelve

3D Modeling

CHAPTER OBJECTIVES

- Create and view a 3D wireframe box
- Define user coordinate systems
- Explore the **3D Basics** workspace
- Create solid boxes and wedges
- Access different visual styles
- Create the union of two solids
- Work with DUCS
- Create composite solids with **SUBTRACT**
- Create chamfers and fillets on solid objects
- Practice 3D gizmo editing
- Render solid models
- Change viewpoints with the ViewCube
- Create layouts with multiple views

Introduction

In this chapter, you take on a step-by-step journey into 3D space and modeling. You begin in the familiar territory of the **Drafting & Annotation** workspace, bring the *Z*-axis into play, and move the viewpoint so the drawing begins to represent objects in 3D space you can present from any angle. Once oriented in three dimensions, you create a wireframe box and then define new user coordinate systems that allow you to draw and edit on any plane in 3D space. From there, you switch to the **3D Basics** workspace to create and edit a 3D model with solids. To complete the trip, you find out how to render the model with lighting and textures to give it a realistic appearance and then use the model to create a layout with multiple views.

Creating and Viewing a 3D Wireframe Box

wireframe model: A three-dimensional model that represents only the edges and boundaries of objects.

It is now time to begin thinking in three dimensions. In the first two sections, you bridge the gap between 2D and 3D by creating a very simple ***wireframe model***. In the "Exploring the 3D Basics Workspace" section, you move on to solid modeling. Like 2D and isometric drawings, wireframe models represent objects by outlining their edges and boundaries. Wireframe models are drawn line by line, edge by edge. Whereas wireframe modeling is the logical extension of 2D drafting into three dimensions, solid modeling uses a completely different logic, as you will see.

In this section, you use the **Drafting & Annotation** workspace. As you work your way into 3D space, you will notice the UCS icon becomes important, so first check to see that it is visible (see Figure 12-1). If not, follow this procedure to turn it on:

5. Type **ucsicon <Enter>**.
6. Select **On** from the dynamic input list or type **on <Enter>** at the command prompt.

Figure 12-1
UCS icon

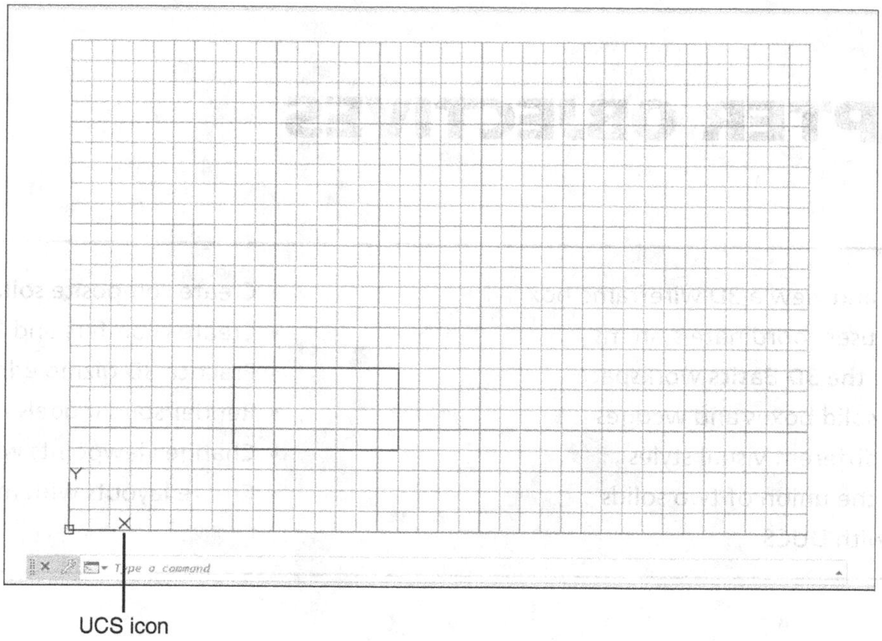

world coordinate system: In AutoCAD, the default coordinate system in which the point of origin is at the intersection of the default *X*-, *Y*-, and *Z*-axes. All user coordinate systems are defined relative to the world coordinate system.

For now, simply observe the icon as you go through the process of creating a three-dimensional box, and be aware that you are currently working in the same coordinate system you have always used in AutoCAD. It is called the ***world coordinate system*** (WCS) to distinguish it from others you create yourself beginning in the "Defining User Coordinate Systems" section.

Currently, the origin of the WCS is at the lower left of your grid. This is the point (0,0,0) when you are thinking 3D, or simply (0,0) when you are in 2D. The *x* coordinates increase to the right horizontally in the drawing, and the *y* coordinates increase vertically in the drawing, as usual. The *Z*-axis, which has been ignored until now, currently extends up and toward you, perpendicular to the *X*- and *Y*-axes and the current plane. This orientation of the three planes is called a *plan view*. Soon, you will switch to a front, right, top, or southeast isometric view.

Let's begin.

✔ Create a new drawing with decimal units and 18 × 12 limits. (Use the 1B template if you have it.)

✔ Type **zoom <Enter>** and then type **a <Enter>** to zoom to the limits of the drawing.

✔ Draw a 4.00 × 2.00 rectangle with the lower-left corner at (4,2,0), as shown in Figure 12-1.

Changing Viewpoints

viewpoint: The point in space from which a three-dimensional object is viewed.

To move immediately into a 3D mode of drawing and thinking, the first step is to change the ***viewpoint*** on the drawing. There are several methods for defining 3D points of view. Of these, the most flexible method is the **View Manager** dialog box. For now, this is the main method to be used.

✔ Type **view <Enter>** or click **View** > **Named Views** > **View Manager** from the ribbon.

*This opens the **View Manager** dialog box, which is used to create named views. In this chapter, you use the **Preset Views** option.*

✔ Click the **+** sign next to **Preset Views** in the **Views** list.

This opens the list of 10 standard preset views shown in Figure 12-2. Imagine your point of view to be perpendicular to the dark blue face of the cube in each case. In the six orthographic views (top, bottom, left, etc.), objects are presented from points of view along each of the six axis directions. You see objects in the drawing from directly above (top, positive Z) or directly below (bottom, negative Z), or by looking in along the positive or negative X-axis (left and right) or the positive or negative Y-axis (front and back).

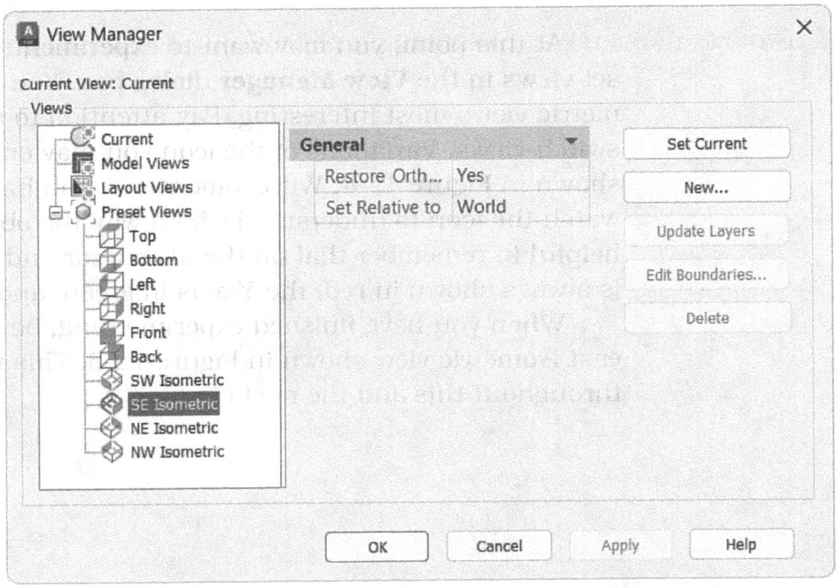

Figure 12-2
View Manager dialog box

The four isometric views present objects at 45° angles from the X- and Y-axes and take you up 30° degrees from the XY plane. Here, you use a southeast isometric view. Imagine a compass; the lower-right quadrant is the southeast. In a southeast isometric view, you are looking in from 45° in this quadrant and down at a 30° angle. Try it.

- ✔ Select **SE Isometric** from the list of views.
- ✔ Click the **Set Current** button.
- ✔ Click **OK**.

The dialog box closes, and the drawing area is redrawn to the view shown in Figure 12-3. Notice how the grid and the coordinate system icon have changed to show the new orientation. These visual aids are extremely helpful in viewing 3D objects on the flat screen and imagining them as if they were positioned in space.

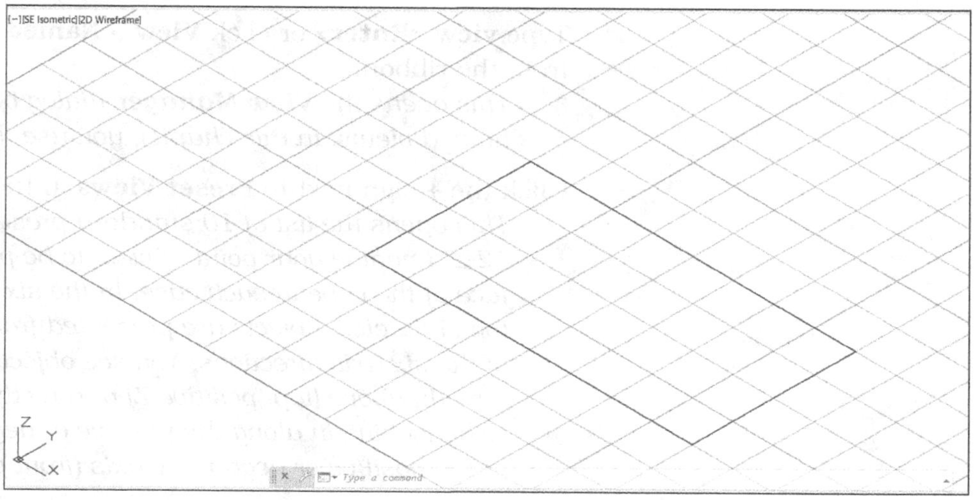

Figure 12-3
Southeast isometric view

At this point, you may want to experiment with the other standard preset views in the **View Manager** dialog box. You will probably find the isometric views most interesting. Pay attention to the grid and the icon as you switch views. Variations of the icon you may encounter here and later are shown in Figure 12-4. With some views, you have to think carefully and watch the icon to understand which way the object is being presented. It is helpful to remember that on the 3D cursor and other 3D icons, the *X*-axis is always shown in red, the *Y*-axis in green, and the *Z*-axis in blue.

When you have finished experimenting, be sure to return to the southeast isometric view shown in Figure 12-3. This view will frequently be used throughout this and the next chapter.

Figure 12-4
Variations of UCS icons as shown in the AutoCAD Online help

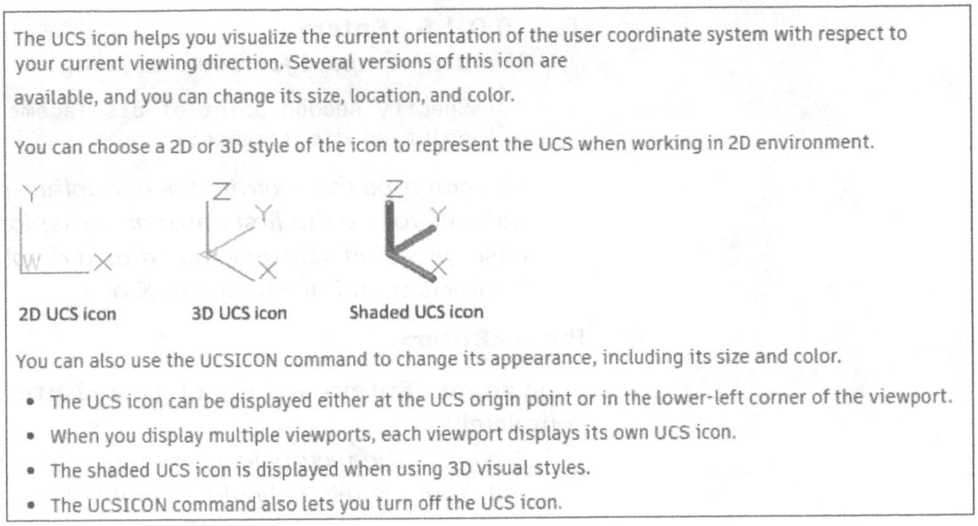
The UCS icon helps you visualize the current orientation of the user coordinate system with respect to your current viewing direction. Several versions of this icon are available, and you can change its size, location, and color.

You can choose a 2D or 3D style of the icon to represent the UCS when working in 2D environment.

2D UCS icon 3D UCS icon Shaded UCS icon

You can also use the UCSICON command to change its appearance, including its size and color.

- The UCS icon can be displayed either at the UCS origin point or in the lower-left corner of the viewport.
- When you display multiple viewports, each viewport displays its own UCS icon.
- The shaded UCS icon is displayed when using 3D visual styles.
- The UCSICON command also lets you turn off the UCS icon.

Entering 3D Coordinates

Next, you create a copy of the rectangle placed 1.50 units above the original. This brings up a basic 3D problem: When specifying points on the *XY* plane, how does one indicate a point or a displacement in the *Z* direction? In wireframe modeling, there are three possibilities: type 3D coordinates, X/Y/Z point filters, and object snaps. Object snaps are useful only if an object has already been drawn above or below the *XY* plane, so it is no help right now. You use typed coordinates first and then you learn how point filters can be used as an alternative later.

3D coordinates can be entered from the keyboard in the same manner as 2D coordinates. Often, this is an impractical way to enter individual points in a drawing. However, within **COPY** or **MOVE**, entering from the keyboard provides a simple method for specifying a displacement in the *Z* direction.

✔ Click **Home** > **Modify** > **Copy** from the ribbon.

You are prompted for object selection.

✔ Select the complete rectangle.

✔ Right-click to end object selection.

You are now prompted for the base point of a vector or displacement value:

```
Specify base point or displacement or [Displacement/mOde]
<Displacement>:
```

Typically, you would respond to this prompt and the next by specifying the two endpoints of a displacement vector. However, you cannot easily specify a displacement in the Z direction by pointing. This is important for understanding and using the coordinate systems. Unless an object snap is used, all points specified with the pointing device are interpreted as being on the XY plane of the current UCS. In wireframe modeling, without an entity outside the XY plane to use in an object snap, there is no way to point to a displacement in the Z direction.

✔ Type **0,0,1.5 <Enter>**.

You are prompted for a second point:

```
Specify second point of displacement, or [Array] <use first
point as displacement>:
```

You can type the coordinates of another point, or press ***<Enter>*** *to indicate to use the first entry as a displacement from (0,0,0). In this case, pressing* ***<Enter>*** *indicates a displacement of 1.50 units in the Z direction and no change in* X *or* Y*.*

✔ Press **<Enter>**.

✔ Type **zoom <Enter>** and then type **a <Enter>** to see both rectangles completely.

A copy of the rectangle is created 1.50 units directly above the original. Your drawing should resemble Figure 12-5.

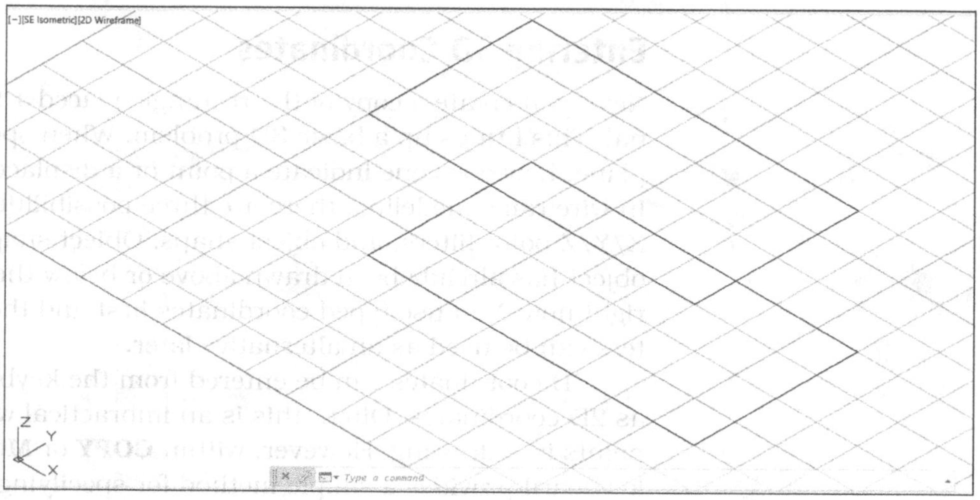

Figure 12-5
Copy of rectangle

X/Y/Z Point Filters

point filter: A system for specifying a point by first filtering one or two coordinate values from a given point and then specifying the other value(s) independently.

Point filters are very useful in 3D. In a point filter, you filter some of a coordinate's values from one point and change others to specify a new point. To see how this works, notice that in the displacement you just entered, the only thing that changed was the *z* value. Note also that you could've specified that same displacement using any point on the *XY* plane as a base point. For example, (3,6,0) to (3,6,1.5) would show the same displacement as (0,0,0) to (0,0,1.5). In fact, you don't even need to know the *x* and *y* values as long as you know they don't change, although the *z* value does.

That is how an .XY point filter works. You borrow, or "filter," the *x* and *y* values from a point, without needing to know what the values actually are, and then specify a new *z* value. Of course, other types of filters are possible, such as .Z, in which *z* is constant while *x* and *y* change. Another example is .YZ, where *y* and *z* are constant and *x* changes.

You can use a point filter, like an object snap, any time you are prompted to specify a point. After a point filter is specified, you are prompted with *of.* In an .XY filter, you are being asked, "You want the *x* and *y* values of what point?" In response, you specify a point, and then you are prompted to fill in a *z value*. You learn to use point filters in the "Rendering Solid Models" section, where they are used to position lights in a model to be rendered.

Using Object Snap

Right now there are two rectangles floating in space. The next job is to connect the corners to form a wireframe box. This is easily managed using **Endpoint** object snaps, and it is a good example of how object snaps allow for the creation of entities not on the *XY* plane of the current coordinate system.

✔ Right-click the **Object Snap** button on the status bar.

*For now, this is the regular **Object Snap** button, not the **3D Object Snap** button.*

✔ Select **Object Snap Settings** from the shortcut menu.

✔ Make sure **Object Snap On** is checked at the top left of the dialog box.

✔ Click the **Clear All** button.

✔ Select the **Endpoint** check box.

✔ Click **OK**.

*The running **Endpoint** object snap is now on and affects all points specified with the pointing device.*

Now, you draw some lines:

✔ Turn **Snap Mode** off.

✔ Click **Home** > **Draw** > **Line** from the ribbon or type **line <Enter>** at the Command prompt. Connect the upper and lower corners of the two rectangles, as shown in Figure 12-6.

Figure 12-6
Connecting corners

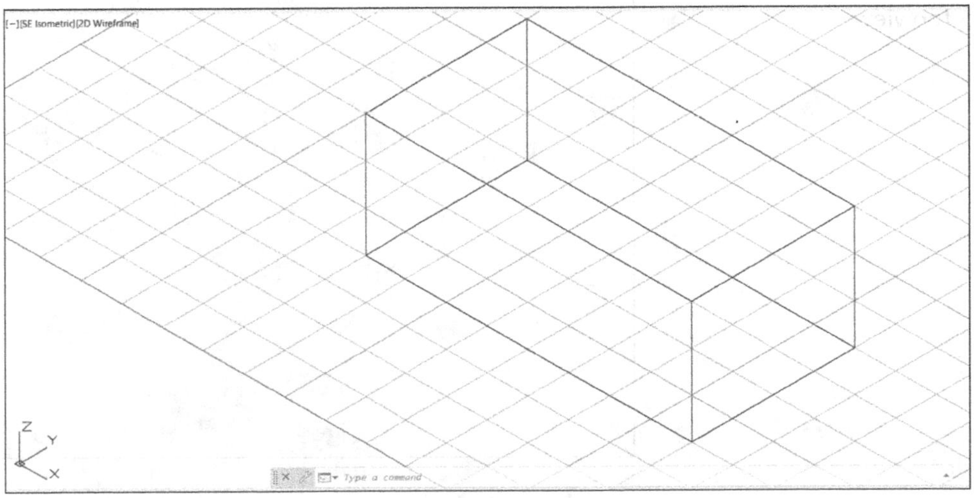

Before proceeding, pause to take note of what you have drawn. The box is a true 3D model. Unlike an isometric drawing, it can be turned, viewed, and plotted from any point in space. It is not, however, a solid model or a surface model. It is only a set of lines in 3D space. Removing hidden lines or shading would have no effect on this model, because no surfaces are represented.

In the next section, you begin to define your own coordinate systems that allow you to perform drawing and editing functions on any plane you choose.

UCS	
Command	UCS
Alias	Uc
Panel	Coordinates
Tool	

Defining User Coordinate Systems

In this exercise, you begin to develop new vocabulary and techniques for working with objects in 3D space. The primary tool is the UCS icon, which can be moved and rotated to create a new user-defined coordinate systems.

Until now, you have worked with only one coordinate system to. All coordinates and displacements have been defined relative to a single point of origin. Keep in mind that a *viewpoint* and *coordinate system* are not the same, although they use similar vocabulary. In the previous section, you changed the point of view, but the UCS icon changed along with it, so that the orientations of the *X*-, *Y*-, and *Z*-axes relative to the object were retained. With the **UCS** command or by direct manipulation of the UCS icon, you can free the coordinate system from the viewpoint and define new coordinate systems at any point and any angle in 3D space. When you do, you can use the coordinate system icon and the grid to help you visualize the plane you are working on, and all commands and drawing aids function relative to the new coordinate system.

The coordinate system you are currently using, WCS (world coordinate system), is unique. It is the one you always begin with. The square at the base of the coordinate system icon indicates that you are working in the WCS. A UCS is nothing more than a new point of origin and a new orientation for the *X*-, *Y*-, and *Z*-axes.

You begin by defining a UCS on the plane, as shown in Figure 12-7.

Figure 12-7
UCS top view

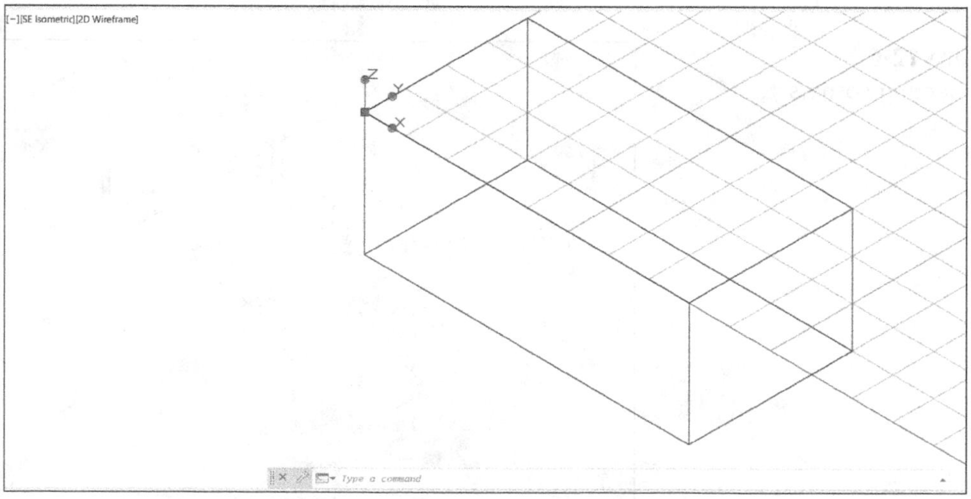

✔ Leave the **Endpoint** object snap on as you begin this exercise.

You can select and manipulate the UCS icon like other objects. When you do, grips will appear that can be used to change the position and orientation of the icon, which, in turn, changes the orientation and origin of the coordinate system.

✔ Move the cursor over the UCS icon. When it is highlighted in yellow, click the left mouse button.

Grips appear at the origin and along each of the three axes, as shown in Figure 12-8. The square grip at the origin is used to move the icon to a new origin point. The circular grips on each axis are used to rotate the icon.

You use the square grip to move the icon to the top-left corner of the box and define a new UCS on the plane of the top of the box.

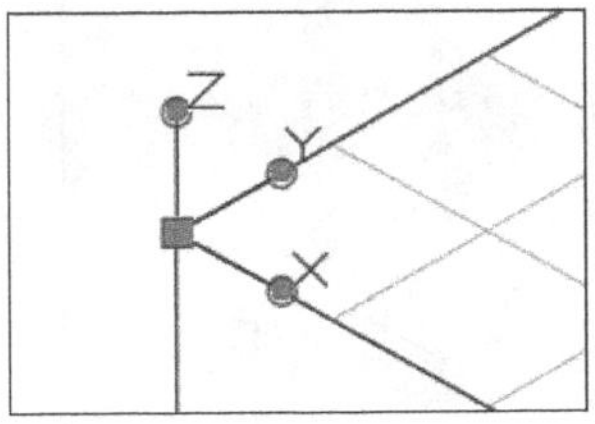

Figure 12-8
Grips appear on UCS icon

✔ Click the square grip at the base of the UCS icon.

As you move the cursor away from the world coordinate system origin, the icon moves with you, and a rubber band is added. Also, if you let the cursor rest, a multifunctional grip message appears, as shown in Figure 12-9. This shows that you can use the grip to move the icon in different ways, with or without changing the alignment of the icon. You can also return the icon back to the WCS origin.

Figure 12-9
Multifunctional grip message appears

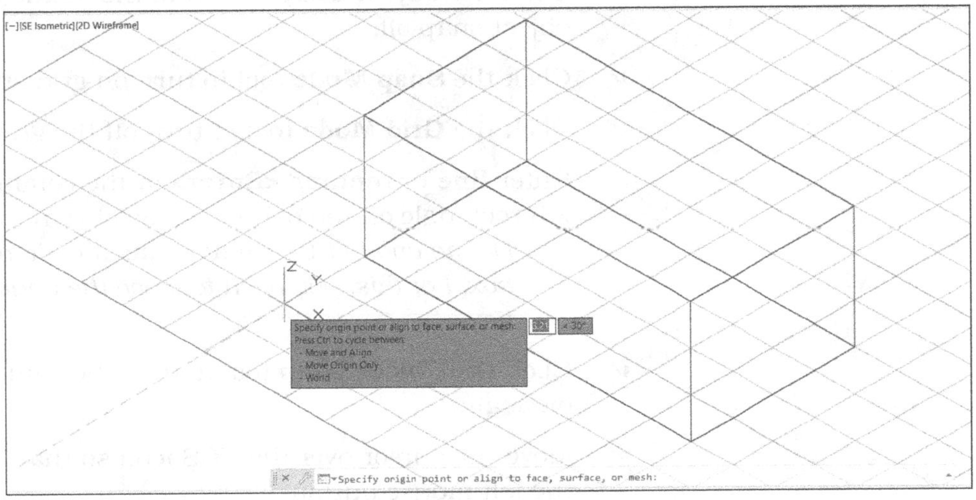

✔ Use the **Endpoint** object snap to specify the top-left corner of the box, as shown by the location of the icon in Figure 12-7.

*The grid origin moves to the corner of the box. The **Endpoint** object snap ensures that you actually specify the top corner. Without it, you can easily specify a point that appears to be the upper corner of the box but is actually a point in the current XY plane.*

✔ Press **<Esc>** to remove grips.

Notice that the box is gone from the UCS icon, indicating that you are no longer in the WCS.

The UCS just created will make it easy to draw and edit entities on the plane of the top of the box. To do this, draw a 1 × 3–unit rectangle on top of the box, as shown in Figure 12-10.

Figure 12-10
Drawing a rectangle on top of the box

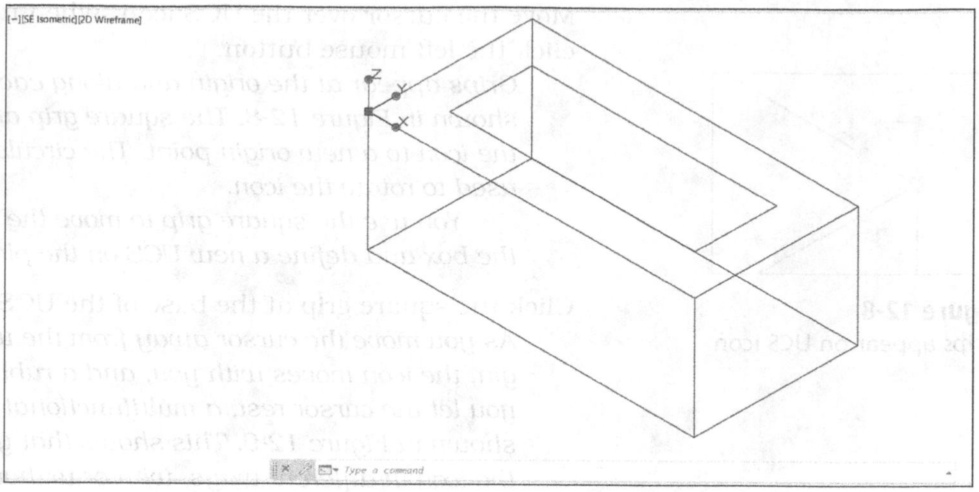

✔ Click the **Object Snap** tool from the status bar to turn the running object snap off.

✔ Click the **Snap Mode** tool to turn on grid snap.

✔ Click the **Grid Mode** tool to turn off the grid display.

✔ Enter **line** or **rectang <Enter>** at the command prompt, and draw a 1 × 3 rectangle on top of the box, as shown in Figure 12-10.

Define another UCS that aligns the XY plane with the left face of the box. For this, you need to move the origin and change the icon rotation.

✔ Click the **Object Snap** tool to turn the running **Endpoint** object snap on again.

✔ Move the cursor over the UCS icon so that it is highlighted and click the left mouse button.

✔ Click the box grip at the origin of the UCS.

✔ Using the **Endpoint** object snap, specify the lower-front left of the wireframe box—P1 in Figure 12-11.

You have moved the origin of the UCS to P1, but you now need to rotate the icon so that the left front of the box is in the XY plane. The X-axis is already aligned with the bottom edge of the box, but you need to rotate Y. The grips are still displayed. Using the circular grip on the Y-axis, along with the ***Endpoint*** *object snap, you can rotate the icon and the coordinate system as desired.*

✔ Click the grip on the *Y*-axis of the UCS icon.

✔ Using the **Endpoint** object snap, specify P2, as shown in Figure 12-11.

The object snap ensures that the new axis aligns with the left side of the object. When this sequence is complete, the coordinate system icon has rotated along with the grid and moved to the new origin, as shown. This UCS is convenient for drawing and editing on the left plane of the box, or editing on any plane parallel to the front plane, such as the back plane.

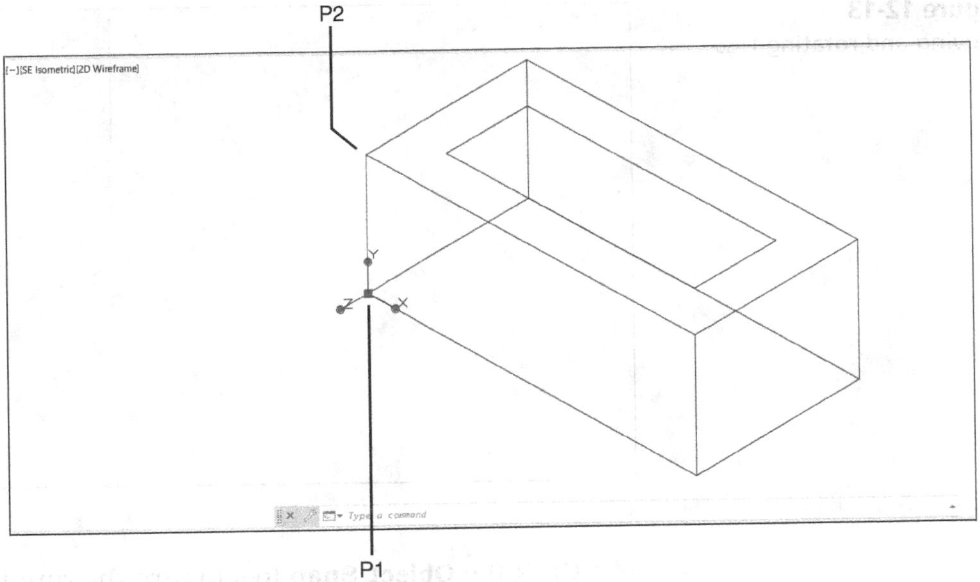

Figure 12-11
UCS origin moved to P1

✔ Turn off the **Object Snap** tool, use the **LINE** or **RECTANG** command, and draw a 0.5 × 3 unit rectangle on the left plane of the box, as shown in Figure 12-12.

Finally, you will use the same procedure to create a UCS on the plane of the right side of the wireframe box.

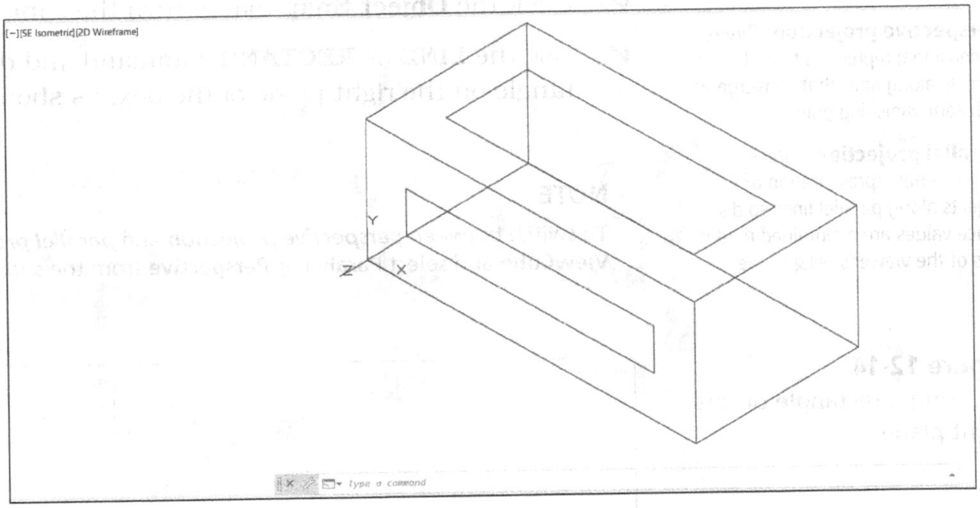

Figure 12-12
Drawing a rectangle on the left plane

✔ Highlight and select the UCS icon.

✔ Click the square grip at the origin of the icon.

✔ Specify the lower-front-right corner of the box for the origin, as shown in Figure 12-13.

There is no need to use an object snap here because this point is on the current XY plane. The UCS icon moves to the specified point. Next, you rotate the icon to align with the right side of the box.

Figure 12-13
Moving and rotating UCS

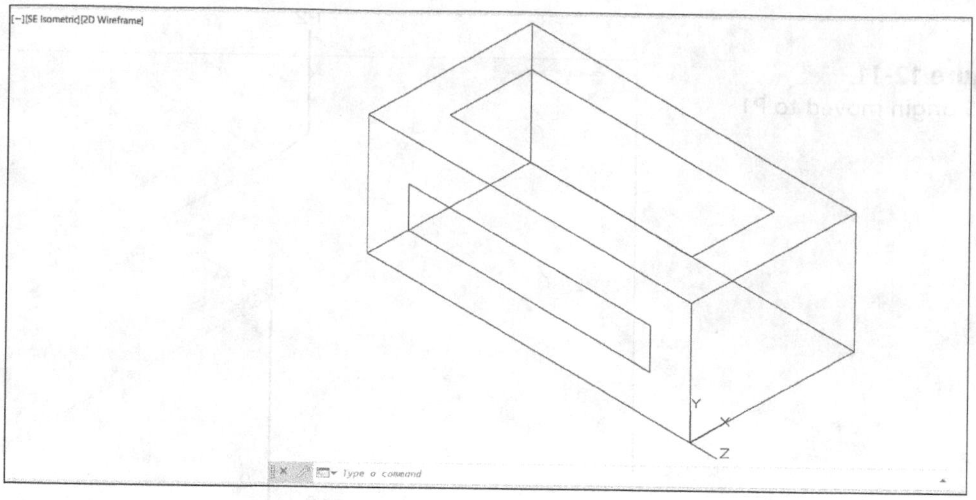

✔ Click the **Object Snap** tool to turn the running **Endpoint** object snap on again.

✔ If necessary, select the UCS icon again.

✔ Click the circular grip on the *X*-axis.

✔ Specify the back-right corner of the box.
You should now have the XY plane of your UCS aligned with the right side of the box, as shown in Figure 12-13.

✔ Click the **Object Snap** tool to turn the running object snap off.

✔ Use the **LINE** or **RECTANG** command and draw a 0.5 × 1.0 unit rectangle on the right plane of the box, as shown in Figure 12-14.

perspective projection: Three-dimensional representation of objects along lines that converge at a distant vanishing point.

parallel projection: Three-dimensional representation of objects along parallel lines so distance values are maintained regardless of the viewer's perspective.

NOTE

To switch between ***perspective projection*** and ***parallel projection***, right-click the **ViewCube** and select **Parallel** or **Perspective** from the shortcut menu.

Figure 12-14
Drawing a rectangle on the right plane

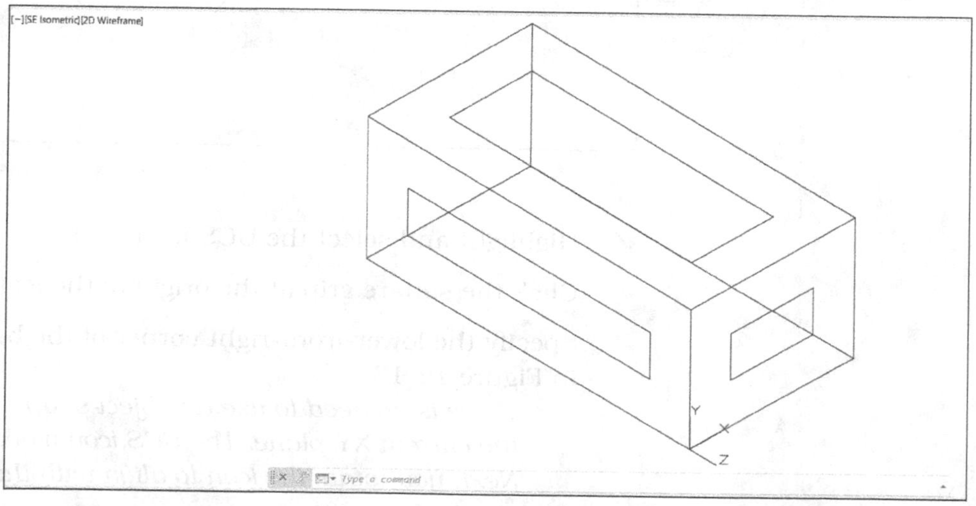

Exploring the 3D Basics Workspace

solid modeling: A system of creating 3D objects from combinations of 3D solid primitive objects.

Solid modeling is, in many ways, easier than wireframe modeling. You can draw a complete solid object in a fraction of the time it would take to draw it line by line. Furthermore, once the object is drawn, it contains more information than a wireframe model and can be manipulated in numerous ways. As you move on to solid modeling in this section, you create a new drawing based on the acad3D template and switch to the **3D Basics** workspace.

✔ Click the **New** tool on the **Quick Access** toolbar. Or you can click the **Start** tab and then open the **Templates** drop-down menu adjacent to the **New** button and select **Browse Templates.**

✔ In the **Select Template** dialog box, select the **acad3D** template and click **Open**.

*This will be just below the **acad** template in the **Templates** list. Even with using the **acad3D** template, you will still be in the **Drafting & Annotation** workspace, but there will be a change in visual style, as shown in Figure 12-15. Notice the 3D coordinate system icon in the middle of the grid with a solid blue arrow for the Z-axis, a solid red arrow for the X-axis, and a solid green arrow for the Y-axis and the 3D cursor with three narrow lines in colors similar to the UCS icon colors.*

*Next, you will switch to the **3D Basics** workspace.*

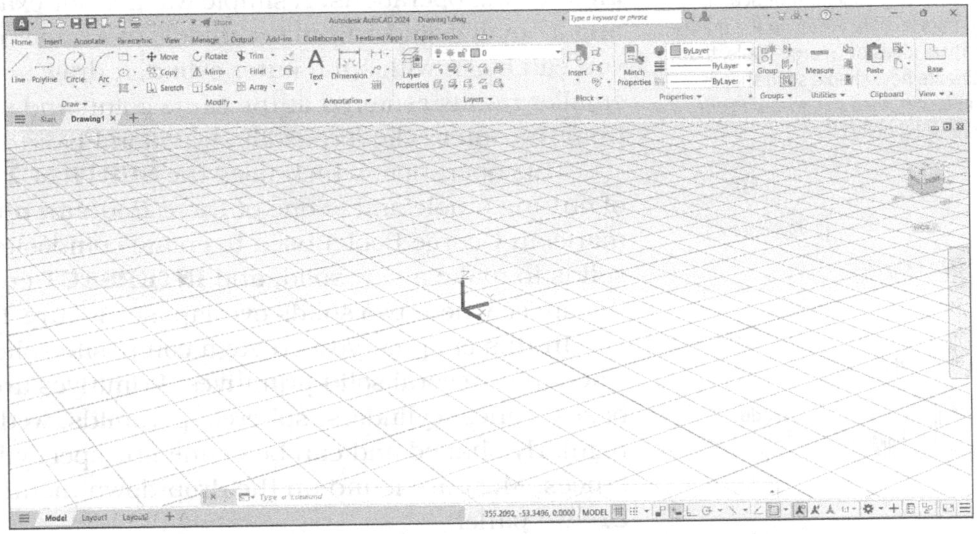

Figure 12-15
New drawing based on the acad3D template

✔ Click the **Workspace** tool from the status bar to select **3D Basics** from the menu.

✔ Your application window should resemble Figure 12-16. This is the ***3D Basics*** workspace. The drawing area has not changed, but you have a new set of tool panels on the ribbon. These are tools devoted to 3D solid modeling and rendering procedures. Notice that there is a new set of tabs and the ***Home*** tab in this workspace is different from the one in ***Drafting & Annotation.***

*In the following sections, you create a solid model using several of the tools on the **3D Basics** workspace ribbon.*

Figure 12-16
3D Basics workspace

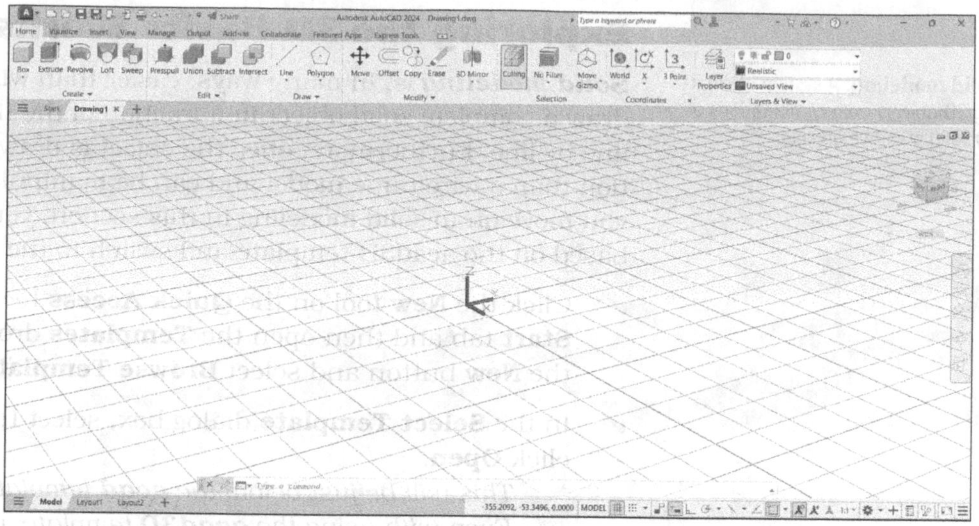

Creating Solid Boxes and Wedges

constructive solid geometry: A system of three-dimensional modeling that represents solid objects as composites made by combining simple shapes called primitives.

Boolean operations: Logical operations, such as union, subtraction, and intersection, based on the mathematical ideas of George Boole, that delineate how simple solid shapes can be combined to construct composite solid objects.

Solid modeling requires a type of thinking different from any of the drawings you have completed so far. Instead of focusing on lines and arcs and edges and surfaces, you need to imagine how 3D objects may be pieced together by combining or subtracting basic solid shapes. This building block process is called ***constructive solid geometry*** and includes unioning, subtracting, and intersecting operations. A simple washer, for example, can be made by cutting a small cylinder from the middle of a larger cylinder. In solid modeling, you can begin with a flat outer cylinder, draw an inner cylinder with a smaller radius centered at the same point, and subtract the inner cylinder from the outer cylinder, as illustrated in Figure 12-17.

This operation, which uses the **SUBTRACT** command, is the equivalent of cutting a hole and is one of three ***Boolean operations*** (after the mathematician George Boole) used to create composite solids. **UNION** joins two solids to make a new solid, and **INTERSECT** creates a composite solid in the space where two solids overlap (see Figure 12-17).

In this chapter, you create a composite solid from the union and subtraction of several solid primitives. Primitives are 3D solid building blocks—boxes, cones, cylinders, spheres, pyramids, wedges, and torus. They all are regularly shaped and can be defined by specifying a few points and distances. Most are found on the drop-down menu on the left side of the **Create** panel.

Before you begin to model, you will want to make two adjustments to the grid.

✔ Type **zoom <Enter>** and then **a <Enter>** to zoom to the limits of this drawing.

*The **acad3D** template drawing has a 12 × 9 limit, but the grid is initially drawn larger to give a fuller perspective. Zooming all will take you closer to the actual limits.*

✔ Click the **Snap Mode** tool on the status bar to turn on grid snap.

✔ Right-click the **Snap Mode** button and select **Snap Settings** from the shortcut menu.

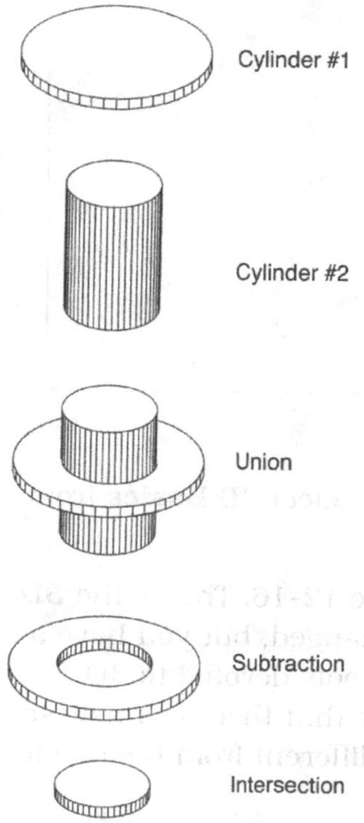

Figure 12-17
Constructive solid geometry

- ✔ Clear the **Adaptive grid** check box in the **Grid behavior** panel.
- ✔ Click **OK**.

  You should now have a grid line at each 0.5000 interval and a bolder grid line at each 2.5000 interval. Snap, like grid, is set at 0.5000. Your drawing should resemble Figure 12-18.

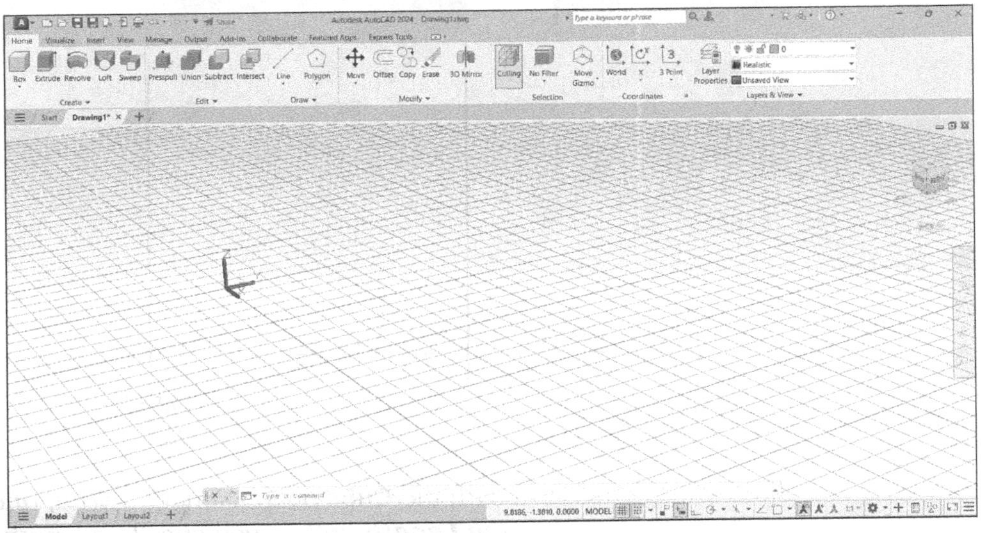

Figure 12-18
Grid lines

The BOX Command

BOX	
Command	BOX
Alias	(none)
Panel	Create
Tool	

- ✔ Zoom in slightly to the area around the 3D UCS icon.
- ✔ Click the **Box** tool from the **Create** panel on the ribbon, as shown in Figure 12-19.

  Boxes can be drawn from the base up or from the center out. In either case, you specify a length and width or two corners and then a height. AutoCAD prompts:

  ```
  Specify first corner or [Center]:
  ```

  You start with the default method—showing two corners of the base—and then typing the height.

- ✔ Specify a first corner point at **(1.0000,1.0000)**—P1 in Figure 12-20.

  AutoCAD prompts for a second corner:

  ```
  Specify second corner or [Cube/Length]:
  ```

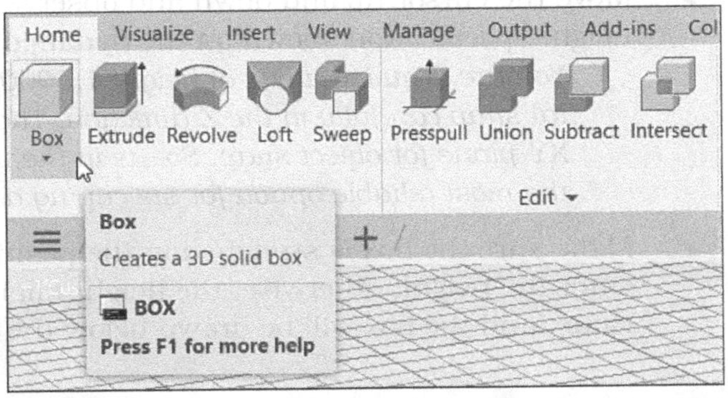

Figure 12-19
Box tool

Figure 12-20
Drawing a box, points P1 and P2

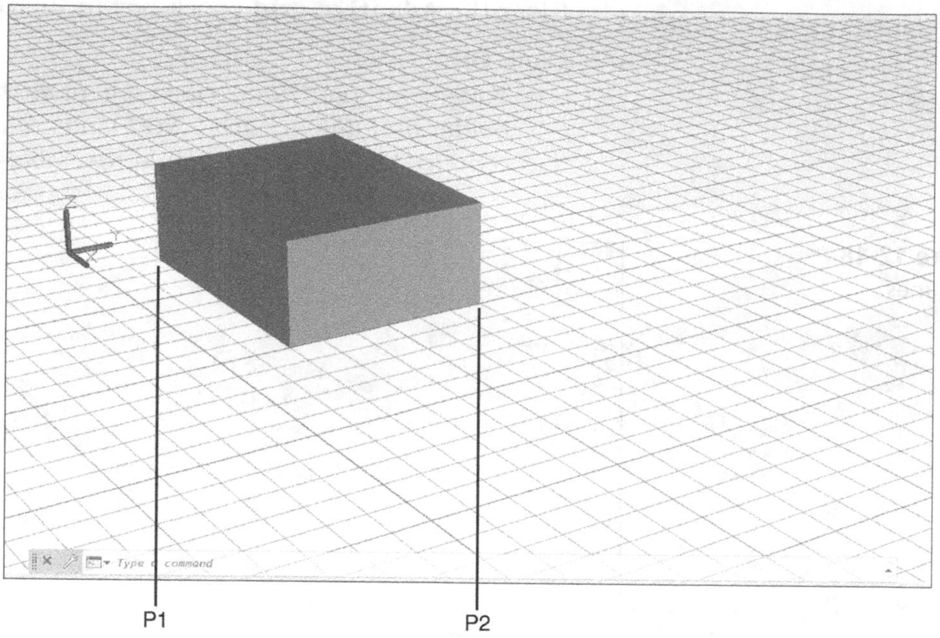

*With the **Cube** option, length, width, and height are all equal. With the **Length** option, you specify a length and width, rather than corners. You draw a box with a length of 4, width of 3, and height of 1.5.*

✔ Specify a point 4.00 units in the *X* direction and 3.00 units in the *Y* direction, as shown by P2 in Figure 12-20.

This is the point (5.0000,4.0000) on the coordinate display. The dynamic input display shows the x and y distances. A box shape is drawn that can be stretched up or down in the Z direction as you are prompted for a height:

```
Specify height or [2Point]:
```

NOTE

Be careful not to rest the cursor on any of the faces of the box so that an outline is highlighted. If this happens, AutoCAD begins creating a wedge on the plane of that face. This is a very powerful capability explored later in this exercise, but it is not helpful right now.

✔ Move the cursor up and down and observe the box. Also observe the height specification shown on the dynamic input display.

You are drawing a box of height 1.5000, but you must use incremental snap carefully in the Z direction. There is also no object above the XY plane for object snap. So, as in the wireframe example, typing is the most reliable option for specifying a height.

✔ Make sure the box is stretched in the positive *Z* direction before you enter the height; otherwise, the height might be taken as a negative value, and the box will be drawn below the *XY* plane.

✔ Type **1.5 <Enter>**.

Your box is complete and should resemble Figure 12-20.

The WEDGE Command

WEDGE	
Command	WEDGE
Alias	We
Panel	Create
Tool	

Next, you create a solid wedge. The process is exactly the same as a box. Again, you use the default option of providing a length and width by specifying two corner points.

✔ Click the **Wedge** tool from the **Solid Primitives** drop-down menu (under **Box**) on the **Create** panel.

AutoCAD prompts:

```
Specify first corner of wedge or [Center]:
```

✔ Specify the front corner point of the box—P1 in Figure 12-21.

*As in the **BOX** command, you are prompted for a cube, length, or the other corner:*

```
Specify corner or [Cube/Length]:
```

✔ Specify a point 4.00 units in the *X* direction and 3.00 units in the *Y* direction, as shown by P2 in Figure 12-21.

This point should be easy to find because the back corner lines up with the back of the box previously drawn.

After you specify the second corner, AutoCAD shows the wedge and prompts for a height.

✔ Move the cursor up and down and watch the wedge stretch. Make sure that you have the wedge stretched in the positive *Z* direction before you enter the height.

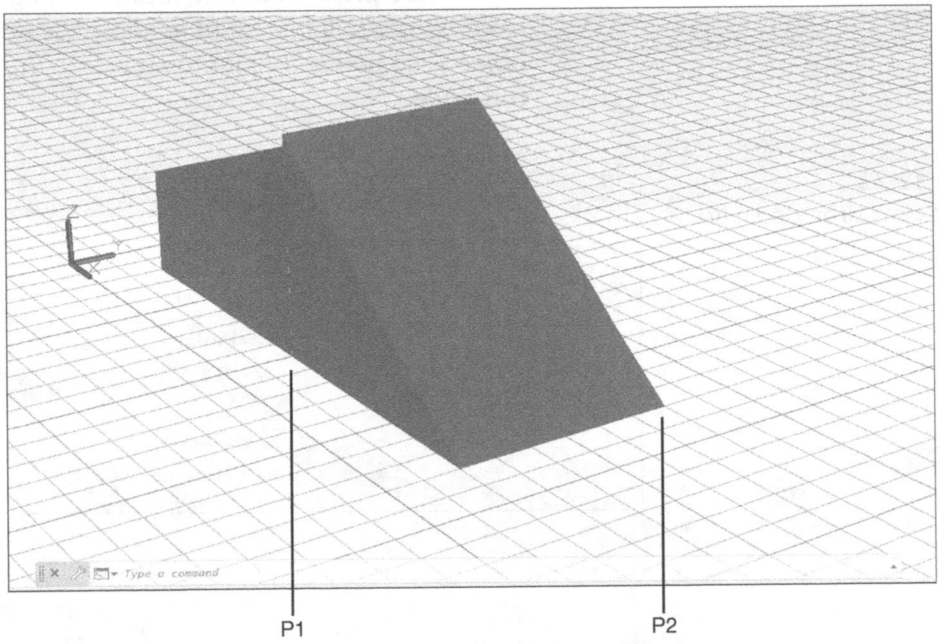

Figure 12-21
Drawing a wedge, points P1 and P2

✔ Type **3 <Enter>**.

AutoCAD draws the wedge you have specified. Notice that a wedge is simply half a box, cut along a diagonal plane.

Your model should resemble Figure 12-21. The box and wedge are true solids and are different from anything you've previously drawn. In the "Creating the Union of Two Solids" section, you join them to form a new composite solid.

Accessing Different Visual Styles

Visual styles are simple, default styles for presenting 3D objects in your drawing. You are familiar with the 2D wireframe visual style. In this chapter, you have used the **Realistic** style, the default visual style in the **acad3D** template. Before moving on, it will be useful to switch to a visual style that more readily displays the borders between objects. Take a minute to view your box and wedge presented in the other predefined styles. At the right end of the ribbon's **Home** tab, on the **Layers & View** panel, there is a drop-down list of visual styles, with **Realistic** showing as the current style.

✔ Move your cursor over the **Layers & View** panel at the right end of the **Home** tab.

*The **Layers & View** panel contains the **Visual Styles** drop-down list shown in Figure 12-22.*

✔ Click anywhere over the **Visual Styles** drop-down list.

*The **Visual Styles** gallery opens as shown in* Figure 12-23. *There are 10 preset styles. Styles vary in how they show edges and treat solid objects. To get a feel for them, select each style and observe the effects.*

✔ One by one, try each of the 10 visual styles.

*You will find some of these styles to be very different from what you are used to seeing. The 10 styles show a great variety in how objects are presented and outlined. As you continue on with the exercises, it will be useful to show the edges around and between objects, so you will want to switch to the **Shaded with Edges** visual style.*

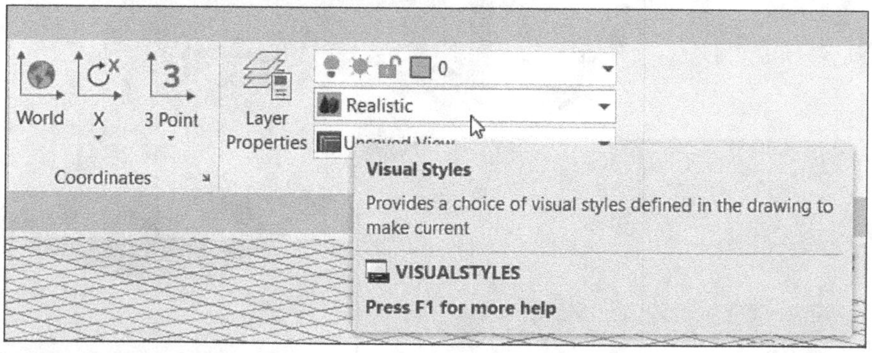

Figure 12-22
Visual Styles drop-down list

Figure 12-23
Gallery of Visual Styles

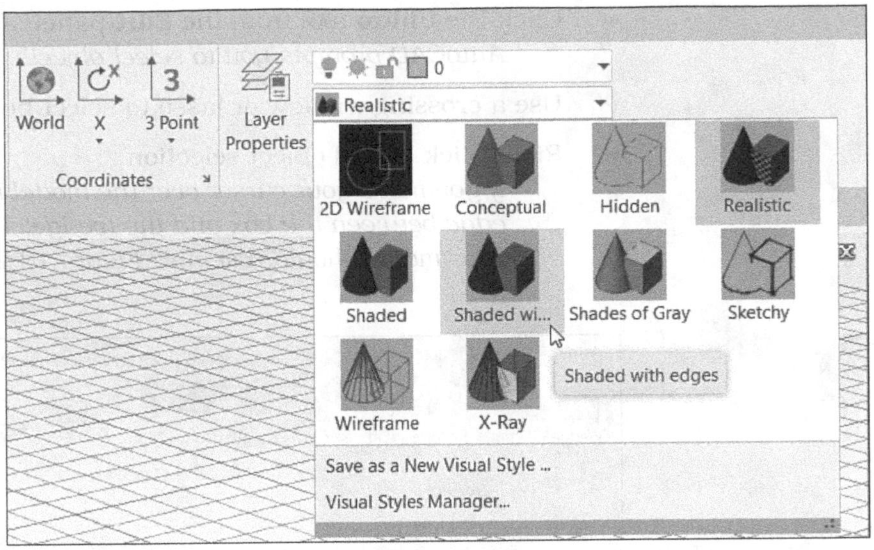

Figure 12-24
Shaded with Edges

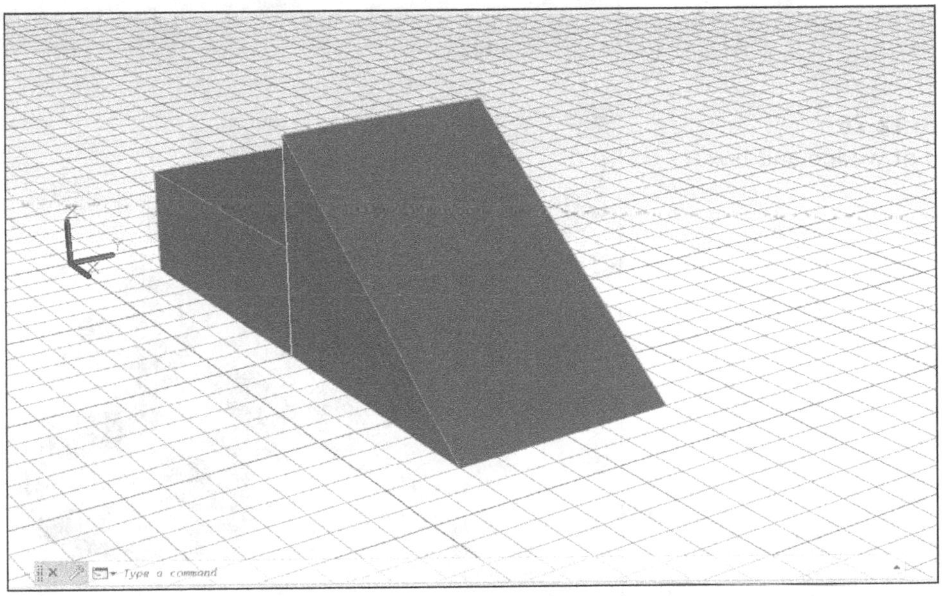

✔ Select **Shaded with Edges** before moving on.

Your drawing window should resemble Figure 12-24. *The color of your model will depend on the layer on which the 3D object was created.*

Creating the Union of Two Solids

UNION	
Command	UNION
Alias	Uni
Panel	Edit
Tool	

Unions are simple to create and usually easy to visualize. The union of two objects is an object that includes all points that are on either of the objects. Unions can be performed just as easily on more than two objects. The union of objects can be created even if the objects have no points in common (i.e., they do not touch or overlap).

Right now, you have two distinct solids in the drawing; with **UNION**, you can join them.

- ✔ Click the **Union** tool from the **Edit** panel, as shown in Figure 12-25.

  AutoCAD prompts you to select objects.

- ✔ Use a crossing window or lasso to select both objects.

- ✔ Right-click to end object selection.

  If you move your cursor over the model now, you see that there is no edge between the box and the wedge. They have become one object. Your model should resemble Figure 12-26.

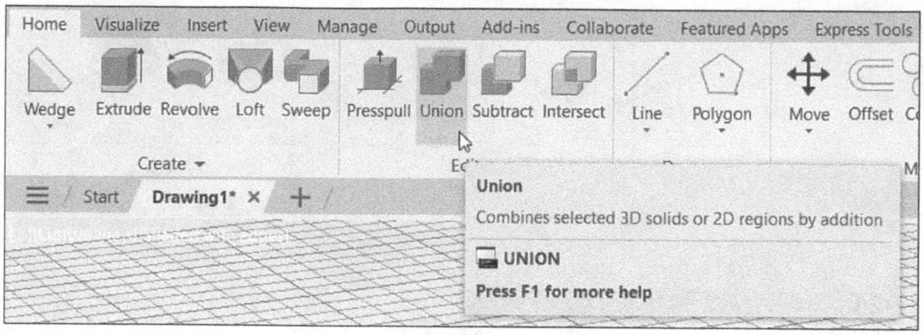

Figure 12-25
Union tool

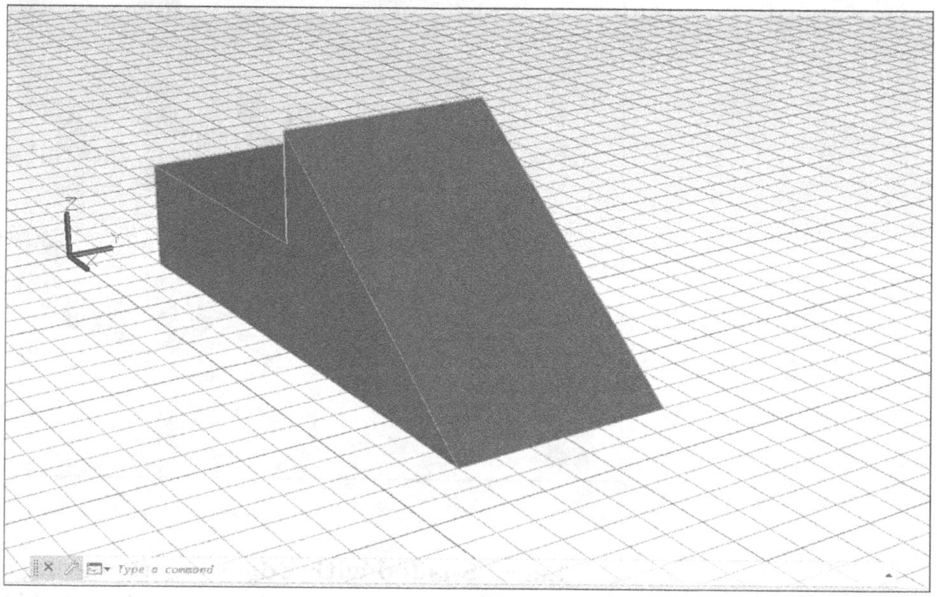

Figure 12-26
Union of wedge and box

Working with DUCS

dynamic user coordinate system (DUCS): In AutoCAD, the 3D system that creates a temporary user coordinate system aligned with the face of a 3D object.

In this exercise, you draw another solid box while using the ***dynamic user coordinate system (DUCS)***. This feature allows you to establish coordinate systems on-the-fly aligned with the faces of previously drawn solids. The thin box is drawn on top of the box from the last section and then moved to the middle of the composite object. In the next section, you move, stretch, and subtract it to form a groove.

- ✔ To begin this exercise, you should have the union of a wedge and a box in your model, as shown in Figure 12-26.

  You begin by drawing a second box positioned on top of the first box.

✔ Click the **Object Snap** tool from the status bar to turn the running object snap off.

✔ Click the **Snap Mode** tool to turn on **Grid Snap** mode.

✔ If necessary, select **Dynamic UCS** from the **Customization** menu located on the right side of the status bar to display the tool on the status bar, shown in Figure 12-27; when enabled, it should be blue.

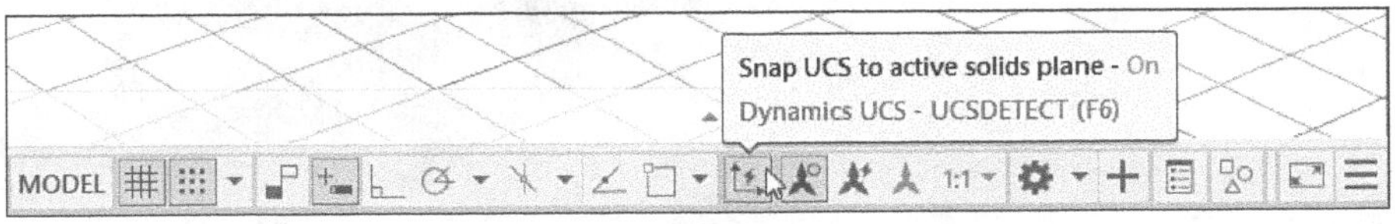

Figure 12-27
Dynamic UCS button

✔ Click the **Box** tool from the **Solid Primitives** drop-down menu on the **Create** panel.

✔ Move the cursor slowly over the faces of the composite object in your model.

As you do this, notice that the faces are highlighted in blue as you cross them. Also notice the 3D cursor. The 3D cursor will turn to align with each face as the face is highlighted. This includes the diagonal face on the wedge, which rotates the cursor on an angle. Notice that the blue Z axis is always normal to the highlighted face.

✔ Move the cursor over the diagonal face on the right side of the wedge and observe the orientation of the 3D cursor.

✔ Let the cursor rest on the top of the box so that it is highlighted, as shown in Figure 12-28.

With this face highlighted, AutoCAD creates a temporary coordinate system aligned with the top of the box.

TIP

Dynamic Input tooltips always display ***X*** and ***Y*** coordinate fields. When working with 3D, you might want to always display the ***Z*** coordinate field. The ***Z*** coordinate field can be displayed by right-clicking in the drawing area and selecting **Options**. In the **Options** dialog box, **3D Modeling** tab, **Dynamic Input** section, check **Show Z Field for Pointer Input**.

✔ With the top face highlighted, carefully move the cursor to the front-left corner of the top of the box and click to specify the corner point.

This creates a coordinate system aligned with the top face and its origin at the specified point, as shown in Figure 12-29. This is similar to the first user coordinate system you created in the "Defining User Coordinate Systems" section. As you move the cursor now, the base plane of the new box you are drawing will be on the plane of the top of the box.

Figure 12-28
Face highlights

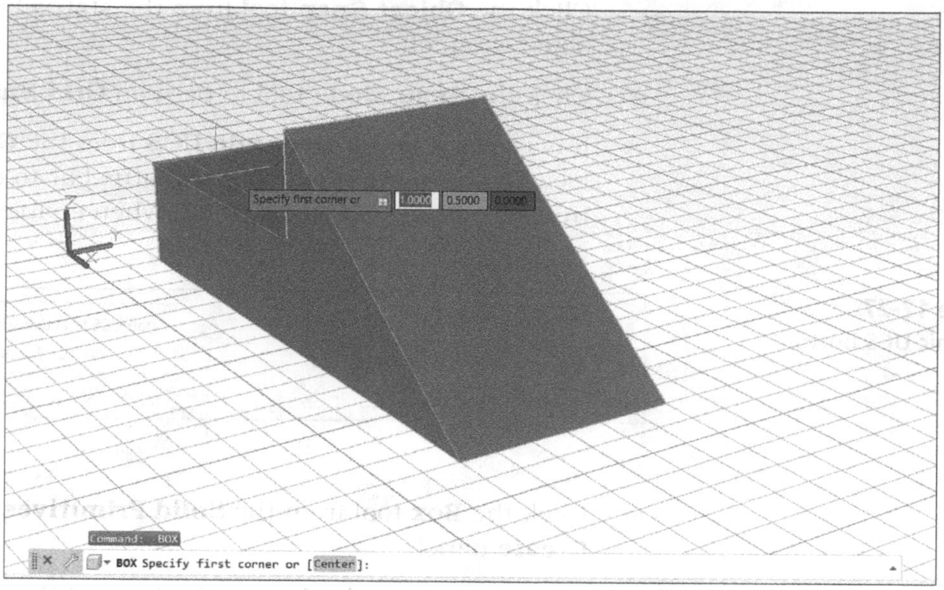

Figure 12-29
Cursor aligns with top face

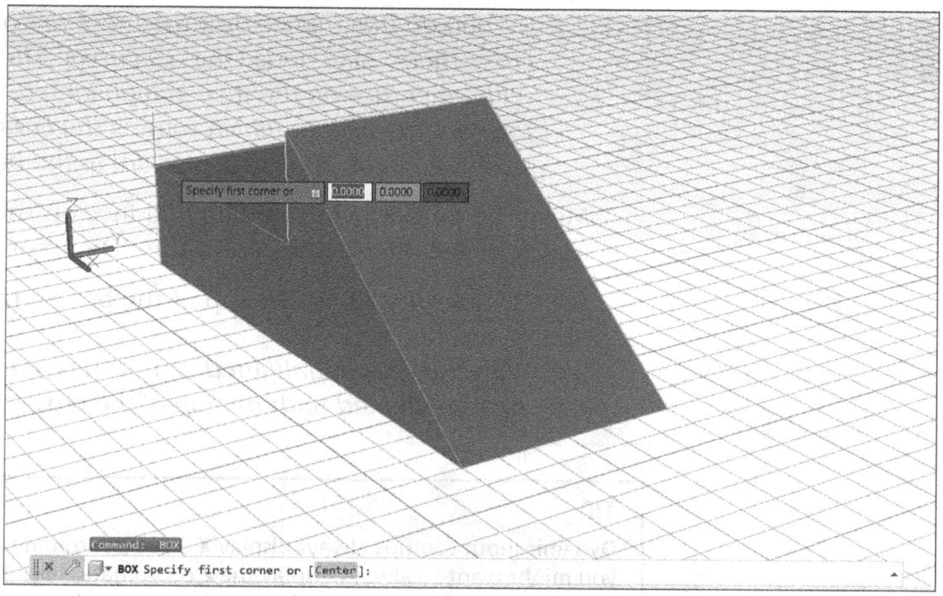

- ✔ Select **Length** from the command line.

  With the ***Length*** *option, you define the length and width of the base separately, rather than specifying the opposite corner. AutoCAD prompts for a length.*

- ✔ Move your cursor along the front edge of the box 4.0000 units to the point where the box and wedge meet.
- ✔ Specify this point to define the length.

  AutoCAD prompts for the width.

- ✔ Move the cursor over 0.5000 units toward the back of the box and specify a point to define the width.

  AutoCAD prompts for a height.

✔ Make sure that the cursor stretches the box in the positive *Z* direction and type **2 <Enter>**.

Your model should resemble Figure 12-30.

Next, you move the new box so that the midpoint of its top front edge is at the midpoint of the top of the wedge.

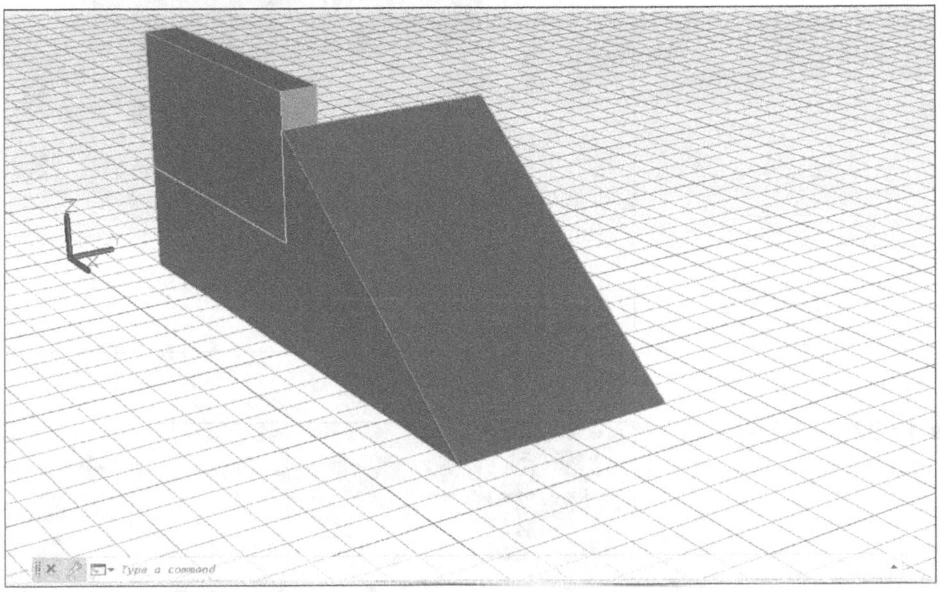

Figure 12-30
Drawing a new box

Creating Composite Solids with SUBTRACT

SUBTRACT	
Command	SUBTRACT
Alias	Su
Panel	Edit
Tool	

SUBTRACT is the logical opposite of **UNION**. In a union operation, all the points contained in one solid are added to the points contained in other solids to form a new composite solid. In a subtraction, all points in the solids to be subtracted are removed from the source solid. A new composite solid is defined by what is left.

In this exercise, you use the objects already in your model to create a slotted wedge. First, you need to move the thin upper box into place, copy it to create a longer slot, and subtract the narrow boxes from the union solid comprised of the box and wedge.

✔ To begin this exercise, you should have the composite box and wedge solid and the thin box in your model, as shown in Figure 12-30.

Before subtracting, you move the box to the position shown in Figure 12-31.

✔ Click the **Move** tool from the **Modify** panel on the ribbon's **Home** tab, as shown in Figure 12-32.

✔ Select the narrow box drawn in the previous exercise.

✔ Right-click to end object selection.

✔ At the ***Specify base point or displacement*** prompt, use a **Midpoint** object snap to specify the midpoint of the top-right edge of the narrow box.

Figure 12-31
Moving box to midpoint of wedge

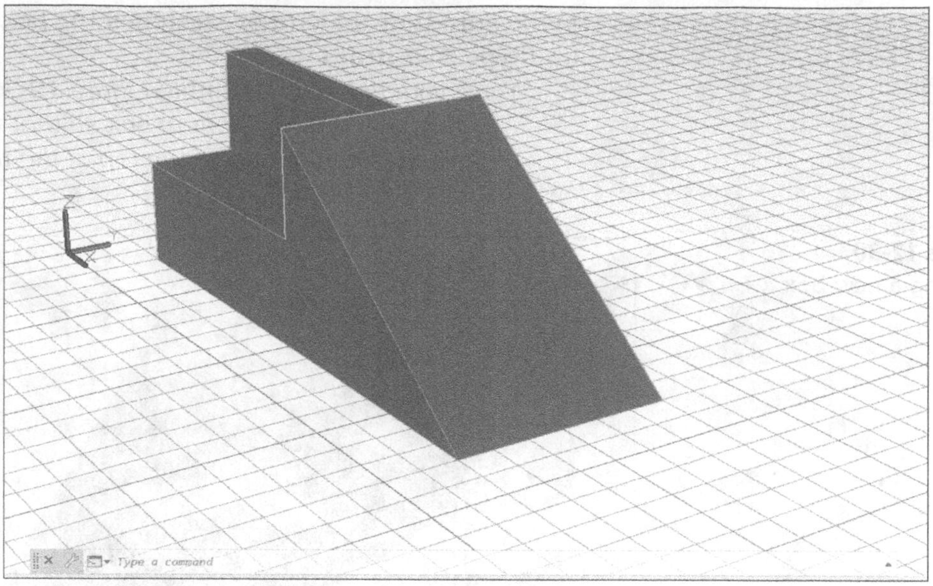

Figure 12-32
Move tool

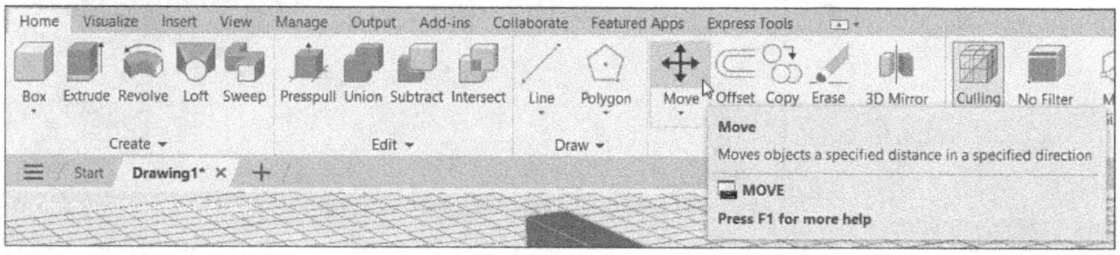

- ✔ At the next ***Specify second point or displacement*** prompt, use the **Midpoint** object snap again to specify the top edge of the wedge.

  This moves the narrow box over and down. If you were to perform the subtraction now, you would create a slot, but it would run only through the box, not the wedge. You can create a longer slot by creating a second copy of the narrow box over to the right.

- ✔ Click the **Copy** tool from the **Modify** panel, as shown in Figure 12-33.
- ✔ Select the narrow box.
- ✔ Right-click to end object selection.

Figure 12-33
Copy tool

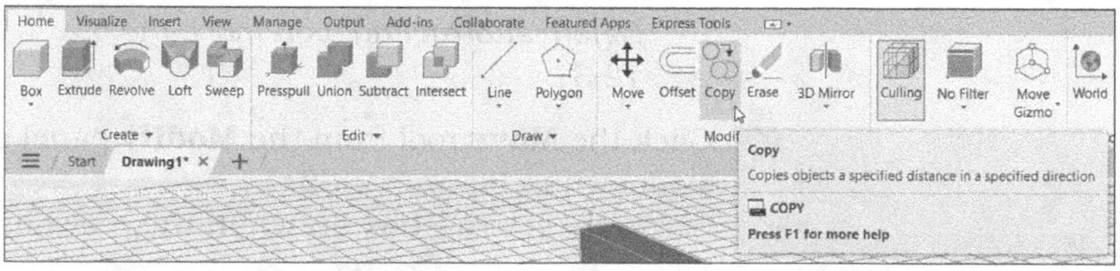

You want to create a copy to the right in a line parallel to the X-axis. This can be easily done by picking the origin for the first point and then picking a point along the X-axis.

- ✔ Press **<Enter>** to use the origin of the WCS for the displacement base point.

✔ Type **4,0,0 <Enter>** for the displacement point.
Your model should resemble Figure 12-34.

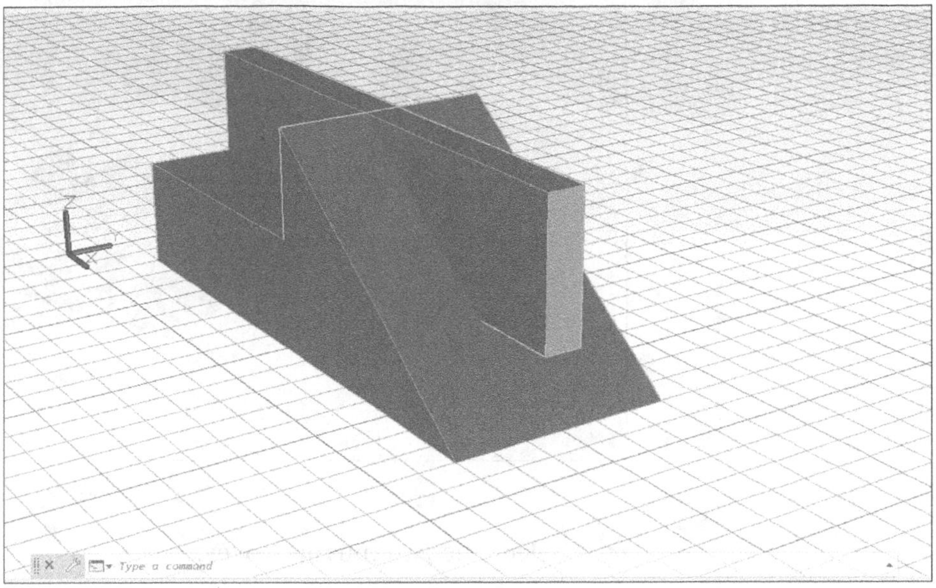

Figure 12-34
Copying the narrow box

Subtraction

The rest is easy. **SUBTRACT** works just like **UNION**, but the results are quite different.

✔ Click the **Subtract** tool from the **Edit** panel on the ribbon's **Home** tab, as shown in Figure 12-35.
AutoCAD prompts you to select objects to subtract from first:

```
Select solids and regions to subtract from . . .
Select objects:
```

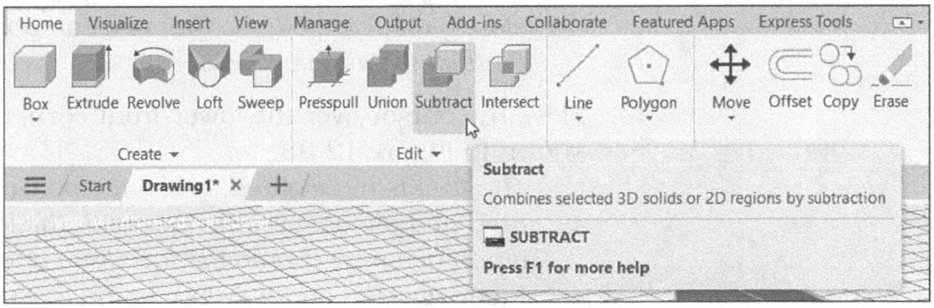

Figure 12-35
Subtract tool

✔ Select the composite of the box and the wedge.

✔ Right-click to end selection of source objects.
AutoCAD prompts for objects to be subtracted:

```
Select solids and regions to subtract . . .
Select objects:
```

Figure 12-36
Subtracting the two narrow boxes

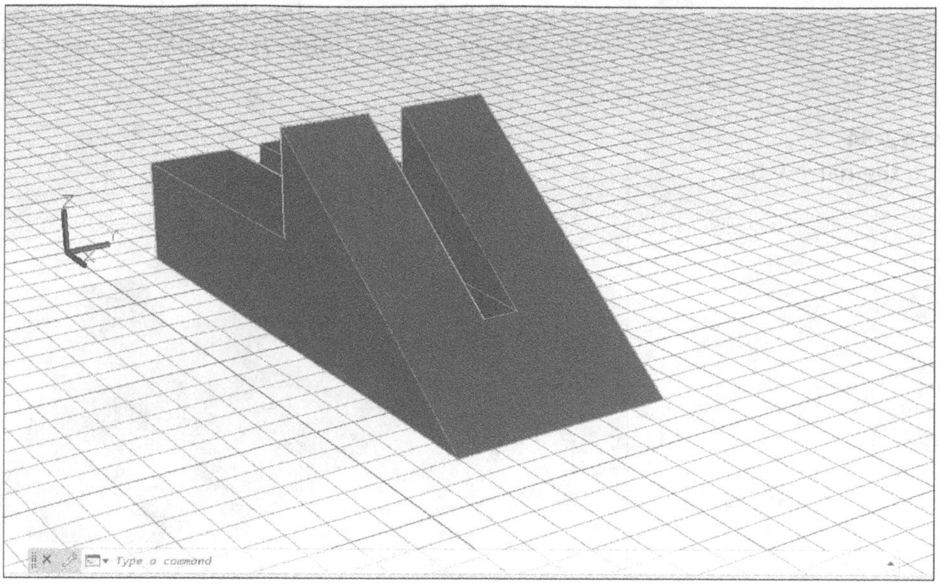

- ✔ Select the two narrow boxes.
- ✔ Right-click to end selection.

  Your model should resemble Figure 12-36.

  To complete this object, you draw a solid cylinder aligned with the diagonal face of the wedge and subtract it to create a hole on the right side below the slot.

- ✔ Click the **Cylinder** tool from the **Solid Primitives** drop-down menu on the ribbon's **Home** tab, as shown in Figure 12-37.

  AutoCAD prompts:

  ```
  Specify center point for base of cylinder or [3P/2P/Ttr/
  Elliptical] <0,0,0>:
  ```

  You use the default method of specifying a center point and then defining a base radius and a height. Be sure to move your cursor slowly and carefully so that you can observe the dynamic user coordinate system in action.

- ✔ Move the cursor over the lower-front corner of the diagonal face, as shown in Figure 12-38.

  The face is highlighted, and a temporary coordinate system is created and aligns with the face with the lower-front corner as the origin. If you moved onto the face from another corner, it would become the temporary origin. Notice in the illustration how the point where the cursor rests has become (0.0000,0.0000,0.0000) in the new coordinate system. You use this coordinate system to locate the center point of the cylinder.

Figure 12-37
Cylinder tool

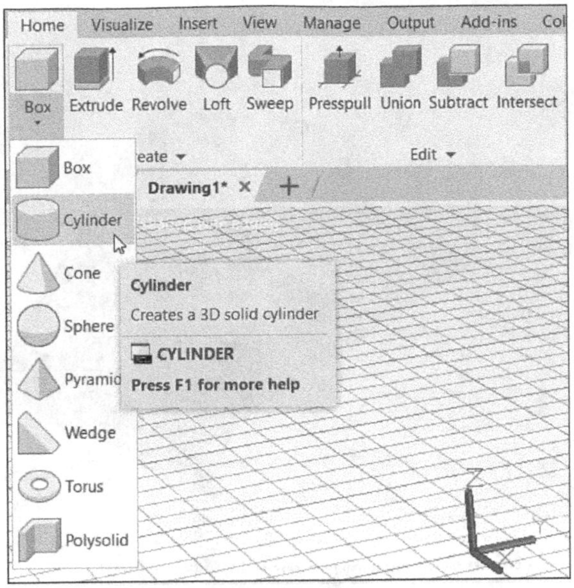

Figure 12-38
Move cursor over the diagonal face

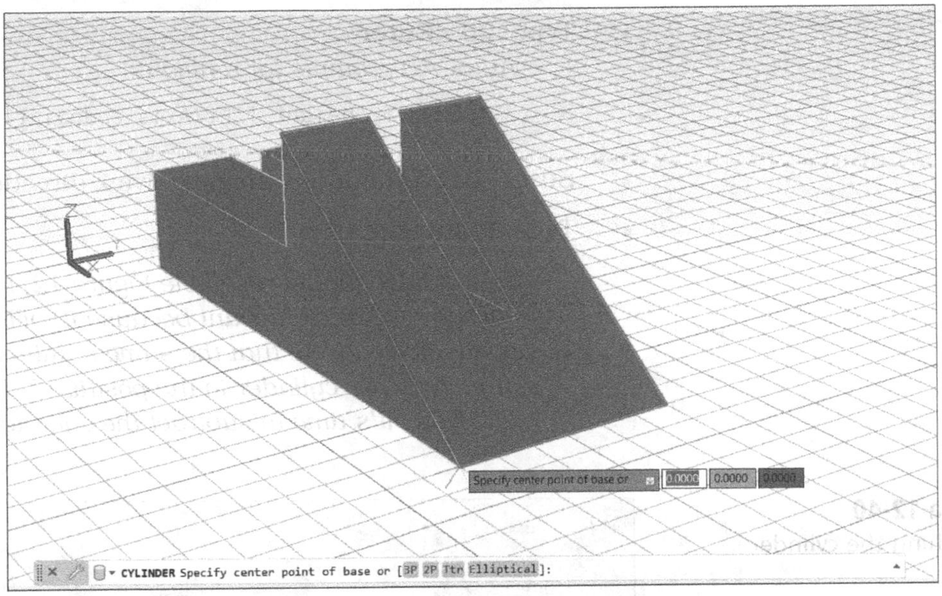

TIP

To ensure that **Dynamic UCS** creates the temporary UCS with the origin at the lower-front corner, bring the cursor onto the angled wedge face from this point. If you enter from another corner, **Dynamic UCS** establishes this as the origin.

✔ Move the cursor over and up to the point (1.5000,1.0000,0.0000) in the new coordinate system and click the left mouse button.

The point is specified, and the 3D cursor moves to this point, aligned with the angle of the face, as shown in Figure 12-39. *This point has been specified as the center point of the base of the cylinder and has also become the origin of another temporary coordinate system. AutoCAD prompts:*

```
Specify base radius [Diameter]:
```

Figure 12-39
Cursor aligns with the angle of face

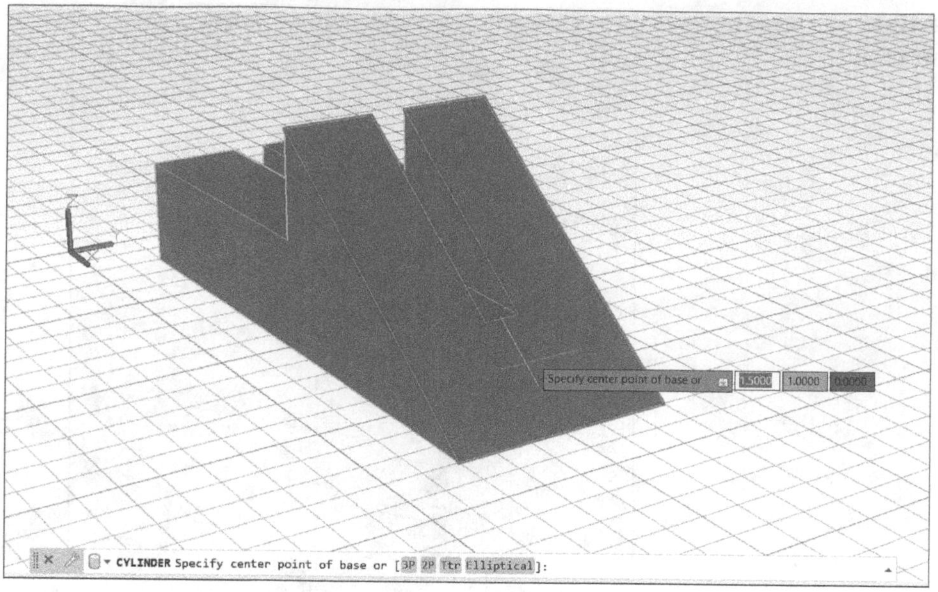

✔ Type **.25 <Enter>**.

AutoCAD prompts for a height:

```
Specify height [2Pt/Axis endpoint] <2.0000>:
```

✔ Stretch the cylinder in the negative *Z* direction.

✔ Type **3 <Enter>**.

Your model should resemble Figure 12-40. The exact height of the cylinder is not significant because it will be subtracted from the composite object. Note that the same results could be achieved by stretching the cylinder in the positive Z direction and typing **–3**.

Now, it's time to subtract the cylinder from the composite solid.

Figure 12-40
Stretching the cylinder

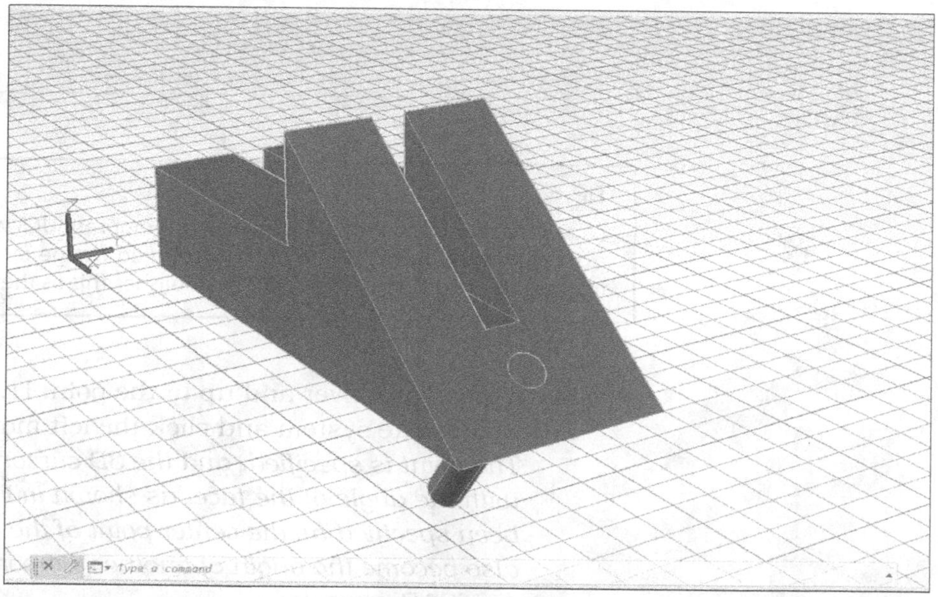

- ✔ Click the **Subtract** tool from the **Edit** panel on the ribbon's **Home** tab.
- ✔ Select the composite object.
- ✔ Right-click to end object selection.
- ✔ Select the cylinder.
- ✔ Right-click to end object selection.

  Your model should resemble Figure 12-41.

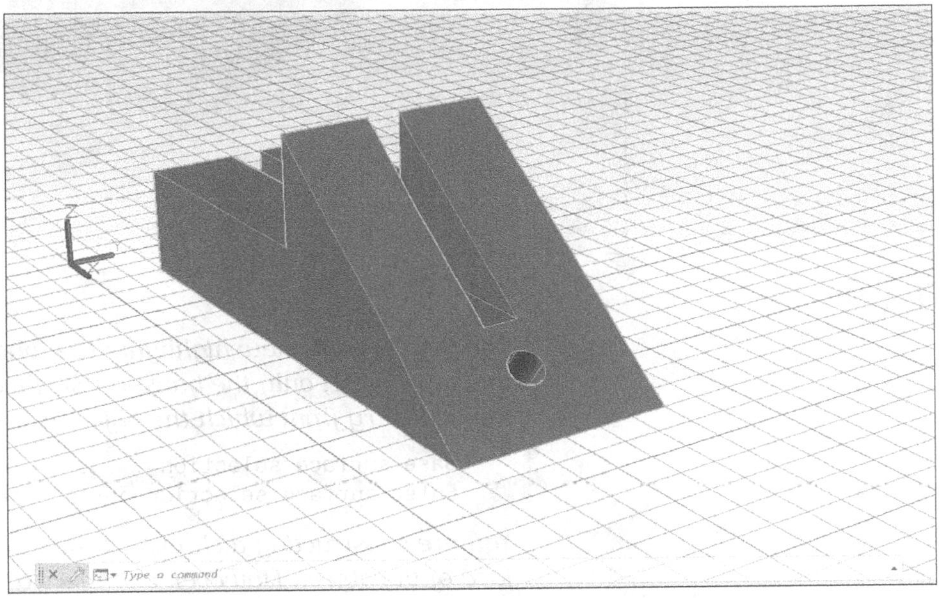

Figure 12-41
Subtracting the cylinder

Creating Chamfers and Fillets on Solid Objects

Chamfering and filleting edges on solids is simple, but the language of the prompts can cause confusion because of some ambiguity in the designation of edges and surfaces to be modified. You begin by putting a chamfer on the back left edge of the model.

- ✔ To begin this exercise, you should have the solid model shown in Figure 12-41.

  *In the **3D Basics** workspace, you will find the **Chamfer** and **Fillet** tools by expanding the **Modify** panel on the **Home** tab.*

- ✔ Expand the **Modify** panel and click the **Chamfer** tool.

  The first chamfer prompt is the same as always:

  ```
  Select first line or [Undo/Polyline/Distance/Angle/Trim/
  mEthod/Multiple]:
  ```

- ✔ Select the edge at **P1**, as shown in Figure 12-42.

Figure 12-42
Select edges P1 and P2

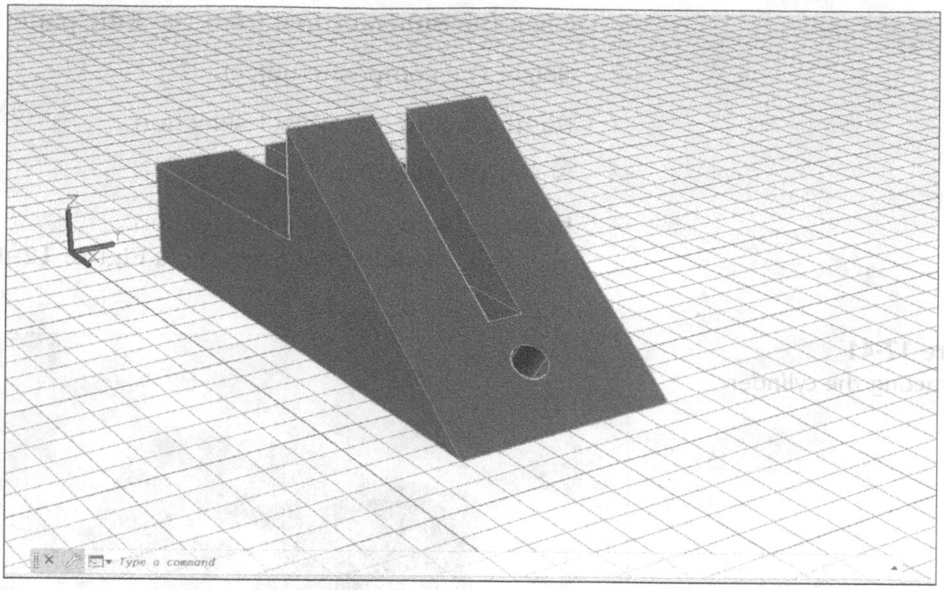

The selection preview highlights the whole solid, but when you select the edge at P1, only the back-left surface is highlighted and displays the geometry from which the object is constructed, and prompts:

```
Base surface selection . . .
Enter surface selection option [Next/OK (current)] <OK>:
```

You are constructing a chamfer that will cut across the front-left surface of the object. However, chamfers and fillets happen along edges that are common to two surfaces. What is a base surface in relation to a chamfered edge? Actually, it refers to either of the two faces that meet at the edge where the chamfer will be. As long as you select this edge, you are bound to select one of these two surfaces, and either will do. Which of the two surfaces is the base surface and which is the adjacent surface does not matter until you enter the chamfer distances, and then only if the distances are unequal. However, you can switch to the other surface that shares this edge by typing ***n*** *for the* ***Next*** *option or selecting* ***Next*** *from the dynamic input menu or at the command line.*

✔ Press **<Enter>**.
AutoCAD prompts:

```
Specify base surface chamfer distance or [Expression]:
```

The ***Expression*** *option allows you to specify chamfer distances with a mathematical expression instead of an actual value.*

✔ Type **.5 <Enter>** for the base surface distance.
Now, AutoCAD prompts:

```
Specify other surface chamfer distance or [Expression]
<0.5000>:
```

Now, you can see the significance of the base surface. The chamfer is created with the first distance on the base surface side and the second distance on the other surface side.

✔ Type **.75 <Enter>** for the other base surface distance.

This constructs a chamfer that cuts 0.5 down into the left side and 0.75 forward along the top side.

Now, AutoCAD prompts for the edge or edges to be chamfered:

```
Select an edge or [Loop]:
```

*The **Loop** option constructs chamfers on all edges of the chosen base surface. Selecting edges allows you to place them only on the selected edges. You have no difficulty selecting edges if you select the edge you want to chamfer again. The only difference is that you need to select twice, once on each side of the slot.*

✔ Select the top-left edge of the model, to one side of the slot (P1 in Figure 12-42 again).

✔ Select the same edge again, but on the other side of the slot (P2 in Figure 12-42).

✔ Press **<Enter>** to end edge selection (right-clicking opens a shortcut menu).

Your model should resemble Figure 12-43.

Figure 12-43
Chamfering edges

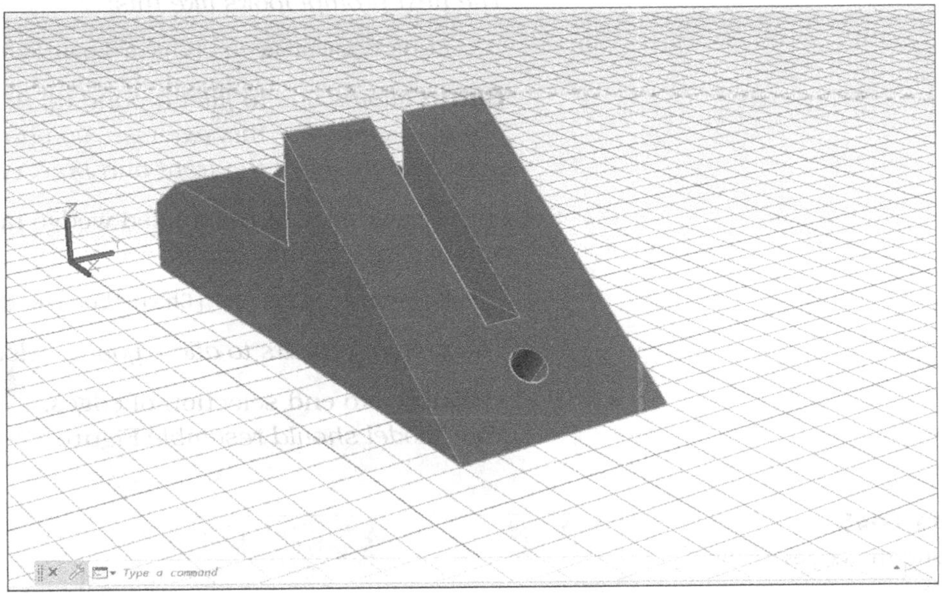

Creating Fillets

The procedure for adding fillets to solids is simpler. There is one step fewer because there is no need to differentiate between base and other surfaces in a fillet.

✔ Click the **Fillet** tool from the expanded **Modify** panel on the **Home** tab.

AutoCAD provides you the current settings and prompts:

```
Select first object or [Undo/Polyline/Radius/Trim/Multiple]:
```

✔ Select the front edge of the angled wedge face, as shown in Figure 12-44.

AutoCAD prompts:

```
Enter fillet radius:
```

Figure 12-44
Select the front edge of the wedge

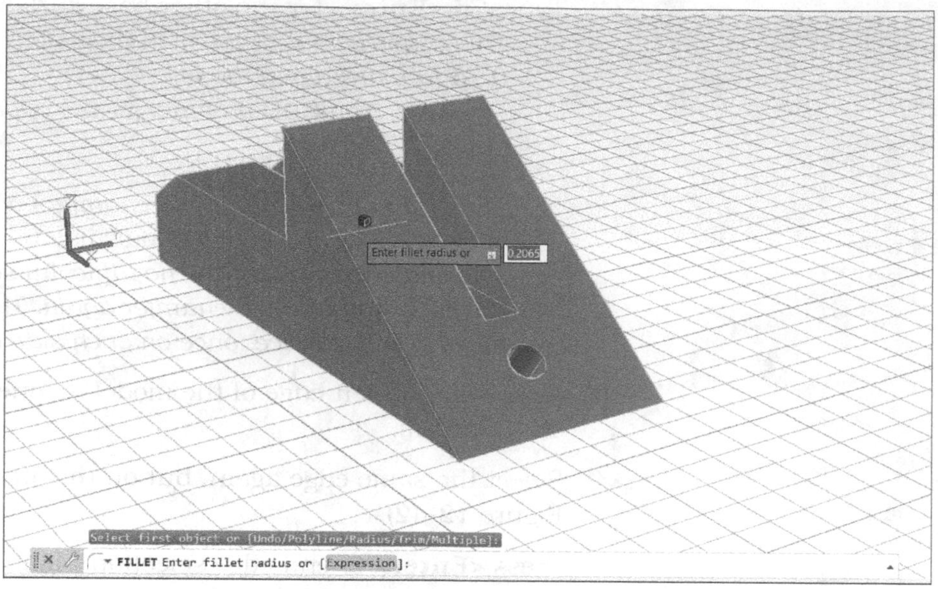

- ✔ Type **.25 <Enter>**.

  The next prompt looks like this:

  ```
  Select an edge or [Chain/Loop/Radius]:
  ```

  Chain *allows you to fillet around all the edges of one side of a solid object at once. For this exercise, you do not want a chain. Instead, you want to select the front and back edges of the diagonal face.*

- ✔ Select the back edge of the angled wedge face.

  You see this prompt again:

  ```
  Select an edge or [Chain/Loop/Radius]:
  ```

  The prompt repeats to allow you to select more edges to fillet.

- ✔ Press **<Enter>** to end selection of edges.

  Your model should resemble Figure 12-45.

Figure 12-45
Filleting the edges of the wedge

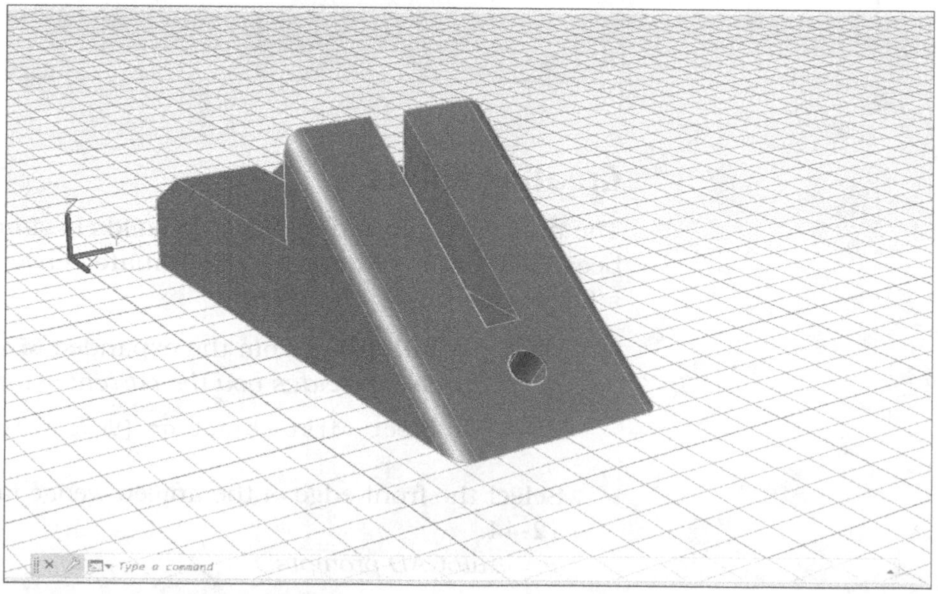

Practicing 3D Gizmo Editing

gizmo: In AutoCAD 3D modeling, one of three tools that facilitate editing of solid models. The three gizmos are for moving, rotating, and scaling models.

Gizmos are 3D icons that facilitate editing in strict relation to the current coordinate system. Using the **Move** gizmo, you can easily move objects parallel to the *X*-, *Y*-, or *Z*-axis. Using the **Rotate** gizmo, you can rotate objects around these same axes. Using the **Scale** gizmo, you can scale along any of the axes, through the plane of any two axes, or uniformly in all directions. Here, you learn to move and rotate objects using 3D gizmos.

✔ Open the **Gizmo** drop-down menu from the **Selection** panel on the ribbon's **Home** tab, as shown in Figure 12-46.

*You see the three gizmos, along with a **No Gizmo** tool. **No Gizmo** is a useful option because you will not always want the visual distraction of gizmos appearing each time you select an object. You begin with the **Move** gizmo.*

Figure 12-46
Gizmo drop-down list

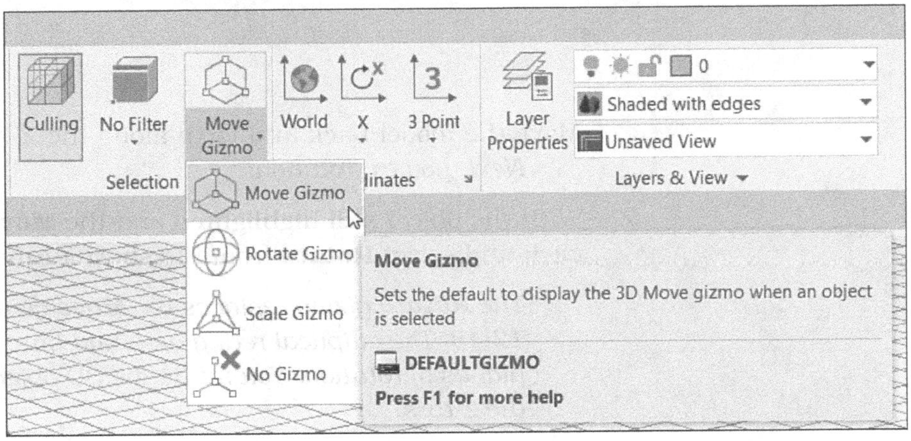

✔ Click the **Move Gizmo** tool.

*This ensures that the **Move** gizmo is active and at the top of the menu, which it might be by default.*

✔ Select the composite 3D object in the model.

*The 3D object is highlighted, and the **Move** gizmo appears at the center, as shown in Figure 12-47.*

✔ Move your cursor over the gizmo slowly.

As you slowly cross over an axis, a construction line is displayed with the color of that axis. Also, the axis is highlighted in gold. In Figure 12-47, you see the X-axis highlighted, with a red construction line extending in both directions. If you move into a quadrant between two axes, the square between those two axes will be highlighted in gold, indicating that you are on the plane of those two axes.

✔ Move the cursor so that the *X*-axis is highlighted.

✔ Click the left mouse button to constrain movement along the *X*-axis.

Figure 12-47
Move Gizmo icon

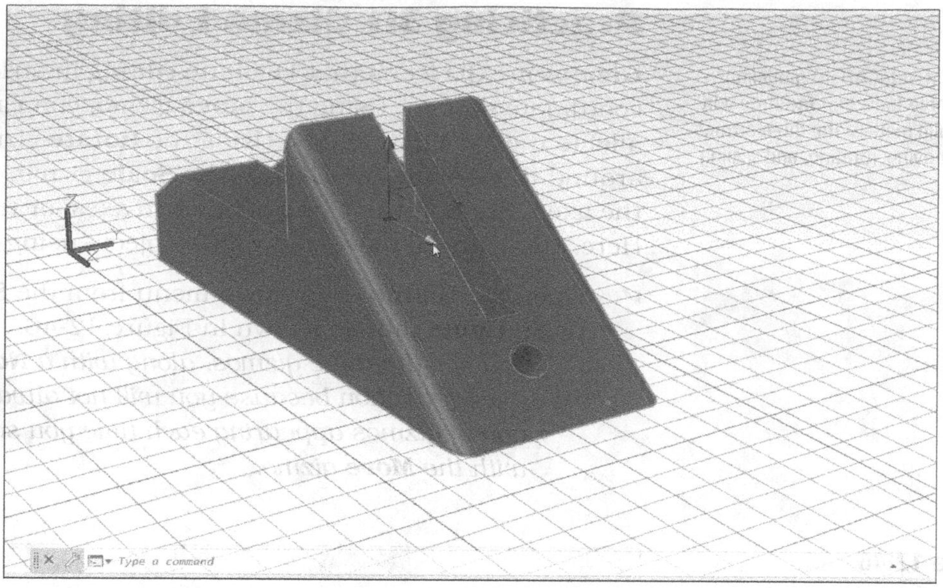

- ✔ Move the model back and forth along the *X*-axis.

  Next, you try rotation.

- ✔ With the object still highlighted and the **Move** gizmo showing, right-click and select **Rotate** from the shortcut menu.

  The ***Rotate*** *gizmo replaces the* ***Move*** *gizmo, as shown in Figure 12-48. The elliptical red, green, and blue circles represent the three planes of rotation. You rotate the 3D object on the XY plane, around the Z-axis.*

Figure 12-48
Rotate Gizmo icon

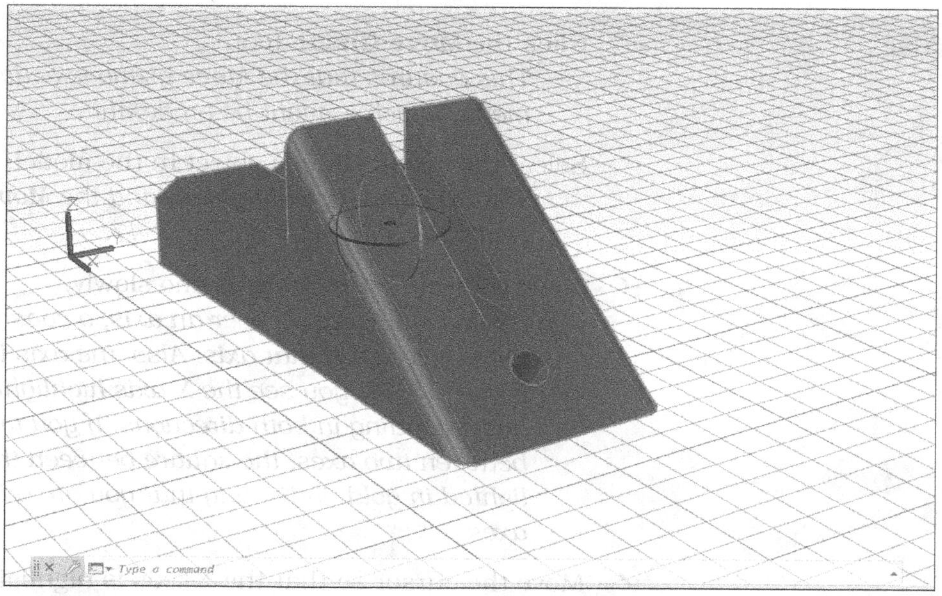

- ✔ Move your cursor over the blue ellipse as shown, so that it turns gold.

  When the blue ellipse is highlighted gold, a blue Z-axis is displayed.

- ✔ Click the left mouse button to constrain rotation around the Z-axis.

- ✔ Move your cursor in the model to perform a rotation around the *Z*-axis.
- ✔ Move the cursor back to a position similar to its original rotation.
- ✔ Click the left mouse button to complete the operation.

The **Scale** gizmo is a bit more complex, and is not covered here. As shown in Figure 12-49, the **Scale** gizmo is similar to the **Move** gizmo, except that it has gold triangulating lines drawn between each pair of axes and boxes at the end. By highlighting an individual axis, you can scale along that axis. By highlighting a bar in the plane between any two axes, you can scale in both of these directions. By highlighting the complete pattern of gold lines and gold boxes all at once, you can uniform scale in all directions.

Figure 12-49
Scale Gizmo icon

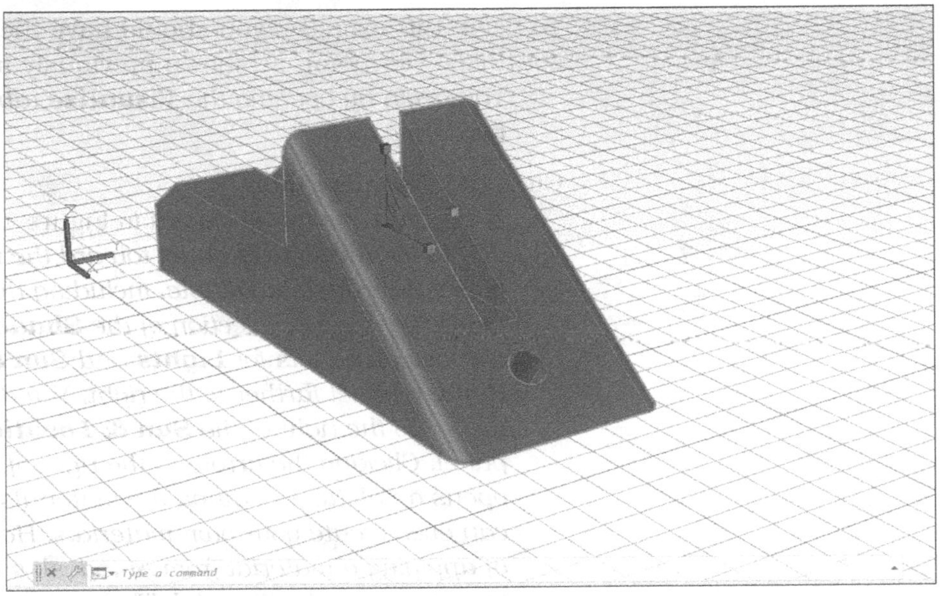

Rendering 3D Models

rendering: The process by which the mathematical data used to describe a 3D model comprised of solids and surfaces are translated into pixels and represented on a computer screen.

Rendering a 3D model can be a very complex process requiring a great deal of time and expertise. The mathematics of rendering programs requires repeated passes over the geometry of the drawing to generate increasingly precise representations. A high-quality rendering of a complex model can easily require an overnight session. The most precise renderings require the most detailed mathematics along with multiple repetitions, called "levels," which translates to significant time. Rendering can be set to perform anywhere from 1 repetition of the least complex formulae to an option that would run the most robust math without a time limit until you are satisfied with the results.

The usual sequence for creating a rendered model is to begin by adding materials to the model, then adding lighting and a background, and finally setting the computer to work to generate the rendering. You follow this course in this exercise, except you learn simple rendering procedures early on so you can see the results of features you add as you develop your rendered model.

Attaching Materials

In this exercise, you follow a simple procedure for adding materials to a model. Here, you have one object, to which to attach a material. The procedure you follow can be used repeatedly to add a variety of materials to different objects in a complex model.

Materials can be selected from a library. Each material definition has its own characteristic color, texture, and response to light. Materials can also be created or modified. Changing an object's material dramatically affects the way it is rendered, so it usually makes sense to attach materials before adjusting light intensity and color. In this exercise, you go through the procedure of loading materials from the installed library and attaching them to an object. When you experiment on your own, you will likely see color effects that cannot be shown here.

✔ To begin this exercise, you should have the composite solid model in a southeast viewpoint, as shown previously in Figure 12-45.

You begin by opening the ***Visualize*** *tab, where you find many of the rendering tools.*

✔ Click the **Visualize** tab.

The ***Visualize*** *tab is shown in* Figure 12-50. *Before turning attention to the* ***Materials*** *panel toward the right side of the ribbon, notice the panels available, including the* ***Visual Styles*** *panel, where your early selection of the* ***Shaded with Edges*** *style is accessible; panels for* ***Lights*** *and* ***Sun & Location****; and the* ***Render*** *panel farther to the right. You delve into all of these momentarily. To the right of the* ***Sun & Location*** *panel is the* ***Materials*** *panel. Clicking the arrow at the right of the* ***Materials*** *panel title bar opens a palette for editing the materials in your drawing. Here, you can even create your own materials. Here, you follow a simpler path of applying a material from Autodesk's* ***Materials Library*** *directly to your composite 3D solid. These materials are found in the* ***Materials Browser****.*

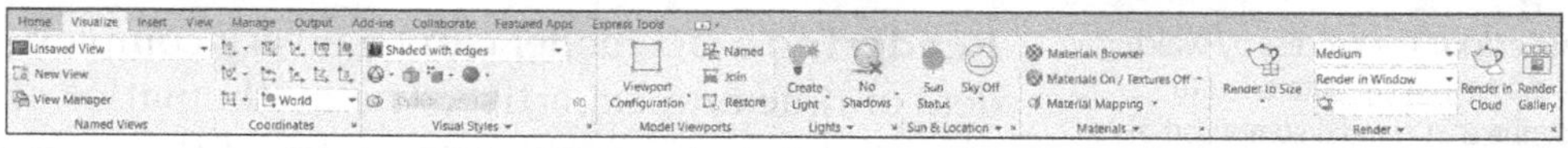

Figure 12-50
Visualize tab

✔ Click the **Materials Browser** tool from the **Materials** panel of the **Visualize** tab, as shown in Figure 12-51.

This opens the ***Materials Browser*** *palette, shown in Figure 12-52. Your palette may look different from the one shown if someone has customized the installed materials library. In the palette on the left, you have the option of browsing through materials of your own creation or through the installed* ***Autodesk Library****.*

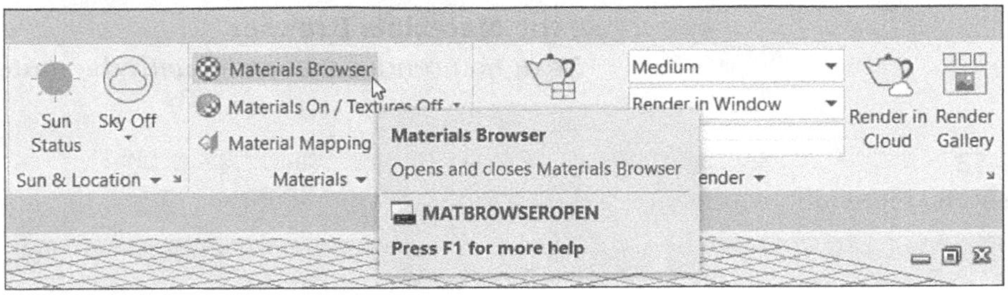

Figure 12-51
Materials Browser tool

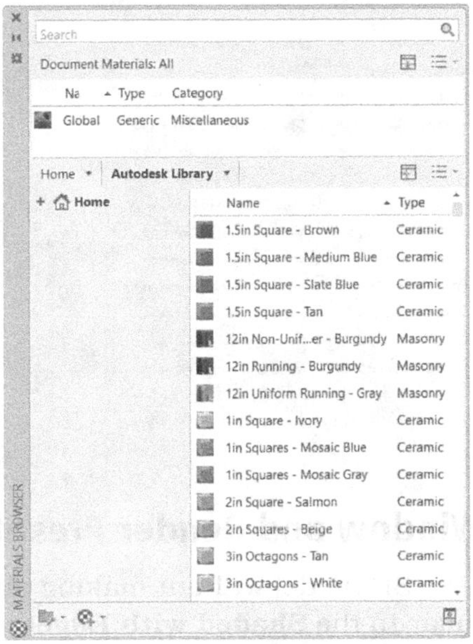

Figure 12-52
Materials Browser palette

NOTE

If the attached material does not appear on your model, try clicking the **Materials and Textures** drop-down menu on the **Materials** panel. There are three settings: **Materials/Textures On, Materials On/Textures Off**, and **Materials/Textures Off**. You need materials and textures on to produce the results shown here.

✔ Click the small arrow to the right of the **Autodesk Library** title.

This opens a list of material types, beginning with ***Ceramic****. Each of these items opens a set of material varieties, represented by a thumbnail to the left of the material name. Here, you will add an anodized blue-gray aluminum to your model.*

✔ Scroll down and select **Metal** from the list, as shown in Figure 12-53.

✔ Select **Anodized – Blue-Gray**, as shown.

You may have to manipulate the width of the column or the palette in order to read the names.

✔ Click the **Anodized – Blue-Gray** image and drag it into the drawing area.

✔ Drag the image over the composite 3D object and release the left mouse button.

Your model and edges will change color, indicating that the material has been attached to the object. However, the qualities of the material attached aren't visible until the object is rendered.

✔ Close the **Materials Browser**.

Next, you render the model with the material attached.

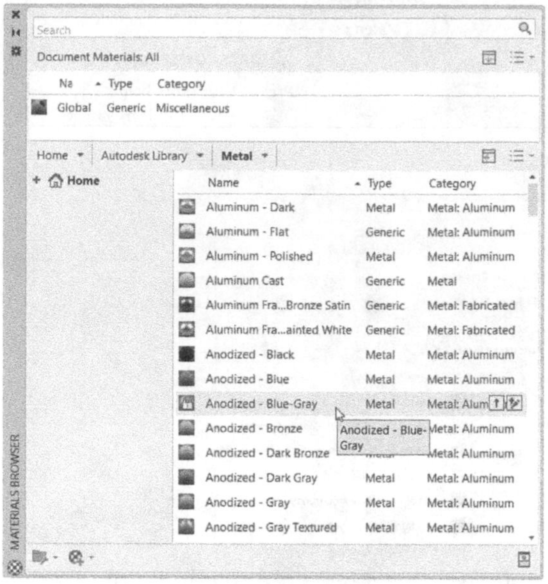

Figure 12-53
Select the **Metal** material

The Render Window and Render Presets

You first render the 3D model without making any lighting changes. The result will be similar to the **Shaded with Edges** visual style you already see in the drawing, with the notable addition of the **Anodized – Blue-Gray** metallic material on the faces of the 3D model. When you render an object, it can be shown in a special render window or within a viewport. The render window is used by default.

Also, you have a choice of several different render settings that control the degree of precision in the rendering. As stated previously, the factors to be specified will be a combination of the amount of time you want the computer to work, the complexity of the math, and the number of levels you want it to perform.

To the right of the **Materials** panel on the **Visualize** tab is the **Render** panel. This is where changes to the actual rendering process, separate from lighting, materials, or background, are specified.

✔ Click the menu arrow below the **Render to Size tool**.

This opens the menu of render size options shown in Figure 12-54. These options are dependent on the quality of your display and graphics adapter. The default setting is 800 × 600 px SVGA, which will work fine for this exercise. Yours may already be set to a higher resolution. In any case, you can leave it set the way it is, or you can change it if you have better information about your display specs.

The ***Render*** *tool above the* ***Render to Size*** *drop-down menu performs a rendering with the current settings. Before you do that, you explore the* ***Render Presets*** drop-down *list and the* ***Render Presets Manager****, where you can specify how you want to perform this rendering. The* ***Render Presets Manager*** *is accessed from the* ***Render Presets*** *drop-down list at the top center of the* ***Render*** *panel, as shown in Figure 12-55.*

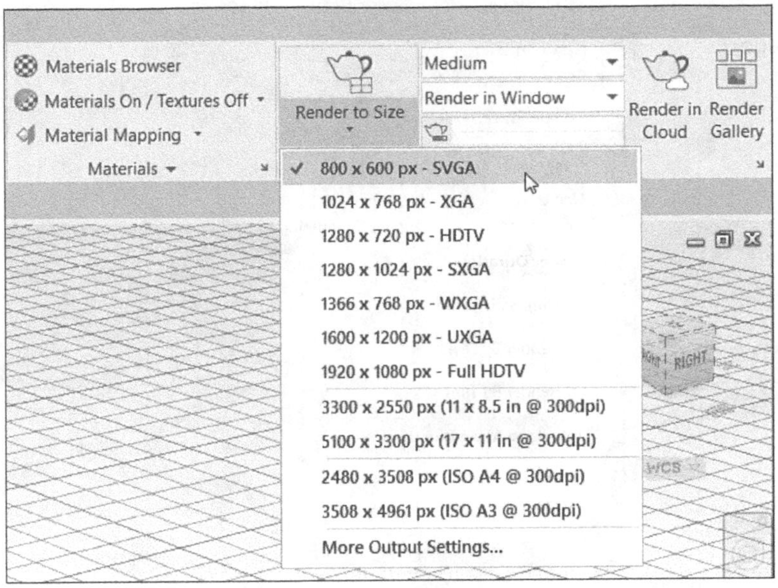

Figure 12-54
Render to Size drop-down menu

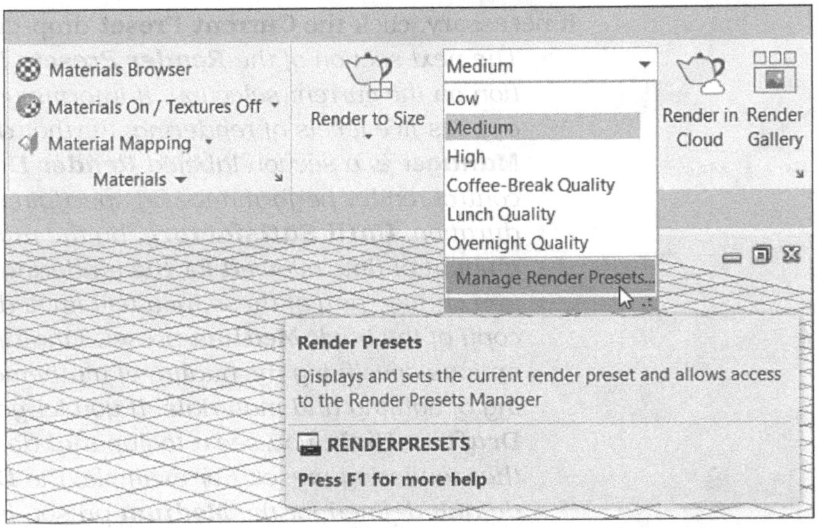

Figure 12-55
Render Presets drop-down list

✔ Click the arrow on the right side of the **Render** panel title bar or click **Manage Render Presets** at the bottom of the **Render Presets** drop-down list, as shown.

This opens the ***Render Presets Manager*** *shown in Figure 12-56. The top three drop-down lists duplicate the choices that are available on the ribbon but in a different arrangement. You can choose to render to the render window, a viewport in the drawing, or a defined region within a viewport. You can choose the size of the rendering to coordinate with the display specifications. And you can choose among six different predefined rendering settings, defined by the amount of time or the number of levels. The default setting is* ***Medium****. The preset rendering options cannot be edited. If you change a setting while a preset option is selected, a copy of the preset is created and given a different name, such as Medium-Copy 1.*

Figure 12-56
Render Presets Manager

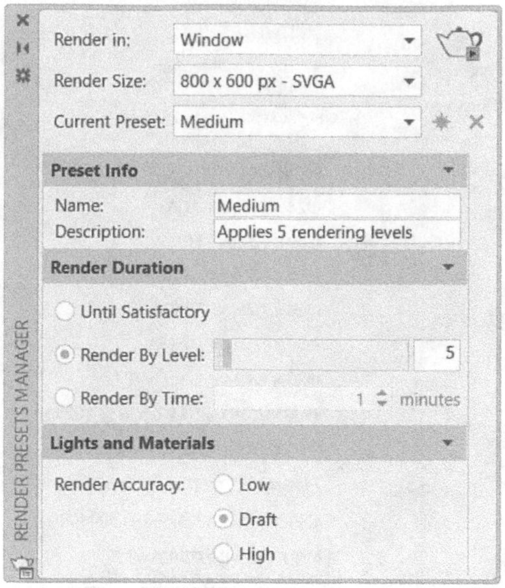

✔ If necessary, click the **Current Preset** drop-down list and select **Medium**.

*The next section of the **Render Presets Manager** provides information on the current selection. It informs you that the **Medium** preset applies five levels of rendering. Further down in the **Render Presets Manager** is a section labeled **Render Duration** that enables you to control render performance by specifying an open-ended render duration, **Until Satisfactory**, by the number of levels, or by the amount of time allowed for the rendering to complete. Notice that if you change any of these, you will immediately be working with a copy of the basic **Medium** preset. Finally, at the bottom, are three options specifying the quality of mathematics applied to the rendering of lighting and materials. If you let your cursor rest on **Low**, **Draft**, or **High**, you see a tooltip that describes the characteristics of that rendering preset. For example, the **Draft** quality tooltip, the default defined for the **Medium** preset, is shown in Figure 12-57.*

Figure 12-57
Draft quality tooltip

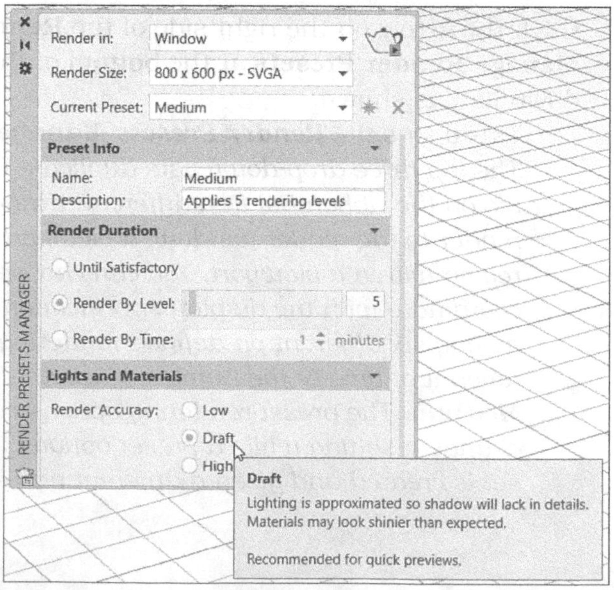

*Proceed with the **Medium** preset, five levels of **Render Duration**, and **Draft** quality. From here, you can use either the **Render** tool in the upper-right corner of the **Render Presets Manager** or the tool on the ribbon.*

✔ Click the **Render** tool from the **Render Presets Manager**, as shown in Figure 12-58.

The render window opens and displays the rendered image shown in Figure 12-59. *Like other windows, the render window can be minimized and maximized. The render window also retains all renderings that are done in this drawing session so that you can switch back and forth and keep a record of what you have done. You can access previous renderings by clicking the down arrow in the bottom-left corner of the window. Rendering requires a lot of trial and error, so this history is useful. Below the rendering is a progress bar that will show the progress of the rendering. In this case, it indicates the five levels. Depending on your computer, the levels should go by quickly with this simple model.*

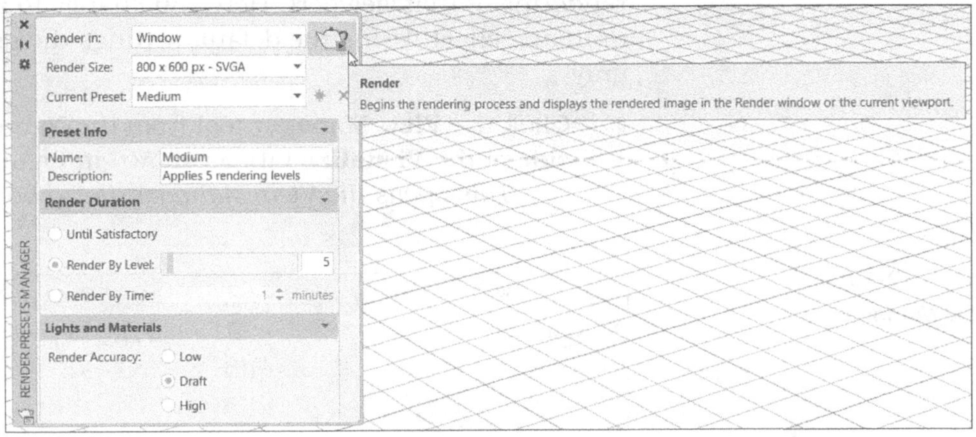

Figure 12-58
Render tool

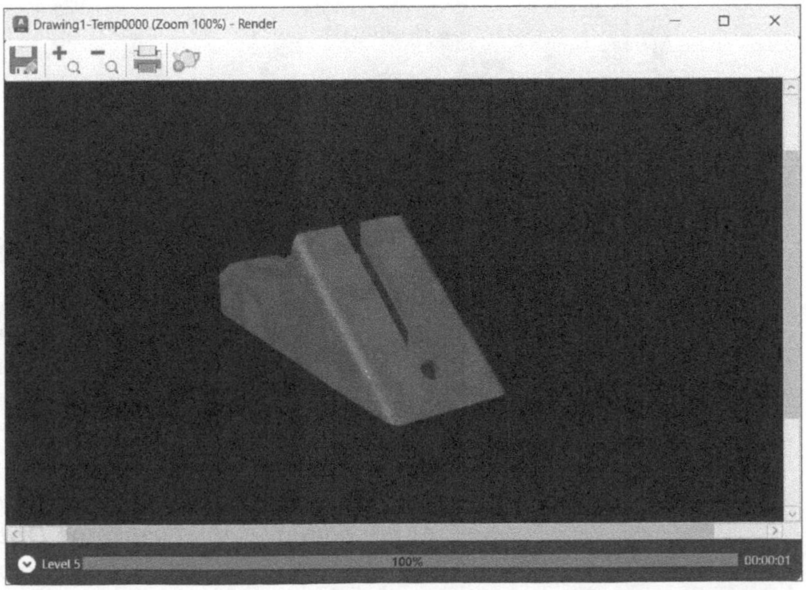

Figure 12-59
Render window

> **NOTE**
>
> Depending on the previous usage of the feature, you may see the message **Autodesk Materials Library - Medium Image library is not installed**. In this case, you have a choice of either downloading and installing the library or continuing to work without using the library. Either way, you can check the **Do not show this dialog again** box to avoid seeing this dialog box each time you proceed to render an image.

✔ Close the render window or click the drawing name label on the Windows taskbar to return to the drawing window.

Next, you add a background to the viewport.

Changing the Background and Naming Views

You may find that certain rendered images are too light or dark against the background color of the drawing window. You can remedy this by changing to a different background through the **View Manager** dialog box with the **VIEW** command or **Background** dialog box with the **BACKGROUND** command. When the background is changed in a viewport, it is retained for the rendering of that viewport. Here you change to a gradient background for dramatic effect. Using the default settings the gradient will be in shades of gray.

✔ Click the **View Manager** tool from the **Named Views** panel on the left side of the **Visualize** tab, as shown in Figure 12-60.

This opens the View Manager dialog box.

Figure 12-60
View Manager tool

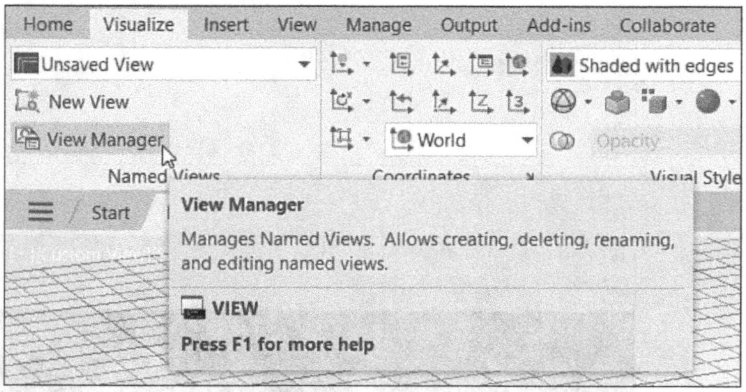

✔ In the **View Manager** dialog box, click the **New** button.

✔ In the **New View/Shot Properties** dialog box, click the **More Options** control in the lower-left corner to expand the dialog box, and then click the drop-down list in the **Background** section at the bottom.

✔ From the drop-down list, select **Gradient**.

*This opens the **Background** dialog box shown in Figure 12-61. You see a **Preview** panel with a gradient pattern from darker to lighter gray. At the bottom is the **Gradient Options** section that allows you to change the gradient colors and to rotate the middle border.*

Figure 12-61
Background dialog box

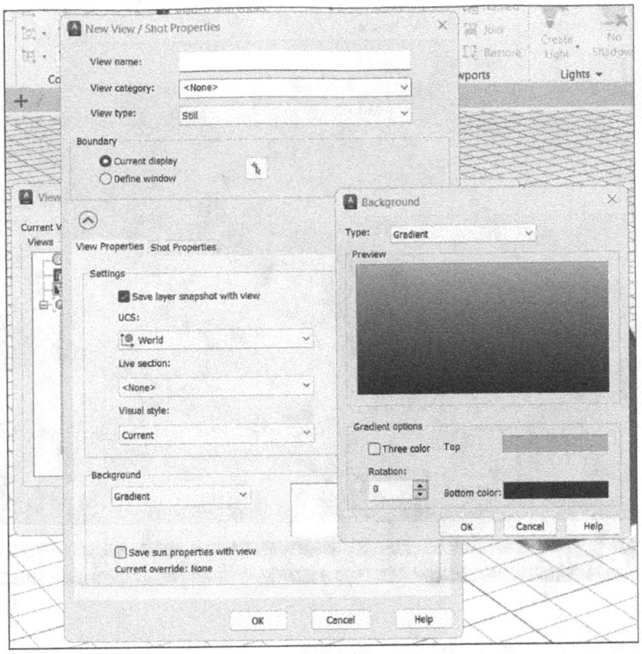

NOTE

The technique of saving named views can also be used to save more complex configurations of lights, materials, and light settings. When you have achieved a scene you wish to keep, it is a good idea to save it as a named view.

✔ Click **OK** to accept the default gradient scheme.

*This returns you to the **New View/Shot Properties** dialog box, where you must name the view before you can apply it.*

✔ In the **View Name** box, type **Gradient**.

✔ Click **OK**.

*You are returned to the **View Manager** dialog box; notice the preview image at the lower-right. To change your viewport to this view, you must set it as current.*

✔ Click the **Set Current** button in the upper-right.

✔ Click **OK**.

You should now see your shaded model with a gradient background.

✔ If **Grid Mode** is on, turn it off.

✔ Click the **Render** tool from the **Render Presets Manager**.

*The gradient background is displayed in the **Render** window, as shown in Figure 12-62.*

Figure 12-62
Render with background

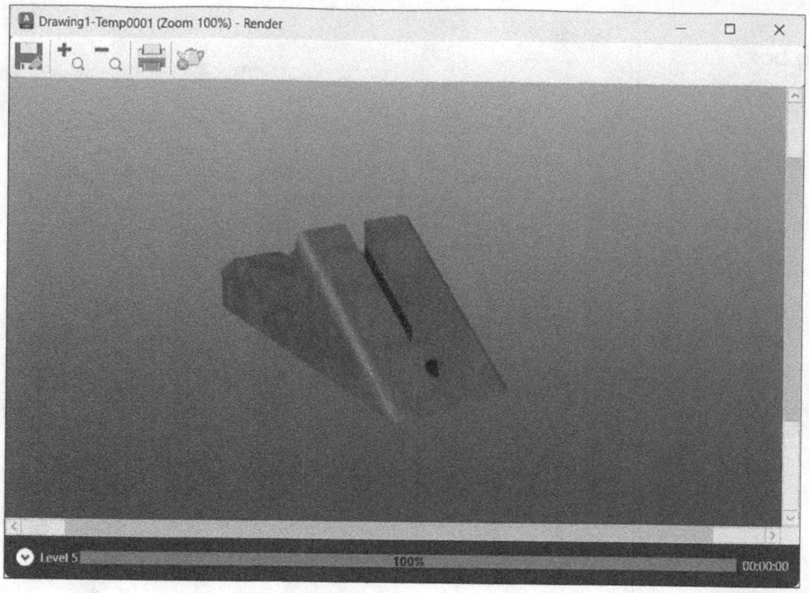

Spotlight

Although you have done nothing to add lights to the current model, there is light present. It is the default viewport lighting and is added automatically. It produces the effect you see. When you add your own lighting, you will have the option of turning off default lighting. You begin by adding a spotlight.

Four types of lights are available from the **Create Light** drop-down menu shown in Figure 12-63. You are going to add a spotlight on the right side of the object, aimed in along the slot. Light placement is probably the most important consideration in rendering. Lights can be placed using point filters or typed coordinates. Keep in mind that lights are usually positioned above the *XY* plane and are often alone in space. Point filters can be very helpful in this situation because there is nothing to snap the lights onto.

✔ Click the **Spot** tool from the **Create Light** drop-down menu on the **Lights** panel, as shown in Figure 12-63.

Figure 12-63
Spotlight tool

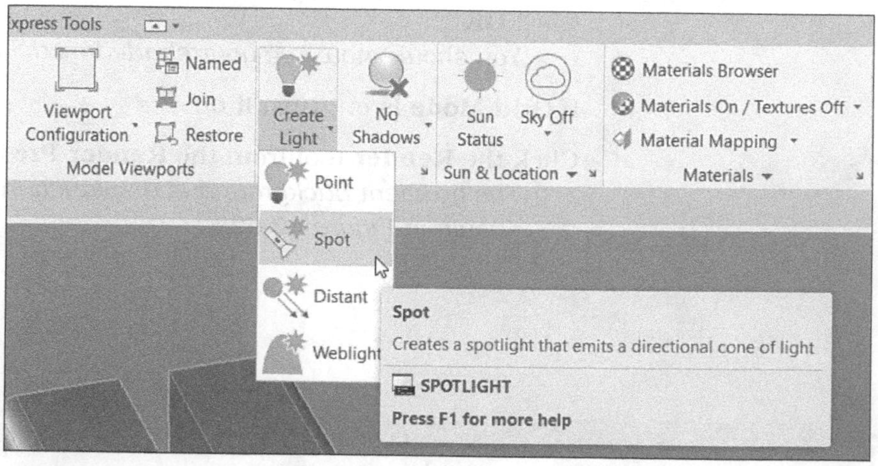

*At this point, a **Lighting – Viewport Lighting mode** message might be presented that asks whether you want to turn off default lighting.*

✔ If necessary, click the **Turn Off the Default Lighting** option.

A spotlight glyph appears at the crosshairs, and you are prompted with

```
Specify source location <0,0,0>:
```

Spotlights have a target and source position. As is the case with real spotlights, AutoCAD-rendered spotlights are carefully placed and aimed at a particular point in the drawing. The light falls in a cone shape and diminishes from the center of the cone. The area of the focal beam is called the hotspot. The surrounding area where the light fades is called the falloff area.

For this exercise, you place a light above and to the right of the composite 3D object, aimed directly into the front of the slot. You use object snap and an .XY filter to place the target and the light source.

✔ At the prompt for a light source, type **.xy <Enter>** or open the **Object Snap** shortcut menu by holding **<Shift>** and right-clicking. Highlight **Point Filters** and select **.XY**.

*AutoCAD prompts **.xy of** and waits for you to specify a point on the XY plane.*

✔ Specify a point 1.0 unit to the right of the composite 3D object the point (10,2.5,0).

AutoCAD now prompts for a Z value:

```
(need Z):
```

✔ Type **4 <Enter>**.

This places the source location of the light to the right and above the composite 3D object. Now, AutoCAD prompts for the target location:

```
Specify target location <0,0,-10>:
```

*Use the **Midpoint** object snap to place the target at the right end of the slot.*

✔ **<Shift> + right-click**, and select **Midpoint** from the **Object Snap** menu.

✔ Use the **Midpoint** object snap to select the midpoint of the right end of the slot.

The target point is now specified, and options are provided to adjust the spotlight. AutoCAD prompts:

```
Enter option to change
[Name/Intensity factor/Status/Photometry/Hotspot/Falloff/
shadow/Attenuation/filter Color/eXit] <eXit>:
```

These same options are shown on the dynamic input display. Don't change any options at this point.

✔ Press **<Enter>** to exit the command.

The composite 3D object is shaded, showing the effect of the spotlight shining on the end of the slot. The shading is rather dark. Next, you add some sunlight.

- ✔ Click the **Visual Styles** gallery on the **Visual Styles** panel, and select **Realistic**.

  The Realistic visual style allows you to see a basic representation of the lighting in your 3D model.
- ✔ Click the **Sun Status** tool on the **Sun & Location** panel, as shown in Figure 12-64, to turn it on.

  *The **Lighting – Sunlight and Exposure** message box is displayed, allowing you to adjust the exposure settings or retain the current settings. For the purpose of this exercise, you retain exposure settings.*

Figure 12-64
Sun Status tool

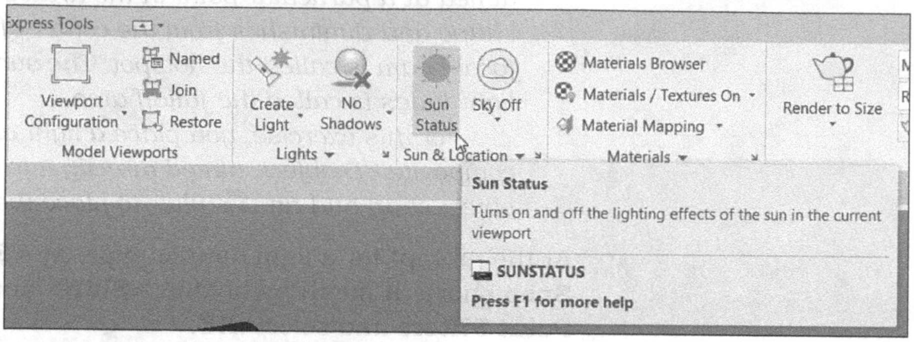

- ✔ Click **Keep Exposure Settings**.

  The shaded image brightens. Your model should resemble Figure 12-65. Sunlight can be edited to represent different locations, times of day, and dates. The default sunlight specification is 3:00 P.M. in your current city on the current date. You explore these settings later.

  Before adding another light, try rendering the object.
- ✔ Click the **Render** tool from the **Render Presets Manager**.

Figure 12-65
Shaded wedge

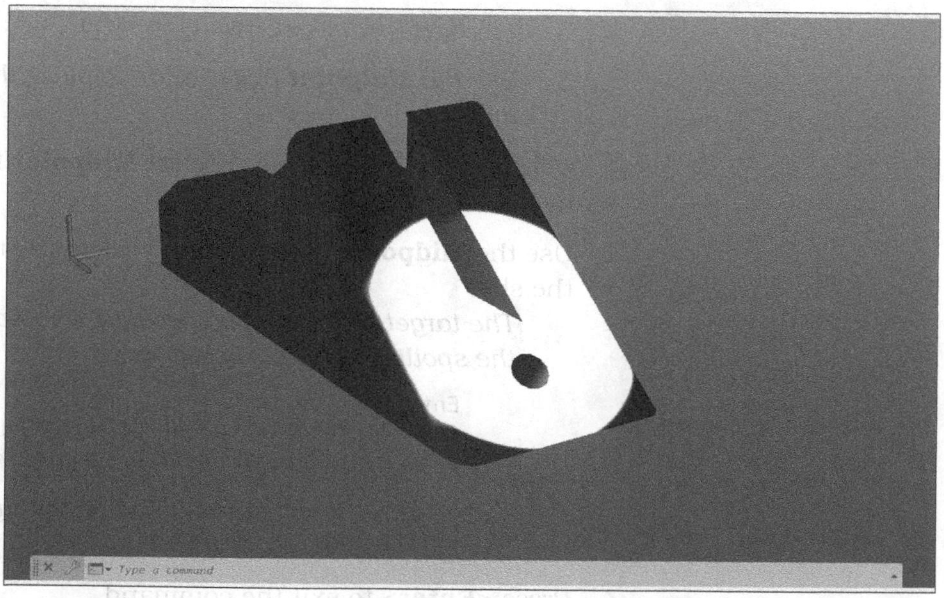

NOTE

Notice the small flashlight image that has been added to the drawing that indicates the placement of lights. This is called a ***glyph***, and its visibility can be turned on or off using the **Light Glyph Display** tool on the expanded **Lights** panel of the **Visualize** tab.

*In a few moments, the image in your render window should resemble Figure 12-66. Notice how the spotlight is treated more precisely in the rendered model. There are numerous ways to adjust the cone of light. You can adjust two settings to achieve the softer lighting effect shown in Figure 12-67—**Hotspot Angle** and **Intensity Factor**.*

Figure 12-66
Rendered spotlight

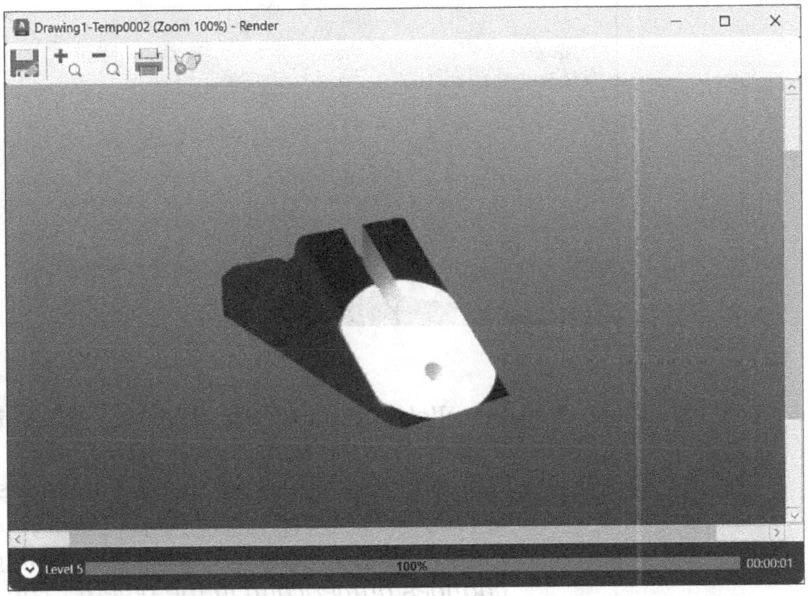

Figure 12-67
Softer lighting effects

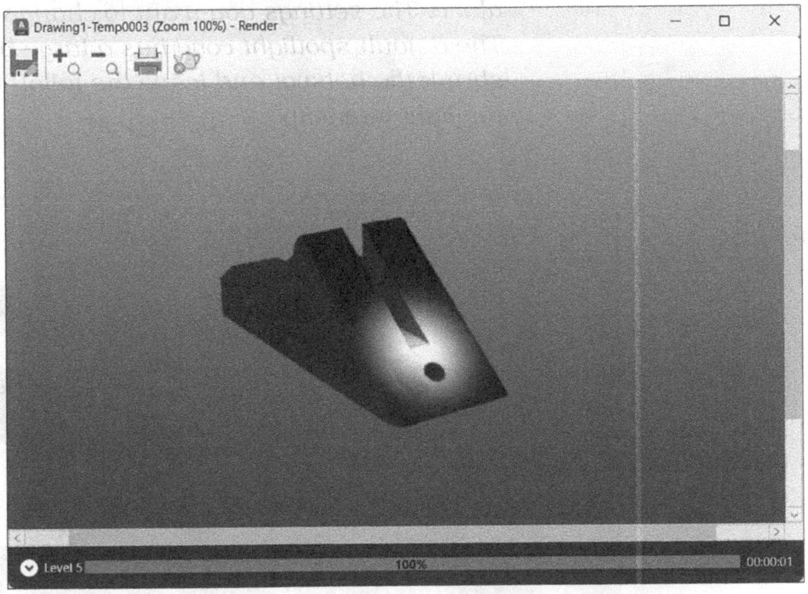

The Lights in Model Palette

The **Lights in Model** tool opens a palette in which you can easily select lights to change their characteristics. Here you open it to select the spotlight you previously added and change its hotspot angle and intensity settings.

- ✔ Close the render window and return to the drawing window.
- ✔ Click the arrow at the right of the **Lights** panel title bar on the **Visualize** tab, as shown in Figure 12-68.

Figure 12-68
Lights in Model tool

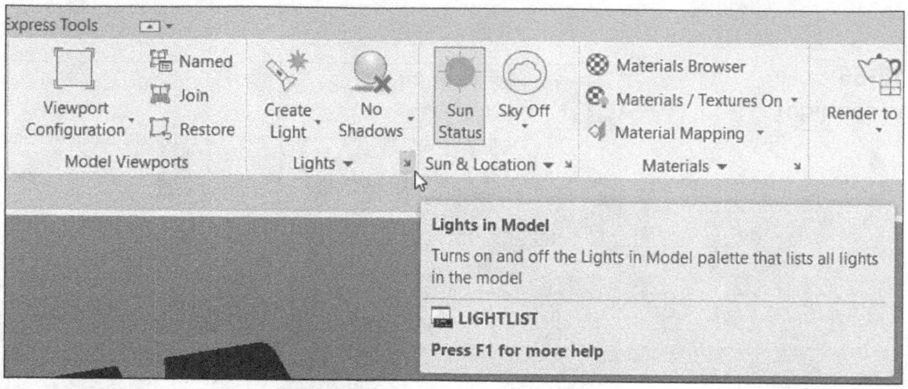

- ✔ Double-click the name **Spotlight1** in the **Lights in Model** palette.

  *This opens the light **Properties** palette, shown in Figure 12-69. It also shows the hotspot and falloff cones in the drawing area for the spotlight. With the cones displayed, you can adjust the light cones by dragging the grips. Rather than using grips, you will make the changes numerically in the palette. The first line of the palette gives you the opportunity to change the name, but for this exercise leave it alone. The settings you want to change are on lines four and six. The default spotlight cone has a large beam with a quick falloff. You shrink the hotspot and leave the falloff where it is. You also lessen the light intensity.*

Figure 12-69
Properties palette

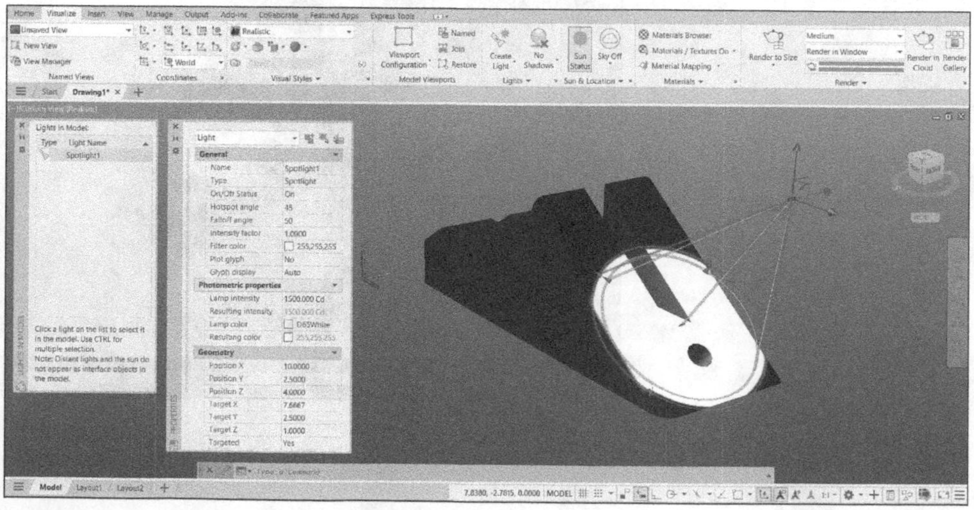

- ✔ Click once in the **Hotspot Angle** edit box.
- ✔ Change the **Hotspot Angle** value to **20** and press **<Enter>**.
  When you make this change, you can see the cone display adjust.
- ✔ Click once in the **Falloff Angle** edit box.
- ✔ Change the **Falloff Angle** value to **70** and press **<Enter>**.
- ✔ Click once in the **Intensity Factor** edit box.
- ✔ Change the **Intensity Factor** value to **0.05** and press **<Enter>**.
- ✔ Close the **Properties** palette.
- ✔ Close the **Lights in Model** palette.
- ✔ Click the **Render** tool.
  In a few moments, your drawing window should resemble Figure 12-67, shown previously. Next, you add a point light.
- ✔ Press **<Esc>**, or click the AutoCAD drawing on the Windows taskbar to return to the drawing.

Point Light

A point light works like a lightbulb with no shade. It radiates outward equally in all directions. The light from a point light is attenuated over distance.

You will place a point light inside the slot of the wedge. This clearly shows the lightbulb effect of a small point of light radiating outward.

- ✔ Click the **Point** tool from the **Create Light** drop-down menu on the **Lights** panel.
  For a point light, you need to specify only a source location because a point light has no direction other than outward from the source. A glyph is created and can be dragged to the source location for the light. The prompt displayed is

```
Specify source location <0,0,0>:
```

  You use typed coordinates to locate this light.

- ✔ At the prompt, type **4,2.5,1.5 <Enter>**.
  Because the slot is at 1.00 from the XY plane, this puts the point light just above the bottom of the slot. This time around, you use the dynamic input display to change the intensity. With point light, there is no hotspot or falloff.
  A familiar prompt is displayed for options to change. The same options are on the dynamic input display.

```
Enter option to change
[Name/Intensity factor/Status/Photometry/Hotspot/Falloff/
shadoW/Attenuation/filter Color/eXit] <eXit>:
```

- ✔ Select **Intensity Factor** from the dynamic input display.
- ✔ Type **.05 <Enter>** for the intensity level.
- ✔ Press **<Enter>** to complete the light specification.
  The effect of the point light appears immediately.

✔ Click the **Render** tool.

Your rendered model should resemble Figure 12-70. In this image, you can clearly see the effect of the point light within the slot along with the spotlight falling on the right side of the object.

Sunlight Editing

Sunlight editing is easy and produces dramatic changes. The arrow to the right of the title bar on the **Sun & Location** panel opens the **Sun Properties** palette, which allows you direct access to many sunlight settings. But even more accessible are the two sliders for date and time that are available when the **Sun & Location** is expanded, as shown in Figure 12-71. You begin by adjusting the time of day using the second slider.

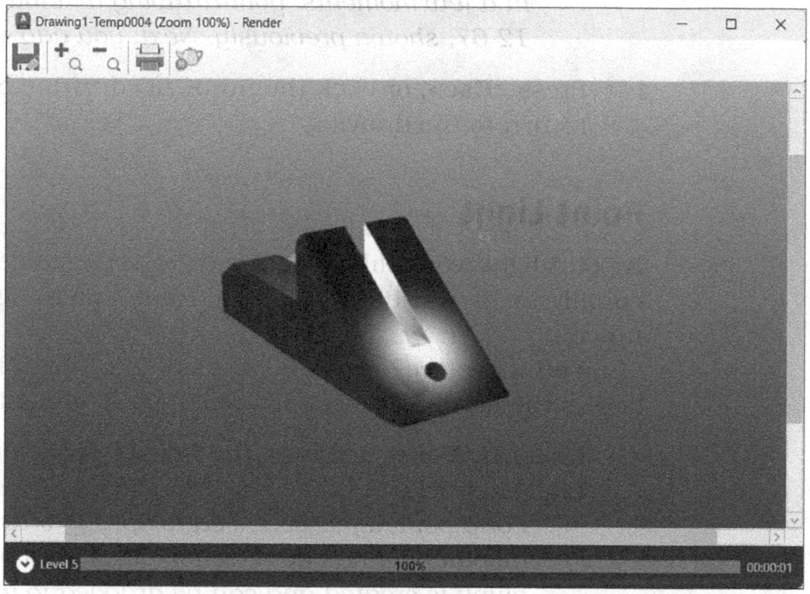

Figure 12-70
The effect of the point light

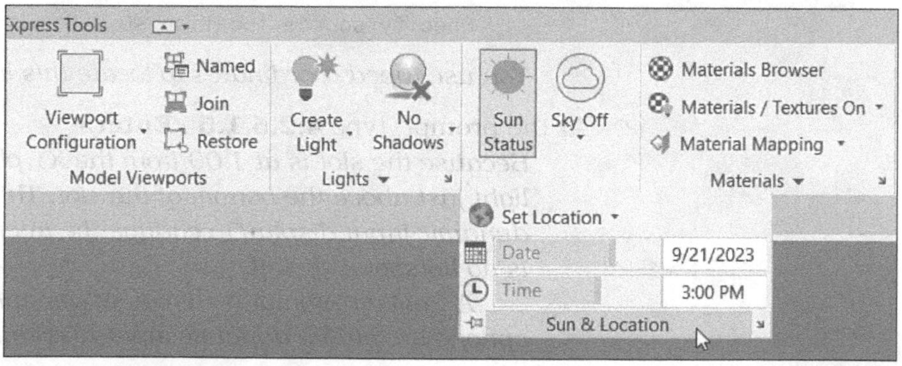

Figure 12-71
Sun & Location panel expanded

✔ Click the title bar of the **Sun & Location** panel to expand it.

✔ Move your cursor into the **Time** text box so that the two-way arrow labeled **SUNPROPERTIES** appears.

- ✔ Hold down the left mouse button and drag the two-way arrow cursor slowly left and right. Observe the effect.

  As you drag the cursor, let it rest here and there and observe the changes to the lighting in your model. As you can see, nighttime hours produce darkened results, whereas daylight hours produce a wide range of sunlit effects. As you drag the cursor, you see the change in lighting moving across the object, as in time-lapse photography.

- ✔ Hold down the left mouse button and move the cursor to the left to specify a time a few minutes past 10:00 A.M.
- ✔ While still holding the left mouse button, let the cursor rest over the **Time** text box and use the arrow keys on your keyboard to adjust the time to 10:00 A.M.
- ✔ Click the **Render** tool.

  The effect is significant, as shown in Figure 12-72.

  In addition to the ***Time*** *slider, there is a* ***Date*** *slider, which adjusts your lighting to replicate different dates in the year.*

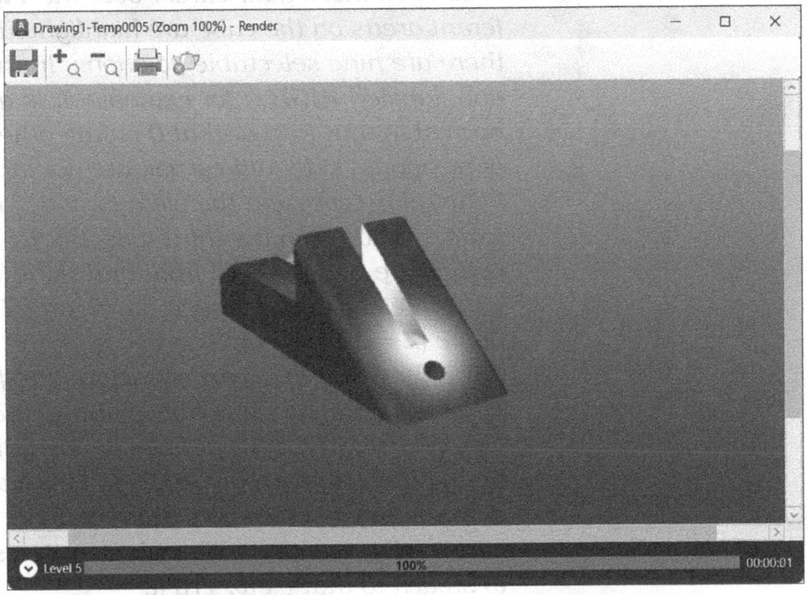

Figure 12-72
Sunlight edited

Geographic Location

Time and date will affect lighting differently at different points on the planet, so geographic information also affects the interpretation of lighting data. Clicking the **Set Location** tool (the globe at the top of the expanded **Sun & Location** panel) allows you to specify a geographic location. The tool opens a dialog box with two choices. First, you can open a map and find locations there. To access online maps, you sign in to your Autodesk account. Second, you can access information from a KML (Keyhole Markup Language) or KMZ (KML zipped) file. These are file formats used by Google Earth to display geographic data.

Changing Viewpoints with the ViewCube

You've probably been wondering about that cube in the upper-right corner of a drawing window. It has been mentioned before, but it is much more useful now that you know something about 3D viewpoints. This is the ***ViewCube*** shown in Figure 12-73. It is a very easy and logical way to change viewpoints in a 3D drawing. Once you understand what the cube represents, all you need do is click the cube area that represents the viewpoint you want to specify. In essence, this is the same cube represented by the **Preset Named Views** you encountered at the beginning of the chapter. The front of the cube corresponds to the front point of view, where you are looking in along the north–south *Y*-axis of your coordinate system. From this perspective, the *X*-axis is running left to right, east to west in front of you, and the *Z*-axis is running vertically, top to bottom. Relative to this position, the viewpoint you have been using throughout this chapter is up and to the right. With the front of the **ViewCube** facing you, it is represented by the upper-right corner.

ViewCube: In AutoCAD, an icon representing standard orthographic and isometric viewpoints used to change viewpoints in a 3D drawing or viewport.

Figure 12-73
ViewCube

✔ Move your cursor over the **ViewCube** without pressing the left mouse button.

*When you move your cursor over the **ViewCube**, you see that the different areas on the cube are highlighted as you go. On each face, there are nine selectable positions. In the middle is the face-on position, labeled **RIGHT**, for example. It is at some point along the axis normal to that face and at 0 on the other two axes. Two other types of positions, side and corner, are not labeled but can be selected. Four sides represent the view from 45° angles between each pair of axes, and 0° from the third axis. So, for example, the front right view is the side between the front and right faces of the cube, and represents a viewpoint between the X- and Y-axes but within the XY plane (Z = 0). The corners represent the isometric views, which are 45° off from all three axes, such as the front-right top view. The small image of a house above and to the left represents the home view, which AutoCAD defines as top-left front in the current drawing. This puts your point of view in the area of the origin of the coordinate system. Once you know how the cube represents coordinate space, all you need do is pick a corner, side, or face of the **ViewCube** to switch to that view. Try it.*

✔ Click the right face of the **ViewCube**, labeled with the word **RIGHT**.

Objects in your drawing aligned to put you at the "right" viewpoint, as shown in Figure 12-74.

✔ Click the edge to the left of the right face of the **ViewCube**.

Your viewpoint aligns to the front-right view shown in Figure 12-75.

✔ Click the front-right top corner of the cube to return to a front right top view.

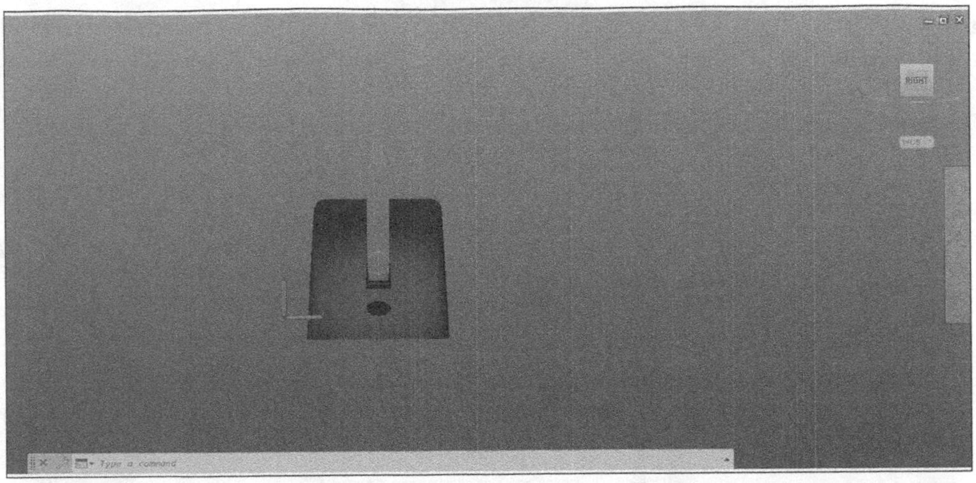

Figure 12-74
Right viewpoint

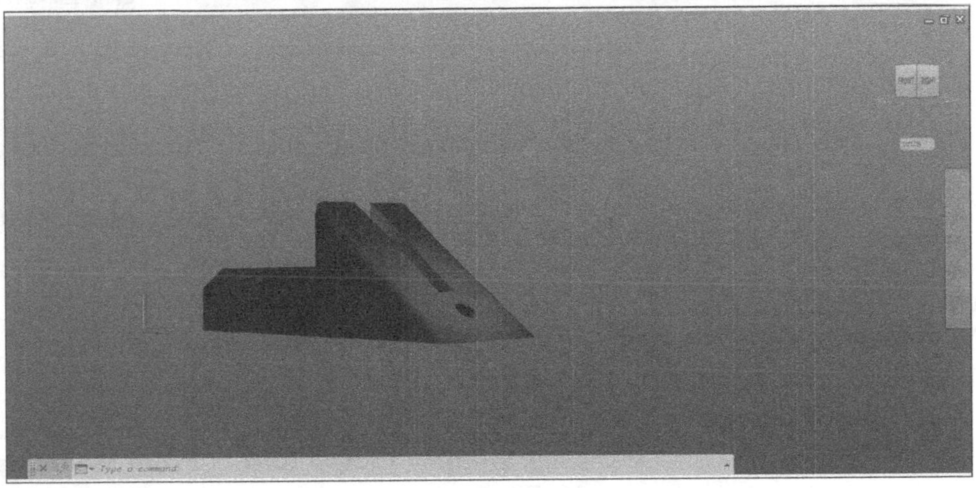

Figure 12-75
Front-right viewpoint

Creating Layouts with Multiple Views

You close this chapter on 3D modeling by creating a paper space layout with orthographic projections of the 3D model. This is an impressive and easy-to-use feature, demonstrating, once again, the power of solid modeling and the flexibility you have with the 3D model.

> **NOTE**
>
> The Model Documentation feature may need to be installed as you work through this exercise. If it needs to be installed, AutoCAD informs you that the feature isn't installed and displays a message box from which you can install it.

✔ To begin, you should have the composite 3D model in the current drawing.

You create a layout with two orthographic projections, one isometric projection, and one detail, as shown in Figure 12-76. This can be best accomplished by first switching to the **3D Modeling** workspace.

Figure 12-76
Creating a layout

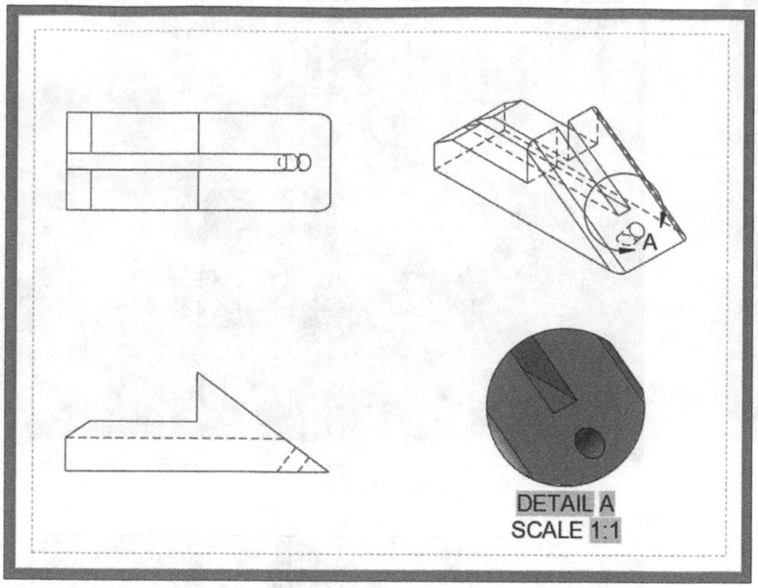

✔ Click the **Workspace** tool on the **status bar** and select **3D Modeling** from the list.

*The **3D Modeling** workspace is set current, as shown in Figure 12-77.*

Figure 12-77
3D Modeling workspace

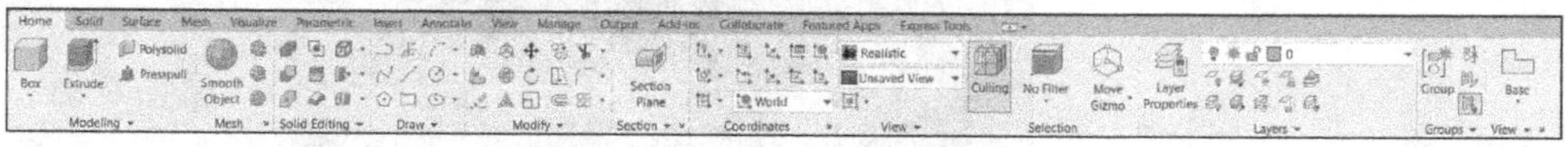

✔ Click **Home** > **View** > **Base** > **From Model Space**, as shown in Figure 12-78.

*Notice that this is the **View** panel at the right end of the ribbon, not the **View** tab. This initiates the **VIEWBASE** command and indicates that you will create the base view in the layout from the objects currently in model space. The other option is to create views from parts and assemblies modeled with Autodesk Inventor, Autodesk's specialized software for three-dimensional mechanical design. AutoCAD prompts:*

```
Select objects or [Entire model] <Entire model>:
```

Figure 12-78
Base View from Model Space

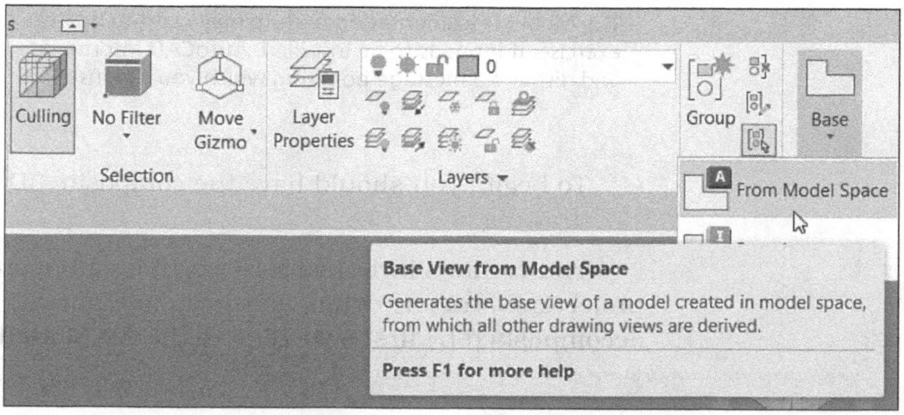

✔ Press **<Enter>** to select the entire model.

AutoCAD prompts for a layout name.

```
Enter new or existing layout name to make current or [?]
<Layout1>:
```

*For the purpose of this exercise, you can accept the default name, **Layout1**.*

✔ Press **<Enter>** to accept the default name for the new layout.

*The layout named **Layout1** is set to current, and a preview of the model is presented. As you drag the preview, position the first projection in the bottom left, as shown in Figure 12-74. The model is placed at (2.50,2.00). To facilitate this, press the F9 key to turn on **Snap Mode** on in the layout. Remember, there is no **Snap Mode** tool available on the status bar in paper space.*

✔ Press **<F9>** on your keyboard (**Fn** + **<F9>** on a laptop) to turn on **Snap Mode** *and* incremental snap.

✔ Move the cursor to position the view in the lower-left corner of the layout, as shown. Click the left mouse button to complete the placement of the projected view. Here, the view was placed at (2.50,2.00).

You are prompted with many options for manipulating your projection:

```
Select option [sElect/Orientation/Hidden lines/Scale/
Visibility/Move/eXit] <eXit>:
```

✔ Press **<Enter>** to exit this prompt.

You are presented with a second projection that can be dragged into place. If you stick to orthogonal directions, you get orthogonal projections. AutoCAD prompts:

```
Specify location of projected view or <exit>:
```

✔ Move the cursor directly upward to create the top view placement shown in Figure 12-79. Here, the view was placed at (2.50,6.00).

You continue to be prompted for view locations.

Figure 12-79
Shaded figures

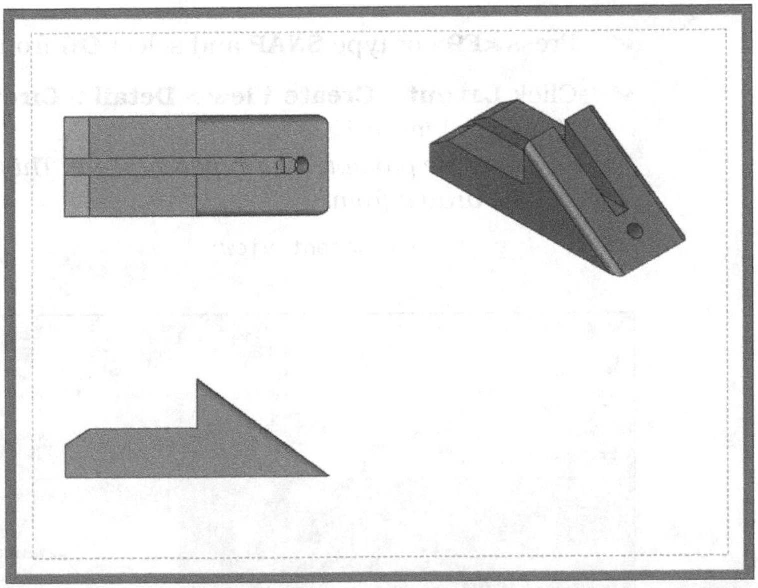

✔ Move the cursor to a position diagonally opposite the first view, as shown by the 3D view in Figure 12-79. Here, the view was placed at (8.00,6.00).

Notice that this diagonal placement creates an isometric projection. At this point, another orthogonal projection to the right could be created, but instead, you place a detail view in this area. To do this, you must leave the ***VIEWBASE*** *command.*

✔ Press **<Enter>** to exit the command.

The projections are adjusted to 2D wireframe images, as shown in Figure 12-80. The final step is to create the detail at the right, as shown previously in Figure 12-76. For this procedure, you want to turn on off ***Snap Mode*** *and make sure to use the* ***Midpoint*** *object snap.*

Figure 12-80
Wireframe figures

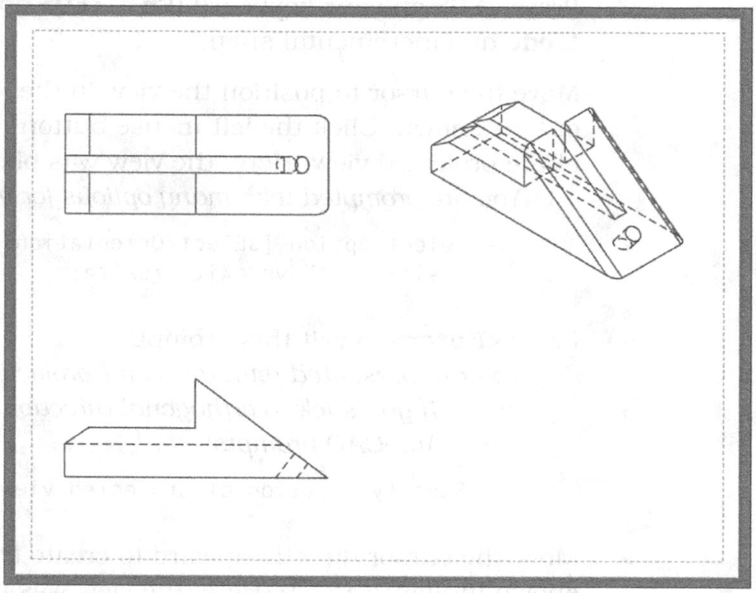

View Details

✔ Press **<F9>** or type **SNAP** and select **Off** from the command line.

✔ Click **Layout** > **Create View** > **Detail** > **Circular** from the ribbon, as shown in Figure 12-81.

You are prompted for a parent view. This is the view the detail will be drawn from.

```
Select parent view:
```

Figure 12-81
Circular Detail tool

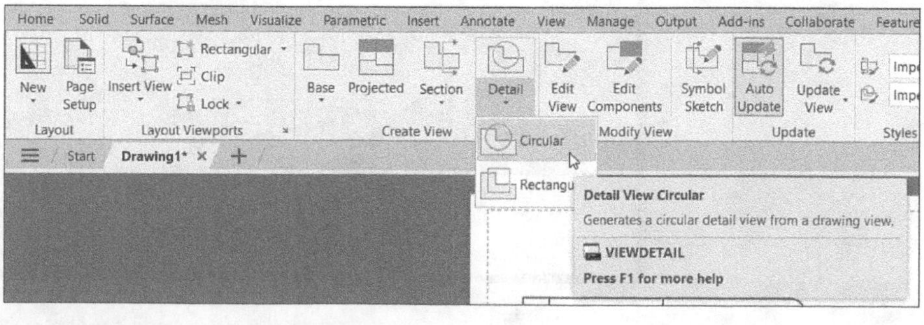

✔ Select the 3D isometric projection in the top-right.

Because you are creating a detail with a circular border, you are prompted for a center point.

✔ Make sure that running **Object Snap** mode is off for the remainder of this exercise.

✔ Hold **<Shift> + right-click** and select **Midpoint** from the shortcut menu.

✔ Carefully select the midpoint of the edge at the bottom front of the slot.

You are prompted for the size of the boundary.

```
Specify size of boundary or [Rectangular/Undo]:
```

This is the radius of the circle surrounding the detail. There are other options here that may be specified before or after you size the boundary. You can drag out the circle or enter a radius value.

✔ Type **.6 <Enter>** for the circular boundary radius.

You are prompted for a location:

```
Specify location of detail.
```

Here again, the prompt includes many of the same options included in the previous prompt.

✔ Specify a location point similar to the one in Figure 12-76. Turn **Snap Mode** on and specify (**7.00,2.50**).

At this point, you could exit the command, and the detail using the same wireframe presentation as the parent view would be drawn. Instead, you will specify a shaded presentation.

✔ Select **Hidden Lines** from the dynamic input display or the command line.

This provides a further set of options:

```
Select style [Visible lines/vIsible and hidden lines/Shaded
with visible lines/sHaded with visible and hidden lines/From
parent] <From parent>:
```

✔ Select **Shaded with Visible Lines** from the dynamic input display or the command line.

AutoCAD returns the same set of options so that you can continue to modify your detail.

✔ Press **<Enter>** to exit the command.

✔ Select the label below the detail and use the square grip to reposition the MText object.

Your drawing should resemble Figure 12-76, as shown previously, with the three views and the detail and callout.

12 chapter twelve

Chapter Summary

In this chapter, you learned a whole new way of creating designs with AutoCAD. You learned to manipulate coordinate systems so that you can create user-defined coordinate systems at any point and any orientation in space. You learned to use dynamic coordinate systems that AutoCAD creates automatically while drawing 3D wireframe and solid models, and to draw and edit on the different planes of these models. You saw how you can easily switch among different visual styles for representing 3D objects in your models. You learned a whole new set of constructive geometry concepts and techniques for creating objects by combining solid primitives in union, subtraction, and intersection procedures. You learned to modify solid objects using familiar editing tools, 3D variations of these tools, and other tools, such as 3D gizmos, that have no counterpart in two dimensions. You used powerful lighting and rendering features to produce realistic 3D shaded models. You learned to change points of view with the **ViewCube** and create base views from a 3D model on named layouts.

Chapter Test Questions

Multiple Choice

Circle the correct answer.

1. In a southwest isometric viewpoint, objects are viewed from a point where

   a. *x* is positive, *y* is positive, *z* is positive.

   b. *x* is negative, *y* is negative, *z* is positive.

   c. *x* is negative, *y* is positive, *z* is negative.

   d. *x* is positive, *y* is negative, *z* is positive.

2. The point (3,3,3) **cannot** be specified by

   a. Typing　　c. Pointing

   b. Point filters　　d. Object snap

3. 3D gizmos are **not** used to

   a. Move solids　　c. Scale solids

   b. Rotate solids　　d. Stretch solids

4. Attaching materials to solids is accomplished through the

   a. **ATTACH** command　　**c. Materials Manager**

   b. **Materials Browser**　　d. **Materials** dialog box

5. The west face of the **ViewCube** is labeled

   a. Left　　c. Front

   b. West　　d. Back

Matching

Write the number of the correct answer on the line.

a. Conceptual _____
b. UCS _____
c. Solid modeling _____
d. Rotate intersection _____
e. Intersection _____

1. Gizmo
2. World
3. Constructive solid geometry
4. Boolean operation
5. Visual style

True or False

Circle the correct answer.

1. **True or False:** The world coordinate system can be rotated.
2. **True or False:** In the standard 3D UCS icon, the *Z*-axis is red.
3. **True or False:** In the acad3D template, the grid is presented in perspective projection.
4. **True or False:** 3D fillets can be created with the same command as 2D fillets.
5. **True or False:** In order to create the union of two solid objects, the objects must overlap.

Questions

1. What 3D solid objects and commands would you use to create a square nut with a bolt hole in the middle?
2. Describe the effects of union, subtraction, and intersection.
3. When is it important to use an object snap to rotate the UCS icon to establish a new coordinate system?
4. How would you use a point filter to place a spotlight 5.0 units above the point (3,5,0)?
5. What are the shapes and qualities of spotlights and point lights?

Drawing Problems

1. Create a new drawing from the acad3D template and change the snap setting to **0.25**. Zoom in as needed.
2. Draw a solid wedge, with a 5.0 × 5.0 unit base and a height of 2.5.
3. Draw a 3.0 × 3.0 box with a height of 2.0, normal to the angled face of the wedge, with the front-left corner in 1.0 and over 1.0 from the two edges of the face of the wedge.
4. Draw a 0.75-radius cylinder with its base aligned and centered at the center of the right-front face of the box drawn in Step 3. This cylinder should have a height of 7.0 extending back through the box in the negative *Z* direction of the DUCS aligned with the right front face of the box.
5. Draw a 0.50-radius cylinder with the same alignment and center point. This cylinder should have a height of 10.0 units extending in the same direction as the first cylinder.
6. Draw a 0.25-radius cylinder with height 13.0. Align and center it with the previous two cylinders.

12 chaptertwelve

Chapter Drawing Projects

M Drawing 12-1: *Flange* [INTERMEDIATE]

You begin with three 3D models for this chapter. They will give you a feel for this whole new way of putting objects together on the screen. Look the objects over and consider what primitive shapes and Boolean processes will be required to complete the models. In each case, the finished drawing is the 3D model itself. The orthographic views are presented to give the information you need to draw the solid models correctly. They may be included as part of your completed drawing, or your instructor may prefer that you just complete the model.

Drawing Suggestions

- You can complete this drawing with two commands.
- Begin with the bottom of the flange in the *XY* plane and draw three cylinders, all with the same center point and different heights.
- Draw four 0.500-diameter holes on the quadrants of a 3.5 circle around the same center point.
- Subtract the middle cylinder and the four small cylinders to create the completed model.

Drawing 12-1
Flange

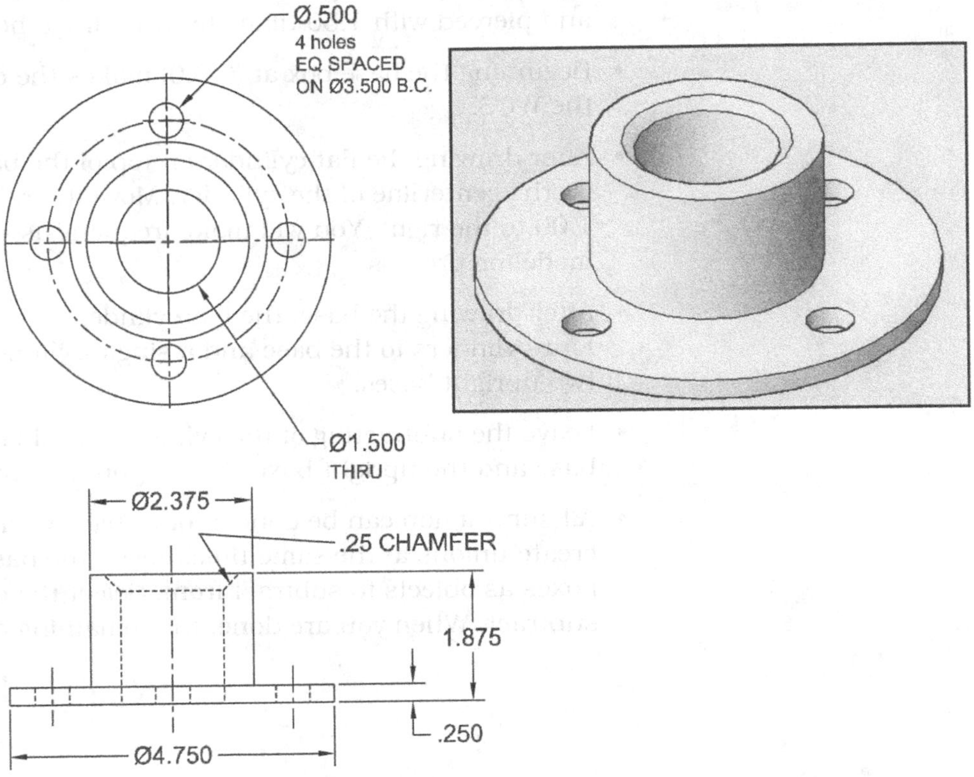

M Drawing 12-2: *Link Mount* [ADVANCED]

This drawing is very manageable with the techniques you learned in this chapter. When you have finished drawing this 3D model, you may want to experiment with adding materials, lights, and changing point of view.

Drawing Suggestions

- You will need a 0.25 snap for this drawing.
- Before you begin, notice what the model consists of, and think ahead to how it will be constructed. You have a filleted 8 × 8 box at the base, with four cylindrical holes. A flat cylinder sits on top of this at the center. On top of the cylinder, you have two upright boxes, filleted across the top and pierced with 1.50-diameter cylindrical holes.
- Beginning the base box at (0,0,0) makes the coordinates easy to read in the WCS.
- After drawing the flat cylinder on top of the base, draw one upright box on the centerline of the cylinder. Move it 0.5 left, and then make a copy 1.00 to the right. You will make frequent use of DUCS throughout the modeling process.
- After drawing the base, the flat cylinder, and the upright boxes, add the four cylinders to the base and a single cylinder through the middle of the two upright boxes.
- Leave the subtracting of the cylinders until last. In particular, fillet the base and the upright boxes before you do any subtraction.
- All subtraction can be done in one step. When you do this, you will also create unions at the same time. Select the base, flat cylinder, and upright boxes as objects to subtract from. Select the other cylinders as objects to subtract. When you are done, the remaining object will be a single object.

Drawing 12-2
Link mount

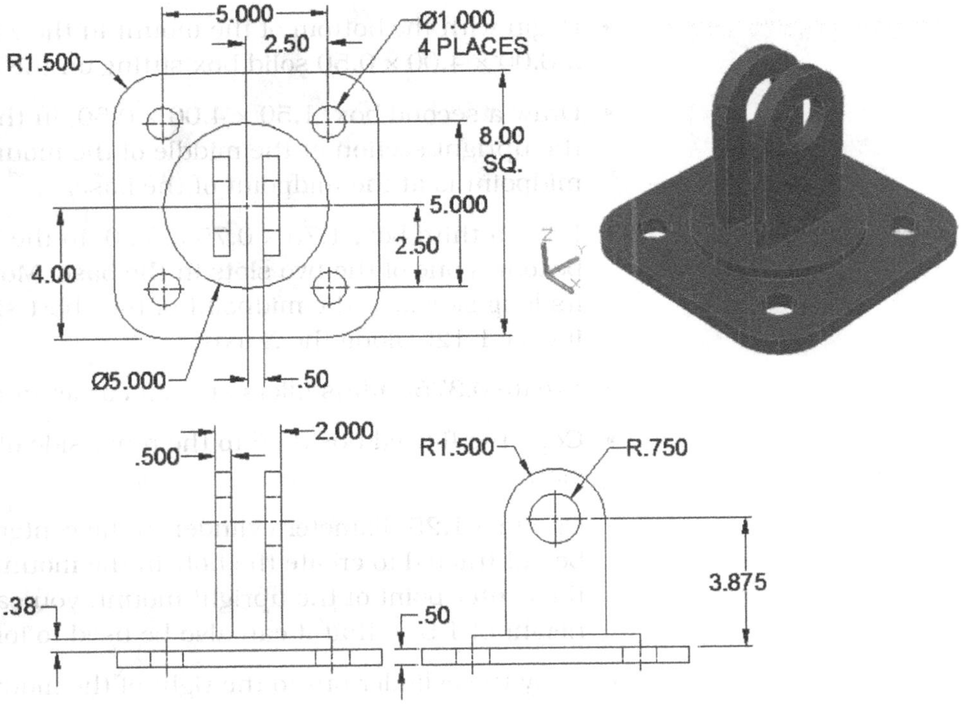

M Drawing 12-3: *Bushing Mount* [ADVANCED]

This drawing gives you more practice in the techniques used in Drawing 12-2. The addition of the bushing is a primary difference. Although the geometry of the bushing can be used to create the hole in the mount, the mount and the bushing should be created and retained as separate objects. Use an efficient sequence in the construction of all composite solids. In general, this means saving union, subtraction, and intersection operations until most of the solid objects have been drawn and positioned. This approach also allows you to continue to use the geometry of the parts for snap points as you position other parts.

Drawing Suggestions

- Begin with the bottom of the mount in the *XY* plane. This means drawing a 6.00 × 4.00 × 0.50 solid box sitting on the *XY* plane.
- Draw a second box, 1.50 × 4.00 × 0.50, in the *XY* plane. This becomes the upright section at the middle of the mount. Move it so that its own midpoint is at the midpoint of the base.
- Draw a third box, 1.75 × 0.75 × 0.50, in the *XY* plane. This is copied and becomes one of the two slots in the base. Move it so that the midpoint of its long side is at the midpoint of the short side of the base. Then, move it over 1.125 along the *X*-axis.
- Create 0.375-radius fillets at each corner of the slot.
- Copy the filleted box 3.75 to the other side of the base to form the other slot.
- Create a 1.25-diameter cylinder in the center of the mount, where it can be subtracted to create the hole in the mount upright. Using DUCS at the center point of the upright mount, you can draw this cylinder with a height of 1.5 so that it can also be used to form the bushing.
- Copy the cylinder out to the right of the mount directly along the center-line of the mount.
- Draw a second cylinder to form the top of the bushing.
- Draw a 0.375 cylinder through the center of the bushing.
- Subtract the 0.375 cylinder from the bushing to create the hole in the center.
- Subtract the boxes and cylinders to form the slots in the base and the bushing-sized cylinder to form the hole in the mount.

Drawing 12-3
Bushing mount

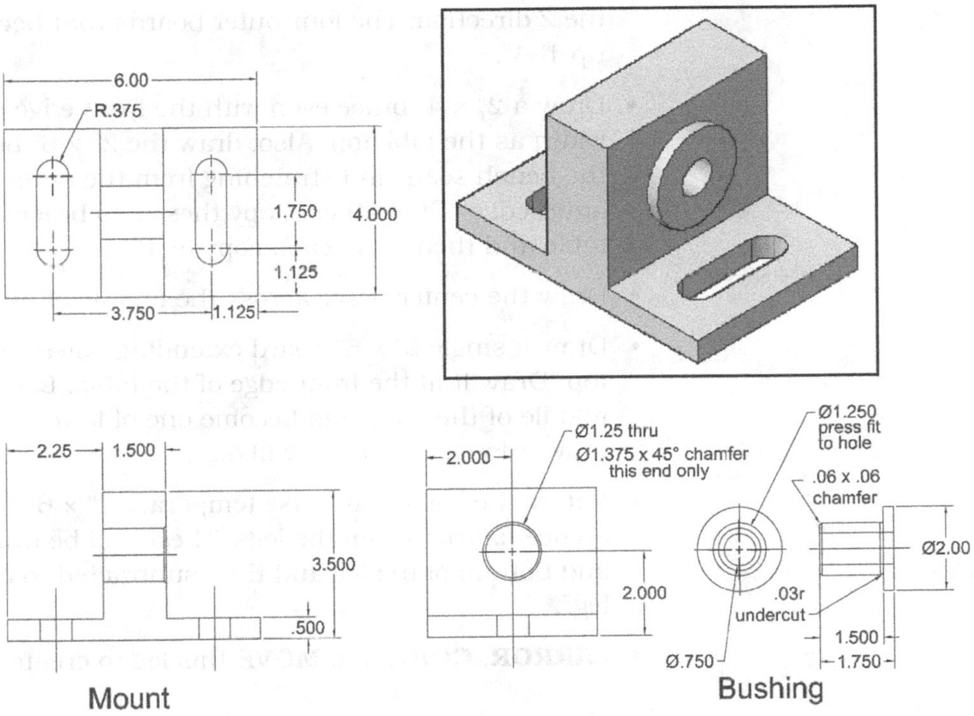

A A Drawing 12-4: *Picnic Table* [ADVANCED]

This drawing is quite different from the previous three. It can be a challenge getting the legs correctly angled and in place. Still, you will find that everything here can be done with techniques learned in this chapter.

Drawing Suggestions

- It is recommended to start with the *XY* plane at the bottom of the table legs and move everything up into the *Z* direction. First, draw nine 2" × 6" boards, 8' long. You can draw one board and array the rest 1" apart.
- The five middle boards that become the tabletop can be copied up 2'-4" in the *Z* direction. The four outer boards that become the bench seats move up 1'-4".
- Draw a 2" × 4" brace even with the front edge of the table and the same width as the tabletop. Also, draw the 2" × 6" board even with the front of the bench seats and stretching from the outer edge of one seat to the outer edge of the other. Copy these two braces to the other end of the table and then move each copy in 1'.
- Draw the center brace across the middle of the five tabletop boards.
- Draw a single 2" × 6" board extending down perpendicular to the tabletop. Draw it at the front edge of the table. Later, this will be moved to the middle of the table and become one of four legs. It will be trimmed, so draw it long: 3' or more will do.
- Rotate the leg 30° and use temporary 2" × 6" blocks as shown in the reference figure to trim the legs. These will be drawn overlapping the top and bottom of the leg and then subtracted to create the correctly angled leg.
- **MIRROR**, **COPY**, and **MOVE** this leg to create the four table legs.

Drawing 12-4
Picnic table

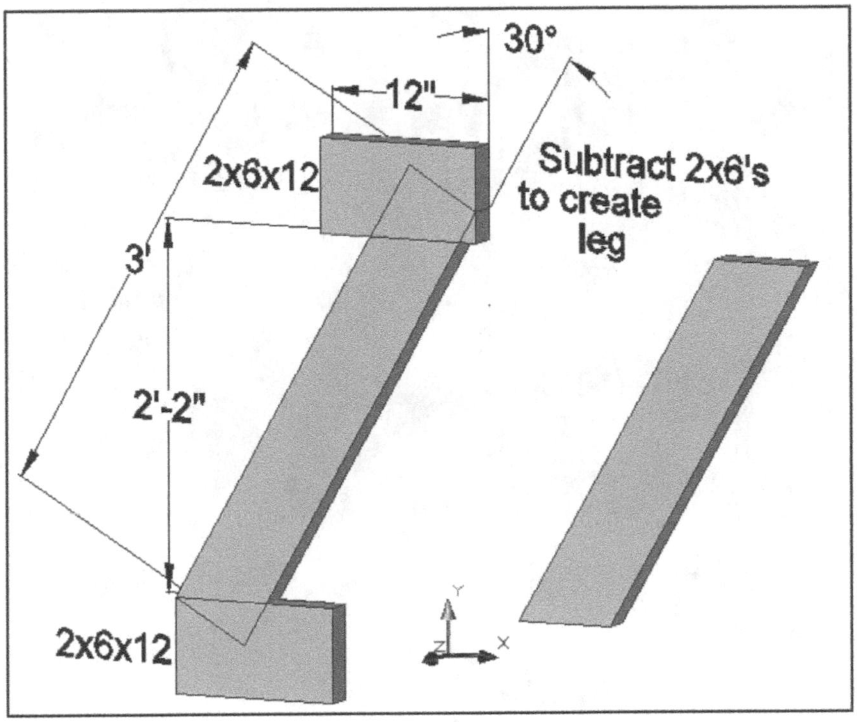

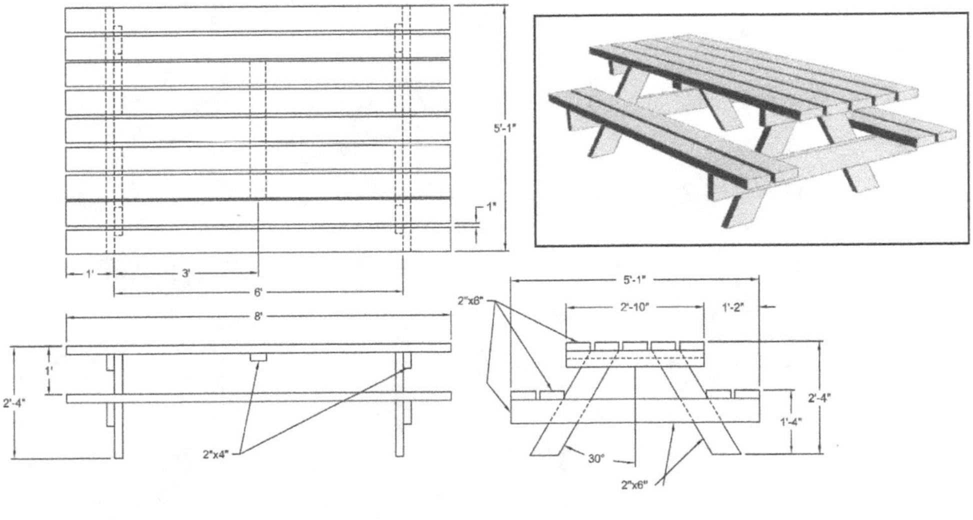

chapter thirteen

More Modeling Techniques and Commands

CHAPTER OBJECTIVES

- Draw polysolids
- Draw cones
- Draw pyramids
- Draw torus
- Slice and section solids
- Perform mesh modeling
- Adjust viewpoints with **3DORBIT**
- Create 3D solids from 2D outlines
- Walk through a 3D landscape
- Create an animated walk-through

Introduction

In addition to the primary methods involved in 3D solid modeling, AutoCAD has numerous other commands and techniques that facilitate the creation of particular 3D shapes. These include commands that produce regular 3D solid primitives, such as cones and spheres, commands that allow you to create 3D objects by revolving or extruding 2D outlines of 3D objects, and commands that create mesh models that can be shaped in ways that solids cannot. The addition of these techniques will make it possible for you to create all kinds of 3D models you cannot create with solid primitives. As you explore these new possibilities, you will also use the **3D Modeling** workspace.

POLYSOLID	
Command	POLYSOLID
Alias	(none)
Panel	Modeling
Tool	

polysolid: A 3D entity similar to a 2D polyline but with the dimension of height added along with width and length.

Drawing Polysolids

Most of this chapter is devoted to introducing commands for drawing shapes other than boxes, wedges, and cylinders. Some are created as simple solid primitives; others are derived from previously drawn meshes, lines, or curves. In this first section, you draw a ***polysolid***. Polysolids are drawn just like 2D polylines, but they have a height as well as a width. Like polylines, they can have both straight and curved segments. Those you create will include both.

✔ Create a new drawing using the acad3D.dwt drawing template file.

✔ Click the **Workspace** list on the status bar, and select **3D Modeling** from the list, if necessary.

Drawing in Multiple Tiled Viewports

tiled viewports: Viewports that cover the drawing area and do not overlap. Tiled viewports may show objects from different points of view, but are not plotted.

A major feature needed to draw effectively in 3D is the ability to view objects from several different points of view simultaneously as you work on them. Here, you create a three-viewport configuration so that you can see what is happening from different viewpoints simultaneously. If you do not continually examine 3D objects from different points of view, it is easy to create entities that appear correct in the current view but are clearly incorrect from other points of view. As you work, remember that these viewports are simple model space ***tiled viewports***. Tiled viewports cover the complete drawing area, do not overlap, and cannot be plotted simultaneously. Plotting multiple viewports is accomplished in paper space layouts with floating viewports.

✔ Click **Visualize** > **Model Viewports** > **Viewport Configuration** > **Three: Right**, as shown in Figure 13-1.

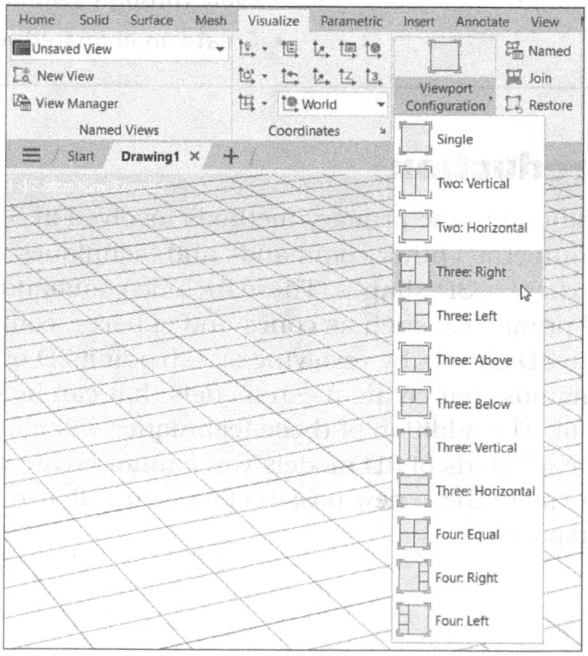

Figure 13-1
Viewport Configuration drop-down menu

You now see three viewports, as shown in Figure 13-2. Each viewport displays the same 3D point of view, as you can verify by clicking in each viewport in succession to make it active. You find that all three show the same viewpoint, but only the active viewport shows the model, the navigation bar, the viewport label, and the USC icon. You alter each viewport to achieve the views you want to work in. For this you use the Named Views drop-down list shown in Figure 13-3.

Notice also the very small gray sliders in the middle of each viewport border. These can be used to adjust the boundaries among the three viewports. Try it if you like. By clicking one of these sliders, you can move the border line horizontally or vertically between any two adjacent viewports.

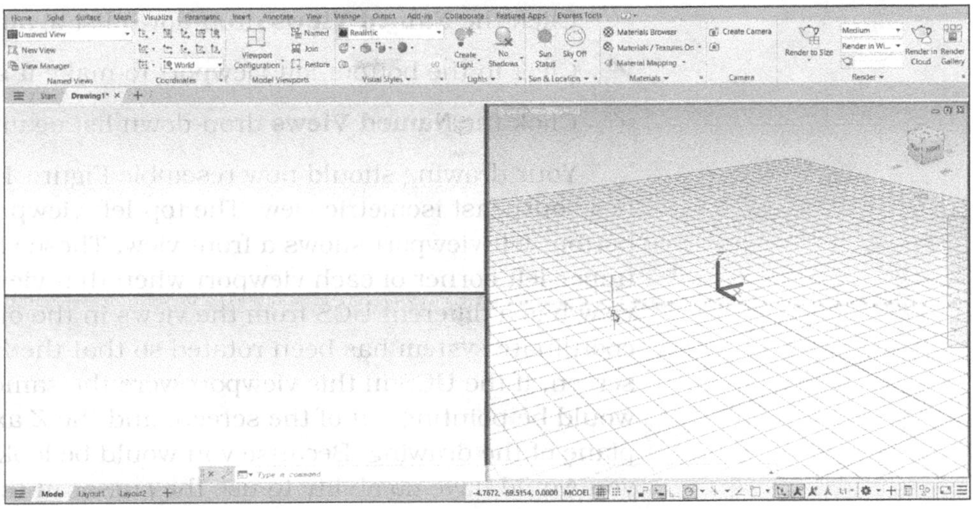

Figure 13-2
Three: Right viewport configuration

- ✔ Make sure that the right, 3D viewport is the active viewport, which it should be by default.
- ✔ Click **Visualize** > **Named Views** > **SE Isometric**, as shown in Figure 13-3.

  AutoCAD changes to a higher angle as shown in the right viewport in Figure 13-4.

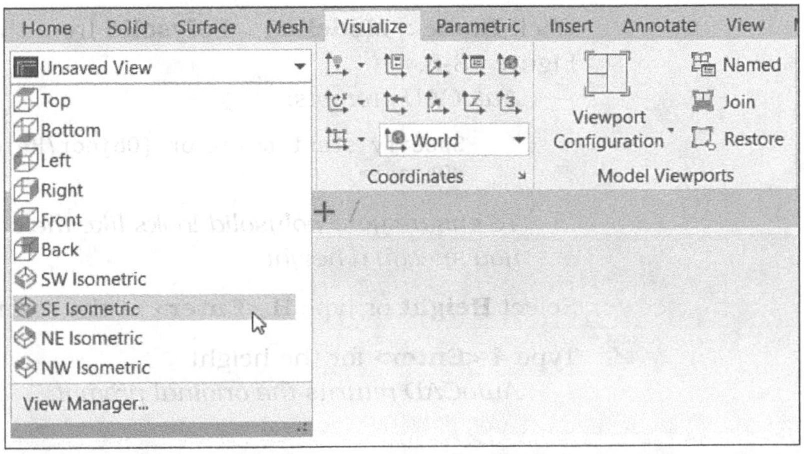

Figure 13-3
Named Views drop-down list

Figure 13-4
Adjusted viewports

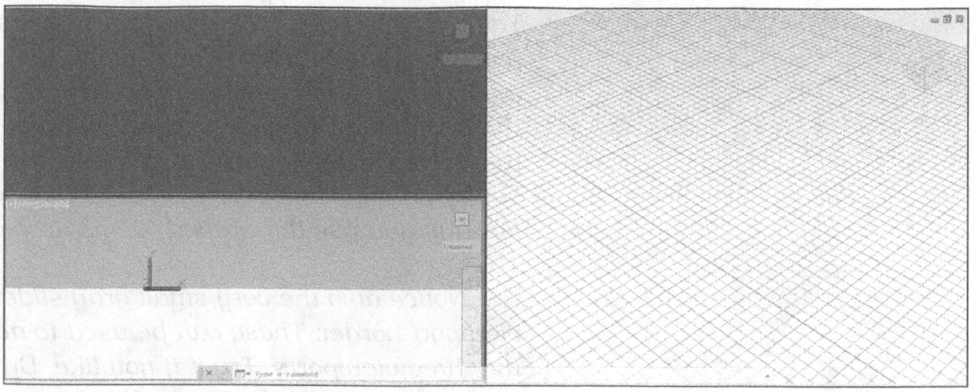

- ✔ Click in the top-left viewport to make it active.
- ✔ Click the **Named Views** drop-down list again and select **Top**.
- ✔ Click in the bottom-left viewport to make it active.
- ✔ Click the **Named Views** drop-down list again and select **Front**.

Your drawing should now resemble Figure 13-4. The view on the right is a southeast isometric view. The top-left viewport is a plan view, and the bottom-left viewport shows a front view. These viewpoints are labeled in the upper-left corner of each viewport when that viewport is active. The front view has a different UCS from the views in the other two viewports. The coordinate system has been rotated so that the *Z*-axis still points out of the screen. If the UCS in this viewport were the same as the others, the *Y*-axis would be pointing out of the screen, and the *Z*-axis would be vertical in the plane of the drawing. Because you would be looking in along the *XY* plane, you would have no ability to use the cursor in this viewport. Still, the change in color in this viewport shows the horizon in the world coordinate system even though the axes are rotated 90°.

- ✔ Click in the right viewport to make it active.
- ✔ Turn on **Snap Mode** and **Ortho Mode**.

  You are now ready to begin drawing in this viewport configuration. Once you have defined viewports, any drawing or editing in the active viewport appears in all the viewports. As you draw, watch what happens in all viewports. You may need to zoom out or pan to get full views in each viewport.

- ✔ Click **Home** > **Modeling** > **Polysolid** from the ribbon, as shown in Figure 13-5.

  AutoCAD prompts:

  ```
  Specify start point or [Object/Height/Width/Justify]
  <Object>:
  ```

  To ensure your polysolid looks like the one shown in Figure 13-6, you specify a height.

- ✔ Select **Height** or type **H <Enter>** at the command line.
- ✔ Type **4 <Enter>** for the height.

  AutoCAD returns the original prompt.

Figure 13-5
Polysolid tool

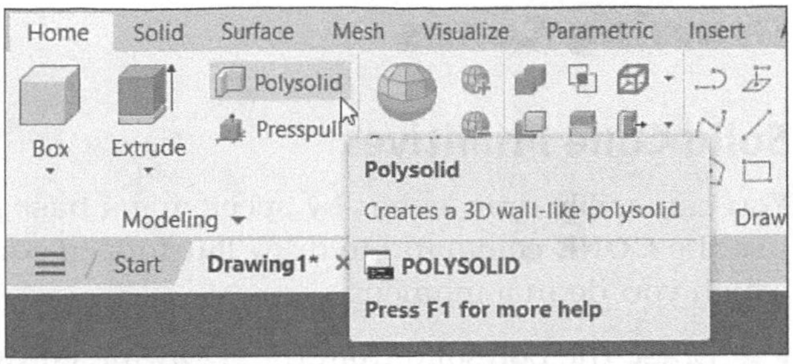

✔ Specify point **(2.5,2.5,0)** for a start point.

AutoCAD shows you a polysolid to drag. It appears like a wall in the 3D viewport and can be stretched out, like drawing a line segment. With **Ortho** *on, it stretches only orthogonally. AutoCAD prompts for the next point.*

✔ Specify the point **(10,2.5,0)** for the next point.

Notice that this makes this segment 7.5 units long. From here, you could continue to draw straight segments, but you switch to an arc.

✔ Right-click and select **Arc** from the shortcut menu.

AutoCAD shows an arc segment and prompts for an endpoint. With **Ortho** *on, you can stretch in only two directions.*

✔ Specify the point **(10,8,0)** for the arc endpoint.

Now, you switch back to drawing line segments.

✔ Right-click and select **Line** from the shortcut menu.

AutoCAD shows a straight segment beginning at the endpoint of the arc and prompts for a next point.

✔ Specify the point **(2.5,8,0)** for the next point. Again this is a length of 7.5 units.

Finally, you switch to arc again and then use the **Close** *option to complete the polysolid.*

✔ Right-click and select **Arc** from the shortcut menu.

✔ Select **Close** or type **c <Enter>** at the command line to close the polysolid.

Your drawing should resemble Figure 13-6.

Figure 13-6
Polysolid

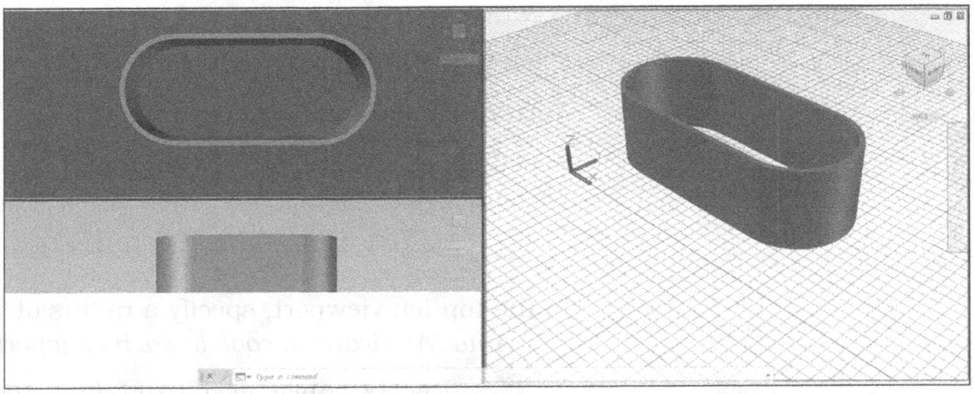

Drawing Cones

CONE	
Command	CONE
Alias	(none)
Panel	Modeling
Tool	

frustum cone: A cone that does not rise to a point. It has a bottom radius and a top radius and is therefore flat-topped.

Solid Cone Primitives

You can easily draw cones by specifying a base and a height. You can also use the **CONE** command to draw flat-topped cones, called ***frustum cones***, which you do in a moment.

✔ Erase the polysolid from the "Drawing Polysolids" section.

✔ Click the **Cone** tool from the **Solid Primitives** drop-down menu on the **Modeling** panel of the **Home** tab, as shown in Figure 13-7.

Notice that this is the same drop-down menu as in the ***3D Basics*** *workspace. AutoCAD prompts:*

```
Specify center point of base or [3P/2P/Ttr/Elliptical]:
```

Notice the other options, including the option to create cones with elliptical bases.

You can specify the base in either the top viewport or the right viewport. Using the top viewport gives you a better view of the base and its coordinates.

Figure 13-7
Cone tool

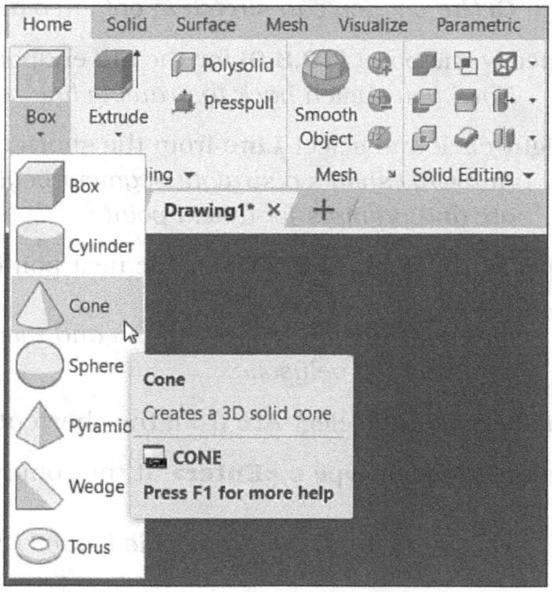

✔ Click in the top-left viewport to make it active.

✔ Turn on **Snap Mode** in this viewport.

✔ Specify point **(5,5,0)** for the center of the cone base.

AutoCAD prompts:

```
Specify base radius or [Diameter] <0.0000>:
```

✔ In the top-left viewport, specify a radius of **2**.

AutoCAD draws a cone in each viewport and prompts for a height:

```
Specify height or [2Point/Axis endpoint/Top radius]
<0.0000>:
```

- Move the cursor and observe the cones in each viewport.

  If you look carefully, you will notice that the cone in the top viewport appears to tilt slightly to the left. This viewport is drawn in perspective projection. The tilt effect is a result of perspective projection. The other viewports show that there is no actual tilt. The perspective projection can cause some problems in plan views such as the upper-left viewport. You fix this later in the "Drawing Torus" section.

- Specify a point to indicate a height of **4**.

  The cone is complete, and your drawing should resemble Figure 13-8.

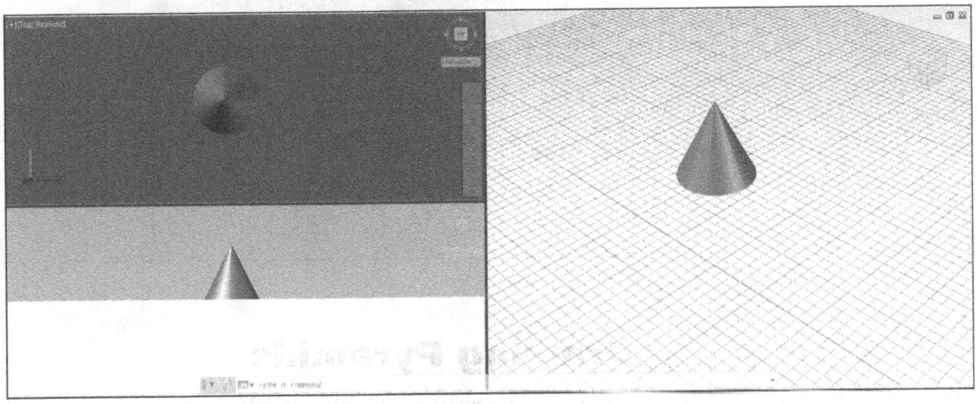

Figure 13-8
Cone

Frustum Cones

Next, you create a cone with a negative *z* height and a different top radius. Cones with different top and bottom radii (that do not rise to a point) are called *frustum cones.*

- Click the **Cone** tool from the **Modeling** panel on the **Home** tab.
- In the top-left viewport, specify the point **(10,5,0)** for the base center.
- As before, specify a radius of **2**.

  Move the cursor and observe the cones in each viewport. You want to create a cone that drops below the XY plane. Notice that you cannot do this in the active top view.

- Click in the right viewport to make it active.
- Drag the cone downward and notice the effects in the right viewport.

  You also want this cone to have a flat top, so you need to specify this before specifying the height.

- Right-click and select **Top radius** from the shortcut menu.

  AutoCAD prompts:

  ```
  Specify top radius <0.0000>:
  ```

  Move the cursor again to see the range of possibilities. You can create anything, from a very large, wide, flat cone to a long, narrow one. The top radius can be larger or smaller than the base radius. Also, the top can be below the base.

✔ Type **5 <Enter>** for a top radius.

AutoCAD prompts again for a height.

✔ Make sure the right viewport is showing the cone in the negative direction, and type **8 <Enter>** for a height.

Your drawing should resemble Figure 13-9. You may need to pan in the viewport to completely see both cones.

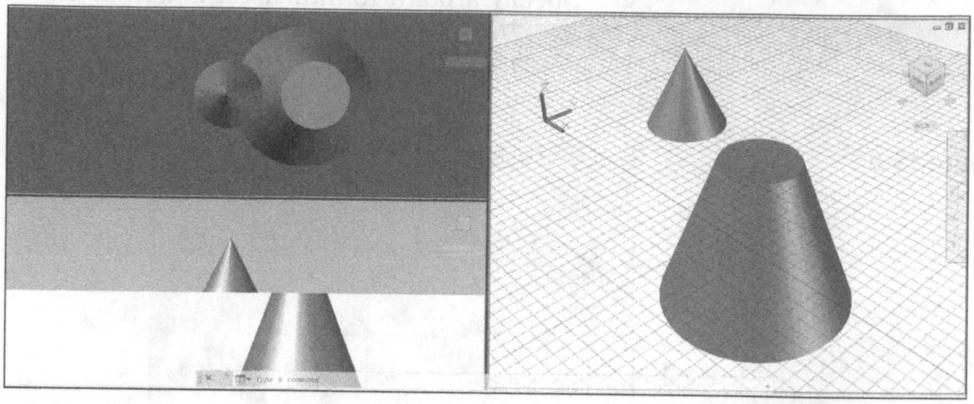

Figure 13-9
Frustum cone with negative *z* height

Drawing Pyramids

PYRAMID	
Command	PYRAMID
Alias	Pyr
Panel	Modeling
Tool	

Drawing pyramids is much like drawing cones. Instead of a circular base, pyramids have polygons at the base and possibly at the top. The process for drawing the base polygon is similar to using the **POLYGON** command.

✔ Click the **Pyramid** tool from the **Solid Primitives** drop-down menu on the **Modeling** panel on the **Home** tab.

AutoCAD prompts:

```
Specify center point of base or [Edge/Sides]:
```

The default is a four-sided base. Here, you specify six sides.

✔ Right-click and select **Sides** from the shortcut menu, or select **Sides** from the command line.

AutoCAD prompts for the number of sides.

✔ Type **6 <Enter>**.

AutoCAD takes this information and repeats the initial prompt. If you specify a center point, it then prompts for the radius to the midpoint of a side, using the default ***Inscribed*** *option. Recall that for an inscribed polygon, the radius is measured from the center to the midpoint of a side; for a circumscribed polygon, the radius is drawn out to a vertex. You proceed with the default* ***Inscribed*** *option.*

✔ Specify **(15,5,0)** for the center point.

AutoCAD prompts for a base radius. The radius is measured from the center point to the point you specify.

NOTE

By default, pyramids are drawn inscribed. If for any reason you have ***Circumscribed*** *as your default, you can switch by selecting* ***Circumscribed*** *from the command prompt. The default switches to* ***Inscribed****. This also works in reverse. Selecting* ***Inscribed*** *from the command prompt switches the option to* ***Circumscribed****.*

✔ Specify the point **(17,5,0)** to define a radius of **2**.

AutoCAD draws the base and prompts for height.

✔ Make sure your pyramid is being drawn in the positive direction, and type **4 <Enter>**.

Your drawing should resemble Figure 13-10.

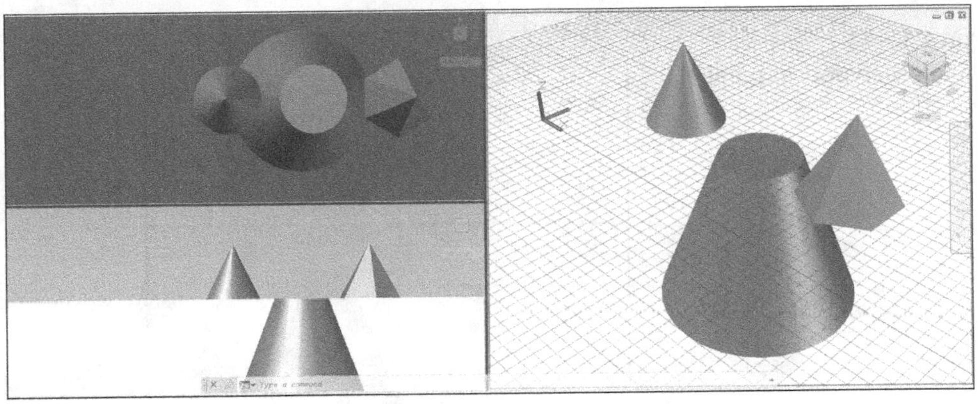

Figure 13-10
Pyramid

Drawing Torus

TORUS	
Command	TORUS
Alias	Tor
Panel	Modeling
Tool	(torus icon)

Torus is another solid primitive shape that is easily drawn. It is like drawing a donut in 2D and requires an outer radius as well as a tube radius. Try this:

✔ Click the **Torus** tool from the bottom of the **Solid Primitives** drop-down menu on the **Modeling** panel of the **Home** tab.

AutoCAD prompts:

```
Specify center point or [3P/2P/Ttr]:
```

The ***Three-point****,* ***Two-point****, and* ***Tangent Tangent Radius*** *options work just as they do in the* ***CIRCLE*** *command. You place a torus behind and above the frustum cone.*

✔ Type **10,10,4 <Enter>** for a center point.

Notice the z coordinate of 4, which places the torus above the XY plane.

AutoCAD prompts for a radius or diameter.

✔ Type **2 <Enter>**.

Now, AutoCAD prompts for a second radius, the radius of the torus tube.

✔ Type **.5 <Enter>**.

Switching to Parallel Projection

Notice how the torus appears off e center in the top- and bottom-left viewports. As mentioned previously, this is caused by perspective projection. Having perspective projection in a plan view is counterproductive. Here, you switch to parallel projection in both of these viewports.

✔ Make sure that the top-left viewport is active.

✔ Right-click the **ViewCube** in the top-left viewport.

✔ Select **Parallel**.

Your top-left viewport should resemble the one in Figure 13-11. This figure also shows the lower-left viewport in parallel projection. The same procedure accomplishes this.

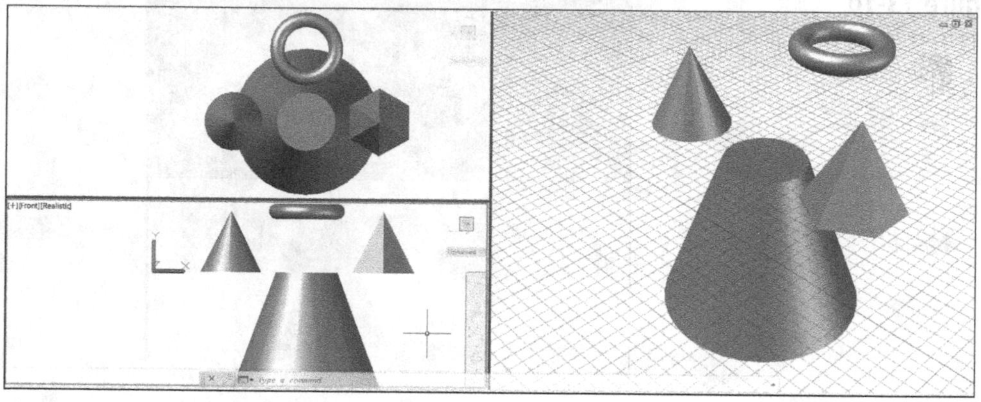

Figure 13-11
Top-left viewport in parallel projection

✔ Make sure that the bottom-left viewport is active.

✔ Right-click the **ViewCube** in the bottom-left viewport.

✔ Select **Parallel**.

As shown in Figure 13-11, the bottom-left viewport is now in parallel perspective, and the horizon is no longer represented.

Slicing and Sectioning Solids

In addition to Boolean operations, there are other methods that create solid shapes by modifying previously drawn objects. In this section, you explore slicing and sectioning.

Slice

SLICE	
Command	SLICE
Alias	Sl
Panel	Solid Editing
Tool	

The **SLICE** command allows easy creation of objects by cutting away portions of drawn solids on one side of a slicing plane. In this exercise, you slice off the tops of a pyramid and a cone. For this purpose, you work in the front view in the bottom-left viewport.

✔ You should begin this exercise with the objects and viewports in your drawing as shown in Figure 13-11.

✔ Click in the bottom-left viewport to make it active.

✔ Check to see that **Snap Mode** and **Ortho Mode** are on in this viewport.

✔ Click the **Slice** tool from the **Solid Editing** panel on the **Home** tab, as shown in Figure 13-12.

AutoCAD prompts for objects to slice.

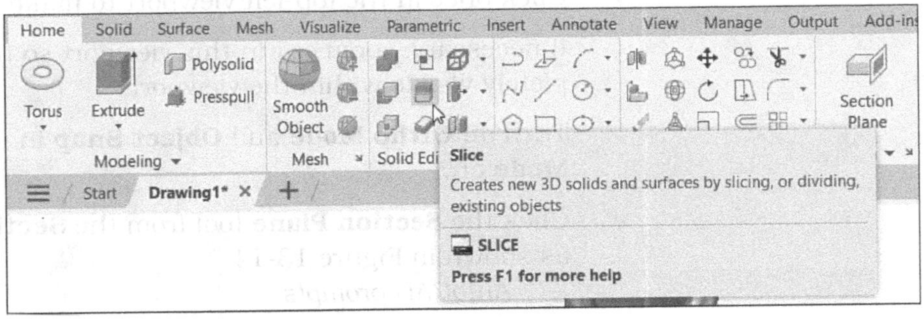

Figure 13-12
Slice tool

✔ Select the cone on the left and the pyramid on the right of the viewport.

✔ Right-click to end object selection.

AutoCAD prompts:

```
Specify start point of slicing plane or [planar Object/
Surface/Zaxis/View/XY/YZ/ZX/3points] <3points>:
```

This prompt allows you to define a plane by pointing, selecting a planar object or object surface, or using one of the planes of the current coordinate system. You can specify a plane with two points in the front view.

✔ Specify point **(2.5,2,0)** to the left of the cone.

✔ Specify point **(17.5,2,0)** to the right of the pyramid.

AutoCAD now has the plane defined but needs to know which side of the plane to cut.

✔ Specify a point below the specified plane.

The tops of the cone and pyramid are sliced off, as shown in Figure 13-13.

Figure 13-13
Tops of pyramid and cone sliced off

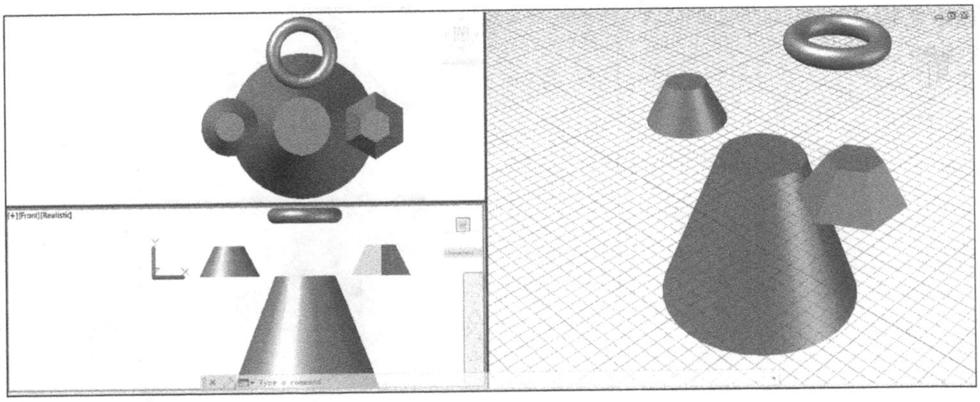

Section

Sectioning is accomplished by creating a section plane and then selecting options from a shortcut menu. Here, you create a section plane through three of the objects in your drawing and then create 3D sections.

- ✔ Click once in the top-left viewport to make it active.
- ✔ If necessary, zoom out in this viewport so that all objects are completely visible within the viewport.
- ✔ Turn off **Ortho Mode** and **Object Snap** in this viewport, but leave **Snap Mode** on.
- ✔ Click the **Section Plane** tool from the **Section** panel on the **Home** tab, as shown in Figure 13-14.

  AutoCAD prompts:

  ```
  Select face or any point to locate section line or [Draw
  section/Orthographic/Type]:
  ```

  You begin by using point selection.

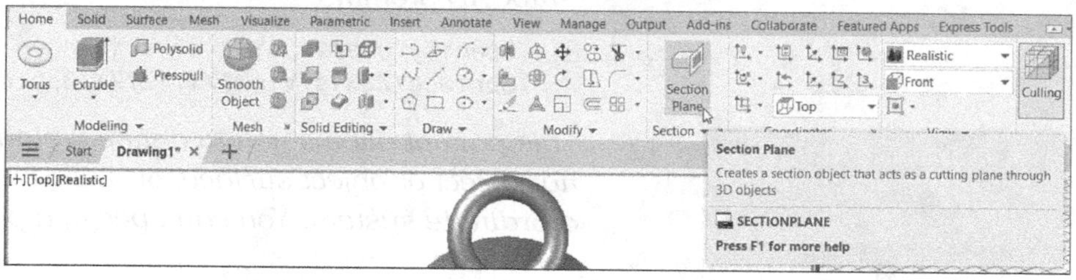

Figure 13-14
Section Plane tool

- ✔ Specify point **(2.5,2.5,0)**.

  AutoCAD shows a plane and prompts for a through point. I draw the plane through the middle of the cone and the torus.

- ✔ Specify point **(12.5,12.5,0)**.

  The section plane is drawn. Your drawing should resemble Figure 13-15.

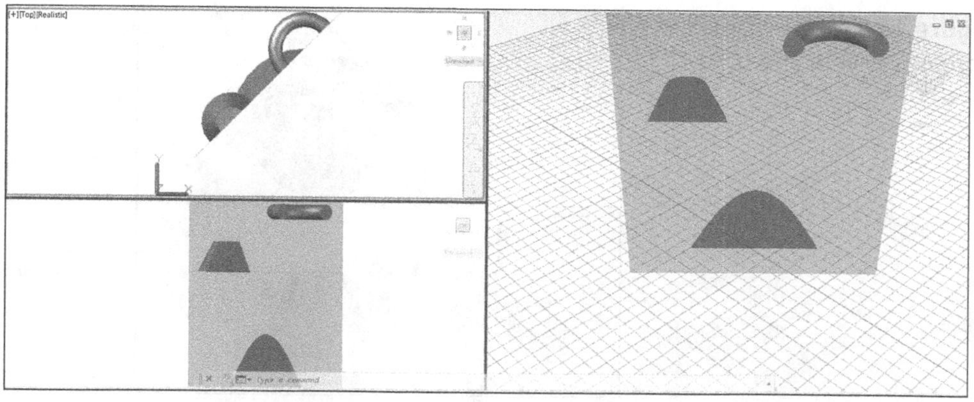

Figure 13-15
Section plane

> **NOTE**
>
> *If all objects are not cut through along the section plane, as shown in Figure 13-15, try regenerating all viewports by typing* **REGENALL <Enter>** *at the command line.*

Adjust Section Plane with Grips

You now have three sectioned objects in your drawing. They may be selected and modified independently. The section plane itself is also an object in your drawing and would be included if you plotted any of the three views represented. To plot the objects without the section plane, you can move the section plane to another layer and turn it off.

You can continue to adjust the location and effect of the section plane using grips. Here's how:

✔ Make the top-left viewport active and then select the section plane in this viewport.

A set of 3D grips and a gizmo are added. The line used to define the section plane is highlighted, as shown in Figure 13-16. Grips are added as shown in the top-left viewport. These are also labeled in Figure 13-16. Taking these grips one at a time starting from the lower left, the first square grip is called the ***base grip****. It is always adjacent to the* ***menu*** *grip, which is the second grip in the section plane view. The menu grip gives you a small set of sectioning options. By default, sectioning is cut along the plane, but you can also create two parallel planes to create a* ***slice*** *of the objects; a four-sided box, called a boundary, to slice the objects along four planes rather than one or two; or you can slice by specifying a* ***volume*** *for the remaining object.*

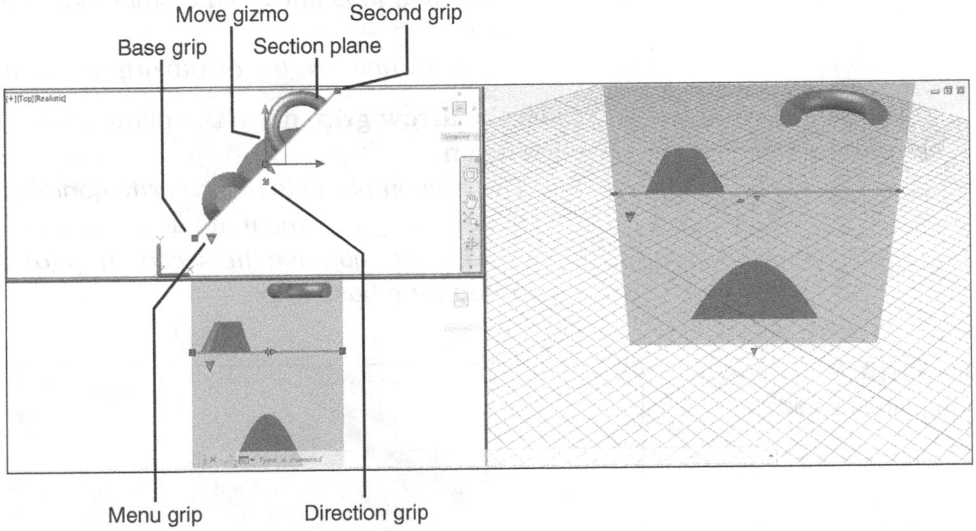

Figure 13-16
Section Plane with labeled grips

In the middle are two differently formed arrow grips. The first is a complete arrow with a small shaft. This is the ***direction grip****. Selecting this grip flips the geometry so that the opposite side of the plane is removed. The other arrow is a regularly shaped arrow grip, called simply the arrow grip. Clicking, holding, and moving this grip* *moves the section plane in a direction normal to its current placement and alters the sectioning of the object accordingly. The box grip at the intersection of the* ***Move*** *gizmo is part of the gizmo and can be used to move the section plane according to standard gizmo editing procedures. Finally, the square grip at the upper-right is called the* ***second grip****. Ordinarily, this grip creates rotation of the plane around the base grip at the other end. If you open the shortcut menu by right-clicking after clicking the grip, you can choose other typical grip mode options.*

Here you learn to use three of these grip features, beginning with the direction grip. You are certainly invited to try out the others as well.

✔ With the section plane selected, click the **direction grip** near its middle.

The sectioned geometry is immediately switched to the opposite side of the section plane, as shown in Figure 13-17.

Figure 13-17
Direction flipped

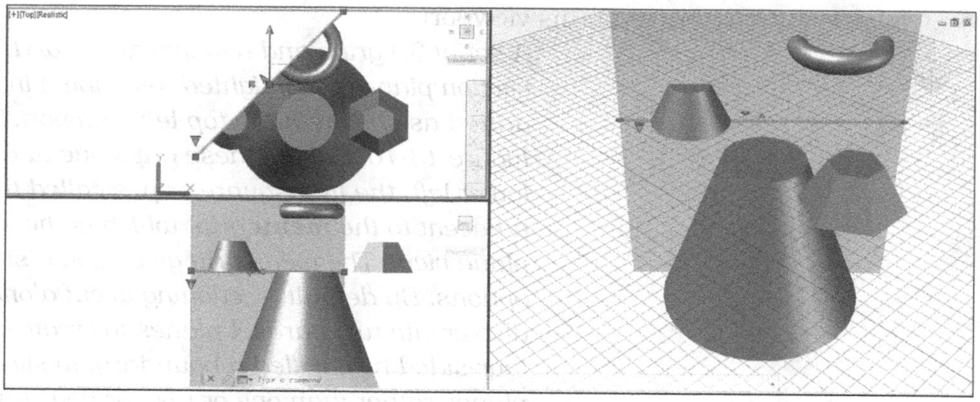

✔ Click the **direction grip** again.

Sectioning flips back to the other side, shown previously in Figure 13-16.

Next, you use the arrow grip in the middle of the plane.

✔ Click the **arrow grip**, move the plane about 2 units to the right, and click again.

The section plane is moved orthogonally, and the objects are sectioned along a plane in its new location, as shown in Figure 13-18.

Finally, you use the second grip (at the top) to rotate the section around the base grip.

Figure 13-18
Section plane moved

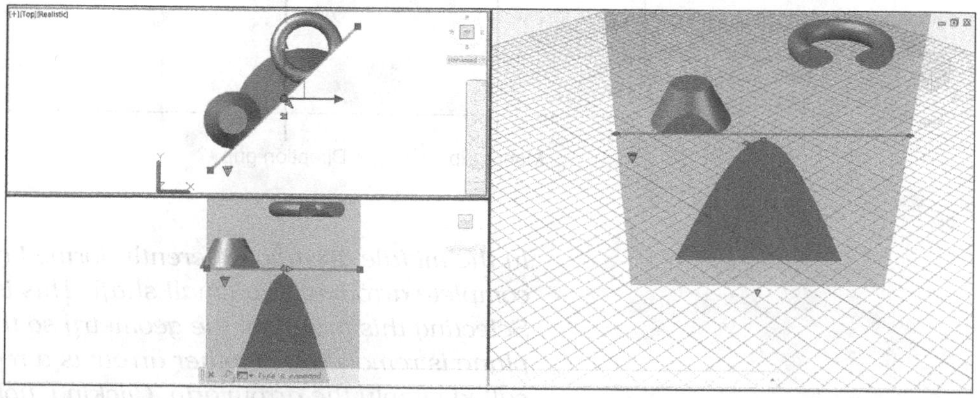

✔ Click the **second grip** and move the cursor downward to change the angle of the plane, as shown in Figure 13-19.

Your top viewport should resemble Figure 13-19.

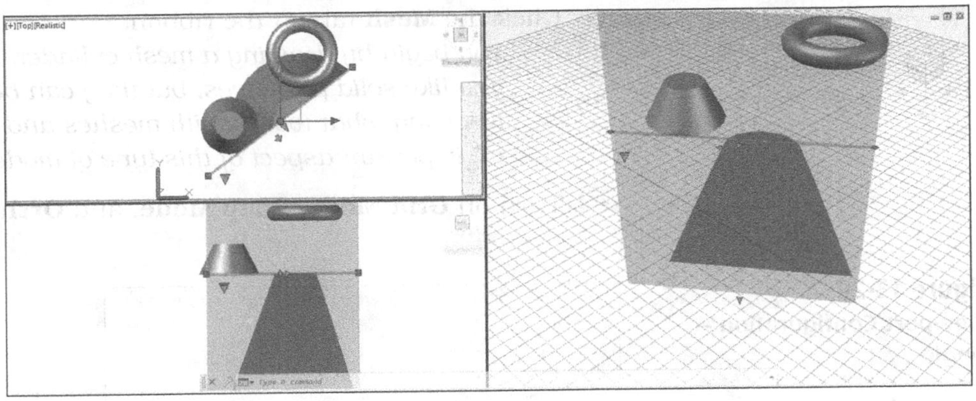

Figure 13-19
Section plane angle changed

> **NOTE**
>
> At times, you may want to add a hatch pattern to highlight the sectioned surfaces. You can use the following procedure:
>
> 1. Click the small diagonal arrow to the right of the **Section** panel title on the **Home** tab in the **3D Modeling** workspace. This opens the tall **Section Settings** dialog box. The second section of this dialog box is labeled **Intersection Fill**. The second item under **Intersection Fill** is **Face Hatch**. By default, this is set to **Predefined/SOLID**.
> 2. Click in the **Face Hatch** edit box and click the list box arrow to the right of this setting to open the list.
> 3. Select **Hatch Pattern Type**.
> 4. Click the **Pattern** button to see thumbnails of each available pattern, or open the drop-down list by clicking the arrow to the right to open a list of pattern names.
> 5. Select a hatch pattern.
> 6. Click **OK** if you are in the **Hatch Pattern Palette** dialog box.
> 7. Click **OK** to close the **Hatch Pattern Type** dialog box.
> 8. Click **OK** to close the **Section Settings** dialog box.

Mesh Modeling

mesh modeling: A 3D modeling system in which 3D mesh objects are created with faces that can be split, creased, refined, moved, and smoothed to create realistic free-form models.

Mesh modeling is a system that allows you to create free-form mesh solids with adjustable levels of smoothness to better represent real objects. This exercise takes you through a complete mesh modeling project, introducing many of the concepts, features, and procedures available in this system of 3D drawing.

✔ To begin, erase all objects from your drawing, or create a new drawing using the **acad3D.dwt** drawing template file.

✔ Type **Zoom <Enter>**, and then select **All** from the command line.

✔ If you continued with the drawing from the previous section, return to a single viewport by making the right viewport active, and then selecting **Visualize** > **Model Viewports** > **Viewport Configuration** > **Single**, as shown in Figure 13-20.

✔ If you are in a new drawing, select **Visualize > Named Views > Named Views > SE Isometric.**

This will take you to a higher angle necessary for some of the steps that follow.

✔ Click the **Mesh** tab on the ribbon.

You begin by drawing a mesh cylinder. Mesh primitives are created just like solid primitives, but they can be edited very differently. Knowing what works with meshes and what works with solids is an important aspect of this type of modeling, as you will see.

✔ Turn on **Grid Mode**, **Snap Mode**, and **Ortho Mode**.

Figure 13-20
Viewport Configuration - Single

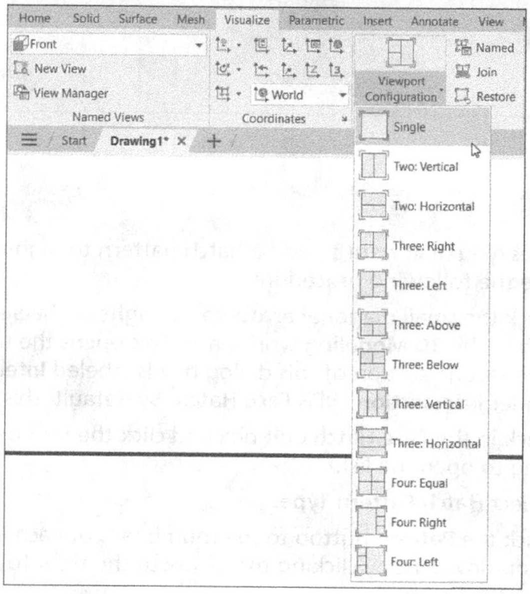

✔ Click the **Mesh Cylinder** tool from the **Mesh Primitives** drop-down menu on the **Mesh** tab's **Primitives** panel, as shown in Figure 13-21.

✔ Specify **(5,5,0)** for the center point of the base.

✔ Stretch the cylinder out to specify a radius of **2.5**.

✔ Make sure that the cylinder is stretched in the positive *Z* direction and type **5 <Enter>**.

You have a complete mesh cylinder, as shown in Figure 13-22. Notice that the cylinder has distinct faces on all sides and that the presentation is faceted, instead of smooth and rounded, as a solid cylinder would be. The faces provide opportunities to shape and mold the object. Smoothness will be added later. In mesh modeling, you begin with faceted images that serve as an outline for the smooth object you want to create. It is also useful to use a visual style with edges visible.

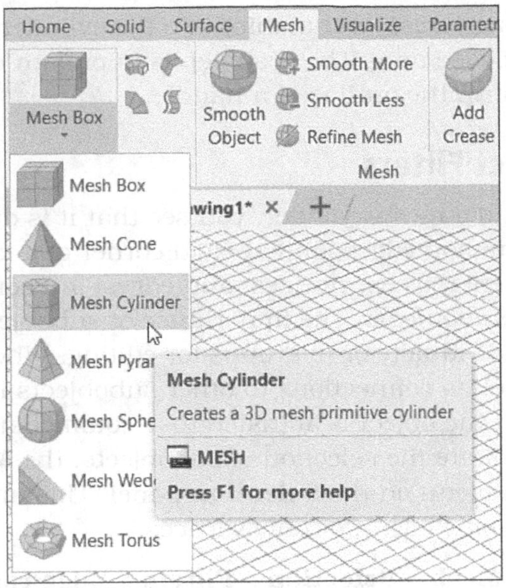

Figure 13-21
Mesh Cylinder tool

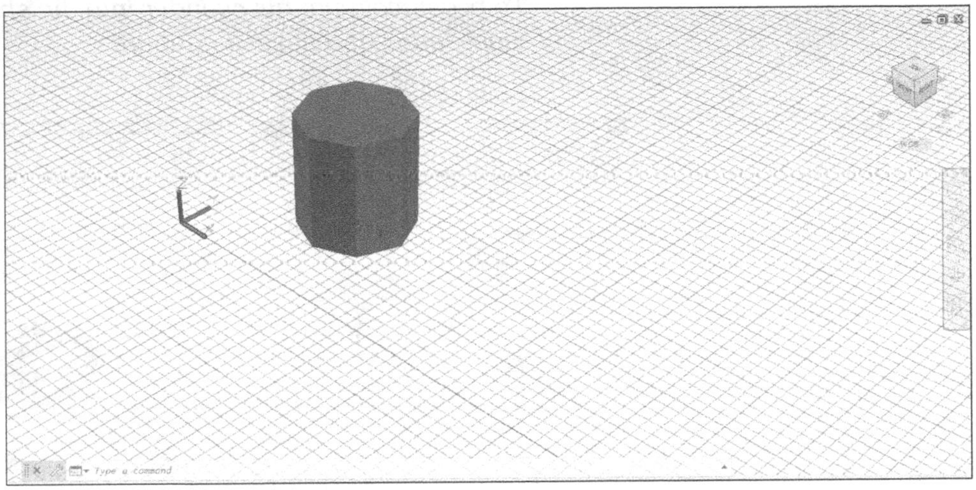

Figure 13-22
Mesh cylinder

✔ Select **Visualize** > **Visual Styles** (not the **Visual Styles** panel extension) > **Shaded with edges**, as shown in Figure 13-23.

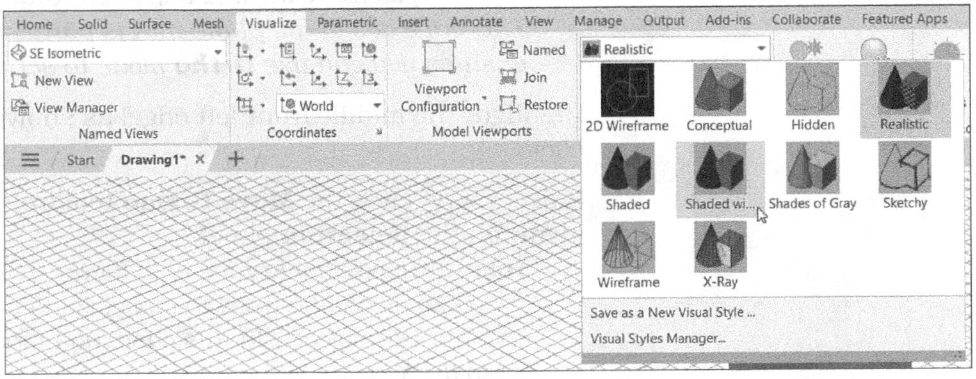

Figure 13-23
Shaded with edges visual style

In this exercise, you manipulate the cylinder to form the semblance of a stylized coffee mug. The first step is to pull an edge out away from the center to form the outline of a handle.

Subobject Filters

subobject: In AutoCAD mesh modeling, a face, edge, or vertex that can be independently selected for editing.

Looking at the mesh cylinder, you see that it is divided into faces. The faces meet at common edges, and at each corner of a face there is a vertex. These three elements, faces, vertices, and edges, are common to all meshes and are called ***subobjects***. The importance of subobjects is that they can be selected individually or in groups for editing. When a subobject is moved, for example, its connections to other subobjects in the mesh are maintained, and the object is adjusted to accommodate the move.

To facilitate the selection of subobjects, the **Mesh** tab has a **Filters** drop-down menu on the **Selection** panel. This menu has tools for selecting only faces, only edges, or only vertices.

✔ Select **Mesh** > **Selection** > **Filters** > **Edge tool**, as shown in Figure 13-24.

To begin molding this cylinder into the shape of a mug, you select a single edge and move it outward.

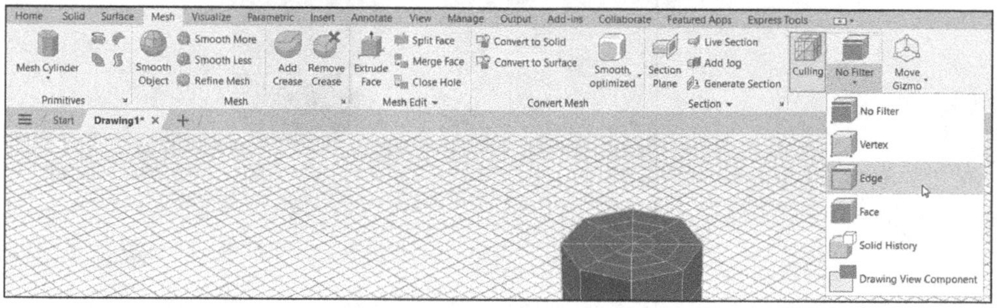

Figure 13-24
Edge tool

✔ Move your cursor over the cylinder.

As you do this, you see an edge badge added to the crosshairs and each edge you cross is highlighted. Some of the edges are not in the front of the cylinder as it is now positioned, so look carefully to see that the edge you want is selected.

*For this exercise, it is important that you select the edge shown. This edge lies in the plane that is parallel to the YZ plane, which ensures you can use **Ortho** mode to get a clean, symmetrical result.*

✔ Highlight the middle front left edge, as shown in Figure 13-25, and click.

✔ If necessary, click the **Move Gizmo** tool from the **3D Gizmo** drop-down menu on the **Selection** panel.

Your drawing should resemble Figure 13-25.

Gizmos can be used to move, rotate, or scale subobjects as well as complete objects. In this case, you move the edge 1.5 units parallel to the Y-axis.

✔ Position your cursor over the *Y*-axis of the **Move** gizmo so that the green axis line is showing.

- ✔ With the *Y*-axis line showing, click.
- ✔ Stretch the edge out to the left, as shown in Figure 13-26.

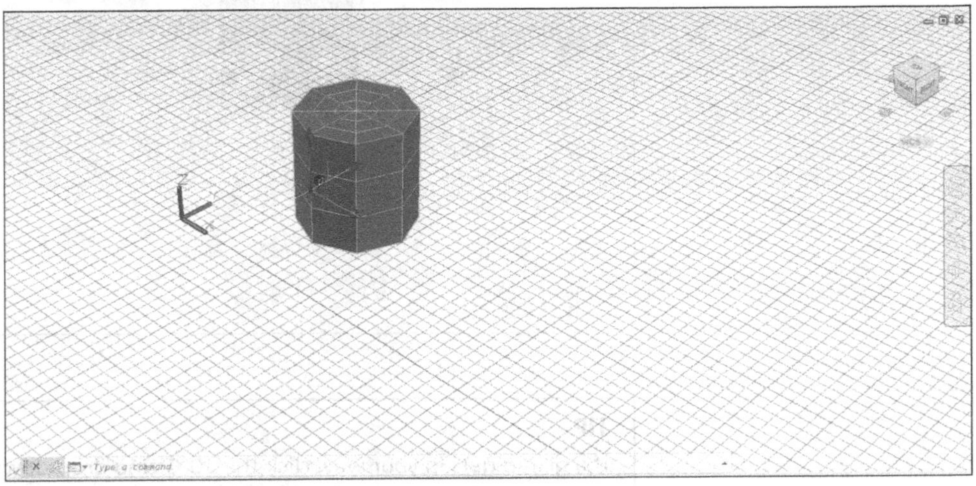

Figure 13-25
Gizmo aligns with selected edge

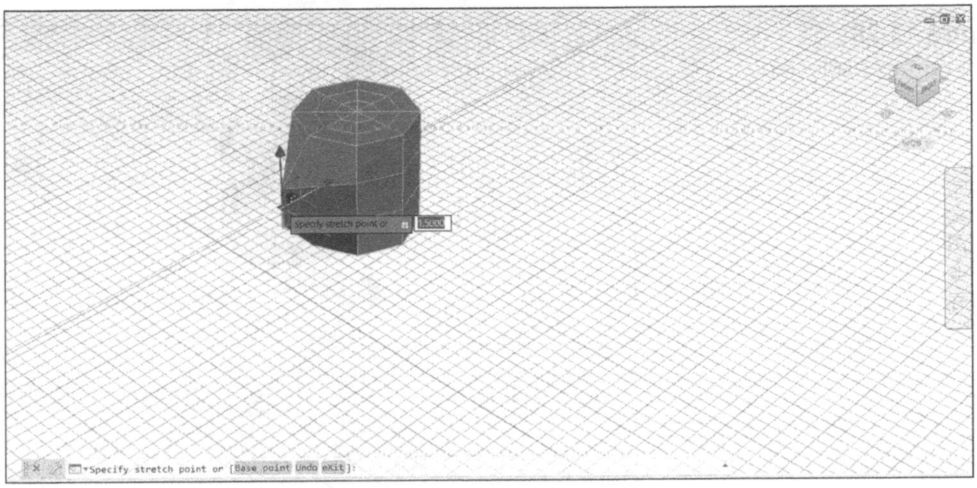

Figure 13-26
Stretch edge out to left

- ✔ Type **1.5 <Enter>**.
- ✔ Press **<Esc>** to clear grips and remove the **Move** gizmo.

  Your drawing should resemble Figure 13-27.

  Next, you select all the faces in the middle two rings on the top of the cylinder and move them down 4.75 to create the inside of the mug.

- ✔ Click the **Face** tool from the **Filters** drop-down menu on the **Selection** panel.

  Now as you move the cursor over the cylinder, faces are highlighted instead of edges.

- ✔ Select each of the sixteen inner faces on the top of the cylinder, as shown in Figure 13-28.

  As each face is selected, a red dot appears, as shown.

Figure 13-27
Stretched edge

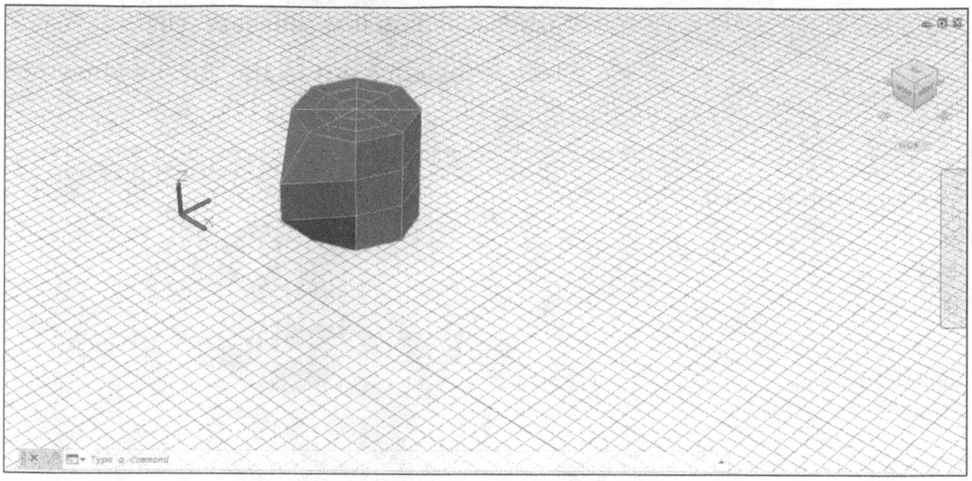

TIP
If a gizmo gets in your way, click the **3D Gizmo** drop-down menu and select **No Gizmo**.

Figure 13-28
Sixteen faces selected

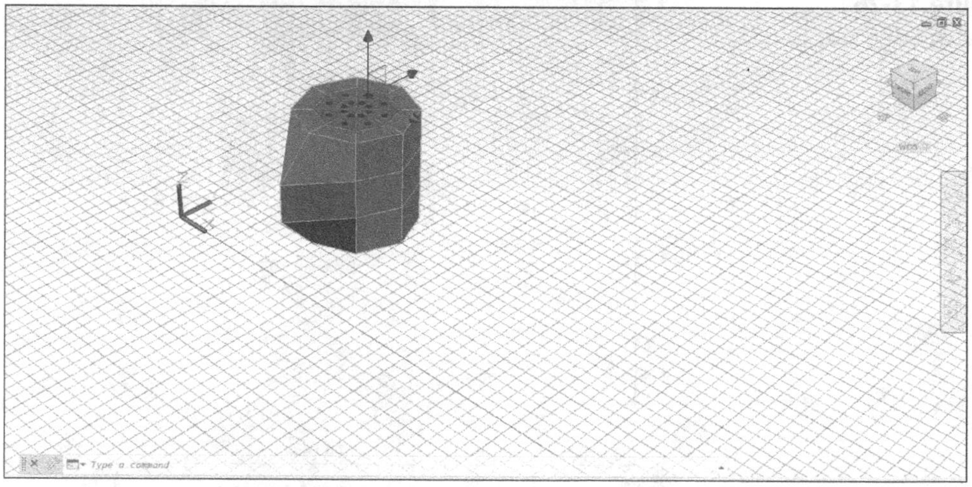

- ✔ If necessary, click the **Move Gizmo** tool from the **3D Gizmo** drop-down menu on the **Selection** panel.
- ✔ With the sixteen faces selected, move your cursor so that the vertical blue line on the **Move** gizmo appears and the blue arrow turns gold.
- ✔ Click the blue arrow and stretch the faces downward.
- ✔ Make sure that **Ortho Mode** is on; if it is not, press **<F8>**.
- ✔ With **Ortho** on and the faces stretched downward, type **4.75 <Enter>**.

  Notice how the outer faces stretch along their edges with the inner faces to maintain the connections, as shown in Figure 13-29.

  To complete this object, you smooth the mesh, convert it to a solid, and then subtract a cylinder to form a hole in the handle. The order in which things are done is important because of the limitations of both solids and meshes. Only mesh primitives can be smoothed, and only solids can be manipulated using Boolean operations. In a task like this exercise, you do all subobject manipulation to the mesh primitive first; then you smooth the mesh. Finally, you convert the mesh to a solid so that you can do a subtraction. Although it is possible to convert either way, a solid converted to a mesh will not have the same clearly organized structure of meshes found in a mesh primitive.

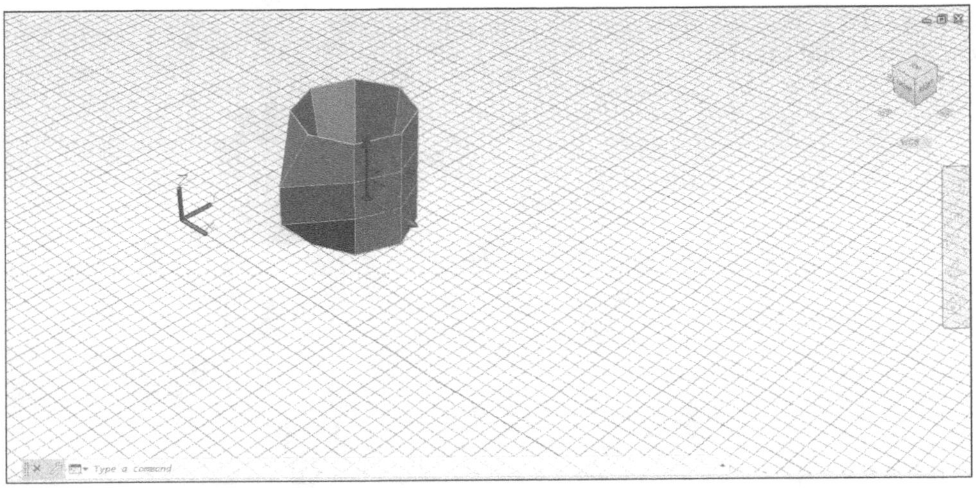

Figure 13-29
Inside faces stretched down

Having completed the structure of the mesh, you can now add smoothness.

Smoothing Meshes

Meshes can be presented with varying levels of smoothness. At each level, the overall outline is maintained, but the number of faces increases until all the faces blend into a smooth surface. Each added level multiplies the number of mesh faces by four. Adding smoothness is simple.

- ✔ Make sure the mesh object is selected. If needed, select **Mesh** > **Selection** > **Filters** > **No Filter tool**.
- ✔ Click the **Smooth More** tool from the **Mesh** panel, as shown in Figure 13-30.

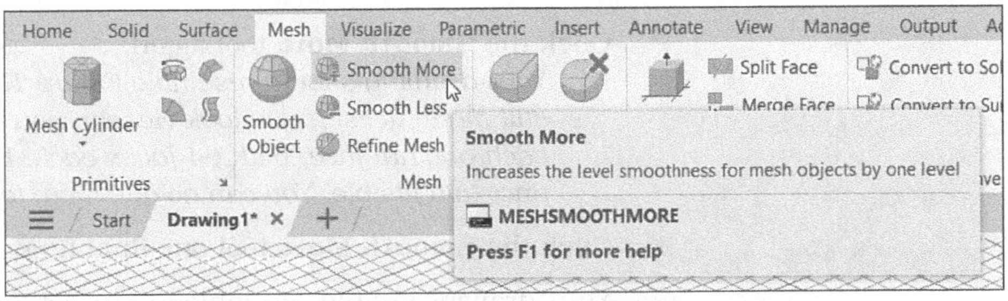

Figure 13-30
Smooth More tool

Your drawing should resemble Figure 13-31. Faces have been multiplied and diminished in size. Edges have been softened, and the object has a more rounded look. The darker lines show the original faces, but each original face is now divided into four faces.

✔ Click the **Smooth More** tool again.

Your drawing should resemble Figure 13-32. The mesh is smoothed further. The number of faces has increased dramatically. Each original face is now divided into 16 faces. The appearance is much smoother, but the new divisions are still clearly visible on the faceted surfaces. You can smooth the mesh even more.

Figure 13-31
Faces divided and smoothed

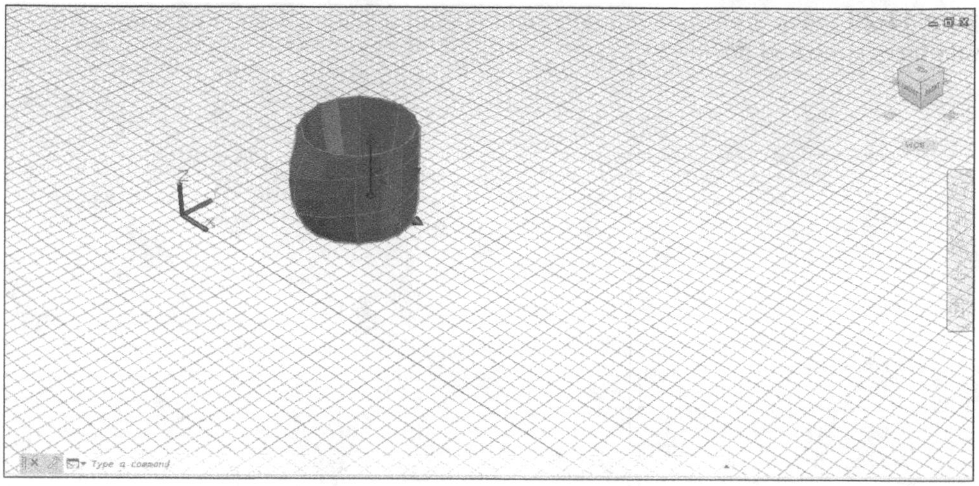

Figure 13-32
Mesh smoothed further

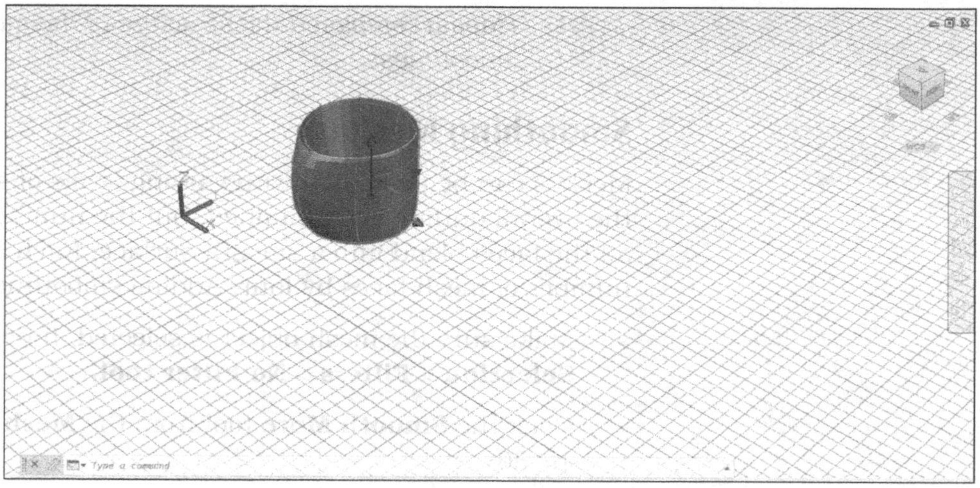

✔ Click the **Smooth More** tool again.

Your drawing should resemble Figure 13-33. It is still smoother, with still more faces. If you look closely, you can see 8 × 8 patterns on each original face, with 64 faces each. But these faces are still distinct and visible. You can go one more level.

✔ Click the **Smooth More** tool one final time.

Your drawing should resemble Figure 13-34. You can no longer see or count the divided faces. The edge lines still show the original faces, but the fourth and final levels of smoothness have been reached. If you attempt to go further, the following message is displayed: "One or more meshes in the current selection cannot be smoothed again."

Figure 13-33
Faces still distinct and visible

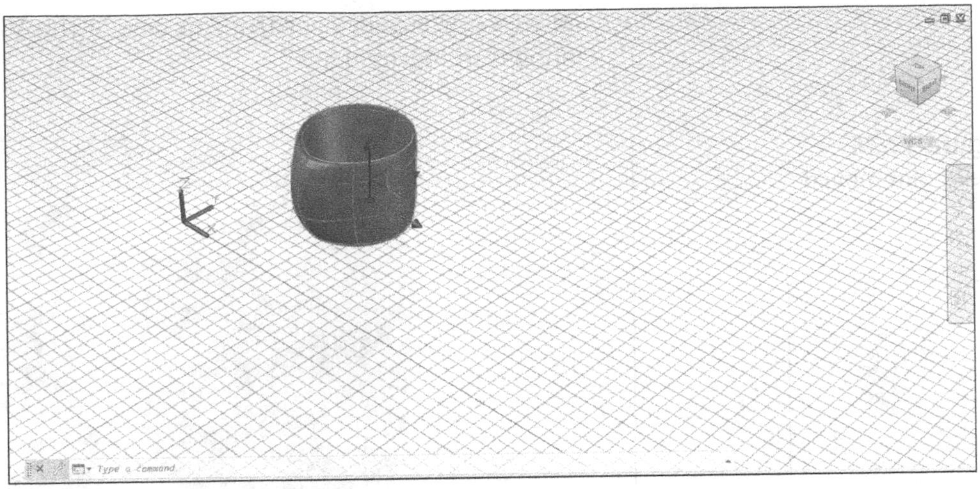

Figure 13-34
Final level of smoothness

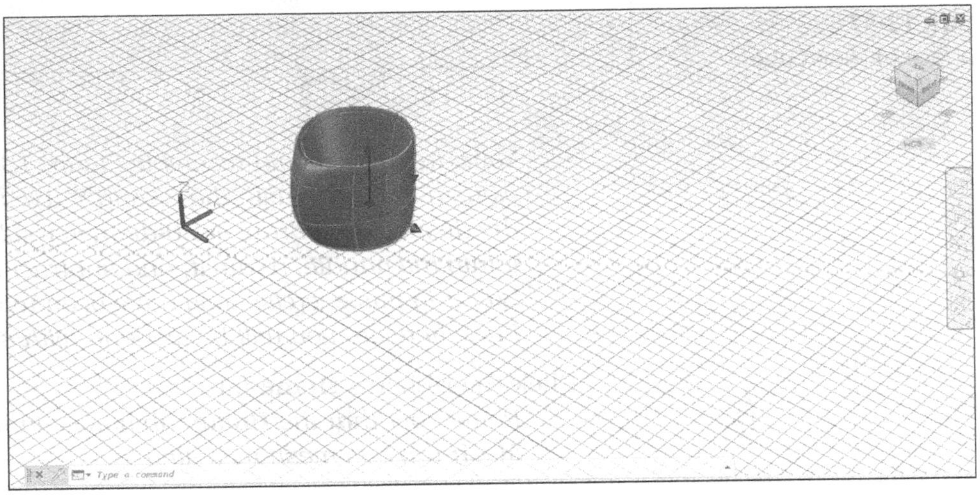

Boolean Operations on Meshes and Solids

Next, you draw a solid cylinder and subtract it from the mesh to create a hole in the handle. To accomplish this, you also need to convert the mesh to a solid. Only meshes can be smoothed; only solids can be manipulated through the Boolean operations. Although you could draw the cylinder in the current view, procedures will be much clearer and more reliable if you temporarily change to a plan view. You use the **ViewCube** and move in two steps. First, switch to the southwest isometric viewpoint. This view is also called the "home" view because it puts the view directly over the origin of the world coordinate system.

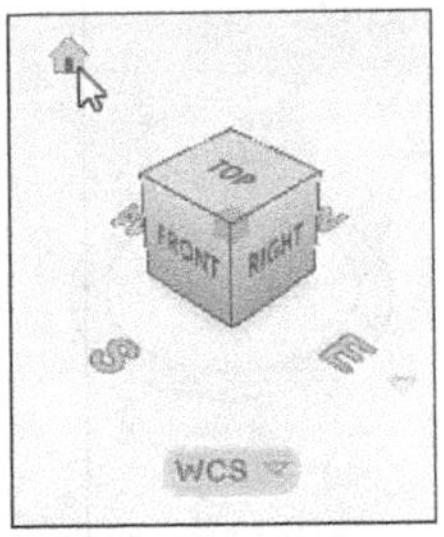

Figure 13-35
House icon appears above ViewCube

✔ Move your cursor over the **ViewCube** so that the small house icon appears above the cube, as shown in Figure 13-35.

✔ Click the house icon.

This switches your viewpoint so that your drawing resembles Figure 13-36. Notice the red X-axis and the green Y-axis that converge off the screen in the direction from which you are looking, putting you roughly at the origin.

The second step is to move to a top, or plan, viewpoint.

✔ Move your cursor over the Top face of the **ViewCube** and click, as shown in Figure 13-37.

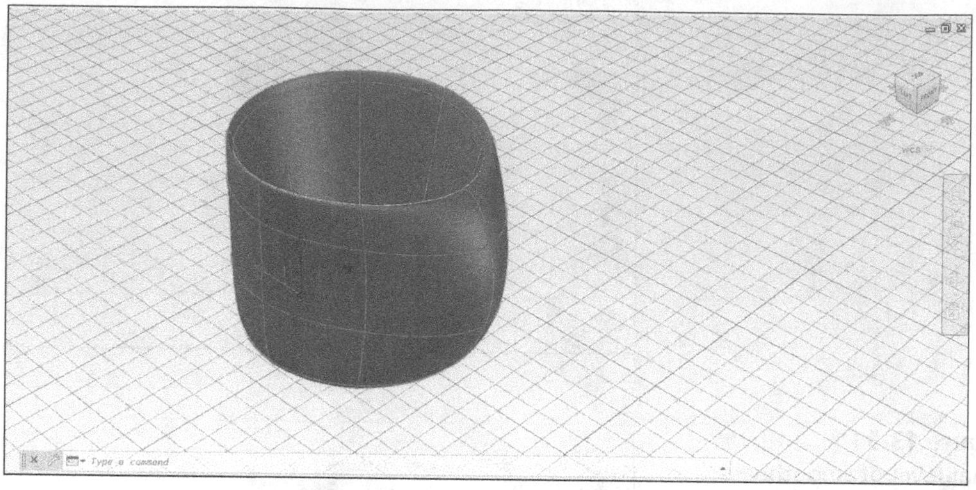

Figure 13-36
Viewpoint moved

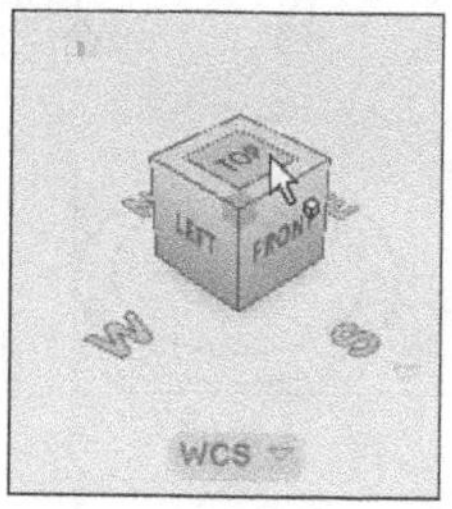

Figure 13-37
Top face of **ViewCube**

Your drawing should resemble Figure 13-38. This is a standard plan view in the WCS, with the X- and Y-axes aligned with the sides of the display. You draw a 1.0-diameter solid cylinder at (0,2.5), move it into the handle, rotate it, and subtract it to complete the drawing. So far in this exercise, you have been working with a mesh object. From here on, you will be working with solids.

✔ Click the ribbon's **Home** tab.

Remember that the ***Home*** *tab has solid modeling tools, whereas the* ***Mesh*** *tab has mesh modeling tools.*

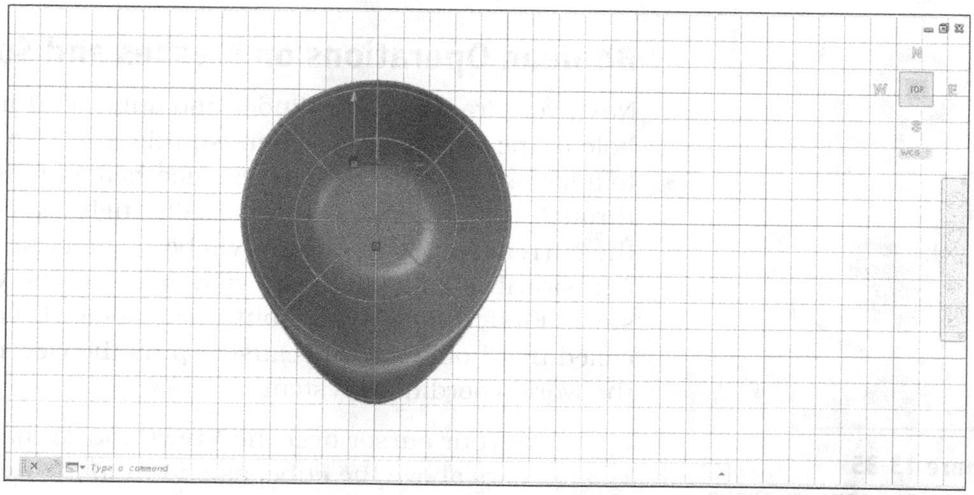

Figure 13-38
Standard plan view

✔ Click the **Cylinder** tool from the **Solid Primitives** drop-down menu on the **Modeling** panel.

✔ Specify **(0,2.5,0)** for the center of the base, as shown in Figure 13-39.

✔ Specify a radius point 0.50 from the center of the cylinder.

Figure 13-39
Drawing a cylinder

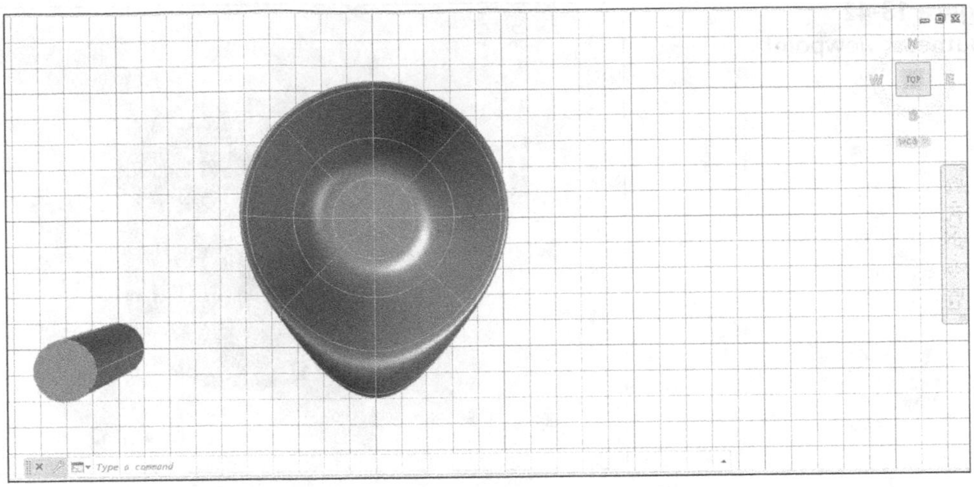

✔ Type **5 <Enter>** for the cylinder height.
Next, you move the cylinder 5 units to the right to center it within the stretched portion of the mesh.

✔ Click the **Move** gizmo from the **3D Gizmo** drop-down menu on the **Selection** panel.

✔ Click the **No Filter** tool from the **Filter** drop-down menu (to the left of the **3D Gizmo** drop-down).

✔ Select the solid cylinder.

✔ Move the cursor to highlight the red *X*-axis on the **Move** gizmo and then click.

✔ Drag the cylinder to the right.

✔ Type **5 <Enter>**, and then press **<Esc>** to remove the gizmo.
Your drawing should resemble Figure 13-40. For the next step, you return to the southeast isometric view.

Figure 13-40
Cylinder moved

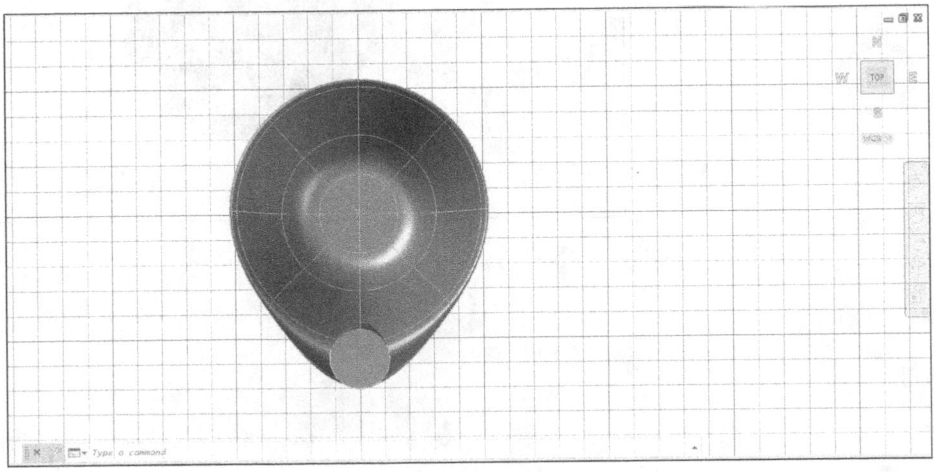

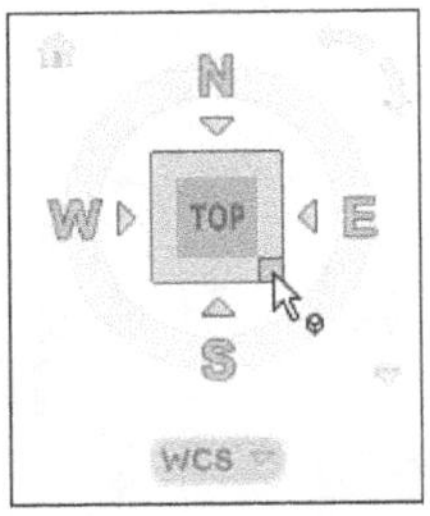

Figure 13-41
Southeast corner of **ViewCube**

✔ Click the southeast corner of the **ViewCube**, as shown in Figure 13-41.
*Your drawing should resemble Figure 13-42. To rotate the cylinder 90°, you switch to the **Rotate** gizmo.*

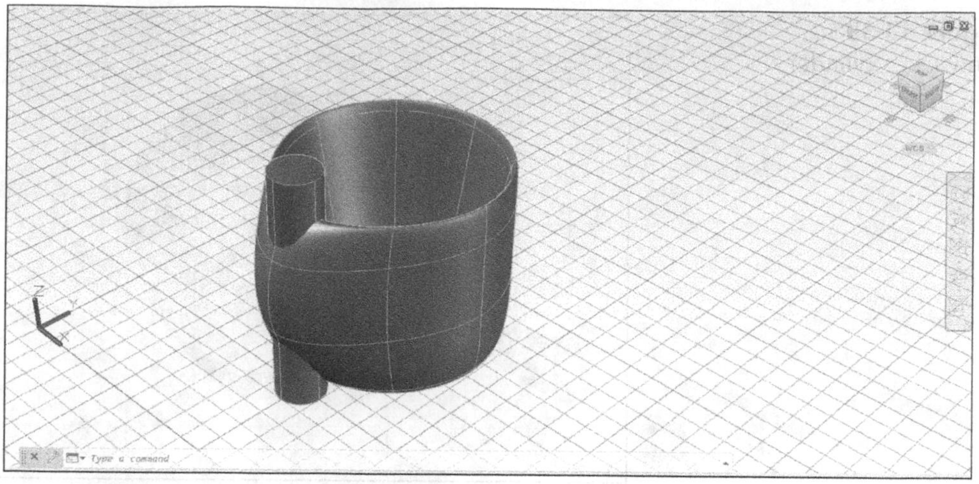

Figure 13-42
Southeast viewpoint

- ✔ Click the **3D Gizmo** drop-down menu on the **Selection** panel and click the **Rotate Gizmo** tool.
- ✔ Select the solid cylinder.
- ✔ Move the cursor to highlight rotation in the green *XZ* plane, around the *Y*-axis, as shown in Figure 13-43.
- ✔ Click the *XZ* plane on the **Rotate** gizmo and then type **90 <Enter>**.
- ✔ Press **<Esc>** to remove the gizmo.

  Your drawing should resemble Figure 13-44.

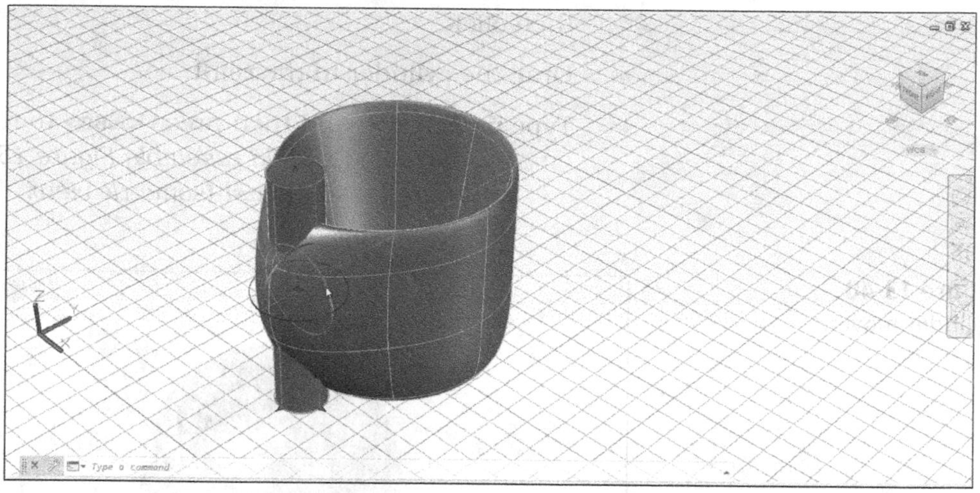

Figure 13-43
Rotate gizmo

Figure 13-44
Cylinder rotated

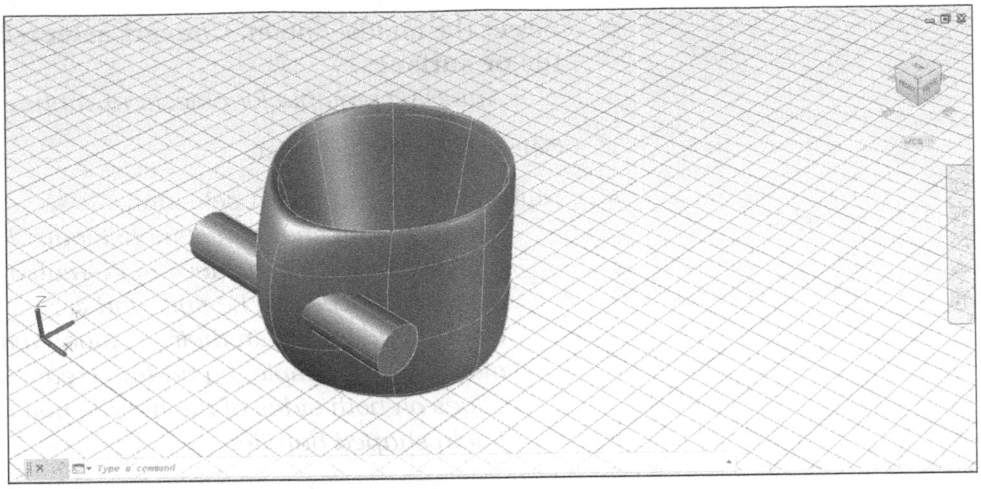

Converting Meshes to Solids

Before you can subtract the solid cylinder from the smoothed mesh, you have to convert the mesh to a solid. This process is simplified by initiating the subtraction first. Before AutoCAD performs the subtraction, it provides the option of converting the mesh to a solid. Conversion is simple, but you should not convert until you are sure that you are satisfied with the shaping of the mesh. If you attempt to convert back to a mesh, the mesh created will not be well organized and will be difficult to shape.

✔ Select **Home** > **Solid Editing** > **Solid, Subtract**.

✔ Select the mesh object.

✔ Right-click to end object selection.

AutoCAD presents the message box shown in Figure 13-45. You have three choices of what to do with the mesh objects in your selection set.

Figure 13-45
Converting to 3D solid

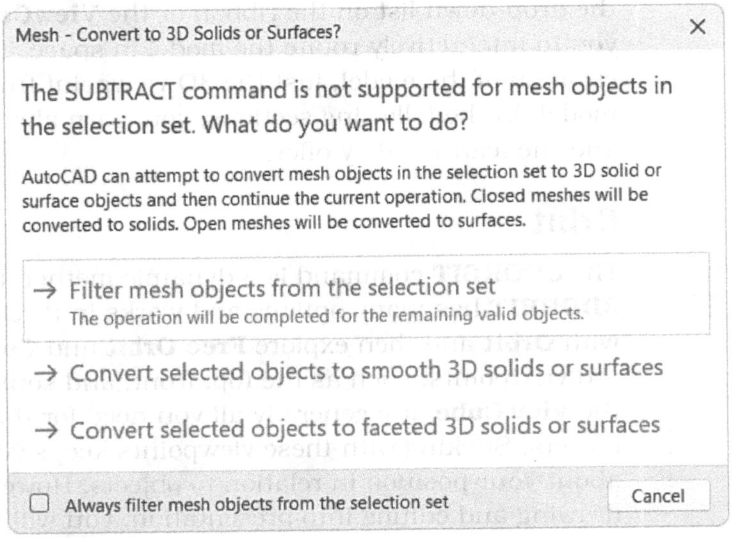
Mesh - Convert to 3D Solids or Surfaces?
The SUBTRACT command is not supported for mesh objects in the selection set. What do you want to do?
AutoCAD can attempt to convert mesh objects in the selection set to 3D solid or surface objects and then continue the current operation. Closed meshes will be converted to solids. Open meshes will be converted to surfaces.
→ Filter mesh objects from the selection set
The operation will be completed for the remaining valid objects.
→ Convert selected objects to smooth 3D solids or surfaces
→ Convert selected objects to faceted 3D solids or surfaces
Always filter mesh objects from the selection set
Cancel

- ✔ Select the middle option, **Convert selected objects to smooth 3D solids or surfaces.**

  AutoCAD prompts for objects to subtract.

- ✔ Select the solid cylinder.
- ✔ Right-click to end object selection.

  Your drawing should resemble Figure 13-46. This is a simple but effective model. To achieve more realism and more definition, consider that faces can be split and creases added before editing. Creased edges retain their positions when adjacent faces are moved. For example, by adding creases and additional faces to the edges on both sides of the handle you could create a narrower, more finely shaped handle.

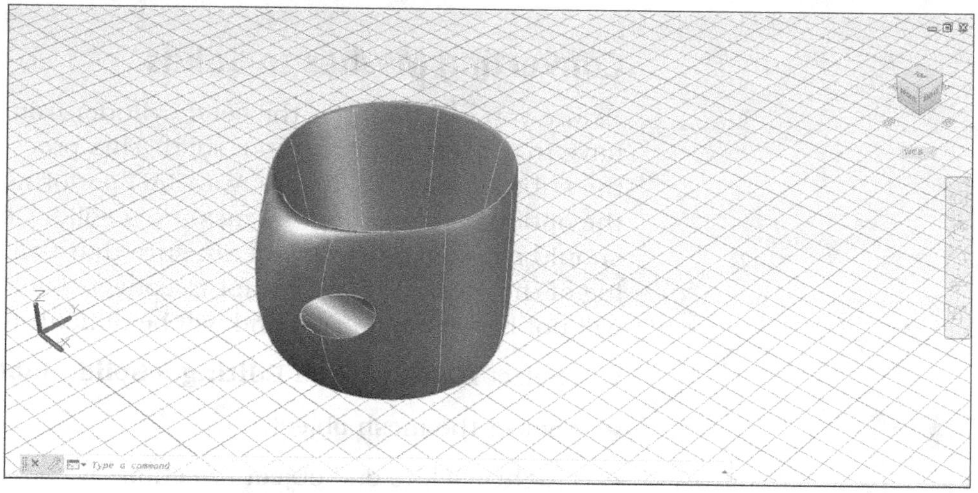

Figure 13-46
Cylinder subtracted

Adjusting Viewpoints with 3DORBIT

Until this point, you have been switching to named isometric views using the drop-down list on the ribbon or the **ViewCube**. The 3D Orbit tools allow you to interactively rotate the model in space. This doesn't change the orientation of the model, just the 3D viewpoint from which you are viewing the model. In the following sections, you learn about the different Orbit tools and the features they offer.

Orbit

3DORBIT	
Command	3DORBIT
Alias	3do
Panel	Navigate
Tool	

The **3DORBIT** command is a dynamic method for adjusting 3D viewpoints. **3DORBIT** has many options and works in three distinct modes. You begin with **Orbit** and then explore **Free Orbit** and **Continuous Orbit**. The standard viewpoints, such as the top, front, and southeast isometric found on the **ViewCube**, are generally all you need for the creation and editing of objects. Sticking with these viewpoints keeps you well-grounded and clear about your position in relation to objects. However, when you change from drawing and editing into presentation, you will find **3DORBIT** vastly more satisfying and freeing than the static viewpoint options.

The model created in the last section works well for a demonstration of **3DORBIT**.

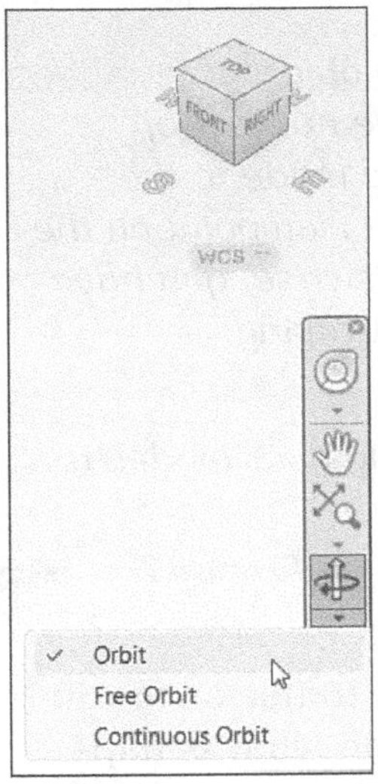

Figure 13-47
Orbit tool on the navigation bar

- ✔ Click the arrow beneath the **Orbit** tool on the **navigation bar** to open the menu shown in Figure 13-47.
  *If, for any reason, your navigation bar has been turned off, turn it on by typing **navbar <Enter>** and selecting **On** from the command line.*
- ✔ Click **Orbit**, as shown.
  Notice the orbit cursor that replaces the crosshairs.
- ✔ Click and hold the left mouse button while slowly move the cursor in any direction.
  The model moves along with the cursor movement.
- ✔ Move the cursor left and right, using mostly horizontal motion.
  Horizontal motion creates movement parallel to the XY plane of the world coordinate system.
- ✔ Move the cursor up and down, using mostly vertical motion.
  *Vertical motion creates movement parallel to the Z-axis of the world coordinate system. You can create any viewpoint on the model using these simple motions. Notice also that the **ViewCube** moves in the same manner as the model.*
- ✔ Move the cursor back to create a viewpoint similar to the one you started with.
- ✔ Press **<Enter>** to exit **3DORBIT**.

Free Orbit

In **Free Orbit** mode, **3DFORBIT** makes use of a tool called an *arcball*, as shown in Figure 13-48. The center of the arcball is the center of the current viewport. Therefore, to place your objects near the center of the arcball, you must place them near the center of the viewport; more precisely, you must place the center point of the objects at the center of the display.

Figure 13-48
Arcball

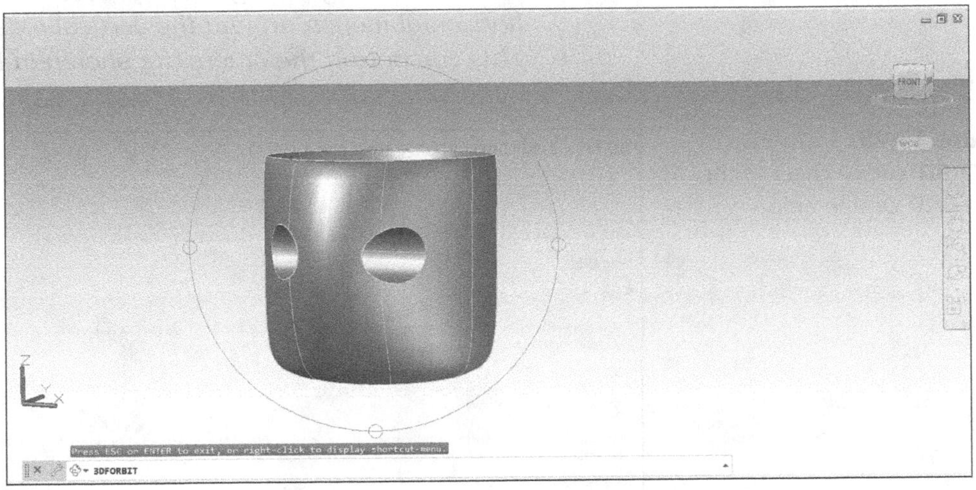

- ✔ If necessary, use **Pan** or pan with the scroll wheel to adjust the model so that it is roughly centered on the center of the viewport.

✔ Turn off **Grid Mode**.

*Before entering **3DFORBIT** you can select viewing objects. **3DFORBIT** performance is improved by limiting the number of objects used in viewing. Whatever adjustments are made to the viewpoint on the selected objects are applied to the viewpoint on the entire drawing when the command is exited. In this case, you have just one object to view, so you can use the whole drawing.*

✔ Click **Free Orbit** from the **Orbit** drop-down menu.

Your screen is updated with the arcball surrounding your model, as shown in Figure 13-48.

The Arcball and Rotation Cursors

The arcball is a somewhat complex tool, but it is very easy to use once you get the hang of it. It also gives you a more precise handle on what is happening than the **Orbit** mode does. You already know that the center of the arcball is the center of the viewport, or the center of the drawing area in this case, because there is only a single viewport. AutoCAD uses a camera-target analogy to explain viewpoint adjustment. Your viewpoint on the drawing is called the *camera position*. The point at which the camera is aimed is called the *target*. In **3DFORBIT**, the target point is fixed at the center of the arcball. As you change viewpoints, you are moving your viewpoint around in relation to this fixed target point.

There are four modes of adjustment, which you take up one at a time. Each mode has its own cursor, and the mode you are in depends on where you start in relation to the arcball. Try the following steps:

✔ Position the cursor in the small circle at the left quadrant of the arcball, as shown in Figure 13-48.

When the cursor is placed within either the right or the left quadrant circle, the horizontal rotation cursor appears. This cursor consists of a horizontal elliptical arrow surrounding a small sphere, with a vertical axis running through the sphere. When this cursor is visible, only horizontal motion around the vertical axis of the arcball is allowed. This cursor and the others are shown in Figure 13-49.

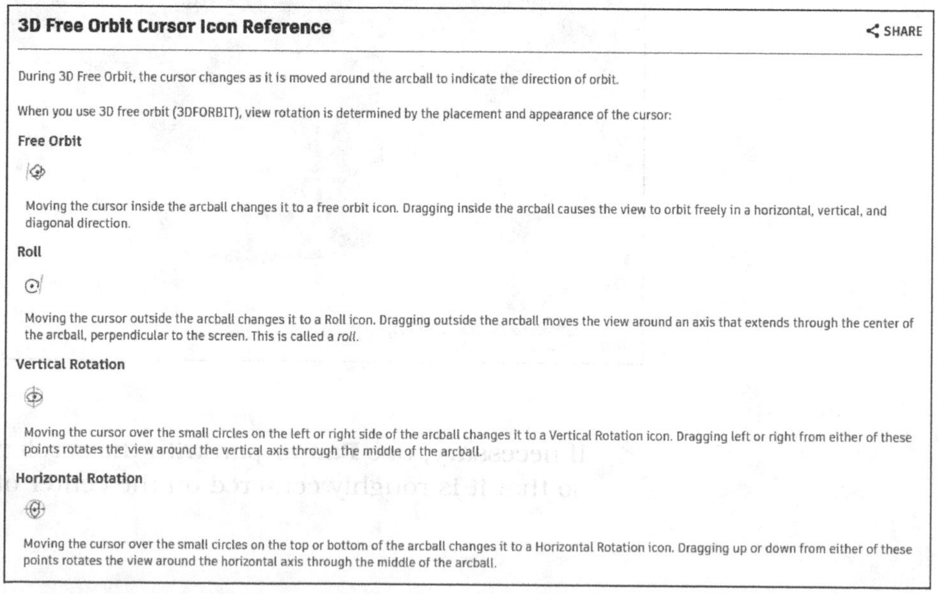
3D Free Orbit Cursor Icon Reference

SHARE

During 3D Free Orbit, the cursor changes as it is moved around the arcball to indicate the direction of orbit.

When you use 3D free orbit (3DFORBIT), view rotation is determined by the placement and appearance of the cursor:

Free Orbit

Moving the cursor inside the arcball changes it to a free orbit icon. Dragging inside the arcball causes the view to orbit freely in a horizontal, vertical, and diagonal direction.

Roll

Moving the cursor outside the arcball changes it to a Roll icon. Dragging outside the arcball moves the view around an axis that extends through the center of the arcball, perpendicular to the screen. This is called a *roll*.

Vertical Rotation

Moving the cursor over the small circles on the left or right side of the arcball changes it to a Vertical Rotation icon. Dragging left or right from either of these points rotates the view around the vertical axis through the middle of the arcball.

Horizontal Rotation

Moving the cursor over the small circles on the top or bottom of the arcball changes it to a Horizontal Rotation icon. Dragging up or down from either of these points rotates the view around the horizontal axis through the middle of the arcball.

Figure 13-49
3DORBIT cursor chart in the AutoCAD Online help

✔ With the cursor in the left quadrant circle and the horizontal cursor displayed, press and hold the left mouse button.

✔ Slowly drag the cursor from the left quadrant circle to the right quadrant circle, observing the model and the 3D UCS icon as you go.

As long as you keep the left mouse button pressed, the horizontal cursor is displayed.

✔ With the cursor in the right quadrant circle, release the left mouse button.

You have created a 180° rotation. Your drawing should resemble Figure 13-50.

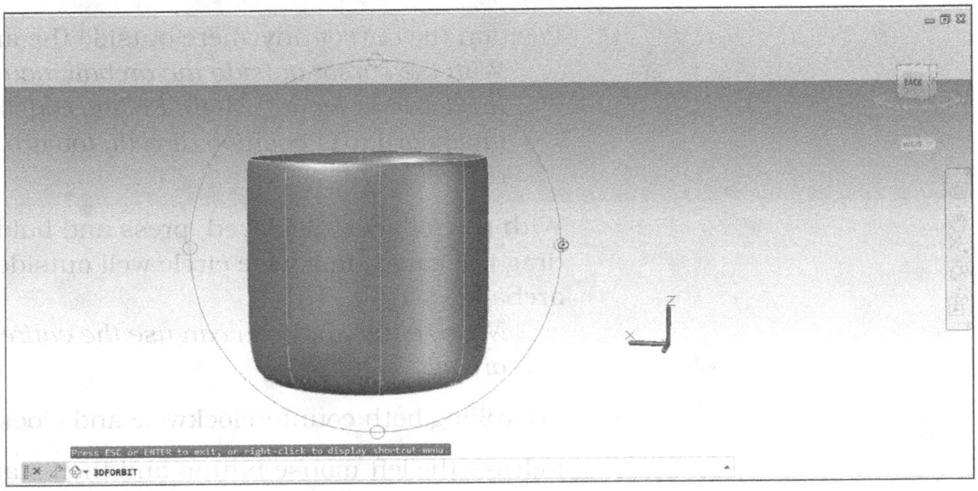

Figure 13-50
180° rotation

✔ With the cursor in the right quadrant circle and the horizontal cursor displayed, press and hold the left mouse button again, and then move the cursor slowly back to the left quadrant circle.

✔ Release the left mouse button.

You have moved the image roughly back to its original position. Now, try a vertical rotation.

✔ Move the cursor into the small circle at the top of the arcball.

The vertical rotation cursor appears. When this cursor is visible, rotation is restricted to around the horizontal axis, as shown in the chart in Figure 13-49.

✔ With the vertical rotation cursor displayed, press and hold the left mouse button, and drag down toward the circle at the lower quadrant.

✔ This time, do not release the left mouse button but continue dragging downward to the bottom of the screen.

The viewpoint continues to adjust, and the vertical cursor is displayed as long as you hold down the left mouse button. Notice that ***3DFORBIT*** *uses the entire screen, not just the drawing area. You can drag all the way down through the command line, the status bar, and the Windows taskbar.*

✔ Spend some time experimenting with vertical and horizontal rotation.

Note that you always have to start in a quadrant to constrain to horizontal or vertical rotation. What happens when you move horizontally with the vertical cursor displayed or vice versa? How much rotation can you achieve in one click-and-drag sequence vertically? What about horizontally? Are they the same amount? Why is there a difference?

✔ When you have finished experimenting, try to rotate the view back to its original viewpoint, shown previously in Figure 13-48.

If you are unable to get back to this viewpoint, don't worry. You learn how to do this easily in a moment. For now, try the other two modes.

✔ Position the cursor anywhere outside the arcball.

With the cursor outside the arcball, you can see the roll icon, the third icon in Figure 13-49. Rolling constrains rotation around an imaginary axis pointing directly toward you out of the center of the arcball.

✔ With the roll icon displayed, press and hold the left mouse button, and drag the cursor in a wide circle well outside the circumference of the arcball.

Notice again that you can use the entire screen, outside of the arcball.

✔ Try rolling both counterclockwise and clockwise.

✔ Release the left mouse button and then start again.

Note that you must be in the drawing area with the roll icon displayed to initiate a roll and that you must stay outside the arcball. Finally, try the free rotation cursor. This is the most powerful, and therefore the trickiest, form of rotation. It is also the same as the ***Orbit*** *mode as long as you remain within the arcball. The free cursor appears when you start inside the arcball or when you cross into the arcball while rolling. It allows rotation horizontally, vertically, and diagonally, depending on the movement of your pointing device.*

✔ Position the cursor inside the arcball and watch for the free rotation icon.

✔ With the free rotation icon displayed, press and hold the left mouse button, and drag the cursor within the arcball.

Make small movements vertically, horizontally, and diagonally. What happens if you move outside the arcball?

The free rotation icon gives you a less restricted type of rotation. Making small adjustments seems to work best. Imagine that you are grabbing the model and turning it a little at a time. Release the left mouse button and click/drag again. You may need to do this several times to reach a desired position.

✔ Try returning the view to approximate the southeast isometric view before proceeding.

Other 3DORBIT Features

3DORBIT is more than an enhanced viewpoint command. While you work within the command, you can adjust visual styles, projections, and even create a continuous-motion effect. **3DORBIT** options are accessed through the shortcut menu shown in Figure 13-51. You explore these from the bottom up, looking at the lower two panels and one option from the second panel.

You should remain in the **3DORBIT** command to begin this section.

✔ Right-click anywhere in the drawing area to open the shortcut menu.

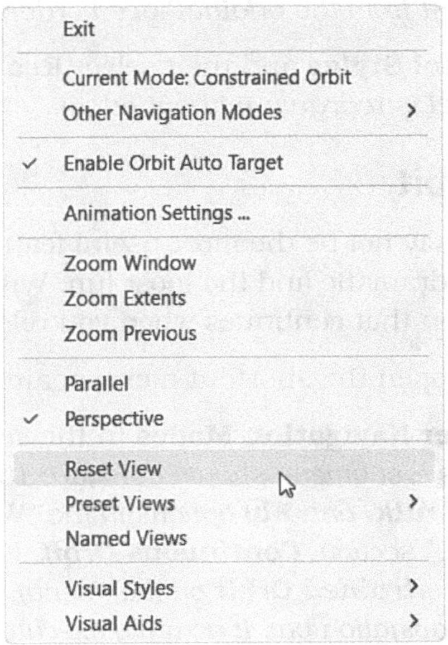

Figure 13-51
Orbit shortcut menu

Preset and Reset Views

In the second-from-the-bottom panel, there is a **Preset Views** option that provides convenient access to the standard ten orthographic and isometric viewpoints, so that you can access these views without leaving the command. Above this is a **Reset View** option. This option quickly returns you to the view that was current when you initially entered **3DORBIT**. This is a great convenience because you can get pretty far out of adjustment and have a difficult time finding your way back.

✔ Select **Reset View** from the shortcut menu.

Regardless of what you have done within the ***3DORBIT*** *command, your viewpoint is immediately returned to the view shown previously in Figure 13-48. If you have not left* ***3DORBIT (or 3DFORBIT)****, the view is reset to whatever view was current when you initially entered the command. If you have attempted to return to this view manually using the command, you can see that there is still a slight adjustment to return your viewpoint to the precise view.*

Visual Aids and Visual Styles

✔ Right-click to open the shortcut menu again.

On the bottom panel, you can see ***Visual Styles*** *and* ***Visual Aids*** *selections. Highlighting* ***Visual Aids*** *opens a submenu with three options:* ***Compass****,* ***Grid****, and* ***UCS icon****. The* ***Grid*** *option is useful* *for turning the grid on and off without leaving the command. The* ***Compass*** *adds an adjustable gyroscope-style overlay to the arcball. There are three rings of dashed ellipses showing the planes of the X-, Y-, and Z-axes of the current UCS. Try this if you like.*

The third option on the submenu turns the 3D UCS icon on and off.

Highlighting ***Visual Styles*** *opens a submenu with the nine 3D visual styles. You have been working in the* ***Shaded with edges*** *style. This allows you to change styles without leaving the command. Switching to* ***Realistic****, for example, would remove the edges that are left from the original face borders. Try it.*

✔ Highlight **Visual Styles** and then select **Realistic** from the submenu.

Your model is redrawn without edges.

Continuous Orbit

Continuous orbit may not be the most useful feature of AutoCAD, but it is probably the most dramatic and the most fun. With continuous orbit, you can set objects in motion that continues when you release the left mouse button.

✔ Right-click to open the shortcut menu again.

✔ Highlight **Other Navigation Modes** in the second panel.

This opens a submenu shown in Figure 13-52. You explore some of the ***Camera****,* ***Walk****, and* ***Fly*** *options in the "Walking Through a 3D Landscape" section.* ***Continuous Orbit****, like* ***Free Orbit*** *and* ***Orbit*** *(called* ***Constrained Orbit*** *on this menu), can also be initiated directly from the navigation bar. It actually executes a different command called* ***3DCORBIT****.*

✔ Select **Continuous Orbit** from the submenu.

The arcball disappears, and the continuous orbit icon is displayed, consisting of a sphere surrounded by two ellipses, as shown in Figure 13-53. The concept is simple: Dragging the cursor creates a motion vector. The direction and speed of the vector are applied to the model to set it in rotated motion around the target point. Motion continues until you press the left mouse button again.

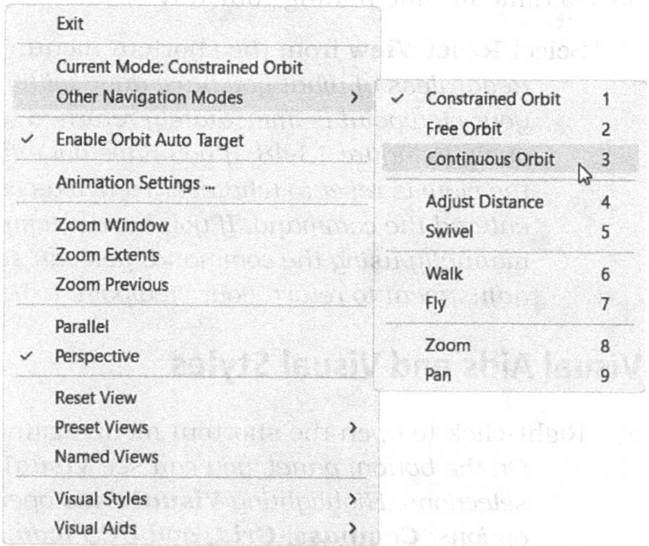

Figure 13-52
Navigation submenu

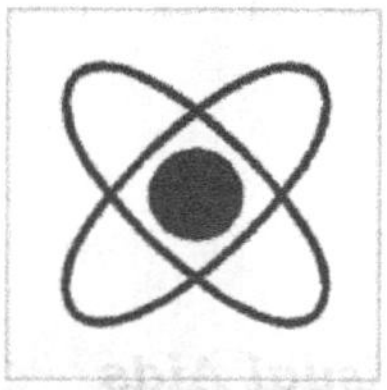

Figure 13-53
Continuous orbit icon

✔ With the continuous orbit cursor displayed, press and hold the left mouse button and then drag the cursor at a moderate speed in any direction.

This effect cannot be illustrated, but if you have done this correctly, your model should now be in continuous rotation. Try it again.

✔ Press the left mouse button at any time to stop rotation.

✔ Press and hold the left mouse button again, and drag the cursor in a different direction, at a different speed.

✔ Press the left mouse button to stop rotation.

✔ Press the left mouse button, drag, and release again.

Now, try changing directions without stopping.

✔ While the model is spinning, press and hold the left mouse button, and then drag in another direction.

Have a ball. Experiment. Play. Try to create gentle, controlled motions in different directions. Try to create fast spins in different directions. Try to create diagonal, horizontal, and vertical spins.

> **TIP**
> The best way to achieve control over continuous orbit is to specify a point actually on the model and imagine you are grabbing and spinning it. It is much easier to communicate the desired speed and direction in this way. Note the similarity between the action of continuous orbit and the free rotation or constrained orbit icon. The grabbing and turning are the same, but continuous orbit keeps rotating when you release the left mouse button, whereas free rotation stops. Also notice that however complex your dragging motion is, continuous orbit registers only one vector—the speed and direction of your last motion before releasing the left mouse button.

Here is one more trick before moving on:

✔ Set your model into a moderate spin in any direction.

✔ With your model spinning, right-click to open the shortcut menu.

The model keeps spinning. Many of the shortcut menu options can be accessed without disrupting continuous orbit.

✔ Select **Reset View** from the shortcut menu.

The model makes an immediate adjustment to the original view and continues to spin without interruption.

✔ Open the shortcut menu again.

✔ Highlight **Visual Styles** and select **Conceptual**.

The style is changed and the model keeps spinning—pretty impressive.

✔ To stop continuous orbit, press the left mouse button once quickly without dragging.

✔ Press **<Enter>** then **<Esc>** or the spacebar to exit **3DCORBIT**.

You return to the command prompt, but any changes you have made in point of view and visual style are retained.

Creating 3D Solids from 2D Outlines

extruding: A method of creating a three-dimensional object by projecting a two-dimensional object along a straight path in the third dimension.

In this chapter, you have created several 3D mesh primitives and one solid model. In this section, you look at three commands that create 3D objects from 2D outlines. You explore ***extruding***, revolving, and sweeping 2D shapes to create complex 3D objects.

Extrude

EXTRUDE	
Command	EXTRUDE
Alias	Ext
Panel	Modeling
Tool	

✔ To begin, erase all objects from your current drawing, or create a new drawing using the **acad3D.dwt** drawing template file.

✔ Type **Zoom <Enter>**, and then select **All** from the command line.

You begin by drawing a square and extruding it.

✔ Select **Home** > **View** > **Visual Styles** > **Realistic**.

✔ Turn **Snap Mode** on, and turn the **Grid** off.

✔ Select **Home** > **Draw** > **Rectangle**.

✔ Specify the point **(5.0,5.0,0)** for the first corner.

✔ Specify the point **(10.0,10.0,0)** for the second corner.

✔ Click the **Extrude** tool from the **Modeling** panel on the **Home** tab, as shown in Figure 13-54.

AutoCAD prompts for objects to extrude.

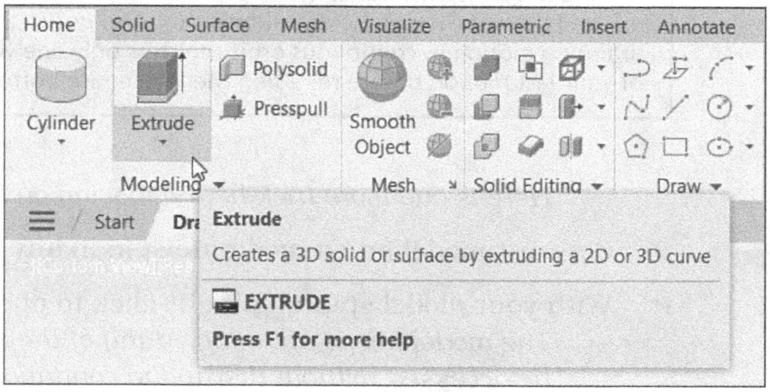

Figure 13-54
Extrude tool

✔ Select the square.

✔ Press **<Enter>** to end object selection.

*The **EXTRUDE** command automatically converts the 2D square to a solid and allow you to stretch in the positive or negative Z direction. The prompts also allow you to extrude in a direction other than along the Z-axis by drawing a directional line or using a preexisting line as a path.*

*You use the **Direction** option to create a slanted solid.*

✔ Select **Direction** from the command line.

AutoCAD prompts for the first point of a direction vector. The vector can be drawn anywhere.

- ✔ Specify the point **(10,10,0)** for the start point.

  To place the endpoint above the XY plane, you use a point filter.

- ✔ At the prompt for an endpoint, type **.xy <Enter>** for an .XY point filter.
- ✔ At the *of* prompt, specify the point **(10,12.5,0)**.
- ✔ At the *need z* prompt, type **2 <Enter>**.

  Your drawing should resemble Figure 13-55. Before moving on to revolving, you learn the technique of pressing and pulling solid objects.

Figure 13-55
Extruded rectangle

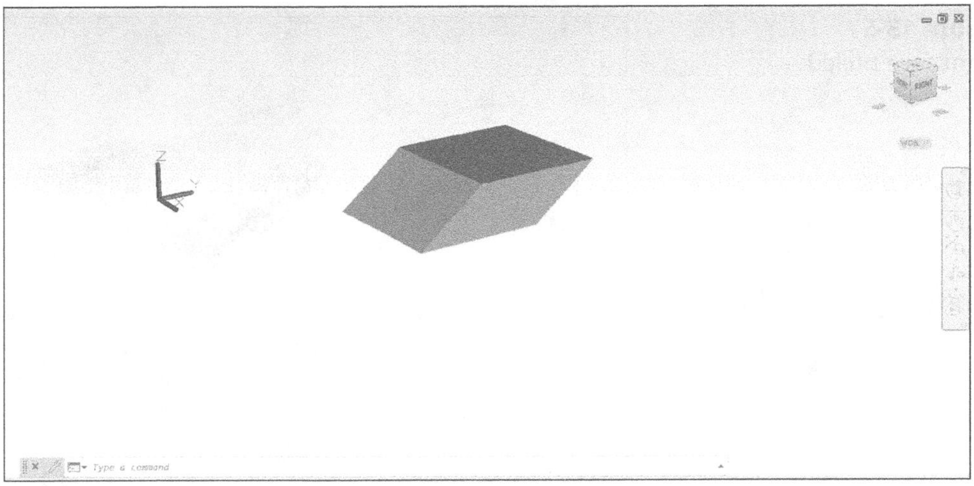

Presspull

PRESSPULL	
Command	PRESSPULL
Alias	(none)
Panel	Modeling
Tool	

The **PRESSPULL** command allows you to extend a solid object in a direction perpendicular to any of its faces.

- ✔ Click the **Presspull** tool from the **Modeling** panel on the **Home** tab, as shown in Figure 13-56.

  AutoCAD prompts you to select a face. The prompt is

  ```
  Select object or bounded area:
  ```

- ✔ Select the front face.

  AutoCAD provides a preview to drag and a dynamic UCS with Z normal to the face.

- ✔ Drag in the positive and negative directions, perpendicular to the selected face.
- ✔ With the object dragged in the positive direction, type **3 <Enter>**.
- ✔ Press **<Enter>** to exit the command.

  Your drawing should resemble Figure 13-57.

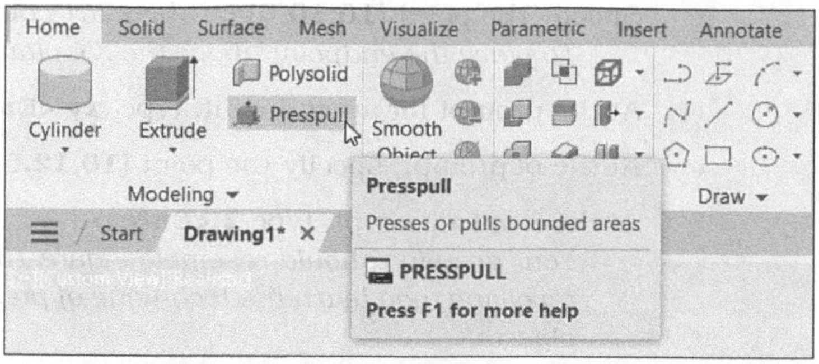

Figure 13-56
Presspull tool

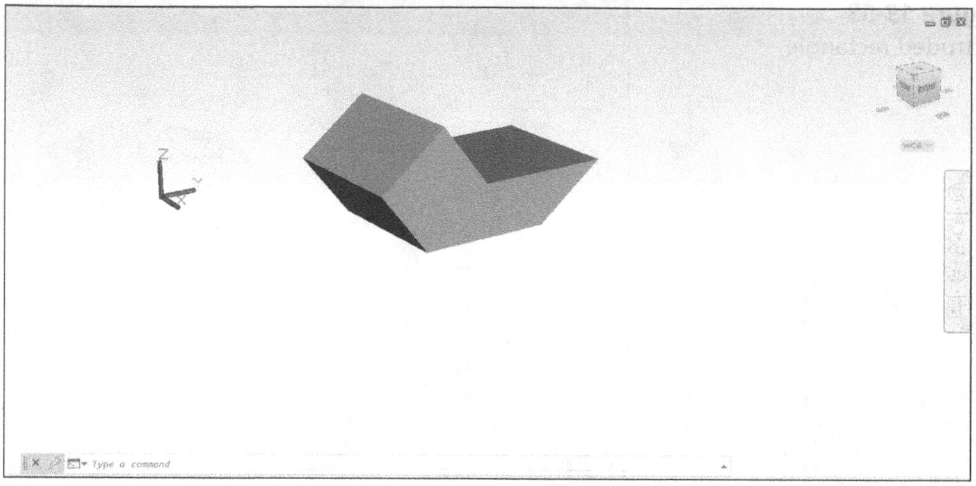

Figure 13-57
Front face pulled

Revolve

REVOLVE	
Command	REVOLVE
Alias	Rev
Panel	Modeling
Tool	

The **REVOLVE** command creates a 3D solid by continuous repetition of a 2D shape along the path of a circle or arc around a specified axis. Here, you draw a rectangle and revolve it 180° to create an arc-shaped model. Along the way you also learn how a 2D object can be converted to a 3D planar surface.

NOTE

Coordinate systems can sometimes get out of order after a DUCS has been in use. To correct this, simply click the **UCS**, **World** tool in the upper-right corner of the **Coordinates** panel on the **Home** tab. This returns you to the world coordinate system.

- ✔ Click the **Rectangle** tool from the **Draw** panel on the **Home** tab.
- ✔ Specify the point **(15,5,0)** for the first corner point.
- ✔ Specify the point **(17.5,10,0)** to create a 2.5 × 5.0 rectangle.

  *Next, you use the **Convert to Surface** tool to make this a rectangular surface rather than a wireframe outline. Note that this is for demonstration only. As in the **EXTRUDE** command, you can create a 3D solid directly from a 2D outline with the **REVOLVE** command.*

✔ Click the **Home** tab, and from the expanded **Solid Editing** panel, select **Convert to Surface** tool from the ribbon, as shown in Figure 13-58.

Notice that there is also a ***Convert to Solid*** *tool, which converts a model made of 3D surfaces to a solid model. AutoCAD prompts for object selection.*

✔ Select the rectangle.

✔ Right-click to end object selection.

The rectangle becomes a 3D surface; your drawing should resemble Figure 13-59.

Figure 13-58
Convert to Surface tool

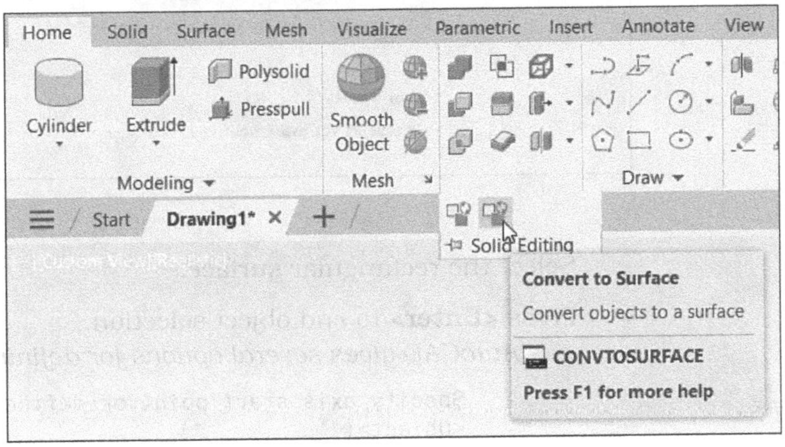

Figure 13-59
Rectangle becomes a 3D surface

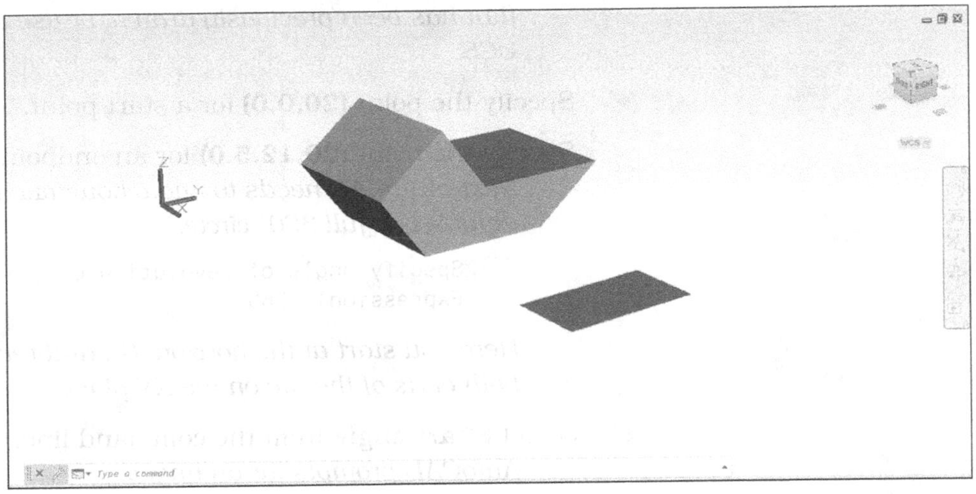

✔ Select **Home > Modeling > Extrude > Revolve**, as shown in Figure 13-60.

AutoCAD prompts for objects to revolve.

Figure 13-60
Revolve tool

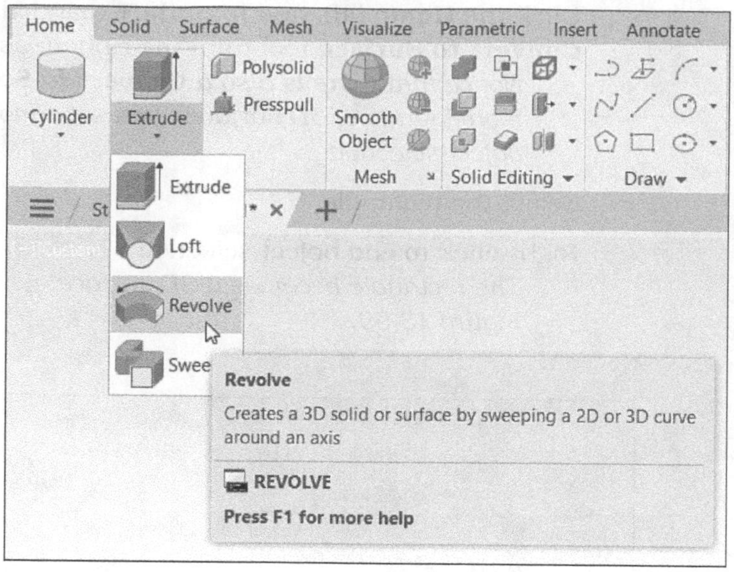

- ✔ Select the rectangular surface.
- ✔ Press **<Enter>** to end object selection.

  AutoCAD gives several options for defining an axis of rotation:

```
Specify axis start point or define axis by [Object/X/Y/Z]
<Object>:
```

  You can specify start points and endpoints, select a line or polyline that has been previously drawn, or use one of the axes of the current UCS.

- ✔ Specify the point **(20,0,0)** for a start point.
- ✔ Specify the point **(20,12.5,0)** for an endpoint.

  Next, AutoCAD needs to know how much revolution you want. The default is a full 360° circle.

```
Specify angle of revolution or [STart angle/Reverse/
EXpression] <360>:
```

  Here you start at the horizon, 0°, and revolve through 180°, placing both ends of the arc on the XY plane.

- ✔ Select **STart angle** from the command line.

  AutoCAD prompts for an angle.

- ✔ Press **<Enter>** to accept the default start angle, or type **0** if your angle has been changed.

  AutoCAD now prompts for an angle of revolution.

- ✔ Type **180 <Enter>**.

  The revolved solid is created and your drawing should resemble Figure 13-61.

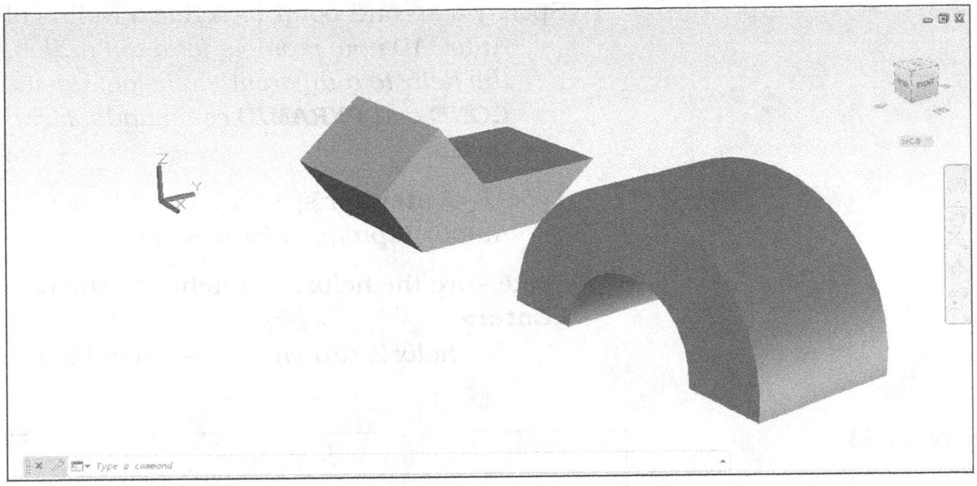

Figure 13-61
Revolved solid

Helix

HELIX	
Command	HELIX
Alias	(none)
Panel	Draw
Tool	

A helix can be drawn as either a 2D or 3D object. Here, you use the **HELIX** command to create a 3D spiral and then use the **SWEEP** command to convert the helix to a solid coil.

✔ Click the **Helix** tool from the expanded **Draw** panel on the **Home** tab, as shown in Figure 13-62.

*Helix characteristics can be changed using the **Properties palette**. Among the default specifications are two shown in the prompt area. Number of turns is the number of times the spiral shape goes around within the height you specify. The twist is either counterclockwise or clockwise.*

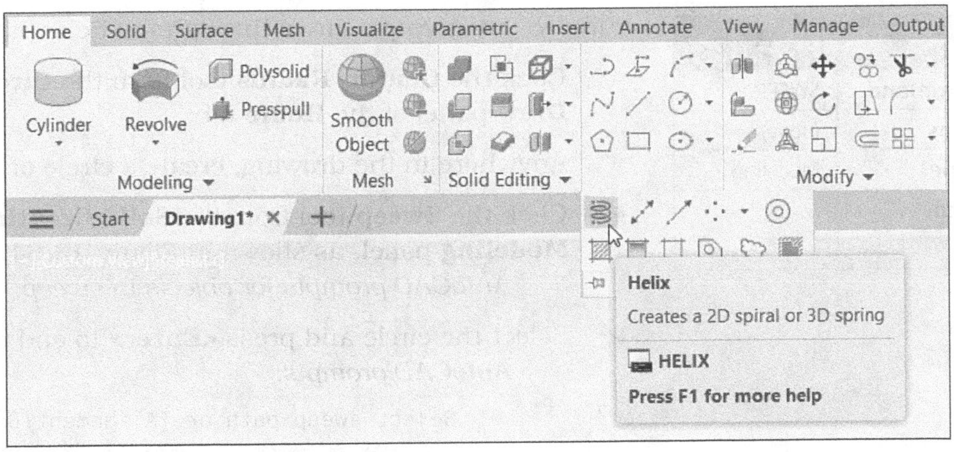

Figure 13-62
Helix tool

✔ Specify the point **(12.5,–5.0,0)** for the center point of the helix base.

AutoCAD prompts for a base radius:

```
Specify base radius or [Diameter] <1.0000>:
```

The default is retained from any previous use of the command in the current drawing session.

✔ Specify a second point to define a radius of **2.5000**.

AutoCAD now prompts for a top radius, showing that you can taper the helix to a different top height, similar to the options with the ***CONE*** *and* ***PYRAMID*** *commands. Here, you specify a smaller top radius.*

✔ Type **1 <Enter>** or specify a point to set a top radius of 1.0000.

AutoCAD prompts for a height.

✔ Make sure the helix is stretched in the positive direction, and type **4 <Enter>**.

The helix is drawn, as shown in Figure 13-63.

Figure 13-63
Helix

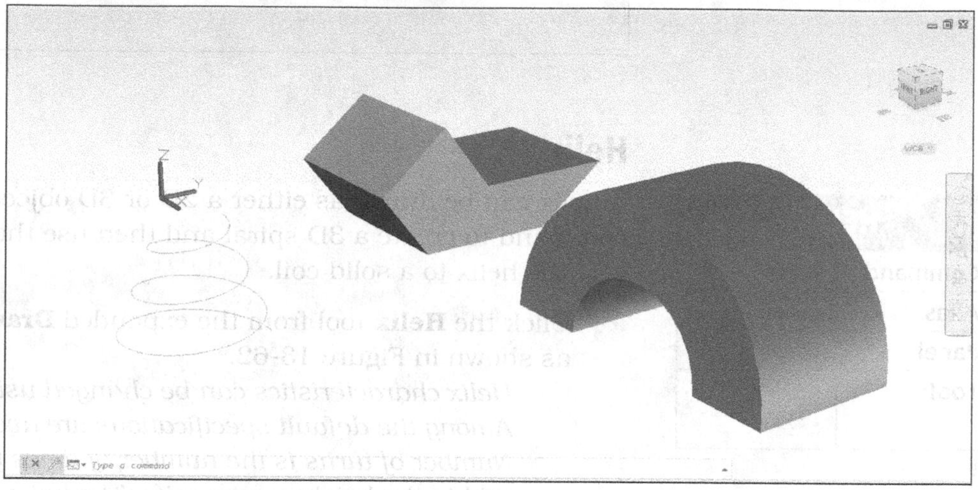

The SWEEP Command

SWEEP	
Command	SWEEP
Alias	(none)
Panel	Modeling
Tool	

Finally, you sweep a circle through the helix path to create a solid coil.

✔ Click the **Center**, **Radius** tool from the **Circle** drop-down menu on the **Draw** panel of the **Home** tab.

✔ Anywhere in the drawing, create a circle of radius 0.5.

✔ Click the **Sweep** tool from the **Solid Creation** drop-down menu on the **Modeling** panel, as shown in Figure 13-64.

AutoCAD prompts for objects to sweep.

✔ Select the circle and press **<Enter>** to end object selection.

AutoCAD prompts:

```
Select sweep path or [Alignment/Base point/Scale/Twist]:
```

The default is to select a path, such as the helix. By default, the object being swept is aligned perpendicular to the sweep path. The ***Alignment*** *option can be used to alter this.* ***Base point*** *allows you to start the sweep at a point other than the beginning of the sweep path.* ***Scale*** *allows you to change the scale of the objects being swept. By default, the object being swept remains perpendicular to the path at every point. To vary this and create a more complex sweep, use the* ***Twist*** *option. Here you use the default sweep path.*

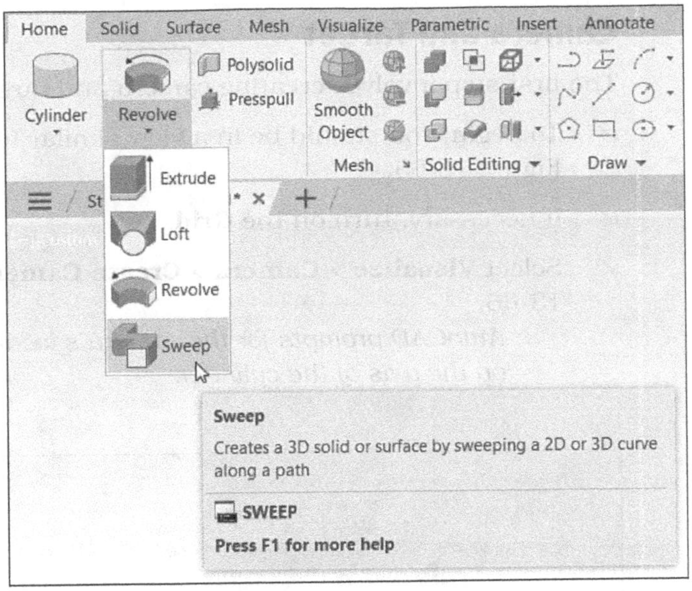

Figure 13-64
Sweep tool

✔ Select the helix.

Your drawing should resemble Figure 13-65.

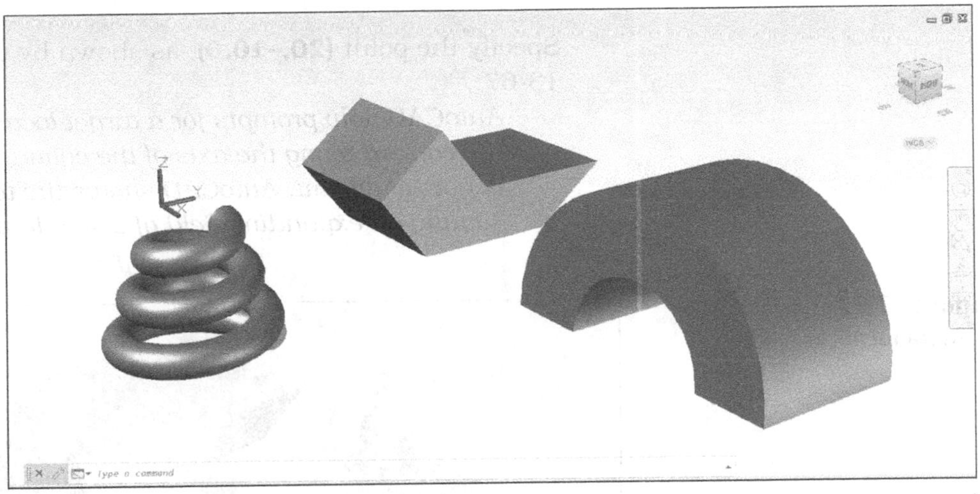

Figure 13-65
Swept helix

That completes this section on modeling techniques. In the final two sections, you learn to use the **CAMERA** and **3DWALK** commands to move your point of view through the 3D landscape, and **ANIPATH** to create an animated walk-through.

Walking Through a 3D Landscape

AutoCAD has features that allow you to move your point of view through the 3D space of a model. This is useful in architectural drawings in which you can create a simulated walk-through of a model. In this section, you use the **3DWALK** command to navigate through the objects in your drawing. The process involves creating a camera and a target, and then using arrow keys to move the camera. The goal is to navigate under the cylinder, as if you were walking under an arch.

Camera and Target

The first step involves creating camera and target locations.

✔ To begin, you should be in a view similar to that shown previously in Figure 13-65.

✔ If necessary, turn on the **Grid**.

✔ Select **Visualize > Camera > Create Camera**, as shown in Figure 13-66.

AutoCAD prompts for the camera's location. You start with a location on the axis of the cylinder.

Figure 13-66
Create Camera tool

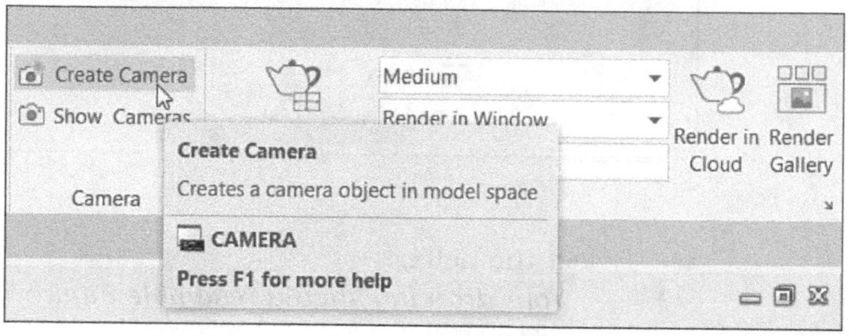

✔ Specify the point **(20,–10,0)**, as shown by the camera glyph in Figure 13-67.

AutoCAD now prompts for a target location. Here, you want to point the camera along the axis of the cylinder. The distance to the target is not significant. AutoCAD shows the target with a preview representing an expanding field of vision in the direction specified.

Figure 13-67
Camera location

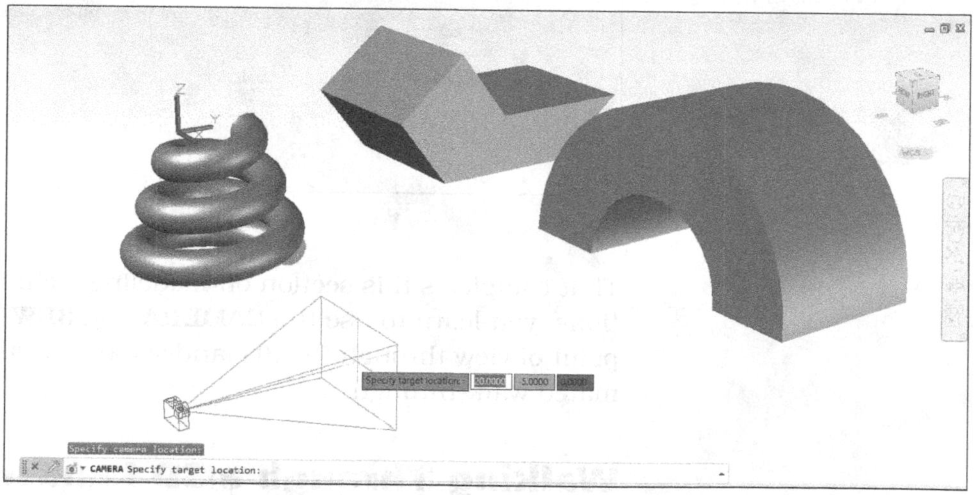

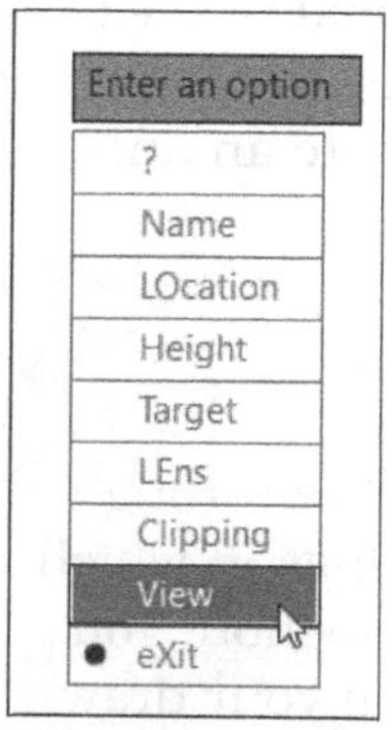

Figure 13-68
Dynamic Input menu

✔ Specify the point **(20,–5,0)**, as shown by the field of vision mechanism in Figure 13-67.

AutoCAD shows you a set of options on the ***Dynamic Input*** *menu in Figure 13-68. You choose the* ***View*** *option, which changes the display to align with the camera's point of view on the target.*

> **TIP**
>
> If you cannot see the **View** option, the **Dynamic Input** menu may be cut off at the bottom and covers the **View** option on the command line. If this happens, click once in any open section of the drawing area to move the menu.

✔ Select **View** from the command line or the **Dynamic Input** menu.

With another small menu, AutoCAD prompts you to verify switching to the camera view.

✔ Select **Yes** from the menu.

This completes the command and switches your view to the camera view shown in Figure 13-69. You are now ready to proceed with walking the model.

Figure 13-69
Camera view

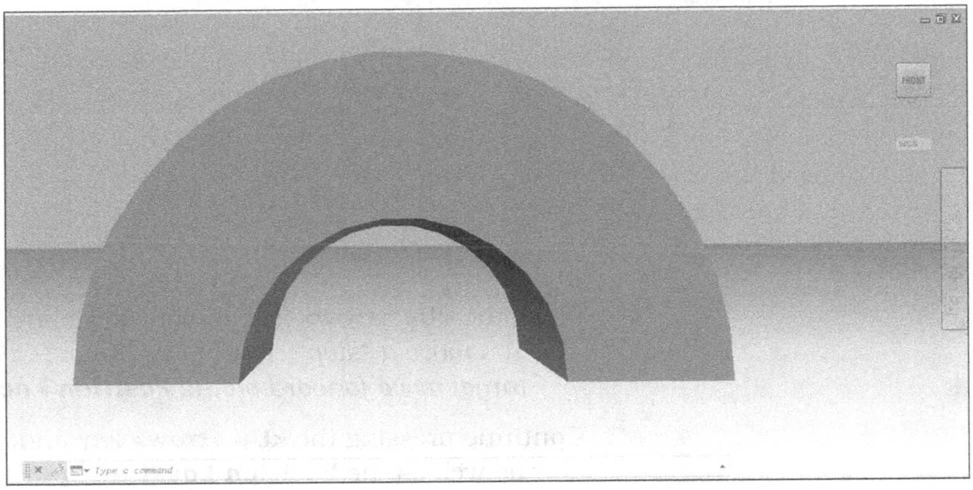

The 3DWALK and 3DFLY Commands

The **3DWALK** and **3DFLY** commands use identical procedures, but **3DWALK** keeps you in the *XY* plane, whereas **3DFLY** allows you to move above or below the plane. Here, **3DWALK** is used to walk beneath the arch, turn left to view the other objects, and then turn around and walk back between the objects.

✔ Type **3DWALK <Enter>**.

*You see the **Position Locator** palette in Figure 13-70. This palette shows a plan view of the objects in the drawing with a red circle representing the camera position and a green triangle representing the target and field of vision. Before you begin to move through the model, it may be helpful to zoom out in the **Position Locator** palette to provide a little more room to work with.*

✔ If necessary, click once on the **Zoom In** or **Zoom Out** tool along the top of the **Position Locator palette**.

*Your objects should appear smaller in the **Position Locator palette**, as shown in Figure 13-70. You use the **<Up arrow>** key to move forward through the arch. Notice that AutoCAD also positions a green cross on the screen, indicating the target position.*

> **TIP**
>
> If your mouse has a scroll wheel, you can press and hold the scroll wheel over the small preview area on the **Position Location palette** to adjust the preview.

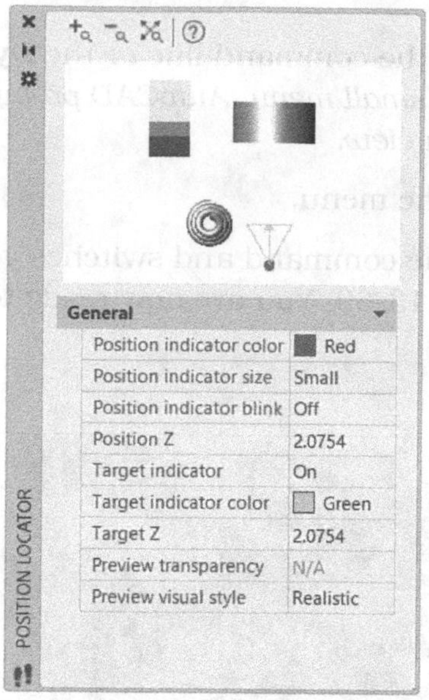

Figure 13-70
Position Locator palette

✔ Press the **<Up arrow>** key on your keyboard once to move forward.

*You move a "step" closer to the arch. Notice also that the camera and target move forward on the **Position Locator** palette.*

✔ Continue pressing the **<Up arrow>** key and observing the drawing window as well as the **Position Locator**.

✔ Walk beneath the arch until you reach the other side. Watch the **Position Locator** palette to ensure that you moved the camera location completely past the arch.

*At this point the camera location on the **Position Locator** palette should be completely beyond the arch, as shown in Figure 13-71.*

✔ Press the **<Left arrow>** key once and observe the **Position Locator** palette.

The camera and target shifts to the left on the palette, and your viewpoint shifts in the drawing, but you see no change because there is nothing but the horizon in this direction.

✔ Press the **<Left arrow>** key again.

Notice that the camera continues to move to the left, but the target is still straight ahead.

✔ Continue moving to the left until the camera and target image is between the cylinder and the boxes to the left.

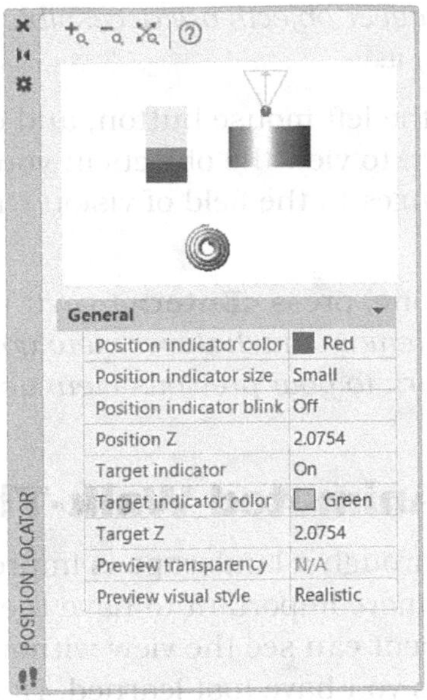

Figure 13-71
Camera location image is beyond arch

✔ Move the cursor over the arrow at the top of the green triangle representing the field of vision in the **Position Locator palette**.

*When the cursor is in this position, it appears as a hand icon, like the **PAN** command. With the hand icon showing, you can move and expand the field of vision.*

✔ With the hand icon showing and resting on the field of vision triangle (not on the red "camera"), press and hold the left mouse button, and drag the triangle around 180°.

Your camera is now pointing toward the coil. Your drawing should resemble Figure 13-72.

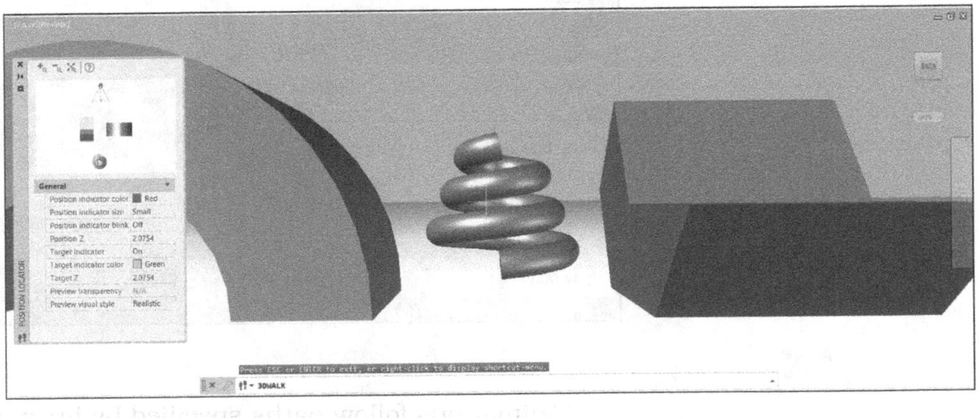

Figure 13-72
Camera pointing toward coil

✔ Continue using the arrow keys and the mouse along with the pan cursor to move through the objects on your model.

*There is one other trick you should try. In addition to changing your field of vision in the **Position Locator palette**, you can change it directly in the drawing by dragging your mouse. Whereas moving the field of vision triangle only creates movement within the XY plane, the mouse can be moved up, down, sideways, and diagonally* *to view whatever objects are accessible from your current camera location. Try it.*

✔ Press and hold the left mouse button, and drag the mouse right and left, up and down to view the objects in your drawing. As you do this, observe the changes in the field of vision triangle in the **Position Locator** palette.

✔ When you are done, press **<Enter>** to exit the command.

The objects remain in whatever view you have created. Of course, you can return to your previous view using the ***U*** *command.*

Creating an Animated Walk-Through

The ability to walk through a landscape is impressive, but for presentation purposes, it may be more important to have the walk-through animated so that any potential client can see the view without having to interact with AutoCAD in the ways you have just learned. Here, you use the **ANIPATH** command to create a simple animation of a walk-through that is slightly different from the one you did manually in the last section. You begin by switching to a plan view.

✔ Select **Visualize** > **Named Views** > **Named Views** > **Top**, as shown in Figure 13-73.

Regardless of what was in your view previously, you should now be in the plan view shown in Figure 13-74.

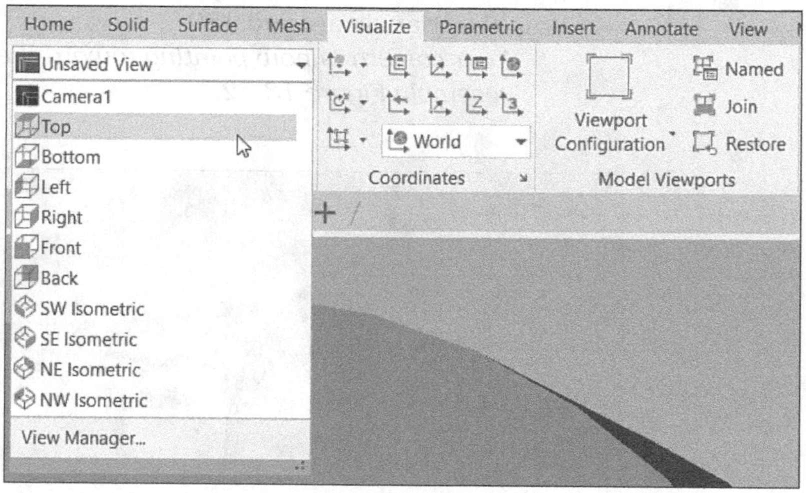

Figure 13-73
Named Views panel

Animations follow paths specified by lines, polylines, or 3D polylines. For this exercise, you draw the simple polyline path shown in Figure 13-75. First, you draw it with right angles and then fillet one corner, as shown.

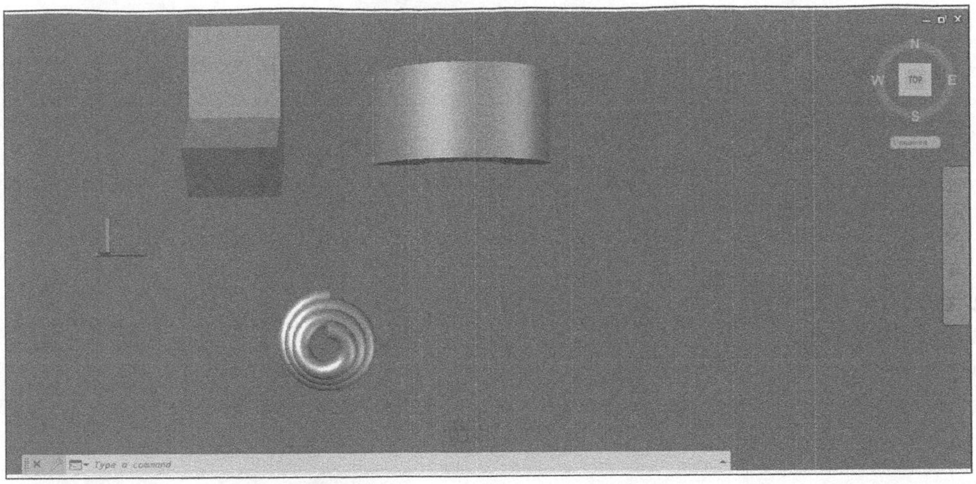

Figure 13-74
Plan view

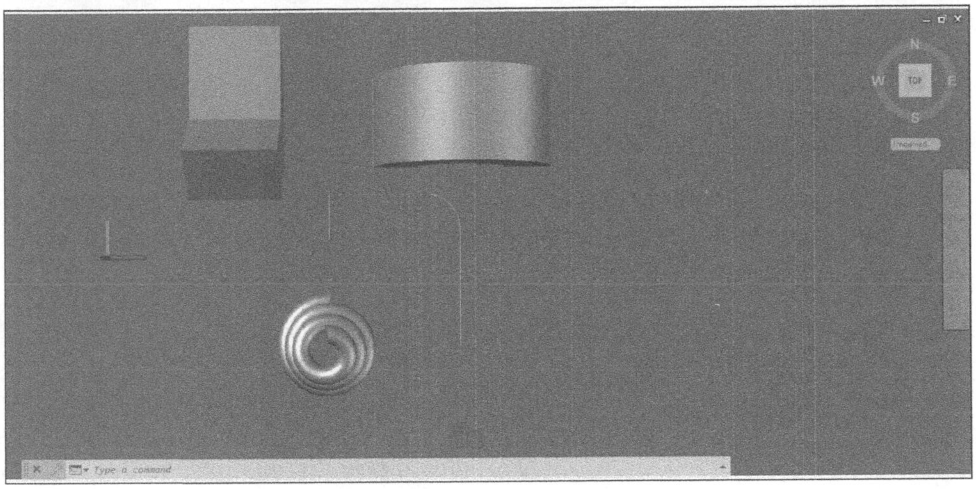

Figure 13-75
Polyline animation path

- ✔ Select **Home** > **Draw** > **Polyline**.
- ✔ Specify the point **(20,–5,0)** for a start point.
- ✔ Specify the point **(20,3.5,0)** for the next point.
- ✔ Specify the point **(12.5,3.5,0)** for the next point.
- ✔ Specify the point **(12.5,1,0)** for the final point.
- ✔ Press **<Enter>** to complete the polyline and exit the command.

  Now, you fillet the right corner to complete the path. The fillet has a significant impact on the animation.
- ✔ Type **F <Enter>** or click the **Fillet** tool from the **Modify** panel on the **Home** tab.
- ✔ Select **Radius** from the command line.
- ✔ Type **2 <Enter>** for a radius specification.
- ✔ At the prompt for a first object, select the vertical line segment on the right.

✔ At the prompt for a second object, select the horizontal segment.

Your drawing should resemble Figure 13-75.

You are now ready to create an animation.

✔ Type **ANIPATH <Enter>**.

*This opens the **Motion Path Animation** dialog box shown in Figure 13-76.*

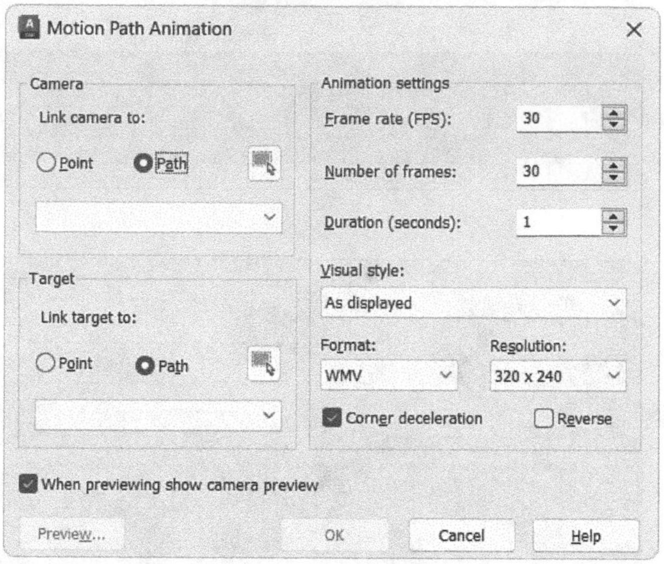

Figure 13-76
Motion Path Animation dialog box

✔ In the dialog box, select the **Path** option in the middle of the **Camera** panel, and then click the **Select** button to its right.

The dialog box disappears, giving you access to the drawing area.

✔ Select the polyline.

*The polyline is selected and AutoCAD prompts for a **Path Name**, as shown in Figure 13-77.*

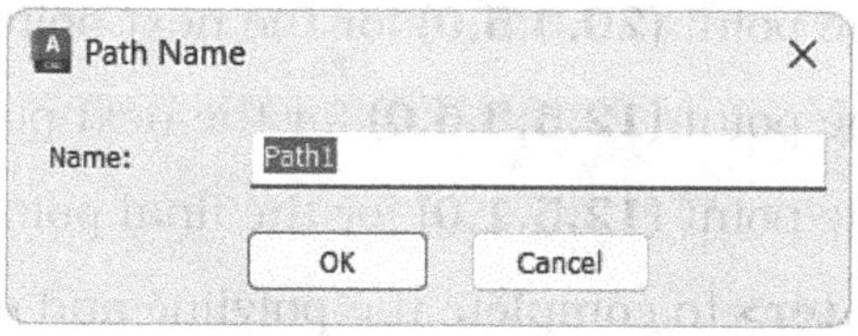

Figure 13-77
Path Name dialog box

✔ Click **OK** to accept the default name (Path1).

This brings you back to the dialog box. You make one more critical adjustment.

✔ In the **Animation settings** panel on the right, change the **Duration** setting to **10**.

If you did not change this setting, the animation would move very quickly, and it would be difficult to see what was happening.

✔ Make sure the **When previewing show camera preview** box is checked (refer to Figure 13-76).

✔ Click the **Preview** button in the bottom left of the **Motion Path Animation** dialog box.

AutoCAD shows you a preview of the path and then the actual animation preview. Watch closely. What you see will be an animation based on moving a camera along the specified path. Notice the difference between the gentle swing to the left along the fillet path and the abrupt left turn at the final right angle. When the animation is done, the ***Animation Preview*** *dialog box should resemble Figure 13-78.*

Figure 13-78
Animation preview

✔ Click the **X** in the upper-right corner to close the **Animation Preview dialog box**.

This brings you back to the ***Motion Path Animation*** *dialog box.*

At this point, you can cancel the animation and return to your drawing, or click ***OK*** *to save it. If you click* ***OK****, AutoCAD initiates a process of creating a video. It's saved as a WMV file that can be played back by other programs such as Windows Media Player. Once created, you can run the video by opening the file and following the Windows Media Player procedure.*

There you have it. Congratulations on your first video.

Chapter Summary

This chapter explained how to draw polysolids, cones, pyramids, torus, and mesh models and to extrude 2D objects to form 3D solids. You can slice and section solids and convert 2D outlines into 3D solids and surfaces. You learned how to use powerful tools for creating and adjusting 3D points of view and present objects in continuous orbit. You also discovered how to create a controlled walk-through of a 3D model and record an animated walk-through for playback in AutoCAD or other media software.

Chapter Test Questions

Multiple Choice

Circle the correct answer.

1. Which of these *cannot* be extruded?

a. Line
b. Polysolid
c. Circle
d. Rectangle

2. Which of these is *not* a solid?

a. Extruded circle
b. Swept rectangle
c. Torus
d. Helix

3. In **3DWALK**, the ______________ is always in the *XY* plane.

a. Camera location
b. Target location
c. Field of vision
d. Viewpoint

4. Unlike **3DWALK** and **3DFLY**, an animated walk-through requires a

a. Camera
b. Target
c. Path
d. Gizmo

5. Mesh models should be converted to solid models

a. Before editing
b. After changing visual styles
c. Before rendering
d. After smoothing

Matching

Write the number of the correct answer on the line.

a. Floating viewport _____
b. Tiled viewport _____
c. Torus _____
d. Face _____
e. Arcball _____

1. Solid primitive
2. Not plotted
3. Plotted
4. Subobject
5. **3DFORBIT**

True or False

Circle the correct answer.

1. **True or False**: Tiled viewports are required for editing 3D models.
2. **True or False**: In a **Three: Right** viewport configuration, all three viewports are in parallel projection by default.
3. **True or False**: In a **Three: Right** viewport configuration, all three viewports are in plan view by default.
4. **True or False**: You can select the face of a solid box without a filter, but the filter makes it easier.
5. **True or False**: Only meshes can be smoothed; only solids can be combined.

Questions

1. Name at least three commands that create 3D models from 2D objects.
2. While still in the **3DORBIT** command, what is the quickest way to return to the view you started with before entering **3DORBIT**? How do you access this feature without leaving the **3DORBIT** command?
3. How many direction vectors are specified by the motion of your mouse in the **Continuous Orbit** mode?
4. What elements must be present in your drawing before you can use the **3DWALK** and **3DFLY** commands?
5. What additional element must be present before you can create an animated walk-through?

Drawing Problems

1. Create a drawing using the acad3D.dwt drawing template file, draw a circle with a radius of **0.5** units anywhere.
2. Draw a helix with a center point at **(0,0,0)**, base radius **5.0**, top radius **1.0**, and height **5.0**.
3. Sweep the circle through the helix path to create a solid coil.
4. Draw a cone with base center at **(0,0,0)**, radius **5.0**, and height **6.5**.
5. Subtract the coil from the cone.
6. Create a section view of the object; cut along the *YZ* plane.

13 chapterthirteen

Chapter Drawing Projects

G Drawing 13-1: *Revolve Designs* [ADVANCED]

The **REVOLVE** command is fascinating and powerful. As you become familiar with it, you might find yourself identifying objects in the world that can be conceived as surfaces of revolution. To encourage this process, this page of 12 revolved objects and designs has been provided. The next drawing is also an application of the **REVOLVE** procedure.

To complete the exercise, you need only the **PLINE** and **REVOLVE** commands. In the first six designs, the path curves and axes of rotation used to create the designs are shown. In the other six, you are on your own.

Exact shapes and dimensions are not important in this exercise, but imagination is. When you have completed the first designs, invent some of your own. Also, consider adding materials and lights to any of your designs and viewing them from different viewpoints using **3DORBIT**.

Drawing 13-1
REVOLVE designs

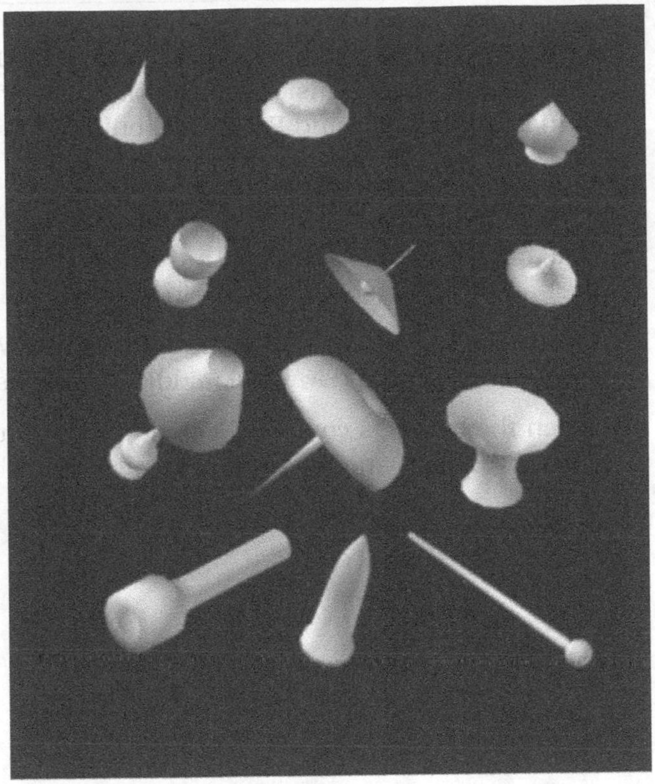

M Drawing 13-2: *Tapered Bushing* [ADVANCED]

This is a more technical application of the **REVOLVE** command. By carefully following the dimensions in the side view, you can create the complete drawing using **PLINE** and **REVOLVE** only.

Drawing Suggestions

- Use at least two viewports with the dimensioned side view in one viewport and the 3D isometric view in another.
- Create the 2D outline as shown and then **REVOLVE** it 270° around a centerline running down the middle of the bushing.
- When the model is complete, consider how you might present it in different views on a paper space layout.

Drawing 13-2
Tapered bushing

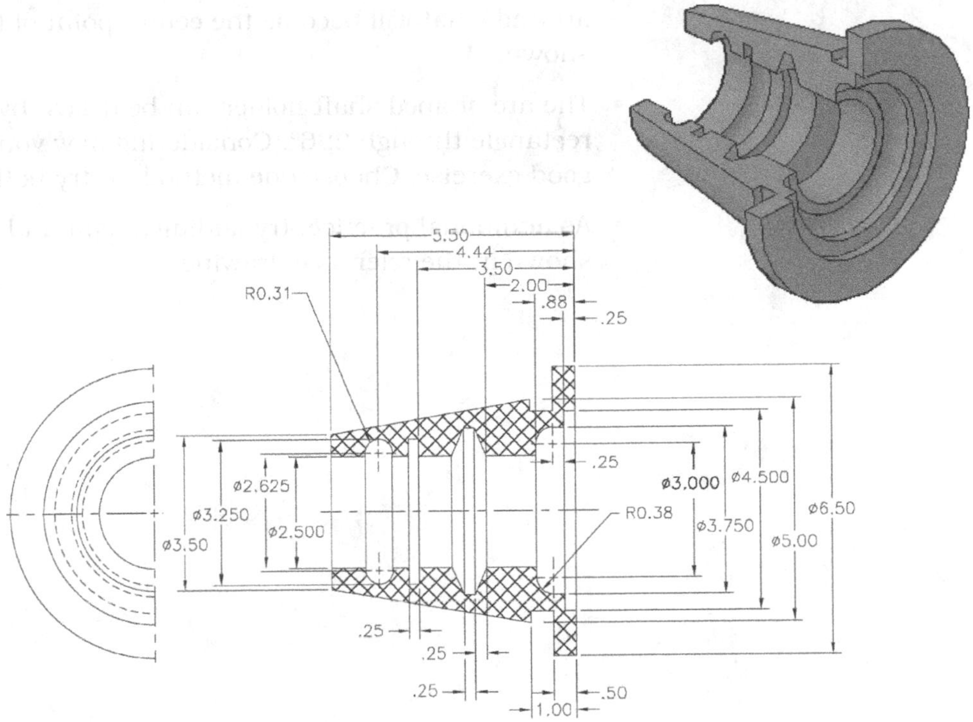

G Drawing 13-3: *Globe* [ADVANCED]

This drawing uses a new command. The **SPHERE** command creates a sphere as a 3D solid, which should be no trouble to learn and use at this point. You can find it on the **Modeling** panel's **Solid Primitives** drop-down menu. Like a circle, it requires only a center point and a radius or diameter.

Drawing Suggestions

- Use a three-viewport configuration with top and front views on the left and an isometric 3D view on the right.
- Use 12-sided pyramids to create the base and the top part of the base.
- Draw the 12.25 cylindrical shaft in vertical position, and then rotate it around what will become the center point of the sphere, using the angle shown.
- The arc-shaped shaft holder can be drawn by sweeping or revolving a rectangle through 226°. Considering how you would do it both ways is a good exercise. Choose one method, or try both.
- As additional practice, try adding a light and rendering the globe as shown in the reference drawing.

Drawing 13-3
Globe

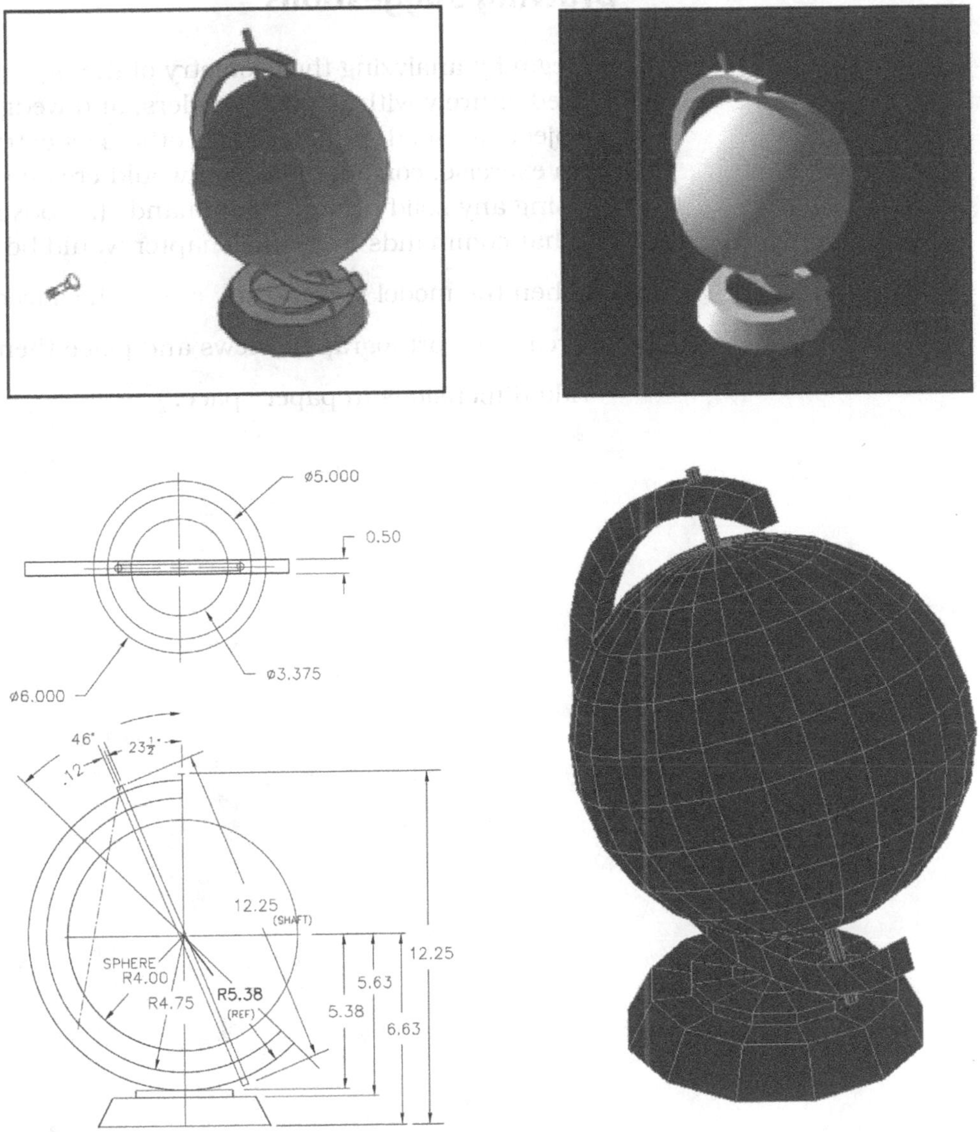

M Drawing 13-4: *Pivot Mount* [ADVANCED]

This drawing gives you a workout in constructive geometry. It is suggested to do this drawing with completely dimensioned orthographic views and the 3D model as shown. Also, create a sliced view of the model as shown in the reference figure.

Drawing Suggestions

- Begin by analyzing the geometry of the figure. Notice that it can be created entirely with boxes, cylinders, and wedges, or you can create some objects as solid primitives and others as extruded or revolved figures. As an exercise, consider how you would create the entire model without using any solid primitive commands (no boxes, wedges, or cylinders). What commands from this chapter would be required?
- When the model is complete, create the sliced view as shown.
- Create the orthographic views and place them in paper space viewports.
- Add dimensions in paper space.

Drawing 13-4
Pivot mount

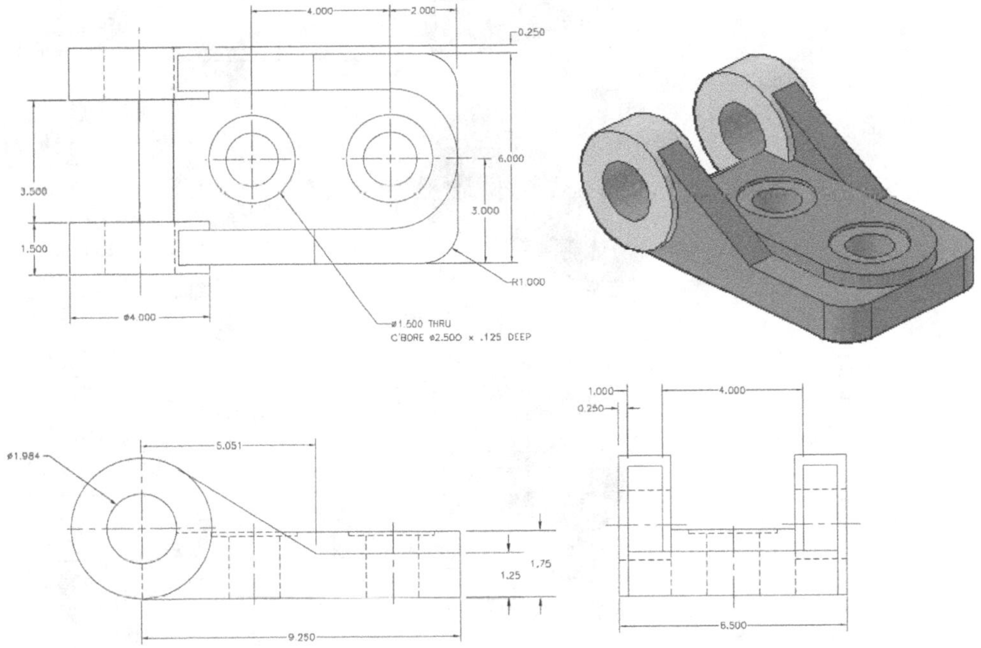

M Drawings 13-5 [ADVANCED]

The drawings that follow are 3D solid models derived from 2D drawings. You can start from scratch or begin with the 2D drawing and use some of the geometry as a guide to your 3D model.

Drawing 13-5a
Flanged bushing, stepped shaft, base plate

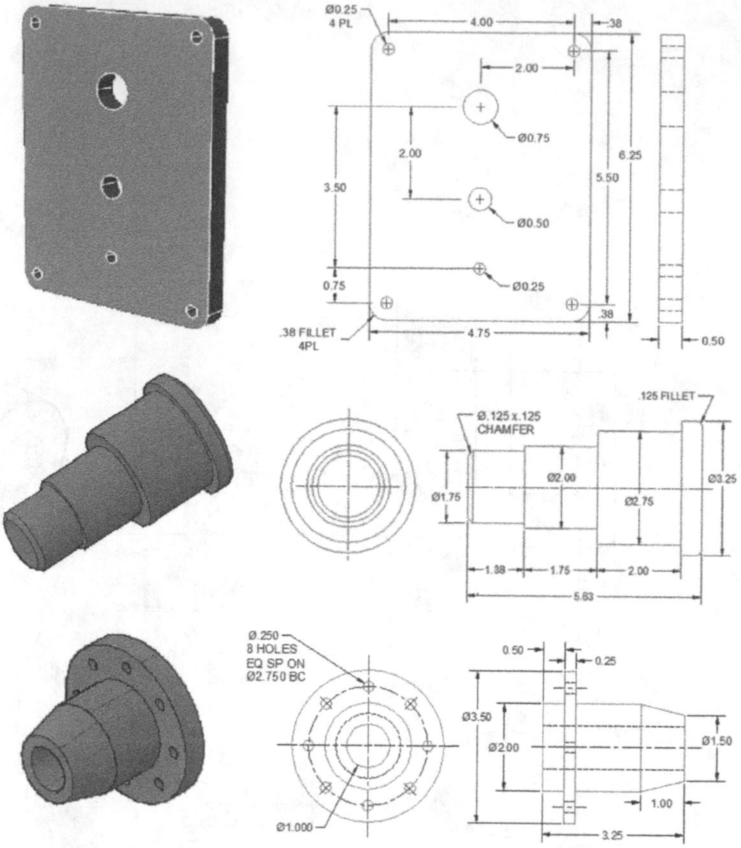

Drawing 13-5b
Test bracket, packing flange

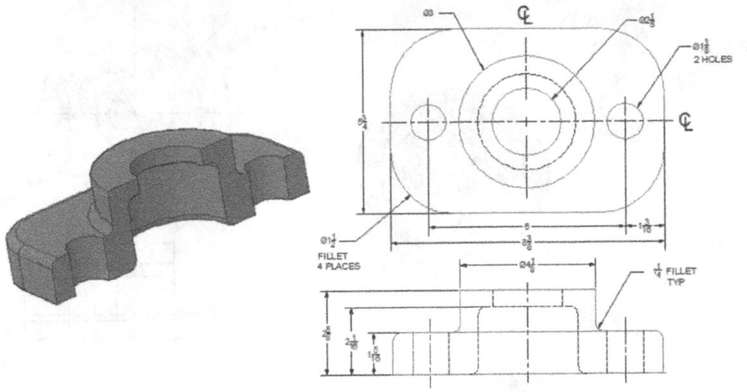

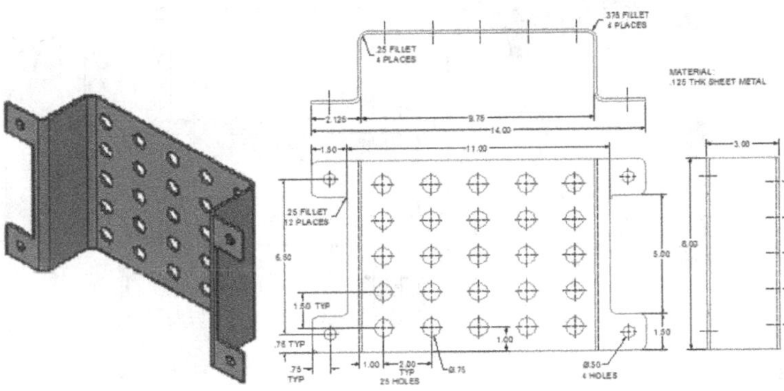

Drawing 13-5c
Alignment wheel, grooved hub

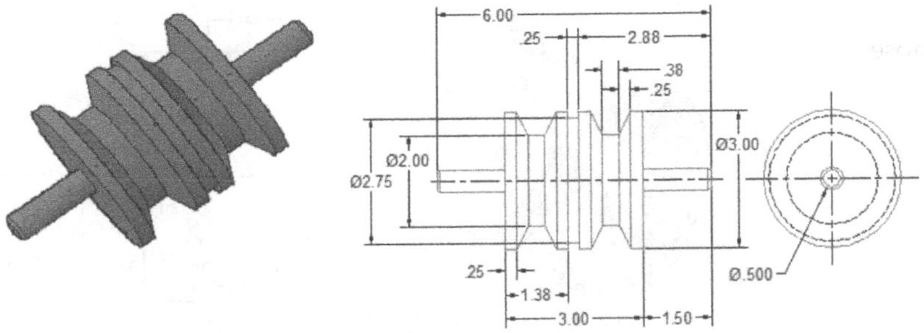

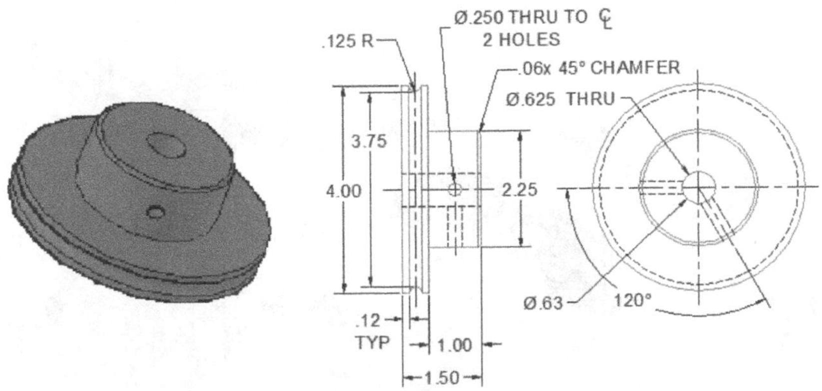

Drawing 13-5d
Slotted flange, tool block

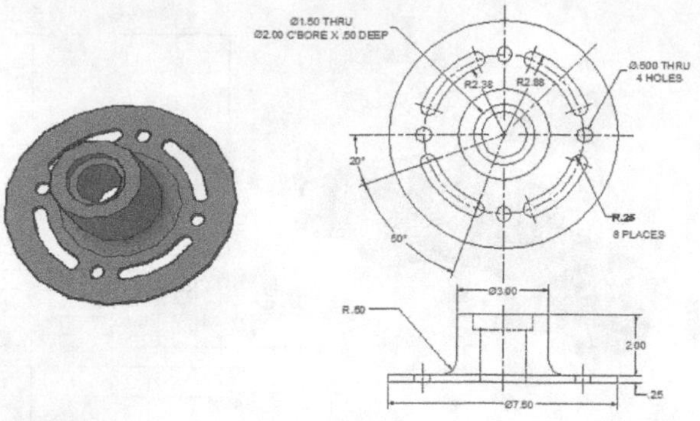

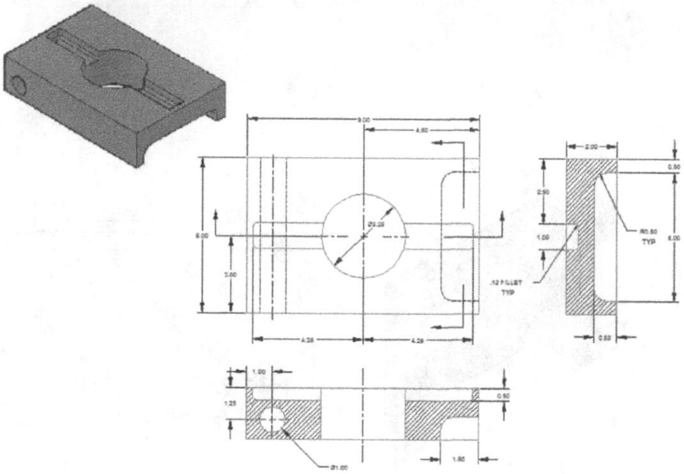

Drawing 13-5e
Flanged wheel, nose adapter

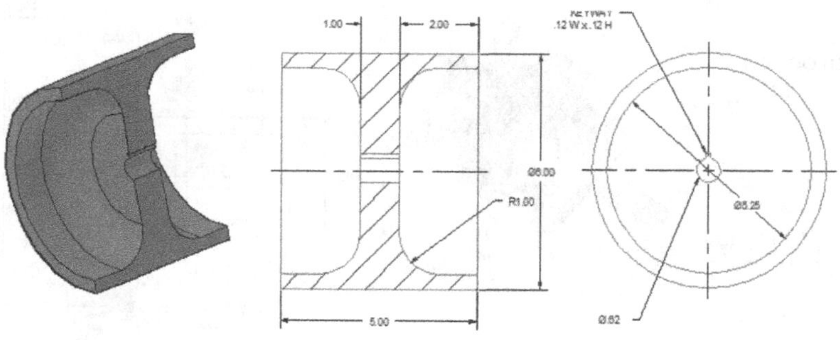

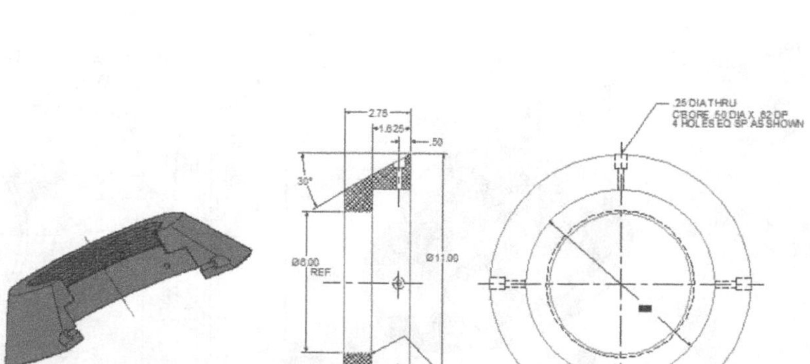

Drawing 13-5f
Angle support, mirror mounting plate

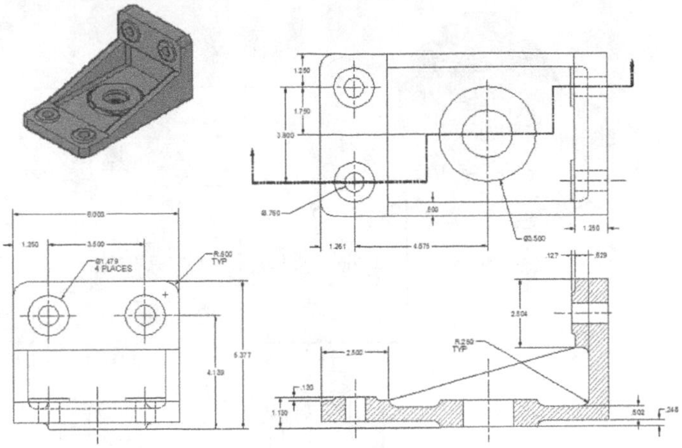

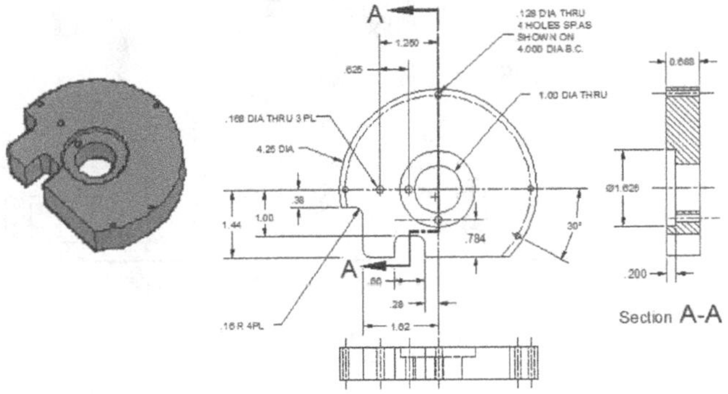

Drawing 13-5g
Double bearing

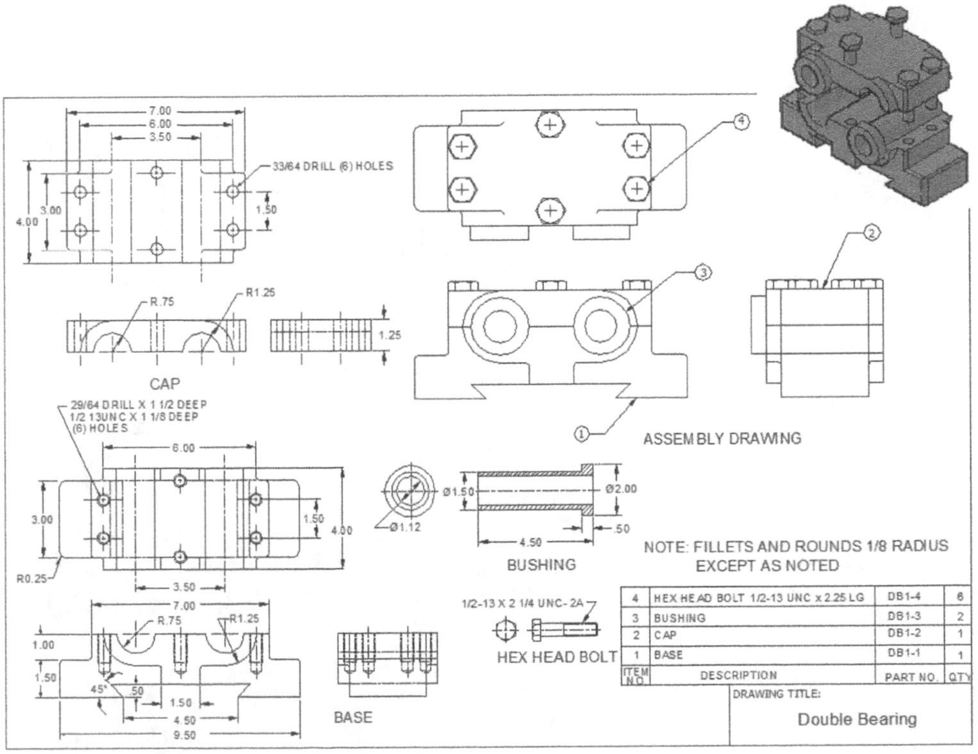

Drawing 13-5h
Base assembly

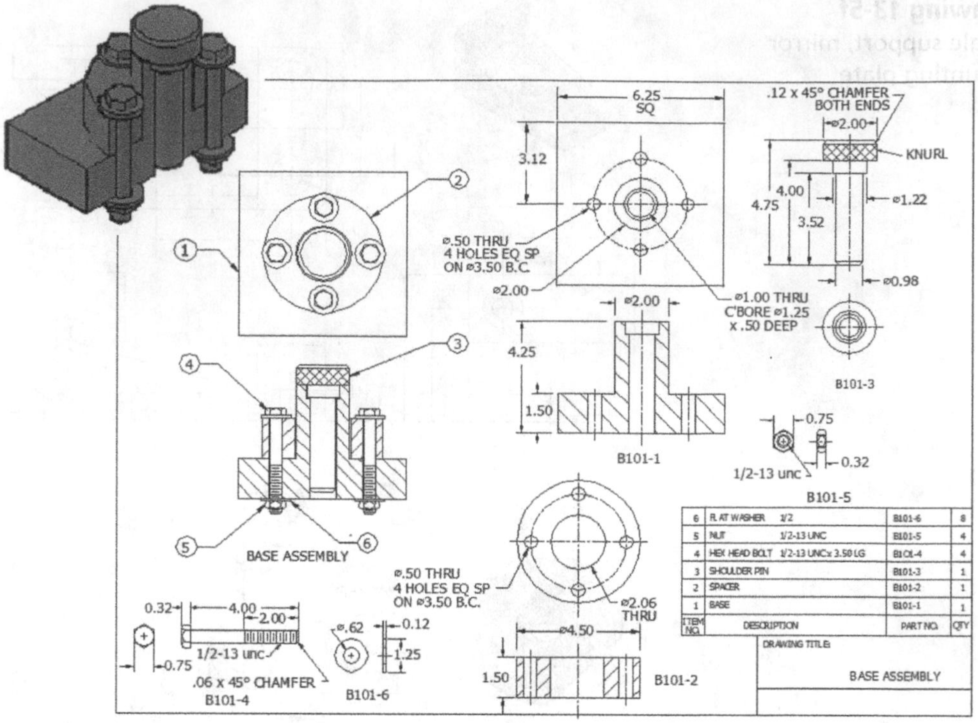

Appendix A

Drawing Projects

The drawings on the following pages are offered as additional challenges and are presented without suggestions. They may be drawn in two or three dimensions and may be presented as multiple-view drawings, hidden-line drawings, or rendered drawings. In short, you are on your own to explore and master everything you have learned.

A

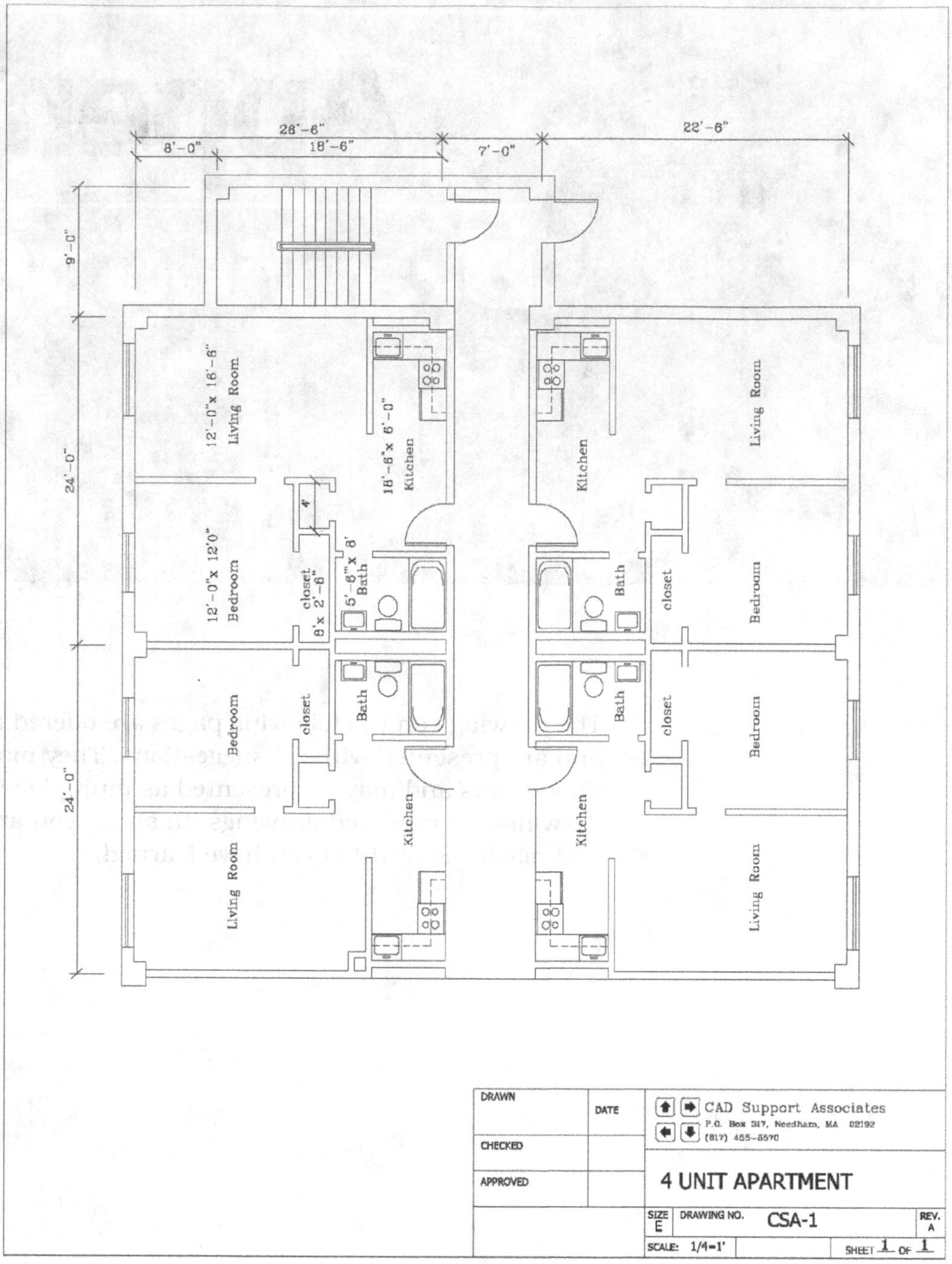
26'-6"
8'-0"
18'-6"
7'-0"
22'-6"
9'-0"
24'-0"
24'-0"
12'-0"x 16'-6"
Living Room
18'-6"x 6'-0"
Kitchen
4'
12'-0"x 12'0"
Bedroom
closet
8'x 2'-6"
5'-8"x 8'
Bath
Kitchen
Living Room
Bath
closet
Bedroom
Bedroom
closet
Bath
Kitchen
Living Room
Bath
closet
Bedroom
Kitchen
Living Room
DRAWN
DATE
CHECKED
APPROVED
CAD Support Associates
P.O. Box 317, Needham, MA 02192
(617) 455-8570
4 UNIT APARTMENT
SIZE
E
DRAWING NO.
CSA-1
REV.
A
SCALE: 1/4=1'
SHEET 1 OF 1

M

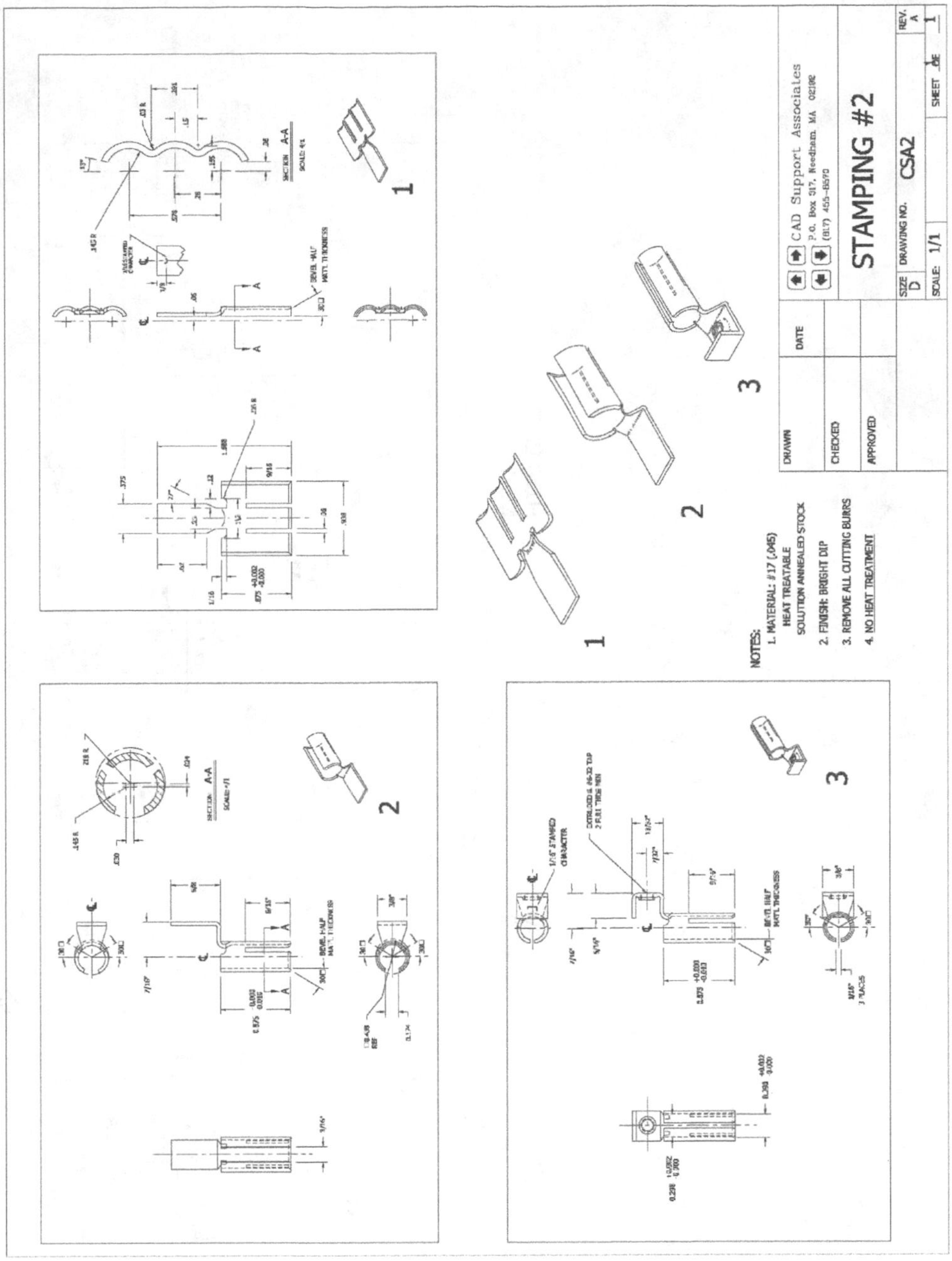
NOTES:
1. MATERIAL: #17 (.045)
HEAT TREATABLE
SOLUTION ANNEALED STOCK
2. FINISH: BRIGHT DIP
3. REMOVE ALL CUTTING BURRS
4. NO HEAT TREATMENT
CAD Support Associates
DRAWN
DATE
CHECKED
APPROVED
STAMPING #2
SIZE D
DRAWING NO. CSA2
REV. A
SCALE: 1/1
SHEET 1 OF 1
SECTION A-A
1
2
3

E

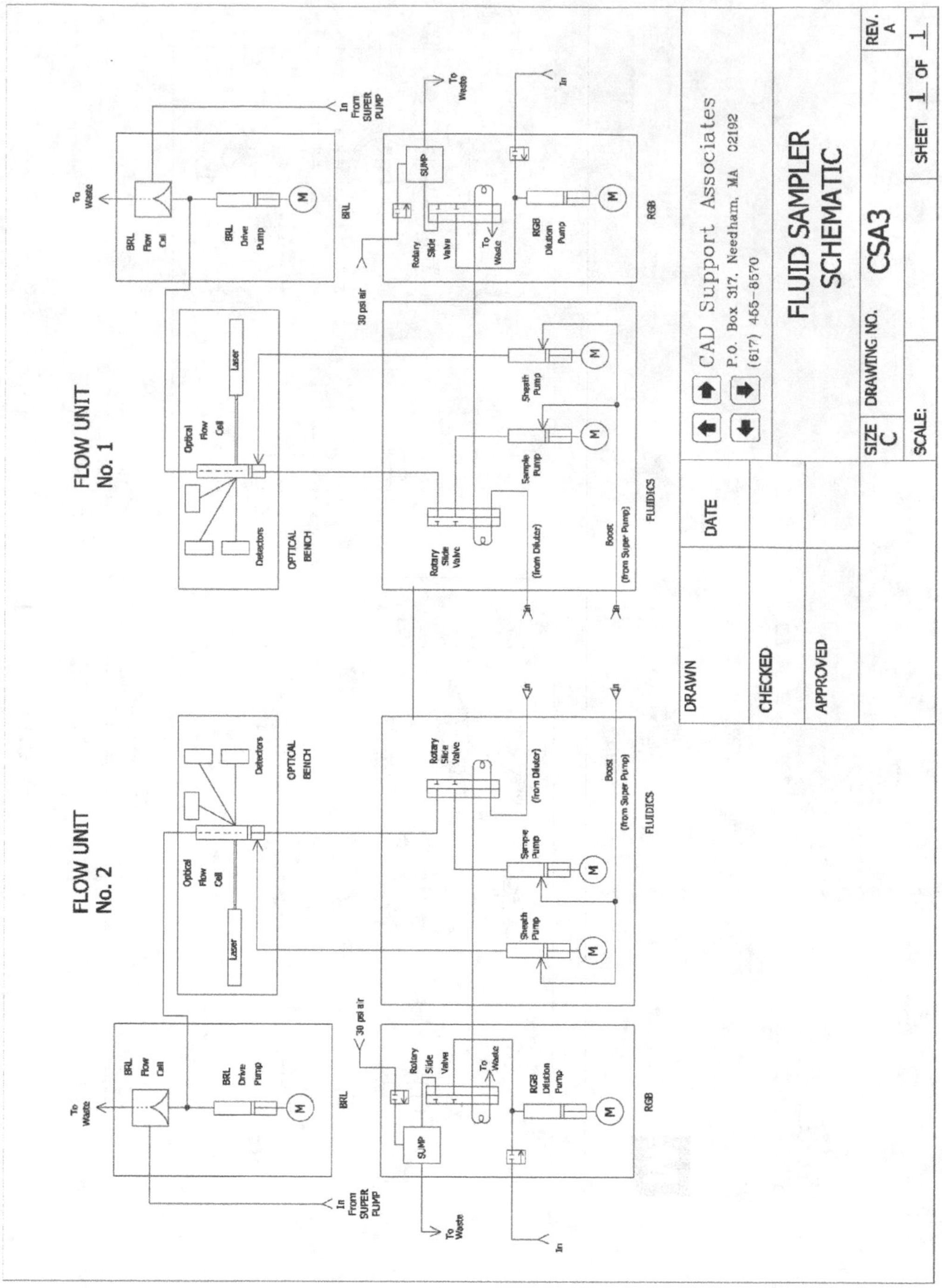
FLOW UNIT No. 1
FLOW UNIT No. 2
OPTICAL BENCH
FLUIDICS
BRL
RGB
Laser
Optical Flow Cell
Detectors
Rotary Slide Valve
Sample Pump
Sheath Pump
(from Diluter)
Boost (from Super Pump)
BRL Flow Cell
BRL Drive Pump
RGB Dilution Pump
SUMP
To Waste
In From SUPER PUMP
30 psi air
In
CAD Support Associates
P.O. Box 317, Needham, MA 02192
(617) 455-8570
FLUID SAMPLER SCHEMATIC
DRAWN
CHECKED
APPROVED
DATE
SIZE C
DRAWING NO. CSA3
REV. A
SCALE:
SHEET 1 OF 1

E

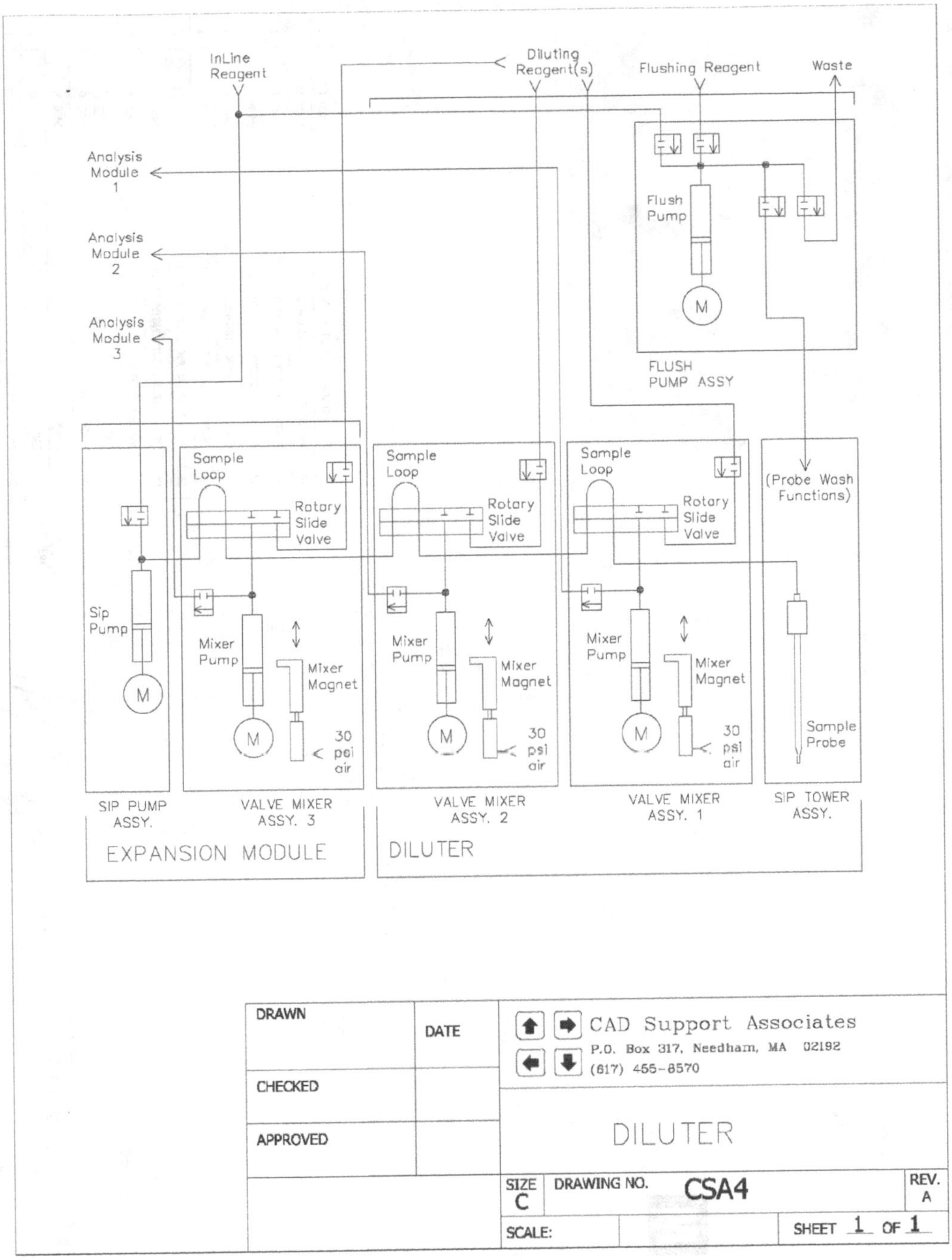
InLine Reagent
Diluting Reagent(s)
Flushing Reagent
Waste
Analysis Module 1
Analysis Module 2
Analysis Module 3
Flush Pump
M
FLUSH PUMP ASSY
Sample Loop
Rotary Slide Valve
Sip Pump
Mixer Pump
Mixer Magnet
30 psi air
(Probe Wash Functions)
Sample Probe
SIP PUMP ASSY.
VALVE MIXER ASSY. 3
VALVE MIXER ASSY. 2
VALVE MIXER ASSY. 1
SIP TOWER ASSY.
EXPANSION MODULE
DILUTER
DRAWN
DATE
CHECKED
APPROVED
CAD Support Associates
P.O. Box 317, Needham, MA 02192
(617) 455-8570
DILUTER
SIZE C
DRAWING NO. CSA4
REV. A
SCALE:
SHEET 1 OF 1

M

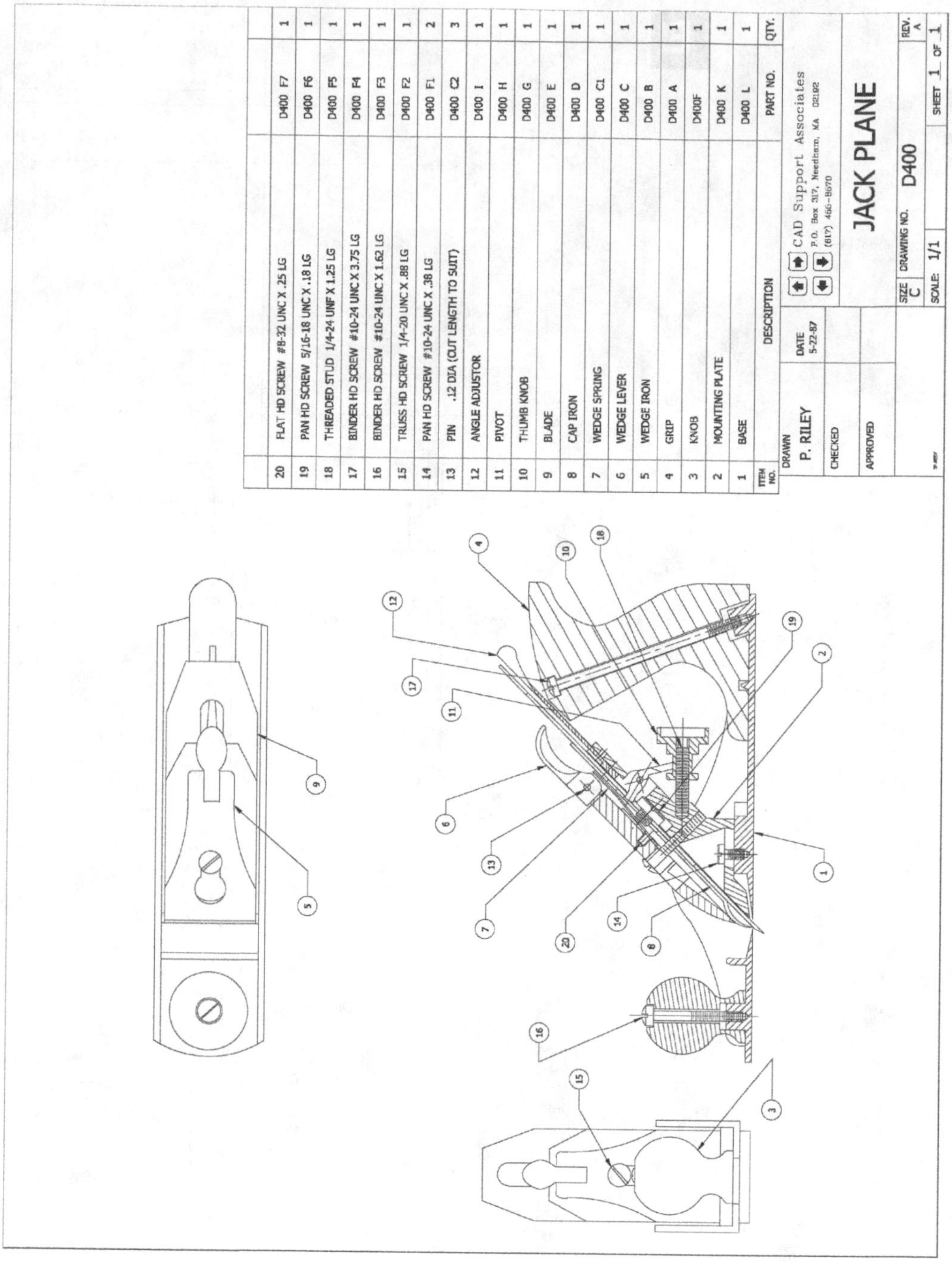

20 FLAT HD SCREW #8-32 UNC X .25 LG D400 F7 1
19 PAN HD SCREW 5/16-18 UNC X .18 LG D400 F6 1
18 THREADED STUD 1/4-24 UNF X 1.25 LG D400 F5 1
17 BINDER HD SCREW #10-24 UNC X 3.75 LG D400 F4 1
16 BINDER HD SCREW #10-24 UNC X 1.62 LG D400 F3 1
15 TRUSS HD SCREW 1/4-20 UNC X .88 LG D400 F2 1
14 PAN HD SCREW #10-24 UNC X .38 LG D400 F1 2
13 PIN .12 DIA (CUT LENGTH TO SUIT) D400 C2 3
12 ANGLE ADJUSTOR D400 I 1
11 PIVOT D400 H 1
10 THUMB KNOB D400 G 1
9 BLADE D400 E 1
8 CAP IRON D400 D 1
7 WEDGE SPRING D400 C1 1
6 WEDGE LEVER D400 C 1
5 WEDGE IRON D400 B 1
4 GRIP D400 A 1
3 KNOB D400F 1
2 MOUNTING PLATE D400 K 1
1 BASE D400 L 1
ITEM NO. DESCRIPTION PART NO. QTY.
DRAWN P. RILEY
DATE 5-22-87
CHECKED
APPROVED
CAD Support Associates
P.O. Box 317, Needham, MA 02192
(617) 456-8670
JACK PLANE
SIZE C
DRAWING NO. D400
REV. A
SCALE: 1/1
SHEET 1 OF 1

M

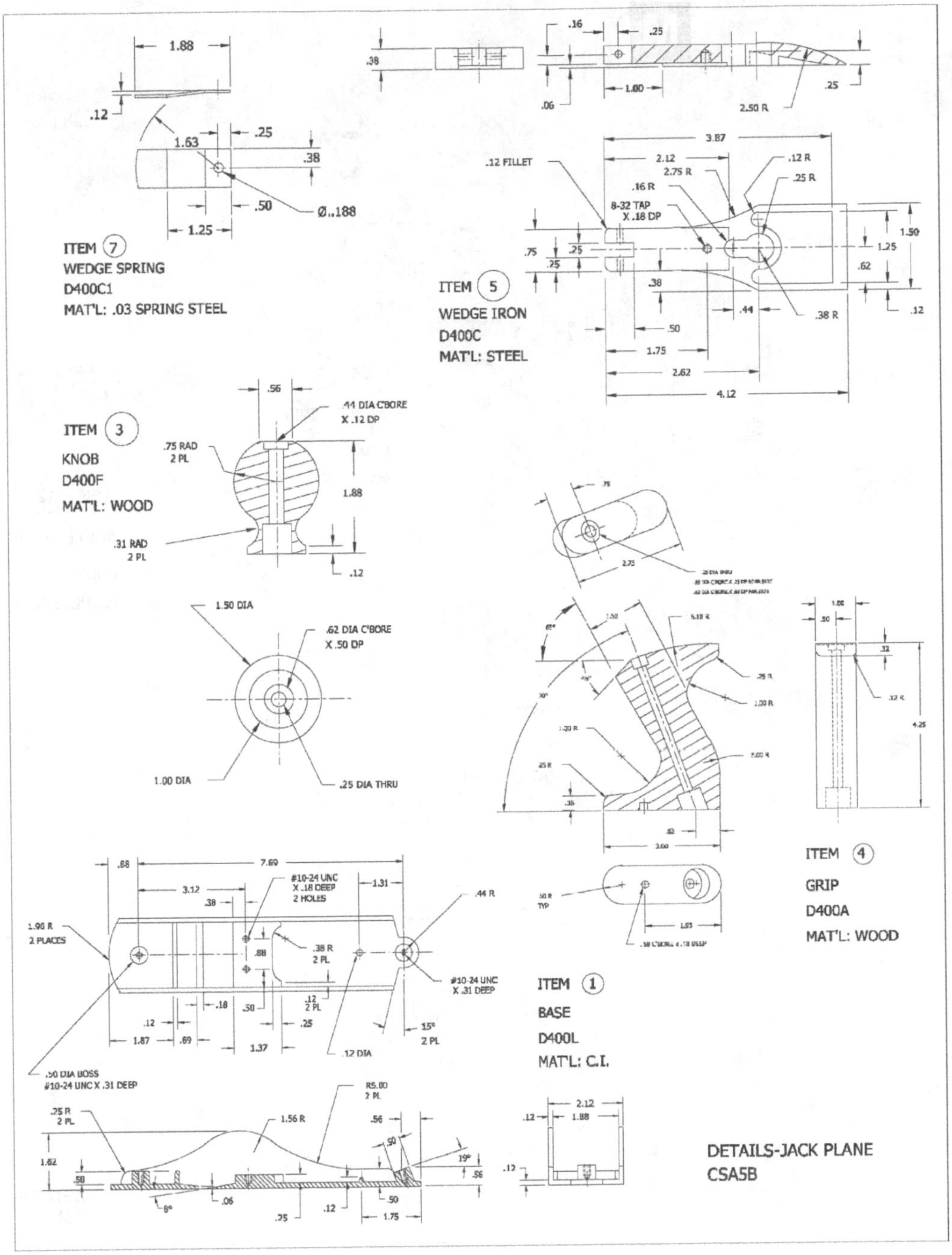

ITEM 7
WEDGE SPRING
D400C1
MAT'L: .03 SPRING STEEL
ITEM 5
WEDGE IRON
D400C
MAT'L: STEEL
.12 FILLET
8-32 TAP X .18 DP
ITEM 3
KNOB
D400F
MAT'L: WOOD
.44 DIA C'BORE X .12 DP
.75 RAD 2 PL
.31 RAD 2 PL
1.50 DIA
.62 DIA C'BORE X .50 DP
1.00 DIA
.25 DIA THRU
ITEM 4
GRIP
D400A
MAT'L: WOOD
#10-24 UNC X .18 DEEP 2 HOLES
1.90 R 2 PLACES
#10-24 UNC X .31 DEEP
.50 DIA BOSS #10-24 UNC X .31 DEEP
ITEM 1
BASE
D400L
MAT'L: C.I.
DETAILS-JACK PLANE
CSA5B

M

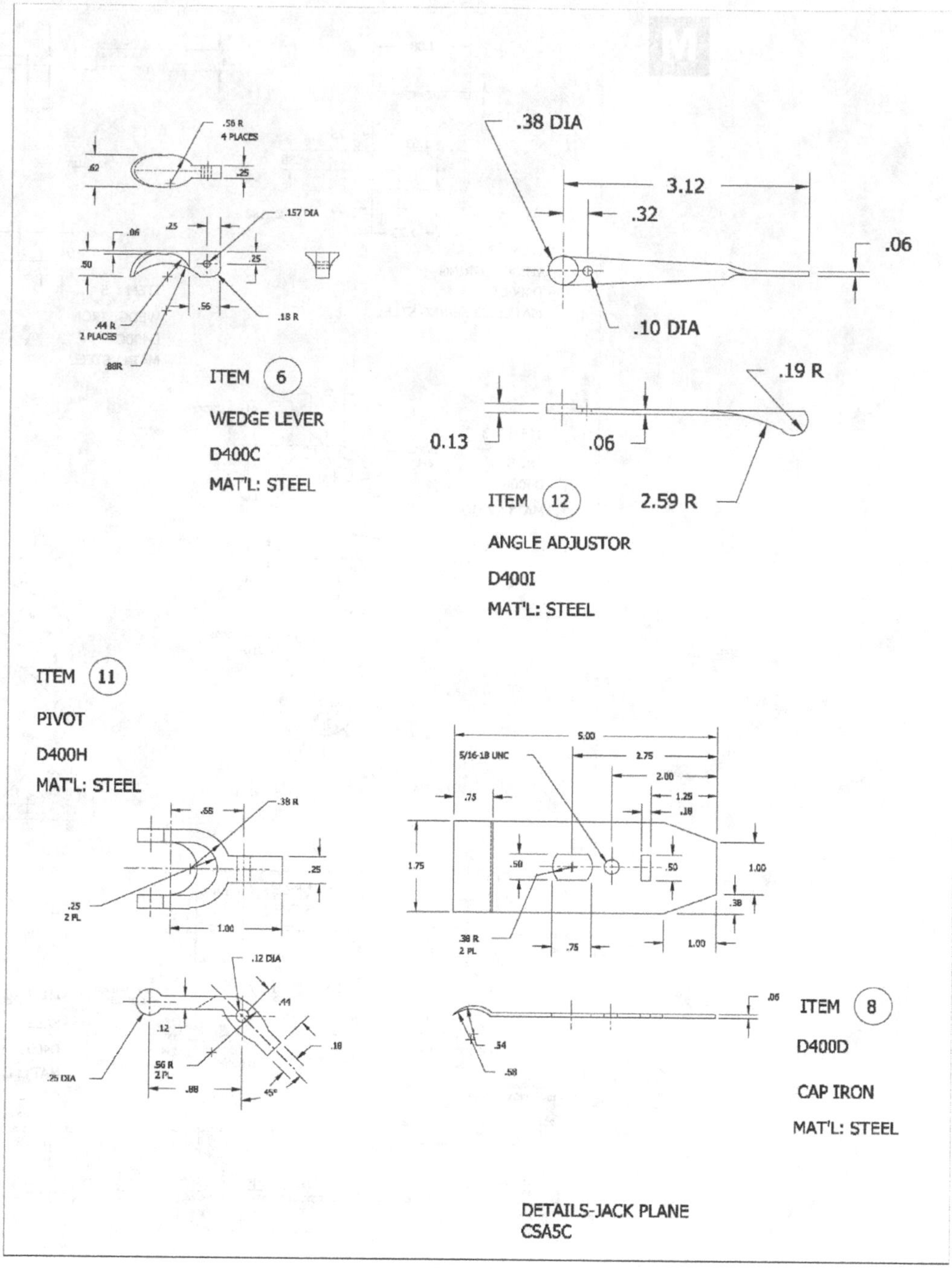
.38 DIA
3.12
.32
.06
.10 DIA
.19 R
0.13
.06
2.59 R
ITEM 6
WEDGE LEVER
D400C
MAT'L: STEEL
ITEM 12
ANGLE ADJUSTOR
D400I
MAT'L: STEEL
ITEM 11
PIVOT
D400H
MAT'L: STEEL
ITEM 8
D400D
CAP IRON
MAT'L: STEEL
DETAILS-JACK PLANE
CSA5C

M

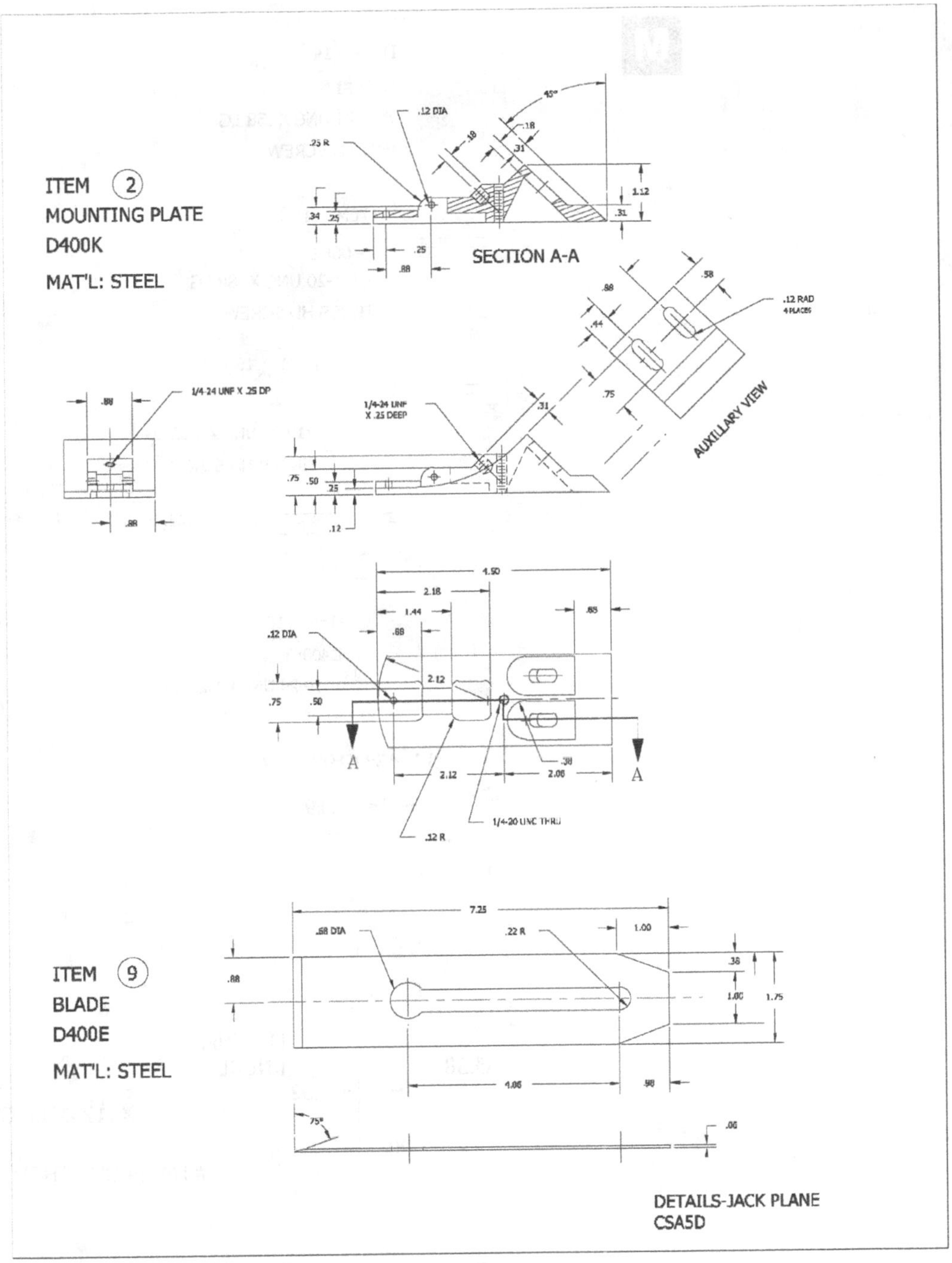
ITEM 2
MOUNTING PLATE
D400K
MAT'L: STEEL
SECTION A-A
AUXILIARY VIEW
1/4-24 UNF X .25 DP
1/4-24 UNF
X .25 DEEP
1/4-20 UNC THRU
ITEM 9
BLADE
D400E
MAT'L: STEEL
DETAILS-JACK PLANE
CSA5D

M

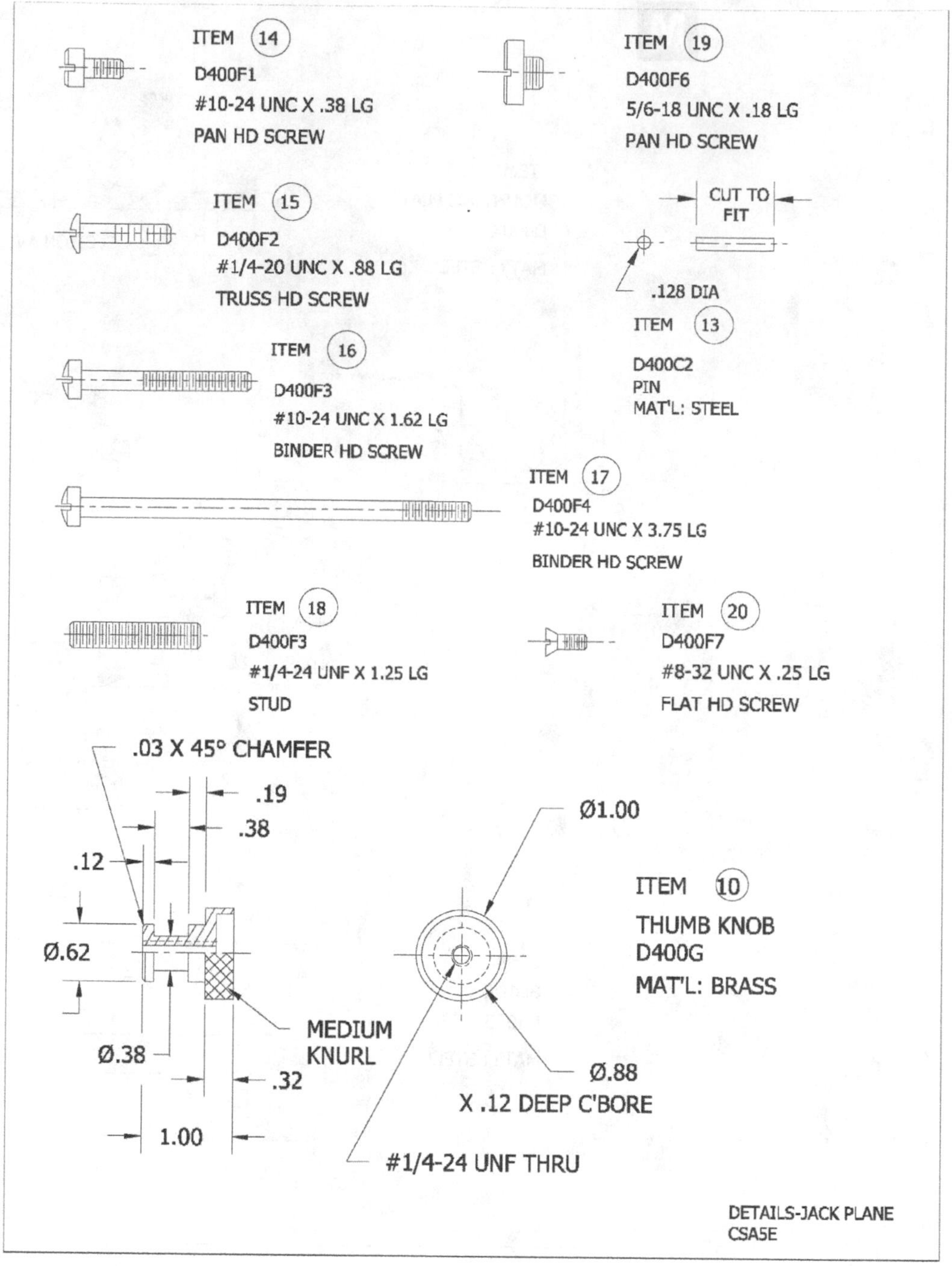
ITEM 14
D400F1
#10-24 UNC X .38 LG
PAN HD SCREW
ITEM 19
D400F6
5/6-18 UNC X .18 LG
PAN HD SCREW
ITEM 15
D400F2
#1/4-20 UNC X .88 LG
TRUSS HD SCREW
CUT TO FIT
.128 DIA
ITEM 13
D400C2
PIN
MAT'L: STEEL
ITEM 16
D400F3
#10-24 UNC X 1.62 LG
BINDER HD SCREW
ITEM 17
D400F4
#10-24 UNC X 3.75 LG
BINDER HD SCREW
ITEM 18
D400F3
#1/4-24 UNF X 1.25 LG
STUD
ITEM 20
D400F7
#8-32 UNC X .25 LG
FLAT HD SCREW
.03 X 45° CHAMFER
.19
.38
.12
Ø.62
Ø.38
MEDIUM
KNURL
.32
1.00
Ø1.00
ITEM 10
THUMB KNOB
D400G
MAT'L: BRASS
Ø.88
X .12 DEEP C'BORE
#1/4-24 UNF THRU
DETAILS-JACK PLANE
CSA5E

M

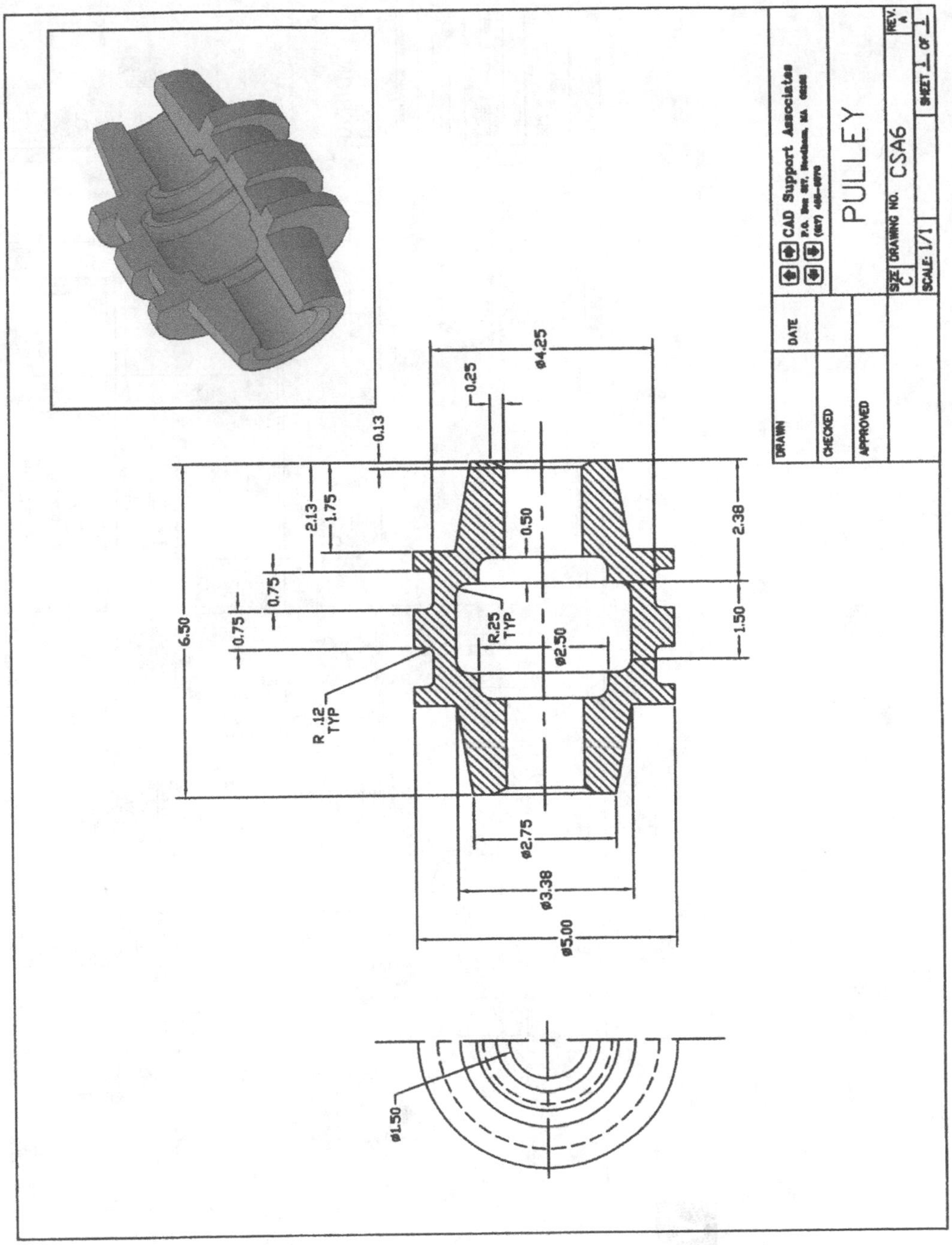
CAD Support Associates
PULLEY
DRAWN
DATE
CHECKED
APPROVED
SIZE C
DRAWING NO. CSA6
REV. A
SCALE: 1/1
6.50
2.13
1.75
0.75
0.75
0.13
0.25
0.50
R.25 TYP
R .12 TYP
ø2.50
ø4.25
2.38
1.50
ø2.75
ø3.38
ø5.00
ø1.50

Chapter A

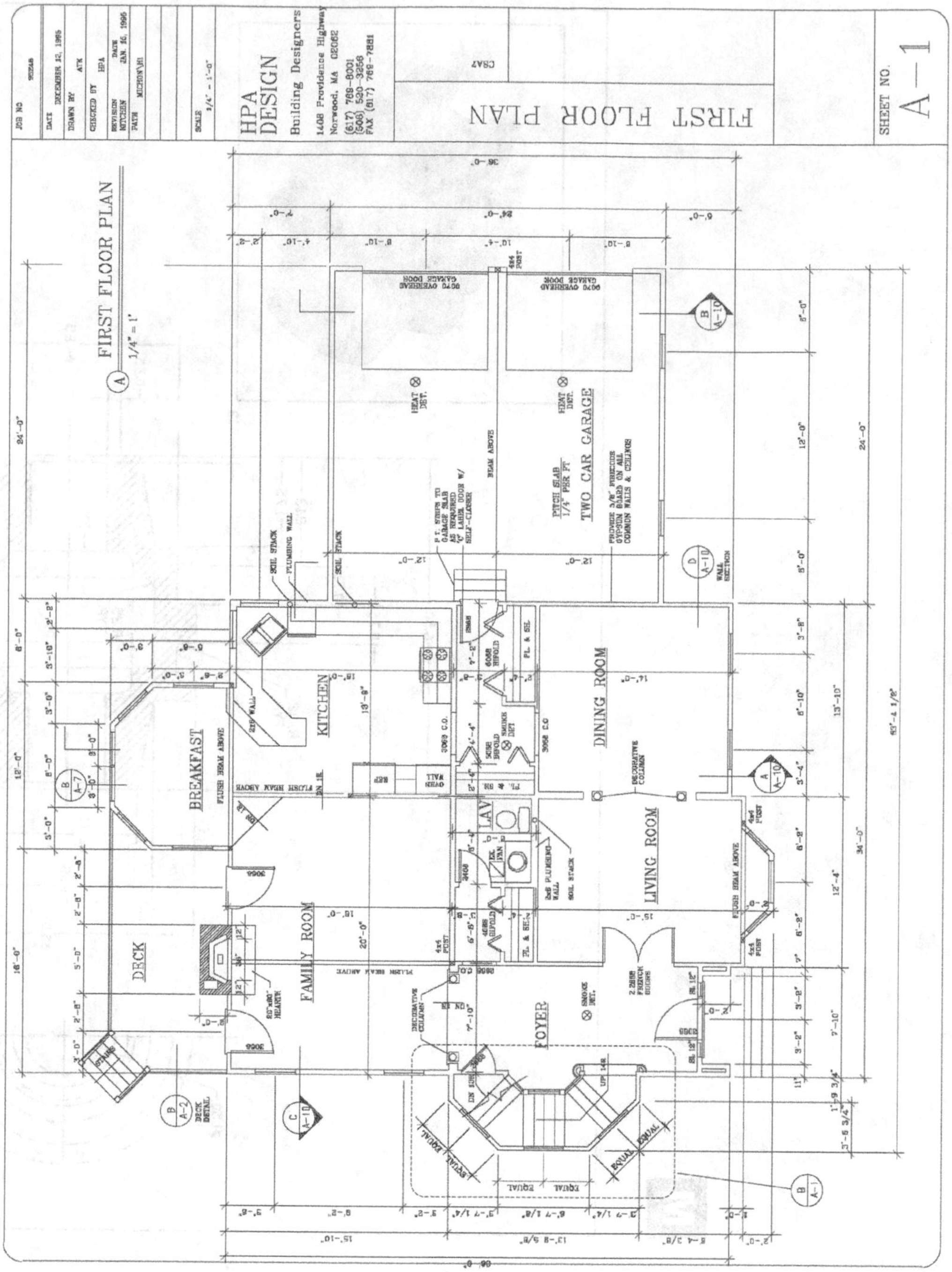
FIRST FLOOR PLAN
1/4" = 1'
HPA
DESIGN
Building Designers
1408 Providence Highway
Norwood, MA 02062
SHEET NO.
A-1
TWO CAR GARAGE
KITCHEN
BREAKFAST
DINING ROOM
LIVING ROOM
FAMILY ROOM
DECK
FOYER
LAV

A

A

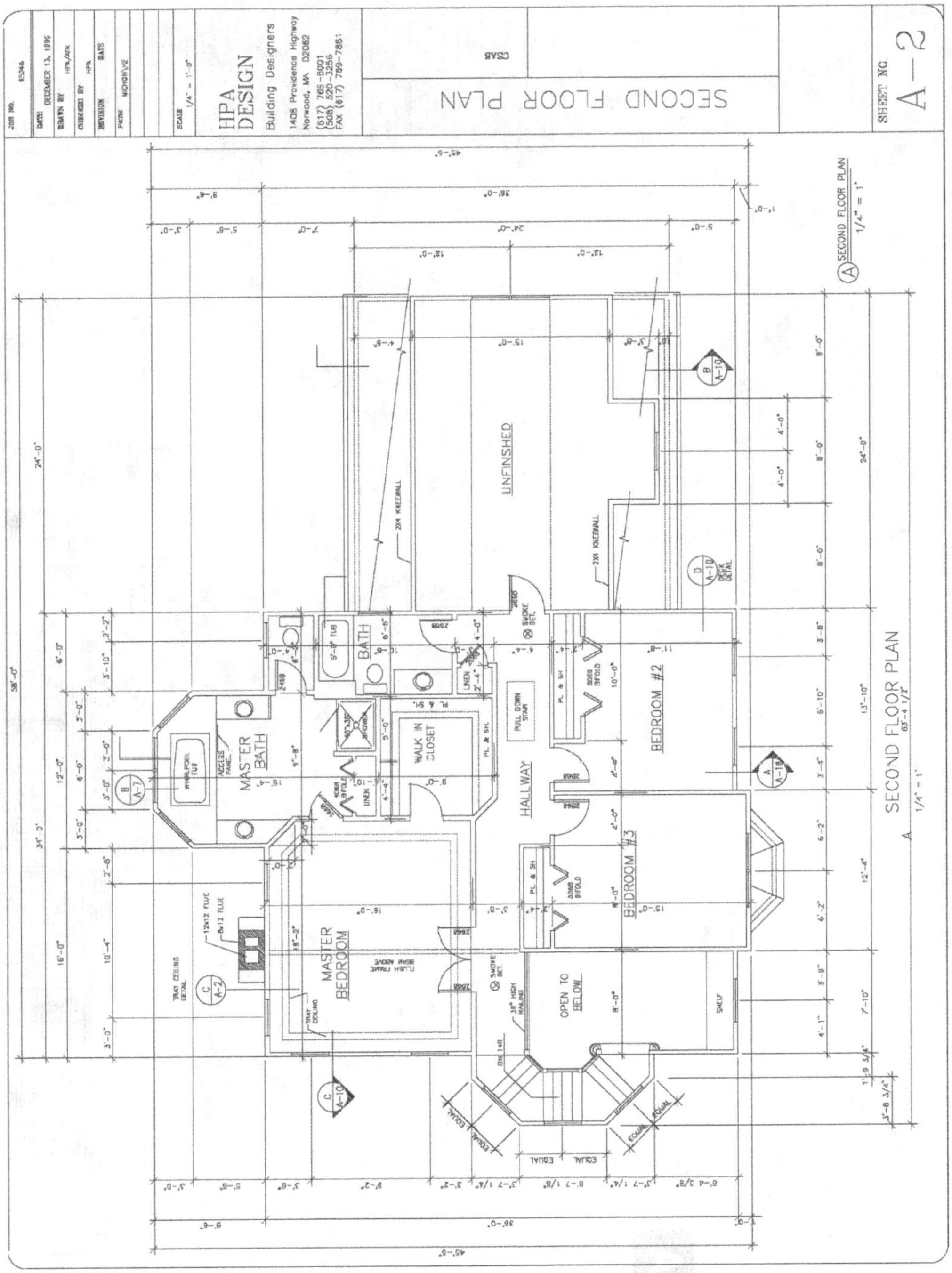
HPA DESIGN
Building Designers
1408 Providence Highway
Norwood, MA 02062
SECOND FLOOR PLAN
SHEET NO
A-2
MASTER BEDROOM
MASTER BATH
WALK IN CLOSET
BATH
HALLWAY
BEDROOM #2
BEDROOM #3
OPEN TO BELOW
UNFINISHED
SECOND FLOOR PLAN
1/4" = 1'

Chapter A

A

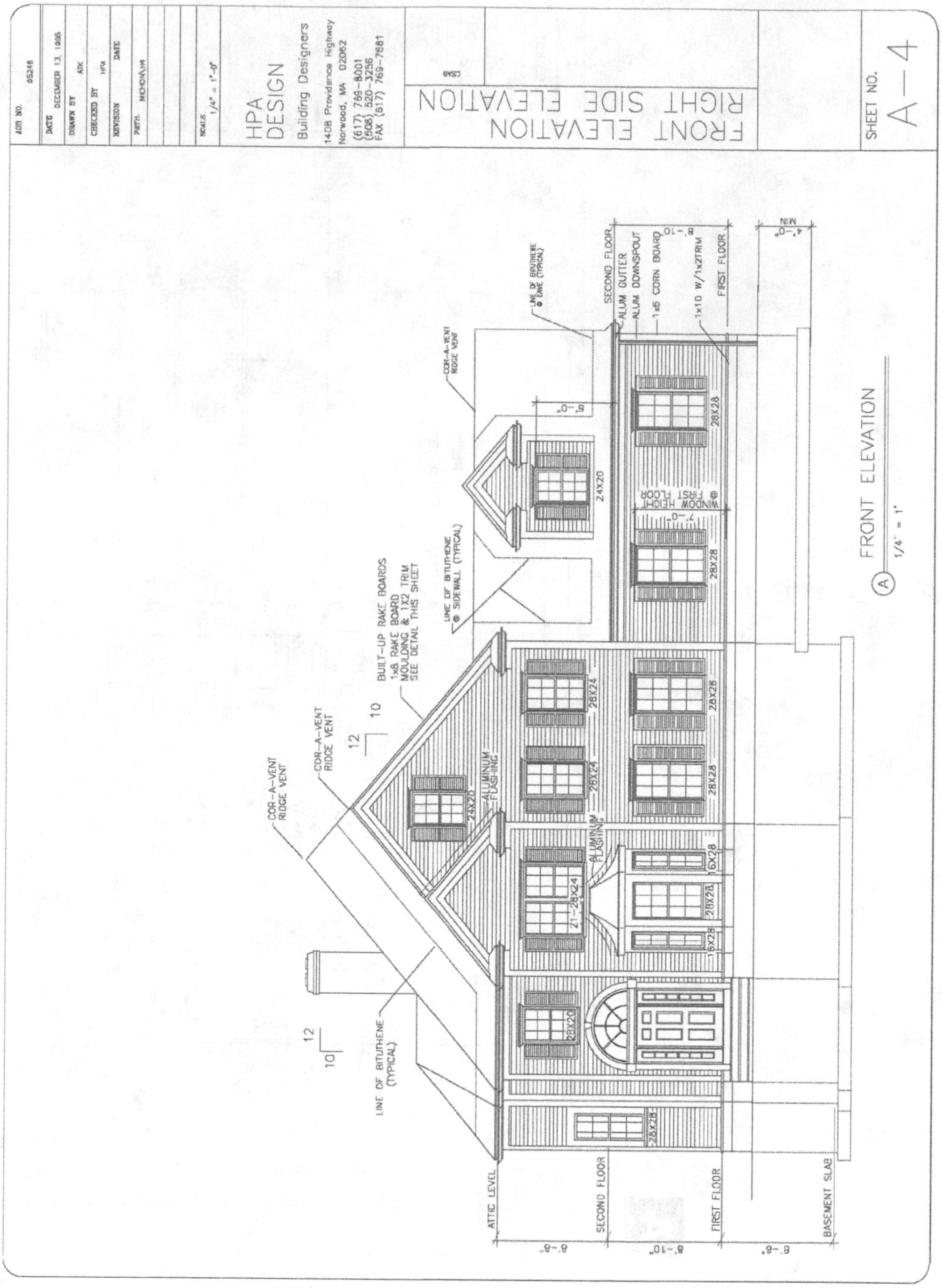

JOB NO. 95248
DATE DECEMBER 13, 1995
DRAWN BY ATK
CHECKED BY HPA
REVISION DATE
SCALE 1/4" = 1'-0"
HPA DESIGN
Building Designers
1408 Providence Highway
Norwood, MA 02062
(617) 769-8001
(508) 520-3256
FAX (617) 769-7881
FRONT ELEVATION
RIGHT SIDE ELEVATION
SHEET NO.
A-4
FRONT ELEVATION
1/4" = 1'
ATTIC LEVEL
SECOND FLOOR
FIRST FLOOR
BASEMENT SLAB
COR-A-VENT RIDGE VENT
BUILT-UP RAKE BOARDS
LINE OF BITUTHENE (TYPICAL)
ALUMINUM FLASHING
ALUM GUTTER
ALUM DOWNSPOUT
1x6 CORN BOARD
1x10 W/1x2TRIM
WINDOW HEIGHT @ FIRST FLOOR

A

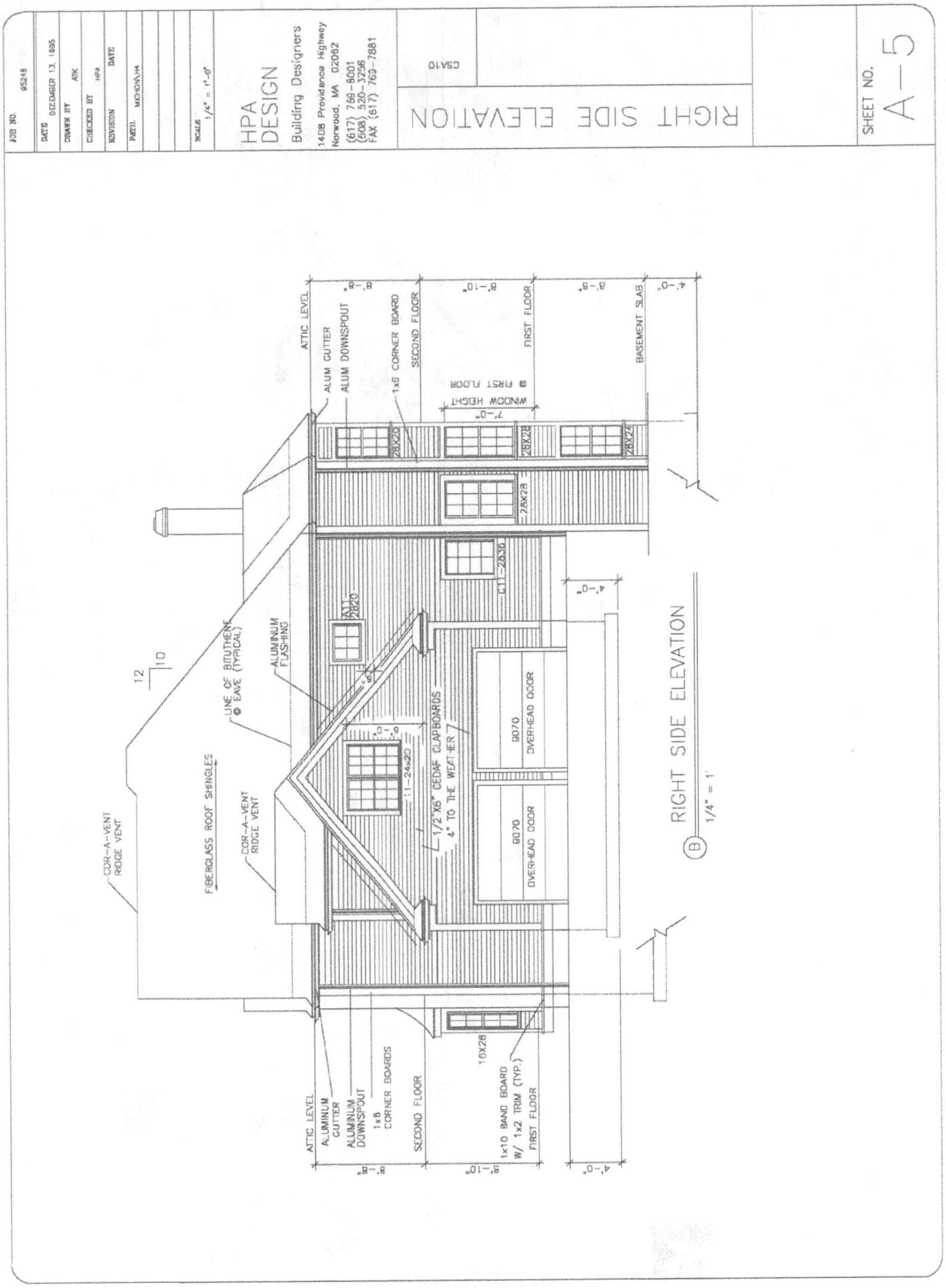

RIGHT SIDE ELEVATION
1/4" = 1'
FIBERGLASS ROOF SHINGLES
COR-A-VENT RIDGE VENT
LINE OF BITUTHENE @ EAVE (TYPICAL)
ALUMINUM FLASHING
1/2"X6" CEDAR CLAPBOARDS 4" TO THE WEATHER
9070 OVERHEAD DOOR
9070 OVERHEAD DOOR
ATTIC LEVEL
ALUMINUM GUTTER
ALUMINUM DOWNSPOUT
1x6 CORNER BOARDS
SECOND FLOOR
1x10 BAND BOARD W/ 1x2 TRIM (TYP.)
FIRST FLOOR
ALUM GUTTER
ALUM DOWNSPOUT
1x6 CORNER BOARD
WINDOW HEIGHT @ FIRST FLOOR
BASEMENT SLAB
HPA DESIGN
Building Designers
1408 Providence Highway
Norwood, MA 02062
(617) 769-8001
(508) 520-3256
FAX (617) 769-7881
RIGHT SIDE ELEVATION
SHEET NO.
A-5

Chapter A

A

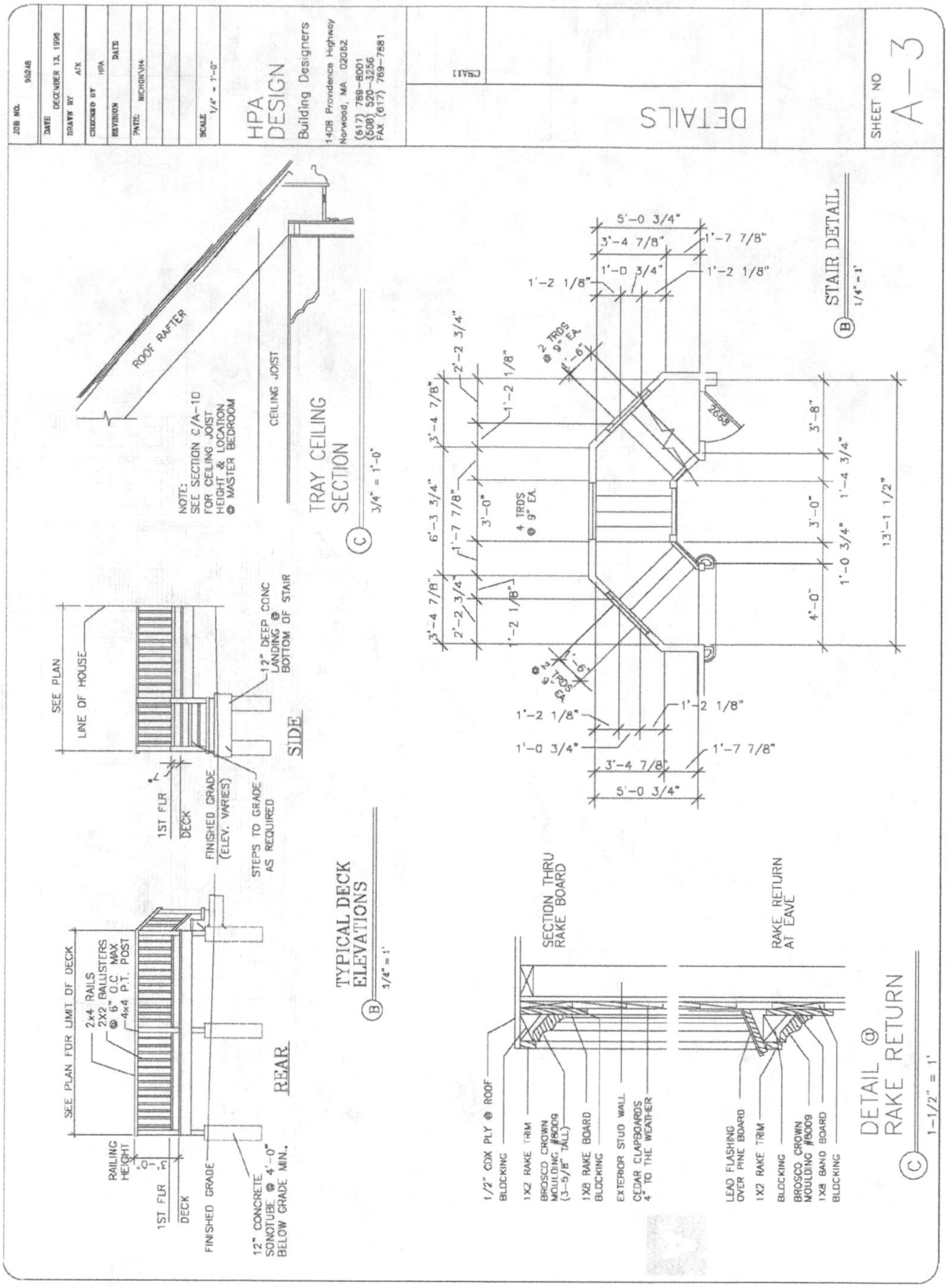
JOB NO. 95248
DATE DECEMBER 13, 1996
DRAWN BY ATK
CHECKED BY HPA
REVISION DATE
PATH: WICHOLYUMA
SCALE 1/4" = 1'-0"
HPA DESIGN
Building Designers
1408 Providence Highway
Norwood, MA 02062
(617) 769-8001
(508) 520-3256
FAX (617) 769-7881
DETAILS
SHEET NO
A-3
ROOF RAFTER
NOTE: SEE SECTION C/A-10 FOR CEILING JOIST HEIGHT & LOCATION @ MASTER BEDROOM
CEILING JOIST
TRAY CEILING SECTION
3/4" = 1'-0"
STAIR DETAIL
1/4"=1'
4 TRDS @ 9" EA.
2 TRDS @ 9" EA.
TYPICAL DECK ELEVATIONS
1/4"=1'
SEE PLAN FOR LIMIT OF DECK
2x4 RAILS
2X2 BALUSTERS @ 6" O.C. MAX
4x4 P.T. POST
RAILING HEIGHT
1ST FLR
DECK
FINISHED GRADE
12" CONCRETE SONOTUBE @ 4'-0" BELOW GRADE MIN.
REAR
SEE PLAN
LINE OF HOUSE
FINISHED GRADE (ELEV. VARIES)
STEPS TO GRADE AS REQUIRED
12" DEEP CONC LANDING @ BOTTOM OF STAIR
SIDE
1/2" CDX PLY @ ROOF
BLOCKING
1X2 RAKE TRIM
BROSCO CROWN MOULDING #8009 (3-5/8" TALL)
1X8 RAKE BOARD
BLOCKING
EXTERIOR STUD WALL
CEDAR CLAPBOARDS 4" TO THE WEATHER
SECTION THRU RAKE BOARD
LEAD FLASHING OVER PINE BOARD
1X2 RAKE TRIM
BLOCKING
BROSCO CROWN MOULDING #8009
1X8 BAND BOARD
BLOCKING
RAKE RETURN AT EAVE
DETAIL @ RAKE RETURN
1-1/2" = 1'

G

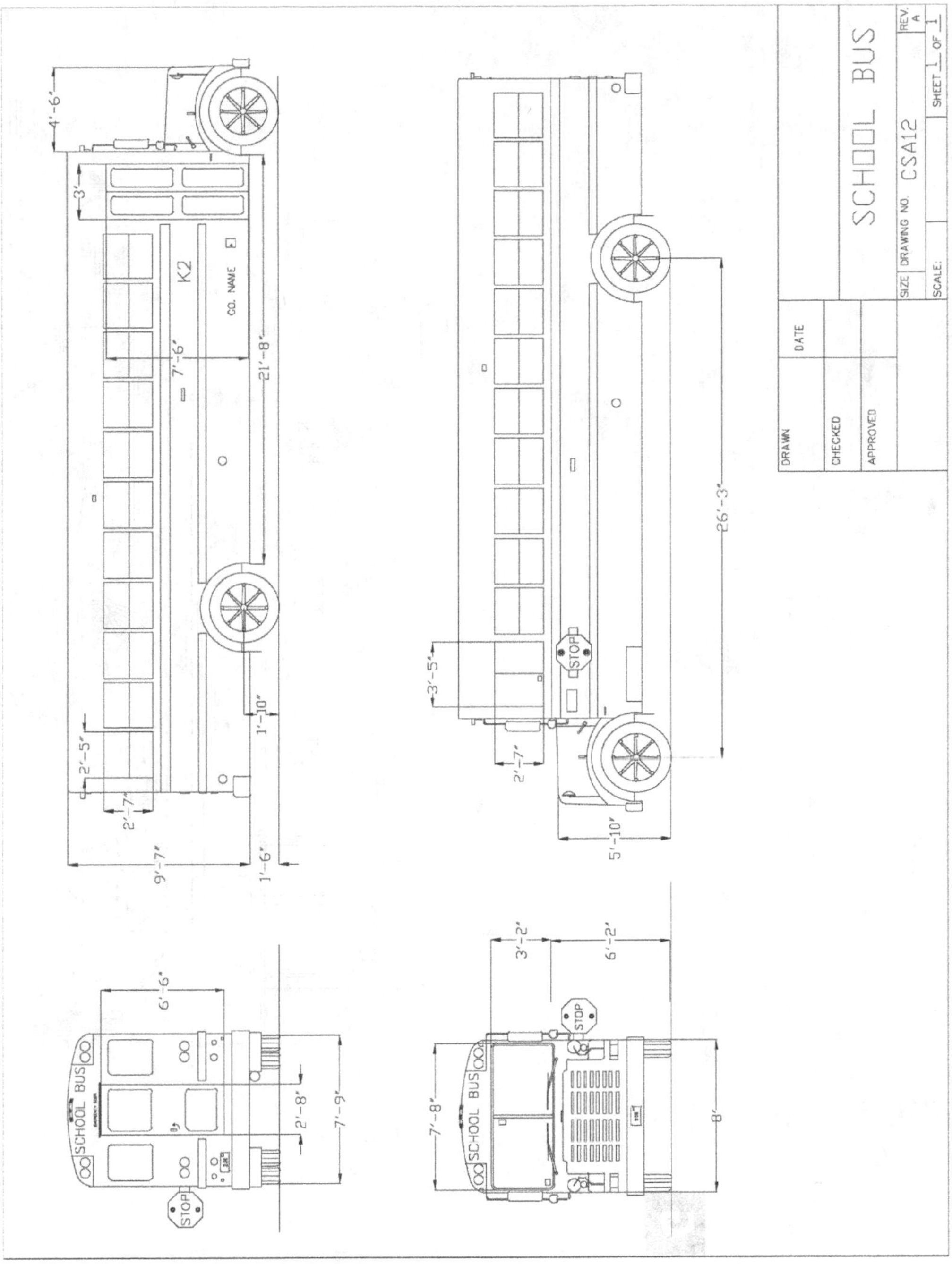

SCHOOL BUS
DRAWN
DATE
CHECKED
APPROVED
SIZE
DRAWING NO. CSA12
REV. A
SCALE:
SHEET 1 OF 1
4'-6"
3'
K2
CO. NAME
7'-6"
21'-8"
2'-5"
2'-7"
9'-7"
1'-10"
1'-6"
3'-5"
STOP
26'-3"
2'-7"
5'-10"
6'-6"
SCHOOL BUS
2'-8"
7'-9"
3'-2"
6'-2"
7'-8"
8'

Chapter A

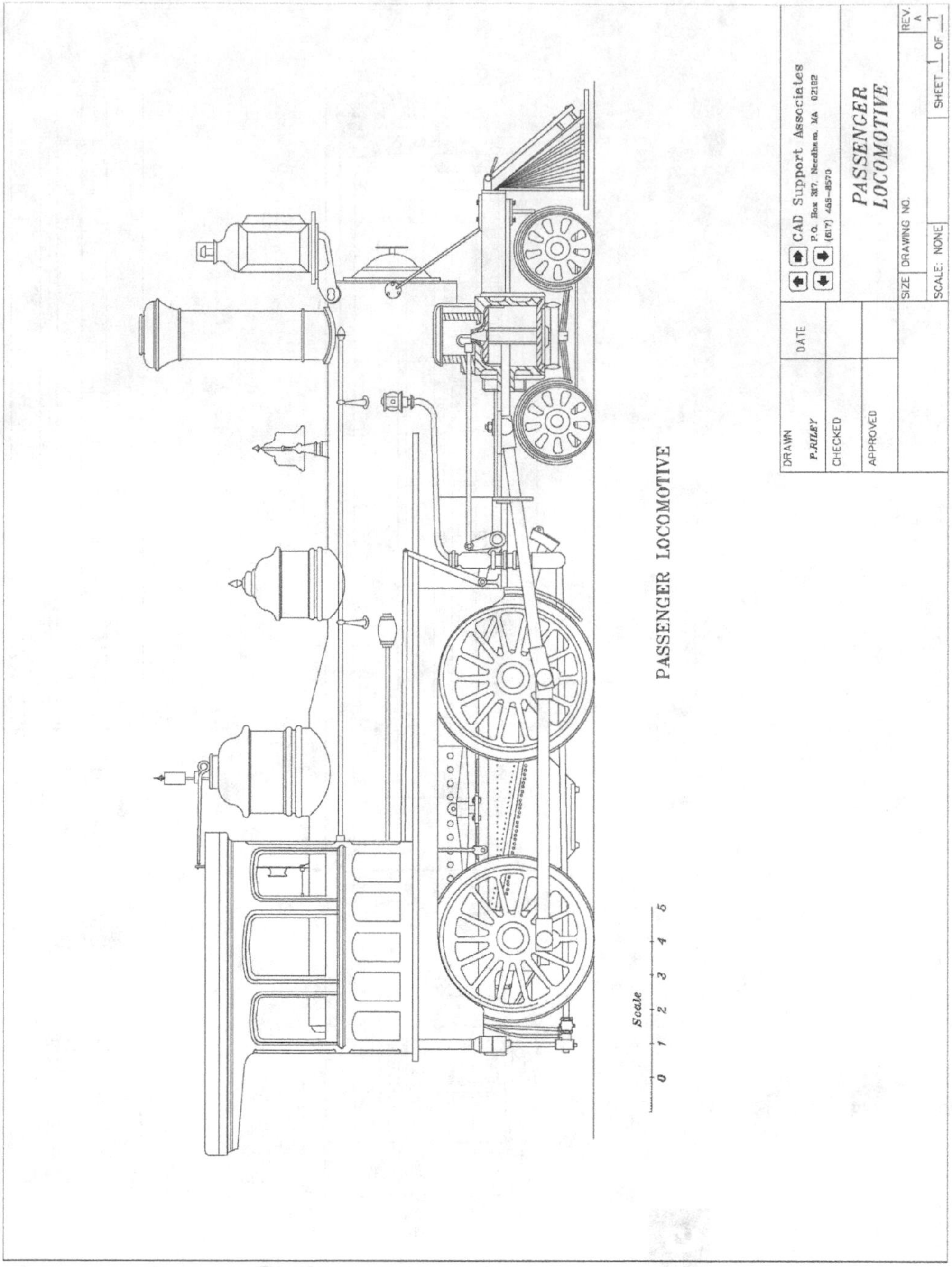
PASSENGER LOCOMOTIVE
Scale
0 1 2 3 4 5
CAD Support Associates
DRAWN
P.RILEY
DATE
CHECKED
APPROVED
PASSENGER LOCOMOTIVE
SIZE
DRAWING NO.
REV.
A
SCALE: NONE
SHEET 1 OF 1

G

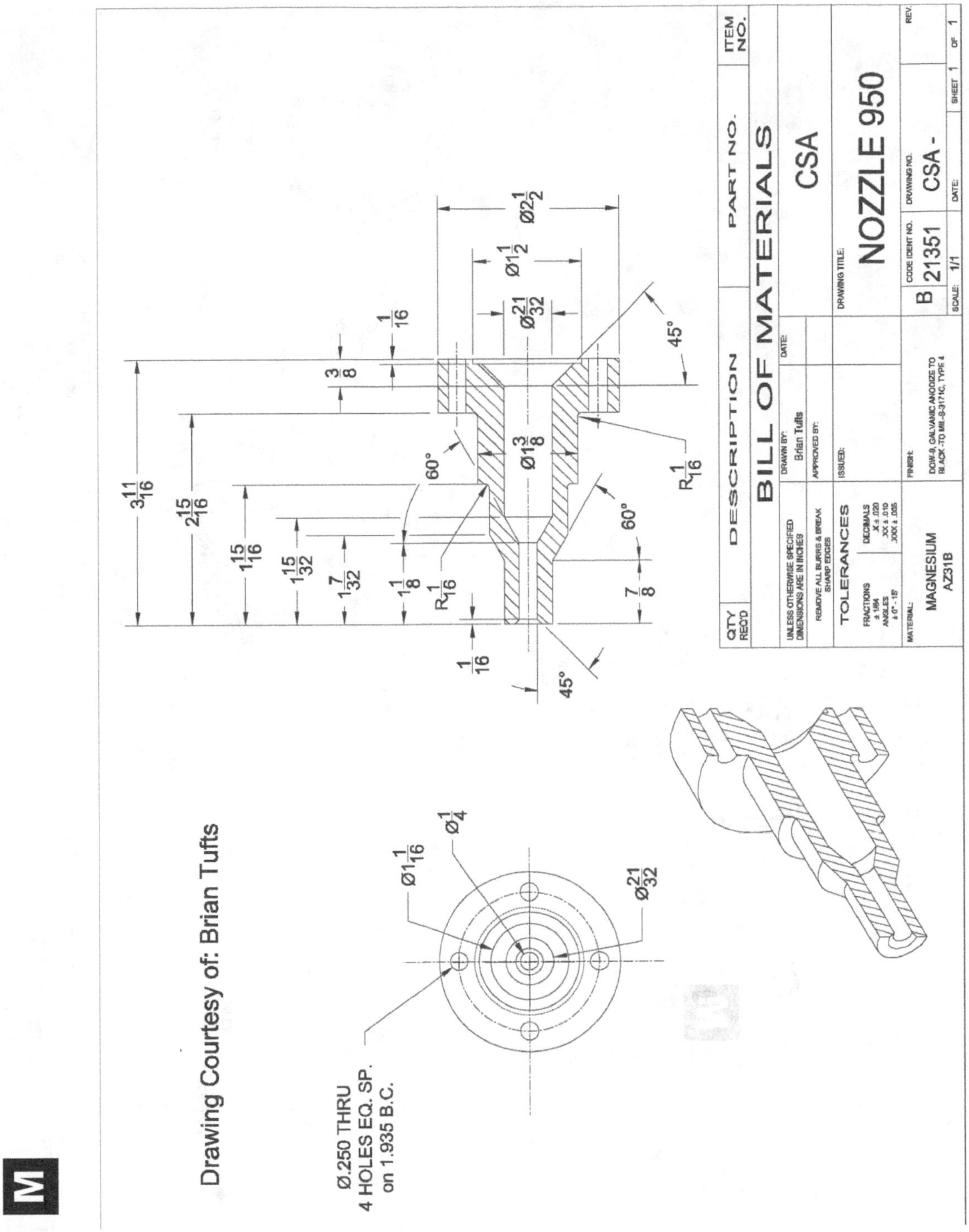
M
Drawing Courtesy of: Brian Tufts
Ø.250 THRU
4 HOLES EQ. SP.
on 1.935 B.C.
Ø1 1/16
Ø1/4
Ø21/32
3 11/16
2 15/16
1 15/16
1 15/32
1 7/32
1 1/8
R 1/16
1/16
7/8
45°
60°
Ø1 3/8
3/8
Ø21/32
Ø1 1/2
Ø2 1/2
ITEM NO.
PART NO.
DESCRIPTION
QTY REQ'D
BILL OF MATERIALS
CSA
UNLESS OTHERWISE SPECIFIED DIMENSIONS ARE IN INCHES
REMOVE ALL BURRS & BREAK SHARP EDGES
TOLERANCES
FRACTIONS ± 1/64
ANGLES ± 0° - 15'
DECIMALS X ± .020 XX ± .010 XXX ± .005
DRAWN BY: Brian Tufts
DATE:
APPROVED BY:
ISSUED:
DRAWING TITLE:
NOZZLE 950
MATERIAL: MAGNESIUM AZ31B
FINISH:
CODE IDENT NO. B 21351
DRAWING NO. CSA -
REV.
SCALE: 1/1
DATE:
SHEET 1 OF 1

M

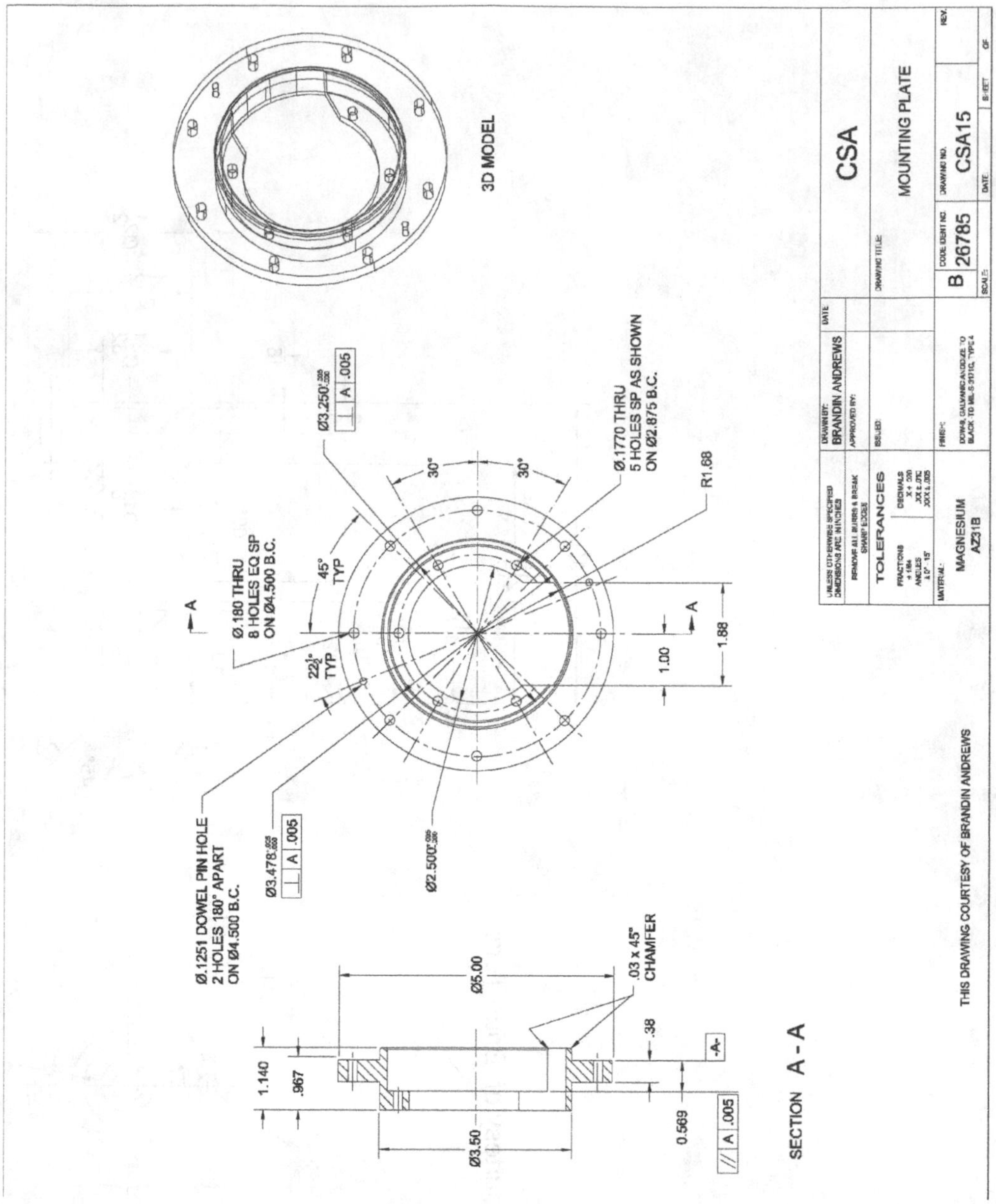
SECTION A - A
Ø5.00
Ø3.50
1.140
.967
.38
0.569
.03 x 45° CHAMFER
Ø.1251 DOWEL PIN HOLE
2 HOLES 180° APART
ON Ø4.500 B.C.
Ø.180 THRU
8 HOLES EQ SP
ON Ø4.500 B.C.
45° TYP
30°
30°
Ø.1770 THRU
5 HOLES SP AS SHOWN
ON Ø2.875 B.C.
R1.68
1.00
1.88
3D MODEL
TOLERANCES
BRANDIN ANDREWS
MAGNESIUM
AZ31B
CSA
MOUNTING PLATE
B
26785
CSA15
THIS DRAWING COURTESY OF BRANDIN ANDREWS

M

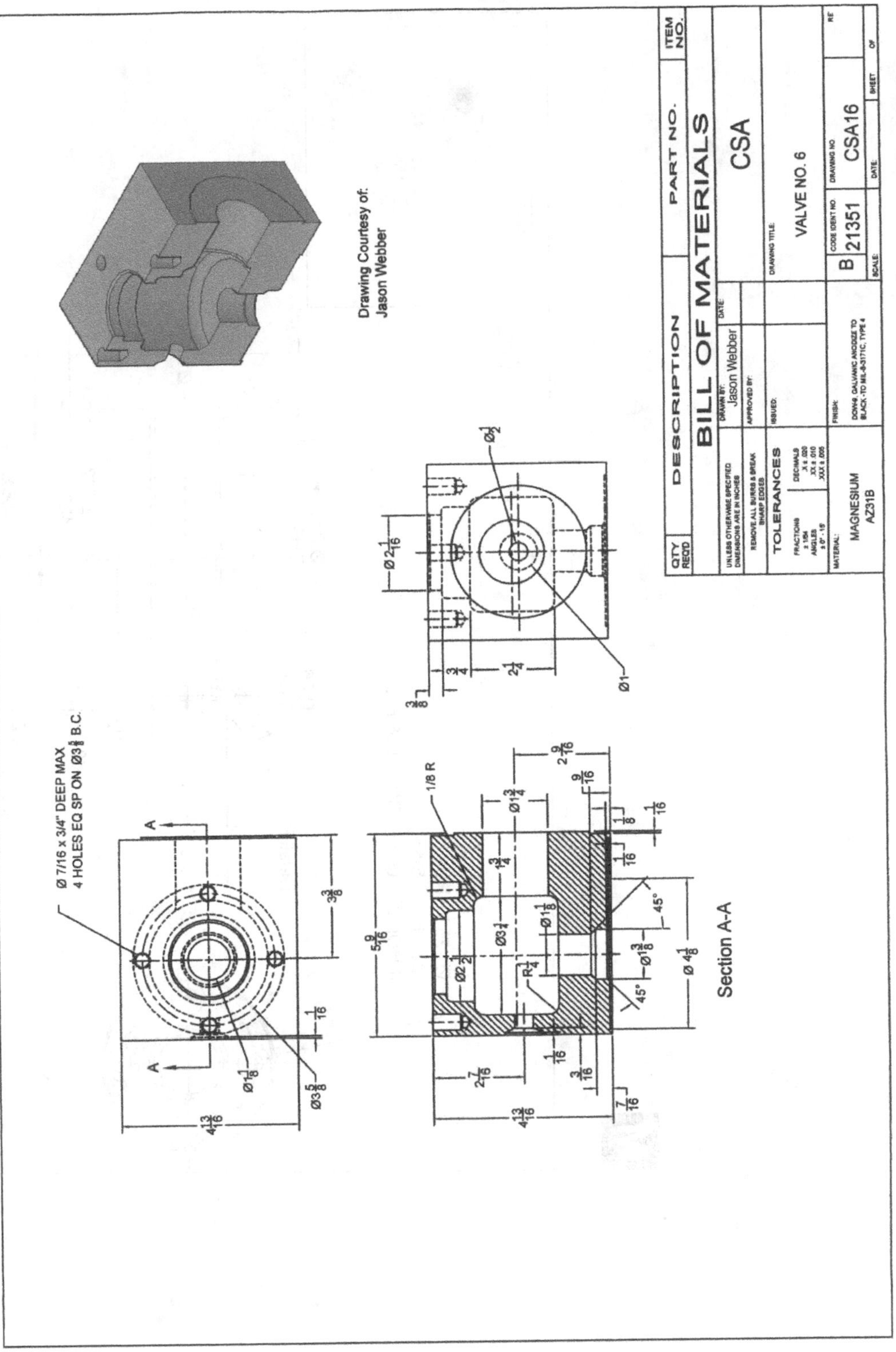

Ø 7/16 x 3/4" DEEP MAX
4 HOLES EQ SP ON Ø3⅜ B.C.
Section A-A
1/8 R
Drawing Courtesy of:
Jason Webber
QTY REQ'D
DESCRIPTION
PART NO.
ITEM NO.
BILL OF MATERIALS
UNLESS OTHERWISE SPECIFIED DIMENSIONS ARE IN INCHES
REMOVE ALL BURRS & BREAK SHARP EDGES
TOLERANCES
DRAWN BY:
Jason Webber
APPROVED BY:
ISSUED:
DATE:
CSA
DRAWING TITLE:
VALVE NO. 6
MATERIAL:
MAGNESIUM
AZ31B
FINISH:
DOW#9 GALVANIC ANODIZE TO BLACK - TO MIL-M-3171C, TYPE 4
B
CODE IDENT NO
21351
DRAWING NO
CSA16
SCALE:
DATE:
SHEET
OF

Chapter A

M

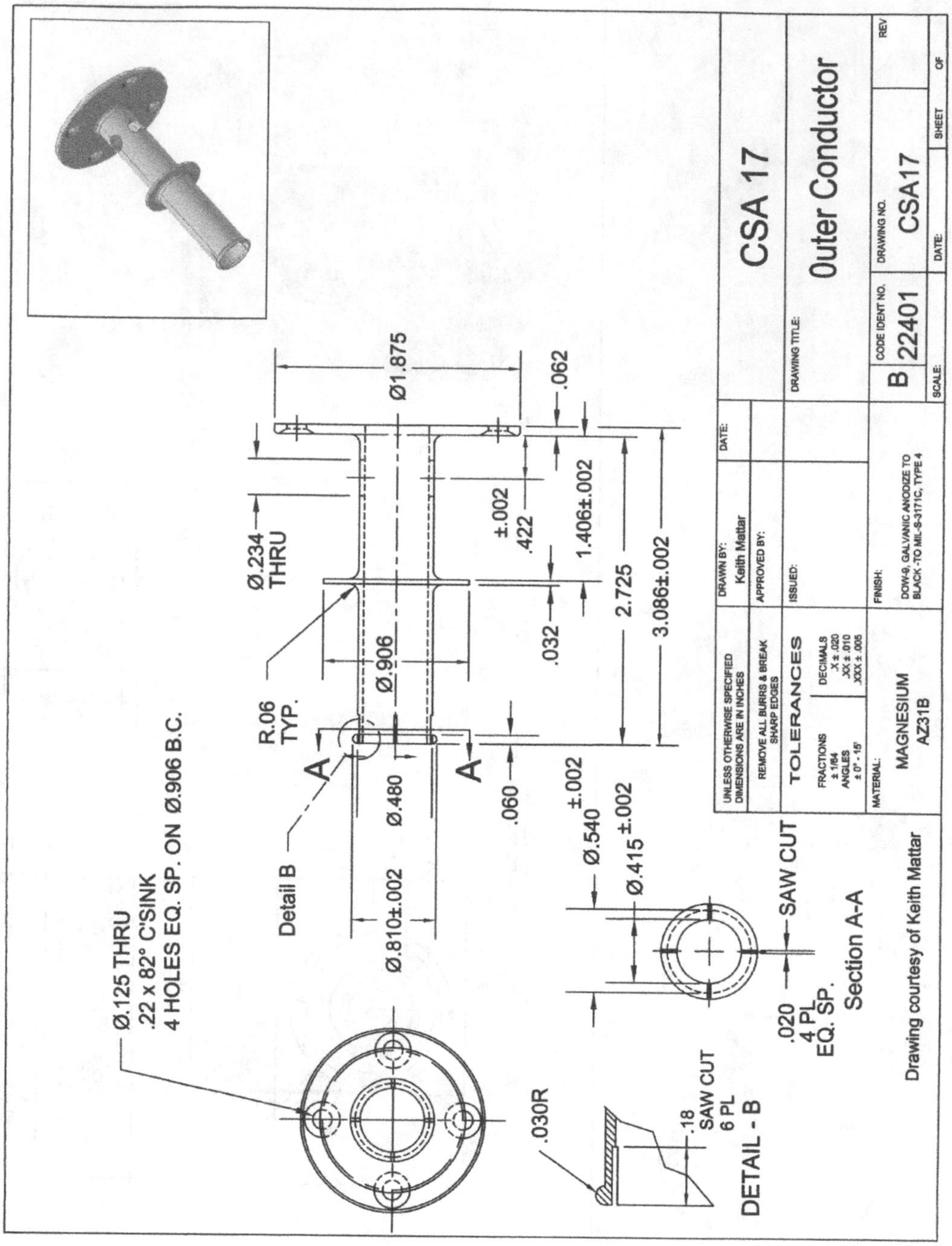
Ø.125 THRU
.22 x 82° C'SINK
4 HOLES EQ. SP. ON Ø.906 B.C.
.030R
.18
SAW CUT
6 PL
DETAIL - B
Ø.810±.002
Detail B
Ø.480
A
A
R.06
TYP.
Ø.906
Ø.234
THRU
Ø1.875
.060
.032
±.002
.422
1.406±.002
2.725
3.086±.002
.062
Ø.540 ±.002
Ø.415 ±.002
.020
4 PL
EQ. SP.
SAW CUT
Section A-A
Drawing courtesy of Keith Mattar
UNLESS OTHERWISE SPECIFIED
DIMENSIONS ARE IN INCHES
REMOVE ALL BURRS & BREAK SHARP EDGES
TOLERANCES
FRACTIONS ± 1/64
ANGLES ± 0° - 15'
DECIMALS .X ± .020 .XX ± .010 .XXX ± .005
DRAWN BY: Keith Mattar
APPROVED BY:
ISSUED:
DATE:
MATERIAL: MAGNESIUM AZ31B
FINISH: DOW-9, GALVANIC ANODIZE TO BLACK - TO MIL-S-3171C, TYPE 4
CSA 17
DRAWING TITLE: Outer Conductor
B
CODE IDENT NO. 22401
DRAWING NO. CSA17
REV
SCALE:
DATE:
SHEET
OF

Appendix B

Creating Custom Ribbon Panels

This appendix provides a partial introduction to some of the many ways in which AutoCAD can be customized to fit the needs of a particular industry, company, or individual user. At this point, you probably know how to create custom tool palettes. Tool palettes give you easy access to libraries of frequently used blocks, symbols, and commands. You can also create custom toolbars and ribbon panels to store sets of frequently used commands or commands that you modify to suit your preferences. Creating your own ribbon panels is a simple and powerful feature that also gives you some idea of the more complex customization options available.

This chapter explains AutoCAD's **Customize User Interface (CUI)** editor, where you can customize many elements of the AutoCAD interface. This appendix takes you through creating your own ribbon panel and modifying the behavior of some basic commands. When you have completed this exercise, you will have added a simple ribbon panel to the **Home** tab and have the knowledge to create other ribbon panels of your own design. The techniques you learn here are also applicable to customizing other elements in the **CUI** editor, which are covered briefly in Appendix C.

> **NOTE**
> The ability to create and customize AutoCAD elements is a powerful feature. Its recommended that you not make changes to the standard AutoCAD set of panels. Adding, removing, or otherwise changing standard tools can lead to confusion and the need to restore the AutoCAD customization (CUIx) file. Less confusion is created if you customize only new elements that you create yourself. You can modify or remove these without disturbing standard AutoCAD workflows.

There are two levels to creating a custom panel. The first level has you simply creating the panel, naming it, and adding the commands you want to put there. This can be handy for putting together sets of tools that would otherwise be located on different panels and menus. The second level has you duplicating a command, modifying its functionality, and then altering its name and the look of its button image so it functions differently from the standard AutoCAD command. In this exercise, you begin by creating a new panel and then adding standard and custom command tools to the ribbon panel.

Creating a Customized Ribbon Panel

You can begin this exercise in any AutoCAD drawing and in any workspace with a ribbon.

> **TIP**
>
> The following is a general procedure for creating a ribbon panel:
>
> 1. Click **Manage** > **Customization** > **User Interface**.
> 2. In the **CUI editor, Customize** tab, **Customizations in All Files** pane, expand the **Ribbon** node.
> 3. Right-click the **Panels** node.
> 4. Select **New Panel** from the shortcut menu.
> 5. Provide the new ribbon panel a name in the **Customizations in All Files** pane.
> 6. In the **Command List** pane, select a category from the **Category** drop-down list.
> 7. Find tools in the **Command List** pane, and drag them to **Row 1** of the new panel in the **Customizations in All Files** pane.
> 8. Click **OK** to exit the editor.

✔ Click **Manage** > **Customization** > **User Interface**, as shown in Figure B-1.

This opens the ***Customize User Interface (CUI)*** *editor shown in Figure B-2, which is an editor for customizing various elements of the AutoCAD interface. Elements that can be customized are listed in the* ***Customizations in All Files*** *pane on the upper-left. These elements are described in Appendix C.*

Figure B-1
User Interface tool

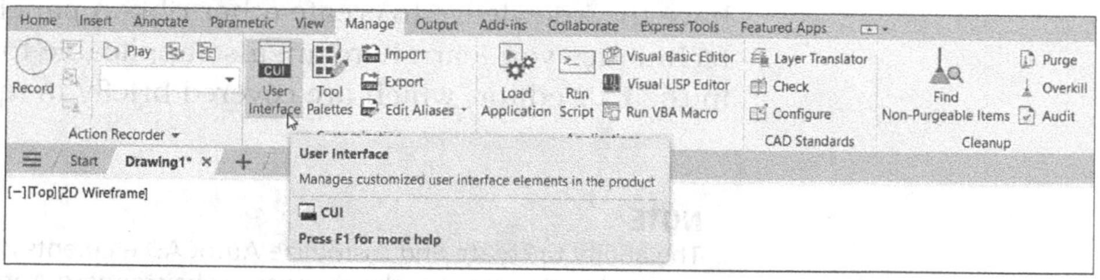

✔ Expand the **Ribbon** node in the **Customizations in All Files** pane on the left.

✔ Right-click on the **Panels** node.

✔ Select **New Panel** from the shortcut menu.

*This opens the **Ribbon** panel's node on the left and displays the **Panel Preview** and **Properties** panes on the right side of the **CUI** editor. A new ribbon panel is added to the bottom of the list. The default name is **Panel1** (or **Panel2** if someone has already created a **Panel1** on your system). This name will do fine for this purpose. Next, you add a command to the new ribbon panel.*

Figure B-2
Customize User Interface (CUI) editor

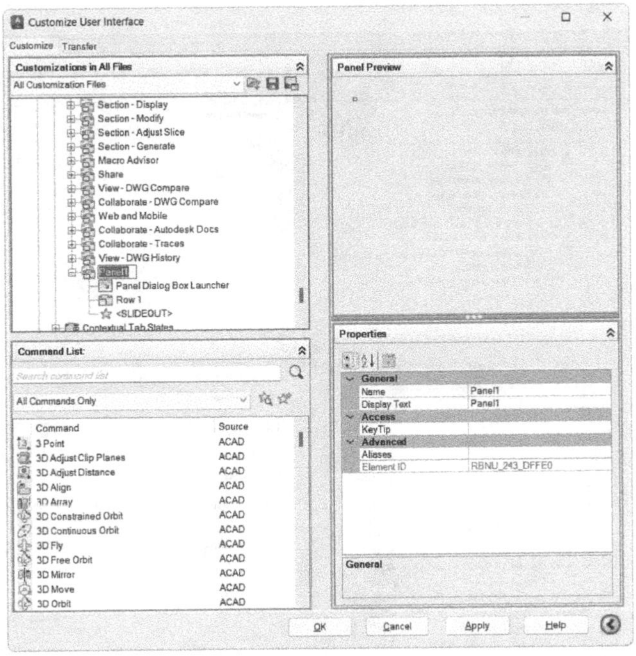

*The procedure for adding commands to a ribbon panel is simple. Select a command from the **Command List** pane and then drag it up to the ribbon panel node. For this exercise, you bring together three very common commands. The first you add without any customization. In the next section, you add two custom commands. The **Command List** pane in the bottom left of the **CUI** editor has a drop-down list that allows you to filter the commands in the list at the bottom. You begin by adding the standard **LINE** command.*

✔ If necessary, click the arrow to open the drop-down list in the **Command List** pane in the bottom left of the editor.

*A list beginning with **All Commands Only** and ending with **Legacy is displayed**.*

✔ In the list of command categories, select **Draw**.

*This filters the Command list to show only the **Draw** commands.*

✔ Scroll down the list until you see the **LINE** command and button image.

*From here, it's a simple matter of dragging the tool up to **Row 1** of **Panel1**.*

✔ Click and drag the **Line** tool up to **Row 1** under **Panel1**.

*When you are in the correct position, you see a blue arrow to the right of **Row 1**.*

✔ With the blue arrow showing to the right of **Row 1**, release the mouse button to drop the command.

*You should now see the **Button Image** and **Properties** panes for this command on the right. The **Line** tool is added to the **Panel Preview**, and **Line** is added to **Panel1**, **Row 1** in the **Customizations in All Files** pane, as shown in Figure B-3. Your new panel currently has one tool and the title bar, showing **Panel1** in the **Panel Preview**.*

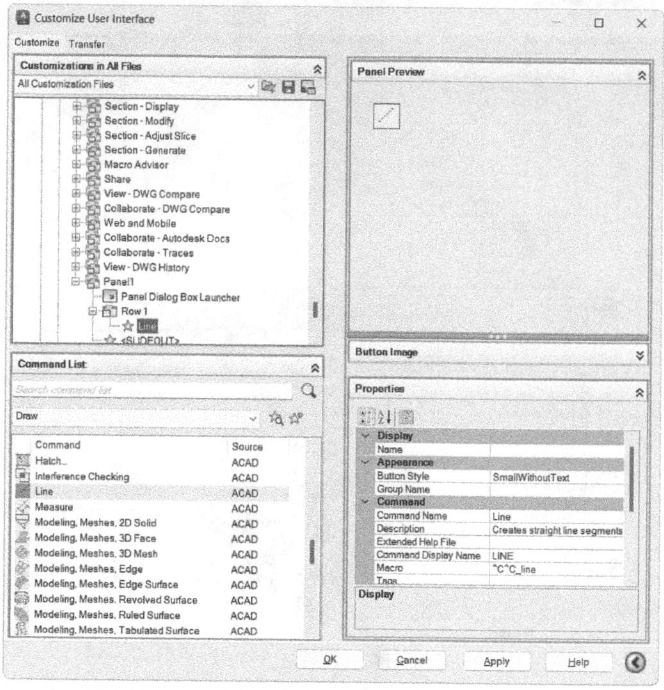

Figure B-3
Line tool in **Panel Preview**

Before you can see the panel in your application window, you need to assign it to a ribbon tab. You could drag the ribbon panel up to a ribbon tab, but the lists are long, so copying and pasting it works best.

✔ Right-click on **Panel1** and select **Copy** from the shortcut menu.

✔ Scroll up in the **Customizations in All Files** pane until you see the **Tabs** node under the **Ribbon** node. (It's a long way up.)

✔ Click the **+** sign next to **Tabs** to expand the node.

*You add **Panel1** to the **Home 2D** tab.*

✔ Right-click **Home – 2D** and select **Paste** from the shortcut menu.

***Panel1** is added to the bottom of the list of panels on the **Home – 2D** tab, just below **Home – Clipboard**.*

✔ Click **OK** to close the **CUI** editor.

✔ If necessary, switch to the **Drafting & Annotation** workspace, and click the **Home** tab on the ribbon.

***Panel1** should be displayed on the right of the ribbon next to the **Touch Mode** or **View** panel, as shown in Figure B-4. The **Touch Mode** panel is displayed only when your computer utilizes a touch-screen for its display.*

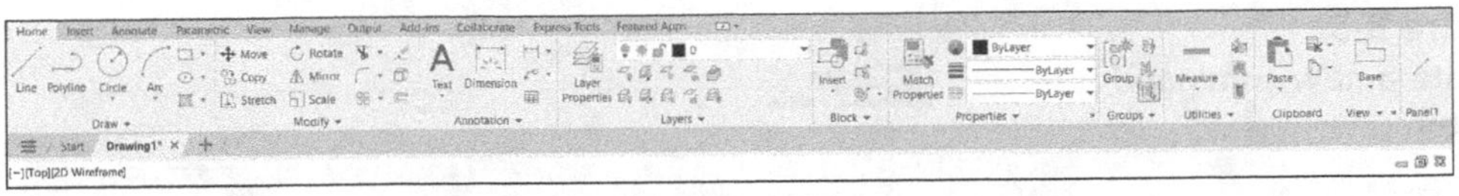

Figure B-4
Panel 1 added to end of ribbon

Creating Customized Tools

In this section, you are introduced to command customization. The "Creating a Customized Ribbon Panel" section describes how to create a new panel with one tool. In this section, you find out how to customize tools. These new tools function differently from standard AutoCAD commands.

> **TIP**
>
> The following is a general procedure for creating a customized tool:
>
> 1. With the **CUI** editor displayed, click the **Create a new command** tool in the **Command List** pane.
> 2. In the **Properties** pane, give the command a new name.
> 3. Edit the command macro associated with the tool.
> 4. In the **Button Image** pane, click **Edit** and edit the button image in the **Button Editor**.
> 5. Save the edited button image.
> 6. Check to see that the tool is defined as you want it to be.

✔ You should be in an AutoCAD drawing with the new panel created in the "Creating a Customized Ribbon Panel" section.

✔ Click **Manage** > **Customization** > **User Interface** to display the **Customize User Interface (CUI)** editor.

*In the **Command List** pane, there are two buttons that look like stars to the right of the drop-down list. The one to the right is the **Create a new command** button.*

✔ Click the **Create a new command** button, as shown in Figure B-5.

*This creates a new tool in the **Command List** pane and displays its properties in the **Properties** pane shown in Figure B-6. This is a very powerful area in the AutoCAD customization system. Here, you can change the name associated with a tool, change the appearance of a tool button, and edit the macro that determines, to an extent, how the tool functions. You do not actually create new commands but can determine default options that are provided automatically as part of the command sequence. For example, it might be useful to have a version of the **Line** tool that draws only one line segment and then returns you to the command line prompt. This is easily accomplished with a little knowledge of the macro language. **Macros** are command sequences that can contain options, values, special characters, and even the use of DIESEL expressions that can be used to make logical decisions based on system variable values. By automatically providing an extra press of the **<Enter>** key after drawing a single line segment, you can complete the command sequence as desired.*

Figure B-5
Create a new command button

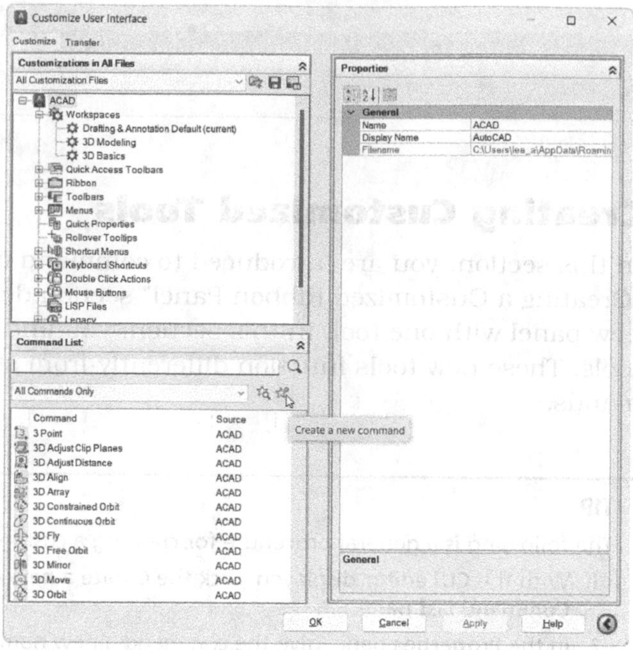

First, though, give this tool a name to differentiate it from the standard ***Line*** *tool.*

✔ Double-click in the **Name** edit box and type **Line1 <Enter>**.

This is a good descriptive name. Notice that ***Line1*** *is also reflected in the* ***Command List*** on the left.

Next, you modify the macro so that the **LINE** command completes after one line segment is drawn. For the purposes of this exercise, you need to know only two items about the macro language. A semicolon (;) is the macro language equivalent to pressing **<Enter>**. When AutoCAD sees a semicolon in a macro, it acts as though the user has pressed **<Enter>** or the spacebar in situations when the spacebar can be used in place of **<Enter>**. The backslash character (\) represents a pause for user input. You can learn about other characters that have special use in macros as part of Appendix C.

When AutoCAD reads a backslash in a macro, it waits for you to provide input at the current prompt only once before continuing on through the keyboard or pointing device. If you provide an invalid response, the macro continues on and could produce an unexpected result. So, it is important to be careful of the input you provide.

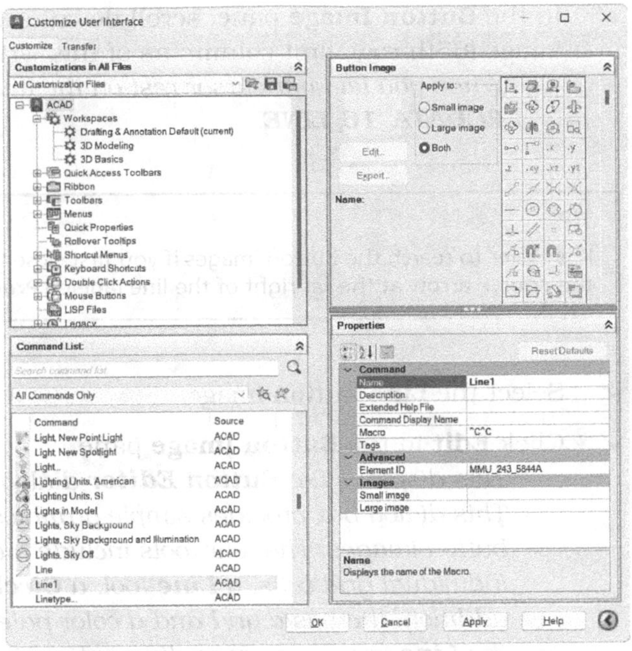

Figure B-6
Properties pane

- ✔ Click in the box next to **Macro** and type **._line;\\;** at the end of the macro, so that the complete macro reads
- ✔ **^C^C._line;\\;**

  It is very important that this be entered exactly as shown, without extra spaces. The macro language, like many programming languages, is very fussy.

  The following table breaks down what the characters are doing in the macro.

^C^C	The macro equivalent of pressing the **<Esc>** key twice, which cancels most commands that might be in progress before starting the **LINE** command
.	Standard definition of the command will be started rather than the redefined definition, if one exists
_	Declares the proceeding command name is the global name of a command and allows the macro to be supported in any language of the product
line	Types **line** at the command line prompt
;	Like pressing **<Enter>** after typing the command
\	Waits for the user to specify the first point
\	Waits for the user to specify a second point
;	Like pressing **<Enter>** or the spacebar, ends the command sequence

In a moment, you can try executing this new command, but first, change the button image to reflect that the command sequence for this custom tool is different from the standard **Line** tool. So that you do not have to start from scratch, you can start with the **Line** button image in the **Button Image** pane. Unfortunately, the selection of images is quite long. The **Line** button image is in the 65th row, first column.

✔ In the **Button Image** pane, scroll down until you see the **Line** button image (65th row, first column as of this writing).

*When you let your cursor rest on the image, the label will be **RCDATA_16_LINE**.*

> **TIP**
>
> It is easier to search the button images if you first close the **Properties** pane by clicking the double arrow at the far right of the line labeled **Properties**.

✔ Select the **Line** button image.

✔ Click **Edit** in the **Button Image** pane.

*This displays the **Button Editor** dialog box illustrated in Figure B-7. This dialog box provides simple graphics tools for creating or editing button images. The four tools include a drawing "pencil" for drawing individual grid cells, a **Line** tool, a **Circle** tool, and an **Erase** tool. In addition, there is a grid and a color palette. Here, you simply shorten the **Line** button image to differentiate it from the regular **Line** tool.*

✔ Click the **Erase** tool from the top right to switch edit tools. Then click and drag over the editing area to erase the lower-left half of the **Line** button image, as shown in Figure B-8.

Figure B-7
Button Editor pane

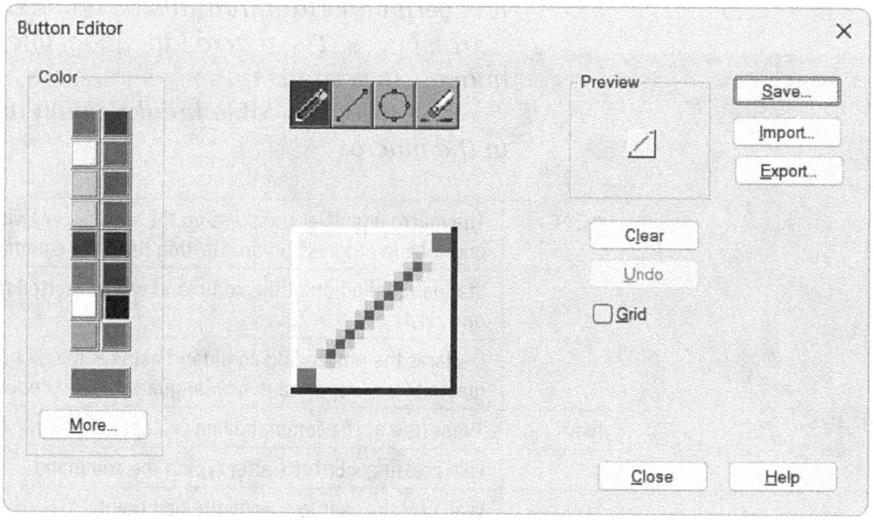

✔ Click **Save** to displays the **Save Image** dialog box.

✔ Type **Line1** for the name of the button image.

*Notice that there are now two aspects of this modified **LINE** command in the CUI file: the **Line1** tool, which uses the **LINE** command in a macro that limits input by using additional macro characters, and the button image stored as a .bmp file. Both of them are referred to as **Line1**.*

Figure B-8
Create new **Line** button image

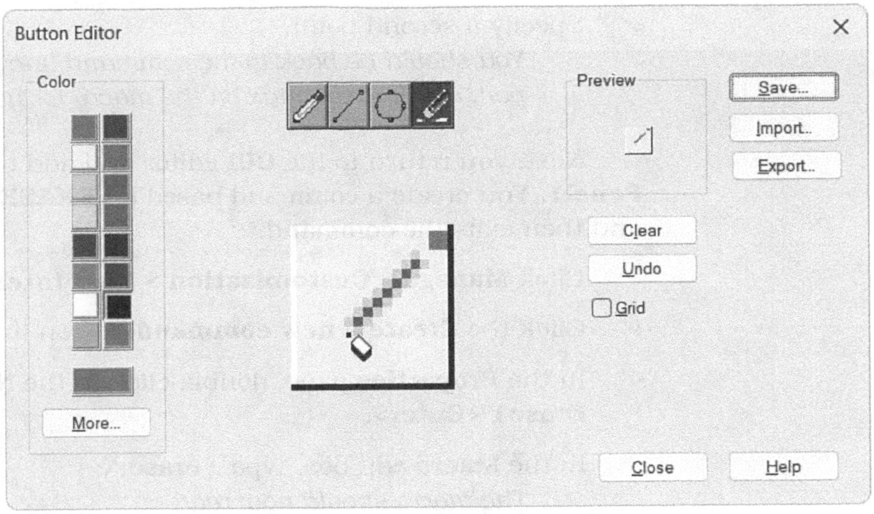

✔ Click **OK** in the **Save Image** dialog box.

✔ Click **Close** to exit the **Button Editor** dialog box and return to the **CUI** editor.

*Finally, you need to add **Line1** to **Panel1** before you leave the **CUI** editor.*

✔ Expand the **Ribbon** node in the **Customizations in All Files** pane.

✔ Expand the **Panels** node underneath the **Ribbon** node.

✔ Scroll to the bottom of the list and expand **Panel1**.

✔ In the **Command List** pane, make sure **All Commands Only** is showing in the drop-down list.

*This is necessary. You will not find the new command **Line1** in the list of **Draw** commands.*

✔ In the **Search Command List** text box, type **Lin**.

✔ If necessary, scroll the list to find **Line1**.

✔ Select the **Line1** tool and drag it up to **Row 1** under **Panel1**.

✔ With the blue arrow showing, drop **Line1** in **Row 1**.

*The **Line1** tool is added to your **Panel Preview**.*

✔ Click **Apply** to execute the changes to your customized tool button.

Now, close the CUI editor and try your new tool.

✔ Click **OK**.

The editor closes, returning you to the drawing area.

✔ If necessary, click the **Home** tab on the ribbon.

***Panel1** should be at the far right with the standard **Line** tool and the new **Line1** tool.*

✔ Click the **Line1** tool from **Panel1**.

✔ Specify a first point anywhere in the drawing area.

✔ Specify a second point.

*You should be back to the command line prompt. If this did not happen, check the syntax on the macro for your **Line1** tool.*

Next, you return to the **CUI** editor and add one more new command to **Panel1**. You create a command based on **ERASE** that erases a single object and then exits the command.

✔ Click **Manage** > **Customization** > **User Interface** from the ribbon.

✔ Click the **Create a new command** button in the **Command List** pane.

✔ In the **Properties** pane, double-click in the **Name** edit box and type **Erase1 <Enter>**.

✔ In the **Macro** edit box, type **._erase;\;**

The macro should now read

^C^C._erase;\;

*Consider how this macro will work. After canceling any other command, it types **erase**, and then the first semicolon enters the **ERASE** command. The \ instructs AutoCAD to wait for input. After the user selects one object, the second semicolon completes the command and returns to the command line prompt.*

✔ If necessary, open the **Button Image** pane and/or close the **Properties** pane.

✔ Scroll down to find the **Erase** button image (20th row, second column as of this writing).

✔ Select the **Erase** button image.

✔ Click **Edit** in the **Button Image** pane to display the **Button Editor dialog box.**

✔ Use the **Erase** and **Line** tools to create the button image shown in Figure B-9.

This image shows the eraser head over a single object. When using the pencil, you may need to click the gray color or another brighter color in the palette to make this part of the image visible.

Figure B-9
Create new **Erase** button image

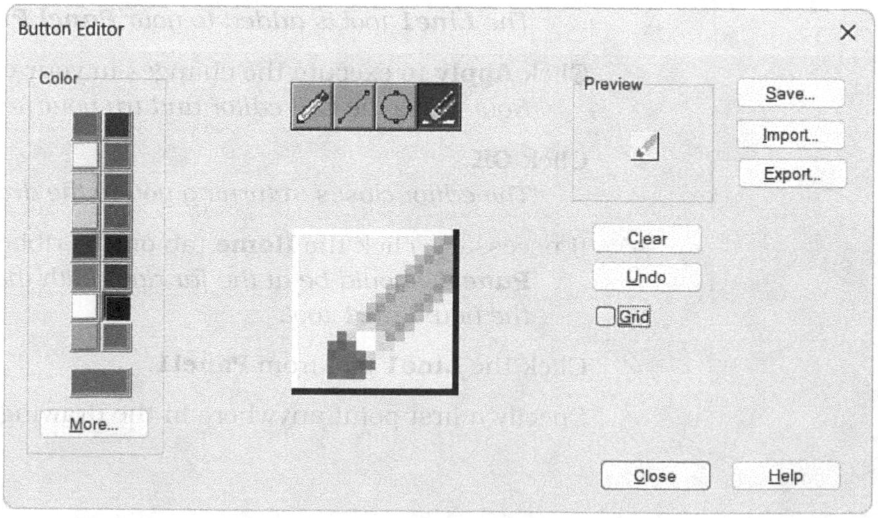

✔ Save the modified image as **Erase1**.

✔ Close the **Button Editor**.

✔ Expand the **Ribbon** node in the **Customizations in All Files** pane.

✔ Expand the **Panels** node.

✔ Scroll down to **Panel1**.

✔ Expand **Panel1**.

✔ Expand **Row 1**.

✔ If necessary, scroll to the **Erase1** command in the **Command List** pane.

✔ Drag **Erase1** up to **Row 1**.

*The **Erase1** tool is added to your **Panel Preview**.*

✔ Click **Apply** to save changes to **Panel1** and the **Erase1** tool.

✔ Click **OK** to close the **CUI** editor.

✔ Move your cursor over the **Panel1** tab to view the three tools, as shown in Figure B-10.

*The **Erase1** tool has been added to **Panel1**, but you need to bring your cursor to the panel to see the three icons, as shown.*

Finally, try your new tools to see that they are working.

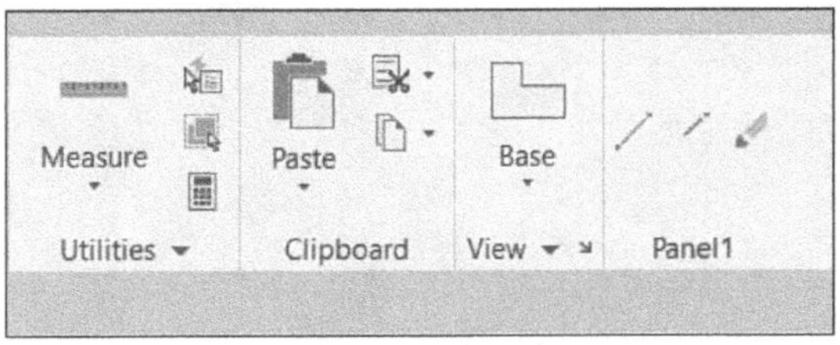

Figure B-10
Panel1 with three tools

✔ Use the **Line1** tool to draw a single line segment.

✔ Use the **Erase1** tool to erase the line.

Be aware that pressing the spacebar to repeat one of these commands repeats the regular AutoCAD command, not the macro you created for your custom panel.

Appendix C

Menus, Macros, and the CUI Dialog Box

When you begin to look below the surface of AutoCAD as it is configured straight out of the box, you find a whole world of customization possibilities. This open architecture, which allows you to create your own menus, commands, toolbars, tool palettes, ribbon panels, and automated routines, is one of the reasons for AutoCAD's success. It is characteristic of all AutoCAD releases and has allowed a vast network of third-party developers to create custom software products tailoring AutoCAD to the particular needs of various industries and tasks.

The **Customize User Interface** (or CUI) dialog box is the largest single resource for customizing elements of the AutoCAD user interface. In this appendix, you briefly explore the vocabulary of the macro language used to start commands from the AutoCAD user interface and find out how it is used with the elements in the **CUI** dialog box. The elements shown in the **CUI** dialog box for editing are stored in customization (CUIx) files. You used the **CUI** dialog box in Appendix B while customizing the ribbon and writing and editing macros. The intention of this chapter is not to make you a customization expert but to expand your knowledge of what is going on in the CUI system. After reading this, you should have a sense of what elements are readily available for customization beyond ribbon tabs and panels introduced in Appendix B.

The CUI Dialog Box

In the **CUI** dialog box, all elements are customized in the same way. All elements are represented by starred entries in the tree view on the left in the **Customizations In** pane with their properties displayed in the **Properties** pane on the right. Some elements also support images that can be modified as part of the **Button Image** pane.

Following is a list of the elements in the tree view with a brief description of each. The "Characters Used in Macros" section further discusses the special characters and sequences that make up the macro language.

✔ To display the **CUI** dialog box, click **Manage** > **Customization** > **User Interface** from the ribbon.

The tree view in the top-left pane allows you to access the elements that can be customized, including workspaces, Quick Access toolbars, the ribbon tabs and panels, toolbars, menus, shortcut menus, keyboard shortcuts, double-click actions, mouse buttons, LISP files, legacy elements, and partial customization files. Click any of the top level nodes to see a description of the element in the **Information** pane on the right. Following is a brief description of each.

Workspaces

Workspaces are a way of controlling which and where elements should be displayed in the AutoCAD user interface. Workspaces consist of ribbon tabs and panels, menus, palettes, Quick Access toolbar, and "legacy" toolbars. By selecting elements to add to or remove from the application window, you can create unique and customized configurations. These can be saved as workspaces and then displayed together as a named workspace. The default workspace includes all the elements you are used to seeing. A simple example of customizing a workspace is to open the menu bar and then save this configuration as a **Menu Bar** workspace. Then, whenever you want to be in this workspace, you click the **Workspace** drop-down list on the status bar and select the **Menu Bar** workspace.

Quick Access Toolbars

A Quick Access toolbar is displayed on the AutoCAD application window title bar. The standard Quick Access toolbar is named **Quick Access Toolbar1** and is displayed in all default workspaces. This toolbar can be customized by clicking the down-arrow button on the right side of the **Quick Access** toolbar and selecting tools from the drop-down list. Other **Quick Access** toolbars can be created in the **CUI** dialog box using the same procedures used to create other elements, such as the procedures used to customize the ribbon in the "Creating Custom Ribbon Panels" section of Appendix B.

Ribbon

The ribbon is the user interface most frequently used for locating and starting AutoCAD commands. Additional ribbon tabs and panels can be created and modified. It's recommended that you not modify the standard AutoCAD ribbon tabs or panels.

Toolbars

Toolbars can be created and added to the tree view list of toolbars. You probably will not use toolbars as much as in the past because the ribbon interface is more efficient. The procedures used for creating panels work the same for creating toolbars. You can also modify existing toolbars using the same techniques used to create new ones. It's recommended that you not modify the standard AutoCAD toolbars.

Menus

These are the standard menus on the menu bar. If you expand the **Menus** node in the **CUI** dialog box, you see the list, from **File** to **Help**. If you expand **File**, you see the list of commands on the **File** menu, from **New** to **Exit**. Most entries on menus refer to commands, and they work exactly like the tool button entries on ribbon panels, Quick Access toolbar, and toolbars. For example, select **New** under the **Menu** node, and you will see the **Button Image** for the **New** command in the top-right pane and the **Properties** pane below that. The macro for this item on the menu is **^C^C_new**.

Quick Properties

This node is used to control which properties are displayed by object type in the **Quick Properties** palette. You can add or remove properties based on those you frequently use.

Rollover Tooltips

This node is used to control which properties are displayed by object type in the tooltip that is displayed when the cursor is hovering over an object in the drawing area. You can add or remove properties of those objects for which you frequently want to know the current value without displaying the **Properties** or **Quick Properties** palettes.

Shortcut Menus

Here, you find the standard shortcut menus. Under **Grips Cursor Menu**, for example, you see familiar grip modes and options that appear when you right-click while in the grip editing system.

Keyboard Shortcuts

This is a good place to explore the complete keyboard shortcuts available. For example, open the tree view, expand the **Keyboard Shortcuts** node, and look at the **New item**. You will find that this is the place where **<Ctrl>+N** is established as the keyboard shortcut for entering the **New** command. There are more than 40 keyboard shortcuts defined here, including many you've probably never noticed. The **Temporary Overrides** node shows key combinations that temporarily override a drafting aid setting without changing it. Most of these use the **<Shift>** key in combination with another key.

Double-Click Actions

This node determines what action is taken when you double-click with the cursor resting on an object in a drawing. The action taken depends on the type of object present and is a customizable feature. By default, when you double-click most objects, the **Quick Properties** panel is displayed. The following are some other examples: double-clicking a polyline starts the **PEDIT** command, double-clicking a multiline starts the **MLEDIT command**, or double-clicking an attribute definition starts the **EATTEDIT command**.

Mouse Buttons

The options for a standard two-button mouse are pretty limited, but this node is used to customize pointing devices with more than two buttons.

LISP Files

AutoCAD allows you to create customized routines in other languages in addition to the macro language presented later in this chapter. AutoLISP is a programming language based on LISP, which is a standard list processing language. You see AutoLISP statements in place of some macros in the **Properties** pane. LISP statements are enclosed in parentheses.

Legacy

Legacy refers to elements of the application that are no longer in common use but are still supported for those who like to use them. This includes tablet menus and buttons and image tile menus. You do not need to know about these unless you are working on a system that uses legacy features.

Partial Customization Files

The preferred way to create custom user interface elements is through the use of partial customization files. Thus, you do not alter the original customization files and can go back to the out-of-box state at any time. If you open this node, you will see that there are currently five or more partial customization files, including one called **CUSTOM**. It contains all the element types of the standard customization file, but there are no entries under the main element nodes. To start creating custom elements, you can start with **CUSTOM** and add commands and macros to any of the elements. If you want to create a new partial customization file, you can use the Transfer tab and the tools in the right pane. Once a new partial customization file has been created, you can load and use that new partial customization file under the **Partial Customization Files** node on the **Customize** tab.

This completes the tour of the **CUI** dialog box. In the next section, you learn more about the characters and their meanings of the macro language. Refer back to Appendix B how you created and modified macros to see which characters you previously used.

Characters Used in Menus and Macros

The following table lists some of the menu and macro characters you find used by many elements in the CUIx file.

Most Common Menu and Macro Characters	
&	Placed before a letter that can be used as an alias; the letter will be underlined on the menu.
;	Same as pressing **<Enter>** while typing.
^C	**<Ctrl>+C;** same as pressing **<Esc>**.
^C^C	Double cancel; cancels most commands and ensures you are returned to the command prompt before a new command is issued.
POP*n*	Section header, where ***n*** is a number between 1 and 16, identifying one of the 16 possible menu areas; POP0 refers to the cursor menu.
[--]	Represents a separator line on a menu.
_	Global command or option name. (underscore character)
'	Transparent command modifier (apostrophe character)
( )	Parentheses encloses **AutoLISP** and **DIESEL** expressions.
****	Pause for user input; allows for keyboard entry, point specification, and object selection; terminated by pressing **<Enter>** or the left mouse button.
~	Defines a menu label that is unavailable; can be used to indicate a function not currently in use.
***^C^C**	Causes the menu item to repeat.

Index

Symbols

A

B

C

D

E

F

G

H

I

J

M

N

T

U

V

W

X–Y–Z